W9-CFC-882

# HYGRADE®

## CATALOG & PRICE GUIDE
## OF TOPPS, DONRUSS, FLEER
## AND SPORTFLICS

# BASEBALL CARDS

**Features card values of virtually every baseball card issued by these manufacturers:**

TOPPS–years 1951 to 1987

DONRUSS–years 1981 to 1987

FLEER–years 1981 to 1987

SPORTFLICS–years 1986 to 1987

Second Edition

**Publisher: HYGRADE SPORTS CARD CO., 5 East 17th Street, New York, N.Y. 10003**

# TABLE OF CONTENTS

## General Information

Card values in this catalog represent approximate retail values as of April, 1987. Due to high demand, the values of popular cards have been fluctuating every few weeks. Keep up-to-date on the latest market values with a monthly price guide. Information on card values was compiled from various sources including dealer ads in card magazines, dealer catalogs, card auctions, offers at card conventions, etc. **The card values in this catalog do not represent an offer to buy or sell by the publisher.**

## What Makes a Card Valuable?

The value of a baseball card is determined by *supply* (how many cards are offered for sale at a certain price), and *demand* (how many cards buyers are willing and able to purchase at a certain price). When the demand is greater than the supply, the card's value *increases;* when supply exceeds demand, the card's value *decreases.* However, as with stamps, coins, and other collectibles, the *condition* of a card also affects its value. Cards which have been preserved in *mint* condition are much more in demand by collectors, and therefore worth more than the same cards in worn condition. If the card shows *very light wear,* its value is usually about 65% to 80% of the price for the same card in mint condition. The more wear or damage the card shows, the less it is worth. So if you eventually hope to sell your collection for a profit, try to buy cards in the best possible condition.

## Rookie Cards

A *rookie* card is a player's first card from the *main* card set of a major card manufacturer. Today, the major card manufacturers are Topps, Donruss, Fleer and Sportflics. Sometimes several players are shown on one rookie card. For example, Pete Rose is pictured with three other players on his 1963 rookie card. Occasionally a rookie card is issued one or more years after the player's actual rookie season. Each of the major manufacturers issues a main card set each year, as well as several special card sets. But in order for a card to qualify as the *rookie* card it must appear in the main card set, which is universally distributed. Sometimes special card sets, like the Topps *Traded Update,* include a player's first card, but this card is not generally considered to be a rookie card. Traded cards are only distributed through card hobby dealers, unlike cards from the main set which are sold everywhere. From 1956 to 1980 Topps was the only major card manufacturer, so each player had only one rookie card. Today there are four major card manufacturers—so each player can have up to four rookie cards.

Topps has announced that its 1987 Traded Card Set will be universally distributed in gum packs. Therefore, for the first time the Topps rookie card can appear in the traded set instead of the main card set.

## Complete Sets

The total cost of the individual cards in a set is always much greater than the complete set price—which makes the complete set an economical purchase. This is because a complete set includes many common cards, and minor-star cards which a dealer will sell at a reduced price when sold as a group. The complete set value does not include any error or variety cards.

## Double-Printed Cards

Baseball cards are not printed individually, but are printed on big sheets that have space for up to 132 cards. Once printed, these sheets are cut apart, and the cards are sorted and packaged. If the number of cards on a sheet is the same as the number of cards in a set, or divides evenly into that set number, then each of the cards on the sheet shows a different player. From 1973 to 1977, Topps issued baseball sets of 660 cards. These were printed on five sheets, each with 132 different cards. But beginning in 1978 and continuing until 1981, Topps changed the number of cards in its sets from 660 to 726, an increase of 66 cards. Rather than print a sixth sheet only half filled, Topps decided to *double-print* (print twice the quantity) 66 cards in each set.

## Common Cards

*Common* cards are the lowest valued cards in a set. They are cards that feature ordinary players, not stars or popular personalities. There is very little demand by collectors for individual common cards. They are often sold in lots and used primarily to assemble card sets. A typical Topps card set includes about 60% *common* cards, 25% *minor star* cards and 15% *star* cards.

## High-Numbers

During the period from 1952 to 1973 Topps released their annual card sets in series, rather than issuing the complete set at one time as they do now. Most Topps sets consisted of six or seven card series, each released a few weeks or months apart. For example, the first series of the 1970 Topps card set had 132 cards, numbers 1 to 132; the second series contained numbers 133 to 263, etc. Since sales of the cards tended to become less and less as the season progressed, Topps usually printed fewer of the later card series, which contained the high number cards. Because the high number cards are scarcer today, they are generally more valuable as a group, than the low number cards of the same set. If the last series is not scarce, compared to other series in the same set, it is not a high number series. Every Topps set issued from 1952 to 1973 has a high number series except years 1954, 1956, 1957, 1958 and 1969.

Several Topps card sets from 1952 to 1973 also have a *semi-high-number* series. This is the next to the last series of a card set in which there is also a high number series, and the semi-high number cards are scarce. Semi-high number cards as a group are generally worth less than high numbers, but more than low numbers. Beginning in 1974 and continuing until today, Topps changed their policy and distributed their card sets all at one time, thus eliminating high numbers.

# RARE & FAMOUS BASEBALL CARDS

1910 Honus Wagner

1933 Goudey Gum

1933 Goudey Gum

1911 Sherry "Magie"

| Year | Manufacturer | Player | Value Mint | |
|------|--------------|--------|-----------:|---|
| 1910 | T-206 Tobacco | Honus Wagner (Pitt) | $35,000.00 | |
| 1910 | T-206 Tobacco | Eddie Plank (Phil) | 7,000.00 | |
| 1910 | T-206 Tobacco | Ray Demmitt (St. L) | 1,000.00 | |
| 1911 | T-206 Tobacco | Sherry "Magie" (misspelled) | 3,500.00 | |
| 1911 | T-3 Tobacco | Ty Cobb | 1,500.00 | |
| 1911 | T-3 Tobacco | Walter Johnson | 750.00 | |
| 1911 | T-3 Tobacco | Christy Mathewson | 750.00 | |
| 1911 | T-205 Tobacco | Ty Cobb | 500.00 | |
| 1912 | T-207 Tobacco | Duffy Lewis (Boston N.) | 1,000.00 | |
| 1914 | Cracker Jack | Ty Cobb | 750.00 | |
| 1933 | Goudey Gum | Napoleon Lajoie | 7,500.00 | |
| 1933 | Goudey Gum | Babe Ruth (4 diff. cards) | 750.00 | each |
| 1933 | De Long Gum | Lou Gegrig | 1,000.00 | |
| 1934 | Goudey Gum | Lou Gehrig (2 diff. cards) | 600.00 | each |
| 1938 | Goudey Gum | Joe DiMaggio (2 diff. cards) | 650.00 | each |
| 1940 | Play Ball (Gum, Inc.) | Joe DiMaggio | 500.00 | |
| 1941 | Play Ball (Gum, Inc.) | Joe DiMaggio | 500.00 | |
| 1948 | Leaf Gum | Satchel Paige | 600.00 | |
| 1951 | Topps All-Stars | Jim Konstanty | 3750.00 | |
| 1951 | Topps All-Stars | Robin Roberts | 4000.00 | |
| 1951 | Topps All-Stars | Eddie Stanky | 4000.00 | |
| 1951 | Bowman Gum | Mickey Mantle | 800.00 | |
| 1951 | Bowman Gum | Willie Mays | 500.00 | |
| 1952 | Topps | Mickey Mantle | 3,000.00 | |
| 1954 | Bowman Gum | Ted Williams | 850.00 | |
| 1963 | Topps | Pete Rose | 550.00 | |
| 1968 | Topps 3-D | Roberto Clemente | 1050.00 | |

1910 Eddie Plank

1934 Goudey Gum

1938 Goudey Gum

1912 Duffy Lewis

# LEGEND

**R**—the player's rookie card. Only rookie cards of "star" players are noted.

**RR**—the manufacturer's first card for that player, which is in the Traded Update set.

**\***—there is a special feature of this card, which can be determined by referring to the headline for the set.

**AS**—a card featuring a player who was on the previous year's all-star team.

**DK**—abbreviation for Diamond King, which is a Donruss card with artwork by the Perez-Steele Gallery.

**Mgr.**—a card featuring the manager of a baseball team.

**MVP**—Most Valuable Player award

## 1951 Topps "Red Backs".... Complete Set of 52 Cards—Value $250.00

This set, as well as the 1951 "Blue Backs", was Topps' first baseball card issue. The backs of the 2" x 2⅝" cards can be used to play a baseball card game. Card 36 was issued as either White Sox or Athletics. Card 52 was issued as either Hartford or Braves.

| NO. PLAYER | MINT |
|---|---|
| 1 Yogi Berra | 30.00 |
| 2 Sid Gordon | 3.00 |
| 3 Ferris Fain | 3.00 |
| 4 Verne Stephens | 3.00 |
| 5 Phil Rizzuto | 14.00 |
| 6 Allie Reynolds | 5.00 |
| 7 Howie Pollet | 3.00 |
| 8 Early Wynn | 10.00 |
| 9 Roy Sievers | 3.00 |
| 10 Mel Parnell | 3.00 |
| 11 Gene Hermanski | 3.00 |
| 12 Jim Hegan | 3.00 |
| 13 Dale Mitchell | 3.00 |

| NO. PLAYER | MINT |
|---|---|
| 14 Wayne Terwilliger | 3.00 |
| 15 Ralph Kiner | 10.00 |
| 16 Preacher Roe | 6.00 |
| 17 Dave Bell | 3.00 |
| 18 Gerry Coleman | 3.00 |
| 19 Dick Kokos | 3.00 |
| 20 Dominick DiMaggio | 5.00 |
| 21 Larry Jansen | 3.00 |
| 22 Bob Feller | 17.00 |
| 23 Ray Boone | 3.00 |
| 24 Hank Bauer | 5.00 |
| 25 Cliff Chambers | 3.00 |
| 26 Luke Easter | 3.00 |

| NO. PLAYER | MINT |
|---|---|
| 27 Wally Westlake | 3.00 |
| 28 Elmer Valo | 3.00 |
| 29 Bob Kennedy | 3.00 |
| 30 Warren Spahn | 13.00 |
| 31 Gil Hodges | 13.00 |
| 32 Henry Thompson | 3.00 |
| 33 William Werle | 3.00 |
| 34 Grady Hatton | 3.00 |
| 35 Al Rosen | 6.00 |
| 36 Gus Zernial* | 8.00 |
| 37 Wes Westrum | 3.00 |
| 38 Duke Snider | 20.00 |
| 39 Ted Kluszewski | 6.00 |

| NO. PLAYER | MINT |
|---|---|
| 40 Mike Garcia | 3.00 |
| 41 Whitey Lockman | 3.00 |
| 42 Ray Scarborough | 3.00 |
| 43 Maurice McDermott | 3.00 |
| 44 Sid Hudson | 3.00 |
| 45 Andy Seminick | 3.00 |
| 46 Billy Goodman | 3.00 |
| 47 Tom Glaviano | 3.00 |
| 48 Ed Stanky | 3.00 |
| 49 Al Zarilla | 3.00 |
| 50 Monte Irvin | 11.00 |
| 51 Eddie Robinson | 3.00 |
| 52 Tommy Holmes* | 9.00 |

## 1951 Topps "Blue Backs".... Complete Set of 52 Cards—Value $550.00

Similar in format to the 1951 "Red Backs." The backs of the 2" x 2⅝" cards can be used to play a baseball card game.

| NO. PLAYER | MINT |
|---|---|
| 1 Eddie Yost | 15.00 |
| 2 Hank Majeski | 10.00 |
| 3 Richie Ashburn | 15.00 |
| 4 Del Ennis | 10.00 |
| 5 Johnny Pesky | 10.00 |
| 6 Al Schoendienst | 12.00 |
| 7 Gerald Staley | 10.00 |
| 8 Dick Sisler | 10.00 |
| 9 Johnny Sain | 13.00 |
| 10 Joe Page | 10.00 |
| 11 Johnny Groth | 10.00 |
| 12 Sam Jethroe | 10.00 |
| 13 Mickey Vernon | 10.00 |

| NO. PLAYER | MINT |
|---|---|
| 14 George Munger | 10.00 |
| 15 Eddie Joost | 10.00 |
| 16 Murry Dickson | 10.00 |
| 17 Roy Smalley | 10.00 |
| 18 Ned Garver | 10.00 |
| 19 Phil Masi | 10.00 |
| 20 Ralph Branca | 10.00 |
| 21 Bill Johnson | 10.00 |
| 22 Bob Kuzava | 10.00 |
| 23 Dizzy Trout | 10.00 |
| 24 Sherman Lollar | 10.00 |
| 25 Sam Mele | 10.00 |
| 26 Chico Carrasquel | 10.00 |

| NO. PLAYER | MINT |
|---|---|
| 27 Andy Pafko | 10.00 |
| 28 Harry Brecheen | 10.00 |
| 29 Granville Hamner | 10.00 |
| 30 Enos Slaughter | 20.00 |
| 31 Lou Brissie | 10.00 |
| 32 Bob Elliott | 10.00 |
| 33 Don Lenhardt | 10.00 |
| 34 Earl Torgeson | 10.00 |
| 35 Tom Byrne (R) | 10.00 |
| 36 Cliff Fannin | 10.00 |
| 37 Bobby Doerr | 15.00 |
| 38 Irv Noren | 10.00 |
| 39 Ed Lopat | 12.00 |

| NO. PLAYER | MINT |
|---|---|
| 40 Vic Wertz | 10.00 |
| 41 Johnny Schmitz | 10.00 |
| 42 Bruce Edwards | 10.00 |
| 43 Willie Jones | 10.00 |
| 44 Johnny Wyrostek | 10.00 |
| 45 Bill Pierce (R) | 12.00 |
| 46 Gerry Priddy | 10.00 |
| 47 Herman Wehmeier | 10.00 |
| 48 Billy Cox | 10.00 |
| 49 Hank Sauer | 10.00 |
| 50 Johnny Mize | 22.00 |
| 51 Ed Waitkus | 10.00 |
| 52 Sam Chapman | 10.00 |

# 1952 Topps.... Complete Set of 407 Cards—Value $17,500.00

Features the rookie cards of Hoyt Wilhelm, Billy Martin and Eddie Mathews. This is Topps' first *major* baseball card set. Cards 1 to 80 were printed with *black* or *red* backs. The high number series is 311 to 407. Semi-high numbers are 251 to 310. Topps introduced a new card size—2⅝" x 3¾", used until 1956. Cards 48 and 49 exist with each other's backs transposed—worth $100.00 each.

| NO. PLAYER | MINT | NO. PLAYER | MINT | NO. PLAYER | MINT | NO. PLAYER | MINT |
|---|---|---|---|---|---|---|---|
| 1 Andy Pafko | 225.00 | 69 Virgil Stallcup | 8.00 | 137 Roy McMillan | 6.00 | 205 Clyde King | 6.00 |
| 2 James Runnels | 12.00 | 70 Al Zarilla | 8.00 | 138 Bill MacDonald | 6.00 | 206 Joe Ostrowski | 6.00 |
| 3 Hank Thompson | 8.00 | 71 Tom Upton | 8.00 | 139 Ken Wood | 6.00 | 207 Mickey Harris | 6.00 |
| 4 Donald Lenhardt | 8.00 | 72 Karl Olson | 8.00 | 140 John Antonelli | 6.00 | 208 Marlin Stuart | 6.00 |
| 5 Larry Jansen | 8.00 | 73 William Werle | 8.00 | 141 Clint Hartung | 6.00 | 209 Howie Fox | 6.00 |
| 6 Grady Hatton | 8.00 | 74 Andy Hansen | 8.00 | 142 Harry Perkowski | 6.00 | 210 Dick Fowler | 6.00 |
| 7 Wayne Terwilliger | 8.00 | 75 Wes Westrum | 8.00 | 143 Les Moss | 6.00 | 211 Ray Coleman | 6.00 |
| 8 Fred Marsh, | 8.00 | 76 Eddie Stanky | 8.00 | 144 Edward Blake | 6.00 | 212 Ned Garver | 6.00 |
| 9 Bob Hogue | 8.00 | 77 Bob Kennedy | 8.00 | 145 Joe Haynes | 6.00 | 213 Nippy Jones | 6.00 |
| 10 Al Rosen | 15.00 | 78 Ellis Kinder | 8.00 | 146 Frank House | 6.00 | 214 Johnny Hopp | 6.00 |
| 11 Phil Rizzuto | 40.00 | 79 Gerald Staley | 8.00 | 147 Bob Young | 6.00 | 215 Hank Bauer | 9.00 |
| 12 Monty Basgall | 8.00 | 80 Herman Wehmeier | 8.00 | 148 John Klippstein | 6.00 | 216 Richie Ashburn | 16.00 |
| 13 Johnny Wyrostek | 8.00 | 81 Vernon Law | 6.00 | 149 Dick Kryhoski | 6.00 | 217 George Stirnweiss | 6.00 |
| 14 Bob Elliott | 8.00 | 82 Duane Pillette | 6.00 | 150 Ted Beard | 6.00 | 218 Clyde McCullough | 6.00 |
| 15 Johnny Pesky | 8.00 | 83 Billy Johnson | 6.00 | 151 Wally Post | 6.00 | 219 Bobby Shantz | 9.00 |
| 16 Gene Hermanski | 8.00 | 84 Vern Stephens | 6.00 | 152 Al Evans | 6.00 | 220 Joe Presko | 6.00 |
| 17 Jim Hegan | 8.00 | 85 Bob Kuzava | 6.00 | 153 Bob Rush | 6.00 | 221 Granny Hamner | 6.00 |
| 18 Merrill Combs | 8.00 | 86 Teddy Gray | 6.00 | 154 Joe Muir | 6.00 | 222 Walter Evers | 6.00 |
| 19 John Bucha | 8.00 | 87 Dale Coogan | 6.00 | 155 Frank Overmire | 6.00 | 223 Del Ennis | 6.00 |
| 20 Billy Loes | 8.00 | 88 Bob Feller | 40.00 | 156 Frank Hiller | 6.00 | 224 Bruce Edwards | 6.00 |
| 21 Ferris Fain | 8.00 | 89 Johnny Lipon | 6.00 | 157 Bob Usher | 6.00 | 225 Frank Baumholtz | 6.00 |
| 22 Dom DiMaggio | 16.00 | 90 Mickey Grasso | 6.00 | 158 Eddie Waitkus | 6.00 | 226 Dave Philley | 6.00 |
| 23 Billy Goodman | 8.00 | 91 Al Schoendienst | 10.00 | 159 Saul Rogovin | 6.00 | 227 Joe Garagiola | 27.00 |
| 24 Luke Easter | 8.00 | 92 Dale Mitchell | 6.00 | 160 Owen Friend | 6.00 | 228 Al Brazle | 6.00 |
| 25 Johnny Groth | 8.00 | 93 Al Sima | 6.00 | 161 Bud Byerly | 6.00 | 229 Gene Bearden | 6.00 |
| 26 Monte Irvin | 18.00 | 94 Sam Mele | 6.00 | 162 Del Crandall | 6.00 | 230 Matt Batts | 6.00 |
| 27 Sam Jethroe | 8.00 | 95 Ken Holcombe | 6.00 | 163 Stan Rojek | 6.00 | 231 Sam Zoldak | 6.00 |
| 28 Jerry Priddy | 8.00 | 96 Willard Marshall | 6.00 | 164 Walt Dubiel | 6.00 | 232 Billy Cox | 6.00 |
| 29 Ted Kluszewski | 16.00 | 97 Earl Torgeson | 6.00 | 165 Ed Kazak | 6.00 | 233 Bob Friend | 6.00 |
| 30 Mel Parnell | 8.00 | 98 Bill Pierce | 6.00 | 166 Paul LaPalme | 6.00 | 234 Steve Souchock | 6.00 |
| 31 Gus Zernial | 8.00 | 99 Gene Woodling | 6.00 | 167 Bill Howerton | 6.00 | 235 Walt Dropo | 6.00 |
| 32 Eddie Robinson | 8.00 | 100 Del Rice | 6.00 | 168 Charlie Silvera | 6.00 | 236 Ed Fitzgerald | 6.00 |
| 33 Warren Spahn | 35.00 | 101 Max Lanier | 6.00 | 169 Howie Judson | 6.00 | 237 Jerry Coleman | 6.00 |
| 34 Elmer Valo | 8.00 | 102 Bill Kennedy | 6.00 | 170 Gus Bell | 6.00 | 238 Art Houtteman | 6.00 |
| 35 Hank Sauer | 12.00 | 103 Cliff Mapes | 6.00 | 171 Ed Erautt | 6.00 | 239 Rocky Bridges | 6.00 |
| 36 Gil Hodges | 35.00 | 104 Don Kolloway | 6.00 | 172 Eddie Miksis | 6.00 | 240 Jack Phillips | 6.00 |
| 37 Duke Snider | 60.00 | 105 John Pramesa | 6.00 | 173 Roy Smalley | 6.00 | 241 Tommy Byrne | 6.00 |
| 38 Wally Westlake | 8.00 | 106 Mickey Vernon | 6.00 | 174 Clarence Marshall | 6.00 | 242 Tom Poholsky | 6.00 |
| 39 Dizzy Trout | 8.00 | 107 Connie Ryan | 6.00 | 175 Billy Martin (R) | 60.00 | 243 Larry Doby | 10.00 |
| 40 Irv Noren | 8.00 | 108 Jimmy Konstanty | 6.00 | 176 Hank Edwards | 6.00 | 244 Vic Wertz | 6.00 |
| 41 Bob Wellman | 8.00 | 109 Ted Wilks | 6.00 | 177 Bill Wight | 6.00 | 245 Sherry Robertson | 6.00 |
| 42 Lou Kretlow | 8.00 | 110 Dutch Leonard | 6.00 | 178 Cass Michaels | 6.00 | 246 George Kell | 15.00 |
| 43 Ray Scarborough | 8.00 | 111 Harry Lowrey | 6.00 | 179 Frank Smith | 6.00 | 247 Randy Gumpert | 6.00 |
| 44 Con Dempsey | 8.00 | 112 Henry Majeski | 6.00 | 180 Charley Maxwell | 6.00 | 248 Frank Shea | 6.00 |
| 45 Ed Joost | 8.00 | 113 Dick Sisler | 6.00 | 181 Bob Swift | 6.00 | 249 Bobby Adams | 6.00 |
| 46 Gordon Goldsberry | 8.00 | 114 Willard Ramsdell | 6.00 | 182 Bill Hitchcock | 5.50 | 250 Carl Erskine | 15.00 |
| 47 Willie Jones | 8.00 | 115 George Munger | 6.00 | 183 Erv Dusak | 6.00 | 251 Chico Carrasquel | 13.50 |
| 48 Joe Page* | 12.00 | 116 Carl Scheib | 6.00 | 184 Bob Ramazzotti | 6.00 | 252 Vern Bickford | 13.50 |
| 49 Johnny Sain* | 15.00 | 117 Sherman Lollar | 6.00 | 185 Bill Nicholson | 6.00 | 253 Johnny Berardino | 13.50 |
| 50 Marv Rickert | 8.00 | 118 Ken Raffensberger | 6.00 | 186 Walt Masterson | 6.00 | 254 Joe Dobson | 13.50 |
| 51 Jim Russell | 8.00 | 119 Maurice McDermott | 6.00 | 187 Bob Miller | 6.00 | 255 Clyde Vollmer | 13.50 |
| 52 Don Mueller | 8.00 | 120 Bob Chakales | 6.00 | 188 Clarence Podbielan | 6.00 | 256 Pete Suder | 13.50 |
| 53 Chris Van Cuyk | 8.00 | 121 Gus Niarhos | 6.00 | 189 Harold Reiser | 6.00 | 257 Bob Avila | 13.50 |
| 54 Leo Kiely | 8.00 | 122 Jack Jensen | 9.00 | 190 Don Johnson | 6.00 | 258 Steve Gromek | 13.50 |
| 55 Ray Boone | 8.00 | 123 Eddie Yost | 6.00 | 191 Yogi Berra | 70.00 | 259 Bob Addis | 13.50 |
| 56 Tom Glaviano | 8.00 | 124 Monte Kennedy | 6.00 | 192 Myron Ginsberg | 6.00 | 260 Pete Castiglione | 13.50 |
| 57 Eddie Lopat | 14.00 | 125 Bill Rigney | 6.00 | 193 Harry Simpson | 6.00 | 261 Willie Mays | 425.00 |
| 58 Bob Mahoney | 8.00 | 126 Fred Hutchinson | 6.00 | 194 Joe Hatten | 6.00 | 262 Virgil Trucks | 13.50 |
| 59 Robin Roberts | 27.00 | 127 Paul Minner | 6.00 | 195 Orestes Minoso (R) | 15.00 | 263 Harry Brecheen | 13.50 |
| 60 Sid Hudson | 8.00 | 128 Don Bollweg | 6.00 | 196 Solly Hemus | 6.00 | 264 Roy Hartsfield | 13.50 |
| 61 Tookie Gilbert | 8.00 | 129 Johnny Mize | 20.00 | 197 George Strickland | 6.00 | 265 Chuck Diering | 13.50 |
| 62 Chuck Stobbs | 8.00 | 130 Sheldon Jones | 6.00 | 198 Phil Haugstad | 6.00 | 266 Murry Dickson | 13.50 |
| 63 Howie Pollett | 8.00 | 131 Morris Martin | 6.00 | 199 George Zuverink | 6.00 | 267 Sid Gordon | 13.50 |
| 64 Roy Sievers | 8.00 | 132 Clyde Klutz | 6.00 | 200 Ralph Houk (R) | 16.00 | 268 Bob Lemon | 55.00 |
| 65 Enos Slaughter | 21.00 | 133 Al Widmar | 6.00 | 201 Alex Kellner | 6.00 | 269 Willard Nixon | 13.50 |
| 66 Preacher Roe | 13.00 | 134 Joe Tipton | 6.00 | 202 Joe Collins | 6.00 | 270 Lou Brissie | 13.50 |
| 67 Allie Reynolds | 12.00 | 135 Dixie Howell | 6.00 | 203 Curt Simmons | 6.00 | 271 Jim Delsing | 13.50 |
| 68 Cliff Chambers | 8.00 | 136 Johnny Schmitz | 6.00 | 204 Ron Northey | 6.00 | 272 Mike Garcia | 13.50 |

| NO. PLAYER | MINT | NO. PLAYER | MINT | NO. PLAYER | MINT | NO. PLAYER | MINT |
|---|---|---|---|---|---|---|---|
| 273 Erv Palica | 13.50 | 307 Frank Campos | 12.00 | 341 Hal Jeffcoat | 60.00 | 375 Jack Merson | 60.00 |
| 274 Ralph Branca | 13.50 | 308 Luis Aloma | 12.00 | 342 Clem Labine | 60.00 | 376 Faye Throneberry | 60.00 |
| 275 Pat Mullin | 13.50 | 309 Jim Busby | 12.00 | 343 Dick Gernert | 60.00 | 377 Chuck Dressen | 60.00 |
| 276 Jim Wilson | 13.50 | 310 George Metkovich | 12.00 | 344 Ewell Blackwell | 60.00 | 378 Les Fusselman | 60.00 |
| 277 Early Wynn | 70.00 | 311 Mickey Mantle | 3000.00 | 345 Sammy White | 60.00 | 379 Joe Rossi | 60.00 |
| 278 Al Clark | 13.50 | 312 Jackie Robinson | 450.00 | 346 George Spencer | 60.00 | 380 Clem Koshorek | 60.00 |
| 279 Ed Stewart | 13.50 | 313 Bobby Thomson | 90.00 | 347 Joe Adcock | 80.00 | 381 Milton Stock | 60.00 |
| 280 Cloyd Boyer | 13.50 | 314 Roy Campanella | 525.00 | 348 Bob Kelly | 60.00 | 382 Samuel Jones | 60.00 |
| 281 Tom Brown | 20.00 | 315 Leo Durocher (Mgr) | 120.00 | 349 Bob Cain | 60.00 | 383 Del Wilber | 60.00 |
| 282 Birdie Tebbetts | 20.00 | 316 Dave Williams | 60.00 | 350 Cal Abrams | 60.00 | 384 Frank Crosetti | 120.00 |
| 283 Phil Masi | 20.00 | 317 Connie Marrerro | 60.00 | 351 Alvin Dark | 70.00 | 385 Herman Franks | 60.00 |
| 284 Hank Arft | 20.00 | 318 Hal Gregg | 60.00 | 352 Karl Drews | 70.00 | 386 Eddie Yuhas | 60.00 |
| 285 Cliff Fannin | 20.00 | 319 Al Walker | 60.00 | 353 Robert Del Greco | 70.00 | 387 Bill Meyer | 60.00 |
| 286 Joe DeMaestri | 20.00 | 320 John Rutherford | 60.00 | 354 Fred Hatfield | 70.00 | 388 Bob Chipman | 60.00 |
| 287 Steve Bilko | 20.00 | 321 Joe Black (R) | 80.00 | 355 Bobby Morgan | 70.00 | 389 Ben Wade | 60.00 |
| 288 Chet Nichols | 20.00 | 322 Randy Jackson | 60.00 | 356 Toby Atwell | 70.00 | 390 Glenn Nelson | 60.00 |
| 289 Tommy Holmes | 20.00 | 323 Bubba Church | 60.00 | 357 Smokey Burgess | 70.00 | 391 Ben Chapman | 60.00 |
| 290 Joe Astroth | 20.00 | 324 Warren Hacker | 60.00 | 358 John Kucab | 70.00 | (photo of Sam Chapman) | |
| 291 Gil Coan | 20.00 | 325 Bill Serena | 60.00 | 359 Dee Fondy | 70.00 | 392 Hoyt Wilhelm (R) | 275.00 |
| 292 Floyd Baker | 20.00 | 326 George Shuba | 60.00 | 360 George Crowe | 70.00 | 393 Ebba St. Claire | 60.00 |
| 293 Sibby Sisti | 20.00 | 327 Archie Wilson | 60.00 | 361 Bill Posedel | 70.00 | 394 Billy Herman | 90.00 |
| 294 Walker Cooper | 20.00 | 328 Bob Borkowski | 60.00 | 362 Kenny Heintzelman | 70.00 | 395 Jake Pitler | 60.00 |
| 295 Phil Cavarretta | 20.00 | 329 Ivan Delock | 60.00 | 363 Dick Rozek | 70.00 | 396 Dick Williams (R) | 105.00 |
| 296 Red Rolfe | 20.00 | 330 Turk Lown | 60.00 | 364 Clyde Sukeforth | 70.00 | 397 Forrest Main | 60.00 |
| 297 Andy Seminick | 20.00 | 331 Tom Morgan | 60.00 | 365 Cookie Lavagetto | 70.00 | 398 Hal Rice | 60.00 |
| 298 Bob Ross | 20.00 | 332 Anthony Bartirome | 60.00 | 366 Dave Madison | 70.00 | 399 Jim Fridley | 60.00 |
| 299 Ray Murray | 20.00 | 333 Pee Wee Reese | 340.00 | 367 Bob Thorpe | 70.00 | 400 Bill Dickey | 275.00 |
| 300 Barney McCosky | 20.00 | 334 Wilmer Mizell | 60.00 | 368 Ed Wright | 70.00 | 401 Bob Schultz | 60.00 |
| 301 Bob Porterfield | 12.00 | 335 Ted Lepcio | 60.00 | 369 Dick Groat (R) | 140.00 | 402 Earl Harrist | 60.00 |
| 302 Max Surkont | 12.00 | 336 Dave Koslo | 60.00 | 370 Bill Hoeft | 60.00 | 403 Bill Miller | 60.00 |
| 303 Harry Dorish | 12.00 | 337 Jim Hearn | 60.00 | 371 Bob Hofman | 60.00 | 404 Dick Brodowski | 60.00 |
| 304 Sam Dente | 12.00 | 338 Sal Yvars | 60.00 | 372 Gil McDougald (R) | 135.00 | 405 Eddie Pellagrini | 60.00 |
| 305 Paul Richards | 12.00 | 339 Russ Meyer | 60.00 | 373 Jim Turner | 60.00 | 406 Joseph Nuxhall (R) | 90.00 |
| 306 Lou Sleater | 12.00 | 340 Bob Hooper | 60.00 | 374 Al Benton | 60.00 | 407 Eddie Mathews (R) | 575.00 |

# 1953 Topps.... Complete Set of 274 Cards—Value $2500.00

Features the rookie cards of Johnny Padres and Jim Gilliam. Although the cards are numbered up to 280, there are only 274 cards in the set. Six cards were not issued—numbers 253, 261, 267, 268, 271 and 275. The high number series is 221 to 280. Card size 2⅝" x 3¾".

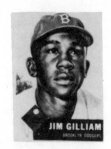
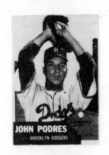

| NO. PLAYER | MINT | NO. PLAYER | MINT | NO. PLAYER | MINT | NO. PLAYER | MINT |
|---|---|---|---|---|---|---|---|
| 1 Jackie Robinson | 110.00 | 23 Toby Atwell | 3.50 | 45 Grady Hatton | 3.50 | 67 Roy Sievers | 3.50 |
| 2 Luke Easter | 3.50 | 24 Ferris Fain | 3.50 | 46 John Klippstein | 3.50 | 68 Del Rice | 3.50 |
| 3 George Crowe | 3.50 | 25 Ray Boone | 3.50 | 47 Bubba Church | 3.50 | 69 Dick Brodowski | 3.50 |
| 4 Benjamin Wade | 3.50 | 26 Dale Mitchell | 3.50 | 48 Bob Del Greco | 3.50 | 70 Eddie Yuhas | 3.50 |
| 5 Joe Dobson | 3.50 | 27 Roy Campanella | 60.00 | 49 Faye Throneberry | 3.50 | 71 Tony Bartirome | 3.50 |
| 6 Sam Jones | 3.50 | 28 Eddie Pellagrini | 3.50 | 50 Chuck Dressen | 3.50 | 72 Fred Hutchison | 3.50 |
| 7 Bob Borkowski | 3.50 | 29 Hal Jeffcoat | 3.50 | 51 Frank Campos | 3.50 | 73 Eddie Robinson | 3.50 |
| 8 Clem Koshorek | 3.50 | 30 Willard Nixon | 3.50 | 52 Ted Gray | 3.50 | 74 Joe Rossi | 3.50 |
| 9 Joe Collins | 3.50 | 31 Ewell Blackwell | 3.50 | 53 Sherman Lollar | 3.50 | 75 Mike Garcia | 3.50 |
| 10 Smokey Burgess | 3.50 | 32 Clyde Vollmer | 3.50 | 54 Bob Feller | 32.00 | 76 Pee Wee Reese | 27.00 |
| 11 Sal Yvars | 3.50 | 33 Bob Kennedy | 3.50 | 55 Maurice McDermott | 3.50 | 77 John Mize | 11.00 |
| 12 Howie Judson | 3.50 | 34 George Shuba | 3.50 | 56 Gerald Staley | 3.50 | 78 Al Schoendienst | 5.00 |
| 13 Connie Marrero | 3.50 | 35 Irv Noren | 3.50 | 57 Carl Scheib | 3.50 | 79 Johnny Wyrostek | 3.50 |
| 14 Clem Labine | 3.50 | 36 Johnny Groth | 3.50 | 58 George Metkovich | 3.50 | 80 Jim Hegan | 3.50 |
| 15 Bobo Newsom | 3.50 | 37 Ed Mathews | 22.00 | 59 Karl Drews | 3.50 | 81 Joe Black | 3.50 |
| 16 Harry Lowrey | 3.50 | 38 Jim Hearn | 3.50 | 60 Cloyd Boyer | 3.50 | 82 Mickey Mantle | 550.00 |
| 17 Billy Hitchcock | 3.50 | 39 Eddie Miksis | 3.50 | 61 Early Wynn | 12.00 | 83 Howie Pollett | 3.50 |
| 18 Ted Lepcio | 3.50 | 40 Johnny Lipon | 3.50 | 62 Monte Irvin | 8.00 | 84 Bob Hooper | 3.50 |
| 19 Melvin Parnell | 3.50 | 41 Enos Slaughter | 13.00 | 63 Gus Niarhos | 3.50 | 85 Bobby Morgan | 3.50 |
| 20 Hank Thompson | 3.50 | 42 Gus Zernial | 3.50 | 64 David Philley | 3.50 | 86 Billy Martin | 22.00 |
| 21 Billy Johnson | 3.50 | 43 Gil McDougald | 5.00 | 65 Earl Harrist | 3.50 | 87 Ed Lopat | 7.00 |
| 22 Howie Fox | 3.50 | 44 Ellis Kinder | 3.50 | 66 Orestes Minoso | 5.00 | 88 Willie Jones | 3.50 |

| NO. | PLAYER | MINT |
|-----|--------|------|
| 89 | Chuck Stobbs | 3.50 |
| 90 | Hank Edwards | 3.50 |
| 91 | Ebba St. Claire | 3.50 |
| 92 | Paul Minner | 3.50 |
| 93 | Hal Rice | 3.50 |
| 94 | William Kennedy | 3.50 |
| 95 | Willard Marshall | 3.50 |
| 96 | Virgil Trucks | 3.50 |
| 97 | Don Kolloway | 3.50 |
| 98 | Cal Abrams | 3.50 |
| 99 | Dave Madison | 3.50 |
| 100 | Bill Miller | 3.50 |
| 101 | Ted Wilks | 3.50 |
| 102 | Connie Ryan | 3.50 |
| 103 | Joe Astroth | 3.50 |
| 104 | Yogi Berra | 50.00 |
| 105 | Joe Nuxhall | 3.50 |
| 106 | John Antonelli | 3.50 |
| 107 | Danny O'Connell | 3.50 |
| 108 | Bob Porterfield | 3.50 |
| 109 | Alvin Dark | 5.00 |
| 110 | Herman Wehmeier | 3.50 |
| 111 | Hank Sauer | 3.50 |
| 112 | Ned Garver | 3.50 |
| 113 | Jerry Priddy | 3.50 |
| 114 | Phil Rizzuto | 22.00 |
| 115 | George Spencer | 3.50 |
| 116 | Frank Smith | 3.50 |
| 117 | Sidney Gordon | 3.50 |
| 118 | Gus Bell | 3.50 |
| 119 | Johnny Sain | 6.00 |
| 120 | Davey Williams | 3.50 |
| 121 | Walt Dropo | 3.50 |
| 122 | Elmer Valo | 3.50 |
| 123 | Tommy Byrne | 3.50 |
| 124 | Sibby Sisti | 3.50 |
| 125 | Dick Williams | 4.00 |
| 126 | Billy Connelly | 3.50 |
| 127 | Clint Courtney | 3.50 |
| 128 | Wilmer Mizell | 3.50 |
| 129 | Keith Thomas | 3.50 |
| 130 | Turk Lown | 3.50 |
| 131 | Harry Byrd | 3.50 |
| 132 | Tom Morgan | 3.50 |
| 133 | Gil Coan | 3.50 |
| 134 | Rube Walker | 3.50 |
| 135 | Al Rosen | 10.00 |
| 136 | Ken Heintzelman | 3.50 |
| 137 | John Rutherford | 3.50 |
| 138 | George Kell | 12.00 |
| 139 | Sammy White | 3.50 |
| 140 | Tommy Glaviano | 3.50 |
| 141 | Allie Reynolds | 6.00 |
| 142 | Vic Wertz | 3.50 |
| 143 | Billy Pierce | 5.00 |
| 144 | Bob Schultz | 3.50 |
| 145 | Harry Dorish | 3.50 |
| 146 | Granville Hamner | 3.50 |
| 147 | Warren Spahn | 27.00 |
| 148 | Mickey Grasso | 3.50 |
| 149 | Dom DiMaggio | 9.00 |
| 150 | Harry Simpson | 3.50 |
| 151 | Hoyt Wilhelm | 14.00 |
| 152 | Bob Adams | 3.50 |
| 153 | Andy Seminick | 3.50 |
| 154 | Dick Groat | 5.00 |
| 155 | Dutch Leonard | 3.50 |
| 156 | Jim Rivera | 3.50 |
| 157 | Bob Addis | 3.50 |
| 158 | John Logan | 3.50 |
| 159 | Wayne Terwilliger | 3.50 |
| 160 | Bob Young | 3.50 |
| 161 | Vern Bickford | 3.50 |
| 162 | Ted Kluszewski | 3.50 |
| 163 | Fred Hatfield | 3.50 |
| 164 | Frank Shea | 3.50 |
| 165 | Billy Hoeft | 3.50 |
| 166 | Bill Hunter | 2.50 |
| 167 | Art Schult | 2.50 |
| 168 | Willard Schmidt | 2.50 |
| 169 | Dizzy Trout | 2.50 |
| 170 | Bill Werle | 2.50 |
| 171 | Bill Glynn | 2.50 |
| 172 | Rip Repulski | 2.50 |
| 173 | Preston Ward | 2.50 |
| 174 | Billy Loes | 2.50 |
| 175 | Ronald Kline | 2.50 |
| 176 | Don Hoak | 2.50 |
| 177 | Jim Dyck | 2.50 |
| 178 | Jim Waugh | 2.50 |
| 179 | Gene Hermanski | 2.50 |
| 180 | Virgil Stallcup | 2.50 |
| 181 | Al Zarilla | 2.50 |
| 182 | Robert Hofman | 2.50 |
| 183 | Stuart Miller | 2.50 |
| 184 | Hal Brown | 2.50 |
| 185 | Jim Pendleton | 2.50 |
| 186 | Charles Bishop | 2.50 |
| 187 | Jim Fridley | 2.50 |
| 188 | Andy Carey | 2.50 |
| 189 | Ray Jablonski | 2.50 |
| 190 | Dixie Walker | 2.50 |
| 191 | Ralph Kiner | 16.00 |
| 192 | Wally Westlake | 2.50 |
| 193 | Mike Clark | 2.50 |
| 194 | Eddie Kazak | 2.50 |
| 195 | Eddie McGhee | 2.50 |
| 196 | Bob Keegan | 2.50 |
| 197 | Del Crandall | 2.50 |
| 198 | Forrest Main | 2.50 |
| 199 | Marion Fricano | 2.50 |
| 200 | Gordon Goldsberry | 2.50 |
| 201 | Paul LaPalme | 2.50 |
| 202 | Carl Sawatski | 2.50 |
| 203 | Cliff Fannin | 2.50 |
| 204 | Dick Bokelmann | 2.50 |
| 205 | Vern Benson | 2.50 |
| 206 | Ed Bailey | 2.50 |
| 207 | Whitey Ford | 27.00 |
| 208 | Jim Wilson | 2.50 |
| 209 | Jim Greengrass | 2.50 |
| 210 | Bob Cerv | 2.50 |
| 211 | J.W. Porter | 2.50 |
| 212 | Jack Dittmer | 2.50 |
| 213 | Ray Scarborough | 2.50 |
| 214 | Bill Bruton | 2.50 |
| 215 | Gene Conley | 2.50 |
| 216 | Jim Hughes | 2.50 |
| 217 | Murray Wall | 2.50 |
| 218 | Les Fusselman | 2.50 |
| 219 | Pete Runnels | 2.50 |
| | (Photo of Don Johnson) | |
| 220 | Satchell Paige | 65.00 |
| 221 | Bob Milliken | 12.00 |
| 222 | Vic Janowicz | 15.00 |
| 223 | John O'Brien | 12.00 |
| 224 | Lou Sleater | 12.00 |
| 225 | Bobby Shantz | 16.00 |
| 226 | Edward Erautt | 12.00 |
| 227 | Morris Martin | 12.00 |
| 228 | Hal Newhouser | 25.00 |
| 229 | Rocky Krsnich | 12.00 |
| 230 | Johnny Lindell | 12.00 |
| 231 | Solly Hemus | 12.00 |
| 232 | Dick Kokos | 12.00 |
| 233 | Al Aber | 12.00 |
| 234 | Ray Murray | 12.00 |
| 235 | John Hetki | 12.00 |
| 236 | Harold Perkowski | 12.00 |
| 237 | Clarence Podbielan | 12.00 |
| 238 | Cal Hogue | 12.00 |
| 239 | Jim Delsing | 12.00 |
| 240 | Fred Marsh | 12.00 |
| 241 | Al Sima | 12.00 |
| 242 | Charlie Silvera | 12.00 |
| 243 | Carlos Bernier | 12.00 |
| 244 | Willie Mays | 550.00 |
| 245 | Bill Norman | 12.00 |
| 246 | Roy Face (R) | 20.00 |
| 247 | Mike Sandlock | 12.00 |
| 248 | Gene Stephens | 12.00 |
| 249 | Ed O'Brien | 12.00 |
| 250 | Bob Wilson | 12.00 |
| 251 | Sid Hudson | 12.00 |
| 252 | Henry Foiles | 12.00 |
| 254 | Preacher Roe | 20.00 |
| 255 | Dixie Howell | 12.00 |
| 256 | Les Peden | 12.00 |
| 257 | Bob Boyd | 12.00 |
| 258 | Jim Gilliam (R) | 75.00 |
| 259 | Roy McMillan | 12.00 |
| 260 | Sam Calderone | 12.00 |
| 262 | Bob Oldis | 12.00 |
| 263 | John Podres (R) | 55.00 |
| 264 | Gene Woodling | 25.00 |
| 265 | Jackie Jensen | 35.00 |
| 266 | Bob Cain | 12.00 |
| 269 | Duane Pillette | 12.00 |
| 270 | Vern Stephens | 12.00 |
| 272 | Bill Antonello | 12.00 |
| 273 | Harvey Haddix (R) | 20.00 |
| 274 | John Riddle | 12.00 |
| 276 | Ken Raffensberger | 12.00 |
| 277 | Don Lund | 12.00 |
| 278 | Willie Miranda | 12.00 |
| 279 | Joe Coleman | 12.00 |
| 280 | Milt Bolling (R) | 45.00 |

## 1954 Topps.... Complete Set of 250 Cards—Value $1250.00

Features the rookie cards of Hank Aaron, Al Kaline and Ernie Banks. Card size 2⅝" x 3¾". Topps' signed Ted Williams to a special contract for this set, and he appears on two cards.

| NO. | PLAYER | MINT |
|-----|--------|------|
| 1 | Ted Williams | 90.00 |
| 2 | Gus Zernial | 1.50 |
| 3 | Monte Irvin | 6.00 |
| 4 | Hank Sauer | 1.50 |
| 5 | Ed Lopat | 3.00 |
| 6 | Pete Runnels | 1.50 |
| 7 | Ted Kluszewski | 4.00 |
| 8 | Bobby Young | 1.50 |
| 9 | Harvey Haddix | 1.50 |
| 10 | Jackie Robinson | 55.00 |
| 11 | Paul Smith | 1.50 |
| 12 | Del Crandall | 1.50 |
| 13 | Billy Martin | 20.00 |
| 14 | Preacher Roe | 3.00 |
| 15 | Al Rosen | 4.00 |
| 16 | Vic Janowicz | 1.50 |
| 17 | Phil Rizzuto | 20.00 |
| 18 | Walt Dropo | 1.50 |
| 19 | Johnny Lipon | 1.50 |
| 20 | Warren Spahn | 20.00 |

| NO. PLAYER | MINT | NO. PLAYER | MINT | NO. PLAYER | MINT | NO. PLAYER | MINT |
|---|---|---|---|---|---|---|---|
| 21 Bobby Shantz | 1.50 | 79 Andy Pafko | 1.50 | 137 Wally Moon | 2.50 | 193 Johnny Hopp | 1.50 |
| 22 Jim Greengrass | 1.50 | 80 Jackie Jensen | 3.00 | 138 Bob Borkowski | 1.50 | 194 Bill Sarni | 1.50 |
| 23 Luke Easter | 1.50 | 81 Dave Hoskins | 1.50 | 139 The O'Brien's: | 3.00 | 195 Bill Consolo | 1.50 |
| 24 Granny Hamner | 1.50 | 82 Milt Bolling | 1.50 | Johnny O'Brien, | | 196 Stan Jok | 1.50 |
| 25 Harvey Kuenn (R) | 5.00 | 83 Joe Collins | 1.50 | Eddie O'Brien | | 197 L. Rowe | 1.50 |
| 26 Ray Jablonski | 1.50 | 84 Dick Cole | 1.50 | 140 Tom Wright | 1.50 | 198 Carl Sawatski | 1.50 |
| 27 Ferris Fain | 1.50 | 85 Bob Turley (R) | 4.00 | 141 Joe Jay | 1.50 | 199 Glenn Nelson | 1.50 |
| 28 Paul Minner | 1.50 | 86 Billy Herman | 3.00 | 142 Tom Poholsky | 1.50 | 200 Larry Jansen | 1.50 |
| 29 Jim Hegan | 1.50 | 87 Roy Face | 1.50 | 143 Rollie Hemsley | 1.50 | 201 Al Kaline (R) | 95.00 |
| 30 Ed Mathews | 16.00 | 88 Matt Batts | 1.50 | 144 Bill Werle | 1.50 | 202 Bob Purkey | 1.50 |
| 31 John Klippstein | 1.50 | 89 Howie Pollet | 1.50 | 145 Elmer Valo | 1.50 | 203 Harry Brecheen | 1.50 |
| 32 Duke Snider | 35.00 | 90 Willie Mays | 110.00 | 146 Don Johnson | 1.50 | 204 Angel Scull | 1.50 |
| 33 Johnny Schmitz | 1.50 | 91 Bob Oldis | 1.50 | 147 John Riddle | 1.50 | 205 Johnny Sain | 4.00 |
| 34 Jim Rivera | 1.50 | 92 Wally Westlake | 1.50 | 148 Bob Trice | 1.50 | 206 Ray Crone | 1.50 |
| 35 Junior Gilliam | 3.00 | 93 Sid Hudson | 1.50 | 149 Jim Robertson | 1.50 | 207 Tom Oliver | 1.50 |
| 36 Hoyt Wilhelm | 8.00 | 94 Ernie Banks (R) | 95.00 | 150 Dick Kryhoski | 1.50 | 208 Grady Hatton | 1.50 |
| 37 Whitey Ford | 20.00 | 95 Hal Rice | 1.50 | 151 Alex Grammas | 1.50 | 209 Charlie Thompson | 1.50 |
| 38 Eddie Stanky | 1.50 | 96 Charlie Silvera | 1.50 | 152 Mike Blyzka | 1.50 | 210 Bob Buhl | 1.50 |
| 39 Sherm Lollar | 1.50 | 97 Jerry Lane | 1.50 | 153 Albert Walker | 1.50 | 211 Don Hoak | 1.50 |
| 40 Mel Parnell | 1.50 | 98 Joe Black | 2.00 | 154 Mike Fornieles | 1.50 | 212 Bob Micelotta | 1.50 |
| 41 Willie Jones | 1.50 | 99 Bob Hofman | 1.50 | 155 Bob Kennedy | 1.50 | 213 John Fitzpatrick | 1.50 |
| 42 Don Mueller | 1.50 | 100 Bob Keegan | 1.50 | 156 Joe Coleman | 1.50 | 214 A. Portocarrero | 1.50 |
| 43 Dick Groat | 2.50 | 101 Gene Woodling | 2.00 | 157 Don Lenhardt | 1.50 | 215 Ed McGhee | 1.50 |
| 44 Ned Garver | 1.50 | 102 Gil Hodges | 20.00 | 158 Peanuts Lowrey | 1.50 | 216 Al Sima | 1.50 |
| 45 Richie Ashburn | 5.00 | 103 Jim Lemon | 1.50 | 159 Dave Philley | 1.50 | 217 Paul Schreiber | 1.50 |
| 46 Ken Raffensberger | 1.50 | 104 Mike Sandlock | 1.50 | 160 Red Kress | 1.50 | 218 Fred Marsh | 1.50 |
| 47 Ellis Kinder | 1.50 | 105 Andy Carey | 1.50 | 161 John Hetki | 1.50 | 219 Charles Kress | 1.50 |
| 48 Bill Hunter | 1.50 | 106 Dick Kokos | 1.50 | 162 Herman Wehmeier | 1.50 | 220 Ruben Gomez | 1.50 |
| 49 Ray Murray | 1.50 | 107 Duane Pillette | 1.50 | 163 Frank House | 1.50 | 221 Dick Brodowski | 1.50 |
| 50 Yogi Berra | 35.00 | 108 Thornton Kipper | 1.50 | 164 Stuart Miller | 1.50 | 222 Bill Wilson | 1.50 |
| 51 Johnny Lindell | 3.00 | 109 Bill Bruton | 1.50 | 165 Jim Pendleton | 1.50 | 223 Joe Haynes | 1.50 |
| 52 Vic Power | 3.00 | 110 Harry Dorish | 1.50 | 166 Johnny Podres | 3.00 | 224 Dick Weik | 1.50 |
| 53 Jack Dittmer | 3.00 | 111 Jim Delsing | 1.50 | 167 Don Lund | 1.50 | 225 Don Liddle | 1.50 |
| 54 Vern Stephens | 3.00 | 112 Bill Renna | 1.50 | 168 Morrie Martin | 1.50 | 226 Jehosie Heard | 1.50 |
| 55 Phil Cavarretta | 3.00 | 113 Bob Boyd | 1.50 | 169 Jim Hughes | 1.50 | 227 Buster Mills | 1.50 |
| 56 Willie Miranda | 3.00 | 114 Dean Stone | 1.50 | 170 Jim Rhodes | 1.50 | 228 Gene Hermanski | 1.50 |
| 57 Luis Aloma | 3.00 | 115 Rip Repulski | 1.50 | 171 Leo Kiely | 1.50 | 229 Bob Talbot | 1.50 |
| 58 Bob Wilson | 3.00 | 116 Steve Bilko | 1.50 | 172 Hal Brown | 1.50 | 230 Bob Kuzava | 1.50 |
| 59 Gene Conley | 3.00 | 117 Solly Hemus | 1.50 | 173 Jack Harshman | 1.50 | 231 Roy Smalley | 1.50 |
| 60 Frank Baumholtz | 3.00 | 118 Carl Scheib | 1.50 | 174 Tom Qualters | 1.50 | 232 Lou Limmer | 1.50 |
| 61 Bob Cain | 3.00 | 119 John Antonelli | 1.50 | 175 Frank Leja | 1.50 | 233 Augie Galan | 1.50 |
| 62 Eddie Robinson | 3.00 | 120 Roy McMillan | 1.50 | 176 Robert Kelley | 1.50 | 234 Jerry Lynch | 1.50 |
| 63 Johnny Pesky | 3.00 | 121 Clem Labine | 1.50 | 177 Bob Milliken | 1.50 | 235 Vernon Law | 1.50 |
| 64 Hank Thompson | 3.00 | 122 Johnny Logan | 1.50 | 178 Bill Glynn | 1.50 | 236 Paul Penson | 1.50 |
| 65 Bob Swift | 3.00 | 123 Bobby Adams | 1.50 | 179 Gair Allie | 1.50 | 237 Mike Ryba | 1.50 |
| 66 Thad Lepcio | 3.00 | 124 Marion Fricano | 1.50 | 180 Wes Westrum | 1.50 | 238 Al Aber | 1.50 |
| 67 Jim Willis | 3.00 | 125 Harry Perkowski | 1.50 | 181 Mel Roach | 1.50 | 239 Bill Skowron (R) | 4.00 |
| 68 Sammy Calderone | 3.00 | 126 Ben Wade | 1.50 | 182 Chuck Harmon | 1.50 | 240 Sam Mele | 1.50 |
| 69 Bud Podbielan | 3.00 | 127 Steve O'Neill | 1.50 | 183 Earle Combs | 3.00 | 241 Bob Miller | 1.50 |
| 70 Larry Doby | 5.00 | 128 Hank Aaron (R) | 275.00 | 184 Ed Bailey | 1.50 | 242 Curt Roberts | 1.50 |
| 71 Frank Smith | 3.00 | 129 Forrest Jacobs | 1.50 | 185 Chuck Stobbs | 1.50 | 243 Ray Blades | 1.50 |
| 72 Preston Ward | 3.00 | 130 Hank Bauer | 3.00 | 186 Karl Olson | 1.50 | 244 Leroy Wheat | 1.50 |
| 73 Wayne Terwilliger | 3.00 | 131 Reno Bertoia | 1.50 | 187 Heinie Manush | 3.00 | 245 Roy Sievers | 1.50 |
| 74 Bill Taylor | 3.00 | 132 Tommy Lasorda (R) | 13.00 | 188 Dave Jolly | 1.50 | 246 Howie Fox | 1.50 |
| 75 Fred Haney | 3.00 | 133 Del Baker | 1.50 | 189 Bob Ross | 1.50 | 247 Ed Mayo | 1.50 |
| 76 Bob Scheffing | 1.50 | 134 Cal Hogue | 1.50 | 190 Ray Herbert | 1.50 | 248 Al Smith | 1.50 |
| 77 Ray Boone | 1.50 | 135 Joe Presko | 1.50 | 191 Dick Schofield | 1.50 | 249 Wilmer Mizell | 1.50 |
| 78 Ted Kazanski | 1.50 | 136 Connie Ryan | 1.50 | 192 Ellis Deal | 1.50 | 250 Ted Williams | 90.00 |

## 1955 Topps.... Complete Set of 206 Cards—Value $1000.00

Features the rookie cards of Roberto Clemente, Sandy Koufax and Harmon Killebrew. Topps' switched to a horizontal format in 1955. Card size 2⅝" x 3¾". Four cards originally intended to be issued—175, 186, 203 and 209 were withdrawn. The high number series is 161 to 210.

# 1955 Topps (Continued)

| NO. | PLAYER | MINT |
|---|---|---|
| 1 | Dusty Rhodes | 5.00 |
| 2 | Ted Williams | 50.00 |
| 3 | Art Fowler | 1.25 |
| 4 | Al Kaline | 20.00 |
| 5 | Jim Gilliam | 3.00 |
| 6 | Stan Hack | 1.25 |
| 7 | Jim Hegan | 1.25 |
| 8 | Hal Smith | 1.25 |
| 9 | Bob Miller | 1.25 |
| 10 | Bob Keegan | 1.25 |
| 11 | Ferris Fain | 1.25 |
| 12 | Vernon Thies | 1.25 |
| 13 | Fred Marsh | 1.25 |
| 14 | Jim Finigan | 1.25 |
| 15 | Jim Pendleton | 1.25 |
| 16 | Roy Sievers | 1.25 |
| 17 | Bobby Hofman | 1.25 |
| 18 | Russ Kemmerer | 1.25 |
| 19 | Billy Herman | 2.50 |
| 20 | Andy Carey | 1.50 |
| 21 | Alex Grammas | 1.25 |
| 22 | Bill Skowron | 2.50 |
| 23 | Jack Parks | 1.25 |
| 24 | Hal Newhouser | 2.00 |
| 25 | Johnny Podres | 2.50 |
| 26 | Dick Groat | 1.50 |
| 27 | Billy Gardner | 1.50 |
| 28 | Ernie Banks | 20.00 |
| 29 | Herman Wehmeier | 1.25 |
| 30 | Vic Power | 1.25 |
| 31 | Warren Spahn | 12.00 |
| 32 | Ed McGhee | 1.25 |
| 33 | Tom Qualters | 1.25 |
| 34 | Wayne Terwilliger | 1.25 |
| 35 | Dave Jolly | 1.25 |
| 36 | Leo Kiely | 1.25 |
| 37 | Joe Cunningham | 1.25 |
| 38 | Bob Turley | 2.50 |
| 39 | Billy Glynn | 1.25 |
| 40 | Don Hoak | 1.25 |
| 41 | Chuck Stobbs | 1.25 |
| 42 | John McCall | 1.25 |
| 43 | Harvey Haddix | 2.00 |
| 44 | Harold Valentine | 1.25 |
| 45 | Hank Sauer | 1.25 |
| 46 | Ted Kazanski | 1.25 |
| 47 | Hank Aaron | 60.00 |
| 48 | Bob Kennedy | 1.25 |
| 49 | J.W. Porter | 1.25 |
| 50 | Jackie Robinson | 40.00 |
| 51 | Jim Hughes | 1.25 |
| 52 | Bill Tremel | 1.25 |

| NO. | PLAYER | MINT |
|---|---|---|
| 53 | Bill Taylor | 1.25 |
| 54 | Lou Limmer | 1.25 |
| 55 | Eldon Repulski | 1.25 |
| 56 | Ray Jablonski | 1.25 |
| 57 | Bill O'Dell | 1.25 |
| 58 | Manuel Rivera | 1.25 |
| 59 | Gair Allie | 1.25 |
| 60 | Dean Stone | 1.25 |
| 61 | Forrest Jacobs | 1.25 |
| 62 | Thornton Kipper | 1.25 |
| 63 | Joe Collins | 1.25 |
| 64 | Gus Triandos | 1.25 |
| 65 | Ray Boone | 1.25 |
| 66 | Ron Jackson | 1.25 |
| 67 | Wally Moon | 1.25 |
| 68 | Jim Davis | 1.25 |
| 69 | Ed Bailey | 1.25 |
| 70 | Al Rosen | 2.50 |
| 71 | Ruben Gomez | 1.25 |
| 72 | Karl Olson | 1.25 |
| 73 | Jack Shepard | 1.25 |
| 74 | Bob Borkowski | 1.25 |
| 75 | Sandy Amoros (R) | 2.50 |
| 76 | Howie Pollet | 1.25 |
| 77 | Arnold Portocarrero | 1.25 |
| 78 | Gordon Jones | 1.25 |
| 79 | Clyde Schell | 1.25 |
| 80 | Bob Grim (R) | 2.00 |
| 81 | Gene Conley | 1.25 |
| 82 | Chuck Harmon | 1.25 |
| 83 | Thomas Brewer | 1.25 |
| 84 | Camilo Pascual (R) | 2.00 |
| 85 | Don Mossi (R) | 2.00 |
| 86 | Bill Wilson | 1.25 |
| 87 | Frank House | 1.25 |
| 88 | Bob Skinner | 1.25 |
| 89 | Joe Frazier | 1.25 |
| 90 | Karl Spooner | 1.25 |
| 91 | Milton Bolling | 1.25 |
| 92 | Don Zimmer (R) | 3.00 |
| 93 | Steve Bilko | 1.25 |
| 94 | Reno Bertoia | 1.25 |
| 95 | Preston Ward | 1.25 |
| 96 | Charlie Bishop | 1.25 |
| 97 | Carlos Paula | 1.25 |
| 98 | Johnny Riddle | 1.25 |
| 99 | Frank Leja | 1.25 |
| 100 | Monte Irvin | 5.00 |
| 101 | Johnny Gray | 1.25 |
| 102 | Wally Westlake | 1.25 |
| 103 | Charlie White | 1.25 |

| NO. | PLAYER | MINT |
|---|---|---|
| 104 | Jack Harshman | 1.25 |
| 105 | Chuck Diering | 1.25 |
| 106 | Frank Sullivan | 1.25 |
| 107 | Curt Roberts | 1.25 |
| 108 | Rube Walker | 1.25 |
| 109 | Ed Lopat | 2.50 |
| 110 | Gus Zernial | 1.25 |
| 111 | Bob Milliken | 1.25 |
| 112 | Nelson King | 1.25 |
| 113 | Harry Brecheen | 1.25 |
| 114 | Louie Ortiz | 1.25 |
| 115 | Ellis Kinder | 1.25 |
| 116 | Tom Hurd | 1.25 |
| 117 | Mel Roach | 1.25 |
| 118 | Bob Purkey | 1.25 |
| 119 | Bob Lennon | 1.25 |
| 120 | Ted Kluszewski | 3.00 |
| 121 | Bill Renna | 1.25 |
| 122 | Carl Sawatski | 1.25 |
| 123 | Sandy Koufax (R) | 110.00 |
| 124 | Harmon Killebrew (R) | 50.00 |
| 125 | Ken Boyer (R) | 5.00 |
| 126 | Dick Hall | 1.25 |
| 127 | Dale Long | 1.25 |
| 128 | Ted Lepcio | 1.25 |
| 129 | Elvin Tappe | 1.25 |
| 130 | Mayo Smith | 1.25 |
| 131 | Grady Hatton | 1.25 |
| 132 | Bob Trice | 1.25 |
| 133 | Dave Hoskins | 1.25 |
| 134 | Joe Jay | 1.25 |
| 135 | Johnny O'Brien | 1.25 |
| 136 | Bunky Stewart | 1.25 |
| 137 | Harry Elliott | 1.25 |
| 138 | Ray Herbert | 1.25 |
| 139 | Steve Kraly | 1.25 |
| 140 | Mel Parnell | 1.25 |
| 141 | Tom Wright | 1.25 |
| 142 | Jerry Lynch | 1.25 |
| 143 | Dick Schofield | 1.25 |
| 144 | Joe Amalfitano | 1.25 |
| 145 | Elmer Valo | 1.25 |
| 146 | Dick Donovan | 1.25 |
| 147 | Laurin Pepper | 1.25 |
| 148 | Hal Brown | 1.25 |
| 149 | Ray Crone | 1.25 |
| 150 | Michael Higgins | 1.25 |
| 151 | Ralph Kress | 2.50 |
| 152 | Harry Agganis (R) | 4.00 |
| 153 | Bud Podbielan | 2.50 |
| 154 | Willie Miranda | 2.50 |

| NO. | PLAYER | MINT |
|---|---|---|
| 155 | Eddie Mathews | 15.00 |
| 156 | Joe Black | 4.00 |
| 157 | Bob Miller | 2.50 |
| 158 | Tommy Carroll | 2.50 |
| 159 | Johnny Schmitz | 2.50 |
| 160 | Raymond Narleski | 2.50 |
| 161 | Chuck Tanner (R) | 5.00 |
| 162 | Joe Coleman | 4.00 |
| 163 | Faye Throneberry | 4.00 |
| 164 | Roberto Clemente (R) | 200.00 |
| 165 | Don Johnson | 4.00 |
| 166 | Hank Bauer | 10.00 |
| 167 | Tom Casagrande | 4.00 |
| 168 | Duane Pillette | 4.00 |
| 169 | Bob Oldis | 4.00 |
| 170 | Jim Pearce | 4.00 |
| 171 | Dick Brodowski | 4.00 |
| 172 | Frank Baumholtz | 4.00 |
| 173 | Bob Kline | 4.00 |
| 174 | Rudy Minarcin | 4.00 |
| 176 | Norm Zauchin | 4.00 |
| 177 | Jim Robertson | 4.00 |
| 178 | Bobby Adams | 4.00 |
| 179 | Jim Bolger | 4.00 |
| 180 | Clem Labine | 4.00 |
| 181 | Roy McMillan | 4.00 |
| 182 | Humberto Robinson | 4.00 |
| 183 | Anthony Jacobs | 4.00 |
| 184 | Harry Perkowski | 4.00 |
| 185 | Don Ferrarese | 4.00 |
| 187 | Gil Hodges | 40.00 |
| 188 | Charlie Silvera | 4.00 |
| 189 | Phil Rizzuto | 30.00 |
| 190 | Gene Woodling | 4.00 |
| 191 | Eddie Stanky | 4.00 |
| 192 | Jim Delsing | 4.00 |
| 193 | Johnny Sain | 6.00 |
| 194 | Willie Mays | 150.00 |
| 195 | Eddie Roebuck | 4.00 |
| 196 | Gale Wade | 4.00 |
| 197 | Al Smith | 4.00 |
| 198 | Yogi Berra | 55.00 |
| 199 | Bert Hamrick | 4.00 |
| 200 | Jack Jensen | 5.00 |
| 201 | Sherman Lollar | 4.00 |
| 202 | Jim Owens | 4.00 |
| 204 | Frank Smith | 4.00 |
| 205 | Gene Freese | 4.00 |
| 206 | Pete Daley | 4.00 |
| 207 | Bill Consolo | 4.00 |
| 208 | Ray Moore | 4.00 |
| 210 | Duke Snider | 120.00 |

## 1956 Topps....Complete Set of 340 Cards—Value $1000.00

In 1956 Topps bought its competitor—Bowman Card Co., including all of its player contracts. Topps card sets would now be larger and more complete. Card size 2⅝" x 3¾". Features the rookie card of Luis Aparicio. Card numbers 1 to 180 were printed with *gray* or *white* backs. The six team cards indicated by an *asterisk* were issued with three different *face* designs. The team card dated *1955* is worth about four times the value of the other team cards. The two checklists are not included in the complete set price.

| NO. | PLAYER | MINT |
|---|---|---|
| 1 | William Harridge (AL President) | 11.00 |
| 2 | Warren Giles (NL President) | 4.00 |

| NO. | PLAYER | MINT |
|---|---|---|
| 3 | Elmer Valo | 1.00 |
| 4 | Carlos Paula | 1.00 |
| 5 | Ted Williams | 50.00 |
| 6 | Ray Boone | 1.00 |

| NO. | PLAYER | MINT |
|---|---|---|
| 7 | Ron Negray | 1.00 |
| 8 | Walter Alston (Mgr) | 5.00 |
| 9 | Ruben Gomez | 1.00 |
| 10 | Warren Spahn | 10.00 |

| NO. | PLAYER | MINT |
|---|---|---|
| 11 | Chicago Cubs* | 3.00 |
| 12 | Andy Carey | 1.00 |
| 13 | Roy Face | 1.00 |
| 14 | Ken Boyer | 2.50 |

12

# 1956 Topps (Continued)

| NO. PLAYER | MINT | NO. PLAYER | MINT | NO. PLAYER | MINT | NO. PLAYER | MINT |
|---|---|---|---|---|---|---|---|
| 15 Ernie Banks | 13.00 | 97 Jerry Lynch | 1.00 | 179 Harry Chiti | 1.25 | 261 Bobby Shantz | 1.50 |
| 16 Hector Lopez | 1.00 | 98 Camilo Pascual | 1.00 | 180 Robin Roberts | 8.00 | 262 Howie Pollett | 1.50 |
| 17 Gene Conley | 1.00 | 99 Don Zimmer | 1.50 | 181 Billy Martin | 11.00 | 263 Bob Miller | 1.50 |
| 18 Dick Donovan | 1.00 | 100 Baltimore Orioles* | 3.00 | 182 Paul Minner | 2.00 | 264 Ray Monzant | 1.50 |
| 19 Chuck Diering | 1.00 | 101 Roy Campanella | 40.00 | 183 Stan Lopata | 2.00 | 265 Sandy Consuegra | 1.50 |
| 20 Al Kaline | 15.00 | 102 Jim Davis | 1.25 | 184 Don Bessent | 2.00 | 266 Don Ferrarese | 1.50 |
| 21 Joe Collins | 1.00 | 103 Willie Miranda | 1.25 | 185 Bill Bruton | 2.00 | 267 Bob Nieman | 1.50 |
| 22 Jim Finigan | 1.00 | 104 Bob Lennon | 1.25 | 186 Ron Jackson | 2.00 | 268 Dale Mitchell | 1.50 |
| 23 Freddie Marsh | 1.00 | 105 Al Smith | 1.25 | 187 Early Wynn | 10.00 | 269 Jack Meyer | 1.50 |
| 24 Dick Groat | 2.00 | 106 Joe Astroth | 1.25 | 188 Chicago White Sox | 3.00 | 270 Billy Loes | 1.50 |
| 25 Ted Kluszewski | 3.00 | 107 Ed Mathews | 10.00 | 189 Ned Garver | 2.00 | 271 Foster Castleman | 1.50 |
| 26 Grady Hatton | 1.00 | 108 Laurin Pepper | 1.25 | 190 Carl Furillo | 5.00 | 272 Danny O'Connell | 1.50 |
| 27 Nelson Burbrink | 1.00 | 109 Enos Slaughter | 5.00 | 191 Frank Lary | 2.50 | 273 Walker Cooper | 1.50 |
| 28 Bobby Hofman | 1.00 | 110 Yogi Berra | 30.00 | 192 Smokey Burgess | 2.00 | 274 Frank Baumholtz | 1.50 |
| 29 Jack Harshman | 1.00 | 111 Boston Red Sox | 4.00 | 193 Wilmer Mizell | 2.00 | 275 Jim Greengrass | 1.50 |
| 30 Jackie Robinson | 45.00 | 112 Dee Fondy | 1.25 | 194 Monte Irvin | 6.00 | 276 George Zuverink | 1.50 |
| 31 Hank Aaron | 50.00 | 113 Phil Rizzuto | 12.00 | 195 George Kell | 7.00 | 277 Daryl Spencer | 1.50 |
| 32 Frank House | 1.00 | 114 Jim Owens | 1.25 | 196 Tom Poholsky | 2.00 | 278 Chet Nichols | 1.50 |
| 33 Roberto Clemente | 40.00 | 115 Jackie Jensen | 2.25 | 197 Granny Hamner | 2.00 | 279 Johnny Groth | 1.50 |
| 34 Tom Brewer | 1.00 | 116 Eddie O'Brien | 1.25 | 198 Ed Fitzgerald | 2.00 | 280 Jim Gilliam | 3.00 |
| 35 Al Rosen | 2.50 | 117 Virgil Trucks | 1.25 | 199 Hank Thompson | 2.00 | 281 Art Houtteman | 1.50 |
| 36 Rudy Minarcin | 1.00 | 118 Nellie Fox | 3.00 | 200 Bob Feller | 25.00 | 282 Warren Hacker | 1.50 |
| 37 Alex Grammas | 1.00 | 119 Larry Jackson | 1.25 | 201 Rip Repulski | 2.00 | 283 Hal Smith | 1.50 |
| 38 Bob Kennedy | 1.00 | 120 Richie Ashburn | 3.00 | 202 Jim Hearn | 2.00 | 284 Ike Delock | 1.50 |
| 39 Don Mossi | 1.00 | 121 Pittsburgh Pirates | 2.50 | 203 Bill Tuttle | 2.00 | 285 Eddie Miksis | 1.50 |
| 40 Bob Turley | 2.00 | 122 Willard Nixon | 1.25 | 204 Arthur Swanson | 2.00 | 286 Bill Wight | 1.50 |
| 41 Hank Sauer | 1.00 | 123 Roy McMillan | 1.25 | 205 Whitey Lockman | 2.00 | 287 Bobby Adams | 1.50 |
| 42 Sandy Amoros | 1.00 | 124 Don Kaiser | 1.25 | 206 Erv Palica | 2.00 | 288 Bob Cerv | 1.50 |
| 43 Ray Moore | 1.00 | 125 Minnie Minoso | 2.50 | 207 Jim Small | 2.00 | 289 Hal Jeffcoat | 1.50 |
| 44 Windy McCall | 1.00 | 126 Jim Brady | 1.25 | 208 Elston Howard | 7.50 | 290 Curt Simmons | 1.50 |
| 45 Gus Zernial | 1.00 | 127 Willie Jones | 1.25 | 209 Max Surkont | 2.00 | 291 Frank Kellert | 1.50 |
| 46 Gene Freese | 1.00 | 128 Eddie Yost | 1.25 | 210 Mike Garcia | 2.00 | 292 Luis Aparicio (R) | 25.00 |
| 47 Art Fowler | 1.00 | 129 Jake Martin | 1.25 | 211 Murry Dickson | 2.00 | 293 Stu Miller | 1.50 |
| 48 Jim Hegan | 1.00 | 130 Willie Mays | 55.00 | 212 Johnny Temple | 2.00 | 294 Ernie Johnson | 1.50 |
| 49 Pedro Ramos | 1.00 | 131 Bob Roselli | 1.25 | 213 Detroit Tigers | 8.00 | 295 Clem Labine | 1.50 |
| 50 Dusty Rhodes | 1.00 | 132 Bobby Avila | 1.25 | 214 Bob Rush | 2.00 | 296 Andy Seminick | 1.50 |
| 51 Ernie Oravetz | 1.00 | 133 Ray Narleski | 1.25 | 215 Tommy Byrne | 2.00 | 297 Bob Skinner | 1.50 |
| 52 Bob Grim | 1.00 | 134 St. Louis Cardinals | 2.50 | 216 Jerry Schoonmaker | 2.00 | 298 Johnny Schmitz | 1.50 |
| 53 Arnold Portocarrero | 1.00 | 135 Mickey Mantle | 210.00 | 217 Billy Klaus | 2.00 | 299 Charley Neal | 1.50 |
| 54 Bob Keegan | 1.00 | 136 Johnny Logan | 1.25 | 218 Joe Nuxhall | 2.00 | 300 Vic Wertz | 1.50 |
| 55 Wally Moon | 1.00 | 137 Al Silvera | 1.25 | 219 Lew Burdette | 4.00 | 301 Marv Grissom | 1.50 |
| 56 Dale Long | 1.00 | 138 Johnny Antonelli | 1.25 | 220 Del Ennis | 2.00 | 302 Eddie Robinson | 1.50 |
| 57 Duke Maas | 1.00 | 139 Tommy Carroll | 1.25 | 221 Bob Friend | 2.00 | 303 Jim Dyck | 1.50 |
| 58 Ed Roebuck | 1.00 | 140 Herb Score (R) | 3.00 | 222 Dave Philley | 2.00 | 304 Frank Malzone | 1.50 |
| 59 Jose Santiago | 1.00 | 141 Joe Frazier | 1.25 | 223 Randy Jackson | 2.00 | 305 Brooks Lawrence | 1.50 |
| 60 Mayo Smith | 1.00 | 142 Gene Baker | 1.25 | 224 Bud Podbielan | 2.00 | 306 Curt Roberts | 1.50 |
| 61 Bill Skowron | 2.50 | 143 Jimmy Piersall | 2.00 | 225 Gil McDougald | 5.00 | 307 Hoyt Wilhelm | 10.00 |
| 62 Hal Smith | 1.00 | 144 Leroy Powell | 1.25 | 226 New York Giants | 8.00 | 308 Charles Harmon | 1.50 |
| 63 Roger Craig (R) | 2.00 | 145 Gil Hodges | 15.00 | 227 Russ Meyer | 2.00 | 309 Don Blasingame | 1.50 |
| 64 Luis Arroyo | 1.00 | 146 Washington Nat'l | 2.00 | 228 Mickey Vernon | 2.00 | 310 Steve Gromek | 1.50 |
| 65 Johnny O'Brien | 1.00 | 147 Earl Torgeson | 1.25 | 229 Harry Brecheen | 2.00 | 311 Hal Naragon | 1.50 |
| 66 Bob Speake | 1.00 | 148 Alvin Dark | 1.25 | 230 Chico Carrasquel | 2.00 | 312 Andy Pafko | 1.50 |
| 67 Vic Power | 1.00 | 149 Dixie Howell | 1.25 | 231 Bob Hale | 2.00 | 313 Gene Stephens | 1.50 |
| 68 Chuck Stobbs | 1.00 | 150 Duke Snider | 40.00 | 232 Toby Atwell | 2.00 | 314 Hobie Landrith | 1.50 |
| 69 Chuck Tanner | 1.00 | 151 Spook Jacobs | 1.25 | 233 Carl Erskine | 5.00 | 315 Milt Bolling | 1.50 |
| 70 Jim Rivera | 1.00 | 152 Billy Hoeft | 1.25 | 234 Pete Runnels | 2.00 | 316 Jerry Coleman | 1.50 |
| 71 Frank Sullivan | 1.00 | 153 Frank Thomas | 1.25 | 235 Don Newcombe | 9.00 | 317 Al Aber | 1.50 |
| 72 Philadelphia Phillies* | 3.00 | 154 David Pope | 1.25 | 236 Kansas C. Athletics | 3.00 | 318 Fred Hatfield | 1.50 |
| 73 Wayne Terwilliger | 1.00 | 155 Harvey Kuenn | 1.25 | 237 Jose Valdivielso | 2.00 | 319 Jack Crimian | 1.50 |
| 74 Jim King | 1.00 | 156 Wes Westrum | 1.25 | 238 Walt Dropo | 2.00 | 320 Joe Adcock | 1.50 |
| 75 Roy Sievers | 1.00 | 157 Dick Brodowski | 1.25 | 239 Harry Simpson | 2.00 | 321 Jim Konstanty | 1.50 |
| 76 Ray Crone | 1.00 | 158 Wally Post | 1.25 | 240 Whitey Ford | 25.00 | 322 Karl Olson | 1.50 |
| 77 Harvey Haddix | 1.00 | 159 Clint Courtney | 1.25 | 241 Don Mueller | 2.00 | 323 Willard Schmidt | 1.50 |
| 78 Herman Wehmeier | 1.00 | 160 Billy Pierce | 1.25 | 242 Hershell Freeman | 2.00 | 324 Rocky Bridges | 1.50 |
| 79 Sandy Koufax | 45.00 | 161 Joe DeMaestri | 1.25 | 243 Sherm Lollar | 2.00 | 325 Don Liddle | 1.50 |
| 80 Gus Triandos | 1.00 | 162 Gus Bell | 1.25 | 244 Bob Buhl | 2.00 | 236 Connie Johnson | 1.50 |
| 81 Wally Westlake | 1.00 | 163 Gene Woodling | 1.25 | 245 Billy Goodman | 2.00 | 327 Bob Wiesler | 1.50 |
| 82 Bill Renna | 1.00 | 164 Harmon Killebrew | 20.00 | 246 Tom Gorman | 2.00 | 328 Preston Ward | 1.50 |
| 83 Karl Spooner | 1.00 | 165 Red Schoendienst | 2.00 | 247 Bill Sarni | 2.00 | 329 Lou Berberet | 1.50 |
| 84 Babe Birrer | 1.00 | 166 Brooklyn Dodgers | 15.00 | 248 Bob Porterfield | 2.00 | 330 Jim Busby | 1.50 |
| 85 Cleveland Indians* | 2.50 | 167 Harry Dorish | 1.25 | 249 Johnny Klippstein | 2.00 | 331 Dick Hall | 1.50 |
| 86 Ray Jablonski | 1.00 | 168 Sammy White | 1.25 | 250 Larry Doby | 4.00 | 332 Don Larsen | 3.00 |
| 87 Dean Stone | 1.00 | 169 Bob Nelson | 1.25 | 251 New York Yankees | 20.00 | 333 Rube Walker | 1.50 |
| 88 Johnny Kucks | 1.00 | 170 Bill Virdon | 2.00 | 252 Vernon Law | 2.00 | 334 Bob Miller | 1.50 |
| 89 Norm Zauchin | 1.00 | 171 Jim Wilson | 1.25 | 253 Irv Noren | 2.00 | 335 Don Hoak | 1.50 |
| 90 Cincinnati Redlegs* | 3.00 | 172 Frank Torre | 1.25 | 254 George Crowe | 2.00 | 336 Ellis Kinder | 1.50 |
| 91 Gail Harris | 1.00 | 173 Johnny Podres | 1.25 | 255 Bob Lemon | 10.00 | 337 Bobby Morgan | 1.50 |
| 92 Red Wilson | 1.00 | 174 Glen Gorbous | 1.25 | 256 Tom Hurd | 2.00 | 338 Jim Delsing | 1.50 |
| 93 George Susce Jr. | 2.50 | 175 Del Crandall | 1.25 | 257 Bobby Thomson | 4.00 | 339 Rance Pless | 1.50 |
| 94 Ronald Kline | 1.00 | 176 Alex Kellner | 1.25 | 258 Art Ditmar | 2.00 | 340 Mickey McDermott | 1.50 |
| 95 Milwaukee Braves* | 2.50 | 177 Hank Bauer | 2.00 | 259 Sam Jones | 2.00 | — Checklist 1/3 | 65.00 |
| 96 Bill Tremel | 1.00 | 178 Joe Black | 1.25 | 260 Pee Wee Reese | 17.50 | — Checklist 2/4 | 65.00 |

# 1957 Topps....Complete Set of 407 Cards—Value $1400.00

Topps' switched to a 2½" x 3½" card size. The 1957 set features the rookie cards of Don Drysdale, Frank Robinson, Tony Kubek and Brooks Robinson. The four checklists are not included in the complete set price.

   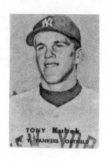 

| NO. PLAYER | MINT | NO. PLAYER | MINT | NO. PLAYER | MINT | NO. PLAYER | MINT |
|---|---|---|---|---|---|---|---|
| 1 Ted Williams | 85.00 | 65 Wally Moon | .75 | 130 Don Newcombe | 3.00 | 196 Larry Jackson | .75 |
| 2 Yogi Berra | 25.00 | 66 Brooks Lawrence | .75 | 131 Milt Bolling | .75 | 197 Hank Sauer | .75 |
| 3 Dale Long | .75 | 67 Chico Carrasquel | .75 | 132 Art Ditmar | .75 | 198 Detroit Tigers | 4.00 |
| 4 Johnny Logan | .75 | 68 Ray Crone | .75 | 133 Del Crandall | .75 | 199 Vernon Law | .75 |
| 5 Sal Maglie | 2.00 | 69 Roy McMillan | .75 | 134 Don Kaiser | .75 | 200 Gil McDougald | 2.25 |
| 6 Hector Lopez | .75 | 70 Richie Ashburn | 3.00 | 135 Bill Skowron | 2.50 | 201 Sandy Amoros | .75 |
| 7 Luis Aparicio | 5.00 | 71 Murry Dickson | .75 | 136 Jim Hegan | .75 | 202 Dick Gernert | .75 |
| 8 Don Mossi | .75 | 72 Bill Tuttle | .75 | 137 Bob Rush | .75 | 203 Hoyt Wilhelm | 6.00 |
| 9 Johnny Temple | .75 | 73 George Crowe | .75 | 138 Minnie Minoso | 2.50 | 204 Kansas C. Athletics | 2.00 |
| 10 Willie Mays | 40.00 | 74 Vito Valentinetti | .75 | 139 Lou Kretlow | .75 | 205 Charlie Maxwell | .75 |
| 11 George Zuverink | .75 | 75 Jim Piersall | 2.00 | 140 Frank Thomas | .75 | 206 Willard Schmidt | .75 |
| 12 Dick Groat | 1.50 | 76 Roberto Clemente | 35.00 | 141 Al Aber | .75 | 207 Bill Hunter | .75 |
| 13 Wally Burnette | .75 | 77 Paul Foytack | .75 | 142 Charley Thompson | .75 | 208 Lew Burdette | 2.00 |
| 14 Bob Nieman | .75 | 78 Vic Wertz | .75 | 143 Andy Pafko | .75 | 209 Bob Skinner | .75 |
| 15 Robin Roberts | 6.00 | 79 Lindy McDaniel | .75 | 144 Ray Narleski | .75 | 210 Roy Campanella | 30.00 |
| 16 Walt Moryn | .75 | 80 Gil Hodges | 13.00 | 145 Al Smith | .75 | 211 Camilo Pascual | .75 |
| 17 Billy Gardner | .75 | 81 Herman Wehmeier | .75 | 146 Don Ferrarese | .75 | 212 Rocco Colavito (R) | 5.00 |
| 18 Don Drysdale (R) | 35.00 | 82 Elston Howard | 3.00 | 147 Al Walker | .75 | 213 Les Moss | .75 |
| 19 Bob Wilson | .75 | 83 Lou Skizas | .75 | 148 Don Mueller | .75 | 214 Philadelphia Phillies | 3.00 |
| 20 Hank Aaron | 45.00 | 84 Moe Drabowsky | .75 | 149 Bob Kennedy | .75 | 215 Enos Slaughter | 6.00 |
| (negative reversed) | | 85 Larry Doby | 1.50 | 150 Bob Friend | .75 | 216 Marv Grissom | .75 |
| 21 Frank Sullivan | .75 | 86 Bill Sarni | .75 | 151 Willie Miranda | .75 | 217 Gene Stephens | .75 |
| 22 Jerry Snyder | .75 | 87 Tom Gorman | .75 | 152 Jack Harshman | .75 | 218 Ray Jablonski | .75 |
| (photo of Ed Fitzgerald) | | 88 Harvey Kuenn | 1.50 | 153 Karl Olson | .75 | 219 Tom Acker | .75 |
| 23 Sherm Lollar | .75 | 89 Roy Sievers | .90 | 154 Red Schoendienst | 2.00 | 220 Jackie Jensen | 2.00 |
| 24 Bill Mazeroski (R) | 5.00 | 90 Warren Spahn | 13.00 | 155 Jim Brosnan | .75 | 221 Dixie Howell | .75 |
| 25 Whitey Ford | 12.00 | 91 Mack Burk | .75 | 156 Gus Triandos | .75 | 222 Alex Grammas | .75 |
| 26 Bob Boyd | .75 | 92 Mickey Vernon | .75 | 157 Wally Post | .75 | 223 Frank House | .75 |
| 27 Ted Kazanski | .75 | 93 Hal Jeffcoat | .75 | 158 Curt Simmons | .75 | 224 Marv Blaylock | .75 |
| 28 Gene Conley | .75 | 94 Bobby Del Greco | .75 | 159 Solly Drake | .75 | 225 Harry Simpson | .75 |
| 29 Whitey Herzog | 2.00 | 95 Mickey Mantle | 225.00 | 160 Billy Pierce | 1.50 | 226 Preston Ward | .75 |
| 30 Pee Wee Reese | 13.00 | 96 Hank Aguirre | .75 | 161 Pittsburgh Pirates | 1.50 | 227 Jerry Staley | .75 |
| 31 Ron Northey | .75 | 97 New York Yankees | 9.00 | 162 Jack Meyer | .75 | 228 Smokey Burgess | .75 |
| 32 Hersh Freeman | .75 | 98 Alvin Dark | 1.50 | 163 Sammy White | .75 | 229 George Susce | .75 |
| 33 Jim Small | .75 | 99 Bob Keegan | .75 | 164 Tommy Carroll | .75 | 230 George Kell | 5.00 |
| 34 Tom Sturdivant | .75 | 100 Giles and Harridge | 2.00 | 165 Ted Kluszewski | 2.50 | 231 Solly Hemus | .75 |
| 35 Frank Robinson (R) | 50.00 | (League Presidents) | | 166 Roy Face | 1.25 | 232 Whitey Lockman | .75 |
| 36 Bob Grim | .75 | 101 Chuck Stobbs | .75 | 167 Vic Power | .75 | 233 Art Fowler | .75 |
| 37 Frank Torre | .75 | 102 Ray Boone | .75 | 168 Frank Lary | .75 | 234 Dick Cole | .75 |
| 38 Nellie Fox | 3.00 | 103 Joe Nuxhall | .75 | 169 Herb Plews | .75 | 235 Tom Poholsky | .75 |
| 39 Al Worthington | .75 | 104 Hank Foiles | .75 | 170 Duke Snider | 25.00 | 236 Joe Ginsberg | .75 |
| 40 Early Wynn | 6.00 | 105 Johnny Antonelli | .75 | 171 Boston Red Sox | 3.00 | 237 Foster Catleman | .75 |
| 41 Hal Smith | .75 | 106 Ray Moore | .75 | 172 Gene Woodling | .90 | 238 Eddie Robinson | .75 |
| 42 Dee Fondy | .75 | 107 Jim Rivera | .75 | 173 Roger Craig | 1.25 | 239 Tom Morgan | .75 |
| 43 Connie Johnson | .75 | 108 Tommy Byrne | .75 | 174 Willie Jones | .75 | 240 Hank Bauer | 3.00 |
| 44 Joe DeMaestri | .75 | 109 Hank Thompson | .75 | 175 Don Larsen | 2.00 | 241 Joe Lonnett | .75 |
| 45 Carl Furillo | 3.00 | 110 Bill Virdon | 2.00 | 176 Gene Baker | .75 | 242 Charlie Neal | .75 |
| 46 Bob Miller | .75 | 111 Hal Smith | .75 | 177 Eddie Yost | .75 | 243 St. Louis Cardinals | 3.00 |
| 47 Don Blasingame | .75 | 112 Tom Brewer | .75 | 178 Don Bessent | .75 | 244 Billy Loes | .75 |
| 48 Bill Bruton | .75 | 113 Wilmer Mizell | .75 | 179 Ernie Oravetz | .75 | 245 Rip Repulski | .75 |
| 49 Daryl Spencer | .75 | 114 Milwaukee Braves | 3.00 | 180 Dave Bell | .75 | 246 Jose Valdivielso | .75 |
| 50 Herb Score | 1.50 | 115 Jim Gilliam | 2.00 | 181 Dick Donovan | .75 | 247 Turk Lown | .75 |
| 51 Clint Courtney | .75 | 116 Mike Fornieles | .75 | 182 Hobie Landrith | .75 | 248 Jim Finigan | .75 |
| 52 Lee Walls | .75 | 117 Joe Adcock | 1.50 | 183 Chicago Cubs | 3.00 | 249 Dave Pope | .75 |
| 53 Clem Labine | .75 | 118 Bob Porterfield | .75 | 184 Tito Francona | .75 | 250 Ed Mathews | 8.00 |
| 54 Elmer Valo | .75 | 119 Stan Lopata | .75 | 185 Johnny Kucks | .75 | 251 Baltimore Orioles | 3.00 |
| 55 Ernie Banks | 15.00 | 120 Bob Lemon | 6.00 | 186 Jim King | .75 | 252 Carl Erskine | 3.00 |
| 56 Dave Sisler | .75 | 121 Cletis Boyer | 1.50 | 187 Virgil Trucks | .75 | 253 Gus Zernial | .75 |
| 57 Jim Lemon | .75 | 122 Ken Boyer | 2.00 | 188 Felix Mantilla | .75 | 254 Ron Negray | .75 |
| 58 Ruben Gomez | .75 | 123 Steve Ridzik | .75 | 189 Willard Nixon | .75 | 255 Charlie Silvera | .75 |
| 59 Dick Williams | .75 | 124 Dave Philley | .75 | 190 Randy Jackson | .75 | 256 Ronnie Kline | .75 |
| 60 Billy Hoeft | .75 | 125 Al Kaline | 13.00 | 191 Joe Margoneri | .75 | 257 Walt Dropo | .75 |
| 61 Dusty Rhodes | .75 | 126 Bob Wiesler | .75 | 192 Gerry Coleman | .75 | 258 Steve Gromek | .75 |
| 62 Billy Martin | 9.00 | 127 Bob Buhl | .75 | 193 Del Rice | .75 | 259 Eddie O'Brien | .75 |
| 63 Ike Delock | .75 | 128 Ed Bailey | .75 | 194 Hal Brown | .75 | 260 Del Ennis | .75 |
| 64 Pete Runnels | .75 | 129 Saul Rogovin | .75 | 195 Bobby Avila | .75 | 261 Bob Chakales | .75 |

| NO. PLAYER | MINT | NO. PLAYER | MINT | NO. PLAYER | MINT | NO. PLAYER | MINT |
|---|---|---|---|---|---|---|---|
| 262 Bobby Thomson | 2.00 | 301 Sam Esposito | 4.00 | 339 Bob Speake | 4.00 | 377 Andre Rodgers | 1.00 |
| 263 George Strickland | .75 | 302 Sandy Koufax | 80.00 | 340 Bill Wight | 4.00 | 378 Elmer Singleton | 1.00 |
| 264 Bob Turley | 2.00 | 303 Billy Goodman | 4.00 | 341 Don Gross | 4.00 | 379 Don Lee | 1.00 |
| 265 Harvey Haddix | 4.00 | 304 Joe Cunningham | 4.00 | 342 Gene Mauch | 6.00 | 380 Walker Cooper | 1.00 |
| 266 Kenny Kuhn | 4.00 | 305 Chico Fernandez | 4.00 | 343 Taylor Phillips | 4.00 | 381 Dean Stone | 1.00 |
| 267 Danny Kravitz | 4.00 | 306 Darrell Johnson | 4.00 | 344 Paul LaPalme | 4.00 | 382 Jim Brideweser | 1.00 |
| 268 Jackie Collum | 4.00 | 307 Jack Phillips | 4.00 | 345 Paul Smith | 4.00 | 383 Juan Pizarro | 1.00 |
| 269 Bob Cerv | 4.00 | 308 Dick Hall | 4.00 | 346 Dick Littlefield | 4.00 | 384 Bobby Smith | 1.00 |
| 270 Washington Senators | 6.00 | 309 Jim Busby | 4.00 | 347 Hal Naragon | 4.00 | 385 Art Houtteman | 1.00 |
| 271 Danny O'Connell | 4.00 | 310 Max Surkont | 4.00 | 348 Jim Hearn | 4.00 | 386 Lyle Luttrell | 1.00 |
| 272 Bobby Shantz | 8.00 | 311 Al Pilarcik | 4.00 | 349 Nelson King | 4.00 | 387 Jack Sanford (R) | 1.50 |
| 273 Jim Davis | 4.00 | 312 Tony Kubek (R) | 30.00 | 350 Eddie Miksis | 4.00 | 388 Pete Daley | 1.00 |
| 274 Don Hoak | 4.00 | 313 Mel Parnell | 4.00 | 351 Dave Hillman | 4.00 | 389 Dave Jolly | 1.00 |
| 275 Cleveland Indians | 6.00 | 314 Ed Bouchee | 4.00 | 352 Ellis Kinder | 4.00 | 390 Reno Bertoia | 1.00 |
| 276 Jim Pyburn | 4.00 | 315 Lou Berberet | 4.00 | 353 Cal Neeman | 1.00 | 391 Ralph Terry (R) | 1.50 |
| 277 Johnny Podres | 15.00 | 316 Billy O'Dell | 4.00 | 354 Rip Coleman | 1.00 | 392 Chuck Tanner | 1.25 |
| 278 Fred Hatfield | 4.00 | 317 New York Giants | 15.00 | 355 Frank Malzone | 1.00 | 393 Raul Sanchez | 1.00 |
| 279 Bob Thurman | 4.00 | 318 Mickey McDermott | 4.00 | 356 Faye Throneberry | 1.00 | 394 Luis Aroyo | 1.00 |
| 280 Alex Kellner | 4.00 | 319 Gino Cimoli | 4.00 | 357 Earl Torgeson | 1.00 | 395 Bubba Phillips | 1.00 |
| 281 Gail Harris | 4.00 | 320 Neil Chrisley | 4.00 | 358 Jerry Lynch | 1.00 | 396 Casey Wise | 1.00 |
| 282 Jack Dittmer | 4.00 | 321 Red Murff | 4.00 | 359 Tom Cheney | 1.00 | 397 Roy Smalley | 1.00 |
| 283 Wes Covington | 4.00 | 322 Cincinnati Redlegs | 15.00 | 360 Johnny Groth | 1.00 | 398 Al Cicotte | 1.00 |
| 284 Don Zimmer | 4.00 | 323 Wes Westrum | 4.00 | 361 Curt Barclay | 1.00 | 399 Billy Consolo | 1.00 |
| 285 Ned Garver | 4.00 | 324 Brooklyn Dodgers | 25.00 | 362 Roman Mejias | 1.00 | 400 Dodgers' Sluggers: | 25.00 |
| 286 Bobby Richardson (R) | 20.00 | 325 Frank Bolling | 4.00 | 363 Eddie Kasko | 1.00 | Carl Furillo, Gil Hodges | |
| 287 Sam Jones | 4.00 | 326 Pedro Ramos | 4.00 | 364 Cal McLish | 1.00 | Duke Snider, | |
| 288 Ted Lepcio | 4.00 | 327 Jim Pendleton | 4.00 | 365 Ossie Virgil | 1.00 | Roy Campanella | |
| 289 Jim Bolger | 4.00 | 328 Brooks Robinson | 105.00 | 366 Ken Lehman | 1.00 | 401 Earl Battey | 1.00 |
| 290 Andy Carey | 4.00 | 329 Chicago White Sox | 9.00 | 367 Ed Fitzgerald | 1.00 | 402 Jim Pisani | 1.00 |
| 291 Windy McCall | 4.00 | 330 Jim Wilson | 4.00 | 368 Bob Purkey | 1.00 | 403 Dick Hyde | 1.00 |
| 292 Bill Klaus | 4.00 | 331 Ray Katt | 4.00 | 369 Milt Graff | 1.00 | 404 Harry Anderson | 1.00 |
| 293 Ted Abernathy | 4.00 | 332 Bpb Bowman | 4.00 | 370 Warren Hacker | 1.00 | 405 Duke Maas | 1.00 |
| 294 Rocky Bridges | 4.00 | 333 Ernie Johnson | 4.00 | 371 Bob Lennon | 1.00 | 406 Bob Hale | 1.00 |
| 295 Joe Collins | 4.00 | 334 Jerry Schoonmaker | 4.00 | 372 Norm Zauchin | 1.00 | 407 Yanks' Power Hitters: | 38.00 |
| 296 Johnny Klippstein | 4.00 | 335 Granny Hamner | 4.00 | 373 Pete Whisenant | 1.00 | Mickey Mantle, Yogi Berra | |
| 297 Jack Crimian | 4.00 | 336 Haywood Sullivan | 4.00 | 374 Don Cardwell | 1.00 | — Checklist 1/2 | 20.00 |
| 298 Irv Noren | 4.00 | 337 Rene Valdes | 4.00 | 375 Jim Landis | 1.00 | — Checklist 2/3 | 35.00 |
| 299 Chuck Harmon | 4.00 | 338 Jim Bunning (R) | 20.00 | 376 Don Elston | 1.00 | — Checklist 3/4 | 75.00 |
| 300 Mike Garcia | 4.00 | | | | | — Checklist 4/5 | 90.00 |

## 1958 Topps....Complete Set of 494 Cards—Value $750.00

Features the rookie cards of Roger Maris and Orlando Cepeda. 33 cards exist with the player's name or team in *yellow* type. These cards are worth more than the cards with *white* type. Card 145 was not issued. Prices for team checklists (377, 397, 408 and 428) are with the teams listed in alphabetical order. Team checklists with the teams in numerical order are worth about $12.00 each.

| NO. PLAYER | MINT | NO. PLAYER | MINT | NO. PLAYER | MINT | NO. PLAYER | MINT |
|---|---|---|---|---|---|---|---|
| 1 Ted Williams | 85.00 | 11 Jim Rivera | 6.00 | 21 Curt Barclay | .75 | 31 Tex Clevenger | .75 |
| 2 Bob Lemon | 5.00 | (yellow type) | | 22 Hal Naragon | .75 | 32 J.W. Porter | .75 |
| 2 Bob Lemon | 12.00 | 12 George Crowe | .75 | 23 Bill Tuttle | .75 | 32 J.W. Porter | 8.00 |
| (yellow type) | | 13 Billy Hoeft | .75 | 23 Bill Tuttle | 7.50 | (yellow letters) | |
| 3 Alex Kellner | .75 | 13 Billy Hoeft | 7.50 | (yellow type) | | 33 Cal Neeman | .75 |
| 4 Hank Foiles | .75 | (yellow type) | | 24 Hobie Landrith | .75 | 33 Cal Neeman | 7.50 |
| 5 Willie Mays | 35.00 | 14 Rip Repulski | .75 | 24 Hobie Landrith | 8.00 | (yellow letters) | |
| 6 George Zuverink | .75 | 15 Jim Lemon | .75 | (yellow type) | | 34 Bob Thurman | .75 |
| 7 Dale Long | .75 | 16 Charley Neal | .75 | 25 Don Drysdale | 8.00 | 35 Don Mossi | .75 |
| 8 Eddie Kasko | .75 | 17 Felix Mantilla | .75 | 26 Ron Jackson | .75 | 35 Don Mossi | 7.50 |
| 8 Eddie Kasko | 7.50 | 18 Frank Sullivan | .75 | 27 Bud Freeman | .75 | (yellow letters) | |
| (yellow type) | | 19 New York Giants | 4.00 | 28 Jim Busby | .75 | 36 Ted Kazanski | .75 |
| 9 Hank Bauer | 1.50 | 20 Gil McDougald | 2.00 | 29 Ted Lepcio | .75 | 37 Mike McCormick | .75 |
| 10 Lou Burdette | 1.50 | 20 Gil McDougald | 11.00 | 30 Hank Aaron | 35.00 | (photo of Ray Monzant) | |
| 11 Jim Rivera | .75 | (yellow type) | | 30 Hank Aaron | 65.00 | 38 Dick Gernert | .75 |
| | | | | (yellow letters) | | | |

# 1958 Topps (Continued)

| NO. PLAYER | MINT |
|---|---|
| 39 Bob Martyn | .75 |
| 40 George Kell | 3.50 |
| 41 Dave Hillman | .75 |
| 42 John Roseboro (R) | 1.50 |
| 43 Sal Maglie | 1.50 |
| 44 Wash Senators | 2.00 |
| 45 Dick Groat | 1.50 |
| 46 Lou Sleater | .75 |
| 46 Lou Sleater (yellow letters) | 7.50 |
| 47 Roger Maris (R) | 45.00 |
| 48 Chuck Harmon | .75 |
| 49 Smokey Burgess | .75 |
| 50 Billy Pierce | 1.50 |
| 50 Billy Pierce (yellow letters) | 7.50 |
| 51 Del Rice | .75 |
| 52 Bob Clemente | 25.00 |
| 52 Bob Clemente (yellow letters) | 50.00 |
| 53 Morrie Martin | .75 |
| 53 Morrie Martin (yellow letters) | 8.00 |
| 54 Norm Siebern | .75 |
| 55 Chico Carrasquel | .75 |
| 56 Bill Fischer | .75 |
| 57 Tim Thompson | .75 |
| 57 Tim Thompson (yellow letters) | 9.00 |
| 58 Art Schult | .75 |
| 58 Art Schult (yellow letters) | 7.50 |
| 59 Dave Sisler | .75 |
| 60 Del Ennis | .75 |
| 60 Del Ennis (yellow letters) | 8.00 |
| 61 Darrell Johnson | .75 |
| 61 Darrell Johnson (yellow letters) | 7.50 |
| 62 Joe DeMaestri | .75 |
| 63 Joe Nuxhall | .75 |
| 64 Joe Lonnett | .75 |
| 65 Von McDaniel | .75 |
| 65 Von McDaniel (yellow letters) | 7.50 |
| 66 Lee Walls | .75 |
| 67 Joe Ginsberg | .75 |
| 68 Daryl Spencer | .75 |
| 69 Wally Burnette | .75 |
| 70 Al Kaline | 12.00 |
| 70 Al Kaline (yellow letters) | 40.00 |
| 71 Brooklyn Dodgers | 5.00 |
| 72 Bud Byerly | .75 |
| 73 Pete Daley | .75 |
| 74 Roy Face | .75 |
| 75 Gus Bell | .75 |
| 76 Dick Farrell | .75 |
| 76 Dick Farrell (yellow letters) | 7.50 |
| 77 Don Zimmer | 1.25 |
| 77 Don Zimmer (yellow letters) | 7.50 |
| 78 Ernie Johnson | .75 |
| 78 Ernie Johnson (yellow letters) | 8.00 |
| 79 Dick Williams | 1.25 |
| 79 Dick Williams (yellow letters) | 7.50 |
| 80 Dick Drott | .75 |
| 81 Steve Boros | .75 |
| 81 Steve Boros (yellow letters) | 7.50 |
| 82 Ronnie Kline | .75 |
| 83 Bob Hazle | .75 |
| 84 Billy O'Dell | .75 |
| 85 Luis Aparicio | 5.00 |
| 85 Luis Aparicio (yellow letters) | 13.50 |
| 86 Valmy Thomas | .75 |
| 87 Johnny Kucks | .75 |
| 88 Duke Snider | 18.00 |
| 89 Bill Klaus | .75 |
| 90 Robin Roberts | 6.00 |
| 91 Chuck Tanner | 1.25 |
| 92 Clint Courtney | .75 |
| 92 Clint Courtney (yellow letters) | 7.50 |
| 93 Sandy Amoros | .75 |
| 94 Bob Skinner | .75 |
| 95 Frank Bolling | .75 |
| 96 Joseph Durham | .75 |
| 97 Larry Jackson | .75 |
| 97 Larry Jackson (yellow letters) | 8.00 |
| 98 Bill Hunter | .75 |
| 98 Bill Hunter (yellow letters) | 7.50 |
| 99 Bobby Adams | .75 |
| 100 Early Wynn | 5.00 |
| 100 Early Wynn (yellow letters) | 12.00 |
| 101 Bob Richardson | 2.50 |
| 101 Bob Richardson (yellow letters) | 10.00 |
| 102 George Strickland | .75 |
| 103 Jerry Lynch | .75 |
| 104 Jim Pendleton | .75 |
| 105 Billy Gardner | .75 |
| 106 Dick Schofield | .75 |
| 107 Ossie Virgil | .75 |
| 108 Jim Landis | .75 |
| 108 Jim Landis (yellow letters) | 7.50 |
| 109 Herb Plews | .75 |
| 110 Johnny Logan | .75 |
| 111 Stu Miller | .75 |
| 112 Gus Zernial | .75 |
| 113 Jerry Walker | .75 |
| 114 Irv Noren | .75 |
| 115 Jim Bunning | 2.50 |
| 116 Dave Philley | .75 |
| 117 Frank Torre | .75 |
| 118 Harvey Haddix | .75 |
| 119 Harry Chiti | .75 |
| 120 Johnny Podres | 2.00 |
| 121 Ed Miksis | .75 |
| 122 Walter Moryn | .75 |
| 123 Dick Tomanek | .75 |
| 124 Bobby Usher | .75 |
| 125 Al Dark | 1.25 |
| 126 Stan Palys | .75 |
| 127 Tom Sturdivant | .75 |
| 128 Willie Kirkland | .75 |
| 129 Jim Derrington | .75 |
| 130 Jackie Jensen | 2.25 |
| 131 Bob Henrich | .75 |
| 132 Vernon Law | .75 |
| 133 Russ Nixon | .75 |
| 134 Philadelphia Phillies | 2.50 |
| 135 Mike Drabowsky | .75 |
| 136 Jim Finigan | .75 |
| 137 Russ Kemmerer | .75 |
| 138 Earl Torgeson | .75 |
| 139 George Brunet | .75 |
| 140 Wes Covington | .75 |
| 141 Ken Lehman | .75 |
| 142 Enos Slaughter | 3.00 |
| 143 Billy Muffett | .75 |
| 144 Bobby Morgan | .75 |
| 146 Dick Gray | .75 |
| 147 Don McMahon | .75 |
| 148 Billy Consolo | .75 |
| 149 Tom Acker | .75 |
| 150 Mickey Mantle | 120.00 |
| 151 Buddy Pritchard | .75 |
| 152 Johnny Antonelli | .75 |
| 153 Les Moss | .75 |
| 154 Harry Byrd | .75 |
| 155 Hector Lopez | .75 |
| 156 Dick Hyde | .75 |
| 157 Dee Fondy | .75 |
| 158 Cleveland Indians | 2.00 |
| 159 Taylor Phillips | .75 |
| 160 Don Hoak | .75 |
| 161 Don Larsen | 2.00 |
| 162 Gil Hodges | 8.00 |
| 163 Jim Wilson | .75 |
| 164 Bob Taylor | .75 |
| 165 Bob Nieman | .75 |
| 166 Danny O'Connell | .75 |
| 167 Frank Baumann | .75 |
| 168 Joe Cunningham | .75 |
| 169 Ralph Terry | .75 |
| 170 Vic Wertz | .75 |
| 171 Harry Anderson | .75 |
| 172 Don Gross | .75 |
| 173 Eddie Yost | .75 |
| 174 Kansas C. Athletics | 2.00 |
| 175 Marv Throneberry (R) | 2.00 |
| 176 Bob Buhl | .75 |
| 177 Al Smith | .75 |
| 178 Ted Kluszewski | 2.00 |
| 179 Willy Miranda | .75 |
| 180 Lindy McDaniel | .60 |
| 181 Willie Jones | .75 |
| 182 Joe Caffie | .75 |
| 183 Dave Jolly | .75 |
| 184 Elvin Tappe | .75 |
| 185 Ray Boone | .75 |
| 186 Jack Meyer | .75 |
| 187 Sandy Koufax | 28.00 |
| 188 Milt Bolling (photo of Lou Berberet) | .75 |
| 189 George Susce | .75 |
| 190 Red Schoendienst | 1.25 |
| 191 Art Ceccarelli | .75 |
| 192 Milt Graff | .75 |
| 193 Jerry Lumpe | .75 |
| 194 Roger Craig | .75 |
| 195 Whitey Lockman | .75 |
| 196 Mike Garcia | .75 |
| 197 Haywood Sullivan | .75 |
| 198 Bill Virdon | 1.25 |
| 199 Don Blasingame | .50 |
| 200 Bob Keegan | .50 |
| 201 Jim Bolger | .50 |
| 202 Woody Held | .50 |
| 203 Al Walker | .50 |
| 204 Leo Kiely | .50 |
| 205 Johnny Temple | .50 |
| 206 Bob Shaw | .50 |
| 207 Solly Hemus | .50 |
| 208 Cal McLish | .50 |
| 209 Bob Anderson | .50 |
| 210 Wally Moon | .50 |
| 211 Pete Burnside | .50 |
| 212 Bubba Phillips | .50 |
| 213 Red Wilson | .50 |
| 214 Willard Schmidt | .50 |
| 215 Jim Gilliam | 1.50 |
| 216 St. Louis Cardinals | 2.50 |
| 217 Jack Harshman | .50 |
| 218 Dick Rand | .50 |
| 219 Camilo Pascual | .50 |
| 220 Tom Brewer | .50 |
| 221 Jerry Kindall | .50 |
| 222 Bud Daley | .50 |
| 223 Andy Pafko | .50 |
| 224 Bob Grim | .50 |
| 225 Billy Goodman | .50 |
| 226 Bob Smith | .50 |
| 227 Gene Stephens | .50 |
| 228 Duke Maas | .50 |
| 229 Frank Zupo | .50 |
| 230 Richie Ashburn | 2.50 |
| 231 Lloyd Merritt | .50 |
| 232 Reno Bertoia | .50 |
| 233 Mickey Vernon | .50 |
| 234 Carl Sawatski | .50 |
| 235 Tom Gorman | .50 |
| 236 Ed Fitzgerald | .50 |
| 237 Bill Wight | .50 |
| 238 Bill Mazeroski | 2.00 |
| 239 Chuck Stobbs | .50 |
| 240 Moose Skowron | 2.00 |
| 241 Dick Littlefield | .50 |
| 242 Johnny Klippstein | .50 |
| 243 Larry Raines | .50 |
| 244 Don Demeter | .50 |
| 245 Frank Lary | .50 |
| 246 New York Yankees | 6.00 |
| 247 Casey Wise | .50 |
| 248 Herm Wehmeier | .50 |
| 249 Ray Moore | .50 |
| 250 Roy Sievers | .50 |
| 251 Warren Hacker | .50 |
| 252 Bob Trowbridge | .50 |
| 253 Don Mueller | .50 |
| 254 Alex Grammas | .50 |
| 255 Bob Turley | 2.00 |
| 256 Chicago White Sox | 2.00 |
| 257 Hal Smith | .50 |
| 258 Carl Erskine | 2.00 |
| 259 Alan Pilarcik | .50 |
| 260 Frank Malzone | .50 |
| 261 Turk Lown | .50 |
| 262 John Groth | .50 |
| 263 Ed Bressoud | .50 |
| 264 Jack Sanford | .60 |
| 265 Pete Runnels | .50 |
| 266 Connie Johnson | .50 |
| 267 Sherm Lollar | .50 |
| 268 Granny Hamner | .50 |
| 269 Paul Smith | .50 |
| 270 Warren Spahn | 8.00 |
| 271 Billy Martin | 3.00 |
| 272 Ray Crone | .50 |
| 273 Hal Smith | .50 |
| 274 Rocky Bridges | .50 |
| 275 Elston Howard | 2.00 |
| 276 Bobby Avila | .50 |
| 277 Virgil Trucks | .50 |
| 278 Mack Burk | .50 |
| 279 Bob Boyd | .50 |
| 280 Jim Piersall | 1.50 |
| 281 Sam Taylor | .50 |
| 282 Paul Foytack | .50 |
| 283 Ray Shearer | .50 |
| 284 Ray Katt | .50 |
| 285 Frank Robinson | 12.00 |
| 286 Gino Cimoli | .50 |
| 287 Sam Jones | .50 |
| 288 Harmon Killebrew | 13.00 |
| 289 Hurling Rivals: Lou Burdette, Bobby Shantz | 2.00 |
| 290 Dick Donovan | .50 |
| 291 Don Landrum | .50 |
| 292 Ned Garver | .50 |
| 293 Gene Freese | .50 |
| 294 Hal Jeffcoat | .50 |
| 295 Minnie Minoso | 2.00 |
| 296 Ryne Duren | 1.00 |
| 297 Don Buddin | .50 |
| 298 Jim Hearn | .50 |
| 299 Harry Simpson | .50 |
| 300 Harridge and Giles League Presidents | 2.00 |
| 301 Randy Jackson | .50 |
| 302 Mike Baxes | .50 |
| 303 Neil Chrisley | .50 |
| 304 Tigers' Big Bats: Harvey Kuenn, Al Kaline | 4.00 |
| 305 Clem Labine | .75 |
| 306 Whammy Douglas | .50 |
| 307 Brooks Robinson | 16.00 |
| 308 Paul Giel | .50 |
| 309 Gail Harris | .50 |
| 310 Ernie Banks | 15.00 |
| 311 Bob Purkey | .50 |
| 312 Boston Red Sox | 2.00 |
| 313 Bob Rush | .50 |
| 314 Boss and Power: Duke Snider, Walt Alston | 6.00 |
| 315 Bob Friend | .50 |
| 316 Tito Francona | .50 |
| 317 Albie Pearson | 1.00 |
| 318 Frank House | .50 |

| NO. PLAYER | MINT | NO. PLAYER | MINT | NO. PLAYER | MINT | NO. PLAYER | MINT |
|---|---|---|---|---|---|---|---|
| 319 Lou Skizas | .50 | 362 Ray Jablonski | .50 | 407 Carlton Willey | .50 | 450 Preston Ward | 2.00 |
| 320 Whitey Ford | 11.00 | 363 Don Elston | .50 | 408 Baltimore Orioles* | 2.50 | 451 Joe Taylor | .50 |
| 321 Sluggers Supreme: | 6.00 | 364 Earl Battey | .50 | 409 Frank Thomas | .50 | 452 Roman Mejias | .50 |
| Ted Kluszewski, | | 365 Tom Morgan | .50 | 410 Murray Wall | .50 | 453 Tom Qualters | .50 |
| Ted Williams | | 366 Gene Green | .50 | 411 Tony Taylor | .50 | 454 Harry Hanebrink | .50 |
| 322 Harding Peterson | .50 | 367 Jack Urban | .50 | 412 Jerry Staley | .50 | 455 Hal Griggs | .50 |
| 323 Elmer Valo | .50 | 368 Rocky Colavito | 2.00 | 413 Jim Davenport | .50 | 456 Dick Brown | .50 |
| 324 Hoyt Wilhelm | 5.00 | 369 Ralph Lumenti | .50 | 414 Sammy White | .50 | 457 Milt Pappas (R) | 1.00 |
| 325 Joe Adcock | 1.00 | 370 Yogi Berra | 15.00 | 415 Bob Bowman | .50 | 458 Julio Becquer | .50 |
| 326 Bob Miller | .50 | 371 Marty Keough | .50 | 416 Foster Castleman | .50 | 459 Ron Blackburn | .50 |
| 327 Chicago Cubs | 2.50 | 372 Don Cardwell | .50 | 417 Carl Furillo | 2.00 | 460 Chuck Essegian | .50 |
| 328 Ike Delock | .50 | 373 Joe Pignatano | .50 | 418 W. Series Batting Foes: | 30.00 | 461 Ed Mayer | .50 |
| 329 Bob Cerv | .50 | 374 Brooks Lawrence | .50 | Mickey Mantle, Hank Aaron | | 462 Gary Geiger | 2.00 |
| 330 Ed Bailey | .50 | 375 Pee Wee Reese | 12.00 | 419 Bobby Shantz | 1.00 | 463 Vito Valentinetti | .50 |
| 331 Pedro Ramos | .50 | 376 Charley Rabe | .50 | 420 Vada Pinson | 3.00 | 464 Curt Flood (R) | 3.00 |
| 332 Jim King | .50 | 377 Milwaukee Braves* | 2.00 | 421 Dixie Howell | .50 | 465 Arnie Portocarrero | .50 |
| 333 Andy Carey | .50 | 378 Hank Sauer | .50 | 422 Norm Zauchin | .50 | 466 Pete Whisenant | .50 |
| 334 Mound Aces: | 1.50 | 379 Ray Herbert | .50 | 423 Phil Clark | .50 | 467 Glen Hobbie | .50 |
| Bob Friend, Billy Pierce | | 380 Charley Maxwell | .50 | 424 Larry Doby | 1.50 | 468 Bob Schmidt | .50 |
| 335 Ruben Gomez | .50 | 381 Hal Brown | .50 | 425 Sam Esposito | .50 | 469 Don Ferrarese | .50 |
| 336 Bert Hamric | .50 | 382 Al Cicotte | .50 | 426 Johnny O'Brien | .50 | 470 R.C. Stevens | .50 |
| 337 Hank Aguirre | .50 | 383 Lou Berberet | .50 | 427 Al Worthington | .50 | 471 Lenny Green | .50 |
| 338 Walter Dropo | .50 | 384 John Goryl | .50 | 428 Cincinnati Redlegs* | 2.50 | 472 Joe Jay | .50 |
| 339 Fred Hatfield | .50 | 385 Wilmer Mizell | .50 | 429 Gus Triandos | .50 | 473 Bill Renna | .50 |
| 340 Don Newcombe | 2.00 | 386 Young Sluggers: | 1.50 | 430 Bobby Thomson | 1.50 | 474 Roman Semproch | .50 |
| 341 Pittsburgh Pirates | 1.50 | Ed Bailey, Birdie Tebbetts, | | 431 Gene Conley | .50 | 475 All-Star Managers: | 3.50 |
| 342 Jim Brosnan | .50 | Frank Robinson | | 432 John Powers | .50 | Stengel, Haney | |
| 343 Orlando Cepeda (R) | 11.00 | 387 Wally Post | .50 | 433 Pancho Herrera | .75 | 476 Stan Musial (AS) | 4.00 |
| 344 Bob Porterfield | .50 | 388 Billy Moran | .50 | 433 Pancho Herrer | 7.50 | 477 Bill Skowron (AS) | .75 |
| 345 Jim Hegan | .50 | 389 Bill Taylor | .50 | (name spelled wrong) | | 478 Johnny Temple (AS) | .75 |
| 346 Steve Bilko | .50 | 390 Del Crandall | .50 | 434 Harvey Kuenn | 1.50 | 479 Nellie Fox (AS) | 1.50 |
| 347 Don Rudolph | .50 | 391 Dave Melton | .50 | 435 Ed Roebuck | .50 | 480 Eddie Mathews (AS) | 3.00 |
| 348 Chico Fernandez | .50 | 392 Bennie Daniels | .50 | 436 Rival Fence Busters: | 17.00 | 481 Frank Malzone (AS) | .75 |
| 349 Murry Dickson | .50 | 393 Tony Kubek | 3.00 | Willie Mays, Duke Snider | | 482 Ernie Banks (AS) | 5.00 |
| 350 Ken Boyer | 2.00 | 394 Jim Grant | .50 | 437 Bob Speake | .50 | 483 Luis Aparicio (AS) | 3.00 |
| 351 Braves Fence Busters: | 6.00 | 395 Willard Nixon | .50 | 438 Whitey Herzog | .50 | 484 Frank Robinson (AS) | 4.00 |
| Del Crandall, Eddie Mathews, | | 396 Dutch Dotterer | .50 | 439 Ray Narleski | .50 | 485 Ted Williams (AS) | 10.00 |
| Hank Aaron, Joe Adcock | | 397 Detroit Tigers* | 3.00 | 440 Eddie Mathews | 8.00 | 486 Willie Mays (AS) | 7.50 |
| 352 Herb Score | 1.25 | 398 Gene Woodling | .50 | 441 Jim Marshall | .50 | 487 Mickey Mantle (AS) | 7.50 |
| 353 Stan Lopata | .50 | 399 Marv Grissom | .50 | 442 Phil Paine | .50 | 488 Hank Aaron (AS) | 7.50 |
| 354 Art Ditmar | .50 | 400 Nellie Fox | 2.00 | 443 Billy Harrell | 2.00 | 489 Jackie Jensen (AS) | .75 |
| 355 Billy Bruton | .50 | 401 Don Bessent | .50 | 444 Danny Kravitz | .50 | 490 Ed Bailey (AS) | .75 |
| 356 Bob Malkmus | .50 | 402 Bobby Gene Smith | .50 | 445 Bob Smith | .50 | 491 Sherm Lollar (AS) | .75 |
| 357 Danny McDevitt | .50 | 403 Steve Korcheck | .50 | 446 Carroll Hardy | 2.00 | 492 Bob Friend (AS) | .75 |
| 358 Gene Baker | .50 | 404 Curt Simmons | .50 | 447 Ray Monzant | .50 | 493 Bob Turley (AS) | .75 |
| 359 Billy Loes | .50 | 405 Ken Aspromonte | .50 | 448 Charlie Lau | .75 | 494 Warren Spahn (AS) | 3.00 |
| 360 Roy McMillan | .50 | 406 Vic Power | .50 | 449 Gene Fodge | .50 | 495 Herb Score (AS) | 1.00 |
| 361 Mike Fornieles | .50 | | | | | | |

# 1959 Topps....Complete Set of 572 Cards—Value $750.00

Includes Bob Gibson's rookie card. The high numbers are 507 to 572. Cards 199 to 286 were issued with *white* or *gray* backs. Cards 316, 321, 322, 336 and 362 exist without the *option* or *traded* line—worth $20.00 each.

    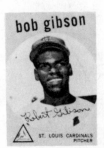

| NO. PLAYER | MINT | NO. PLAYER | MINT | NO. PLAYER | MINT | NO. PLAYER | MINT |
|---|---|---|---|---|---|---|---|
| 1 BB Commissioner: | 5.00 | 10 Mickey Mantle | 90.00 | 18 Jack Urban | .50 | 28 Red Worthington | .50 |
| Ford Frick | | 11 Billy Hunter | .50 | 19 Ed Bressoud | .50 | 29 Jim Bolger | .50 |
| 2 Eddie Yost | .50 | 12 Vern Law | .50 | 20 Duke Snider | 13.00 | 30 Nellie Fox | 2.50 |
| 3 Don McMahon | .50 | 13 Dick Gernert | .50 | 21 Connie Johnson | .50 | 31 Ken Lehman | .50 |
| 4 Albie Pearson | .50 | 14 Pete Whisenant | .50 | 22 Al Smith | .50 | 32 Don Buddin | .50 |
| 5 Dick Donovan | .50 | 15 Dick Drott | .50 | 23 Murry Dickson | .50 | 33 Ed Fizgerald | .50 |
| 6 Alex Grammas | .50 | 16 Joe Pignatano | .50 | 24 Red Wilson | .50 | 34 Pitchers Beware: | 2.00 |
| 7 Al Pilarcik | .50 | 17 Danny's All-Stars: | 1.00 | 25 Don Hoak | .50 | Al Kaline, Charley Maxwell | |
| 8 Philadelphia Phillies | 2.00 | Frank Thomas, Danny | | 26 Chuck Stobbs | .50 | 35 Ted Kluszewski | 1.50 |
| 9 Paul Giel | .50 | Murtaugh, Ted Kluszewski | | 27 Andy Pafko | .50 | 36 Hank Aguirre | .50 |

# 1959 Topps (Continued)

| NO. PLAYER | MINT |
|---|---|
| 37 Gene Green | .50 |
| 38 Morrie Martin | .50 |
| 39 Ed Bouchee | .50 |
| 40 Warren Spahn | 9.00 |
| 41 Bob Martyn | .50 |
| 42 Murray Wall | .50 |
| 43 Steven Bilko | .50 |
| 44 Vito Valentinetti | .50 |
| 45 Andy Carey | .50 |
| 46 Bill Henry | .50 |
| 47 Jim Finigan | .50 |
| 48 Baltimore Orioles | 2.00 |
| 49 Bill Hall | .50 |
| 50 Willie Mays | 30.00 |
| 51 Rip Coleman | .50 |
| 52 Coot Veal | .50 |
| 53 Stan Williams | .50 |
| 54 Mel Roach | .50 |
| 55 Tom Brewer | .50 |
| 56 Carl Sawatski | .50 |
| 57 Al Cicotte | .50 |
| 58 Eddie Miksis | .50 |
| 59 Irv Noren | .50 |
| 60 Bob Turley | 1.00 |
| 61 Dick Brown | .50 |
| 62 Tony Taylor | .50 |
| 63 Jim Hearn | .50 |
| 64 Joe DeMaestri | .50 |
| 65 Frank Torre | .50 |
| 66 Joe Ginsberg | .50 |
| 67 Brooks Lawrence | .50 |
| 68 Dick Schofield | .50 |
| 69 San F. Giants | 2.00 |
| 70 Harvey Kuenn | 1.50 |
| 71 Don Bessent | .50 |
| 72 Bill Renna | .50 |
| 73 Ron Jackson | .50 |
| 74 Directing the Power: | .75 |
|   Jim Lemon, Cookie | |
|   Lavagetto, Roy Sievers | |
| 75 Sam Jones | .50 |
| 76 Bobby Richardson | 2.00 |
| 77 John Goryl | .50 |
| 78 Pedro Ramos | .50 |
| 79 Harry Chiti | .50 |
| 80 Minnie Minoso | 1.50 |
| 81 Hal Jeffcoat | .50 |
| 82 Bob Boyd | .50 |
| 83 Bob Smith | .50 |
| 84 Reno Bertoia | .50 |
| 85 Harry Anderson | .50 |
| 86 Bob Keegan | .50 |
| 87 Danny O'Connell | .50 |
| 88 Herb Score | .50 |
| 89 Billy Gardner | .50 |
| 90 Bill Skowron | 1.50 |
| 91 Herb Moford | .50 |
| 92 David Philley | .50 |
| 93 Julio Becquer | .50 |
| 94 Chicago White Sox | 2.00 |
| 95 Carl Willey | .50 |
| 96 Lou Berberet | .50 |
| 97 Jerry Lynch | .50 |
| 98 Arnie Portocarrero | .50 |
| 99 Ted Kazanski | .50 |
| 100 Bob Cerv | .50 |
| 101 Alex Kellner | .50 |
| 102 Felipe Alou (R) | 1.75 |
| 103 Billy Goodman | .50 |
| 104 Del Rice | .50 |
| 105 Lee Walls | .50 |
| 106 Hal Woodeshick | .50 |
| 107 Norm Larker | .50 |
| 108 Zack Monroe | .50 |
| 109 Bob Schmidt | .50 |
| 110 George Witt | .50 |
| 111 Cincinnati Redlegs | 2.50 |
| 112 Billy Consolo | .50 |
| 113 Taylor Phillips | .50 |
| 114 Earl Battey | .50 |
| 115 Mickey Vernon | .50 |

**No. 116 to 146 Rookie Stars**

| NO. PLAYER | MINT |
|---|---|
| 116 Bob Allison | 2.00 |
| 117 John Blanchard | .50 |
| 118 John Buzhardt | .50 |
| 119 John Callison | 1.50 |
| 120 Chuck Coles | .50 |
| 121 Bob Conley | .50 |
| 122 Bennie Daniels | .50 |
| 123 Donald Dillard | .50 |
| 124 Dan Dobbek | .50 |
| 125 Ron Fairly | .75 |
| 126 Eddie Haas | .50 |
| 127 Kent Hadley | .50 |
| 128 Bob Hartman | .50 |
| 129 Frank Herrera | .50 |
| 130 Lou Jackson | .50 |
| 131 Deron Johnson | .50 |
| 132 Don Lee | .50 |
| 133 Bob Lillis | .75 |
| 134 Jim McDaniel | .50 |
| 135 Gene Oliver | .50 |
| 136 Jim O'Toole | .50 |
| 137 Dick Ricketts | .50 |
| 138 John Romano | .50 |
| 139 Ed Sadowski | .50 |
| 140 Charlie Secrest | .50 |
| 141 Joe Shipley | .50 |
| 142 Dick Stigman | .50 |
| 143 Willie Tasby | .50 |
| 144 Jerry Walker | .50 |
| 145 Dom Zanni | .50 |
| 146 Jerry Zimmerman | .50 |
| 147 Cubs' Clubbers: | 2.00 |
|   Dale Long, Ernie Banks, | |
|   Walt Moryn | |
| 148 Mike McCormick | .50 |
| 149 Jim Bunning | 2.00 |
| 150 Stan Musial | 20.00 |
| 151 Bob Malkmus | .50 |
| 152 Johnny Klippstein | .50 |
| 153 Jim Marshall | .50 |
| 154 Ray Herbert | .50 |
| 155 Enos Slaughter | 3.00 |
| 156 Ace Hurlers: | 1.00 |
|   Billy Pierce, Robin Roberts | |
| 157 Felix Mantilla | .50 |
| 158 Walt Dropo | .50 |
| 159 Bob Shaw | .50 |
| 160 Dick Groat | 1.00 |
| 161 Frank Baumann | .50 |
| 162 Bobby Smith | .50 |
| 163 Sandy Koufax | 27.00 |
| 164 Johnny Groth | .50 |
| 165 Bill Bruton | .50 |
| 166 Destruction Crew: | 1.00 |
|   Minnie Minoso, Rocky | |
|   Colavito, Larry Doby | |
| 167 Duke Maas | .50 |
| 168 Carroll Hardy | .50 |
| 169 Ted Abernathy | .50 |
| 170 Gene Woodling | .50 |
| 171 Willard Schmidt | .50 |
| 172 Kansas C. Athletics | 1.50 |
| 173 Bill Monbouquette | .50 |
| 174 Jim Pendleton | .50 |
| 175 Dick Farrell | .50 |
| 176 Preston Ward | .50 |
| 177 John Briggs | .50 |
| 178 Ruben Amaro | .50 |
| 179 Don Rudolph | .50 |
| 180 Yogi Berra | 15.00 |
| 181 Bob Porterfield | .50 |
| 182 Milt Graff | .50 |
| 183 Stu Miller | .50 |
| 184 Harvey Haddix | .50 |
| 185 Jim Busby | .50 |
| 186 Mudcat Grant | .50 |
| 187 Bubba Phillips | .50 |
| 188 Juan Pizarro | .50 |
| 189 Neil Chrisley | .50 |
| 190 Bill Virdon | 1.00 |

| NO. PLAYER | MINT |
|---|---|
| 191 Russ Kemmerer | .50 |
| 192 Charley Beamon | .50 |
| 193 Sammy Taylor | .50 |
| 194 Jim Brosnan | .50 |
| 195 Rip Repulski | .50 |
| 196 Billy Moran | .50 |
| 197 Ray Semproch | .50 |
| 198 Jim Davenport | .50 |
| 199 Leo Kiely | .50 |
| 200 NL President: | |
|   Warren Giles | 1.50 |
| 201 Tom Acker | .50 |
| 202 Roger Maris | 10.00 |
| 203 Ozzie Virgil | .50 |
| 204 Casey Wise | .50 |
| 205 Don Larsen | 1.50 |
| 206 Carl Furillo | 1.50 |
| 207 George Strickland | .50 |
| 208 Willie Jones | .40 |
| 209 Lenny Green | .50 |
| 210 Ed Bailey | .50 |
| 211 Bob Blaylock | .50 |
| 212 Fence Busters: | 5.00 |
|   Hank Aaron, Eddie Mathews | |
| 213 Jim Rivera | .50 |
| 214 Marcelino Solis | .50 |
| 215 Jim Lemon | .50 |
| 216 Andre Rodgers | .50 |
| 217 Carl Erskine | 1.50 |
| 218 Roman Mejias | .50 |
| 219 George Zuverink | .50 |
| 220 Frank Malzone | .50 |
| 221 Bob Bowman | .50 |
| 222 Bobby Shantz | .50 |
| 223 St. Louis Cardinals | 2.00 |
| 224 Claude Osteen (R) | 1.00 |
| 225 Johnny Logan | .50 |
| 226 Art Ceccarelli | .50 |
| 227 Hal Smith | .50 |
| 228 Don Gross | .50 |
| 229 Vic Power | .50 |
| 230 Bill Fischer | .50 |
| 231 Ellis Burton | .50 |
| 232 Eddie Kasko | .50 |
| 233 Paul Foytack | .50 |
| 234 Chuck Tanner | .50 |
| 235 Valmy Thomas | .50 |
| 236 Ted Bowsfield | .50 |
| 237 Run Preventers: | 1.50 |
|   Gil McDougald, Bob Turley, | |
|   Bobby Richardson | |
| 238 Gene Baker | .50 |
| 239 Bob Trowbridge | .50 |
| 240 Hank Bauer | 1.50 |
| 241 Billy Muffett | .50 |
| 242 Ron Samford | .50 |
| 243 Marv Grissom | .50 |
| 244 Dick Gray | .50 |
| 245 Ned Garver | .50 |
| 246 J.W. Porter | .50 |
| 247 Don Ferrarese | .50 |
| 248 Boston Red Sox | 2.00 |
| 249 Bobby Adams | .50 |
| 250 Billy O'Dell | .50 |
| 251 Cletis Boyer | .50 |
| 252 Ray Boone | .50 |
| 253 Seth Morehead | .50 |
| 254 Zeke Bella | .50 |
| 255 Del Ennis | .50 |
| 256 Jerry Davie | .50 |
| 257 Leon Wagner | .50 |
| 258 Fred Kipp | .50 |
| 259 Jim Pisoni | .50 |
| 260 Early Wynn | 4.00 |
| 261 Gene Stephens | .50 |
| 262 Hitters' Foes: | 1.50 |
|   Johnny Podres, Clem | |
|   Labine, Don Drysdale | |
| 263 Buddy Daley | .50 |
| 264 Chico Carrasquel | .50 |
| 265 Ron Kline | .50 |

| NO. PLAYER | MINT |
|---|---|
| 266 Woody Held | .50 |
| 267 John Romonosky | .50 |
| 268 Tito Francona | .50 |
| 269 Jack Mayer | .50 |
| 270 Gil Hodges | 5.00 |
| 271 Orlando Pena | .50 |
| 272 Jerry Lumpe | .50 |
| 273 Joey Jay | .50 |
| 274 Jerry Kindall | .50 |
| 275 Jack Sanford | .50 |
| 276 Pete Daley | .50 |
| 277 Turk Lown | .50 |
| 278 Chuck Essegian | .50 |
| 279 Ernie Johnson | .50 |
| 280 Frank Bolling | .50 |
| 281 Walt Craddock | .50 |
| 282 R.C. Stevens | .50 |
| 283 Russ Heman | .50 |
| 284 Steve Korcheck | .50 |
| 285 Joe Cunningham | .50 |
| 286 Dean Stone | .50 |
| 287 Don Zimmer | .75 |
| 288 Dutch Dotterer | .50 |
| 289 Johnny Kucks | .50 |
| 290 Wes Covington | .50 |
| 291 Pitching Partners: | .75 |
|   Pedro Ramos, | |
|   Camilo Pascual | |
| 292 Dick Williams | .50 |
| 293 Ray Moore | .50 |
| 294 Hank Foiles | .50 |
| 295 Billy Martin | 3.00 |
| 296 Ernie Broglio | .50 |
| 297 Jackie Brandt | .50 |
| 298 Tex Clevenger | .50 |
| 299 Billy Klaus | .50 |
| 300 Richie Ashburn | 2.50 |
| 301 Earl Averill | .50 |
| 302 Don Mossi | .50 |
| 303 Marty Keough | .50 |
| 304 Chicago Cubs | 2.50 |
| 305 Curt Raydon | .50 |
| 306 Jim Gilliam | 1.50 |
| 307 Curt Barclay | .50 |
| 308 Norm Siebern | .50 |
| 309 Sal Maglie | .75 |
| 310 Luis Aparicio | 4.00 |
| 311 Norm Zauchin | .50 |
| 312 Don Newcombe | 1.25 |
| 313 Frank House | .50 |
| 314 Don Cardwell | .50 |
| 315 Joe Adcock | 1.00 |
| 316 Ralph Lumenti* | .50 |
|   (photo of Camilo Pascual) | |
| 317 Hitting Kings: | 5.00 |
|   Willie Mays, Richie Ashburn | |
| 318 Rocky Bridges | .50 |
| 319 Dave Hillmann | .50 |
| 320 Bob Skinner | .50 |
| 321 Bob Giallombardo* | .50 |
| 322 Harry Hanebrink* | .50 |
| 323 Frank Sullivan | .50 |
| 324 Donald Demeter | .50 |
| 325 Ken Boyer | 1.50 |
| 326 Marv Throneberry | 1.25 |
| 327 Gary Bell | .50 |
| 328 Lou Skizas | .50 |
| 329 Detroit Tigers | 2.50 |
| 330 Gus Triandos | .50 |
| 331 Steve Boros | .50 |
| 332 Ray Monzant | .50 |
| 333 Harry Simpson | .50 |
| 334 Glen Hobbie | .50 |
| 335 Johnny Temple | .50 |
| 336 Billy Loes* | .50 |
| 337 George Crowe | .50 |
| 338 Sparky Anderson (R) | 2.50 |
| 339 Roy Face | .50 |
| 340 Roy Sievers | .50 |
| 341 Tom Qualters | .50 |
| 342 Ray Jablonski | .50 |

| NO. PLAYER | MINT |
|---|---|
| 343 Billy Hoeft | .50 |
| 344 Russ Nixon | .50 |
| 345 Gil McDougald | 1.50 |
| 346 Batter Bafflers: | .50 |
| Tom Brewer, Dave Sisler | |
| 347 Bob Buhl | .50 |
| 348 Ted Lepcio | .50 |
| 349 Hoyt Wilhelm | 3.00 |
| 350 Ernie Banks | 13.00 |
| 351 Earl Torgeson | .50 |
| 352 Robin Roberts | 4.00 |
| 353 Curt Flood | 1.00 |
| 354 Pete Burnside | .50 |
| 355 Jim Piersall | 1.00 |
| 356 Bob Mabe | .50 |
| 357 Dick Stuart (R) | 1.00 |
| 358 Ralph Terry | .50 |
| 359 Bill White (R) | 1.50 |
| 360 Al Kaline | 10.00 |
| 361 Willard Nixon | .50 |
| 362 Dolan Nichols* | .50 |
| 363 Bobby Avila | .50 |
| 364 Danny McDevitt | .50 |
| 365 Gus Bell | .50 |
| 366 Humberto Robinson | .50 |
| 367 Cal Neeman | .50 |
| 368 Don Mueller | .50 |
| 369 Dick Tomanek | .50 |
| 370 Pete Runnels | .50 |
| 371 Dick Brodowski | .50 |
| 372 Jim Hegan | .50 |
| 373 Herb Plews | .50 |
| 374 Art Ditmar | .50 |
| 375 Bob Nieman | .50 |
| 376 Hal Naragon | .50 |
| 377 Johnny Antonelli | .50 |
| 378 Gail Harris | .50 |
| 379 Bob Miller | .50 |
| 380 Hank Aaron | 30.00 |
| 381 Mike Baxes | .50 |
| 382 Curt Simmons | .50 |
| 383 Words of Wisdom: | 2.50 |
| Don Larsen, Casey Stengel | |
| 384 Dave Sisler | .50 |
| 385 Sherm Lollar | .50 |
| 386 Jim Delsing | .50 |
| 387 Don Drysdale | 8.00 |
| 388 Bob Will | .50 |
| 389 Joe Nuxhall | .50 |
| 390 Orlando Cepeda | 2.50 |
| 391 Milt Pappas | .50 |
| 392 Whitey Herzog | .75 |
| 393 Frank Lary | .50 |
| 394 Randy Jackson | .50 |
| 395 Elston Howard | 2.00 |
| 396 Bob Rush | .50 |
| 397 Washington Senators | 1.50 |
| 398 Wally Post | .50 |
| 399 Larry Jackson | .50 |
| 400 Jackie Jensen | .75 |

| NO. PLAYER | MINT |
|---|---|
| 401 Ron Blackburn | .50 |
| 402 Hector Lopez | .50 |
| 403 Clem Labine | .50 |
| 404 Hank Sauer | .50 |
| 405 Roy McMillan | .50 |
| 406 Solly Drake | .50 |
| 407 Moe Drabowsky | .50 |
| 408 Keystone Combo: | 2.00 |
| Nellie Fox, Luis Aparicio | |
| 409 Gus Zernial | .50 |
| 410 Billy Pierce | .50 |
| 411 Whitey Lockman | .50 |
| 412 Stan Lopata | .50 |
| 413 Camillo Pascual | .50 |
| 414 Dale Long | .50 |
| 415 Bill Mazeroski | 1.50 |
| 416 Haywood Sullivan | .50 |
| 417 Virgil Trucks | .50 |
| 418 Gino Cimoli | .50 |
| 419 Milwaukee Braves | 2.00 |
| 420 Rocky Colavito | 1.50 |
| 421 Herm Wehmeier | .50 |
| 422 Hobie Landrith | .50 |
| 423 Bob Grim | .50 |
| 424 Ken Aspromonte | .50 |
| 425 Del Crandall | .50 |
| 426 Jerry Staley | .50 |
| 427 Charlie Neal | .50 |
| 428 Buc Hill Aces: | 1.00 |
| Ron Kline, Bob Friend, | |
| Vernon Law, Roy Face | |
| 429 Bobby Thomson | .50 |
| 430 Whitey Ford | 10.00 |
| 431 Whammy Douglas | .50 |
| 432 Smokey Burgess | .50 |
| 433 Billy Harrell | .50 |
| 434 Hal Griggs | .50 |
| 435 Frank Robinson | 11.00 |
| 436 Granny Hamner | .50 |
| 437 Ike Delock | .50 |
| 438 Sam Esposito | .50 |
| 439 Brooks Robinson | 13.00 |
| 440 Lou Burdette | 2.00 |
| 441 John Roseboro | .50 |
| 442 Ray Narleski | .50 |
| 443 Daryl Spencer | .50 |
| 444 Ronnie Hansen | .50 |
| 445 Cal McLish | .50 |
| 446 Rocky Nelson | .50 |
| 447 Bob Anderson | .50 |
| 448 Vada Pinson | 1.50 |
| 449 Tom Gorman | .50 |
| 450 Ed Mathews | 6.00 |
| 451 Jimmy Constable | .50 |
| 452 Chico Fernandez | .50 |
| 453 Les Moss | .50 |
| 454 Phil Clark | .50 |
| 455 Larry Doby | 1.00 |
| 456 Jerry Casale | .50 |
| 457 Los Angeles Dodgers | 4.00 |

| NO. PLAYER | MINT |
|---|---|
| 458 Gordon Jones | .50 |
| 459 Bill Tuttle | .50 |
| 460 Bob Friend | .50 |
| 461 Mantle Hits 42nd HR | 9.00 |
| 462 Colavito's Catch | 1.00 |
| 463 Kaline Bat Champ | 2.00 |
| 464 Mays' Series Catch | 4.00 |
| 465 Sievers HR Mark | .75 |
| 466 Pierce All-Star | .75 |
| 467 Aaron Clubs Homer | 4.00 |
| 468 Snider's Play | 3.00 |
| 469 Banks MVP | 3.00 |
| 470 Musial's 3000 Hits | 3.00 |
| 471 Tom Sturdivant | .50 |
| 472 Gene Freese | .50 |
| 473 Mike Fornieles | .50 |
| 474 Moe Thacker | .50 |
| 475 Jack Harshman | .50 |
| 476 Cleveland Indians | 1.50 |
| 477 Barry Latman | .50 |
| 478 Bob Clemente | 20.00 |
| 479 Lindy McDaniel | .50 |
| 480 Red Schoendienst | 1.00 |
| 481 Charlie Maxwell | .50 |
| 482 Russ Meyer | .50 |
| 483 Clint Courtney | .50 |
| 484 Willie Kirkland | .50 |
| 485 Ryne Duren | .50 |
| 486 Sammy White | .50 |
| 487 Hal Brown | .50 |
| 488 Walt Moryn | .50 |
| 489 John Powers | .50 |
| 490 Frank Thomas | .50 |
| 491 Don Blasingame | .50 |
| 492 Gene Conley | .50 |
| 493 Jim Landis | .50 |
| 494 Don Pavletich | .50 |
| 495 Johnny Podres | 1.00 |
| 496 Wayne Terwilliger | .50 |
| 497 Hal R. Smith | .50 |
| 498 Dick Hyde | .50 |
| 499 Johnny O'Brien | .50 |
| 500 Vic Wertz | .50 |
| 501 Bobby Tiefenauer | .50 |
| 502 Al Dark | .50 |
| 503 Jim Owens | .50 |
| 504 Ossie Alvarez | .50 |
| 505 Tony Kubek | 2.00 |
| 506 Bob Purkey | .50 |
| 507 Bob Hale | 2.00 |
| 508 Art Fowler | 2.00 |
| 509 Norm Cash (R) | 4.00 |
| 510 New York Yankees | 10.00 |
| 511 George Susce | 2.00 |
| 512 George Altman | 2.00 |
| 513 Tommy Carroll | 2.00 |
| 514 Bob Gibson (R) | 50.00 |
| 515 Harmon Killebrew | 22.00 |
| 516 Mike Garcia | 2.00 |
| 517 Joe Koppe | 2.00 |

| NO. PLAYER | MINT |
|---|---|
| 518 Mike Cueller (R) | 3.00 |
| 519 Infield Power: | 2.50 |
| Pete Runnels, Dick | |
| Gernert, Frank Malzone | |
| 520 Don Elston | 2.00 |
| 521 Gary Geiger | 2.00 |
| 522 Gene Snyder | 2.00 |
| 523 Harry Bright | 2.00 |
| 524 Larry Osborne | 2.00 |
| 525 Jim Coates | 2.00 |
| 526 Bob Speake | 2.00 |
| 527 Solly Hemus | 2.00 |
| 528 Pittsburgh Pirates | 4.00 |
| 529 George Bamberger (R) | 4.00 |
| 530 Wally Moon | 2.00 |
| 531 Ray Webster | 2.00 |
| 532 Mark Freeman | 2.00 |
| 533 Darrell Johnson | 2.00 |
| 534 Faye Throneberry | 2.00 |
| 535 Ruben Gomez | 2.00 |
| 536 Dan Kravitz | 2.00 |
| 537 Rudolph Arias | 2.00 |
| 538 Chick King | 2.00 |
| 539 Gary Blaylock | 2.00 |
| 540 Willie Miranda | 2.00 |
| 541 Bob Thurman | 2.00 |
| 542 Jim Perry (R) | 2.00 |
| 543 Corsair Outfield Trio: | 10.00 |
| Bob Skinner, Bll Virdon, | |
| Roberto Clemente | |
| 544 Lee Tate | 2.00 |
| 545 Tom Morgan | 2.00 |
| 546 Al Schroll | 2.00 |
| 547 Jim Baxes | 2.00 |
| 548 Elmer Singleton | 2.00 |
| 549 Howie Nunn | 2.00 |
| 550 Symbol of Courage: | 30.00 |
| Roy Campanella | |
| 551 F. Haney—Mgr.(AS) | 2.50 |
| 552 C. Stengel—Mgr. (AS) | 5.00 |
| 553 Orlando Cepeda (AS) | 2.50 |
| 554 Bll Skowron (AS) | 2.50 |
| 555 Bill Mazeroski (AS) | 2.50 |
| 556 Nellie Fox (AS) | 2.50 |
| 557 Ken Boyer (AS) | 2.50 |
| 558 Frank Malzone (AS) | 2.50 |
| 559 Ernie Banks (AS) | 7.50 |
| 560 Luis Aparicio (AS) | 4.00 |
| 561 Hank Aaron (AS) | 15.00 |
| 562 Al Kaline (AS) | 7.50 |
| 563 Willie Mays (AS) | 16.00 |
| 564 Mickey Mantle (AS) | 40.00 |
| 565 Wes Covington (AS) | 2.50 |
| 566 Roy Sievers (AS) | 2.50 |
| 567 Del Crandall (AS) | 2.50 |
| 568 Gus Triandos (AS) | 2.50 |
| 569 Bob Friend (AS) | 2.50 |
| 570 Bob Turley (AS) | 2.50 |
| 571 Warren Spahn (AS) | 5.00 |
| 572 Billy Pierce (AS) | 2.50 |

## 1960 Topps. . . .Complete Set of 572 Cards—Value $750.00

This set features the rookie cards of Willie McCovey and Carl Yastrzemski. The high numbers are 507 to 572. Semi-high numbers are 441 to 506. Topps' switched to a predominately horizontal format, and used it for the last time. Cards 375 to 440 exist with *gray* or *white* backs.

| NO. | PLAYER | MINT |
|---|---|---|
| 1 | Early Wynn | 6.00 |
| 2 | Roman Mejias | .40 |
| 3 | Joe Adcock | .75 |
| 4 | Bob Purkey | .40 |
| 5 | Wally Moon | .40 |
| 6 | Lou Berberet | .40 |
| 7 | Master & Mentor: | 3.50 |
| | Willie Mays, Bill Rigney | |
| 8 | Bud Daley | .40 |
| 9 | Faye Throneberry | .40 |
| 10 | Ernie Banks | 7.00 |
| 11 | Norm Siebern | .40 |
| 12 | Milt Pappas | .40 |
| 13 | Wally Post | .40 |
| 14 | Jim Grant | .40 |
| 15 | Pete Runnels | .40 |
| 16 | Ernie Broglio | .40 |
| 17 | John Callison | .40 |
| 18 | Los Angeles Dodgers | 3.00 |
| 19 | Felix Mantilla | .40 |
| 20 | Roy Face | .75 |
| 21 | Dutch Dotterer | .40 |
| 22 | Rocky Bridges | .40 |
| 23 | Eddie Fisher | .40 |
| 24 | Dick Gray | .40 |
| 25 | Roy Sievers | .40 |
| 26 | Wayne Terwilliger | .40 |
| 27 | Dick Drott | .40 |
| 28 | Brooks Robinson | 10.00 |
| 29 | Clem Labine | .40 |
| 30 | Tito Francona | .40 |
| 31 | Sammy Esposito | .40 |
| 32 | Sophomore Stalwarts: | .60 |
| | Jim O'Toole, Vada Pinson | |
| 33 | Tom Morgan | .40 |
| 34 | Sparky Anderson | 1.00 |
| 35 | Whitey Ford | 6.00 |
| 36 | Russ Nixon | .40 |
| 37 | Bill Bruton | .40 |
| 38 | Jerry Casale | .40 |
| 39 | Earl Averill | .40 |
| 40 | Joe Cunningham | .40 |
| 41 | Barry Latman | .40 |
| 42 | Hobie Landrith | .40 |
| 43 | Washington Senators | 1.00 |
| 44 | Bobby Locke | .40 |
| 45 | Roy McMillan | .40 |
| 46 | Jack Fisher | .40 |
| 47 | Don Zimmer | .75 |
| 48 | Hal Smith | .40 |
| 49 | Curt Raydon | .40 |
| 50 | Al Kaline | 7.50 |
| 51 | Jim Coates | .40 |
| 52 | Dave Philley | .40 |
| 53 | Jackie Brandt | .40 |
| 54 | Mike Fornieles | .40 |
| 55 | Bill Mazeroski | 1.25 |
| 56 | Steve Korcheck | .40 |
| 57 | Win Savers: | .60 |
| | Turk Lown, Jerry Staley | |
| 58 | Gino Cimoli | .40 |
| 59 | Juan Pizarro | .40 |
| 60 | Gus Triandos | .40 |
| 61 | Eddie Kasko | .40 |
| 62 | Roger Craig | .40 |
| 63 | George Strickland | .40 |
| 64 | Jack Meyer | .40 |
| 65 | Elston Howard | 1.50 |
| 66 | Bob Trowbridge | .40 |
| 67 | Jose Pagan | .40 |
| 68 | Dave Hillman | .40 |
| 69 | Billy Goodman | .40 |
| 70 | Lou Burdette | 1.00 |
| 71 | Marty Keough | .40 |
| 72 | Detroit Tigers | 2.00 |
| 73 | Bob Gibson | 7.00 |
| 74 | Walt Moryn | .40 |
| 75 | Vic Power | .40 |
| 76 | Bill Fischer | .40 |
| 77 | Hank Foiles | .40 |
| 78 | Bob Grim | .40 |
| 79 | Walt Dropo | .40 |

| NO. | PLAYER | MINT |
|---|---|---|
| 80 | Johnny Antonelli | .40 |
| 81 | Russ Snyder | .40 |
| 82 | Ruben Gomez | .40 |
| 83 | Tony Kubek | 1.50 |
| 84 | Hal Smith | .40 |
| 85 | Frank Lary | .40 |
| 86 | Dick Gernert | .40 |
| 87 | John Romonosky | .40 |
| 88 | John Roseboro | .40 |
| 89 | Hal Brown | .40 |
| 90 | Bobby Avila | .40 |
| 91 | Bennie Daniels | .40 |
| 92 | Whitey Herzog | .75 |
| 93 | Art Schult | .40 |
| 94 | Leo Kiely | .40 |
| 95 | Frank Thomas | .40 |
| 96 | Ralph Terry | .40 |
| 97 | Ted Lepcio | .40 |
| 98 | Gordon Jones | .40 |
| 99 | Lenny Green | .40 |
| 100 | Nellie Fox | 1.50 |
| 101 | Bob Miller | .40 |
| 102 | Kent Hadley | .40 |
| 103 | Dick Farrell | .40 |
| 104 | Dick Schofield | .40 |
| 105 | Larry Sherry (R) | .75 |
| 106 | Billy Gardner | .40 |
| 107 | Carl Willey | .40 |
| 108 | Pete Daley | .40 |
| 109 | Cletis Boyer | .40 |
| 110 | Cal McLish | .40 |
| 111 | Vic Wertz | .40 |
| 112 | Jack Harshman | .40 |
| 113 | Bob Skinner | .40 |
| 114 | Ken Aspromonte | .40 |
| 115 | Fork & Knuckler: | 1.50 |
| | Roy Face, Hoyt Wilhelm | |
| 116 | Jim Rivera | .40 |

**No. 117 to 148—ROOKIE STARS**

| NO. | PLAYER | MINT |
|---|---|---|
| 117 | Tom Borland | .40 |
| 118 | Bob Bruce | .40 |
| 119 | Chico Cardenas | .40 |
| 120 | Duke Carmel | .40 |
| 121 | Camilo Carreon | .40 |
| 122 | Don Dillard | .40 |
| 123 | Dan Dobbek | .40 |
| 124 | Jim Donohue | .40 |
| 125 | Dick Ellsworth | .40 |
| 126 | Chuck Estrada (R) | .75 |
| 127 | Ronnie Hansen | .40 |
| 128 | Bill Harris | .40 |
| 129 | Bob Hartman | .40 |
| 130 | Frank Herrera | .40 |
| 131 | Ed Hobaugh | .40 |
| 132 | Frank Howard (R) | 3.00 |
| 133 | Manuel Javier | .40 |
| 134 | Deron Johnson | .40 |
| 135 | Ken Johnson | .40 |
| 136 | Jim Kaat (R) | 10.00 |
| 137 | Lou Klimchock | .40 |
| 138 | Art Mahaffey | .50 |
| 139 | Carl Mathias | .40 |
| 140 | Julio Navarro | .40 |
| 141 | Jim Proctor | .40 |
| 142 | Bill Short | .40 |
| 143 | Al Spangler | .40 |
| 144 | Al Stieglitz | .40 |
| 145 | Jim Umbricht | .40 |
| 146 | Ted Wieand | .40 |
| 147 | Bob Will | .40 |
| 148 | Carl Yastrzemski (R) | 120.00 |
| 149 | Bob Nieman | .40 |
| 150 | Billy Pierce | .75 |
| 151 | San F. Giants | 1.50 |
| 152 | Gail Harris | .40 |
| 153 | Bobby Thomson | .75 |
| 154 | Jim Davenport | .40 |
| 155 | Charlie Neal | .40 |
| 156 | Art Ceccarelli | .40 |
| 157 | Rocky Nelson | .40 |
| 158 | Wes Covington | .40 |

| NO. | PLAYER | MINT |
|---|---|---|
| 159 | Jim Piersall | .75 |
| 160 | Rival All-Stars: | 7.00 |
| | Mickey Mantle, Ken Boyer | |
| 161 | Ray Narleski | .40 |
| 162 | Sammy Taylor | .40 |
| 163 | Hector Lopez | .40 |
| 164 | Cincinnati Reds | 2.00 |
| 165 | Jack Sanford | .40 |
| 166 | Chuck Essegian | .40 |
| 167 | Valmy Thomas | .40 |
| 168 | Alex Grammas | .40 |
| 169 | Jake Striker | .40 |
| 170 | Del Crandall | .40 |
| 171 | Johnny Groth | .40 |
| 172 | Willie Kirkland | .40 |
| 173 | Billy Martin | 2.00 |
| 174 | Cleveland Indians | 1.50 |
| 175 | Pedro Ramos | .40 |
| 176 | Vada Pinson | 1.00 |
| 177 | Johnny Kucks | .40 |
| 178 | Woody Held | .40 |
| 179 | Rip Coleman | .40 |
| 180 | Harry Simpson | .40 |
| 181 | Billy Loes | .40 |
| 182 | Glen Hobbie | .40 |
| 183 | Eli Grba | .40 |
| 184 | Gary Geiger | .40 |
| 185 | Jim Owens | .40 |
| 186 | Dave Sisler | .40 |
| 187 | Jay Hook | .40 |
| 188 | Dick Williams | .40 |
| 189 | Don McMahon | .40 |
| 190 | Gene Woodling | .40 |
| 191 | Johnny Klippstein | .40 |
| 192 | Danny O'Connell | .40 |
| 193 | Dick Hyde | .40 |
| 194 | Bobby Gene Smith | .40 |
| 195 | Lindy McDaniel | .40 |
| 196 | Andy Carey | .40 |
| 197 | Ron Kline | .40 |
| 198 | Jerry Lynch | .40 |
| 199 | Dick Donovan | .40 |
| 200 | Willie Mays | 25.00 |
| 201 | Larry Osborne | .40 |
| 202 | Fred Kipp | .40 |
| 203 | Sammy White | .40 |
| 204 | Ryne Duren | .75 |
| 205 | Johnny Logan | .40 |
| 206 | Claude Osteen | .40 |
| 207 | Bob Boyd | .40 |
| 208 | Chicago White Sox | 1.50 |
| 209 | Ron Blackburn | .40 |
| 210 | Hamon Killebrew | 7.00 |
| 211 | Taylor Phillips | .40 |
| 212 | Walt Alston (Mgr.) | 2.00 |
| 213 | Chuck Dressen (Mgr.) | .40 |
| 214 | Jim Dykes (Mgr.) | .40 |
| 215 | Bob Elliott (Mgr.) | .40 |
| 216 | Joe Gordon (Mgr.) | .40 |
| 217 | Charley Grimm (Mgr.) | .40 |
| 218 | Solly Hemus (Mgr.) | .40 |
| 219 | Fred Hutchinson (Mgr.) | .40 |
| 220 | Billy Jurges (Mgr.) | .40 |
| 221 | Cookie Lavagetto (Mgr.) | .40 |
| 222 | Al Lopez (Mgr.) | 1.25 |
| 223 | Danny Murtaugh (Mgr.) | .40 |
| 224 | Paul Richards (Mgr.) | .40 |
| 225 | Bill Rigney (Mgr.) | .40 |
| 226 | Eddie Sawyer (Mgr.) | .40 |
| 227 | Casey Stengel (Mgr.) | 5.00 |
| 228 | Ernie Johnson | .40 |
| 229 | Joe Morgan | .40 |
| 230 | Mound Magicians: | 3.00 |
| | Lou Burdette, Warren | |
| | Spahn, Bob Buhl | |
| 231 | Hal Naragon | .40 |
| 232 | Jim Busby | .40 |
| 233 | Don Elston | .40 |
| 234 | Don Demeter | .40 |
| 235 | Gus Bell | .40 |
| 236 | Dick Ricketts | .40 |
| 237 | Elmer Valo | .40 |

| NO. | PLAYER | MINT |
|---|---|---|
| 238 | Danny Kravitz | .40 |
| 239 | Joe Shipley | .40 |
| 240 | Luis Aparicio | 4.00 |
| 241 | Albie Pearson | .40 |
| 242 | St. Louis Cardinals | 1.50 |
| 243 | Bubba Phillips | .40 |
| 244 | Hal Griggs | .40 |
| 245 | Eddie Yost | .40 |
| 246 | Lee Maye | .40 |
| 247 | Gil McDougald | 1.00 |
| 248 | Del Rice | .40 |
| 249 | Earl Wilson | .40 |
| 250 | Stan Musial | 15.00 |
| 251 | Bobby Malkmus | .40 |
| 252 | Ray Herbert | .40 |
| 253 | Eddie Bressoud | .40 |
| 254 | Arnie Portocarrero | .40 |
| 255 | Jim Gilliam | 1.00 |
| 256 | Dick Brown | .40 |
| 257 | Gordy Coleman | .40 |
| 258 | Dick Groat | 1.50 |
| 259 | George Altman | .40 |
| 260 | Power Plus: | .75 |
| | Rocky Colavito, | |
| | Tito Francona | |
| 261 | Pete Burnside | .40 |
| 262 | Hank Bauer | .75 |
| 263 | Darrell Johnson | .40 |
| 264 | Robin Roberts | 4.00 |
| 265 | Rip Repulski | .40 |
| 266 | Joe Jay | .40 |
| 267 | Jim Marshall | .40 |
| 268 | Al Worthington | .40 |
| 269 | Gene Green | .40 |
| 270 | Bob Turley | .75 |
| 271 | Julio Bequer | .40 |
| 272 | Fred Green | .40 |
| 273 | Neil Chrisley | .40 |
| 274 | Tom Acker | .40 |
| 275 | Curt Flood | .75 |
| 276 | Ken McBride | .40 |
| 277 | Harry Bright | .40 |
| 278 | Stan Williams | .40 |
| 279 | Chuck Tanner | .40 |
| 280 | Frank Sullivan | .40 |
| 281 | Ray Boone | .40 |
| 282 | Joe Nuxhall | .40 |
| 283 | John Blanchard | .40 |
| 284 | Don Gross | .40 |
| 285 | Harry Anderson | .40 |
| 286 | Ray Semproch | .40 |
| 287 | Felipe Alou | .40 |
| 288 | Bob Mabe | .40 |
| 289 | Willie Jones | .40 |
| 290 | Jerry Lumpe | .40 |
| 291 | Bob Keegan | .40 |
| 292 | Dodger Backstops: | .60 |
| | Joe Pignatano, | |
| | John Roseboro | |
| 293 | Gene Conley | .40 |
| 294 | Tony Taylor | .40 |
| 295 | Gil Hodges | 5.00 |
| 296 | Nelson Chittum | .40 |
| 297 | Reno Bertoia | .40 |
| 298 | George Witt | .40 |
| 299 | Earl Torgeson | .40 |
| 300 | Hank Aaron | 30.00 |
| 301 | Jerry Davie | .40 |
| 302 | Philadelphia Phillies | 1.50 |
| 303 | Billy O'Dell | .40 |
| 304 | Joe Ginsberg | .40 |
| 305 | Richie Ashburn | 1.50 |
| 306 | Frank Baumann | .40 |
| 307 | Gene Oliver | .40 |
| 308 | Dick Hall | .40 |
| 309 | Bob Hale | .40 |
| 310 | Frank Malzone | .40 |
| 311 | Raul Sanchez | .40 |
| 312 | Charlie Lau | .40 |
| 313 | Turk Lown | .40 |
| 314 | Chico Fernandez | .40 |
| 315 | Bobby Shantz | .75 |

| NO. PLAYER | MINT |
|---|---|
| 316 Willie McCovey (R) | 50.00 |
| 317 Pumpsie Green | .40 |
| 318 Jim Baxes | .40 |
| 319 Joe Koppe | .40 |
| 320 Bob Allison | .40 |
| 321 Ron Fairly | .40 |
| 322 Willie Tasby | .40 |
| 323 Johnny Romano | .40 |
| 324 Jim Perry | .40 |
| 325 Jim O'Toole | .40 |
| 326 Bob Clemente | 20.00 |
| 327 Ray Sadecki | .40 |
| 328 Earl Battey | .40 |
| 329 Zack Monroe | .40 |
| 330 Harvey Kuenn | 1.00 |
| 331 Henry Mason | .40 |
| 332 New York Yankees | 7.00 |
| 333 Danny McDevitt | .40 |
| 334 Ted Abernathy | .40 |
| 335 Red Schoendienst | 1.00 |
| 336 Ike Delock | .40 |
| 337 Cal Neeman | .40 |
| 338 Ray Monzant | .40 |
| 339 Harry Chiti | .40 |
| 340 Harvey Haddix | .75 |
| 341 Carroll Hardy | .40 |
| 342 Casey Wise | .40 |
| 343 Sandy Koufax | 15.00 |
| 344 Clint Courtney | .40 |
| 345 Don Newcombe | .75 |
| 346 J.C. Martin | .40 |
| (photo of Gary Peters) | |
| 347 Ed Bouchee | .40 |
| 348 Barry Shetrone | .40 |
| 349 Moe Drabowsky | .40 |
| 350 Mickey Mantle | 75.00 |
| 351 Don Nottebart | .40 |
| 352 Cincy Clouters: | 2.00 |
| Gus Bell, Frank | |
| Robinson, Jerry Lynch | |
| 353 Don Larsen | .75 |
| 354 Bob Lillis | .40 |
| 355 Bill White | .40 |
| 356 Joe Amalfitano | .40 |
| 357 Al Schroll | .40 |
| 358 Joe DeMaestri | .40 |
| 359 Buddy Gilbert | .40 |
| 360 Herb Score | .40 |
| 361 Bob Oldis | .40 |
| 362 Russ Kemmerer | .40 |
| 363 Gene Stephens | .40 |
| 364 Paul Foytack | .40 |
| 365 Minnie Minoso | 1.00 |
| 366 Dallas Green (R) | 1.25 |
| 367 Bill Tuttle | .40 |
| 368 Daryl Spencer | .40 |
| 369 Billy Hoeft | .40 |
| 370 Bill Skowron | 1.50 |
| 371 Bud Byerly | .40 |
| 372 Frank House | .40 |
| 373 Don Hoak | .40 |
| 374 Bob Buhl | .40 |
| 375 Dale Long | .40 |
| 376 Johnny Briggs | .40 |
| 377 Roger Maris | 15.00 |
| 378 Stu Miller | .40 |
| 379 Red Wilson | .40 |
| 380 Bob Shaw | .40 |
| 381 Milwakee Braves | 1.50 |
| 382 Ted Bowsfield | .40 |
| 383 Leon Wagner | .40 |
| 384 Don Cardwell | .40 |
| 385 World Series Game 1 | 1.50 |
| Neal Steals Second | |

| NO. PLAYER | MINT |
|---|---|
| 386 World Series Game 2 | 1.50 |
| Neal Belts 2nd Homer | |
| 387 World Series Game 3 | 1.50 |
| Furillo Breaks Up Game | |
| 388 World Series Game 4 | 1.50 |
| Hodges' Winning Homer | |
| 389 World Series Game 5 | 1.50 |
| Luis Swipes Base | |
| 390 World Series Game 6 | 1.50 |
| Scrambling After Ball | |
| 391 World Series | 1.50 |
| The Champs Celebrate | |
| 392 Tex Clevenger | .40 |
| 393 Smokey Burgess | .40 |
| 394 Norm Larker | .40 |
| 395 Hoyt Wilhelm | 4.00 |
| 396 Steve Bilko | .40 |
| 397 Don Blasingame | .40 |
| 398 Mike Cuellar | .40 |
| 399 Young Hill Stars: | .40 |
| Milt Pappas, Jack Fisher, | |
| Jerry Walker | |
| 400 Rocky Colavito | 1.00 |
| 401 Bob Duliba | .40 |
| 402 Dick Stuart | .40 |
| 403 Ed Sadowski | .40 |
| 404 Bob Rush | .40 |
| 405 Bobby Richardson | 1.00 |
| 406 Billy Klaus | .40 |
| 407 Gary Peters | .40 |
| (photo of J.C. Martin) | |
| 408 Carl Furillo | 1.50 |
| 409 Ron Samford | .40 |
| 410 Sam Jones | .40 |
| 411 Ed Bailey | .40 |
| 412 Bob Anderson | .40 |
| 413 Kansas C. Athletics | 1.25 |
| 414 Don Williams | .40 |
| 415 Bob Cerv | .40 |
| 416 Humberto Robinson | .40 |
| 417 Chuck Cottier (R) | .75 |
| 418 Don Mossi | .40 |
| 419 George Crowe | .40 |
| 420 Ed Mathews | 4.00 |
| 421 Duke Maas | .40 |
| 422 Johnny Powers | .40 |
| 423 Ed Fitzgerald | .40 |
| 424 Pete Whisenant | .40 |
| 425 Johnny Podres | 1.00 |
| 426 Ron Jackson | .40 |
| 427 Al Grunwald | .40 |
| 428 Al Smith | .40 |
| 429 Amer. League Kings: | 1.25 |
| Nellie Fox, Harvey Kuenn | |
| 430 Art Ditmar | .40 |
| 431 Andre Rodgers | .40 |
| 432 Chuck Stobbs | .40 |
| 433 Irv Noren | .40 |
| 434 Brooks Lawrence | .40 |
| 435 Gene Freese | .40 |
| 436 Marv Throneberry | 1.00 |
| 437 Bob Friend | .40 |
| 438 Jim Coker | .40 |
| 439 Tom Brewer | .40 |
| 440 Jim Lemon | .40 |
| 441 Gary Bell | .60 |
| 442 Joe Pignatano | .60 |
| 443 Charlie Maxwell | .60 |
| 444 Jerry Kindall | .60 |
| 445 Warren Spahn | 7.50 |
| 446 Ellis Burton | .60 |
| 447 Ray Moore | .60 |
| 448 Jim Gentile | .75 |

| NO. PLAYER | MINT |
|---|---|
| 449 Jim Brosnan | .75 |
| 450 Orlando Cepeda | 2.50 |
| 451 Curt Simmons | .60 |
| 452 Ray Webster | .60 |
| 453 Vern Law | 1.00 |
| 454 Hal Woodeschick | .60 |
| 455 Orioles Coaches: | .75 |
| Robinson, Brecheen, Harris | |
| 456 Red Sox Coaches: | 1.25 |
| York, Herman, Maglie, Baker | |
| 457 Cubs Coaches: | .75 |
| Klein, Tappe, Root | |
| 458 White Sox Coaches: | .75 |
| Cooney, Gutteridge, | |
| Cuccinello, Berres | |
| 459 Reds Coaches: | .75 |
| Deal, Moses, Otero | |
| 460 Indians Coaches: | .75 |
| White, Lemon, Harder, Kress | |
| 461 Tigers Coaches: | 1.50 |
| Ferrick, Appling, Hitchcock | |
| 462 Athletics Coaches: | .75 |
| Cooper, Fitzsimmons, | |
| Heffner | |
| 463 Dodgers Coaches: | 1.50 |
| Bragan, Reiser, | |
| Becker, Mulleavy | |
| 464 Braves Coaches: | .75 |
| Scheffing, Myatt, | |
| Wyatt, Pafko | |
| 465 Yankees Coaches: | 2.50 |
| Dickey, Houk, | |
| Lopat, Crosetti | |
| 466 Phillies Coaches: | .75 |
| Silvestri, Cohen, Carter | |
| 467 Pirates Coaches: | .75 |
| Vernon, Oceak, | |
| Narron, Burwell | |
| 468 Cardinals Coaches: | .75 |
| Keane, Pollet, | |
| Katt, Walker | |
| 469 Giants Coaches: | .75 |
| Westrum, Parker, Posedel | |
| 470 Senators Coaches: | .75 |
| Swift, Mele, Clary | |
| 471 Ned Garver | .60 |
| 472 Al Dark | .75 |
| 473 Al Cicotte | .60 |
| 474 Haywood Sullivan | .60 |
| 475 Don Drysdale | 7.50 |
| 476 Lou Johnson | .60 |
| 477 Don Ferrarese | .60 |
| 478 Frank Torre | .60 |
| 479 Georges Maranda | .60 |
| 480 Yogi Berra | 13.00 |
| 481 Wes Stock | .75 |
| 482 Frank Bolling | .60 |
| 483 Camilo Pascual | .60 |
| 484 Pittsburgh Pirates | 3.00 |
| 485 Ken Boyer | 1.50 |
| 486 Bobby Del Greco | .60 |
| 487 Tom Sturdivant | .60 |
| 488 Norm Cash | 1.50 |
| 489 Steve Ridzik | .60 |
| 490 Frank Robinson | 9.00 |
| 491 Mel Roach | .60 |
| 492 Larry Jackson | .60 |
| 493 Duke Snider | 12.00 |
| 494 Baltimore Orioles | 2.50 |
| 495 Sherm Lollar | .60 |
| 496 Bill Virdon | 1.10 |
| 497 John Tsitouris | .60 |
| 498 Al Pilarcik | .60 |

| NO. PLAYER | MINT |
|---|---|
| 499 Johnny James | .60 |
| 500 Johnny Temple | .60 |
| 501 Bob Schmidt | .60 |
| 502 Jim Bunning | 2.00 |
| 503 Don Lee | .60 |
| 504 Seth Morehead | .60 |
| 505 Ted Kluszewski | 1.50 |
| 506 Lee Walls | .60 |
| 507 Dick Stigman | 2.00 |
| 508 Billy Consolo | 2.00 |
| 509 Tommy Davis (R) | 4.00 |
| 510 Jerry Staley | 2.00 |
| 511 Ken Walters | 2.00 |
| 512 Joe Gibbon | 2.00 |
| 513 Chicago Cubs | 4.00 |
| 514 Steve Barber | 2.00 |
| 515 Stan Lopata | 2.00 |
| 516 Marty Kutyna | 2.00 |
| 517 Charley James | 2.00 |
| 518 Tony Gonzalez | 2.00 |
| 519 Ed Roebuck | 2.00 |
| 520 Don Buddin | 2.00 |
| 521 Mike Lee | 2.00 |
| 522 Ken Hunt | 2.00 |
| 523 Clay Dalrymple | 2.00 |
| 524 Bill Henry | 2.00 |
| 525 Marv Breeding | 2.00 |
| 526 Paul Giel | 2.00 |
| 527 Jose Valdivielso | 2.00 |
| 528 Ben Johnson | 2.00 |
| 529 Norm Sherry (R) | 2.00 |
| 530 Mike McCormick | 2.00 |
| 531 Sandy Amoros | 2.00 |
| 532 Mike Garcia | 2.00 |
| 533 L. Clinton | 2.00 |
| 534 Ken Mackenzie | 2.00 |
| 535 Whitey Lockman | 2.00 |
| 536 Wynn Hawkins | 2.00 |
| 537 Boston Red Sox | 4.00 |
| 538 Frank Barnes | 2.00 |
| 539 Gene Baker | 2.00 |
| 540 Jerry Walker | 2.00 |
| 541 Tony Curry | 2.00 |
| 542 Ken Hamlin | 2.00 |
| 543 Elio Chacon | 2.00 |
| 544 Bill Monbouquette | 2.00 |
| 545 Carl Sawatski | 2.00 |
| 546 Hank Aguirre | 2.00 |
| 547 Bob Aspromonte | 2.00 |
| 548 Don Mincher | 2.00 |
| 549 John Buzhardt | 2.00 |
| 550 Jim Landis | 2.00 |
| 551 Ed Rakow | 2.00 |
| 552 Walt Bond | 2.00 |
| 553 Bill Skowron (AS) | 2.00 |
| 554 Willie McCovey (AS) | 12.00 |
| 555 Nellie Fox (AS) | 3.00 |
| 556 Charlie Neal (AS) | 2.00 |
| 557 Frank Malzone (AS) | 2.00 |
| 558 Eddie Mathews (AS) | 5.00 |
| 559 Luis Aparicio (AS) | 4.00 |
| 560 Ernie Banks (AS) | 8.00 |
| 561 Al Kaline (AS) | 8.00 |
| 562 Joe Cunningham (AS) | 2.00 |
| 563 Mickey Mantle (AS) | 35.00 |
| 564 Willie Mays (AS) | 17.00 |
| 565 Roger Maris (AS) | 9.00 |
| 566 Hank Aaron (AS) | 20.00 |
| 567 Sherm Lollar (AS) | 2.00 |
| 568 Del Crandall (AS) | 2.00 |
| 569 Camilo Pascual (AS) | 2.00 |
| 570 Don Drysdale (AS) | 4.00 |
| 571 Billy Pierce (AS) | 2.00 |
| 572 Johnny Antonelli (AS) | 2.00 |

# 1961 Topps....Complete Set of 587 Cards—Value $1150.00

Juan Marichal and Billy Williams' rookie cards are in this set. The high numbers are 523 to 589. Cards 587 and 588 were not issued. Card 426 (Braves team) was mistakenly numbered 463.

| NO. PLAYER | MINT |
|---|---|
| 1 Dick Groat | 3.00 |
| 2 Roger Maris | 15.00 |
| 3 John Buzhardt | .35 |
| 4 Lenny Green | .35 |
| 5 Johnny Romano | .35 |
| 6 Ed Roebuck | .35 |
| 7 Chicago White Sox | .75 |
| 8 Dick Williams | .35 |
| 9 Bob Purkey | .35 |
| 10 Brooks Robinson | 8.00 |
| 11 Curt Simmons | .35 |
| 12 Moe Thacker | .35 |
| 13 Chuck Cottier | .35 |
| 14 Don Mossi | .35 |
| 15 Willie Kirkland | .35 |
| 16 Billy Muffett | .35 |
| 17 Checklist No. 1 | 1.50 |
| 18 Jim Grant | .35 |
| 19 Cletis Boyer | .35 |
| 20 Robin Roberts | 3.00 |
| 21 Zorro Versalles | .35 |
| 22 Clem Labine | .35 |
| 23 Don Demeter | .35 |
| 24 Ken Johnson | .35 |
| 25 Reds' Heavy Artillery: | 1.50 |
| Vada Pinson, Gus Bell, | |
| Frank Robinson | |
| 26 Wes Stock | .35 |
| 27 Jerry Kindall | .35 |
| 28 Hector Lopez | .35 |
| 29 Don Nottebart | .35 |
| 30 Nellie Fox | 1.50 |
| 31 Bob Schmidt | .35 |
| 32 Ray Sadecki | .35 |
| 33 Gary Geiger | .35 |
| 34 Wynn Hawkins | .35 |
| 35 Ron Santo (R) | 2.00 |
| 36 Jack Kralick | .35 |
| 37 Charlie Maxwell | .35 |
| 38 Bob Lillis | .35 |
| 39 Leo Posada | .35 |
| 40 Bob Turley | .75 |
| 41 NL Batting Leaders: | 1.50 |
| Willie Mays, Dick Gorat, | |
| Norm Larker, | |
| Roberto Clemente | |
| 42 AL Batting Leaders: | .75 |
| Pete Runnels, | |
| Minnie Minoso, Al Smith, | |
| Bill Skowron | |
| 43 NL Home Run Leaders: | 1.25 |
| Ernie Banks, Ed Mathews, | |
| Hank Aaron, Ken Boyer | |
| 44 AL Home Run Leaders: | 3.00 |
| Mickey Mantle, Roger Maris, | |
| Jim Lemon, Rocky Colavito | |
| 45 NL ERA Leaders: | .75 |
| Mike McCormick, Ernie | |
| Broglio, Don Drysdale, | |
| Bob Friend, Stan Williams | |
| 46 AL ERA Leaders: | .75 |
| Frank Baumann, Jim | |
| Bunning, Art Ditmar, | |
| Hal Brown | |
| 47 NL Pitching Leaders: | .75 |
| E. Broglio, W. Spahn, | |
| Vern Law, Lou Burdette | |

| NO. PLAYER | MINT |
|---|---|
| 48 AL Pitching Leaders: | .75 |
| Chuck Estrada, Jim Perry, | |
| Bud Daley, Art Ditmar, | |
| Frank Lary, Milt Pappas | |
| 49 NL Strikeout Leaders: | 1.00 |
| Don Drysdale, Sandy | |
| Koufax, Sam Jones, | |
| Ernie Broglio | |
| 50 AL Strikeout Leaders: | .75 |
| Jim Bunning, Pedro Ramos, | |
| Early Wynn, Frank Lary | |
| 51 Detroit Tigers | 1.50 |
| 52 George Crowe | .35 |
| 53 Russ Nixon | .35 |
| 54 Earl Francis | .35 |
| 55 Jim Davenport | .35 |
| 56 Russ Kemmerer | .35 |
| 57 Marv Throneberry | .60 |
| 58 Joe Schaffernoth | .35 |
| 59 Jim Woods | .35 |
| 60 Woodie Held | .35 |
| 61 Ron Piche | .35 |
| 62 Al Pilarcik | .35 |
| 63 Jim Kaat | 2.50 |
| 64 Alex Grammas | .35 |
| 65 Ted Kluszewski | 1.00 |
| 66 Bill Henry | .35 |
| 67 Ossie Virgil | .35 |
| 68 Deron Johnson | .35 |
| 69 Earl Wilson | .35 |
| 70 Bill Virdon | .75 |
| 71 Jerry Adair | .35 |
| 72 Stu Miller | .35 |
| 73 Al Spangler | .35 |
| 74 Joe Pignatano | .35 |
| 75 Lindy Shows Larry: | .35 |
| Lindy McDaniel, | |
| Larry Jackson | |
| 76 Harry Anderson | .35 |
| 77 Dick Stigman | .35 |
| 78 Lee Walls | .35 |
| 79 Joe Ginsberg | .35 |
| 80 Harmon Killebrew | 5.00 |
| 81 Tracy Stallard | .35 |
| 82 Joe Christopher | .35 |
| 83 Bob Bruce | .35 |
| 84 Lee Maye | .35 |
| 85 Jerry Walker | .35 |
| 86 Los Angeles Dodgers | 2.00 |
| 87 Joe Amalfitano | .35 |
| 88 Richie Ashburn | 1.50 |
| 89 Billy Martin | 2.00 |
| 90 Jerry Staley | .35 |
| 91 Walt Moryn | .35 |
| 92 Hal Naragon | .35 |
| 93 Tony Gonzalez | .35 |
| 94 John Kucks | .35 |
| 95 Norm Cash | 1.00 |
| 96 Bill O'Dell | .35 |
| 97 Jerry Lynch | .35 |
| 98 Checklist No. 2 | 1.50 |
| 99 Don Buddin | .35 |
| 100 Harvey Haddix | .55 |
| 101 Bubba Phillips | .35 |
| 102 Gene Stephens | .35 |
| 103 Ruben Amaro | .35 |
| 104 John Blanchard | .35 |

| NO. PLAYER | MINT |
|---|---|
| 105 Carl Willey | .35 |
| 106 Whitey Herzog | .35 |
| 107 Seth Morehead | .35 |
| 108 Dan Dobbek | .35 |
| 109 Johnny Podres | 1.00 |
| 110 Vada Pinson | 1.00 |
| 111 Jack Meyer | .35 |
| 112 Chico Fernandez | .35 |
| 113 Mike Fornieles | .35 |
| 114 Hobie Landrith | .35 |
| 115 Johnny Antonelli | .35 |
| 116 Joe DeMaestri | .35 |
| 117 Dale Long | .35 |
| 118 Chris Cannizzaro | .35 |
| 119 A's Big Armor: | .50 |
| Norm Siebern, Hank Bauer, | |
| Jerry Lumpe | |
| 120 Ed Mathews | 4.00 |
| 121 Eli Grba | .35 |
| 122 Chicago Cubs | 1.00 |
| 123 Billy Gardner | .35 |
| 124 J.C. Martin | .35 |
| 125 Steve Barber | .35 |
| 126 Dick Stuart | .35 |
| 127 Ron Kline | .35 |
| 128 Rip Repulski | .35 |
| 129 Ed Hobaugh | .35 |
| 130 Norm Larker | .35 |
| 131 Paul Richards (Mgr.) | .50 |
| 132 Al Lopez (Mgr.) | 1.00 |
| 133 Ralph Houk (Mgr.) | .75 |
| 134 Mickey Vernon (Mgr.) | .50 |
| 135 Fred Hutchinson (Mgr.) | .50 |
| 136 Walt Alston (Mgr.) | 2.00 |
| 137 Chuck Dressen (Mgr.) | .50 |
| 138 Danny Murtaugh (Mgr.) | .50 |
| 139 Solly Hemus (Mgr.) | .50 |
| 140 Gus Triandos | .35 |
| 141 Billy Williams (R) | 20.00 |
| 142 Luis Arroyo | .35 |
| 143 Russ Snyder | .35 |
| 144 Jim Coker | .35 |
| 145 Bob Buhl | .35 |
| 146 Marty Keough | .35 |
| 147 Ed Rakow | .35 |
| 148 Julian Javier | .35 |
| 149 Bob Oldis | .35 |
| 150 Willie Mays | 22.00 |
| 151 Jim Donohue | .35 |
| 152 Earl Torgeson | .35 |
| 153 Don Lee | .35 |
| 154 Bobby Del Greco | .35 |
| 155 Johnny Temple | .35 |
| 156 Ken Hunt | .35 |
| 157 Cal McLish | .35 |
| 158 Pete Daley | .35 |
| 159 Baltimore Orioles | 1.00 |
| 160 Whitey Ford | 10.00 |
| 161 Sherman Jones | .40 |
| 162 Jay Hook | .40 |
| 163 Ed Sadowski | .40 |
| 164 Felix Mantilla | .40 |
| 165 Gino Cimoli | .40 |
| 166 Danny Kravitz | .40 |
| 167 San F. Giants | 1.00 |
| 168 Tommy Davis | 1.00 |
| 169 Don Elston | .40 |

| NO. PLAYER | MINT |
|---|---|
| 170 Al Smith | .40 |
| 171 Paul Foytack | .40 |
| 172 Don Dillard | .40 |
| 173 Beantown Bombers: | .60 |
| Frank Malzone, Vic Wertz, | |
| Jackie Jensen | |
| 174 Ray Semproch | .35 |
| 175 Gene Freese | .35 |
| 176 Ken Aspromonte | .35 |
| 177 Don Larsen | .50 |
| 178 Bob Nieman | .35 |
| 179 Joe Koppe | .35 |
| 180 Bobby Richardson | 1.50 |
| 181 Fred Green | .35 |
| 182 Dave Nicholson | .35 |
| 183 Andre Rodgers | .35 |
| 184 Steve Bilko | .35 |
| 185 Herb Score | .35 |
| 186 Elmer Valo | .35 |
| 187 Billy Klaus | .35 |
| 188 Jim Marshall | .35 |
| 189 Checklist No. 3 | 1.50 |
| 190 Stan Williams | .35 |
| 191 Mike De La Hoz | .35 |
| 192 Dick Brown | .35 |
| 193 Gene Conley | .35 |
| 194 Gordy Coleman | .35 |
| 195 Jerry Casale | .35 |
| 196 Ed Bouchee | .35 |
| 197 Dick Hall | .35 |
| 198 Carl Sawatski | .35 |
| 199 Bob Boyd | .35 |
| 200 Warren Spahn | 6.00 |
| 201 Pete Whisenant | .35 |
| 202 Al Neiger | .35 |
| 203 Eddie Bressoud | .35 |
| 204 Bob Skinner | .35 |
| 205 Bill Pierce | .60 |
| 206 Gene Green | .35 |
| 207 Dodger Southpaws: | 3.00 |
| Sandy Koufax, J. Podres | |
| 208 Larry Osborne | .35 |
| 209 Ken McBride | .35 |
| 210 Pete Runnels | .35 |
| 211 Bob Gibson | 6.00 |
| 212 Haywood Sullivan | .35 |
| 213 Bill Stafford | .35 |
| 214 Danny Murphy | .35 |
| 215 Gus Bell | .35 |
| 216 Ted Bowsfield | .35 |
| 217 Mel Roach | .35 |
| 218 Hal Brown | .35 |
| 219 Gene Mauch (Mgr.) | .50 |
| 220 Al Dark (Mgr.) | .50 |
| 221 Mike Higgins (Mgr.) | .35 |
| 222 Jimmie Dykes (Mgr.) | .35 |
| 223 Bob Scheffing (Mgr.) | .35 |
| 224 Joe Gordon (Mgr.) | .50 |
| 225 Bill Rigney (Mgr.) | .35 |
| 226 Harry Lavagetto (Mgr.) | .35 |
| 227 Juan Pizarro | .35 |
| 228 New York Yankees | 4.50 |
| 229 Rudy Hernandez | .35 |
| 230 Don Hoak | .35 |
| 231 Dick Drott | .35 |
| 232 Bill White | .35 |
| 233 Joe Jay | .35 |

| NO. PLAYER | MINT |
|---|---|
| 234 Ted Lepcio | .35 |
| 235 Camilo Pascual | .35 |
| 236 Don Gile | .35 |
| 237 Billy Loes | .35 |
| 238 Jim Gilliam | 1.00 |
| 239 Dave Sisler | .35 |
| 240 Ron Hansen | .35 |
| 241 Al Cicotte | .35 |
| 242 Hal Smith | .35 |
| 243 Frank Lary | .35 |
| 244 Chico Cardenas | .35 |
| 245 Joe Adcock | .75 |
| 246 Bob Davis | .35 |
| 247 Billy Goodman | .35 |
| 248 Ed Keegan | .35 |
| 249 Cincinnati Reds | 1.50 |
| 250 Buc Hill Aces: | .50 |
|     Vern Law, Roy Face | |
| 251 Bill Bruton | .35 |
| 252 Bill Short | .35 |
| 253 Sammy Taylor | .35 |
| 254 Ted Sadowski | .35 |
| 255 Vic Power | .35 |
| 256 Billy Hoeft | .35 |
| 257 Carroll Hardy | .35 |
| 258 Jack Sanford | .35 |
| 259 John Schaive | .35 |
| 260 Don Drysdale | 4.00 |
| 261 Charlie Lau | .35 |
| 262 Tony Curry | .35 |
| 263 Ken Hamlin | .35 |
| 264 Glen Hobbie | .35 |
| 265 Tony Kubek | 2.00 |
| 266 Lindy McDaniel | .35 |
| 267 Norm Siebern | .35 |
| 268 Ike Delock | .35 |
| 269 Harry Chiti | .35 |
| 270 Bob Friend | .35 |
| 271 Jim Landis | .35 |
| 272 Tom Morgan | .35 |
| 273 Checklist No. 4 | 1.50 |
| 274 Gary Bell | .35 |
| 275 Gene Woodling | .35 |
| 276 Ray Rippelmeyer | .35 |
| 277 Hank Foiles | .35 |
| 278 Don McMahon | .35 |
| 279 Jose Pagan | .35 |
| 280 Frank Howard | 1.00 |
| 281 Frank Sullivan | .35 |
| 282 Faye Throneberry | .35 |
| 283 Bob Anderson | .35 |
| 284 Dick Gernert | .35 |
| 285 Sherm Lollar | .35 |
| 286 George Witt | .35 |
| 287 Carl Yastrzemski | 60.00 |
| 288 Albie Pearson | .35 |
| 289 Ray Moore | .35 |
| 290 Stan Musial | 17.00 |
| 291 Tex Clevenger | .35 |
| 292 Jim Baumer | .35 |
| 293 Tom Sturdivant | .35 |
| 294 Don Blasingame | .35 |
| 295 Milt Pappas | .35 |
| 296 Wes Covington | .35 |
| 297 Kansas C. Athletics | 1.00 |
| 298 Jim Golden | .35 |
| 299 Clay Dalrymple | .35 |
| 300 Mickey Mantle | 75.00 |
| 301 Chet Nichols | .35 |
| 302 Al Heist | .35 |
| 303 Gary Peters | .35 |
| 304 Rocky Nelson | .35 |
| 305 Mike McCormick | .35 |
| 306 World Series Game 1 | 1.50 |
|     Virdon Saves Game | |
| 307 World Series Game 2 | 5.00 |
|     Mantle Slams 2 Homers | |
| 308 World Series Game 3 | 1.50 |
|     Richardson is Hero | |
| 309 World Series Game 4 | 1.50 |
|     Cimoli Safe | |

| NO. PLAYER | MINT |
|---|---|
| 310 World Series Game 5 | 1.50 |
|     Face Saves the Day | |
| 311 World Series Game 6 | 1.50 |
|     Ford Shutout | |
| 312 World Series Game 7 | 1.50 |
|     Mazeroski's Homer | |
| 313 W.S. Celebration | 1.50 |
| 314 Bob Miller | .35 |
| 315 Earl Battey | .35 |
| 316 Bobby Gene Smith | .35 |
| 317 Jim Brewer | .35 |
| 318 Danny O'Connell | .35 |
| 319 Valmy Thomas | .35 |
| 320 Lou Burdette | 1.00 |
| 321 Marv Breeding | .35 |
| 322 Bill Kunkel | .35 |
| 323 Sammy Esposito | .35 |
| 324 Hank Aguirre | .35 |
| 325 Wally Moon | .35 |
| 326 Dave Hillman | .35 |
| 327 Matty Alou (R) | 1.00 |
| 328 Jim O'Toole | .35 |
| 329 Julio Becquer | .35 |
| 330 Rocky Colavito | 1.25 |
| 331 Ned Garver | .35 |
| 332 Dutch Dotterer | .35 |
|     (photo of Tommy Dotterer) | |
| 333 Fritz Brickell | .35 |
| 334 Walt Bond | .35 |
| 335 Frank Bolling | .35 |
| 336 Don Mincher | .35 |
| 337 Al's Aces: | 1.50 |
|     Herb Score, Early Wynn, | |
|     Al Lopez | |
| 338 Don Landrum | .35 |
| 339 Gene Baker | .35 |
| 340 Vic Wertz | .35 |
| 341 Jim Owens | .35 |
| 342 Clint Courtney | .35 |
| 343 Earl Robinson | .35 |
| 344 Sandy Koufax | 18.00 |
| 345 Jim Piersall | .75 |
| 346 Howie Nunn | .35 |
| 347 St. Louis Cardinals | 1.00 |
| 348 Steve Boros | .45 |
| 349 Danny McDevitt | .35 |
| 350 Ernie Banks | 7.00 |
| 351 Jim King | .35 |
| 352 Bob Shaw | .35 |
| 353 Howie Bedell | .35 |
| 354 Billy Harrell | .35 |
| 355 Bob Allison | .35 |
| 356 Ryne Duren | .35 |
| 357 Daryl Spencer | .35 |
| 358 Earl Averill | .35 |
| 359 Dallas Green | .75 |
| 360 Frank Robinson | 10.00 |
| 361 Checklist No. 5 | 2.00 |
| 362 Frank Funk | .35 |
| 363 John Roseboro | .35 |
| 364 Moe Drabowski | .35 |
| 365 Jerry Lumpe | .35 |
| 366 Eddie Fisher | .35 |
| 367 Jim Rivera | .35 |
| 368 Bennie Daniels | .35 |
| 369 Dave Philley | .35 |
| 370 Roy Face | .60 |
| 371 Bill Skowron | 2.00 |
| 372 Bob Hendley | .45 |
| 373 Boston Red Sox | 1.00 |
| 374 Paul Giel | .45 |
| 375 Ken Boyer | 2.00 |
| 376 Mike Roarke | .45 |
| 377 Ruben Gomez | .45 |
| 378 Wally Post | .45 |
| 379 Bobby Shantz | .85 |
| 380 Minnie Minoso | 1.00 |
| 381 Dave Wickersham | .35 |
| 382 Frank Thomas | .40 |
| 383 Frisco First Liners: | .50 |
|     Mike McCormick, Jack | |
|     Sanford, Billy O'Dell | |

| NO. PLAYER | MINT |
|---|---|
| 384 Chuck Essegian | .45 |
| 385 Jim Perry | .75 |
| 386 Joe Hicks | .45 |
| 387 Duke Maas | .45 |
| 388 Bob Clemente | 17.00 |
| 389 Ralph Terry | .45 |
| 390 Del Crandall | .45 |
| 391 Winston Brown | .45 |
| 392 Reno Bertoia | .45 |
| 393 Batter Bafflers: | .45 |
|     Don Cardwell, Glen Hobbie | |
| 394 Ken Walters | .45 |
| 395 Chuck Estrada | .45 |
| 396 Bob Aspromonte | .45 |
| 397 Hal Woodeschick | .45 |
| 398 Hank Bauer | .75 |
| 399 Cliff Cook | .45 |
| 400 Vern Law | .60 |
| 401 Ruth 60th Homer | 5.00 |
| 402 Larsen—Perfect Game | 1.50 |
| 403 26 Inning Tie | 1.00 |
| 404 Honsby .424 Average | 1.50 |
| 405 Gehrig—2,130 Games | 4.00 |
| 406 Mantle 565 Ft. HR | 6.00 |
| 407 Chesbro Wins 41 | 1.00 |
| 408 Mathewson 267 SO's | 2.50 |
| 409 Johnson Shutouts | 2.50 |
| 410 Haddix Perfect Game | 1.00 |
| 411 Tony Taylor | .45 |
| 412 Larry Sherry | .45 |
| 413 Eddie Yost | .45 |
| 414 Dick Donovan | .45 |
| 415 Hank Aaron | 25.00 |
| 416 Dick Howser (R) | 1.00 |
| 417 Juan Marichal (R) | 35.00 |
| 418 Ed Bailey | .45 |
| 419 Tom Borland | .45 |
| 420 Ernie Broglio | .45 |
| 421 Ty Cline | .45 |
| 422 Bud Daley | .45 |
| 423 Charlie Neal | .45 |
| 424 Turk Lown | .45 |
| 425 Yogi Berra | 15.00 |
| 426 Milwaukee Braves | 2.00 |
|     (error—numbered 463) | |
| 427 Dick Ellsworth | .45 |
| 428 Ray Barker | .45 |
| 429 Al Kaline | 9.00 |
| 430 Bill Mazeroski | 1.50 |
| 431 Chuck Stobbs | .45 |
| 432 Coot Veal | .45 |
| 433 Art Mahaffey | .45 |
| 434 Tom Brewer | .45 |
| 435 Orlando Cepeda | 2.00 |
| 436 Jim Maloney (R) | 1.00 |
| 437 Checklist No. 6 | 1.50 |
| 438 Curt Flood | .75 |
| 439 Phil Regan | .45 |
| 440 Luis Aparicio | 3.00 |
| 441 Dick Bertell | .45 |
| 442 Gordon Jones | .45 |
| 443 Duke Snider | 8.00 |
| 444 Joe Nuxhall | .45 |
| 445 Frank Malzone | .45 |
| 446 Bob Taylor | .45 |
| 447 Harry Bright | .45 |
| 448 Del Rice | .45 |
| 449 Bobby Bolin | .45 |
| 450 Jim Lemon | .45 |
| 451 Power for Ernie: | .45 |
|     Daryl Spencer, Bill White, | |
|     Ernie Broglio | |
| 452 Bob Allen | .45 |
| 453 Dick Schofield | .45 |
| 454 Pumpsie Green | .45 |
| 455 Early Wynn | 3.00 |
| 456 Hal Bevan | .45 |
| 457 Johnny James | .45 |
| 458 Willie Tasby | .45 |
| 459 Terry Fox | .45 |
| 460 Gil Hodges | 4.00 |
| 461 Smoky Burgess | .45 |

| NO. PLAYER | MINT |
|---|---|
| 462 Lou Klimchock | .45 |
| 463 Jack Fisher (see #426) | .50 |
| 464 Leroy Thomas | .45 |
| 465 Roy McMillan | .45 |
| 466 Ron Moeller | .45 |
| 467 Cleveland Indians | 1.00 |
| 468 John Callison | .45 |
| 469 Ralph Lumenti | .45 |
| 470 Roy Sievers | .45 |
| 471 Phil Rizzuto (MVP) | 3.00 |
| 472 Yogi Berra (MVP) | 5.00 |
| 473 Bobby Shantz (MVP) | .75 |
| 474 Al Rosen (MVP) | 1.00 |
| 475 Mickey Mantle (MVP) | 15.00 |
| 476 Jackie Jensen (MVP) | .75 |
| 477 Nellie Fox (MVP) | 1.00 |
| 478 Roger Maris (MVP) | 4.00 |
| 479 Jim Konstanty (MVP) | .75 |
| 480 R. Campanella (MVP) | 6.00 |
| 481 Hank Sauer (MVP) | .75 |
| 482 Willie Mays (MVP) | 7.50 |
| 483 Don Newcombe (MVP) | .75 |
| 484 Hank Aaron (MVP) | 7.50 |
| 485 Ernie Banks (MVP) | 4.00 |
| 486 Dick Groat (MVP) | .75 |
| 487 Gene Oliver | .45 |
| 488 Joe McClain | .45 |
| 489 Walt Bond | .45 |
| 490 Jim Bunning | 1.50 |
| 491 Philadelphia Phillies | 1.00 |
| 492 Ron Fairly | .45 |
| 493 Don Zimmer | .60 |
| 494 Tom Cheney | .45 |
| 495 Elston Howard | 1.50 |
| 496 Ken MacKenzie | .45 |
| 497 Willie Jones | .45 |
| 498 Ray Herbert | .45 |
| 499 Chuck Schilling | .45 |
| 500 Harvey Kuenn | 1.00 |
| 501 John DeMerit | .45 |
| 502 Clarence Coleman | .45 |
| 503 Tito Francona | .45 |
| 504 Billy Consolo | .45 |
| 505 Red Schoendienst | 1.00 |
| 506 Willie Davis (R) | 1.50 |
| 507 Pete Burnside | .45 |
| 508 Rocky Bridges | .45 |
| 509 Camilo Carreon | .45 |
| 510 Art Ditmar | .45 |
| 511 Joe Morgan | .45 |
| 512 Bob Will | .45 |
| 513 Jim Brosnan | .45 |
| 514 Jake Wood | .45 |
| 515 Jackie Brandt | .45 |
| 516 Checklist No. 7 | 1.50 |
| 517 Willie McCovey | 12.00 |
| 518 Andy Carey | .45 |
| 519 Jim Pagliaroni | .45 |
| 520 Joe Cunningham | .45 |
| 521 Brother Battery: | .50 |
|     Norm Sherry, Larry Sherry | |
| 522 Dick Farrell | .45 |
| 523 Joe Gibbon | 6.00 |
| 524 Johnny Logan | 6.00 |
| 525 Ron Perranoski | 6.00 |
| 526 R.C. Stevens | 6.00 |
| 527 Gene Leek | 6.00 |
| 528 Pedro Ramos | 6.00 |
| 529 Bob Roselli | 6.00 |
| 530 Bobby Malkmus | 6.00 |
| 531 Jim Coates | 6.00 |
| 532 Bob Hale | 6.00 |
| 533 Jack Curtis | 6.00 |
| 534 Eddie Kasko | 6.00 |
| 535 Larry Jackson | 6.00 |
| 536 Bill Tuttle | 6.00 |
| 537 Bobby Locke | 6.00 |
| 538 Chuck Hiller | 6.00 |
| 539 John Klippstein | 6.00 |
| 540 Jackie Jensen | 7.50 |
| 541 Roland Sheldon | 6.00 |
| 542 Minnesota Twins | 9.00 |

| NO. PLAYER | MINT | NO. PLAYER | MINT | NO. PLAYER | MINT | NO. PLAYER | MINT |
|---|---|---|---|---|---|---|---|
| 543 Roger Craig | 7.00 | 555 Sam Jones | 6.00 | 566 P. Richards—Mgr. (AS) | 6.00 | 577 Hank Aaron (AS) | 50.00 |
| 544 George Thomas | 6.00 | 556 Ken R. Hunt | 6.00 | 567 D. Murtaugh—Mgr. (AS) | 6.00 | 578 Mickey Mantle (AS) | 90.00 |
| 545 Hoyt Wilhelm | 18.00 | 557 Jose Valdivielso | 6.00 | 568 Bill Skowron (AS) | 7.00 | 579 Willie Mays (AS) | 50.00 |
| 546 Marty Kutyna | 6.00 | 558 Don Ferrarese | 6.00 | 569 Frank Herrera (AS) | 6.00 | 580 Al Kaline (AS) | 20.00 |
| 547 Leon Wagner | 6.00 | 559 Jim Gentile | 6.00 | 570 Nellie Fox (AS) | 9.00 | 581 Frank Robinson (AS) | 20.00 |
| 548 Ted Wills | 6.00 | 560 Barry Latman | 6.00 | 571 Bill Mazeroski (AS) | 7.00 | 582 Earl Battey (AS) | 6.00 |
| 549 Hal R. Smith | 6.00 | 561 Charley James | 6.00 | 572 Brooks Robinson | 20.00 | 583 Del Crandall (AS) | 6.00 |
| 550 Frank Baumann | 6.00 | 562 Bill Monbouquette | 6.00 | 573 Ken Boyer (AS) | 7.00 | 584 Jim Perry (AS) | 6.00 |
| 551 George Altman | 6.00 | 563 Bob Cerv | 6.00 | 574 Luis Aparicio (AS) | 15.00 | 585 Bob Friend (AS) | 6.00 |
| 552 Jim Archer | 6.00 | 564 Don Cardwell | 6.00 | 575 Ernie Banks (AS) | 20.00 | 586 Whitey Ford (AS) | 20.00 |
| 553 Bill Fischer | 6.00 | 565 Felipe Alou | 6.00 | 576 Roger Maris (AS) | 20.00 | 589 Warren Spahn (AS) | 20.00 |
| 554 Pittsburgh Pirates | 8.00 | | | | | | |

# 1962 Topps....Complete Set of 598 Cards—Value $800.00

The rookie cards of Lou Brock, Gaylord Perry and Bob Uecker are in this set. The high numbers are 523 to 598. Nine cards were reprinted with different photos. These are worth a premium. The value of the complete set does not include the *variety* cards.

| NO. PLAYER | MINT | NO. PLAYER | MINT | NO. PLAYER | MINT | NO. PLAYER | MINT |
|---|---|---|---|---|---|---|---|
| 1 Roger Maris | 27.00 | 42 Jim King | .40 | 62 Steve Boros | .40 | 104 Ted Savage | .40 |
| 2 Jim Brosnan | .40 | 43 Los Angeles Dodgers | 1.50 | 63 Tony Cloninger | .40 | 105 Don Mossi | .40 |
| 3 Pete Runnels | .40 | 44 Don Taussig | .40 | 64 Russ Snyder | .40 | 106 Carl Sawatski | .40 |
| 4 John DeMerit | .40 | 45 Brooks Robinson | 7.50 | 65 Bobby Richardson | 1.00 | 107 Mike McCormick | .40 |
| 5 Sandy Koufax | 16.00 | 46 Jack Baldschun | .40 | 66 Cuno Barragon | .40 | 108 Willie Davis | .40 |
| 6 Marv Breeding | .40 | 47 Bob Will | .40 | 67 Harvey Haddix | .40 | 109 Bob Shaw | .40 |
| 7 Frank Thomas | .40 | 48 Ralph Terry | .40 | 68 Ken Hunt | .40 | 110 Bill Skowron | 1.50 |
| 8 Ray Herbert | .40 | 49 Hal Jones | .40 | 69 Phil Ortega | .40 | 111 Dallas Green | .40 |
| 9 Jim Davenport | .40 | 50 Stan Musial | 18.00 | 70 Harmon Killebrew | 6.00 | 112 Hank Foiles | .40 |
| 10 Bob Clemente | 17.00 | 51 AL Batting Leaders: | 1.00 | 71 Dick Le May | .40 | 113 Chicago White Sox | 1.00 |
| 11 Tom Morgan | .40 | Al Kaline, Norm Cash, | | 72 Bob's Pupils: | .50 | 114 Howie Koplitz | .40 |
| 12 Harry Craft (Mgr.) | .40 | Jim Piersall, Elston Howard | | Steve Boros, Bob | | 115 Bob Skinner | .40 |
| 13 Dick Howser | .40 | 52 NL Batting Leaders: | 1.00 | Scheffing, Jake Wood | | 116 Herb Score | .40 |
| 14 Bill White | .40 | Wally Moon, Bob Clemente, | | 73 Nellie Fox | 1.50 | 117 Gary Geiger | .40 |
| 15 Dick Donovan | .40 | Vada Pinson, Ken Boyer | | 74 Bob Lillis | .40 | 118 Julian Javier | .40 |
| 16 Darrell Johnson | .40 | 53 AL Home Run Leaders: | 3.00 | 75 Milt Pappas | .40 | 119 Danny Murphy | .40 |
| 17 Johnny Callison | .40 | Jim Gentile, Roger | | 76 Howie Bedell | .40 | 120 Bob Purkey | .40 |
| 18 Managers' Dream: | 16.00 | Maris, Mickey Mantle, | | 77 Tony Taylor | .40 | 121 Billy Hitchcock | .40 |
| Mickey Mantle, Willie Mays | | Harmon Killebrew | | 78 Gene Green | .40 | 122 Norm Bass | .40 |
| 19 Ray Washburn | .40 | 54 NL Home Run Leaders: | 1.00 | 79 Ed Hobaugh | .40 | 123 Mike De La Hoz | .40 |
| 20 Rocky Colavito | 1.00 | Orlando Cepeda, Willie | | 80 Vada Pinson | 1.00 | 124 Bill Pleis | .40 |
| 21 Jim Kaat | 1.50 | Mays, Frank Robinson | | 81 Jim Pagliaroni | .40 | 125 Gene Woodling | .40 |
| 22 Checklist No. 1 | 1.50 | 55 AL ERA Leaders: | 1.00 | 82 Deron Johnson | .40 | 126 Al Cicotte | .40 |
| 23 Norm Larker | .40 | Dick Donovan, Bill Stafford, | | 83 Larry Jackson | .40 | 127 Pride of A's: | .40 |
| 24 Detroit Tigers | 1.50 | Don Mossi, Milt Pappas | | 84 Lenny Green | .40 | Norm Siebern, Hank Bauer, |
| 25 Ernie Banks | 6.00 | 56 NL ERA Leaders: | 1.00 | 85 Gil Hodges | 4.00 | Jerry Lumpe |
| 26 Chris Cannizzaro | .40 | Warren Spahn, Jim | | 86 Donn Clendenon | .60 | 128 Art Fowler | .40 |
| 27 Chuck Cottier | .40 | O'Toole, Curt Simmons, | | 87 Mike Roarke | .40 | 129 Lee Walls (faces right) | .75 |
| 28 Minnie Minoso | 1.00 | Mike McCormick | | 88 Ralph Houk | .60 | 129 Lee Walls (faces left) | 4.50 |
| 29 Casey Stengel (Mgr.) | 4.00 | 57 AL Win Leaders: | 1.00 | 89 Barney Schultz | .40 | 130 Frank Bolling | .40 |
| 30 Ed Mathews | 4.00 | Frank Lary, Whitey Ford, | | 90 Jim Piersall | .60 | 131 Pete Richert | .40 |
| 31 Tom Tresh (R) | 2.00 | Steve Barber, Jim Bunning | | 91 J.C. Martin | .40 | 132 Los Angeles Angels* | 1.00 |
| 32 John Roseboro | .40 | 58 NL Win Leaders: | 1.00 | 92 Sam Jones | .40 | 133 Felipe Alou | .40 |
| 33 Don Larsen | .40 | Warren Spahn, Joe Jay, | | 93 John Blanchard | .40 | 134 Billy Hoeft (faces right) | .75 |
| 34 Johnny Temple | .40 | Jim O'Toole | | 94 Jay Hook | .40 | 134 Billy Hoeft (faces front) | 4.50 |
| 35 Don Schwall | .40 | 59 AL Strikeout Leaders: | 1.00 | 95 Don Hoak | .40 | 135 Babe Ruth Special: | 4.00 |
| 36 Don Leppert | .40 | Camilo Pascual, Whitey | | 96 Eli Grba | .40 | Babe as a Boy |
| 37 Tribe Hill Trio: | .40 | Ford, Jim Bunning, | | 97 Tito Francona | .40 | 136 Babe Ruth Special: | 4.00 |
| Barry Latman, Dick | | Juan Pizzaro | | 98 Checklist No. 2 | 1.50 | Babe Joins Yanks |
| Stigman, Jim Perry | | 60 NL Strikeout Leaders: | 1.00 | 99 John Powell (R) | 3.00 | 137 Babe Ruth Special: | 4.00 |
| 38 Gene Stephens | .40 | Sandy Koufax, Stan | | 100 Warren Spahn | 5.00 | Babe and Mgr. Huggins |
| 39 Joe Koppe | .40 | Williams, Don Drysdale, | | 101 Carroll Hardy | .40 | 138 Babe Ruth Special: | 4.00 |
| 40 Orlando Cepeda | 1.50 | Jim O'Toole | | 102 Al Schroll | .40 | Famous Slugger |
| 41 Cliff Cook | .40 | 61 St. Louis Cardinals | 1.00 | 103 Don Blasingame | .40 | | |

| NO. PLAYER | MINT |
|---|---|
| 139 Babe Ruth Special | 4.00 |
| Babe Hits 60 | |
| See Card no. 159 | |
| 140 Babe Ruth Special: | 4.00 |
| Gehrig and Ruth | |
| 141 Babe Ruth Special: | 4.00 |
| Twilight Years | |
| 142 Babe Ruth Special: | 4.00 |
| Coaching for Dodgers | |
| 143 Babe Ruth Special: | 4.00 |
| Greatest Sports Hero | |
| 144 Babe Ruth Special: | 4.00 |
| Farewell Speech | |
| 145 Barry Latman | .40 |
| 146 Don Demeter | .40 |
| 147 Bill Kunkel (head shot) | .75 |
| 147 Bill Kunkel (pitching) | 4.50 |
| 148 Wally Post | .40 |
| 149 Bob Duliba | .40 |
| 150 Al Kaline | 5.00 |
| 151 Johnny Klippstein | .40 |
| 152 Mickey Vernon (Mgr.) | .40 |
| 153 Pumpsie Green | .40 |
| 154 Lee Thomas | .40 |
| 155 Stu Miller | .40 |
| 156 Merritt Ranew | .40 |
| 157 Wes Covington | .40 |
| 158 Milwaukee Braves | 1.00 |
| 159 Hal Reniff | .75 |
| 159 Hal Reniff (head shot) | 7.50 |
| Error—reads no. 139 | |
| 159 Hal Reniff (pitching) | 25.00 |
| Error—reads no. 139 | |
| 160 Dick Stuart | .40 |
| 161 Frank Baumann | .40 |
| 162 Sammy Drake | .40 |
| 163 Hot Corner Guardians: | .50 |
| Billy Gardner, Cletis Boyer | |
| 164 Hal Naragon | .40 |
| 165 Jackie Brandt | .40 |
| 166 Don Lee | .40 |
| 167 Tim McCarver (R) | 2.50 |
| 168 Leo Posada | .40 |
| 169 Bob Cerv | .40 |
| 170 Ron Santo | 1.00 |
| 171 Dave Sisler | .40 |
| 172 Fred Hutchinson (Mgr.) | .40 |
| 173 Chico Fernandez | .40 |
| 174 Carl Willey (no hat) | .75 |
| 174 Carl Willey (with hat) | 4.50 |
| 175 Frank Howard | 1.00 |
| 176 Eddie Yost (head shot) | .75 |
| 176 Eddie Yost (with bat) | 4.50 |
| 177 Bobby Shantz | .40 |
| 178 Camilo Carreon | .40 |
| 179 Tom Sturdivant | .40 |
| 180 Bob Allison | .40 |
| 181 Paul Brown | .40 |
| 182 Bob Nieman | .40 |
| 183 Roger Craig | .40 |
| 184 Haywood Sullivan | .40 |
| 185 Roland Sheldon | .40 |
| 186 Mack Jones | .40 |
| 187 Gene Conley | .40 |
| 188 Chuck Hiller | .40 |
| 189 Dick Hall | .40 |
| 190 Wally Moon (head shot) | .75 |
| 190 Wally Moon (with bat) | 4.50 |
| 191 Jim Brewer | .40 |
| 192 Checklist No. 3 | 1.50 |
| 193 Eddie Kasko | .40 |
| 194 Dean Chance | .40 |
| 195 Joe Cunningham | .40 |
| 196 Terry Fox | .40 |
| 197 Daryl Spencer | .40 |
| 198 Johnny Keane (Mgr.) | .40 |
| 199 Gaylord Perry (R) | 40.00 |
| 200 Mickey Mantle | 80.00 |
| 201 Ike Delock | .40 |
| 202 Carl Warwick | .40 |
| 203 Jack Fisher | .40 |
| 204 Johnny Weekly | .40 |

| NO. PLAYER | MINT |
|---|---|
| 205 Gene Freese | .40 |
| 206 Washington Senators | 1.00 |
| 207 Pete Burnside | .40 |
| 208 Billy Martin | 2.00 |
| 209 Jim Fregosi (R) | 1.50 |
| 210 Roy Face | .60 |
| 211 Midway Masters: | .40 |
| Frank Bolling, Roy McMillan | |
| 212 Jim Owens | .40 |
| 213 Richie Ashburn | 1.00 |
| 214 Dom Zanni | .40 |
| 215 Woody Held | .40 |
| 216 Ron Kline | .40 |
| 217 Walt Alston (Mgr.) | 1.25 |
| 218 Joe Torre (R) | 4.00 |
| 219 Al Downing (R) | .75 |
| 220 Roy Sievers | .40 |
| 221 Bill Short | .40 |
| 222 Jerry Zimmerman | .40 |
| 223 Alex Grammas | .40 |
| 224 Don Rudolph | .40 |
| 225 Frank Malzone | .40 |
| 226 San F. Giants | 1.00 |
| 227 Bobby Tiefenauer | .40 |
| 228 Dale Long | .40 |
| 229 Jesus McFarlane | .40 |
| 230 Camilo Pascual | .40 |
| 231 Ernie Bowman | .40 |
| 232 World Series Game 1: | 1.50 |
| Yanks Win Opener | |
| 233 World Series Game 2: | 1.50 |
| Jay Ties It Up | |
| 234 World Series Game 3: | 2.50 |
| Maris Wins In 9th | |
| 235 World Series Game 4: | 2.50 |
| Ford Sets New Mark | |
| 236 World Series Game 5: | 1.50 |
| Yanks Crush Reds | |
| 237 World Series | 1.50 |
| Winners Celebrate | |
| 238 Norm Sherry | .40 |
| 239 Cecil Butler | .40 |
| 240 George Altman | .40 |
| 241 Johnny Kucks | .40 |
| 242 Mel McGaha (Mgr.) | .40 |
| 243 Robin Roberts | 3.00 |
| 244 Don Gile | .40 |
| 245 Ron Hansen | .40 |
| 246 Art Ditmar | .40 |
| 247 Joe Pignatano | .40 |
| 248 Bob Aspromonte | .40 |
| 249 Ed Keegan | .40 |
| 250 Norm Cash | 1.00 |
| 251 New York Yankees | 3.00 |
| 252 Earl Francis | .40 |
| 253 Harry Chiti | .40 |
| 254 Gordon Windhorn | .40 |
| 255 Joan Pizarro | .40 |
| 256 Elio Chacon | .40 |
| 257 Jack Spring | .40 |
| 258 Marty Keough | .40 |
| 259 Lou Klimchock | .40 |
| 260 Bill Pierce | .50 |
| 261 George Alusik | .40 |
| 262 Bob Schmidt | .40 |
| 263 The Right Pitch: | .40 |
| Bob Purkey, Jim Turner, | |
| Joe Jay | |
| 264 Dick Ellsworth | .40 |
| 265 Joe Adcock | .60 |
| 266 John Anderson | .40 |
| 267 Dan Dobbek | .40 |
| 268 Ken McBride | .40 |
| 269 Bob Oldis | .40 |
| 270 Dick Groat | 1.00 |
| 271 Ray Rippelmeyer | .40 |
| 272 Earl Robinson | .40 |
| 273 Gary Bell | .40 |
| 274 Sammy Taylor | .40 |
| 275 Norm Siebern | .40 |
| 276 Hal Kolstad | .40 |
| 277 Checklist No. 4 | 1.50 |

| NO. PLAYER | MINT |
|---|---|
| 278 Ken Johnson | .40 |
| 279 Hobie Landrith | .40 |
| 280 Johnny Podres | 1.00 |
| 281 Jake Gibbs | .40 |
| 282 Dave Hillman | .40 |
| 283 Charlie Smith | .40 |
| 284 Ruben Amaro | .40 |
| 285 Curt Simmons | .40 |
| 286 Al Lopez (Mgr.) | 1.00 |
| 287 George Witt | .40 |
| 288 Billy Williams | 3.00 |
| 289 Mike Krsnich | .40 |
| 290 Jim Gentile | .40 |
| 291 Hal Stowe | .40 |
| 292 Jerry Kindall | .40 |
| 293 Bob Miller | .40 |
| 294 Philadelphia Phillies | 1.00 |
| 295 Vern Law | .40 |
| 296 Ken Hamlin | .40 |
| 297 Ron Perranoski | .40 |
| 298 Bill Tuttle | .40 |
| 299 Don Wert | .40 |
| 300 Willie Mays | 35.00 |
| 301 Galen Cisco | .40 |
| 302 John Edwards | .40 |
| 303 Frank Torre | .40 |
| 304 Dick Farrell | .40 |
| 305 Jerry Lumpe | .40 |
| 306 Redbird Rippers: | .40 |
| Lindy McDaniel, | |
| Larry Jackson | |
| 307 Jim Grant | .40 |
| 308 Neil Chrisley | .40 |
| 309 Moe Morhardt | .40 |
| 310 Whitey Ford | 6.00 |
| 311 Kubek Double Play | 1.00 |
| 312 Spahn No-Hit | 2.00 |
| 313 Maris Blasts 61 HR | 2.00 |
| 314 Colavito's Power | 1.00 |
| 315 Ford Curveball | 2.50 |
| 316 Killebrew's Orbit | 2.00 |
| 317 Musial's 21st Season | 3.00 |
| 318 Switch Hitter Mantle | 8.00 |
| 319 McCormick in Action | .75 |
| 320 Hank Aaron | 35.00 |
| 321 Lee Stange | .40 |
| 322 Al Dark (Mgr.) | .40 |
| 323 Don Landrum | .40 |
| 324 Joe McClain | .40 |
| 325 Luis Aparicio | 3.50 |
| 326 Tom Parsons | .40 |
| 327 Ozzie Virgil | .40 |
| 328 Ken Walters | .40 |
| 329 Bob Bolin | .40 |
| 330 Johnny Romano | .40 |
| 331 Moe Drabowsky | .40 |
| 332 Don Buddin | .40 |
| 333 Frank Cipriani | .40 |
| 334 Boston Red Sox | 1.50 |
| 335 Bill Bruton | .40 |
| 336 Billy Muffett | .40 |
| 337 Jim Marshall | .40 |
| 338 Billy Gardner | .40 |
| 339 Jose Valdivielso | .40 |
| 340 Don Drysdale | 6.00 |
| 341 Mike Hershberger | .40 |
| 342 Ed Rakow | .40 |
| 343 Albie Pearson | .40 |
| 344 Ed Bauta | .40 |
| 345 Chuck Schilling | .40 |
| 346 Jack Kralick | .40 |
| 347 Chuck Hinton | .40 |
| 348 Larry Burright | .40 |
| 349 Paul Foytack | .40 |
| 350 Frank Robinson | 7.50 |
| 351 Braves' Backstops: | .75 |
| Joe Torre, Del Crandall | |
| 352 Frank Sullivan | .40 |
| 353 Bill Mazeroski | 1.00 |
| 354 Roman Mejias | .40 |
| 355 Steve Barber | .40 |
| 356 Tom Haller | .40 |

| NO. PLAYER | MINT |
|---|---|
| 357 Jerry Walker | .40 |
| 358 Tommy Davis | .75 |
| 359 Bobby Locke | .40 |
| 360 Yogi Berra | 10.00 |
| 361 Bob Hendley | .40 |
| 362 Ty Cline | .40 |
| 363 Bob Roselli | .40 |
| 364 Ken Hunt | .40 |
| 365 Charley Neal | .40 |
| 366 Phil Regan | .40 |
| 367 Checklist No. 5 | 1.50 |
| 368 Bob Tillman | .40 |
| 369 Ted Bowsfield | .40 |
| 370 Ken Boyer | 1.50 |
| 371 Earl Battey | .60 |
| 372 Jack Curtis | .60 |
| 373 Al Heist | .60 |
| 374 Gene Mauch (Mgr.) | .60 |
| 375 Ron Fairly | .60 |
| 376 Bud Daley | .60 |
| 377 Johnny Orsino | .60 |
| 378 Bennie Daniels | .60 |
| 379 Chuck Essegian | .60 |
| 380 Lou Burdette | 1.00 |
| 381 Chico Cardenas | .60 |
| 382 Dick Williams | .60 |
| 383 Ray Sadecki | .60 |
| 384 K.C. Athletics | 1.00 |
| 385 Early Wynn | 3.00 |
| 386 Don Mincher | .60 |
| 387 Lou Brock (R) | 48.00 |
| 388 Ryne Duren | .60 |
| 389 Smoky Burgess | .60 |
| 390 Orlando Cepeda (AS) | 1.00 |
| 391 Bill Mazeroski (AS) | .75 |
| 392 Ken Boyer (AS) | .60 |
| 393 Roy McMillan (AS) | .60 |
| 394 Hank Aaron (AS) | 7.50 |
| 395 Willie Mays (AS) | 7.50 |
| 396 Frank Robinson (AS) | 4.00 |
| 397 John Roseboro (AS) | .60 |
| 398 Don Drysdale (AS) | 3.00 |
| 399 Warren Spahn (AS) | 3.00 |
| 400 Elston Howard | 1.50 |
| 401 AL & NL Homer Kings: | 4.00 |
| Roger Maris, O. Cepeda | |
| 402 Gino Cimoli | .60 |
| 403 Chet Nichols | .60 |
| 404 Tim Harkness | .60 |
| 405 Jim Perry | .75 |
| 406 Bob Taylor | .60 |
| 407 Hank Aguirre | .60 |
| 408 Gus Bell | .60 |
| 409 Pittsburgh Pirates | 1.25 |
| 410 Al Smith | .60 |
| 411 Danny O'Connell | .60 |
| 412 Charlie James | .60 |
| 413 Matty Alou | .60 |
| 414 Joe Gaines | .60 |
| 415 Bill Virdon | .60 |
| 416 Bob Scheffing (Mgr.) | .60 |
| 417 Joe Azcue | .60 |
| 418 Andy Carey | .60 |
| 419 Bob Bruce | .60 |
| 420 Gus Triandos | .60 |
| 421 Ken MacKenzie | .60 |
| 422 Steve Bilko | .60 |
| 423 Rival Relief Aces: | 1.50 |
| Roy Face, Hoyt Wilhelm | |
| 424 Al McBean | .60 |
| 425 Carl Yastrzemski | 75.00 |
| 426 Bob Farley | .60 |
| 427 Jake Wood | .60 |
| 428 Joe Hicks | .60 |
| 429 Billy O'Dell | .60 |
| 430 Tony Kubek | 2.50 |
| 431 Bob Rodgers | .60 |
| 432 Jim Pendleton | .60 |
| 433 Jim Archer | .60 |
| 434 Clay Dalrymple | .60 |
| 435 Larry Sherry | .60 |
| 436 Felix Mantilla | .60 |

# 1962 Topps (Continued)

| NO. PLAYER | MINT |
|---|---|
| 437 Ray Moore | .60 |
| 438 Dick Brown | .60 |
| 439 Jerry Buchek | .60 |
| 440 Joe Jay | .60 |
| 441 Checklist No. 6 | 1.50 |
| 442 Wes Stock | .60 |
| 443 Del Crandall | .60 |
| 444 Ted Wills | .60 |
| 445 Vic Power | .60 |
| 446 Don Elston | .60 |
| 447 Willie Kirland | .60 |
| 448 Joe Gibbon | .60 |
| 449 Jerry Adair | .60 |
| 450 Jim O'Toole | .60 |
| 451 Jose Tartabull | .60 |
| 452 Earl Averill | .60 |
| 453 Cal McLish | .60 |
| 454 Floyd Robinson | .60 |
| 455 Luis Arroyo | .60 |
| 456 Joe Amalfitano | .60 |
| 457 Lou Clinton | .60 |
| 458 Bob Buhl ("M" on hat) | .75 |
| 458 Bob Buhl | 10.00 |
| (without "M" on hat) | |
| 459 Ed Bailey | .60 |
| 460 Jim Bunning | 2.00 |
| 461 Ken Hubbs (R) | 2.00 |
| 462 Willie Tasby | .75 |
| ("W" on hat) | |
| 462 Willie Tasby | 10.00 |
| (without "W" on hat) | |
| 463 Hank Bauer (Mgr.) | .60 |
| 464 Al Jackson | .60 |
| 465 Cincinnati Reds | 1.50 |
| 466 Norm Cash (AS) | 1.00 |
| 467 Chuck Schilling (AS) | 1.00 |
| 468 Brooks Robinson (AS) | 4.00 |
| 469 Luis Aparicio (AS) | 2.00 |
| 470 Al Kaline (AS) | 4.00 |
| 471 Mickey Mantle (AS) | 16.00 |
| 472 Rocky Colavito (AS) | 1.00 |
| 473 Elston Howard (AS) | 1.00 |
| 474 Frank Lary (AS) | 1.00 |
| 475 Whitey Ford (AS) | 4.00 |
| 476 Baltimore Orioles | 1.00 |
| 477 Andre Rodgers | .60 |
| 478 Don Zimmer | .60 |
| 479 Joel Horlen | .60 |
| 480 Harvey Kuenn | 1.00 |
| 481 Vic Wertz | .60 |
| 482 Sam Mele | .60 |
| 483 Don McMahon | .60 |
| 484 Dick Schofield | .60 |
| 485 Pedro Ramos | .60 |
| 486 Jim Gilliam | 2.00 |
| 487 Jerry Lynch | .60 |
| 488 Hal Brown | .60 |
| 489 Julio Gotay | .60 |
| 490 Clete Boyer | 1.00 |
| 491 Leon Wagner | .60 |
| 492 Hal Smith | .60 |
| 493 Danny McDevitt | .60 |
| 494 Sammy White | .60 |
| 495 Don Cardwell | .60 |
| 496 Wayne Causey | .60 |
| 497 Ed Bouchee | .60 |
| 498 Jim Donohue | .60 |
| 499 Zoilo Versalles | .60 |
| 500 Duke Snider | 13.00 |
| 501 Claude Osteen | .60 |
| 502 Hector Lopez | .60 |
| 503 Danny Murtaugh (Mgr.) | .60 |
| 504 Eddie Bressoud | .60 |
| 505 Juan Marichal | 8.00 |
| 506 Charley Maxwell | .60 |
| 507 Ernie Broglio | .60 |
| 508 Gordy Coleman | .60 |
| 509 Dave Giusti | .60 |
| 510 Jim Lemon | .60 |
| 511 Bubba Phillips | .60 |
| 512 Mike Fornieles | .60 |
| 513 Whitey Herzog | .60 |
| 514 Sherm Lollar | .60 |
| 515 Stan Williams | .60 |
| 516 Checklist No. 7 | 2.00 |
| 517 Dave Wickersham | .60 |
| 518 Lee Maye | .60 |
| 519 Bob Johnson | .60 |
| 520 Bob Friend | .60 |
| 521 Jacke Davis | .60 |
| 522 Lindy McDaniel | .60 |
| 523 Russ Nixon | 2.00 |
| 524 Howie Nunn | 2.00 |
| 525 George Thomas | 2.00 |
| 526 Hal Woodeschick | 2.00 |
| 527 Dick McAuliffe | 2.00 |
| 528 Turk Lown | 2.00 |
| 529 John Schaive | 2.00 |
| 530 Bob Gibson | 38.00 |
| 531 Bobby G. Smith | 2.00 |
| 532 Dick Stigman | 2.00 |
| 533 Charley Lau | 2.00 |
| 534 Tony Gonzalez | 2.00 |
| 535 Ed Roebuck | 2.00 |
| 536 Dick Gernert | 2.00 |
| 537 Cleveland Indians | 3.50 |
| 538 Jack Sanford | 2.00 |
| 539 Billy Moran | 2.00 |
| 540 Jim Landis | 2.00 |
| 541 Don Nottebart | 2.00 |
| 542 Dave Philley | 2.00 |
| 543 Bob Allen | 2.00 |
| 544 Willie McCovey | 36.00 |
| 545 Hoyt Wilhelm | 15.00 |
| 546 Moe Thacker | 2.00 |
| 547 Don Ferrarese | 2.00 |
| 548 Bobby Del Greco | 2.00 |
| 549 Bill Rigney (Mgr.) | 2.00 |
| 550 Art Mahaffey | 2.00 |
| 551 Harry Bright | 2.00 |
| 552 Chicago Cubs | 3.50 |
| 553 Jim Coates | 2.00 |
| 554 Bubba Morton | 2.00 |
| 555 John Buzhardt | 2.00 |
| 556 Al Spangler | 2.00 |
| 557 Bob Anderson | 2.00 |
| 558 John Goryl | 2.00 |
| 559 Mike Higgins (Mgr.) | 2.00 |
| 560 Chuck Estrada | 2.00 |
| 561 Gene Oliver | 2.00 |
| 562 Bill Henry | 2.00 |
| 563 Ken Aspromonte | 2.00 |
| 564 Bob Grim | 2.00 |
| 565 Jose Pagan | 2.00 |
| 566 Marty Kutyna | 2.00 |
| 567 Tracy Stallard | 2.00 |
| 568 Jim Golden | 2.00 |
| 569 Ed Sadowski | 2.00 |
| 570 Bill Stafford | 2.00 |
| 571 Billy Klaus | 2.00 |
| 572 Bob Miller | 2.00 |
| 573 Johnny Logan | 2.00 |
| 574 Dean Stone | 2.00 |
| 575 Red Schoendienst | 3.00 |
| 576 Russ Kemmerer | 2.00 |
| 577 Dave Nicholson | 2.00 |
| 578 Jim Duffalo | 2.00 |
| 579 Jim Schaffer | 2.00 |
| 580 Bill Monbouquette | 2.00 |
| 581 Mel Roach | 2.00 |
| 582 Ron Piche | 2.00 |
| 583 Larry Osborne | 2.00 |
| 584 Minnesota Twins | 3.50 |
| 585 Glen Hobbie | 2.00 |
| 586 Sammy Esposito | 2.00 |
| 587 Frank Funk | 2.00 |
| 588 Birdie Tebbetts (Mgr.) | 2.00 |
| 589 Bob Turley | 2.00 |
| 590 Curt Flood | 3.00 |
| 591 Rookie Pitchers: | 5.00 |
| Sam McDowell, D. Radatz, Ron Taylor, Ron Nischwitz, Art Quirk | |
| 592 Rookie Pitchers: | 7.00 |
| D. Stenhouse, Dan Pfister, Bo Belinsky, Jim Bouton, Joe Bonikowski | |
| 593 Rookie Pitchers: | 4.00 |
| Bob Moorhead, Jack Lamabe, Jack Hamilton, Bob Veale, Craig Anderson | |
| 594 Rookie Catchers: | 30.00 |
| Bob Uecker, Doc Edwards, Ken Retzer, Doug Camilli, Don Pavletich | |
| 595 Rookie Infielders: | 4.00 |
| Bob Sadowski, Marlan Coughtry, Ed Charles, Felix Torres | |
| 596 Rookie Infielders: | 7.00 |
| Bernie Allen, Phil Linz, Rich Rollins, Joe Pepitone | |
| 597 Rookie Infielders: | 4.00 |
| Denis Menke, Jim McKnight, Rod Kanehl, Amado Samuel | |
| 598 Rookie Outfielders: | 5.00 |
| Al Luplow, Danny Jimenez, Ed Olivares, Howie Gross, Jim Hickman | |

## 1963 Topps....Complete Set of 576 Cards—Value $1200.00

Pete Rose's rookie card is in this set. Cards 507 to 576 are the high numbers. Also includes the rookie cards of Willie Stargell, Tony Oliva, and Rusty Staub. Cards 29 and 54 exist with the error "1962 Rookie Stars" instead of "1963 Rookie Stars"—worth $3.00 each.

| NO. PLAYER | MINT |
|---|---|
| 1 NL Batting Leaders: | 3.00 |
| Frank Robinson, Stan Musial, Tommy Davis, Bill White, Hank Aaron | |
| 2 AL Batting Leaders: | 2.00 |
| Norm Siebern, Pete Runnels, Floyd Robinson, C. Hinton, Mickey Mantle | |
| 3 NL Home Run Leaders: | 2.50 |
| O. Cepeda, Hank Aaron, Ernie Banks, Frank Robinson, Willie Mays | |
| 4 AL Home Run Leaders: | 1.00 |
| Roger Maris, R. Colavito, Harmon Killebrew, Norm Cash, J. Gentile, L. Wagner | |
| 5 NL ERA Leaders: | 1.50 |
| Bob Purkey, Bob Shaw, Sandy Koufax, Bob Gibson, Don Drysdale | |
| 6 AL ERA Leaders: | 1.00 |
| Whitey Ford, Robin Roberts, Eddie Fisher, Hank Aguirre, Dean Chance | |
| 7 NL Pitching Leaders: | 1.00 |
| Don Drysdale, Billy O'Dell, Jack Sanford, Art Mahaffey, Joe Jay | |
| 8 AL Pitching Leaders: | 1.00 |
| Dick Donovan, Ray Herbert, Ralph Terry, Jim Bunning, Camilo Pascual | |

| NO. PLAYER | MINT |
|---|---|
| 9 NL Strikeout Leaders: | 1.50 |
| Sandy Koufax, Bob Gibson, Don Drysdale, Billy O'Dell, Dick Farrell | |
| 10 AL Strikeout Leaders: | 1.00 |
| Ralph Terry, Juan Pizarro, Camilo Pascual, Jim Bunning, Jim Kaat | |
| 11 Lee Walls | .25 |
| 12 Steve Barber | .25 |
| 13 Philadelphia Phillies | .75 |
| 14 Pedro Ramos | .25 |
| 15 Ken Hubbs | .60 |
| 16 Al Smith | .25 |
| 17 Ryne Duren | .25 |
| 18 Buc Blasters: | 1.50 |
| Smoky Burgess, Dick Stuart, Bob Clemente, Bob Skinner | |
| 19 Pete Burnside | .25 |
| 20 Tony Kubek | 1.50 |
| 21 Marty Keough | .25 |
| 22 Curt Simmons | .25 |
| 23 Ed Lopat (Mgr.) | .35 |
| 24 Bob Bruce | .25 |
| 25 Al Kaline | 5.00 |
| 26 Ray Moore | .25 |
| 27 Choo Choo Coleman | .25 |
| 28 Mike Fornieles | .25 |
| 29 Rookie Stars:* | .40 |
| Sammy Ellis, Jesse Gonder, Ray Culp, John Boozer | |
| 30 Harvey Kuenn | .45 |
| 31 Cal Koonce | .25 |
| 32 Tony Gonzalez | .25 |
| 33 Bo Belinsky | .25 |
| 34 Dick Schofield | .25 |
| 35 John Buzhardt | .25 |
| 36 Jerry Kindall | .25 |
| 37 Jerry Lynch | .25 |
| 38 Bud Daley | .25 |
| 39 Los Angeles Angels | .75 |
| 40 Vic Power | .25 |
| 41 Charlie Lau | .25 |
| 42 Stan Williams | .25 |
| 43 Veteran Masters: | 1.50 |
| C. Stengel, G. Woodling | |
| 44 Terry Fox | .25 |
| 45 Bob Aspromonte | .25 |
| 46 Tommie Aaron | .25 |
| 47 Don Lock | .25 |
| 48 Birdie Tebbetts (Mgr.) | .25 |
| 49 Dal Maxvill | .25 |
| 50 Bill Pierce | .45 |
| 51 George Alusik | .25 |
| 52 Chuck Schilling | .25 |
| 53 Joe Moeller | .25 |
| 54 Rookie Stars:* | 2.50 |
| N. Mathews, D. DeBusschere, Harry Fanok, J. Cullen | |
| 55 Bill Virdon | .75 |
| 56 Dennis Bennett | .25 |
| 57 Billy Moran | .25 |
| 58 Bob Will | .25 |
| 59 Craig Anderson | .25 |
| 60 Elston Howard | 2.00 |
| 61 Ernie Bowman | .25 |
| 62 Bob Hendley | .25 |
| 63 Cincinnati Reds | 1.00 |
| 64 Dick McAuliffe | .25 |
| 65 Jackie Brandt | .25 |
| 66 Mike Joyce | .25 |
| 67 Ed Charles | .25 |
| 68 Friendly Foes: | 3.50 |
| Duke Snider, Gil Hodges | |
| 69 Bud Zipfel | .25 |
| 70 Jim O'Toole | .25 |
| 71 Bobby Wine | .25 |
| 72 Johnny Romano | .25 |
| 73 Bob Bragan (Mgr.) | .25 |
| 74 Denver Lemaster | .25 |
| 75 Bobby Allison | .25 |
| 76 Earl Wilson | .25 |
| 77 Al Spangler | .25 |
| 78 Marv Throneberry | .45 |
| 79 Checklist No. 1 | 1.50 |
| 80 Jim Gilliam | 1.25 |
| 81 Jim Schaffer | .25 |
| 82 Ed Rakow | .25 |
| 83 Charley James | .25 |
| 84 Ron Kline | .25 |
| 85 Tom Haller | .25 |
| 86 Charley Maxwell | .25 |
| 87 Bob Veale | .25 |
| 88 Ron Hansen | .25 |
| 89 Dick Stigman | .25 |
| 90 Gordy Coleman | .25 |
| 91 Dallas Green | .25 |
| 92 Hector Lopez | .25 |
| 93 Galen Cisco | .25 |
| 94 Bob Schmidt | .25 |
| 95 Larry Jackson | .25 |
| 96 Lou Clinton | .25 |
| 97 Bob Duliba | .25 |
| 98 George Thomas | .25 |
| 99 Jim Umbricht | .25 |
| 100 Joe Cunningham | .25 |
| 101 Joe Gibbon | .25 |
| 102 Checklist No. 2 | 1.25 |
| 103 Chuck Essegian | .25 |
| 104 Lew Krausse | .25 |
| 105 Ron Fairly | .25 |
| 106 Bob Bolin | .25 |
| 107 Jim Hickman | .25 |
| 108 Hoyt Wilhelm | 3.00 |
| 109 Lee Maye | .25 |
| 110 Rich Rollins | .25 |
| 111 Al Jackson | .25 |
| 112 Dick Brown | .25 |
| 113 Don Landrum | .25 |
| (photo of Ron Santo) | |
| 114 Dan Osinski | .25 |
| 115 Carl Yastrzemski | 35.00 |
| 116 Jim Brosnan | .25 |
| 117 Jacke Davis | .25 |
| 118 Sherm Lollar | .25 |
| 119 Bob Lillis | .25 |
| 120 Roger Maris | 7.00 |
| 121 Jim Hannan | .25 |
| 122 Julio Gotay | .25 |
| 123 Frank Howard | .75 |
| 124 Dick Howser | .25 |
| 125 Robin Roberts | 2.50 |
| 126 Bob Uecker | 6.00 |
| 127 Bill Tuttle | .25 |
| 128 Matty Alou | .25 |
| 129 Gary Bell | .25 |
| 130 Dick Groat | .45 |
| 131 Washington Senators | .75 |
| 132 Jack Hamilton | .25 |
| 133 Gene Freese | .25 |
| 134 Bob Scheffing (Mgr.) | .25 |
| 135 Richie Ashburn | 1.50 |
| 136 Ike Delock | .25 |
| 137 Mack Jones | .25 |
| 138 Pride Of N.L.: | 6.00 |
| Willie Mays, Stan Musial | |
| 139 Earl Averill | .25 |
| 140 Frank Lary | .25 |
| 141 Manny Mota (R) | 1.50 |
| 142 World Series Game 1 | 2.00 |
| Ford Wins Opener | |
| 143 World Series Game 2 | 1.50 |
| Sanford Shutout | |
| 144 World Series Game 3 | 2.00 |
| Maris Sparks Rally | |
| 145 World Series Game 4 | 1.50 |
| Hiller Grand Slam | |
| 146 World Series Game 5 | 1.50 |
| Tresh's Homer | |
| 147 World Series Game 6 | 1.50 |
| Pierce Victory | |
| 148 World Series Game 7 | 1.50 |
| Yanks Celebrate | |
| 149 Marv Breeding | .25 |
| 150 Johnny Podres | .75 |
| 151 Pittsburgh Pirates | .75 |
| 152 Ron Nischwitz | .25 |
| 153 Hal Smith | .25 |
| 154 Walt Alston (Mgr.) | 1.00 |
| 155 Bill Stafford | .25 |
| 156 Roy McMillan | .25 |
| 157 Diego Segui | .25 |
| 158 Rookie Stars: | .45 |
| Bob Saverine, Rogelio Alvarez, Dave Roberts, Tommy Harper | |
| 159 Jim Pagliaroni | .25 |
| 160 Juan Pizarro | .25 |
| 161 Frank Torre | .25 |
| 162 Minnesota Twins | .75 |
| 163 Don Larsen | .35 |
| 164 Bubba Morton | .25 |
| 165 Jim Kaat | 1.50 |
| 166 Johnny Keane (Mgr.) | .25 |
| 167 Jim Fregosi | .35 |
| 168 Russ Nixon | .25 |
| 169 Rookie Stars: | 8.00 |
| Gaylord Perry, Dick Egan, Julio Navarro, Tommie Sisk | |
| 170 Joe Adcock | .25 |
| 171 Steve Hamilton | .25 |
| 172 Gene Oliver | .25 |
| 173 Bombers' Best: | 7.00 |
| Tom Tresh, Mickey Mantle, Bobby Richardson | |
| 174 Larry Burright | .25 |
| 175 Bob Buhl | .25 |
| 176 Jim King | .25 |
| 177 Bubba Phillips | .25 |
| 178 Johnny Edwards | .25 |
| 179 Ron Pich | .25 |
| 180 Bill Skowron | .75 |
| 181 Sammy Esposito | .25 |
| 182 Albie Pearson | .25 |
| 183 Joe Pepitone | .50 |
| 184 Vern Law | .25 |
| 185 Chuck Hiller | .25 |
| 186 Jerry Zimmerman | .25 |
| 187 Willie Kirkland | .25 |
| 188 Eddie Bressoud | .25 |
| 189 Dave Giusti | .25 |
| 190 Minnie Minoso | .75 |
| 191 Checklist No. 3 | 1.50 |
| 192 Clay Dalrymple | .25 |
| 193 Andre Rodgers | .25 |
| 194 Joe Nuxhall | .25 |
| 195 Manny Jimenez | .25 |
| 196 Doug Camilli | .25 |
| 197 Roger Craig | .40 |
| 198 Lenny Green | .40 |
| 199 Joe Amalfitano | .40 |
| 200 Mickey Mantle | 65.00 |
| 201 Cecil Butler | .40 |
| 202 Boston Red Sox | 1.50 |
| 203 Chico Cardenas | .40 |
| 204 Don Nottebart | .40 |
| 205 Luis Aparicio | 3.00 |
| 206 Ray Washburn | .40 |
| 207 Ken Hunt | .40 |
| 208 Rookie Stars: | .40 |
| Ron Herbel, John Miller, Ron Taylor, Wally Wolf | |
| 209 Hobie Landrith | .40 |
| 210 Sandy Koufax | 25.00 |
| 211 Fred Whitfield | .40 |
| 212 Glen Hobbie | .40 |
| 213 Billy Hitchcock (Mgr.) | .40 |
| 214 Orlando Pena | .40 |
| 215 Bob Skinner | .40 |
| 216 Gene Conley | .40 |
| 217 Joe Christopher | .40 |
| 218 Tiger Twirlers: | 1.00 |
| Frank Lary, Don Mossi, Jim Bunning | |
| 219 Chuck Cottier | .40 |
| 220 Camilo Pascual | .40 |
| 221 Cookie Rojas | .40 |
| 222 Chicago Cubs | 1.00 |
| 223 Eddie Fisher | .40 |
| 224 Mike Roarke | .40 |
| 225 Joe Jay | .40 |
| 226 Julian Javier | .40 |
| 227 Jim Grant | .40 |
| 228 Rookie Stars: | 6.00 |
| Max Alvis, Bob Bailey, Pedro Oliva, Ed Kranepool | |
| 229 Willie Davis | .40 |
| 230 Pete Runnels | .40 |
| 231 Eli Grba | .40 |
| (photo of Ryne Duren) | |
| 232 Frank Malzone | .40 |
| 233 Casey Stengel (Mgr.) | 4.00 |
| 234 Dave Nicholson | .40 |
| 235 Bill O'Dell | .40 |
| 236 Bill Bryan | .40 |
| 237 Jim Coates | .40 |
| 238 Lou Johnson | .40 |
| 239 Harvey Haddix | .40 |
| 240 Rocky Colavito | 1.00 |
| 241 Billy Smith | .40 |
| 242 Power Plus: | 4.00 |
| Ernie Banks, Hank Aaron | |
| 243 Don Leppert | .40 |
| 244 John Tsitouris | .40 |
| 245 Gil Hodges | 3.00 |
| 246 Lee Stange | .40 |
| 247 New York Yankees | 3.50 |
| 248 Tito Francona | .40 |
| 249 Leo Burke | .40 |
| 250 Stan Musial | 20.00 |
| 251 Jack Lamabe | .40 |
| 252 Ron Santo | 1.00 |
| 253 Rookie Stars; | .40 |
| Len Gabrielson, Pete Jernigan, Deacon Jones, John Wojcik | |
| 254 Mike Hershberger | .40 |
| 255 Bob Shaw | .40 |
| 256 Jerry Lumpe | .40 |
| 257 Hank Aguirre | .40 |
| 258 Alvin Dark (Mgr.) | .40 |
| 259 Johnny Logan | .40 |
| 260 Jim Gentile | .40 |
| 261 Bob Miller | .40 |
| 262 Ellis Burton | .40 |
| 263 Dave Stenhouse | .40 |
| 264 Phil Linz | .40 |
| 265 Vada Pinson | 1.00 |
| 266 Bob Allen | .40 |
| 267 Carl Sawatski | .40 |
| 268 Don Demter | .40 |
| 269 Don Mincher | .40 |
| 270 Felipe Alou | .40 |
| 271 Dean Stone | .40 |
| 272 Danny Murphy | .40 |
| 273 Sammy Taylor | .40 |
| 274 Checklist No. 4 | 1.50 |
| 275 Ed Mathews | 4.50 |
| 276 Barry Shetrone | .40 |
| 277 Dick Farrell | .40 |
| 278 Chico Fernandez | .40 |
| 279 Wally Moon | .40 |
| 280 Bob Rodgers | .40 |
| 281 Tom Sturdivant | .40 |
| 282 Bob Del Greco | .40 |
| 283 Roy Sievers | .40 |
| 284 Dave Sisler | .40 |
| 285 Dick Stuart | .40 |
| 286 Stu Miller | .40 |
| 287 Dick Bertell | .40 |
| 288 Chicago White Sox | 1.00 |
| 289 Hal Brown | .40 |
| 290 Bill White | .40 |
| 291 Don Rudolph | .40 |
| 292 Pumpsie Green | .40 |
| 293 Bill Pleis | .40 |
| 294 Bill Rigney (Mgr.) | .40 |
| 295 Ed Roebuck | .40 |

| NO. PLAYER | MINT | NO. PLAYER | MINT | NO. PLAYER | MINT | NO. PLAYER | MINT |
|---|---|---|---|---|---|---|---|
| 296 Doc Edwards | .40 | 369 Jim Lemon | .40 | 440 Juan Marichal | 5.00 | 514 Larry Osborne | 1.50 |
| 297 Jim Golden | .40 | 370 Dick Donovan | .40 | 441 Lee Thomas | .40 | 515 Don Elston | 1.50 |
| 298 Don Dillard | .40 | 371 Rod Kanehl | .40 | 442 J.C. Hartman | .40 | 516 Purnal Goldy | 1.50 |
| 299 Rookie Stars: | .40 | 372 Don Lee | .40 | 443 Jim Piersall | .75 | 517 Hal Woodeschick | 1.50 |
| Dave Morehead, Bob Dustal, | | 373 Jim Campbell | .40 | 444 Jim Maloney | .40 | 518 Don Blasingame | 1.50 |
| Dan Schenider, Tom Butters | | 374 Claude Osteen | .40 | 445 Norm Cash | 1.50 | 519 Claude Raymond | 1.50 |
| 300 Willie Mays | 35.00 | 375 Ken Boyer | 1.50 | 446 Whitey Ford | 11.00 | 520 Orlando Cepeda | 5.00 |
| 301 Bill Fischer | .40 | 376 John Wyatt | .40 | 447 Felix Mantilla | 2.00 | 521 Dan Pfister | 2.00 |
| 302 Whitey Herzog | .75 | 377 Baltimore Orioles | 1.00 | 448 Jack Kralick | 2.00 | 522 Rookie Stars: | 2.00 |
| 303 Earl Francis | .40 | 378 Bill Henry | .40 | 449 Jose Tartabull | 2.00 | Mel Nelson, Gary Peters, | |
| 304 Harry Bright | .40 | 379 Bob Anderson | .40 | 450 Bob Friend | 2.00 | Art Quirk, Jim Roland | |
| 305 Don Hoak | .40 | 380 Ernie Banks | 15.00 | 451 Cleveland Indians | 3.00 | 523 Bill Kunkel | 2.00 |
| 306 Star Receivers: | .75 | 381 Frank Baumann | .40 | 452 Barney Schultz | 2.00 | 524 St. Louis Cards | 3.50 |
| Earl Battey, Elston Howard | | 382 Ralph Houk (Mgr.) | .60 | 453 Jake Wood | 2.00 | 525 Nellie Fox | 3.50 |
| 307 Chet Nichols | .40 | 383 Pete Richert | .40 | 454 Art Fowler | 2.00 | 526 Dick Hall | 2.00 |
| 308 Camilo Carreon | .40 | 384 Bob Tillman | .40 | 455 Ruben Amaro | 2.00 | 527 Ed Sadowski | 2.00 |
| 309 Jim Brewer | .40 | 385 Art Mahaffey | .40 | 456 Jim Coker | 2.00 | 528 Carl Willey | 2.00 |
| 310 Tommy Davis | .75 | 386 Rookie Stars: | .60 | 457 Tex Clevenger | 2.00 | 529 Wes Covington | 2.00 |
| 311 Joe McClain | .40 | Ed Kirkpatrick, J. Bateman, | | 458 Al Lopez (Mgr.) | 3.00 | 530 Don Mossi | 2.00 |
| 312 Houston Colts | 2.50 | G. Roggenburk, L. Bearnarth | | 459 Dick LeMay | 2.00 | 531 Sam Mele (Mgr.) | 2.00 |
| 313 Ernie Broglio | .40 | 387 Al McBean | .40 | 460 Del Crandall | 2.00 | 532 Steve Boros | 2.00 |
| 314 John Goryl | .40 | 388 Jim Davenport | .40 | 461 Norm Bass | 2.00 | 533 Bobby Shantz | 2.00 |
| 315 Ralph Terry | .40 | 389 Frank Sullivan | .40 | 462 Wally Post | 2.00 | 534 Ken Walters | 2.00 |
| 316 Norm Sherry | .40 | 390 Hank Aaron | 35.00 | 463 Joe Schaffernoth | 2.00 | 535 Jim Perry | 2.00 |
| 317 Sam McDowell | .50 | 391 Bill Dailey | .40 | 464 Ken Aspromonte | 2.00 | 536 Norm Larker | 2.00 |
| 318 Gene Mauch (Mgr.) | .50 | 392 Tribe Thumpers: | .40 | 465 Chuck Estrada | 2.00 | 537 Rookie Stars: | 550.00 |
| 319 Joe Gaines | .40 | Johnny Romano, | | 466 Rookie Stars: | 3.00 | Pedro Gonzalez, Pete Rose, | |
| 320 Warren Spahn | 6.00 | Tito Francona | | Tony Martinez, Bill Freehan, | | Ken McMullen, Al Weis | |
| 321 Gino Cimoli | .40 | 393 Ken MacKenzie | .40 | Jerry Robinson, Nate Oliver | | 538 George Brunet | 2.00 |
| 322 Bob Turley | .50 | 394 Tim McCarver | .75 | 467 Phil Ortega | 2.00 | 539 Wayne Causey | 2.00 |
| 323 Bill Mazeroski | .75 | 395 Don McMahon | .40 | 468 Carroll Hardy | 2.00 | 540 Bob Clemente | 50.00 |
| 324 Rookie Stars: | .75 | 396 Joe Koppe | .40 | 469 Jay Hook | 2.00 | 541 Ron Moeller | 2.00 |
| G. Williams, Vic Davalillo, | | 397 Kansas C. Athletics | 1.00 | 470 Tom Tresh | 5.00 | 542 Lou Klimchock | 2.00 |
| P. Ward, Phil Roof | | 398 Boog Powell | 1.75 | 471 Ken Retzer | 2.00 | 543 Russ Snyder | 2.00 |
| 325 Jack Sanford | .40 | 399 Dick Ellsworth | .40 | 472 Lou Brock | 45.00 | 544 Rookie Stars: | 15.00 |
| 326 Hank Foiles | .40 | 400 Frank Robinson | 12.00 | 473 New York Mets | 5.00 | Rusty Staub, Duke Carmel, | |
| 327 Paul Foytack | .40 | 401 Jim Bouton | 1.00 | 474 Jack Fisher | 2.00 | Bill Haas, Dick Phillips | |
| 328 Dick Williams | .60 | 402 Mickey Vernon (Mgr.) | .40 | 475 Gus Triandos | 2.00 | 545 Jose Pagan | 2.00 |
| 329 Lindy McDaniel | .40 | 403 Ron Perranoski | .40 | 476 Frank Funk | 2.00 | 546 Hal Reniff | 2.00 |
| 330 Chuck Hinton | .40 | 404 Bob Oldis | .40 | 477 Donn Clendenon | 2.00 | 547 Gus Bell | 2.00 |
| 331 Series Foes: | .40 | 405 Floyd Robinson | .40 | 478 Paul Brown | 2.00 | 548 Tom Satriano | 2.00 |
| Bill Stafford, Bill Pierce | | 406 Howie Koplitz | .40 | 479 Ed Brinkman | 2.00 | 549 Rookie Stars: | 2.00 |
| 332 Joel Horlen | .40 | 407 Rookie Stars: | | 480 Bill Monbouquette | 2.00 | Paul Ratliff, Marcelino | |
| 333 Carl Warwick | .40 | Dick Simpson, Frank Kostro, | | 481 Bob Taylor | 2.00 | Lopez, Pete Lovrich, | |
| 334 Wynn Hawkins | .40 | Chico Ruiz, Larry Elliot | | 482 Felix Torres | 2.00 | Elmo Plaskett | |
| 335 Leon Wagner | .40 | 408 Billy Gardner | .40 | 483 Jim Owens | 2.00 | 550 Duke Snider | 25.00 |
| 336 Ed Bauta | .40 | 409 Roy Face | .40 | 484 Dale Long | 2.00 | 551 Billy Klaus | 2.00 |
| 337 Los Angeles Dodgers | 2.50 | 410 Earl Battey | .40 | 485 Jim Landis | 2.00 | 552 Detroit Tigers | 6.00 |
| 338 Russ Kemmerer | .40 | 411 Jim Constable | .40 | 486 Ray Sadecki | 2.00 | 553 Rookie Stars: | 55.00 |
| 339 Ted Bowsfield | .40 | 412 Dodger Big Three: | 6.50 | 487 John Roseboro | 2.00 | Brock Davis, Jim Gosger, | |
| 340 Yogi Berra | 15.00 | Sandy Koufax, Johnny | | 488 Jerry Adair | 2.00 | W. Stargell, J. Herrnstein | |
| 341 Jack Baldschun | .40 | Podres, Don Drysdale | | 489 Paul Toth | 2.00 | 554 Hank Fischer | 2.00 |
| 342 Gene Woodling | .40 | 413 Jerry Walker | .40 | 490 Willie McCovey | 35.00 | 555 John Blanchard | 2.00 |
| 343 Johnny Pesky (Mgr.) | .40 | 414 Ty Cline | .40 | 491 Harry Craft (Mgr.) | 2.00 | 556 Al Worthington | 2.00 |
| 344 Don Schwall | .40 | 415 Bob Gibson | 11.00 | 492 Dave Wickersham | 2.00 | 557 Cuno Barragan | 2.00 |
| 345 Brooks Robinson | 11.00 | 416 Alex Grammas | .40 | 493 Walt Bond | 2.00 | 558 Rookie Stars: | 2.00 |
| 346 Billy Hoeft | .40 | 417 San F. Giants | 1.00 | 494 Phil Regan | 2.00 | Bill Faul, Ron Hunt, | |
| 347 Joe Torre | 1.50 | 418 Johnny Orsino | .40 | 495 Frank Thomas | 2.00 | Bob Lipski, Al Moran | |
| 348 Vic Wertz | .40 | 419 Tracy Stallard | .40 | 496 Rookie Stars: | 2.00 | 559 Danny Murtaugh (Mgr.) | 2.00 |
| 349 Zoilo Versalles | .40 | 420 Bobby Richardson | 1.50 | Steve Dalkowski, Carl | | 560 Ray Herbert | 2.00 |
| 350 Bob Purkey | .40 | 421 Tom Morgan | .40 | Bouldin, Fred Newman, | | 561 Mike De La Hoz | 2.00 |
| 351 Al Luplow | .40 | 422 Fred Hutchinson (Mgr.) | .40 | Jack Smith | | 562 Rookie Stars: | 3.00 |
| 352 Ken Johnson | .40 | 423 Ed Hobaugh | .40 | 497 Bennie Daniels | 2.00 | Don Rowe, Randy Cardinal, | |
| 353 Billy Williams | 2.50 | 424 Charley Smith | .40 | 498 Eddie Kasko | 2.00 | Dave McNally, Ken Rowe | |
| 354 Dom Zanni | .40 | 425 Smokey Burgess | .40 | 499 J.C. Martin | 2.00 | 563 Mike McCormick | 2.00 |
| 355 Dean Chance | .40 | 426 Barry Latman | .40 | 500 Harmon Killebrew | 25.00 | 564 George Banks | 2.00 |
| 356 John Schaive | .40 | 427 Bernie Allen | .40 | 501 Joe Azcue | 2.00 | 565 Larry Sherry | 2.00 |
| 357 George Altman | .40 | 428 Carl Boles | .40 | 502 Daryl Spencer | 2.00 | 566 Clif Cook | 2.00 |
| 358 Milt Pappas | .40 | 429 Lou Burdette | 1.00 | 503 Milwaukee Braves | 4.00 | 567 Jim Duffalo | 2.00 |
| 359 Haywood Sullivan | .40 | 430 Norm Siebern | .40 | 504 Bob Johnson | 2.00 | 568 Bob Sadowski | 2.00 |
| 360 Don Drysdale | 6.00 | 431 Checklist No. 6 | 1.50 | 505 Curt Flood | 4.00 | 569 Luis Arroyo | 2.00 |
| 361 Clete Boyer | .60 | 432 Roman Mejias | .40 | 506 Gene Green | 2.00 | 570 Frank Bolling | 2.00 |
| 362 Checklist No. 5 | 1.50 | 433 Denis Menke | .40 | 507 Roland Sheldon | 1.50 | 571 Johnny Klippstein | 2.00 |
| 363 Dick Radatz | .40 | 434 Johnny Callison | .40 | 508 Ted Savage | 1.50 | 572 Jack Spring | 2.00 |
| 364 Howie Goss | .40 | 435 Woody Held | .40 | 509 Checklist No. 7 | 4.50 | 573 Coot Veal | 2.00 |
| 365 Jim Bunning | 2.00 | 436 Tim Harkness | .40 | 510 Ken McBride | 1.50 | 574 Hal Kolstad | 2.00 |
| 366 Tony Taylor | .40 | 437 Bill Bruton | .40 | | | 575 Don Cardwell | 2.00 |
| 367 Tony Cloninger | .40 | 438 Wes Stock | .40 | 512 Cal McLish | 1.50 | 576 Johnny Temple | 2.00 |
| 368 Ed Bailey | .40 | 439 Don Zimmer | .60 | 513 Gary Geiger | 1.50 | | |

# 1964 Topps....Complete Set of 587 Cards—Value $650.00

Phil Niekro's rookie card is in this set. The high numbers are 523 to 587. For the first time a card was issued for a deceased player—Ken Hubbs.

 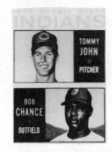 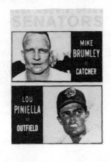 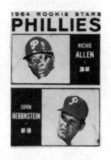 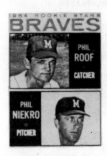

| NO. PLAYER | MINT |
|---|---|
| 1 NL ERA Leaders: ........2.50 | |
| Sandy Koufax, Dick | |
| Ellsworth, Bob Friend | |
| 2 AL ERA Leaders: ........85 | |
| Gary Peters, Juan Pizarro, | |
| Camilo Pascual | |
| 3 NL Pitching Leaders: ....1.50 | |
| S. Koufax, Juan Marichal, | |
| W. Spahn, Jim Maloney | |
| 4 AL Pitching Leaders: ......85 | |
| Whitey Ford, Camilo | |
| Pascual, Jim Bouton | |
| 5 NL Strikeout Leaders: ...1.50 | |
| Sandy Koufax, Jim | |
| Maloney, Don Drysdale | |
| 6 AL Strikeout Leaders:......85 | |
| Camilo Pascual, Jim | |
| Bunning, Dick Stigman | |
| 7 NL Batting Leaders: .......85 | |
| T. Davis, Bob Clemente, | |
| D. Groat, Hank Aaron | |
| 8 AL Batting Leaders: .....1.50 | |
| Carl Yastrzemski, Al Kaline, | |
| Rich Rollins | |
| 9 NL Home Run Leaders: ..2.50 | |
| Hank Aaron, W. McCovey, | |
| W. Mays, Orlando Cepeda | |
| 10 AL Home Run Leaders: ....85 | |
| Harmon Killebrew, Dick | |
| Stuart, Bob Allison | |
| 11 NL RBI Leaders:.........85 | |
| Hank Aaron, Ken Boyer, | |
| Bill White | |
| 12 AL RBI Leaders: ........85 | |
| Dick Stuart, Al Kaline, | |
| Harmon Killebrew | |
| 13 Hoyt Wilhelm ..........2.50 | |
| 14 Dodgers Rookies:.........30 | |
| Dick Nen, Nick Willhite | |
| 15 Zoilo Versalles ...........30 | |
| 16 John Boozer ............30 | |
| 17 Willie Kirkland ...........30 | |
| 18 Bill O'Dell ..............30 | |
| 19 Don Wert ...............30 | |
| 20 Bob Friend ..............30 | |
| 21 Yogi Berra (Mgr.).......9.00 | |
| 22 Jerry Adair ..............30 | |
| 23 Chris Zachary ...........30 | |
| 24 Carl Sawatski............30 | |
| 25 Bill Monbouquette........30 | |
| 26 Gino Cimoli .............30 | |
| 27 New York Mets ..........1.00 | |
| 28 Claude Osteen ...........30 | |
| 29 Lou Brock ...........12.00 | |
| 30 Ron Perranoski ..........30 | |
| 31 Dave Nicholson ..........30 | |
| 32 Dean Chance ............45 | |
| 33 Reds Rookies:............30 | |
| Sammy Ellis, Mel Queen | |
| 34 Jim Perry ...............30 | |
| 35 Ed Mathews.............3.50 | |
| 36 Hal Reniff ..............30 | |
| 37 Smoky Burgess ..........30 | |
| 38 Jim Wynn (R) ............75 | |
| 39 Hank Aguirre ............30 | |
| 40 Dick Groat ..............50 | |

| NO. PLAYER | MINT |
|---|---|
| 41 Friendly Foes:..........1.00 | |
| W. McCovey, Leon Wagner | |
| 42 Moe Drabowski ..........30 | |
| 43 Roy Sievers .............30 | |
| 44 Duke Carmel ............30 | |
| 45 Milt Pappas .............30 | |
| 46 Ed Brinkman ............30 | |
| 47 Giants Rookies:..........50 | |
| Jesus Alou, Ron Herbel | |
| 48 Bob Perry ...............30 | |
| 49 Bill Henry ..............30 | |
| 50 Mickey Mantle .........60.00 | |
| 51 Pete Richert ............30 | |
| 52 Chuck Hinton ...........30 | |
| 53 Denis Menke ............30 | |
| 54 Sam Mele ...............30 | |
| 55 Ernie Banks ............5.00 | |
| 56 Hal Brown ...............30 | |
| 57 Tim Harkness ...........30 | |
| 58 Don Demeter ............30 | |
| 59 Ernie Broglio ............30 | |
| 60 Frank Malzone ...........30 | |
| 61 Angel Backstops:.........30 | |
| Bob Rodgers, Ed Sadowski | |
| 62 Ted Savage ..............30 | |
| 63 Johnny Orsino ...........30 | |
| 64 Ted Abernathy ...........30 | |
| 65 Felipe Alou ..............30 | |
| 66 Eddie Fisher .............30 | |
| 67 Detroit Tigers ............75 | |
| 68 Willie Davis .............45 | |
| 69 Clete Boyer .............30 | |
| 70 Joe Torre ..............1.00 | |
| 71 Jack Spring .............30 | |
| 72 Chico Cardenas .........30 | |
| 73 Jimmie Hall .............30 | |
| 74 Pirates Rookies:.........30 | |
| Bob Priddy, Tom Butters | |
| 75 Wayne Causey ...........30 | |
| 76 Checklist No. 1 .........1.50 | |
| 77 Jerry Walker .............30 | |
| 78 Merritt Ranew ...........30 | |
| 79 Bob Heffner.............30 | |
| 80 Vada Pinson ...........1.00 | |
| 81 All-Star Vets:...........2.25 | |
| Nellie Fox, H. Killebrew | |
| 82 Jim Davenport ...........30 | |
| 83 Gus Triandos ............30 | |
| 84 Carl Willey ..............30 | |
| 85 Pete Ward ..............30 | |
| 86 Al Doning ...............30 | |
| 87 St. Louis Cardinals .......75 | |
| 88 John Roseboro ...........30 | |
| 89 Boog Powell ............1.00 | |
| 90 Earl Battey .............30 | |
| 91 Bob Bailey ..............30 | |
| 92 Steve Ridzik ............30 | |
| 93 Gary Geiger .............30 | |
| 94 Braves Rookies:..........30 | |
| Jim Britton, Larry Maxie | |
| 95 George Altman ...........30 | |
| 96 Bob Buhl ...............30 | |
| 97 Jim Fregosi .............30 | |
| 98 Bill Bruton ..............30 | |
| 99 Al Stanek ...............30 | |
| 100 Elston Howard .........1.25 | |

| NO. PLAYER | MINT |
|---|---|
| 101 Walt Alston (Mgr.) ....1.00 | |
| 102 Checklist No. 2 ........1.50 | |
| 103 Curt Flood .............65 | |
| 104 Art Mahaffey ...........30 | |
| 105 Woody Held ............30 | |
| 106 Joe Nuxhall ............30 | |
| 107 White Sox Rookies: .....30 | |
| B. Howard, F. Kreutzer | |
| 108 John Wyatt .............30 | |
| 109 Rusty Staub ...........2.00 | |
| 110 Albie Pearson ..........30 | |
| 111 Don Elston .............30 | |
| 112 Bob Tillman ............30 | |
| 113 Grover Powell ..........30 | |
| 114 Don Lock ...............30 | |
| 115 Frank Bolling ...........30 | |
| 116 Twins Rookies: ........2.50 | |
| Jay Ward, Tony Oliva | |
| 117 Earl Francis ............30 | |
| 118 John Blanchard .........30 | |
| 119 Gary Kolb ..............30 | |
| 120 Don Drysdale ..........3.75 | |
| 121 Pete Runnels............30 | |
| 122 Don McMahon ..........30 | |
| 123 Jose Pagan .............30 | |
| 124 Orlando Pena ...........30 | |
| 125 Pete Rose ...........110.00 | |
| 126 Russ Snyder ............30 | |
| 127 Angels Rookies:..........30 | |
| Dick Simpson, | |
| Aubrey Gatewood | |
| 128 Mickey Lolich (R) ......2.50 | |
| 129 Amado Samuel ..........30 | |
| 130 Gary Peters ............30 | |
| 131 Steve Boros ............30 | |
| 132 Milwaukee Braves ........75 | |
| 133 Jim Grant ..............30 | |
| 134 Don Zimmer ............50 | |
| 135 Johnny Callison .........30 | |
| 136 World Series Game 1 ....2.75 | |
| Koufax Strikes Out 15 | |
| 137 World Series Game 2 ....1.50 | |
| Davis Sparks Rally | |
| 138 World Series Game 3 ....1.50 | |
| LA Takes 3 Straight | |
| 139 World Series Game 4 ....1.50 | |
| Sealing Yanks' Doom | |
| 140 World Series ...........1.50 | |
| Dodgers Celebrate | |
| 141 Danny Murtaugh (Mgr.) ...30 | |
| 142 John Bateman ...........30 | |
| 143 Bubba Phillips ..........30 | |
| 144 Al Worthington .........30 | |
| 145 Norm Siebern ...........30 | |
| 146 Indians Rookies: .......8.00 | |
| Tommy John, Bob Chance | |
| 147 Ray Sadecki ............30 | |
| 148 J.C. Martin .............30 | |
| 149 Paul Foytack ...........30 | |
| 150 Willie Mays ..........22.00 | |
| 151 K.C. Athletics ...........75 | |
| 152 Denver LeMaster ........30 | |
| 153 Dick Williams ...........30 | |
| 154 Dick Tracewski..........30 | |
| 155 Duke Snider ...........7.50 | |
| 156 Bill Dailey ..............30 | |

| NO. PLAYER | MINT |
|---|---|
| 157 Gene Mauch .............30 | |
| 158 Ken Johnson............30 | |
| 159 Charlie Dees ............30 | |
| 160 Ken Boyer .............2.00 | |
| 161 Dave McNally ...........30 | |
| 162 Hitting Area: ...........30 | |
| Dick Sisler, Vada Pinson | |
| 163 Donn Clendenon .........30 | |
| 164 Bud Daley ..............30 | |
| 165 Jerry Lumpe ............30 | |
| 166 Marty Keough ..........30 | |
| 167 Senators Rookies: .......6.00 | |
| Mike Brumley, Lou Piniella | |
| 168 Al Weis ................30 | |
| 169 Del Crandall ............30 | |
| 170 Dick Radatz.............30 | |
| 171 Ty Cline ...............30 | |
| 172 Cleveland Indians ........70 | |
| 173 Ryne Duren .............30 | |
| 174 Doc Edwards ............30 | |
| 175 Billy Williams ..........2.00 | |
| 176 Tracy Stallard ...........30 | |
| 177 Harmon Killebrew .......4.50 | |
| 178 Hank Bauer (Mgr.) .......30 | |
| 179 Carl Warwick ...........30 | |
| 180 Tommy Davis ............50 | |
| 181 Dave Wickersham ........30 | |
| 182 Sox Sockers: ..........2.25 | |
| C. Schilling, C. Yastrzemski | |
| 183 Ron Taylor..............30 | |
| 184 Al Luplow ..............30 | |
| 185 Jim O'Toole ............30 | |
| 186 Roman Mejias ...........30 | |
| 187 Ed Roebuck .............30 | |
| 188 Checklist No. 3 .........1.50 | |
| 189 Bob Hendley ............30 | |
| 190 Bobby Richardson .....1.00 | |
| 191 Clay Dalrymple ..........30 | |
| 192 Cubs Rookies:...........30 | |
| J. Boccabella, B. Cowan | |
| 193 Jerry Lynch .............30 | |
| 194 John Goryl ..............30 | |
| 195 Floyd Robinson ..........30 | |
| 196 Jim Gentile .............30 | |
| 197 Frank Lary ..............30 | |
| 198 Len Gabrielson ..........30 | |
| 199 Joe Azcue ..............30 | |
| 200 Sandy Koufax .........15.00 | |
| 201 Orioles Rookies:.........30 | |
| Wally Bunker, Sam Bowens | |
| 202 Galen Cisco ............30 | |
| 203 John Kennedy ...........30 | |
| 204 Matty Alou .............30 | |
| 205 Nellie Fox..............1.00 | |
| 206 Steve Hamilton ..........30 | |
| 207 Fred Hutchinson (Mgr.) ...30 | |
| 208 Wes Covington ..........30 | |
| 209 Bob Allen ..............30 | |
| 210 Carl Yastrzemski......35.00 | |
| 211 Jim Coker ..............30 | |
| 212 Pete Lovrich ............30 | |
| 213 L.A. Angels .............75 | |
| 214 Ken McMullen ..........30 | |
| 215 Ray Herbert ............30 | |
| 216 Mike De La Hoz .........30 | |
| 217 Jim King................30 | |

# 1964 Topps (Continued)

| NO. | PLAYER | MINT |
|---|---|---|
| 218 | Hank Fischer | .30 |
| 219 | Young Aces: Al Downing, Jim Bouton | .30 |
| 220 | Dick Ellsworth | .30 |
| 221 | Bob Saverine | .30 |
| 222 | Bill Pierce | .50 |
| 223 | George Banks | .30 |
| 224 | Tommie Sisk | .30 |
| 225 | Roger Maris | 7.00 |
| 226 | Colts Rookies: Gerald Grote, Larry Yellen | .30 |
| 227 | Barry Latman | .30 |
| 228 | Felix Mantilla | .30 |
| 229 | Charley Lau | .30 |
| 230 | Brooks Robinson | 9.00 |
| 231 | Dick Calmus | .30 |
| 232 | Al Lopez (Mgr.) | 1.00 |
| 233 | Hal Smith | .30 |
| 234 | Gary Bell | .30 |
| 235 | Ron Hunt | .30 |
| 236 | Bill Faul | .30 |
| 237 | Chicago Cubs | 1.00 |
| 238 | Roy McMillan | .30 |
| 239 | Herm Starrette | .30 |
| 240 | Bill White | .30 |
| 241 | Jim Owens | .30 |
| 242 | Harvey Kuenn | .60 |
| 243 | Phillies Rookies (R): Richie Allen, J. Herrnstein | 4.00 |
| 244 | Tony LaRussa (R) | 1.00 |
| 245 | Dick Stigman | .30 |
| 246 | Manny Mota | .75 |
| 247 | Dave DeBusschere | 1.00 |
| 248 | Johnny Pesky | .30 |
| 249 | Doug Camili | .30 |
| 250 | Al Kaline | 5.00 |
| 251 | Choo Choo Coleman | .30 |
| 252 | Ken Aspromonte | .30 |
| 253 | Wally Post | .30 |
| 254 | Don Hoak | .30 |
| 255 | Lee Thomas | .30 |
| 256 | Johnny Weekly | .30 |
| 257 | San F. Giants | .75 |
| 258 | Garry Roggenburk | .30 |
| 259 | Harry Bright | .30 |
| 260 | Frank Robinson | 5.00 |
| 261 | Jim Hannan | .30 |
| 262 | Cardinals Rookies: Harry Fanok, Mike Shannon | .75 |
| 263 | Chuck Estrada | .30 |
| 264 | Jim Lndis | .30 |
| 265 | Jim Bunning | 1.00 |
| 266 | Gene Freese | .30 |
| 267 | Wilbur Wood | .50 |
| 268 | Bill's Got It: Bill Virdon, D. Murtaugh | .30 |
| 269 | Ellis Burton | .30 |
| 270 | Rich Rollins | .30 |
| 271 | Bob Sadowski | .30 |
| 272 | Jake Wood | .30 |
| 273 | Mel Nelson | .30 |
| 274 | Checklist No. 4 | 1.50 |
| 275 | John Tsitouris | .30 |
| 276 | Jose Tartabull | .30 |
| 277 | Ken Retzer | .30 |
| 278 | Bobby Shantz | .30 |
| 279 | Joe Koppe | .30 |
| 280 | Juan Marichal | 4.00 |
| 281 | Yankees Rookies: Jake Gibbs, Tom Metcalf | .50 |
| 282 | Bob Bruce | .30 |
| 283 | Tommy McCraw | .30 |
| 284 | Dick Schofield | .30 |
| 285 | Robin Roberts | 3.00 |
| 286 | Don Landrum | .30 |
| 287 | Red Sox Rookies: T. Conigliaro, B. Spanswick | 2.00 |
| 288 | Al Moran | .30 |
| 289 | Frank Funk | .30 |
| 290 | Bob Allison | .30 |
| 291 | Phil Ortega | .30 |
| 292 | Mike Roarke | .30 |
| 293 | Philadelphia Phillies | .75 |
| 294 | Ken Hunt | .30 |
| 295 | Roger Craig | .30 |
| 296 | Ed Kirkpatrick | .30 |
| 297 | Ken MacKenzie | .30 |
| 298 | Harry Craft (Mgr.) | .30 |
| 299 | Bill Stafford | .30 |
| 300 | Hank Aaron | 25.00 |
| 301 | Larry Brown | .30 |
| 302 | Dan Pfister | .30 |
| 303 | Jim Campbell | .30 |
| 304 | Bob Johnson | .30 |
| 305 | Jack Lamabe | .30 |
| 306 | Giant Gunners: Willie Mays, O. Cepeda | 4.00 |
| 307 | Joe Gibbon | .30 |
| 308 | Gene Stephens | .30 |
| 309 | Paul Toth | .30 |
| 310 | Jim Gilliam | 1.00 |
| 311 | Tom Brown | .30 |
| 312 | Tigers Rookies: Fred Gladding, Fritz Fisher | .30 |
| 313 | Chuck Hiller | .30 |
| 314 | Jerry Buchek | .30 |
| 315 | Bo Belinsky | .30 |
| 316 | Gene Oliver | .30 |
| 317 | Al Smith | .30 |
| 318 | Minnesota Twins | .75 |
| 319 | Paul Brown | .30 |
| 320 | Rocky Colavito | 1.00 |
| 321 | Bob Lillis | .30 |
| 322 | George Brunet | .30 |
| 323 | John Buzhardt | .30 |
| 324 | Casey Stengel (Mgr.) | 4.00 |
| 325 | Hector Lopez | .30 |
| 326 | Ron Brand | .30 |
| 327 | Don Blasingame | .30 |
| 328 | Bob Shaw | .30 |
| 329 | Russ Nixon | .30 |
| 330 | Tommy Harper | .30 |
| 331 | AL Bombers: Mickey Mantle, R. Maris, Norm Cash, Al Kaline | 16.00 |
| 332 | Ray Washburn | .30 |
| 333 | Billy Moran | .30 |
| 334 | Lew Krausse | .30 |
| 335 | Don Mossi | .30 |
| 336 | Andre Rodgers | .30 |
| 337 | Dodgers Rookies: Al Ferrara, Jeff Torborg | .60 |
| 338 | Jack Kralick | .30 |
| 339 | Walt Bond | .30 |
| 340 | Joe Cunningham | .30 |
| 341 | Jim Roland | .30 |
| 342 | Willie Stargell | 8.00 |
| 343 | Washington Senators | .60 |
| 344 | Phil Linz | .30 |
| 345 | Frank Thomas | .30 |
| 346 | Joe Jay | .30 |
| 347 | Bobby Wine | .30 |
| 348 | Ed Lopat | .50 |
| 349 | Art Fowler | .30 |
| 350 | Willie McCovey | 7.00 |
| 351 | Dan Schneider | .30 |
| 352 | Eddie Bressoud | .30 |
| 353 | Wally Moon | .30 |
| 354 | Dave Giusti | .30 |
| 355 | Vic Power | .30 |
| 356 | Reds Rookies: Bill McCool, Chico Ruiz | .30 |
| 357 | Charley James | .30 |
| 358 | Ron Kline | .30 |
| 359 | Jim Schaffer | .30 |
| 360 | Joe Pepitone | .60 |
| 361 | Jay Hook | .30 |
| 362 | Checklist No. 5 | 1.50 |
| 363 | Dick McAuliffe | .30 |
| 364 | Joe Gaines | .30 |
| 365 | Cal McLish | .30 |
| 366 | Nelson Mathews | .30 |
| 367 | Fred Whitfield | .30 |
| 368 | White Sox Rookies: Fritz Ackley, Don Buford | .30 |
| 369 | Jerry Zimmerman | .30 |
| 370 | Hal Woodeschick | .30 |
| 371 | Frank Howard | 1.25 |
| 372 | Howie Koplitz | .40 |
| 373 | Pittsburgh Pirates | 1.00 |
| 374 | Bobby Bolin | .40 |
| 375 | Ron Santo | 1.00 |
| 376 | Dave Morehead | .40 |
| 377 | Bob Skinner | .40 |
| 378 | Braves Rookies: W. Woodward, Jack Smith | .40 |
| 379 | Tony Gonzalez | .40 |
| 380 | Whitey Ford | 7.50 |
| 381 | Bob Taylor | .40 |
| 382 | Wes Stock | .40 |
| 383 | Bill Rigney (Mgr.) | .40 |
| 384 | Ron Hansen | .40 |
| 385 | Curt Simmons | .50 |
| 386 | Lenny Green | .40 |
| 387 | Terry Fox | .40 |
| 388 | A's Rookies: G. Williams, J. O'Donoghue | .40 |
| 389 | Jim Umbricht | .40 |
| 390 | Orlando Cepeda | 2.00 |
| 391 | Sam McDowell | .60 |
| 392 | Jim Pagliaroni | .40 |
| 393 | Casey Teaches: C. Stengel, Ed Kranepool | 2.00 |
| 394 | Bob Miller | .40 |
| 395 | Tom Tresh | .90 |
| 396 | Dennis Bennett | .40 |
| 397 | Chuck Cottier | .55 |
| 398 | Mets Rookies: Bill Haas, Dick Smith | .40 |
| 399 | Jackie Brandt | .40 |
| 400 | Warren Spahn | 7.00 |
| 401 | Charlie Maxwell | .40 |
| 402 | Tom Sturdivant | .40 |
| 403 | Cincinnati Reds | 1.25 |
| 404 | Tony Martinez | .40 |
| 405 | Ken McBride | .40 |
| 406 | Al Spangler | .40 |
| 407 | Bill Freehan | 1.00 |
| 408 | Cubs Rookies: Jim Stewart, Fred Burdette | .40 |
| 409 | Bill Fischer | .40 |
| 410 | Dick Stuart | .60 |
| 411 | Lee Walls | .40 |
| 412 | Ray Culp | .40 |
| 413 | Johnny Keane (Mgr.) | .40 |
| 414 | Jack Sanford | .40 |
| 415 | Tony Kubek | 1.75 |
| 416 | Lee Maye | .40 |
| 417 | Don Cardwell | .40 |
| 418 | Orioles Rookies: Les Narum, D. Knowles | .75 |
| 419 | Ken Harrelson (R) | 2.00 |
| 420 | Jim Maloney | .60 |
| 421 | Camilo Carreon | .40 |
| 422 | Jack Fisher | .40 |
| 423 | Tops in N.L.: Hank Aaron, Willie Mays | 9.00 |
| 424 | Dick Bertell | .40 |
| 425 | Norm Cash | 1.00 |
| 426 | Bob Rodgers | .40 |
| 427 | Don Rudolph | .40 |
| 428 | Red Sox Rookies: Archie Skeen, Pete Smith | .40 |
| 429 | Tim McCarver | 1.00 |
| 430 | Juan Pizarro | .40 |
| 431 | George Alusik | .40 |
| 432 | Ruben Amaro | .40 |
| 433 | New York Yankees | 3.00 |
| 434 | Don Nottebart | .40 |
| 435 | Vic Davalillo | .40 |
| 436 | Charlie Neal | .40 |
| 437 | Ed Bailey | .40 |
| 438 | Checklist No. 6 | 1.50 |
| 439 | Harvey Haddix | .60 |
| 440 | Bob Clemente | 18.00 |
| 441 | Bob Duliba | .40 |
| 442 | Pumpsie Green | .40 |
| 443 | Chuck Dressen (Mgr.) | .40 |
| 444 | Larry Jackson | .40 |
| 445 | Bill Skowron | 1.00 |
| 446 | Julian Javier | .40 |
| 447 | Ted Bowsfield | .40 |
| 448 | Cookie Rojas | .40 |
| 449 | Deron Johnson | .40 |
| 450 | Steve Barber | .40 |
| 451 | Joe Amalfitano | .40 |
| 452 | Giants Rookies: Gil Garrido, Jim Hart | .90 |
| 453 | Frank Baumann | .40 |
| 454 | Tommie Aaron | .40 |
| 455 | Bernie Allen | .40 |
| 456 | Dodgers Rookies: John Werhas, Wes Parker | .90 |
| 457 | Jesse Gonder | .40 |
| 458 | Ralph Terry | .40 |
| 459 | Red Sox Rookies: Pete Charton, D. Jones | .40 |
| 460 | Bob Gibson | 7.50 |
| 461 | George Thomas | .40 |
| 462 | Birdie Tebbetts | .40 |
| 463 | Don Leppert | .40 |
| 464 | Dallas Green | .70 |
| 465 | Mike Hershberger | .40 |
| 466 | A's Rookies: D. Green, A. Monteagudo | .40 |
| 467 | Bob Aspromonte | .40 |
| 468 | Gaylord Perry | 7.50 |
| 469 | Cubs Rookies: S. Slaughter, Fred Norman | .60 |
| 470 | Jim Bouton | 1.00 |
| 471 | Gates Brown (R) | .80 |
| 472 | Vern Law | .60 |
| 473 | Baltimore Orioles | 1.00 |
| 474 | Larry Sherry | .40 |
| 475 | Ed Charles | .40 |
| 476 | Braves Rookies: Rico Carty, Dick Kelley | 2.00 |
| 477 | Mike Joyce | .40 |
| 478 | Dick Howser | .75 |
| 479 | Cardinals Rookies: D. Bakenhaster, J. Lewis | .40 |
| 480 | Bob Purkey | .40 |
| 481 | Chuck Schilling | .40 |
| 482 | Phillies Rookies: John Briggs, Danny Cater | .60 |
| 483 | Fred Valentine | .40 |
| 484 | Bill Pleis | .40 |
| 485 | Tom Haller | .40 |
| 486 | Bob Kennedy | .40 |
| 487 | Mike McCormick | .40 |
| 488 | Yankees Rookies: Pete Mikkelsen, Bob Meyer | .40 |
| 489 | Julio Navarro | .40 |
| 490 | Ron Fairly | .40 |
| 491 | Ed Rakow | .40 |
| 492 | Colts Rookies: Jim Beauchamp, M. White | .40 |
| 493 | Don Lee | .40 |
| 494 | Al Jackson | .40 |
| 495 | Bill Virdon | 1.00 |
| 496 | Chicago White Sox | .90 |
| 497 | Jeoff Long | .40 |
| 498 | Dave Stenhouse | .40 |
| 499 | Indians Rookies: Chico Salmon, G. Seyfried | .40 |
| 500 | Camilo Pascual | .60 |
| 501 | Bob Veale | .40 |
| 502 | Angels Rookies: Bobby Knoop, Bob Lee | .40 |
| 503 | Earl Wilson | .40 |
| 504 | Claude Raymond | .40 |
| 505 | Stan Williams | .40 |
| 506 | Bobby Bragan (Mgr.) | .40 |
| 507 | John Edwards | .40 |

# 1964 Topps (Continued)

| NO. PLAYER | MINT |
|---|---|
| 508 Diego Segui | .40 |
| 509 Pirates Rookies: | .80 |
| Gene Alley, O. McFarlane | |
| 510 Lindy McDaniel | .40 |
| 511 Lou Jackson | .40 |
| 512 Tigers Rookies: | 2.00 |
| Joe Sparma, Willie Horton | |
| 513 Don Larsen | .65 |
| 514 Jim Hickman | .40 |
| 515 Johnny Romano | .40 |
| 516 Twins Rookies: | .90 |
| Dwight Siebler, Jerry Arrigo | |
| 517 Checklist No. 7 | 1.75 |
| 518 Carl Bouldin | .40 |
| 519 Charlie Smith | .40 |
| 520 Jack Baldschun | .40 |
| 521 Tom Satriano | .40 |
| 522 Bobby Tiefenauer | .40 |
| 523 Lou Burdette | 1.75 |
| 524 Reds Rookies: | .90 |
| Jim Dickson, Bobby Klaus | |
| 525 Al McBean | .90 |
| 526 Lou Clinton | l90 |
| 527 Larry Bearnarth | .90 |
| 528 A's Rookies: | .90 |
| D. Duncan, Tom Reynolds | |

| NO. PLAYER | MINT |
|---|---|
| 529 Al Dark | .90 |
| 530 Leon Wagner | .90 |
| 531 L.A. Dodgers | 2.50 |
| 532 Twins Rookies: | .90 |
| Bud Bloomfield (wrong photo), Joe Nossek | |
| 533 John Klippstein | .90 |
| 534 Gus Bell | .90 |
| 535 Phil Regan | .90 |
| 536 Mets Rookies: | .90 |
| Larry Elliot, J. Stephenson | |
| 537 Dan Osinski | .90 |
| 538 Minnie Minoso | 2.00 |
| 539 Roy Face | 1.25 |
| 540 Luis Aparicio | 4.00 |
| 541 Braves Rookies: | 35.00 |
| Phil Niekro, Phil Roof | |
| 542 Don Mincher | 1.00 |
| 543 Bob Uecker | 9.00 |
| 544 Colts Rookies: | .90 |
| Steve Hertz, Joe Hoerner | |
| 545 Max Alvis | .90 |
| 546 Joe Christopher | .90 |
| 547 Gil Hodges (Mgr.) | 4.00 |
| 548 NL Rookies: | .90 |
| W. Schurr, P. Speckenbach | |

| NO. PLAYER | MINT |
|---|---|
| 549 Joe Moeller | .85 |
| 550 Ken Hubbs | 3.00 |
| (In Memoriam) | |
| 551 Billy Hoeft | .90 |
| 552 Indians Rookies: | .90 |
| Tom Kelley, Sonny Siebert | |
| 553 Jim Brewer | .90 |
| 554 Hank Foiles | .90 |
| 555 Lee Stange | .90 |
| 556 Mets Rookies: | .90 |
| Steve Dillon, Ron Locke | |
| 557 Leo Burke | .90 |
| 558 Don Schwall | .90 |
| 559 Dick Phillips | .90 |
| 560 Dick Farrell | .90 |
| 561 Phillies Rookies: | 1.50 |
| Dave Bennett, Rick Wise | |
| 562 Pedro Ramos | .90 |
| 563 Dal Maxvill | .90 |
| 564 AL Rookies: | .90 |
| Joe McCabe, J. McNertney | |
| 565 Stu Miller | .90 |
| 566 Ed Kranepool | 1.25 |
| 567 Jim Kaat | 3.00 |

| NO. PLAYER | MINT |
|---|---|
| 568 NL Rookies: | .90 |
| Phil Gagliano, Cap Peterson | |
| 569 Fred Newman | .90 |
| 570 Bill Mazeroski | 2.00 |
| 571 Gene Conley | .90 |
| 572 AL Rookies: | .90 |
| Dave Gray, Dick Egan | |
| 573 Jim Duffalo | .90 |
| 574 Manny Jimenez | .90 |
| 575 Tony Cloninger | .90 |
| 576 Mets Rookies: | .90 |
| J. Hinsley, Bill Wakefield | |
| 577 Gordy Coleman | .90 |
| 578 Glen Hobbie | .90 |
| 579 Boston Red Sox | 2.50 |
| 580 Johnny Podres | 2.00 |
| 581 Yankees Rookies: | 1.25 |
| P. Gonzalez, Archie Moore | |
| 582 Rod Kanehl | .90 |
| 583 Tito Francona | .90 |
| 584 Joel Horlen | .90 |
| 585 Tony Taylor | .90 |
| 586 Jim Piersall | 1.25 |
| 587 Bennie Daniels | 1.00 |

# 1965 Topps.... Complete Set of 598 Cards—Value $750.00

This set includes the rookie cards of Steve Carlton, Joe Morgan, Tony Perez and "Catfish" Hunter. Cards 523 to 598 are the high numbers. Semi-high numbers are 447 to 522.

| NO. PLAYER | MINT |
|---|---|
| 1 AL Batting Leaders: | 2.00 |
| Elston Howard, Tony Oliva, Brooks Robinson | |
| 2 NL Batting Leaders: | 2.00 |
| Hank Aaron, Bob Clemente, Rico Carty | |
| 3 AL Home Run Leaders: | 2.00 |
| Boog Powell, Harmon Killebrew, Mickey Mantle | |
| 4 NL Home Run Leaders: | 1.50 |
| Willie Mays, Billy Williams, Johnny Callison, Jim Hart, Orlando Cepeda | |
| 5 AL RBI Leaders: | 2.00 |
| Brooks Robinson, Dick Stuart, Harmon Killebrew, Mickey Mantle | |
| 6 NL RBI Leaders: | 1.25 |
| Ken Boyer, Willie Mays, Ron Santo | |
| 7 AL ERA Leaders: | 1.00 |
| Dean Chance, Joel Horlen | |
| 8 NL ERA Leaders: | 2.00 |
| S. Koufax, Don Drysdale | |
| 9 AL Pitching Leaders: | 1.00 |
| D. Chance, G. Peters, J. Pizarro, W. Bunker, D. Wickersham | |
| 10 NL Pitching Leaders: | 1.00 |
| L. Jackson, Juan Marichal, Ray Sadecki | |

| NO. PLAYER | MINT |
|---|---|
| 11 AL Strikeout Leaders: | 1.00 |
| A. Downing, D. Chance, C. Pascual | |
| 12 NL Strikeout Leaders: | 1.25 |
| Bob Gibson, B. Veale, Don Drysdale | |
| 13 Pedro Ramos | .25 |
| 14 Len Gabrielson | .25 |
| 15 Robin Roberts | 2.50 |
| 16 Houston Rookies: | 20.00 |
| Joe Morgan, Sonny Jackson | |
| 17 John Romano | .25 |
| 18 Bill McCool | .25 |
| 19 Gates Brown | '25 |
| 20 Jim Bunning | 1.00 |
| 21 Don Blasingame | .25 |
| 22 Charlie Smith | .25 |
| 23 Bob Tiefenauer | .25 |
| 24 Twins—6th Place | .90 |
| 25 Al McBean | .25 |
| 26 Bob Knoop | .25 |
| 27 Dick Bertell | .25 |
| 28 Barney Schultz | .25 |
| 29 Felix Mantilla | .25 |
| 30 Jim Bouton | .50 |
| 31 Mike White | .25 |
| 32 Herman Franks | .25 |
| 33 Jackie Brandt | .25 |
| 34 Cal Koonce | .25 |
| 35 Ed Charles | .25 |
| 36 Bobby Wine | .25 |

| NO. PLAYER | MINT |
|---|---|
| 37 Fred Gladding | .25 |
| 38 Jim King | .25 |
| 39 Gerry Arrigo | .25 |
| 40 Frank Howard | .75 |
| 41 White Sox Rookies: | .25 |
| Bruce Howard, Marv Staehle | |
| 42 Earl Wilson | .25 |
| 43 Mike Shannon | .50 |
| 44 Wade Blasingame | .25 |
| 45 Roy McMillan | .25 |
| 46 Bob Lee | .25 |
| 47 Tommy Harper | .25 |
| 48 Claude Raymond | .25 |
| 49 Orioles Rookies: | .50 |
| John Miller, Curt Blefary | |
| 50 Juan Marichal | 3.00 |
| 51 Billy Bryan | .25 |
| 52 Ed Roebuck | .25 |
| 53 Dick McAuliffe | .25 |
| 54 Joe Gibbon | .25 |
| 55 Tony Conigliaro | .75 |
| 56 Ron Kline | .25 |
| 57 Cardinals—1st Place | .75 |
| 58 Fred Talbot | .25 |
| 59 Nate Oiver | .25 |
| 60 Jim O'Toole | .25 |
| 61 Chris Cannizzaro | .25 |
| 62 Jim Kaat | 2.00 |
| 63 Ty Cline | .25 |
| 64 Lou Burdette | .75 |
| 65 Tony Kubek | 1.25 |

| NO. PLAYER | MINT |
|---|---|
| 66 Bill Rigney | .25 |
| 67 Harvey Haddix | .25 |
| 68 Del Crandall | .25 |
| 69 Bill Virdon | .60 |
| 70 Bill Skowron | .60 |
| 71 John O'Donoghue | .25 |
| 72 Tony Gonzalez | .25 |
| 73 Dennis Ribant | .25 |
| 74 Red Sox Rookies: | 1.00 |
| R. Petrocelli, J. Stephenson | |
| 75 Deron Johnson | .25 |
| 76 Sam McDowell | .25 |
| 77 Doug Camilli | .25 |
| 78 Dal Maxvill | .25 |
| 79 Checklist No. 1 | 1.50 |
| 80 Turk Farrell | .25 |
| 81 Don Buford | .25 |
| 82 Braves Rookies: | .25 |
| Santos Alomar, John Braun | |
| 83 George Thomas | .25 |
| 84 Ron Herbel | .25 |
| 85 Willie Smith | .25 |
| 86 Les Narum | .25 |
| 87 Nelson Mathews | .25 |
| 88 Jack Lamabe | .25 |
| 89 Mike Hershberger | .25 |
| 90 Rich Rollins | .25 |
| 91 Cubs—8th Place | .75 |
| 92 Dick Howser | .40 |
| 93 Jack Fisher | .25 |
| 94 Charlie Lau | .25 |

| NO. PLAYER | MINT |
|---|---|
| 95 Bill Mazeroski | 1.00 |
| 96 Sonny Siebert | .25 |
| 97 Pedro Gonzalez | .25 |
| 98 Bob Miller | .25 |
| 99 Gil Hodges | 2.50 |
| 100 Ken Boyer | 1.00 |
| 101 Fred Newman | .25 |
| 102 Steve Boros | .25 |
| 103 Harvey Kuenn | .60 |
| 104 Checklist No. 2 | 1.50 |
| 105 Chico Salmon | .25 |
| 106 Gene Oliver | .20 |
| 107 Phillies Rookies: | .60 |
| C. Shockley, Pat Corrales | |
| 108 Don Mincher | .25 |
| 109 Walt Bond | .25 |
| 110 Ron Santo | .70 |
| 111 Lee Thomas | .25 |
| 112 Derrell Griffith | .25 |
| 113 Steve Barber | .25 |
| 114 Jim Hickman | .25 |
| 115 Bob Richardson | 1.00 |
| 116 Cardinals Rookies: | .60 |
| Dave Dowling, Bob Tolan | |
| 117 Wes Stock | .25 |
| 118 Hal Lanier | .25 |
| 119 John Kennedy | .25 |
| 120 Frank Robinson | 4.50 |
| 121 Gene Alley | .25 |
| 122 Bill Pleis | .25 |
| 123 Frank Thomas | .25 |
| 124 Tom Satriano | .25 |
| 125 Juan Pizarro | .25 |
| 126 Dodgers—6th Place | 1.25 |
| 127 Frank Lary | .25 |
| 128 Vic Davalillo | .25 |
| 129 Bennie Daniels | .25 |
| 130 Al Kaline | 5.00 |
| 131 Johnny Keane (Mgr.) | .25 |
| 132 World Series Game 1 | 1.00 |
| Cards Take Opener | |
| 133 World Series Game 2 | 1.00 |
| Stottlemyre Wins | |
| 134 World Series Game 3 | 5.00 |
| Mantle's Clutch Homer | |
| 135 World Series Game 4 | 1.00 |
| Boyer's Grand-Slam | |
| 136 World Series Game 5 | 1.00 |
| 10th Inning Triumph | |
| 137 World Series Game 6 | 1.00 |
| Bouton Wins Again | |
| 138 World Series Game 7 | 2.00 |
| Gibson Wins Finale | |
| 139 World Series | 1.00 |
| The Cards Celebrate | |
| 140 Dean Chance | .25 |
| 141 Charlie James | .25 |
| 142 Bill Monbouquette | .25 |
| 143 Pirates Rookies: | .25 |
| John Gelnar, Jerry May | |
| 144 Ed Kranepool | .25 |
| 145 Luis Tiant (R) | 2.50 |
| 146 Ron Hansen | .25 |
| 147 Dennis Bennett | .25 |
| 148 Willie Kirkland | .25 |
| 149 Wayne Schurr | .25 |
| 150 Brooks Robinson | 6.00 |
| 151 Athletics—10th Place | .75 |
| 152 Phil Ortega | .25 |
| 153 Norm Cash | .75 |
| 154 Bob Humphreys | .25 |
| 155 Roger Maris | 6.00 |
| 156 Bob Sadowski | .25 |
| 157 Zoilo Versalles | .75 |
| 158 Dick Sisler (Mgr.) | .25 |
| 159 Jim Duffalo | .25 |
| 160 Bob Clemente | 11.00 |
| 161 Frank Baumann | .25 |
| 162 Russ Nixon | .25 |
| 163 John Briggs | .25 |
| 164 Al Spangler | .25 |
| 165 Dick Ellsworth | .25 |
| 166 Indians Rookies: | .50 |
| G. Culver, Tommie Agee | |
| 167 Bill Wakefield | .25 |

| NO. PLAYER | MINT |
|---|---|
| 168 Dick Green | .25 |
| 169 Dave Vineyard | .25 |
| 170 Hank Aaron | 20.00 |
| 171 Jim Roland | .25 |
| 172 Jim Piersall | .60 |
| 173 Tigers—4th Place | 1.00 |
| 174 Joe Jay | .25 |
| 175 Bob Aspromonte | .25 |
| 176 Willie McCovey | 5.00 |
| 177 Pete Mikkelsen | .25 |
| 178 Dalton Jones | .25 |
| 179 Hal Woodeschick | .25 |
| 180 Bob Allison | .25 |
| 181 Senators Rookies: | .25 |
| Don Loun, Joe McCabe | |
| 182 Mike De La Hoz | .25 |
| 183 Dave Nicholson | .25 |
| 184 John Boozer | .25 |
| 185 Max Alvis | .25 |
| 186 Bill Cowan | .25 |
| 187 Casey Stengel (Mgr.) | 3.50 |
| 188 Sam Bowens | .25 |
| 189 Checklist No. 3 | 1.25 |
| 190 Bill White | .25 |
| 191 Phil Regan | .25 |
| 192 Jim Coker | .25 |
| 193 Gaylord Perry | 4.00 |
| 194 Angels Rookies: | .25 |
| Rick Reichardt, Bill Kelso | |
| 195 Bob Veale | .25 |
| 196 Ron Fairly | .25 |
| 197 Diego Segui | .25 |
| 198 Smoky Burgess | .25 |
| 199 Bob Heffner | .25 |
| 200 Joe Torre | 1.00 |
| 201 Twins Rookies: | .50 |
| S. Valdespino, Cesar Tovar | |
| 202 Leo Burke | .25 |
| 203 Dallas Green | .25 |
| 204 Russ Snyder | .25 |
| 205 Warren Spahn | 5.00 |
| 206 Willie Horton | .50 |
| 207 Pete Rose | 105.00 |
| 208 Tommy John | 2.00 |
| 209 Pirates—6th Place | .75 |
| 210 Jim Fregosi | .25 |
| 211 Steve Ridzik | .25 |
| 212 Ron Brand | .25 |
| 213 Jim Davenport | .25 |
| 214 Bob Purkey | .25 |
| 215 Pete Ward | .25 |
| 216 Al Worthington | .25 |
| 217 Walt Alston (Mgr.) | 1.00 |
| 218 Dick Schofield | .25 |
| 219 Bob Meyer | .25 |
| 220 Billy Williams | 2.50 |
| 221 John Tsitouris | .25 |
| 222 Bob Tillman | .25 |
| 223 Dan Osinski | .25 |
| 224 Bob Chance | .25 |
| 225 Bo Belinsky | .25 |
| 226 Yankees Rookies: | .50 |
| Elvio Jimenez, Jake Gibbs | |
| 227 Bobby Klaus | .25 |
| 228 Jack Sanford | .25 |
| 229 Lou Clinton | .25 |
| 230 Ray Sadecki | .25 |
| 231 Jerry Adair | .25 |
| 232 Steve Blass (R) | .60 |
| 233 Don Zimmer | .50 |
| 234 White Sox—2nd Place | .55 |
| 235 Chuck Hinton | .25 |
| 236 Dennis McLain (R) | 3.00 |
| 237 Bernie Allen | .25 |
| 238 Joe Moeller | .25 |
| 239 Doc Edwards | .25 |
| 240 Bob Bruce | .25 |
| 241 Mack Jones | .25 |
| 242 George Brunet | .25 |
| 243 Reds Rookies: | .50 |
| T. Helms, Ted Davidson | |
| 244 Lindy McDaniel | .25 |
| 245 Joe Pepitone | .50 |
| 246 Tom Butters | .25 |
| 247 Wally Moon | .25 |

| NO. PLAYER | MINT |
|---|---|
| 248 Gus Triandos | .25 |
| 249 Dave McNally | .50 |
| 250 Willie Mays | 20.00 |
| 251 Billy Herman (Mgr.) | .75 |
| 252 Pete Richert | .25 |
| 253 Danny Cater | .25 |
| 254 Roland Sheldon | .25 |
| 255 Camilo Pascual | .25 |
| 256 Tito Francona | .25 |
| 257 Jim Wynn | .50 |
| 258 Larry Bearnarth | .25 |
| 259 Tigers Rookies: | .75 |
| Jim Northrup, Ray Oyler | |
| 260 Don Drysdale | 4.50 |
| 261 Duke Carmel | .25 |
| 262 Bud Daley | .25 |
| 263 Marty Keough | .25 |
| 264 Bob Buhl | .25 |
| 265 Jim Pagliaroni | .25 |
| 266 Bert Campaneris | 1.00 |
| 267 Senators—9th Place | .50 |
| 268 Ken McBride | .25 |
| 269 Frank Bolling | .25 |
| 270 Milt Pappas | .25 |
| 271 Don Wert | .25 |
| 272 Chuck Schilling | .25 |
| 273 Checklist No. 4 | 1.25 |
| 274 Lum Harris (Mgr.) | .25 |
| 275 Dick Groat | .50 |
| 276 Hoyt Wilhelm | 2.50 |
| 277 Johnny Lewis | .25 |
| 278 Ken Retzer | .25 |
| 279 Dick Tracewski | .25 |
| 280 Dick Stuart | .25 |
| 281 Bill Stafford | .25 |
| 282 Giants Rookies: | .60 |
| Dick Estelle, M. Murakami | |
| 283 Fred Whitfield | .25 |
| 284 Nick Willhite | .25 |
| 285 Ron Hunt | .25 |
| 286 Athletics Rookies: | .25 |
| J. Dickson, A. Monteagudo | |
| 287 Gary Kolb | .25 |
| 288 Jack Hamilton | .25 |
| 289 Gordy Coleman | .25 |
| 290 Wally Bunker | .25 |
| 291 Jerry Lynch | .25 |
| 292 Larry Yellen | .25 |
| 293 Angels—5th Place | .60 |
| 294 Tim McCarver | .75 |
| 295 Dick Radatz | .25 |
| 296 Tony Taylor | .25 |
| 297 Dave Debusschere | 1.25 |
| 298 Jim Stewart | .25 |
| 299 Jerry Zimmerman | .25 |
| 300 Sandy Koufax | 16.00 |
| 301 Birdie Tebbetts | .25 |
| 302 Al Stanek | .25 |
| 303 John Orsino | .25 |
| 304 Dave Stenhouse | .25 |
| 305 Rico Carty | .60 |
| 306 Bubba Phillips | .25 |
| 307 Barry Latman | .25 |
| 308 Mets Rookies: | .25 |
| Tom Parsons, Cleon Jones | |
| 309 Steve Hamilton | .25 |
| 310 Johnny Callison | .25 |
| 311 Orlando Pena | .25 |
| 312 Joe Nuxhall | .25 |
| 313 Jim Schaffer | .25 |
| 314 Sterling Slaughter | .25 |
| 315 Frank Malzone | .25 |
| 316 Reds—2nd Place | .90 |
| 317 Don McMahon | .25 |
| 318 Matty Alou | .25 |
| 319 Ken McMullen | .25 |
| 320 Bob Gibson | 4.50 |
| 321 Rusty Staub | 1.50 |
| 322 Rick Wise | .25 |
| 323 Hank Bauer (Mgr.) | .25 |
| 324 Bobby Locke | .25 |
| 325 Donn Clendenon | .25 |
| 326 Dwight Siebler | .25 |
| 327 Dennis Menke | .25 |
| 328 Eddie Fisher | .25 |

| NO. PLAYER | MINT |
|---|---|
| 329 Hawk Taylor | .25 |
| 330 Whitey Ford | 5.00 |
| 331 Dodgers Rookies: | .45 |
| Al Ferrara, John Purdin | |
| 332 Ted Abernathy | .25 |
| 333 Tommie Reynolds | .25 |
| 334 Vic Roznovsky | .25 |
| 335 Mickey Lolich | 1.00 |
| 336 Woody Held | .25 |
| 337 Mike Cuellar | .25 |
| 338 Phillies—2nd Place | .75 |
| 339 Ryne Duren | .25 |
| 340 Tony Oliva | 2.00 |
| 341 Bobby Bolin | .25 |
| 342 Bob Rodgers | .25 |
| 343 Mike McCormick | .25 |
| 344 Wes Parker | .25 |
| 345 Floyd Robinson | .25 |
| 346 Bob Bragan (Mgr.) | .25 |
| 347 Roy Face | .35 |
| 348 George Banks | .25 |
| 349 Larry Miller | .25 |
| 350 Mickey Mantle | 70.00 |
| 351 Jim Perry | .40 |
| 352 Alex Johnson | .25 |
| 353 Jerry Lumpe | .25 |
| 354 Cubs Rookies: | .25 |
| Billy Ott, Jack Warner | |
| 355 Vada Pinson | 1.00 |
| 356 Bill Spanswick | .25 |
| 357 Carl Warwick | .25 |
| 358 Albie Pearson | .25 |
| 359 Ken Johnson | .25 |
| 360 Orlando Cepeda | 1.75 |
| 361 Checklist No. 5 | 1.25 |
| 362 Don Schwall | .25 |
| 363 Bob Johnson | .25 |
| 364 Galen Cisco | .25 |
| 365 Jim Gentile | .25 |
| 366 Dan Schneider | .25 |
| 367 Leon Wagner | .25 |
| 368 White Sox Rookies: | .40 |
| Ken Berry, Joel Gibson | |
| 369 Phil Linz | .25 |
| 370 Tommy Davis | .50 |
| 371 Frank Kreutzer | .25 |
| 372 Clay Dalrymple | .25 |
| 373 Curt Simmons | .25 |
| 374 Angels Rookies: | .50 |
| J. Cardenal, D. Simpson | |
| 375 Dave Wickersham | .25 |
| 376 Jim Landis | .25 |
| 377 Willie Stargell | 5.00 |
| 378 Chuck Estrada | .25 |
| 379 Giants—4th Place | .60 |
| 380 Rocky Colavito | 1.00 |
| 381 Al Jackson | .25 |
| 382 J.C. Martin | .25 |
| 383 Felipe Alou | .25 |
| 384 Johnny Klippstein | .25 |
| 385 Carl Yastrzemski | 30.00 |
| 386 Cubs Rookies: | .50 |
| Paul Jaeckel, Fred Norman | |
| 387 Johnny Podres | 1.00 |
| 388 John Blanchard | .25 |
| 389 Don Larsen | .50 |
| 390 Bill Freehan | .60 |
| 391 Mel McGaha | .25 |
| 392 Bob Friend | .25 |
| 393 Ed Kirkpatrck | .25 |
| 394 Jim Hannan | .25 |
| 395 Jim Hart | .25 |
| 396 Frank Bertaina | .25 |
| 397 Jerry Buchek | .25 |
| 398 Reds Rookies: | .25 |
| Art Shamsky, Dan Neville | |
| 399 Ray Herbert | .25 |
| 400 Harmon Killebrew | 5.00 |
| 401 Carl Willey | .25 |
| 402 Joe Amalfitano | .25 |
| 403 Red Sox—8th Place | .75 |
| 404 Stan Williams | .25 |
| 405 John Roseboro | .25 |
| 406 Ralph Terry | .25 |
| 407 Lee Maye | .25 |

| NO. PLAYER | MINT |
|---|---|
| 408 Larry Sherry | .25 |
| 409 Astros Rookies: | .50 |
| Jim Beauchamp, L. Dierker | |
| 410 Luis Aparicio | 2.50 |
| 411 Roger Craig | .25 |
| 412 Bob Bailey | .25 |
| 413 Hal Reniff | .25 |
| 414 Al Lopez | 1.00 |
| 415 Curt Flood | .60 |
| 416 Jim Brewer | .25 |
| 417 Ed Brinkman | .25 |
| 418 Johnny Edwards | .25 |
| 419 Ruben Amaro | .25 |
| 420 Larry Jackson | .25 |
| 421 Twins Rookies: | .25 |
| Gary Dotter, Jay Ward | |
| 422 Aubrey Gatewood | .25 |
| 423 Jesse Gonder | .25 |
| 424 Gary Bell | .25 |
| 425 Wayne Causey | .25 |
| 426 Braves—5th Place | .60 |
| 427 Bob Saverine | .25 |
| 428 Bob Shaw | .25 |
| 429 Don Demeter | .25 |
| 430 Gary Peters | .25 |
| 431 Cards Rookies: | .50 |
| Nelson Briles, W. Spiezio | |
| 432 Jim Grant | .25 |
| 433 John Bateman | .25 |
| 434 Dave Morehead | .25 |
| 435 Willie Davis | .25 |
| 436 Don Elston | .25 |
| 437 Chico Cardenas | .25 |
| 438 Harry Walker (Mgr.) | .25 |
| 439 Moe Drabowsky | .25 |
| 440 Tom Tresh | .25 |
| 441 Denver LeMaster | .25 |
| 442 Vic Power | .25 |
| 443 Checklist No. 6 | 1.25 |
| 444 Bob Hendley | .25 |
| 445 Don Lock | .25 |
| 446 Art Mahaffey | .25 |
| 447 Julian Javier | .50 |
| 448 Lee Stange | .50 |
| 449 Mets Rookies: | .50 |
| Jerry Hinsley, Gary Kroll | |
| 450 Elston Howard | 1.50 |
| 451 Jim Owens | .50 |
| 452 Gary Geiger | .50 |
| 453 Dodgers Rookies: | .75 |
| W. Crawford, J. Werhas | |
| 454 Ed Rakow | .50 |
| 455 Norm Siebern | .50 |
| 456 Bill Henry | .50 |
| 457 Bob Kennedy—Coach | .50 |
| 458 John Buzhardt | .50 |
| 459 Frank Kostro | .50 |
| 460 Richie Allen | 2.00 |

| NO. PLAYER | MINT |
|---|---|
| 461 Braves Rookies: | 10.00 |
| Clay Carroll, Phil Niekro | |
| 462 Lew Krausse | .50 |
| (photo of Pete Lovrich) | |
| 463 Manny Mota | 1.00 |
| 464 Ron Piche | .50 |
| 465 Tom Haller | .50 |
| 466 Senators Rookies: | .50 |
| Pete Craig, Dick Nen | |
| 467 Ray Washburn | .50 |
| 468 Larry Brown | .50 |
| 469 Don Nottebart | .50 |
| 470 Yogi Berra | 12.00 |
| 471 Billy Hoeft | .50 |
| 472 Don Pavletich | .50 |
| 473 Orioles Rookies: | 3.00 |
| Paul Blair, Dave Johnson | |
| 474 Cookie Rojas | .50 |
| 475 Clete Boyer | .75 |
| 476 Billy O'Dell | .50 |
| 477 Cards Rookies: | 125.00 |
| Fritz Ackley, Steve Carlton | |
| 478 Wilbur Wood | .50 |
| 479 Ken Harrelson | 1.00 |
| 480 Joel Horlen | .50 |
| 481 Indians—7th Place | 1.00 |
| 482 Bob Priddy | .50 |
| 483 George Smith | .50 |
| 484 Ron Perranoski | .75 |
| 485 Nellie Fox | 1.50 |
| 486 Angels Rookies: | .75 |
| Pat Rogan Tom Egan | |
| 487 Woody Woodward | .50 |
| 488 Ted Wills | .50 |
| 489 Gene Mauch (Mgr.) | .75 |
| 490 Earl Battey | .50 |
| 491 Tracy Stallard | .50 |
| 492 Gene Freese | .50 |
| 493 Tigers Rookies: | .50 |
| Bill Roman, Bruce Brubaker | |
| 494 Jay Ritchie | .50 |
| 495 Joe Christopher | .50 |
| 496 Joe Cunningham | .50 |
| 497 Giants Rookies: | .75 |
| Ken Henderson, Jack Hiatt | |
| 498 Gene Stephens | .50 |
| 499 Stu Miller | .50 |
| 500 Ed Mathews | 6.00 |
| 501 Indians Rookies: | .50 |
| Jim Rittwage, R. Gagliano | |
| 502 Don Cardwell | .50 |
| 503 Phil Gagliano | .50 |
| 504 Jerry Grote | .50 |
| 505 Ray Culp | .50 |
| 506 Sam Mele | .50 |
| 507 Sammy Ellis | .50 |
| 508 Checklist No. 7 | 1.75 |
| 509 Red Sox Rookies: | .50 |
| Bob Guindon, G. Vezendy | |

| NO. PLAYER | MINT |
|---|---|
| 510 Ernie Banks | 15.00 |
| 511 Ron Locke | .50 |
| 512 Cap Peterson | .50 |
| 513 Yankees—1st Place | 2.50 |
| 514 Joe Azcue | .50 |
| 515 Vern Law | .50 |
| 516 Al Weis | .50 |
| 517 Angels Rookies: | .50 |
| Paul Schaal, Jack Warner | |
| 518 Ken Rowe | .50 |
| 519 Bob Uecker | 8.00 |
| 520 Tony Cloninger | .50 |
| 521 Phillies Rookies: | .50 |
| Dave Bennett, M. Steevens | |
| 522 Hank Aguirre | .50 |
| 523 Mike Brumley | .75 |
| 524 Dave Giusti | .75 |
| 525 Ed Bressoud | .75 |
| 526 Athletics Rookies: | 16.00 |
| S. Lockwood, R. Lachemann, | |
| Johnny Odom, Jim Hunter | |
| 527 Jeff Torborg | .75 |
| 528 George Altman | .75 |
| 529 Jerry Fosnow | .75 |
| 530 Jim Maloney | .75 |
| 531 Chuck Hiller | .75 |
| 532 Hector Lopez | .75 |
| 533 Mets Rookies: | 4.00 |
| Dan Napoleon, Ron | |
| Swoboda, Jim Bethke, | |
| Tug McGraw | |
| 534 John Herrnstein | .75 |
| 535 Jack Kralick | .75 |
| 536 Andre Rodgers | .75 |
| 537 Angels Rookies: | 1.00 |
| Marcelino Lopez, Rudy | |
| May, Phil Roof | |
| 538 Chuck Dressen (Mgr.) | .75 |
| 539 Herm Starrette | .75 |
| 540 Lou Brock | 12.00 |
| 541 White Sox Rookies: | .75 |
| Bob Locker, Greg Bollo | |
| 542 Lou Klimchock | .75 |
| 543 Ed Connolly | .75 |
| 544 Howie Reed | .75 |
| 545 Jesus Alou | .75 |
| 546 Indians Rookies: | .75 |
| Floyd Weaver, Bill Davis, | |
| Mike Hedlund, Ray Barker | |
| 547 Jake Wood | .75 |
| 548 Dick Stigman | .75 |
| 549 Cubs Rookies: | 1.25 |
| R. Pena, Glenn Beckert | |
| 550 Mel Stottlemyre (R) | 2.50 |
| 551 Mets—10th Place | 2.00 |
| 552 Julio Gotay | .75 |
| 553 Astros Rookies: | .75 |
| Gene Ratliff, Dan Coombs, | |
| Jack McClure | |

| NO. PLAYER | MINT |
|---|---|
| 554 Chico Ruiz | .75 |
| 555 Jack Baldschun | .75 |
| 556 Red Schoendienst | 1.25 |
| 557 Jose Santiago | .75 |
| 558 Tommie Sisk | .75 |
| 559 Ed Bailey | .75 |
| 560 Boog Powell | 1.50 |
| 561 Dodgers Rookies: | 1.50 |
| D. Daboll, Mike Kekich, | |
| H. Valle, Jim Lefebvre | |
| 562 Billy Moran | .75 |
| 563 Julio Navarro | .75 |
| 564 Mel Nelson | .75 |
| 565 Ernie Broglio | .75 |
| 566 Yankees Rookies: | .75 |
| Art Lopez, Gil Blanco, | |
| Ross Moschitto | |
| 567 Tommie Aaron | .75 |
| 568 Ron Taylor | .75 |
| 569 Gino Cimoli | .75 |
| 570 Claude Osteen | .75 |
| 571 Ossie Virgil | .75 |
| 572 Orioles—3rd Place | 1.50 |
| 573 Red Sox Rookies: | 1.50 |
| Jim Lonborg, Mike Ryan, | |
| G. Moses, Bill Schlesinger | |
| 574 Roy Sievers | .75 |
| 575 Jose Pagan | .75 |
| 576 Terry Fox | 75 |
| 577 AL Rookie Stars: | .75 |
| D. Knowles, R. Scheinblum, | |
| Don Buschhorn | |
| 578 Camilo Carreon | .75 |
| 579 Dick Smith | .75 |
| 580 Jimmie Hall | .75 |
| 581 NL Rookie Stars: | 20.00 |
| Tony Perez, Dave Ricketts, | |
| Kevin Collins | |
| 582 Bob Schmidt | .75 |
| 583 Wes Covington | .75 |
| 584 Harry Bright | .75 |
| 585 Hank Fischer | .75 |
| 586 Tommy McCraw | .75 |
| 587 Joe Sparma | .75 |
| 588 Lenny Green | .75 |
| 589 Giants Rookies: | .75 |
| Frank Linzy, B. Schroder | |
| 590 Johnnie Wyatt | .75 |
| 591 Bob Skinner | .75 |
| 592 Frank Bork | .75 |
| 593 Tigers Rookies: | .75 |
| Jackie Moore, John Sullivan | |
| 594 Joe Gaines | .75 |
| 595 Don Lee | .75 |
| 596 Don Landrum | .75 |
| 597 Twins Rookies: | .75 |
| Dick Reese, Joe Nossek, | |
| John Sevcik | |
| 598 Al Downing | 1.50 |

# 1966 Topps....Complete Set of 598 Cards—Value $850.00

Features the rookie cards of Jim Palmer, and Don Sutton. The high numbers are 523 to 598. Cards 62, 91, 103 and 104 exist without a *traded* or *sold* line—worth $7.50 each. Card 101 (checklist) exists identifying card 115 as either Bill Henry—worth $1.25 or Warren Spahn—worth $5.00.

FERGUSON JENKINS p    BILL SORRELL 1b-of

JIM PALMER    pitcher

WILLIE McCOVEY    1st base

GAYLORD PERRY    pitcher

BILL SINGER pitcher    DON SUTTON pitcher

| NO. | PLAYER | MINT |
|---|---|---|
| 1 | Willie Mays | 35.00 |
| 2 | Ted Abernathy | .20 |
| 3 | Sam Mele (Mgr.) | .20 |
| 4 | Ray Culp | .20 |
| 5 | Jim Fregosi | .20 |
| 6 | Chuck Schilling | .20 |
| 7 | Tracy Stallard | .20 |
| 8 | Floyd Robinson | .20 |
| 9 | Clete Boyer | .20 |
| 10 | Tony Cloninger | .20 |
| 11 | Senators Rookies: | .20 |
| | Brant Alyea, Pete Craig | |
| 12 | John Tsitouris | .20 |
| 13 | Lou Johnson | .20 |
| 14 | Norm Siebern | .20 |
| 15 | Vern Law | .25 |
| 16 | Larry Brown | .20 |
| 17 | John Stephenson | .20 |
| 18 | Roland Sheldon | .20 |
| 19 | Giants—2nd Place | .60 |
| 20 | Willie Horton | .40 |
| 21 | Don Nottebart | .20 |
| 22 | Joe Nossek | .20 |
| 23 | Jack Sanford | .20 |
| 24 | Don Kessinger (R) | .50 |
| 25 | Pete Ward | .20 |
| 26 | Ray Sadecki | .20 |
| 27 | Orioles Rookies: | .30 |
| | D. Knowles, A. Etchebarren | |
| 28 | Phil Niekro | 4.00 |
| 29 | Mike Brumley | .20 |
| 30 | Pete Rose | 40.00 |
| 31 | Jack Cullen | .20 |
| 32 | Adolfo Phillips | .20 |
| 33 | Jim Pagliaroni | .20 |
| 34 | Checklist No. 1 | 1.00 |
| 35 | Ron Swoboda | .20 |
| 36 | Jim Hunter | 3.50 |
| 37 | Billy Herman | .60 |
| 38 | Ron Nischwitz | .20 |
| 39 | Ken Henderson | .20 |
| 40 | Jim Grant | .20 |
| 41 | Don LeJohn | .20 |
| 42 | Aubrey Gatewood | .20 |
| 43 | Don Landrum | .20 |
| 44 | Indians Rookies: | .20 |
| | Bill Davis, Tom Kelley | |
| 45 | Jim Gentile | .25 |
| 46 | Howie Koplitz | .20 |
| 47 | J.C. Martin | .20 |
| 48 | Paul Blair | .20 |
| 49 | Woody Woodward | .20 |
| 50 | Mickey Mantle | 55.00 |
| 51 | Gordon Richardson | .20 |
| 52 | Power Plus: | .30 |
| | W. Covington, J. Callison | |
| 53 | Bob Duliba | .20 |
| 54 | Jose Pagan | .20 |
| 55 | Ken Harrelson | .45 |
| 56 | Sandy Valdespino | .20 |
| 57 | Jim Lefebvre | .20 |
| 58 | Dave Wickersham | .20 |
| 59 | Reds—4th Place | .75 |
| 60 | Curt Flood | .60 |
| 61 | Bob Bolin | .20 |
| 62 | Merritt Ranew* | .20 |
| 63 | Jim Stewart | .20 |
| 64 | Bob Bruce | .20 |
| 65 | Leon Wagner | .20 |
| 66 | Al Weis | .20 |
| 67 | Mets Rookies: | .20 |
| | Cleon Jones, Dick Selma | |
| 68 | Hal Reniff | .20 |
| 69 | Ken Hamlin | .20 |
| 70 | Carl Yastrzemski | 30.00 |
| 71 | Frank Carpin | .20 |
| 72 | Tony Perez | 3.00 |
| 73 | Jerry Zimmerman | .20 |
| 74 | Don Mossi | .20 |
| 75 | Tommy Davis | .50 |
| 76 | R. Schoendienst (Mgr.) | .50 |
| 77 | Johnny Orsino | .20 |
| 78 | Frank Linzy | .20 |
| 79 | Joe Pepitone | .50 |
| 80 | Richie Allen | 1.00 |
| 81 | Ray Oyler | .20 |
| 82 | Bob Hendley | .20 |
| 83 | Albie Pearson | .20 |
| 84 | Braves Rookies: | .20 |
| | J. Beauchamp, D. Kelley | |
| 85 | Eddie Fisher | .20 |
| 86 | John Bateman | .20 |
| 87 | Dan Napoleon | .20 |
| 88 | Fred Whitfield | .20 |
| 89 | Ted Davidson | .20 |
| 90 | Luis Aparicio | 2.50 |
| 91 | Bob Uecker* | 4.00 |
| 92 | Yankees—6th Place | 1.25 |
| 93 | Jim Lonborg | .40 |
| 94 | Matty Alou | .25 |
| 95 | Pete Richert | .20 |
| 96 | Felipe Alou | .25 |
| 97 | Jim Merritt | .20 |
| 98 | Don Demeter | .20 |
| 99 | Buc Belters: | 1.00 |
| | W. Stargell, D. Clendenon | |
| 100 | Sandy Koufax | 15.00 |
| 101 | Checklist No. 2* | 1.25 |
| 102 | Ed Kirkpatrick | .20 |
| 103 | Dick Groat* | .40 |
| 104 | Alex Johnson* | .30 |
| 105 | Milt Pappas | .20 |
| 106 | Rusty Staub | 1.00 |
| 107 | A's Rookies: | .20 |
| | L. Stahl, Ron Tompkins | |
| 108 | Bobby Klaus | .20 |
| 109 | Ralph Terry | .20 |
| 110 | Ernie Banks | 5.00 |
| 111 | Gary Peters | .30 |
| 112 | Manny Mota | .30 |
| 113 | Hank Aguirre | .30 |
| 114 | Jim Gosger | .30 |
| 115 | Bill Henry* | .30 |
| 116 | Walt Alston (Mgr.) | 1.00 |
| 117 | Jake Gibbs | .30 |
| 118 | Mike McCormick | .30 |
| 119 | Art Shamsky | .30 |
| 120 | Harmon Killebrew | 4.00 |
| 121 | Ray Herbert | .30 |
| 122 | Joe Gaines | .30 |
| 123 | Pirates Rookies: | .30 |
| | Frank Bork, Jerry May | |
| 124 | Tug McGraw | 1.00 |
| 125 | Lou Brock | 5.00 |
| 126 | Jim Palmer (R) | 35.00 |
| 127 | Ken Berry | .30 |
| 128 | Jim Landis | .30 |
| 129 | Jack Kralick | .30 |
| 130 | Joe Torre | .75 |
| 131 | Angels—7th Place | .75 |
| 132 | Orlando Cepeda | 1.25 |
| 133 | Don McMahon | .30 |
| 134 | Wes Parker | .30 |
| 135 | Dave Morehead | .30 |
| 136 | Woody Held | .30 |
| 137 | Pat Corrales | .30 |
| 138 | Roger Repoz | .30 |
| 139 | Cubs Rookies: | .30 |
| | Byron Browne, Don Young | |
| 140 | Jim Maloney | .30 |
| 141 | Tom McCraw | .30 |
| 142 | Don Dennis | .30 |
| 143 | Jose Tartabull | .30 |
| 144 | Don Schwall* | .30 |
| 145 | Bill Freehan | .30 |
| 146 | George Altman | .30 |
| 147 | Lum Harris (Mgr.) | .30 |
| 148 | Bob Johnson | .30 |
| 149 | Dick Nen | .30 |
| 150 | Rocky Colavito | .60 |
| 151 | Gary Wagner | .30 |
| 152 | Frank Malzone | .30 |
| 153 | Rico Carty | .60 |
| 154 | Chuck Hiller | .30 |
| 155 | Marcelino Lopez | .30 |
| 156 | Double Play Combo: | .30 |
| | Dick Schofield, Hal Lanier | |
| 157 | Rene Lachemann | .30 |
| 158 | Jim Brewer | .30 |
| 159 | Chico Ruiz | .30 |
| 160 | Whitey Ford | 4.00 |
| 161 | Jerry Lumpe | .30 |
| 162 | Lee Maye | .30 |
| 163 | Tito Francona | .30 |
| 164 | White Sox Rookies: | .30 |
| | Tommie Agee, M. Staehle | |
| 165 | Don Lock | .30 |
| 166 | Chris Krug | .30 |
| 167 | Boog Powell | 1.00 |
| 168 | Dan Osinski | .30 |
| 169 | Duke Sims | .30 |
| 170 | Cookie Rojas | .30 |
| 171 | Nick Willhite | .30 |
| 172 | Mets—10th Place | .75 |
| 173 | Al Spangler | .30 |
| 174 | Ron Taylor | .30 |
| 175 | Bert Campaneris | .50 |
| 176 | Jim Davenport | .30 |
| 177 | Hector Lopez | .30 |
| 178 | Bob Tillman | .30 |
| 179 | Cards Rookies: | .30 |
| | Dennis Aust, Bob Tolan | |
| 180 | Vada Pinson | .75 |
| 181 | Al Worthington | .0 |
| 182 | Jerry Lynch | .30 |
| 183 | Checklist No. 3 | 1.25 |
| 184 | Denis Menke | .30 |
| 185 | Bob Buhl | .30 |
| 186 | Ruben Amaro | .30 |
| 187 | Chuck Dressen (Mgr.) | .30 |
| 188 | Al Luplow | .30 |
| 189 | John Roseboro | .30 |
| 190 | Jimmie Hall | .30 |
| 191 | Darrell Sutherland | .30 |
| 192 | Vic Power | .30 |
| 193 | Dave McNally | .30 |
| 194 | Senators—8th Place | .50 |
| 195 | Joe Morgan | 5.00 |
| 196 | Don Pavletich | .30 |
| 197 | Sonny Siebert | .30 |
| 198 | Mickey Stanley | .50 |
| 199 | Chisox Clubbers: | .30 |
| | Bill Skowron, Johnny | |
| | Romano, Floyd Robinson | |
| 200 | Ed Mathews | 3.00 |
| 201 | Jim Dickson | .30 |
| 202 | Clay Dalrymple | .30 |
| 203 | Jose Santiago | .30 |
| 204 | Cubs—8th Place | .75 |
| 205 | Tom Tresh | .45 |
| 206 | Alvin Jackson | .30 |
| 207 | Frank Quilici | .30 |
| 208 | Bob Miller | .30 |
| 209 | Tigers Rookies: | 1.00 |
| | Fritz Fisher, John Hiller | |
| 210 | Bill Mazeroski | .75 |
| 211 | Frank Kreutzer | .30 |
| 212 | Ed Kranepool | .30 |
| 213 | Fred Newman | .30 |
| 214 | Tommy Harper | .30 |
| 215 | NL Batting Leaders: | 3.00 |
| | Willie Mays, Bob | |
| | Clemente, Hank Aaron | |
| 216 | AL Batting Leaders: | 1.50 |
| | Tony Oliva, Carl | |
| | Yastrzemski, Vic Davalillo | |
| 217 | NL Home Run Leaders: | 1.50 |
| | Willie McCovey, Willie | |
| | Mays, Billy Williams | |
| 218 | AL Home Run Leaders: | 1.00 |
| | Norm Cash, Willie | |
| | Horton, Tony Conigliaro | |
| 219 | NL RBI Leaders: | 1.25 |
| | Frank Robinson, Deron | |
| | Johnson, Willie Mays | |
| 220 | AL RBI Leaders: | 1.00 |
| | Rocky Colavito, Willie | |
| | Horton, Tony Oliva | |
| 221 | NL ERA Leaders: | 1.50 |
| | Sandy Koufax, Vern | |
| | Law, Juan Marichal | |
| 222 | AL ERA Leaders: | 1.00 |
| | Sam McDowell, Sonny | |
| | Siebert, Eddie Fisher | |
| 223 | NL Pitching Leaders: | 1.50 |
| | Sandy Koufax, Tony | |
| | Cloninger, Don Drysdale | |
| 224 | AL Pitching Leaders: | 1.00 |
| | Mel Stottlemyre, | |
| | Jim Grant, Jim Kaat | |
| 225 | NL Strikeout Leaders: | 1.50 |
| | Bob Gibson, Sandy Koufax, | |
| | Bob Veale | |
| 226 | AL Strikeout Leaders: | 1.00 |
| | Sam McDowell, Mickey | |
| | Lolich, Denny McLain, | |
| | Sonny Siebert | |
| 227 | Russ Nixon | .30 |
| 228 | Larry Dierker | .30 |
| 229 | Hank Bauer | .30 |
| 230 | Johnny Callison | .30 |
| 231 | F. Weaver | .30 |
| 232 | Glenn Beckert | .30 |
| 233 | Dom Zanni | .30 |
| 234 | Yankees Rookies: | 1.50 |
| | Roy White, Rich Beck | |
| 235 | Don Cardwell | .30 |
| 236 | Mike Hershberger | .30 |
| 237 | Billy O'Dell | .30 |
| 238 | Dodgers—1st Place | 1.00 |
| 239 | Orlando Pena | .30 |
| 240 | Earl Battey | .30 |
| 241 | Dennis Ribant | .30 |
| 242 | Jesus Alou | .30 |
| 243 | Nelson Briles | .30 |
| 244 | Astros Rookies: | .30 |
| | C. Harrison, S. Jackson | |
| 245 | John Buzhardt | .30 |
| 246 | Ed Bailey | .30 |
| 247 | Carl Warwick | .30 |
| 248 | Pete Mikkelsen | .30 |
| 249 | Bill Rigney (Mgr.) | .30 |
| 250 | Sam Ellis | .30 |
| 251 | Ed Brinkman | .30 |
| 252 | Denver Lemaster | .30 |
| 253 | Don Wert | .30 |
| 254 | Phillies Rookies: | 10.00 |
| | Ferguson Jenkins, | |
| | Bill Sorrell | |
| 255 | Willie Stargell | 4.50 |
| 256 | Lew Krausse | .30 |
| 257 | Jeff Torborg | .30 |
| 258 | Dave Giusti | .30 |
| 259 | Red Sox—9th Place | .65 |
| 260 | Bob Shaw | .30 |
| 261 | Ron Hansen | .30 |
| 262 | Jack Hamilton | .30 |
| 263 | Tom Egan | .30 |
| 264 | Twins Rookies: | .30 |
| | Ted Uhlaender, Andy Kosco | |
| 265 | Stu Miller | .30 |
| 266 | Pedro Gonzalez | .30 |
| 267 | Joe Sparma | .30 |
| 268 | John Blanchard | .30 |
| 269 | Don Heffner (Mgr.) | .30 |
| 270 | Claude Osteen | .30 |
| 271 | Hal Lanier | .30 |
| 272 | Jack Baldschun | .30 |
| 273 | Astro Aces: | .60 |
| | Bob Aspromonte, | |
| | Rusty Staub | |
| 274 | Buster Narum | .30 |
| 275 | Tim McCarver | .75 |
| 276 | Jim Bouton | .40 |
| 277 | George Thomas | .30 |
| 278 | Calvin Koonce | .30 |
| 279 | Checklist No. 4 | 1.25 |
| 280 | Bobby Knoop | .30 |
| 281 | Bruce Howard | .30 |
| 282 | Johnny Lewis | .30 |
| 283 | Jim Perry | .30 |
| 284 | Bobby Wine | .30 |
| 285 | Luis Tiant | 1.00 |
| 286 | Gary Geiger | .30 |
| 287 | Jack Aker | .30 |
| 288 | Dodgers Rookies: | 22.00 |
| | Bill Singer, Don Sutton | |
| 289 | Larry Sherry | .30 |
| 290 | Ron Santo | .50 |
| 291 | Moe Drabowsky | .30 |
| 292 | Jim Coker | .30 |

| NO. | PLAYER | MINT | NO. | PLAYER | MINT | NO. | PLAYER | MINT | NO. | PLAYER | MINT |
|---|---|---|---|---|---|---|---|---|---|---|---|
| 293 | Mike Shannon | .30 | 374 | Bob Locker | .30 | 455 | Mickey Lolich | 1.00 | 531 | Joe Cunningham | 3.50 |
| 294 | Steve Ridzik | .30 | 375 | Donn Clendenon | .30 | 456 | Red Sox Rookies: | .60 | 532 | Aurelio Monteagudo | 3.50 |
| 295 | Jim Hart | .30 | 376 | Paul Schaal | .30 | | Darrell Brandon, Joe Foy | | 533 | Jerry Adair | 3.50 |
| 296 | Johnny Keane (Mgr.) | .30 | 377 | Turk Farrell | .30 | 457 | Joe Gibbon | .60 | 534 | Mets Rookies: | 3.50 |
| 297 | Jim Owens | .30 | 378 | Dick Tracewski | .30 | 458 | Manny Jimenez | .60 | | Dave Eilers, Rob Gardner | |
| 298 | Rico Petrocelli | .30 | 379 | Cardinal—7th Place | .75 | 459 | Bill McCool | .60 | 535 | Willie Davis | 4.50 |
| 299 | Lou Burdette | .50 | 380 | Tony Conigliaro | .60 | 460 | Curt Blefary | .60 | 536 | Dick Egan | 3.50 |
| 300 | Bob Clemente | 22.00 | 381 | Hank Fischer | .30 | 461 | Roy Face | .90 | 537 | Herman Franks (Mgr.) | 3.50 |
| 301 | Greg Bollo | .30 | 382 | Phil Roof | .30 | 462 | Bob Rodgers | .60 | 538 | Bob Allen | 3.50 |
| 302 | Ernie Bowman | .30 | 383 | Jack Brandt | .30 | 463 | Phillies—6th Place | 1.25 | 539 | Astros Rookies: | 3.50 |
| 303 | Indians—5th Place | .60 | 384 | Al Downing | .30 | 464 | Larry Bearnarth | .60 | | Bill Heath, Carroll Sembera | |
| 304 | John Herrnstein | .30 | 385 | Ken Boyer | 1.00 | 465 | Don Buford | .60 | 540 | Denny McLain | 11.00 |
| 305 | Camilo Pascual | .30 | 386 | Gil Hodges (Mgr.) | 2.50 | 466 | Ken Johnson | .60 | 541 | Gene Oliver | 3.50 |
| 306 | Ty Cline | .30 | 387 | Howie Reed | .30 | 467 | Vic Roznovsky | .60 | 542 | George Smith | 3.50 |
| 307 | Clay Carroll | .30 | 388 | Don Mincher | .30 | 468 | Johnny Podres | 1.00 | 543 | Roger Craig | 3.50 |
| 308 | Tom Haller | .30 | 389 | Jim O'Toole | .30 | 469 | Yankees Rookies: | 4.00 | 544 | Cardinals Rookies: | 3.50 |
| 309 | Diego Segui | .30 | 390 | Brooks Robinson | 5.00 | | Bobby Murcer, | | | J. Williams, J. Hoerner, | |
| 310 | Frank Robinson | 10.00 | 391 | Chuck Hinton | .30 | | Dooley Womack | | | George Kernek | |
| 311 | Reds Rookies: | .30 | 392 | Cubs Rookies: | .30 | 470 | Sam McDowell | .60 | 545 | Dick Green | 3.50 |
| | D. Simpson, T. Helms | | | Bill Hands, Randy Hundley | | 471 | Bob Skinner | .60 | 546 | Dwight Siebler | 3.50 |
| 312 | Bob Saverine | .30 | 393 | George Brunet | .30 | 472 | Terry Fox | .60 | 547 | Horace Clarke (R) | 4.50 |
| 313 | Chris Zachary | .30 | 394 | Ron Brand | .30 | 473 | Rich Rollins | .60 | 548 | Gary Kroll | 3.50 |
| 314 | Hector Valle | .30 | 395 | Len Gabrielson | .30 | 474 | Dick Schofield | .60 | 549 | Senators Rookies: | 3.50 |
| 315 | Norm Cash | .75 | 396 | Jerry Stephenson | .30 | 475 | Dick Radatz | .60 | | Al Closter, Casey Cox | |
| 316 | Jack Fisher | .30 | 397 | Bill White | .30 | 476 | Bobby Bragan | .60 | 550 | Willie McCovey | 50.00 |
| 317 | Dalton Jones | .30 | 398 | Danny Cater | .30 | 477 | Steve Barber | .60 | 551 | Bob Purkey | 3.50 |
| 318 | Harry Walker | .30 | 399 | Ray Washburn | .30 | 478 | Tony Gonzalez | .60 | 552 | Birdie Tebbetts | 3.50 |
| 319 | Gene Freese | .30 | 400 | Zoilo Versalles | .30 | 479 | Jim Hannan | .60 | 553 | Rookie Stars: | 3.50 |
| 320 | Bob Gibson | 4.50 | 401 | Ken McMullen | .30 | 480 | Dick Stuart | .60 | | Pat Garrett, Jackie Warner | |
| 321 | Rick Reichardt | .30 | 402 | Jim Hickman | .30 | 481 | Bob Lee | .60 | 554 | Jim Northrup | 3.50 |
| 322 | Bill Faul | .30 | 403 | Fred Talbot | .30 | 482 | Cubs Rookies: | .60 | 555 | Ron Perranoski | 4.00 |
| 323 | Ray Barker | .30 | 404 | Pirates—3rd Place | .60 | | J. Boccabella, D. Dowling | | 556 | Mel Queen | 3.50 |
| 324 | John Boozer | .30 | 405 | Elston Howard | 1.25 | 483 | Joe Nuxhall | .60 | 557 | Felix Mantilla | 3.50 |
| 325 | Vic Davalillo | .30 | 406 | Joe Jay | .30 | 484 | Wes Covington | .60 | 558 | Red Sox Rookies: | 6.00 |
| 326 | Braves—5th Place | .60 | 407 | John Kennedy | .30 | 485 | Bob Bailey | .60 | | Pete Magrini, Guido Grilli, | |
| 327 | Bernie Allen | .30 | 408 | Lee Thomas | .30 | 486 | Tommy John | 2.50 | | George Scott | |
| 328 | Jerry Grote | .30 | 409 | Billy Hoeft | .30 | 487 | Al Ferrara | .60 | 559 | Roberto Pena | 3.50 |
| 329 | Pete Charton | .30 | 410 | Al Kaline | 5.00 | 488 | George Banks | .60 | 560 | Joel Horlen | 3.50 |
| 330 | Ron Fairly | .30 | 411 | Gene Mauch (Mgr.) | .40 | 489 | Curt Simmons | .60 | 561 | Choo Choo Coleman | 3.50 |
| 331 | Ron Herbel | .30 | 412 | Sam Bowens | .30 | 490 | Bobby Richardson | 2.00 | 562 | Russ Snyder | 3.50 |
| 332 | Billy Bryan | .30 | 413 | John Romano | .30 | 491 | Dennis Bennett | .60 | 563 | Twins Rookies: | 4.50 |
| 333 | Senators Rookies: | .30 | 414 | Dan Coombs | .30 | 492 | Athletics—10th Place | 1.00 | | Pete Cimino, Cesar Tovar | |
| | Joe Coleman, Jim French | | 415 | Max Alvis | .30 | 493 | John Klippstein | .60 | 564 | Bob Chance | 3.50 |
| 334 | Marty Keough | .30 | 416 | Phil Ortega | .30 | 494 | Gordon Coleman | .60 | 565 | Jimmy Piersall | 6.00 |
| 335 | Juan Pizarro | .30 | 417 | Angels Rookies: | .30 | 495 | Dick McAuliffe | .60 | 566 | Mike Cuellar | 3.50 |
| 336 | Gene Alley | .30 | | Jim McGlothlin, Ed Sukla | | 496 | Lindy McDaniel | .60 | 567 | Dick Howser | 3.50 |
| 337 | Fred Gladding | .30 | 418 | Phil Gagliano | .30 | 497 | Chris Cannizzaro | .60 | 568 | Athletics Rookies: | 3.50 |
| 338 | Dal Maxvill | .30 | 419 | Mike Ryan | .30 | 498 | Pirates Rookies: | .60 | | Paul Lindblad, Ron Stone | |
| 339 | Del Crandall | .30 | 420 | Juan Marichal | 4.00 | | Luke Walker, W. Fryman | | 569 | Orlando McFarlane | 3.50 |
| 340 | Dean Chance | .35 | 421 | Roy McMillan | .30 | 499 | Wally Bunker | .60 | 570 | Art Mahaffey | 3.50 |
| 341 | Wes Westrum | .30 | 422 | Ed Charles | .30 | 500 | Hank Aaron | 24.00 | 571 | Dave Roberts | 3.50 |
| 342 | Bob Humphreys | .30 | 423 | Ernie Broglio | .30 | 501 | John O'Donoghue | .60 | 572 | Bob Priddy | 3.50 |
| 343 | Joe Christopher | .30 | 424 | Reds Rookies: | 1.00 | 502 | Lenny Green | .60 | 573 | Derrell Griffith | 3.50 |
| 344 | Steve Blass | .30 | | Lee May, Darrell Osteen | | 503 | Steve Hamilton | .60 | 574 | Mets Rookies: | 3.50 |
| 345 | Bob Allison | .30 | 425 | Bob Veale | .30 | 504 | Grady Hatton | .60 | | Billy Hepler, Bill Murphy | |
| 346 | Mike De La Hoz | .30 | 426 | White Sox—2nd Place | .60 | 505 | Jose Cardenal | .60 | 575 | Earl Wilson | 3.50 |
| 347 | Phil Regan | .30 | 427 | John Miller | .30 | 506 | Bo Belinsky | .60 | 576 | Dave Nicholson | 3.50 |
| 348 | Orioles—3rd Place | .75 | 428 | Sandy Alomar | .30 | 507 | John Edwards | .60 | 577 | Jack Lamabe | 3.50 |
| 349 | Cap Peterson | .30 | 429 | Bill Monbouquette | .30 | 508 | Steve Hargan | .60 | 578 | Chi Chi Olivo | 3.50 |
| 350 | Mel Stottlemyre | .50 | 430 | Don Drysdale | 3.50 | 509 | Jake Wood | .60 | 579 | Orioles Rookies: | 3.50 |
| 351 | Fred Valentine | .30 | 431 | Walt Bond | .30 | 510 | Hoyt Wilhelm | 4.00 | | F. Bertaina, G. Brabender, | |
| 352 | Bob Aspromonte | .30 | 432 | Bob Heffner | .30 | 511 | Giants Rookies: | .60 | | Dave Johnson | |
| 353 | Al McBean | .30 | 433 | Alvin Dark (Mgr.) | .30 | | Bob Barton, Tito Fuentes | | 580 | Billy Williams | 15.00 |
| 354 | Smoky Burgess | .30 | 434 | Willie Kirkland | .30 | 512 | Dick Stigman | .60 | 581 | Tony Martinez | 3.50 |
| 355 | Wade Blasingame | .30 | 435 | Jim Bunning | 1.25 | 513 | Camilo Carreon | .60 | 582 | Garry Roggenburk | 3.50 |
| 356 | Red Sox Rookies: | .30 | 436 | Julian Javier | .30 | 514 | Hal Woodeschick | .60 | 583 | Tigers—3rd Place | 9.00 |
| | Owen Johnson, | | 437 | Al Stanek | .30 | 515 | Frank Howard | 1.50 | 584 | Yankees Rookies: | 5.00 |
| | Ken Sanders | | 438 | Willie Smith | .30 | 516 | Eddie Bressoud | .60 | | F. Fernandez, F. Peterson | |
| 357 | Gerry Arrigo | .30 | 439 | Pedro Ramos | .30 | 517 | Checklist No. 7 | 3.00 | 585 | Tony Taylor | 3.50 |
| 358 | Charlie Smith | .30 | 440 | Deron Johnson | .30 | 518 | Braves Rookies: | .60 | 586 | Claude Raymond | 3.50 |
| 359 | Johnny Briggs | .30 | 441 | Tommie Sisk | .30 | | Arnie Umbach, H. Hippauf | | 587 | Dick Bertell | 3.50 |
| 360 | Ron Hunt | .30 | 442 | Orioles Rookies: | .30 | 519 | Bob Friend | .60 | 588 | Athletics Rookies: | 3.50 |
| 361 | Tom Satriano | .30 | | Ed Barnowski, Eddie Watt | | 520 | Jim Wynn | .60 | | Ken Suarez, Chuck Dobson | |
| 362 | Gates Brown | .30 | 443 | Bill Wakefield | .30 | 521 | John Wyatt | .60 | 589 | Lou Klimchock | 3.50 |
| 363 | Checklist No. 5 | 1.25 | 444 | Checklist No. 6 | 1.25 | 522 | Phil Linz | .60 | 590 | Bill Skowron | 5.00 |
| 364 | Nate Oliver | .30 | 445 | Jim Kaat | 2.00 | 523 | Bob Sadowski | 3.50 | 591 | NL Rookie Stars | 4.50 |
| 365 | Roger Maris | 5.00 | 446 | Mack Jones | .30 | 524 | Giants Rookies: | 3.50 | | Bart Shirley, Grant Jackson | |
| 366 | Wayne Causey | .30 | 447 | Dick Ellsworth | .55 | | Ollie Brown, Don Mason | | 592 | Andre Rodgers | 3.50 |
| 367 | Mel Nelson | .30 | | (photo of Ken Hubbs) | | 525 | Gary Bell | 3.50 | 593 | Doug Camilli | 3.50 |
| 368 | Charlie Lau | .30 | 448 | Eddie Stanky | .60 | 526 | Twins—1st Place | 6.00 | 594 | Chico Salmon | 3.50 |
| 369 | Jim King | .30 | 449 | Joe Moeller | .60 | 527 | Julio Navarro | 3.50 | 595 | Larry Jackson | 3.50 |
| 370 | Chico Cardenas | .30 | 450 | Tony Oliva | 1.50 | 528 | Jesse Gonder | 3.50 | 596 | John Sullivan | 3.50 |
| 371 | Lee Stange | .30 | 451 | Barry Latman | .60 | 529 | White Sox Rookies: | 4.50 | 597 | Astros Rookies: | 4.50 |
| 372 | Harvey Kuenn | .30 | 452 | Joe Azcue | .60 | | Dennis Higgins, Lee Elia, | | | Nate Colbert, Greg Sims | |
| 373 | Giants Rookies: | .40 | 453 | Ron Kline | .60 | | Bill Voss | | 598 | Gaylord Perry | 60.00 |
| | Jack Hiatt, Dick Estelle | | 454 | Jerry Buchek | .60 | 530 | Robin Roberts | 12.00 | | | |

# 1967 Topps....Complete Set of 609 Cards—Value $1250.00

Features the rookie cards of Tom Seaver and Rod Carew. Cards 534 to 609 are high numbers. Cards 458 to 533 are semi-high numbers. Cards 26 and 86 exist without the *traded* line—worth $7.00 each. Card 191 exists identifying card 214 as either Dick Kelley—worth $5.00 or Tom Kelley—worth $1.50.

| NO. | PLAYER | MINT |
|---|---|---|
| 1 | The Champs: | 3.00 |
|  | Frank Robinson, Hank | |
|  | Bauer, Brooks Robinson | |
| 2 | Jack Hamilton | .25 |
| 3 | Duke Sims | .25 |
| 4 | Hal Lanier | .25 |
| 5 | Whitey Ford | 4.50 |
| 6 | Dick Simpson | .25 |
| 7 | Don McMahon | .25 |
| 8 | Chuck Harrison | .25 |
| 9 | Ron Hansen | .25 |
| 10 | Matty Alou | .25 |
| 11 | Barry Moore | .25 |
| 12 | Dodgers Rookies: | .45 |
|  | J. Campanis, Bill Singer | |
| 13 | Joe Sparma | .25 |
| 14 | Phil Linz | .25 |
| 15 | Earl Battey | .25 |
| 16 | Bill Hands | .25 |
| 17 | Jim Gosger | .25 |
| 18 | Gene Oliver | .25 |
| 19 | Jim McGlothlin | .25 |
| 20 | Orlando Cepeda | 2.00 |
| 21 | Dave Bristol (Mgr.) | .25 |
| 22 | Gene Brabender | .25 |
| 23 | Larry Elliot | .25 |
| 24 | Bob Allen | .25 |
| 25 | Elston Howard | 1.00 |
| 26 | Bob Priddy* | .25 |
| 27 | Bob Saverine | .25 |
| 28 | Barry Latman | .25 |
| 29 | Tom McCraw | .25 |
| 30 | Al Kaline | 4.00 |
| 31 | Jim Brewer | .25 |
| 32 | Bob Bailey | .25 |
| 33 | Athletic Rookies: | .75 |
|  | Sal Bando, R. Schwartz | |
| 34 | Pete Cimino | .30 |
| 35 | Rico Carty | .50 |
| 36 | Bob Tillman | .25 |
| 37 | Rick Wise | .25 |
| 38 | Bob Johnson | .25 |
| 39 | Curt Simmons | .25 |
| 40 | Rick Reichardt | .25 |
| 41 | Joe Hoerner | .25 |
| 42 | Mets Team | 1.00 |
| 43 | Chico Salmon | .25 |
| 44 | Joe Nuxhall | .25 |
| 45 | Roger Maris | 4.00 |
| 46 | Lindy McDaniel | .25 |
| 47 | Ken McMullen | .25 |
| 48 | Bill Freehan | .45 |
| 49 | Roy Face | .45 |
| 50 | Tony Oliva | 1.00 |
| 51 | Astros Rookies: | .25 |
|  | Dave Adlesh, W. Bales | |
| 52 | Dennis Higgins | .25 |
| 53 | Clay Dalrymple | .25 |
| 54 | Dick Green | .25 |
| 55 | Don Drysdale | 3.00 |
| 56 | Jose Tartabull | .25 |
| 57 | Pat Jarvis | .25 |
| 58 | Paul Schaal | .25 |
| 59 | Ralph Terry | .25 |
| 60 | Luis Aparicio | 2.50 |
| 61 | Gordy Coleman | .25 |

| NO. | PLAYER | MINT |
|---|---|---|
| 62 | Checklist No. 1 | 1.25 |
| 63 | Cards Clubbers | 1.50 |
|  | Lou Brock, Curt Flood | |
| 64 | Fred Valentine | .25 |
| 65 | Tom Haller | .25 |
| 66 | Manny Mota | .35 |
| 67 | Ken Berry | .25 |
| 68 | Bob Buhl | .25 |
| 69 | Vic Davalillo | .25 |
| 70 | Ron Santo | .50 |
| 71 | Camilo Pascual | .25 |
| 72 | Tigers Rookies: | .35 |
|  | George Korince (Photo of | |
|  | John Brown), J. Matchick | |
| 73 | Rusty Staub | 1.00 |
| 74 | Wes Stock | .25 |
| 75 | George Scott | .25 |
| 76 | Jim Barbieri | .25 |
| 77 | Dooley Womack | .25 |
| 78 | Pat Corrales | .25 |
| 79 | Bubba Morton | .25 |
| 80 | Jim Maloney | .25 |
| 81 | Eddie Stanky (Mgr.) | .25 |
| 82 | Steve Barber | .25 |
| 83 | Ollie Brown | .25 |
| 84 | Tommie Sisk | .25 |
| 85 | Johnny Callison | .25 |
| 86 | Mike McCormick* | .25 |
| 87 | George Altman | .25 |
| 88 | Mickey Lolich | .75 |
| 89 | Felix Millan | .25 |
| 90 | Jim Nash | .25 |
| 91 | Johnny Lewis | .25 |
| 92 | Ray Washburn | .25 |
| 93 | Yankees Rookies: | 1.25 |
|  | Stan Bahnsen, B. Murcer | |
| 94 | Ron Fairly | .25 |
| 95 | Sonny Siebert | .25 |
| 96 | Art Shamsky | .25 |
| 97 | Mike Cuellar | .25 |
| 98 | Rich Rollins | .25 |
| 99 | Lee Stange | .25 |
| 100 | Frank Robinson | 4.00 |
| 101 | Ken Johnson | .25 |
| 102 | Phillies Team | .60 |
| 103 | Checklist No. 2 | 2.00 |
| 104 | Minnie Rojas | .25 |
| 105 | Ken Boyer | .65 |
| 106 | Randy Hundley | .25 |
| 107 | Joel Horlen | .25 |
| 108 | Alex Johnson | .25 |
| 109 | Tribe Thumpers: | .25 |
|  | R. Colavito, Leon Wagner | |
| 110 | Jack Aker | .25 |
| 111 | John Kennedy | .25 |
| 112 | Dave Wickersham | .25 |
| 113 | Dave Nicholson | .25 |
| 114 | Jack Baldschun | .25 |
| 115 | Paul Casanova | .25 |
| 116 | Herman Franks | .25 |
| 117 | Darrell Brandon | .25 |
| 118 | Bernie Allen | .25 |
| 119 | Wade Blasingame | .25 |
| 120 | Floyd Robinson | .25 |
| 121 | Ed Bressoud | .25 |
| 122 | George Brunet | .25 |

| NO. | PLAYER | MINT |
|---|---|---|
| 123 | Pirates Rookies: | .25 |
|  | Jim Price, L. Walker | |
| 124 | Jim Stewart | .25 |
| 125 | Moe Drabowsky | .25 |
| 126 | Tony Taylor | .25 |
| 127 | John O'Donoghue | .25 |
| 128 | Ed Spiezio | .25 |
| 129 | Phil Roof | .25 |
| 130 | Phil Regan | .25 |
| 131 | Yankees Team | 1.00 |
| 132 | Ozzie Virgil | .25 |
| 133 | Ron Kline | .25 |
| 134 | Gates Brown | .25 |
| 135 | Deron Johnson | .25 |
| 136 | Carroll Sembera | .25 |
| 137 | Twins Rookies: | .25 |
|  | Ron Clark, Jim Ollum | |
| 138 | Dick Kelley | .25 |
| 139 | Dalton Jones | .25 |
| 140 | Willie Stargell | 4.00 |
| 141 | John Miller | .25 |
| 142 | Jackie Brandt | .25 |
| 143 | Sox Sockers: | .35 |
|  | Don Buford, Pete Ward | |
| 144 | Bill Hepler | .25 |
| 145 | Larry Brown | .25 |
| 146 | Steve Carlton | 30.00 |
| 147 | Tom Egan | .25 |
| 148 | Adolfo Phillips | .25 |
| 149 | Joe Moeller | .25 |
| 150 | Mickey Mantle | 50.00 |
| 151 | World Series Game 1: | 1.00 |
|  | Moe Mows Down 11 | |
| 152 | World Series Game 2: | 1.50 |
|  | Palmer Blanks Dodgers | |
| 153 | World Series Game 3: | 1.00 |
|  | Blair's Homer Defeats L.A. | |
| 154 | World Series Game 4: | 1.00 |
|  | Orioles Win 4 Straight | |
| 155 | World Series: | 1.00 |
|  | The Winners Celebrate | |
| 156 | Ron Herbel | .25 |
| 157 | Danny Cater | .25 |
| 158 | Jimmy Coker | .25 |
| 159 | Bruce Howard | .25 |
| 160 | Willie Davis | .25 |
| 161 | Dick Williams (Mgr.) | .35 |
| 162 | Billy O'Dell | .25 |
| 163 | Vic Roznovsky | .25 |
| 164 | Dwight Siebler | .25 |
| 165 | Cleon Jones | .25 |
| 166 | Ed Mathews | 3.00 |
| 167 | Senators Rookies: | .25 |
|  | Joe Coleman, Tim Cullen | |
| 168 | Ray Culp | .25 |
| 169 | Horace Clarke | .25 |
| 170 | Dick McAuliffe | .25 |
| 171 | Calvin Koonce | .25 |
| 172 | Bill Heath | .25 |
| 173 | Cardinals Team | .60 |
| 174 | Dick Radatz | .25 |
| 175 | Bobby Knoop | .25 |
| 176 | Sammy Ellis | .25 |
| 177 | Tito Fuentes | .25 |
| 178 | John Buzhardt | .25 |
| 179 | Braves Rookies: | .25 |
|  | C. Vaughan, Cecil Upshaw | |

| NO. | PLAYER | MINT |
|---|---|---|
| 180 | Curt Blefary | .25 |
| 181 | Terry Fox | .25 |
| 182 | Ed Charles | .25 |
| 183 | Jim Pagliaroni | .25 |
| 184 | George Thomas | .25 |
| 185 | Ken Holtzman (R) | .75 |
| 186 | Mets Maulers | .35 |
|  | Ed Kranepool, R. Swoboda | |
| 187 | Pedro Ramos | .25 |
| 188 | Ken Harrelson | .60 |
| 189 | Chuck Hinton | .25 |
| 190 | Turk Farrell | .25 |
| 191 | Checklist No. 3* | 1.50 |
| 192 | Fred Gladding | .25 |
| 193 | Jose Cardenal | .25 |
| 194 | Bob Allison | .25 |
| 195 | Al Jackson | .25 |
| 196 | Johnny Romano | .25 |
| 197 | Ron Perranoski | .25 |
| 198 | Chuck Hiller | .25 |
| 199 | Billy Hitchcock | .25 |
| 200 | Willie Mays | 20.00 |
| 201 | Hal Reniff | .25 |
| 202 | Johnny Edwards | .25 |
| 203 | Al McBean | .25 |
| 204 | Orioles Rookies: | .35 |
|  | Mike Epstein, Tom Phoebus | |
| 205 | Dick Groat | .40 |
| 206 | Dennis Bennett | .25 |
| 207 | John Orsino | .25 |
| 208 | Jack Lamabe | .25 |
| 209 | Joe Nossek | .25 |
| 210 | Bob Gibson | 3.50 |
| 211 | Twins Team | .60 |
| 212 | Chris Zachary | .25 |
| 213 | Jay Johnstone | .25 |
| 214 | Tom Kelley | .25 |
| 215 | Ernie Banks | 5.00 |
| 216 | Bengal Belters: | 2.00 |
|  | Norm Cash, Al Kaline | |
| 217 | Rob Gardner | .25 |
| 218 | Wes Parker | .25 |
| 219 | Clay Carroll | .25 |
| 220 | Jim Hart | .25 |
| 221 | Woody Fryman | .25 |
| 222 | Reds Rookies: | .50 |
|  | Darrell Osteen, Lee May | |
| 227 | Mike Ryan | .25 |
| 224 | Walt Bond | .25 |
| 225 | Mel Stottlemyre | .50 |
| 226 | Julian Javier | .25 |
| 227 | Paul Lindblad | .25 |
| 228 | Gil Hodges (Mgr.) | 2.00 |
| 229 | Larry Jackson | .25 |
| 230 | Boog Powell | .75 |
| 231 | John Bateman | .25 |
| 232 | Don Buford | .25 |
| 233 | AL ERA Leaders: | .75 |
|  | Joel Horlen, Gary Peters, | |
|  | Steve Hargan | |
| 234 | NL ERA Leaders: | 2.00 |
|  | Sandy Koufax, Mike | |
|  | Cuellar, Juan Marichal | |
| 235 | AL Pitching Leaders: | .75 |
|  | Earl Wilson, Jim Kaat, | |
|  | Denny McLain | |

| NO. PLAYER | MINT |
| --- | --- |
| 236 NL Pitching Leaders: Sandy Koufax, Juan Marichal, Gaylord Perry, Bob Gibson | 2.50 |
| 237 AL Strikeout Leaders: Jim Kaat, Earl Wilson, Sam McDowell | .75 |
| 238 NL Strikeout Leaders: Sandy Koufax, Jim Bunning, Bob Veale | 1.50 |
| 239 AL Batting Leaders: Al Kaline, Frank Robinson, Tony Oliva | 1.50 |
| 240 NL Batting Leaders: Matty Alou, Felipe Alou, Rico Carty | .75 |
| 241 AL RBI Leaders: Frank Robinson, Boog Powell, Harmon Killebrew | 1.50 |
| 242 NL RBI Leaders: Bob Clemente, Richie Allen, Hank Aaron | 1.50 |
| 243 AL Home Run Leaders: Frank Robinson, Harmon Killebrew, Boog Powell | 1.50 |
| 244 NL Home Run Leaders: Hank Aaron, Richie Allen, Willie Mays | 1.50 |
| 245 Curt Flood | .50 |
| 246 Jim Perry | .40 |
| 247 Jerry Lumpe | .25 |
| 248 Gene Mauch (Mgr.) | .40 |
| 249 Nick Willhite | .25 |
| 250 Hank Aaron | 20.00 |
| 251 Woody Held | .25 |
| 252 Bob Bolin | .25 |
| 253 Indians Rookies: Bill Davis, Gus Gil | .25 |
| 254 Milt Pappas | .25 |
| 255 Frank Howard | .75 |
| 256 Bob Hendley | .25 |
| 257 Charley Smith | .25 |
| 258 Lee Maye | .25 |
| 259 Don Dennis | .25 |
| 260 Jim Lefebvre | .25 |
| 261 John Wyatt | .25 |
| 262 Athletics Team | .50 |
| 263 Hank Aguirre | .25 |
| 264 Ron Swoboda | .25 |
| 265 Lou Burdette | .25 |
| 266 Pitt Power: W. Stargell, D. Clendenon | 1.25 |
| 267 Don Schwall | .25 |
| 268 John Briggs | .25 |
| 269 Don Nottebart | .25 |
| 270 Zoilo Versalles | .25 |
| 271 Eddie Watt | .25 |
| 272 Cubs Rookies: Bill Connors, Dave Dowling | .25 |
| 273 Dick Lines | .25 |
| 274 Bob Aspromonte | .25 |
| 275 Fred Whitfield | .25 |
| 276 Bruce Brubaker | .25 |
| 277 Steve Whitaker | .25 |
| 278 Checklist No. 4 | 1.00 |
| 279 Frank Linzy | .25 |
| 280 Tony Conigliaro | .50 |
| 281 Bob Rodgers | .25 |
| 282 Johnny Odom | .25 |
| 283 Gene Alley | .25 |
| 284 Johnny Podres | .50 |
| 285 Lou Brock | 4.00 |
| 286 Wayne Causey | .25 |
| 287 Mets Rookies: Greg Goossen, Bart Shirley | .25 |
| 288 Denver Lemaster | .25 |
| 289 Tom Tresh | .35 |
| 290 Bill White | .40 |
| 291 Jim Hannan | .25 |
| 292 Don Pavletich | .25 |
| 293 Ed Kirkpatrick | .25 |
| 294 Walt Alston (Mgr.) | 1.00 |
| 295 Sam McDowell | .40 |
| 296 Glenn Beckert | .30 |
| 297 Dave Morehead | .25 |

| NO. PLAYER | MINT |
| --- | --- |
| 298 Ron Davis | .25 |
| 299 Norm Siebern | .25 |
| 300 Jim Kaat | 1.00 |
| 301 Jesse Gonder | .25 |
| 302 Orioles Team | .60 |
| 303 Gil Blanco | .25 |
| 304 Phil Gagliano | .25 |
| 305 Earl Wilson | .25 |
| 306 Bud Harrelson | .25 |
| 307 Jim Beauchamp | .25 |
| 308 Al Downing | .25 |
| 309 Hurlers Beware: J. Callison, Richie Allen | .50 |
| 310 Gary Peters | .25 |
| 311 Ed Brinkman | .25 |
| 312 Don Mincher | .25 |
| 313 Bob Lee | .25 |
| 314 Red Sox Rookies: Mike Andrews, R. Smith | 1.50 |
| 315 Billy Williams | 1.50 |
| 316 Jack Kralick | .25 |
| 317 Cesar Tovar | .25 |
| 318 Dave Giusti | .25 |
| 319 Paul Blair | .25 |
| 320 Gaylord Perry | 3.00 |
| 321 Mayo Smith (Mgr.) | .25 |
| 322 Jose Pagan | .25 |
| 323 Mike Hershberger | .25 |
| 324 Hal Woodeschick | .25 |
| 325 Chico Cardenas | .25 |
| 326 Bob Uecker | 4.00 |
| 327 Angels Team | .60 |
| 328 Clete Boyer | .25 |
| 329 Charlie Lau | .25 |
| 330 Claude Osteen | .25 |
| 331 Joe Foy | .25 |
| 332 Jesus Alou | .25 |
| 333 Ferguson Jenkins | 1.50 |
| 334 Twin Terrors: Bob Allison, H. Killebrew | 1.50 |
| 335 Bob Veale | .25 |
| 336 Joe Azcue | .25 |
| 337 Joe Morgan | 4.00 |
| 338 Bob Locker | .25 |
| 339 Chico Ruiz | .25 |
| 340 Joe Pepitone | .40 |
| 341 Giants Rookies: Dick Dietz, Bill Sorrell | .35 |
| 342 Hank Fischer | .25 |
| 343 Tom Satriano | .25 |
| 344 Ossie Chavarria | .25 |
| 345 Stu Miller | .25 |
| 346 Jim Hickman | .25 |
| 347 Grady Hatton (Mgr.) | .25 |
| 348 Tug McGraw | .75 |
| 349 Bob Chance | .25 |
| 350 Joe Torre | .75 |
| 351 Vern Law | .25 |
| 352 Ray Oyler | .25 |
| 353 Bill McCool | .25 |
| 354 Cubs Team | .75 |
| 355 Carl Yastrzemski | 40.00 |
| 356 Larry Jaster | .25 |
| 357 Bill Skowron | .50 |
| 358 Ruben Amaro | .25 |
| 359 Dick Ellsworth | .25 |
| 360 Leon Wagner | .25 |
| 361 Checklist No. 5 | 1.25 |
| 362 Darold Knowles | .25 |
| 363 Dave Johnson | .35 |
| 364 Claude Raymond | .25 |
| 365 John Roseboro | .25 |
| 366 Andy Kosco | .25 |
| 367 Angels Rookies: Bill Kelso, Don Wallace | .25 |
| 368 Jack Hiatt | .25 |
| 369 Jim Hunter | 2.50 |
| 370 Tommy Davis | .35 |
| 371 Jim Lonborg | .60 |
| 372 Mike De La Hoz | .25 |
| 373 White Sox Rookies: D. Josephson, F. Klages | .25 |
| 374 Mel Queen | .25 |
| 375 Jake Gibbs | .25 |
| 376 Don Lock | .25 |

| NO. PLAYER | MINT |
| --- | --- |
| 377 Luis Tiant | .75 |
| 378 Tigers Team | 1.00 |
| 379 Jerry May | .25 |
| 380 Dean Chance | .25 |
| 381 Dick Schofield | .25 |
| 382 Dave McNally | .40 |
| 383 Ken Henderson | .25 |
| 384 Cardinals Rookies: Dick Hughes, Jim Cosman | .40 |
| 385 Jim Fregosi | .35 |
| 386 Dick Selma | .25 |
| 387 Cap Peterson | .25 |
| 388 Arnold Earley | .25 |
| 389 Al Dark (Mgr.) | .40 |
| 390 Jim Wynn | .35 |
| 391 Wilbur Wood | .40 |
| 392 Tommy Harper | .30 |
| 393 Jim Bouton | .75 |
| 394 Jake Wood | .40 |
| 395 Chris Short | .25 |
| 396 Atlanta Aces: D. Meke, T. Cloninger | .35 |
| 397 Willie Smith | .25 |
| 398 Jeff Torborg | .40 |
| 399 Al Worthington | .25 |
| 400 Bob Clemente | 16.00 |
| 401 Jim Coates | .25 |
| 402 Phillies Rookies: Grant Jackson, Billy Wilson | .40 |
| 403 Dick Nen | .25 |
| 404 Nelson Briles | .25 |
| 405 Russ Snyder | .25 |
| 406 Lee Elia | .25 |
| 407 Reds Team | .75 |
| 408 Jim Northrup | .35 |
| 409 Ray Sadecki | .25 |
| 410 Lou Johnson | .25 |
| 411 Dick Howser | .50 |
| 412 Astros Rookies: Norm Miller, Doug Rader | .75 |
| 413 Jerry Grote | .25 |
| 414 Casey Cox | .25 |
| 415 Sonny Jackson | .25 |
| 416 Roger Repoz | .25 |
| 417 Bob Bruce | .25 |
| 418 Sam Mele (Mgr.) | .25 |
| 419 Don Kessinger | .25 |
| 420 Denny McLain | 1.00 |
| 421 Dal Maxvill | .25 |
| 422 Hoyt Wilhelm | 2.50 |
| 423 Fence Busters: Willie Mays, Willie McCovey | 4.00 |
| 424 Pedro Gonzalez | .25 |
| 425 Pete Mikkelsen | .25 |
| 426 Lou Clinton | .25 |
| 427 Ruben Gomez | .25 |
| 428 Dodgers Rookies: Tom Hutton, Gene Michael | .60 |
| 429 Garry Roggenburk | .25 |
| 430 Pete Rose | 45.00 |
| 431 Ted Uhlaender | .25 |
| 432 Jimmie Hall | .25 |
| 433 Al Luplow | .25 |
| 434 Eddie Fisher | .25 |
| 435 Mack Jones | .25 |
| 436 Pete Ward | .25 |
| 437 Senators Team | .50 |
| 438 Chuck Dobson | .25 |
| 439 Byron Browne | .25 |
| 440 Steve Hargan | .25 |
| 441 Jim Davenport | .25 |
| 442 Yankees Rookies: Bill Robinson, Joe Verbanic | .50 |
| 443 Tito Francona | .35 |
| 444 George Smith | .25 |
| 445 Don Sutton | 2.50 |
| 446 Russ Nixon | .25 |
| 447 Bo Belinsky | .25 |
| 448 Harry Walker (Mgr.) | .25 |
| 449 Orlando Pena | .25 |
| 450 Richie Allen | 1.00 |
| 451 Fred Newman | .25 |
| 452 Ed Kranepool | .50 |
| 453 Aurelio Monteagudo | .25 |
| 454 Checklist No. 6 | 1.25 |

| NO. PLAYER | MINT |
| --- | --- |
| 455 Tommy Agee | .25 |
| 456 Phil Niekro | 3.00 |
| 457 Andy Etchebarren | .25 |
| 458 Lee Thomas | .75 |
| 459 Senators Rookies: Dick Bosman, Pete Craig | .75 |
| 460 Harmon Killebrew | 8.00 |
| 461 Bob Miller | .75 |
| 462 Bob Barton | .75 |
| 463 Hill Aces: Sam McDowell, S. Siebert | 1.00 |
| 464 Dan Coombs | .75 |
| 465 Willie Horton | .75 |
| 466 Bobby Wine | .75 |
| 467 Jim O'Toole | .75 |
| 468 Ralph Houk (Mgr.) | .85 |
| 469 Len Gabrielson | .75 |
| 470 Bob Shaw | .75 |
| 471 Rene Lachemann | .75 |
| 472 Rookies Pirates: John Gelnar, G. Spriggs | .75 |
| 473 Jose Santiago | .75 |
| 474 Bob Tolan | .75 |
| 475 Jim Palmer | 12.00 |
| 476 Tony Perez | 13.00 |
| 477 Braves Team | 1.00 |
| 478 Bob Humphreys | .75 |
| 479 Gary Bell | .75 |
| 480 Willie McCovey | 9.00 |
| 481 Leo Durocher (Mgr.) | 1.00 |
| 482 Bill Monbouquette | .75 |
| 483 Jim Landis | .75 |
| 484 Jerry Adair | .75 |
| 485 Tim McCarver | 1.25 |
| 486 Twins Rookies: Rich Reese, Bill Whitby | .75 |
| 487 Tom Reynolds | .75 |
| 488 Gerry Arrigo | .75 |
| 489 Doug Clemens | .75 |
| 490 Tony Cloninger | .75 |
| 491 Sam Bowens | .75 |
| 492 Pirates Team | .75 |
| 493 Phil Ortega | .75 |
| 494 Bill Rigney (Mgr.) | .75 |
| 495 Fritz Peterson | .75 |
| 496 Orlando McFarlane | .75 |
| 497 Ron Campbell | .75 |
| 498 Larry Dierker | .75 |
| 499 Indians Rookies: George Culver, Jose Vidal | .75 |
| 500 Juan Marichal | 4.00 |
| 501 Jerry Zimmerman | .75 |
| 502 Derrell Griffith | .75 |
| 503 Dodgers Team | 2.00 |
| 504 Orlando Martinez | .75 |
| 505 Tommy Helms | .75 |
| 506 Smoky Burgess | .75 |
| 507 Orioles Rookies: Ed Barnowski, Larry Haney | .75 |
| 508 Dick Hall | .75 |
| 509 Jim King | .75 |
| 510 Bill Mazeroski | 1.25 |
| 511 Don Wert | .75 |
| 512 R. Schoendienst (Mgr.) | 1.00 |
| 513 Marcelino Lopez | .75 |
| 514 John Werhas | .75 |
| 515 Bert Campaneris | .75 |
| 516 Giants Team | .75 |
| 517 Fred Talbot | .75 |
| 518 Denis Menke | .75 |
| 519 Ted Davidson | .75 |
| 520 Max Alvis | .75 |
| 521 Bird Bombers: Boog Powell, Curt Blefary | .75 |
| 522 John Stephenson | .75 |
| 523 Jim Merritt | .75 |
| 524 Felix Mantilla | .75 |
| 525 Ron Hunt | .75 |
| 526 Tigers Rookies: Pat Dobson, G. Korince | 1.25 |
| 527 Dennis Ribant | .75 |
| 528 Rico Petrocelli | .75 |
| 529 Gary Wagner | .75 |
| 530 Felipe Alou | .75 |
| 531 Checklist No. 7 | 3.00 |

# 1967 Topps (Continued)

| NO. | PLAYER | MINT |
|---|---|---|
| 532 | Jim Hicks | .75 |
| 533 | Jack Fisher | .75 |
| 534 | Hank Bauer (Mgr.) | 2.50 |
| 535 | Donn Clendenon | 2.50 |
| 536 | Cubs Rookies: | 4.00 |
| | Joe Niekro, Paul Popovich | |
| 537 | Chuck Estrada | 2.00 |
| 538 | J.C. Martin | 2.00 |
| 539 | Dick Egan | 2.00 |
| 540 | Norm Cash | 5.00 |
| 541 | Joe Gibbon | 2.00 |
| 542 | Athletics Rookies: | 3.00 |
| | Tony Pierce, Rick Monday | |
| 543 | Dan Schneider | 2.00 |
| 544 | Indians Team | 3.00 |
| 545 | Jim Grant | 2.00 |
| 546 | Woody Woodward | 2.00 |
| 547 | Red Sox Rookies: | 2.00 |
| | Russ Gibson, Bill Rohr | |
| 548 | Tony Gonzalez | 2.00 |
| 549 | Jack Sanford | 2.00 |
| 550 | Vada Pinson | 3.00 |
| 551 | Doug Camilli | 2.00 |

| NO. | PLAYER | MINT |
|---|---|---|
| 552 | Ted Savage | 2.00 |
| 553 | Yankees Rookies: | 4.00 |
| | Mike Hegan, Thad Tillotson | |
| 554 | Andre Rodgers | 2.00 |
| 555 | Don Cardwell | 2.00 |
| 556 | Al Weis | 2.00 |
| 557 | Al Ferrara | 2.00 |
| 558 | Orioles Rookies: | 6.00 |
| | Mark Belanger, Bill Dillman | |
| 559 | Dick Tracewski | 2.00 |
| 560 | Jim Bunning | 9.00 |
| 561 | Sandy Alomar | 2.00 |
| 562 | Steve Blass | 2.00 |
| 563 | Joe Adcock (Mgr.) | 5.00 |
| 564 | Astros Rookies: | 2.50 |
| | Alonzo Harris, A. Pointer | |
| 565 | Lew Krausse | 2.00 |
| 566 | Gary Geiger | 2.00 |
| 567 | Steve Hamilton | 2.00 |
| 568 | John Sullivan | 2.00 |
| 569 | AL Rookies: | 120.00 |
| | Rod Carew, Hank Allen | |
| 570 | Maury Wills | 60.00 |

| NO. | PLAYER | MINT |
|---|---|---|
| 571 | Larry Sherry | 2.00 |
| 572 | Don Demeter | 2.00 |
| 573 | White Sox Team | 4.00 |
| 574 | Jerry Buchek | 2.00 |
| 575 | Dave Boswell | 2.00 |
| 576 | NL Rookies: | 2.00 |
| | R. Hernandez, Norm Gigon | |
| 577 | Bill Short | 2.00 |
| 578 | John Boccabella | 2.00 |
| 579 | Bill Henry | 2.00 |
| 580 | Rocky Colavito | 8.00 |
| 581 | Mets Rookies: | 250.00 |
| | Bill Denehy, Tom Seaver | |
| 582 | Jim Owens | 2.00 |
| 583 | Ray Barker | 2.00 |
| 584 | Jim Piersall | 5.00 |
| 585 | Wally Bunker | 2.00 |
| 586 | Manny Jimenez | 2.00 |
| 587 | NL Rookies: | 2.00 |
| | Don Shaw, Gary Sutherland | |
| 588 | Johnny Klippstein | 2.00 |
| 589 | Dave Ricketts | 2.00 |
| 590 | Pete Richert | 2.00 |

| NO. | PLAYER | MINT |
|---|---|---|
| 591 | Ty Cline | 2.00 |
| 592 | NL Rookies: | 2.00 |
| | Jim Shellenback, Ron Willis | |
| 593 | Wes Westrum (Mgr.) | 2.00 |
| 594 | Dan Osinski | 2.00 |
| 595 | Cookie Rojas | 2.00 |
| 596 | Galen Cisco | 2.00 |
| 597 | Ted Abernathy | 2.00 |
| 598 | White Sox Rookies: | 2.00 |
| | Ed Stroud, Walt Williams | |
| 599 | Bob Duliba (Mgr.) | 2.00 |
| 600 | Brooks Robinson | 125.00 |
| 601 | Bill Bryan | 2.00 |
| 602 | Juan Pizarro | 2.00 |
| 603 | Athletics Rookies: | 2.00 |
| | Tim Talton, Ramon Webster | |
| 604 | Red Sox Team | 7.50 |
| 605 | Mike Shannon | 2.00 |
| 606 | Ron Taylor | 2.00 |
| 607 | Mickey Stanley | 2.00 |
| 608 | Cubs Rookies: | 2.00 |
| | John Upham, Rich Nye | |
| 609 | Tommy John | 28.00 |

# 1968 Topps....Complete Set of 598 Cards—Value $550.00

Features the rookie cards of Johnny Bench and Nolan Ryan. High numbers are 534 to 598. Card 66 exists with "Senators" in *white*—worth $.20 and "Senators" in *yellow*—worth $4.50. Card 518 (checklist) exists identifying card 539 as "Maj. L. Rookies"—worth $1.25 or "Am. L. Rookies"—worth $5.00.

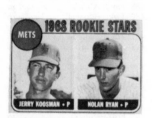

| NO. | PLAYER | MINT |
|---|---|---|
| 1 | NL Batting Leaders: | 2.00 |
| | Bob Clemente, Matty Alou, Tony Gonzalez | |
| 2 | AL Batting Leaders: | 1.50 |
| | Frank Robinson, Al Kaline, Carl Yastrzemski | |
| 3 | NL RBI Leaders: | 1.50 |
| | Hank Aaron, O. Cepeda, Bob Clemente | |
| 4 | AL RBI Leaders: | 1.50 |
| | C. Yastrzemski, H. Killebrew, F. Robinson | |
| 5 | NL Home Run Leaders: | 1.50 |
| | Ron Santo, Hank Aaron, Jim Wynn, Willie McCovey | |
| 6 | AL Home Run Leaders: | 1.50 |
| | C. Yastrzemski, H. Killebrew, F. Howard | |
| 7 | NL ERA Leaders: | .75 |
| | Jim Bunning, Chris Short, Phil Niekro | |
| 8 | AL ERA Leaders: | .75 |
| | Joe Horlen, Sonny Siebert, Gary Peters | |
| 9 | NL Pitching Leaders: | .75 |
| | C. Osteen, M. McCormick, F. Jenkins, J. Bunning | |
| 10 | AL Pitching Leaders: | .75 |
| | Jim Lonborg, Earl Wilson, Dean Chance | |
| 11 | NL Strikeout Leaders: | .75 |
| | Ferguson Jenkins, Gaylord Perry, Jim Bunning | |
| 12 | AL Strikeout Leaders: | .75 |
| | Jim Lonborg, Dean Chance, Sam McDowell | |

| NO. | PLAYER | MINT |
|---|---|---|
| 13 | Chuck Hartenstein | .20 |
| 14 | Jerry McNertney | .20 |
| 15 | Ron Hunt | .20 |
| 16 | Indians Rookies: | 1.50 |
| | Lou Piniella, R. Schienblum | |
| 17 | Dick Hall | .20 |
| 18 | Mike Hershberger | .20 |
| 19 | Juan Pizarro | .20 |
| 20 | Brooks Robinson | 4.50 |
| 21 | Ron Davis | .20 |
| 22 | Pat Dobson | .30 |
| 23 | Chico Cardenas | .20 |
| 24 | Bobby Locke | .20 |
| 25 | Julian Javier | .20 |
| 26 | Darrell Brandon | .20 |
| 27 | Gil Hodges (Mgr.) | 2.00 |
| 28 | Ted Uhlaender | .20 |
| 29 | Joe Verbanic | .20 |
| 30 | Joe Torre | .75 |
| 31 | Ed Stroud | .20 |
| 32 | Joe Gibbon | .20 |
| 33 | Pete Ward | .20 |
| 34 | Al Ferrara | .20 |
| 35 | Steve Hargan | .20 |
| 36 | Pirates Rookies: | .35 |
| | Bob Moose, B. Robertson | |
| 37 | Billy Williams | 1.50 |
| 38 | Tony Pierce | .20 |
| 39 | Cookie Rojas | .20 |
| 40 | Denny McLain | 1.75 |
| 41 | Julio Gotay | .20 |
| 42 | Larry Haney | .20 |
| 43 | Gary Bell | .20 |
| 44 | Frank Kostro | .20 |
| 45 | Tom Seaver | 30.00 |
| 46 | Dave Ricketts | .20 |

| NO. | PLAYER | MINT |
|---|---|---|
| 47 | Ralph Houk (Mgr.) | .40 |
| 48 | Ted Davidson | .20 |
| 49 | Ed Brinkman | .20 |
| 50 | Willie Mays | 16.00 |
| 51 | Bob Locker | .20 |
| 52 | Hawk Taylor | .20 |
| 53 | Gene Alley | .20 |
| 54 | Stan Williams | .20 |
| 55 | Felipe Alou | .30 |
| 56 | Orioles Rookies: | .30 |
| | Dave May, Dave Leonhard | |
| 57 | Dan Schneider | .20 |
| 58 | Ed Mathews | 2.50 |
| 59 | Don Lock | .20 |
| 60 | Ken Holtzman | .30 |
| 61 | Reggie Smith | .75 |
| 62 | Chuck Dobson | .20 |
| 63 | Dick Kenworthy | .20 |
| 64 | Jim Merritt | .20 |
| 65 | John Roseboro | .20 |
| 66 | Casey Cox* | .20 |
| 67 | Checklist No. 1 | 1.00 |
| 68 | Ron Willis | .20 |
| 69 | Tom Tresh | .25 |
| 70 | Bob Veale | .20 |
| 71 | Vern Fuller | .20 |
| 72 | Tommy John | 1.50 |
| 73 | Jim Hart | .20 |
| 74 | Milt Pappas | .20 |
| 75 | Don Mincher | .20 |
| 76 | Braves Rookies: | .20 |
| | Jim Britton, Ron Reed | |
| 77 | Don Wilson | .20 |
| 78 | Jim Northrup | .20 |
| 79 | Ted Kubiak | .20 |
| 80 | Rod Carew | 20.00 |

| NO. | PLAYER | MINT |
|---|---|---|
| 81 | Larry Jackson | .20 |
| 82 | Sam Bowens | .20 |
| 83 | John Stephenson | .20 |
| 84 | Bob Tolan | .20 |
| 85 | Gaylord Perry | 2.50 |
| 86 | Willie Stargell | 3.00 |
| 87 | Dick Williams (Mgr.) | .30 |
| 88 | Phil Regan | .20 |
| 89 | Jake Gibbs | .20 |
| 90 | Vada Pinson | .60 |
| 91 | Jim Ollom | .20 |
| 92 | Ed Kranepool | .20 |
| 93 | Tony Cloninger | .20 |
| 94 | Lee Maye | .20 |
| 95 | Bob Aspromonte | .20 |
| 96 | Senator Rookies: | .20 |
| | Frank Coggins, Dick Nold | |
| 97 | Tom Phoebus | .20 |
| 98 | Gary Sutherland | .20 |
| 99 | Rocky Colavito | .75 |
| 100 | Bob Gibson | 4.00 |
| 101 | Glenn Beckert | .20 |
| 102 | Jose Cardenal | .20 |
| 103 | Don Sutton | 1.50 |
| 104 | Dick Dietz | .20 |
| 105 | Al Downing | .20 |
| 106 | Dalton Jones | .20 |
| 107 | Checklist No. 2 | 1.00 |
| 108 | Don Pavletich | .20 |
| 109 | Bert Campaneris | .30 |
| 110 | Hank Aaron | 15.00 |
| 111 | Rich Reese | .20 |
| 112 | Woody Fryman | .20 |
| 113 | Tigers Rookies: | .20 |
| | T. Matchick, D. Patterson | |
| 114 | Ron Swoboda | .20 |

| NO. | PLAYER | MINT |
|---|---|---|
| 115 | Sam McDowell | .20 |
| 116 | Ken McMullen | .20 |
| 117 | Larry Jaster | .20 |
| 118 | Mark Belanger | .30 |
| 119 | Ted Savage | .20 |
| 120 | Mel Stottlemyre | .30 |
| 121 | Jimmie Hall | .20 |
| 122 | Gene Mauch (Mgr.) | .30 |
| 123 | Jose Santiago | .20 |
| 124 | Nate Oliver | .20 |
| 125 | Joe Horlen | .20 |
| 126 | Bobby Etheridge | .20 |
| 127 | Paul Lindblad | .20 |
| 128 | Astros Rookies: | .20 |
|  | Alonzo Harris, Tom Dukes | |
| 129 | Mickey Stanley | .20 |
| 130 | Tony Perez | 2.00 |
| 131 | Frank Bertaina | .20 |
| 132 | Bud Harrelson | .20 |
| 133 | Fred Whitfield | .20 |
| 134 | Pat Jarvis | .20 |
| 135 | Paul Blair | .20 |
| 136 | Randy Hundley | .20 |
| 137 | Minnesota Twins | .40 |
| 138 | Ruben Amaro | .20 |
| 139 | Chris Short | .20 |
| 140 | Tony Conigliaro | .45 |
| 141 | Dal Maxvill | .20 |
| 142 | White Sox Rookies: | .20 |
|  | Bill Voss, B. Bradford | |
| 143 | Pete Cimino | .20 |
| 144 | Joe Morgan | 2.50 |
| 145 | Don Drysdale | 3.00 |
| 146 | Sal Bando | .35 |
| 147 | Frank Linzy | .20 |
| 148 | Dave Bristol (Mgr.) | .20 |
| 149 | Bob Saverine | .20 |
| 150 | Bob Clemente | 12.00 |
| 151 | World Series Game 1: | 2.00 |
|  | Brock Socks 4 Hits | |
| 152 | World Series Game 2: | 2.00 |
|  | Yaz Smashes 2 Homers | |
| 153 | World Series Game 3: | 1.00 |
|  | Briles Cools Off Boston | |
| 154 | World Series Game 4: | 2.00 |
|  | Gibson Hurls Shutout | |
| 155 | World Series Game 5: | 1.00 |
|  | Lonborg Wins Again | |
| 156 | World Series Game 6: | 1.00 |
|  | Petrocelli 2 Homers | |
| 157 | World Series Game 7: | 1.00 |
|  | St. Louis Wins It | |
| 158 | World Series: | 1.00 |
|  | The Cardinal Celebrate | |
| 159 | Don Kessinger | .20 |
| 160 | Earl Wilson | .20 |
| 161 | Norm Miller | .20 |
| 162 | Cardinals Rookies: | .60 |
|  | Hal Gilson, Mike Torrez | |
| 163 | Gene Brabender | .20 |
| 164 | Ramon Webster | .20 |
| 165 | Tony Oliva | 1.00 |
| 166 | Claude Raymond | .20 |
| 167 | Elston Howard | 1.00 |
| 168 | Los Angeles Dodgers | 1.00 |
| 169 | Bob Bolin | .20 |
| 170 | Jim Fregosi | .20 |
| 171 | Don Nottebart | .20 |
| 172 | Walt Williams | .20 |
| 173 | John Boozer | .20 |
| 174 | Bob Tillman | .20 |
| 175 | Maury Wills | 1.00 |
| 176 | Bob Allen | .20 |
| 177 | Mets Rookies: | 75.00 |
|  | J. Koosman, Nolan Ryan | |
| 178 | Don Wert | .20 |
| 179 | Bill Stoneman | .20 |
| 180 | Curt Flood | .40 |
| 181 | Jerry Zimmerman | .20 |
| 182 | Dave Guisti | .20 |
| 183 | Bob Kennedy | .20 |
| 184 | Lou Johnson | .20 |
| 185 | Tom Haller | .20 |
| 186 | Eddie Watt | .20 |
| 187 | Sonny Jackson | .20 |
| 188 | Cap Peterson | .20 |
| 189 | Bill Landis | .20 |
| 190 | Bill White | .35 |
| 191 | Dan Frisella | .20 |
| 192 | Checklist No. 3 | 1.25 |
| 193 | Jack Hamilton | .20 |
| 194 | Don Buford | .20 |
| 195 | Joe Pepitone | .30 |
| 196 | Gary Nolan | .20 |
| 197 | Larry Brown | .20 |
| 198 | Roy Face | .30 |
| 199 | A's Rookies: | .25 |
|  | R. Rodriquez, D. Osteen | |
| 200 | Orlando Cepeda | 1.50 |
| 201 | Mike Marshall (R) | .75 |
| 202 | Adolfo Phillips | .20 |
| 203 | Dick Kelley | .20 |
| 204 | Andy Etchebarren | .20 |
| 205 | Juan Marichal | 2.50 |
| 206 | Cal Ermer | .20 |
| 207 | Carroll Sembera | .20 |
| 208 | Willie Davis | .35 |
| 209 | Tim Cullen | .20 |
| 210 | Gary Peters | .20 |
| 211 | J.C. Martin | .20 |
| 212 | Dave Morehead | .20 |
| 213 | Chico Ruiz | .20 |
| 214 | Yankees Rookies: | .30 |
|  | S. Bahnsen, F. Fernandez | |
| 215 | Jim Bunning | 1.00 |
| 216 | Bubba Morton | .20 |
| 217 | Turk Farrell | .20 |
| 218 | Ken Suarez | .20 |
| 219 | Rob Gardner | .20 |
| 220 | Harmon Killebrew | 3.50 |
| 221 | Atlanta Braves | .50 |
| 222 | Jim Hardin | .20 |
| 223 | Ollie Brown | .20 |
| 224 | Jack Aker | .20 |
| 225 | Richie Allen | .65 |
| 226 | Jimmie Price | .20 |
| 227 | Joe Hoerner | .20 |
| 228 | Dodgers Rookies: | .35 |
|  | Jack Billingham, Jim Fairey | |
| 229 | Fred Klages | .20 |
| 230 | Pete Rose | 40.00 |
| 231 | Dave Baldwin | .20 |
| 232 | Denis Menke | .20 |
| 233 | George Scott | .20 |
| 234 | Bill Monbouquette | .20 |
| 235 | Ron Santo | .50 |
| 236 | Tug McGraw | .75 |
| 237 | Alvin Dark (Mgr.) | .30 |
| 238 | Tom Satriano | .20 |
| 239 | Bill Henry | .20 |
| 240 | Al Kaline | 4.00 |
| 241 | Felix Millan | .20 |
| 242 | Moe Drabowsky | .20 |
| 243 | Rich Rollins | .20 |
| 244 | John Donaldson | .20 |
| 245 | Tony Gonzalez | .20 |
| 246 | Fritz Peterson | .20 |
| 247 | Reds Rookies: | 75.00 |
|  | Johnny Bench, R. Tompkins | |
| 248 | Fred Valentine | .20 |
| 249 | Bill Singer | .20 |
| 250 | Carl Yastrzemski | 18.00 |
| 251 | Manny Sanguillen (R) | .75 |
| 252 | Angels Team | .50 |
| 253 | Dick Hughes | .20 |
| 254 | Cleon Jones | .20 |
| 255 | Dean Chance | .20 |
| 256 | Norm Cash | .75 |
| 257 | Phil Niekro | 2.00 |
| 258 | Cubs Rookies: | .30 |
|  | J. Arcia, B. Schlesinger | |
| 259 | Ken Boyer | .60 |
| 260 | Jim Wynn | .35 |
| 261 | Dave Duncan | .20 |
| 262 | Rick Wise | .20 |
| 263 | Horace Clarke | .20 |
| 264 | Ted Abernathy | .20 |
| 265 | Tommy Davis | .30 |
| 266 | Paul Popovich | .20 |
| 267 | Herman Franks (Mgr.) | .20 |
| 268 | Bob Humphreys | .20 |
| 269 | Bob Tiefenauer | .20 |
| 270 | Matty Alou | .30 |
| 271 | Bobby Knoop | .20 |
| 272 | Ray Culp | .20 |
| 273 | Dave Johnson | .30 |
| 274 | Mike Cuellar | .30 |
| 275 | Tim McCarver | .50 |
| 276 | Jim Roland | .20 |
| 277 | Jerry Buchek | .20 |
| 278 | Checklist No. 4 | .75 |
| 279 | Bill Hands | .20 |
| 280 | Mickey Mantle | 40.00 |
| 281 | Jim Campanis | .20 |
| 282 | Rick Monday | .35 |
| 283 | Mel Queen | .20 |
| 284 | John Briggs | .20 |
| 285 | Dick McAuliffe | .20 |
| 286 | Cecil Upshaw | .20 |
| 287 | White Sox Rookies: | .25 |
|  | Mickey Abarbanel, Cisco Carlos | |
| 288 | Dave Wickersham | .20 |
| 289 | Woody Held | .20 |
| 290 | Willie McCovey | 4.00 |
| 291 | Dick Lines | .20 |
| 292 | Art Shamsky | .20 |
| 293 | Bruce Howard | .20 |
| 294 | Red Schoendienst | .50 |
| 295 | Sonny Siebert | .20 |
| 296 | Byron Browne | .20 |
| 297 | Russ Gibson | .20 |
| 298 | Jim Brewer | .20 |
| 299 | Gene Michael | .20 |
| 300 | Rusty Staub | .75 |
| 301 | Twins Rookies: | .25 |
|  | G. Mitterwald, R. Renick | |
| 302 | Gerry Arrigo | .20 |
| 303 | Dick Green | .20 |
| 304 | Sandy Valdespino | .20 |
| 305 | Minnie Rojas | .20 |
| 306 | Mike Ryan | .20 |
| 307 | John Hiller | .20 |
| 308 | Pittsburgh Pirates | .50 |
| 309 | Ken Henderson | .20 |
| 310 | Luis Aparicio | 2.00 |
| 311 | Jack Lamabe | .20 |
| 312 | Curt Blefary | .20 |
| 313 | Al Weis | .20 |
| 314 | Red Sox Rookies: | .20 |
|  | Bill Rohr, George Spriggs | |
| 315 | Zoilo Versalles | .20 |
| 316 | Steve Barber | .20 |
| 317 | Ron Brand | .20 |
| 318 | Chico Salmon | .20 |
| 319 | George Culver | .20 |
| 320 | Frank Howard | .65 |
| 321 | Leo Durocher (Mgr.) | .75 |
| 322 | Dave Boswell | .20 |
| 323 | Deron Johnson | .20 |
| 324 | Jim Nash | .20 |
| 325 | Manny Mota | .30 |
| 326 | Denny Ribant | .20 |
| 327 | Tony Taylor | .20 |
| 328 | Angels Rookies: | .20 |
|  | Chuck Vinson, Jim Weaver | |
| 329 | Duane Josephson | .20 |
| 330 | Roger Maris | 4.00 |
| 331 | Dan Osinski | .20 |
| 332 | Doug Rader | .20 |
| 333 | Ron Herbel | .20 |
| 334 | Baltimore Orioles | .60 |
| 335 | Bob Allison | .20 |
| 336 | John Purdin | .20 |
| 337 | Bill Robinson | .20 |
| 338 | Bob Johnson | .20 |
| 339 | Rich Nye | .20 |
| 340 | Max Alvis | .20 |
| 341 | Jim Lemon (Mgr.) | .20 |
| 342 | Ken Johnson | .20 |
| 343 | Jim Gosger | .20 |
| 344 | Don Clendenon | .20 |
| 345 | Bob Hendley | .20 |
| 346 | Jerry Adair | .20 |
| 347 | George Brunet | .20 |
| 348 | Phillies Rookies: | .20 |
|  | Larry Colton, Dick Thoenen | |
| 349 | Ed Spiezio | .20 |
| 350 | Hoyt Wilhelm | 2.00 |
| 351 | Bob Barton | .20 |
| 352 | Jackie Hernandez | .20 |
| 353 | Mack Jones | .20 |
| 354 | Pete Richert | .20 |
| 355 | Ernie Banks | 3.50 |
| 356 | Checklist No. 5 | 1.00 |
| 357 | Len Gabrielson | .20 |
| 358 | Mike Epstein | .20 |
| 359 | Joe Moeller | .20 |
| 360 | Willie Horton | .50 |
| 361 | Harmon Killebrew (AS) | 1.50 |
| 362 | Orlando Cepeda (AS) | .75 |
| 363 | Rod Carew (AS) | 2.50 |
| 364 | Joe Morgan (AS) | 1.50 |
| 365 | Brooks Robinson (AS) | 2.50 |
| 366 | Ron Santo (AS) | .50 |
| 367 | Jim Fregosi (AS) | .35 |
| 368 | Gene Alley (AS) | .35 |
| 369 | Carl Yastrzemski (AS) | 4.00 |
| 370 | Hank Aaron (AS) | 4.50 |
| 371 | Tony Oliva (AS) | .50 |
| 372 | Lou Brock (AS) | 2.50 |
| 373 | Frank Robinson (AS) | 2.50 |
| 374 | Bob Clemente (AS) | 3.50 |
| 375 | Bill Freehan (AS) | .35 |
| 376 | Tim McCarver (AS) | .50 |
| 377 | Joe Horlen (AS) | .30 |
| 378 | Bob Gibson (AS) | 2.50 |
| 379 | Gary Peters (AS) | .30 |
| 380 | Ken Holtzman (AS) | .30 |
| 381 | Boog Powell | .75 |
| 382 | Ramon Hernandez | .30 |
| 383 | Steve Whitaker | .30 |
| 384 | Reds Rookies: | 2.00 |
|  | Bill Henry, Hal McRae | |
| 385 | Jim Hunter | 2.50 |
| 386 | Greg Goossen | .20 |
| 387 | Joe Foy | .20 |
| 388 | Ray Washburn | .20 |
| 389 | Jay Johnstone | .20 |
| 390 | Bill Mazeroski | .50 |
| 391 | Bob Priddy | .20 |
| 392 | Grady Hatton (Mgr.) | .20 |
| 393 | Jim Perry | .30 |
| 394 | Tommie Aaron | .20 |
| 395 | Camilo Pascual | .20 |
| 396 | Bobby Wine | .20 |
| 397 | Vic Davalillo | .20 |
| 398 | Jim Grant | .20 |
| 399 | Ray Oyler | .20 |
| 400 | Mike McCormick | .20 |
| 401 | New York Mets | 1.00 |
| 402 | Mike Hegan | .20 |
| 403 | John Buzhardt | .20 |
| 404 | Floyd Robinson | .20 |
| 405 | Tommy Helms | .20 |
| 406 | Dick Ellsworth | .20 |
| 407 | Gary Kolb | .20 |
| 408 | Steve Carlton | 25.00 |
| 409 | Orioles Rookies: | .30 |
|  | Frank Peters, Don Stone | |
| 410 | Ferguson Jenkins | 1.50 |
| 411 | Ron Hansen | .20 |
| 412 | Clay Carroll | .20 |
| 413 | Tommy McCraw | .20 |
| 414 | Mickey Lolich | 1.00 |
| 415 | Johnny Callison | .20 |
| 416 | Bill Rigney (Mgr.) | .20 |
| 417 | Willie Crawford | .20 |
| 418 | Eddie Fisher | .20 |
| 419 | Jack Hiatt | .20 |
| 420 | Cesar Tovar | .20 |
| 421 | Ron Taylor | .20 |
| 422 | Rene Lacheman | .20 |
| 423 | Fred Gladding | .20 |
| 424 | Chicago White Sox | .50 |
| 425 | Jim Maloney | .20 |
| 426 | Hank Allen | .20 |
| 427 | Dick Calmus | .20 |
| 428 | Vic Roznovsky | .20 |
| 429 | Tommie Sisk | .20 |

# 1968 Topps (Continued)

| NO. PLAYER | MINT |
|---|---|
| 430 Rico Petrocelli | .25 |
| 431 Dooley Womack | .20 |
| 432 Indians Rookies: | .20 |
| Bill Davis, Jose Vidal | |
| 433 Bob Rodgers | .20 |
| 434 Ricardo Joseph | .20 |
| 435 Ron Perranoski | .20 |
| 436 Hal Lanier | .20 |
| 437 Don Cardwell | .20 |
| 438 Lee Thomas | .20 |
| 439 Luman Harris (Mgr.) | .20 |
| 440 Claude Osteen | .20 |
| 441 Alex Johnson | .20 |
| 442 Dick Bosman | .20 |
| 443 Joe Azcue | .20 |
| 444 Jack Fisher | .20 |
| 445 Mike Shannon | .20 |
| 446 Ron Kline | .20 |
| 447 Tigers Rookies: | .20 |
| G. Korince, F. Lasher | |
| 448 Gary Wagner | .20 |
| 449 Gene Oliver | .20 |
| 450 Jim Kaat | 1.00 |
| 451 Al Spangler | .20 |
| 452 Jesus Alou | .20 |
| 453 Sammy Ellis | .20 |
| 454 Checklist No. 6 | 1.25 |
| 455 Rico Carty | .40 |
| 456 John O'Donoghue | .20 |
| 457 Jim Lefebvre | .20 |
| 458 Lew Krausse | .30 |
| 459 Dick Simpson | .30 |
| 460 Jim Lonborg | .30 |
| 461 Chuck Hiller | .30 |
| 462 Barry Moore | .30 |
| 463 Jimmie Schaffer | .30 |
| 464 Don McMahon | .30 |
| 465 Tommie Agee | .30 |
| 466 Bill Dillman | .30 |
| 467 Dick Howser | .30 |
| 468 Larry Sherry | .30 |
| 469 Ty Cline | .30 |
| 470 Bill Freehan | .45 |
| 471 Orlando Pena | .30 |
| 472 Walt Alston (Mgr.) | .75 |
| 473 Al Worthington | .30 |

| NO. PLAYER | MINT |
|---|---|
| 474 Paul Schaal | .30 |
| 475 Joe Niekro | 1.00 |
| 476 Woody Woodward | .30 |
| 477 Philadelphia Phillies | .60 |
| 478 Dave McNally | .30 |
| 479 Phil Gagliano | .30 |
| 480 Manager's Dream: | 4.00 |
| Tony Oliva, Chico | |
| Cardenas, Bob Clemente | |
| 481 John Wyatt | .30 |
| 482 Jose Pagan | .30 |
| 483 Darold Knowles | .30 |
| 484 Phil Roof | .30 |
| 485 Ken Berry | .30 |
| 486 Cal Koonce | .30 |
| 487 Lee May | .30 |
| 488 Dick Tracewski | .30 |
| 489 Wally Bunker | .30 |
| 490 Super Stars: | 10.00 |
| Harmon Killebrew, Willie | |
| Mays, Mickey Mantle | |
| 491 Denny LeMaster | .30 |
| 492 Jeff Torborg | .30 |
| 493 Jim McGlothlin | .30 |
| 494 Ray Sadecki | .30 |
| 495 Leon Wagner | .30 |
| 496 Steve Hamilton | .30 |
| 497 St. Louis Cardinals | .75 |
| 498 Bill Bryan | .30 |
| 499 Steve Blass | .30 |
| 500 Frank Robinson | 4.50 |
| 501 John Odom | .30 |
| 502 Mike Andrews | .30 |
| 503 Al Jackson | .30 |
| 504 Russ Snyder | .30 |
| 505 Joe Sparma | .30 |
| 506 Clarence Jones | .30 |
| 507 Wade Blasingame | .30 |
| 508 Duke Sims | .30 |
| 509 Dennis Higgins | .30 |
| 510 Ron Fairly | .30 |
| 511 Bill Kelso | .30 |
| 512 Grant Jackson | .30 |
| 513 Hank Bauer (Mgr.) | .30 |
| 514 Al McBean | .30 |
| 515 Russ Nixon | .30 |

| NO. PLAYER | MINT |
|---|---|
| 516 Pete Mikkelsen | .30 |
| 517 Diego Segui | .30 |
| 518 Checklist No. 7* | 1.25 |
| 519 Jerry Stephenson | .30 |
| 520 Lou Brock | 4.00 |
| 521 Don Shaw | .30 |
| 522 Wayne Causey | .30 |
| 523 John Tsitouris | .30 |
| 524 Andy Kosco | .30 |
| 525 Jim Davenport | .30 |
| 526 Bill Denehy | .30 |
| 527 Tito Francona | .30 |
| 528 Detroit Tigers | 2.50 |
| 529 Bruce Von Hoff | .30 |
| 530 Bird Belters: | 3.50 |
| Frank Robinson, | |
| Brooks Robinson | |
| 531 Chuck Hinton | .30 |
| 532 Luis Tiant | .75 |
| 533 Wes Parker | .30 |
| 534 Bob Miller | .30 |
| 535 Danny Cater | .30 |
| 536 Bill Short | .30 |
| 537 Norm Siebern | .30 |
| 538 Manny Jimenez | .30 |
| 539 Major League Rookies: | .30 |
| Jim Ray, Mike Ferraro | |
| 540 Nelson Briles | .30 |
| 541 Sandy Alomar | .30 |
| 542 John Boccabella | .30 |
| 543 Bob Lee | .30 |
| 544 Mayo Smith (Mgr.) | .30 |
| 545 Lindy McDaniel | .30 |
| 546 Roy White | .45 |
| 547 Dan Coombs | .30 |
| 548 Bernie Allen | .30 |
| 549 Orioles Rookies: | .30 |
| Curt Motton, Roger Nelson | |
| 550 Clete Boyer | .30 |
| 551 Darrell Sutherland | .30 |
| 552 Ed Kirkpatrick | .30 |
| 553 Hank Aguirre | .30 |
| 554 Oakland A's | .75 |
| 555 Jose Tartabull | .30 |
| 556 Dick Selma | .30 |
| 557 Frank Quilici | .30 |

| NO. PLAYER | MINT |
|---|---|
| 558 John Edwards | .30 |
| 559 Pirates Rookies: | .30 |
| Carl Taylor, Luke Walker | |
| 560 Paul Casanova | .30 |
| 561 Lee Elia | .30 |
| 562 Jim Bouton | .50 |
| 563 Ed Charles | .30 |
| 564 Eddie Stanky | .30 |
| 565 Larry Dierker | .30 |
| 566 Ken Harrelson | .50 |
| 567 Clay Dalrymple | .30 |
| 568 Willie Smith | .30 |
| 569 NL Rookies: | .30 |
| Ivan Murrell, Les Rohr | |
| 570 Rick Reichardt | .30 |
| 571 Tony LaRussa | .30 |
| 572 Don Bosch | .30 |
| 573 Joe Coleman | .30 |
| 574 Cincinnati Reds | 1.00 |
| 575 Jim Palmer | 6.00 |
| 576 Dave Adlesh | .30 |
| 577 Fred Talbot | .30 |
| 578 Orlando Martinez | .30 |
| 579 NL Rookies: | .75 |
| Larry Hisle, Mike Lum | |
| 580 Bob Bailey | .30 |
| 581 Garry Roggenburk | .30 |
| 582 Jerry Grote | .30 |
| 583 Gates Brown | .30 |
| 584 Larry Shepard | .30 |
| 585 Wilbur Wood | .30 |
| 586 Jim Pagliaroni | .30 |
| 587 Roger Repoz | .30 |
| 588 Dick Schofield | .30 |
| 589 Twins Rookies: | .30 |
| Ron Clark, Moe Ogier | |
| 590 Tommy Harper | .30 |
| 591 Dick Nen | .30 |
| 592 John Bateman | .30 |
| 593 Lee Stange | .30 |
| 594 Phil Linz | .30 |
| 595 Phil Ortega | .30 |
| 596 Charlie Smith | .30 |
| 597 Bill McCool | .30 |
| 598 Jerry May | .60 |

## 1969 Topps....Complete Set of 664 Cards—Value $600.00

Includes the rookie cards of Reggie Jackson, Al Oliver and Rollie Fingers. The high numbers are 513 to 664. The values listed for the 23 cards with an *asterisk* are with the player's entire name in *yellow* letters. These cards also exist with the player's name in *white* letters—worth $4.00 each, except card no. 440—$30.00, no. 485—$15.00 and no. 500—$95.00.

    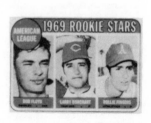

| NO. PLAYER | MINT |
|---|---|
| 1 AL Batting Leaders: | 2.00 |
| Carl Yastrzemski, Tony Oliva, Danny Cater | |
| 2 NL Batting Leaders: | 1.50 |
| Matty Alou, Felipe Alou, Pete Rose | |
| 3 AL RBI Leaders: | .75 |
| Frank Howard, Ken Harrelson, Jim Northrup | |

| NO. PLAYER | MINT |
|---|---|
| 4 NL RBI Leaders: | .75 |
| Willie McCovey, Ron Santo, Billy Williams | |
| 5 AL Home Run Leaders: | .75 |
| Frank Howard, Willie Horton, Ken Harrelson | |
| 6 NL Home Run Leaders: | 1.50 |
| Willie McCovey, Richie Allen, Ernie Banks | |

| NO. PLAYER | MINT |
|---|---|
| 7 AL ERA Leaders: | .50 |
| Luis Tiant, Sam McDowell, Dave McNally | |
| 8 NL ERA Leaders: | .75 |
| Bobby Bolin, Bob Gibson, Bob Veale | |
| 9 AL Pitching Leaders: | .50 |
| Mel Stottlemyre, Denny McLain, Dave McNally, Luis Tiant | |

| NO. PLAYER | MINT |
|---|---|
| 10 NL Pitching Leaders: | 1.50 |
| Juan Marichal, Bob Gibson, Fergie Jenkins | |
| 11 AL Strikeout Leaders: | .50 |
| Sam McDowell, Denny McLain, Luis Tiant | |
| 12 NL Strikeout Leaders: | .75 |
| Bob Gibson, Fergie Jenkins, Bill Singer | |

| NO. PLAYER | MINT |
|---|---|
| 13 Mickey Stanley | .25 |
| 14 Al McBean | .25 |
| 15 Boog Powell | .75 |
| 16 Giants Rookies: | .35 |
| C. Gutierrez, R. Robertson | |
| 17 Mike Marshall | .40 |
| 18 Dick Schofield | .25 |
| 19 Ken Suarez | .25 |
| 20 Ernie Banks | 3.00 |
| 21 Jose Santiago | .25 |
| 22 Jesus Alou | .25 |
| 23 Lew Krause | .25 |
| 24 Walt Alston (Mgr.) | .75 |
| 25 Roy White | .25 |
| 26 Clay Carroll | .25 |
| 27 Bernie Allen | .25 |
| 28 Mike Ryan | .25 |
| 29 Dave Morehead | .25 |
| 30 Bob Allison | .25 |
| 31 Mets Rookies: | 1.00 |
| Gary Gentry, Amos Otis | |
| 32 Sammy Ellis | .25 |
| 33 Wayne Causey | .25 |
| 34 Gary Peters | .25 |
| 35 Joe Morgan | 2.50 |
| 36 Luke Walker | .25 |
| 37 Curt Motton | .25 |
| 38 Zoilo Versalles | .25 |
| 39 Dick Hughes | .25 |
| 40 Mayo Smith (Mgr.) | .25 |
| 41 Bob Barton | .25 |
| 42 Tommy Harper | .25 |
| 43 Joe Niekro | .50 |
| 44 Danny Cater | .25 |
| 45 Maury Wills | 1.00 |
| 46 Fritz Peterson | .25 |
| 47 Paul Popovich | .25 |
| (without "C" on helmet) | |
| 47 Paul Popovich | 6.00 |
| (with "C" on helmet) | |
| 48 Brant Alyea | .25 |
| 49 Royals Rookies | .25 |
| Steve Jones, E. Rodriguez | |
| 49 Royals Rookies | 6.00 |
| Error—name misspelled | |
| "Rodriquez" | |
| 50 Bob Clemente | 12.00 |
| 51 Woody Fryman | .25 |
| 52 Mike Andrews | .25 |
| 53 Sonny Jackson | .25 |
| 54 Cisco Carlos | .25 |
| 55 Jerry Grote | .25 |
| 56 Rich Reese | .25 |
| 57 Checklist No. 1 | 1.00 |
| 58 Fred Gladding | .25 |
| 59 Jay Johnstone | .25 |
| 60 Nelson Briles | .25 |
| 61 Jimmie Hall | .25 |
| 62 Chico Salmon | .25 |
| 63 Jim Hickman | .25 |
| 64 Bill Monbouquette | .25 |
| 65 Willie Davis | .40 |
| 66 Orioles Rookies: | .35 |
| M. Adamson, M. Rettenmund | |
| 67 Bill Stoneman | .25 |
| 68 Dave Duncan | .25 |
| 69 Steve Hamilton | .25 |
| 70 Tommy Helms | .25 |
| 71 Steve Whitaker | .25 |
| 72 Ron Taylor | .25 |
| 73 Johnny Briggs | .25 |
| 74 Preston Gomez (Mgr.) | .25 |
| 75 Luis Aparicio | 2.00 |
| 76 Norm Miller | .25 |
| 77 Ron Perranoski | .25 |
| (no team logo on hat) | |
| 77 Ron Perranoski | 4.00 |
| (with team logo on hat) | |
| 78 Tom Satriano | .25 |
| 79 Milt Pappas | .25 |
| 80 Norm Cash | .75 |
| 81 Mel Queen | .25 |
| 82 Pirates Rookies: | 12.50 |
| Rich Hebner, Al Oliver | |
| 83 Mike Ferraro | .25 |

| NO. PLAYER | MINT |
|---|---|
| 84 Bob Humphreys | .25 |
| 85 Lou Brock | 4.00 |
| 86 Pete Richert | .25 |
| 87 Horace Clarke | .25 |
| 88 Rich Nye | .25 |
| 89 Russ Gibson | .25 |
| 90 Jerry Koosman | .75 |
| 91 Al Dark (Mgr.) | .25 |
| 92 Jack Billingham | .25 |
| 93 Joe Foy | .25 |
| 94 Hank Aguirre | .25 |
| 95 Johnny Bench | 25.00 |
| 96 Denver LeMaster | .25 |
| 97 Buddy Bradford | .25 |
| 98 Dave Giusti | .25 |
| 99 Twins Rookies: | 9.00 |
| Danny Morris, Graig Nettles | |
| 100 Hank Aaron | 12.00 |
| 101 Daryl Patterson | .25 |
| 102 Jim Davenport | .25 |
| 103 Roger Repoz | .25 |
| 104 Steve Blass | .25 |
| 105 Rick Monday | .25 |
| 106 Jim Hannan | .25 |
| 107 Checklist No.2 | 1.00 |
| (error—#161 Jim Purdin) | |
| 107 Checklist No.2 | 4.00 |
| (correct—#161 John Purdin) | |
| 108 Tony Taylor | .25 |
| 109 Jim Lonborg | .25 |
| 110 Mike Shannon | .25 |
| 111 Johnny Morris | .25 |
| 112 J.C. Martin | .25 |
| 113 Dave May | .25 |
| 114 Yankees Rookies: | .25 |
| A. Closter, J. Cumberland | |
| 115 Bill Hands | .25 |
| 116 Chuck Harrison | .25 |
| 117 Jim Fairey | .25 |
| 118 Stan Williams (Mgr.) | .25 |
| 119 Doug Rader | .25 |
| 120 Pete Rose | 30.00 |
| 121 Joe Grzenda | .25 |
| 122 Ron Fairly | .25 |
| 123 Wilbur Wood | .25 |
| 124 Hank Bauer (Mgr.) | .25 |
| 125 Ray Sadecki | .25 |
| 126 Dick Tracewski | .25 |
| 127 Kevin Collins | .25 |
| 128 Tommie Aaron | .25 |
| 129 Bill McCool | .25 |
| 130 Carl Yastrzemski | 18.00 |
| 131 Chris Cannizzaro | .25 |
| 132 Dave Baldwin | .25 |
| 133 Johnny Callison | .25 |
| 134 Jim Weaver | .25 |
| 135 Tommy Davis | .35 |
| 136 Cards Rookies: | .35 |
| Steve Huntz, Mike Torrez | |
| 137 Wally Bunker | .25 |
| 138 John Bateman | .25 |
| 139 Andy Kosco | .25 |
| 140 Jim Lefebvre | .25 |
| 141 Bill Dillman | .25 |
| 142 Woody Woodward | .25 |
| 143 Joe Nossek | .25 |
| 144 Bob Hendley | .25 |
| 145 Max Alvis | .25 |
| 146 Jim Perry | .40 |
| 147 Leo Durocher (Mgr.) | .75 |
| 148 Lee Stange | .25 |
| 149 Ollie Brown | .25 |
| 150 Denny McLain | 1.00 |
| 151 Clay Dalrymple | .25 |
| (Orioles Team) | |
| 151 Clay Dalrymple | 5.00 |
| (Phillies Team) | |
| 152 Tommie Sisk | .25 |
| 153 Ed Brinkman | .25 |
| 154 Jim Britton | .25 |
| 155 Pete Ward | .25 |
| 156 Houston Rookies: | .25 |
| Hal Gilson, Leon McFadden | |
| 157 Bob Rodgers | .25 |
| 158 Joe Gibbon | .25 |

| NO. PLAYER | MINT |
|---|---|
| 159 Jerry Adair | .25 |
| 160 Vada Pinson | .75 |
| 161 John Purdin | .25 |
| 162 World Series Game 1: | 2.00 |
| Gibson Fans 17 | |
| 163 World Series Game 2: | 1.00 |
| Tigers Deck Cards | |
| 164 World Series Game 3: | 1.00 |
| McCarver's Homer | |
| 165 World Series Game 4: | 2.00 |
| Brock Lead-Off HR | |
| 166 World Series Game 5: | 2.00 |
| Kaline's Key Hit | |
| 167 World Series Game 6: | 1.00 |
| Tigers 10-Run Inning | |
| 168 World Series Game 7: | 2.00 |
| Lolich Outduels Gibson | |
| 169 World Series: | 1.00 |
| Tigers Celebrate Victory | |
| 170 Frank Howard | .75 |
| 171 Glenn Beckert | .25 |
| 172 Jerry Stephenson | .25 |
| 173 White Sox Rookies: | .25 |
| B. Christian, G. Nyman | |
| 174 Grant Jackson | .25 |
| 175 Jim Bunning | .75 |
| 176 Joe Azcue | .25 |
| 177 Ron Reed | .25 |
| 178 Ray Oyler | .25 |
| 179 Don Pavletich | .25 |
| 180 Willie Horton | .35 |
| 181 Mel Nelson | .25 |
| 182 Bill Rigney (Mgr.) | .25 |
| 183 Don Shaw | .25 |
| 184 Roberto Pena | .25 |
| 185 Tom Phoebus | .25 |
| 186 John Edwards | .25 |
| 187 Leon Wagner | .25 |
| 188 Rick Wise | .25 |
| 189 Red Sox Rookies: | .35 |
| J. Lahoud, J. Thibadeau | |
| 190 Willie Mays | 15.00 |
| 191 Lindy McDaniel | .25 |
| 192 Jose Pagan | .25 |
| 193 Don Cardwell | .25 |
| 194 Ted Uhlaender | .25 |
| 195 John Odom | .25 |
| 196 Lum Harris (Mgr.) | .25 |
| 197 Dick Selma | .25 |
| 198 Willie Smith | .25 |
| 199 Jim French | .25 |
| 200 Bob Gibson | 3.00 |
| 201 Russ Snyder | .25 |
| 202 Don Wilson | .25 |
| 203 Dave Johnson | .35 |
| 204 Jack Hiatt | .25 |
| 205 Rick Reichardt | .25 |
| 206 Phillies Rookies: | .35 |
| Larry Hisle, Barry Lersch | |
| 207 Roy Face | .35 |
| 208 Donn Clendenon | .25 |
| (Astros Team) | |
| 208 Donn Clendenon | 5.00 |
| (Expos Team) | |
| 209 Larry Haney | .25 |
| (negative reversed) | |
| 210 Felix Millan | .25 |
| 211 Galen Cisco | .25 |
| 212 Tom Tresh | .25 |
| 213 Gerry Arrigo | .25 |
| 214 Checklist No. 3 | 1.00 |
| 215 Rico Petrocelli | .25 |
| 216 Don Sutton | 1.50 |
| 217 John Donaldson | .25 |
| 218 John Roseboro | .25 |
| 219 Freddie Patek | .35 |
| 220 Sam McDowell | .35 |
| 221 Art Shamsky | .35 |
| 222 Duane Josephson | .35 |
| 223 Tom Dukes | .35 |
| 224 Angels Rookies: | .45 |
| B. Harrelson, S. Kealey | |
| 225 Don Kessinger | .35 |
| 226 Bruce Howard | .35 |
| 227 Frank Johnson | .35 |

| NO. PLAYER | MINT |
|---|---|
| 228 Dave Leonhard | .35 |
| 229 Don Lock | .35 |
| 230 Rusty Staub | .75 |
| 231 Pat Dobson | .35 |
| 232 Dave Ricketts | .35 |
| 233 Steve Barber | .35 |
| 234 Dave Bristol (Mgr.) | .35 |
| 235 Jim Hunter | 2.00 |
| 236 Manny Mota | .50 |
| 237 Bobby Cox | .45 |
| 238 Ken Johnson | .35 |
| 239 Bob Taylor | .35 |
| 240 Ken Harrelson | .50 |
| 241 Jim Brewer | .35 |
| 242 Frank Kostro | .35 |
| 243 Ron Kline | .35 |
| 244 Indians Rookies: | .50 |
| R. Fosse, G. Woodson | |
| 245 Ed Charles | .35 |
| 246 Joe Coleman | .35 |
| 247 Gene Oliver | .35 |
| 248 Bob Priddy | .35 |
| 249 Ed Spiezio | .35 |
| 250 Frank Robinson | 7.50 |
| 251 Ron Herbel | .35 |
| 252 Chuck Cottier | .35 |
| 253 Jerry Johnson | .35 |
| 254 Joe Schultz (Mgr.) | .35 |
| 255 Steve Carlton | 24.00 |
| 256 Gates Brown | .35 |
| 257 Jim Ray | .35 |
| 258 Jackie Hernandez | .35 |
| 259 Bill Short | .35 |
| 260 Reggie Jackson (R) | 110.00 |
| 261 Bob Johnson | .35 |
| 262 Mike Kekich | .35 |
| 263 Jerry May | .35 |
| 264 Bill Landis | .35 |
| 265 Chico Cardenas | .35 |
| 266 Dodger Rookies: | .50 |
| Tom Hutton, Alan Foster | |
| 267 Vicente Romo | .35 |
| 268 Al Spangler | .35 |
| 269 Al Weis | .35 |
| 270 Mickey Lolich | 1.00 |
| 271 Larry Stahl | .35 |
| 272 Ed Stroud | .35 |
| 273 Ron Willis | .35 |
| 274 Clyde King (Mgr.) | .35 |
| 275 Vic Davalillo | .35 |
| 276 Gary Wagner | .35 |
| 277 Ron Hendricks | .35 |
| 278 Gary Geiger | .35 |
| 279 Roger Nelson | .35 |
| 280 Alex Johnson | .35 |
| 281 Ted Kubiak | .35 |
| 282 Pat Jarvis | .35 |
| 283 Sandy Alomar | .35 |
| 284 Expos Rookies: | .40 |
| M. Wegener, J. Robertson | |
| 285 Don Mincher | .35 |
| 286 Dock Ellis | .35 |
| 287 Jose Tartabull | .35 |
| 288 Ken Holtzman | .35 |
| 289 Bart Shirley | .35 |
| 290 Jim Kaat | 1.50 |
| 291 Vern Fuller | .35 |
| 292 Al Downing | .35 |
| 293 Dick Dietz | .35 |
| 294 Jim Lemon | .35 |
| 295 Tony Perez | 2.00 |
| 296 Andy Messersmith (R) | .50 |
| 297 Deron Johnson | .35 |
| 298 Dave Nicholson | .35 |
| 299 Mark Belanger | .50 |
| 300 Felipe Alou | .50 |
| 301 Darrell Brandon | .35 |
| 302 Jim Pagliaroni | .35 |
| 303 Cal Koonce | .35 |
| 304 Padres Rookies: | .35 |
| Bill Davis, Clarence Gaston | |
| 305 Dick McAuliffe | .35 |
| 306 Jim Grant | .35 |
| 307 Gary Kolb | .35 |
| 308 Wade Blasingame | .35 |

| NO. PLAYER | MINT |
|---|---|
| 309 Walt Williams | .35 |
| 310 Tom Haller | .35 |
| 311 Sparky Lyle (R) | 1.50 |
| 312 Lee Elia | .35 |
| 313 Bill Robinson | .35 |
| 314 Checklist No. 4 | 1.00 |
| 315 Eddie Fisher | .35 |
| 316 Hal Lanier | .35 |
| 317 Bruce Look | .35 |
| 318 Jack Fisher | .35 |
| 319 Ken McMullen | .35 |
| 320 Dal Maxvill | .35 |
| 321 Jim McAndrew | .35 |
| 322 Jose Vidal | .35 |
| 323 Larry Miller | .35 |
| 324 Tiger Rookies: | .50 |
|     Les Cain, Dave Campbell | |
| 325 Jose Cardenal | .35 |
| 326 Gary Sutherland | .35 |
| 327 Willie Crawford | .35 |
| 328 Joe Horlen | .25 |
| 329 Rick Joseph | .25 |
| 330 Tony Conigliaro | .50 |
| 331 Braves Rookies: | .35 |
|     Tom House, Gil Garrido | |
| 332 Fred Talbot | .25 |
| 333 Ivan Murrell | .25 |
| 334 Phil Roof | .25 |
| 335 Bill Mazeroski | .50 |
| 336 Jim Roland | .25 |
| 337 Marty Martinez | .25 |
| 338 Del Unser | .25 |
| 339 Reds Rookies: | .35 |
|     Steve Mingori, Jose Pena | |
| 340 Dave McNally | .30 |
| 341 Dave Adlesh | .25 |
| 342 Bubba Morton | .25 |
| 343 Dan Frisella | .25 |
| 344 Tom Matchick | .25 |
| 345 Frank Linzy | .25 |
| 346 Wayne Comer | .25 |
| 347 Randy Hundley | .25 |
| 348 Steve Hargan | .25 |
| 349 Dick Williams (Mgr.) | .25 |
| 350 Richie Allen | .60 |
| 351 Carroll Sembera | .25 |
| 352 Paul Schaal | .25 |
| 353 Jeff Torborg | .25 |
| 354 Nate Oliver | .25 |
| 355 Phil Niekro | 2.00 |
| 356 Frank Quilici | .25 |
| 357 Carl Taylor | .25 |
| 358 Athletics Rookies: | .25 |
|     George Lauzerique, | |
|     Roberto Rodriguez | |
| 359 Dick Kelley | .25 |
| 360 Jim Wynn | .25 |
| 361 Gary Holman | .25 |
| 362 Jim Maloney | .25 |
| 363 Russ Nixon | .25 |
| 364 Tommie Agee | .25 |
| 365 Jim Fregosi | .25 |
| 366 Bo Belinsky | .25 |
| 367 Lou Johnson | .25 |
| 368 Vic Roznovsky | .25 |
| 369 Bob Skinner (Mgr.) | .25 |
| 370 Juan Marichal | 2.50 |
| 371 Sal Bando | .50 |
| 372 Adolfo Phillips | .25 |
| 373 Fred Lasher | .25 |
| 374 Bob Tillman | .25 |
| 375 Harmon Killebrew | 5.00 |
| 376 Royals Rookies: | .35 |
|     Mike Fiore, Jim Rooker | |
| 377 Gary Bell | .25 |
| 378 Jose Herrera | .25 |
| 379 Ken Boyer | .75 |
| 380 Stan Bahnsen | .25 |
| 381 Ed Kranepool | .25 |
| 382 Pat Corrales | .25 |
| 383 Casey Cox | .25 |
| 384 Larry Shepard | .25 |
| 385 Orlando Cepeda | 1.25 |
| 386 Jim McGlothlin | .25 |

| NO. PLAYER | MINT |
|---|---|
| 387 Bobby Klaus | .25 |
| 388 Tom McCraw | .25 |
| 389 Dan Coombs | .25 |
| 390 Bill Freehan | .35 |
| 391 Ray Culp | .25 |
| 392 Bob Burda | .25 |
| 393 Gene Brabender | .25 |
| 394 Pilots Rookies: | 1.00 |
|     Lou Piniella, M. Staehle | |
| 395 Chris Short | .25 |
| 396 Jim Campanis | .25 |
| 397 Chuck Dobson | .25 |
| 398 Tito Francona | .25 |
| 399 Bob Bailey | .25 |
| 400 Don Drysdale | 3.00 |
| 401 Jake Gibbs | .25 |
| 402 Ken Boswell | .25 |
| 403 Bob Miller | .25 |
| 404 Cubs Rookies: | .35 |
|     Vic LaRose, Gary Ross | |
| 405 Lee May | .25 |
| 406 Phil Ortega | .25 |
| 407 Tom Egan | .25 |
| 408 Nate Colbert | .25 |
| 409 Bob Moose | .25 |
| 410 Al Kaline | 3.50 |
| 411 Larry Dierker | .25 |
| 412 Checklist No. 5 | 2.00 |
| 413 Roland Sheldon | .25 |
| 414 Duke Sims | .25 |
| 415 Ray Washburn | .25 |
| 416 Willie McCovey (AS) | 2.00 |
| 417 Ken Harrelson (AS) | .35 |
| 418 Tommy Helms (AS) | .35 |
| 419 Rod Carew (AS) | 3.00 |
| 420 Ron Santo (AS) | .35 |
| 421 Brooks Robinson (AS) | 2.50 |
| 422 Don Kessinger (AS) | .35 |
| 423 Bert Campaneris (AS) | .35 |
| 424 Pete Rose (AS) | 6.00 |
| 425 Carl Yastrzemski (AS) | 4.00 |
| 426 Curt Flood (AS) | .35 |
| 427 Tony Oliva (AS) | .50 |
| 428 Lou Brock (AS) | 2.00 |
| 429 Willie Horton (AS) | .35 |
| 430 Johnny Bench (AS) | 3.00 |
| 431 Bill Freehan (AS) | .35 |
| 432 Bob Gibson (AS) | 2.00 |
| 433 Denny McLain (AS) | .50 |
| 434 Jerry Koosman (AS) | .35 |
| 435 Sam McDowell (AS) | .35 |
| 436 Gene Alley | .25 |
| 437 Luis Alcaraz | .25 |
| 438 Gary Waslewski | .25 |
| 439 White Sox Rookies: | .35 |
|     Ed Herrmann, Dan Lazar | |
| 440 Willie McCovey* | 6.00 |
| 441 Dennis Higgins* | .25 |
| 442 Ty Cline | .25 |
| 443 Don Wert | .25 |
| 444 Joe Moeller* | .25 |
| 445 Bobby Knoop | .25 |
| 446 Claude Raymond | .25 |
| 447 Ralph Houk (Mgr.)* | .50 |
| 448 Bob Tolan | .25 |
| 449 Paul Lindblad | .25 |
| 450 Billy Williams | 1.50 |
| 451 Rich Rollins* | .25 |
| 452 Al Ferrara* | .25 |
| 453 Mike Cuellar | .50 |
| 454 Phillies Rookies:* | .35 |
|     Larry Colton, Don Money | |
| 455 Sonny Siebert | .25 |
| 456 Bud Harrelson | .25 |
| 457 Dalton Jones | .25 |
| 458 Curt Blefary | .25 |
| 459 Dave Boswell | .25 |
| 460 Joe Torre | .60 |
| 461 Mike Epstein* | .25 |
| 462 Red Schoendienst | .50 |
| 463 Dennis Ribant | .25 |
| 464 Dave Marshall* | .25 |
| 465 Tommy John* | 1.25 |
| 466 John Boccabella | .25 |

| NO. PLAYER | MINT |
|---|---|
| 467 Tom Reynolds | .25 |
| 468 Pirates Rookies:* | .35 |
|     Bruce Del Canton, | |
|     Bob Robertson | |
| 469 Chico Ruiz | .25 |
| 470 Mel Stottlemyre* | .50 |
| 471 Ted Savage* | .25 |
| 472 Jim Price | .25 |
| 473 Jose Arcia* | .25 |
| 474 Tom Murphy | .25 |
| 475 Tim McCarver | .40 |
| 476 Boston Rookies:* | .35 |
|     Ken Brett, Gerry Moses | |
| 477 Jeff James | .25 |
| 478 Don Buford | .25 |
| 479 Richie Scheinblum | .25 |
| 480 Tom Seaver | 25.00 |
| 481 Bill Melton | .25 |
| 482 Jim Gosger* | .25 |
| 483 Ted Abernathy | .25 |
| 484 Joe Gordon | .25 |
| 485 Gaylord Perry* | 2.50 |
| 486 Paul Casanova* | .25 |
| 487 Denis Menke | .25 |
| 488 Joe Sparma | .25 |
| 489 Clete Boyer | .35 |
| 490 Matty Alou | .25 |
| 491 Twins Rookies:* | .35 |
|     Jerry Crider, | |
|     George Mitterwald | |
| 492 Tony Cloninger | .25 |
| 493 Wes Parker* | .25 |
| 494 Ken Berry | .25 |
| 495 Bert Campaneris | .35 |
| 496 Larry Jaster | .25 |
| 497 Julian Javier | .25 |
| 498 Juan Pizarro | .25 |
| 499 Astro Rookies: | .35 |
|     Don Bryant, Steve Shea | |
| 500 Mickey Mantle | 45.00 |
| 501 Tony Gonzalez* | .25 |
| 502 Minnie Rojas | .25 |
| 503 Larry Brown | .25 |
| 504 Checklist No. 6 | 1.25 |
| 505 Bobby Bolin* | .25 |
| 506 Paul Blair | .25 |
| 507 Cookie Rojas | .25 |
| 508 Moe Drabowsky | .25 |
| 509 Manny Sanguillen | .35 |
| 510 Rod Carew | 20.00 |
| 511 Diego Segui* | .25 |
| 512 Cleon Jones | .25 |
| 513 Camilo Pascual | .25 |
| 514 Mike Lum | .25 |
| 515 Dick Green | .25 |
| 516 Earl Weaver (Mgr.) | 2.00 |
| 517 Mike McCormick | .25 |
| 518 Fred Whitfield | .25 |
| 519 Yankees Rookies: | .35 |
|     G. Kenney, Len Boehmer | |
| 520 Bob Veale | .25 |
| 521 George Thomas | .25 |
| 522 Joe Hoerner | .25 |
| 523 Bob Chance | .25 |
| 524 Expos Rookies: | .25 |
|     Jose Laboy, Floyd Wicker | |
| 525 Earl Wilson | .25 |
| 526 Hector Torres | .25 |
| 527 Al Lopez (Mgr.) | .75 |
| 528 Claude Osteen | .25 |
| 529 Ed Kirkpatrick | .25 |
| 530 Cesar Tovar | .25 |
| 531 Dick Farrell | .25 |
| 532 Bird Bird Aces: | .50 |
|     D. McNally, T. Phoebus, | |
|     J. Hardin, M. Cuellar | |
| 533 Nolan Ryan | 18.00 |
| 534 Jerry McNertney | .25 |
| 535 Phil Regan | .25 |
| 536 Padres Rookies: | .35 |
|     D. Breeden, Dave Roberts | |
| 537 Mike Paul | .25 |
| 538 Charlie Smith | .25 |
| 539 Ted Shows How: | 1.50 |
|     Mike Epstein, Ted Williams | |

| NO. PLAYER | MINT |
|---|---|
| 540 Curt Flood | .50 |
| 541 Joe Verbanic | .25 |
| 542 Bob Aspromonte | .25 |
| 543 Fred Newman | .25 |
| 544 Tigers Rookies: | .45 |
|     Mike Kilkenny, Ron Woods | |
| 545 Willie Stargell | 3.00 |
| 546 Jim Nash | .25 |
| 547 Billy Martin (Mgr.) | 1.00 |
| 548 Bob Locker | .25 |
| 549 Ron Brand | .25 |
| 550 Brooks Robinson | 6.00 |
| 551 Wayne Granger | .25 |
| 552 Dodgers Rookies: | .50 |
|     Ted Sizemore, Bill Sudakis | |
| 553 Ron Davis | .25 |
| 554 Frank Bertaina | .25 |
| 555 Jim Hart | .25 |
| 556 A's Stars: | .50 |
|     Bert Campaneris, Sal | |
|     Bando, Danny Cater | |
| 557 Frank Fernandez | .25 |
| 558 Tom Burgmeier | .25 |
| 559 Cardinals Rookies: | .35 |
|     Joe Hague, Jim Hicks | |
| 560 Luis Tiant | .50 |
| 561 Ron Clark | .25 |
| 562 Bob Watson (R) | .75 |
| 563 Marty Pattin | .25 |
| 564 Gil Hodges (Mgr.) | 2.50 |
| 565 Hoyt Wilhelm | 2.50 |
| 566 Ron Hansen | .25 |
| 567 Pirates Rookies: | .35 |
|     Elvio Jimenez, | |
|     Jim Shellenback | |
| 568 Cecil Upshaw | .25 |
| 569 Billy Harris | .25 |
| 570 Ron Santo | .50 |
| 571 Cap Peterson | .25 |
| 572 Giants Heroes: | 3.00 |
|     Willie McCovey, | |
|     Juan Marichal | |
| 573 Jim Palmer | 6.00 |
| 574 George Scott | .25 |
| 575 Bill Singer | .25 |
| 576 Phillies Rookies: | .35 |
|     Ron Stone, Bill Wilson | |
| 577 Mike Hegan | .25 |
| 578 Don Bosch | .25 |
| 579 Dave Nelson | .25 |
| 580 Jim Northrup | .25 |
| 581 Gary Nolan | .25 |
| 582 Checklist No. 7 | 1.00 |
| 583 Clyde Wright | .25 |
| 584 Don Mason | .25 |
| 585 Ron Swoboda | .35 |
| 586 Tim Cullen | .25 |
| 587 Joe Rudi (R) | .75 |
| 588 Bill White | .35 |
| 589 Joe Pepitone | .45 |
| 590 Rico Carty | .35 |
| 591 Mike Hedlund | .25 |
| 592 Padres Rookies: | .35 |
|     R. Robles, Al Santorini | |
| 593 Don Nottebart | .25 |
| 594 Dooley Womack | .25 |
| 595 Lee Maye | .25 |
| 596 Chuck Hartenstein | .25 |
| 597 AL Rookies: | 13.00 |
|     Bob Floyd, Larry Burchart, | |
|     Rollie Fingers | |
| 598 Ruben Amaro | .25 |
| 599 John Boozer | .25 |
| 600 Tony Oliva | 1.00 |
| 601 Tug McGraw | .75 |
| 602 Cubs Rookies: | .35 |
|     Alec Distaso, Jim Qualls, | |
|     Don Young | |
| 603 Joe Keough | .25 |
| 604 Bobby Etheridge | .25 |
| 605 Dick Ellsworth | .25 |
| 606 Gene Mauch (Mgr.) | .35 |
| 607 Dick Bosman | .25 |
| 608 Dick Simpson | .25 |

| NO. | PLAYER | MINT |
|---|---|---|
| 609 | Phil Gagliano | .25 |
| 610 | Jim Hardin | .25 |
| 611 | Braves Rookies: Bob Didier, Walt Hriniak, Gary Neibauer | .35 |
| 612 | Jack Aker | .25 |
| 613 | Jim Beauchamp | .25 |
| 614 | Houston Rookies: Tom Griffin, Skip Guinn | .35 |
| 615 | Len Gabrielson | .25 |
| 616 | Don McMahon | .25 |
| 617 | Jesse Gonder | .25 |
| 618 | Ramon Webster | .25 |
| 619 | Royals Rookies: Pat Kelly, Juan Rios, Bill Butler | .50 |
| 620 | Dean Chance | .25 |
| 621 | Bill Voss | .25 |
| 622 | Dan Osinski | .25 |
| 623 | Hank Allen | .25 |

| NO. | PLAYER | MINT |
|---|---|---|
| 624 | NL Rookies: Darrel Chaney, Duffy Dyer, Terry Harmon | .25 |
| 625 | Mack Jones | .25 |
| 626 | Gene Michael | .25 |
| 627 | George Stone | .25 |
| 628 | Red Sox Rookies: Bill Conigliaro, Syd O'Brien, Fred Wenz | .50 |
| 629 | Jack Hamilton | .25 |
| 630 | Bobby Bonds (R) | 2.00 |
| 631 | John Kennedy | .25 |
| 632 | Jon Warden | .25 |
| 633 | Harry Walker (Mgr.) | .25 |
| 634 | Andy Etchebarren | .25 |
| 635 | George Culver | .25 |
| 636 | Woodie Held | .25 |
| 637 | Padres Rookies: Jerry DaVanon, Frank Reberger, Clay Kirby | .35 |

| NO. | PLAYER | MINT |
|---|---|---|
| 638 | Ed Sprague | .25 |
| 639 | Barry Moore | .25 |
| 640 | Fergie Jenkins | 1.50 |
| 641 | NL Rookies: Bobby Darwin, John Miller, Tommy Dean | .25 |
| 642 | John Hiller | .25 |
| 643 | Billy Cowan | .25 |
| 644 | Chuck Hinton | .25 |
| 645 | George Brunet | .25 |
| 646 | Expos Rookies: Carl Morton, Dan McGinn | .25 |
| 647 | Dave Wickersham | .25 |
| 648 | Bobby Wine | .25 |
| 649 | Al Jackson | .25 |
| 650 | Ted Williams (Mgr.) | 2.50 |
| 651 | Gus Gil | .25 |
| 652 | Eddie Watt | .25 |
| 653 | Aurelio Rodriguez (Photo of Angels Batboy) | 1.00 |

| NO. | PLAYER | MINT |
|---|---|---|
| 654 | White Sox Rookies: Carlos May, Don Secrist, Rich Morales | .35 |
| 655 | Mike Hershberger | .25 |
| 656 | Dan Schneider | .25 |
| 657 | Bobby Murcer | .75 |
| 658 | AL Rookies: Tom Hall, Bill Burbach, Jim Miles | .25 |
| 659 | Johnny Podres | .50 |
| 660 | Reggie Smith | .75 |
| 661 | Jim Merritt | .25 |
| 662 | Royals Rookies: Dick Drago, Bob Oliver, George Spriggs | .35 |
| 663 | Dick Radatz | .25 |
| 664 | Ron Hunt | .50 |

## 1970 Topps....Complete Set of 720 Cards—Value $650.00

Features the rookie cards of Thurman Munson, Darrell Evans, Vida Blue, and Bill Buckner. The high numbers are 634 to 720. Card 588 (checklist) exists with *Adolpho* misspelled *Adolfo*—worth $3.00.

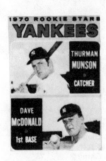
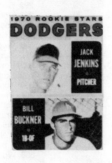

| NO. | PLAYER | MINT |
|---|---|---|
| 1 | World Champion Mets | 2.50 |
| 2 | Diego Segui | .20 |
| 3 | Darrel Chaney | .20 |
| 4 | Tom Egan | .20 |
| 5 | Wes Parker | .20 |
| 6 | Grant Jackson | .20 |
| 7 | Indians Rookies: Gary Boyd, Russ Nagelson | .20 |
| 8 | Jose Martinez | .20 |
| 9 | Checklist No. 1 | .75 |
| 10 | Carl Yastrzemski | 18.00 |
| 11 | Nate Colbert | .20 |
| 12 | John Hiller | .20 |
| 13 | Jack Hiatt | .20 |
| 14 | Hank Allen | .20 |
| 15 | Larry Dierker | .20 |
| 16 | Charlie Metro | .20 |
| 17 | Hoyt Wilhelm | 2.00 |
| 18 | Carlos May | .20 |
| 19 | John Boccabella | .20 |
| 20 | Dave McNally | .20 |
| 21 | A's Rookies: Gene Tenace, Vida Blue | 2.00 |
| 22 | Ray Washburn | .20 |
| 23 | Bill Robinson | .20 |
| 24 | Dick Selma | .20 |
| 25 | Cesar Tovar | .20 |
| 26 | Tug McGraw | .50 |
| 27 | Chuck Hinton | .20 |
| 28 | Billy Wilson | .20 |
| 29 | Sandy Alomar | .20 |
| 30 | Matty Alou | .20 |
| 31 | Marty Pattin | .20 |
| 32 | Harry Walker | .20 |
| 33 | Don Wert | .20 |
| 34 | Willie Crawford | .20 |
| 35 | Joe Horlen | .20 |

| NO. | PLAYER | MINT |
|---|---|---|
| 36 | Red Rookies: D. Breeden, B. Carbo | .20 |
| 37 | Dick Drago | .20 |
| 38 | Mack Jones | .20 |
| 39 | Mike Nagy | .20 |
| 40 | Rich Allen | .50 |
| 41 | George Lauzerique | .20 |
| 42 | Tito Fuentes | .20 |
| 43 | Jack Aker | .20 |
| 44 | Roberto Pena | .20 |
| 45 | Dave Johnson | .20 |
| 46 | Ken Rudolph | .20 |
| 47 | Bob Miller | .20 |
| 48 | Gil Garrido | .20 |
| 49 | Tim Cullen | .20 |
| 50 | Tommie Agee | .20 |
| 51 | Bob Christian | .20 |
| 52 | Bruce Dal Canton | .20 |
| 53 | John Kennedy | .20 |
| 54 | Jeff Torborg | .20 |
| 55 | John Odom | .20 |
| 56 | Phillies Rookies: Joe Lis, Scott Reid | .20 |
| 57 | Pat Kelly | .20 |
| 58 | Dave Marshall | .20 |
| 59 | Dick Ellsworth | .20 |
| 60 | Jim Wynn | .20 |
| 61 | NL Batting Leaders: Cleon Jones, Pete Rose, Bob Clemente | 2.50 |
| 62 | AL Batting Leaders: Rod Carew, Reggie Smith, Tony Oliva | 1.00 |
| 63 | NL RBI Leaders: Ron Santo, Tony Perez, Willie McCovey | 1.00 |

| NO. | PLAYER | MINT |
|---|---|---|
| 64 | AL RBI Leaders: Harmon Killebrew, Boog Powell, Reggie Jackson | 1.00 |
| 65 | NL Home Run Leaders: Hank Aaron, Willie McCovey, Lee May | 1.00 |
| 66 | AL Home Run Leaders: Harmon Killebrew, Frank Howard, Reggie Jackson | 1.00 |
| 67 | NL ERA Leaders: Bob Gibson, Juan Marichal, Steve Carlton | 1.50 |
| 68 | AL ERA Leaders: Dick Bosman, Jim Palmer, Mike Cuellar | .75 |
| 69 | NL Pitching Leaders: Phil Niekro, Tom Seaver, F. Jenkins, Juan Marichal | 1.50 |
| 70 | AL Pitching Leaders: Dennis McLain, Mike Cuellar, Dave McNally, Jim Perry, Dave Boswell, Mel Stottlemyre | .50 |
| 71 | NL Strikeout Leaders: Fergie Jenkins, Bob Gibson, Bill Singer | .75 |
| 72 | AL Strikeout Leaders: Andy Messersmith, Sam McDowell, Mickey Lolich | .50 |
| 73 | Wayne Granger | .20 |
| 74 | Angels Rookies: Greg Washburn, Wally Wolf | .30 |
| 75 | Jim Kaat | .75 |
| 76 | Carl Taylor | .20 |
| 77 | Frank Linzy | .20 |
| 78 | Joe Lahoud | .20 |
| 79 | Clay Kirby | .20 |

| NO. | PLAYER | MINT |
|---|---|---|
| 80 | Don Kessinger | .20 |
| 81 | Dave May | .20 |
| 82 | Frank Fernandez | .20 |
| 83 | Don Cardwell | .20 |
| 84 | Paul Casanova | .20 |
| 85 | Max Alvis | .20 |
| 86 | Lum Harris (Mgr.) | .20 |
| 87 | Steve Renko | .20 |
| 88 | Pilots Rookies: Miguel Fuentes, Dick Baney | .20 |
| 89 | Juan Rios | .20 |
| 90 | Tim McCarver | .50 |
| 91 | Rich Morales | .20 |
| 92 | George Culver | .20 |
| 93 | Rick Renick | .20 |
| 94 | Fred Patek | .20 |
| 95 | Earl Wilson | .20 |
| 96 | Cardinals Rookies: Leron Lee, Jerry Reuss | 1.50 |
| 97 | Joe Moeller | .20 |
| 98 | Gates Brown | .20 |
| 99 | Bobby Pfeil | .20 |
| 100 | Mel Stottlemyre | .20 |
| 101 | Bobby Floyd | .20 |
| 102 | Joe Rudi | .20 |
| 103 | Frank Reberger | .20 |
| 104 | Gerry Moses | .20 |
| 105 | Tony Gonzalez | .20 |
| 106 | Darold Knowles | .20 |
| 107 | Bobby Etheridge | .20 |
| 108 | Tom Burgmeier | .20 |
| 109 | Expos Rookies: Garry Jestadt, Carl Morton | .20 |
| 110 | Bob Moose | .20 |
| 111 | Mike Hegan | .20 |
| 112 | Dave Nelson | .20 |
| 113 | Jim Ray | .20 |

| NO. PLAYER | MINT |
|---|---|
| 114 Gene Michael | .20 |
| 115 Alex Johnson | .20 |
| 116 Sparky Lyle | .40 |
| 117 Don Young | .20 |
| 118 George Mitterwald | .20 |
| 119 Chuck Taylor | .20 |
| 120 Sal Bando | .35 |
| 121 Orioles Rookies: | .30 |
| Fred Beene, Terry Crowley | |
| 122 George Stone | .20 |
| 123 Don Gutteridge (Mgr.) | .20 |
| 124 Larry Jaster | .20 |
| 125 Deron Johnson | .20 |
| 126 Marty Martinez | .20 |
| 127 Joe Coleman | .20 |
| 128 Checklist No. 2 | .75 |
| 129 Jimmie Price | .20 |
| 130 Ollie Brown | .20 |
| 131 Dodgers Rookies: | .30 |
| Ray Lamb, Bob Stinson | |
| 132 Jim McGlothlin | .20 |
| 133 Clay Carroll | .20 |
| 134 Danny Walton | .20 |
| 135 Dick Dietz | .20 |
| 136 Steve Hargan | .20 |
| 137 Art Shamsky | .20 |
| 138 Joe Foy | .20 |
| 139 Rich Nye | .20 |
| 140 Reggie Jackson | 22.00 |
| 141 Pirates Rookies: | .30 |
| Dave Cash, Johnny Jeter | |
| 142 Fritz Peterson | .20 |
| 143 Phil Gagliano | .20 |
| 144 Ray Culp | .20 |
| 145 Rico Carty | .35 |
| 146 Danny Murphy | .20 |
| 147 Angel Hermoso | .20 |
| 148 Earl Weaver (Mgr.) | .75 |
| 149 Billy Champion | .20 |
| 150 Harmon Killebrew | 3.00 |
| 151 Dave Roberts | .20 |
| 152 Ike Brown | .20 |
| 153 Gary Gentry | .20 |
| 154 Senators Rookies: | .25 |
| Jim Miles, Jan Dukes | |
| 155 Denis Menke | .20 |
| 156 Eddie Fisher | .20 |
| 157 Manny Mota | .30 |
| 158 Jerry McNertney | .20 |
| 159 Tommy Helms | .20 |
| 160 Phil Niekro | 2.00 |
| 161 Richie Scheinblum | .20 |
| 162 Jerry Johnson | .20 |
| 163 Syd O'Brien | .20 |
| 164 Ty Cline | .20 |
| 165 Ed Kirkpatrick | .20 |
| 166 Al Oliver | 2.50 |
| 167 Bill Burbach | .20 |
| 168 Dave Watkins | .20 |
| 169 Tom Hall | .20 |
| 170 Billy Williams | 1.50 |
| 171 Jim Nash | .20 |
| 172 Braves Rookies: | .50 |
| Garry Hill, Ralph Garr | |
| 173 Jim Hicks | .20 |
| 174 Ted Sizemore | .20 |
| 175 Dick Bosman | .20 |
| 176 Jim Hart | .20 |
| 177 Jim Northrup | .20 |
| 178 Denny Lemaster | .20 |
| 179 Ivan Murrell | .20 |
| 180 Tommy John | 1.25 |
| 181 Sparky Anderson | .40 |
| 182 Dick Hall | .20 |
| 183 Jerry Grote | .20 |
| 184 Ray Fosse | .20 |
| 185 Don Mincher | .20 |
| 186 Rick Joseph | .20 |
| 187 Mike Hedlund | .20 |
| 188 Manny Sanguillen | .20 |
| 189 Yankees Rookies: | 20.00 |
| Thurman Munson, Dave McDonald | |
| 190 Joe Torre | .50 |
| 191 Vicente Romo | .20 |

| NO. PLAYER | MINT |
|---|---|
| 192 Jim Qualls | .20 |
| 193 Mike Wegener | .20 |
| 194 Chuck Manuel | .20 |
| 195 NL Playoff Game 1: | 1.25 |
| Seaver Wins Opener | |
| 196 NL Playoff Game 2: | .75 |
| Mets Show Muscle | |
| 197 NL Playoff Game 3: | 1.25 |
| Ryan Saves the Day | |
| 198 We're Number One | .75 |
| Mets Celebrate | |
| 199 AL Playoff Game 1: | .75 |
| Orioles Win Squeaker | |
| 200 AL Playoff Game 2: | .75 |
| Powell Scores Winning Run | |
| 201 AL Playoff Game 3: | .75 |
| Birds Wrap it Up | |
| 202 Sweep Twins in Three! | .75 |
| Orioles Celebrate | |
| 203 Rudy May | .20 |
| 204 Len Gabrielson | .20 |
| 205 Bert Campaneris | .30 |
| 206 Clete Boyer | .20 |
| 207 Tigers Rookies: | .35 |
| Norman McRae, Bob Reed | |
| 208 Fred Gladding | .20 |
| 209 Ken Suarez | .20 |
| 210 Juan Marichal | 2.00 |
| 211 Ted Williams (Mgr.) | 2.00 |
| 212 Al Santorini | .20 |
| 213 Andy Etchebarren | .20 |
| 214 Ken Boswell | .20 |
| 215 Reggie Smith | .75 |
| 216 Chuck Hartenstein | .20 |
| 217 Ron Hansen | .20 |
| 218 Ron Stone | .20 |
| 219 Jerry Kenney | .20 |
| 220 Steve Carlton | 10.00 |
| 221 Ron Brand | .20 |
| 222 Jim Rooker | .20 |
| 223 Nate Oliver | .20 |
| 224 Steve Barber | .20 |
| 225 Lee May | .30 |
| 226 Ron Perranoski | .30 |
| 227 Astros Rookies: | .75 |
| J. Mayberry, B. Watkins | |
| 228 Aurelio Rodriguez | .20 |
| 229 Rich Robertson | .20 |
| 230 Brooks Robinson | 4.00 |
| 231 Luis Tiant | .50 |
| 232 Bob Didier | .20 |
| 233 Lew Krausse | .20 |
| 234 Tommy Dean | .20 |
| 235 Mike Epstein | .20 |
| 236 Bob Veale | .20 |
| 237 Russ Gibson | .20 |
| 238 Jose Laboy | .20 |
| 239 Ken Berry | .20 |
| 240 Fergie Jenkins | 1.00 |
| 241 Royals Rookies: | .30 |
| A. Fitzmorris, S. Northey | |
| 242 Walter Alston (Mgr.) | .75 |
| 243 Joe Sparma | .20 |
| 244 Checklist No. 4 | .75 |
| 245 Leo Cardenas | .20 |
| 246 Jim McAndrew | .20 |
| 247 Lou Klimchock | .20 |
| 248 Jesus Alou | .20 |
| 249 Bob Locker | .20 |
| 250 Willie McCovey | 4.00 |
| 251 Dick Schofield | .20 |
| 252 Lowell Palmer | .20 |
| 253 Ron Woods | .20 |
| 254 Camilo Pascual | .20 |
| 255 Jim Spencer | .20 |
| 256 Vic Davalillo | .20 |
| 257 Dennis Higgins | .20 |
| 258 Paul Popovich | .20 |
| 259 Tommie Reynolds | .20 |
| 260 Claude Osteen | .20 |
| 261 Curt Motton | .20 |
| 262 Twins Rookies: | .25 |
| Jerry Morales, Jim Williams | |
| 263 Duane Josephson | .20 |
| 264 Rich Hebner | .20 |

| NO. PLAYER | MINT |
|---|---|
| 265 Randy Hundley | .20 |
| 266 Wally Bunker | .20 |
| 267 Twins Rookies: | .25 |
| Paul Ratliff, Herman Hill | |
| 268 Claude Raymond | .20 |
| 269 Cesar Gutierrez | .20 |
| 270 Chris Short | .20 |
| 271 Greg Goossen | .20 |
| 272 Hector Torres | .20 |
| 273 Ralph Houk (Mgr.) | .30 |
| 274 Gerry Arrigo | .20 |
| 275 Duke Sims | .20 |
| 276 Ron Hunt | .20 |
| 277 Paul Doyle | .20 |
| 278 Tommie Aaron | .20 |
| 279 Bill Lee | .20 |
| 280 Donn Clendenon | .20 |
| 281 Casey Cox | .20 |
| 282 Steve Huntz | .20 |
| 283 Angel Bravo | .20 |
| 284 Jack Baldschun | .20 |
| 285 Paul Blair | .20 |
| 286 Dodgers Rookies: | 4.00 |
| Bill Buckner, Jack Jenkins | |
| 287 Fred Talbot | .20 |
| 288 Larry Hisle | .30 |
| 289 Gene Brabender | .20 |
| 290 Rod Carew | 11.00 |
| 291 Leo Durocher (Mgr.) | .75 |
| 292 Eddie Leon | .20 |
| 293 Bob Bailey | .20 |
| 294 Jose Azcue | .20 |
| 295 Cecil Upshaw | .20 |
| 296 Woody Woodward | .20 |
| 297 Curt Blefary | .20 |
| 298 Ken Henderson | .20 |
| 299 Buddy Bradford | .20 |
| 300 Tom Seaver | 18.00 |
| 301 Chico Salmon | .20 |
| 302 Jeff James | .20 |
| 303 Brant Alyea | .20 |
| 304 Bill Russell (R) | 1.25 |
| 305 World Series Game 1 | .75 |
| Buford's Leadoff Homer | |
| 306 World Series Game 2 | .75 |
| Clendenon's Homer | |
| 307 World Series Game 3 | .75 |
| Agee's Catch | |
| 308 World Series Game 4 | .75 |
| Martin's Bunt | |
| 309 World Series Game 5 | .75 |
| Koosman Shuts Door | |
| 310 World Series Celebration | .75 |
| Mets Whoop it Up | |
| 311 Dick Green | .20 |
| 312 Mike Torrez | .30 |
| 313 Mayo Smith (Mgr.) | .20 |
| 314 Bill McCool | .20 |
| 315 Luis Aparicio | 2.00 |
| 316 Skip Guinn | .20 |
| 317 Red Sox Rookies: | .40 |
| B. Conigliaro, L. Alvarado | |
| 318 Willie Smith | .20 |
| 319 Clay Dalrymple | .20 |
| 320 Jim Maloney | .20 |
| 321 Lou Piniella | 1.00 |
| 322 Luke Walker | .20 |
| 323 Wayne Comer | .20 |
| 324 Tony Taylor | .20 |
| 325 Dave Boswell | .20 |
| 326 Bill Voss | .20 |
| 327 Hal King | .20 |
| 328 George Brunet | .20 |
| 329 Chris Cannizzaro | .20 |
| 330 Lou Brock | 3.50 |
| 331 Chuck Dobson | .20 |
| 332 Bobby Wine | .20 |
| 333 Bobby Murcer | .50 |
| 334 Phil Regan | .20 |
| 335 Bill Freehan | .30 |
| 336 Del Unser | .20 |
| 337 Mike McCormick | .20 |
| 338 Paul Schaal | .20 |
| 339 Johnny Edwards | .20 |
| 340 Tony Conigliaro | .35 |

| NO. PLAYER | MINT |
|---|---|
| 341 Bill Sudakis | .20 |
| 342 Wilbur Wood | .20 |
| 343 Checklist No. 4 | .75 |
| 344 Marcelino Lopez | .20 |
| 345 Al Ferrara | .20 |
| 346 Red Schoendienst | .40 |
| 347 Russ Snyder | .20 |
| 348 Mets Rookies: | .35 |
| M. Jorgensen, J. Hudson | |
| 349 Steve Hamilton | .20 |
| 350 Roberto Clemente | 13.00 |
| 351 Tom Murphy | .20 |
| 352 Bob Barton | .20 |
| 353 Stan Williams | .20 |
| 354 Amos Otis | .30 |
| 355 Doug Rader | .20 |
| 356 Fred Lasher | .20 |
| 357 Bob Burda | .20 |
| 358 Pedro Borbon | .20 |
| 359 Phil Roof | .20 |
| 360 Curt Flood | .30 |
| 361 Ray Jarvis | .20 |
| 362 Joe Hague | .20 |
| 363 Tom Shopay | .20 |
| 364 Dan McGinn | .20 |
| 365 Zoilo Versalles | .20 |
| 366 Barry Moore | .20 |
| 367 Mike Lum | .20 |
| 368 Ed Herrmann | .20 |
| 369 Alan Foster | .20 |
| 370 Tommy Harper | .20 |
| 371 Rod Gaspar | .20 |
| 372 Dave Guisti | .20 |
| 373 Roy White | .20 |
| 374 Tommie Sisk | .20 |
| 375 Johnny Callison | .20 |
| 376 Lefty Phillips (Mgr.) | .20 |
| 377 Bill Butler | .20 |
| 378 Jim Davenport | .20 |
| 379 Tom Tischinski | .20 |
| 380 Tony Perez | 1.50 |
| 381 Athletics Rookies: | .25 |
| Bobby Brooks, Mike Olivo | |
| 382 Jack DiLauro | .20 |
| 383 Mickey Stanley | .20 |
| 384 Gary Neibauer | .20 |
| 385 George Scott | .20 |
| 386 Bill Dillman | .20 |
| 387 Baltimore Orioles | .75 |
| 388 Byron Browne | .20 |
| 389 Jim Shellenback | .20 |
| 390 Willie Davis | .30 |
| 391 Larry Brown | .20 |
| 392 Walt Hriniak | .20 |
| 393 John Gelnar | .20 |
| 394 Gil Hodges (Mgr.) | 2.00 |
| 395 Walt Williams | .20 |
| 396 Steve Blass | .20 |
| 397 Roger Repoz | .20 |
| 398 Bill Stoneman | .20 |
| 399 New York Yankees | 1.00 |
| 400 Denny McLain | .60 |
| 401 Giants Rookies: | .25 |
| John Harrell, B. Williams | |
| 402 Ellie Rodriguez | .20 |
| 403 Jim Bunning | .75 |
| 404 Rich Reese | .20 |
| 405 Bill Hands | .20 |
| 406 Mike Andrews | .20 |
| 407 Bob Watson | .30 |
| 408 Paul Lindblad | .20 |
| 409 Bob Tolan | .20 |
| 410 Boog Powell | 1.00 |
| 411 L.A. Dodgers | 1.00 |
| 412 Larry Burchart | .20 |
| 413 Sonny Jackson | .20 |
| 414 Paul Edmondson | .20 |
| 415 Julian Javier | .20 |
| 416 Joe Verbanic | .20 |
| 417 John Bateman | .20 |
| 418 John Donaldson | .20 |
| 419 Ron Taylor | .20 |
| 420 Ken McMullen | .20 |
| 421 Pat Dobson | .20 |
| 422 Kansas City Royals | .55 |

# 1970 Topps (Continued)

| NO. PLAYER | MINT | NO. PLAYER | MINT | NO. PLAYER | MINT | NO. PLAYER | MINT |
|---|---|---|---|---|---|---|---|
| 423 Jerry May | .20 | 500 Hank Aaron | 12.50 | 575 Cleon Jones | .40 | 650 Sam McDowell | .75 |
| 424 Mike Kilkenny | .20 | 501 Chicago White Sox | .50 | 576 Milt Pappas | .40 | 651 Jim Gosger | .75 |
| 425 Bobby Bonds | .50 | 502 Rollie Fingers | 2.50 | 577 Bernie Allen | .40 | 652 Rich Rollins | .75 |
| 426 Bill Rigney (Mgr.) | .20 | 503 Dal Maxvill | .20 | 578 Tom Griffin | .40 | 653 Moe Drabowsky | .75 |
| 427 Fred Norman | .20 | 504 Don Pavletich | .20 | 579 Detroit Tigers | 1.00 | 654 NL Rookies: | 2.00 |
| 428 Don Buford | .20 | 505 Ken Holtzman | .25 | 580 Pete Rose | 45.00 | Oscar Gamble, Boots Day, | |
| 429 Cubs Rookies: | .35 | 506 Ed Stroud | .20 | 581 Tom Satriano | .40 | Angel Mangual | |
| Randy Bobb, Jim Cosman | | 507 Pat Corrales | .20 | 582 Mike Paul | .40 | 655 John Roseboro | .75 |
| 430 Andy Messersmith | .35 | 508 Joe Niekro | .50 | 583 Hal Lanier | .40 | 656 Jim Hardin | .75 |
| 431 Ron Swoboda | .20 | 509 Montreal Expos | .50 | 584 Al Downing | .40 | 657 San Diego Padres | 2.00 |
| 432 Checklist No. 5 | .75 | 510 Tony Oliva | 1.00 | 585 Rusty Staub | 1.00 | 658 Ken Tatum | .75 |
| 433 Ron Bryant | .20 | 511 Joe Hoerner | .20 | 586 Rickey Clark | .40 | 659 Pete Ward | .75 |
| 434 Felipe Alou | .20 | 512 Billy Harris | .20 | 587 Jose Arcia | .40 | 660 Johnny Bench | 60.00 |
| 435 Nelson Briles | .20 | 513 Preston Gomez (Mgr.) | .20 | 588 Checklist No. 7* | 1.50 | 661 Jerry Robertson | .75 |
| 436 Philadelphia Phillies | .55 | 514 Steve Hovley | .20 | 589 Joe Keough | .40 | 662 Frank Lucchesi | .75 |
| 437 Danny Cater | .20 | 515 Don Wilson | .20 | 590 Mike Cuellar | .40 | 663 Tito Francona | .75 |
| 438 Pat Jarvis | .20 | 516 Yankees Rookies: | .40 | 591 Mike Ryan | .40 | 664 Bob Robertson | .75 |
| 439 Lee Maye | .20 | John Ellis, Jim Lyttle | | 592 Daryl Patterson | .40 | 665 Jim Lonborg | .75 |
| 440 Bill Mazeroski | .35 | 517 Joe Gibbon | .20 | 593 Chicago Cubs | 1.00 | 666 Adolfo Phillips | .75 |
| 441 John O'Donoghue | .20 | 518 Bill Melton | .20 | 594 Jake Gibbs | .40 | 667 Bob Meyer | .75 |
| 442 Gene Mauch (Mgr.) | .20 | 519 Don McMahon | .20 | 595 Maury Wills | 1.00 | 668 Bob Tillman | .75 |
| 443 Al Jackson | .20 | 520 Willie Horton | .30 | 596 Mike Hershberger | .40 | 669 White Sox Rookies: | 1.00 |
| 444 White Sox Rookies: | .25 | 521 Cal Koonce | .20 | 597 Sonny Siebert | .40 | Bart Johnson, Dan Lazar, | |
| Billy Farmer, John Matias | | 522 California Angels | .60 | 598 Joe Pepitone | .40 | Mickey Scott | |
| 445 Vada Pinson | .50 | 523 Jose Pena | .20 | 599 Senators Rookies: | .40 | 670 Ron Santo | 1.50 |
| 446 B. Grabarkewitz | .20 | 524 Alvin Dark (Mgr.) | .20 | Dick Such, Gene Martin, | | 671 Jim Campanis | .75 |
| 447 Lee Stange | .20 | 525 Jerry Adair | .20 | Dick Stelmaszek, | | 672 Leon McFadden | .75 |
| 448 Houston Astros | .50 | 526 Ron Herbel | .20 | 600 Willie Mays | 13.50 | 673 Ted Uhlaender | .75 |
| 449 Jim Palmer | 5.00 | 527 Don Bosch | .20 | 601 Pete Richert | .40 | 674 Dave Leonhard | .75 |
| 450 Willie McCovey (AS) | 2.00 | 528 Elrod Hendricks | .20 | 602 Ted Savage | .40 | 675 Jose Cardenal | 1.00 |
| 451 Boog Powell (AS) | .50 | 529 Bob Aspromonte | .20 | 603 Ray Oyler | .40 | 676 Washington Senators | 1.00 |
| 452 Felix Millan (AS) | .30 | 530 Bob Gibson | 3.50 | 604 Clarence Gaston | .40 | 677 Woodie Fryman | .75 |
| 453 Rod Carew (AS) | 3.00 | 531 Ron Clark | .20 | 605 Rick Wise | .40 | 678 Dave Duncan | .75 |
| 454 Ron Santo (AS) | .30 | 532 Danny Murtaugh (Mgr.) | .20 | 606 Chico Ruiz | .40 | 679 Ray Sadecki | .75 |
| 455 Brooks Robinson (AS) | 2.50 | 533 Buzz Stephen | .20 | 607 Gary Waslewski | .40 | 680 Rico Petrocelli | 1.00 |
| 456 Don Kessinger (AS) | .30 | 534 Minnesota Twins | .50 | 608 Pittsburgh Pirates | .75 | 681 Bob Garibaldi | .75 |
| 457 Rico Petrocelli (AS) | .30 | 535 Andy Kosco | .20 | 609 Buck Martinez | .40 | 682 Dalton Jones | .75 |
| 458 Pete Rose (AS) | 7.50 | 536 Mike Kekich | .20 | 610 Jerry Koosman | .75 | 683 Reds Rookies: | 2.00 |
| 459 Reggie Jackson (AS) | 4.00 | 537 Joe Morgan | 2.50 | 611 Norm Cash | .60 | Wayne Simpson, Vern | |
| 460 Matty Alou (AS) | .30 | 538 Bob Humphreys | .20 | 612 Jim Hickman | .40 | Geishert, Hal McRae | |
| 461 Carl Yastrzemski (AS) | 4.00 | 539 Phillies Rookies: | 2.00 | 613 Dave Baldwin | .40 | 684 Jack Fisher | .75 |
| 462 Hank Aaron (AS) | 4.00 | Larry Bowa, Dennis Doyle | | 614 Mike Shannon | .40 | 685 Tom Haller | .75 |
| 463 Frank Robinson (AS) | 2.50 | 540 Gary Peters | .20 | 615 Mark Belanger | .40 | 686 Jackie Hernandez | .75 |
| 464 Johnny Bench (AS) | 3.00 | 541 Bill Heath | .20 | 616 Jim Merritt | .40 | 687 Bob Priddy | .75 |
| 465 Bill Freehan (AS) | .30 | 542 Checklist No. 6 | .75 | 617 Jim French | .40 | 688 Ted Kubiak | .75 |
| 466 Juan Marichal (AS) | 2.00 | 543 Clyde Wright | .20 | 618 Billy Wynne | .40 | 689 Frank Tepedino | .75 |
| 467 Denny McLain (AS) | .40 | 544 Cincinnati Reds | 1.00 | 619 Norm Miller | .40 | 690 Ron Fairly | .75 |
| 468 Jerry Koosman (AS) | .30 | 545 Ken Harrelson | .40 | 620 Jim Perry | 1.00 | 691 Joe Grzenda | .75 |
| 469 Sam McDowell (AS) | .30 | 546 Ron Reed | .20 | 621 Braves Rookies: | 3.00 | 692 Duffy Dyer | .75 |
| 470 Willie Stargell | 3.50 | 547 Rick Monday | .40 | Darrell Evans, Mike | | 693 Bob Johnson | .75 |
| 471 Chris Zachary | .20 | 548 Howie Reed | .20 | McQueen, Rick Kester | | 694 Gary Ross | .75 |
| 472 Atlanta Braves | .50 | 549 St. Louis Cardinals | .75 | 622 Don Sutton | 2.00 | 695 Bobby Knoop | .75 |
| 473 Don Bryant | .20 | 550 Frank Howard | .60 | 623 Horace Clarke | .40 | 696 S.F. Giants | 1.25 |
| 474 Dick Kelley | .20 | 551 Dock Ellis | .40 | 624 Clyde King | .40 | 697 Jim Hannan | .75 |
| 475 Dick McAuliffe | .20 | 552 Royals Rookies: | .50 | 625 Dean Chance | .40 | 698 Tom Tresh | 1.00 |
| 476 Don Shaw | .20 | Dennis Paepke, Fred Rico, | | 626 Dave Ricketts | .40 | 699 Hank Aguirre | .75 |
| 477 Orioles Rookies: | .30 | Don O'Riley | | 627 Gary Wagner | .40 | 700 Frank Robinson | 12.00 |
| Roger Freed, Al Severinsen | | 553 Jim LeFebvre | .40 | 628 Wayne Garrett | .40 | 701 Jack Billingham | .75 |
| 478 Bob Heise | .20 | 554 Tom Timmermann | .40 | 629 Merv Rettenmund | .40 | 702 AL Rookies: | .75 |
| 479 Dick Woodson | .20 | 555 Orlando Cepeda | 2.00 | 630 Ernie Banks | 8.50 | Bob Johnson, Ron | |
| 480 Glen Beckert | .20 | 556 Dave Bristol | .40 | 631 Oakland Athletics | .75 | Klimkowski, Bill Zepp | |
| 481 Jose Tartabull | .20 | 557 Ed Kranepool | .40 | 632 Gary Sutherland | .40 | 703 Lou Marone | .75 |
| 482 Tom Hilgendorf | .20 | 558 Vern Fuller | .40 | 633 Roger Nelson | .40 | 704 Frank Baker | .75 |
| 483 Gail Hopkins | .20 | 559 Tommy Davis | .40 | 634 Bud Harrelson | .75 | 705 Tony Cloninger | .75 |
| 484 Gary Nolan | .20 | 560 Gaylord Perry | 3.00 | 635 Bob Allison | .75 | 706 John McNamara (R) | 1.50 |
| 485 Jay Johnstone | .20 | 561 Tom McCraw | .40 | 636 Jim Stewart | .75 | 707 Kevin Collins | .75 |
| 486 Terry Harmon | .20 | 562 Ted Abernathy | .40 | 637 Cleveland Indians | 1.50 | 708 Jose Santiago | .75 |
| 487 Cisco Carlos | .20 | 563 Boston Red Sox | 1.00 | 638 Frank Bertaina | .75 | 709 Mike Fiore | .75 |
| 488 J.C. Martin | .20 | 564 Johnny Briggs | .40 | 639 Dave Campbell | .75 | 710 Felix Millan | .75 |
| 489 Eddie Kasko (Mgr.) | .20 | 565 Jim Hunter | 2.50 | 640 Al Kaline | 12.00 | 711 Ed Brinkman | .75 |
| 490 Bill Singer | .20 | 566 Gene Alley | .40 | 641 Al McBean | .75 | 712 Nolan Ryan | 22.00 |
| 491 Graig Nettles | 2.00 | 567 Bob Oliver | .40 | 642 Angels Rookies: | 1.00 | 713 Seattle Pilots | 4.00 |
| 492 Astros Rookies: | .30 | 568 Stan Bahnsen | .40 | Greg Garrett, Jarvis Tatum, | | 714 Al Spangler | .75 |
| K. Lampard, S. Spinks | | 569 Cookie Rojas | .40 | Gordon Lund | | 715 Mickey Lolich | 2.00 |
| 493 Lindy McDaniel | .20 | 570 Jim Fregosi | .40 | 643 Jose Pagan | .75 | 716 Cardinals Rookies: | 1.00 |
| 494 Larry Stahl | .20 | 571 Jim Brewer | .40 | 644 Gerry Nyman | .75 | Sal Campisi, R. Cleveland, | |
| 495 Dave Morehead | .20 | 572 Frank Quilici | .40 | 645 Don Money | .75 | Santiago Guzman | |
| 496 Steve Whitaker | .20 | 573 Padres Rookies: | .50 | 646 Jim Britton | .75 | 717 Tom Phoebus | .75 |
| 497 Eddie Watt | .20 | Mike Corkins, Rafael | | 647 Tom Matchick | .75 | 718 Ed Spiezio | .75 |
| 498 Al Weis | .20 | Robles, Ron Slocum | | 648 Larry Haney | .75 | 719 Jim Roland | .75 |
| 499 Skip Lockwood | .20 | 574 Bobby Bolin | .40 | 649 Jimmie Hall | .75 | 720 Rick Reichardt | 1.25 |

# 1971 Topps....Complete Set of 752 Cards—Value $600.00

Features the rookie cards of Steve Garvey, Don Baylor and George Foster. The high numbers are 644 to 752. Semi-high numbers are 524 to 643. The cards in this set are more difficult to find in *mint* condition because the black border scratches easily.

| NO. PLAYER | MINT |
|---|---|
| 1 World Champions | 2.50 |
| 2 Dock Ellis | .25 |
| 3 Dick McAuliffe | .25 |
| 4 Vic Davalillo | .25 |
| 5 Thurman Munson | 10.00 |
| 6 Ed Spiezio | .25 |
| 7 Jim Holt | .25 |
| 8 Mike McQueen | .25 |
| 9 George Scott | .25 |
| 10 Claude Osteen | .25 |
| 11 Elliott Maddox | .25 |
| 12 Johnny Callison | .25 |
| 13 White Sox Rookies: | .30 |
| C. Brinkman, D. Moloney | |
| 14 Dave Concepcion (R) | 3.50 |
| 15 Andy Messersmith | .25 |
| 16 Ken Singleton (R) | 2.00 |
| 17 Billy Sorrell | .25 |
| 18 Norm Miller | .25 |
| 19 Skip Pitlock | .25 |
| 20 Reggie Jackson | 16.50 |
| 21 Dan McGinn | .25 |
| 22 Phil Roof | .25 |
| 23 Oscar Gamble | .35 |
| 24 Rich Hand | .25 |
| 25 Clarence Gaston | .25 |
| 26 Bert Blyleven (R) | 5.00 |
| 27 Pirates Rookies | .30 |
| Fred Cambria, Gene Clines | |
| 28 Ron Klimkowski | .25 |
| 29 Don Buford | .25 |
| 30 Phil Niekro | 2.00 |
| 31 Eddie Kasko | .25 |
| 32 Jerry Da Vanon | .25 |
| 33 Del Unser | .25 |
| 34 Sandy Vance | .25 |
| 35 Lou Piniella | .50 |
| 36 Dean Chance | .25 |
| 37 Rich McKinney | .25 |
| 38 Jim Colborn | .25 |
| 39 Tiger Rookies: | .40 |
| L. LaGrow, Gene Lamont | |
| 40 Lee May | .25 |
| 41 Rick Austin | .25 |
| 42 Boots Day | .25 |
| 43 Steve Kealey | .25 |
| 44 Johnny Edwards | .25 |
| 45 Jim Hunter | 2.00 |
| 46 Dave Campbell | .25 |
| 47 Johnny Jeter | .25 |
| 48 Dave Baldwin | .25 |
| 49 Don Money | .25 |
| 50 Willie McCovey | 3.00 |
| 51 Steve Kline | .25 |
| 52 Braves Rookies: | .35 |
| Oscar Brown, Earl Williams | |
| 53 Paul Blair | .25 |
| 54 Checklist No. 1 | .75 |
| 55 Steve Carlton | 10.00 |
| 56 Duane Josephson | .25 |
| 57 Von Joshua | .25 |
| 58 Bill Lee | .25 |
| 59 Gene Mauch (Mgr.) | .25 |
| 60 Dick Bosman | .25 |
| 61 AL Batting Leaders: | .75 |
| Alex Johnson, Carl Yastrzemski, Tony Oliva | |

| NO. PLAYER | MINT |
|---|---|
| 62 NL Batting Leaders: | .60 |
| Joe Torre, Rico Carty, Manny Sanguillen | |
| 63 AL RBI Leaders: | .75 |
| Boog Powell, Frank Robinson, Tony Conigliaro | |
| 64 NL RBI Leaders: | .75 |
| Johnny Bench, Billy Williams, Tony Perez | |
| 65 AL HR Leaders: | .75 |
| Frank Howard, Harmon Killebrew, C. Yastrzemski | |
| 66 NL HR Leaders: | .75 |
| Johnny Bench, Billy Williams, Tony Perez | |
| 67 AL ERA Leaders: | .60 |
| Clyde Wright, Diego Segui, Jim Palmer | |
| 68 NL ERA Leaders: | .75 |
| Wayne Simpson, Luke Walker, Tom Seaver | |
| 69 AL Pitching Leaders: | .60 |
| Mike Cuellar, Dave McNally, Jim Perry | |
| 70 NL Pitching Leaders: | 1.00 |
| Gaylord Perry, Bob Gibson, Fergie Jenkins | |
| 71 AL Strikeout Leaders: | .60 |
| Sam McDowell, Mickey Lolich, Bob Johnson | |
| 72 NL Strikeout Leaders: | 1.00 |
| Bob Gibson, Tom Seaver, Fergie Jenkins | |
| 73 George Brunet | .25 |
| 74 Twins Rookies: | .30 |
| Pete Hamm, Jim Nettles | |
| 75 Gary Nolan | .25 |
| 76 Ted Savage | .25 |
| 77 Mike Compton | .25 |
| 78 Jim Spencer | .25 |
| 79 Wade Blasingame | .25 |
| 80 Bill Melton | .25 |
| 81 Felix Millan | .25 |
| 82 Casey Cox | .25 |
| 83 Met Rookies: | .35 |
| Tim Foli, Randy Bobb | |
| 84 Marcel Lachemann | .25 |
| 85 Bill Grabarkewitz | .25 |
| 86 Mike Kilkenny | .25 |
| 87 Jack Heidemann | .25 |
| 88 Hal King | .25 |
| 89 Ken Brett | .25 |
| 90 Joe Pepitone | .35 |
| 91 Bob Lemon (Mgr.) | .75 |
| 92 Fred Wenz | .25 |
| 93 Senators Rookies: | .25 |
| Norm McRae, Denny Riddleberger | |
| 94 Don Hahn | .25 |
| 95 Luis Tiant | .50 |
| 96 Joe Hague | .25 |
| 97 Floyd Wicker | .25 |
| 98 Joe Decker | .25 |
| 99 Mark Belanger | .25 |
| 100 Pete Rose | 27.00 |
| 101 Les Cain | .25 |

| NO. PLAYER | MINT |
|---|---|
| 102 Astros Rookies: | .50 |
| Ken Forsch, Larry Howard | |
| 103 Rich Severson | .25 |
| 104 Dan Frisella | .25 |
| 105 Tony Conigliaro | .35 |
| 106 Tom Dukes | .25 |
| 107 Roy Foster | .25 |
| 108 John Cumberland | .25 |
| 109 Steve Hovley | .25 |
| 110 Bill Mazeroski | .40 |
| 111 Yankee Rookies: | .35 |
| L. Colson, B. Mitchell | |
| 112 Manny Mota | .30 |
| 113 Jerry Crider | .25 |
| 114 Billy Conigliaro | .25 |
| 115 Donn Clendenon | .25 |
| 116 Ken Sanders | .25 |
| 117 Ted Simmons (R) | 5.00 |
| 118 Cookie Rojas | .25 |
| 119 Frank Lucchesi (Mgr.) | .25 |
| 120 Willie Horton | .30 |
| 121 Cubs Rookies: | .35 |
| J. Dunegan, R. Skidmore | |
| 122 Eddie Watt | .25 |
| 123 Checklist No. 2 | .75 |
| 124 Don Gullett | .25 |
| 125 Ray Fosse | .25 |
| 126 Danny Coombs | .25 |
| 127 Danny Thompson | .25 |
| 128 Frank Johnson | .25 |
| 129 Aurelio Monteagudo | .25 |
| 130 Denis Menke | .25 |
| 131 Curt Blefary | .25 |
| 132 Jose Laboy | .25 |
| 133 Mickey Lolich | .40 |
| 134 Jose Arcia | .25 |
| 135 Rick Monday | .25 |
| 136 Duffy Dyer | .25 |
| 137 Marcelino Lopez | .25 |
| 138 Phillies Rookies: | .35 |
| Joe Lis, W. Montanez | |
| 139 Paul Casanova | .25 |
| 140 Gaylord Perry | 2.50 |
| 141 Frank Quilici | .25 |
| 142 Mack Jones | .25 |
| 143 Steve Blass | .25 |
| 144 Jackie Hernandez | .25 |
| 145 Bill Singer | .25 |
| 146 Ralph Houk (Mgr.) | .30 |
| 147 Bob Priddy | .25 |
| 148 John Mayberry | .25 |
| 149 Mike Hershberger | .25 |
| 150 Sam McDowell | .25 |
| 151 Tommy Davis | .30 |
| 152 Angels Rookies: | .30 |
| Lloyd Allen, Winston Llenas | |
| 153 Gary Ross | .25 |
| 154 Cesar Gutierrez | .25 |
| 155 Ken Henderson | .25 |
| 156 Bart Johnson | .25 |
| 157 Bob Bailey | .25 |
| 158 Jerry Reuss | .45 |
| 159 Jarvis Tatum | .25 |
| 160 Tom Seaver | 14.00 |
| 161 Coins Checklist | .75 |
| 162 Jack Billingham | .25 |

| NO. PLAYER | MINT |
|---|---|
| 163 Buck Martinez | .25 |
| 164 Reds Rookies: | .60 |
| Frank Duffy, Milt Wilcox | |
| 165 Cesar Tovar | .25 |
| 166 Joe Hoerner | .25 |
| 167 Tom Grieve | .25 |
| 168 Bruce Dal Canton | .25 |
| 169 Ed Herrmann | .25 |
| 170 Mike Cuellar | .25 |
| 171 Bobby Wine | .25 |
| 172 Duke Sims | .25 |
| 173 Gil Garrido | .25 |
| 174 Dave LaRoche | .25 |
| 175 Jim Hickman | .25 |
| 176 Red Sox Rookies: | .35 |
| Bob Montgomery, Doug Griffin | |
| 177 Hal McRae | .35 |
| 178 Dave Duncan | .25 |
| 179 Mike Corkins | .25 |
| 180 Al Kaline | 3.50 |
| 181 Hal Lanier | .25 |
| 182 Al Downing | .25 |
| 183 Gil Hodges (Mgr.) | 2.00 |
| 184 Stan Bahnsen | .25 |
| 185 Julian Javier | .25 |
| 186 Bob Spence | .25 |
| 187 Ted Abernathy | .25 |
| 188 Dodgers Rookies: | .60 |
| Mike Strahler, Bob Valentine | |
| 189 George Mitterwald | .25 |
| 190 Bob Tolan | .25 |
| 191 Mike Andrews | .25 |
| 192 Billy Wilson | .25 |
| 193 Bob Grich (R) | 1.50 |
| 194 Mike Lum | .25 |
| 195 AL Playoff Game 1 | .75 |
| Powell Muscles Twins | |
| 196 AL Playoff Game 2 | .75 |
| McNally's Two Straight | |
| 197 AL Playoff Game 3 | .75 |
| Palmer Mows 'Em Down | |
| 198 Orioles Celebrate | .75 |
| A Team Effort | |
| 199 NL Playoff Game 1 | .75 |
| Cline Pinch-Triple | |
| 200 NL Playoff Game 2 | .75 |
| Tolan Scores Third Time | |
| 201 NL Playoff Game 3 | .75 |
| Cline Scores Winning Run | |
| 202 Reds Celebrate | .75 |
| World Series Bound | |
| 203 Larry Gura (R) | 1.00 |
| 204 Brewers Rookies: | .30 |
| B. Smith, G. Kopacz | |
| 205 Gerry Moses | .25 |
| 206 Checklist No. 3 | .75 |
| 207 Alan Foster | .25 |
| 208 Billy Martin | 1.00 |
| 209 Steve Renko | .25 |
| 210 Rod Carew | 12.00 |
| 211 Phil Hennigan | .25 |
| 212 Rich Hebner | .25 |
| 213 Frank Baker | .25 |
| 214 Al Ferrara | .25 |
| 215 Diego Segui | .25 |

| NO. | PLAYER | MINT |
|-----|--------|------|
| 216 | Cards Rookies: | .30 |
| | Reggie Cleveland, | |
| | Luis Melendez | |
| 217 | Ed Stroud | .25 |
| 218 | Tony Cloninger | .25 |
| 219 | Elrod Hendricks | .25 |
| 220 | Ron Santo | .35 |
| 221 | Dave Morehead | .25 |
| 222 | Bob Watson | .30 |
| 223 | Cecil Upshaw | .25 |
| 224 | Alan Gallagher | .25 |
| 225 | Gary Peters | .25 |
| 226 | Bill Russell | .25 |
| 227 | Floyd Weaver | .25 |
| 228 | Wayne Garrett | .25 |
| 229 | Jim Hannan | .25 |
| 230 | Willie Stargell | 3.00 |
| 231 | Indians Rookies: | .35 |
| | Vince Colbert, | |
| | John Lowenstein | |
| 232 | John Strohmayer | .25 |
| 233 | Larry Bowa | .75 |
| 234 | Jim Lyttle | .25 |
| 235 | Nate Colbert | .25 |
| 236 | Bob Humphreys | .25 |
| 237 | Cesar Cedeno (R) | 2.00 |
| 238 | Chuck Dobson | .25 |
| 239 | R. Schoendienst (Mgr.) | .40 |
| 240 | Clyde Wright | .25 |
| 241 | Dave Nelson | .25 |
| 242 | Jim Ray | .25 |
| 243 | Carlos May | .25 |
| 244 | Bob Tillman | .25 |
| 245 | Jim Kaat | 1.00 |
| 246 | Tony Taylor | .25 |
| 247 | Royals Rookies: | .50 |
| | Jerry Cram, Paul Splittorff | |
| 248 | Hoyt Wilhelm | 2.00 |
| 249 | Chico Salmon | .25 |
| 250 | Johnny Bench | 15.00 |
| 251 | Frank Reberger | .25 |
| 252 | Eddie Leon | .25 |
| 253 | Bill Sudakis | .25 |
| 254 | Cal Koonce | .25 |
| 255 | Bob Robertson | .25 |
| 256 | Tony Gonzalez | .25 |
| 257 | Nelson Briles | .25 |
| 258 | Dick Green | .25 |
| 259 | Dave Marshall | .25 |
| 260 | Tommy Harper | .25 |
| 261 | Darold Knowles | .25 |
| 262 | Padres Rookies: | .30 |
| | D. Robinson, J. Williams | |
| 263 | John Ellis | .25 |
| 264 | Joe Morgan | 2.00 |
| 265 | Jim Northrup | .25 |
| 266 | Bill Stoneman | .25 |
| 267 | Rich Morales | .25 |
| 268 | Philadelphia Phillies | .40 |
| 269 | Gail Hopkins | .25 |
| 270 | Rico Carty | .25 |
| 271 | Bill Zepp | .25 |
| 272 | Tommy Helms | .25 |
| 273 | Pete Richert | .25 |
| 274 | Ron Slocum | .25 |
| 275 | Vada Pinson | .50 |
| 276 | Giants Rookies: | 5.00 |
| | M. Davison, George Foster | |
| 277 | Gary Waslewski | .25 |
| 278 | Jerry Grote | .25 |
| 279 | Lefty Phillips (Mgr.) | .25 |
| 280 | Fergie Jenkins | 1.00 |
| 281 | Danny Walton | .25 |
| 282 | Jose Pagan | .25 |
| 283 | Dick Such | .25 |
| 284 | Jim Gosger | .25 |
| 285 | Sal Bando | .25 |
| 286 | Jerry McNertney | .25 |
| 287 | Mike Fiore | .25 |
| 288 | Joe Moeller | .25 |
| 289 | Chicago White Sox | .40 |
| 290 | Tony Oliva | .75 |
| 291 | George Culver | .25 |
| 292 | Jay Johnstone | .25 |
| 293 | Pat Corrales | .25 |

| NO. | PLAYER | MINT |
|-----|--------|------|
| 294 | Steve Dunning | .25 |
| 295 | Bobby Bonds | .50 |
| 296 | Tom Timmermann | .25 |
| 297 | Johnny Briggs | .25 |
| 298 | Jim Nelson | .25 |
| 299 | Ed Kirkpatrick | .25 |
| 300 | Brooks Robinson | 4.50 |
| 301 | Earl Wilson | .25 |
| 302 | Phil Gagliano | .25 |
| 303 | Lindy McDaniel | .25 |
| 304 | Ron Brand | .25 |
| 305 | Reggie Smith | .50 |
| 306 | Jim Nash | .25 |
| 307 | Don Wert | .25 |
| 308 | St. Louis Cardinals | .50 |
| 309 | Dick Ellsworth | .25 |
| 310 | Tommie Agee | .25 |
| 311 | Lee Stange | .25 |
| 312 | Harry Walker | .25 |
| 313 | Tom Hall | .25 |
| 314 | Jeff Torborg | .25 |
| 315 | Ron Fairly | .25 |
| 316 | Fred Scherman | .25 |
| 317 | Athletic Rookies: | .25 |
| | Angel Mangual, Jim Driscoll | |
| 318 | Rudy May | .25 |
| 319 | Ty Cline | .25 |
| 320 | Dave McNally | .25 |
| 321 | Tom Matchick | .25 |
| 322 | Jim Beauchamp | .25 |
| 323 | Billy Champion | .25 |
| 324 | Graig Nettles | 1.50 |
| 325 | Juan Marichal | 2.00 |
| 326 | Richie Scheinblum | .25 |
| 327 | World Series Game 1 | .75 |
| | Powell Homers | |
| 328 | World Series Game 2 | .75 |
| | Buford Goes 2 For 4 | |
| 329 | World Series Game 3 | 1.25 |
| | F. Robinson Shows Muscle | |
| 330 | World Series Game 4 | .75 |
| | Reds Stay Alive | |
| 331 | World Series Game 5 | 1.25 |
| | B. Robinson Robbery | |
| 332 | World Series Celebration | 1.00 |
| | Convincing Performance | |
| 333 | Clay Kirby | .25 |
| 334 | Roberto Pena | .25 |
| 335 | Jerry Koosman | .50 |
| 336 | Detroit Tigers | .60 |
| 337 | Jesus Alou | .25 |
| 338 | Gene Tenace | .25 |
| 339 | Wayne Simpson | .25 |
| 340 | Rico Petrocelli | .25 |
| 341 | Steve Garvey (R) | 50.00 |
| 342 | Frank Tepedino | .25 |
| 343 | Pirates Rookies: | .30 |
| | Ed Acosta, M. May | |
| 344 | Ellie Rodriguez | .25 |
| 345 | Joe Horlen | .25 |
| 346 | Lum Harris | .25 |
| 347 | Ted Uhlaender | .25 |
| 348 | Fred Norman | .25 |
| 349 | Rich Reese | .25 |
| 350 | Billy Williams | 1.25 |
| 351 | Jim Shellenback | .25 |
| 352 | Denny Doyle | .25 |
| 353 | Carl Taylor | .25 |
| 354 | Don McMahon | .25 |
| 355 | Bud Harrelson | .25 |
| 356 | Bob Locker | .25 |
| 357 | Cincinnati Reds | .75 |
| 358 | Danny Cater | .25 |
| 359 | Ron Reed | .25 |
| 360 | Jim Fregosi | .25 |
| 361 | Don Sutton | 1.00 |
| 362 | Orioles Rookies: | .35 |
| | Mike Adamson, R. Freed | |
| 363 | Mike Nagy | .25 |
| 364 | Tommy Dean | .25 |
| 365 | Bob Johnson | .25 |
| 366 | Ron Stone | .25 |
| 367 | Dalton Jones | .25 |
| 368 | Bob Veale | .25 |
| 369 | Checklist No. 4 | .75 |

| NO. | PLAYER | MINT |
|-----|--------|------|
| 370 | Joe Torre | 1.00 |
| 371 | Jack Hiatt | .25 |
| 372 | Lew Krausse | .25 |
| 373 | Tom McCraw | .25 |
| 374 | Clete Boyer | .25 |
| 375 | Steve Hargan | .25 |
| 376 | Expos Rookies: | .25 |
| | C. Mashore, E. McAnally | |
| 377 | Greg Garrett | .25 |
| 378 | Tito Fuentes | .25 |
| 379 | Wayne Granger | .25 |
| 380 | Ted Williams (Mgr.) | 2.50 |
| 381 | Fred Gladding | .25 |
| 382 | Jake Gibbs | .25 |
| 383 | Rod Gaspar | .25 |
| 384 | Rollie Fingers | 2.00 |
| 385 | Maury Wills | 1.00 |
| 386 | Boston Red Sox | 1.00 |
| 387 | Ron Herbel | .25 |
| 388 | Al Oliver | 2.00 |
| 389 | Ed Brinkman | .25 |
| 390 | Glenn Beckert | .25 |
| 391 | Twins Rookies: | .25 |
| | Steve Brye, Cotton Nash | |
| 392 | Grant Jackson | .25 |
| 393 | Merv Rettenmund | .25 |
| 394 | Clay Carroll | .25 |
| 395 | Roy White | .25 |
| 396 | Dick Schofield | .25 |
| 397 | Alvin Dark (Mgr.) | .25 |
| 398 | Howie Reed | .25 |
| 399 | Jim French | .25 |
| 400 | Hank Aaron | 11.00 |
| 401 | Tom Murphy | .25 |
| 402 | Los Angeles Dodgers | 1.00 |
| 403 | Joe Coleman | .25 |
| 404 | Astros Rookies: | .25 |
| | B. Harris, R. Metzger | |
| 405 | Leo Cardenas | .25 |
| 406 | Ray Sadecki | .25 |
| 407 | Joe Rudi | .25 |
| 408 | Rafael Robles | .25 |
| 409 | Don Pavletich | .25 |
| 410 | Ken Holtzman | .25 |
| 411 | George Spriggs | .25 |
| 412 | Jerry Johnson | .25 |
| 413 | Pat Kelly | .25 |
| 414 | Woodie Fryman | .25 |
| 415 | Mike Hegan | .25 |
| 416 | Gene Alley | .25 |
| 417 | Dick Hall | .25 |
| 418 | Adolfo Phillips | .25 |
| 419 | Ron Hansen | .25 |
| 420 | Jim Merritt | .25 |
| 421 | John Stephenson | .25 |
| 422 | Frank Bertaina | .25 |
| 423 | Tigers Rookies: | .45 |
| | T. Marting, D. Saunders | |
| 424 | Roberto Rodriquez | .25 |
| 425 | Doug Rader | .25 |
| 426 | Chris Cannizzaro | .25 |
| 427 | Bernie Allen | .25 |
| 428 | Jim McAndrew | .25 |
| 429 | Chuck Hinton | .25 |
| 430 | Wes Parker | .25 |
| 431 | Tom Burgmeier | .25 |
| 432 | Bob Didier | .25 |
| 433 | Skip Lockwood | .25 |
| 434 | Gary Sutherland | .25 |
| 435 | Jose Cardenal | .25 |
| 436 | Wilbur Wood | .25 |
| 437 | Danny Murtaugh (Mgr.) | .25 |
| 438 | Mike McCormick | .25 |
| 439 | Phillies Rookies: | 2.00 |
| | Greg Luzinski, Scott Reid | |
| 440 | Bert Campaneris | .25 |
| 441 | Milt Pappas | .25 |
| 442 | California Angels | .50 |
| 443 | Rich Robertson | .25 |
| 444 | Jimmie Price | .25 |
| 445 | Art Shamsky | .25 |
| 446 | Bobby Bolin | .25 |
| 447 | Cesar Geronimo | .25 |
| 448 | Dave Roberts | .25 |
| 449 | Brant Alyea | .25 |

| NO. | PLAYER | MINT |
|-----|--------|------|
| 450 | Bob Gibson | 3.50 |
| 451 | Joe Keough | .25 |
| 452 | John Boccabella | .25 |
| 453 | Terry Crowley | .25 |
| 454 | Mike Paul | .25 |
| 455 | Don Kessinger | .25 |
| 456 | Bob Meyer | .25 |
| 457 | Willie Smith | .25 |
| 458 | White Sox Rookies: | .30 |
| | Ron Lolich, Dave Lemonds | |
| 459 | Jim LeFebvre | .25 |
| 460 | Fritz Peterson | .25 |
| 461 | Jim Hart | .25 |
| 462 | Senators Team | .35 |
| 463 | Tom Kelley | .25 |
| 464 | Aurelio Rodriguez | .25 |
| 465 | Tim McCarver | .50 |
| 466 | Ken Berry | .25 |
| 467 | Al Santorini | .25 |
| 468 | Frank Fernandez | .25 |
| 469 | Bob Aspromonte | .25 |
| 470 | Bob Oliver | .25 |
| 471 | Tom Griffin | .25 |
| 472 | Ken Rudolph | .25 |
| 473 | Gary Wagner | .25 |
| 474 | Jim Fairey | .25 |
| 475 | Ron Perranoski | .25 |
| 476 | Dal Maxvill | .25 |
| 477 | Earl Weaver (Mgr.) | .75 |
| 478 | Bernie Carbo | .25 |
| 479 | Dennis Higgins | .25 |
| 480 | Manny Sanguillen | .25 |
| 481 | Daryl Patterson | .25 |
| 482 | San Diego Padres | .35 |
| 483 | Gene Michael | .25 |
| 484 | Don Wilson | .25 |
| 485 | Ken McMullen | .25 |
| 486 | Steve Huntz | .25 |
| 487 | Paul Schaal | .25 |
| 488 | Jerry Stephenson | .25 |
| 489 | Luis Alvarado | .25 |
| 490 | Deron Johnson | .25 |
| 491 | Jim Hardin | .25 |
| 492 | Ken Boswell | .25 |
| 493 | Dave May | .25 |
| 494 | Braves Rookies: | .35 |
| | Ralph Garr, Rick Kester | |
| 495 | Felipe Alou | .25 |
| 496 | Woody Woodward | .25 |
| 497 | Horacio Pina | .25 |
| 498 | John Kennedy | .25 |
| 499 | Checklist No. 5 | .75 |
| 500 | Jim Perry | .30 |
| 501 | Andy Etchebarren | .25 |
| 502 | Chicago Cubs | .60 |
| 503 | Gates Brown | .25 |
| 504 | Ken Wright | .25 |
| 505 | Ollie Brown | .25 |
| 506 | Bobby Knoop | .25 |
| 507 | George Stone | .25 |
| 508 | Roger Repoz | .25 |
| 509 | Jim Grant | .25 |
| 510 | Ken Harrelson | .35 |
| 511 | Chris Short | .25 |
| 512 | Red Sox Rookies: | .35 |
| | Dick Mills, Mike Garman | |
| 513 | Nolan Ryan | 12.00 |
| 514 | Ron Woods | .25 |
| 515 | Carl Morton | .25 |
| 516 | Ted Kubiak | .25 |
| 517 | Charlie Fox (Mgr.) | .25 |
| 518 | Joe Grzenda | .25 |
| 519 | Willie Crawford | .25 |
| 520 | Tommy John | 1.50 |
| 521 | Leron Lee | .25 |
| 522 | Minnesota Twins | .60 |
| 523 | John Odom | .25 |
| 524 | Mickey Stanley | .35 |
| 525 | Ernie Banks | 7.00 |
| 526 | Ray Jarvis | .50 |
| 527 | Cleon Jones | .50 |
| 528 | Wally Bunker | .50 |
| 529 | NL Rookies: | 2.50 |
| | Enzo, Hernandez, Bill | |
| | Buckner, Marty Perez | |

| NO. | PLAYER | MINT |
|---|---|---|
| 530 | Carl Yastrzemski | 15.00 |
| 531 | Mike Torrez | .40 |
| 532 | Bill Rigney (Mgr.) | .40 |
| 533 | Mike Ryan | .40 |
| 534 | Luke Walker | .40 |
| 535 | Curt Flood | .50 |
| 536 | Claude Raymond | .40 |
| 537 | Tom Egan | .40 |
| 538 | Angel Bravo | .40 |
| 539 | Larry Brown | .40 |
| 540 | Larry Dierker | .40 |
| 541 | Bob Burda | .40 |
| 542 | Bob Miller | .40 |
| 543 | New York Yankees | 1.25 |
| 544 | Vida Blue | 2.00 |
| 545 | Dick Dietz | .40 |
| 546 | John Matias | .40 |
| 547 | Pat Dobson | .40 |
| 548 | Don Mason | .40 |
| 549 | Jim Brewer | .40 |
| 550 | Harmon Killebrew | 4.50 |
| 551 | Frank Linzy | .40 |
| 552 | Buddy Bradford | .40 |
| 553 | Kevin Collins | .40 |
| 554 | Lowell Palmer | .40 |
| 555 | Walt Williams | .40 |
| 556 | Jim McGlothlin | .40 |
| 557 | Tom Satriano | .40 |
| 558 | Hector Torres | .40 |
| 559 | AL Rookies: | .40 |
|  | Gary Jones, Terry Cox, |  |
|  | Bill Gogolewski |  |
| 560 | Rusty Staub | 1.00 |
| 561 | Syd O'Brien | .40 |
| 562 | Dave Giusti | .40 |
| 563 | Giants Team | 1.25 |
| 564 | Al Fitzmorris | .40 |
| 565 | Jim Wynn | .60 |
| 566 | Tim Cullen | .40 |
| 567 | Walt Alston (Mgr.) | 1.00 |
| 568 | Sal Campisi | .40 |
| 569 | Ivan Murrell | .40 |
| 570 | Jim Palmer | 5.00 |
| 571 | Ted Sizemore | .40 |
| 572 | Jerry Kenney | .40 |
| 573 | Ed Kranepool | .40 |
| 574 | Jim Bunning | 1.00 |
| 575 | Bill Freehan | .50 |
| 576 | Cubs Rookies: | .60 |
|  | Brock Davis, Adrian |  |
|  | Garrett, Garry Jestadt |  |
| 577 | Jim Lonborg | .40 |
| 578 | Ron Hunt | .40 |
| 579 | Marty Pattin | .40 |
| 580 | Tony Perez | 1.50 |
| 581 | Roger Nelson | .40 |
| 582 | Dave Cash | .40 |
| 583 | Ron Cook | .40 |
| 584 | Cleveland Indians | 1.25 |
| 585 | Willie Davis | .40 |
| 586 | Dick Woodson | .40 |

| NO. | PLAYER | MINT |
|---|---|---|
| 587 | Sonny Jackson | .40 |
| 588 | Tom Bradley | .40 |
| 589 | Bob Barton | .40 |
| 590 | Alex Johnson | .40 |
| 591 | Jackie Brown | .40 |
| 592 | Randy Hundley | .40 |
| 593 | Jack Aker | .40 |
| 594 | Cardinals Rookies: | 1.00 |
|  | Bob Chlupsa, Bob Stinson, |  |
|  | Al Hrabosky |  |
| 595 | Dave Johnson | .75 |
| 596 | Mike Jorgensen | .40 |
| 597 | Ken Suarez | .40 |
| 598 | Rick Wise | .45 |
| 599 | Norm Cash | .75 |
| 600 | Willie Mays | 15.00 |
| 601 | Ken Tatum | .40 |
| 602 | Marty Martinez | .40 |
| 603 | Pittsburgh Pirates | 1.00 |
| 604 | John Gelnar | .40 |
| 605 | Orlando Cepeda | 1.50 |
| 606 | Chuck Taylor | .40 |
| 607 | Paul Ratliff | .40 |
| 608 | Mike Wegener | .40 |
| 609 | Leo Durocher (Mgr.) | .75 |
| 610 | Amos Otis | .60 |
| 611 | Tom Phoebus | .40 |
| 612 | Indians Rookies: | .50 |
|  | Ted Ford, Steve Mingori, |  |
|  | Lou Camilli |  |
| 613 | Pedro Borbon | .40 |
| 614 | Billy Cowan | .40 |
| 615 | Mel Stottlemyre | .60 |
| 616 | Larry Hisle | .50 |
| 617 | Clay Dalrymple | .40 |
| 618 | Tug McGraw | 1.00 |
| 619 | Checklist No. 6 | 1.25 |
| 620 | Frank Howard | .80 |
| 621 | Ron Bryant | .40 |
| 622 | Joe LaHoud | .40 |
| 623 | Pat Jarvis | .40 |
| 624 | Oakland Athletics | 1.25 |
| 625 | Lou Brock | 6.00 |
| 626 | Freddie Patek | .40 |
| 627 | Steve Hamilton | .40 |
| 628 | John Bateman | .40 |
| 629 | John Hiller | .40 |
| 630 | Roberto Clemente | 12.00 |
| 631 | Eddie Fisher | .40 |
| 632 | Darrel Chaney | .40 |
| 633 | AL Rookies: | .40 |
|  | Pete Koegel, Bobby Brooks, |  |
|  | Scott Northey |  |
| 634 | Phil Regan | .40 |
| 635 | Bobby Murcer | 1.00 |
| 636 | Denny LeMaster | .40 |
| 637 | Dave Bristol (Mgr.) | .40 |
| 638 | Stan Williams | .40 |
| 639 | Tom Haller | .40 |
| 640 | Frank Robinson | 7.00 |
| 641 | New York Mets | 1.50 |

| NO. | PLAYER | MINT |
|---|---|---|
| 642 | Jim Roland | .40 |
| 643 | Rick Reichardt | .40 |
| 644 | Jim Stewart | 1.00 |
| 645 | Jim Maloney | 1.00 |
| 646 | Bobby Floyd | 1.00 |
| 647 | Juan Pizarro | 1.00 |
| 648 | Mets Rookies: | 2.00 |
|  | Rich Folkers, Ted Martinez, |  |
|  | John Matlack |  |
| 649 | Sparky Lyle | 1.50 |
| 650 | Rich Allen | 3.00 |
| 651 | Jerry Robertson | 1.00 |
| 652 | Atlanta Braves | 1.50 |
| 653 | Russ Snyder | 1.00 |
| 654 | Don Shaw | 1.00 |
| 655 | Mike Epstein | 1.00 |
| 656 | Gerry Nyman | 1.00 |
| 657 | Jose Azcue | 1.00 |
| 658 | Paul Lindblad | 1.00 |
| 659 | Byron Browne | 1.00 |
| 660 | Ray Culp | 1.00 |
| 661 | Chuck Tanner (Mgr.) | 1.50 |
| 662 | Mike Hedlund | 1.00 |
| 663 | Marv Staehle | 1.00 |
| 664 | Rookies Pitchers: | 1.00 |
|  | Archie Reynolds, Bob |  |
|  | Reynolds, K. Reynolds |  |
| 665 | Ron Swoboda | 1.00 |
| 666 | Gene Brabender | 1.00 |
| 667 | Pete Ward | 1.00 |
| 668 | Gary Neibauer | 1.00 |
| 669 | Ike Brown | 1.00 |
| 670 | Bill Hands | 1.00 |
| 671 | Bill Voss | 1.00 |
| 672 | Ed Crosby | 1.00 |
| 673 | Gerry Janeski | 1.00 |
| 674 | Montreal Expos | 1.50 |
| 675 | Dave Boswell | 1.00 |
| 676 | Tommie Reynolds | 1.00 |
| 677 | Jack DiLauro | 1.00 |
| 678 | George Thomas | 1.00 |
| 679 | Don O'Riley | 1.00 |
| 680 | Don Mincher | 1.00 |
| 681 | Bill Butler | 1.00 |
| 682 | Terry Harmon | 1.00 |
| 683 | Bill Burbach | 1.00 |
| 684 | Curt Motton | 1.00 |
| 685 | Moe Drabowsky | 1.00 |
| 686 | Chico Ruiz | 1.00 |
| 687 | Ron Taylor | 1.00 |
| 688 | S. Anderson (Mgr.) | 1.50 |
| 689 | Frank Baker | 1.00 |
| 690 | Bob Moose | 1.00 |
| 691 | Bob Heise | 1.00 |
| 692 | AL Rookies Pitchers: | 1.00 |
|  | Hal Haydel, Rogelio Moret, |  |
|  | Wayne Twitchell |  |
| 693 | Jose Pena | 1.00 |
| 694 | Rick Renick | 1.00 |
| 695 | Joe Niekro | 1.50 |
| 696 | Jerry Morales | 1.00 |

| NO. | PLAYER | MINT |
|---|---|---|
| 697 | Rickey Clark | 1.00 |
| 698 | Milwaukee Brewers | 2.00 |
| 699 | Jim Britton | 1.00 |
| 700 | Boog Powell | 2.00 |
| 701 | Bob Garibaldi | 1.00 |
| 702 | Milt Ramirez | 1.00 |
| 703 | Mike Kekich | 1.00 |
| 704 | J.C. Martin | 1.00 |
| 705 | Dick Selma | 1.00 |
| 706 | Joe Foy | 1.00 |
| 707 | Fred Lasher | 1.00 |
| 708 | Russ Nagelson | 1.00 |
| 709 | Rookie Outfielders: | 15.00 |
|  | Don Baylor, Tom Paciorek, |  |
|  | Dusty Baker |  |
| 710 | Sonny Siebert | 1.00 |
| 711 | Larry Stahl | 1.00 |
| 712 | Jose Martinez | 1.00 |
| 713 | Mike Marshall | 1.00 |
| 714 | Dick Williams (Mgr.) | 1.00 |
| 715 | Horace Clarke | 1.00 |
| 716 | Dave Leonhard | 1.00 |
| 717 | Tommie Aaron | 1.00 |
| 718 | Billy Wynne | 1.00 |
| 719 | Jerry May | 1.00 |
| 720 | Matty Alou | 1.00 |
| 721 | John Morris | 1.00 |
| 722 | Houston Astros | 1.50 |
| 723 | Vicente Romo | 1.00 |
| 724 | Tom Tischinski | 1.00 |
| 725 | Gary Gentry | 1.00 |
| 726 | Paul Popovich | 1.00 |
| 727 | Ray Lamb | 1.00 |
| 728 | NL Rookie Outfielders: | 1.00 |
|  | Wayne Redmond, Keith |  |
|  | Lampard, Bernie Williams |  |
| 729 | Dick Billings | 1.00 |
| 730 | Jim Rooker | 1.00 |
| 731 | Jim Qualls | 1.00 |
| 732 | Bob Reed | 1.00 |
| 733 | Lee Maye | 1.00 |
| 734 | Rob Gardner | 1.00 |
| 735 | Mike Shannon | 1.00 |
| 736 | Mel Queen | 1.00 |
| 737 | Preston Gomez (Mgr.) | 1.00 |
| 738 | Russ Gibson | 1.00 |
| 739 | Barry Lersch | 1.00 |
| 740 | Luis Aparicio | 5.00 |
| 741 | Skip Guinn | 1.00 |
| 742 | Kansas City Royals | 1.75 |
| 743 | John O'Donoghue | 1.00 |
| 744 | Chuck Manuel | 1.00 |
| 745 | Sandy Alomar | 1.00 |
| 746 | Andy Kosco | 1.00 |
| 747 | NL Rookie Pitchers: | 1.00 |
|  | Al Severinsen, Scipio |  |
|  | Spinks, Balor Moore |  |
| 748 | John Purdin | 1.00 |
| 749 | Ken Szotkiewicz | 1.00 |
| 750 | Denny McLain | 2.00 |
| 751 | Al Weis | 1.00 |
| 752 | Dick Drago | 1.00 |

## 1972 Topps....Complete Set of 787 Cards—Value $650.00

Features the rookie cards of Carlton Fisk and Ben Oglivie. The high numbers are 657 to 787. Semi-high numbers are 526 to 656.

| NO. PLAYER | MINT | NO. PLAYER | MINT | NO. PLAYER | MINT | NO. PLAYER | MINT |
|---|---|---|---|---|---|---|---|
| 1 Pirates—Champs | 1.50 | 79 Red Sox Rookies: | 17.50 | 132 Joe Morgan | 2.00 | 209 Joe Rudi | .20 |
| 2 Ray Culp | .15 | Carlton Fisk, Mike Garman, | | 133 Joe Keough | .15 | 210 Denny McLain | .50 |
| 3 Bob Tolan | .15 | Cecil Cooper | | 134 Carl Morton | .15 | 211 Gary Sutherland | .15 |
| 4 Checklist No. 1 | .75 | 80 Tony Perez | 1.00 | 135 Vada Pinson | .25 | 212 Grant Jackson | .15 |
| 5 John Bateman | .15 | 81 Mike Hedlund | .15 | 136 Darrel Chaney | .15 | 213 Angels Rookies: | .20 |
| 6 Fred Scherman | .15 | 82 Ron Woods | .15 | 137 Dick Williams | .25 | Tom Silverio, Billy Parker, |
| 7 Enzo Hernandez | .15 | 83 Dalton Jones | .15 | 138 Mike Kekich | .15 | Art Kusnyer |
| 8 Ron Swoboda | .15 | 84 Vince Colbert | .15 | 139 Tim McCarver | .40 | 214 Mike McQueen | .15 |
| 9 Stan Williams | .15 | 85 NL Batting Leaders: | .75 | 140 Pat Dobson | .20 | 215 Alex Johnson | .15 |
| 10 Amos Otis | .25 | Ralph Garr, Glenn Beckert, | | 141 Mets Rookies: | .40 | 216 Joe Niekro | .40 |
| 11 Bobby Valentine | .25 | Joe Torre | | Buzz Capra, Leroy Stanton, | | 217 Roger Metzger | .15 |
| 12 Jose Cardenal | .15 | 86 AL Batting Leaders: | .75 | Jon Matlack | | 218 Eddie Kasko | .15 |
| 13 Joe Grzenda | .15 | Tony Oliva, Bobby Murcer, | | 142 Chris Chambliss (R) | 2.00 | 219 Rennie Stennett | .20 |
| 14 Phillies Rookies: | .20 | Merv Rettenmund | | 143 Garry Jestadt | .15 | 220 Jim Perry | .20 |
| Pete Koegel, Mike | | 87 NL RBI Leaders: | 1.00 | 144 Marty Pattin | .15 | 221 NL Playoffs: | .75 |
| Anderson, W. Twitchell | | Joe Torre, Willie Stargell, | | 145 Don Kessinger | .20 | Bucs Champs |
| 15 Walt Williams | .15 | Hank Aaron | | 146 Steve Kealey | .15 | 222 AL Playoffs: | 1.25 |
| 16 Mike Jorgensen | .15 | 88 AL RBI Leaders: | .75 | 147 Dave Kingman (R) | 3.50 | Orioles Champs |
| 17 Dave Duncan | .15 | Harmon Killebrew, Frank | | 148 Dick Billings | .15 | 223 World Series Game 1 | .75 |
| 18 Juan Pizarro | .15 | Robinson, Reggie Smith | | 149 Gary Neibauer | .15 | 224 World Series Game 2 | .75 |
| 19 Billy Cowan | .15 | 89 NL Home Run Leaders: | 1.00 | 150 Norm Cash | .25 | 225 World Series Game 3 | .75 |
| 20 Don Wilson | .15 | Willie Stargell, Lee May, | | 151 Jim Brewer | .15 | 226 World Series Game 4 | 1.50 |
| 21 Atlanta Braves | .50 | Hank Aaron | | 152 Gene Clines | .15 | 227 World Series Game 5 | .75 |
| 22 Rob Gardner | .15 | 90 AL Home Run Leaders: | .75 | 153 Rick Auerbach | .15 | 228 World Series Game 6 | .75 |
| 23 Ted Kubiak | .15 | Reggie Jackson, Bill | | 154 Ted Simmons | 1.25 | 229 World Series Game 7 | .75 |
| 24 Ted Ford | .15 | Melton, Norm Cash | | 155 Larry Dierker | .20 | 230 World S. Celebration | .75 |
| 25 Bill Singer | .15 | 91 NL ERA Leaders: | .75 | 156 Minnesota Twins | .35 | 231 Casey Cox | .15 |
| 26 Andy Etchebarren | .15 | Tom Seaver, Dave Roberts | | 157 Don Gullett | .25 | 232 Giants Rookies: | .20 |
| 27 Bob Johnson | .15 | (wrong photo), D. Wilson | | 158 Jerry Kenney | .15 | Chris Arnold, Jim Barr, |
| 28 Twins Rookies: | .20 | 92 AL ERA Leaders: | .75 | 159 John Boccabella | .15 | Dave Rader |
| Steve Brye, Bob Gebhard, | | Vida Blue, Wilbur Wood, | | 160 Andy Messersmith | .25 | 233 Jay Johnstone | .20 |
| Hal Haydel | | Jim Palmer | | 161 Brock Davis | .15 | 234 Ron Taylor | .15 |
| 29 Bill Bonham | .15 | 93 NL Pitching Leaders: | 1.00 | 162 Brewers Rookies: | 1.00 | 235 Merv Rettenmund | .15 |
| 30 Rico Petrocelli | .20 | Tom Seaver, Fergie | | Darrell Porter, Jerry Bell, | | 236 Jim McGlothlin | .15 |
| 31 Cleon Jones | .15 | Jenkins, Steve Carlton, | | Bob Reynolds (Bell and | | 237 New York Yankees | .75 |
| 32 C. Jones (In Action) | .15 | Al Downing | | Porter photos switched) | | 238 Leron Lee | .15 |
| 33 Billy Martin | .75 | 94 AL Pitching Leaders: | .50 | 163 Tug McGraw | .50 | 239 Tom Timmermann | .15 |
| 34 B. Martin (In Action) | .50 | Mickey Lolich, Vida Blue, | | 164 T. McGraw (In Action) | .25 | 240 Rich Allen | .75 |
| 35 Jerry Johnson | .15 | Wilbur Wood | | 165 Chris Speier | .15 | 241 Rollie Fingers | 1.75 |
| 36 J. Johnson (In Action) | .15 | 95 NL Strikeout Leaders: | .75 | 166 C. Speier (In Action) | .15 | 242 Don Mincher | .15 |
| 37 Carl Yastrzemski | 7.50 | Bill Stoneman, Tom Seaver, | | 167 Deron Johnson | .15 | 243 Frank Linzy | .15 |
| 38 Yastrzemski (In Action) | 3.50 | Fergie Jenkins | | 168 D. Johnson (In Action) | .15 | 244 Steve Braun | .15 |
| 39 Bob Barton | .15 | 96 AL Strikeout Leaders: | .50 | 169 Vida Blue | .60 | 245 Tommie Agee | .15 |
| 40 B. Barton (In Action) | .15 | Mickey Lolich, Vida Blue, | | 170 V. Blue (In Action) | .30 | 246 Tom Burgmeier | .15 |
| 41 Tommy Davis | .20 | Joe Coleman | | 171 Darrell Evans | .50 | 247 Milt May | .15 |
| 42 T. Davis (In Action) | .20 | 97 Tom Kelley | .15 | 172 D. Evans (In Action) | .30 | 248 Tom Bradley | .15 |
| 43 Rick Wise | .25 | 98 Chuck Tanner | .25 | 173 Clay Kirby | .15 | 249 Garry Walker | .15 |
| 44 R. Wise (In Action) | .25 | 99 Ross Grimsley | .15 | 174 C. Kirby (In Action) | .15 | 250 Boog Powell | .60 |
| 45 Glenn Beckert | .25 | 100 Frank Robinson | 2.50 | 175 Tom Haller | .15 | 251 Checklist No. 3 | .75 |
| 46 G. Beckert (In Action) | .25 | 101 Astros Rookies: | 1.00 | 176 T. Haller (In Action) | .15 | 252 Ken Reynolds | .15 |
| 47 John Ellis | .15 | B. Greif, J.R. Richard, | | 177 Paul Schaal | .15 | 253 Sandy Alomar | .15 |
| 48 J. Ellis (In Action) | .15 | Ray Busse | | 178 P. Schaal (In Action) | .15 | 254 Boots Day | .15 |
| 49 Willie Mays | 7.50 | 102 Lloyd Allen | .15 | 179 Dock Ellis | .15 | 255 Jim Lonborg | .20 |
| 50 W. Mays (In Action) | 3.50 | 103 Checklist No. 2 | .55 | 180 D. Ellis (In Action) | .15 | 256 George Foster | 1.50 |
| 51 Harmon Killebrew | 2.00 | 104 Toby Harrah (R) | 1.50 | 181 Ed Kranepool | .20 | 257 Tigers Rookies: | .30 |
| 52 H. Killebrew (In Action) | 1.00 | 105 Gary Gentry | .15 | 182 E. Kranepool (In Action) | .20 | Paul Jata, Jim Foor, |
| 53 Bud Harrelson | .20 | 106 Milwaukee Brewers | .50 | 183 Bill Melton | .15 | Tim Hosley |
| 54 B. Harrelson (In Action) | .20 | 107 Jose Cruz (R) | 2.50 | 184 B. Melton (In Action) | .15 | 258 Randy Hundley | .15 |
| 55 Clyde Wright | .15 | 108 Gary Waslewski | .15 | 185 Ron Bryant | .15 | 259 Sparky Lyle | .25 |
| 56 Rich Chiles | .15 | 109 Jerry May | .15 | 186 R. Bryant (In Action) | .15 | 260 Ralph Garr | .15 |
| 57 Bob Oliver | .15 | 110 Ron Hunt | .15 | 187 Gates Brown | .15 | 261 Steve Mingori | .15 |
| 58 Ernie McAnally | .15 | 111 Jim Grant | .15 | 188 Frank Lucchesi | .15 | 262 San Diego Padres | .40 |
| 59 Fred Stanley | .15 | 112 Greg Luzinski | 1.00 | 189 Gene Tenace | .20 | 263 Felipe Alou | .20 |
| 60 Manny Sanguillen | .25 | 113 Rogelio Moret | .15 | 190 Dave Giusti | .15 | 264 Tommy John | 1.25 |
| 61 Cubs Rookies: | .75 | 114 Bill Buckner | .75 | 191 Jeff Burroughs | .40 | 265 Wes Parker | .15 |
| Burt Hooton, Gene Hiser, | | 115 Jim Fregosi | .25 | 192 Chicago Cubs | .60 | 266 Bobby Bolin | .15 |
| Earl Stephenson | | 116 Ed Farmer | .15 | 193 Kurt Bevacqua | .15 | 267 Dave Concepcion | 1.25 |
| 62 Angel Mangual | .15 | 117 Cleo James | .15 | 194 Fred Norman | .15 | 268 A's Rookies: | .20 |
| 63 Duke Sims | .15 | 118 Skip Lockwood | .15 | 195 Orlando Cepeda | .75 | Dwain Anderson, C. Floethe |
| 64 Pete Broberg | .15 | 119 Marty Perez | .15 | 196 Mel Queen | .15 | 269 Don Hahn | .15 |
| 65 Cesar Cedeno | .75 | 120 Bill Freehan | .25 | 197 Johnny Briggs | .15 | 270 Jim Palmer | 3.00 |
| 66 Ray Corbin | .15 | 121 Ed Sprague | .15 | 198 Dodgers Rookies: | .50 | 271 Ken Rudolph | .15 |
| 67 Red Schoendienst | .35 | 122 Larry Biittner | .15 | Charlie Hough, Bob | | 272 Mickey Rivers | 1.00 |
| 68 Jim York | .15 | 123 Ed Acosta | .15 | O'Brien, Mike Strahler | | 273 Bobby Floyd | .15 |
| 69 Roger Freed | .15 | 124 Yankees Rookies: | .25 | 199 Mike Fiore | .15 | 274 Al Severinsen | .15 |
| 70 Mike Cuellar | .15 | Alan Closter, Rusty | | 200 Lou Brock | 2.50 | 275 Cesar Tovar | .15 |
| 71 Angels Team | .50 | Torres, R. Hambright | | 201 Phil Roof | .15 | 276 Gene Mauch | .15 |
| 72 Bruce Kison (R) | .50 | 125 Dave Cash | .15 | 202 Scipio Spinks | .15 | 277 Eliott Maddox | .15 |
| 73 Steve Huntz | .15 | 126 Bart Johnson | .15 | 203 Ron Blomberg | .15 | 278 Dennis Higgins | .15 |
| 74 Cecil Upshaw | .15 | 127 Duffy Dyer | .15 | 204 Tommy Helms | .15 | 279 Larry Brown | .15 |
| 75 Bert Campaneris | .25 | 128 Eddie Watt | .15 | 205 Dick Drago | .15 | 280 Willie McCovey | 3.00 |
| 76 Don Carrithers | .15 | 129 Charlie Fox | .15 | 206 Dal Maxvill | .15 | 281 Bill Parsons | .15 |
| 77 Ron Theobald | .15 | 130 Bob Gibson | 2.00 | 207 Tom Egan | .15 | 282 Houston Astros | .45 |
| 78 Steve Arlin | .15 | 131 Jim Nettles | .15 | 208 Milt Pappas | .15 | 283 Darrell Brandon | .15 |

| NO. PLAYER | MINT |
|---|---|
| 284 Ike Brown | .15 |
| 285 Gaylord Perry | 2.50 |
| 286 Gene Alley | .15 |
| 287 Jim Hardin | .15 |
| 288 Johnny Jeter | .15 |
| 289 Syd O'Brien | .15 |
| 290 Sonny Siebert | .15 |
| 291 Hal McRae | .25 |
| 292 H. McRae (In Action) | .20 |
| 293 Danny Frisella | .15 |
| 294 D. Frisella (In Action) | .15 |
| 295 Dick Dietz (In Action) | .15 |
| 296 D. Dietz (In Action) | .15 |
| 297 Claude Osteen | .15 |
| 298 C. Osteen (In Action) | .15 |
| 299 Hank Aaron | 9.00 |
| 300 H. Aaron (In Action) | 5.00 |
| 301 George Mitterwald | .15 |
| 302 Mitterwald (In Action) | .15 |
| 303 Joe Pepitone | .25 |
| 304 J. Pepitone (In Action) | .20 |
| 305 Ken Boswell | .15 |
| 306 K. Boswell (In Action) | .15 |
| 307 Steve Renko | .15 |
| 308 S. Renko (In Action) | .15 |
| 309 Roberto Clemente | 7.50 |
| 310 Clemente (In Action) | 3.50 |
| 311 Clay Carroll | .15 |
| 312 C. Carroll (In Action) | .15 |
| 313 Luis Aparicio | 2.00 |
| 314 L. Aparicio (In Action) | 1.00 |
| 315 Paul Splittorff | .20 |
| 316 Cardinals Rookies: | .40 |
| Jim Bibby, Jorge Roque, | |
| Santiago Guzman | |
| 317 Rich Hand | .15 |
| 318 Sonny Jackson | .15 |
| 319 Aurelio Rodriguez | .15 |
| 320 Steve Blass | .15 |
| 321 Joe LaHoud | .15 |
| 322 Jose Pena | .15 |
| 323 Earl Weaver | .35 |
| 324 Mike Ryan | .15 |
| 325 Mel Stottlemyre | .30 |
| 326 Pat Kelly | .15 |
| 327 Steve Stone (R) | .50 |
| 328 Boston Red Sox | .60 |
| 329 Roy Foster | .15 |
| 330 Jim Hunter | 1.50 |
| 331 Stan Swanson | .15 |
| 332 Buck Martinez | .15 |
| 333 Steve Barber | .15 |
| 334 Rangers Rookies: | .20 |
| Bill Fahey, Jim Mason, | |
| Tom Ragland | |
| 335 Bill Hands | .15 |
| 336 Marty Martinez | .15 |
| 337 Mike Kilkenny | .15 |
| 338 Bob Grich | .50 |
| 339 Ron Cook | .15 |
| 340 Roy White | .15 |
| 341 Joe Torre (Boyhood) | .20 |
| 342 Wilbur Wood (Boyhood) | .20 |
| 343 W. Stargell (Boyhood) | .60 |
| 344 D. McNally (Boyhood) | .20 |
| 345 Rick Wise (Boyhood) | .20 |
| 346 Jim Fregosi (Boyhood) | .20 |
| 347 Tom Seaver (Boyhood) | 1.00 |
| 348 Sal Bando (Boyhood) | .20 |
| 349 Al Fitzmorris | .15 |
| 350 Frank Howard | .50 |
| 351 Braves Rookies: | .20 |
| Tom House, Rick Kester, | |
| Jimmy Britton | |
| 352 Dave LaRoche | .15 |
| 353 Art Shamsky | .15 |
| 354 Tom Murphy | .15 |
| 355 Bob Watson | .30 |
| 356 Gerry Moses | .15 |
| 357 Woodie Fryman | .15 |
| 358 Sparky Anderson | .30 |
| 359 Don Pavletich | .15 |
| 360 Dave Roberts | .15 |
| 361 Mike Andrews | .15 |
| 362 New York Mets | .75 |

| NO. PLAYER | MINT |
|---|---|
| 363 Ron Klimkowski | .15 |
| 364 Johnny Callison | .15 |
| 365 Dick Bosman | .15 |
| 366 Jimmy Rosario | .15 |
| 367 Ron Perranoski | .15 |
| 368 Danny Thompson | .15 |
| 369 Jim LeFebvre | .15 |
| 370 Don Buford | .15 |
| 371 Denny LeMaster | .15 |
| 372 Royals Rookies: | .15 |
| Lance Clemons, | |
| Monty Montgomery | |
| 373 John Mayberry | .25 |
| 374 Jack Heidemann | .15 |
| 375 Reggie Cleveland | .15 |
| 376 Andy Kosco | .15 |
| 377 Terry Harmon | .15 |
| 378 Checklist No. 4 | .75 |
| 379 Ken Berry | .15 |
| 380 Earl Williams | .15 |
| 381 Chicago White Sox | .50 |
| 382 Joe Gibbon | .15 |
| 383 Brant Alyea | .15 |
| 384 Dave Campbell | .15 |
| 385 Mickey Stanley | .15 |
| 386 Jim Colborn | .15 |
| 387 Horace Clarke | .15 |
| 388 Charlie Williams | .15 |
| 389 Bill Rigney | .15 |
| 390 Willie Davis | .25 |
| 391 Kan Sanders | .15 |
| 392 Pirates Rookies: | .75 |
| Fred Cambria, Richie Zisk | |
| 393 Curt Motton | .15 |
| 394 Ken Forsch | .20 |
| 395 Matty Alou | .20 |
| 396 Paul Lindblad | .20 |
| 397 Philadelphia Phillies | .75 |
| 398 Larry Hisle | .30 |
| 399 Milt Wilcox | .20 |
| 400 Tony Oliva | 1.00 |
| 401 Jim Nash | .20 |
| 402 Bobby Heise | .20 |
| 403 John Cumberland | .20 |
| 404 Jeff Torborg | .20 |
| 405 Ron Fairly | .20 |
| 406 George Hendrick (R) | 1.50 |
| 407 Chuck Taylor | .20 |
| 408 Jim Northrup | .20 |
| 409 Frank Baker | .20 |
| 410 Fergie Jenkins | .75 |
| 411 Bob Montgomery | .20 |
| 412 Dick Kelley | .20 |
| 413 White Sox Rookies: | .30 |
| Don Eddy, Dave Lemonds | |
| 414 Bob Miller | .20 |
| 415 Cookie Rojas | .20 |
| 416 Johnny Edwards | .20 |
| 417 Tom Hall | .20 |
| 418 Tom Shopay | .20 |
| 419 Jim Spencer | .20 |
| 420 Steve Carlton | 10.00 |
| 421 Ellie Rodriguez | .20 |
| 422 Ray Lamb | .20 |
| 423 Oscar Gamble | .25 |
| 424 Bill Gogolewski | .20 |
| 425 Ken Singleton | .50 |
| 426 K. Singleton (In Action) | .25 |
| 427 Tito Fuentes | .20 |
| 428 T. Fuentes (In Action) | .20 |
| 429 Bob Robertson | .20 |
| 430 B. Robertson (In Action) | .20 |
| 431 Clarence Gaston | .20 |
| 432 C. Gaston (In Action) | .20 |
| 433 Johnny Bench | 11.00 |
| 434 J. Bench (In Action) | 5.00 |
| 435 Reggie Jackson | 10.00 |
| 436 R. Jackson (In Action) | 5.00 |
| 437 Maury Wills | 1.00 |
| 438 M. Wills (In Action) | .50 |
| 439 Billy Williams | 1.25 |
| 440 B. Williams (In Action) | .60 |
| 441 Thurman Munson | 6.00 |
| 442 T. Munson (In Action) | 2.50 |
| 443 Ken Henderson | .20 |

| NO. PLAYER | MINT |
|---|---|
| 444 Henderson (In Action) | .20 |
| 445 Tom Seaver | 7.50 |
| 446 T. Seaver (In Action) | 3.00 |
| 447 Willie Stargell | 3.00 |
| 448 W. Stargell (In Action) | 1.50 |
| 449 Bob Lemon | .60 |
| 450 Mickey Lolich | .50 |
| 451 Tony LaRussa | .30 |
| 452 Ed Herrmann | .20 |
| 453 Barry Lersch | .20 |
| 454 Oakland A's | .40 |
| 455 Tommy Harper | .20 |
| 456 Mark Belanger | .20 |
| 457 Padres Rookies: | .30 |
| Darcy Fast, Derrel Thomas, | |
| Mike Ivie | |
| 458 Aurelio Monteagudo | .20 |
| 459 Rick Renick | .20 |
| 460 Al Downing | .20 |
| 461 Tim Cullen | .20 |
| 462 Rickey Clark | .20 |
| 463 Bernie Carbo | .20 |
| 464 Jim Roland | .20 |
| 465 Gil Hodges | 1.50 |
| 466 Norm Miller | .20 |
| 467 Steve Kline | .20 |
| 468 Richie Scheinblum | .20 |
| 469 Ron Herbel | .20 |
| 470 Ray Fosse | .20 |
| 471 Luke Walker | .20 |
| 472 Phil Gagliano | .20 |
| 473 Dan McGinn | .20 |
| 474 Orioles Rookies: | 1.50 |
| Johnny Oates, Don Baylor, | |
| Roric Harrison | |
| 475 Gary Nolan | .20 |
| 476 Lee Richard | .20 |
| 477 Tom Phoebus | .20 |
| 478 Checklist No. 5 | .75 |
| 479 Don Shaw | .20 |
| 480 Lee May | .20 |
| 481 Billy Conigliaro | .20 |
| 482 Joe Hoerner | .20 |
| 483 Ken Suarez | .20 |
| 484 Lum Harris | .20 |
| 485 Phil Regan | .20 |
| 486 John Lowenstein | .20 |
| 487 Detroit Tigers | .75 |
| 488 Mike Nagy | .20 |
| 489 Expos Rookies: | .20 |
| T. Humphrey, K. Lampard | |
| 490 Dave McNally | .20 |
| 491 Lou Piniella (Boyhood) | .30 |
| 492 M. Stottlemyre (Boyhood) | .30 |
| 493 Bob Bailey (Boyhood) | .30 |
| 494 Willie Horton (Boyhood) | .30 |
| 495 Bill Melton (Boyhood) | .30 |
| 496 B. Harrelson (Boyhood) | .30 |
| 497 Jim Perry (Boyhood) | .30 |
| 498 B. Robinson (Boyhood) | 1.00 |
| 499 Vicente Romo | .20 |
| 500 Joe Torre | .50 |
| 501 Pete Hamm | .20 |
| 502 Jackie Hernandez | .20 |
| 503 Gary Peters | .20 |
| 504 Ed Spiezio | .20 |
| 505 Mike Marshall | .25 |
| 506 Indians Rookies: | .30 |
| Terry Ley, Dick Tidrow, | |
| Jim Moyer | |
| 507 Fred Gladding | .20 |
| 508 Ellie Hendricks | .20 |
| 509 Don McMahon | .20 |
| 510 Ted Williams (Mgr.) | 3.00 |
| 511 Tony Taylor | .20 |
| 512 Paul Popovich | .20 |
| 513 Lindy McDaniel | .20 |
| 514 Ted Sizemore | .20 |
| 515 Bert Blyleven | 1.50 |
| 516 Oscar Brown | .20 |
| 517 Ken Brett | .20 |
| 518 Wayne Garrett | .20 |
| 519 Ted Abernathy | .20 |
| 520 Larry Bowa | .75 |
| 521 Alan Foster | .20 |

| NO. PLAYER | MINT |
|---|---|
| 522 Los Angeles Dodgers | 1.00 |
| 523 Chuck Dobson | .20 |
| 524 Reds Rookies: | .35 |
| Ed Armbrister, Mel Behney | |
| 525 Carlos May | .20 |
| 526 Bob Bailey | .40 |
| 527 Dave Leonhard | .40 |
| 528 Ron Stone | .40 |
| 529 Dave Nelson | .40 |
| 530 Don Sutton | 1.50 |
| 531 Freddie Patek | .40 |
| 532 Fred Kendall | .40 |
| 533 Ralph Houk (Mgr.) | .60 |
| 534 Jim Hickman | .40 |
| 535 Ed Brinkman | .40 |
| 536 Doug Rader | .40 |
| 537 Bob Locker | .40 |
| 538 Charlie Sands | .40 |
| 539 Terry Forster (R) | 1.00 |
| 540 Felix Milan | .40 |
| 541 Roger Repoz | .40 |
| 542 Jack Billingham | .40 |
| 543 Duane Josephson | .40 |
| 544 Ted Martinez | .40 |
| 545 Wayne Granger | .40 |
| 546 Joe Hague | .40 |
| 547 Cleveland Indians | .75 |
| 548 Frank Reberger | .40 |
| 549 Dave May | .40 |
| 550 Brooks Robinson | 5.00 |
| 551 Ollie Brown | .40 |
| 552 O. Brown (In Action) | .40 |
| 553 Wilbur Wood | .40 |
| 554 W. Wood (In Action) | .40 |
| 555 Ron Santo | .65 |
| 556 R. Santo (In Action) | .40 |
| 557 John Odom | .40 |
| 558 J. Odom (In Action) | .40 |
| 559 Pete Rose | 40.00 |
| 560 P. Rose (In Action) | 20.00 |
| 561 Leo Cardenas | .40 |
| 562 L. Cardenas (In Action) | .40 |
| 563 Ray Sadecki | .40 |
| 564 R. Sadecki (In Action) | .40 |
| 565 Reggie Smith | .60 |
| 566 R. Smith (In Action) | .40 |
| 567 Juan Marichal | 2.50 |
| 568 J. Marichal (In Action) | 1.50 |
| 569 Ed Kirkpatrick | .40 |
| 570 Kirkpatrick (In Action) | .40 |
| 571 Nate Colbert | .40 |
| 572 N. Colbert (In Action) | .40 |
| 573 Fritz Peterson | .40 |
| 574 F. Peterson (In Action) | .40 |
| 575 Al Oliver | 2.00 |
| 576 Leo Durocher | .75 |
| 577 Mike Paul | .40 |
| 578 Billy Grabarkewitz | .40 |
| 579 Doyle Alexander (R) | 1.00 |
| 580 Lou Piniella | 1.25 |
| 581 Wade Blasingame | .40 |
| 582 Montreal Expos | .60 |
| 583 Darold Knowles | .40 |
| 584 Jerry McNertney | .40 |
| 585 George Scott | .40 |
| 586 Denis Menke | .40 |
| 587 Billy Wilson | .40 |
| 588 Jim Holt | .40 |
| 589 Hal Lanier | .40 |
| 590 Graig Nettles | 1.50 |
| 591 Paul Casanova | .40 |
| 592 Lew Krausse | .40 |
| 593 Rich Morales | .40 |
| 594 Jim Beauchamp | .40 |
| 595 Nolan Ryan | 7.50 |
| 596 Manny Mota | .50 |
| 597 Jim Magnuson | .40 |
| 598 Hal King | .40 |
| 599 Billy Champion | .40 |
| 600 Al Kaline | 5.00 |
| 601 George Stone | .40 |
| 602 Dave Bristol | .40 |
| 603 Jim Ray | .40 |
| 604 Checklist No. 6 | 2.00 |
| 605 Nelson Briles | .40 |

| NO. PLAYER | MINT | NO. PLAYER | MINT | NO. PLAYER | MINT | NO. PLAYER | MINT |
|---|---|---|---|---|---|---|---|
| 606 Luis Melendez | .40 | 653 Jim Fairey | .40 | 700 B. Murcer (In Action) | 2.00 | 744 Jim Slaton | 1.00 |
| 607 Frank Duffy | .40 | 654 Horacio Pina | .40 | 701 Jose Pagan | 1.00 | 745 Julian Javier | 1.00 |
| 608 Mike Corkins | .40 | 655 Jerry Grote | .40 | 702 J. Pagan (In Action) | 1.00 | 746 Lowell Palmer | 1.00 |
| 609 Tom Grieve | .40 | 656 Rudy May | .40 | 703 Doug Griffin | 1.00 | 747 Jim Stewart | 1.00 |
| 610 Bill Stoneman | .40 | 657 Bobby Wine | 1.00 | 704 D. Griffin (In Action) | 1.00 | 748 Phil Hennigan | 1.00 |
| 611 Rich Reese | .40 | 658 Steve Dunning | 1.00 | 705 Pat Corrales | 1.00 | 749 Walter Alston (Mgr.) | 2.50 |
| 612 Joe Decker | .40 | 659 Bob Aspromonte | 1.00 | 706 P. Corrales (In Action) | 1.00 | 750 Willie Horton | 1.50 |
| 613 Mike Ferraro | .40 | 660 Paul Blair | 1.00 | 707 Tim Foli | 1.00 | 751 S. Carlton (Traded) | 25.00 |
| 614 Ted Uhlaender | .40 | 661 Bill Virdon | 1.25 | 708 T. Foli (In Action) | 1.00 | 752 Joe Morgan (Traded) | 10.00 |
| 615 Steve Hargan | .40 | 662 Stan Bahnsen | 1.00 | 709 Jim Kaat | 4.00 | 753 D. McLain (Traded) | 2.50 |
| 616 Joe Ferguson (R) | .50 | 663 Fran Healy | 1.00 | 710 J. Kaat (In Action) | 2.00 | 754 F. Robinson (Traded) | 7.50 |
| 617 Kansas City Royals | .75 | 664 Bobby Knoop | 1.00 | 711 Bobby Bonds | 4.00 | 755 Jim Fregosi (Traded) | 1.25 |
| 618 Rich Robertson | .40 | 665 Chris Short | 1.00 | 712 B. Bonds (In Action) | 2.00 | 756 Rick Wise (Traded) | 1.00 |
| 619 Rich McKinney | .40 | 666 Hector Torres | 1.00 | 713 Gene Michael | 1.00 | 757 J. Cardenal (Traded) | 1.00 |
| 620 Phil Niekro | 2.00 | 667 Ray Newman | 1.00 | 714 G. Michael (In Action) | 1.00 | 758 Gil Garrido | 1.00 |
| 621 Commissioners Award | .75 | 668 Texas Rangers | 2.00 | 715 Mike Epstein | 1.00 | 759 Chris Cannizzaro | 1.00 |
| 622 MVP Award | .75 | 669 Willie Crawford | 1.00 | 716 Jesus Alou | 1.00 | 760 Bill Mazeroski | 2.00 |
| 623 Cy Young Award | .75 | 670 Ken Holtzman | 1.50 | 717 Bruce Dal Canton | 1.00 | 761 Rookie Stars: | 12.50 |
| 624 Minor League Player of the Year | .60 | 671 Donn Clendenon | 1.00 | 718 Del Rice | 1.00 |   Bernie Williams, Ben Oglivie, Ron Cey |  |
| 625 Rookie of the Year | .75 | 672 Archie Reynolds | 1.00 | 719 Cesar Geronimo | 1.00 | 762 Wayne Simpson | 1.00 |
| 626 Babe Ruth Award | .75 | 673 Dave Marshall | 1.00 | 720 Sam McDowell | 1.00 | 763 Ron Hansen | 1.00 |
| 627 Moe Drabowsky | .40 | 674 John Kennedy | 1.00 | 721 Eddie Leon | 1.00 | 764 Dusty Baker | 3.00 |
| 628 Terry Crowley | .40 | 675 Pat Jarvis | 1.00 | 722 Bill Sudakis | 1.00 | 765 Ken McMullen | 1.00 |
| 629 Paul Doyle | .40 | 676 Danny Cater | 1.00 | 723 Al Santorini | 1.00 | 766 Steve Hamilton | 1.00 |
| 630 Rich Hebner | .40 | 677 Ivan Murrell | 1.00 | 724 AL Rookie Pitchers: | 1.25 | 767 Tom McCraw | 1.00 |
| 631 John Strohmayer | .40 | 678 Steve Luebber | 1.00 |   John Curtis, Rich Hinton, Mickey Scott |  | 768 Denny Doyle | 1.00 |
| 632 Mike Hegan | .40 | 679 Astros Rookies: | 1.25 | 725 Dick McAuliffe | 1.00 | 769 Jack Aker | 1.00 |
| 633 Jack Hiatt | .40 |   Bob Fenwick, Bob Stinson |  | 726 Dick Selma | 1.00 | 770 Jim Wynn | 1.00 |
| 634 Dick Woodson | .40 | 680 Dave Johnson | 1.50 | 727 Jose LaBoy | 1.00 | 771 San Francisco Giants | 1.50 |
| 635 Don Money | .40 | 681 Bobby Pfeil | 1.00 | 728 Gail Hopkins | 1.00 | 772 Ken Tatum | 1.00 |
| 636 Bill Lee | .40 | 682 Mike McCormick | 1.00 | 729 Bob Veale | 1.00 | 773 Ron Brand | 1.00 |
| 637 Preston Gomez | .40 | 683 Steve Hovley | 1.00 | 730 Rick Monday | 1.50 | 774 Luis Alvarado | 1.00 |
| 638 Ken Wright | .40 | 684 Hal Breeden | 1.00 | 731 Baltimore Orioles | 1.50 | 775 Jerry Reuss | 2.00 |
| 639 J.C. Martin | .40 | 685 Joe Horlen | 1.00 | 732 George Culver | 1.00 | 776 Bill Voss | 1.00 |
| 640 Joe Coleman | .40 | 686 Steve Garvey | 65.00 | 733 Jim Hart | 1.00 | 777 Hoyt Wilhelm | 5.00 |
| 641 Mike Lum | .40 | 687 Del Unser | 1.00 | 734 Bob Burda | 1.00 | 778 Twins Rookies: | 1.50 |
| 642 Dennis Riddleberger | .40 | 688 St. Louis Cardinals | 1.50 | 735 Diego Segui | 1.00 |   Vic Albury, Rick Dempsey, Jim Strickland |  |
| 643 Russ Gibson | .40 | 689 Eddie Fisher | 1.00 | 736 Bill Russell | 1.50 | 779 Tony Cloninger | 1.00 |
| 644 Bernie Allen | .40 | 690 Willie Montanez | 1.00 | 737 Lenny Randle | 1.00 | 780 Dick Green | 1.00 |
| 645 Jim Maloney | .40 | 691 Curt Blefary | 1.00 | 738 Jim Merritt | 1.00 | 781 Jim McAndrew | 1.00 |
| 646 Chico Salmon | .40 | 692 C. Blefary (In Action) | 1.00 | 739 Don Mason | 1.00 | 792 Larry Stahl | 1.00 |
| 647 Bob Moose | .40 | 693 Alan Gallagher | 1.00 | 740 Rico Carty | 1.25 | 783 Les Cain | 1.00 |
| 648 Jim Lyttle | .40 | 694 Gallagher (In Action) | 1.00 | 741 Rookie Stars: | 1.50 | 784 Ken Aspromonte | 1.00 |
| 649 Pete Richert | .40 | 695 Rod Carew | 55.00 |   Tom Hutton, John Milner, Rick Miller |  | 785 Vic Davalillo | 1.00 |
| 650 Sal Bando | .50 | 696 R. Carew (In Action) | 25.00 | 742 Jim Rooker | 1.00 | 786 Chuck Brinkman | 1.00 |
| 651 Cincinnati Reds | 1.00 | 697 Jerry Koosman | 4.00 | 743 Cesar Gutierrez | 1.00 | 787 Ron Reed | 1.50 |
| 652 Marcelino Lopez | .40 | 698 J. Koosman (In Action) | 2.00 |  |  |  |  |
|  |  | 699 Bobby Murcer | 4.00 |  |  |  |  |

## 1973 Topps....Complete Set of 660 Cards—Value $325.00

Includes the rookie cards of Mike Schmidt, Darrell Evans and Davey Lopes. The high numbers are 529 to 660. This was the last Topps' set to be issued in *series*. Starting in 1974 the entire set was issued at one time.

| NO. PLAYER | MINT | NO. PLAYER | MINT | NO. PLAYER | MINT | NO. PLAYER | MINT |
|---|---|---|---|---|---|---|---|
| 1 All-Time HR Leaders: | 6.00 | 10 Don Sutton | 1.00 | 21 Randy Hundley | .15 | 32 Fred Norman | .15 |
|   Babe Ruth, Hank Aaron, Willie Mays |  | 11 Chris Chambliss | .30 | 22 Ted Abernathy | .15 | 33 Jim Breazeale | .15 |
| 2 Rich Hebner | .15 | 12 Don Zimmer (Mgr.) | .25 | 23 Dave Kingman | 1.00 | 34 Pat Dobson | .15 |
| 3 Jim Lonborg | .15 | 13 George Hendrick | .50 | 24 Al Santorini | .15 | 35 Willie Davis | .25 |
| 4 John Milner | .15 | 14 Sonny Siebert | .15 | 25 Roy White | .20 | 36 Steve Barber | .15 |
| 5 Ed Brinkman | .15 | 15 Ralph Garr | .15 | 26 Pittsburgh Pirates | .45 | 37 Bill Robinson | .15 |
| 6 Mac Scarce | .15 | 16 Steve Braun | .15 | 27 Bill Gogolewski | .15 | 38 Mike Epstein | .15 |
| 7 Texas Rangers | .25 | 17 Fred Gladding | .15 | 28 Hal McRae | .30 | 39 Dave Roberts | .15 |
| 8 Tom Hall | .15 | 18 Leroy Stanton | .15 | 29 Tony Taylor | .15 | 40 Reggie Smith | .50 |
| 9 Johnny Oates | .15 | 19 Tim Foli | .15 | 30 Tug McGraw | .50 | 41 Tom Walker | .15 |
|  |  | 20 Stan Bahnsen | .15 | 31 Buddy Bell (R) | 2.50 | 42 Mike Andrews | .15 |

| NO. PLAYER | MINT |
|---|---|
| 43 Randy Moffitt | .15 |
| 44 Rick Monday | .20 |
| 45 Ellie Rodriguez (wrong photo) | .15 |
| 46 Lindy McDaniel | .15 |
| 47 Luis Melendez | .15 |
| 48 Paul Splittorff | .25 |
| 49 Frank Quilici (Mgr.) | .20 |
| 50 Roberto Clemente | 7.50 |
| 51 Chuck Seelbach | .15 |
| 52 Denis Menke | .15 |
| 53 Steve Dunning | .15 |
| 54 Checklist No. 1 | .60 |
| 55 Jon Matlack | .20 |
| 56 Merv Rettenmund | .15 |
| 57 Derrel Thomas | .15 |
| 58 Mike Paul | .15 |
| 59 Steve Yeager (R) | .50 |
| 60 Ken Holtzman | .20 |
| 61 Batting Leaders: Billy Williams, Rod Carew | 1.00 |
| 62 Home Run Leaders: Johnny Bench, Dick Allen | 1.00 |
| 63 RBI Leaders: Johnny Bench, Dick Allen | 1.00 |
| 64 Stolen Base Leaders: B. Campaneris, L. Brock | .50 |
| 65 ERA Leaders: Steve Carlton, Luis Tiant | .75 |
| 66 Victory Leaders: Wilbur Wood, Steve Carlton, Gaylord Perry | 1.00 |
| 67 Strikeout Leaders: Steve Carlton, Nolan Ryan | 1.50 |
| 68 Leading Firemen: Clay Carroll, Sparky Lyle | .25 |
| 69 Phil Gagliano | .15 |
| 70 Milt Pappas | .15 |
| 71 Johnny Briggs | .15 |
| 72 Ron Reed | .15 |
| 73 Ed Herrmann | .15 |
| 74 Billy Champion | .15 |
| 75 Vada Pinson | .30 |
| 76 Doug Rader | .15 |
| 77 Mike Torrez | .20 |
| 78 Richie Scheinblum | .15 |
| 79 Jim Willoughby | .15 |
| 80 Tony Oliva | .60 |
| 81 Whitey Lockman (Mgr.) | .45 |
| 82 Fritz Peterson | .15 |
| 83 Leron Lee | .15 |
| 84 Rollie Fingers | 1.25 |
| 85 Ted Simmons | 1.00 |
| 86 Tom McCraw | .15 |
| 87 Ken Boswell | .15 |
| 88 Mickey Stanley | .15 |
| 89 Jack Billingham | .15 |
| 90 Brooks Robinson | 3.00 |
| 91 Los Angeles Dodgers | .75 |
| 92 Jerry Bell | .15 |
| 93 Jesus Alou | .15 |
| 94 Dick Billings | .15 |
| 95 Steve Blass | .15 |
| 96 Doug Griffin | .15 |
| 97 Willie Montanez | .15 |
| 98 Dick Woodson | .15 |
| 99 Carl Taylor | .15 |
| 100 Hank Aaron | 7.50 |
| 101 Ken Henderson | .15 |
| 102 Rudy May | .15 |
| 103 Celerino Sanchez | .15 |
| 104 Reggie Cleveland | .15 |
| 105 Carlos May | .15 |
| 106 Terry Humphrey | .15 |
| 107 Phil Hennigan | .15 |
| 108 Bill Russell | .15 |
| 109 Doyle Alexander | .15 |
| 110 Bob Watson | .20 |
| 111 Dave Nelson | .15 |
| 112 Gary Ross | .15 |
| 113 Jerry Grote | .15 |
| 114 Lynn McGlothen | .15 |
| 115 Ron Santo | .25 |
| 116 Ralph Houk (Mgr.) | .50 |
| 117 Ramon Hernandez | .15 |

| NO. PLAYER | MINT |
|---|---|
| 118 John Mayberry | .20 |
| 119 Larry Bowa | .40 |
| 120 Joe Coleman | .15 |
| 121 Dave Rader | .15 |
| 122 Jim Strickland | .15 |
| 123 Sandy Alomar | .15 |
| 124 Jim Hardin | .15 |
| 125 Ron Fairly | .15 |
| 126 Jim Brewer | .15 |
| 127 Milwaukee Brewers | .45 |
| 128 Ted Sizemore | .15 |
| 129 Terry Forster | .25 |
| 130 Pete Rose | 14.00 |
| 131 Eddie Kasko (Mgr.) | .30 |
| 132 Matty Alou | .20 |
| 133 Dave Roberts | .15 |
| 134 Milt Wilcox | .20 |
| 135 Lee May | .20 |
| 136 Earl Weaver (Mgr.) | .50 |
| 137 Jim Beauchamp | .15 |
| 138 Horacio Pina | .15 |
| 139 Carmen Fanzone | .15 |
| 140 Lou Piniella | .50 |
| 141 Bruce Kison | .20 |
| 142 Thurman Munson | 3.50 |
| 143 John Curtis | .15 |
| 144 Marty Perez | .15 |
| 145 Bobby Bonds | .25 |
| 146 Woodie Fryman | .15 |
| 147 Mike Anderson | .15 |
| 148 Dave Goltz | .15 |
| 149 Ron Hunt | .15 |
| 150 Wilbur Wood | .15 |
| 151 Wes Parker | .15 |
| 152 Dave May | .15 |
| 153 Al Hrabosky | .20 |
| 154 Jeff Torborg | .15 |
| 155 Sal Bando | .25 |
| 156 Cesar Geronimo | .15 |
| 157 Denny Riddleberger | .15 |
| 158 Houston Astros | .45 |
| 159 Clarence Gaston | .15 |
| 160 Jim Palmer | 3.00 |
| 161 Ted Martinez | .15 |
| 162 Pete Broberg | .15 |
| 163 Vic Davalillo | .15 |
| 164 Monty Montgomery | .15 |
| 165 Luis Aparicio | 1.75 |
| 166 Terry Harmon | .15 |
| 167 Steve Stone | .20 |
| 168 Jim Northrup | .15 |
| 169 Ron Schueler | .15 |
| 170 Harmon Killebrew | 2.00 |
| 171 Bernie Carbo | .15 |
| 172 Steve Kline | .15 |
| 173 Hal Breeden | .15 |
| 174 Rich Gossage (R) | 6.50 |
| 175 Frank Robinson | 2.50 |
| 176 Chuck Taylor | .15 |
| 177 Bill Plummer | .15 |
| 178 Don Rose | .15 |
| 179 Dick Williams (Mgr.) | .35 |
| 180 Fergie Jenkins | .75 |
| 181 Jack Brohamer | .15 |
| 182 Mike Caldwell (R) | .40 |
| 183 Don Buford | .15 |
| 184 Jerry Koosman | .30 |
| 185 Jim Wynn | .20 |
| 186 Bill Fahey | .15 |
| 187 Luke Walker | .15 |
| 188 Cookie Rojas | .15 |
| 189 Greg Luzinski | .75 |
| 190 Bob Gibson | 2.00 |
| 191 Detroit Tigers | .60 |
| 192 Pat Jarvis | .15 |
| 193 Carlton Fisk | 2.00 |
| 194 Jorge Orta | .15 |
| 195 Clay Carroll | .15 |
| 196 Ken McMullen | .15 |
| 197 Ed Goodson | .15 |
| 198 Horace Clarke | .15 |
| 199 Bert Blyleven | .75 |
| 200 Billy Williams | 1.00 |
| 201 AL Playoffs: Hendrick Scores | .75 |

| NO. PLAYER | MINT |
|---|---|
| 202 NL Playoffs: Foster's Run Decides It | .75 |
| 203 World Series Game 1 Tenace the Menace | .75 |
| 204 World Series Game 2 A's Make It Two Straight | .75 |
| 205 World Series Game 3 Reds Win Squeaker | .75 |
| 206 World Series Game 4 Tenace Singles In Ninth | .75 |
| 207 World Series Game 5 Odom Out at Plate | .75 |
| 208 World Series Game 6 Red's Ties Series | .75 |
| 209 World Series Game 7 Campy Stars Rally | .75 |
| 210 World Series A's— World Champions | .75 |
| 211 Balor Moore | .15 |
| 212 Joe LaHoud | .15 |
| 213 Steve Garvey | 7.50 |
| 214 Steve Hamilton | .15 |
| 215 Dusty Baker | .75 |
| 216 Toby Harrah | .25 |
| 217 Don Wilson | .15 |
| 218 Aurelio Rodriguez | .15 |
| 219 St. Louis Cardinals | .45 |
| 220 Nolan Ryan | 4.00 |
| 221 Fred Kendall | .15 |
| 222 Rob Gardner | .15 |
| 223 Bud Harrelson | .15 |
| 224 Bill Lee | .15 |
| 225 Al Oliver | 1.25 |
| 226 Ray Fosse | .15 |
| 227 Wayne Twitchell | .15 |
| 228 Bobby Darwin | .15 |
| 229 Roric Harrison | .15 |
| 230 Joe Morgan | 1.50 |
| 231 Bill Parsons | .15 |
| 232 Ken Singleton | .40 |
| 233 Ed Kirkpatrick | .15 |
| 234 Bill North | .15 |
| 235 Jim Hunter | 1.25 |
| 236 Tito Fuentes | .15 |
| 237 Eddie Mathews (Mgr.) | .15 |
| 238 Tony Muser | .15 |
| 239 Pete Richert | .15 |
| 240 Bobby Murcer | .50 |
| 241 Dwain Anderson | .15 |
| 242 George Culver | .15 |
| 243 California Angels | .15 |
| 244 Ed Acosta | .15 |
| 245 Carl Yastrzemski | 7.50 |
| 246 Ken Sanders | .15 |
| 247 Del Unser | .15 |
| 248 Jerry Johnson | .15 |
| 249 Larry Biittner | .15 |
| 250 Manny Sanguillen | .20 |
| 251 Roger Nelson | .15 |
| 252 Charlie Fox (Mgr.) | .30 |
| 253 Mark Belanger | .20 |
| 254 Bill Stoneman | .15 |
| 255 Reggie Jackson | 7.50 |
| 256 Chris Zachary | .15 |
| 257 Yogi Berra (Mgr.) | .75 |
| 258 Tommy John | .75 |
| 259 Jim Holt | .15 |
| 260 Gary Nolan | .15 |
| 261 Pat Kelly | .15 |
| 262 Jack Aker | .15 |
| 263 George Scott | .15 |
| 264 Checklist No. 2 | .60 |
| 265 Gene Michael | .15 |
| 266 Mike Lum | .15 |
| 267 Lloyd Allen | .15 |
| 268 Jerry Morales | .15 |
| 269 Tim McCarver | .40 |
| 270 Luis Tiant | .30 |
| 271 Tom Hutton | .15 |
| 272 Ed Farmer | .15 |
| 273 Chris Speier | .15 |
| 274 Darold Knowles | .15 |
| 275 Tony Perez | .75 |
| 276 Joe Lovitto | .15 |
| 277 Bob Miller | .15 |

| NO. PLAYER | MINT |
|---|---|
| 278 Baltimore Orioles | .50 |
| 279 Mike Strahler | .15 |
| 280 Al Kaline | 3.00 |
| 281 Mike Jorgensen | .15 |
| 282 Steve Hovley | .15 |
| 283 Ray Sadecki | .15 |
| 284 Glenn Borgmann | .15 |
| 285 Don Kessinger | .15 |
| 286 Frank Linzy | .15 |
| 287 Eddie Leon | .15 |
| 288 Gary Gentry | .15 |
| 289 Bob Oliver | .15 |
| 290 Cesar Cedeno | .40 |
| 291 Rogelio Moret | .15 |
| 292 Jose Cruz | .60 |
| 293 Bernie Allen | .15 |
| 294 Steve Arlin | .15 |
| 295 Bert Campaneris | .25 |
| 296 Sparky Anderson (Mgr.) | .40 |
| 297 Walt Williams | .15 |
| 298 Ron Bryant | .15 |
| 299 Ted Ford | .15 |
| 300 Steve Carlton | 6.00 |
| 301 Billy Grabarkewitz | .15 |
| 302 Terry Crowley | .15 |
| 303 Nelson Briles | .15 |
| 304 Duke Sims | .15 |
| 305 Willie Mays | 7.50 |
| 306 Tom Burgmeier | .15 |
| 307 Boots Day | .15 |
| 308 Skip Lockwood | .15 |
| 309 Paul Popovich | .15 |
| 310 Dick Allen | .30 |
| 311 Joe Decker | .15 |
| 312 Oscar Brown | .15 |
| 313 Jim Ray | .15 |
| 314 Ron Swoboda | .15 |
| 315 John Odom | .15 |
| 316 San Diego Padres | .40 |
| 317 Danny Cater | .15 |
| 318 Jim McGlothlin | .15 |
| 319 Jim Spencer | .15 |
| 320 Lou Brock | 2.50 |
| 321 Rich Hinton | .15 |
| 322 Garry Maddox (R) | .75 |
| 323 Billy Martin (Mgr.) | .50 |
| 324 Al Downing | .15 |
| 325 Boog Powell | .50 |
| 326 Darrell Brandon | .15 |
| 327 John Lowenstein | .15 |
| 328 Bill Bonham | .15 |
| 329 Ed Kranepool | .15 |
| 330 Rod Carew | 6.50 |
| 331 Carl Morton | .15 |
| 332 John Felske | .15 |
| 333 Gene Clines | .15 |
| 334 Freddie Patek | .15 |
| 335 Bob Tolan | .15 |
| 336 Tom Bradley | .15 |
| 337 Dave Duncan | .15 |
| 338 Checklist No. 3 | .60 |
| 339 Dick Tidrow | .15 |
| 340 Nate Colbert | .15 |
| 341 Jim Palmer (Boyhood) | 1.00 |
| 342 S. McDowell (Boyhood) | .25 |
| 343 B. Murcer (Boyhood) | .25 |
| 344 Jim Hunter (Boyhood) | .50 |
| 345 Chris Speier (Boyhood) | .25 |
| 346 G. Perry (Boyhood) | .60 |
| 347 Kansas City Royals | .50 |
| 348 Rennie Stennett | .15 |
| 349 Dick McAuliffe | .15 |
| 350 Tom Seaver | 6.50 |
| 351 Jimmy Stewart | .15 |
| 352 Don Stanhouse | .15 |
| 353 Steve Brye | .15 |
| 354 Billy Parker | .15 |
| 355 Mike Marshall | .25 |
| 356 Chuck Tanner (Mgr.) | .35 |
| 357 Ross Grimsley | .15 |
| 358 Jim Nettles | .15 |
| 359 Cecil Upshaw | .15 |
| 360 Joe Rudi (photo of Gene Tenace) | .45 |
| 361 Fran Healy | .15 |

| NO. PLAYER | MINT |
|---|---|
| 362 Eddie Watt | .15 |
| 363 Jackie Hernandez | .15 |
| 364 Rick Wise | .15 |
| 365 Rico Petrocelli | .15 |
| 366 Brock Davis | .15 |
| 367 Burt Hooton | .15 |
| 368 Bill Buckner | .60 |
| 369 Lerrin LaGrow | .15 |
| 370 Willie Stargell | 2.50 |
| 371 Mike Kekich | .15 |
| 372 Oscar Gamble | .20 |
| 373 Clyde Wright | .15 |
| 374 Darrell Evans | .35 |
| 375 Larry Dierker | .15 |
| 376 Frank Duffy | .15 |
| 377 Gene Mauch (Mgr.) | .25 |
| 378 Lenny Randle | .15 |
| 379 Cy Acosta | .15 |
| 380 Johnny Bench | 7.00 |
| 381 Vicente Romo | .15 |
| 382 Mike Hegan | .15 |
| 383 Diego Segui | .15 |
| 384 Don Baylor | .75 |
| 385 Jim Perry | .25 |
| 386 Don Money | .15 |
| 387 Jim Barr | .15 |
| 388 Ben Oglivie | .50 |
| 389 New York Mets | 1.00 |
| 390 Mickey Lolich | .40 |
| 391 Lee Lacy (R) | 1.00 |
| 392 Dick Drago | .15 |
| 393 Jose Cardenal | .15 |
| 394 Sparky Lyle | .25 |
| 395 Roger Metzger | .15 |
| 396 Grant Jackson | .15 |
| 397 Dave Cash | .20 |
| 398 Rich Hand | .20 |
| 399 George Foster | 1.50 |
| 400 Gaylord Perry | 1.75 |
| 401 Clyde Mashore | .20 |
| 402 Jack Hiatt | .20 |
| 403 Sonny Jackson | .20 |
| 404 Chuck Brinkman | .20 |
| 405 Cesar Tovar | .20 |
| 406 Paul Lindblad | .20 |
| 407 Felix Millan | .20 |
| 408 Jim Colborn | .20 |
| 409 Ivan Murrell | .20 |
| 410 Willie McCovey | 2.50 |
| 411 Ray Corbin | .20 |
| 412 Manny Mota | .25 |
| 413 Tom Timmerman | .20 |
| 414 Ken Rudolph | .20 |
| 415 Marty Pattin | .20 |
| 416 Paul Schaal | .20 |
| 417 Scipio Spinks | .20 |
| 418 Bobby Grich | .35 |
| 419 Casey Cox | .20 |
| 420 Tommie Agee | .20 |
| 421 Bobby Winkles (Mgr.) | .30 |
| 422 Bob Robertson | .20 |
| 423 Johnny Jeter | .20 |
| 424 Denny Doyle | .20 |
| 425 Alex Johnson | .20 |
| 426 Dave LaRoche | .20 |
| 427 Rick Auerbach | .20 |
| 428 Wayne Simpson | .20 |
| 429 Jim Fairey | .20 |
| 430 Vida Blue | .40 |
| 431 Gerry Moses | .20 |
| 432 Dan Frisella | .20 |
| 433 Willie Horton | .25 |
| 434 San F. Giants | .40 |
| 435 Rico Carty | .35 |
| 436 Jim McAndrew | .20 |
| 437 John Kennedy | .20 |
| 438 Enzo Hernandez | .20 |
| 439 Eddie Fisher | .20 |
| 440 Glenn Beckert | .20 |
| 441 Gail Hopkins | .20 |
| 442 Dick Dietz | .20 |
| 443 Danny Thompson | .20 |
| 444 Ken Brett | .20 |
| 445 Ken Berry | .20 |
| 446 Jerry Reuss | .35 |

| NO. PLAYER | MINT |
|---|---|
| 447 Joe Hague | .20 |
| 448 John Hiller | .20 |
| 449 Ken Aspromonte (Mgr.) | .40 |
| 450 Joe Torre | .50 |
| 451 John Vuckovich | .20 |
| 452 Paul Casanova | .20 |
| 453 Checklist No. 4 | .75 |
| 454 Tom Haller | .20 |
| 455 Bill Melton | .20 |
| 456 Dick Green | .20 |
| 457 John Strohmayer | .20 |
| 458 Jim Mason | .20 |
| 459 Jimmy Howarth | .20 |
| 460 Bill Freehan | .25 |
| 461 Mike Corkins | .20 |
| 462 Ron Blomberg | .20 |
| 463 Ken Tatum | .20 |
| 464 Chicago Cubs | .60 |
| 465 Dave Giusti | .20 |
| 466 Jose Arcia | .20 |
| 467 Mike Ryan | .20 |
| 468 Tom Griffin | .20 |
| 469 Dan Monzon | .20 |
| 470 Mike Cuellar | .25 |
| 471 All-Time Hits | 2.00 |
| Ty Cobb (4,191) | |
| 472 All-Time Grand Slams: | 2.00 |
| Lou Gehrig (23) | |
| 473 All-Time Total Bases | 2.00 |
| hank Aaron (6,172) | |
| 474 All-Time RBI's | 2.50 |
| Babe Ruth (2,209) | |
| 475 All-Time Batting: | 2.00 |
| Ty Cobb (.367) | |
| 476 All-Time Shutouts: | 1.50 |
| Walter Johnson (113) | |
| 477 All-Time Victory Ldrs. | 1.50 |
| Cy Young (511) | |
| 478 All-Time Strikeouts: | 1.50 |
| Walter Johnson (3,508) | |
| 479 Hal Lanier | .20 |
| 480 Juan Marichal | 2.00 |
| 481 Chicago White Sox | .50 |
| 482 Rick Reuschel (R) | .80 |
| 483 Dal Maxvill | .20 |
| 484 Ernie McAnally | .20 |
| 485 Norm Cash | .30 |
| 486 Danny Ozark (Mgr.) | .40 |
| 487 Bruce Dal Canton | .20 |
| 488 Dave Campbell | .20 |
| 489 Jeff Burroughs | .20 |
| 490 Claude Osteen | .20 |
| 491 Bob Montgomery | .20 |
| 492 Pedro Borbon | .20 |
| 493 Duffy Dyer | .20 |
| 494 Rich Morales | .20 |
| 495 Tommy Helms | .20 |
| 496 Ray Lamb | .20 |
| 497 R. Schoendienst (Mgr.) | .50 |
| 498 Graig Nettles | 1.50 |
| 499 Bob Moose | .20 |
| 500 Oakland A's | .40 |
| 501 Larry Gura | .25 |
| 502 Bobby Valentine | .25 |
| 503 Phil Niekro | 1.50 |
| 504 Earl Williams | .20 |
| 505 Bob Bailey | .20 |
| 506 Bart Johnson | .20 |
| 507 Darrel Chaney | .20 |
| 508 Gates Brown | .20 |
| 509 Jim Nash | .20 |
| 510 Amos Otis | .30 |
| 511 Sam McDowell | .20 |
| 512 Dalton Jones | .20 |
| 513 Dave Marshall | .20 |
| 514 Jerry Kenney | .20 |
| 515 Andy Messersmith | .30 |
| 516 Danny Walton | .20 |
| 517 Bill Virdon (Mgr.) | .35 |
| 518 Bob Veale | .20 |
| 519 John Edwards | .20 |
| 520 Mel Stottlemyre | .35 |
| 521 Atlanta Braves | .50 |
| 522 Leo Cardenas | .20 |

| NO. PLAYER | MINT |
|---|---|
| 523 Wayne Granger | .20 |
| 524 Gene Tenace | .20 |
| 525 Jim Fregosi | .20 |
| 526 Ollie Brown | .20 |
| 527 Dan McGinn | .20 |
| 528 Paul Blair | .20 |
| 529 Milt May | .65 |
| 530 Jim Kaat | 1.50 |
| 531 Ron Woods | .65 |
| 532 Steve Mingori | .65 |
| 533 Larry Stahl | .65 |
| 534 Dave Lemonds | .65 |
| 535 John Callison | .90 |
| 536 Philadelphia Phillies | 1.25 |
| 537 Bill Slayback | .60 |
| 538 Jim Hart | .60 |
| 539 Tom Murphy | .60 |
| 540 Cleon Jones | .60 |
| 541 Bob Bolin | .60 |
| 542 Pat Corrales | .60 |
| 543 Alan Foster | .60 |
| 544 Von Joshua | .60 |
| 545 Orlando Cepeda | 1.50 |
| 546 Jim York | .60 |
| 547 Bobby Heise | .60 |
| 548 Don Durham | .60 |
| 549 Whitey Herzog (Mgr.) | 1.25 |
| 550 Dave Johnson | 1.50 |
| 551 Mike Kilkenny | .60 |
| 552 J.C. Martin | .60 |
| 553 Mickey Scott | .60 |
| 554 Dave Concepcion | 1.50 |
| 555 Bill Hands | .60 |
| 556 New York Yankees | 2.25 |
| 557 Bernie Williams | .60 |
| 558 Jerry May | .60 |
| 559 Barry Lersch | .60 |
| 560 Frank Howard | 1.50 |
| 561 Jim Geddes | .60 |
| 562 Wayne Garrett | .60 |
| 563 Larry Haney | .60 |
| 564 Mike Thompson | .60 |
| 565 Jim Hickman | .60 |
| 566 Lew Krausse | .60 |
| 567 Bob Fenwick | .60 |
| 568 Ray Newman | .60 |
| 569 Walt Alston (Mgr.) | 1.50 |
| 570 Bill Singer | .60 |
| 571 Rusty Torres | .60 |
| 572 Gary Sutherland | .60 |
| 573 Fred Beene | .60 |
| 574 Bob Didier | .60 |
| 575 Dock Ellis | .60 |
| 576 Montreal Expos | 1.25 |
| 577 Eric Soderholm | .60 |
| 578 Ken Wright | .60 |
| 579 Tom Grieve | .60 |
| 580 Joe Pepitone | .75 |
| 581 Steve Kealey | .60 |
| 582 Darrell Porter | 1.00 |
| 583 Bill Grief | .60 |
| 584 Chris Arnold | .60 |
| 585 Joe Niekro | 1.25 |
| 586 Bill Sudakis | .60 |
| 587 Rich McKinney | .60 |
| 588 Checklist No. 5 | 6.00 |
| 589 Ken Forsch | .60 |
| 590 Deron Johnson | .60 |
| 591 Mike Hedlund | .60 |
| 592 John Boccabella | .60 |
| 593 Jack McKeon (Mgr.) | .60 |
| 594 Vic Harris | .60 |
| 595 Don Gullett | .60 |
| 596 Boston Red Sox | 1.50 |
| 597 Mickey Rivers | 1.25 |
| 598 Phil Roof | .60 |
| 599 Ed Crosby | .60 |
| 600 Dave McNally | .60 |
| 601 Rookie Catchers: | .75 |
| George Pena, Sergio Robles, R. Stelmaszek | |
| 602 Rookie Pitchers: | .75 |
| Doug Rau, Mel Behney, Ralph Garcia | |

| NO. PLAYER | MINT |
|---|---|
| 603 Rookie 3rd Basemen: | .75 |
| Billy McNulty, Ken Reitz, Terry Hughes | |
| 604 Rookie Pitchers: | .75 |
| Jesse Jefferson, Dennis O'Toole, Bob Strampe | |
| 605 Rookie 1st Basemen: | .75 |
| Pat Bourque, Enos Cabell, Gonzalo Marquez | |
| 606 Rookie Outfielders: | 2.50 |
| Jorge Roque, Gary Matthews, T. Paciorek | |
| 607 Rookie Shortstops: | .75 |
| Pepe Frias, Ray Busse, Mario Guerrero | |
| 608 Rookie Pitchers: | .75 |
| S. Busby, G. Medich, Dick Colpaert | |
| 609 Rookie 2nd Basemen: | 3.00 |
| Larvell Blanks, P. Garcia, Dave Lopes | |
| 610 Rookie Pitchers: | 1.50 |
| Hank Webb, J. Freeman, Charlie Hough | |
| 611 Rookie Outfielders: | 1.50 |
| Richie Zisk, Rich Coggins, J. Wohlford | |
| 612 Rookie Pitchers: | .75 |
| Steve Lawson, Bob Reynolds, Brent Strom | |
| 613 Rookie Catchers: | 1.50 |
| Bob Boone, S. Jutze, Mike Ivie | |
| 614 Rookie Outfielders: | 7.50 |
| A. Bumbry, Dwight Evans, Charlie Spikes | |
| 615 Rookie 3rd Basemen: | 105.00 |
| Ron Cey, Mike Schmidt, John Hilton | |
| 616 Rookie Pitchers: | .75 |
| S. Blateric, Norm Angelini, Mike Garman | |
| 617 Rich Chiles | .60 |
| 618 Andy Etchebarren | .60 |
| 619 Billy Wilson | .60 |
| 620 Tommy Harper | .60 |
| 621 Joe Ferguson | .60 |
| 622 Larry Hisle | .60 |
| 623 Steve Renko | .60 |
| 624 Leo Durocher (Mgr.) | 1.00 |
| 625 Angel Mangual | .60 |
| 626 Bob Barton | .60 |
| 627 Luis Alvarado | .60 |
| 628 Jim Slaton | .60 |
| 629 Cleveland Indians | 1.25 |
| 630 Denny McLain | 1.50 |
| 631 Tom Matchick | .60 |
| 632 Dick Selma | .60 |
| 633 Ike Brown | .60 |
| 634 Alan Closter | .60 |
| 635 Gene Alley | .60 |
| 636 Rick Clark | .60 |
| 637 Norm Miller | .60 |
| 638 Ken Reynolds | .60 |
| 639 Willie Crawford | .60 |
| 640 Dick Bosman | .60 |
| 641 Cincinnati Reds | 1.25 |
| 642 Jose LaBoy | .60 |
| 643 Al Fitzmorris | .60 |
| 644 Jack Heidemann | .60 |
| 645 Bob Locker | .60 |
| 646 Del Crandall (Mgr.) | 1.00 |
| 647 George Stone | .60 |
| 648 Tom Egan | .60 |
| 649 Rich Folkers | .60 |
| 650 Felipe Alou | .60 |
| 651 Don Carrithers | .60 |
| 652 Ted Kubiak | .60 |
| 653 Joe Hoerner | .60 |
| 654 Minnesota Twins | 1.25 |
| 655 Clay Kirby | .60 |
| 656 John Ellis | .60 |
| 657 Bob Johnson | .60 |
| 658 Elliott Maddox | .60 |
| 659 Jose Pagan | .60 |
| 660 Fred Scherman | 1.00 |

# 1974 Topps....Complete Set of 660 Cards—Value $250.00

Features the rookie cards of Dave Parker and Dave Winfield. This was Topps' first card set to be released all at one time. Previous card sets were released in series, several weeks or months apart. Fifteen Padres cards were printed either "San Diego" or "Washington". Because of a false rumor that the Padres were moving, Topps printed "Washington" on the cards, but it was quickly corrected.

| NO. PLAYER | MINT |
|---|---|
| 1 Hank Aaron | 10.00 |
| Home Run King | |
| 2 Aaron Special (1954-57) | 2.50 |
| 3 Aaron Special (1958-61) | 2.50 |
| 4 Aaron Special (1962-65) | 2.50 |
| 5 Aaron Special (1966-69) | 2.50 |
| 6 Aaron Special (1970-73) | 2.50 |
| 7 Jim Hunter | 1.25 |
| 8 George Theodore | .15 |
| 9 Mickey Lolich | .30 |
| 10 Johnny Bench | 4.25 |
| 11 Jim Bibby | .15 |
| 12 Dave May | .15 |
| 13 Tom Hilgendorf | .15 |
| 14 Paul Popovich | .15 |
| 15 Joe Torre | .45 |
| 16 Baltimore Orioles | .45 |
| 17 Doug Bird | .15 |
| 18 Gary Thomasson | .15 |
| 19 Gerry Moses | .15 |
| 20 Nolan Ryan | 3.50 |
| 21 Bob Gallagher | .15 |
| 22 Cy Acosta | .15 |
| 23 Craig Robinson | .15 |
| 24 John Hiller | .20 |
| 25 Ken Singleton | .25 |
| 26 Bill Campbell (R) | .25 |
| 27 George Scott | .15 |
| 28 Manny Sanguillen | .15 |
| 29 Phil Niekro | 1.00 |
| 30 Bobby Bonds | .25 |
| 31 Preston Gomez (Mgr.) | .20 |
| 32 John Grubb (SD) | .40 |
| 32 John Grubb (Wash) | 3.00 |
| 33 Don Newhauser | .15 |
| 34 Andy Kosco | .15 |
| 35 Gaylord Perry | 1.50 |
| 36 St. Louis Cardinals | .45 |
| 37 Dave Sells | .15 |
| 38 Don Kessinger | .15 |
| 39 Ken Suarez | .15 |
| 40 Jim Palmer | 2.75 |
| 41 Bobby Floyd | .15 |
| 42 Claude Osteen | .15 |
| 43 Jim Wynn | .15 |
| 44 Mel Stottlemyre | .20 |
| 45 Dave Johnson | .20 |
| 46 Pat Kelly | .15 |
| 47 Dick Ruthven | .15 |
| 48 Dick Sharon | .15 |
| 49 Steve Renko | .15 |
| 50 Rod Carew | 4.75 |
| 51 Bob Heise | .15 |
| 52 Al Oliver | 1.00 |
| 53 Fred Kendall (SD) | .25 |
| 53 Fred Kendall (Wash) | 3.00 |
| 54 Elias Sosa | .15 |
| 55 Frank Robinson | 2.50 |
| 56 New York Mets | .75 |
| 57 Darold Knowles | .15 |
| 58 Charlie Spikes | .15 |
| 59 Ross Grimsley | .15 |
| 60 Lou Brock | 2.25 |
| 61 Luis Aparicio | 1.50 |
| 62 Bob Locker | .15 |
| 63 Bill Sudakis | .15 |

| NO. PLAYER | MINT |
|---|---|
| 64 Doug Rau | .15 |
| 65 Amos Otis | .25 |
| 66 Sparky Lyle | .25 |
| 67 Tommy Helms | .15 |
| 68 Grant Jackson | .15 |
| 69 Del Unser | .15 |
| 70 Dick Allen | .25 |
| 71 Dan Frisella | .15 |
| 72 Aurelio Rodriguez | .15 |
| 73 Mike Marshall | .40 |
| 74 Minnesota Twins | .35 |
| 75 Jim Colborn | .15 |
| 76 Mickey Rivers | .25 |
| 77 Rich Troedson (SD) | .25 |
| 77 Rich Troedson (Wash) | 3.00 |
| 78 Charlie Fox (Mgr.) | .20 |
| 79 Gene Tenace | .15 |
| 80 Tom Seaver | 4.00 |
| 81 Frank Duffy | .15 |
| 82 Dave Giusti | .15 |
| 83 Orlando Cepeda | .60 |
| 84 Rick Wise | .15 |
| 85 Joe Morgan | 1.50 |
| 86 Joe Ferguson | .15 |
| 87 Fergie Jenkins | .75 |
| 88 Freddie Patek | .15 |
| 89 Jackie Brown | .15 |
| 90 Bobby Murcer | .40 |
| 91 Ken Forsch | .15 |
| 92 Paul Blair | .15 |
| 93 Rod Gilbreath | .15 |
| 94 Detroit Tigers | .60 |
| 95 Steve Carlton | 5.50 |
| 96 Jerry Hairston | .15 |
| 97 Bob Bailey | .15 |
| 98 Bert Blyleven | .50 |
| 99 Del Crandall (Mgr.) | .25 |
| 100 Willie Stargell | 2.00 |
| 101 Bobby Valentine | .20 |
| 102 Bill Greif (SD) | .30 |
| 102 Bill Greif (Wash.) | 3.00 |
| 103 Sal Bando | .30 |
| 104 Ron Bryant | .15 |
| 105 Carlton Fisk | 1.00 |
| 106 Harry Parker | .15 |
| 107 Alex Johnson | .15 |
| 108 Al Hrabosky | .15 |
| 109 Bob Grich | .25 |
| 110 Billy Williams | .75 |
| 111 Clay Carroll | .15 |
| 112 Dave Lopes | .25 |
| 113 Dick Drago | .15 |
| 114 California Angels | .40 |
| 115 Willie Horton | .20 |
| 116 Jerry Reuss | .25 |
| 117 Ron Blomberg | .15 |
| 118 Bill Lee | .15 |
| 119 Danny Ozark (Mgr.) | .25 |
| 120 Wilbur Wood | .15 |
| 121 Larry Lintz | .15 |
| 122 Jim Holt | .15 |
| 123 Nellie Briles | .15 |
| 124 Bobby Coluccio | .15 |
| 125 Nate Colbert (SD) | .30 |
| 125 Nate Colbert (Wash.) | 3.00 |
| 126 Checklist No. 1 | .50 |

| NO. PLAYER | MINT |
|---|---|
| 127 Tom Paciorek | .20 |
| 128 John Ellis | .15 |
| 129 Chris Speier | .15 |
| 130 Reggie Jackson | 5.00 |
| 131 Bob Boone | .20 |
| 132 Felix Milan | .15 |
| 133 David Clyde | .15 |
| 134 Denis Menke | .15 |
| 135 Roy White | .15 |
| 136 Rick Reuschel | .20 |
| 137 Al Bumbry | .15 |
| 138 Ed Brinkman | .15 |
| 139 Aurelio Monteagudo | .15 |
| 140 Darrell Evans | .30 |
| 141 Pat Bourque | .15 |
| 142 Pedro Garcia | .15 |
| 143 Dick Woodson | .15 |
| 144 Walter Alston (Mgr.) | .65 |
| 145 Dock Ellis | .15 |
| 146 Ron Fairly | .15 |
| 147 Bart Johnson | .15 |
| 148 Dave Hilton (SD) | .30 |
| 148 Dave Hilton (Wash.) | 3.00 |
| 149 Mac Scarce | .15 |
| 150 John Mayberry | .20 |
| 151 Diego Segui | .15 |
| 152 Oscar Gamble | .25 |
| 153 Jon Matlack | .20 |
| 154 Houston Astros | .35 |
| 155 Bert Campaneris | .25 |
| 156 Randy Moffitt | .15 |
| 157 Vic Harris | .15 |
| 158 Jack Billingham | .15 |
| 159 Jim Hart | .15 |
| 160 Brooks Robinson | 2.50 |
| 161 Ray Burris (R) | .45 |
| 162 Bill Freehan | .20 |
| 163 Ken Berry | .15 |
| 164 Tom House | .15 |
| 165 Willie Davis | .15 |
| 166 Jack McKeon (Mgr.) | .25 |
| 167 Luis Tiant | .25 |
| 168 Danny Thompson | .15 |
| 169 Steve Rogers (R) | 1.00 |
| 170 Bill Melton | .15 |
| 171 Eduardo Rodriguez | .15 |
| 172 Gene Clines | .15 |
| 173 Randy Jones (SD) | .50 |
| 173 Randy Jones (Wash.) | 3.50 |
| 174 Bill Robinson | .15 |
| 175 Reggie Cleveland | .15 |
| 176 John Lowenstein | .15 |
| 177 Dave Roberts | .15 |
| 178 Garry Maddox | .15 |
| 179 Yogi Berra (Mgr.) | .60 |
| 180 Ken Holtzman | .20 |
| 181 Cesar Geronimo | .20 |
| 182 Lindy McDaniel | .20 |
| 183 Johnny Oates | .20 |
| 184 Texas Rangers | .25 |
| 185 Jose Cardenal | .15 |
| 186 Fred Scherman | .15 |
| 187 Don Baylor | .50 |
| 188 Rudy Meoli | .15 |
| 189 Jim Brewer | .15 |
| 190 Tony Oliva | .50 |

| NO. PLAYER | MINT |
|---|---|
| 191 Al Fitzmorris | .15 |
| 192 Mario Guerrero | .15 |
| 193 Tom Walker | .15 |
| 194 Darrell Porter | .15 |
| 195 Carlos May | .15 |
| 196 Jim Fregosi | .20 |
| 197 Vicente Romo (SD) | .30 |
| 197 Vicente Romo (Wash.) | 3.00 |
| 198 Dave Cash | .15 |
| 199 Mike Kekich | .15 |
| 200 Cesar Cedeno | .40 |
| 201 Batting Leaders: | 2.00 |
| Rod Carew, Pete Rose | |
| 202 Home Run Leaders: | 1.25 |
| R. Jackson, Willie Stargell | |
| 203 RBI Leaders: | 1.25 |
| R. Jackson, Willie Stargell | |
| 204 Stolen Base Leaders: | .75 |
| Tommy Harper, Lou Brock | |
| 205 Victory Leaders: | .45 |
| Wilbur Wood, Ron Bryant | |
| 206 ERA Leaders: | 1.25 |
| Jim Palmer, T. Seaver | |
| 207 Strikeout Leaders: | 1.25 |
| Nolan Ryan, Tom Seaver | |
| 208 Leading Firemen: | .40 |
| John Hiller, M. Marshall | |
| 209 Ted Sizemore | .15 |
| 210 Bill Singer | .15 |
| 211 Chicago Cubs | .50 |
| 212 Rollie Fingers | 1.00 |
| 213 Dave Rader | .15 |
| 214 Bill Grabarkewitz | .15 |
| 215 Al Kaline | 2.25 |
| 216 Ray Sadecki | .15 |
| 217 Tim Foli | .15 |
| 218 Johnny Briggs | .15 |
| 219 Doug Griffin | .15 |
| 220 Don Sutton | .75 |
| 221 Chuck Tanner (Mgr.) | .30 |
| 222 Ramon Hernandez | .15 |
| 223 Jeff Burroughs | .40 |
| 224 Roger Metzger | .15 |
| 225 Paul Splittorff | .20 |
| 226 Padres Team (SD) | .45 |
| 226 Padres Team (Wash.) | 3.50 |
| 227 Mike Lum | .15 |
| 228 Ted Kubiak | .15 |
| 229 Fritz Peterson | .15 |
| 230 Tony Perez | .60 |
| 231 Dick Tidrow | .15 |
| 232 Steve Brye | .15 |
| 233 Jim Barr | .15 |
| 234 John Milner | .15 |
| 235 Dave McNally | .15 |
| 236 R. Schoendienst (Mgr.) | .30 |
| 237 Ken Brett | .15 |
| 238 Fran Healy | .15 |
| 239 Bill Russell | .15 |
| 240 Joe Coleman | .15 |
| 241 Glenn Beckert (SD) | .15 |
| 241 Glenn Beckert (Wash.) | 3.00 |
| 242 Bill Gogolewski | .15 |
| 243 Bob Oliver | .15 |
| 244 Carl Morton | .15 |
| 245 Cleon Jones | .15 |

# 1974 Topps (Continued)

| NO. | PLAYER | MINT |
|---|---|---|
| 246 | Oakland Athletics | .30 |
| 247 | Rick Miller | .15 |
| 248 | Tom Hall | .15 |
| 249 | George Mitterwald | .15 |
| 250 | W. McCovey (SD) | 3.50 |
| 250 | W. McCovey (Wash.) | 12.50 |
| 251 | Graig Nettles | 1.25 |
| 252 | Dave Parker (R) | 15.00 |
| 253 | John Boccabella | .15 |
| 254 | Stan Bahnsen | .15 |
| 255 | Larry Bowa | .40 |
| 256 | Tom Griffin | .15 |
| 257 | Buddy Bell | .75 |
| 258 | Jerry Morales | .15 |
| 259 | Bob Reynolds | .15 |
| 260 | Ted Simmons | .85 |
| 261 | Jerry Bell | .15 |
| 262 | Ed Kirkpatrick | .15 |
| 263 | Checklist No. 2 | .50 |
| 264 | Joe Rudi | .25 |
| 265 | Tug McGraw | .40 |
| 266 | Jim Northrup | .15 |
| 267 | Andy Messersmith | .20 |
| 268 | Tom Grieve | .15 |
| 269 | Bob Johnson | .15 |
| 270 | Ron Santo | .25 |
| 271 | Bill Hands | .15 |
| 272 | Paul Casanova | .15 |
| 273 | Checklist No. 3 | .50 |
| 274 | Fred Beene | .15 |
| 275 | Ron Hunt | .15 |
| 276 | Bobby Winkles (Mgr.) | .25 |
| 277 | Gary Nolan | .15 |
| 278 | Cookie Rojas | .15 |
| 279 | Jim Crawford | .15 |
| 280 | Carl Yastrzemski | 6.00 |
| 281 | San F. Giants | .30 |
| 282 | Doyle Alexander | .15 |
| 283 | Mike Schmidt | 14.00 |
| 284 | Dave Duncan | .15 |
| 285 | Reggie Smith | .40 |
| 286 | Tony Muser | .15 |
| 287 | Clay Kirby | .15 |
| 288 | Gorman Thomas (R) | 2.50 |
| 289 | Rick Auerback | .15 |
| 290 | Vida Blue | .35 |
| 291 | Don Hahn | .15 |
| 292 | Chuck Seelbach | .15 |
| 293 | Milt May | .15 |
| 294 | Steve Foucault | .15 |
| 295 | Rick Monday | .15 |
| 296 | Ray Corbin | .15 |
| 297 | Hal Breeden | .15 |
| 298 | Roric Harrison | .15 |
| 299 | Gene Michael | .15 |
| 300 | Pete Rose | 12.50 |
| 301 | Bob Montgomery | .15 |
| 302 | Rudy May | .15 |
| 303 | George Hendrick | .45 |
| 304 | Don Wilson | .15 |
| 305 | Tito Fuentes | .15 |
| 306 | Earl Weaver (Mgr.) | .60 |
| 307 | Luis Melendez | .15 |
| 308 | Bruce Dal Canton | .15 |
| 309 | Dave Roberts (SD) | .30 |
| 309 | Dave Roberts (Wash.) | 3.00 |
| 310 | Terry Forster | .15 |
| 311 | Jerry Grote | .15 |
| 312 | Deron Johnson | .15 |
| 313 | Barry Lersch | .15 |
| 314 | Milwaukee Brewers | .30 |
| 315 | Ron Cey | 1.00 |
| 316 | Jim Perry | .15 |
| 317 | Richie Zisk | .20 |
| 318 | Jim Merritt | .15 |
| 319 | Randy Hundley | .15 |
| 320 | Dusty Baker | .50 |
| 321 | Steve Braun | .15 |
| 322 | Ernie McAnally | .15 |
| 323 | Richie Scheinblum | .15 |
| 324 | Steve Kline | .15 |
| 325 | Tommy Harper | .15 |
| 326 | Sparky Anderson (Mgr.) | .45 |
| 327 | Tom Timmermann | .15 |
| 328 | Skip Jutze | .15 |
| 329 | Mark Belanger | .15 |
| 330 | Juan Marichal | 1.50 |
| 331 | All-Star Catchers: Carlton Fisk, Johnny Bench | 1.00 |
| 332 | AS 1st Baseman: Dick Allen, Hank Aaron | 1.00 |
| 333 | AS 2nd Baseman: Rod Carew, Joe Morgan | 1.00 |
| 334 | AS 3rd Baseman: B. Robinson, Ron Santo | .75 |
| 335 | AS Shortstops: B. Campaneris, C. Speier | .25 |
| 336 | AS Left Fielders: Pete Rose, Bobby Mercer | 2.50 |
| 337 | AS Center Fielders: Amos Otis, Cesar Cedeno | .25 |
| 338 | AS Right Fielders: R. Jackson, B. Williams | 1.25 |
| 339 | AS Pitchers: Jim Hunter, Rick Wise | .50 |
| 340 | Thurman Munson | 4.00 |
| 341 | Dan Driessen | .50 |
| 342 | Jim Lonborg | .15 |
| 343 | Kansas City Royals | .30 |
| 344 | Mike Caldwell | .15 |
| 345 | Bill North | .15 |
| 346 | Ron Reed | .15 |
| 347 | Sandy Alomar | .15 |
| 348 | Pete Richert | .15 |
| 349 | John Vukovich | .15 |
| 350 | Bob Gibson | 2.00 |
| 351 | Dwight Evans | 1.25 |
| 352 | Bill Stoneman | .15 |
| 353 | Rich Coggins | .15 |
| 354 | Whitey Lockman (Mgr.) | .25 |
| 355 | Dave Nelson | .15 |
| 356 | Jerry Koosman | .25 |
| 357 | Buddy Bradford | .15 |
| 358 | Dal Maxvill | .15 |
| 359 | Brent Strom | .15 |
| 360 | Greg Luzinski | .75 |
| 361 | Don Carrithers | .15 |
| 362 | Hal King | .15 |
| 363 | New York Yankees | .75 |
| 364 | C. Gaston (SD) | .30 |
| 364 | C. Gaston (Wash.) | 3.00 |
| 365 | Steve Busby | .20 |
| 366 | Larry Hisle | .25 |
| 367 | Norm Cash | .20 |
| 368 | Manny Mota | .20 |
| 369 | Paul Lindblad | .15 |
| 370 | Bob Watson | .25 |
| 371 | Jim Slaton | .15 |
| 372 | Ken Reitz | .15 |
| 373 | John Curtis | .15 |
| 374 | Marty Perez | .15 |
| 375 | Earl Williams | .15 |
| 376 | Jorge Orta | .15 |
| 377 | Ron Woods | .15 |
| 378 | Burt Hooton | .15 |
| 379 | Billy Martin (Mgr.) | .50 |
| 380 | Bud Harrelson | .15 |
| 381 | Charlies Sands | .15 |
| 382 | Bob Moose | .15 |
| 383 | Phil. Phillies | .35 |
| 384 | Chris Chambliss | .25 |
| 385 | Don Gullett | .20 |
| 386 | Gary Matthews | .50 |
| 387 | Rich Morales (SD) | .30 |
| 387 | Rich Morales (Wash.) | 3.00 |
| 388 | Phil Roof | .15 |
| 389 | Gates Brown | .15 |
| 390 | Lou Piniella | .50 |
| 391 | Billy Champion | .15 |
| 392 | Dick Green | .15 |
| 393 | Orlando Pena | .15 |
| 394 | Ken Henderson | .15 |
| 395 | Doug Rader | .15 |
| 396 | Tommy Davis | .15 |
| 397 | George Stone | .15 |
| 398 | Duke Sims | .15 |
| 399 | Mike Paul | .15 |
| 400 | Harmon Killebrew | 2.00 |
| 401 | Elliott Maddox | .15 |
| 402 | Jim Rooker | .15 |
| 403 | Darrell Johnson (Mgr.) | .30 |
| 404 | Jim Howarth | .15 |
| 405 | Ellie Rodriguez | .15 |
| 406 | Steve Arlin | .15 |
| 407 | Jim Wohlford | .15 |
| 408 | Charlie Hough | .15 |
| 409 | Ike Brown | .15 |
| 410 | Pedro Borbon | .15 |
| 411 | Frank Baker | .15 |
| 412 | Chuck Taylor | .15 |
| 413 | Don Money | .15 |
| 414 | Checklist No. 4 | .50 |
| 415 | Gary Gentry | .15 |
| 416 | Chicago White Sox | .35 |
| 417 | Rich Folkers | .15 |
| 418 | Walt Williams | .15 |
| 419 | Wayne Twitchell | .15 |
| 420 | Ray Fosse | .15 |
| 421 | Dan Fife | .15 |
| 422 | Gonzalo Marquez | .15 |
| 423 | Fred Stanley | .15 |
| 424 | Jim Beauchamp | .15 |
| 425 | Pete Broberg | .15 |
| 426 | Rennie Stennett | .15 |
| 427 | Bobby Bolin | .15 |
| 428 | Gary Sutherland | .15 |
| 429 | Dick Lange | .15 |
| 430 | Matty Alou | .15 |
| 431 | Gene Garber | .15 |
| 432 | Chris Arnold | .15 |
| 433 | Lerrin LaGrow | .15 |
| 434 | Ken McMullen | .15 |
| 435 | Dave Concepcion | .50 |
| 436 | Don Hood | .15 |
| 437 | Jim Lyttle | .15 |
| 438 | Ed Herrmann | .15 |
| 439 | Norm Miller | .15 |
| 440 | Jim Kaat | .75 |
| 441 | Tom Ragland | .15 |
| 442 | Alan Foster | .15 |
| 443 | Tom Hutton | .15 |
| 444 | Vic Davalillo | .15 |
| 445 | George Medich | .15 |
| 446 | Len Randle | .15 |
| 447 | Frank Quilici (Mgr.) | .25 |
| 448 | Ron Hodges | .15 |
| 449 | Tom McCraw | .15 |
| 450 | Rich Hebner | .15 |
| 451 | Tommy John | 1.00 |
| 452 | Gene Hiser | .15 |
| 453 | Balor Moore | .15 |
| 454 | Kurt Bevacqua | .15 |
| 455 | Tom Bradley | .15 |
| 456 | Dave Winfield (R) | 22.00 |
| 457 | Chuck Goggin | .15 |
| 458 | Jim Ray | .15 |
| 459 | Cincinnati Reds | .50 |
| 460 | Boog Powell | .45 |
| 461 | John Odom | .15 |
| 462 | Luis Alvarado | .15 |
| 463 | Pat Dobson | .15 |
| 464 | Jose Cruz | .50 |
| 465 | Dick Bosman | .15 |
| 466 | Dick Billings | .15 |
| 467 | Winston Llenas | .15 |
| 468 | Pepe Frias | .15 |
| 469 | Joe Decker | .15 |
| 470 | A.L. Playoffs: A's Beat Orioles | 1.50 |
| 471 | N.L. Playoffs: Mets Beat Reds | .50 |
| 472 | World Series Game 1: Oakland 2, N.Y. 1 | .50 |
| 473 | World Series Game 2: N.Y. 10, Oakland 7 | 1.50 |
| 474 | World Series Game 3: Oakland 3, N.Y. 2 | .50 |
| 475 | World Series Game 4: N.Y. 6, Oakland 1 | .50 |
| 476 | World Series Game 5: N.Y. 2, Oakland 0 | .50 |
| 477 | World Series Game 6: Oakland 3, N.Y. 1 | 1.50 |
| 478 | World Series Game 7: Oakland 5, N.Y. 2 | .50 |
| 479 | World Series: A's Win | .50 |
| 480 | Willie Crawford | .15 |
| 481 | Jerry Terrell | .15 |
| 482 | Bob Didier | .15 |
| 483 | Atlanta Braves | .35 |
| 484 | Carmen Fanzone | .15 |
| 485 | Felipe Alou | .15 |
| 486 | Steve Stone | .15 |
| 487 | Ted Martinez | .15 |
| 488 | Andy Etchebarren | .15 |
| 489 | Danny Murtaugh (Mgr.) | .25 |
| 490 | Vada Pinson | .25 |
| 491 | Roger Nelson | .15 |
| 492 | Mike Rogodzinski | .15 |
| 493 | Joe Hoerner | .15 |
| 494 | Ed Goodson | .15 |
| 495 | Dick McAuliffe | .15 |
| 496 | Tom Murphy | .15 |
| 497 | Bobby Mitchell | .15 |
| 498 | Pat Corrales | .15 |
| 499 | Rusty Torres | .15 |
| 500 | Lee May | .20 |
| 501 | Eddie Leon | .15 |
| 502 | Dave LaRoche | .15 |
| 503 | Eric Soderholm | .15 |
| 504 | Joe Niekro | .25 |
| 505 | Bill Buckner | .50 |
| 506 | Ed Farmer | .15 |
| 507 | Larry Stahl | .15 |
| 508 | Montreal Expos | .30 |
| 509 | Jesse Jefferson | .15 |
| 510 | Wayne Garrett | .15 |
| 511 | Toby Harrah | .20 |
| 512 | Joe Lahoud | .15 |
| 513 | Jim Campanis | .15 |
| 514 | Paul Schaal | .15 |
| 515 | Willie Montanez | .15 |
| 516 | Horacio Pina | .15 |
| 517 | Mike Hegan | .15 |
| 518 | Derrel Thomas | .15 |
| 519 | Bill Sharp | .15 |
| 520 | Tim McCarver | .40 |
| 521 | Ken Aspromonte (Mgr.) | .25 |
| 522 | J.R. Richard | .40 |
| 523 | Cecil Cooper | 2.00 |
| 524 | Bill Plummer | .15 |
| 525 | Clyde Wright | .15 |
| 526 | Frank Tepedino | .15 |
| 527 | Bobby Darwin | .15 |
| 528 | Bill Bonham | .15 |
| 529 | Horace Clarke | .15 |
| 530 | Mickey Stanley | .15 |
| 531 | Gene Mauch (Mgr.) | .15 |
| 532 | Skip Lockwood | .15 |
| 533 | Mike Phillips | .15 |
| 534 | Eddie Watt | .15 |
| 535 | Bob Tolan | .15 |
| 536 | Duffy Dyer | .15 |
| 537 | Steve Mingori | .15 |
| 538 | Cesar Tovar | .15 |
| 539 | Lloyd Allen | .15 |
| 540 | Bob Robertson | .15 |
| 541 | Cleveland Indians | .30 |
| 542 | Rich Gossage | 2.00 |
| 543 | Danny Cater | .15 |
| 544 | Ron Schueler | .15 |
| 545 | Billy Conigliaro | .15 |
| 546 | Mike Corkins | .15 |
| 547 | Glenn Borgmann | .15 |
| 548 | Sonny Siebert | .15 |
| 549 | Mike Jorgensen | .15 |
| 550 | Sam McDowell | .15 |
| 551 | Von Joshua | .15 |
| 552 | Denny Doyle | .15 |
| 553 | Jim Willoughby | .15 |
| 554 | Tim Johnson | .15 |
| 555 | Woodie Fryman | .15 |
| 556 | Dave Campbell | .15 |
| 557 | Jim McGlothlin | .15 |
| 558 | Bill Fahey | .15 |
| 559 | Darrell Chaney | .15 |
| 560 | Mike Cuellar | .15 |
| 561 | Ed Kranepool | .15 |
| 562 | Jack Aker | .15 |

| NO. | PLAYER | MINT |
|---|---|---|
| 563 | Hal McRae | .20 |
| 564 | Mike Ryan | .15 |
| 565 | Milt Wilcox | .20 |
| 566 | Jackie Hernandez | .15 |
| 567 | Boston Red Sox | .40 |
| 568 | Mike Torrez | .20 |
| 569 | Rick Dempsey | .15 |
| 570 | Ralph Garr | .15 |
| 571 | Rich Hand | .15 |
| 572 | Enzo Hernandez | .15 |
| 573 | Mike Adams | .15 |
| 574 | Bill Parsons | .15 |
| 575 | Steve Garvey | 6.00 |
| 576 | Scipio Spinks | .15 |
| 577 | Mike Sadek | .15 |
| 578 | Ralph Houk (Mgr.) | .20 |
| 579 | Cecil Upshaw | .15 |
| 580 | Jim Spencer | .15 |
| 581 | Fred Norman | .15 |
| 582 | Bucky Dent (R) | .50 |
| 583 | Marty Pattin | .15 |
| 584 | Ken Rudolph | .15 |
| 585 | Merv Rettenmund | .15 |
| 586 | Jack Brohamer | .15 |
| 587 | Larry Christenson | .15 |
| 588 | Hal Lanier | .15 |
| 589 | Boots Day | .15 |
| 590 | Roger Moret | .15 |
| 591 | Sonny Jackson | .15 |
| 592 | Ed Bane | .15 |
| 593 | Steve Yeager | .15 |
| 594 | Leroy Stanton | .15 |
| 595 | Steve Blass | .15 |
| 596 | Rookie Pitchers: | .40 |
| | Wayne Garland, Fred Holdsworth, Dick Pole, Mark Littell | |

| NO. | PLAYER | MINT |
|---|---|---|
| 597 | Rookie Shortstops: | 1.00 |
| | John Gamble, Pete MacKanin, Dave Chalk, Manny Trillo | |
| 598 | Rookie Outfielders: | 2.00 |
| | Steve Ontiveros, Dave Augustine, Ken Griffey, Jim Tyrone | |
| 599 | Rookie Pitchers | 5.00 |
| | "San Diego"—small type Ron Diorio, D. Freisleben, F. Riccelli, G. Shanahan | |
| 599 | Rookie Pitchers | 2.50 |
| | "San Diego"—large type | |
| 599 | Rookie Pitchers | 1.00 |
| | "Washington" Ron Diorio, D. Freisleben, F. Riccelli, G. Shanahan | |
| 600 | Rookie Infielders: | 7.50 |
| | Ron Cash, Jim Cox, Bill Madlock, Reggie Sanders | |
| 601 | Rookie Outfielders: | .75 |
| | Ed Armbrister, Rich Bladt, B. Downing, B. McBride | |
| 602 | Rookie Pitchers | .50 |
| | Glenn Abbott, Craig Swan R. Henninger, D. Vossler | |
| 603 | Rookie Catchers: | .40 |
| | B. Foote, T. Lundstedt, C. Moore, S. Robles | |
| 604 | Rookie Infielders: | 2.00 |
| | Terry Hughes, John Knox, A. Thornton, F. White | |

| NO. | PLAYER | MINT |
|---|---|---|
| 605 | Rookie Pitchers: | .65 |
| | Vic Albury, Ken Frailing, Kevin Kobel, Frank Tanana | |
| 606 | Rookie Outfielders: | .30 |
| | Jim Fuller, Wilbur Howard, Tommy Smith, Otto Velez | |
| 607 | Rookie Shortstops: | .30 |
| | Leo Foster, Dave Rosello, T. Heintzelman, F. Taveras | |
| 608 | Rookie Pitchers: | .40 |
| | Bob Apodaca, Mike Wallace D. Baney, J. D'Acquisto | |
| 608 | "Apodaca"—error misspelled "Apodoco" | 2.00 |
| 609 | Rico Petrocelli | .15 |
| 610 | Dave Kingman | .75 |
| 611 | Rich Stelmaszek | .15 |
| 612 | Luke Walker | .15 |
| 613 | Dan Monzon | .15 |
| 614 | Adrian Devine | .15 |
| 615 | John Jeter | .15 |
| 616 | Larry Gura | .20 |
| 617 | Ted Ford | .15 |
| 618 | Jim Mason | .15 |
| 619 | Mike Anderson | .15 |
| 620 | Al Downing | .15 |
| 621 | Bernie Carbo | .15 |
| 622 | Phil Gagliano | .15 |
| 623 | Celerino Sanchez | .15 |
| 624 | Bob Miller | .15 |
| 625 | Ollie Brown | .15 |
| 626 | Pittsburgh Pirates | .40 |
| 627 | Carl Taylor | .15 |
| 628 | Ivan Murrell | .15 |

| NO. | PLAYER | MINT |
|---|---|---|
| 629 | Rusty Staub | .50 |
| 630 | Tommie Agee | .15 |
| 631 | Steve Barber | .15 |
| 632 | George Culver | .15 |
| 633 | Dave Hamilton | .15 |
| 634 | Eddie Mathews (Mgr.) | .50 |
| 635 | John Edwards | .15 |
| 636 | Dave Goltz | .15 |
| 637 | Checklist No. 5 | .50 |
| 638 | Ken Sanders | .15 |
| 639 | Joe Lovitto | .15 |
| 640 | Milt Pappas | .15 |
| 641 | Chuck Brinkman | .15 |
| 642 | Terry Harmon | .15 |
| 643 | Los Angeles Dodgers | .75 |
| 644 | Wayne Granger | .15 |
| 645 | Ken Boswell | .15 |
| 646 | George Foster | 1.50 |
| 647 | Juan Beniquez | .60 |
| 648 | Terry Crowley | .15 |
| 649 | Fernando Gonzalez | .15 |
| 650 | Mike Epstein | .15 |
| 651 | Leron Lee | .15 |
| 652 | Gail Hopkins | .15 |
| 653 | Bob Stinson | .15 |
| 654 | Jesus Alou | .40 |
| 654 | Jesus Alou | 5.00 |
| | "outfield" deleted on front | |
| 655 | Mike Tyson | .15 |
| 656 | Adrian Garrett | .15 |
| 657 | Jim Shellenback | .15 |
| 658 | Lee Lacy | .20 |
| 659 | Joe Lis | .15 |
| 660 | Larry Dierker | .35 |

# 1974 Topps Traded.... Complete Set of 44 Cards—Value $6.00

Topps' first Traded set. Topps issued another in 1976, and beginning in 1981 issued a Traded set every year. The traded set features players who were traded after the main set was printed. This set uses the same numbers as the regular set, followed by a "T".

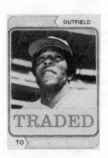    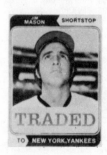

| NO. | | PLAYER | MINT |
|---|---|---|---|
| 23 | T | Craig Robinson | .10 |
| 42 | T | Claude Osteen | .12 |
| 43 | T | Jim Wynn | .15 |
| 51 | T | Bobby Heise | .10 |
| 59 | T | Ross Grimsley | .10 |
| 62 | T | Bob Locker | .10 |
| 63 | T | Bill Sudakis | .10 |
| 73 | T | Mike Marshall | .15 |
| 123 | T | Nelson Briles | .10 |
| 139 | T | Aurelio Monteagudo | .10 |
| 151 | T | Diego Segui | .10 |

| NO. | | PLAYER | MINT |
|---|---|---|---|
| 165 | T | Willie Davis | .25 |
| 175 | T | Reggie Cleveland | .10 |
| 182 | T | Lindy McDaniel | .10 |
| 186 | T | Fred Scherman | .10 |
| 249 | T | George Mitterwald | .10 |
| 262 | T | Ed Kirkpatrick | .10 |
| 269 | T | Bob Johnson | .10 |
| 270 | T | Ron Santo | .25 |
| 313 | T | Barry Lersch | .10 |
| 319 | T | Randy Hundley | .10 |
| 330 | T | Juan Marichal | 1.00 |

| NO. | | PLAYER | MINT |
|---|---|---|---|
| 348 | T | Pete Richert | .10 |
| 373 | T | John Curtis | .10 |
| 390 | T | Lou Piniella | .40 |
| 428 | T | Gary Sutherland | .10 |
| 454 | T | Kurt Bevacqua | .10 |
| 458 | T | Jim Ray | .10 |
| 485 | T | Felipe Alou | .15 |
| 486 | T | Steve Stone | .12 |
| 496 | T | Tom Murphy | .10 |
| 516 | T | Horacio Pina | .10 |
| 534 | T | Eddie Watt | .10 |

| NO. | | PLAYER | MINT |
|---|---|---|---|
| 538 | T | Cesar Tovar | .10 |
| 544 | T | Ron Schueler | .10 |
| 579 | T | Cecil Upshaw | .10 |
| 585 | T | Merv Rettenmund | .10 |
| 612 | T | Luke Walker | .10 |
| 616 | T | Larry Gura | .20 |
| 618 | T | Jim Mason | .10 |
| 630 | T | Tommie Agee | .10 |
| 648 | T | Terry Crowley | .10 |
| 649 | T | Fernando Gonzalez | .10 |
| — | | Traded Checklist | .60 |

# 1975 Topps. . . .Complete Set of 660 Cards—Value $350.00

Features the rookie cards of Robin Yount, George Brett, Jim Rice, Gary Carter, Fred Lynn and Keith Hernandez. The set was also issued in a mini-size (2¼" x 3⅛") which was tested in a section of the country. The mini-size cards are worth 2 to 2½ times more than the regular size cards.

| NO. PLAYER | MINT | NO. PLAYER | MINT | NO. PLAYER | MINT | NO. PLAYER | MINT |
|---|---|---|---|---|---|---|---|
| 1 Highlights: Aaron Sets Homer Mark | 5.50 | 59 Ken Henderson | .20 | 124 Jerry Reuss | .25 | 188 Tom Griffin | .20 |
| 2 Highlights: Brock Steals 118 Bases | 1.50 | 60 Fergie Jenkins | .75 | 125 Ken Singleton | .30 | 189 1951 MVP's: Y. Berra, R. Campanella | 1.00 |
| 3 Highlights: Gibson's 3000th Strikeout | 1.25 | 61 Dave Winfield | 5.00 | 126 Checklist No.1 | .50 | 190 1952 MVP's: B. Shantz, Hank Bauer | .35 |
| 4 Highlights: Kaline's 3000th Hit | 1.25 | 62 Fritz Peterson | .20 | 127 Glenn Borgmann | .20 | 191 1953 MVP's: Al Rosen, R. Campanella | .50 |
| 5 Highlights: Ryan Fans 300—3rd Year | 1.50 | 63 Steve Swisher | .20 | 128 Bill Lee | .20 | 192 1954 MVP's: Yogi Berra, Willie Mays | 1.00 |
| 6 Highlights: Marshall Hurls 106 Games | .50 | 64 Dave Chalk | .20 | 129 Rick Monday | .20 | 193 1955 MVP's: Y. Berra, R. Campanella | 1.00 |
| 7 Highlights: No Hitters: Nolan Ryan, Dick Bosman, Steve Busby | .75 | 65 Don Gullett | .20 | 130 Phil Niekro | 1.00 | 194 1956 MVP's: M. Mantle, D. Newcombe | 1.25 |
| 8 Rogelio Moret | .20 | 66 Willie Horton | .25 | 131 Toby Harrah | .25 | 195 1957 MVP's: Hank Aaron, M. Mantle | 2.00 |
| 9 Frank Tepedino | .20 | 67 Tug McGraw | .40 | 132 Randy Moffitt | .20 | 196 1958 MVP's: J. Jensen, Ernie Banks | .60 |
| 10 Willie Davis | .20 | 68 Ron Blomberg | .20 | 133 Dan Driessen | .20 | 197 1959 MVP's: Nellie Fox, Ernie Banks | .75 |
| 11 Bill Melton | .20 | 69 John Odom | .20 | 134 Ron Hodges | .20 | 198 1960 MVP's: Roger Maris, Dick Groat | .60 |
| 12 David Clyde | .20 | 70 Mike Schmidt | 13.00 | 135 Charlie Spikes | .20 | 199 1961 MVP's: F. Robinson, Roger Maris | 1.00 |
| 13 Gene Locklear | .20 | 71 Charlie Hough | .20 | 136 Jim Mason | .20 | 200 1962 MVP's: M. Mantle, Maury Wills | 1.50 |
| 14 Milt Wilcox | .20 | 72 Royals/J. McKeon (Mgr.) | .40 | 137 Terry Forster | .20 | 201 1963 MVP's: Elston Howard, S. Koufax | .50 |
| 15 Jose Cardenal | .20 | 73 J.R. Richard | .30 | 138 Del Unser | .20 | 202 1964 MVP's: Ken Boyer, B. Robinson | .60 |
| 16 Frank Tanana | .25 | 74 Mark Belanger | .20 | 139 Horacio Pina | .20 | 203 1965 MVP's: Zoilo Versalles, W. Mays | .75 |
| 17 Dave Concepcion | .50 | 75 Ted Simmons | .75 | 140 Steve Garvey | 4.50 | 204 1966 MVP's: F. Robinson, Bob Clemente | .75 |
| 18 Tigers/R. Houk (Mgr.) | .50 | 76 Ed Sprague | .20 | 141 Mickey Stanley | .20 | 205 1967 MVP's: C. Yastrzemski, O. Cepeda | .75 |
| 19 Jerry Koosman | .25 | 77 Richie Zisk | .20 | 142 Bob Reynolds | .20 | 206 1968 MVP's: D. McLain, Bob Gibson | .75 |
| 20 Thurman Munson | 3.50 | 78 Ray Corbin | .20 | 143 Cliff Johnson | .20 | 207 1969 MVP's: W. McCovey, H. Killebrew | .75 |
| 21 Rollie Fingers | 1.00 | 79 Gary Matthews | .40 | 144 Jim Wohlford | .20 | 208 1970 MVP's: Boog Powell, J. Bench | .65 |
| 22 Dave Cash | .20 | 80 Carlton Fisk | 1.25 | 145 Ken Holtzman | .20 | 209 1971 MVP's: Vida Blue, Joe Torre | .50 |
| 23 Bill Russell | .20 | 81 Ron Reed | .20 | 146 San Diego Padres J. McNamara (Mgr.) | .20 | 210 1972 MVP's: Richie Allen, J. Bench | .50 |
| 24 Al Fitzmorris | .20 | 82 Pat Kelly | .20 | 147 Pedro Garcia | .20 | 211 1973 MVP's: Pete Rose, R. Jackson | 2.00 |
| 25 Lee May | .20 | 83 Jim Merritt | .20 | 148 Jim Rooker | .20 | 212 1974 MVP's: J. Burroughs, S. Garvey | .60 |
| 26 Dave McNally | .20 | 84 Enzo Hernandez | .20 | 149 Tim Foli | .20 | 213 Oscar Gamble | .25 |
| 27 Ken Reitz | .20 | 85 Bill Bonham | .20 | 150 Bob Gibson | 2.00 | 214 Harry Parker | .20 |
| 28 Tom Murphy | .20 | 86 Joe Lis | .20 | 151 Steve Brye | .20 | 215 Bobby Valentine | .20 |
| 29 Dave Parker | 3.00 | 87 George Foster | 1.50 | 152 Mario Guerrero | .20 | 216 San Francisco Giants Wes Westrum (Mgr.) | .35 |
| 30 Bert Blyleven | .50 | 88 Tom Egan | .20 | 153 Rick Reuschel | .25 | 217 Lou Piniella | .45 |
| 31 Dave Rader | .20 | 89 Jim Ray | .20 | 154 Mike Lum | .20 | 218 Jerry Johnson | .20 |
| 32 Reggie Cleveland | .20 | 90 Rusty Staub | .45 | 155 Jim Bibby | .20 | 219 Ed Herrmann | .20 |
| 33 Dusty Baker | .50 | 91 Dick Green | .20 | 156 Dave Kingman | .75 | 220 Don Sutton | .75 |
| 34 Steve Renko | .20 | 92 Cecil Upshaw | .20 | 157 Pedro Borbon | .20 | 221 Aurelio Rodriguez | .20 |
| 35 Ron Santo | .30 | 93 Dave Lopes | .35 | 158 Jerry Grote | .20 | 222 Dan Spillner | .20 |
| 36 Joe Lovitto | .20 | 94 Jim Lonborg | .20 | 159 Steve Arlin | .20 | 223 Robin Yount (R) | 20.00 |
| 37 Dave Freisleben | .20 | 95 John Mayberry | .25 | 160 Graig Nettles | 1.00 | 224 Ramon Hernandez | .20 |
| 38 Buddy Bell | .75 | 96 Mike Cosgrove | .20 | 161 Stan Bahnsen | .20 | 225 Bob Grich | .25 |
| 39 Andy Thornton | .75 | 97 Earl Williams | .20 | 162 Willie Montanez | .20 | 226 Bill Campbell | .20 |
| 40 Bill Singer | .20 | 98 Rich Folkers | .20 | 163 Jim Brewer | .20 | 227 Bob Watson | .25 |
| 41 Cesar Geronimo | .20 | 99 Mike Hegan | .20 | 164 Mickey Rivers | .20 | 228 George Brett (R) | 45.00 |
| 42 Joe Coleman | .20 | 100 Willie Stargell | 2.00 | 165 Doug Rader | .20 | | |
| 43 Cleon Jones | .20 | 101 Expos/G. Mauch (Mgr.) | .35 | 166 Woodie Fryman | .20 | | |
| 44 Pat Dobson | .20 | 102 Joe Decker | .20 | 167 Rich Coggins | .20 | | |
| 45 Joe Rudi | .20 | 103 Rick Miller | .20 | 168 Bill Greif | .20 | | |
| 46 Phillies/D. Ozark (Mgr.) | .40 | 104 Bill Madlock | 1.75 | 169 Cookie Rojas | .20 | | |
| 47 Tommy John | .75 | 105 Buzz Capra | .20 | 170 Bert Campaneris | .25 | | |
| 48 Freddie Patek | .20 | 106 Mike Hargrove (R) | .60 | 171 Ed Kirkpatrick | .20 | | |
| 49 Larry Dierker | .20 | 107 Jim Barr | .20 | 172 Boston Red Sox D. Johnson (Mgr.) | .45 | | |
| 50 Brooks Robinson | 2.50 | 108 Tom Hall | .20 | 173 Steve Rogers | .40 | | |
| 51 Bob Forsch | .20 | 109 George Hendrick | .40 | 174 Bake McBride | .20 | | |
| 52 Darrell Porter | .20 | 110 Wilbur Wood | .20 | 175 Don Money | .20 | | |
| 53 Dave Giusti | .20 | 111 Wayne Garrett | .20 | 176 Burt Hooton | .20 | | |
| 54 Eric Soderholm | .20 | 112 Larry Hardy | .20 | 177 Vic Correll | .20 | | |
| 55 Bobby Bonds | .25 | 113 Elliot Maddox | .20 | 178 Cesar Tovar | .20 | | |
| 56 Rick Wise | .20 | 114 Dick Lange | .20 | 179 Tom Bradley | .20 | | |
| 57 Dave Johnson | .25 | 115 Joe Ferguson | .20 | 180 Joe Morgan | 2.50 | | |
| 58 Chuck Taylor | .20 | 116 Lerrin LaGrow | .20 | 181 Fred Beene | .20 | | |
| | | 117 Orioles/E. Weaver (Mgr.) | .60 | 182 Don Hahn | .20 | | |
| | | 118 Mike Anderson | .20 | 183 Mel Stottlemyre | .25 | | |
| | | 119 Tommy Helms | .20 | 184 Jorge Orta | .20 | | |
| | | 120 Steve Busby (photo of Fran Healy) | .20 | 185 Steve Carlton | 5.00 | | |
| | | 121 Bill North | .20 | 186 Willie Crawford | .20 | | |
| | | 122 Al Hrabosky | .20 | 187 Denny Doyle | .20 | | |
| | | 123 Johnny Briggs | .20 | | | | |

| NO. | PLAYER | MINT | NO. | PLAYER | MINT | NO. | PLAYER | MINT | NO. | PLAYER | MINT |
|---|---|---|---|---|---|---|---|---|---|---|---|
| 229 | Barry Foote | .20 | 308 | RBI Leaders: J. Burroughs, J. Bench | .60 | 381 | John Curtis | .20 | 462 | World Series Game 2: Los Angeles 3, Oakland 2 | .40 |
| 230 | Jim Hunter | 1.00 | 309 | Stolen Base Leaders: Bill North, Lou Brock | .50 | 382 | Don Baylor | .75 | 463 | World Series Game 3: Oakland 3, Los Angeles 2 | .65 |
| 231 | Mike Tyson | .20 | 310 | Victory Leaders: Andy Messersmith, Jim Hunter, Fergie Jenkins, Phil Niekro | .50 | 383 | Jim York | .20 | 464 | World Series Game 4: Oakland 5, Los Angeles 2 | .35 |
| 232 | Diego Segui | .20 | 311 | ERA Leaders: Jim Hunter, Buzz Capra | .40 | 384 | Milwaukee Brewers Del Crandall (Mgr.) | .40 | 465 | World Series Game 5 Oakland 3, Los Angeles 2 | .35 |
| 233 | Billy Grabarkewitz | .20 | 312 | Strikeout Leaders: Nolan Ryan, Steve Carlton | 1.00 | 385 | Dock Ellis | .20 | 466 | A's Win 3rd World Series | .40 |
| 234 | Tom Grieve | .20 | 313 | Leading Firemen: Mike Marshall, Terry Forster | .30 | 386 | Checklist: No. 3 | .50 | 467 | Ed Halicki | .20 |
| 235 | Jack Billingham | .20 | 314 | Buck Martinez | .20 | 387 | Jim Spencer | .20 | 468 | Bobby Mitchell | .20 |
| 236 | Angels/D. Williams (Mgr.) | .45 | 315 | Don Kessinger | .20 | 388 | Steve Stone | .20 | 469 | Tom Dettore | .20 |
| 237 | Carl Morton | .20 | 316 | Jackie Brown | .20 | 389 | Tony Solaita | .20 | 470 | Jeff Burroughs | .20 |
| 238 | Dave Duncan | .20 | 317 | Joe LaHoud | .20 | 390 | Ron Cey | .75 | 471 | Bob Stinson | .20 |
| 239 | George Stone | .20 | 318 | Ernie McAnally | .20 | 391 | Don DeMola | .20 | 472 | Bruce Dal Canton | .20 |
| 240 | Garry Maddox | .20 | 319 | Johnny Oates | .20 | 392 | Bruce Bochte (R) | .50 | 473 | Ken McMullen | .20 |
| 241 | Dick Tidrow | .20 | 320 | Pete Rose | 15.00 | 393 | Gary Gentry | .20 | 474 | Luke Walker | .20 |
| 242 | Jay Johnstone | .20 | 321 | Rudy May | .20 | 394 | Larvell Blanks | .20 | 475 | Darrell Evans | .40 |
| 243 | Jim Kaat | .75 | 322 | Ed Goodson | .20 | 395 | Bud Harrelson | .20 | 476 | Eduardo Figueroa | .20 |
| 244 | Bill Buckner | .50 | 323 | Fred Holdsworth | .20 | 396 | Fred Norman | .20 | 477 | Tom Hutton | .20 |
| 245 | Mickey Lolich | .25 | 324 | Ed Kranepool | .20 | 397 | Bill Freehan | .20 | 478 | Tom Burgmeier | .20 |
| 246 | St. Louis Cardinals Red Schoendienst (Mgr.) | .40 | 325 | Tony Oliva | .50 | 398 | Elias Sosa | .20 | 479 | Ken Boswell | .20 |
| 247 | Enos Cabell | .20 | 326 | Wayne Twitchell | .20 | 399 | Terry Harmon | .20 | 480 | Carlos May | .20 |
| 248 | Randy Jones | .20 | 327 | Jerry Hairston | .20 | 400 | Dick Allen | .35 | 481 | Will McEnaney | .20 |
| 249 | Danny Thompson | .20 | 328 | Sonny Siebert | .20 | 401 | Mike Wallace | .20 | 482 | Tom McCraw | .20 |
| 250 | Ken Brett | .20 | 329 | Ted Kubiak | .20 | 402 | Bob Tolan | .20 | 483 | Steve Ontiveros | .20 |
| 251 | Fran Healy | .20 | 330 | Mike Marshall | .20 | 403 | Tom Buskey | .20 | 484 | Glenn Beckert | .20 |
| 252 | Fred Scherman | .20 | 331 | Cleveland Indians Frank Robinson (Mgr.) | .50 | 404 | Ted Sizemore | .20 | 485 | Sparky Lyle | .25 |
| 253 | Jesus Alou | .20 | 332 | Fred Kendall | .20 | 405 | John Montague | .20 | 486 | Ray Fosse | .20 |
| 254 | Mike Torrez | .20 | 333 | Dick Drago | .20 | 406 | Bob Gallagher | .20 | 487 | Astros/P. Gomez (Mgr.) | .40 |
| 255 | Dwight Evans | .75 | 334 | Greg Gross | .20 | 407 | Herb Washington | .20 | 488 | Bill Travers | .20 |
| 256 | Billy Champion | .20 | 335 | Jim Palmer | 2.50 | 408 | Clyde Wright | .20 | 489 | Cecil Cooper | 1.50 |
| 257 | Checklist No. 2 | .50 | 336 | Rennie Stennett | .20 | 409 | Bob Robertson | .20 | 490 | Reggie Smith | .30 |
| 258 | Dave LaRoche | .20 | 337 | Kevin Kobel | .20 | 410 | Mike Cueller | .20 | 491 | Doyle Alexander | .20 |
| 259 | Len Randle | .20 | 338 | Rick Stelmaszek | .20 | 411 | George Mitterwald | .20 | 492 | Rich Hebner | .20 |
| 260 | Johnny Bench | 5.00 | 339 | Jim Fregosi | .20 | 412 | Bill Hands | .20 | 493 | Don Stanhouse | .20 |
| 261 | Andy Hassler | .20 | 340 | Paul Splittorff | .20 | 413 | Marty Pattin | .20 | 494 | Pete LaCock | .20 |
| 262 | Rowland Office | .20 | 341 | Hal Breeden | .20 | 414 | Manny Mota | .20 | 495 | Nelson Briles | .20 |
| 263 | Jim Perry | .20 | 342 | Leroy Stanton | .20 | 415 | John Hiller | .20 | 496 | Pepe Frias | .20 |
| 264 | John Milner | .20 | 343 | Danny Frisella | .20 | 416 | Larry Lintz | .20 | 497 | Jim Nettles | .20 |
| 265 | Ron Bryant | .20 | 344 | Ben Oglivie | .30 | 417 | Skip Lockwood | .20 | 498 | Al Downing | .20 |
| 266 | Sandy Alomar | .20 | 345 | Clay Carroll | .20 | 418 | Leo Foster | .20 | 499 | Marty Perez | .20 |
| 267 | Dick Ruthven | .20 | 346 | Bobby Darwin | .20 | 419 | Dave Goltz | .20 | 500 | Nolan Ryan | 3.50 |
| 268 | Hal McRae | .25 | 347 | Mike Caldwell | .20 | 420 | Larry Bowa | .30 | 501 | Bill Robinson | .20 |
| 269 | Doug Rau | .20 | 348 | Tony Muser | .20 | 421 | Mets/Y. Berra (Mgr.) | .60 | 502 | Pat Bourque | .20 |
| 270 | Ron Fairly | .20 | 349 | Ray Sadecki | .20 | 422 | Brian Downing | .20 | 503 | Fred Stanley | .20 |
| 271 | Jerry Moses | .20 | 350 | Bobby Murcer | .50 | 423 | Clay Kirby | .20 | 504 | Buddy Bradford | .20 |
| 272 | Lynn McGlothen | .20 | 351 | Bob Boone | .25 | 424 | John Lowenstein | .20 | 505 | Chris Speier | .20 |
| 273 | Steve Braun | .20 | 352 | Darold Knowles | .20 | 425 | Tito Fuentes | .20 | 506 | Leron Lee | .20 |
| 274 | Vincente Romo | .20 | 353 | Luis Melendez | .20 | 426 | Geroge Medich | .20 | 507 | Tom Carroll | .20 |
| 275 | Paul Blair | .20 | 354 | Dick Bosman | .20 | 427 | Clarence Gaston | .20 | 508 | Bob Hansen | .20 |
| 276 | Chicago White Sox Chuck Tanner (Mgr.) | .40 | 355 | Chris Cannizzaro | .20 | 428 | Dave Hamilton | .20 | 509 | Dave Hilton | .20 |
| 277 | Frank Taveras | .20 | 356 | Rico Petrocelli | .20 | 429 | Jim Dwyer | .20 | 510 | Vida Blue | .20 |
| 278 | Paul Lindblad | .20 | 357 | Ken Frosch | .20 | 430 | Luis Tiant | .30 | 511 | Rangers/B. Martin (Mgr.) | .60 |
| 279 | Milt May | .20 | 358 | Al Bumbry | .20 | 431 | Rod Gilbreath | .20 | 512 | Larry Milbourne | .20 |
| 280 | Carl Yastrzemski | 6.00 | 359 | Paul Popovich | .20 | 432 | Ken Berry | .20 | 513 | Dick Pole | .20 |
| 281 | Jim Slaton | .20 | 360 | George Scott | .20 | 433 | Larry Demery | .20 | 514 | Jose Cruz | .50 |
| 282 | Jerry Morales | .20 | 361 | Los Angeles Dodgers Walter Alston (Mgr.) | .60 | 434 | Bob Locker | .20 | 515 | Manny Sanguillen | .25 |
| 283 | Steve Foucault | .20 | 362 | Steve Hargan | .20 | 435 | Dave Nelson | .20 | 516 | Don Hood | .20 |
| 284 | Ken Griffey | .60 | 363 | Carmen Fanzone | .20 | 436 | Ken Frailing | .20 | 517 | Checklist: No. 4 | .50 |
| 285 | Ellie Rodriguez | .20 | 364 | Doug Bird | .20 | 437 | Al Cowens (R) | .50 | 518 | Leo Cardenas | .20 |
| 286 | Mike Jorgensen | .20 | 365 | Bob Bailey | .20 | 438 | Don Carrithers | .20 | 519 | Jim Todd | .20 |
| 287 | Roric Harrison | .20 | 366 | Ken Sanders | .20 | 439 | Ed Brinkman | .20 | 520 | Amos Otis | .25 |
| 288 | Bruce Ellingsen | .20 | 367 | Craig Robinson | .20 | 440 | Andy Messersmith | .20 | 521 | Dennis Blair | .20 |
| 289 | Ken Rudolph | .20 | 368 | Vic Albury | .20 | 441 | Bobby Heise | .20 | 522 | Gary Sutherland | .20 |
| 290 | Jon Matlack | .20 | 369 | Merv Rettenmund | .20 | 442 | Maximino Leon | .20 | 523 | Tom Paciorek | .20 |
| 291 | Bill Sudakis | .20 | 370 | Tom Seaver | 5.00 | 443 | Twins/F. Quilici (Mgr.) | .40 | 524 | John Doherty | .20 |
| 292 | Ron Schueler | .20 | 371 | Gates Brown | .20 | 444 | Gene Garber | .20 | 525 | Tom House | .20 |
| 293 | Dick Sharon | .20 | 372 | John D'Acquisto | .20 | 445 | Felix Millan | .20 | 526 | Larry Hisle | .20 |
| 294 | Geoff Zahn | .20 | 373 | Bill Sharp | .20 | 446 | Bart Johnson | .20 | 527 | Mac Scarce | .20 |
| 295 | Vada Pinson | .25 | 374 | Eddie Watt | .20 | 447 | Terry Crowley | .20 | 528 | Eddie Leon | .20 |
| 296 | Alan Foster | .20 | 375 | Roy White | .20 | 448 | Frank Duffy | .20 | 529 | Gary Thomasson | .20 |
| 297 | Craig Kusick | .20 | 376 | Steve Yeager | .20 | 449 | Charlie Williams | .20 | 530 | Gaylord Perry | 1.50 |
| 298 | Johnny Grubb | .20 | 377 | Tom Hilgendorf | .20 | 450 | Willie McCovey | 2.00 | 531 | Cincinnati Reds Sparky Anderson (Mgr.) | .60 |
| 299 | Bucky Dent | .25 | 378 | Derrel Thomas | .20 | 451 | Rick Dempsey | .25 | 532 | Gorman Thomas | .75 |
| 300 | Reggie Jackson | 6.00 | 379 | Bernie Carbo | .20 | 452 | Angel Mangual | .20 | 533 | Rudy Meoli | .20 |
| 301 | Dave Roberts | .20 | 380 | Sal Bando | .20 | 453 | Claude Osteen | .20 | 534 | Alex Johnson | .20 |
| 302 | Rick Burleson (R) | .50 | | | | 454 | Doug Griffin | .20 | 535 | Gene Tenace | .20 |
| 303 | Grant Jackson | .20 | | | | 455 | Don Wilson | .20 | 536 | Bob Moose | .20 |
| 304 | Pittsburgh Pirates Danny Murtaugh (Mgr.) | .40 | | | | 456 | Bob Coluccio | .20 | 537 | Tommy Harper | .20 |
| 305 | Jim Colborn | .20 | | | | 457 | Mario Mendoza | .20 | 538 | Duffy Dyer | .20 |
| 306 | Batting Leaders: Rod Carew, Ralph Garr | .50 | | | | 458 | Ross Grimsley | .20 | 539 | Jesse Jefferson | .20 |
| 307 | Home Run Leaders: Dick Allen, Mike Schmidt | .75 | | | | 459 | 1974 AL Champs: A's over Orioles | .40 | 540 | Lou Brock | 2.00 |
| | | | | | | 460 | 1974 NL Champs: Dodgers over Pirates | .60 | | | |
| | | | | | | 461 | World Series Game 1: Oakland 3, Los Angeles 2 | 1.25 | | | |

| NO. | PLAYER | MINT |
|---|---|---|
| 541 | Roger Metzger | .20 |
| 542 | Pete Broberg | .20 |
| 543 | Larry Biittner | .20 |
| 544 | Steve Mingori | .20 |
| 545 | Billy Williams | .75 |
| 546 | John Knox | .20 |
| 547 | Von Joshua | .20 |
| 548 | Charlie Sands | .20 |
| 549 | Bill Butler | .20 |
| 550 | Ralph Garr | .20 |
| 551 | Larry Christenson | .20 |
| 552 | Jack Brohamer | .20 |
| 553 | John Boccabella | .20 |
| 554 | Rich Gossage | 1.25 |
| 555 | Al Oliver | .75 |
| 556 | Tim Johnson | .20 |
| 557 | Larry Gura | .20 |
| 558 | Dave Roberts | .20 |
| 559 | Bob Montgomery | .20 |
| 560 | Tony Perez | .75 |
| 561 | A's/Alvin Dark (Mgr.) | .40 |
| 562 | Gary Nolan | .20 |
| 563 | Wilbur Howard | .20 |
| 564 | Tommy Davis | .20 |
| 565 | Joe Torre | .50 |
| 566 | Ray Burris | .20 |
| 567 | Jim Sundberg (R) | .75 |
| 568 | Dale Murray | .20 |
| 569 | Frank White | .30 |
| 570 | Jim Wynn | .20 |
| 571 | Dave Lemanczyk | .20 |
| 572 | Roger Nelson | .20 |
| 573 | Orlando Pena | .20 |
| 574 | Tony Taylor | .20 |
| 575 | Gene Clines | .20 |
| 576 | Phil Roof | .20 |
| 577 | John Morris | .20 |
| 578 | Dave Tomlin | .20 |
| 579 | Skip Pitlock | .20 |
| 580 | Frank Robinson | 2.00 |
| 581 | Darrel Chaney | .20 |
| 582 | Eduardo Rodriguez | .20 |
| 583 | Andy Etchebarren | .20 |
| 584 | Mike Garman | .20 |
| 585 | Chris Chambliss | .25 |
| 586 | Tim McCarver | .35 |
| 587 | Chris Ward | .20 |
| 588 | Rick Auerbach | .20 |
| 589 | Braves/C. King (Mgr.) | .40 |
| 590 | Cesar Cedeno | .35 |
| 591 | Glenn Abbott | .20 |
| 592 | Balor Moore | .20 |
| 593 | Gene Lamont | .20 |
| 594 | Jim Fuller | .20 |
| 595 | Joe Niekro | .35 |
| 596 | Ollie Brown | .20 |
| 597 | Winston Llenas | .20 |
| 598 | Bruce Kison | .20 |
| 599 | Nate Colbert | .20 |
| 600 | Rod Carew | 4.00 |
| 601 | Juan Beniquez | .20 |
| 602 | John Vukovich | .20 |
| 603 | Lew Krausse | .20 |
| 604 | Oscar Zamora | .20 |
| 605 | John Ellis | .20 |
| 606 | Bruce Miller | .20 |
| 607 | Jim Holt | .20 |
| 608 | Gene Michael | .20 |
| 609 | Ellie Hendricks | .20 |
| 610 | Ron Hunt | .20 |
| 611 | Yankees/B. Virdon (Mgr.) | .50 |
| 612 | Terry Hughes | .20 |
| 613 | Bill Parsons | .20 |
| 614 | Rookie Pitchers: Jack Kucek, Dyar Miller, Paul Siebert, Vern Ruhle | .20 |
| 615 | Rookie Pitchers: Dennis Leonard, Tom Underwood, Hank Webb, Pat Darcy | .75 |
| 616 | Rookie Outfielders: Jim Rice, D. Augustine, Pepe Mangual, J. Scott | 30.00 |
| 617 | Rookie Infielders: Mike Cubbage, Reggie Sanders, Manny Trillo, Doug DeCinces | 2.00 |
| 618 | Rookie Pitchers: Tom Johnson, Jamie Easterly, Scott McGregor, Rick Rhoden | 2.00 |
| 619 | Rookie Outfielders: Benny Ayala, Nyls Nyman, Tommy Smith, Jerry Turner | .30 |
| 620 | Rookie Catchers/OF's: Gary Carter, Marc Hill, Danny Meyer, Leon Roberts | 25.00 |
| 621 | Rookie Pitchers: John Denny, Rawly Eastwick, Jim Kern, Juan Veintidos | 2.00 |
| 622 | Rookie Outfielders: Ed Armbrister, Fred Lynn, T. Whitfield, Tom Poquette | 10.00 |
| 623 | Rookie Infielders: Phil Garner, Bob Sheldon, K. Hernandez, T. Veryzer | 18.00 |
| 624 | Rookie Pitchers: Doug Konieczny, Gary Lavelle, Jim Otten, Eddie Solomon | .40 |
| 625 | Boog Powell | .50 |
| 626 | Larry Haney (Photo of Dave Duncan) | .20 |
| 627 | Tom Walker | .20 |
| 628 | Ron LeFlore (R) | .60 |
| 629 | Joe Hoerner | .20 |
| 630 | Greg Luzinski | .75 |
| 631 | Lee Lacy | .20 |
| 632 | Morris Nettles | .20 |
| 633 | Paul Casanova | .20 |
| 634 | Cy Acosta | .20 |
| 635 | Chuck Dobson | .20 |
| 636 | Charlie Moore | .20 |
| 637 | Ted Martinez | .20 |
| 638 | Cubs/J. Marshall (Mgr.) | .40 |
| 639 | Steve Kline | .20 |
| 640 | Harmon Killebrew | 1.75 |
| 641 | Jim Northrup | .20 |
| 642 | Mike Phillips | .20 |
| 643 | Brent Strom | .20 |
| 644 | Bill Fahey | .20 |
| 645 | Danny Cater | .20 |
| 646 | Checklist No. 5 | .50 |
| 647 | Claudell Washington | 1.50 |
| 648 | Dave Pagan | .20 |
| 649 | Jack Heidemann | .20 |
| 650 | Dave May | .20 |
| 651 | John Morlan | .20 |
| 652 | Lindy McDaniel | .20 |
| 653 | Lee Richards | .20 |
| 654 | Jerry Terrell | .20 |
| 655 | Rico Carty | .20 |
| 656 | Bill Plummer | .20 |
| 657 | Bob Oliver | .20 |
| 658 | Vic Harris | .20 |
| 659 | Bob Apodaca | .20 |
| 660 | Hank Aaron | 8.00 |

## 1976 Topps....Complete Set of 660 Cards—Value $180.00

Features the rookie card of Ron Guidry. This set includes the only card ever issued for the Joe Garagiola and Bazooka "Bubble Gum Blowing Champ". Topps added a 44-card Traded set later in the season.

| NO. | PLAYER | MINT |
|---|---|---|
| 1 | Record—Aaron Most RBI's—2,262 | 5.00 |
| 2 | Record—Bonds Most Lead-Off Homers—32; Most Seasons of 30 HR's; and 30 Stolen Bases | .30 |
| 3 | Record—Lolich Most Strikeouts Lefthander—2,679 | .30 |
| 4 | Record—Lopes Most Consecutive Steal Attempts—38 | .30 |
| 5 | Record—Seaver Most Consecutive Seasons of 200 Strikeouts—8 | 1.25 |
| 6 | Record—Stennett Most Hits in a Nine Inning Game—7 | .30 |
| 7 | Jim Umbarger | .15 |
| 8 | Tito Fuentes | .15 |
| 9 | Paul Lindblad | .15 |
| 10 | Lou Brock | 1.50 |
| 11 | Jim Hughes | .15 |
| 12 | Richie Zisk | .15 |
| 13 | Johnny Wockenfuss | .15 |
| 14 | Gene Garber | .15 |
| 15 | George Scott | .15 |
| 16 | Bob Apodaca | .15 |
| 17 | New York Yankees | .75 |
| 18 | Dale Murray | .15 |
| 19 | George Brett | 10.00 |
| 20 | Bob Watson | .15 |
| 21 | Dave LaRoche | .15 |
| 22 | Bill Russell | .15 |
| 23 | Brian Downing | .15 |
| 24 | Cesar Geronimo | .15 |
| 25 | Mike Torrez | .15 |
| 26 | Andy Thornton | .25 |
| 27 | Ed Figueroa | .15 |
| 28 | Dusty Baker | .30 |
| 29 | Rick Burleson | .25 |
| 30 | John Montefusco (R) | .35 |
| 31 | Len Randle | .15 |
| 32 | Danny Frisella | .15 |
| 33 | Bill North | .15 |
| 34 | Mike Garman | .15 |
| 35 | Tony Oliva | .50 |
| 36 | Frank Taveras | .15 |
| 37 | John Hiller | .15 |
| 38 | Garry Maddox | .15 |
| 39 | Pete Broberg | .15 |
| 40 | Dave Kingman | .60 |
| 41 | Tippy Martinez (R) | .75 |
| 42 | Barry Foote | .15 |
| 43 | Paul Splittorff | .15 |
| 44 | Doug Rader | .15 |
| 45 | Boog Powell | .40 |
| 46 | Los Angeles Dodgers | .65 |
| 47 | Jesse Jefferson | .15 |
| 48 | Dave Concepcion | .40 |
| 49 | Dave Duncan | .15 |
| 50 | Fred Lynn | 1.50 |
| 51 | Ray Buris | .15 |
| 52 | Dave Chalk | .15 |
| 53 | Mike Beard | .15 |
| 54 | Dave Rader | .15 |
| 55 | Gaylord Perry | 1.25 |
| 56 | Bob Toaln | .15 |
| 57 | Phil Garner | .20 |
| 58 | Ron Reed | .15 |
| 59 | Larry Hisle | .15 |
| 60 | Jerry Reuss | .20 |
| 61 | Ron LeFlore | .20 |
| 62 | Johnny Oates | .15 |
| 63 | Bobby Darwin | .15 |
| 64 | Jerry Koosman | .20 |
| 65 | Chris Chambliss | .20 |
| 66 | Father & Son: Gus Bell, Buddy Bell | .40 |

| NO. | PLAYER | MINT |
|---|---|---|
| 67 | Father & Son: | .20 |
| | Ray Boone, | |
| | Bob Boone | |
| 68 | Father & Son: | .20 |
| | Joe Coleman, | |
| | Joe Coleman, Jr. | |
| 69 | Father & Son: | .20 |
| | Jim Hegan, | |
| | Mike Hegan | |
| 70 | Father & Son: | .20 |
| | Roy Smalley, | |
| | Roy Smalley Jr. | |
| 71 | Steve Rogers | .30 |
| 72 | Hal McRae | .25 |
| 73 | Baltimore Orioles | .50 |
| 74 | Oscar Gamble | .20 |
| 75 | Larry Dierker | .15 |
| 76 | Willie Crawford | .15 |
| 77 | Pedro Borbon | .15 |
| 78 | Cecil Cooper | 1.00 |
| 79 | Jerry Morales | .15 |
| 80 | Jim Kaat | .50 |
| 81 | Darrell Evans | .30 |
| 82 | Von Joshua | .15 |
| 83 | Jim Spencer | .15 |
| 84 | Brent Strom | .15 |
| 85 | Mickey Rivers | .20 |
| 86 | Mike Tyson | .15 |
| 87 | Tom Burgmeier | .15 |
| 88 | Duffy Dyer | .15 |
| 89 | Vern Ruhle | .15 |
| 90 | Sal Bando | .20 |
| 91 | Tom Hutton | .15 |
| 92 | Eduardo Rodriguez | .15 |
| 93 | Mike Phillips | .15 |
| 94 | Jim Dwyer | .15 |
| 95 | Brooks Robinson | 2.00 |
| 96 | Doug Bird | .15 |
| 97 | Wilbur Howard | .15 |
| 98 | Dennis Eckersley (R) | 1.00 |
| 99 | Lee Lacy | .20 |
| 100 | Jim Hunter | .75 |
| 101 | Pete LaCock | .15 |
| 102 | Jim Willoughby | .15 |
| 103 | Biff Pocoroba | .15 |
| 104 | Cincinnati Reds | .60 |
| 105 | Gary Lavelle | .15 |
| 106 | Tom Grieve | .15 |
| 107 | Dave Roberts | .15 |
| 108 | Don Kirkwood | .15 |
| 109 | Larry Lintz | .15 |
| 110 | Carlos May | .15 |
| 111 | Danny Thompson | .15 |
| 112 | Kent Tekulve (R) | .75 |
| 113 | Gary Sutherland | .15 |
| 114 | Jay Johnstone | .15 |
| 115 | Ken Holtzman | .15 |
| 116 | Charlie Moore | .15 |
| 117 | Mike Jorgensen | .15 |
| 118 | Boston Red Sox | .65 |
| 119 | Checklist No. 1 | .40 |
| 120 | Rusty Staub | .35 |
| 121 | Tony Solaita | .15 |
| 122 | Mike Cosgrove | .15 |
| 123 | Walt Williams | .15 |
| 124 | Doug Rau | .15 |
| 125 | Don Baylor | .50 |
| 126 | Tom Dettore | .15 |
| 127 | Larvell Blanks | .15 |
| 128 | Ken Griffey | .40 |
| 129 | Andy Etchebarren | .15 |
| 130 | Luis Tiant | .25 |
| 131 | Bill Stein | .15 |
| 132 | Don Hood | .15 |
| 133 | Gary Matthews | .30 |
| 134 | Mike Ivie | .15 |
| 135 | Bake McBride | .15 |
| 136 | Dave Goltz | .15 |
| 137 | Bill Robinson | .15 |
| 138 | Lerrin LaGrow | .15 |
| 139 | Gorman Thomas | .50 |
| 140 | Vida Blue | .30 |
| 141 | Larry Parrish (R) | 1.00 |
| 142 | Dick Drago | .12 |
| 143 | Jerry Grote | .15 |
| 144 | Al Fitzmorris | .15 |
| 145 | Larry Bowa | .35 |
| 146 | George Medich | .15 |
| 147 | Houston Astros | .40 |
| 148 | Stan Thomas | .15 |
| 149 | Tommy Davis | .15 |
| 150 | Steve Garvey | 4.00 |
| 151 | Bill Bonham | .15 |
| 152 | Leroy Stanton | .15 |
| 153 | Buzz Capra | .15 |
| 154 | Bucky Dent | .20 |
| 155 | Jack Billingham | .15 |
| 156 | Rico Carty | .20 |
| 157 | Mike Caldwell | .15 |
| 158 | Ken Reitz | .15 |
| 159 | Jerry Terrell | .15 |
| 160 | Dave Winfield | 4.00 |
| 161 | Bruce Kison | .15 |
| 162 | Jack Pierce | .15 |
| 163 | Jim Staton | .15 |
| 164 | Pepe Mangual | .15 |
| 165 | Gene Tenace | .15 |
| 166 | Skip Lockwood | .15 |
| 167 | Freddie Patek | .15 |
| 168 | Tom Hilgendorf | .15 |
| 169 | Graig Nettles | 1.00 |
| 170 | Rick Wise | .15 |
| 171 | Greg Gross | .15 |
| 172 | Texas Rangers | .40 |
| 173 | Steve Swisher | .15 |
| 174 | Charlie Hough | .15 |
| 175 | Ken Singleton | .25 |
| 176 | Dick Lange | .15 |
| 177 | Marty Perez | .15 |
| 178 | Tom Buskey | .15 |
| 179 | George Foster | 1.50 |
| 180 | Rich Gossage | 1.25 |
| 181 | Willie Montanez | .15 |
| 182 | Harry Rasmussen | .15 |
| 183 | Steve Braun | .15 |
| 184 | Bill Greif | .15 |
| 185 | Dave Parker | 2.00 |
| 186 | Tom Walker | .15 |
| 187 | Pedro Garcia | .15 |
| 188 | Fred Scherman | .15 |
| 189 | Claudell Washington | .45 |
| 190 | Jon Matlack | .15 |
| 191 | NL Batting Leaders: | .50 |
| | Ted Simmons, Bill Madlock, | |
| | Manny Sanguillen | |
| 192 | AL Batting Leaders: | 1.00 |
| | Fred Lynn, Rod Carew, | |
| | Thurman Munson | |
| 193 | NL Home Run Leaders: | .60 |
| | Mike Schmidt, Greg | |
| | Luzinski, Dave Kingman | |
| 194 | AL Home Run Leaders: | .60 |
| | John Mayberry, Reggie | |
| | Jackson, George Scott | |
| 195 | NL RBI Leaders: | .50 |
| | Greg Luzinski, Johnny | |
| | Bench, Tony Perez | |
| 196 | AL RBI Leaders: | .40 |
| | John Mayberry, George | |
| | Scott, Fred Lynn | |
| 197 | NL Stolen Base Leaders: | .60 |
| | Dave Lopes, Lou Brock, | |
| | Joe Morgan | |
| 198 | AL Stolen Base Leaders: | .30 |
| | Mickey Rivers, Claudell | |
| | Washington, Amos Otis | |
| 199 | NL Victory Leaders: | .50 |
| | Tom Seaver, Randy Jones, | |
| | Andy Messersmith | |
| 200 | AL Victory Leaders: | .60 |
| | Jim Palmer, Jim Hunter, | |
| | Vida Blue | |
| 201 | NL ERA Leaders: | .50 |
| | Randy Jones, Andy | |
| | Messersmith, Tom Seaver | |
| 202 | AL ERA Leaders: | .50 |
| | Jim Hunter, Dennis | |
| | Eckersley, Jim Palmer | |
| 203 | NL Strikeout Leaders: | .50 |
| | John Montefusco, Andy | |
| | Messersmith, Tom Seaver | |
| 204 | AL Strikeout Leaders: | .50 |
| | Frank Tanana, Gaylord | |
| | Perry, Bert Blyleven | |
| 205 | Leading Firemen: | .35 |
| | Al Hrabosky, Rich Gossage | |
| 206 | Manny Trillo | .25 |
| 207 | Andy Hassler | .15 |
| 208 | Mike Lum | .15 |
| 209 | Alan Ashby | .15 |
| 210 | Lee May | .20 |
| 211 | Clay Carroll | .15 |
| 212 | Pat Kelly | .15 |
| 213 | Dave Heaverlo | .15 |
| 214 | Eric Soderholm | .15 |
| 215 | Reggie Smith | .35 |
| 216 | Montreal Expos | .35 |
| 217 | Dave Freisleben | .15 |
| 218 | John Knox | .15 |
| 219 | Tom Murphy | .15 |
| 220 | Manny Sanguillen | .15 |
| 221 | Jim Todd | .15 |
| 222 | Wayne Garrett | .15 |
| 223 | Ollie Brown | .15 |
| 224 | Jim York | .15 |
| 225 | Roy White | .15 |
| 226 | Jim Sundberg | .20 |
| 227 | Oscar Zamora | .15 |
| 228 | John Hale | .15 |
| 229 | Jerry Remy (R) | .30 |
| 230 | Carl Yastrzemski | 5.00 |
| 231 | Tom House | .15 |
| 232 | Frank Duffy | .15 |
| 233 | Grant Jackson | .15 |
| 234 | Mike Sadek | .15 |
| 235 | Bert Blyleven | .50 |
| 236 | Kansas City Royals | .40 |
| 237 | Dave Hamilton | .15 |
| 238 | Larry Biittner | .15 |
| 239 | John Curtis | .15 |
| 240 | Pete Rose | 12.00 |
| 241 | Hector Torres | .15 |
| 242 | Dan Meyer | .15 |
| 243 | Jim Rooker | .15 |
| 244 | Bill Sharp | .15 |
| 245 | Felix Millan | .15 |
| 246 | Cesar Tovar | .15 |
| 247 | Terry Harmon | .15 |
| 248 | Dick Tidrow | .15 |
| 249 | Cliff Johnson | .15 |
| 250 | Fergie Jenkins | .45 |
| 251 | Rick Monday | .15 |
| 252 | Tim Nordbrook | .15 |
| 253 | Bill Buckner | .40 |
| 254 | Rudy Meoli | .15 |
| 255 | Fritz Peterson | .15 |
| 256 | Rowland Office | .15 |
| 257 | Ross Grimsley | .15 |
| 258 | Nyls Nyman | .15 |
| 259 | Darrel Chaney | .15 |
| 260 | Steve Busby | .15 |
| 261 | Gary Thomasson | .15 |
| 262 | Checklist No. 2 | .45 |
| 263 | Lyman Bostock (R) | .50 |
| 264 | Steve Renko | .15 |
| 265 | Willie Davis | .15 |
| 266 | Alan Foster | .15 |
| 267 | Aurelio Rodriguez | .15 |
| 268 | Del Unser | .15 |
| 269 | Rick Austin | .15 |
| 270 | Willie Stargell | 1.50 |
| 271 | Jim Lonborg | .15 |
| 272 | Rick Dempsey | .20 |
| 273 | Joe Niekro | .25 |
| 274 | Tommy Harper | .15 |
| 275 | Rick Manning (R) | .30 |
| 276 | Mickey Scott | .15 |
| 277 | Chicago Cubs | .50 |
| 278 | Bernie Carbo | .15 |
| 279 | Roy Howell | .15 |
| 280 | Burt Hooton | .15 |
| 281 | Dave May | .15 |
| 282 | Dan Osborn | .15 |
| 283 | Merv Rettenmund | .15 |
| 284 | Steve Ontiveros | .15 |
| 285 | Mike Cuellar | .15 |
| 286 | Jim Wohlford | .15 |
| 287 | Pete Mackanin | .15 |
| 288 | Bill Campbell | .15 |
| 289 | Enzo Hernandez | .15 |
| 290 | Ted Simmons | .50 |
| 291 | Ken Sanders | .15 |
| 292 | Leon Roberts | .15 |
| 293 | Bill Castro | .15 |
| 294 | Ed Kirkpatrick | .15 |
| 295 | Dave Cash | .15 |
| 296 | Pat Dobson | .15 |
| 297 | Roger Metzger | .15 |
| 298 | Dick Bosman | .15 |
| 299 | Champ Summers | .15 |
| 300 | Johnny Bench | 4.00 |
| 301 | Jackie Brown | .15 |
| 302 | Rick Miller | .15 |
| 303 | Steve Foucault | .15 |
| 304 | California Angels | .40 |
| 305 | Andy Messersmith | .20 |
| 306 | Rod Gilbreath | .15 |
| 307 | Al Bumbry | .15 |
| 308 | Jim Barr | .15 |
| 309 | Bill Melton | .15 |
| 310 | Randy Jones | .20 |
| 311 | Cookie Rojas | .15 |
| 312 | Don Carrithers | .15 |
| 313 | Dan Ford (R) | .35 |
| 314 | Ed Kranepool | .15 |
| 315 | Al Hrabosky | .15 |
| 316 | Robin Yount | 4.00 |
| 317 | John Candelaria (R) | 1.75 |
| 318 | Bob Boone | .15 |
| 319 | Larry Gura | .15 |
| 320 | Willie Horton | .20 |
| 321 | Jose Cruz | .40 |
| 322 | Glenn Abbott | .15 |
| 323 | Rob Sperring | .15 |
| 324 | Jim Bibby | .15 |
| 325 | Tony Perez | .50 |
| 326 | Dick Pole | .15 |
| 327 | Dave Moates | .15 |
| 328 | Carl Morton | .15 |
| 329 | Joe Ferguson | .15 |
| 330 | Nolan Ryan | 3.50 |
| 331 | San Diego Padres | .40 |
| 332 | Charlie Williams | .15 |
| 333 | Bob Coluccio | .15 |
| 334 | Dennis Leonard | .20 |
| 335 | Bob Grich | .20 |
| 336 | Vic Albury | .15 |
| 337 | Bud Harrelson | .15 |
| 338 | Bob Bailey | .15 |
| 339 | John Denny | .65 |
| 340 | Jim Rice | 7.00 |
| 341 | All-Time 1B: | 1.50 |
| | Lou Gehrig | |
| 342 | All-Time 2B: | 1.00 |
| | Rogers Hornsby | |
| 343 | All-Time 3B: | .75 |
| | Pie Traynor | |
| 344 | All-Time SS: | 1.00 |
| | Honus Wagner | |
| 345 | All-Time OF: | 2.50 |
| | Babe Ruth | |
| 346 | All-Time OF: | 2.00 |
| | Ty Cobb | |
| 347 | All-Time OF: | 2.00 |
| | Ted Williams | |
| 348 | All-Time Catcher: | .75 |
| | Mickey Cochrane | |
| 349 | All-Time Pitcher (Right) | 1.00 |
| | Walter Johnson | |
| 350 | All-Time Pitcher (Left) | .75 |
| | Lefty Grove | |
| 351 | Randy Hundley | .15 |
| 352 | Dave Giusti | .15 |
| 353 | Sixto Lezcano (R) | .40 |
| 354 | Ron Blomberg | .15 |
| 355 | Steve Carlton | 4.00 |
| 356 | Ted Martinez | .15 |
| 357 | Ken Forsch | .15 |
| 358 | Buddy Bell | .50 |
| 359 | Rick Reuschel | .20 |
| 360 | Jeff Burroughs | .15 |

| NO. PLAYER | MINT |
|---|---|
| 361 Detroit Tigers | .60 |
| 362 Will McEnaney | .15 |
| 363 Dave Collins (R) | 1.00 |
| 364 Elias Sosa | .15 |
| 365 Carlton Fisk | 1.25 |
| 366 Bobby Valentine | .15 |
| 367 Bruce Miller | .15 |
| 368 Wilbur Wood | .15 |
| 369 Frank White | .25 |
| 370 Ron Cey | .75 |
| 371 Ellie Hendricks | .15 |
| 372 Rick Baldwin | .15 |
| 373 Johnny Briggs | .15 |
| 374 Dan Warthen | .15 |
| 375 Ron Fairly | .15 |
| 376 Rich Hebner | .15 |
| 377 Mike Hegan | .15 |
| 378 Steve Stone | .15 |
| 379 Ken Boswell | .15 |
| 380 Bobby Bonds | .25 |
| 381 Denny Doyle | .15 |
| 382 Matt Alexander | .15 |
| 383 John Ellis | .15 |
| 384 Philadelphia Phillies | .45 |
| 385 Mickey Lolich | .25 |
| 386 Ed Goodson | .15 |
| 387 Mike Miley | .15 |
| 388 Stan Perzanowski | .15 |
| 389 Glenn Adams | .15 |
| 390 Don Gullett | .15 |
| 391 Jerry Hariston | .15 |
| 392 Checklist No. 3 | .40 |
| 393 Paul Mitchell | .15 |
| 394 Fran Healy | .15 |
| 395 Jim Wynn | .15 |
| 396 Bill Lee | .15 |
| 397 Tim Foli | .15 |
| 398 Dave Tomlin | .15 |
| 399 Luis Melendez | .15 |
| 400 Rod Carew | 3.50 |
| 401 Ken Brett | .15 |
| 402 Don Money | .15 |
| 403 Geoff Zahn | .15 |
| 404 Enos Cabell | .15 |
| 405 Rollie Fingers | .75 |
| 406 Ed Herrmann | .15 |
| 407 Tom Underwood | .15 |
| 408 Charlie Spikes | .15 |
| 409 Dave Lemanczyk | .15 |
| 410 Ralph Garr | .15 |
| 411 Bill Singer | .15 |
| 412 Toby Harrah | .15 |
| 413 Pete Varney | .15 |
| 414 Wayne Garland | .15 |
| 415 Vada Pinson | .20 |
| 416 Tommy John | .75 |
| 417 Gene Clines | .15 |
| 418 Jose Morales | .15 |
| 419 Reggie Cleveland | .15 |
| 420 Joe Morgan | 2.25 |
| 421 Oakland A's | .40 |
| 422 Johnny Grubb | .15 |
| 423 Ed Halicki | .15 |
| 424 Phil Roof | .15 |
| 425 Rennie Stennett | .15 |
| 426 Bob Forsch | .15 |
| 427 Kurt Bevacqua | .15 |
| 428 Jim Crawford | .15 |
| 429 Fred Stanley | .15 |
| 430 Jose Cardenal | .15 |
| 431 Dick Ruthven | .15 |
| 432 Tom Veryzer | .15 |
| 433 Rick Waits | .15 |
| 434 Morris Nettles | .15 |
| 435 Phil Niekro | .80 |
| 436 Bill Fahey | .15 |
| 437 Terry Forster | .15 |
| 438 Doug DeCinces | .60 |
| 439 Rick Rhoden | .25 |
| 440 John Mayberry | .15 |
| 441 Gary Carter | 7.50 |
| 442 Hank Webb | .15 |

| NO. PLAYER | MINT |
|---|---|
| 443 S.F. Giants | .40 |
| 444 Gary Nolan | .15 |
| 445 Rico Petrocelli | .15 |
| 446 Larry Haney | .15 |
| 447 Gene Locklear | .15 |
| 448 Tom Johnson | .15 |
| 449 Bob Robertson | .15 |
| 450 Jim Palmer | 2.50 |
| 451 Buddy Bradford | .15 |
| 452 Tom Hausman | .15 |
| 453 Lou Piniella | .35 |
| 454 Tom Griffin | .15 |
| 455 Dick Allen | .25 |
| 456 Joe Coleman | .15 |
| 457 Ed Crosby | .15 |
| 458 Earl Williams | .15 |
| 459 Jim Brewer | .15 |
| 460 Cesar Cedeno | .25 |
| 461 Championships: | .50 |
| Reds Sweep Bucs, | |
| Bosox Surprise A's | |
| 462 World Series: | .50 |
| Reds Champs! | |
| 463 Steve Hargan | .15 |
| 464 Ken Henderson | .15 |
| 465 Mike Marshall | .15 |
| 466 Bob Stinson | .15 |
| 467 Woodie Fryman | .15 |
| 468 Jesus Alou | .15 |
| 469 Rawly Eastwick | .15 |
| 470 Bobby Murcer | .40 |
| 471 Jim Burton | .15 |
| 472 Bob Davis | .15 |
| 473 Paul Blair | .15 |
| 474 Ray Corbin | .15 |
| 475 Joe Rudi | .15 |
| 476 Bob Moose | .15 |
| 477 Cleveland Indians | .40 |
| 478 Lynn McGlothen | .15 |
| 479 Bobby Mitchell | .15 |
| 480 Mike Schmidt | 6.00 |
| 481 Rudy May | .15 |
| 482 Tim Hosley | .15 |
| 483 Mickey Stanley | .15 |
| 484 Eric Raich | .15 |
| 485 Mike Hargrove | .15 |
| 486 Bruce Dal Canton | .15 |
| 487 Leron Lee | .15 |
| 488 Claude Osteen | .15 |
| 489 Skip Jutze | .15 |
| 490 Frank Tanana | .20 |
| 491 Terry Crowley | .15 |
| 492 Marty Pattin | .15 |
| 493 Derrel Thomas | .15 |
| 494 Craig Swan | .15 |
| 495 Nate Colbert | .15 |
| 496 Juan Beniquez | .15 |
| 497 Joe McIntosh | .15 |
| 498 Glenn Borgmann | .15 |
| 499 Mario Guerrero | .15 |
| 500 Reggie Jackson | 6.00 |
| 501 Billy Champion | .15 |
| 502 Tim McCarver | .30 |
| 503 Elliott Maddox | .15 |
| 504 Pittsburgh Pirates | .40 |
| 505 Mark Belanger | .15 |
| 506 George Mitterwald | .15 |
| 507 Ray Bare | .15 |
| 508 Duane Kuiper | .15 |
| 509 Bill Hands | .15 |
| 510 Amos Otis | .15 |
| 511 Jamie Easterley | .15 |
| 512 Ellie Rodriguez | .15 |
| 513 Bart Johnson | .15 |
| 514 Dan Driessen | .15 |
| 515 Steve Yeager | .15 |
| 516 Wayne Granger | .15 |
| 517 John Milner | .15 |
| 518 Doug Flynn | .15 |
| 519 Steve Brye | .15 |
| 520 Willie McCovey | 1.50 |

| NO. PLAYER | MINT |
|---|---|
| 521 Jim Colborn | .15 |
| 522 Ted Sizemore | .15 |
| 523 Bob Montgomery | .15 |
| 524 Pete Falcone | .15 |
| 525 Billy Williams | .75 |
| 526 Checklist No. 4 | .45 |
| 527 Mike Anderson | .15 |
| 528 Dock Ellis | .15 |
| 529 Deron Johnson | .15 |
| 530 Don Sutton | .60 |
| 531 New York Mets | .75 |
| 532 Milt May | .15 |
| 533 Lee Richard | .15 |
| 534 Stan Bahnsen | .15 |
| 535 Dave Nelson | .15 |
| 536 Mike Thompson | .15 |
| 537 Tony Muser | .15 |
| 538 Pat Darcy | .15 |
| 539 John Balaz | .15 |
| 540 Bill Freehan | .15 |
| 541 Steve Mingori | .15 |
| 542 Keith Hernandez | 4.00 |
| 543 Wayne Twitchell | .15 |
| 544 Pepe Frias | .15 |
| 545 Sparky Lyle | .20 |
| 546 Dave Rosello | .15 |
| 547 Roric Harrison | .15 |
| 548 Manny Mota | .15 |
| 549 Randy Tate | .15 |
| 550 Hank Aaron | 5.00 |
| 551 Jerry DaVanon | .15 |
| 552 Terry Humphrey | .15 |
| 553 Randy Moffitt | .15 |
| 554 Ray Fosse | .15 |
| 555 Dyar Miller | .15 |
| 556 Minnesota Twins | .40 |
| 557 Dan Spillner | .15 |
| 558 Clarence Gaston | .15 |
| 559 Clyde Wright | .15 |
| 560 Jorge Orta | .15 |
| 561 Tom Carroll | .15 |
| 562 Adrian Garrett | .15 |
| 563 Larry Demery | .15 |
| 564 Gum Blowing Champ: | .15 |
| Kurt Bevacqua | |
| 565 Tug McGraw | .35 |
| 566 Ken McMullen | .15 |
| 567 George Stone | .15 |
| 568 Rob Andrews | .15 |
| 569 Nelson Briles | .15 |
| 570 George Hendrick | .30 |
| 571 Don DeMola | .15 |
| 572 Rich Coggins | .15 |
| 573 Bill Travers | .15 |
| 574 Don Kessinger | .15 |
| 575 Dwight Evans | .50 |
| 576 Maximino Leon | .15 |
| 577 Marc Hill | .15 |
| 578 Ted Kubiak | .15 |
| 579 Clay Kirby | .15 |
| 580 Bert Campaneris | .15 |
| 581 St. Louis Cardinals | .60 |
| 582 Mike Kekich | .15 |
| 583 Tommy Helms | .15 |
| 584 Stan Wall | .15 |
| 585 Joe Torre | .35 |
| 586 Ron Schueler | .15 |
| 587 Leo Cardenas | .15 |
| 588 Kevin Kobel | .15 |
| 589 Rookie Pitchers: | 1.25 |
| Joe Pactwa, Santo Alcala, | |
| Mike Flanagan, P. Torrealba | |
| 590 Rookie Outfielders: | 1.50 |
| Henry Cruz, Ellis Valentine, | |
| Chet Lemon, T. Whitfield | |
| 591 Rookie Pitchers: | .30 |
| Steve Grilli, C. Mitchell, | |
| Jose Sosa, George Throop | |
| 592 Rookie Infielders | 1.50 |
| W. Randolph, D. McKay, | |
| J. Royster, R. Staiger | |

| NO. PLAYER | MINT |
|---|---|
| 593 Rookie Pitchers: | .30 |
| Larry Anderson, M. Littell, | |
| Butch Metzger, Ken Crosby | |
| 594 Rookie Catchers & OF's | .30 |
| Andy Merchant, Ed Ott, | |
| R. Stillman, Jerry White | |
| 595 Rookie Pitchers: | .30 |
| Art DeFillipis, R. Lerch, | |
| Sid Monge, Steve Barr | |
| 596 Rookie Infielders: | .50 |
| C. Reynolds, L. Johnson, | |
| J. LeMaster, J. Manuel | |
| 597 RooKie Pitchers: | .50 |
| D. Aase, Jack Kucek, | |
| Frank LaCorte, Mike Pazik | |
| 598 Rookie Outfielders: | .30 |
| Hector Cruz, J. Quirk, | |
| Jerry Turner, Joe Wallis | |
| 599 Rookie Pitchers: | 11.00 |
| Rob Dressler, Ron Guidry, | |
| Bob McClure, Pat Zachry | |
| 600 Tom Seaver | 4.00 |
| 601 Ken Rudolph | .15 |
| 602 Doug Konieczny | .15 |
| 603 Jim Holt | .15 |
| 604 Joe Lovitto | .15 |
| 605 Al Downing | .15 |
| 606 Milwaukee Brewers | .40 |
| 607 Rich Hinton | .15 |
| 608 Vic Correll | .15 |
| 609 Fred Norman | .15 |
| 610 Greg Luzinski | .50 |
| 611 Rich Folkers | .15 |
| 612 Joe Lahoud | .15 |
| 613 Tim Johnson | .15 |
| 614 Fernando Arroyo | .15 |
| 615 Mike Cubbage | .15 |
| 616 Buck Martinez | .15 |
| 617 Darold Knowles | .15 |
| 618 Jack Brohamer | .15 |
| 619 Bill Butler | .15 |
| 620 Al Oliver | .75 |
| 621 Tom Hall | .15 |
| 622 Rick Auerbach | .15 |
| 623 Bob Allietta | .15 |
| 624 Tony Taylor | .15 |
| 625 J.R. Richard | .20 |
| 626 Bob Sheldon | .15 |
| 627 Bill Plummer | .15 |
| 628 John D'Acquisto | .15 |
| 629 Sandy Alomar | .15 |
| 630 Chris Speier | .15 |
| 631 Atlanta Braves | .40 |
| 632 Rogelio Moret | .15 |
| 633 John Stearns (R) | .25 |
| 634 Larry Christenson | .15 |
| 635 Jim Fregosi | .15 |
| 636 Joe Decker | .15 |
| 637 Bruce Bochte | .15 |
| 638 Doyle Alexander | .15 |
| 639 Fred Kendall | .15 |
| 640 Bill Madlock | 1.25 |
| 641 Tom Paciorek | .15 |
| 642 Dennis Blair | .15 |
| 643 Checklist No. 5 | .40 |
| 644 Tom Bradley | .15 |
| 645 Darrell Porter | .15 |
| 646 John Lowenstein | .15 |
| 647 Ramon Hernandez | .15 |
| 648 Al Cowens | .15 |
| 649 Dave Roberts | .15 |
| 650 Thurman Munson | 3.00 |
| 651 John Odom | .15 |
| 652 Ed Armbrister | .15 |
| 653 Mike Norris (R) | .25 |
| 654 Doug Griffin | .15 |
| 655 Mike Vail | .15 |
| 656 Chicago White Sox | .40 |
| 657 Roy Smalley (R) | .40 |
| 658 Jerry Johnson | .15 |
| 659 Ben Oglivie | .30 |
| 660 Dave Lopes | .50 |

# 1976 Topps Traded....Complete Set of 44 Cards—Value $6.50

This set features players who were traded after the regular 1976 set was printed. The card numbers are the same as the main set, with the addition of "T" after the number.

| NO. | PLAYER | MINT | NO. | PLAYER | MINT | NO. | PLAYER | MINT | NO. | PLAYER | MINT |
|---|---|---|---|---|---|---|---|---|---|---|---|
| 27 T | Ed Figueroa | .10 | 146 T | George Medich | .10 | 380 T | Bobby Bonds | .15 | 527 T | Mike Anderson | .10 |
| 28 T | Dusty Baker | .35 | 158 T | Ken Reitz | .10 | 383 T | John Ellis | .10 | 528 T | Dock Ellis | .10 |
| 44 T | Doug Rader | .15 | 208 T | Mike Lum | .10 | 385 T | Mickey Lolich | .25 | 532 T | Milt May | .10 |
| 58 T | Ron Reed | .12 | 211 T | Clay Carroll | .10 | 401 T | Ken Brett | .15 | 554 T | Ray Fosse | .10 |
| 74 T | Oscar Gamble | .20 | 231 T | Tom House | .10 | 410 T | Ken Brett | .15 | 579 T | Clay Kirby | .10 |
| 80 T | Jim Kaat | .50 | 250 T | Fergie Jenkins | .45 | 411 T | Bill Singer | .10 | 583 T | Tommy Helms | .10 |
| 83 T | Jim Spencer | .10 | 259 T | Darrel Chaney | .10 | 428 T | Jim Crawford | .10 | 592 T | Willie Randolph | .35 |
| 85 T | Mickey Rivers | .20 | 292 T | Leon Roberts | .10 | 434 T | Morris Nettles | .10 | 618 T | Jack Brohamer | .10 |
| 99 T | Lee Lacy | .15 | 296 T | Pat Dobson | .10 | 464 T | Ken Henderson | .10 | 632 T | Rogelio Moret | .10 |
| 120 T | Rusty Staub | .35 | 309 T | Bill Melton | .10 | 497 T | Joe McIntosh | .10 | 649 T | Dave Roberts | .10 |
| 127 T | Larvell Blanks | .10 | 338 T | Bob Bailey | .10 | 524 T | Pete Falcone | .10 | — | Checklist | .45 |

# 1977 Topps....Complete Set of 660 Cards—Value $175.00

Dale Murphy, Tony Armas, and Andre Dawson's rookie cards are in this set. There is an error on card 634—the photos are switched.

   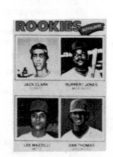 

| NO. | PLAYER | MINT | NO. | PLAYER | MINT | NO. | PLAYER | MINT | NO. | PLAYER | MINT |
|---|---|---|---|---|---|---|---|---|---|---|---|
| 1 | Batting Leaders: George Brett, Bill Madlock | 1.50 | 21 | Ken Frosch | .12 | 50 | Ron Cey | .60 | 78 | Bob Davis | .12 |
| 2 | Home Run Leaders: Graig Nettles, Mike Schmidt | .75 | 22 | Bill Freehan | .12 | 51 | Milwaukee Brewers/ Alex Grammas (Mgr.) | .50 | 79 | Don Money | .12 |
| 3 | RBI Leaders: Lee May, George Foster | .40 | 23 | Dan Driessen | .12 | 52 | Ellis Valentine | .12 | 80 | Andy Messersmith | .15 |
| 4 | Stolen Base Leaders: B. North, Dave Lopes | .30 | 24 | Carl Morton | .12 | 53 | Paul Mitchell | .12 | 81 | Juan Beniquez | .15 |
| 5 | Victory Leaders: Jim Palmer, Randy Jones | .50 | 25 | Dwight Evans | .50 | 54 | Sandy Alomar | .12 | 82 | Jim Rooker | .12 |
| 6 | Strikeout Leaders: Nolan Ryan, Tom Seaver | .60 | 26 | Ray Sadecki | .12 | 55 | Jeff Burroughs | .12 | 83 | Kevin Bell | .12 |
| 7 | ERA Leaders: Mark Fidrych, J. Denny | .30 | 27 | Bill Buckner | .35 | 56 | Rudy May | .12 | 84 | Ollie Brown | .12 |
| 8 | Leading Firemen: B. Campbell, R. Eastwick | .25 | 28 | Woodie Fryman | .12 | 57 | Marc Hill | .12 | 85 | Duane Kuiper | .12 |
| 9 | Doug Rader | .12 | 29 | Bucky Dent | .20 | 58 | Chet Lemon | .50 | 86 | Pat Zachry | .12 |
| 10 | Reggie Jackson | 5.50 | 30 | Greg Luzinski | .50 | 59 | Larry Christenson | .12 | 87 | Glenn Borgmann | .12 |
| 11 | Rob Dressler | .12 | 31 | Jim Todd | .12 | 60 | Jim Rice | 6.00 | 88 | Stan Wall | .12 |
| 12 | Larry Haney | .12 | 32 | Checklist No. 1 | .45 | 61 | Manny Sanguillen | .12 | 89 | Butch Hobson | .12 |
| 13 | Luis Gomez | .12 | 33 | Wayne Garland | .12 | 62 | Eric Raich | .12 | 90 | Cesar Cedeno | .25 |
| 14 | Tommy Smith | .12 | 34 | Angels/Norm Sherry (Mgr.) | .40 | 63 | Tito Fuentes | .12 | 91 | John Verhoeven | .12 |
| 15 | Don Gullett | .12 | 35 | Rennie Stennett | .12 | 64 | Larry Biittner | .12 | 92 | Dave Rosello | .12 |
| 16 | Bob Jones | .12 | 36 | John Ellis | .12 | 65 | Skip Lockwood | .12 | 93 | Tom Poquette | .12 |
| 17 | Steve Stone | .12 | 37 | Steve Hargan | .12 | 66 | Roy Smalley | .12 | 94 | Craig Swan | .12 |
| 18 | Cleveland Indians/ Frank Robinson (Mgr.) | .40 | 38 | Craig Kusick | .12 | 67 | Joaquin Andujar (R) | 2.00 | 95 | Keith Hernandez | 3.00 |
| 19 | John D'Acquisto | .12 | 39 | Tom Griffin | .12 | 68 | Bruce Bochte | .12 | 96 | Lou Piniella | .35 |
| 20 | Graig Nettles | .75 | 40 | Bobby Murcer | .40 | 69 | Jim Crawford | .12 | 97 | Dave Heaverlo | .12 |
| | | | 41 | Jim Kern | .12 | 70 | Johnny Bench | 2.50 | 98 | Milt May | .12 |
| | | | 42 | Jose Cruz | .35 | 71 | Dock Ellis | .12 | 99 | Tom Hausman | .12 |
| | | | 43 | Ray Bare | .12 | 72 | Mike Anderson | .12 | 100 | Joe Morgan | 1.25 |
| | | | 44 | Bud Harrelson | .12 | 73 | Charlie Williams | .12 | 101 | Dick Bosman | .12 |
| | | | 45 | Rawly Eastwick | .12 | 74 | A's/J. McKeon (Mgr.) | .40 | 102 | Jose Morales | .12 |
| | | | 46 | Buck Martinez | .12 | 75 | Dennis Leonard | .12 | 103 | Mike Bacsik | .12 |
| | | | 47 | Lynn McGlothen | .12 | 76 | Tim Foli | .12 | 104 | Omar Moreno (R) | .50 |
| | | | 48 | Tom Paciorek | .12 | 77 | Dyar Miller | .12 | 105 | Steve Yeager | .15 |
| | | | 49 | Grant Jackson | .12 | | | | 106 | Mike Flanagan | .30 |

| NO. | PLAYER | MINT |
|---|---|---|
| 107 | Bill Melton | .12 |
| 108 | Alan Foster | .12 |
| 109 | Jorge Orta | .12 |
| 110 | Steve Carlton | 4.00 |
| 111 | Rico Petrocelli | .12 |
| 112 | Bill Greif | .12 |
| 113 | Toronto Blue Jays/ | .35 |
|  | Roy Hartsfield (Mgr.) |  |
| 114 | Bruce Dal Canton | .12 |
| 115 | Rick Manning | .12 |
| 116 | Joe Niekro | .25 |
| 117 | Frank White | .20 |
| 118 | Rick Jone | .12 |
| 119 | John Stearns | .12 |
| 120 | Rod Carew | 3.50 |
| 121 | Gary Nolan | .12 |
| 122 | Ben Oglivie | .20 |
| 123 | Fred Stanley | .12 |
| 124 | George Mitterwald | .12 |
| 125 | Bill Travers | .12 |
| 126 | Rod Gilbreath | .12 |
| 127 | Ron Fairly | .12 |
| 128 | Tommy John | .75 |
| 129 | Mike Sadek | .12 |
| 130 | Al Oliver | .75 |
| 131 | Orlando Ramirez | .12 |
| 132 | Chip Lang | .12 |
| 133 | Ralph Garr | .12 |
| 134 | San Diego Padres/ | .45 |
|  | John McNamara (Mgr.) |  |
| 135 | Mark Belanger | .12 |
| 136 | Jerry Mumphrey (R) | .50 |
| 137 | Jeff Terpko | .12 |
| 138 | Bob Stinson | .12 |
| 139 | Fred Norman | .12 |
| 140 | Mike Schmidt | 6.00 |
| 141 | Mark Littell | .12 |
| 142 | Steve Dillard | .12 |
| 143 | Ed Herrmann | .12 |
| 144 | Bruce Sutter (R) | 4.00 |
| 145 | Tom Veryzer | .12 |
| 146 | Dusty Baker | .30 |
| 147 | Jackie Brown | .12 |
| 148 | Fran Healy | .12 |
| 149 | Mike Cubbage | .12 |
| 150 | Tom Seaver | 3.50 |
| 151 | Johnnie LeMaster | .12 |
| 152 | Gaylord Perry | 1.00 |
| 153 | Ron Jackson | .12 |
| 154 | Dave Guisti | .12 |
| 155 | Joe Rudi | .12 |
| 156 | Pete Mackanin | .12 |
| 157 | Ken Brett | .12 |
| 158 | Ted Kubiak | .12 |
| 159 | Bernie Carbo | .12 |
| 160 | Will McEnaney | .12 |
| 161 | Garry Templeton (R) | 1.75 |
| 162 | Mike Cuellar | .12 |
| 163 | Dave Hilton | .12 |
| 164 | Tug McGraw | .20 |
| 165 | Jim Wynn | .12 |
| 166 | Bill Campbell | .12 |
| 167 | Rich Hebner | .12 |
| 168 | Charlie Spikes | .12 |
| 169 | Darold Knowles | .12 |
| 170 | Thurman Munson | 2.00 |
| 171 | Ken Sanders | .12 |
| 172 | John Milner | .12 |
| 173 | Chuck Scrivener | .12 |
| 174 | Nelson Briles | .12 |
| 175 | Butch Wynegar (R) | .75 |
| 176 | Bob Robertson | .12 |
| 177 | Bart Johnson | .12 |
| 178 | Bombo Rivera | .12 |
| 179 | Paul Hartzell | .12 |
| 180 | Dave Lopes | .25 |
| 181 | Ken McMullen | .12 |
| 182 | Dan Spillner | .12 |
| 183 | Cardinals/V. Rapp (Mgr.) | .50 |
| 184 | Bo McLaughlin | .12 |
| 185 | Sixto Lezcano | .12 |
| 186 | Doug Flynn | .12 |
| 187 | Dick Pole | .12 |
| 188 | Bob Tolan | .12 |
| 189 | Rick Dempsey | .15 |

| NO. | PLAYER | MINT |
|---|---|---|
| 190 | Ray Burris | .12 |
| 191 | Doug Griffin | .12 |
| 192 | Clarence Gaston | .12 |
| 193 | Larry Gura | .12 |
| 194 | Gary Matthews | .30 |
| 195 | Ed Figueroa | .12 |
| 196 | Len Randle | .12 |
| 197 | Ed Ott | .12 |
| 198 | Wilbur Wood | .12 |
| 199 | Pepe Frias | .12 |
| 200 | Frank Tanana | .15 |
| 201 | Ed Kranepool | .12 |
| 202 | Tom Johnson | .12 |
| 203 | Ed Armbrister | .12 |
| 204 | Jeff Newman | .12 |
| 205 | Pete Falcone | .12 |
| 206 | Boog Powell | .12 |
| 207 | Glenn Abbott | .12 |
| 208 | Checklist No. 2 | .45 |
| 209 | Rob Andrews | .12 |
| 210 | Fred Lynn | 1.50 |
| 211 | San Francisco Giants/ | .40 |
|  | Joe Altobelli (Mgr.) |  |
| 212 | Jim Mason | .12 |
| 213 | Maximino Leon | .12 |
| 214 | Darrell Porter | .20 |
| 215 | Butch Metzger | .12 |
| 216 | Doug DeCinces | .40 |
| 217 | Tom Underwood | .12 |
| 218 | John Wathan | .25 |
| 219 | Joe Coleman | .12 |
| 220 | Chris Chambliss | .20 |
| 221 | Bob Bailey | .12 |
| 222 | Francisco Barrios | .12 |
| 223 | Earl Williams | .12 |
| 224 | Rusty Torres | .12 |
| 225 | Bob Apodaca | .12 |
| 226 | Leroy Stanton | .12 |
| 227 | Joe Sambito | .12 |
| 228 | Minnesota Twins/ | .40 |
|  | Gene Mauch (Mgr.) |  |
| 229 | Don Kessinger | .12 |
| 230 | Vida Blue | .25 |
| 231 | Record—Brett | 1.50 |
|  | Most Consecutive Games |  |
|  | with 3 or More Hits |  |
| 232 | Record—Minoso | .25 |
|  | Oldest Player to Hit Safely |  |
| 233 | Record—Morales | .20 |
|  | Most Pinch-Hits for Season |  |
| 234 | Record—Ryan | 1.00 |
|  | Most Seasons 300 SO's |  |
| 235 | Cecil Cooper | 1.00 |
| 236 | Tom Buskey | .12 |
| 237 | Gene Clines | .12 |
| 238 | Tippy Martinez | .12 |
| 239 | Bill Plummer | .12 |
| 240 | Ron LeFlore | .15 |
| 241 | Dave Tomlin | .12 |
| 242 | Ken Henderson | .12 |
| 243 | Ron Reed | .12 |
| 244 | John Mayberry | .15 |
| 245 | Rick Rhoden | .15 |
| 246 | Mike Vail | .12 |
| 247 | Chris Knapp | .12 |
| 248 | Wilbur Howard | .12 |
| 249 | Pete Redfern | .12 |
| 250 | Bill Madlock | .85 |
| 251 | Tony Muser | .12 |
| 252 | Dale Murray | .12 |
| 253 | John Hale | .12 |
| 254 | Doyle Alexander | .12 |
| 255 | George Scott | .12 |
| 256 | Joe Hoerner | .12 |
| 257 | Mike Miley | .12 |
| 258 | Luis Tiant | .15 |
| 259 | Mets/J. Frazier (Mgr.) | .60 |
| 260 | J.R. Richard | .20 |
| 261 | Phil Garner | .12 |
| 262 | Al Cowens | .12 |
| 263 | Mike Marshall | .12 |
| 264 | Tom Hutton | .12 |
| 265 | Mark Fidrych (R) | .50 |
| 266 | Derrel Thomas | .12 |
| 267 | Ray Fosse | .12 |

| NO. | PLAYER | MINT |
|---|---|---|
| 268 | Rick Sawyer | .12 |
| 269 | Joe Lis | .12 |
| 270 | Dave Parker | 2.00 |
| 271 | Terry Forster | .20 |
| 272 | Lee Lacy | .15 |
| 273 | Eric Soderholm | .12 |
| 274 | Don Stanhouse | .12 |
| 275 | Mike Hargrove | .12 |
| 276 | A.L. Championship: | .40 |
|  | Chambliss' Homer |  |
| 277 | N.L. Championship: | .45 |
|  | Reds Sweep Phillies in 3 |  |
| 278 | Danny Frisella | .12 |
| 279 | Joe Wallis | .12 |
| 280 | Jim Hunter | .60 |
| 281 | Roy Staiger | .12 |
| 282 | Sid Monge | .12 |
| 283 | Jerry DaVanon | .12 |
| 284 | Mike Norris | .12 |
| 285 | Brooks Robinson | 2.00 |
| 286 | Johnny Grubb | .12 |
| 287 | Cincinnati Reds | .50 |
|  | Sparky Anderson (Mgr.) |  |
| 288 | Bob Montgomery | .12 |
| 289 | Gene Garber | .12 |
| 290 | Amos Otis | .15 |
| 291 | Jason Thompson (R) | 1.00 |
| 292 | Rogelio Moret | .12 |
| 293 | Jack Brohamer | .12 |
| 294 | George Medich | .12 |
| 295 | Gary Carter | 5.00 |
| 296 | Don Hood | .12 |
| 297 | Ken Reitz | .12 |
| 298 | Charlie Hough | .12 |
| 299 | Otto Velez | .12 |
| 300 | Jerry Koosman | .20 |
| 301 | Toby Harrah | .15 |
| 302 | Mike Garman | .12 |
| 303 | Gene Tenace | .12 |
| 304 | Jim Hughes | .12 |
| 305 | Mickey Rivers | .20 |
| 306 | Rick Waits | .12 |
| 307 | Gary Sutherland | .12 |
| 308 | Gene Pentz | .12 |
| 309 | Boston Red Sox/ | .50 |
|  | Don Zimmer (Mgr.) |  |
| 310 | Larry Bowa | .20 |
| 311 | Vern Ruhle | .12 |
| 312 | Rob Belloir | .12 |
| 313 | Paul Blair | .12 |
| 314 | Steve Mingori | .12 |
| 315 | Dave Chalk | .12 |
| 316 | Steve Rogers | .20 |
| 317 | Kurt Bevacqua | .12 |
| 318 | Duffy Dyer | .12 |
| 319 | Rich Gossage | .75 |
| 320 | Ken Griffey | .25 |
| 321 | Dave Goltz | .12 |
| 322 | Bill Russell | .12 |
| 323 | Larry Lintz | .12 |
| 324 | John Curtis | .12 |
| 325 | Mike Ivie | .12 |
| 326 | Jesse Jefferson | .12 |
| 327 | Astros/B. Virdon (Mgr.) | .40 |
| 328 | Tommy Boggs | .12 |
| 329 | Ron Hodges | .12 |
| 330 | George Hendrick | .25 |
| 331 | Jim Colborn | .12 |
| 332 | Elliott Maddox | .12 |
| 333 | Paul Reuschel | .12 |
| 334 | Bill Stein | .12 |
| 335 | Bill Robinson | .12 |
| 336 | Denny Doyle | .12 |
| 337 | Ron Schueler | .12 |
| 338 | Dave Duncan | .12 |
| 339 | Adrian Devine | .12 |
| 340 | Hal McRae | .15 |
| 341 | Joe Kerrigan | .12 |
| 342 | Jerry Remy | .12 |
| 343 | Ed Halicki | .12 |
| 344 | Brian Downing | .12 |
| 345 | Reggie Smith | .25 |
| 346 | Bill Singer | .12 |
| 347 | George Foster | 1.25 |
| 348 | Brent Strom | .12 |

| NO. | PLAYER | MINT |
|---|---|---|
| 349 | Jim Holt | .12 |
| 350 | Larry Dierker | .12 |
| 351 | Jim Sundberg | .12 |
| 352 | Mike Phillips | .12 |
| 353 | Stan Thomas | .12 |
| 354 | Pirates/C. Tanner (Mgr.) | .40 |
| 355 | Lou Brock | 1.25 |
| 356 | Checklist No. 3 | .40 |
| 357 | Tim McCarver | .35 |
| 358 | Tom House | .12 |
| 359 | Willie Randolph | .25 |
| 360 | Rick Monday | .12 |
| 361 | Eduardo Rodriguez | .12 |
| 362 | Tommy Davis | .12 |
| 363 | Dave Roberts | .12 |
| 364 | Vic Correll | .12 |
| 365 | Mike Torrez | .12 |
| 366 | Ted Sizemore | .12 |
| 367 | Dave Hamilton | .12 |
| 368 | Mike Jorgensen | .12 |
| 369 | Terry Humphrey | .12 |
| 370 | John Montefusco | .12 |
| 371 | Royals/W. Herzog (Mgr.) | .50 |
| 372 | Rich Folkers | .12 |
| 373 | Bert Campaneris | .15 |
| 374 | Kent Tekulve | .15 |
| 375 | Larry Hisle | .15 |
| 376 | Nino Espinosa | .12 |
| 377 | Dave McKay | .12 |
| 378 | Jim Umbarger | .12 |
| 379 | Larry Cox | .12 |
| 380 | Lee May | .20 |
| 381 | Bob Forsch | .12 |
| 382 | Charlie Moore | .12 |
| 383 | Stan Bahnsen | .12 |
| 384 | Darrel Chaney | .12 |
| 385 | Dave LaRoche | .12 |
| 386 | Manny Mota | .15 |
| 387 | New York Yankees/ | .60 |
|  | Billy Martin (Mgr.) |  |
| 388 | Terry Harmon | .12 |
| 389 | Ken Kravec | .12 |
| 390 | Dave Winfield | 3.00 |
| 391 | Dan Warthen | .12 |
| 392 | Phil Roof | .12 |
| 393 | John Lowenstein | .12 |
| 394 | Bill Laxton | .12 |
| 395 | Manny Trillo | .12 |
| 396 | Tom Murphy | .12 |
| 397 | Larry Herndon (R) | .60 |
| 398 | Tom Burgmeier | .12 |
| 399 | Bruce Boisclair | .12 |
| 400 | Steve Garvey | 3.00 |
| 401 | Mickey Scott | .12 |
| 402 | Tommy Helms | .12 |
| 403 | Tom Grieve | .12 |
| 404 | Eric Rasmussen | .12 |
| 405 | Claudell Washington | .20 |
| 406 | Tim Johnson | .12 |
| 407 | Dave Freisleben | .12 |
| 408 | Cesar Tovar | .12 |
| 409 | Pete Broberg | .12 |
| 410 | Willie Montanez | .12 |
| 411 | World Series | .50 |
|  | Morgan Homers, |  |
|  | Bench Stars for Reds |  |
| 412 | World Series # 1 & 2 | .50 |
|  | Reds' Defense, |  |
|  | Bench's Two Homers |  |
| 413 | World Series # 3 & 4 | .50 |
|  | Cincy Wins |  |
| 414 | Tommy Harper | .12 |
| 415 | Jay Johnstone | .12 |
| 416 | Chuck Hartenstein | .12 |
| 417 | Wayne Garrett | .12 |
| 418 | Chicago White Sox/ | .40 |
|  | Bob Lemon (Mgr.) |  |
| 419 | Steve Swisher | .12 |
| 420 | Rusty Staub | .25 |
| 421 | Doug Rau | .12 |
| 422 | Freddie Patek | .12 |
| 423 | Gary Lavelle | .12 |
| 424 | Steve Brye | .12 |
| 425 | Joe Torre | .25 |
| 426 | Dick Drago | .12 |

| NO. PLAYER | MINT |
|---|---|
| 427 Dave Rader | .12 |
| 428 Texas Rangers/ | .40 |
| Frank Lucchesi (Mgr.) | |
| 429 Ken Boswell | .12 |
| 430 Fergie Jenkins | .40 |
| 431 Dave Collins | .20 |
| (photo of Bobby Jones) | |
| 432 Buzz Capra | .12 |
| 433 Turn Back Clock (1972) | .20 |
| Colbert Hits 5 Homers | |
| 434 Turn Back Clock (1967) | 1.50 |
| Yaz Wins Triple Crown | |
| 435 Turn Back Clock (1962) | .50 |
| Wills 104 Steals | |
| 436 Turn Back Clock (1957) | .20 |
| Keegan No-Hitter | |
| 437 Turn Back Clock (1952) | .50 |
| Kiner Leads NL | |
| 438 Marty Perez | .12 |
| 439 Gorman Thomas | .40 |
| 440 Jon Matlack | .12 |
| 441 Larvell Blanks | .12 |
| 442 Atlanta Braves/ | .40 |
| Dave Bristol (Mgr.) | |
| 443 Lamar Johnson | .12 |
| 444 Wayne Twitchell | .12 |
| 445 Ken Singleton | .30 |
| 446 Bill Bonham | .12 |
| 447 Jerry Turner | .12 |
| 448 Ellie Rodriguez | .12 |
| 449 Al Fitzmorris | .12 |
| 450 Pete Rose | 7.50 |
| 451 Checklist No. 4 | .45 |
| 452 Mike Caldwell | .12 |
| 453 Pedro Garcia | .12 |
| 454 Andy Etchebarren | .12 |
| 455 Rick Wise | .12 |
| 456 Leon Roberts | .12 |
| 457 Steve Luebber | .12 |
| 458 Leo Foster | .12 |
| 459 Steve Foucault | .12 |
| 460 Willie Stargell | 1.50 |
| 461 Dick Tidrow | .12 |
| 462 Don Baylor | .50 |
| 463 Jamie Quirk | .12 |
| 464 Randy Moffitt | .12 |
| 465 Rico Carty | .12 |
| 466 Fred Holdsworth | .12 |
| 467 Philadelphia Phillies/ | .45 |
| Danny Ozark (Mgr.) | |
| 468 Ramon Hernandez | .12 |
| 469 Pat Kelly | .12 |
| 470 Ted Simmons | .50 |
| 471 Del Unser | .12 |
| 472 Rookie Pitchers: | .40 |
| Bob McClure, Don Aase, | |
| Gil Patterson, Dave | |
| Wehrmeister | |
| 473 Rookie Outfielders: | 10.00 |
| Gene Richards, John Scott, | |
| D. Walling, A. Dawson | |
| 474 Rookie Shortstops: | .30 |
| Bob Bailor, Kiko Garcia, | |
| C. Reynolds, A. Taveras | |
| 475 Rookie Pitchers: | .50 |
| Chris Batton, Rick Camp | |
| S. McGregor, M. Sarmiento | |
| 476 Rookie Catchers: | 50.00 |
| Dale Murphy, Rick Cerone, | |
| G. Alexander, K. Pasley | |
| 477 Rookie Infielders: | .30 |
| R. Dauer, O. Gonzalez, | |
| D. Ault, P. Mankowski | |

| NO. PLAYER | MINT |
|---|---|
| 478 Rookie Pitchers: | .30 |
| Leon Hooten, Jim Gideon, | |
| Mark Lemongello, | |
| Dave Johnson, | |
| 479 Rookie Outfielders: | .30 |
| A. Woods, Wayne Gross, | |
| B. Asselstine, S. Mejias | |
| 480 Carl Yastrzemski | 3.50 |
| 481 Roger Metzger | .12 |
| 482 Tony Solaita | .12 |
| 483 Richie Zisk | .12 |
| 484 Burt Hooton | .12 |
| 485 Roy White | .12 |
| 486 Ed Bane | .12 |
| 487 Rookie Pitchers: | .30 |
| Joe Henderson, Ed Glynn, | |
| L. Anderson, G. Terlecky | |
| 488 Rookie Outfielders: | 7.00 |
| Lee Mazzilli, Jack Clark, | |
| R. Jones, D. Thomas | |
| 489 Rookie Pitchers: | 1.00 |
| Len Barker, Randy Lerch, | |
| Greg Minton, Mike Overy | |
| 490 Rookie Shortstops: | .30 |
| T. McMillan, B. Almon, | |
| M. Klutts, M. Wagner | |
| 491 Rookie Pitchers: | .40 |
| Mike Dupree, Bob Sykes, | |
| D. Martinez, C. Mitchell | |
| 492 Rookie Outfielders: | 4.50 |
| Tony Armas, Steve Kemp, | |
| C. Lopez, Gary Woods | |
| 493 Rookie Pitchers: | .50 |
| G. Wheelock, M. Krukow, | |
| Jim Otten, Mike Willis | |
| 494 Rookie Infielders: | .50 |
| Juan Bernhardt, J. Gantner, | |
| M. Champion, B. Wills | |
| 495 Al Hrabosky | .12 |
| 496 Gary Thomasson | .12 |
| 497 Clay Carroll | .12 |
| 498 Sal Bando | .15 |
| 499 Pablo Torealba | .12 |
| 500 Dave Kingman | .50 |
| 501 Jim Bibby | .12 |
| 502 Randy Hundley | .12 |
| 503 Bill Lee | .12 |
| 504 Los Angeles Dodgers/ | .60 |
| Tom Lasorda (Mgr.) | |
| 505 Oscar Gamble | .20 |
| 506 Steve Grilli | .12 |
| 507 Mike Hegan | .12 |
| 508 Dave Pagan | .12 |
| 509 Cookie Rojas | .12 |
| 510 John Candelaria | .25 |
| 511 Bill Fahey | .12 |
| 512 Jack Billingham | .12 |
| 513 Jerry Terrell | .12 |
| 514 Cliff Johnson | .12 |
| 515 Chris Speier | .12 |
| 516 Bake McBride | .15 |
| 517 Pete Vuckovich (R) | .75 |
| 518 Chicago Cubs/ | .45 |
| Herman Franks (Mgr.) | |
| 519 Don Kirkwood | .12 |
| 520 Garry Maddox | .15 |
| 521 Bob Grich | .20 |
| 522 Enzo Hernandez | .12 |
| 523 Rollie Fingers | .60 |
| 524 Rowland Office | .12 |
| 525 Dennis Eckersley | .20 |
| 526 Larry Parrish | .20 |

| NO. PLAYER | MINT |
|---|---|
| 527 Dan Meyer | .12 |
| 528 Bill Castro | .12 |
| 529 Jim Essian | .12 |
| 530 Rick Reuschel | .15 |
| 531 Lyman Bostock | .25 |
| 532 Jim Willoughby | .12 |
| 533 Mickey Stanley | .12 |
| 534 Paul Splittorff | .12 |
| 535 Cesar Geronimo | .12 |
| 536 Vic Albury | .12 |
| 537 Dave Roberts | .12 |
| 538 Frank Taveras | .12 |
| 539 Mike Wallace | .12 |
| 540 Bob Watson | .12 |
| 541 John Denny | .35 |
| 542 Frank Duffy | .12 |
| 543 Ron Blomberg | .12 |
| 544 Gary Ross | .12 |
| 545 Bob Boone | .15 |
| 546 Baltimore Orioles/ | .50 |
| Earl Weaver (Mgr.) | |
| 547 Willie McCovey | 1.50 |
| 548 Joel Youngblood | .12 |
| 549 Jerry Royster | .12 |
| 550 Randy Jones | .12 |
| 551 Bill North | .12 |
| 552 Pepe Mangual | .12 |
| 553 Jack Heidemann | .12 |
| 554 Bruce Kimm | .12 |
| 555 Dan Ford | .12 |
| 556 Doug Bird | .12 |
| 557 Jerry White | .12 |
| 558 Elias Sosa | .12 |
| 559 Alan Bannister | .12 |
| 560 Dave Concepcion | .40 |
| 561 Pete LaCock | .12 |
| 562 Checklist No. 5 | .45 |
| 563 Bruce Kison | .12 |
| 564 Alan Ashby | .12 |
| 565 Mickey Lolich | .15 |
| 566 Rick Miller | .12 |
| 567 Enos Cabell | .12 |
| 568 Carlos May | .12 |
| 569 Jim Lonborg | .12 |
| 570 Bobby Bonds | .20 |
| 571 Darrell Evans | .25 |
| 572 Ross Grimsley | .12 |
| 573 Joe Ferguson | .12 |
| 574 Aurelio Rodriguez | .12 |
| 575 Dick Ruthven | .12 |
| 576 Fred Kendall | .12 |
| 577 Jerry Augustine | .12 |
| 578 Bob Randall | .12 |
| 579 Don Carrithers | .12 |
| 580 George Brett | 7.00 |
| 581 Pedro Borbon | .12 |
| 582 Ed Kirkpatrick | .12 |
| 583 Paul Lindblad | .12 |
| 584 Ed Goodson | .12 |
| 585 Rick Burleson | .12 |
| 586 Steve Renko | .12 |
| 587 Rick Baldwin | .12 |
| 588 Dave Moates | .12 |
| 589 Mike Cosgrove | .12 |
| 590 Buddy Bell | .40 |
| 591 Chris Arnold | .12 |
| 592 Dan Briggs | .12 |
| 593 Dennis Blair | .12 |
| 594 Biff Pocoroba | .12 |
| 595 John Hiller | .12 |
| 596 Jerry Martin | .12 |

| NO. PLAYER | MINT |
|---|---|
| 597 Seattle Mariners/ | .35 |
| Darrell Johnson (Mgr.) | |
| 598 Sparky Lyle | .30 |
| 599 Mike Tyson | .12 |
| 600 Jim Palmer | 1.50 |
| 601 Mike Lum | .12 |
| 602 Andy Hassler | .12 |
| 603 Willie Davis | .12 |
| 604 Jim Slaton | .12 |
| 605 Felix Millan | .12 |
| 606 Steve Braun | .12 |
| 607 Larry Demery | .12 |
| 608 Roy Howell | .12 |
| 609 Jim Barr | .12 |
| 610 Jose Cardenal | .12 |
| 611 Dave Lemanczyk | .12 |
| 612 Barry Foote | .12 |
| 613 Reggie Cleveland | .12 |
| 614 Greg Gross | .12 |
| 615 Phil Niekro | .75 |
| 616 Tommy Sandt | .12 |
| 617 Bobby Darwin | .12 |
| 618 Pat Dobson | .12 |
| 619 Johnny Oates | .12 |
| 620 Don Sutton | .50 |
| 621 Detroit Tigers/ | .50 |
| Ralph Houk (Mgr.) | |
| 622 Jim Wohlford | .12 |
| 623 Jack Kucek | .12 |
| 624 Hector Cruz | .12 |
| 625 Ken Holtzman | .12 |
| 626 Al Bumbry | .12 |
| 627 Bob Myrick | .12 |
| 628 Mario Guerrero | .12 |
| 629 Bobby Valentine | .40 |
| 630 Bert Blyleven | .40 |
| 631 Big League Brothers: | 1.25 |
| George Brett, Ken Brett | |
| 632 Big League Brothers: | .30 |
| Ken Forsch, Bob Forsch | |
| 633 Big League Brothers: | .30 |
| Lee May, Carlos May | |
| 634 Big League Brothers: | .30 |
| Paul Reuschel, Rick | |
| Reuschel (photos switched) | |
| 635 Robin Yount | 3.00 |
| 636 Santo Alcala | .12 |
| 637 Alex Johnson | .12 |
| 638 Jim Kaat | .45 |
| 639 Jerry Morales | .12 |
| 640 Carlton Fisk | .65 |
| 641 Dan Larson | .12 |
| 642 Willie Crawford | .12 |
| 643 Mike Pazik | .12 |
| 644 Matt Alexander | .12 |
| 645 Jerry Reuss | .15 |
| 646 Andres Mora | .12 |
| 647 Montreal Expos/ | .40 |
| Dick Williams (Mgr.) | |
| 648 Jim Spencer | .12 |
| 649 Dave Cash | .12 |
| 650 Nolan Ryan | 2.50 |
| 651 Von Joshua | .12 |
| 652 Tom Walker | .12 |
| 653 Diego Segui | .12 |
| 654 Ron Pruitt | .12 |
| 655 Tony Perez | .50 |
| 656 Ron Guidry | 2.00 |
| 657 Mick Kelleher | .12 |
| 658 Marty Pattin | .12 |
| 659 Merv Rettenmund | .12 |
| 660 Willie Horton | .30 |

# 1978 Topps....Complete Set of 726 Cards—Value $135.00

After five consecutive years of issuing sets of 660 cards, Topps increased the size of its main set to 726 cards. 66 cards were double printed. Eddie Murray, Paul Molitar and Lou Whitaker's rookie cards are in this set.

| NO. PLAYER | MINT | NO. PLAYER | MINT | NO. PLAYER | MINT | NO. PLAYER | MINT |
|---|---|---|---|---|---|---|---|
| 1 Record — L. Brock | 1.25 | 60 Thurman Munson | 1.50 | 126 Paul Moskau | .10 | 192 San Diego Padres | .30 |
| Most Career Steals | | 61 Larvell Blanks | .10 | 127 Chet Lemon | .15 | 193 Rich Chiles | .10 |
| 2 Record — S. Lyle | .25 | 62 Jim Barr | .10 | 128 Bill Russell | .10 | 194 Derrel Thomas | .10 |
| Most Career Relief | | 63 Don Zimmer (Mgr.) | .10 | 129 Jim Colborn | .10 | 195 Larry Dierker | .10 |
| 3 Record — W. McCovey | .60 | 64 Gene Pentz | .10 | 130 Jeff Burroughs | .10 | 196 Bob Bailor | .10 |
| Most 2 HR's in Inning | | 65 Ken Singleton | .20 | 131 Bert Blyleven | .30 | 197 Nino Espinosa | .10 |
| 4 Record — B. Robinson | .75 | 66 Chicago White Sox | .35 | 132 Enos Cabell | .10 | 198 Ron Pruitt | .10 |
| Most Seasons — Same Club | | 67 Claudell Washington | .15 | 133 Jerry Augustine | .10 | 199 Craig Reynolds | .10 |
| 5 Record — P. Rose | 1.75 | 68 Steve Foucault | .10 | 134 Steve Henderson | .10 | 200 Reggie Jackson | 3.00 |
| Most Hits — Switch Hitter | | 69 Mike Vail | .10 | 135 Ron Guidry | .60 | 201 Batting Leaders: | .50 |
| 6 Record — N. Ryan | .75 | 70 Rich Gossage | .50 | 136 Ted Sizemore | .10 | Dave Parker, Rod Carew | |
| Games 10 or More SO's | | 71 Terry Humphrey | .10 | 137 Craig Kusick | .10 | 202 Home Run Leaders: | .20 |
| 7 Record — R. Jackson | 1.00 | 72 Andre Dawson | 1.50 | 138 Larry Demery | .10 | George Foster, Jim Rice | |
| Most Homers — W. Series | | 73 Andy Hassler | .10 | 139 Wayne Gross | .10 | 203 RBI Leaders: | .20 |
| 8 Mike Sadek | .10 | 74 Checklist No. 1 | .25 | 140 Rollie Fingers | .50 | George Foster, Larry Hisle | |
| 9 Doug DeCinces | .25 | 75 Dick Ruthven | .10 | 141 Ruppert Jones | .10 | 204 Stolen Base Leaders: | .15 |
| 10 Phil Niekro | .60 | 76 Steve Ontiveros | .10 | 142 John Montefusco | .10 | F. Tavaras, Freddie Patek | |
| 11 Rick Manning | .10 | 77 Ed Kirpatrick | .10 | 143 Keith Hernandez | 1.75 | 205 Victory Leaders: | .50 |
| 12 Don Aase | .10 | 78 Pablo Torrealba | .10 | 144 Jesse Jefferson | .10 | Steve Carlton, D. Goltz, | |
| 13 Art Howe | .10 | 79 Darrell Johnson (Mgr.) | .10 | 145 Rick Monday | .10 | D. Leonard, J. Palmer | |
| 14 Lerrin LaGrow | .10 | 80 Ken Griffey | .25 | 146 Doyle Alexander | .10 | 206 Strikeout Leaders: | .20 |
| 15 Tony Perez | .15 | 81 Pete Redfern | .10 | 147 Lee Mazzilli | .15 | Phil Niekro, Nolan Ryan | |
| 16 Roy White | .10 | 82 San Fran. Giants | .35 | 148 Andre Thornton | .20 | 207 ERA Leaders: | .15 |
| 17 Mike Krukow | .10 | 83 Bob Montgomery | .10 | 149 Dale Murray | .10 | J. Candelaria, F. Tanana | |
| 18 Bob Grich | .15 | 84 Kent Tekulve | .15 | 150 Bobby Bonds | .15 | 208 Leading Firemen: | .25 |
| 19 Darrell Porter | .15 | 85 Ron Fairly | .10 | 151 Milt Wilcox | .10 | R. Fingers, B. Campbell | |
| 20 Pete Rose | 3.00 | 86 Dave Tomlin | .10 | 152 Ivan DeJesus | .10 | 209 Dock Ellis | .10 |
| 21 Steve Kemp | .30 | 87 John Lowenstein | .10 | 153 Steve Stone | .10 | 210 Jose Cardenal | .10 |
| 22 Charlie Hough | .10 | 88 Mike Phillips | .10 | 154 Cecil Cooper | .30 | 211 Earl Weaver (Mgr.) | .10 |
| 23 Bump Wills | .10 | 89 Ken Clay | .10 | 155 Butch Hobson | .10 | 212 Mike Caldwell | .10 |
| 24 Don Money | .10 | 90 Larry Bowa | .20 | 156 Andy Messersmith | .10 | 213 Alan Bannister | .10 |
| 25 Jon Matlack | .10 | 91 Oscar Zamora | .10 | 157 Pete LaCock | .10 | 214 California Angels | .35 |
| 26 Rich Hebner | .10 | 92 Adrian Devine | .10 | 158 Joaquin Andujar | .50 | 215 Darrell Evans | .25 |
| 27 Geoff Zahn | .10 | 93 Bobby Cox (Mgr.) | .10 | 159 Lou Piniella | .40 | 216 Mike Paxton | .10 |
| 28 Ed Ott | .10 | 94 Chuck Scrivener | .10 | 160 Jim Palmer | 1.25 | 217 Rod Gilbreath | .10 |
| 29 Bob Lacey | .10 | 95 Jamie Quirk | .10 | 161 Bob Boone | .15 | 218 Marty Pattin | .10 |
| 30 George Hendrick | .20 | 96 Baltimore Orioles | .40 | 162 Paul Thormodsgard | .10 | 219 Mike Cubbage | .10 |
| 31 Glenn Abbott | .10 | 97 Stan Bahnsen | .10 | 163 Bill North | .10 | 220 Pedro Borbon | .10 |
| 32 Garry Templeton | .40 | 98 Jim Essian | .10 | 164 Bob Owchinko | .10 | 221 Chris Speier | .10 |
| 33 Dave Lemanczyk | .10 | 99 Willie Hernandez (R) | 2.00 | 165 Rennie Stennett | .10 | 222 Jerry Martin | .10 |
| 34 Willie McCovey | 1.00 | 100 George Brett | 4.00 | 166 Carlos Lopez | .10 | 223 Bruce Kison | .10 |
| 35 Sparky Lyle | .15 | 101 Sid Monge | .10 | 167 Tim Foli | .10 | 224 Jerry Tabb | .10 |
| 36 Eddie Murray (R) | 30.00 | 102 Matt Alexander | .10 | 168 Reggie Smith | .25 | 225 Don Gullett | .10 |
| 37 Rick Waits | .10 | 103 Tom Murphy | .10 | 169 Jerry Johnson | .10 | 226 Joe Ferguson | .10 |
| 38 Willie Montanez | .10 | 104 Lee Lacy | .10 | 170 Lou Brock | 1.25 | 227 Al Fitzmorris | .10 |
| 39 Floyd Bannister (R) | 1.00 | 105 Reggie Cleveland | .10 | 171 Pat Zachry | .10 | 228 Manny Mota | .10 |
| 40 Carl Yastrzemski | 2.50 | 106 Bill Plummer | .10 | 172 Mike Hargrove | .10 | 229 Leo Foster | .10 |
| 41 Burt Hooton | .10 | 107 Ed Halicki | .10 | 173 Robin Yount | 1.75 | 230 Al Hrabosky | .10 |
| 42 Jorge Orta | .10 | 108 Von Joshua | .10 | 174 Wayne Garland | .10 | 231 Wayne Nordhagen | .10 |
| 43 Bill Atkinson | .10 | 109 Joe Torre (Mgr.) | .20 | 175 Jerry Morales | .10 | 232 Mickey Stanley | .10 |
| 44 Toby Harrah | .10 | 110 Richie Zisk | .10 | 176 Milt May | .10 | 233 Dick Pole | .10 |
| 45 Mark Fidrych | .20 | 111 Mike Tyson | .10 | 177 Gene Garber | .10 | 234 Herman Franks (Mgr.) | .10 |
| 46 Al Cowens | .15 | 112 Houston Astros | .30 | 178 Dave Chalk | .10 | 235 Tim McCarver | .25 |
| 47 Jack Billingham | .10 | 113 Don Carrithers | .10 | 179 Dick Tidrow | .10 | 236 Terry Whitfield | .10 |
| 48 Don Baylor | .40 | 114 Paul Blair | .10 | 180 Dave Concepcion | .25 | 237 Rich Dauer | .10 |
| 49 Ed Kranepool | .10 | 115 Gary Nolan | .10 | 181 Ken Forsch | .10 | 238 Juan Beniquez | .10 |
| 50 Rick Reuschel | .15 | 116 Tucker Ashford | .10 | 182 Jim Spencer | .10 | 239 Dyar Miller | .10 |
| 51 Charlie Moore | .10 | 117 John Montague | .10 | 183 Doug Bird | .10 | 240 Gene Tenance | .10 |
| 52 Jim Lonborg | .10 | 118 Terry Harmon | .10 | 184 Checklist No. 2 | .25 | 241 Pete Vuckovich | .15 |
| 53 Phil Garner | .10 | 119 Denny Martinez | .10 | 185 Ellis Valentine | .10 | 242 Barry Bonnell | .10 |
| 54 Tom Johnson | .10 | 120 Gary Carter | 3.00 | 186 Bob Stanley (R) | .35 | 243 Bob McClure | .10 |
| 55 Mitchell Page | .10 | 121 Alvis Woods | .10 | 187 Jerry Royster | .10 | 244 Montreal Expos | .25 |
| 56 Randy Jones | .10 | 122 Dennis Eckersley | .10 | 188 Al Bumbry | .10 | 245 Rick Burleson | .10 |
| 57 Dan Meyer | .10 | 123 Manny Trillo | .10 | 189 Tom Lasorda (Mgr.) | .20 | 246 Dan Driessen | .10 |
| 58 Bob Forsch | .10 | 124 Dave Rozema | .10 | 190 John Candelaria | .15 | 247 Larry Christenson | .10 |
| 59 Otto Velez | .10 | 125 George Scott | .10 | 191 Rodney Scott | .10 | 248 Frank White | .10 |

# 1978 Topps (Continued)

| NO. | PLAYER | MINT |
|---|---|---|
| 249 | Dave Goltz | .10 |
| 250 | Graig Nettles | .20 |
| 251 | Don Kirkwood | .10 |
| 252 | Steve Swisher | .10 |
| 253 | Jim Kern | .10 |
| 254 | Dave Collins | .15 |
| 255 | Jerry Reuss | .15 |
| 256 | Joe Altobelli (Mgr.) | .10 |
| 257 | Hector Cruz | .10 |
| 258 | John Hiller | .10 |
| 259 | Los Angeles Dodgers | .50 |
| 260 | Bert Campaneris | .15 |
| 261 | Tim Hosely | .10 |
| 262 | Rudy May | .10 |
| 263 | Danny Walton | .10 |
| 264 | Jamie Easterly | .10 |
| 265 | Sal Bando | .10 |
| 266 | Bob Shirley | .10 |
| 267 | Doug Ault | .10 |
| 268 | Gil Flores | .10 |
| 269 | Wayne Twitchell | .10 |
| 270 | Carlton Fisk | .60 |
| 271 | Randy Lerch | .10 |
| 272 | Royle Stillman | .10 |
| 273 | Fred Norman | .10 |
| 274 | Freddie Patek | .10 |
| 275 | Dan Ford | .10 |
| 276 | Bill Bonham | .10 |
| 277 | Bruce Boisclair | .10 |
| 278 | Enrique Romo | .10 |
| 279 | Bill Virdon (Mgr.) | .15 |
| 280 | Buddy Bell | .30 |
| 281 | Eric Rasmussen | .10 |
| 282 | New York Yankees | .60 |
| 283 | Omar Moreno | .15 |
| 284 | Randy Moffitt | .10 |
| 285 | Steve Yeager | .10 |
| 286 | Ben Oglivie | .15 |
| 287 | Kiko Garcia | .10 |
| 288 | Dave Hamilton | .10 |
| 289 | Checklist No. 3 | .25 |
| 290 | Willie Horton | .15 |
| 291 | Gary Ross | .10 |
| 292 | Gene Richards | .10 |
| 293 | Mike Willis | .10 |
| 294 | Larry Parrish | .20 |
| 295 | Bill Lee | .10 |
| 296 | Biff Pocoroba | .10 |
| 297 | Warren Brusstar | .10 |
| 298 | Tony Armas | .75 |
| 299 | Whitey Herzog (Mgr.) | .15 |
| 300 | Joe Morgan | .75 |
| 301 | Buddy Schultz | .10 |
| 302 | Chicago Cubs | .45 |
| 303 | Sam Hinds | .10 |
| 304 | John Milner | .10 |
| 305 | Rico Carty | .10 |
| 306 | Joe Niekro | .20 |
| 307 | Glenn Borgmann | .10 |
| 308 | Jim Rooker | .10 |
| 309 | Cliff Johnson | .10 |
| 310 | Don Sutton | .50 |
| 311 | Jose Baez | .10 |
| 312 | Greg Minton | .10 |
| 313 | Andy Etchebarren | .10 |
| 314 | Paul Lindblad | .10 |
| 315 | Mark Belanger | .10 |
| 316 | Henry Cruz | .10 |
| 317 | Dave Johnson | .15 |
| 318 | Tom Griffin | .10 |
| 319 | Alan Ashby | .10 |
| 320 | Fred Lynn | 1.00 |
| 321 | Santo Alcala | .10 |
| 322 | Tom Paciorek | .10 |
| 323 | Jim Fregosi | .10 |
| 324 | Vern Rapp (Mgr.) | .10 |
| 325 | Bruce Sutter | 1.25 |
| 326 | Mike Lum | .10 |
| 327 | Rick Langford | .10 |
| 328 | Milwaukee Brewers | .40 |
| 329 | John Verhoeven | .10 |
| 330 | Bob Watson | .10 |
| 331 | Mark Littell | .10 |
| 332 | Duane Kuiper | .10 |
| 333 | Jim Todd | .10 |
| 334 | John Stearns | .10 |
| 335 | Bucky Dent | .15 |
| 336 | Steve Busby | .10 |
| 337 | Tom Grieve | .10 |
| 338 | Dave Heaverlo | .10 |
| 339 | Mario Guerrero | .10 |
| 340 | Bake McBride | .10 |
| 341 | Mike Flanagan | .20 |
| 342 | Aurelio Rodriguez | .10 |
| 343 | John Wathan | .10 |
| 344 | Sam Ewing | .10 |
| 345 | Luis Tiant | .10 |
| 346 | Larry Biittner | .10 |
| 347 | Terry Forster | .15 |
| 348 | Del Unser | .10 |
| 349 | Rick Camp | .10 |
| 350 | Steve Garvey | 2.25 |
| 351 | Jeff Torborg (Mgr.) | .10 |
| 352 | Tony Scott | .10 |
| 353 | Doug Bair | .10 |
| 354 | Cesar Geronimo | .10 |
| 355 | Bill Travers | .10 |
| 356 | New York Mets | .50 |
| 357 | Tom Poquette | .10 |
| 358 | Mark Lemongello | .10 |
| 359 | Marc Hill | .10 |
| 360 | Mike Schmidt | 3.00 |
| 361 | Chris Knapp | .10 |
| 362 | Dave May | .10 |
| 363 | Bob Randall | .10 |
| 364 | Jerry Turner | .10 |
| 365 | Ed Figueroa | .10 |
| 366 | Larry Milbourne | .10 |
| 367 | Rick Dempsey | .15 |
| 368 | Balor Moore | .10 |
| 369 | Tim Nordbrook | .10 |
| 370 | Rusty Staub | .20 |
| 371 | Ray Burris | .10 |
| 372 | Brian Asselstine | .10 |
| 373 | Jim Willoughby | .10 |
| 374 | Jose Morales | .10 |
| 375 | Tommy John | .50 |
| 376 | Jim Wohlford | .10 |
| 377 | Manny Sarmiento | .10 |
| 378 | Bobby Winkles (Mgr.) | .10 |
| 379 | Skip Lockwood | .10 |
| 380 | Ted Simmons | .40 |
| 381 | Philadelphia Phillies | .35 |
| 382 | Joe Lahoud | .10 |
| 383 | Mario Mendoza | .10 |
| 384 | Jack Clark | 1.00 |
| 385 | Tito Fuentes | .10 |
| 386 | Bob Gorinski | .10 |
| 387 | Ken Holtzman | .10 |
| 388 | Bill Fahey | .10 |
| 389 | Julio Gonzalez | .10 |
| 390 | Oscar Gamble | .10 |
| 391 | Larry Haney | .10 |
| 392 | Billy Almon | .10 |
| 393 | Tippy Martinez | .10 |
| 394 | Roy Howell | .10 |
| 395 | Jim Hughes | .10 |
| 396 | Bob Stinson | .10 |
| 397 | Greg Gross | .10 |
| 398 | Don Hood | .10 |
| 399 | Pete Mackanin | .10 |
| 400 | Nolan Ryan | 1.50 |
| 401 | Sparky Anderson (Mgr.) | .15 |
| 402 | Dave Campbell | .10 |
| 403 | Bud Harrelson | .10 |
| 404 | Detroit Tigers | .60 |
| 405 | Rawly Eastwick | .10 |
| 406 | Mike Jorgensen | .10 |
| 407 | Odell Jones | .10 |
| 408 | Joe Zdeb | .10 |
| 409 | Ron Schueler | .10 |
| 410 | Bill Madlock | .75 |
| 411 | AL Championships: Yankees Defeat Royals | .60 |
| 412 | NL Championships: Dodgers Defeat Phillies | .60 |
| 413 | World Series: Yankees Reign Supreme | 1.00 |
| 414 | Darold Knowles | .10 |
| 415 | Ray Fosse | .10 |
| 416 | Jack Brohamer | .10 |
| 417 | Mike Garman | .10 |
| 418 | Tony Muser | .10 |
| 419 | Jerry Garvin | .10 |
| 420 | Greg Luzinski | .30 |
| 421 | Junior Moore | .10 |
| 422 | Steve Braun | .10 |
| 423 | Dave Rosello | .10 |
| 424 | Boston Red Sox | .40 |
| 425 | Steve Rogers | .10 |
| 426 | Fred Kendall | .10 |
| 427 | Mario Soto (R) | 2.50 |
| 428 | Joel Youngblood | .10 |
| 429 | Mike Barlow | .10 |
| 430 | Al Oliver | .50 |
| 431 | Butch Metzger | .10 |
| 432 | Terry Bulling | .10 |
| 433 | Fernando Gonzalez | .10 |
| 434 | Mike Norris | .10 |
| 435 | Checklist No. 4 | .25 |
| 436 | Vic Harris | .10 |
| 437 | Bo McLaughlin | .10 |
| 438 | John Ellis | .10 |
| 439 | Ken Kravec | .10 |
| 440 | Dave Lopes | .15 |
| 441 | Larry Gura | .15 |
| 442 | Elliott Maddox | .10 |
| 443 | Darrell Chaney | .10 |
| 444 | Roy Hartsfield (Mgr.) | .10 |
| 445 | Mike Ivie | .10 |
| 446 | Tug McGraw | .20 |
| 447 | Leroy Stanton | .10 |
| 448 | Bill Castro | .10 |
| 449 | Tim Blackwell | .10 |
| 450 | Tom Seaver | 1.50 |
| 451 | Minnesota Twins | .35 |
| 452 | Jerry Mumphrey | .10 |
| 453 | Doug Flynn | .10 |
| 454 | Dave LaRoche | .10 |
| 455 | Bill Robinson | .10 |
| 456 | Vern Ruhle | .10 |
| 457 | Bob Bailey | .10 |
| 458 | Jeff Newman | .10 |
| 459 | Charlie Spikes | .10 |
| 460 | Jim Hunter | .50 |
| 461 | Rob Andrews | .10 |
| 462 | Rogelio Moret | .10 |
| 463 | Kevin Bell | .10 |
| 464 | Jerry Grote | .10 |
| 465 | Hal McRae | .15 |
| 466 | Dennis Blair | .10 |
| 467 | Alvin Dark (Mgr.) | .10 |
| 468 | Warren Cromartie | .10 |
| 469 | Rick Cerone | .10 |
| 470 | J.R. Richard | .15 |
| 471 | Roy Smalley | .10 |
| 472 | Ron Reed | .10 |
| 473 | Bill Buckner | .25 |
| 474 | Jim Slaton | .10 |
| 475 | Gary Matthews | .20 |
| 476 | Bill Stein | .10 |
| 477 | Doug Capilla | .10 |
| 478 | Jerry Remy | .10 |
| 479 | St. Louis Cardinals | .40 |
| 480 | Ron LeFlore | .15 |
| 481 | Jackson Todd | .10 |
| 482 | Rick Miller | .10 |
| 483 | Ken Macha | .10 |
| 484 | Jim Norris | .10 |
| 485 | Chris Chambliss | .15 |
| 486 | John Curtis | .10 |
| 487 | Jim Tyrone | .10 |
| 488 | Dan Spillner | .10 |
| 489 | Rudy Meoli | .10 |
| 490 | Amos Otis | .15 |
| 491 | Scott McGregor | .15 |
| 492 | Jim Sundberg | .10 |
| 493 | Steve Renko | .10 |
| 494 | Chuck Tanner (Mgr.) | .10 |
| 495 | Dave Cash | .10 |
| 496 | Jim Clancy | .10 |
| 497 | Glenn Adams | .10 |
| 498 | Joe Sambito | .10 |
| 499 | Seattle Mariners | .25 |
| 500 | George Foster | 1.00 |
| 501 | Dave Roberts | .10 |
| 502 | Pat Rockett | .10 |
| 503 | Ike Hampton | .10 |
| 504 | Roger Freed | .10 |
| 505 | Felix Millan | .10 |
| 506 | Ron Blomberg | .10 |
| 507 | Willie Crawford | .10 |
| 508 | Johnny Oates | .10 |
| 509 | Brent Strom | .10 |
| 510 | Willie Stargell | 1.00 |
| 511 | Frank Duffy | .10 |
| 512 | Larry Herndon | .15 |
| 513 | Barry Foote | .10 |
| 514 | Rob Sperring | .10 |
| 515 | Tim Corcoran | .10 |
| 516 | Gary Beare | .10 |
| 517 | Andres Mora | .10 |
| 518 | Tommy Boggs | .10 |
| 519 | Brian Downing | .10 |
| 520 | Larry Hisle | .10 |
| 521 | Steve Staggs | .10 |
| 522 | Dick Williams (Mgr.) | .15 |
| 523 | Donnie Moore (R) | .60 |
| 524 | Bernie Carbo | .10 |
| 525 | Jerry Terrell | .10 |
| 526 | Cincinnati Reds | .45 |
| 527 | Vic Correll | .10 |
| 528 | Rob Picciolo | .10 |
| 529 | Paul Hartzell | .10 |
| 530 | Dave Winfield | 2.00 |
| 531 | Tom Underwood | .10 |
| 532 | Skip Jutze | .10 |
| 533 | Sandy Alomar | .10 |
| 534 | Wilbur Howard | .10 |
| 535 | Checklist No. 5 | .25 |
| 536 | Roric Harrison | .10 |
| 537 | Bruce Bochte | .10 |
| 538 | Johnnie LeMaster | .10 |
| 539 | Vic Davalillo | .10 |
| 540 | Steve Carlton | 2.00 |
| 541 | Larry Cox | .10 |
| 542 | Tim Johnson | .10 |
| 543 | Larry Harlow | .10 |
| 544 | Len Randle | .10 |
| 545 | Bill Campbell | .10 |
| 546 | Ted Martinez | .10 |
| 547 | John Scott | .10 |
| 548 | Billy Hunter (Mgr.) | .10 |
| 549 | Joe Kerrigan | .10 |
| 550 | John Mayberry | .15 |
| 551 | Atlanta Braves | .35 |
| 552 | Francisco Barrios | .10 |
| 553 | Terry Puhl (R) | .45 |
| 554 | Joe Coleman | .10 |
| 555 | Butch Wynegar | .15 |
| 556 | Ed Armbrister | .10 |
| 557 | Tony Solaita | .10 |
| 558 | Paul Mitchell | .10 |
| 559 | Phil Mankowski | .10 |
| 560 | Dave Parker | 1.25 |
| 561 | Charlie Williams | .10 |
| 562 | Glenn Burke | .10 |
| 563 | Dave Rader | .10 |
| 564 | Mick Kelleher | .10 |
| 565 | Jerry Koosman | .15 |
| 566 | Merv Rettenmund | .10 |
| 567 | Dick Drago | .10 |
| 568 | Tom Hutton | .10 |
| 569 | Lary Sorensen | .10 |
| 570 | Dave Kingman | .50 |
| 571 | Buck Martinez | .10 |
| 572 | Rick Wise | .10 |
| 573 | Luis Gomez | .10 |
| 574 | Bob Lemon (Mgr.) | .25 |
| 575 | Pat Dobson | .10 |
| 576 | Sam Mejias | .10 |
| 577 | Oakland A's | .30 |
| 578 | Buzz Capra | .10 |
| 579 | Rance Mulliniks | .10 |
| 580 | Rod Carew | 1.50 |
| 581 | Lynn McGlothen | .10 |
| 582 | Fran Healy | .10 |
| 583 | George Medich | .10 |
| 584 | John Hale | .10 |
| 585 | Woodie Fryman | .10 |

| NO. PLAYER | MINT |
|---|---|
| 586 Ed Goodson | .10 |
| 587 John Urrea | .10 |
| 588 Jim Mason | .10 |
| 589 Bob Knepper (R) | .50 |
| 590 Bobby Murcer | .25 |
| 591 George Zeber | .10 |
| 592 Bob Apodaca | .10 |
| 593 Dave Skaggs | .10 |
| 594 Dave Freisleben | .10 |
| 595 Sixto Lezcano | .10 |
| 596 Gary Wheelock | .10 |
| 597 Steve Dillard | .10 |
| 598 Eddie Solomon | .10 |
| 599 Gary Woods | .10 |
| 600 Frank Tanana | .15 |
| 601 Gene Mauch (Mgr.) | .15 |
| 602 Eric Soderholm | .10 |
| 603 Will McEnaney | .10 |
| 604 Earl Williams | .10 |
| 605 Rick Rhoden | .10 |
| 606 Pittsburgh Pirates | .35 |
| 607 Fernando Arroyo | .10 |
| 608 Johnny Grubb | .10 |
| 609 John Denny | .25 |
| 610 Garry Maddox | .15 |
| 611 Pat Scanlon | .10 |
| 612 Ken Henderson | .10 |
| 613 Marty Perez | .10 |
| 614 Joe Wallis | .10 |
| 615 Clay Carroll | .10 |
| 616 Pat Kelly | .10 |
| 617 Joe Nolan | .10 |
| 618 Tommy Helms | .10 |
| 619 Thad Bosley | .10 |
| 620 Willie Randolph | .20 |
| 621 Craig Swan | .10 |
| 622 Champ Summers | .10 |
| 623 Eduardo Rodriquez | .10 |
| 624 Gary Alexander | .10 |
| 625 Jose Cruz | .35 |
| 626 Toronto Blue Jays | .20 |
| 627 Dave Johnson | .10 |

| NO. PLAYER | MINT |
|---|---|
| 628 Ralph Garr | .10 |
| 629 Don Stanhouse | .10 |
| 630 Ron Cey | .40 |
| 631 Danny Ozark (Mgr.) | .15 |
| 632 Rowland Office | .10 |
| 633 Tom Veryzer | .10 |
| 634 Len Barker | .10 |
| 635 Joe Rudi | .10 |
| 636 Jim Bibby | .10 |
| 637 Duffy Dyer | .10 |
| 638 Paul Splittorff | .10 |
| 639 Gene Clines | .10 |
| 640 Lee May | .10 |
| 641 Doug Rau | .10 |
| 642 Denny Doyle | .10 |
| 643 Tom House | .10 |
| 644 Jim Dwyer | .10 |
| 645 Mike Torrez | .10 |
| 646 Rick Auerbach | .10 |
| 647 Steve Dunning | .10 |
| 648 Gary Thomasson | .10 |
| 649 Moose Haas (R) | .45 |
| 650 Cesar Cedeno | .20 |
| 651 Doug Rader | .10 |
| 652 Checklist No. 6 | .25 |
| 653 Ron Hodges | .10 |
| 654 Pepe Frias | .10 |
| 655 Lyman Bostock | .15 |
| 656 Dave Garcia (Mgr.) | .10 |
| 657 Bombo Rivera | .10 |
| 658 Manny Sanguillen | .10 |
| 659 Texas Rangers | .35 |
| 660 Jason Thompson | .25 |
| 661 Grant Jackson | .10 |
| 662 Paul Dade | .10 |
| 663 Paul Reuschel | .10 |
| 664 Fred Stanley | .10 |
| 665 Dennis Leonard | .15 |
| 666 Billy Smith | .10 |
| 667 Jeff Byrd | .10 |
| 668 Dusty Baker | .20 |

| NO. PLAYER | MINT |
|---|---|
| 669 Pete Falcone | .10 |
| 670 Jim Rice | 3.00 |
| 671 Gary Lavelle | .10 |
| 672 Don Kessinger | .10 |
| 673 Steve Brye | .10 |
| 674 Ray Knight (R) | .35 |
| 675 Jay Johnstone | .10 |
| 676 Bob Myrick | .10 |
| 677 Ed Herrmann | .10 |
| 678 Tom Burgmeier | .10 |
| 679 Wayne Garrett | .10 |
| 680 Vida Blue | .15 |
| 681 Rob Belloir | .10 |
| 682 Ken Brett | .10 |
| 683 Mike Champion | .10 |
| 684 Ralph Houk (Mgr.) | .15 |
| 685 Frank Taveras | .10 |
| 686 Gaylord Perry | 1.00 |
| 687 Julio Cruz (R) | .40 |
| 688 George Mitterwald | .10 |
| 689 Cleveland Indians | .35 |
| 690 Mickey Rivers | .15 |
| 691 Ross Grimsley | .10 |
| 692 Ken Reitz | .10 |
| 693 Lamar Johnson | .10 |
| 694 Elias Sosa | .10 |
| 695 Dwight Evans | .35 |
| 696 Steve Mingori | .10 |
| 697 Roger Metzger | .10 |
| 698 Juan Bernhardt | .10 |
| 699 Jackie Brown | .10 |
| 700 Johnny Bench | 2.00 |
| 701 Rookie Pitchers: | .40 |
|     Larry Landreth, Tom Hume, | |
|     Steve McCatty, B. Taylor | |
| 702 Rookie Catchers: | .20 |
|     Rick Sweet, Bill Nahordony | |
|     Kevin Pasley, Don Werner | |
| 703 Rookie Pitchers: | 4.00 |
|     Jack Morris, L. Andersen, | |
|     Tim Jones, M. Mahler | |

| NO. PLAYER | MINT |
|---|---|
| 704 Rookie 2nd Basemen: | 5.00 |
|     Garth Iorg, Sam Perlozzo, | |
|     Dave Oliver, Lou Whitaker | |
| 705 Rookie Outfielders: | .40 |
|     D. Bergman, W. Norwood, | |
|     M. Dilone, C. Hurdle | |
| 706 Rookie 1st Basemen: | .30 |
|     Wayne Cage, Ted Cox, | |
|     P. Putnam, D. Revering | |
| 707 Rookie Shortstops: | 12.50 |
|     Mickey Klutts, Paul Molitor, | |
|     Alan Trammell, | |
|     U.L. Washington | |
| 708 Rookie Catchers: | 25.00 |
|     Bo Diaz, Dale Murphy, | |
|     Ernie Whitt, Lance Parrish | |
| 709 Rookie Pitchers: | .30 |
|     Steve Burke, Lance | |
|     Rautzhan, Matt Keough, | |
|     Dan Schatzeder | |
| 710 Rookie Outfielders: | 1.50 |
|     Dell Alston, Rick Bosetti, | |
|     Mike Easler, Keith Smith | |
| 711 Rookie Pitchers: | .25 |
|     C. Camper, D. Lamp, | |
|     R. Thomas, C. Mitchell | |
| 712 Bobby Valentine | .10 |
| 713 Bob Davis | .10 |
| 714 Mike Anderson | .10 |
| 715 Jim Kaat | .40 |
| 716 Clarence Gaston | .10 |
| 717 Nelson Briles | .10 |
| 718 Ron Jackson | .10 |
| 719 Randy Elliott | .10 |
| 720 Fergie Jenkins | .30 |
| 721 Billy Martin (Mgr.) | .35 |
| 722 Pete Broberg | .10 |
| 723 John Wockenfuss | .10 |
| 724 K.C. Royals | .40 |
| 725 Kurt Bevacqua | .10 |
| 726 Wilbur Wood | .10 |

# 1979 Topps....Complete Set of 726 Cards—Value $90.00

Features the rookie cards of Pedro Guerrero and Bob Horner. 66 cards were double printed. Card 369 (Bump Wills) was originally issued in error as a "Blue Jay". A corrected card was issued showing Wills as a "Ranger".

| NO. PLAYER | MINT |
|---|---|
| 1 Batting Leaders: | 1.00 |
|     Rod Carew, Dave Parker | |
| 2 Home Run Leaders: | .50 |
|     Jim Rice, George Foster | |
| 3 RBI Leaders: | .50 |
|     Jim Rice, George Foster | |
| 4 Stolen Base Leaders: | .25 |
|     Ron LeFlore, Omar Moreno | |
| 5 Victory Leaders: | .40 |
|     Ron Guidry, Gaylord Perry | |
| 6 Stikeout Leaders: | .40 |
|     Nolan Ryan, J.R. Richard | |
| 7 ERA Leaders: | .25 |
|     Ron Guidry, Craig Swan | |
| 8 Leading Firemen: | .35 |
|     R. Gossage, R. Fingers | |

| NO. PLAYER | MINT |
|---|---|
| 9 Dave Campbell | .10 |
| 10 Lee May | .10 |
| 11 Marc Hill | .10 |
| 12 Dick Drago | .10 |
| 13 Paul Dade | .10 |
| 14 Rafael Landestoy | .10 |
| 15 Ross Grimsley | .10 |
| 16 Fred Stanley | .10 |
| 17 Donnie Moore | .15 |
| 18 Tony Solaita | .10 |
| 19 Larry Gura | .10 |
| 20 Joe Morgan | .40 |
| 21 Kevin Kobel | .10 |
| 22 Mike Jorgensen | .10 |
| 23 Terry Forster | .15 |
| 24 Paul Molitor | .80 |

| NO. PLAYER | MINT |
|---|---|
| 25 Steve Carlton | 1.50 |
| 26 Jamie Quirk | .10 |
| 27 Dave Goltz | .10 |
| 28 Steve Brye | .10 |
| 29 Rick Langford | .10 |
| 30 Dave Winfield | 2.00 |
| 31 Tom House | .10 |
| 32 Jerry Mumphrey | .15 |
| 33 Dave Rozema | .10 |
| 34 Rob Andrews | .10 |
| 35 Ed Figueroa | .10 |
| 36 Alan Ashby | .10 |
| 37 Joe Kerrigan | .10 |
| 38 Bernie Carbo | .10 |
| 39 Dale Murphy | 5.00 |
| 40 Dennis Eckersley | .15 |

| NO. PLAYER | MINT |
|---|---|
| 41 Minnesota Twins/ | .25 |
|     Gene Mauch (Mgr.) | |
| 42 Ron Blomberg | .10 |
| 43 Wayne Twitchell | .10 |
| 44 Kurt Bevacqua | .10 |
| 45 Al Hrabosky | .10 |
| 46 Ron Hodges | .10 |
| 47 Fred Norman | .10 |
| 48 Merv Rettenmund | .10 |
| 49 Vern Ruhle | .10 |
| 50 Steve Garvey | 1.25 |
| 51 Ray Fosse | .10 |
| 52 Randy Lerch | .10 |
| 53 Mick Kelleher | .10 |
| 54 Del Alston | .10 |
| 55 Wllie Stargell | 1.00 |

# 1979 Topps (Continued)

| NO. PLAYER | MINT |
|---|---|
| 56 John Hale | .10 |
| 57 Eric Rasmussen | .10 |
| 58 Bob Randall | .10 |
| 59 John Denny | .10 |
| 60 Mickey Rivers | .15 |
| 61 Bo Diaz | .15 |
| 62 Randy Moffitt | .10 |
| 63 Jack Brohamer | .10 |
| 64 Tom Underwood | .10 |
| 65 Mark Belanger | .10 |
| 66 Tigers/L. Moss (Mgr.) | .50 |
| 67 Jim Mason | .10 |
| 68 Joe Niekro | .10 |
| 69 Elliott Maddox | .10 |
| 70 John Candelaria | .15 |
| 71 Brian Downing | .15 |
| 72 Steve Mingori | .10 |
| 73 Ken Henderson | .10 |
| 74 Shane Rawley (R) | .50 |
| 75 Steve Yeager | .10 |
| 76 Warren Cromartie | .10 |
| 77 Dan Briggs | .10 |
| 78 Elias Sosa | .10 |
| 79 Ted Cox | .10 |
| 80 Jason Thompson | .15 |
| 81 Roger Erickson | .10 |
| 82 Mets/J. Torre (Mgr.) | .40 |
| 83 Fred Kendall | .10 |
| 84 Greg Minton | .10 |
| 85 Gary Matthews | .20 |
| 86 Rodney Scott | .10 |
| 87 Pete Falcone | .10 |
| 88 Bob Molinaro | .10 |
| 89 Dick Tidrow | .10 |
| 90 Bob Boone | .10 |
| 91 Terry Crowley | .10 |
| 92 Jim Bibby | .10 |
| 93 Phil Mankowski | .10 |
| 94 Len Barker | .15 |
| 95 Robin Yount | 1.50 |
| 96 Cleveland Indians/ Jeff Torborg (Mgr.) | .25 |
| 97 Sam Mejias | .10 |
| 98 Ray Burris | .10 |
| 99 John Wathan | .10 |
| 100 Tom Seaver | .75 |
| 101 Roy Howell | .10 |
| 102 Mike Anderson | .10 |
| 103 Jim Todd | .10 |
| 104 Johnny Oates | .10 |
| 105 Rick Camp | .10 |
| 106 Frank Duffy | .10 |
| 107 Jesus Alou | .10 |
| 108 Eduardo Rodriguez | .10 |
| 109 Joel Youngblood | .10 |
| 110 Vida Blue | .15 |
| 111 Roger Freed | .10 |
| 112 Philadelphia Phillies/ Danny Ozark (Mgr.) | .35 |
| 113 Pete Redfern | .10 |
| 114 Cliff Johnson | .10 |
| 115 Nolan Ryan | 1.25 |
| 116 Ozzie Smith (R) | 3.00 |
| 117 Grant Jackson | .10 |
| 118 Bud Harrelson | .10 |
| 119 Don Stanhouse | .10 |
| 120 Jim Sundberg | .10 |
| 121 Checklist No. 1 | .20 |
| 122 Mike Paxton | .10 |
| 123 Lou Whitaker | 1.50 |
| 124 Dan Schatzeder | .10 |
| 125 Rick Burleson | .10 |
| 126 Doug Bair | .10 |
| 127 Thad Bosley | .10 |
| 128 Ted Martinez | .10 |
| 129 Marty Pattin | .10 |
| 130 Bob Watson | .10 |
| 131 Jim Clancy | .10 |
| 132 Rowland Office | .10 |
| 133 Bill Castro | .10 |
| 134 Alan Bannister | .10 |
| 135 Bobby Murcer | .20 |
| 136 Jim Kaat | .25 |
| 137 Larry Wolfe | .10 |
| 138 Mark Lee | .10 |
| 139 Luis Pujols | .10 |
| 140 Don Gullett | .10 |
| 141 Tom Paciorek | .10 |
| 142 Charlie Williams | .10 |
| 143 Tony Scott | .10 |
| 144 Sandy Alomar | .10 |
| 145 Rick Rhoden | .10 |
| 146 Duane Kuiper | .10 |
| 147 Dave Hamilton | .10 |
| 148 Bruce Boisclair | .10 |
| 149 Manny Sarmiento | .10 |
| 150 Wayne Cage | .10 |
| 151 John Hiller | .10 |
| 152 Rick Cerone | .10 |
| 153 Dennis Lamp | .10 |
| 154 Jim Gantner | .10 |
| 155 Dwight Evans | .35 |
| 156 Buddy Solomon | .10 |
| 157 U.L. Washington | .10 |
| 158 Joe Sambito | .10 |
| 159 Roy White | .10 |
| 160 Mike Flanagan | .25 |
| 161 Barry Foote | .10 |
| 162 Tom Johnson | .10 |
| 163 Glenn Burke | .10 |
| 164 Mickey Lolich | .15 |
| 165 Frank Taveras | .10 |
| 166 Leon Roberts | .10 |
| 167 Roger Metzger | .10 |
| 168 Dave Freisleben | .10 |
| 169 Bill Nahorodny | .10 |
| 170 Don Sutton | .35 |
| 171 Gene Clines | .10 |
| 172 Mike Bruhert | .10 |
| 173 John Lowenstein | .10 |
| 174 Rick Auerbach | .10 |
| 175 George Hendrick | .15 |
| 176 Aurelio Rodriguez | .10 |
| 177 Ron Reed | .10 |
| 178 Alvis Woods | .10 |
| 179 Jim Beattie | .10 |
| 180 Larry Hisle | .10 |
| 181 Mike Garman | .10 |
| 182 Tim Johnson | .10 |
| 183 Paul Splittorff | .10 |
| 184 Darrel Chaney | .10 |
| 185 Mike Torrez | .10 |
| 186 Eric Soderholm | .10 |
| 187 Mark Lemongello | .10 |
| 188 Pat Kelly | .10 |
| 189 Eddie Whitson (R) | .50 |
| 190 Ron Cey | .40 |
| 191 Mike Norris | .10 |
| 192 St. Louis Cardinals/ Ken Boyer (Mgr.) | .35 |
| 193 Glenn Adams | .10 |
| 194 Randy Jones | .10 |
| 195 Bill Madlock | .40 |
| 196 Steve Kemp | .10 |
| 197 Bob Apodaca | .10 |
| 198 Johnny Grubb | .10 |
| 199 Larry Milbourne | .10 |
| 200 Johnny Bench | 1.00 |
| 201 Record — M. Edwards Most Unassisted DP's by 2nd Baseman | .15 |
| 202 Record — R. Guidry Most Strikeouts, Lefthander, 9 Inning Game | .25 |
| 203 Record — J.R. Richard Most Season Stikeouts, Righthander | .25 |
| 204 Record — P. Rose Most Consecutive Games Batting Safely | 1.25 |
| 205 Record — J. Stearns Most Steals by Catcher, Season | .20 |
| 206 Record — S. Stewart 7 Straight Stikeouts, First Major League Game | .20 |
| 207 Dave Lemanczyk | .10 |
| 208 Clarence Gaston | .10 |
| 209 Reggie Cleveland | .10 |
| 210 Larry Bowa | .15 |
| 211 Denny Martinez | .10 |
| 212 Carney Lansford (R) | 1.50 |
| 213 Bill Travers | .10 |
| 214 Boston Red Sox/ Don Zimmer (Mgr.) | .45 |
| 215 Willie McCovey | 1.00 |
| 216 Wilbur Wood | .10 |
| 217 Steve Dillard | .10 |
| 218 Dennis Leonard | .10 |
| 219 Roy Smalley | .10 |
| 220 Cesar Geronimo | .10 |
| 221 Jesse Jefferson | .10 |
| 222 Bob Beall | .10 |
| 223 Kent Tekulve | .15 |
| 224 Dave Revering | .10 |
| 225 Rich Gossage | .60 |
| 226 Ron Pruitt | .10 |
| 227 Steve Stone | .10 |
| 228 Vic Davalillo | .10 |
| 229 Doug Flynn | .10 |
| 230 Bob Forsch | .10 |
| 231 Johnny Wockenfuss | .10 |
| 232 Jimmy Sexton | .10 |
| 233 Paul Mitchell | .10 |
| 234 Toby Harrah | .10 |
| 235 Steve Rogers | .15 |
| 236 Jim Dwyer | .10 |
| 237 Billy Smith | .10 |
| 238 Balor Moore | .10 |
| 239 Willie Horton | .10 |
| 240 Rick Reuschel | .10 |
| 241 Checklist No. 2 | .20 |
| 242 Pablo Torrealba | .10 |
| 243 Buck Martinez | .10 |
| 244 Pittsburgh Pirates/ Chuck Tanner (Mgr.) | .25 |
| 245 Jeff Burroughs | .10 |
| 246 Darrell Jackson | .10 |
| 247 Tucker Ashford | .10 |
| 248 Pete LaCock | .10 |
| 249 Paul Thormodsgard | .10 |
| 250 Willie Randolph | .15 |
| 251 Jack Morris | 1.25 |
| 252 Bob Stinson | .10 |
| 253 Rick Wise | .10 |
| 254 Luis Gomez | .10 |
| 255 Tommy John | .40 |
| 256 Mike Sadek | .10 |
| 257 Adrian Devine | .10 |
| 258 Mike Phillips | .10 |
| 259 Cincinnati Reds/ Sparky Anderson (Mgr.) | .40 |
| 260 Richie Zisk | .10 |
| 261 Mario Guerrero | .10 |
| 262 Nelson Briles | .10 |
| 263 Oscar Gamble | .10 |
| 264 Don Robinson (R) | .30 |
| 265 Don Money | .10 |
| 266 Jim Willoughby | .10 |
| 267 Joe Rudi | .10 |
| 268 Julio Gonzalez | .10 |
| 269 Woodie Fryman | .10 |
| 270 Butch Hobson | .10 |
| 271 Rawly Eastwick | .10 |
| 272 Tim Corcoran | .10 |
| 273 Jerry Terrell | .10 |
| 274 Willie Norwood | .10 |
| 275 Junior Moore | .10 |
| 276 Jim Colborn | .10 |
| 277 Tom Grieve | .10 |
| 278 Andy Messersmith | .10 |
| 279 Jerry Grote | .10 |
| 280 Andre Thornton | .15 |
| 281 Vic Correll | .10 |
| 282 Toronto Blue Jays/ Roy Hartsfield (Mgr.) | .20 |
| 283 Ken Kravec | .10 |
| 284 Johnnie LeMaster | .10 |
| 285 Bobby Bonds | .15 |
| 286 Duffy Dyer | .10 |
| 287 Andres Mora | .10 |
| 288 Milt Wilcox | .10 |
| 289 Jose Cruz | .25 |
| 290 Dave Lopes | .20 |
| 291 Tom Griffin | .10 |
| 292 Don Reynolds | .10 |
| 293 Jerry Garvin | .10 |
| 294 Pepe Frias | .10 |
| 295 Mitchell Page | .10 |
| 296 Preston Hanna | .10 |
| 297 Ted Sizemore | .10 |
| 298 Rich Gale | .10 |
| 299 Steve Ontiveros | .10 |
| 300 Rod Carew | 1.25 |
| 301 Tom Hume | .10 |
| 302 Atlanta Braves/ Bobby Cox (Mgr.) | .35 |
| 303 Lary Sorensen | .10 |
| 304 Steve Swisher | .10 |
| 305 Willie Montanez | .10 |
| 306 Floyd Bannister | .15 |
| 307 Larvell Blanks | .10 |
| 308 Bert Blyleven | .30 |
| 309 Ralph Garr | .10 |
| 310 Thurman Munson | 1.50 |
| 311 Gary Lavelle | .10 |
| 312 Bob Robertson | .10 |
| 313 Dyar Miller | .10 |
| 314 Larry Harlow | .10 |
| 315 John Matlack | .10 |
| 316 Milt May | .10 |
| 317 Jose Cardenal | .10 |
| 318 Bob Welch (R) | 1.00 |
| 319 Wayne Garrett | .10 |
| 320 Carl Yastrzemski | 2.00 |
| 321 Gaylord Perry | .75 |
| 322 Danny Goodwin | .10 |
| 323 Lynn McGlothen | .10 |
| 324 Mike Tyson | .10 |
| 325 Cecil Cooper | .60 |
| 326 Pedro Borbon | .10 |
| 327 Art Howe | .10 |
| 328 Oakland A's/ Jack McKeon (Mgr.) | .20 |
| 329 Joe Coleman | .10 |
| 330 George Brett | 2.50 |
| 331 Mickey Mahler | .10 |
| 332 Gary Alexander | .10 |
| 333 Chet Lemon | .35 |
| 334 Craig Swan | .10 |
| 335 Chris Chambliss | .15 |
| 336 Bobby Thompson | .10 |
| 337 John Montague | .10 |
| 338 Vic Harris | .10 |
| 339 Ron Jackson | .10 |
| 340 Jim Palmer | 1.00 |
| 341 Willie Upshaw (R) | 2.00 |
| 342 Dave Roberts | .10 |
| 343 Ed Glynn | .10 |
| 344 Jerry Royster | .10 |
| 345 Tug McGraw | .15 |
| 346 Bill Buckner | .20 |
| 347 Doug Rau | .10 |
| 348 Andre Dawson | 1.50 |
| 349 Jim Wright | .10 |
| 350 Garry Templeton | .30 |
| 351 Wayne Nordhagen | .10 |
| 352 Steve Renko | .10 |
| 353 Checklist No. 3 | .20 |
| 354 Bill Bonham | .10 |
| 355 Lee Mazzilli | .15 |
| 356 San Francisco Giants/ Joe Altobelli (Mgr.) | .25 |
| 357 Jerry Augustine | .10 |
| 358 Alan Trammell | 1.50 |
| 359 Dan Spillner | .15 |
| 360 Amos Otis | .15 |
| 361 Tom Dixon | .10 |
| 362 Mike Cubbage | .10 |
| 363 Craig Skok | .10 |
| 364 Gene Richards | .10 |
| 365 Sparky Lyle | .15 |
| 366 Juan Bernhardt | .10 |
| 367 Dave Skaggs | .10 |
| 368 Don Aase | .10 |
| 369 Bump Wills (error) (Blue Jays) | 3.00 |
| 369 Bump Wills (correct) (Rangers) | 4.00 |
| 370 Dave Kingman | .40 |

| NO. PLAYER | MINT |
|---|---|
| 371 Jeff Holly | .10 |
| 372 Lamar Johnson | .10 |
| 373 Lance Rautzhan | .10 |
| 374 Ed Herrmann | .10 |
| 375 Bill Campbell | .10 |
| 376 Gorman Thomas | .35 |
| 377 Paul Moskau | .10 |
| 378 Rob Picciolo | .10 |
| 379 Dale Murray | .10 |
| 380 John Mayberry | .10 |
| 381 Houston Astros/ Bill Virdon (Mgr.) | .25 |
| 382 Jerry Martin | .10 |
| 383 Phil Garner | .10 |
| 384 Tommy Boggs | .10 |
| 385 Dan Ford | .10 |
| 386 Francisco Barrios | .10 |
| 387 Gary Thomasson | .10 |
| 388 Jack Billingham | .10 |
| 389 Joe Zdeb | .10 |
| 390 Rollie Fingers | .35 |
| 391 Al Oliver | .35 |
| 392 Doug Ault | .10 |
| 393 Scott McGregor | .15 |
| 394 Randy Stein | .10 |
| 395 Dave Cash | .10 |
| 396 Bill Plummer | .10 |
| 397 Sergio Ferrer | .10 |
| 398 Ivan DeJesus | .10 |
| 399 David Clyde | .10 |
| 400 Jim Rice | 2.50 |
| 401 Ray Knight | .15 |
| 402 Paul Hartzell | .10 |
| 403 Tim Foli | .10 |
| 404 Chicago White Sox/ Don Kessinger (Mgr.) | .25 |
| 405 Butch Wynegar | .10 |
| 406 Joe Wallis | .10 |
| 407 Pete Vuckovich | .10 |
| 408 Charlie Moore | .10 |
| 409 Willie Wilson (R) | 2.25 |
| 410 Darrell Evans | .30 |
| 411 All-Time Hits: Season — George Sisler, Career — Ty Cobb | .50 |
| 412 All-Time RBI's: Season — Hack Wilson Career — Hank Aaron | .50 |
| 413 All-Time Home Runs: Season — Roger Maris Career — Hank Aaron | .50 |
| 414 All-Time Batting Avg.: Career — Ty Cobb Season — R. Hornsby | .50 |
| 415 All-Time Stolen Bases: Career — Lou Brock Season — Lou Brock | .50 |
| 416 All-Time Wins: Career: Cy Young Season: J. Chesbro | .25 |
| 417 All-Time Strikeouts: Career: Walter Johnson Season: Nolan Ryan | .25 |
| 418 All-Time ERA: Career: W. Johnson Season: Dutch Leonard | .25 |
| 419 Dick Ruthven | .10 |
| 420 Ken Griffey | .15 |
| 421 Doug DeCinces | .20 |
| 422 Ruppert Jones | .15 |
| 423 Bob Montgomery | .10 |
| 424 California Angels/ Jim Fregosi (Mgr.) | .30 |
| 425 Rick Manning | .10 |
| 426 Chris Speier | .10 |
| 427 Andy Replogle | .10 |
| 428 Bobby Valentine | .10 |
| 429 John Urrea | .10 |
| 430 Dave Parker | .75 |
| 431 Glenn Borgmann | .10 |
| 432 Dave Heaverlo | .10 |
| 433 Larry Biittner | .10 |
| 434 Ken Clay | .10 |
| 435 Gene Tenace | .10 |
| 436 Hector Cruz | .10 |
| 437 Rick Williams | .10 |
| 438 Horace Speed | .10 |
| 439 Frank White | .15 |
| 440 Rusty Staub | .20 |
| 441 Lee Lacy | .15 |
| 442 Doyle Alexander | .10 |
| 443 Bruce Bochte | .10 |
| 444 Aurelio Lopez (R) | .35 |
| 445 Steve Henderson | .10 |
| 446 Jim Lonborg | .10 |
| 447 Manny Sanguillen | .10 |
| 448 Moose Haas | .10 |
| 449 Bombo Rivera | .10 |
| 450 Dave Concepcion | .25 |
| 451 Kansas City Royals/ Whitey Herzog (Mgr.) | .25 |
| 452 Jerry Morales | .10 |
| 453 Chris Knapp | .10 |
| 454 Len Randle | .10 |
| 455 Bill Lee | .10 |
| 456 Chuck Baker | .10 |
| 457 Bruce Sutter | .75 |
| 458 Jim Essian | .10 |
| 459 Sid Monge | .10 |
| 460 Graig Nettles | .30 |
| 461 Jim Barr | .10 |
| 462 Otto Velez | .10 |
| 463 Steve Comer | .10 |
| 464 Joe Nolan | .10 |
| 465 Reggie Smith | .20 |
| 466 Mark Littell | .10 |
| 467 Don Kessinger | .10 |
| 468 Stan Bahnsen | .10 |
| 469 Lance Parrish | 2.00 |
| 470 Garry Maddox | .10 |
| 471 Joaquin Andujar | .35 |
| 472 Craig Kusick | .10 |
| 473 Dave Roberts | .10 |
| 474 Dick Davis | .10 |
| 475 Dan Driessen | .10 |
| 476 Tom Poquette | .10 |
| 477 Bob Grich | .15 |
| 478 Juan Beniquez | .10 |
| 479 San Diego Padres/ Roger Craig (Mgr.) | .25 |
| 480 Fred Lynn | .75 |
| 481 Skip Lockwood | .10 |
| 482 Craig Reynolds | .10 |
| 483 Checklist No. 4 | .20 |
| 484 Rick Waits | .10 |
| 485 Bucky Dent | .15 |
| 486 Bob Knepper | .15 |
| 487 Miguel Dilone | .10 |
| 488 Bob Owchinko | .10 |
| 489 Larry Cox (photo of Dave Rader) | .10 |
| 490 Al Cowens | .10 |
| 491 Tippy Martinez | .10 |
| 492 Bob Bailor | .10 |
| 493 Larry Christenson | .10 |
| 494 Jerry White | .10 |
| 495 Tony Perez | .35 |
| 496 Barry Bonnell | .10 |
| 497 Glenn Abbott | .10 |
| 498 Rich Chiles | .10 |
| 499 Texas Rangers/ Pat Corrales (Mgr.) | .25 |
| 500 Ron Guidry | .75 |
| 501 Junior Kennedy | .10 |
| 502 Steve Braun | .10 |
| 503 Terry Humphrey | .10 |
| 504 Larry McWilliams (R) | .50 |
| 505 Ed Kranepool | .10 |
| 506 John D'Acquisto | .10 |
| 507 Tony Armas | .60 |
| 508 Charlie Hough | .10 |
| 509 Mario Mendoza | .10 |
| 510 Ted Simmons | .35 |
| 511 Paul Reuschel | .10 |
| 512 Jack Clark | .85 |
| 513 Dave Johnson | .10 |
| 514 Mike Proly | .10 |
| 515 Enos Cabell | .10 |
| 516 Champ Summers | .10 |
| 517 Al Bumbry | .10 |
| 518 Jim Umbarger | .10 |
| 519 Ben Oglivie | .15 |
| 520 Gary Carter | 2.00 |
| 521 Sam Ewing | .10 |
| 522 Ken Holtzman | .10 |
| 523 John Milner | .10 |
| 524 Tom Burgmeier | .10 |
| 525 Freddie Patek | .10 |
| 526 Los Angeles Dodgers/ Tom Lasorda (Mgr.) | .50 |
| 527 Lerrin LaGrow | .10 |
| 528 Wayne Gross | .10 |
| 529 Brian Asselstine | .10 |
| 530 Frank Tanana | .15 |
| 531 Fernando Gonzalez | .10 |
| 532 Buddy Schultz | .10 |
| 533 Leroy Stanton | .10 |
| 534 Ken Forsch | .10 |
| 535 Ellis Valentine | .10 |
| 536 Jerry Reuss | .15 |
| 537 Tom Veryzer | .10 |
| 538 Mike Ivie | .10 |
| 539 John Ellis | .10 |
| 540 Greg Luzinski | .25 |
| 541 Jim Slaton | .10 |
| 542 Rick Bosetti | .10 |
| 543 Kiko Garcia | .10 |
| 544 Fergie Jenkins | .25 |
| 545 John Stearns | .10 |
| 546 Bill Russell | .10 |
| 547 Clint Hurdle | .10 |
| 548 Enrique Romo | .10 |
| 549 Bob Bailey | .10 |
| 550 Sal Bando | .10 |
| 551 Chicago Cubs/ Herman Franks (Mgr.) | .35 |
| 552 Jose Morales | .10 |
| 553 Denny Walling | .10 |
| 554 Matt Keough | .10 |
| 555 Biff Pocoroba | .10 |
| 556 Mike Lum | .10 |
| 557 Ken Brett | .10 |
| 558 Jay Johnstone | .10 |
| 559 Greg Pryor | .10 |
| 560 John Montefusco | .10 |
| 561 Ed Ott | .10 |
| 562 Dusty Baker | .20 |
| 563 Roy Thomas | .10 |
| 564 Jerry Turner | .10 |
| 565 Rico Carty | .10 |
| 566 Nino Espinosa | .10 |
| 567 Rich Hebner | .10 |
| 568 Carlos Lopez | .10 |
| 569 Bob Sykes | .10 |
| 570 Cesar Cedeno | .20 |
| 571 Darrell Porter | .15 |
| 572 Rod Gilbreath | .10 |
| 573 Jim Kern | .10 |
| 574 Claudell Washington | .15 |
| 575 Luis Tiant | .15 |
| 576 Mike Parrott | .10 |
| 577 Milwaukee Brewers/ George Bamberger (Mgr.) | .30 |
| 578 Pete Broberg | .10 |
| 579 Greg Gross | .10 |
| 580 Ron Fairly | .10 |
| 581 Darold Knowles | .10 |
| 582 Paul Blair | .10 |
| 583 Julio Cruz | .10 |
| 584 Jim Rooker | .10 |
| 585 Hal McRae | .15 |
| 586 Bob Horner (R) | 5.00 |
| 587 Ken Reitz | .10 |
| 588 Tom Murphy | .10 |
| 589 Terry Whitfield | .10 |
| 590 J.R. Richard | .15 |
| 591 Mike Hargrove | .10 |
| 592 Mike Krukow | .10 |
| 593 Rick Dempsey | .10 |
| 594 Bob Shirley | .10 |
| 595 Phil Niekro | .60 |
| 596 Jim Wohlford | .10 |
| 597 Bob Stanley | .15 |
| 598 Mark Wagner | .10 |
| 599 Jim Spencer | .10 |
| 600 George Foster | .75 |
| 601 Dave LaRoche | .10 |
| 602 Checklist No. 5 | .20 |
| 603 Rudy May | .10 |
| 604 Jeff Newman | .10 |
| 605 Rick Monday | .10 |
| 606 Montreal Expos/ Dick Williams (Mgr.) | .25 |
| 607 Omar Moreno | .10 |
| 608 Dave McKay | .10 |
| 609 Silvio Martinez | .10 |
| 610 Mike Schmidt | 3.50 |
| 611 Jim Norris | .10 |
| 612 Rick Honeycutt (R) | .60 |
| 613 Mike Edwards | .10 |
| 614 Willie Hernandez | .65 |
| 615 Ken Singleton | .15 |
| 616 Billy Almon | .10 |
| 617 Terry Puhl | .10 |
| 618 Jerry Remy | .10 |
| 619 Ken Landreaux | .30 |
| 620 Bert Campaneris | .10 |
| 621 Pat Zachry | .10 |
| 622 Dave Collins | .15 |
| 623 Bob McClure | .10 |
| 624 Larry Herndon | .10 |
| 625 Mark Fidrych | .15 |
| 626 New York Yankees/ Bob Lemon (Mgr.) | .40 |
| 627 Gary Serum | .10 |
| 628 Del Unser | .10 |
| 629 Gene Garber | .10 |
| 630 Bake McBride | .10 |
| 631 Jorge Orta | .10 |
| 632 Don Kirkwood | .10 |
| 633 Rob Wilfong | .10 |
| 634 Paul Lindblad | .10 |
| 635 Don Baylor | .75 |
| 636 Wayne Garland | .10 |
| 637 Bill Robinson | .10 |
| 638 Al Fitzmorris | .10 |
| 639 Manny Trillo | .10 |
| 640 Eddie Murray | 4.00 |
| 641 Bobby Castillo | .10 |
| 642 Wilbur Howard | .10 |
| 643 Tom Hausman | .10 |
| 644 Manny Mota | .10 |
| 645 George Scott | .10 |
| 646 Rick Sweet | .10 |
| 647 Bob Lacey | .10 |
| 648 Lou Piniella | .30 |
| 649 John Curtis | .10 |
| 650 Pete Rose | 3.50 |
| 651 Mike Caldwell | .10 |
| 652 Stan Papi | .10 |
| 653 Warren Brusstar | .10 |
| 654 Rick Miller | .10 |
| 655 Jerry Koosman | .15 |
| 656 Hosken Powell | .10 |
| 657 George Medich | .10 |
| 658 Taylor Duncan | .10 |
| 659 Seattle Mariners/ Darrell Johnson (Mgr.) | .20 |
| 660 Ron LeFlore | .10 |
| 661 Bruce Kison | .10 |
| 662 Kevin Bell | .10 |
| 663 Mike Vail | .10 |
| 664 Doug Bird | .10 |
| 665 Lou Brock | 1.00 |
| 666 Rich Dauer | .10 |
| 667 Don Hood | .10 |
| 668 Bill North | .10 |
| 669 Checklist No. 6 | .20 |
| 670 Jim Hunter | .15 |
| 671 Joe Ferguson | .10 |
| 672 Ed Halicki | .10 |
| 673 Tom Hutton | .10 |
| 674 Dave Tomlin | .10 |
| 675 Tim McCarver | .15 |
| 676 Johnny Sutton | .10 |
| 677 Larry Parrish | .10 |
| 678 Geoff Zahn | .10 |
| 679 Derrel Thomas | .10 |
| 680 Carlton Fisk | .50 |
| 681 John Johnson | .10 |
| 682 Dave Chalk | .10 |

| NO. PLAYER | MINT | NO. PLAYER | MINT | NO. PLAYER | MINT | NO. PLAYER | MINT |
|---|---|---|---|---|---|---|---|
| 683 Dan Meyer | 10 | 703 Angels Prospects: | 15 | 711 A's Prospects: | 75 | 719 Dodgers Prospects: | 6.00 |
| 684 Jamie Easterly | 10 | Bob Slater, J. Anderson, | | Dwayne Murphy, Bruce | | Pedro Guerrero, Rudy Law, | |
| 685 Sixto Lezcano | 10 | Dave Frost | | Robinson, Alan Wirth | | Joe Simpson | |
| 686 Ron Schueler | 10 | 704 White Sox Prospects: | 15 | 712 Mariners Prospects: | 15 | 720 Expos Prospects: | 30 |
| 687 Rennie Stennett | 10 | Ross Baumgarten, Mike | | Greg Biercevicz, | | Jerry Fry, Jerry Pirtle, | |
| 688 Mike Willis | 10 | Colbern, Mike Squires | | B. McLaughlin, B. Anderson | | Scott Sanderson | |
| 689 Baltimore Orioles/ | 35 | 705 Indians Prospects: | 75 | 713 Rangers Prospects: | 40 | 721 Mets Prospects: | 25 |
| Earl Weaver (Mgr.) | | Tim Norrid, D. Oliver, | | Danny Darwin, Pat Putnam, | | Dwight Bernard, Juan | |
| 690 Buddy Bell | 10 | Alfredo Griffin | | Billy Sample | | Berenguer, Dan Norman | |
| 691 Dock Ellis | 10 | 706 Tigers Prospects: | 20 | 714 Blue Jays Prospects: | 15 | 722 Phillies Prospects: | 1.25 |
| 692 Mickey Stanley | 10 | Dave Stegman, Dave Tobik, | | Victor Cruz, Pat Kelly, | | Jim Morrison, Lonnie | |
| 693 Dave Rader | 10 | Kip Young | | Ernie Whitt | | Smith, Jim Wright | |
| 694 Burt Hooton | 10 | 707 Royals Prospects: | 15 | 715 Braves Prospects: | 50 | 723 Pirates Prospects: | 35 |
| 695 Keith Hernandez | 1.50 | Randy Bass, Jim Gaudet, | | Larry Whisenton, Bruce | | Eugenio Cotes, | |
| 696 Andy Hassler | 10 | R. McGilberry | | Benedict, Glenn Hubbard | | B. Wiltbank, Dale Berra | |
| 697 Dave Bergman | 10 | 708 Brewers Prospects: | 20 | Cubs Prospects: | 20 | 724 Cardinals Prospects: | 1.25 |
| 698 Bill Stein | 10 | Kevin Bass, Ned Yost, | | S. Thompson, Dave Geisel, | | Tom Bruno, George | |
| 699 Hal Dues | 10 | Eddie Romero | | Karl Pagel | | Frazier, Terry Kennedy | |
| 700 Reggie Jackson | 1.00 | 709 Twins Prospects: | 15 | 717 Reds Prospects: | 50 | 725 Padres Prospects: | 15 |
| 701 Orioles Prospects: | 35 | R. Sofield, Kevin Stanfield, | | M. LaCoss, Ron Oester, | | Jim Beswick, Broderick | |
| Mark Corey, John Flinn, | | Sam Perlozzo | | Harry Spilman | | Perkins, Steve Mura | |
| Sammy Stewart | | 710 Yankees Prospects: | 40 | 718 Astros Prospects: | 15 | 726 Giants Prospects: | 20 |
| 702 Red Sox Prospects: | 20 | Mike Heath, D. Rajsich, | | Mike Fischlin, Bruce Bochy, | | J. Tamargo, Greg | |
| Garry Hancock, Joel Finch, | | Brian Doyle | | Don Pisker | | Johnston, Joe Strain | |
| Allen Ripley | | | | | | | |

# 1980 Topps....Complete Set of 726 Cards—Value $95.00

Features the rookie cards of Rickey Henderson, Dan Quisenberry, Rick Sutcliffe and Dave Stieb. 66 cards were double printed.

| NO. PLAYER | MINT | NO. PLAYER | MINT | NO. PLAYER | MINT | NO. PLAYER | MINT |
|---|---|---|---|---|---|---|---|
| 1 Highlights: Brock and | 1.00 | 30 Vida Blue | 15 | 64 Joe Nolan | 08 | 96 Oakland A's/ | 25 |
| Yaz Get 3000 Hits | | 31 Jay Johnstone | 08 | 65 Al Bumbry | 08 | Jim Marshall (Mgr.) | |
| 2 Highlights: McCovey | 50 | 32 Julio Cruz | 08 | 66 Kansas City Royals/ | 25 | 97 Bill Lee | 08 |
| 512 Home Runs | | 33 Tony Scott | 08 | Jim Frey (Mgr.) | | 98 Jerry Terrell | 08 |
| 3 Highlights: Manny Mota | 15 | 34 Jeff Newman | 08 | 67 Doyle Alexander | 08 | 99 Victor Cruz | 08 |
| 145 Pinch Hits | | 35 Luis Tiant | 12 | 68 Larry Harlow | 08 | 100 Johnny Bench | 1.00 |
| 4 Highlights: Pete Rose | 1.00 | 36 Rusty Torres | 08 | 69 Rick Williams | 08 | 101 Aurelio Lopez | 08 |
| 10th 200 Hit Season | | 37 Kiko Garcia | 08 | 70 Gary Carter | 1.50 | 102 Rich Dauer | 08 |
| 5 Highlights: G. Templeton | 25 | 38 Dan Spillner | 08 | 71 John Milner | 08 | 103 Bill Caudill (R) | 75 |
| 100 Lefty and Righty Hits | | 39 Rowland Office | 08 | 72 Fred Howard | 08 | 104 Manny Mota | 08 |
| 6 Highlights: Del Unser | 15 | 40 Carlton Fisk | 40 | 73 Dave Collins | 08 | 105 Frank Tanana | 12 |
| 3rd Consec. Pinch Homer | | 41 Texas Rangers/ | 20 | 74 Sid Monge | 08 | 106 Jeff Leonard (R) | 75 |
| 7 Mike Lum | 08 | Pat Corrales (Mgr.) | | 75 Bill Russell | 08 | 107 Francisco Barrios | 08 |
| 8 Craig Swan | 08 | 42 Dave Palmer (R) | 30 | 76 John Stearns | 08 | 108 Bob Horner | 80 |
| 9 Steve Braun | 08 | 43 Bombo Rivera | 08 | 77 Dave Stieb (R) | 2.50 | 109 Bill Travers | 08 |
| 10 Denny Martinez | 08 | 44 Bill Fahey | 08 | 78 Ruppert Jones | 08 | 110 Fred Lynn | 35 |
| 11 Jimmy Sexton | 08 | 45 Frank White | 12 | 79 Bob Owchinko | 08 | 111 Bob Knepper | 08 |
| 12 John Curtis | 08 | 46 Rico Carty | 08 | 80 Ron LeFlore | 08 | 112 Chicago White Sox/ | 25 |
| 13 Ron Pruitt | 08 | 47 Bill Bonham | 08 | 81 Ted Sizemore | 08 | Tony LaRussa (Mgr.) | |
| 14 Dave Cash | 08 | 48 Rick Miller | 08 | 82 Houston Astros/ | 25 | 113 Geoff Zahn | 08 |
| 15 Bill Campbell | 08 | 49 Mario Guerrero | 08 | Bill Virdon (Mgr.) | | 114 Juan Beniquez | 08 |
| 16 Jerry Narron | 08 | 50 J.R. Richard | 12 | 83 Steve Trout (R) | 60 | 115 Sparky Lyle | 15 |
| 17 Bruce Sutter | 50 | 51 Joe Ferguson | 08 | 84 Gary Lavelle | 08 | 116 Larry Cox | 08 |
| 18 Ron Jackson | 08 | 52 Warren Brusstar | 08 | 85 Ted Simmons | 30 | 117 Dock Ellis | 08 |
| 19 Balor Moore | 08 | 53 Ben Oglivie | 12 | 86 Dave Hamilton | 08 | 118 Phil Garner | 08 |
| 20 Dan Ford | 08 | 54 Dennis Lamp | 08 | 87 Pepe Frias | 08 | 119 Sammy Stewart | 08 |
| 21 Manny Sarmiento | 08 | 55 Bill Madlock | 40 | 88 Ken Landreaux | 08 | 120 Greg Luzinski | 25 |
| 22 Pat Putnam | 08 | 56 Bobby Valentine | 08 | 89 Don Hood | 08 | 121 Checklist No. 1 | 25 |
| 23 Derrel Thomas | 08 | 57 Pete Vuckovich | 12 | 90 Manny Trillo | 08 | 122 Dave Rosello | 08 |
| 24 Jim Slaton | 08 | 58 Doug Flynn | 08 | 91 Rick Dempsey | 08 | 123 Lynn Jones | 08 |
| 25 Lee Mazzilli | 08 | 59 Eddy Putman | 08 | 92 Rick Rhoden | 08 | 124 Dave Lemanczyk | 08 |
| 26 Marty Pattin | 08 | 60 Bucky Dent | 12 | 93 Dave Roberts | 08 | 125 Tony Perez | 30 |
| 27 Del Unser | 08 | 61 Gary Serum | 08 | 94 Neil Allen (R) | 40 | 126 Dave Tomlin | 08 |
| 28 Bruce Kison | 08 | 62 Mike Ivie | 08 | 95 Cecil Cooper | 40 | 127 Gary Thomasson | 08 |
| 29 Mark Wagner | 08 | 63 Bob Stanley | 12 | | | 128 Tom Burgmeier | 08 |

| NO. | PLAYER | MINT |
|---|---|---|
| 129 | Craig Reynolds | .08 |
| 130 | Amos Otis | .08 |
| 131 | Paul Mitchell | .08 |
| 132 | Biff Pocoroba | .08 |
| 133 | Jerry Turner | .08 |
| 134 | Matt Keough | .08 |
| 135 | Bill Buckner | .20 |
| 136 | Dick Ruthven | .08 |
| 137 | John Castino | .20 |
| 138 | Ross Baumgarten | .08 |
| 139 | Dane Iorg | .20 |
| 140 | Rich Gossage | .50 |
| 141 | Gary Alexander | .08 |
| 142 | Phil Huffman | .08 |
| 143 | Bruce Bochte | .08 |
| 144 | Steve Comer | .08 |
| 145 | Darrell Evans | .20 |
| 146 | Bob Welch | .15 |
| 147 | Terry Puhl | .08 |
| 148 | Manny Sanguillen | .08 |
| 149 | Tom Hume | .08 |
| 150 | Jason Thompson | .15 |
| 151 | Tom Hausman | .08 |
| 152 | John Fulgham | .08 |
| 153 | Tim Blackwell | .08 |
| 154 | Lary Sorensen | .08 |
| 155 | Jerry Remy | .08 |
| 156 | Tony Brizzolara | .08 |
| 157 | Willie Wilson | .25 |
| 158 | Rob Picciolo | .08 |
| 159 | Ken Clay | .08 |
| 160 | Eddie Murray | 2.50 |
| 161 | Larry Christenson | .08 |
| 162 | Bob Randall | .08 |
| 163 | Steve Swisher | .08 |
| 164 | Greg Pryor | .08 |
| 165 | Omar Moreno | .08 |
| 166 | Glenn Abbott | .08 |
| 167 | Jack Clark | .50 |
| 168 | Rick Waits | .08 |
| 169 | Luis Gomez | .08 |
| 170 | Burt Hooton | .08 |
| 171 | Fernando Gonzalez | .08 |
| 172 | Ron Hodges | .08 |
| 173 | John Henry Johnson | .08 |
| 174 | Ray Knight | .08 |
| 175 | Rick Reuschel | .12 |
| 176 | Champ Summers | .08 |
| 177 | Dave Heaverlo | .08 |
| 178 | Tim McCarver | .20 |
| 179 | Ron Davis (R) | .40 |
| 180 | Warren Cromartie | .08 |
| 181 | Moose Haas | .08 |
| 182 | Ken Reitz | .08 |
| 183 | Jim Anderson | .08 |
| 184 | Steve Renko | .08 |
| 185 | Hal McRae | .12 |
| 186 | Junior Moore | .08 |
| 187 | Alan Ashby | .08 |
| 188 | Terry Crowley | .08 |
| 189 | Kevin Kobel | .08 |
| 190 | Buddy Bell | .20 |
| 191 | Ted Martinez | .08 |
| 192 | Atlanta Braves/ Bobby Cox (Mgr.) | .25 |
| 193 | Dave Goltz | .08 |
| 194 | Mike Easler | .25 |
| 195 | John Montefusco | .08 |
| 196 | Lance Parrish | .75 |
| 197 | Byron McLaughlin | .08 |
| 198 | Dell Alston | .08 |
| 199 | Mike LaCoss | .08 |
| 200 | Jim Rice | 1.50 |
| 201 | Batting Leaders: K. Hernandez, Fred Lynn | .30 |
| 202 | Home Run Leaders: Dave Kingman, G. Thomas | .30 |
| 203 | RBI Leaders: Don Baylor, Dave Winfield | .30 |
| 204 | Stolen Base Leaders: Omar Moreno, Willie Wilson | .15 |
| 205 | Victory Leaders: Phil Niekro, Joe Niekro, Mike Flanagan | .25 |
| 206 | Strikeout Leaders: J.R. Richard, Nolan Ryan | .25 |
| 207 | ERA Leaders: J.R. Richard, Ron Guidry | .20 |
| 208 | Wayne Cage | .08 |
| 209 | Von Joshua | .08 |
| 210 | Steve Carlton | 1.50 |
| 211 | Dave Skaggs | .08 |
| 212 | Dave Roberts | .08 |
| 213 | Mike Jorgensen | .08 |
| 214 | California Angels/ Jim Fregosi (Mgr.) | .25 |
| 215 | Sixto Lezcano | .08 |
| 216 | Phil Mankowski | .08 |
| 217 | Ed Halicki | .08 |
| 218 | Jose Morales | .08 |
| 219 | Steve Mingori | .08 |
| 220 | Dave Concepcion | .25 |
| 221 | Joe Cannon | .08 |
| 222 | Ron Hassey | .08 |
| 223 | Bob Sykes | .08 |
| 224 | Willie Montanez | .08 |
| 225 | Lou Piniella | .25 |
| 226 | Bill Stein | .08 |
| 227 | Len Barker | .08 |
| 228 | Johnny Oates | .08 |
| 229 | Jim Bibby | .08 |
| 230 | Dave Winfield | 1.50 |
| 231 | Steve McCatty | .08 |
| 232 | Alan Trammell | 1.00 |
| 233 | LaRue Washington | .08 |
| 234 | Vern Ruhle | .08 |
| 235 | Andre Dawson | .80 |
| 236 | Marc Hill | .08 |
| 237 | Scott McGregor | .12 |
| 238 | Rob Wilfong | .08 |
| 239 | Don Aase | .08 |
| 240 | Dave Kingman | .35 |
| 241 | Checklist No. 2 | .25 |
| 242 | Lamar Johnson | .08 |
| 243 | Jerry Augustine | .08 |
| 244 | St. Louis Cardinals/ Ken Boyer (Mgr.) | .25 |
| 245 | Phil Niekro | .50 |
| 246 | Tim Foli | .08 |
| 247 | Frank Riccelli | .08 |
| 248 | Jamie Quirk | .08 |
| 249 | Jim Clancy | .08 |
| 250 | Jim Kaat | .30 |
| 251 | Kip Young | .08 |
| 252 | Ted Cox | .08 |
| 253 | John Montague | .08 |
| 254 | Paul Dade | .08 |
| 255 | Dusty Baker | .08 |
| 256 | Roger Erickson | .08 |
| 257 | Larry Herndon | .08 |
| 258 | Paul Moskau | .08 |
| 259 | New York Mets/ Joe Torre (Mgr.) | .40 |
| 260 | Al Oliver | .35 |
| 261 | Dave Chalk | .08 |
| 262 | Benny Ayala | .08 |
| 263 | Dave LaRoche | .08 |
| 264 | Bill Robinson | .08 |
| 265 | Robin Yount | 1.25 |
| 266 | Bernie Carbo | .08 |
| 267 | Dan Schatzeder | .08 |
| 268 | Rafael Landestoy | .08 |
| 269 | Dave Tobik | .08 |
| 270 | Mike Schmidt | 1.00 |
| 271 | Dick Drago | .08 |
| 272 | Ralph Garr | .08 |
| 273 | Eduardo Rodriguez | .08 |
| 274 | Dale Murphy | 4.00 |
| 275 | Jerry Koosman | .12 |
| 276 | Tom Veryzer | .08 |
| 277 | Rick Bosetti | .08 |
| 278 | Jim Spencer | .08 |
| 279 | Rob Andrews | .08 |
| 280 | Gaylord Perry | .50 |
| 281 | Paul Blair | .08 |
| 282 | Seattle Mariners/ Darrell Johnson (Mgr.) | .20 |
| 283 | John Ellis | .08 |
| 284 | Larry Murray | .08 |
| 285 | Don Baylor | .35 |
| 286 | Darold Knowles | .08 |
| 287 | John Lowenstein | .08 |
| 288 | Dave Rozema | .08 |
| 289 | Bruce Bochy | .08 |
| 290 | Steve Garvey | 1.25 |
| 291 | Randy Scarberry | .08 |
| 292 | Dale Berra | .08 |
| 293 | Elias Sosa | .08 |
| 294 | Charlie Spikes | .08 |
| 295 | Larry Gura | .08 |
| 296 | Dave Rader | .08 |
| 297 | Tim Johnson | .08 |
| 298 | Ken Holtzman | .08 |
| 299 | Steve Henderson | .08 |
| 300 | Ron Guidry | .60 |
| 301 | Mike Edwards | .08 |
| 302 | Los Angeles Dodgers/ Tom Lasorda (Mgr.) | .40 |
| 303 | Bill Castro | .08 |
| 304 | Butch Wynegar | .08 |
| 305 | Randy Jones | .08 |
| 306 | Denny Walling | .08 |
| 307 | Rick Honeycutt | .12 |
| 308 | Mike Hargrove | .08 |
| 309 | Larry McWilliams | .12 |
| 310 | Dave Parker | .75 |
| 311 | Roger Metzger | .08 |
| 312 | Mike Barlow | .08 |
| 313 | Johnny Grubb | .08 |
| 314 | Tim Stoddard | .20 |
| 315 | Steve Kemp | .15 |
| 316 | Bob Lacey | .08 |
| 317 | Mike Anderson | .08 |
| 318 | Jerry Reuss | .12 |
| 319 | Chris Speier | .08 |
| 320 | Dennis Eckersley | .08 |
| 321 | Keith Hernandez | 1.00 |
| 322 | Claudell Washington | .15 |
| 323 | Mick Kelleher | .08 |
| 324 | Tom Underwood | .08 |
| 325 | Dan Driessen | .08 |
| 326 | Bo McLaughlin | .08 |
| 327 | Ray Fosse | .08 |
| 328 | Minnesota Twins/ Gene Mauch (Mgr.) | .20 |
| 329 | Bert Roberge | .08 |
| 330 | Al Cowens | .08 |
| 331 | Rich Hebner | .08 |
| 332 | Enrique Romo | .08 |
| 333 | Jim Norris | .08 |
| 334 | Jim Beattie | .08 |
| 335 | Willie McCovey | .75 |
| 336 | George Medich | .08 |
| 337 | Carney Lansford | .35 |
| 338 | Johnny Wockenfuss | .08 |
| 339 | John D'Acquisto | .08 |
| 340 | Ken Singleton | .15 |
| 341 | Jim Essian | .08 |
| 342 | Odell Jones | .08 |
| 343 | Mike Vail | .08 |
| 344 | Randy Lerch | .08 |
| 345 | Larry Parrish | .12 |
| 346 | Buddy Solomon | .08 |
| 347 | Harry Chappas | .08 |
| 348 | Checklist No. 3 | .25 |
| 349 | Jack Brohamer | .08 |
| 350 | George Hendrick | .15 |
| 351 | Bob Davis | .08 |
| 352 | Dan Briggs | .08 |
| 353 | Andy Hassler | .08 |
| 354 | Rick Auerbach | .08 |
| 355 | Gary Matthews | .15 |
| 356 | San Diego Padres/ Jerry Coleman (Mgr.) | .20 |
| 357 | Bob McClure | .08 |
| 358 | Lou Whitaker | .75 |
| 359 | Randy Moffitt | .08 |
| 360 | Darrell Porter | .08 |
| 361 | Wayne Garland | .08 |
| 362 | Danny Goodwin | .08 |
| 363 | Wayne Gross | .08 |
| 364 | Ray Burris | .08 |
| 365 | Bobby Murcer | .15 |
| 366 | Rob Dressler | .08 |
| 367 | Billy Smith | .08 |
| 368 | Willie Aikens (R) | .25 |
| 369 | Jim Kern | .08 |
| 370 | Cesar Cedeno | .15 |
| 371 | Jack Morris | .75 |
| 372 | Joel Youngblood | .08 |
| 373 | Dan Petry (R) | 2.00 |
| 374 | Jim Gantner | .08 |
| 375 | Ross Grimsley | .08 |
| 376 | Gary Allenson | .15 |
| 377 | Junior Kennedy | .08 |
| 378 | Jerry Mumphrey | .08 |
| 379 | Kevin Bell | .08 |
| 380 | Garry Maddox | .09 |
| 381 | Chicago Cubs/ Preston Gomez (Mgr.) | .35 |
| 382 | Dave Freisleben | .08 |
| 383 | Ed Ott | .08 |
| 384 | Joey McLaughlin | .08 |
| 385 | Enos Cabell | .08 |
| 386 | Darrell Jackson | .08 |
| 387 | Fred Stanley | .08 |
| 388 | Mike Paxton | .08 |
| 389 | Pete LaCock | .08 |
| 390 | Fergie Jenkins | .25 |
| 391 | Tony Armas | .12 |
| 392 | Milt Wilcox | .08 |
| 393 | Ozzie Smith | .60 |
| 394 | Reggie Cleveland | .08 |
| 395 | Ellis Valentine | .08 |
| 396 | Dan Meyer | .08 |
| 397 | Roy Thomas | .08 |
| 398 | Barry Foote | .08 |
| 399 | Mike Proly | .08 |
| 400 | George Foster | .50 |
| 401 | Pete Falcone | .08 |
| 402 | Merv Rettenmund | .08 |
| 403 | Pete Redfern | .08 |
| 404 | Baltimore Orioles/ Earl Weaver (Mgr.) | .35 |
| 405 | Dwight Evans | .30 |
| 406 | Paul Molitor | .35 |
| 407 | Tony Solaita | .08 |
| 408 | Bill North | .08 |
| 409 | Paul Splittorff | .08 |
| 410 | Bobby Bonds | .12 |
| 411 | Frank LaCorte | .08 |
| 412 | Thad Bosley | .08 |
| 413 | Allen Ripley | .08 |
| 414 | George Scott | .08 |
| 415 | Bill Atkinson | .08 |
| 416 | Tom Brookens | .08 |
| 417 | Craig Chamberlain | .08 |
| 418 | Roger Freed | .08 |
| 419 | Vic Correll | .08 |
| 420 | Butch Hobson | .08 |
| 421 | Doug Bird | .08 |
| 422 | Larry Milbourne | .08 |
| 423 | Dave Frost | .08 |
| 424 | New York Yankees/ Dick Howser (Mgr.) | .40 |
| 425 | Mark Belanger | .08 |
| 426 | Grant Jackson | .08 |
| 427 | Tom Hutton | .08 |
| 428 | Pat Zachry | .08 |
| 429 | Duane Kuiper | .08 |
| 430 | Larry Hisle | .08 |
| 431 | Mike Krukow | .08 |
| 432 | Willie Norwood | .08 |
| 433 | Rich Gale | .08 |
| 434 | Johnnie LeMaster | .08 |
| 435 | Don Gullett | .08 |
| 436 | Billy Almon | .08 |
| 437 | Joe Niekro | .15 |
| 438 | Dave Revering | .08 |
| 439 | Mike Phillips | .08 |
| 440 | Don Sutton | .35 |
| 441 | Eric Soderholm | .08 |
| 442 | Jorge Orta | .08 |
| 443 | Mike Parrott | .08 |
| 444 | Alvis Woods | .08 |
| 445 | Mark Fidrych | .12 |

| NO. | PLAYER | MINT |
|-----|--------|------|
| 446 | Duffy Dyer | .08 |
| 447 | Nino Espinosa | .08 |
| 448 | Jim Wohlford | .08 |
| 449 | Doug Bair | .08 |
| 450 | George Brett | 3.50 |
| 451 | Cleveland Indians/ Dave Garcia (Mgr.) | .25 |
| 452 | Steve Dillard | .08 |
| 453 | Mike Bacsik | .08 |
| 454 | Tom Donohue | .08 |
| 455 | Mike Torrez | .08 |
| 456 | Frank Taveras | .08 |
| 457 | Bert Blyleven | .30 |
| 458 | Billy Sample | .08 |
| 459 | Mickey Lolich | .08 |
| 460 | Willie Randolph | .12 |
| 461 | Dwayne Murphy | .15 |
| 462 | Mike Sadek | .08 |
| 463 | Jerry Royster | .08 |
| 464 | John Denny | .15 |
| 465 | Rick Monday | .08 |
| 466 | Mike Squires | .08 |
| 467 | Jesse Jefferson | .08 |
| 468 | Aurelio Rodriquez | .08 |
| 469 | Randy Niemann | .08 |
| 470 | Bob Boone | .08 |
| 471 | Hosken Powell | .08 |
| 472 | Willie Hernandez | .50 |
| 473 | Bump Wills | .08 |
| 474 | Steve Busby | .08 |
| 475 | Cesar Geronimo | .08 |
| 476 | Bob Shirley | .08 |
| 477 | Buck Martinez | .08 |
| 478 | Gil Flores | .08 |
| 479 | Montreal Expos/ Dick Williams (Mgr.) | .20 |
| 480 | Bob Watson | .08 |
| 481 | Tom Paciorek | .08 |
| 482 | R. Henderson (R) | 22.00 |
| 483 | Bo Diaz | .08 |
| 484 | Checklist No. 4 | .20 |
| 485 | Mickey Rivers | .08 |
| 486 | Mike Tyson | .08 |
| 487 | Wayne Nordhagen | .08 |
| 488 | Roy Howell | .08 |
| 489 | Preston Hanna | .08 |
| 490 | Lee May | .08 |
| 491 | Steve Mura | .08 |
| 492 | Todd Cruz | .08 |
| 493 | Jerry Martin | .08 |
| 494 | Craig Minetto | .08 |
| 495 | Bake McBride | .08 |
| 496 | Silvio Martinez | .08 |
| 497 | Jim Mason | .08 |
| 498 | Danny Darwin | .08 |
| 499 | San Francisco Giants/ Dave Bristol (Mgr.) | .25 |
| 500 | Tom Seaver | 1.25 |
| 501 | Rennie Stennett | .08 |
| 502 | Rich Wortham | .08 |
| 503 | Mike Cubbage | .08 |
| 504 | Gener Garber | .08 |
| 505 | Bert Campaneris | .08 |
| 506 | Tom Buskey | .08 |
| 507 | Leon Roberts | .08 |
| 508 | U.L. Washington | .08 |
| 509 | Ed Glynn | .08 |
| 510 | Ron Cey | .40 |
| 511 | Eric Wilkins | .08 |
| 512 | Jose Cardenal | .08 |
| 513 | Tom Dixon | .08 |
| 514 | Steve Ontiveros | .08 |
| 515 | Mike Caldwell | .08 |
| 516 | Hector Cruz | .08 |
| 517 | Don Stanhouse | .08 |
| 518 | Nelson Norman | .08 |
| 519 | Steve Nicosia | .08 |
| 520 | Steve Rogers | .15 |
| 521 | Ken Brett | .08 |
| 522 | Jim Morrison | .08 |
| 523 | Ken Henderson | .08 |
| 524 | Jim Wright | .08 |
| 525 | Clint Hurdle | .08 |
| 526 | Philadelphia Phillies/ Dallas Green (Mgr.) | .25 |
| 527 | Doug Rau | .08 |

| NO. | PLAYER | MINT |
|-----|--------|------|
| 528 | Adrian Devine | .08 |
| 529 | Jim Barr | .08 |
| 530 | Jim Sundberg | .08 |
| 531 | Eric Rasmussen | .08 |
| 532 | Willie Horton | .12 |
| 533 | Checklist No. 5 | .20 |
| 534 | Andre Thornton | .15 |
| 535 | Bob Forsch | .12 |
| 536 | Lee Lacy | .12 |
| 537 | Alex Trevino | .12 |
| 538 | Joe Strain | .08 |
| 539 | Rudy May | .08 |
| 540 | Pete Rose | 3.00 |
| 541 | Miguel Dilone | .08 |
| 542 | Joe Coleman | .08 |
| 543 | Pat Kelly | .08 |
| 544 | Rick Sutcliffe (R) | 2.00 |
| 545 | Jeff Burroughs | .08 |
| 546 | Rick Langford | .08 |
| 547 | John Wathan | .08 |
| 548 | Dave Rajsich | .08 |
| 549 | Larry Wolfe | .08 |
| 550 | Ken Griffey | .12 |
| 551 | Pittsburgh Pirates/ Chuck Tanner (Mgr.) | .25 |
| 552 | Bill Nahorodny | .08 |
| 553 | Dick Davis | .08 |
| 554 | Art Howe | .08 |
| 555 | Ed Figueroa | .08 |
| 556 | Joe Rudi | .08 |
| 557 | Mark Lee | .08 |
| 558 | Alfredo Griffin | .15 |
| 559 | Dale Murray | .08 |
| 560 | Dave Lopes | .15 |
| 561 | Eddie Whitson | .12 |
| 562 | Joe Wallis | .08 |
| 563 | Will McEnaney | .08 |
| 564 | Rick Manning | .08 |
| 565 | Dennis Leonard | .12 |
| 566 | Bud Harrelson | .08 |
| 567 | Skip Lockwood | .08 |
| 568 | Gary Roenicke (R) | .30 |
| 569 | Terry Kennedy | .30 |
| 570 | Roy Smalley | .08 |
| 571 | Joe Sambito | .08 |
| 572 | Jerry Morales | .08 |
| 573 | Kent Tekulve | .12 |
| 574 | Scot Thompson | .08 |
| 575 | Ken Kravec | .08 |
| 576 | Jim Dwyer | .08 |
| 577 | Toronto Blue Jays/ Bobby Mattick (Mgr.) | .20 |
| 578 | Scott Sanderson | .08 |
| 579 | Charlie Moore | .08 |
| 580 | Nolan Ryan | 1.00 |
| 581 | Bob Bailor | .08 |
| 582 | Brian Doyle | .08 |
| 583 | Bob Stinson | .08 |
| 584 | Kurt Bevacqua | .08 |
| 585 | Al Hrabosky | .08 |
| 586 | Mitchell Page | .08 |
| 587 | Garry Templeton | .25 |
| 588 | Greg Minton | .08 |
| 589 | Chet Lemon | .15 |
| 590 | Jim Palmer | .75 |
| 591 | Rick Cerone | .08 |
| 592 | Jon Matlack | .08 |
| 593 | Jesus Alou | .08 |
| 594 | Dick Tidrow | .08 |
| 595 | Don Money | .08 |
| 596 | Rick Matula | .08 |
| 597 | Tom Poquette | .08 |
| 598 | Fred Kendall | .08 |
| 599 | Mike Norris | .08 |
| 600 | Reggie Jackson | 2.00 |
| 601 | Buddy Schultz | .08 |
| 602 | Brian Downing | .08 |
| 603 | Jack Billingham | .08 |
| 604 | Glenn Adams | .08 |
| 605 | Terry Forster | .12 |
| 606 | Cincinnati Reds/ John McNamara (Mgr.) | .30 |
| 607 | Woodie Fryman | .08 |
| 608 | Alan Bannister | .08 |
| 609 | Ron Reed | .08 |
| 610 | Willie Stargell | .65 |

| NO. | PLAYER | MINT |
|-----|--------|------|
| 611 | Jerry Garvin | .08 |
| 612 | Cliff Johnson | .08 |
| 613 | Randy Stein | .08 |
| 614 | John Hiller | .08 |
| 615 | Doug DeCinces | .20 |
| 616 | Gene Richards | .08 |
| 617 | Joaquin Andujar | .30 |
| 618 | Bob Montgomery | .08 |
| 619 | Sergio Ferrer | .08 |
| 620 | Richie Zisk | .08 |
| 621 | Bob Grich | .12 |
| 622 | Mario Soto | .20 |
| 623 | Gorman Thomas | .25 |
| 624 | Lerrin LaGrow | .08 |
| 625 | Chris Chambliss | .12 |
| 626 | Detroit Tigers/ S. Anderson (Mgr.) | .50 |
| 627 | Pedro Borbon | .08 |
| 628 | Doug Capilla | .08 |
| 629 | Jim Todd | .08 |
| 630 | Larry Bowa | .15 |
| 631 | Mark Littell | .08 |
| 632 | Barry Bonnell | .08 |
| 633 | Bob Apodaca | .08 |
| 634 | Glenn Borgmann | .08 |
| 635 | John Candelaria | .12 |
| 636 | Toby Harrah | .08 |
| 637 | Joe Simpson | .08 |
| 638 | Mark Clear (R) | .30 |
| 639 | Larry Biittner | .08 |
| 640 | Mike Flanagan | .12 |
| 641 | Ed Kranepool | .08 |
| 642 | Ken Forsch | .08 |
| 643 | John Mayberry | .08 |
| 644 | Charlie Hough | .08 |
| 645 | Rick Burleson | .12 |
| 646 | Checklist No. 6 | .20 |
| 647 | Milt May | .08 |
| 648 | Roy White | .08 |
| 649 | Tom Griffin | .08 |
| 650 | Joe Morgan | .50 |
| 651 | Rollie Fingers | .40 |
| 652 | Mario Mendoza | .08 |
| 653 | Stan Bahnsen | .08 |
| 654 | Bruce Boisclair | .08 |
| 655 | Tug McGraw | .15 |
| 656 | Larvell Blanks | .08 |
| 657 | Dave Edwards | .08 |
| 658 | Chris Knapp | .08 |
| 659 | Milwaukee Brewers/ George Bamberger (Mgr.) | .25 |
| 660 | Rusty Staub | .15 |
| 661 | Orioles Rookies: Wayne Krenchicki, Mark Corey, D. Ford | .15 |
| 662 | Red Sox Rookies: J. Finch, Mike O'Berry, Chuck Rainey | .15 |
| 663 | Angels Rookies: Ralph Botting, Bob Clark, Dickey Thon | .85 |
| 664 | White Sox Rookies: Guy Hoffman, M. Colbern, Dewey Robinson | .15 |
| 665 | Indians Rookies: Larry Anderson, Bobby Cuellar, Randy Wihtol | .15 |
| 666 | Tigers Rookies: M. Chris, Bruce Robbins, Al Greene | .25 |
| 667 | Royals Rookies: R. Martin, Bill Paschall, Dan Quisenberry | 3.50 |
| 668 | Brewers Rookies: Danny Boitano, W. Mueller, Lenn Sakata | .15 |
| 669 | Twin Rookies: Rick Sofield, Dan Graham, Gary Ward | .60 |
| 670 | Yankee Rookies: B. Brown, Brad Gulden, Darryl Jones | .25 |
| 671 | A's Rookies: Derek Bryant, B. Kingman, Mike Morgan | .25 |

| NO. | PLAYER | MINT |
|-----|--------|------|
| 672 | Mariners Rookies: Rodney Craig, Charlie Beamon, Rafael Vasquez | .15 |
| 673 | Rangers Rookies: Brian Allard, Jerry Don Gleaton, Greg Mahlberg | .15 |
| 674 | Blue Jays Rookies: Butch Edge, Pat Kelly, Ted Wilborn | .15 |
| 675 | Braves Rookies: Bruce Benedict, Eddie Miller, Larry Bradford | .20 |
| 676 | Cubs Rookies: Steve Macko, Dave Geisel, Karl Pagel | .20 |
| 677 | Reds Rookies: Art DeFreites, Harry Spilman, Frank Pastore | .15 |
| 678 | Astros Rookies: Reggie Baldwin, A. Knicely, Pete Ladd | .20 |
| 679 | Dodgers Rookies: Joe Beckwith, Mickey Hatcher, Dave Patterson | .50 |
| 680 | Expos Rookies: Randy Miller, Tony Bernazard, John Tamargo | .40 |
| 681 | Mets Rookies: Dan Norman, J. Orosco, Mike Scott | 5.00 |
| 682 | Phillies Rookies: Kevin Saucier, Ramon Aviles, Dickie Noles | .25 |
| 683 | Pirates Rookies: D. Boyland, Alberto Lois, Harry Saferight | .15 |
| 684 | Cardinals Rookies: George Frazier, Tom Herr, Dan O'Brien | 1.00 |
| 685 | Padres Rookies: Brian Greer, Tim Flannery, Jim Wilhelm | .15 |
| 686 | Giants Rookies: Greg Johnston, D. Littlejohn, Phil Nastu | .15 |
| 687 | Mike Heath | .08 |
| 688 | Steve Stone | .12 |
| 689 | Boston Red Sox/ Don Zimmer (Mgr.) | .25 |
| 690 | Tommy John | .30 |
| 691 | Ivan DeJesus | .08 |
| 692 | Rawly Eastwick | .08 |
| 693 | Craig Kusick | .08 |
| 694 | Jim Rooker | .08 |
| 695 | Reggie Smith | .15 |
| 696 | Julio Gonzalez | .08 |
| 697 | David Clyde | .08 |
| 698 | Oscar Gamble | .08 |
| 699 | Floyd Bannister | .12 |
| 700 | Rod Carew | .50 |
| 701 | Ken Oberkfell | .30 |
| 702 | Ed Farmer | .08 |
| 703 | Otto Velez | .08 |
| 704 | Gene Tenace | .08 |
| 705 | Freddie Patek | .08 |
| 706 | Tippy Martinez | .08 |
| 707 | Elliott Maddox | .08 |
| 708 | Bob Tolan | .08 |
| 709 | Pat Underwood | .08 |
| 710 | Graig Nettles | .25 |
| 711 | Bob Galasso | .08 |
| 712 | Rodney Scott | .08 |
| 713 | Terry Whitfield | .08 |
| 714 | Fred Norman | .08 |
| 715 | Sal Bando | .08 |
| 716 | Lynn McGlothen | .08 |
| 717 | Mickey Klutts | .08 |
| 718 | Greg Gross | .08 |
| 719 | Don Robinson | .08 |
| 720 | Carl Yastrzemski | .75 |
| 721 | Paul Hartzell | .08 |
| 722 | Jose Cruz | .25 |
| 723 | Shane Rawley | .08 |
| 724 | Jerry White | .08 |
| 725 | Rick Wise | .08 |
| 726 | Steve Yeager | .12 |

# 1981 Topps....Complete Set of 726 Cards—Value $65.00

Features the rookie cards of Fernando Valenzuela, Kirk Gibson, Harold Baines and Tim Raines. 66 cards were double printed. In 1981 Topps began getting competition from two other card manufacturers—Donruss and Fleer.

| NO. PLAYER | MINT |
|---|---|
| 1 Batting Leaders: | .50 |
| Bill Buckner, George Brett | |
| 2 Home Run Leaders: | .25 |
| Reggie Jackson, Ben | |
| Oglivie, M. Schmidt | |
| 3 RBI Leaders: | .25 |
| Cecil Cooper, Mike | |
| Schmidt | |
| 4 Stolen Base Leaders: | .20 |
| Rickey Henderson, | |
| Ron LeFlore | |
| 5 Victory Leaders: | .15 |
| Steve Carlton, Steve Stone | |
| 6 Strikeout Leaders: | .15 |
| Len Barker, Steve Carlton | |
| 7 ERA Leaders: | .10 |
| Don Sutton, Rudy May | |
| 8 Leading Firemen: | .15 |
| Dan Quisenberry, Tom | |
| Hume, Rollie Fingers | |
| 9 Pete LaCock | .07 |
| 10 Mike Flanagan | .12 |
| 11 Jim Wohlford | .07 |
| 12 Mark Clear | .07 |
| 13 Joe Charboneau | .12 |
| 14 John Tudor (R) | 1.00 |
| 15 Larry Parrish | .10 |
| 16 Ron Davis | .10 |
| 17 Cliff Johnson | .07 |
| 18 Glenn Adams | .07 |
| 19 Jim Clancy | .07 |
| 20 Jeff Burroughs | .07 |
| 21 Ron Oester | .07 |
| 22 Danny Darwin | .07 |
| 23 Alex Trevino | .07 |
| 24 Don Stanhouse | .07 |
| 25 Sixto Lezcano | .07 |
| 26 U.L. Washington | .07 |
| 27 Champ Summers | .07 |
| 28 Enrique Romo | .07 |
| 29 Gene Tenace | .07 |
| 30 Jack Clark | .50 |
| 31 Checklist No. 1 | .15 |
| 32 Ken Oberkfell | .07 |
| 33 Rick Honeycutt | .07 |
| 34 Aurelio Rodriquez | .07 |
| 35 Mitchell Page | .07 |
| 36 Ed Farmer | .07 |
| 37 Gary Roenicke | .07 |
| 38 Win Remmerswaal | .07 |
| 39 Tom Veryzer | .07 |
| 40 Tug McGraw | .12 |
| 41 Ranger Rookies: | .30 |
| Bob Babcock, J. Butcher, | |
| Jerry Don Gleaton | |
| 42 Jerry White | .07 |
| 43 Jose Morales | .07 |
| 44 Larry McWilliams | .07 |
| 45 Enos Cabell | .07 |
| 46 Rick Bosetti | .07 |
| 47 Ken Brett | .07 |
| 48 Dave Skaggs | .07 |
| 49 Bob Shirley | .07 |
| 50 Dave Lopes | .12 |
| 51 Bill Robinson | .07 |
| 52 Hector Cruz | .07 |

| NO. PLAYER | MINT |
|---|---|
| 53 Kevin Saucler | .07 |
| 54 Ivan DeJesus | .07 |
| 55 Mike Norris | .07 |
| 56 Buck Martinez | .07 |
| 57 Dave Roberts | .07 |
| 58 Joel Youngblood | .07 |
| 59 Dan Petry | .40 |
| 60 Willie Randolph | .12 |
| 61 Butch Wynegar | .10 |
| 62 Joe Pettini | .07 |
| 63 Steve Renko | .07 |
| 64 Brian Asselstine | .07 |
| 65 Scott McGregor | .10 |
| 66 Royals Rookies: | .15 |
| Tim Ireland, Manny | |
| Castillo, Mike Jones | |
| 67 Ken Kravec | .07 |
| 68 Matt Alexander | .07 |
| 69 Ed Halicki | .07 |
| 70 Al Oliver | .12 |
| 71 Hal Dues | .07 |
| 72 Barry Evans | .07 |
| 73 Doug Bair | .07 |
| 74 Mike Hargrove | .07 |
| 75 Reggie Smith | .12 |
| 76 Mario Mendoza | .07 |
| 77 Mike Barlow | .07 |
| 78 Steve Dillard | .07 |
| 79 Bruce Robbins | .07 |
| 80 Rusty Staub | .15 |
| 81 Dave Stapleton | .15 |
| 82 Astros Rookies: | .10 |
| Bobby Sprowl, Danny | |
| Heep, Alan Knicely | |
| 83 Mike Proly | .07 |
| 84 Johnnie LeMaster | .07 |
| 85 Mike Caldwell | .07 |
| 86 Wayne Gross | .07 |
| 87 Rick Camp | .07 |
| 88 Joe LeFebvre | .15 |
| 89 Darrell Jackson | .07 |
| 90 Bake McBride | .07 |
| 91 Tim Stoddard | .07 |
| 92 Mike Easler | .12 |
| 93 Ed Glynn | .07 |
| 94 Harry Spilman | .07 |
| 95 Jim Sundberg | .07 |
| 96 A's Rookies: | .12 |
| Dave Beard, Pat Dempsey, | |
| E. Camacho | |
| 97 Chris Speier | .07 |
| 98 Clint Hurdle | .07 |
| 99 Eric Wilkins | .07 |
| 100 Rod Carew | 1.00 |
| 101 Benny Ayala | .07 |
| 102 Dave Tobik | .07 |
| 103 Jerry Martin | .07 |
| 104 Terry Forster | .12 |
| 105 Jose Cruz | .20 |
| 106 Don Money | .07 |
| 107 Rich Wortham | .07 |
| 108 Bruce Benedict | .07 |
| 109 Mike Scott | .75 |
| 110 Carl Yastrzemski | 1.00 |
| 111 Greg Minton | .07 |

| NO. PLAYER | MINT |
|---|---|
| 112 White Sox Rookies: | .15 |
| Rusty Kuntz, F. Mullin, | |
| Leo Sutherland | |
| 113 Mike Phillips | .07 |
| 114 Tom Underwood | .07 |
| 115 Roy Smalley | .07 |
| 116 Joe Simpson | .07 |
| 117 Pete Falcone | .07 |
| 118 Kurt Bevacqua | .07 |
| 119 Tippy Martinez | .07 |
| 120 Larry Bowa | .12 |
| 121 Larry Harlow | .07 |
| 122 John Denny | .15 |
| 123 Al Cowens | .07 |
| 124 Jerry Garvin | .07 |
| 125 Andre Dawson | .50 |
| 126 Charlie Leibrandt (R) | .75 |
| 127 Rudy Law | .07 |
| 128 Garry Allenson | .07 |
| 129 Art Howe | .07 |
| 130 Larry Gura | .07 |
| 131 Keith Moreland (R) | .60 |
| 132 Tommy Boggs | .07 |
| 133 Jeff Cox | .07 |
| 134 Steve Mura | .07 |
| 135 Gorman Thomas | .20 |
| 136 Doug Capilla | .07 |
| 137 Hosken Powell | .07 |
| 138 Rich Dotson (R) | .50 |
| 139 Oscar Gamble | .07 |
| 140 Bob Forsch | .07 |
| 141 Miguel Dilone | .07 |
| 142 Jackson Todd | .07 |
| 143 Dan Meyer | .07 |
| 144 Allen Ripley | .07 |
| 145 Mickey Rivers | .10 |
| 146 Bobby Castillo | .07 |
| 147 Dale Berra | .07 |
| 148 Randy Niemann | .07 |
| 149 Joe Nolan | .07 |
| 150 Mark Fidrych | .10 |
| 151 Claudell Washington | .10 |
| 152 John Urrea | .07 |
| 153 Tom Poquette | .07 |
| 154 Rick Langford | .07 |
| 155 Chris Chambliss | .10 |
| 156 Bob McClure | .07 |
| 157 John Wathan | .07 |
| 158 Fergie Jenkins | .20 |
| 159 Brian Doyle | .07 |
| 160 Garry Maddox | .07 |
| 161 Dan Graham | .07 |
| 162 Doug Corbett | .12 |
| 163 Billy Almon | .07 |
| 164 LaMarr Hoyt (R) | .60 |
| 165 Tony Scott | .07 |
| 166 Floyd Bannister | .07 |
| 167 Terry Whitfield | .07 |
| 168 Don Robinson | .07 |
| 169 John Mayberry | .07 |
| 170 Ross Grimsley | .07 |
| 171 Gene Richards | .07 |
| 172 Gary Woods | .07 |
| 173 Bump Wills | .07 |
| 174 Doug Rau | .07 |
| 175 Dave Collins | .07 |

| NO. PLAYER | MINT |
|---|---|
| 176 Mike Krukow | .07 |
| 177 Rick Peters | .07 |
| 178 Jim Essian | .07 |
| 179 Rudy May | .07 |
| 180 Pete Rose | 2.25 |
| 181 Elias Sosa | .07 |
| 182 Bob Grich | .12 |
| 183 Dick Davis | .07 |
| 184 Jim Dwyer | .07 |
| 185 Dennis Leonard | .07 |
| 186 Wayne Nordhagen | .07 |
| 187 Mike Parrott | .07 |
| 188 Doug DeCinces | .15 |
| 189 Craig Swan | .07 |
| 190 Cesar Cedeno | .15 |
| 191 Rick Sutcliffe | .40 |
| 192 Braves Rookies: | .35 |
| Terry Harper, Rafael | |
| Ramirez, Ed Miller | |
| 193 Pete Vuckovich | .12 |
| 194 Rod Scurry | .07 |
| 195 Rich Murray | .07 |
| 196 Duffy Dyer | .07 |
| 197 Jim Kern | .07 |
| 198 Jerry Dybzinski | .07 |
| 199 Chuck Rainey | .07 |
| 200 George Foster | .40 |
| 201 Record—J. Bench | .35 |
| Most HR's, Catcher, Career | |
| 202 Record—S. Carlton | .35 |
| Strikeouts, Lefty, Career | |
| 203 Record—B. Gullickson | .12 |
| Strikeouts, Game, Rookie | |
| 204 Rec.—LeFlore, Scott | .12 |
| SB's, Teammates, Season | |
| 205 Record—P. Rose | .75 |
| Most Consecutive Seasons, | |
| 600 or More At-Bats | |
| 206 Record—M. Schmidt | .35 |
| Homers, 3B, Season | |
| 207 Record—O. Smith | .15 |
| Assists, SS, Season | |
| 208 Record—W. Wilson | .15 |
| Most At-Bats, Season | |
| 209 Dickie Thon | .07 |
| 210 Jim Palmer | .50 |
| 211 Derrel Thomas | .07 |
| 212 Steve Nicosia | .07 |
| 213 Al Holland (R) | .40 |
| 214 Angels Rookies: | .15 |
| John Harris, Ralph Botting, | |
| Jim Dorsey | |
| 215 Larry Hisle | .07 |
| 216 John Henry Johnson | .07 |
| 217 Rich Hebner | .07 |
| 218 Paul Splittorff | .07 |
| 219 Ken Landreaux | .07 |
| 220 Tom Seaver | 1.00 |
| 221 Bob Davis | .07 |
| 222 Jorge Orta | .07 |
| 223 Roy Lee Jackson | .07 |
| 224 Pat Zachry | .07 |
| 225 Ruppert Jones | .07 |
| 226 Manny Sanguillen | .07 |
| 227 Fred Martinez | .07 |
| 228 Tom Paciorek | .07 |

| NO. | PLAYER | MINT |
|---|---|---|
| 229 | Rollie Fingers | .50 |
| 230 | George Hendrick | .12 |
| 231 | Joe Beckwith | .07 |
| 232 | Mickey Klutts | .07 |
| 233 | Skip Lockwood | .07 |
| 234 | Lou Whitaker | .40 |
| 235 | Scott Sanderson | .07 |
| 236 | Mike Ivie | .07 |
| 237 | Charlie Moore | .07 |
| 238 | Willie Hernandez | .35 |
| 239 | Rick Miller | .07 |
| 240 | Nolan Ryan | .50 |
| 241 | Checklist No. 2 | .15 |
| 242 | Chet Lemon | .12 |
| 243 | Sal Butera | .07 |
| 244 | Cardinals Rookies: Andy Rincon, T. Landrum, Al Olmsted | .20 |
| 245 | Ed Figueroa | .07 |
| 246 | Ed Ott | .07 |
| 247 | Glenn Hubbard | .07 |
| 248 | Joey McLaughlin | .07 |
| 249 | Larry Cox | .07 |
| 250 | Ron Guidry | .40 |
| 251 | Tom Brookens | .07 |
| 252 | Victor Cruz | .07 |
| 253 | Dave Bergman | .07 |
| 254 | Ozzie Smith | .50 |
| 255 | Mark Littell | .07 |
| 256 | Bombo Rivera | .07 |
| 257 | Rennie Stennett | .07 |
| 258 | Joe Price | .07 |
| 259 | Mets Rookies: Juan Berenguer, H. Brooks, Mookie Wilson | 2.00 |
| 260 | Ron Cey | .30 |
| 261 | Ricky Henderson | 3.00 |
| 262 | Sammy Stewart | .07 |
| 263 | Brian Downing | .07 |
| 264 | Jim Norris | .07 |
| 265 | John Candelaria | .10 |
| 266 | Tom Herr | .30 |
| 267 | Stan Bahnsen | .07 |
| 268 | Jerry Royster | .07 |
| 269 | Ken Forsch | .07 |
| 270 | Greg Luzinski | .15 |
| 271 | Bill Castro | .07 |
| 272 | Bruce Kimm | .07 |
| 273 | Stan Papi | .07 |
| 274 | Craig Chamberlain | .07 |
| 275 | Dwight Evans | .25 |
| 276 | Dan Spillner | .07 |
| 277 | Alfredo Griffin | .07 |
| 278 | Rick Sofield | .07 |
| 279 | Bob Knepper | .07 |
| 280 | Ken Griffey | .12 |
| 281 | Fred Stanley | .07 |
| 282 | Mariners Rookies: Rick Anderson, Rodney Craig, Greg Biercevicz | .15 |
| 283 | Billy Sample | .07 |
| 284 | Brian Kingman | .07 |
| 285 | Jerry Turner | .07 |
| 286 | Dave Frost | .07 |
| 287 | Lenn Sakata | .07 |
| 288 | Bob Clark | .07 |
| 289 | Mickey Hatcher | .07 |
| 290 | Bob Boone | .07 |
| 291 | Aurelio Lopez | .07 |
| 292 | Mike Squires | .07 |
| 293 | Charlie Lea (R) | .40 |
| 294 | Mike Tyson | .07 |
| 295 | Hal McRae | .10 |
| 296 | Bill Nahorodny | .07 |
| 297 | Bob Bailor | .07 |
| 298 | Buddy Solomon | .07 |
| 299 | Elliott Maddox | .07 |
| 300 | Paul Molitor | .25 |
| 301 | Matt Keough | .07 |
| 302 | Dodgers Rookies: Mike Scioscia, Jack Perconte, F. Valenzuela | 7.00 |
| 303 | Johnny Oates | .07 |
| 304 | John Castino | .07 |
| 305 | Ken Clay | .07 |
| 306 | Juan Beniquez | .07 |
| 307 | Gene Garber | .07 |
| 308 | Rick Manning | .07 |
| 309 | Luis Salazar | .15 |
| 310 | Vida Blue | .15 |
| 311 | Freddie Patek | .07 |
| 312 | Rick Rhoden | .07 |
| 313 | Luis Pujols | .07 |
| 314 | Rich Dauer | .07 |
| 315 | Kirk Gibson (R) | 4.00 |
| 316 | Craig Minetto | .07 |
| 317 | Lonnie Smith | .15 |
| 318 | Steve Yeager | .07 |
| 319 | Rowland Office | .07 |
| 320 | Tom Burgmeier | .07 |
| 321 | Leon Durham (R) | 1.25 |
| 322 | Neil Allen | .07 |
| 323 | Jim Morrison | .07 |
| 324 | Mike Willis | .07 |
| 325 | Ray Knight | .07 |
| 326 | Biff Pocoroba | .07 |
| 327 | Moose Haas | .07 |
| 328 | Twins Rookies: Dave Engle, G. Johnston, Gary Ward | .35 |
| 329 | Joaquin Andujar | .30 |
| 330 | Frank White | .12 |
| 331 | Dennis Lamp | .07 |
| 332 | Lee Lacy | .07 |
| 333 | Sid Monge | .07 |
| 334 | Dane Iorg | .07 |
| 335 | Rick Cerone | .07 |
| 336 | Eddie Whitson | .10 |
| 337 | Lynn Jones | .05 |
| 338 | Checklist No.3 | .15 |
| 339 | John Ellis | .07 |
| 340 | Bruce Kison | .07 |
| 341 | Dwayne Murphy | .12 |
| 342 | Eric Rasmussen | .07 |
| 343 | Frank Taveras | .07 |
| 344 | Byron McLaughlin | .07 |
| 345 | Warren Cromartie | .07 |
| 346 | Larry Christenson | .07 |
| 347 | Harold Baines (R) | 4.50 |
| 348 | Bob Sykes | .02 |
| 349 | Glenn Hoffman | .15 |
| 350 | J.R. Richard | .12 |
| 351 | Otto Velez | .07 |
| 352 | Dick Tidrow | .07 |
| 353 | Terry Kennedy | .20 |
| 354 | Mario Soto | .20 |
| 355 | Bob Horner | .40 |
| 356 | Padres Rookies: George Stablein, C. Stimac, Tom Tellmann | .15 |
| 357 | Jim Slaton | .07 |
| 358 | Mark Wagner | .07 |
| 359 | Tom Hausman | .07 |
| 360 | Willie Wilson | .40 |
| 361 | Joe Strain | .07 |
| 362 | Bo Diaz | .07 |
| 363 | Geoff Zahn | .07 |
| 364 | Mike Davis (R) | .75 |
| 365 | Graig Nettles | .40 |
| 366 | Mike Ramsey | .07 |
| 367 | Denny Martinez | .07 |
| 368 | Leon Roberts | .07 |
| 369 | Frank Tanana | .07 |
| 370 | Dave Winfield | .75 |
| 371 | Charlie Hough | .07 |
| 372 | Jay Johnstone | .07 |
| 373 | Pat Underwood | .07 |
| 374 | Tom Hutton | .07 |
| 375 | Dave Concepcion | .15 |
| 376 | Ron Reed | .07 |
| 377 | Jerry Morales | .07 |
| 378 | Dave Rader | .07 |
| 379 | Lary Sorensen | .07 |
| 380 | Willie Stargell | .50 |
| 381 | Cubs Rookies: Carlos Lezcano, Steve Macko, Randy Martz | .20 |
| 382 | Paul Mirabella | .07 |
| 383 | Eric Soderholm | .07 |
| 384 | Mike Sadek | .07 |
| 385 | Joe Sambito | .07 |
| 386 | Dave Edwards | .07 |
| 387 | Phil Niekro | .35 |
| 388 | Andre Thornton | .15 |
| 389 | Marty Pattin | .07 |
| 390 | Cesar Geronimo | .07 |
| 391 | Dave Lemanczyk | .07 |
| 392 | Lance Parrish | .40 |
| 393 | Broderick Perkins | .07 |
| 394 | Woodie Fryman | .07 |
| 395 | Scot Thompson | .07 |
| 396 | Bill Campbell | .07 |
| 397 | Julio Cruz | .07 |
| 398 | Ross Baumgarten | .07 |
| 399 | Orioles Rookies: Mike Boddicker, Mark Corey, Floyd Rayford | 1.75 |
| 400 | Reggie Jackson | 1.50 |
| 401 | A.L. Championships: Royals Sweep Yanks | .40 |
| 402 | N.L. Championships: Phillies Beat Astros | .25 |
| 403 | 1980 World Series: Phillies Beat Royals | .25 |
| 404 | 1980 World Series: Phillies Win | .25 |
| 405 | Nino Espinosa | .07 |
| 406 | Dickie Noles | .07 |
| 407 | Ernie Whitt | .07 |
| 408 | Fernando Arroyo | .07 |
| 409 | Larry Herndon | .07 |
| 410 | Bert Campaneris | .07 |
| 411 | Terry Puhl | .07 |
| 412 | Britt Burns (R) | .60 |
| 413 | Tony Bernazard | .07 |
| 414 | John Pacella | .07 |
| 415 | Ben Oglivie | .12 |
| 416 | Gary Alexander | .07 |
| 417 | Dan Schatzeder | .07 |
| 418 | Bobby Brown | .07 |
| 419 | Tom Hume | .07 |
| 420 | Keith Hernandez | .60 |
| 421 | Bob Stanley | .07 |
| 422 | Dan Ford | .07 |
| 423 | Shane Rawley | .07 |
| 424 | Yankees Rookies: Tim Lollar, Bruce Robinson, Dennis Werth | .40 |
| 425 | Al Bumbry | .07 |
| 426 | Warren Brusstar | .07 |
| 427 | Jonn D'Acquisto | .07 |
| 428 | John Stearns | .07 |
| 429 | Mick Kelleher | .07 |
| 430 | Jim Bibby | .07 |
| 431 | Dave Roberts | .07 |
| 432 | Len Barker | .12 |
| 433 | Rance Mulliniks | .07 |
| 434 | Roger Erickson | .07 |
| 435 | Jim Spencer | .07 |
| 436 | Gary Lucas | .12 |
| 437 | Mike Heath | .07 |
| 438 | John Montefusco | .07 |
| 439 | Denny Walling | .07 |
| 440 | Jerry Reuss | .07 |
| 441 | Ken Reitz | .07 |
| 442 | Ron Pruitt | .07 |
| 443 | Jim Beattie | .07 |
| 444 | Garth Iorg | .07 |
| 445 | Ellis Valentine | .07 |
| 446 | Checklist No. 4 | .15 |
| 447 | Junior Kennedy | .07 |
| 448 | Tim Corcoran | .07 |
| 449 | Paul Mitchell | .07 |
| 450 | Dave Kingman | .15 |
| 451 | Indians Rookies: Chris Bando, Tom Brennan, Sandy Wihtol | .25 |
| 452 | Renie Martin | .07 |
| 453 | Rob Wilfong | .07 |
| 454 | Andy Hassler | .07 |
| 455 | Rick Burleson | .07 |
| 456 | Jeff Reardon (R) | .75 |
| 457 | Mike Lum | .07 |
| 458 | Randy Jones | .07 |
| 459 | Greg Gross | .07 |
| 460 | Rich Gossage | .35 |
| 461 | Dave McKay | .07 |
| 462 | Jack Brohamer | .07 |
| 463 | Milt May | .07 |
| 464 | Adrian Devine | .07 |
| 465 | Bill Russell | .07 |
| 466 | Bob Molinaro | .07 |
| 467 | Dave Stieb | .60 |
| 468 | Johnny Wockenfuss | .07 |
| 469 | Jeff Leonard | .15 |
| 470 | Manny Trillo | .07 |
| 471 | Mike Vail | .07 |
| 472 | Dyar Miller | .07 |
| 473 | Jose Cardenal | .07 |
| 474 | Mike LaCoss | .07 |
| 475 | Buddy Bell | .20 |
| 476 | Jerry Koosman | .15 |
| 477 | Luis Gomez | .07 |
| 478 | Juan Eichelberger | .07 |
| 479 | Expos Rookies: B. Pate, Tim Raines, Roberto Ramos | 6.00 |
| 480 | Carlton Fisk | .40 |
| 481 | Bob Lacey | .07 |
| 482 | Jim Gantner | .07 |
| 483 | Mike Griffin | .07 |
| 484 | Max Venable | .07 |
| 485 | Garry Templeton | .20 |
| 486 | Marc Hill | .07 |
| 487 | Dewey Robinson | .07 |
| 488 | Damaso Garcia (R) | 1.00 |
| 489 | John Littlefield | .07 |
| 490 | Eddie Murray | 1.25 |
| 491 | Gordy Pladson | .07 |
| 492 | Barry Foote | .07 |
| 493 | Dan Quisenberry | .50 |
| 494 | Bob Walk | .07 |
| 495 | Dusty Baker | .12 |
| 496 | Paul Dade | .07 |
| 497 | Fred Norman | .07 |
| 498 | Pat Putnam | .07 |
| 499 | Frank Pastore | .07 |
| 500 | Jim Rice | .75 |
| 501 | Tim Foli | .07 |
| 502 | Giants Rookies: Chris Bourjos, Mike Rowland, A. Hargesheimer | .15 |
| 503 | Steve McCatty | .07 |
| 504 | Dale Murphy | 2.50 |
| 505 | Jason Thompson | .12 |
| 506 | Phil Huffman | .07 |
| 507 | Jamie Quirk | .07 |
| 508 | Rob Dressler | .07 |
| 509 | Pete Mackanin | .07 |
| 510 | Lee Mazzilli | .07 |
| 511 | Wayne Garland | .07 |
| 512 | Gary Thomasson | .07 |
| 513 | Frank LaCorte | .07 |
| 514 | George Riley | .07 |
| 515 | Robin Yount | .65 |
| 516 | Doug Bird | .07 |
| 517 | Richie Zisk | .07 |
| 518 | Grant Jackson | .07 |
| 519 | John Tamargo | .07 |
| 520 | Steve Stone | .07 |
| 521 | Sam Mejias | .07 |
| 522 | Mike Colbern | .07 |
| 523 | John Fulgham | .07 |
| 524 | Willie Aikens | .10 |
| 525 | Mike Torrez | .07 |
| 526 | Phillies Rookies: Marty Bystrom, Jay Loviglio, J. Wright | .25 |
| 527 | Danny Goodwin | .07 |
| 528 | Gary Matthews | .12 |
| 529 | Dave LaRoche | .07 |
| 530 | Steve Garvey | 1.00 |
| 531 | John Curtis | .07 |
| 532 | Bill Stein | .07 |
| 533 | Jesus Figueroa | .07 |
| 534 | Dave Smith | .07 |
| 535 | Omar Moreno | .07 |
| 536 | Bob Owchinko | .07 |
| 537 | Ron Hodges | .07 |
| 538 | Tom Griffin | .07 |

| NO. | PLAYER | MINT |
|---|---|---|
| 539 | Rodney Scott | .07 |
| 540 | Mike Schmidt | .75 |
| 541 | Steve Swisher | .07 |
| 542 | Larry Bradford | .07 |
| 543 | Terry Crowley | .07 |
| 544 | Rich Gale | .07 |
| 545 | Johnny Grubb | .07 |
| 546 | Paul Moskau | .07 |
| 547 | Mario Guerrero | .07 |
| 548 | Dave Goltz | .07 |
| 549 | Jerry Remy | .07 |
| 550 | Tommy John | .30 |
| 551 | Pirates Rookies: | 2.00 |
| | Vance Law, Pascual Perez | |
| | Tony Pena | |
| 552 | Steve Trout | .07 |
| 553 | Tim Blackwell | .07 |
| 554 | Bert Blyleven | .25 |
| 555 | Cecil Cooper | .30 |
| 556 | Jerry Mumphrey | .07 |
| 557 | Chris Knapp | .07 |
| 558 | Barry Bonnell | .07 |
| 559 | Willie Montanez | .07 |
| 560 | Joe Morgan | .35 |
| 561 | Dennis Littlejohn | .07 |
| 562 | Checklist No. 5 | .15 |
| 563 | Jim Kaat | .25 |
| 564 | Ron Hassey | .07 |
| 565 | Burt Hooton | .07 |
| 566 | Del Unser | .07 |
| 567 | Mark Bomback | .07 |
| 568 | Dave Revering | .07 |
| 569 | Al Williams | .07 |
| 570 | Ken Singleton | .12 |
| 571 | Todd Cruz | .07 |
| 572 | Jack Morris | .40 |
| 573 | Phil Garner | .07 |
| 574 | Bill Caudill | .15 |
| 575 | Tony Perez | .25 |
| 576 | Reggie Cleveland | .07 |
| 577 | Blue Jays Rookies: | .40 |
| | Luis Leal, Brian Miller, | |
| | Ken Schrom | |
| 578 | Bill Gullickson | .60 |
| 579 | Tim Flannery | .07 |
| 580 | Don Baylor | .30 |
| 581 | Roy Howell | .07 |
| 582 | Gaylord Perry | .40 |
| 583 | Larry Milbourne | .07 |
| 584 | Randy Lerch | .07 |

| NO. | PLAYER | MINT |
|---|---|---|
| 585 | Amos Otis | .12 |
| 586 | Silvio Martinez | .07 |
| 587 | Jeff Newman | .07 |
| 588 | Gary Lavelle | .07 |
| 589 | Lamar Johnson | .07 |
| 590 | Bruce Sutter | .50 |
| 591 | John Lowenstein | .07 |
| 592 | Steve Comer | .07 |
| 593 | Steve Kemp | .15 |
| 594 | Preston Hanna | .07 |
| 595 | Butch Hobson | .07 |
| 596 | Jerry Augustine | .07 |
| 597 | Rafael Landestoy | .07 |
| 598 | George Vukovich | .07 |
| 599 | Dennis Kinney | .07 |
| 600 | Johnny Bench | .60 |
| 601 | Don Aase | .07 |
| 602 | Bobby Murcer | .15 |
| 603 | John Verhoeven | .07 |
| 604 | Rob Picciolo | .07 |
| 605 | Don Sutton | .25 |
| 606 | Reds Rookies: | .15 |
| | Bruce Berenyi, Geoff | |
| | Combe, P. Householder | |
| 607 | Dave Palmer | .07 |
| 608 | Greg Pryor | .07 |
| 609 | Lynn McGlothen | .07 |
| 610 | Darrell Porter | .07 |
| 611 | Rick Matula | .07 |
| 612 | Duane Kuiper | .07 |
| 613 | Jim Anderson | .07 |
| 614 | Dave Rozema | .07 |
| 615 | Rick Dempsey | .07 |
| 616 | Rick Wise | .07 |
| 617 | Craig Reynolds | .07 |
| 618 | John Milner | .07 |
| 619 | Steve Henderson | .07 |
| 620 | Dennis Eckersley | .07 |
| 621 | Tom Donohue | .07 |
| 622 | Randy Moffitt | .07 |
| 623 | Sal Bando | .07 |
| 624 | Bob Welch | .12 |
| 625 | Bill Buckner | .15 |
| 626 | Tigers Rookies: | .20 |
| | D. Steffen, Jerry Ujdur, | |
| | Roger Weaver | |
| 627 | Luis Tiant | .12 |
| 628 | Vic Correll | .07 |
| 629 | Tony Armas | .20 |
| 630 | Steve Carlton | .75 |

| NO. | PLAYER | MINT |
|---|---|---|
| 631 | Ron Jackson | .07 |
| 632 | Alan Bannister | .07 |
| 633 | Bill Lee | .07 |
| 634 | Doug Flynn | .07 |
| 635 | Bobby Bonds | .12 |
| 636 | Al Hrabosky | .07 |
| 637 | Jerry Narron | .07 |
| 638 | Checklist No. 6 | .15 |
| 639 | Carney Lansford | .20 |
| 640 | Dave Parker | .50 |
| 641 | Mark Belanger | .07 |
| 642 | Vern Ruhle | .07 |
| 643 | Lloyd Moseby (R) | 2.00 |
| 644 | Ramon Aviles | .07 |
| 645 | Rick Reuschel | .07 |
| 646 | Marvis Foley | .07 |
| 647 | Dick Drago | .07 |
| 648 | Darrell Evans | .15 |
| 649 | Manny Sarmiento | .07 |
| 650 | Bucky Dent | .12 |
| 651 | Pedro Guerrero | 1.00 |
| 652 | John Montague | .07 |
| 653 | Bill Fahey | .07 |
| 654 | Ray Burris | .07 |
| 655 | Dan Driessen | .07 |
| 656 | Jon Matlack | .07 |
| 657 | Mike Cubbage | .07 |
| 658 | Milt Wilcox | .07 |
| 659 | Brewers Rookies: | .07 |
| | Ned Yost, J. Flinn, | |
| | Ed Romero | |
| 660 | Gary Carter | 1.00 |
| 661 | Orioles Team | .20 |
| 662 | Red Sox Team | .20 |
| 663 | Angels Team | .20 |
| 664 | White Sox Team | .20 |
| 665 | Indians Team | .20 |
| 666 | Tigers Team | .25 |
| 667 | Royals Team | .20 |
| 668 | Brewers Team | .20 |
| 669 | Twins Team | .20 |
| 670 | Yankees Team | .25 |
| 671 | A's Team | .20 |
| 672 | Mariners Team | .15 |
| 673 | Rangers Team | .20 |
| 674 | Blue Jays Team | .20 |
| 675 | Braves Team | .20 |
| 676 | Cubs Team | .20 |
| 677 | Reds Team | .20 |
| 678 | Astros Team | .20 |

| NO. | PLAYER | MINT |
|---|---|---|
| 679 | Dodgers Team | .25 |
| 680 | Expos Team | .15 |
| 681 | Mets Team | .20 |
| 682 | Phillies Team | .20 |
| 683 | Pirates Team | .20 |
| 684 | Cardinals Team | .20 |
| 685 | Padres Team | .20 |
| 686 | Giants Team | .20 |
| 687 | Jeff Jones | .10 |
| 688 | Kiko Garcia | .07 |
| 689 | Red Sox Rookies: | .75 |
| | Bruce Hurst, Reid Nichols, | |
| | Keith MacWhorter | |
| 690 | Bob Watson | .07 |
| 691 | Dick Ruthven | .07 |
| 692 | Lenny Randle | .07 |
| 693 | Steve Howe (R) | .30 |
| 694 | Bud Harrelson | .07 |
| 695 | Kent Tekulve | .07 |
| 696 | Alan Ashby | .07 |
| 697 | Rick Waits | .07 |
| 698 | Mike Jorgensen | .07 |
| 699 | Glenn Abbott | .07 |
| 700 | George Brett | 2.00 |
| 701 | Joe Rudi | .07 |
| 702 | George Medich | .07 |
| 703 | Alvis Woods | .07 |
| 704 | Bill Travers | .07 |
| 705 | Ted Simmons | .25 |
| 706 | Dave Ford | .07 |
| 707 | Dave Cash | .07 |
| 708 | Doyle Alexander | .07 |
| 709 | Alan Trammell | .12 |
| 710 | Ron LeFlore | .07 |
| 711 | Joe Ferguson | .07 |
| 712 | Bill Bonham | .07 |
| 713 | Bill North | .07 |
| 714 | Pete Redfern | .07 |
| 715 | Bill Madlock | .30 |
| 716 | Glenn Borgmann | .07 |
| 717 | Jim Barr | .07 |
| 718 | Larry Biittner | .07 |
| 719 | Sparky Lyle | .12 |
| 720 | Fred Lynn | .35 |
| 721 | Toby Harrah | .07 |
| 722 | Joe Niekro | .12 |
| 723 | Bruce Bochte | .07 |
| 724 | Lou Piniella | .15 |
| 725 | Steve Rogers | .12 |
| 726 | Rick Monday | .12 |

## 1981 Topps Traded....Complete Set of 132 Cards—Value $25.00

This was the first Topps "traded" set issued since 1976. It updates the main 1981 card set with players who had changed teams during the season and rookies who joined their teams early in the season. The first card in the traded set is numbered 727. It begins where the main set ends: The complete set was packaged in a printed box and only distributed through card hobby dealers.

| NO. | PLAYER | MINT |
|---|---|---|
| 727 | Danny Ainge (RR) | .40 |
| 728 | Doyle Alexander | .08 |
| 729 | Gary Alexander | .08 |
| 730 | Billy Almon | .08 |
| 731 | Joaquin Andujar | .20 |
| 732 | Bob Bailor | .08 |
| 733 | Juan Beniquez | .12 |

| NO. | PLAYER | MINT |
|---|---|---|
| 734 | Dave Bergman | .08 |
| 735 | Tony Bernazard | .08 |
| 736 | Larry Biittner | .08 |
| 737 | Doug Bird | .08 |
| 738 | Bert Blyleven | .25 |
| 739 | Mark Bomback | .08 |
| 740 | Bobby Bonds | .10 |

| NO. | PLAYER | MINT |
|---|---|---|
| 741 | Rick Bosetti | .08 |
| 742 | Hubie Brooks | 1.25 |
| 743 | Rick Burleson | .10 |
| 744 | Ray Burris | .08 |
| 745 | Jeff Burroughs | .10 |
| 746 | Enos Cabell | .08 |
| 747 | Ken Clay | .08 |

| NO. | PLAYER | MINT |
|---|---|---|
| 748 | Mark Clear | .08 |
| 749 | Larry Cox | .08 |
| 750 | Hector Cruz | .08 |
| 751 | Victor Cruz | .08 |
| 752 | Mike Cubbage | .08 |
| 753 | Dick Davis | .08 |
| 754 | Brian Doyle | .08 |

# 1981 Topps Traded (Continued)

| NO. | PLAYER | MINT |
|---|---|---|
| 755 | Dick Drago | .08 |
| 756 | Leon Durham | 1.25 |
| 757 | Jim Dwyer | .08 |
| 758 | Dave Edwards | .08 |
| 759 | Jim Essian | .08 |
| 760 | Bill Fahey | .08 |
| 761 | Rollie Ringers | .75 |
| 762 | Carlton Fisk | .60 |
| 763 | Barry Foote | .08 |
| 764 | Ken Forsch | .08 |
| 765 | Kiko Garcia | .08 |
| 766 | Cesar Geronimo | .08 |
| 767 | Gary Gray | .08 |
| 768 | Mickey Hatcher | .08 |
| 769 | Steve Henderson | .12 |
| 770 | Marc Hill | .08 |
| 771 | Butch Hobson | .08 |
| 772 | Rick Honeycutt | .12 |
| 773 | Roy Howell | .08 |
| 774 | Mike Ivie | .08 |
| 775 | Roy Lee Jackson | .08 |
| 776 | Cliff Johnson | .08 |
| 777 | Randy Jones | .10 |
| 778 | Ruppert Jones | .08 |
| 779 | Mick Kelleher | .08 |
| 780 | Terry Kennedy | .30 |

| NO. | PLAYER | MINT |
|---|---|---|
| 781 | Dave Kingman | .30 |
| 782 | Bob Knepper | .12 |
| 783 | Ken Kravec | .08 |
| 784 | Bob Lacey | .08 |
| 785 | Dennis Lamp | .08 |
| 786 | Rafael Landestoy | .08 |
| 787 | Ken Landreaux | .12 |
| 788 | Carney Lansford | .40 |
| 789 | Dave LaRoche | .08 |
| 790 | Joe LeFebvre | .08 |
| 791 | Ron LeFlore | .12 |
| 792 | Randy Lerch | .08 |
| 793 | Sixto Lezcano | .12 |
| 794 | John Littlefield | .08 |
| 795 | Mike Lum | .08 |
| 796 | Greg Luzinski | .30 |
| 797 | Fred Lynn | .65 |
| 798 | Jerry Martin | .08 |
| 799 | Buck Martinez | .08 |
| 800 | Gary Matthews | .12 |
| 801 | Mario Mendoza | .08 |
| 802 | Larry Milbourne | .08 |
| 803 | Rick Miller | .08 |
| 804 | John Montefusco | .12 |
| 805 | Jerry Morales | .08 |
| 806 | Jose Morales | .08 |

| NO. | PLAYER | MINT |
|---|---|---|
| 807 | Joe Morgan | 1.25 |
| 808 | Jerry Mumphrey | .12 |
| 809 | Gene Nelson (RR) | .25 |
| 810 | Ed Ott | .08 |
| 811 | Bob Owchinko | .08 |
| 812 | Gaylord Perry | .85 |
| 813 | Mike Phillips | .08 |
| 814 | Darrell Porter | .12 |
| 815 | Mike Proly | .08 |
| 816 | Tim Raines | 4.00 |
| 817 | Lenny Randle | .08 |
| 818 | Doug Rau | .08 |
| 819 | Jeff Reardon | .35 |
| 820 | Ken Reitz | .08 |
| 821 | Steve Renko | .08 |
| 822 | Rick Reuschel | .12 |
| 823 | Dave Revering | .08 |
| 824 | Dave Roberts | .08 |
| 825 | Leon Roberts | .08 |
| 826 | Joe Rudi | .12 |
| 827 | Kevin Saucier | .08 |
| 828 | Tony Scott | .08 |
| 829 | Bob Shirley | .08 |
| 830 | Ted Simmons | .40 |
| 831 | Lary Sorensen | .08 |
| 832 | Jim Spencer | .08 |

| NO. | PLAYER | MINT |
|---|---|---|
| 833 | Harry Spilman | .08 |
| 834 | Fred Stanley | .08 |
| 835 | Rusty Staub | .25 |
| 836 | Bill Stein | .08 |
| 837 | Joe Strain | .08 |
| 838 | Bruce Sutter | 1.00 |
| 839 | Don Sutton | .75 |
| 840 | Steve Swisher | .08 |
| 841 | Frank Tanana | .08 |
| 842 | Gene Tenace | .08 |
| 843 | Jason Thompson | .15 |
| 844 | Dickie Thon | .25 |
| 845 | Bill Travers | .08 |
| 846 | Tom Underwood | .08 |
| 847 | John Urrea | .08 |
| 848 | Mike Vail | .08 |
| 849 | Ellis Valentine | .12 |
| 850 | Fernando Valenzuela | 5.00 |
| 851 | Pete Vuckovich | .12 |
| 852 | Mark Wagner | .08 |
| 853 | Bob Walk | .08 |
| 854 | Claudell Washington | .12 |
| 855 | Dave Winfield | 2.00 |
| 856 | Geoff Zahn | .08 |
| 857 | Richie Zisk | .12 |
| 858 | Traded Checklist | .20 |

# 1982 Topps....Complete Set of 792 Cards—Value $60.00

The complete set was increased to 792 cards. Double printed cards were eliminated (66 double prints were in each set from 1978 to 1981). Includes the rookie cards of Cal Ripken, Jesse Barfield, Kent Hrbek and Steve Sax. Card 342 exists with the *autograph* deleted.

| NO. | PLAYER | MINT |
|---|---|---|
| 1 | Highlights—Carlton | .40 |
| | Sets NL Strikeout Record | |
| 2 | Highlights—Davis | .10 |
| | Fans 8 Straight | |
| 3 | Highlights—Raines | .15 |
| | Swipes 71 Bases, Rookie | |
| 4 | Highlights—Rose | .60 |
| | Sets NL Career Hit Mark | |
| 5 | Highlights—Ryan | .25 |
| | 5th Career No-Hitter | |
| 6 | Highlights—Valenzuela | .25 |
| | 8 Rookie Shutouts | |
| 7 | Scott Sanderson | .07 |
| 8 | Rich Dauer | .07 |
| 9 | Ron Guidry | .30 |
| 10 | Guidry (Action) | .15 |
| 11 | Gary Alexander | .07 |
| 12 | Moose Haas | .07 |
| 13 | Lamar Johnson | .07 |
| 14 | Steve Howe | .07 |
| 15 | Ellis Valentine | .07 |
| 16 | Steve Comer | .07 |
| 17 | Darrell Evans | .15 |
| 18 | Fernando Arroyo | .07 |
| 19 | Ernie Whitt | .07 |
| 20 | Garry Maddox | .07 |
| 21 | Orioles Rookies: | 10.00 |
| | Bob Bonner, Cal Ripken, | |
| | Jeff Schneider | |
| 22 | Jim Beattie | .07 |
| 23 | Willie Hernandez | .35 |
| 24 | Dave Frost | .07 |
| 25 | Jerry Remy | .07 |
| 26 | Jorge Orta | .07 |

| NO. | PLAYER | MINT |
|---|---|---|
| 27 | Tom Herr | .25 |
| 28 | John Urrea | .07 |
| 29 | Dwayne Murphy | .07 |
| 30 | Tom Seaver | .50 |
| 31 | Seaver (Action) | .25 |
| 32 | Gene Garber | .07 |
| 33 | Jerry Morales | .07 |
| 34 | Joe Sambito | .07 |
| 35 | Willie Aikens | .10 |
| 36 | Rangers Leaders: | .15 |
| | Al Oliver, George Medich | |
| 37 | Dan Graham | .07 |
| 38 | Charlie Lea | .07 |
| 39 | Lou Whitaker | .40 |
| 40 | Dave Parker | .35 |
| 41 | Parker (Action) | .20 |
| 42 | Rick Sofield | .07 |
| 43 | Mike Cubbage | .07 |
| 44 | Britt Burns | .10 |
| 45 | Rick Cerone | .07 |
| 46 | Jerry Augustine | .07 |
| 47 | Jeff Leonard | .07 |
| 48 | Bobby Castillo | .07 |
| 49 | Alvis Woods | .07 |
| 50 | Buddy Bell | .15 |
| 51 | Cubs Rookies: | .60 |
| | Jay Howell, C. Lezcano, | |
| | Ty Waller | |
| 52 | Larry Andersen | .07 |
| 53 | Greg Gross | .07 |
| 54 | Ron Hassey | .07 |
| 55 | Rick Burleson | .07 |
| 56 | Mark Littell | .07 |
| 57 | Craig Reynolds | .07 |

| NO. | PLAYER | MINT |
|---|---|---|
| 58 | John D'Acquisto | .07 |
| 59 | Rich Gedman (R) | 1.00 |
| 60 | Tony Armas | .25 |
| 61 | Tommy Boggs | .07 |
| 62 | Mike Tyson | .07 |
| 63 | Mario Soto | .15 |
| 64 | Lynn Jones | .07 |
| 65 | Terry Kennedy | .15 |
| 66 | Astros Leaders: | .15 |
| | Art Howe, Nolan Ryan | |
| 67 | Rich Gale | .07 |
| 68 | Roy Howell | .07 |
| 69 | Al Williams | .07 |
| 70 | Tim Raines | 1.00 |
| 71 | Roy Lee Jackson | .07 |
| 72 | Rick Auerbach | .07 |
| 73 | Buddy Solomon | .07 |
| 74 | Bob Clark | .07 |
| 75 | Tommy John | .25 |
| 76 | Greg Pryor | .07 |
| 77 | Miguel Dilone | .07 |
| 78 | George Medich | .07 |
| 79 | Bob Bailor | .07 |
| 80 | Jim Palmer | .35 |
| 81 | Palmer (Action) | .15 |
| 82 | Bob Welch | .10 |
| 83 | Yankees Rookies: | 1.00 |
| | S. Balboni, A. Robertson, | |
| | A. McGaffigan | |
| 84 | Rennie Stennett | .07 |
| 85 | Lynn McGlothen | .07 |
| 86 | Dane Iorg | .07 |
| 87 | Matt Keough | .07 |
| 88 | Biff Pocoroba | .07 |

| NO. | PLAYER | MINT |
|---|---|---|
| 89 | Steve Henderson | .07 |
| 90 | Nolan Ryan | .50 |
| 91 | Carney Lansford | .15 |
| 92 | Brad Havens | .07 |
| 93 | Larry Hisle | .07 |
| 94 | Andy Hassler | .07 |
| 95 | Ozzie Smith | .15 |
| 96 | Royals Leaders: | .20 |
| | G. Brett, L. Gura | |
| 97 | Paul Moskau | .07 |
| 98 | Terry Bulling | .07 |
| 99 | Barry Bonnell | .07 |
| 100 | Mike Schmidt | 1.00 |
| 101 | Schmidt (Action) | .40 |
| 102 | Dan Briggs | .07 |
| 103 | Bob Lacey | .07 |
| 104 | Rance Mulliniks | .07 |
| 105 | Kirk Gibson | .60 |
| 106 | Enrique Romo | .07 |
| 107 | Wayne Krenchicki | .07 |
| 108 | Bob Sykes | .07 |
| 109 | Dave Revering | .07 |
| 110 | Carlton Fisk | .30 |
| 111 | Fisk (Action) | .15 |
| 112 | Billy Sample | .07 |
| 113 | Steve McCatty | .07 |
| 114 | Ken Landreaux | .07 |
| 115 | Gaylord Perry | .25 |
| 116 | Jim Wohlford | .07 |
| 117 | Rawly Eastwick | .07 |
| 118 | Expos Rookies: | .50 |
| | Brad Mills, Terry Francona, | |
| | Bryn Smith | |
| 119 | Joe Pittman | .07 |

| NO. PLAYER | MINT |
|---|---|
| 120 Gary Lucas | .07 |
| 121 Ed Lynch | .20 |
| 122 Jamie Easterly | .07 |
| 123 Danny Goodwin | .07 |
| 124 Reid Nichols | .07 |
| 125 Danny Ainge | .07 |
| 126 Braves Leaders: | .15 |
| C. Washington, Rick Mahler | |
| 127 Lonnie Smith | .12 |
| 128 Frank Pastore | .07 |
| 129 Checklist No. 1 | .15 |
| 130 Julio Cruz | .07 |
| 131 Stan Bahnsen | .07 |
| 132 Lee May | .07 |
| 133 Pat Underwood | .07 |
| 134 Dan Ford | .07 |
| 135 Adny Rincon | .07 |
| 136 Lenn Sakata | .07 |
| 137 George Cappuzzello | .07 |
| 138 Tony Pena | .25 |
| 139 Jeff Jones | .07 |
| 140 Ron Leflore | .07 |
| 141 Indians Rookies: | 1.50 |
| Chris Bando, Von Hayes, Tom Brennan | |
| 142 Dave LaRoche | .07 |
| 143 Mookie Wilson | .15 |
| 144 Fred Breining | .12 |
| 145 Bob Horner | .40 |
| 146 Mike Griffin | .07 |
| 147 Denny Walling | .07 |
| 148 Mickey Klutts | .07 |
| 149 Pat Putnam | .07 |
| 150 Ted Simmons | .15 |
| 151 Dave Edwards | .07 |
| 152 Ramon Aviles | .07 |
| 153 Roger Erickson | .07 |
| 154 Dennis Werth | .07 |
| 155 Otto Velez | .07 |
| 156 A's Leaders: | .15 |
| Rickey Henderson, Steve McCatty | |
| 157 Steve Crawford | .07 |
| 158 Brian Downing | .07 |
| 159 Larry Biittner | .07 |
| 160 Luis Tiant | .10 |
| 161 Batting Leaders: | .15 |
| B. Madlock, C. Lansford | |
| 162 Home Run Leaders: | .25 |
| Bobby Grich, Mike Schmidt, T. Armas, Dwight Evans, Eddie Murray | |
| 163 RBI Leaders: | .25 |
| M. Schmidt, E. Murray | |
| 164 Stolen Base Leaders: | .25 |
| R. Henderson, T. Raines | |
| 165 Victory Leaders: | .25 |
| Tom Seaver, D. Martinez, Steve McCatty, Pete Vuckovich, Jack Morris | |
| 166 Strikeout Leaders: | .20 |
| F. Valenzuela, L. Barker | |
| 167 ERA Leaders: | .20 |
| Steve McCatty, Nolan Ryan | |
| 168 Leading Relievers: | .25 |
| Bruce Sutter, Rollie Fingers | |
| 169 Charlie Leibrandt | .10 |
| 170 Jim Bibby | .07 |
| 171 Giants Rookies: | 1.00 |
| Bob Tufts, Bob Brenly, Chili Davis | |
| 172 Bill Gullickson | .07 |
| 173 Jamie Quirk | .07 |
| 174 Dave Ford | .07 |
| 175 Jerry Mumphrey | .07 |
| 176 Dewey Robinson | .07 |
| 177 John Ellis | .07 |
| 178 Dyar Miller | .07 |
| 179 Steve Garvey | .60 |
| 180 Garvey (Action) | .30 |
| 181 Silvio Martinez | .07 |
| 182 Larry Herndon | .07 |
| 183 Mike Proly | .07 |
| 184 Mick Kelleher | .07 |
| 185 Phil Niekro | .25 |
| 186 Cardinals Leaders: | .15 |
| K. Hernandez, B. Forsch | |
| 187 Jeff Newman | .07 |
| 188 Randy Martz | .07 |
| 189 Glenn Hoffman | .07 |
| 190 J.R. Richard | .10 |
| 191 Tim Wallach (R) | .80 |
| 192 Broderick Perkins | .07 |
| 193 Darrell Jackson | .07 |
| 194 Mike Vail | .07 |
| 195 Paul Molitor | .25 |
| 196 Willie Upshaw | .25 |
| 197 Shane Rawley | .07 |
| 198 Chris Speier | .07 |
| 199 Don Aase | .07 |
| 200 George Brett | 1.50 |
| 201 Brett (Action) | .60 |
| 202 Rick Manning | .07 |
| 203 Blue Jays Rookies: | 3.50 |
| Jesse Barfield, Brian Milner, Boomer Wells | |
| 204 Gray Roenicke | .07 |
| 205 Neil Allen | .07 |
| 206 Tony Bernazard | .07 |
| 207 Rod Scurry | .07 |
| 208 Bobby Murcer | .12 |
| 209 Gary Lavelle | .07 |
| 210 Keith Hernandez | .50 |
| 211 Dan Petry | .25 |
| 212 Mario Mendoza | .07 |
| 213 Dave Stewart | .20 |
| 214 Brian Asselstine | .07 |
| 215 Mike Krukow | .07 |
| 216 White Sox Leaders: | .15 |
| Chet Lemon, Dennis Lamp | |
| 217 Bo McLaughlin | .07 |
| 218 Dave Roberts | .07 |
| 219 John Curtis | .07 |
| 220 Manny Trillo | .07 |
| 221 Jim Slaton | .07 |
| 222 Butch Wynegar | .07 |
| 223 Lloyd Moseby | .25 |
| 224 Bruce Bochte | .07 |
| 225 Mike Torrez | .07 |
| 226 Checklist No. 2 | .15 |
| 227 Ray Burris | .07 |
| 228 Sam Mejias | .07 |
| 229 Geoff Zahn | .07 |
| 230 Willie Wilson | .25 |
| 231 Phillies Rookies: | .60 |
| Ozzie Virgil, Bob Dernier, Mark Davis | |
| 232 Terry Crowley | .07 |
| 233 Duane Kuiper | .07 |
| 234 Ron Hodges | .07 |
| 235 Mike Easler | .10 |
| 236 John Martin | .07 |
| 237 Rusty Kuntz | .07 |
| 238 Kevin Saucier | .07 |
| 239 Jon Matlack | .07 |
| 240 Bucky Dent | .10 |
| 241 Dent (Action) | .07 |
| 242 Milt May | .07 |
| 243 Bob Owchinko | .07 |
| 244 Rufino Linares | .07 |
| 245 Ken Reitz | .07 |
| 246 Mets Leaders: | .20 |
| Hubie Brooks, Mike Scott | |
| 247 Pedro Guerrero | .50 |
| 248 Frank LaCorte | .07 |
| 249 Tim Flannery | .07 |
| 250 Tug McGraw | .10 |
| 251 Fred Lynn | .35 |
| 252 Lynn (Action) | .20 |
| 253 Chuck Baker | .07 |
| 254 Jorge Bell (R) | 3.50 |
| 255 Tony Perez | .20 |
| 256 Perez (Action) | .12 |
| 257 Larry Harlow | .07 |
| 258 Bo Diaz | .10 |
| 259 Rodney Scott | .07 |
| 260 Bruce Sutter | .35 |
| 261 Tigers Rookies: | .20 |
| Howard Bailey, M. Castillo, Dave Rucker | |
| 262 Doug Bair | .07 |
| 263 Victor Cruz | .07 |
| 264 Dan Quisenberry | .30 |
| 265 Al Bumbry | .07 |
| 266 Rick Leach | .07 |
| 267 Kurt Bevacqua | .07 |
| 268 Rickey Keeton | .07 |
| 269 Jim Essian | .07 |
| 270 Rusty Staub | .10 |
| 271 Larry Bradford | .07 |
| 272 Bump Wills | .07 |
| 273 Doug Bird | .07 |
| 274 Bob Ojeda (R) | 1.25 |
| 275 Bob Watson | .07 |
| 276 Angels Leaders: | .20 |
| Ken Forsch, Rod Carew | |
| 277 Terry Puhl | .07 |
| 278 John Littlefield | .07 |
| 279 Bill Russell | .07 |
| 280 Ben Oglivie | .10 |
| 281 John Verhoeven | .07 |
| 282 Ken Macha | .07 |
| 283 Brian Allard | .07 |
| 284 Bob Grich | .10 |
| 285 Sparky Lyle | .10 |
| 286 Bill Fahey | .07 |
| 287 Alan Bannister | .07 |
| 288 Garry Templeton | .15 |
| 289 Bob Stanley | .07 |
| 290 Ken Singleton | .15 |
| 291 Pirates Rookies: | 1.00 |
| Vance Law, Bob Long, Johnny Ray | |
| 292 David Palmer | .07 |
| 293 Rob Picciolo | .07 |
| 294 Mike LaCoss | .07 |
| 295 Jason Thompson | .10 |
| 296 Bob Walk | .07 |
| 297 Clint Hurdle | .07 |
| 298 Danny Darwin | .07 |
| 299 Steve Trout | .07 |
| 300 Reggie Jackson | .75 |
| 301 Jackson (Action) | .40 |
| 302 Doug Flynn | .07 |
| 303 Bill Caudill | .10 |
| 304 Johnnie LeMaster | .07 |
| 305 Don Sutton | .20 |
| 306 Sutton (Action) | .10 |
| 307 Randy Bass | .07 |
| 308 Charlie Moore | .07 |
| 309 Pete Redfern | .07 |
| 310 Mike Hargrove | .10 |
| 311 Dodgers Leaders: | .20 |
| Dusty Baker, Burt Hooton | |
| 312 Lenny Randle | .07 |
| 313 John Harris | .07 |
| 314 Buck Martinez | .07 |
| 315 Burt Hooten | .07 |
| 316 Steve Braun | .07 |
| 317 Dick Ruthven | .07 |
| 318 Mike Heath | .07 |
| 319 Dave Rozema | .07 |
| 320 Chris Chambliss | .10 |
| 321 Chambliss (Action) | .07 |
| 322 Garry Hancock | .07 |
| 323 Bill Lee | .07 |
| 324 Steve Dillard | .07 |
| 325 Jose Cruz | .15 |
| 326 Pete Falcone | .07 |
| 327 Joe Nolan | .07 |
| 328 Ed Farmer | .07 |
| 329 U.L. Washington | .07 |
| 330 Rick Wise | .07 |
| 331 Benny Ayala | .07 |
| 332 Don Robinson | .07 |
| 333 Brewers Rookies: | .20 |
| Frank DiPino, M. Edwards, Chuck Porter | |
| 334 Aurelio Rodriguez | .07 |
| 335 Jim Sundberg | .07 |
| 336 Mariners Leaders: | .15 |
| G. Abbott, T. Paciorek | |
| 337 Pete Rose (AS) | .75 |
| 338 Dave Lopes (AS) | .10 |
| 339 Mike Schmidt (AS) | .45 |
| 340 Dave Concepcion (AS) | .15 |
| 341 Andre Dawson (AS) | .20 |
| 342 George Foster (AS) | .25 |
| 342 George Foster | 3.00 |
| (autograph deleted) | |
| 343 Dave Parker (AS) | .25 |
| 344 Gary Carter (AS) | .25 |
| 345 F. Valenzuela (AS) | .25 |
| 346 Tom Seaver (AS) | .25 |
| 347 Bruce Sutter (AS) | .15 |
| 348 Derrel Thomas | .07 |
| 349 George Frazier | .07 |
| 350 Thad Bosley | .07 |
| 351 Reds Rookies: | .15 |
| Geoff Coumbe, Scott Brown, P. Householder | |
| 352 Dick Davis | .07 |
| 353 Jack O'Connor | .07 |
| 354 Roberto Ramos | .07 |
| 355 Dwight Evans | .15 |
| 356 Denny Lewallyn | .07 |
| 357 Butch Hobson | .07 |
| 358 Mike Parrott | .07 |
| 359 Jim Dwyer | .07 |
| 360 Len Barker | .07 |
| 361 Rafael Landestoy | .07 |
| 362 Jim Wright | .07 |
| (wrong autograph) | |
| 363 Bob Molinaro | .07 |
| 364 Doyle Alexander | .07 |
| 365 Bill Madlock | .25 |
| 366 Padres Leaders: | .15 |
| L. Salazar, J. Eichelberger | |
| 367 Jim Kaat | .15 |
| 368 Alex Trevino | .07 |
| 369 Champ Summers | .07 |
| 370 Mike Norris | .07 |
| 371 Jerry Don Gleaton | .07 |
| 372 Luis Gomez | .07 |
| 373 Gene Nelson | .10 |
| 374 Tim Blackwell | .07 |
| 375 Dusty Baker | .12 |
| 376 Chris Welsh | .07 |
| 377 Kiko Garcia | .07 |
| 378 Mike Caldwell | .07 |
| 379 Rob Wilfong | .07 |
| 380 Dave Stieb | .35 |
| 381 Red Sox Rookies: | .20 |
| D. Schmidt, Julio Valdez, Bruce Hurst | |
| 382 Joe Simpson | .07 |
| 383 Pascual Perez | .10 |
| 384 Keith Moreland | .07 |
| 385 Ken Forsch | .07 |
| 386 Jerry White | .07 |
| 387 Tom Veryzer | .07 |
| 388 Joe Rudi | .07 |
| 389 George Vukovich | .07 |
| 390 Eddie Murray | 1.00 |
| 391 Dave Tobik | .07 |
| 392 Rick Bosetti | .07 |
| 393 Al Hrabosky | .07 |
| 394 Checklist No. 3 | .12 |
| 395 Omar Moreno | .10 |
| 396 Twins Leaders: | .15 |
| John Castino, F. Arroyo | |
| 397 Ken Brett | .07 |
| 398 Mike Squires | .07 |
| 399 Pat Zachry | .07 |
| 400 Johnny Bench | .60 |
| 401 Bench (Action) | .35 |
| 402 Bill Stein | .07 |
| 403 Jim Tracy | .07 |
| 404 Dickie Thon | .10 |
| 405 Rick Reuschel | .07 |
| 406 Al Holland | .07 |
| 407 Danny Boone | .07 |
| 408 Ed Romero | .07 |
| 409 Don Cooper | .07 |
| 410 Ron Cey | .15 |
| 411 Cey (Action) | .10 |
| 412 Luis Leal | .07 |
| 413 Dan Meyer | .07 |
| 414 Elias Sosa | .07 |
| 415 Don Baylor | .15 |

| NO. | PLAYER | MINT |
|---|---|---|
| 416 | Marty Bystrom | .07 |
| 417 | Pat Kelly | .07 |
| 418 | Rangers Rookies: John Butcher, B. Johnson, Dave Schmidt | .15 |
| 419 | Steve Stone | .10 |
| 420 | George Hendrick | .10 |
| 421 | Mark Clear | .07 |
| 422 | Cliff Johnson | .07 |
| 423 | Stan Papi | .07 |
| 424 | Bruce Benedict | .07 |
| 425 | John Candelaria | .10 |
| 426 | Orioles Leaders: Eddie Murray, S. Stewart | .15 |
| 427 | Ron Oester | .07 |
| 428 | LaMarr Hoyt | .15 |
| 429 | John Wathan | .07 |
| 430 | Vida Blue | .10 |
| 431 | Blue (Action) | .07 |
| 432 | Mike Scott | .07 |
| 433 | Alan Ashby | .07 |
| 434 | Joe LeFebvre | .07 |
| 435 | Robin Yount | .60 |
| 436 | Joe Strain | .07 |
| 437 | Juan Berenguer | .07 |
| 438 | Pete Mackanin | .07 |
| 439 | Dave Righetti (R) | 1.50 |
| 440 | Jeff Burroughs | .07 |
| 441 | Astros Rookies: Danny Heep, Billy Smith, Bobby Sprowl | .15 |
| 442 | Bruce Kison | .07 |
| 443 | Mark Wagner | .07 |
| 444 | Terry Forster | .10 |
| 445 | Larry Parrish | .10 |
| 446 | Wayne Garland | .07 |
| 447 | Darrell Porter | .12 |
| 448 | Porter (Action) | .07 |
| 449 | Luis Aguayo | .07 |
| 450 | Jack Morris | .50 |
| 451 | Ed Miller | .07 |
| 452 | Lee Smith (R) | .70 |
| 453 | Art Howe | .07 |
| 454 | Rick Langford | .07 |
| 455 | Tom Burgmeier | .07 |
| 456 | Cubs Leaders: R. Martz, Bill Buckner | .15 |
| 457 | Tim Stoddard | .07 |
| 458 | Willie Montanez | .07 |
| 459 | Bruce Berenyi | .07 |
| 460 | Jack Clark | .35 |
| 461 | Rich Dotson | .10 |
| 462 | Dave Chalk | .07 |
| 463 | Jim Kern | .07 |
| 464 | Juan Bonilla | .07 |
| 465 | Lee Mazzilli | .07 |
| 466 | Randy Lerch | .07 |
| 467 | Mickey Hatcher | .07 |
| 468 | Floyd Bannister | .10 |
| 469 | Ed Ott | .07 |
| 470 | John Mayberry | .07 |
| 471 | Royals Rookies: Mike Jones, Atlee Hammaker, Darryl Motley | .50 |
| 472 | Oscar Gamble | .07 |
| 473 | Mike Stanton | .07 |
| 474 | Ken Oberkfell | .07 |
| 475 | Alan Trammell | .50 |
| 476 | Brian Kingman | .07 |
| 477 | Steve Yeager | .10 |
| 478 | Ray Searage | .10 |
| 479 | Rowland Office | .07 |
| 480 | Steve Carlton | .60 |
| 481 | Carlton (Action) | .30 |
| 482 | Glenn Hubbard | .07 |
| 483 | Gary Woods | .07 |
| 484 | Ivan DeJesus | .07 |
| 485 | Kent Tekulve | .10 |
| 486 | Yankees Leaders: J. Mumphrey, Tommy John | .20 |
| 487 | Bob McClure | .07 |
| 488 | Ron Jackson | .07 |
| 489 | Rick Dempsey | .07 |
| 490 | Dennis Eckersley | .07 |
| 491 | Checklist No. 4 | .15 |
| 492 | Joe Price | .07 |
| 493 | Chet Lemon | .10 |
| 494 | Hubie Brooks | .12 |
| 495 | Dennis Leonard | .07 |
| 496 | Johnny Grubb | .07 |
| 497 | Jim Anderson | .07 |
| 498 | Dave Bergman | .07 |
| 499 | Paul Mirabella | .07 |
| 500 | Rod Carew | .60 |
| 501 | Carew (Action) | .30 |
| 502 | Braves Rookies: Steve Bedrosian, B. Butler, Larry Owen | .75 |
| 503 | Julio Gonzalez | .07 |
| 504 | Rick Peters | .07 |
| 505 | Graig Nettles | .20 |
| 506 | Nettles (Action) | .15 |
| 507 | Terry Harper | .07 |
| 508 | Jody Davis (R) | .75 |
| 509 | Harry Spilman | .07 |
| 510 | Fernando Valenzuela | 1.75 |
| 511 | Ruppert Jones | .07 |
| 512 | Jerry Dybzinski | .07 |
| 513 | Rick Rhoden | .07 |
| 514 | Joe Ferguson | .07 |
| 515 | Larry Bowa | .10 |
| 516 | Bowa (Action) | .07 |
| 517 | Mark Brouhard | .07 |
| 518 | Garth Iorg | .07 |
| 519 | Glenn Adams | .07 |
| 520 | Mike Flanagan | .10 |
| 521 | Billy Almon | .07 |
| 522 | Chuck Rainey | .07 |
| 523 | Gary Gray | .07 |
| 524 | Tom Hausman | .07 |
| 525 | Ray Knight | .07 |
| 526 | Expos Leaders: W. Cromartie, Bill Gullickson | .15 |
| 527 | John Henry Johnson | .07 |
| 528 | Matt Alexander | .07 |
| 529 | Allen Ripley | .07 |
| 530 | Dickie Noles | .07 |
| 531 | A's Rookies: Rich Bordi, M. Budaska, Kelvin Moore | .12 |
| 532 | Toby Harrah | .07 |
| 533 | Joaquin Andujar | .15 |
| 534 | Dave McKay | .07 |
| 535 | Lance Parrish | .40 |
| 536 | Rafael Ramirez | .07 |
| 537 | Doug Capilla | .07 |
| 538 | Lou Piniella | .15 |
| 539 | Vern Ruhle | .07 |
| 540 | Andre Dawson | .30 |
| 541 | Barry Evans | .07 |
| 542 | Ned Yost | .07 |
| 543 | Bill Robinson | .07 |
| 544 | Larry Christenson | .07 |
| 545 | Reggie Smith | .10 |
| 546 | Smith (Action) | .07 |
| 547 | Rod Carew (AS) | .25 |
| 548 | Willie Randolph (AS) | .12 |
| 549 | George Brett (AS) | .40 |
| 550 | Bucky Dent (AS) | .12 |
| 551 | Reggie Jackson (AS) | .40 |
| 552 | Ken Singleton (AS) | .12 |
| 553 | Dave Winfield (AS) | .35 |
| 554 | Carlton Fisk (AS) | .20 |
| 555 | Scott McGregor (AS) | .12 |
| 556 | Jack Morris (AS) | .15 |
| 557 | Rich Gossage (AS) | .20 |
| 558 | John Tudor | .25 |
| 559 | Indians Leaders: M. Hargrove, B. Blyleven | .15 |
| 560 | Doug Corbett | .07 |
| 561 | Cardinals Rookies: Glenn Brummer, Luis DeLeon, Gene Roof | .20 |
| 562 | Mike O'Berry | .07 |
| 563 | Ross Baumgarten | .07 |
| 564 | Doug DeCinces | .15 |
| 565 | Jackson Todd | .07 |
| 566 | Mike Jorgensen | .07 |
| 567 | Bob Babcock | .07 |
| 568 | Joe Pettini | .07 |
| 569 | Willie Randolph | .10 |
| 570 | Randolph (Action) | .07 |
| 571 | Glenn Abbott | .07 |
| 572 | Juan Beniquez | .07 |
| 573 | Rick Waits | .07 |
| 574 | Mike Ramsey | .07 |
| 575 | Al Cowens | .07 |
| 576 | Giants Leaders: Milt May, Vida Blue | .12 |
| 577 | Rick Monday | .07 |
| 578 | Shooty Babitt | .07 |
| 579 | Rick Mahler (R) | .35 |
| 580 | Bobby Bonds | .10 |
| 581 | Ron Reed | .07 |
| 582 | Luis Pujols | .07 |
| 583 | Tippy Martinez | .07 |
| 584 | Hosken Powell | .07 |
| 585 | Rollie Fingers | .25 |
| 586 | Fingers (Action) | .15 |
| 587 | Tim Lollar | .07 |
| 588 | Dale Berra | .07 |
| 589 | Dave Stapleton | .07 |
| 590 | Al Oliver | .25 |
| 591 | Oliver (Action) | .15 |
| 592 | Craig Swan | .07 |
| 593 | Billy Smith | .07 |
| 594 | Renie Martin | .07 |
| 595 | Dave Collins | .07 |
| 596 | Damaso Garcia | .12 |
| 597 | Wayne Nordhagen | .07 |
| 598 | Bob Galasso | .07 |
| 599 | White Sox Rookies: Jay Loviglio, R. Patterson, Leo Sutherland | .12 |
| 600 | Dave Winfield | .50 |
| 601 | Sid Monge | .07 |
| 602 | Freddie Patek | .07 |
| 603 | Rich Hebner | .07 |
| 604 | Orlando Sanchez | .07 |
| 605 | Steve Rogers | .10 |
| 606 | Blue Jays Leaders: John Mayberry, Dave Stieb | .10 |
| 607 | Leon Durham | .35 |
| 608 | Jerry Royster | .07 |
| 609 | Rick Sutcliffe | .30 |
| 610 | Rickey Henderson | 2.00 |
| 611 | Joe Niekro | .12 |
| 612 | Gary Ward | .07 |
| 613 | Jim Gantner | .07 |
| 614 | Juan Eichelberger | .07 |
| 615 | Bob Boone | .07 |
| 616 | Boone (Action) | .07 |
| 617 | Scott McGregor | .10 |
| 618 | Tim Foli | .07 |
| 619 | Bill Campbell | .07 |
| 620 | Ken Griffey | .12 |
| 621 | Griffey (Action) | .07 |
| 622 | Dennis Lamp | .07 |
| 623 | Mets Rookies: Ron Gardenhire, T. Leach, Tim Leary | .25 |
| 624 | Fergie Jenkins | .15 |
| 625 | Hal McRae | .10 |
| 626 | Randy Jones | .07 |
| 627 | Enos Cabell | .07 |
| 628 | Bill Travers | .07 |
| 629 | Johnny Wockenfuss | .07 |
| 630 | Joe Charboneau | .07 |
| 631 | Gene Tenace | .07 |
| 632 | Bryan Clark | .07 |
| 633 | Mitchell Page | .07 |
| 634 | Checklist No. 5 | .15 |
| 635 | Ron Davis | .07 |
| 636 | Phillies Leaders: Pete Rose, Steve Carlton | .25 |
| 637 | Rick Camp | .07 |
| 638 | John Milner | .07 |
| 639 | Ken Kravec | .07 |
| 640 | Cesar Cedeno | .10 |
| 641 | Steve Mura | .07 |
| 642 | Mike Scioscia | .07 |
| 643 | Pete Vuckovich | .12 |
| 644 | John Castino | .07 |
| 645 | Frank White | .10 |
| 646 | White (Action) | .07 |
| 647 | Warren Brusstar | .07 |
| 648 | Jose Morales | .07 |
| 649 | Ken Clay | .07 |
| 650 | Carl Yastrzemski | 1.00 |
| 651 | Yastrzemski (Action) | .50 |
| 652 | Steve Nicosia | .07 |
| 653 | Angels Rookies: Luis Sanchez, Tom Brunansky, Daryl Sconiers | 2.50 |
| 654 | Jim Morrison | .07 |
| 655 | Joel Youngblood | .07 |
| 656 | Eddie Whitson | .10 |
| 657 | Tom Poquette | .07 |
| 658 | Tito Landrum | .07 |
| 659 | Fred Martinez | .07 |
| 660 | Dave Concepcion | .12 |
| 661 | Concepcion (Action) | .07 |
| 662 | Luis Salazar | .07 |
| 663 | Hector Cruz | .07 |
| 664 | Dan Spillner | .07 |
| 665 | Jim Clancy | .07 |
| 666 | Tigers Leaders: Steve Kemp, Dan Petry | .20 |
| 667 | Jeff Reardon | .10 |
| 668 | Dale Murphy | 2.50 |
| 669 | Larry Milbourne | .07 |
| 670 | Steve Kemp | .10 |
| 671 | Mike Davis | .15 |
| 672 | Bob Knepper | .07 |
| 673 | Keith Drumright | .07 |
| 674 | Dave Goltz | .07 |
| 675 | Cecil Cooper | .25 |
| 676 | Sal Butera | .07 |
| 677 | Alfredo Griffin | .10 |
| 678 | Tom Paciorek | .07 |
| 679 | Sammy Stewart | .07 |
| 680 | Gary Matthews | .10 |
| 681 | Dodgers Rookies: Steve Sax, Mike Marshall, Ron Roenicke | 4.00 |
| 682 | Jesse Jefferson | .07 |
| 683 | Phil Garner | .07 |
| 684 | Harold Baines | .75 |
| 685 | Bert Blyleven | .15 |
| 686 | Gary Allenson | .07 |
| 687 | Greg Minton | .07 |
| 688 | Leon Roberts | .07 |
| 689 | Lary Sorensen | .07 |
| 690 | Dave Kingman | .20 |
| 691 | Dan Schatzeder | .07 |
| 692 | Wayne Gross | .07 |
| 693 | Cesar Geronimo | .07 |
| 694 | Dave Wehrmeister | .07 |
| 695 | Warren Cromartie | .07 |
| 696 | Pirates Leaders: Bill Madlock, B. Solomon | .15 |
| 697 | John Montefusco | .07 |
| 698 | Tony Scott | .07 |
| 699 | Dick Tidrow | .07 |
| 700 | George Foster | .25 |
| 701 | Foster (Action) | .15 |
| 702 | Steve Renko | .07 |
| 703 | Brewers Leaders: Cecil Cooper, P. Vuckovich | .25 |
| 704 | Mickey Rivers | .07 |
| 705 | Rivers (Action) | .07 |
| 706 | Barry Foote | .07 |
| 707 | Mark Bomback | .07 |
| 708 | Gene Richards | .07 |
| 709 | Don Money | .07 |
| 710 | Jerry Reuss | .10 |
| 711 | Mariners Rookies: Dave Edler, Reggie Walton, Dave Henderson | .50 |
| 712 | Denny Martinez | .07 |
| 713 | Del Unser | .07 |
| 714 | Jerry Koosman | .10 |
| 715 | Willie Stargell | .35 |
| 716 | Stargell (Action) | .20 |
| 717 | Rick Miller | .07 |
| 718 | Charlie Hough | .07 |
| 719 | Jerry Narron | .07 |
| 720 | Greg Luzinski | .15 |
| 721 | Luzinski (Action) | .10 |

| NO. PLAYER | MINT | NO. PLAYER | MINT | NO. PLAYER | MINT | NO. PLAYER | MINT |
|---|---|---|---|---|---|---|---|
| 722 Jerry Martin | .07 | 740 Dave Lopes | .10 | 758 Claudell Washington | .12 | 775 Bob Forsch | .07 |
| 723 Junior Kennedy | .07 | 741 Lopes (Action) | .07 | 759 Paul Splittorff | .07 | 776 Mark Belanger | .07 |
| 724 Dave Rosello | .07 | 742 Dick Drago | .07 | 760 Bill Buckner | .15 | 777 Tom Griffin | .07 |
| 725 Amos Otis | .10 | 743 John Stearns | .07 | 761 Dave Smith | .07 | 778 Kevin Hickey | .07 |
| 726 Otis (Action) | .07 | 744 Mike Witt (R) | 2.00 | 762 Mike Phillips | .07 | 779 Grant Jackson | .07 |
| 727 Sixto Lezcano | .07 | 745 Bake McBride | .07 | 763 Tom Hume | .07 | 780 Pete Rose | 2.50 |
| 728 Aurelio Lopez | .07 | 746 Andre Thornton | .12 | 764 Steve Swisher | .07 | 781 Rose (Action) | .85 |
| 729 Jim Spencer | .07 | 747 John Lowenstein | .07 | 765 Gorman Thomas | .12 | 782 Frank Taveras | .07 |
| 730 Gary Carter | .50 | 748 Marc Hill | .07 | 766 Twins Rookies: | 4.00 | 783 Greg Harris | .07 |
| 731 Padres Rookies: | .15 | 749 Bob Shirley | .07 |   Lenny Faedo, Kent Hrbek, | | 784 Milt Wilcox | .07 |
|   Doug Gwosdz, Mike | | 750 Jim Rice | .75 |   Tim Laudner | | 785 Dan Driessen | .07 |
|   Armstrong, Fred Kuhaulua | | 751 Rick Honeycutt | .07 | 767 Roy Smalley | .07 | 786 Red Sox Leaders: | .20 |
| 732 Mike Lum | .07 | 752 Lee Lacy | .07 | 768 Jerry Garvin | .07 |   C. Lansford, M. Torrez | |
| 733 Larry McWilliams | .10 | 753 Tom Brookens | .07 | 769 Richie Zisk | .07 | 787 Fred Stanley | .07 |
| 734 Mike Ivie | .07 | 754 Joe Morgan | .35 | 770 Rich Gossage | .25 | 788 Woodie Fryman | .07 |
| 735 Rudy May | .07 | 755 Morgan (Action) | .20 | 771 Gossage (Action) | .15 | 789 Checklist No. 6 | .15 |
| 736 Jerry Turner | .07 | 756 Reds Leaders: | .20 | 772 Bert Campaneris | .07 | 790 Larry Gura | .07 |
| 737 Reggie Cleveland | .07 |   Ken Griffey, Tom Seaver | | 773 John Denny | .10 | 791 Bobby Brown | .07 |
| 738 Dave Engle | .07 | 757 Tom Underwood | .07 | 774 Jay Johnstone | .07 | 792 Frank Tanana | .10 |
| 739 Joey McLaughlin | .07 | | | | | | |

## 1982 Topps Traded....Complete Set of 132 Cards—Value $25.00

Updates the main 1982 card set with players who changed teams during the season and rookies. Unlike the 1981 Traded set, the cards are numbered from 1T to 132T. The complete set was packaged in a printed box and only distributed through card hobby dealers.

| NO. PLAYER | MINT | NO. PLAYER | MINT | NO. PLAYER | MINT | NO. PLAYER | MINT |
|---|---|---|---|---|---|---|---|
| 1 T Doyle Alexander | .15 | 34 T Tim Foli | .10 | 67 T John Mayberry | .10 | 100 T Bill Robinson | .10 |
| 2 T Jesse Barfield | 2.50 | 35 T Dan Ford | .10 | 68 T Lee Mazzilli | .10 | 101 T Aurelio Rodriquez | .10 |
| 3 T Ross Baumgarten | .10 | 36 T George Foster | .25 | 69 T Bake McBride | .15 | 102 T Joe Rudi | .10 |
| 4 T Steve Bedrosian | .15 | 37 T Dave Frost | .10 | 70 T Dan Meyer | .10 | 103 T Steve Sax | 2.50 |
| 5 T Mark Belanger | .10 | 38 T Rich Gale | .10 | 71 T Larry Milbourne | .10 | 104 T Dan Schatzeder | .10 |
| 6 T Kurt Bevacqua | .10 | 39 T Ron Gardenhire | .10 | 72 T Eddie Milner | .25 | 105 T Bob Shirley | .10 |
| 7 T Tim Blackwell | .10 | 40 T Ken Griffey | .15 | 73 T Sid Monge | .10 | 106 T Eric Show (RR) | .50 |
| 8 T Vida Blue | .15 | 41 T Greg Harris | .10 | 74 T John Montefusco | .10 | 107 T Roy Smalley | .10 |
| 9 T Bob Boone | .10 | 42 T Von Hayes | .75 | 75 T Jose Morales | .10 | 108 T Lonnie Smith | .15 |
| 10 T Larry Bowa | .12 | 43 T Larry Herndon | .10 | 76 T Keith Moreland | .15 | 109 T Ozzie Smith | .45 |
| 11 T Dan Briggs | .10 | 44 T Kent Hrbek | 2.50 | 77 T Jim Morrison | .10 | 110 T Reggie Smith | .20 |
| 12 T Bobby Brown | .10 | 45 T Mike Ivie | .10 | 78 T Rance Mulliniks | .10 | 111 T Lary Sorensen | .10 |
| 13 T Tom Brunansky | 1.00 | 46 T Grant Jackson | .10 | 79 T Steve Mura | .10 | 112 T Elias Sosa | .10 |
| 14 T Jeff Burroughs | .12 | 47 T Reggie Jackson | 2.00 | 80 T Gene Nelson | .10 | 113 T Mike Stanton | .10 |
| 15 T Enos Cabell | .10 | 48 T Ron Jackson | .10 | 81 T Joe Nolan | .10 | 114 T Steve Stroughter | .10 |
| 16 T Bill Campbell | .10 | 49 T Fergie Jenkins | .20 | 82 T Dickie Noles | .10 | 115 T Champ Summers | .10 |
| 17 T Bobby Castillo | .10 | 50 T Lamar Johnson | .10 | 83 T Al Oliver | .35 | 116 T Rick Sutcliffe | .50 |
| 18 T Bill Caudill | .15 | 51 T Randy Johnson | .10 | 84 T Jorge Orta | .10 | 117 T Frank Tanana | .10 |
| 19 T Cesar Cedeno | .15 | 52 T Jay Johnstone | .10 | 85 T Tom Paciorek | .10 | 118 T Frank Taveras | .10 |
| 20 T Dave Collins | .12 | 53 T Mick Kelleher | .10 | 86 T Larry Parrish | .12 | 119 T Garry Templeton | .20 |
| 21 T Doug Corbett | .10 | 54 T Steve Kemp | .12 | 87 T Jack Perconte | .10 | 120 T Alex Trevino | .10 |
| 22 T Al Cowens | .15 | 55 T Junior Kennedy | .10 | 88 T Gaylord Perry | .60 | 121 T Jerry Turner | .10 |
| 23 T Chili Davis | 1.00 | 56 T Jim Kern | .10 | 89 T Rob Picciolo | .10 | 122 T Ed VandeBerg (RR) | .25 |
| 24 T Dick Davis | .10 | 57 T Ray Knight | .10 | 90 T Joe Pittman | .10 | 123 T Tom Veryzer | .10 |
| 25 T Ron Davis | .10 | 58 T Wayne Krenchicki | .10 | 91 T Hosken Powell | .10 | 124 T Ron Washington | .10 |
| 26 T Doug DeCinces | .25 | 59 T Mike Krukow | .10 | 92 T Mike Proly | .10 | 125 T Bob Watson | .10 |
| 27 T Ivan DeJesus | .12 | 60 T Duane Kuiper | .10 | 93 T Greg Pryor | .10 | 126 T Dennis Werth | .10 |
| 28 T Bob Dernier | .20 | 61 T Mike LaCoss | .10 | 94 T Charlie Puleo | .10 | 127 T Eddie Whitson | .10 |
| 29 T Bo Diaz | .10 | 62 T Chet Lemon | .15 | 95 T Shane Rawley | .12 | 128 T Rob Wilfong | .10 |
| 30 T Roger Erickson | .10 | 63 T Sixto Lezcano | .10 | 96 T Johnny Ray | .75 | 129 T Bump Wills | .10 |
| 31 T Jim Essian | .10 | 64 T Dave Lopes | .15 | 97 T Dave Revering | .10 | 130 T Gary Woods | .10 |
| 32 T Ed Farmer | .10 | 65 T Jerry Martin | .10 | 98 T Cal Ripken | 6.50 | 131 T Butch Wynegar | .10 |
| 33 T Doug Flynn | .10 | 66 T Renie Martin | .10 | 99 T Allen Ripley | .10 | 132 T Traded Checklist | .25 |

# 1983 Topps....Complete Set of 792 Cards—Value $60.00

Features the rookie cards of Willie McGee, Ryne Sandberg, Wade Boggs, and Tony Gwynn.

| NO. PLAYER | MINT |
|---|---|
| 1 Record—T. Armas | .20 |
| 11 Rightfield Putouts | |
| 2 Record—R. Henderson | .30 |
| Stolen Base Record | |
| 3 Record—G. Minton | .08 |
| No HR's in 269⅓ Innings | |
| 4 Record—L. Parrish | .15 |
| Threw Out 3 in AS Game | |
| 5 Record—Trillo | .08 |
| 479 Errorless Chances | |
| 6 Record—J. Wathan | .08 |
| 31st Stolen Base, Catcher | |
| 7 Gene Richards | .06 |
| 8 Steve Balboni | .10 |
| 9 Joey McLaughlin | .06 |
| 10 Gorman Thomas | .15 |
| 11 Billy Gardner (Mgr.) | .06 |
| 12 Paul Mirabella | .06 |
| 13 Larry Herndon | .08 |
| 14 Frank LaCorte | .06 |
| 15 Ron Cey | .15 |
| 16 George Vukovich | .06 |
| 17 Kent Tekulve | .06 |
| 18 Tekulve (Veteran) | .06 |
| 19 Oscar Gamble | .08 |
| 20 Carlton Fisk | .20 |
| 21 Orioles Leaders: | .20 |
| Eddie Murray, Jim Palmer | |
| 22 Randy Martz | .06 |
| 23 Mike Heath | .06 |
| 24 Steve Mura | .06 |
| 25 Hal McRae | .06 |
| 26 Jerry Royster | .06 |
| 27 Doug Corbett | .06 |
| 28 Bruce Bochte | .06 |
| 29 Randy Jones | .06 |
| 30 Jim Rice | .50 |
| 31 Bill Gullickson | .08 |
| 32 Dave Bergman | .06 |
| 33 Jack O'Connor | .06 |
| 34 Paul Householder | .06 |
| 35 Rollie Fingers | .25 |
| 36 Fingers (Veteran) | .15 |
| 37 Darrell Johnson (Mgr.) | .06 |
| 38 Tim Flannery | .06 |
| 39 Terry Puhl | .06 |
| 40 Fernando Valenzuela | .40 |
| 41 Jerry Turner | .06 |
| 42 Dale Murray | .06 |
| 43 Bob Dernier | .08 |
| 44 Don Robinson | .06 |
| 45 John Mayberry | .06 |
| 46 Richard Dotson | .06 |
| 47 Dave McKay | .06 |
| 48 Lary Sorensen | .06 |
| 49 Willie McGee (R) | 3.50 |
| 50 Bob Horner | .25 |
| 51 Cubs Leaders: | .06 |
| Leon Durham, F. Jenkins | |
| 52 Onix Concepcion | .15 |
| 53 Mike Witt | .12 |
| 54 Jim Maler | .06 |
| 55 Mookie Wilson | .08 |
| 56 Chuck Rainey | .06 |
| 57 Tim Blackwell | .06 |
| 58 Al Holland | .06 |

| NO. PLAYER | MINT |
|---|---|
| 59 Benny Ayala | .06 |
| 60 Johnny Bench | .50 |
| 61 Bench (Veteran) | .30 |
| 62 Bob McClure | .06 |
| 63 Rick Monday | .06 |
| 64 Bill Stein | .06 |
| 65 Jack Morris | .25 |
| 66 Bob Lillis (Mgr.) | .06 |
| 67 Sal Butera | .06 |
| 68 Eric Show (R) | .30 |
| 69 Lee Lacy | .08 |
| 70 Steve Carlton | .50 |
| 71 Carlton (Veteran) | .25 |
| 72 Tom Paciorek | .06 |
| 73 Allen Ripley | .06 |
| 74 Julio Gonzalez | .06 |
| 75 Amos Otis | .06 |
| 76 Rick Mahler | .06 |
| 77 Hosken Powell | .06 |
| 78 Bill Caudill | .08 |
| 79 Mick Kelleher | .06 |
| 80 George Foster | .25 |
| 81 Yankees Leaders: | .20 |
| J. Mumphrey, D. Righetti | |
| 82 Bruce Hurst | .06 |
| 83 Ryne Sandberg (R) | 5.50 |
| 84 Milt May | .06 |
| 85 Ken Singleton | .08 |
| 86 Tom Hume | .06 |
| 87 Joe Rudi | .06 |
| 88 Jim Gantner | .06 |
| 89 Leon Roberts | .06 |
| 90 Jerry Reuss | .08 |
| 91 Larry Milbourne | .06 |
| 92 Mike LaCoss | .06 |
| 93 John Castino | .06 |
| 94 Dave Edwards | .06 |
| 95 Alan Trammell | .35 |
| 96 Dick Howser (Mgr.) | .06 |
| 97 Ross Baumgarten | .06 |
| 98 Vance Law | .06 |
| 99 Dickie Noles | .06 |
| 100 Pete Rose | 2.00 |
| 101 Rose (Veteran) | .60 |
| 102 Dave Beard | .06 |
| 103 Darrell Porter | .08 |
| 104 Bob Walk | .06 |
| 105 Don Baylor | .20 |
| 106 Gene Nelson | .06 |
| 107 Mike Jorgensen | .06 |
| 108 Glenn Hoffman | .06 |
| 109 Luis Leal | .06 |
| 110 Ken Griffey | .15 |
| 111 Expos Leaders: | .15 |
| Al Oliver, Steve Rogers | |
| 112 Bob Shirley | .06 |
| 113 Ron Roenicke | .06 |
| 114 Jim Slaton | .06 |
| 115 Chili Davis | .15 |
| 116 Dave Schmidt | .06 |
| 117 Alan Knicely | .06 |
| 118 Chris Welsh | .06 |
| 119 Tom Brookens | .06 |
| 120 Len Barker | .06 |
| 121 Mickey Hatcher | .06 |
| 122 Jimmy Smith | .06 |

| NO. PLAYER | MINT |
|---|---|
| 123 George Frazier | .06 |
| 124 Marc Hill | .06 |
| 125 Leon Durham | .25 |
| 126 Joe Torre (Mgr.) | .08 |
| 127 Preston Hanna | .06 |
| 128 Mike Ramsey | .06 |
| 129 Checklist No. 1 | .12 |
| 130 Dave Stieb | .25 |
| 131 Ed Ott | .06 |
| 132 Todd Cruz | .06 |
| 133 Jim Barr | .06 |
| 134 Hubie Brooks | .10 |
| 135 Dwight Evans | .15 |
| 136 Willie Aikens | .06 |
| 137 Woodie Fryman | .06 |
| 138 Rick Dempsey | .08 |
| 139 Bruce Berenyi | .06 |
| 140 Willie Randolph | .10 |
| 141 Indians Leaders: | .12 |
| Toby Harrah, Rick Sutcliffe | |
| 142 Mike Caldwell | .06 |
| 143 Joe Pettini | .06 |
| 144 Mark Wagner | .06 |
| 145 Don Sutton | .15 |
| 146 Don Sutton (Veteran) | .10 |
| 147 Rick Leach | .06 |
| 148 Dave Roberts | .06 |
| 149 Johnny Ray | .15 |
| 150 Bruce Sutter | .20 |
| 151 B. Sutter (Veteran) | .15 |
| 152 Jay Johnstone | .06 |
| 153 Jerry Koosman | .06 |
| 154 Johnnie LeMaster | .06 |
| 155 Dan Quisenberry | .25 |
| 156 Billy Martin (Mgr.) | .15 |
| 157 Steve Bedrosian | .08 |
| 158 Rob Wilfong | .06 |
| 159 Mike Stanton | .06 |
| 160 Dave Kingman | .15 |
| 161 D. Kingman (Veteran) | .10 |
| 162 Mark Clear | .06 |
| 163 Cal Ripken | 2.00 |
| 164 David Palmer | .06 |
| 165 Dan Driessen | .06 |
| 166 John Pacella | .06 |
| 167 Mark Brouhard | .06 |
| 168 Juan Eichelberger | .06 |
| 169 Doug Flynn | .06 |
| 170 Steve Howe | .06 |
| 171 Giants Leaders: | .12 |
| Bill Laskey, Joe Morgan | |
| 172 Vern Ruhle | .06 |
| 173 Jim Morrison | .06 |
| 174 Jerry Ujdur | .06 |
| 175 Bo Diaz | .06 |
| 176 Dave Righetti | .15 |
| 177 Harold Baines | .30 |
| 178 Luis Tiant | .08 |
| 179 Luis Tiant (Veteran) | .06 |
| 180 Rickey Henderson | .75 |
| 181 Terry Felton | .06 |
| 182 Mike Fischlin | .06 |
| 183 Ed VandeBerg (R) | .25 |
| 184 Bob Clark | .06 |
| 185 Tim Lollar | .06 |
| 186 Whitey Herzog (Mgr.) | .06 |

| NO. PLAYER | MINT |
|---|---|
| 187 Terry Leach | .06 |
| 188 Rick Miller | .06 |
| 189 Dan Schatzeder | .06 |
| 190 Cecil Cooper | .25 |
| 191 Joe Price | .06 |
| 192 Floyd Rayford | .06 |
| 193 Harry Spilman | .06 |
| 194 Cesar Geronimo | .06 |
| 195 Bob Stoddard | .06 |
| 196 Bill Fahey | .06 |
| 197 Jim Eisenreich | .15 |
| 198 Kiko Garcia | .06 |
| 199 Marty Bystrom | .06 |
| 200 Rod Carew | .40 |
| 201 Rod Carew (Veteran) | .25 |
| 202 Blue Jays Leaders: | .12 |
| Damaso Garcia, Dave Stieb | |
| 203 Mike Morgan | .06 |
| 204 Junior Kennedy | .06 |
| 205 Dave Parker | .25 |
| 206 Ken Oberkfell | .06 |
| 207 Rick Camp | .06 |
| 208 Dan Meyer | .06 |
| 209 Mike Moore (R) | .30 |
| 210 Jack Clark | .25 |
| 211 John Denny | .15 |
| 212 John Stearns | .06 |
| 213 Tom Burgmeier | .06 |
| 214 Jerry White | .06 |
| 215 Mario Soto | .10 |
| 216 Tony LaRussa (Mgr.) | .08 |
| 217 Tim Stoddard | .06 |
| 218 Roy Howell | .06 |
| 219 Mike Armstrong | .06 |
| 220 Dusty Baker | .12 |
| 221 Joe Niekro | .08 |
| 222 Damaso Garcia | .15 |
| 223 John Montefusco | .06 |
| 224 Mickey Rivers | .06 |
| 225 Enos Cabell | .06 |
| 226 Enrique Romo | .06 |
| 227 Chris Bando | .06 |
| 228 Joaquin Andujar | .12 |
| 229 Phillies Leaders: | .12 |
| Bo Diaz, Steve Carlton | |
| 230 Fergie Jenkins | .12 |
| 231 F. Jenkins (Veteran) | .08 |
| 232 Tom Brunansky | .25 |
| 233 Wayne Gross | .06 |
| 234 Larry Andersen | .06 |
| 235 Claudell Washington | .15 |
| 236 Steve Renko | .06 |
| 237 Dan Norman | .06 |
| 238 Bud Black (R) | .40 |
| 239 Dave Stapleton | .06 |
| 240 Rich Gossage | .25 |
| 241 Gossage (Veteran) | .15 |
| 242 Joe Nolan | .06 |
| 243 Duane Walker | .12 |
| 244 Dwight Bernard | .06 |
| 245 Steve Sax | .20 |
| 246 G. Bamberger (Mgr.) | .06 |
| 247 Dave Smith | .06 |
| 248 Bake McBride | .06 |
| 249 Checklist No. 2 | .12 |
| 250 Bill Buckner | .15 |

| NO. | PLAYER | MINT |
|---|---|---|
| 251 | Alan Wiggins (R) | .40 |
| 252 | Luis Aguayo | .06 |
| 253 | Larry McWilliams | .06 |
| 254 | Rick Cerone | .06 |
| 255 | Gene Garber | .06 |
| 256 | G. Garber (Veteran) | .06 |
| 257 | Jesse Barfield | .20 |
| 258 | Manny Castillo | .06 |
| 259 | Jeff Jones | .06 |
| 260 | Steve Kemp | .08 |
| 261 | Tigers Leaders: | .12 |
| | L. Herndon, Dan Petry | |
| 262 | Ron Jackson | .06 |
| 263 | Renie Martin | .06 |
| 264 | Jamie Quirk | .06 |
| 265 | Joel Youngblood | .06 |
| 266 | Paul Boris | .06 |
| 267 | Terry Francona | .06 |
| 268 | Storm Davis (R) | .60 |
| 269 | Ron Oester | .06 |
| 270 | Dennis Eckersley | .06 |
| 271 | Ed Romero | .06 |
| 272 | Frank Tanana | .06 |
| 273 | Mark Belanger | .06 |
| 274 | Terry Kennedy | .10 |
| 275 | Ray Knight | .06 |
| 276 | Gene Mauch (Mgr.) | .06 |
| 277 | Rance Mulliniks | .06 |
| 278 | Kevin Hickey | .06 |
| 279 | Greg Gross | .06 |
| 280 | Bert Blyleven | .15 |
| 281 | Andre Robertson | .06 |
| 282 | Reggie Smith | .10 |
| 283 | R. Smith (Veteran) | .08 |
| 284 | Jeff Lahti | .15 |
| 285 | Lance Parrish | .35 |
| 286 | Rick Langford | .06 |
| 287 | Bobby Brown | .06 |
| 288 | Joe Cowley (R) | .50 |
| 289 | Jerry Dybzinski | .06 |
| 290 | Jeff Reardon | .08 |
| 291 | Pirates Leaders: | .12 |
| | B. Madlock, J. Candelaria | |
| 292 | Craig Swan | .06 |
| 293 | Glen Gulliver | .06 |
| 294 | Dave Engle | .06 |
| 295 | Jerry Remy | .06 |
| 296 | Greg Harris | .06 |
| 297 | Ned Yost | .06 |
| 298 | Floyd Chiffer | .06 |
| 299 | George Wright | .20 |
| 300 | Mike Schmidt | .75 |
| 301 | M. Schmidt (Veteran) | .25 |
| 302 | Ernie Whitt | .06 |
| 303 | Miguel Dilone | .06 |
| 304 | Dave Rucker | .06 |
| 305 | Larry Bowa | .10 |
| 306 | Tom Lasorda (Mgr.) | .10 |
| 307 | Lou Piniella | .12 |
| 308 | Jesus Vega | .06 |
| 309 | Jeff Leonard | .06 |
| 310 | Greg Luzinski | .15 |
| 311 | Glenn Brummer | .06 |
| 312 | Brian Kingman | .06 |
| 313 | Gary Gray | .06 |
| 314 | Ken Dayley | .06 |
| 315 | Rick Burleson | .06 |
| 316 | Paul Splittorff | .06 |
| 317 | Gary Rajsich | .06 |
| 318 | John Tudor | .20 |
| 319 | Lenn Sakata | .06 |
| 320 | Steve Rogers | .08 |
| 321 | Brewers Leaders: | .15 |
| | P. Vuckovich, R. Yount | |
| 322 | Dave Van Gorder | .06 |
| 323 | Luis DeLeon | .06 |
| 324 | Mike Marshall | .25 |
| 325 | Von Hayes | .20 |
| 326 | Garth Iorg | .06 |
| 327 | Bobby Castillo | .06 |
| 328 | Craig Reynolds | .06 |
| 329 | Randy Niemann | .06 |
| 330 | Buddy Bell | .15 |
| 331 | Mike Krukow | .06 |
| 332 | Glenn Wilson (R) | .75 |
| 333 | Dave LaRoche | .06 |
| 334 | D. LaRoche (Veteran) | .06 |
| 335 | Steve Henderson | .06 |
| 336 | R. Lachemann (Mgr.) | .06 |
| 337 | Tito Landrum | .06 |
| 338 | Bob Owchinko | .06 |
| 339 | Terry Harper | .06 |
| 340 | Larry Gura | .06 |
| 341 | Doug DeCinces | .15 |
| 342 | Atlee Hammaker | .08 |
| 343 | Bob Bailor | .06 |
| 344 | Roger LaFrancois | .06 |
| 345 | Jim Clancy | .06 |
| 346 | Joe Pittman | .06 |
| 347 | Sammy Stewart | .06 |
| 348 | Alan Bannister | .06 |
| 349 | Checklist No. 3 | .12 |
| 350 | Robin Yount | .30 |
| 351 | Reds Leaders: | .12 |
| | Cesar Cedeno, Mario Soto | |
| 352 | Mike Scioscia | .06 |
| 353 | Steve Comer | .06 |
| 354 | Randy Johnson | .06 |
| 355 | Jim Bibby | .06 |
| 356 | Gary Woods | .06 |
| 357 | Len Matuszek | .15 |
| 358 | Jerry Garvin | .06 |
| 359 | Dave Collins | .08 |
| 360 | Nolan Ryan | .35 |
| 361 | N. Ryan (Veteran) | .20 |
| 362 | Bill Almon | .06 |
| 363 | John Stuper | .15 |
| 364 | Bret Butler | .15 |
| 365 | Dave Lopes | .07 |
| 366 | Dick Williams (Mgr.) | .06 |
| 367 | Bud Anderson | .06 |
| 368 | Richie Zisk | .06 |
| 369 | Jesse Orosco | .10 |
| 370 | Gary Carter | .40 |
| 371 | Mike Richardt | .06 |
| 372 | Terry Crowley | .06 |
| 373 | Kevin Saucier | .06 |
| 374 | Wayne Krenchicki | .06 |
| 375 | Pete Vuckovich | .06 |
| 376 | Ken Landreaux | .06 |
| 377 | Lee May | .06 |
| 378 | Lee May (Veteran) | .06 |
| 379 | Guy Sularz | .06 |
| 380 | Ron Davis | .06 |
| 381 | Red Sox Leaders: | .15 |
| | Bob Stanley, Jim Rice | |
| 382 | Bob Knepper | .06 |
| 383 | Ozzie Virgil | .06 |
| 384 | Dave Dravecky (R) | .50 |
| 385 | Mike Easler | .06 |
| 386 | Rod Carew (AS) | .25 |
| 387 | Bob Grich (AS) | .08 |
| 388 | George Brett (AS) | .40 |
| 389 | Robin Yount (AS) | .25 |
| 390 | Reggie Jackson (AS) | .30 |
| 391 | Rickey Henderson (AS) | .35 |
| 392 | Fred Lynn (AS) | .15 |
| 393 | Carlton Fisk (AS) | .15 |
| 394 | Pete Vuckovich (AS) | .08 |
| 395 | Larry Gura (AS) | .08 |
| 396 | Dan Quisenberry (AS) | .12 |
| 397 | Pete Rose (AS) | .60 |
| 398 | Manny Trillo (AS) | .08 |
| 399 | Mike Schmidt (AS) | .35 |
| 400 | Dave Concepcion (AS) | .10 |
| 401 | Dale Murphy (AS) | .50 |
| 402 | Andre Dawson (AS) | .20 |
| 403 | Tim Raines (AS) | .18 |
| 404 | Gary Carter (AS) | .25 |
| 405 | Steve Rogers (AS) | .08 |
| 406 | Steve Carlton (AS) | .25 |
| 407 | Bruce Sutter (AS) | .20 |
| 408 | Rudy May | .06 |
| 409 | Marvis Foley | .06 |
| 410 | Phil Niekro | .25 |
| 411 | P. Niekro (Veteran) | .12 |
| 412 | Rangers Leaders: | .10 |
| | Buddy Bell, Charlie Hough | |
| 413 | Matt Keough | .06 |
| 414 | Julio Cruz | .06 |
| 415 | Bob Forsch | .06 |
| 416 | Joe Ferguson | .06 |
| 417 | Tom Hausman | .06 |
| 418 | Greg Pryor | .06 |
| 419 | Steve Crawford | .06 |
| 420 | Al Oliver | .15 |
| 421 | Al Oliver (Veteran) | .08 |
| 422 | George Cappuzzello | .06 |
| 423 | Tom Lawless | .06 |
| 424 | Jerry Augustine | .06 |
| 425 | Pedro Guerrero | .35 |
| 426 | Earl Weaver (Mgr.) | .12 |
| 427 | Roy Lee Jackson | .06 |
| 428 | Champ Summers | .06 |
| 429 | Eddie Whitson | .08 |
| 430 | Kirk Gibson | .30 |
| 431 | Gary Gaetti (R) | .75 |
| 432 | Porfirio Altamirano | .06 |
| 433 | Dale Berra | .06 |
| 434 | Dennis Lamp | .06 |
| 435 | Tony Armas | .15 |
| 436 | Bill Campbell | .06 |
| 437 | Rick Sweet | .06 |
| 438 | Dave LaPoint (R) | .25 |
| 439 | Rafael Ramirez | .06 |
| 440 | Ron Guidry | .25 |
| 441 | Astros Leaders: | .12 |
| | Joe Niekro, Ray Knight | |
| 442 | Brian Downing | .06 |
| 443 | Don Hood | .06 |
| 444 | Wally Backman | .06 |
| 445 | Mike Flanagan | .08 |
| 446 | Reid Nichols | .06 |
| 447 | Bryn Smith | .06 |
| 448 | Darrell Evans | .12 |
| 449 | Eddie Milner | .12 |
| 450 | Ted Simmons | .15 |
| 451 | Ted Simmons (Veteran) | .10 |
| 452 | Lloyd Moseby | .15 |
| 453 | Lamar Johnson | .06 |
| 454 | Bob Welch | .06 |
| 455 | Sixto Lezcano | .06 |
| 456 | Lee Elia (Mgr.) | .06 |
| 457 | Milt Wilcox | .06 |
| 458 | Ron Washington | .06 |
| 459 | Ed Farmer | .06 |
| 460 | Roy Smalley | .06 |
| 461 | Steve Trout | .06 |
| 462 | Steve Nicosia | .06 |
| 463 | Gaylord Perry | .25 |
| 464 | G. Perry (Veteran) | .12 |
| 465 | Lonnie Smith | .12 |
| 466 | Tom Underwood | .06 |
| 467 | Rufino Linares | .06 |
| 468 | Dave Goltz | .06 |
| 469 | Ron Gardenhire | .06 |
| 470 | Greg Minton | .06 |
| 471 | Royals Leaders: | .12 |
| | Willie Wilson, Vida Blue | |
| 472 | Gary Allenson | .06 |
| 473 | John Lowenstein | .06 |
| 474 | Ray Burris | .06 |
| 475 | Cesar Cedeno | .12 |
| 476 | Rob Picciolo | .06 |
| 477 | Tom Niedenfuer | .12 |
| 478 | Phil Garner | .06 |
| 479 | Charlie Hough | .06 |
| 480 | Toby Harrah | .06 |
| 481 | Scot Thompson | .06 |
| 482 | Tony Gwynn (R) | 7.00 |
| 483 | Lynn Jones | .06 |
| 484 | Dick Ruthven | .06 |
| 485 | Omar Moreno | .06 |
| 486 | Clyde King (Mgr.) | .06 |
| 487 | Jerry Hariston | .06 |
| 488 | Alfredo Griffin | .06 |
| 489 | Tom Herr | .20 |
| 490 | Jim Palmer | .25 |
| 491 | Jim Palmer (Veteran) | .15 |
| 492 | Paul Serna | .06 |
| 493 | Steve McCatty | .06 |
| 494 | Bob Brenly | .08 |
| 495 | Warren Cromartie | .06 |
| 496 | Tom Veryzer | .06 |
| 497 | Rick Sutcliffe | .20 |
| 498 | Wade Boggs (R) | 24.00 |
| 499 | Jeff Little | .06 |
| 500 | Reggie Jackson | .75 |
| 501 | R. Jackson (Veteran) | .25 |
| 502 | Braves Leaders: | .15 |
| | Dale Murphy, Phil Niekro | |
| 503 | Moose Haas | .06 |
| 504 | Don Werner | .06 |
| 505 | Garry Templeton | .15 |
| 506 | Jim Gott | .08 |
| 507 | Tony Scott | .06 |
| 508 | Tom Filer (R) | .20 |
| 509 | Lou Whitaker | .25 |
| 510 | Tug McGraw | .08 |
| 511 | Tug McGraw (Veteran) | .06 |
| 512 | Doyle Alexander | .06 |
| 513 | Fred Stanley | .06 |
| 514 | Rudy Law | .06 |
| 515 | Gene Tenace | .06 |
| 516 | Bill Virdon (Mgr.) | .06 |
| 517 | Gary Ward | .06 |
| 518 | Bill Laskey (R) | .25 |
| 519 | Terry Bulling | .06 |
| 520 | Fred Lynn | .25 |
| 521 | Bruce Benedict | .06 |
| 522 | Pat Zachry | .06 |
| 523 | Carney Lansford | .15 |
| 524 | Tom Brennan | .06 |
| 525 | Frank White | .06 |
| 526 | Checklist No. 4 | .12 |
| 527 | Larry Biittner | .06 |
| 528 | Jamie Easterly | .06 |
| 529 | Tim Laudner | .06 |
| 530 | Eddie Murray | .60 |
| 531 | A's Leaders: | .12 |
| | R. Henderson, R. Langford | |
| 532 | Dave Stewart | .06 |
| 533 | Luis Salazar | .06 |
| 534 | John Butcher | .06 |
| 535 | Manny Trillo | .08 |
| 536 | Johnny Wockenfuss | .06 |
| 537 | Rod Scurry | .06 |
| 538 | Danny Heep | .06 |
| 539 | Roger Erickson | .06 |
| 540 | Ozzie Smith | .15 |
| 541 | Britt Burns | .08 |
| 542 | Jody Davis | .10 |
| 543 | Alan Fowlkes | .06 |
| 544 | Larry Whisenton | .06 |
| 545 | Floyd Bannister | .06 |
| 546 | Dave Garcia (Mgr.) | .06 |
| 547 | Geoff Zahn | .06 |
| 548 | Brian Giles | .06 |
| 549 | Charlie Puleo | .06 |
| 550 | Carl Yastrzemski | .60 |
| 551 | Yastrzemski (Veteran) | .30 |
| 552 | Tim Wallach | .12 |
| 553 | Denny Martinez | .06 |
| 554 | Mike Vail | .06 |
| 555 | Steve Yeager | .06 |
| 556 | Willie Upshaw | .15 |
| 557 | Rick Honeycutt | .06 |
| 558 | Dickie Thon | .08 |
| 559 | Peter Redfern | .06 |
| 560 | Ron LeFlore | .08 |
| 561 | Cardinals Leaders: | .12 |
| | L. Smith, J. Andujar | |
| 562 | Dave Rozema | .06 |
| 563 | Juan Bonilla | .06 |
| 564 | Sid Monge | .06 |
| 565 | Bucky Dent | .06 |
| 566 | Manny Sarmiento | .06 |
| 567 | Joe Simpson | .06 |
| 568 | Willie Hernandez | .20 |
| 569 | Jack Perconte | .06 |
| 570 | Vida Blue | .08 |
| 571 | Mickey Klutts | .06 |
| 572 | Bob Watson | .06 |
| 573 | Andy Hassler | .06 |
| 574 | Glenn Adams | .06 |
| 575 | Neil Allen | .06 |
| 576 | Frank Robinson (Mgr.) | .15 |
| 577 | Luis Aponte | .06 |
| 578 | David Green | .15 |
| 579 | Rich Dauer | .06 |

| NO. | PLAYER | MINT |
|---|---|---|
| 580 | Tom Seaver | .75 |
| 581 | T. Seaver (Veteran) | .15 |
| 582 | Marshall Edwards | .06 |
| 583 | Terry Forster | .08 |
| 584 | Dave Hostetler | .12 |
| 585 | Jose Cruz | .12 |
| 586 | Frank Viola (R) | .60 |
| 587 | Ivan DeJesus | .06 |
| 588 | Pat Underwood | .06 |
| 589 | Alvis Woods | .06 |
| 590 | Tony Pena | .15 |
| 591 | White Sox Leaders: | .12 |
|  | Greg Luzinski, LaMarr Hoyt | |
| 592 | Shane Rawley | .06 |
| 593 | Broderick Perkins | .06 |
| 594 | Eric Rasmussen | .06 |
| 595 | Tim Raines | .50 |
| 596 | Randy Johnson | .06 |
| 597 | Mike Proly | .06 |
| 598 | Dwayne Murphy | .06 |
| 599 | Don Aase | .06 |
| 600 | George Brett | .85 |
| 601 | Ed Lynch | .06 |
| 602 | Rich Gedman | .06 |
| 603 | Joe Morgan | .25 |
| 604 | Joe Morgan (Veteran) | .15 |
| 605 | Gary Roenicke | .06 |
| 606 | Bobby Cox (Mgr.) | .06 |
| 607 | Charlie Leibrandt | .08 |
| 608 | Don Money | .06 |
| 609 | Danny Darwin | .06 |
| 610 | Steve Garvey | .50 |
| 611 | Bert Roberge | .06 |
| 612 | Steve Swisher | .06 |
| 613 | Mike Ivie | .06 |
| 614 | Ed Glynn | .08 |
| 615 | Garry Maddox | .06 |
| 616 | Bill Nahorodny | .06 |
| 617 | Butch Wynegar | .06 |
| 618 | LaMarr Hoyt | .15 |
| 619 | Keith Moreland | .08 |
| 620 | Mike Norris | .06 |
| 621 | Mets Leaders: | .12 |
|  | Mookie Wilson, Craig Swan | |
| 622 | Dave Edler | .06 |
| 623 | Luis Sanchez | .06 |
| 624 | Glenn Hubbard | .06 |
| 625 | Ken Forsch | .06 |
| 626 | Jerry Martin | .06 |
| 627 | Doug Bair | .06 |
| 628 | Julio Valdez | .06 |
| 629 | Charlie Lea | .06 |
| 630 | Paul Molitor | .15 |
| 631 | Tippy Martinez | .06 |
| 632 | Alex Trevino | .06 |
| 633 | Vicente Romo | .06 |
| 634 | Max Venable | .06 |
| 635 | Graig Nettles | .15 |

| NO. | PLAYER | MINT |
|---|---|---|
| 636 | G. Nettles (Veteran) | .10 |
| 637 | Pat Corrales (Mgr.) | .06 |
| 638 | Dan Petry | .15 |
| 639 | Art Howe | .06 |
| 640 | Andre Thornton | .10 |
| 641 | Billy Sample | .06 |
| 642 | Checklist: No. 5 | .12 |
| 643 | Bump Wills | .06 |
| 644 | Joe LeFebvre | .06 |
| 645 | Bill Madlock | .15 |
| 646 | Jim Essian | .06 |
| 647 | Bobby Mitchell | .06 |
| 648 | Jeff Burroughs | .06 |
| 649 | Tommy Boggs | .06 |
| 650 | George Hendrick | .10 |
| 651 | Angels Leaders: | .12 |
|  | Rod Carew, Mike Witt | |
| 652 | Butch Hobson | .06 |
| 653 | Ellis Valentine | .06 |
| 654 | Bob Ojeda | .06 |
| 655 | Al Bumbry | .06 |
| 656 | Dave Frost | .06 |
| 657 | Mike Gates | .06 |
| 658 | Frank Pastore | .06 |
| 659 | Charlie Moore | .06 |
| 660 | Mike Hargrove | .06 |
| 661 | Bill Russell | .06 |
| 662 | Joe Sambito | .06 |
| 663 | Tom O'Malley (R) | .12 |
| 664 | Bob Molinaro | .06 |
| 665 | Jim Sundberg | .06 |
| 666 | Sparky Anderson (Mgr.) | .06 |
| 667 | Dick Davis | .06 |
| 668 | Larry Christenson | .06 |
| 669 | Mike Squires | .06 |
| 670 | Jerry Mumphrey | .06 |
| 671 | Lenny Faedo | .06 |
| 672 | Jim Kaat | .10 |
| 673 | Jim Kaat (Veteran) | .06 |
| 674 | Kurt Bevacqua | .06 |
| 675 | Jim Beattie | .06 |
| 676 | Biff Pocoroba | .06 |
| 677 | Dave Revering | .06 |
| 678 | Juan Beniquez | .06 |
| 679 | Mike Scott | .06 |
| 680 | Andre Dawson | .30 |
| 681 | Dodgers Leaders: | .15 |
|  | Fernando Valenzuela, Pedro Guerrero | |
| 682 | Bob Stanley | .06 |
| 683 | Dan Ford | .06 |
| 684 | Rafael Landestoy | .06 |
| 685 | Lee Mazzilli | .06 |
| 686 | Randy Lerch | .06 |
| 687 | U.L. Washington | .06 |
| 688 | Jim Wohlford | .06 |
| 689 | Ron Hassey | .06 |
| 690 | Kent Hrbek | .60 |

| NO. | PLAYER | MINT |
|---|---|---|
| 691 | Dave Tobik | .06 |
| 692 | Denny Walling | .06 |
| 693 | Sparky Lyle | .08 |
| 694 | S. Lyle (Veteran) | .06 |
| 695 | Ruppert Jones | .06 |
| 696 | Chuck Tanner (Mgr.) | .06 |
| 697 | Barry Foote | .06 |
| 698 | Tony Bernazard | .06 |
| 699 | Lee Smith | .10 |
| 700 | Keith Hernandez | .40 |
| 701 | Batting Leaders: | .15 |
|  | Willie Wilson, Al Oliver | |
| 702 | Home Run Leaders: | .15 |
|  | Gorman Thomas, Reggie Jackson, Dave Kingman | |
| 703 | RBI Leaders: | .15 |
|  | Hal McRae, Al Oliver Dale Murphy | |
| 704 | Stolen Base Leaders: | .25 |
|  | R. Henderson, T. Raines | |
| 705 | Victory Leaders: | .15 |
|  | LaMarr Hoyt, Steve Carlton | |
| 706 | Strikeout Leaders: | .15 |
|  | F. Bannister, Steve Carlton | |
| 707 | ERA Leaders: | .12 |
|  | Rick Sutcliffe, Steve Rogers | |
| 708 | Leading Firemen: | .12 |
|  | D. Quisenberry, B. Sutter | |
| 709 | Jimmy Sexton | .06 |
| 710 | Willie Wilson | .20 |
| 711 | Mariners Leaders: | .10 |
|  | Bruce Bochte, Jim Beattie | |
| 712 | Bruce Kison | .06 |
| 713 | Ron Hodges | .06 |
| 714 | Wayne Nordhagen | .06 |
| 715 | Tony Perez | .15 |
| 716 | T. Perez (Veteran) | .10 |
| 717 | Scott Sanderson | .06 |
| 718 | Jim Dwyer | .06 |
| 719 | Rich Gale | .06 |
| 720 | Dave Concepcion | .12 |
| 721 | John Martin | .06 |
| 722 | Jorge Orta | .06 |
| 723 | Randy Moffitt | .06 |
| 724 | Johnny Grubb | .06 |
| 725 | Dan Spillner | .06 |
| 726 | Harvey Kuenn (Mgr.) | .06 |
| 727 | Chet Lemon | .10 |
| 728 | Ron Reed | .06 |
| 729 | Jerry Morales | .06 |
| 730 | Jason Thompson | .12 |
| 731 | Al Williams | .06 |
| 732 | Dave Henderson | .06 |
| 733 | Buck Martinez | .06 |
| 734 | Steve Braun | .06 |
| 735 | Tommy John | .15 |
| 736 | T. John (Veteran) | .08 |
| 737 | Mitchell Page | .06 |

| NO. | PLAYER | MINT |
|---|---|---|
| 738 | Tim Foli | .06 |
| 739 | Rick Ownbey | .08 |
| 740 | Rusty Staub | .12 |
| 741 | R. Staub (Veteran) | .08 |
| 742 | Padres Leaders: | .10 |
|  | Terry Kennedy, Tim Lollar | |
| 743 | Mike Torrez | .06 |
| 744 | Brad Mills | .06 |
| 745 | Scott McGregor | .18 |
| 746 | John Wathan | .06 |
| 747 | Fred Breining | .06 |
| 748 | Derrel Thomas | .06 |
| 749 | Jon Matlack | .06 |
| 750 | Ben Oglivie | .10 |
| 751 | Brad Havens | .06 |
| 752 | Luis Pujols | .06 |
| 753 | Elias Sosa | .06 |
| 754 | Bill Robinson | .06 |
| 755 | John Candelaria | .06 |
| 756 | Russ Nixon (Mgr.) | .06 |
| 757 | Rick Manning | .06 |
| 758 | Aurelio Rodriguez | .06 |
| 759 | Doug Bird | .06 |
| 760 | Dale Murphy | 1.50 |
| 761 | Gary Lucas | .06 |
| 762 | Cliff Johnson | .06 |
| 763 | Al Cowens | .06 |
| 764 | Pete Falcone | .06 |
| 765 | Bob Boone | .06 |
| 766 | Barry Bonnell | .06 |
| 767 | Duane Kuiper | .06 |
| 768 | Chris Speier | .06 |
| 769 | Checklist No. 6 | .12 |
| 770 | Dave Winfield | .40 |
| 771 | Twins Leaders: | .10 |
|  | Kent Hrbek, Bobby Castillo | |
| 772 | Jim Kern | .06 |
| 773 | Larry Hisle | .06 |
| 774 | Alan Ashby | .06 |
| 775 | Burt Hooton | .06 |
| 776 | Larry Parrish | .06 |
| 777 | John Curtis | .06 |
| 778 | Rich Hebner | .06 |
| 779 | Rick Waits | .06 |
| 780 | Gary Matthews | .10 |
| 781 | Rick Rhoden | .06 |
| 782 | Bobby Murcer | .08 |
| 783 | B. Murcer (Veteran) | .06 |
| 784 | Jeff Newman | .06 |
| 785 | Dennis Leonard | .06 |
| 786 | Ralph Houk (Mgr.) | .06 |
| 787 | Dick Tidrow | .06 |
| 788 | Dane Iorg | .06 |
| 789 | Bryan Clark | .06 |
| 790 | Bob Grich | .06 |
| 791 | Gary Lavelle | .06 |
| 792 | Chris Chambliss | .08 |

## 1983 Topps Traded....Complete Set of 132 Cards—Value $35.00

Updates the main 1983 card set with players who changed teams during the season, and rookies. Features the first Topps card of Darryl Strawberry. The complete set was packaged in a printed box and only distributed through card hobby dealers.

# 1983 Topps Traded (Continued)

| NO. | PLAYER | MINT |
|---|---|---|
| 1 T | Neil Allen | .12 |
| 2 T | Bill Almon | .09 |
| 3 T | Joe Altobelli (Mgr.) | .09 |
| 4 T | Tony Armas | .25 |
| 5 T | Doug Bair | .09 |
| 6 T | Steve Baker | .09 |
| 7 T | Floyd Bannister | .12 |
| 8 T | Don Baylor | .25 |
| 9 T | Tony Bernazard | .09 |
| 10 T | Larry Biittner | .09 |
| 11 T | Dann Bilardello | .09 |
| 12 T | Doug Bird | .09 |
| 13 T | Steve Boros (Mgr.) | .09 |
| 14 T | Greg Brock (RR) | .50 |
| 15 T | Mike Brown | .12 |
| 16 T | Tom Burgmeier | .09 |
| 17 T | Randy Bush | .09 |
| 18 T | Bert Campaneris | .12 |
| 19 T | Ron Cey | .25 |
| 20 T | Chris Codiroli | .12 |
| 21 T | Dave Collins | .15 |
| 22 T | Terry Crowley | .09 |
| 23 T | Julio Cruz | .09 |
| 24 T | Mike Davis | .15 |
| 25 T | Frank DiPino | .12 |
| 26 T | Bill Doran (RR) | 1.00 |
| 27 T | Jerry Dybzinski | .09 |
| 28 T | Jamie Easterly | .09 |
| 29 T | Juan Eichelberger | .09 |
| 30 T | Jim Essian | .09 |
| 31 T | Pete Falcone | .09 |
| 32 T | Mike Ferraro (Mgr.) | .09 |
| 33 T | Terry Forster | .12 |

| NO. | PLAYER | MINT |
|---|---|---|
| 34 T | Julio Franco (RR) | 1.25 |
| 35 T | Rich Gale | .09 |
| 36 T | Kiko Garcia | .09 |
| 37 T | Steve Garvey | 1.25 |
| 38 T | Johnny Grubb | .09 |
| 39 T | Mel Hall | .75 |
| 40 T | Von Hayes | .50 |
| 41 T | Danny Heep | .09 |
| 42 T | Steve Henderson | .09 |
| 43 T | Keith Hernandez | .75 |
| 44 T | Leo Hernandez | .20 |
| 45 T | Willie Hernandez | .40 |
| 46 T | Al Holland | .12 |
| 47 T | F. Howard (Mgr.) | .09 |
| 48 T | Bobby Johnson | .09 |
| 49 T | Cliff Johnson | .09 |
| 50 T | Odell Jones | .09 |
| 51 T | Mike Jorgensen | .09 |
| 52 T | Bob Kearney | .09 |
| 53 T | Steve Kemp | .12 |
| 54 T | Matt Keough | .09 |
| 55 T | Ron Kittle (RR) | .75 |
| 56 T | Mickey Klutts | .09 |
| 57 T | Alan Knicely | .09 |
| 58 T | Mike Krukow | .09 |
| 59 T | Rafael Landestoy | .09 |
| 60 T | Carney Lansford | .20 |
| 61 T | Joe Lefebvre | .09 |
| 62 T | Bryan Little | .12 |
| 63 T | Aurelio Lopez | .15 |
| 64 T | Mike Madden | .25 |
| 65 T | Rick Manning | .09 |
| 66 T | Billy Martin (Mgr.) | .15 |

| NO. | PLAYER | MINT |
|---|---|---|
| 67 T | Lee Mazzilli | .12 |
| 68 T | Andy McGaffigan | .09 |
| 69 T | Craig McMurtry | .25 |
| 70 T | J. McNamara (Mgr.) | .09 |
| 71 T | Orlando Mercado | .09 |
| 72 T | Larry Milbourne | .09 |
| 73 T | Randy Moffitt | .09 |
| 74 T | Sid Monge | .09 |
| 75 T | Jose Morales | .09 |
| 76 T | Omar Moreno | .12 |
| 77 T | Joe Morgan | .60 |
| 78 T | Mike Morgan | .09 |
| 79 T | Dale Murray | .09 |
| 80 T | Jeff Newman | .09 |
| 81 T | Pete O'Brien (RR) | 1.00 |
| 82 T | Jorge Orta | .09 |
| 83 T | Alejandro Pena (RR) | .50 |
| 84 T | Pascual Perez | .12 |
| 85 T | Tony Perez | .30 |
| 86 T | Broderick Perkins | .09 |
| 87 T | Tony Phillips | .09 |
| 88 T | Charlie Puleo | .09 |
| 89 T | Pat Putnam | .09 |
| 90 T | Jamie Quirk | .09 |
| 91 T | Doug Rader (Mgr.) | .12 |
| 92 T | Chuck Rainey | .09 |
| 93 T | Bobby Ramos | .09 |
| 94 T | Gary Redus (RR) | .60 |
| 95 T | Steve Renko | .09 |
| 96 T | Leon Roberts | .09 |
| 97 T | Aurelio Rodriquez | .09 |
| 98 T | Dick Ruthven | .09 |
| 99 T | Daryl Sconiers | .09 |

| NO. | PLAYER | MINT |
|---|---|---|
| 100 T | Mike Scott | .08 |
| 101 T | Tom Seaver | 1.25 |
| 102 T | John Shelby (RR) | .20 |
| 103 T | Bob Shirley | .08 |
| 104 T | Joe Simpson | .08 |
| 105 T | Doug Sisk | .15 |
| 106 T | Mike Smithson (RR) | .25 |
| 107 T | Elias Sosa | .06 |
| 108 T | D. Strawberry (RR) | 20.00 |
| 109 T | Tom Tellmann | .08 |
| 110 T | Gene Tenace | .08 |
| 111 T | Gorman Thomas | .25 |
| 112 T | Dick Tidrow | .08 |
| 113 T | Dave Tobik | .08 |
| 114 T | Wayne Tolleson | .12 |
| 115 T | Mike Torrez | .10 |
| 116 T | Manny Trillo | .12 |
| 117 T | Steve Trout | .10 |
| 118 T | Lee Tunnell | .12 |
| 119 T | Mike Vail | .08 |
| 120 T | Ellis Valentine | .15 |
| 121 T | Tom Veryzer | .08 |
| 122 T | George Vukovich | .08 |
| 123 T | Rick Waits | .08 |
| 124 T | Greg Walker (RR) | 2.00 |
| 125 T | Chris Welsh | .08 |
| 126 T | Len Whitehouse | .08 |
| 127 T | Eddie Whitson | .10 |
| 128 T | Jim Wohlford | .08 |
| 129 T | Matt Young (RR) | .35 |
| 130 T | Joel Youngblood | .08 |
| 131 T | Pat Zachry | .08 |
| 132 T | Traded Checklist | .25 |

# 1984 Topps....Complete Set of 792 Cards—Value $60.00
Features the rookie cards of Don Mattingly and Darryl Strawberry.

| NO. | PLAYER | MINT |
|---|---|---|
| 1 | Highlight—S. Carlton 300th Win and SO King | .25 |
| 2 | Highlight—Henderson 100 SB's, 3 Seasons | .30 |
| 3 | Highlight—Quisenberry Save Record | .15 |
| 4 | Highlight—N. Ryan, G. Perry, S. Carlton— Surpass Walter Johnson | .25 |
| 5 | Highlight—D. Righetti, B. Forsch, B. Warren— No Hitters | .15 |
| 6 | Highlight—Bench, Yaz, Perry,—All Retire | .25 |
| 7 | Gary Lucas | .06 |
| 8 | Don Mattingly (R) | 28.00 |
| 9 | Jim Gott | .06 |
| 10 | Robin Yount | .35 |
| 11 | Twins Leaders: Kent Hrbek, Ken Schrom | .10 |
| 12 | Billy Sample | .06 |
| 13 | Scott Holman | .06 |
| 14 | Tom Brookens | .06 |
| 15 | Burt Hooton | .06 |
| 16 | Omar Moreno | .08 |
| 17 | John Denny | .08 |

| NO. | PLAYER | MINT |
|---|---|---|
| 18 | Dale Berra | .06 |
| 19 | Ray Fontenot | .15 |
| 20 | Greg Luzinski | .12 |
| 21 | Joe Altobelli (Mgr.) | .06 |
| 22 | Bryan Clark | .06 |
| 23 | Keith Moreland | .06 |
| 24 | John Martin | .06 |
| 25 | Glenn Hubbard | .08 |
| 26 | Bud Black | .06 |
| 27 | Daryl Sconiers | .06 |
| 28 | Frank Viola | .08 |
| 29 | Danny Heep | .06 |
| 30 | Wade Boggs | 4.00 |
| 31 | Andy McGaffigan | .06 |
| 32 | Bobby Ramos | .06 |
| 33 | Tom Burgmeier | .06 |
| 34 | Eddie Milner | .06 |
| 35 | Don Sutton | .12 |
| 36 | Denny Walling | .06 |
| 37 | Rangers Leaders: Buddy Bell, Rick Honeycutt | .10 |
| 38 | Luis DeLeon | .06 |
| 39 | Garth Iorg | .06 |
| 40 | Dusty Baker | .10 |
| 41 | Tony Bernazard | .06 |
| 42 | Johnny Grubb | .06 |

| NO. | PLAYER | MINT |
|---|---|---|
| 43 | Ron Reed | .06 |
| 44 | Jim Morrison | .06 |
| 45 | Jerry Mumphrey | .06 |
| 46 | Ray Smith | .06 |
| 47 | Rudy Law | .06 |
| 48 | Julio Franco | .40 |
| 49 | John Stuper | .06 |
| 50 | Chris Chambliss | .08 |
| 51 | Jim Frey (Mgr.) | .06 |
| 52 | Paul Splittorff | .06 |
| 53 | Juan Beniquez | .08 |
| 54 | Jesse Orosco | .10 |
| 55 | Dave Concepcion | .15 |
| 56 | Gary Allenson | .06 |
| 57 | Dan Schatzeder | .06 |
| 58 | Max Venable | .06 |
| 59 | Sammy Stewart | .06 |
| 60 | Paul Molitor | .15 |
| 61 | Chris Codiroli (R) | .15 |
| 62 | Dave Hostetler | .06 |
| 63 | Ed VandeBerg | .08 |
| 64 | Mike Scioscia | .06 |
| 65 | Kirk Gibson | .25 |
| 66 | Astros Leaders: Nolan Ryan, Jose Cruz | .10 |
| 67 | Gary Ward | .06 |

| NO. | PLAYER | MINT |
|---|---|---|
| 68 | Luis Salazar | .06 |
| 69 | Rod Scurry | .06 |
| 70 | Gary Matthews | .08 |
| 71 | Leo Hernandez | .15 |
| 72 | Mike Squires | .06 |
| 73 | Jody Davis | .10 |
| 74 | Jerry Martin | .06 |
| 75 | Bob Forsch | .06 |
| 76 | Alfredo Griffin | .06 |
| 77 | Brett Butler | .08 |
| 78 | Mike Torrez | .06 |
| 79 | Rob Wilfong | .06 |
| 80 | Steve Rogers | .08 |
| 81 | Billy Martin (Mgr.) | .15 |
| 82 | Doug Bird | .06 |
| 83 | Richie Zisk | .08 |
| 84 | Lenny Faedo | .06 |
| 85 | Atlee Hammaker | .06 |
| 86 | John Shelby | .15 |
| 87 | Frank Pastore | .06 |
| 88 | Rob Picciolo | .06 |
| 89 | Mike Smithson | .15 |
| 90 | Pedro Guerrero | .40 |
| 91 | Dan Spillner | .06 |
| 92 | Lloyd Moseby | .20 |
| 93 | Bob Knepper | .06 |

| NO. | PLAYER | MINT |
|---|---|---|
| 94 | Mario Ramirez | .06 |
| 95 | Aurelio Lopez | .06 |
| 96 | Royals Leaders: | .10 |
| | Hal McRae, Larry Gura | |
| 97 | LaMarr Hoyt | .15 |
| 98 | Steve Nicosia | .06 |
| 99 | Criag Lefferts (R) | .15 |
| 100 | Reggie Jackson | .50 |
| 101 | Porfirio Altamirano | .06 |
| 102 | Ken Oberkfell | .06 |
| 103 | Dwayne Murphy | .08 |
| 104 | Ken Dayley | .06 |
| 105 | Tony Armas | .15 |
| 106 | Tim Stoddard | .06 |
| 107 | Ned Yost | .06 |
| 108 | Randy Moffitt | .06 |
| 109 | Brad Wellman | .06 |
| 110 | Ron Guidry | .20 |
| 111 | Bill Virdon (Mgr.) | .06 |
| 112 | Tom Niedenfuer | .08 |
| 113 | Kelly Paris | .12 |
| 114 | Checklist No. 1 | .08 |
| 115 | Andre Thornton | .08 |
| 116 | George Bjorkman | .06 |
| 117 | Tom Veryzer | .06 |
| 118 | Charlie Hough | .06 |
| 119 | Johnny Wockenfuss | .06 |
| 120 | Keith Hernandez | .35 |
| 121 | Pat Sheridan | .15 |
| 122 | Cecilio Guante | .06 |
| 123 | Butch Wynegar | .06 |
| 124 | Damaso Garcia | .10 |
| 125 | Britt Burns | .08 |
| 126 | Braves Leaders: | .10 |
| | Dale Murphy, C. McMurtry | |
| 127 | Mike Madden | .15 |
| 128 | Rick Manning | .06 |
| 129 | Bill Laskey | .06 |
| 130 | Ozzie Smith | .15 |
| 131 | Batting Leaders: | .35 |
| | Bill Madlock, Wade Boggs | |
| 132 | Home Run Leaders: | .25 |
| | Mike Schmidt, Jim Rice | |
| 133 | RBI Leaders: | .25 |
| | Dale Murphy, C. Cooper, | |
| | Jim Rice | |
| 134 | Stolen Base Leaders: | .25 |
| | T. Raines, R. Henderson | |
| 135 | Victory Leaders: | .15 |
| | John Denny, LaMarr Hoyt | |
| 136 | Stikeout Leaders: | .15 |
| | Steve Carlton, Jack Morris | |
| 137 | ERA Leaders: | .08 |
| | A. Hammaker, R. Honeycutt | |
| 138 | Leading Firemen: | .10 |
| | A. Holland, D. Quisenberry | |
| 139 | Bert Campaneris | .06 |
| 140 | Storm Davis | .12 |
| 141 | Pat Corrales (Mgr.) | .06 |
| 142 | Rich Gale | .06 |
| 143 | Jose Morales | .06 |
| 144 | Brian Harper | .15 |
| 145 | Gary Lavelle | .06 |
| 146 | Ed Romero | .06 |
| 147 | Dan Petry | .15 |
| 148 | Joe Lefebvre | .06 |
| 149 | Jon Matlack | .06 |
| 150 | Dale Murphy | 1.00 |
| 151 | Steve Trout | .06 |
| 152 | Glenn Brummer | .06 |
| 153 | Dick Tidrow | .06 |
| 154 | Dave Henderson | .06 |
| 155 | Frank White | .06 |
| 156 | A's Leaders: | .10 |
| | R. Henderson, T. Conroy | |
| 157 | Gary Gaetti | .06 |
| 158 | John Curtis | .06 |
| 159 | Darryl Cias | .06 |
| 160 | Mario Soto | .08 |
| 161 | Junior Ortiz | .06 |
| 162 | Bob Ojeda | .06 |
| 163 | Lorenzo Gray | .06 |
| 164 | Scott Sanderson | .06 |
| 165 | Ken Singleton | .08 |
| 166 | Jamie Nelson | .12 |
| 167 | Marshall Edwards | .06 |
| 168 | Juan Bonilla | .06 |
| 169 | Larry Parrish | .08 |
| 170 | Jerry Reuss | .08 |
| 171 | Frank Robinson (Mgr.) | .12 |
| 172 | Frank DiPino | .06 |
| 173 | Marvell Wynne | .15 |
| 174 | Juan Berenguer | .06 |
| 175 | Graig Nettles | .15 |
| 176 | Lee Smith | .10 |
| 177 | Jerry Hairston | .06 |
| 178 | Bill Krueger | .12 |
| 179 | Buck Martinez | .06 |
| 180 | Manny Trillo | .08 |
| 181 | Roy Thomas | .06 |
| 182 | Darryl Strawberry (R) | 6.00 |
| 183 | Al Williams | .06 |
| 184 | Mike O'Berry | .06 |
| 185 | Sixto Lezcano | .06 |
| 186 | Cardinal Leaders: | .10 |
| | Lonnie Smith, John Stuper | |
| 187 | Luis Aponte | .06 |
| 188 | Bryan Little | .06 |
| 189 | Tim Conroy | .12 |
| 190 | Ben Oglivie | .08 |
| 191 | Mike Boddicker | .15 |
| 192 | Nick Esasky (R) | .35 |
| 193 | Darrell Brown | .06 |
| 194 | Domingo Ramos | .06 |
| 195 | Jack Morris | .20 |
| 196 | Don Slaught | .06 |
| 197 | Garry Hancock | .06 |
| 198 | Bill Doran (R) | .75 |
| 199 | Willie Hernandez | .30 |
| 200 | Andre Dawson | .25 |
| 201 | Bruce Kison | .06 |
| 202 | Bobby Cox (Mgr.) | .06 |
| 203 | Matt Keough | .06 |
| 204 | Bobby Meacham (R) | .35 |
| 205 | Greg Minton | .06 |
| 206 | Andy Van Slyke (R) | .50 |
| 207 | Donnie Moore | .08 |
| 208 | Jose Oquendo | .08 |
| 209 | Manny Sarmiento | .06 |
| 210 | Joe Morgan | .20 |
| 211 | Rick Sweet | .06 |
| 212 | Broderick Perkins | .06 |
| 213 | Bruce Hurst | .06 |
| 214 | Paul Householder | .06 |
| 215 | Tippy Martinez | .06 |
| 216 | White Sox Leaders: | .10 |
| | C. Fisk, R. Dotson | |
| 217 | Alan Ashby | .06 |
| 218 | Rick Waits | .06 |
| 219 | Joe Simpson | .06 |
| 220 | Fernando Valenzuela | .40 |
| 221 | Cliff Johnson | .06 |
| 222 | Rick Honeycutt | .08 |
| 223 | Wayne Krenchicki | .06 |
| 224 | Sid Monge | .06 |
| 225 | Lee Mazzilli | .06 |
| 226 | Juan Eichelberger | .06 |
| 227 | Steve Braun | .06 |
| 228 | John Rabb | .15 |
| 229 | Paul Owens (Mgr.) | .06 |
| 230 | Rickey Henderson | .60 |
| 231 | Gary Woods | .06 |
| 232 | Tim Wallach | .10 |
| 233 | Checklist No. 2 | .08 |
| 234 | Rafael Ramirez | .06 |
| 235 | Matt Young | .10 |
| 236 | Ellis Valentine | .06 |
| 237 | John Castino | .06 |
| 238 | Reid Nichols | .06 |
| 239 | Jay Howell | .06 |
| 240 | Eddie Murray | .50 |
| 241 | Billy Almon | .06 |
| 242 | Alex Trevino | .06 |
| 243 | Pete Ladd | .06 |
| 244 | Candy Maldonado | .10 |
| 245 | Rick Sutcliffe | .25 |
| 246 | Mets Leaders: | .12 |
| | M. Wilson, Tom Seaver | |
| 247 | Onix Concepcion | .06 |
| 248 | Bill Dawley (R) | .20 |
| 249 | Jay Johnstone | .06 |
| 250 | Bill Madlock | .15 |
| 251 | Tony Gwynn | 1.00 |
| 252 | Larry Christenson | .06 |
| 253 | Jim Wohlford | .06 |
| 254 | Shane Rawley | .06 |
| 255 | Bruce Benedict | .06 |
| 256 | Dave Geisel | .06 |
| 257 | Julio Cruz | .06 |
| 258 | Luis Sanchez | .06 |
| 259 | Sparky Anderson (Mgr.) | .08 |
| 260 | Scott McGregor | .08 |
| 261 | Bobby Brown | .06 |
| 262 | Tom Candiotti | .06 |
| 263 | Jack Fimple | .06 |
| 264 | Doug Frobel | .12 |
| 265 | Donnie Hill (R) | .15 |
| 266 | Steve Lubratich | .06 |
| 267 | Carmelo Martinez (R) | .40 |
| 268 | Jack O'Connor | .06 |
| 269 | Aurelio Rodriquez | .06 |
| 270 | Jeff Russell | .12 |
| 271 | Moose Haas | .06 |
| 272 | Rick Dempsey | .06 |
| 273 | Charlie Puleo | .06 |
| 274 | Rick Monday | .06 |
| 275 | Len Matuszek | .06 |
| 276 | Angels Leaders: | .10 |
| | Rod Carew, Geoff Zahn | |
| 277 | Eddie Whitson | .06 |
| 278 | Jorge Bell | .10 |
| 279 | Ivan DeJesus | .06 |
| 280 | Floyd Bannister | .10 |
| 281 | Larry Milbourne | .06 |
| 282 | Jim Barr | .06 |
| 283 | Larry Biittner | .06 |
| 284 | Howard Bailey | .06 |
| 285 | Darrell Porter | .06 |
| 286 | Lary Sorensen | .06 |
| 287 | Warren Cromartie | .06 |
| 288 | Jim Beattie | .06 |
| 289 | Randy Johnson | .06 |
| 290 | Dave Dravecky | .08 |
| 291 | Chuck Tanner (Mgr.) | .06 |
| 292 | Tony Scott | .06 |
| 293 | Ed Lynch | .06 |
| 294 | U.L. Washington | .06 |
| 295 | Mike Flanagan | .08 |
| 296 | Jeff Newman | .06 |
| 297 | Bruce Berenyi | .06 |
| 298 | Jim Gantner | .06 |
| 299 | John Butcher | .06 |
| 300 | Pete Rose | 1.25 |
| 301 | Frank LaCorte | .06 |
| 302 | Barry Bonnell | .06 |
| 303 | Marty Castillo | .06 |
| 304 | Warren Brusstar | .06 |
| 305 | Roy Smalley | .06 |
| 306 | Dodgers Leaders: | .12 |
| | Pedro Guerrero, Bob Welch | |
| 307 | Bobby Mitchell | .06 |
| 308 | Ron Hassey | .06 |
| 309 | Tony Phillips | .06 |
| 310 | Willie McGee | .40 |
| 311 | Jerry Koosman | .06 |
| 312 | Jorge Orta | .06 |
| 313 | Mike Jorgensen | .06 |
| 314 | Orlando Mercado | .06 |
| 315 | Bob Grich | .06 |
| 316 | Mark Bradley | .08 |
| 317 | Greg Pryor | .06 |
| 318 | Bill Gullickson | .08 |
| 319 | Al Bumbry | .06 |
| 320 | Bob Stanley | .06 |
| 321 | Harvey Kuenn (Mgr.) | .06 |
| 322 | Ken Schrom | .06 |
| 323 | Alan Knicely | .06 |
| 324 | Alejandro Pena (R) | .30 |
| 325 | Darrell Evans | .12 |
| 326 | Bob Kearney | .06 |
| 327 | Ruppert Jones | .06 |
| 328 | Vern Ruhle | .06 |
| 329 | Pat Tabler | .06 |
| 330 | John Candelaria | .06 |
| 331 | Bucky Dent | .06 |
| 332 | Kevin Gross (R) | .30 |
| 333 | Larry Herndon | .06 |
| 334 | Chuck Rainey | .06 |
| 335 | Don Baylor | .12 |
| 336 | Mariners Leaders: | .10 |
| | Pat Putnam, M. Young | |
| 337 | Kevin Hagen | .06 |
| 338 | Mike Warren | .12 |
| 339 | Roy Lee Jackson | .06 |
| 340 | Hal McRae | .06 |
| 341 | Dave Tobik | .06 |
| 342 | Tim Foli | .06 |
| 343 | Mark Davis | .06 |
| 344 | Rick Miller | .06 |
| 345 | Kent Hrbek | .30 |
| 346 | Kurt Bevacqua | .06 |
| 347 | Allan Ramirez | .06 |
| 348 | Toby Harrah | .06 |
| 349 | Bob Gibson | .12 |
| 350 | George Foster | .20 |
| 351 | Russ Nixon (Mgr.) | .06 |
| 352 | Dave Stewart | .06 |
| 353 | Jim Anderson | .06 |
| 354 | Jeff Burroughs | .06 |
| 355 | Jason Thompson | .08 |
| 356 | Glenn Abbott | .06 |
| 357 | Ron Cey | .15 |
| 358 | Bob Dernier | .08 |
| 359 | Jim Acker (R) | .15 |
| 360 | Willie Randolph | .08 |
| 361 | Dave Smith | .06 |
| 362 | David Green | .06 |
| 363 | Tim Laudner | .06 |
| 364 | Scott Fletcher | .06 |
| 365 | Steve Bedrosian | .06 |
| 366 | Padres Leaders: | .10 |
| | T. Kennedy, D. Dravecky | |
| 367 | Jamie Easterly | .06 |
| 368 | Hubie Brooks | .10 |
| 369 | Steve McCatty | .06 |
| 370 | Tim Raines | .30 |
| 371 | Dave Gumpert | .06 |
| 372 | Gary Roenicke | .06 |
| 373 | Bill Scherrer | .06 |
| 374 | Don Money | .06 |
| 375 | Dennis Leonard | .06 |
| 376 | Dave Anderson | .15 |
| 377 | Danny Darwin | .06 |
| 378 | Bob Brenly | .06 |
| 379 | Checklist No.3 | .08 |
| 380 | Steve Garvey | .40 |
| 381 | Ralph Houk (Mgr.) | .06 |
| 382 | Chris Nyman | .06 |
| 383 | Terry Puhl | .06 |
| 384 | Lee Tunnell | .12 |
| 385 | Tony Perez | .15 |
| 386 | George Hendrick (AS) | .10 |
| 387 | Johnny Ray (AS) | .10 |
| 388 | Mike Schmidt (AS) | .30 |
| 389 | Ozzie Smith (AS) | .12 |
| 390 | Tim Raines (AS) | .20 |
| 391 | Dale Murphy (AS) | .40 |
| 392 | Andre Dawson (AS) | .25 |
| 393 | Gary Carter (AS) | .30 |
| 394 | Steve Rogers (AS) | .12 |
| 395 | Steve Carlton (AS) | .30 |
| 396 | Jesse Orosco (AS) | .08 |
| 397 | Eddie Murray (AS) | .35 |
| 398 | Lou Whitaker (AS) | .12 |
| 399 | George Brett (AS) | .40 |
| 400 | Cal Ripken (AS) | .30 |
| 401 | Jim Rice (AS) | .25 |
| 402 | Dave Winfield (AS) | .25 |
| 403 | Lloyd Moseby (AS) | .12 |
| 404 | Ted Simmons (AS) | .12 |
| 405 | LaMarr Hoyt (AS) | .12 |
| 406 | Ron Guidry (AS) | .15 |
| 407 | Dan Quisenberry (AS) | .15 |
| 408 | Lou Piniella | .10 |
| 409 | Juan Agosto | .06 |
| 410 | Claudell Washington | .08 |
| 411 | Houston Jimenez | .06 |
| 412 | Doug Rader (Mgr.) | .06 |
| 413 | Spike Owen (R) | .20 |
| 414 | Mitchell Page | .06 |

# 1984 Topps (Continued)

| NO. PLAYER | MINT |
|---|---|
| 415 Tommy John | .15 |
| 416 Dane Iorg | .06 |
| 417 Mike Armstrong | .06 |
| 418 Ron Hodges | .06 |
| 419 John Johnson | .06 |
| 420 Cecil Cooper | .20 |
| 421 Charlie Lea | .06 |
| 422 Jose Cruz | .12 |
| 423 Mike Morgan | .06 |
| 424 Dann Bilardello | .06 |
| 425 Steve Howe | .06 |
| 426 Orioles Leaders: | .12 |
| M. Boddicker, C. Ripken | |
| 427 Rick Leach | .06 |
| 428 Fred Breining | .06 |
| 429 Randy Bush | .06 |
| 430 Rusty Staub | .10 |
| 431 Chris Bando | .06 |
| 432 Charlie Hudson (R) | .20 |
| 433 Rich Hebner | .06 |
| 434 Harold Baines | .20 |
| 435 Neil Allen | .06 |
| 436 Rick Peters | .06 |
| 437 Mike Proly | .06 |
| 438 Biff Pocoroba | .06 |
| 439 Bob Stoddard | .06 |
| 440 Steve Kemp | .06 |
| 441 Bob Lillis (Mgr.) | .06 |
| 442 Byron McLaughlin | .06 |
| 443 Benny Ayala | .06 |
| 444 Steve Renko | .06 |
| 445 Jerry Remy | .06 |
| 446 Luis Pujols | .06 |
| 447 Tom Brunansky | .20 |
| 448 Ben Hayes | .06 |
| 449 Joe Pettini | .06 |
| 450 Gary Carter | .45 |
| 451 Bob Jones | .06 |
| 452 Chuck Porter | .06 |
| 453 Willie Upshaw | .15 |
| 454 Joe Beckwith | .06 |
| 455 Terry Kennedy | .10 |
| 456 Cubs Leaders: | .12 |
| F. Jenkins, K. Moreland | |
| 457 Dave Rozema | .06 |
| 458 Kiko Garcia | .06 |
| 459 Kevin Hickey | .06 |
| 460 Dave Winfield | .40 |
| 461 Jim Maler | .06 |
| 462 Lee Lacy | .06 |
| 463 Dave Engle | .06 |
| 464 Jeff Jones | .06 |
| 465 Mookie Wilson | .08 |
| 466 Gene Garber | .06 |
| 467 Mike Ramsey | .06 |
| 468 Geoff Zahn | .06 |
| 469 Tom O'Malley | .06 |
| 470 Nolan Ryan | .30 |
| 471 Dick Howser (Mgr.) | .06 |
| 472 Mike Brown | .06 |
| 473 Jim Dwyer | .06 |
| 474 Greg Bargar | .06 |
| 475 Gary Redus (R) | .40 |
| 476 Tom Tellmann | .06 |
| 477 Rafael Landestoy | .06 |
| 478 Alan Bannister | .06 |
| 479 Frank Tanana | .06 |
| 480 Ron Kittle | .25 |
| 481 Mark Thurmond (R) | .30 |
| 482 Enos Cabell | .06 |
| 483 Fergie Jenkins | .15 |
| 484 Ozzie Virgil | .06 |
| 485 Rick Rhoden | .06 |
| 486 Yankees Leaders: | .12 |
| Don Baylor, Ron Guidry | |
| 487 Ricky Adams | .06 |
| 488 Jesse Barfield | .12 |
| 489 Dave Von Ohlen | .06 |
| 490 Cal Ripken | .50 |
| 491 Bobby Castillo | .06 |
| 492 Tucker Ashford | .06 |
| 493 Mike Norris | .06 |
| 494 Chili Davis | .15 |
| 495 Rollie Fingers | .15 |
| 496 Terry Francona | .06 |

| NO. PLAYER | MINT |
|---|---|
| 497 Bud Anderson | .06 |
| 498 Rich Gedman | .06 |
| 499 Mike Witt | .06 |
| 500 George Brett | .60 |
| 501 Steve Henderson | .06 |
| 502 Joe Torre (Mgr.) | .08 |
| 503 Elias Sosa | .06 |
| 504 Mickey Rivers | .08 |
| 505 Pete Vuckovich | .08 |
| 506 Ernie Whitt | .06 |
| 507 Mike LaCoss | .06 |
| 508 Mel Hall | .12 |
| 509 Brad Havens | .06 |
| 510 Alan Trammell | .30 |
| 511 Marty Bystrom | .06 |
| 512 Oscar Gamble | .08 |
| 513 Dave Beard | .06 |
| 514 Floyd Rayford | .06 |
| 515 Gorman Thomas | .15 |
| 516 Expos Leaders: | .10 |
| Al Oliver, Charlie Lea | |
| 517 John Moses | .06 |
| 518 Greg Walker (R) | .75 |
| 519 Ron Davis | .06 |
| 520 Bob Boone | .06 |
| 521 Pete Falcone | .06 |
| 522 Dave Bergman | .06 |
| 523 Glenn Hoffman | .06 |
| 524 Carlos Diaz | .06 |
| 525 Willie Wilson | .20 |
| 526 Ron Oester | .06 |
| 527 Checklist No. 4 | .08 |
| 528 Mark Brouhard | .06 |
| 529 Keith Atherton | .06 |
| 530 Dan Ford | .06 |
| 531 Steve Boros (Mgr.) | .06 |
| 532 Eric Show | .06 |
| 533 Ken Landreaux | .06 |
| 534 Pete O'Brien (R) | 1.00 |
| 535 Bo Diaz | .06 |
| 536 Doug Bair | .06 |
| 537 Johnny Ray | .12 |
| 538 Kevin Bass | .06 |
| 539 George Frazier | .06 |
| 540 George Hendrick | .08 |
| 541 Dennis Lamp | .06 |
| 542 Duane Kuiper | .06 |
| 543 Craig McMurtry (R) | .15 |
| 544 Cesar Geronimo | .06 |
| 545 Bill Buckner | .10 |
| 546 Indians Leaders: | .08 |
| Mike Hargrove, L. Sorensen | |
| 547 Mike Moore | .06 |
| 548 Ron Jackson | .06 |
| 549 Walt Terrell (R) | .30 |
| 550 Jim Rice | .40 |
| 551 Scott Ullger | .06 |
| 552 Ray Burris | .06 |
| 553 Joe Nolan | .06 |
| 554 Ted Power | .06 |
| 555 Greg Brock | .10 |
| 556 Joey McLaughlin | .06 |
| 557 Wayne Tolleson | .06 |
| 558 Mike Davis | .08 |
| 559 Mike Scott | .06 |
| 560 Carlton Fisk | .20 |
| 561 Whitey Herzog (Mgr.) | .08 |
| 562 Manny Castillo | .06 |
| 563 Glenn Wilson | .12 |
| 564 Al Holland | .06 |
| 565 Leon Durham | .20 |
| 566 Jim Bibby | .06 |
| 567 Mike Heath | .06 |
| 568 Pete Filson | .06 |
| 569 Bake McBride | .06 |
| 570 Dan Quisenberry | .20 |
| 571 Bruce Bochy | .06 |
| 572 Jerry Royster | .06 |
| 573 Dave Kingman | .10 |
| 574 Brian Downing | .06 |
| 575 Jim Clancy | .06 |
| 576 Giants Leaders: | .07 |
| J. Leonard, A. Hammaker | |
| 577 Mark Clear | .06 |
| 578 Lenn Sakata | .06 |

| NO. PLAYER | MINT |
|---|---|
| 579 Bob James (R) | .30 |
| 580 Lonnie Smith | .08 |
| 581 Jose DeLeon (R) | .25 |
| 582 Bob McClure | .06 |
| 583 Derrel Thomas | .06 |
| 584 Dave Schmidt | .06 |
| 585 Dan Driessen | .06 |
| 586 Joe Niekro | .08 |
| 587 Von Hayes | .20 |
| 588 Milt Wilcox | .06 |
| 589 Mike Easler | .08 |
| 590 Dave Stieb | .20 |
| 591 Tony LaRussa (Mgr.) | .06 |
| 592 Andre Robertson | .06 |
| 593 Jeff Lahti | .06 |
| 594 Gene Richards | .06 |
| 595 Jeff Reardon | .08 |
| 596 Ryne Sandberg | 1.00 |
| 597 Rick Camp | .06 |
| 598 Rusty Kuntz | .06 |
| 599 Doug Sisk (R) | .15 |
| 600 Rod Carew | .30 |
| 601 John Tudor | .15 |
| 602 John Wathan | .06 |
| 603 Renie Martin | .06 |
| 604 John Lowenstein | .06 |
| 605 Mike Caldwell | .06 |
| 606 Blue Jays Leaders: | .10 |
| Lloyd Moseby, Dave Stieb | |
| 607 Tom Hume | .06 |
| 608 Bobby Johnson | .06 |
| 609 Dan Meyer | .06 |
| 610 Steve Sax | .20 |
| 611 Chet Lemon | .08 |
| 612 Harry Spilman | .06 |
| 613 Greg Gross | .06 |
| 614 Len Barker | .06 |
| 615 Garry Templeton | .12 |
| 616 Don Robinson | .06 |
| 617 Rick Cerone | .06 |
| 618 Dickie Noles | .06 |
| 619 Jerry Dybzinski | .06 |
| 620 Al Oliver | .15 |
| 621 Frank Howard (Mgr.) | .06 |
| 622 Al Cowens | .06 |
| 623 Ron Washington | .06 |
| 624 Terry Harper | .06 |
| 625 Larry Gura | .06 |
| 626 Bob Clark | .06 |
| 627 Dave LaPoint | .06 |
| 628 Ed Jurak | .06 |
| 629 Rick Langford | .06 |
| 630 Ted Simmons | .12 |
| 631 Denny Martinez | .06 |
| 632 Tom Foley | .12 |
| 633 Mike Krukow | .06 |
| 634 Mike Marshall | .15 |
| 635 Dave Righetti | .15 |
| 636 Pat Putnam | .06 |
| 637 Phillies Leaders: | .10 |
| G. Matthews, J. Denny | |
| 638 George Vuckovich | .06 |
| 639 Rick Lysander | .06 |
| 640 Lance Parrish | .25 |
| 641 Mike Richardt | .06 |
| 642 Tom Underwood | .06 |
| 643 Mike Brown (R) | .30 |
| 644 Tim Lollar | .06 |
| 645 Tony Pena | .12 |
| 646 Checklist No.5 | .08 |
| 647 Ron Roenicke | .06 |
| 648 Len Whitehouse | .06 |
| 649 Tom Herr | .12 |
| 650 Phil Niekro | .15 |
| 651 J. McNamara (Mgr.) | .06 |
| 652 Rudy May | .06 |
| 653 Dave Stapleton | .06 |
| 654 Bob Bailor | .06 |
| 655 Amos Otis | .06 |
| 656 Bryn Smith | .06 |
| 657 Thad Bosley | .06 |
| 658 Jerry Augustine | .06 |
| 659 Duane Walker | .06 |
| 660 Ray Knight | .06 |
| 661 Steve Yeager | .06 |

| NO. PLAYER | MINT |
|---|---|
| 662 Tom Brennan | .06 |
| 663 Johnnie LeMaster | .06 |
| 664 Dave Stegman | .06 |
| 665 Buddy Bell | .15 |
| 666 Tigers Leaders: | .12 |
| Lou Whitaker, J. Morris | |
| 667 Vance Law | .06 |
| 668 Larry McWilliams | .06 |
| 669 Dave Lopes | .08 |
| 670 Rich Gossage | .20 |
| 671 Jamie Quirk | .06 |
| 672 Ricky Nelson | .12 |
| 673 Mike Walters | .12 |
| 674 Tim Flannery | .06 |
| 675 Pascual Perez | .08 |
| 676 Brian Giles | .06 |
| 677 Doyle Alexander | .06 |
| 678 Chris Speier | .06 |
| 679 Art Howe | .06 |
| 680 Fred Lynn | .20 |
| 681 Tom Lasorda (Mgr.) | .08 |
| 682 Dan Morogiello | .06 |
| 683 Marty Barrett (R) | 1.50 |
| 684 Bob Shirley | .06 |
| 685 Willie Aikens | .06 |
| 686 Joe Price | .06 |
| 687 Roy Howell | .06 |
| 688 George Wright | .06 |
| 689 Mike Fischlin | .06 |
| 690 Jack Clark | .20 |
| 691 Steve Lake | .06 |
| 692 Dickie Thon | .06 |
| 693 Alan Wiggins | .08 |
| 694 Mike Stanton | .06 |
| 695 Lou Whitaker | .20 |
| 696 Pirates Leaders: | .08 |
| Bill Madlock, Rick Rhoden | |
| 697 Dale Murray | .06 |
| 698 Marc Hill | .06 |
| 699 Dave Rucker | .06 |
| 700 Mike Schmidt | .40 |
| 701 Batting Leaders: | .30 |
| Bill Madlock, Dave Parker, Pete Rose | |
| 702 Hit Leaders: | .30 |
| Pete Rose, Rusty Staub, Tony Perez | |
| 703 Home Run Leaders: | .25 |
| Mike Schmidt, Tony Perez, D. Kingman | |
| 704 RBI Leaders: | .15 |
| Rusty Staub, Tony Perez, Al Oliver | |
| 705 Stolen Bases Leaders: | .12 |
| Larry Bowa, Joe Morgan, Cesar Cedeno | |
| 706 Victory Leaders: | .15 |
| Steve Carlton, F. Jenkins, Tom Seaver | |
| 707 Strikeout Leaders: | .20 |
| Tom Seaver, Steve Carlton, Nolan Ryan | |
| 708 ERA Leaders: | .15 |
| Tom Seaver, Steve Rogers, Steve Carlton | |
| 709 Save Leaders: | .12 |
| Bruce Sutter, Tug McGraw, G. Garber | |
| 710 Batting Leaders: | .25 |
| Rod Carew, Cecil Cooper, George Brett | |
| 711 Hit Leaders: | .20 |
| Reggie Jackson, Rod Carew, Bert Campaneris | |
| 712 Home Run Leaders: | .20 |
| Graig Nettles, Reggie Jackson, Greg Luzinski | |
| 713 RBI Leaders: | .20 |
| Reggie Jackson, Ted Simmons, Graig Nettles | |
| 714 Stolen Bases Leaders: | .12 |
| Bert Campaneris, D. Lopes, Omar Moreno | |
| 715 Victory Leaders: | .15 |
| Jim Palmer, Don Sutton, Tommy John | |

| NO. PLAYER | MINT | NO. PLAYER | MINT | NO. PLAYER | MINT | NO. PLAYER | MINT |
|---|---|---|---|---|---|---|---|
| 716 Strikeouts Leaders: | .12 | 731 Lynn Jones | .06 | 752 Phil Garner | .06 | 772 Jim Slaton | .06 |
| Don Sutton, Jerry | | 732 Terry Crowley | .06 | 753 Doug Gwosdz | .06 | 773 Todd Cruz | .06 |
| Koosman, Bert Blyleven | | 733 Dave Collins | .06 | 754 Kent Tekulve | .06 | 774 Tom Gorman | .12 |
| 717 ERA Leaders: | .15 | 734 Odell Jones | .06 | 755 Garry Maddox | .06 | 775 Dave Parker | .20 |
| Jim Palmer, R. Fingers, | | 735 Rick Burleson | .06 | 756 Reds Leaders: | .08 | 776 Craig Reynolds | .06 |
| Ron Guidry | | 736 Dick Ruthven | .06 | Ron Oester, Mario Soto | | 777 Tom Paciorek | .06 |
| 718 Save Leaders: | .15 | 737 Jim Essian | .06 | 757 Larry Bowa | .08 | 778 Andy Hawkins (R) | .50 |
| Rollie Fingers, R. Gossage, | | 738 Bill Schroeder (R) | .30 | 758 Bill Stein | .06 | 779 Jim Sundberg | .06 |
| Dan Quisenberry | | 739 Bob Watson | .06 | 759 Richard Dotson | .08 | 780 Steve Carlton | .35 |
| 719 Andy Hassler | .06 | 740 Tom Seaver | .35 | 760 Bob Horner | .25 | 781 Checklist No. 6 | .08 |
| 720 Dwight Evans | .15 | 741 Wayne Gross | .06 | 761 John Montefusco | .06 | 782 Steve Balboni | .06 |
| 721 Del Crandall (Mgr.) | .06 | 742 Dick Williams (Mgr.) | .06 | 762 Rance Mulliniks | .06 | 783 Luis Leal | .06 |
| 722 Bob Welch | .06 | 743 Don Hood | .06 | 763 Craig Swan | .06 | 784 Leon Roberts | .06 |
| 723 Rich Dauer | .06 | 744 Jamie Allen | .12 | 764 Mike Hargrove | .06 | 785 Joaquin Andujar | .12 |
| 724 Eric Rasmussen | .06 | 745 Dennis Eckersley | .06 | 765 Ken Forsch | .06 | 786 Red Sox Leaders: | .20 |
| 725 Cesar Cedeno | .08 | 746 Mickey Hatcher | .06 | 766 Mike Vail | .06 | Bob Ojeda, Wade Boggs | |
| 726 Brewers Leaders: | .10 | 747 Pat Zachry | .06 | 767 Carney Lansford | .08 | 787 Bill Campbell | .06 |
| Ted Simmons, Moose Haas | | 748 Jeff Leonard | .06 | 768 Champ Summers | .06 | 788 Milt May | .06 |
| 727 Joel Youngblood | .06 | 749 Doug Flynn | .06 | 769 Bill Caudill | .08 | 789 Bert Blyleven | .08 |
| 728 Tug McGraw | .08 | 750 Jim Palmer | .25 | 770 Ken Griffey | .08 | 790 Doug DeCinces | .08 |
| 729 Gene Tenace | .06 | 751 Charlie Moore | .06 | 771 Billy Gardner (Mgr.) | .06 | 791 Terry Forster | .06 |
| 730 Bruce Sutter | .20 | | | | | 792 Bill Russell | .06 |

## 1984 Topps Traded. . .Complete Set of 132 Cards—Value $85.00

Updates the main 1984 card set with players who changed teams during the season and rookies. Features the first Topps card for Dwight Gooden and Bret Saberhagen. The complete set was packaged in a printed box and only distributed through card hobby dealers.

| NO. PLAYER | MINT | NO. PLAYER | MINT | NO. PLAYER | MINT | NO. PLAYER | MINT |
|---|---|---|---|---|---|---|---|
| 1 T Willie Aikens | .15 | 34 T Dennis Eckersley | .12 | 67 T R. Lachemann (Mgr.) | .10 | 100 T Jose Rijo (RR) | .50 |
| 2 T Luis Aponte | .10 | 35 T Jim Essian | .08 | 68 T Frank LaCorte | .10 | 101 T Jeff Robinson | .15 |
| 3 T Mike Armstrong | .10 | 36 T Darrell Evans | .25 | 69 T Dennis Lamp | .10 | 102 T Ron Romanick (RR) | .75 |
| 4 T Bob Bailor | .10 | 37 T Mike Fitzgerald | .15 | 70 T Mark Langston (RR) | 1.75 | 103 T Pete Rose | 5.00 |
| 5 T Dusty Baker | .12 | 38 T Tim Foli | .10 | 71 T Rich Leach | .10 | 104 T B. Saberhagen (RR) | 3.00 |
| 6 T Steve Balboni | .15 | 39 T George Frazier | .10 | 72 T Craig Lefferts | .10 | 105 T Juan Samuel (RR) | 2.00 |
| 7 T Alan Bannister | .10 | 40 T Rich Gale | .10 | 73 T Gary Lucas | .10 | 106 T Scott Sandefson | .12 |
| 8 T Dave Beard | .10 | 41 T Barbaro Garbey | .20 | 74 T Jerry Martin | .10 | 107 T Dick Schofield | .50 |
| 9 T Joe Beckwith | .10 | 42 T D. Gooden (RR) | 40.00 | 75 T Carmelo Martinez | .25 | 108 T Tom Seaver | 2.50 |
| 10 T Bruce Berenyi | .10 | 43 T Rich Gossage | .30 | 76 T Mike Mason | .20 | 109 T Jim Slaton | .08 |
| 11 T Dave Bergman | .10 | 44 T Wayne Gross | .10 | 77 T Gary Matthews | .15 | 110 T Mike Smithson | .08 |
| 12 T Tony Bernazard | .10 | 45 T Mark Gubicza (RR) | .50 | 78 T Andy McGaffigan | .10 | 111 T Lary Sorensen | .08 |
| 13 T Yogi Berra (Mgr.) | .30 | 46 T Jackie Gutierrez | .15 | 79 T Larry Milbourne | .10 | 112 T Tim Stoddard | .08 |
| 14 T Barry Bonnell | .10 | 47 T Mel Hall | .20 | 80 T Sid Monge | .10 | 113 T Champ Summers | .08 |
| 15 T Phil Bradley (RR) | 4.50 | 48 T Toby Harrah | .12 | 81 T Jackie Moore (Mgr.) | .10 | 114 T Jim Sundberg | .08 |
| 16 T Fred Breining | .10 | 49 T Ron Hassey | .10 | 82 T Joe Morgan | .75 | 115 T Rick Sutcliffe | .50 |
| 17 T Bill Buckner | .25 | 50 T Rich Hebner | .10 | 83 T Graig Nettles | 1.00 | 116 T Craig Swan | .10 |
| 18 T Ray Burris | .10 | 51 T Willie Hernandez | .40 | 84 T Phil Niekro | .50 | 117 T Tim Teufel (RR) | .40 |
| 19 T John Butcher | .10 | 52 T Ricky Horton (RR) | .35 | 85 T Ken Oberkfell | .12 | 118 T Derrel Thomas | .10 |
| 20 T Brett Butler | .35 | 53 T Art Howe | .10 | 86 T Mike O'Berry | .10 | 119 T Gorman Thomas | .15 |
| 21 T Enos Cabell | .10 | 54 T Dane Iorg | .10 | 87 T Al Oliver | .20 | 120 T Alex Trevino | .08 |
| 22 T Bill Campbell | .10 | 55 T Brook Jacoby (RR) | 1.00 | 88 T Jorge Orta | .10 | 121 T Manny Trillo | .12 |
| 23 T Bill Caudill | .10 | 56 T Mike Jeffcoat | .10 | 89 T Amos Otis | .15 | 122 T John Tudor | .30 |
| 24 T Bob Clark | .10 | 57 T D. Johnson (Mgr.) | .12 | 90 T Dave Parker | .75 | 123 T Tom Underwood | .10 |
| 25 T Bryan Clark | .10 | 58 T Lynn Jones | .10 | 91 T Tony Perez | .30 | 124 T Mike Vail | .10 |
| 26 T Jaime Cocanower | .12 | 59 T Ruppert Jones | .10 | 92 T Gerald Perry | .25 | 125 T Tom Waddell | .10 |
| 27 T Ron Darling (RR) | 6.00 | 60 T Mike Jorgensen | .10 | 93 T Gary Pettis (RR) | .50 | 126 T Gary Ward | .10 |
| 28 T Alvin Davis (RR) | 4.00 | 61 T Bob Kearney | .10 | 94 T Rob Picciolo | .08 | 127 T Curt Wilkerson | .10 |
| 29 T Ken Dayley | .12 | 62 T Jimmy Key (RR) | .75 | 95 T Vern Rapp (Mgr.) | .08 | 128 T Frank Williams | .10 |
| 30 T Jeff Dedmon | .12 | 63 T Dave Kingman | .15 | 96 T Floyd Rayford | .08 | 129 T Glenn Wilson | .25 |
| 31 T Bob Dernier | .10 | 64 T Jerry Koosman | .15 | 97 T Randy Ready (RR) | .35 | 130 T Johnny Wockenfuss | .10 |
| 32 T Carlos Diaz | .10 | 65 T Wayne Krenchicki | .10 | 98 T Ron Reed | .10 | 131 T Ned Yost | .10 |
| 33 T Mike Easler | .12 | 66 T Rusty Kuntz | .10 | 99 T Gene Richards | .10 | 132 T Traded Checklist | .15 |

# 1985 Topps....Complete Set of 792 Cards—Value $50.00

Features the rookie cards of Dwight Gooden, Roger Clemens, Alvin Davis, Bret Saberhagen, Orel Hershiser, and Kirby Puckett. Includes players and coaches of the 1984 USA Olympic Baseball Team.

| NO. PLAYER | MINT | NO. PLAYER | MINT | NO. PLAYER | MINT | NO. PLAYER | MINT |
|---|---|---|---|---|---|---|---|
| 1 Record—C. Fisk | .15 | 57 Pat Zachry | .05 | 123 Dave Smith | .05 | 176 Bill Schroeder | .05 |
| Longest Game, Catcher | | 58 Orlando Mercado | .05 | 124 Rich Hebner | .05 | 177 Dave Von Ohlen | .05 |
| 2 Record—S. Garvey | .20 | 59 Rick Waits | .05 | 125 Ken Tekulve | .05 | 178 Miguel Dilone | .05 |
| Errorless Games, 18 | | 60 George Hendrick | .08 | 126 Ruppert Jones | .05 | 179 Tommy John | .15 |
| 3 Record—D. Gooden | 1.50 | 61 Curt Kaufman (R) | .15 | 127 Mark Gubicza (R) | .25 | 180 Dave Winfield | .30 |
| Most Strikeouts, Rookie | | 62 Mike Ramsey | .05 | 128 Ernie Whitt | .05 | 181 Roger Clemens (R) | 7.00 |
| 4 Record—C. Johnson | .08 | 63 Steve McCatty | .05 | 129 Gene Garber | .05 | 182 Tim Flannery | .05 |
| Most Pinch Homers | | 64 Mark Bailey (R) | .15 | 130 Al Oliver | .10 | 183 Larry McWilliams | .05 |
| 5 Record—J. Morgan | .15 | 65 Bill Buckner | .10 | 131 Father & Son: | .07 | 184 Carmen Castillo | .05 |
| Most Homers, 2B | | 66 Dick Williams (Mgr.) | .05 | Gus and Buddy Bell | | 185 Al Holland | .05 |
| 6 Record—P. Rose | .50 | 67 Rafael Santana (R) | .20 | 132 Father & Son: | .07 | 186 Bob Lillis (Mgr.) | .05 |
| Most Singles, Career | | 68 Von Hayes | .15 | Yogi and Dale Berra | | 187 Mike Walters | .05 |
| 7 Record—N. Ryan | .20 | 69 Jim Winn | .12 | 133 Father & Son: | .07 | 188 Greg Pryor | .05 |
| Most Strikeouts, Career | | 70 Don Baylor | .10 | Ray and Bob Boone | | 189 Warren Brusstar | .05 |
| 8 Record—J. Samuel | .15 | 71 Tim Laudner | .05 | 134 Father & Son: | .07 | 190 Rusty Staub | .08 |
| Stolen Bases, Rookie | | 72 Rick Sutcliffe | .15 | Tito and Terry Francona | | 191 Steve Nicosia | .05 |
| 9 Record—B. Sutter | .12 | 73 Rusty Kuntz | .05 | 135 Father & Son: | .07 | 192 Howard Johnson | .05 |
| Most Saves, Season | | 74 Mike Krukow | .05 | Bob and Terry Kennedy | | 193 Jimmy Key (R) | .40 |
| 10 Record—D. Sutton | .12 | 75 Willie Upshaw | .10 | 136 Father & Son: | .07 | 194 Dave Stegman | .05 |
| 100 Strikeout Seasons | | 76 Alan Bannister | .05 | Jim and Jeff Kunkel | | 195 Glenn Hubbard | .05 |
| 11 Ralph Houk (Mgr.) | .05 | 77 Joe Beckwith | .05 | 137 Father & Son: | .07 | 196 Pete O'Brien | .05 |
| 12 Dave Lopes | .08 | 78 Scott Fletcher | .05 | Vern and Vance Law | | 197 Mike Warren | .05 |
| 13 Tim Lollar | .05 | 79 Rick Mahler | .05 | 138 Father & Son: | .07 | 198 Eddie Milner | .05 |
| 14 Chris Bando | .05 | 80 Keith Hernandez | .30 | Dick and Dick Schofield | | 199 Denny Martinez | .05 |
| 15 Jerry Koosman | .07 | 81 Lenn Sakata | .05 | 139 Father & Son: | .07 | 200 Reggie Jackson | .40 |
| 16 Bobby Meacham | .05 | 82 Joe Price | .05 | Bob and Joel Skinner | | 201 Burt Hooton | .05 |
| 17 Mike Scott | .05 | 83 Charlie Moore | .05 | 140 Father & Son: | .07 | 202 Gorman Thomas | .08 |
| 18 Mickey Hatcher | .05 | 84 Spike Owen | .05 | Roy and Roy Smalley | | 203 Bob McClure | .05 |
| 19 Geroge Frazier | .05 | 85 Mike Marshall | .12 | 141 Father & Son: | .07 | 204 Art Howe | .05 |
| 20 Chet Lemon | .08 | 86 Don Aase | .05 | Dave and Mike Stenhouse | | 205 Steve Rogers | .05 |
| 21 Lee Tunnell | .05 | 87 David Green | .05 | 142 Father & Son: | .07 | 206 Phil Garner | .05 |
| 22 Duane Kuiper | .05 | 88 Bryn Smith | .05 | Dizzy and Steve Trout | | 207 Mark Clear | .05 |
| 23 Bret Saberhagen (R) | 1.50 | 89 Jackie Gutierrez | .12 | 143 Father & Son: | .07 | 208 Champ Summers | .05 |
| 24 Jesse Barfield | .15 | 90 Rich Gossage | .15 | Ossie and Ozzie Virgil | | 209 Bill Campbell | .05 |
| 25 Steve Bedrosian | .07 | 91 Jeff Burroughs | .05 | 144 Ron Gardenhire | .05 | 210 Gary Matthews | .08 |
| 26 Roy Smalley | .05 | 92 Paul Owens (Mgr.) | .05 | 145 Alvin Davis (R) | 2.00 | 211 Clay Christiansen | .15 |
| 27 Bruce Berenyi | .05 | 93 Don Schulze | .10 | 146 Gary Redus | .08 | 212 George Vukovich | .05 |
| 28 Dann Bilardello | .05 | 94 Toby Harrah | .05 | 147 Bill Swaggerty | .12 | 213 Billy Gardner (Mgr.) | .05 |
| 29 Odell Jones | .05 | 95 Jose Cruz | .08 | 148 Steve Yeager | .05 | 214 John Tudor | .10 |
| 30 Cal Ripken | .40 | 96 Johnny Ray | .12 | 149 Dickie Noles | .05 | 215 Bob Brenly | .08 |
| 31 Terry Whitfield | .05 | 97 Pete Filson | .05 | 150 Jim Rice | .30 | 216 Jerry Don Gleaton | .05 |
| 32 Chuck Porter | .05 | 98 Steve Lake | .05 | 151 Moose Haas | .05 | 217 Leon Roberts | .05 |
| 33 Tito Landrum | .05 | 99 Milt Wilcox | .05 | 152 Steve Braun | .05 | 218 Doyle Alexander | .05 |
| 34 Ed Nunez | .10 | 100 George Brett | .40 | 153 Frank LaCorte | .05 | 219 Gerald Perry | .08 |
| 35 Graig Nettles | .12 | 101 Jim Acker | .05 | 154 Argenis Salazar (R) | .12 | 220 Fred Lynn | .15 |
| 36 Fred Breining | .05 | 102 Tommy Dunbar | .08 | 155 Yogi Berra (Mgr.) | .12 | 221 Ron Reed | .05 |
| 37 Reid Nichols | .05 | 103 Randy Lerch | .05 | 156 Craig Reynolds | .05 | 222 Hubie Brooks | .08 |
| 38 Jackie Moore (Mgr.) | .05 | 104 Mike Fitzgerald | .07 | 157 Tug McGraw | .08 | 223 Tom Hume | .05 |
| 39 Johnny Wockenfuss | .05 | 105 Ron Kittle | .15 | 158 Pat Tabler | .05 | 224 Al Cowens | .05 |
| 40 Phil Niekro | .15 | 106 Pascual Perez | .05 | 159 Carlos Diaz | .05 | 225 Mike Boddicker | .10 |
| 41 Mike Fischlin | .05 | 107 Tom Foley | .05 | 160 Lance Parrish | .25 | 226 Juan Beniquez | .05 |
| 42 Luis Sanchez | .05 | 108 Darnell Coles | .15 | 161 Ken Schrom | .05 | 227 Danny Darwin | .05 |
| 43 Andre David | .12 | 109 Gary Roenicke | .05 | 162 Benny Distefano | .15 | 228 Dion James | .10 |
| 44 Dickie Thon | .07 | 110 Alejandro Pena | .05 | 163 Dennis Eckersley | .05 | 229 Dave LaPoint | .05 |
| 45 Greg Minton | .05 | 111 Doug DeCinces | .10 | 164 Jorge Orta | .05 | 230 Gary Carter | .30 |
| 46 Gary Woods | .05 | 112 Tom Tellmann | .05 | 165 Dusty Baker | .08 | 231 Dwayne Murphy | .08 |
| 47 Dave Rozema | .05 | 113 Tom Herr | .15 | 166 Keith Atherton | .05 | 232 Dave Beard | .05 |
| 48 Tony Fernandez | .75 | 114 Bob James | .05 | 167 Rufino Linares | .05 | 233 Ed Jurak | ./05 |
| 49 Butch Davis | .05 | 115 Rickey Henderson | .45 | 168 Garth Iorg | .05 | 234 Jerry Narron | .05 |
| 50 John Candelaria | .08 | 116 Dennis Boyd | .25 | 169 Dan Spillner | .05 | 235 Garry Maddox | .05 |
| 51 Bob Watson | .05 | 117 Greg Gross | .05 | 170 George Foster | .15 | 236 Mark Thurmond | .08 |
| 52 Jerry Dybzinski | .05 | 118 Eric Show | .08 | 171 Bill Stein | .05 | 237 Julio Franco | .15 |
| 53 Tom Gorman | .07 | 119 Pat Corrales (Mgr.) | .05 | 172 Jack Perconte | .05 | 238 Jose Rijo (R) | .25 |
| 54 Cesar Cedeno | .08 | 120 Steve Kemp | .05 | 173 Mike Young | .40 | 239 Tim Teufel | .20 |
| 55 Frank Tanana | .05 | 121 Checklist No. 1 | .08 | 174 Rick Honeycutt | .05 | 240 Dave Stieb | .15 |
| 56 Jim Dwyer | .05 | 122 Tom Brunansky | .15 | 175 Dave Parker | .25 | 241 Jim Frey (Mgr.) | .05 |

Card values from this set fluctuate considerably.

| NO. | PLAYER | MINT |
|---|---|---|
| 242 | Greg Harris | .05 |
| 243 | Barbaro Garbey | .12 |
| 244 | Mike Jones | .05 |
| 245 | Chili Davis | .08 |
| 246 | Mike Norris | .05 |
| 247 | Wayne Tolleston | .05 |
| 248 | Terry Forster | .05 |
| 249 | Harold Baines | .15 |
| 250 | Jesse Orosco | .05 |
| 251 | Brad Gulden | .05 |
| 252 | Dan Ford | .05 |
| 253 | Sid Bream (R) | .25 |
| 254 | Pete Vuckovich | .08 |
| 255 | Lonnie Smith | .08 |
| 256 | Mike Stanton | .05 |
| 257 | Bryan Little | .05 |
| 258 | Mike Brown | .05 |
| 259 | Gary Allenson | .05 |
| 260 | Dave Righetti | .12 |
| 261 | Checklist No. 2 | .08 |
| 262 | Greg Booker | .12 |
| 263 | Mel Hall | .10 |
| 264 | Joe Sambito | .05 |
| 265 | Juan Samuel | .50 |
| 266 | Frank Viola | .07 |
| 267 | Henry Cotto | .12 |
| 268 | Chuck Tanner (Mgr.) | .05 |
| 269 | Doug Baker | .12 |
| 270 | Dan Quisenberry | .15 |

**No. 271 to 282 (# 1 Draft Picks)**

| NO. | PLAYER | MINT |
|---|---|---|
| 271 | Tim Foli (1968) | .05 |
| 272 | Jeff Burroughs (1969) | .05 |
| 273 | Bill Almon (1974) | .05 |
| 274 | Floyd Bannister (1976) | .05 |
| 275 | Harold Baines (1977) | .12 |
| 276 | Bob Horner (1978) | .12 |
| 277 | Al Chambers (1979) | .05 |
| 278 | D. Strawberry (1980) | .60 |
| 279 | Mike Moore (1981) | .05 |
| 280 | S. Dunston (R) (1982) | .75 |
| 281 | Tim Belcher (R) (1983) | .12 |
| 282 | S. Abner (R) (1984) | .25 |
| 283 | Fran Mullins | .05 |
| 284 | Marty Bystrom | .05 |
| 285 | Dan Driessen | .05 |
| 286 | Rudy Law | .05 |
| 287 | Walt Terrell | .05 |
| 288 | Jeff Kunkel | .12 |
| 289 | Tom Underwood | .05 |
| 290 | Cecil Cooper | .15 |
| 291 | Bob Welch | .05 |
| 292 | Brad Komminsk | .10 |
| 293 | Curt Young | .15 |
| 294 | Tom Nieto | .12 |
| 295 | Joe Niekro | .05 |
| 296 | Ricky Nelson | .05 |
| 297 | Gary Lucas | .05 |
| 298 | Marty Barrett | .05 |
| 299 | Andy Hawkins | .08 |
| 300 | Rod Carew | .35 |
| 301 | John Montefusco | .05 |
| 302 | Tim Corcoran | .05 |
| 303 | Mike Jeffcoat | .05 |
| 304 | Gary Gaetti | .05 |
| 305 | Dale Berra | .05 |
| 306 | Rick Reuschel | .05 |
| 307 | Sparky Anderson (Mgr.) | .05 |
| 308 | John Wathan | .05 |
| 309 | Mike Witt | .08 |
| 310 | Manny Trillo | .05 |
| 311 | Jim Gott | .05 |
| 312 | Marc Hill | .05 |
| 313 | Dave Schmidt | .05 |
| 314 | Ron Oester | .05 |
| 315 | Doug Sisk | .05 |
| 316 | John Lowenstein | .05 |
| 317 | Jack Lazorko | .12 |
| 318 | Ted Simmons | .10 |
| 319 | Jeff Jones | .05 |
| 320 | Dale Murphy | .50 |
| 321 | Ricky Horton (R) | .25 |
| 322 | Dave Stapleton | .05 |
| 323 | Andy McGaffigan | .05 |
| 324 | Bruce Bochy | .05 |
| 325 | John Denny | .05 |

| NO. | PLAYER | MINT |
|---|---|---|
| 326 | Kevin Bass | .05 |
| 327 | Brook Jacoby | .25 |
| 328 | Bob Shirley | .05 |
| 329 | Ron Washington | .05 |
| 330 | Leon Durham | .15 |
| 331 | Bill Laskey | .05 |
| 332 | Brian Harper | .05 |
| 333 | Willie Hernandez | .15 |
| 334 | Dick Howser (Mgr.) | .05 |
| 335 | Bruce Benedict | .05 |
| 336 | Rance Mulliniks | .05 |
| 337 | Billy Sample | .05 |
| 338 | Britt Burns | .05 |
| 339 | Danny Heep | .05 |
| 340 | Robin Yount | .30 |
| 341 | Floyd Rayford | .05 |
| 342 | Ted Power | .05 |
| 343 | Bill Russell | .05 |
| 344 | Dave Henderson | .05 |
| 345 | Charlie Lea | .05 |
| 346 | Terry Pendleton (R) | .30 |
| 347 | Rick Langford | .05 |
| 348 | Bob Boone | .05 |
| 349 | Domingo Ramos | .05 |
| 350 | Wade Boggs | 2.50 |
| 351 | Juan Agosto | .05 |
| 352 | Joe Morgan | .15 |
| 353 | Julio Solano | .12 |
| 354 | Andre Robertson | .05 |
| 355 | Bert Blyleven | .10 |
| 356 | Dave Meier | .12 |
| 357 | Rich Bordi | .05 |
| 358 | Tony Pena | .12 |
| 359 | Pat Sheridan | .05 |
| 360 | Steve Carlton | .30 |
| 361 | Alfredo Griffin | .05 |
| 362 | Craig McMurtry | .05 |
| 363 | Ron Hodges | .05 |
| 364 | Richard Dotson | .05 |
| 365 | Danny Ozark (Mgr.) | .05 |
| 366 | Todd Cruz | .05 |
| 367 | Keefe Cato | .12 |
| 368 | Dave Bergman | .05 |
| 369 | R.J. Reynolds (R) | .25 |
| 370 | Bruce Sutter | .15 |
| 371 | Mickey Rivers | .05 |
| 372 | Roy Howell | .05 |
| 373 | Mike Moore | .07 |
| 374 | Brian Downing | .05 |
| 375 | Jeff Reardon | .05 |
| 376 | Jeff Newman | .05 |
| 377 | Checklist No.3 | .08 |
| 378 | Alan Wiggins | .08 |
| 379 | Charles Hudson | .05 |
| 380 | Ken Griffey | .08 |
| 381 | Roy Smith | .12 |
| 382 | Denny Walling | .05 |
| 383 | Rick Lysander | .05 |
| 384 | Jody Davis | .10 |
| 385 | Jose DeLeon | .05 |
| 386 | Dan Gladden (R) | .30 |
| 387 | Buddy Biancalana | .12 |
| 388 | Bert Roberge | .05 |

**No. 389 to 404 (U.S. Olympic Team)**

| NO. | PLAYER | MINT |
|---|---|---|
| 389 | Rod Dedeaux (Coach) | .05 |
| 390 | Sid Akins | .10 |
| 391 | Flavio Alfaro | .10 |
| 392 | Don August | .10 |
| 393 | Scott Bankhead | .10 |
| 394 | Bob Caffrey | .10 |
| 395 | Mike Dunne | .10 |
| 396 | Gary Green | .10 |
| 397 | John Hoover | .10 |
| 398 | Shane Mack | .20 |
| 399 | John Marzano | .10 |
| 400 | Oddibe McDowell (R) | 1.50 |
| 401 | Mark McGwire | .10 |
| 402 | Pat Pacillo | .10 |
| 403 | Cory Snyder (R) | 6.00 |
| 404 | Billy Swift | .10 |
| 405 | Tom Veryzer | .05 |
| 406 | Len Whitehouse | .05 |
| 407 | Bobby Ramos | .05 |
| 408 | Sid Monge | .05 |
| 409 | Brad Wellman | .05 |

| NO. | PLAYER | MINT |
|---|---|---|
| 410 | Bob Horner | .15 |
| 411 | Bobby Cox (Mgr.) | .05 |
| 412 | Bud Black | .05 |
| 413 | Vance Law | .05 |
| 414 | Gary Ward | .05 |
| 415 | Ron Darling | 1.00 |
| 416 | Wayne Gross | .05 |
| 417 | John Franco (R) | .50 |
| 418 | Ken Landreaux | .05 |
| 419 | Mike Caldwell | .05 |
| 420 | Andre Dawson | .20 |
| 421 | Dave Rucker | .05 |
| 422 | Carney Lansford | .10 |
| 423 | Barry Bonnell | .05 |
| 424 | Al Nipper (R) | .35 |
| 425 | Mike Hargrove | .05 |
| 426 | Vern Ruhle | .05 |
| 427 | Mario Ramirez | .05 |
| 428 | Larry Andersen | .05 |
| 429 | Rick Cerone | .05 |
| 430 | Ron Davis | .05 |
| 431 | U.L. Washington | .05 |
| 432 | Thad Bosley | .05 |
| 433 | Jim Morrison | .05 |
| 434 | Gene Richards | .05 |
| 435 | Dan Petry | .12 |
| 436 | Willie Aikens | .05 |
| 437 | Al Jones | .12 |
| 438 | Joe Torre (Mgr.) | .07 |
| 439 | Junior Ortiz | .05 |
| 440 | Fernando Valenzuela | .40 |
| 441 | Duane Walker | .05 |
| 442 | Ken Forsch | .05 |
| 443 | George Wright | .05 |
| 444 | Tony Phillips | .05 |
| 445 | Tippy Martinez | .05 |
| 446 | Jim Sundberg | .05 |
| 447 | Jeff Lahti | .05 |
| 448 | Derrel Thomas | .05 |
| 449 | Phil Bradley (R) | 1.00 |
| 450 | Steve Garvey | .40 |
| 451 | Bruce Hurst | .05 |
| 452 | John Castino | .05 |
| 453 | Tom Waddell | .12 |
| 454 | Glenn Wilson | .10 |
| 455 | Bob Knepper | .05 |
| 456 | Tim Foli | .05 |
| 457 | Cecillio Guante | .05 |
| 458 | Randy Johnson | .05 |
| 459 | Charlie Leibrandt | .05 |
| 460 | Ryne Sandberg | .40 |
| 461 | Marty Castillo | .05 |
| 462 | Gary Lavelle | .05 |
| 463 | Dave Collins | .05 |
| 464 | Mike Mason | .12 |
| 465 | Bob Grich | .07 |
| 466 | Tony LaRussa (Mgr.) | .05 |
| 467 | Ed Lynch | .05 |
| 468 | Wayne Krenchicki | .05 |
| 469 | Sammy Stewart | .05 |
| 470 | Steve Sax | .15 |
| 471 | Pete Ladd | .05 |
| 472 | Jim Essian | .05 |
| 473 | Tim Wallach | .08 |
| 474 | Kurt Kepshire | .12 |
| 475 | Andre Thornton | .08 |
| 476 | Jeff Stone (R) | .30 |
| 477 | Bob Ojeda | .05 |
| 478 | Kurt Bevacqua | .05 |
| 479 | Mike Madden | .05 |
| 480 | Lou Whitaker | .15 |
| 481 | Dale Murray | .05 |
| 482 | Harry Spilman | .05 |
| 483 | Mike Smithson | .05 |
| 484 | Larry Bowa | .05 |
| 485 | Matt Young | .06 |
| 486 | Steve Balboni | .06 |
| 487 | Frank Williams | .12 |
| 488 | Joel Skinner | .12 |
| 489 | Bryan Clark | .05 |
| 490 | Jason Thompson | .08 |
| 491 | Rick Camp | .05 |
| 492 | Dave Johnson (Mgr.) | .05 |
| 493 | Orel Hershiser (R) | 2.00 |
| 494 | Rich Dauer | .05 |

| NO. | PLAYER | MINT |
|---|---|---|
| 495 | Mario Soto | .08 |
| 496 | Donnie Scott | .12 |
| 497 | Gary Pettis (wrong photo—It's his brother—Lynn) | .40 |
| 498 | Ed Romero | .05 |
| 499 | Danny Cox | .20 |
| 500 | Mike Schmidt | .35 |
| 501 | Dan Schatzeder | .05 |
| 502 | Rick Miller | .05 |
| 503 | Tim Conroy | .05 |
| 504 | Jerry Willard | .08 |
| 505 | Jim Beattie | .05 |
| 506 | Franklin Stubbs (R) | 1.00 |
| 507 | Ray Fontenot | .05 |
| 508 | John Shelby | .05 |
| 509 | Milt May | .05 |
| 510 | Kent Hrbek | .30 |
| 511 | Lee Smith | .08 |
| 512 | Tom Brookens | .05 |
| 513 | Lynn Jones | .05 |
| 514 | Jeff Cornell | .12 |
| 515 | Dave Concepcion | .08 |
| 516 | Roy Lee Jackson | .05 |
| 517 | Jerry Martin | .05 |
| 518 | Chris Chambliss | .05 |
| 519 | Doug Rader (Mgr.) | .05 |
| 520 | LaMarr Hoyt | .08 |
| 521 | Rick Dempsey | .05 |
| 522 | Paul Molitor | .10 |
| 523 | Candy Maldonado | .05 |
| 524 | Rob Wilfong | .05 |
| 525 | Darrell Porter | .05 |
| 526 | Dave Palmer | .05 |
| 527 | Checklist No. 4 | .08 |
| 528 | Bill Krueger | .05 |
| 529 | Rich Gedman | .08 |
| 530 | Dave Dravecky | .08 |
| 531 | Joe Lefebvre | .05 |
| 532 | Frank DiPino | .05 |
| 533 | Tony Bernazard | .05 |
| 534 | Brian Dayett | .08 |
| 535 | Pat Putnam | .05 |
| 536 | Kirby Puckett (R) | 4.00 |
| 537 | Don Robinson | .05 |
| 538 | Keith Moreland | .05 |
| 539 | Aurelio Lopez | .05 |
| 540 | Claudell Washington | .08 |
| 541 | Mark Davis | .05 |
| 542 | Don Slaught | .05 |
| 543 | Mike Squires | .05 |
| 544 | Bruce Kison | .05 |
| 545 | Lloyd Moseby | .15 |
| 546 | Brent Gaff | .05 |
| 547 | Pete Rose (Mgr.) | .50 |
| 548 | Larry Parrish | .07 |
| 549 | Mike Scioscia | .05 |
| 550 | Scott McGregor | .07 |
| 551 | Andy Van Slyke | .08 |
| 552 | Chris Codiroli | .05 |
| 553 | Bob Clark | .05 |
| 554 | Doug Flynn | .05 |
| 555 | Bob Stanley | .05 |
| 556 | Sixto Lezcano | .05 |
| 557 | Len Barker | .05 |
| 558 | Carmelo Martinez | .05 |
| 559 | Jay Howell | .05 |
| 560 | Bill Madlock | .15 |
| 561 | Darryl Motley | .05 |
| 562 | Houston Jimenez | .05 |
| 563 | Dick Ruthven | .05 |
| 564 | Alan Ashby | .05 |
| 565 | Kirk Gibson | .25 |
| 566 | Ed Vande Berg | .05 |
| 567 | Joel Youngblood | .05 |
| 568 | Cliff Johnson | .05 |
| 569 | Ken Oberkfell | .05 |
| 570 | Darryl Strawberry | 1.25 |
| 571 | Charlie Hough | .05 |
| 572 | Tom Paciorek | .05 |
| 573 | Jay Tibbs (R) | .30 |
| 574 | Joe Altobelli (Mgr.) | .05 |
| 575 | Pedro Guerrero | .25 |
| 576 | Jaime Cocanower | .12 |
| 577 | Chris Speier | .05 |

| NO. PLAYER | MINT | NO. PLAYER | MINT | NO. PLAYER | MINT | NO. PLAYER | MINT |
|---|---|---|---|---|---|---|---|
| 578 Terry Francona | .05 | 632 Bruce Bochte | .05 | 686 Mike Easler | .05 | 740 Jack Clark | .15 |
| 579 Ron Romanick (R) | .40 | 633 Glenn Hoffman | .05 | 687 Bill Gullickson | .05 | 741 John Butcher | .05 |
| 580 Dwight Evans | .12 | 634 Bill Dawley | .05 | 688 Len Matuszek | .05 | 742 Ron Hassey | .05 |
| 581 Mark Wagner | .05 | 635 Terry Kennedy | .08 | 689 Luis DeLeon | .05 | 743 Frank White | .05 |
| 582 Ken Phelps | .05 | 636 Shane Rawley | .05 | 690 Alan Trammell | .25 | 744 Doug Bair | .05 |
| 583 Bobby Brown | .05 | 637 Brett Butler | .08 | 691 Dennis Rasmussen | .25 | 745 Buddy Bell | .10 |
| 584 Kevin Gross | .05 | 638 Mike Pagliarulo (R) | 2.00 | 692 Randy Bush | .05 | 746 Jim Clancy | .05 |
| 585 Butch Wynegar | .05 | 639 Ed Hodge | .10 | 693 Tim Stoddard | .05 | 747 Alex Trevino | .05 |
| 586 Bill Scherrer | .05 | 640 Steve Henderson | .05 | 694 Joe Carter | 2.50 | 748 Lee Mazzilli | .05 |
| 587 Doug Frobel | .05 | 641 Rod Scurry | .05 | 695 Rick Rhoden | .05 | 749 Julio Cruz | .05 |
| 588 Bobby Castillo | .05 | 642 Dave Owen | .10 | 696 John Rabb | .05 | 750 Rollie Fingers | .15 |
| 589 Bob Dernier | .05 | 643 Johnny Grubb | .05 | 697 Onix Concepcion | .05 | 751 Kelvin Chapman | .12 |
| 590 Ray Knight | .05 | 644 Mark Huismann | .10 | 698 Jorge Bell | .08 | 752 Bob Owchinko | .05 |
| 591 Larry Herndon | .05 | 645 Damaso Garcia | .08 | 699 Donnie Moore | .08 | 753 Greg Brock | .08 |
| 592 Jeff Robinson | .12 | 646 Scot Thompson | .05 | 700 Eddie Murray | .35 | 754 Larry Milbourne | .05 |
| 593 Rick Leach | .05 | 647 Rafael Ramierz | .05 | 701 Eddie Murray (AS) | .25 | 755 Ken Singleton | .08 |
| 594 Curt Wilkerson | .08 | 648 Bob Jones | .05 | 702 Damaso Garcia (AS) | .08 | 756 Rob Picciolo | .05 |
| 595 Larry Gura | .05 | 649 Sid Fernandez | 1.50 | 703 George Brett (AS) | .30 | 757 Willie McGee | .35 |
| 596 Jerry Hairston | .05 | 650 Greg Luzinski | .08 | 704 Cal Ripken (AS) | .25 | 758 Ray Burris | .05 |
| 597 Brad Lesley | .05 | 651 Jeff Russell | .05 | 705 Dave Winfield (AS) | .20 | 759 Jim Fanning (Mgr.) | .05 |
| 598 Jose Oquendo | .05 | 652 Joe Nolan | .05 | 706 Rickey Henderson (AS) | .30 | 760 Nolan Ryan | .30 |
| 599 Storm Davis | .08 | 653 Mark Brouhard | .05 | 707 Tony Armas (AS) | .08 | 761 Jerry Remy | .05 |
| 600 Pete Rose | 1.25 | 654 Dave Anderson | .05 | 708 Lance Parrish (AS) | .15 | 762 Eddie Whitson | .05 |
| 601 Tom Lasorda (Mgr.) | .08 | 655 Joaquin Andujar | .08 | 709 Mike Boddicker (AS) | .08 | 763 Kiko Garcia | .05 |
| 602 Jeff Dedmon | .12 | 656 Chuck Cottier (Mgr.) | .05 | 710 Frank Viola (AS) | .08 | 764 Jamie Easterly | .05 |
| 603 Rick Manning | .05 | 657 Jim Slaton | .05 | 711 Dan Quisenberry (AS) | .15 | 765 Willie Randolph | .05 |
| 604 Daryl Sconiers | .05 | 658 Mike Stenhouse | .05 | 712 Keith Hernandez (AS) | .20 | 766 Paul Mirabella | .05 |
| 605 Ozzie Smith | .10 | 659 Checklist No. 5 | .08 | 713 Ryne Sandberg (AS) | .25 | 767 Darrell Brown | .05 |
| 606 Rich Gale | .05 | 660 Tony Gwynn | .35 | 714 Mike Schmidt (AS) | .25 | 768 Ron Cey | .10 |
| 607 Bill Almon | .05 | 661 Steve Crawford | .05 | 715 Ozzie Smith (AS) | .08 | 769 Joe Cowley | .05 |
| 608 Craig Lefferts | .05 | 662 Mike Heath | .05 | 716 Dale Murphy (AS) | .30 | 770 Carlton Fisk | .15 |
| 609 Broderick Perkins | .05 | 663 Luis Aguayo | .05 | 717 Tony Gwynn (AS) | .25 | 771 Geoff Zahn | .05 |
| 610 Jack Morris | .15 | 664 Steve Farr | .12 | 718 Jeff Leonard (AS) | .08 | 772 Johnnie LeMaster | .05 |
| 611 Ozzie Virgil | .05 | 665 Don Mattingly | 9.00 | 719 Gary Carter (AS) | .20 | 773 Hal McRae | .05 |
| 612 Mike Armstrong | .05 | 666 Mike LaCoss | .05 | 720 Rick Sutcliffe (AS) | .15 | 774 Dennis Lamp | .05 |
| 613 Terry Puhl | .05 | 667 Dave Engle | .05 | 721 Bob Knepper (AS) | .08 | 775 Mookie Wilson | .08 |
| 614 Al Williams | .05 | 668 Steve Trout | .05 | 722 Bruce Sutter (AS) | .15 | 776 Jerry Royster | .05 |
| 615 Marvell Wynne | .05 | 669 Lee Lacy | .05 | 723 Dave Stewart | .05 | 777 Ned Yost | .05 |
| 616 Scott Sanderson | .05 | 670 Tom Seaver | .25 | 724 Oscar Gamble | .05 | 778 Mike Davis | .08 |
| 617 Willie Wilson | .15 | 671 Dane Iorg | .05 | 725 Floyd Bannister | .05 | 779 Nick Esasky | .05 |
| 618 Pete Falcone | .05 | 672 Juan Berenguer | .05 | 726 Al Bumbry | .05 | 780 Mike Flanagan | .05 |
| 619 Jeff Leonard | .05 | 673 Buck Martinez | .05 | 727 Frank Pastore | .05 | 781 Jim Gantner | .05 |
| 620 Dwight Gooden (R) | 8.00 | 674 Atlee Hammaker | .05 | 728 Bob Bailor | .05 | 782 Tom Niedenfuer | .05 |
| 621 Marvis Foley | .05 | 675 Tony Perez | .15 | 729 Don Sutton | .12 | 783 Mike Jorgensen | .05 |
| 622 Luis Leal | .05 | 676 Albert Hall | .12 | 730 Dave Kingman | .10 | 784 Checklist No. 6 | .08 |
| 623 Greg Walker | .12 | 677 Wally Backman | .05 | 731 Neil Allen | .05 | 785 Tony Armas | .12 |
| 624 Benny Ayala | .05 | 678 Joey McLaughlin | .05 | 732 John McNamara (Mgr.) | .05 | 786 Enos Cabell | .05 |
| 625 Mark Langston (R) | .40 | 679 Bob Kearney | .05 | 733 Tony Scott | .05 | 787 Jim Wohlford | .05 |
| 626 German Rivera | .15 | 680 Jerry Reuss | .05 | 734 John Henry Johnson | .05 | 788 Steve Comer | .05 |
| 627 Eric Davis (R) | 6.00 | 681 Ben Oglivie | .05 | 735 Garry Templeton | .10 | 789 Luis Salazar | .05 |
| 628 R. Lachemann (Mgr.) | .05 | 682 Doug Corbett | .05 | 736 Jerry Mumphrey | .05 | 790 Ron Guidry | .20 |
| 629 Dick Schofield | .08 | 683 Whitey Herzog (Mgr.) | .05 | 737 Bo Diaz | .05 | 791 Ivan DeJesus | .05 |
| 630 Tim Raines | .25 | 684 Bill Doran | .05 | 738 Omar Moreno | .05 | 792 Darrell Evans | .12 |
| 631 Bob Forsch | .05 | 685 Bill Caudill | .08 | 739 Ernie Camacho | .05 | | |

## 1985 Topps Traded....Complete Set of 132 Cards—Value $16.00

Updates the main 1985 card set with players who changed teams during the season and rookies who joined their teams early in the season. Features the first Topps card of Vince Coleman, Chris Brown, and Jim Presley. The complete set was packaged in a printed box and only distributed through card hobby dealers. Topps tested a small quantity of wax packs.

| NO. PLAYER | MINT | NO. PLAYER | MINT | NO. PLAYER | MINT | NO. PLAYER | MINT |
|---|---|---|---|---|---|---|---|
| 1 T Don Aase | .08 | 5 T G. Bamberger (Mgr.) | .06 | 9 T Hubie Brooks | .12 | 13 T Ray Burris | .06 |
| 2 T Bill Almon | .06 | 6 T Dale Berra | .10 | 10 T Chris Brown (RR) | 2.00 | 14 T Jeff Burroughs | .06 |
| 3 T Benny Ayala | .06 | 7 T Rich Bordi | .06 | 11 T T. Browning (RR) | 1.00 | 15 T Bill Campbell | .06 |
| 4 T Dusty Baker | .12 | 8 T Daryl Boston (RR) | .20 | 12 T Al Bumbry | .06 | 16 T Don Carman | .25 |

| NO. PLAYER | MINT | NO. PLAYER | MINT | NO. PLAYER | MINT | NO. PLAYER | MINT |
|---|---|---|---|---|---|---|---|
| 17 T Gary Carter | .75 | 46 T Toby Harrah | .08 | 75 T Sixto Lezcano | .06 | 104 T Rick Schu | .25 |
| 18 T Bobby Castillo | .06 | 47 T Greg Harris | .06 | 76 T Tim Lollar | .06 | 105 T Donnie Scott | .06 |
| 19 T Bill Caudill | .10 | 48 T Ron Hassey | .06 | 77 T Fred Lynn | .20 | 106 T Larry Sheets | .40 |
| 20 T Rick Cerone | .08 | 49 T Rickey Henderson | .75 | 78 T Billy Martin (Mgr.) | .15 | 107 T Don Slaught | .06 |
| 21 T Bryan Clark | .06 | 50 T Steve Henderson | .06 | 79 T Ron Mathis | .15 | 108 T Roy Smalley | .08 |
| 22 T Jack Clark | .30 | 51 T George Hendrick | .12 | 80 T Len Matuszek | .06 | 109 T Lonnie Smith | .12 |
| 23 T Pat Clements | .25 | 52 T Joe Hesketh (RR) | .35 | 81 T Gene Mauch (Mgr.) | .06 | 110 T Nate Snell | .20 |
| 24 T V. Coleman (RR) | 4.00 | 53 T T. Higuera (RR) | 2.00 | 82 T Oddibe McDowell | 1.25 | 111 T Chris Speier | .06 |
| 25 T Dave Collins | .08 | 54 T Donnie Hill | .06 | 83 T R. McDowell (RR) | 1.00 | 112 T Mike Stenhouse | .06 |
| 26 T Danny Darwin | .06 | 55 T Al Holland | .08 | 84 T J. McNamara (Mgr.) | .06 | 113 T Tim Stoddard | .06 |
| 27 T J. Davenport (Mgr.) | .06 | 56 T Burt Hooton | .06 | 85 T Donnie Moore | .08 | 114 T Jim Sundberg | .08 |
| 28 T Jerry Davis | .12 | 57 T Jay Howell | .08 | 86 T Gene Nelson | .06 | 115 T Bruce Sutter | .25 |
| 29 T Brian Dayett | .06 | 58 T Ken Howell | .20 | 87 T Steve Nicosia | .06 | 116 T Don Sutton | .30 |
| 30 T Ivan DeJesus | .06 | 59 T LaMarr Hoyt | .12 | 88 T Al Oliver | .12 | 117 T Kent Tekulve | .08 |
| 31 T Ken Dixon | .25 | 60 T Tim Hulett | .20 | 89 T Joe Orsulak | .25 | 118 T Tom Tellmann | .06 |
| 32 T M. Duncan (RR) | .75 | 61 T Bob James | .06 | 90 T Rob Picciolo | .06 | 119 T Walt Terrell | .08 |
| 33 T John Felske (Mgr.) | .06 | 62 T Steve Jeltz (RR) | .25 | 91 T Chris Pittaro | .15 | 120 T Mickey Tettleton | .12 |
| 34 T Mike Fitzgerald | .06 | 63 T Cliff Johnson | .06 | 92 T Jim Presley (RR) | 2.00 | 121 T Derrel Thomas | .06 |
| 35 T Ray Fontenot | .06 | 64 T Howard Johnson | .15 | 93 T Rick Reuschel | .06 | 122 T Rich Thompson | .15 |
| 36 T Greg Gagne | .20 | 65 T Ruppert Jones | .08 | 94 T Bert Roberge | .06 | 123 T Alex Trevino | .06 |
| 37 T Oscar Gamble | .10 | 66 T Steve Kemp | .06 | 95 T Bob Rodgers (Mgr.) | .06 | 124 T John Tudor | .20 |
| 38 T Scott Garrelts (RR) | .40 | 67 T Bruce Kison | .06 | 96 T Jerry Royster | .06 | 125 T Jose Uribe | .12 |
| 39 T Bob Gibson | .06 | 68 T Alan Knicely | .06 | 97 T Dave Rozema | .06 | 126 T B. Valentine (Mgr.) | .10 |
| 40 T Jim Gott | .06 | 69 T Mike LaCoss | .06 | 98 T Dave Rucker | .06 | 127 T Dave Von Ohlen | .06 |
| 41 T David Green | .12 | 70 T Lee Lacy | .08 | 99 T Vern Ruhle | .06 | 128 T U.L. Washington | .06 |
| 42 T Alfredo Griffin | .12 | 71 T Dave LaPoint | .06 | 100 T Paul Runge | .15 | 129 T Earl Weaver (Mgr.) | .12 |
| 43 T Ozzie Guillen (RR) | .75 | 72 T Gary Lavelle | .06 | 101 T Mark Salas (R) | .50 | 130 T Eddie Whitson | .08 |
| 44 T Eddie Haas (Mgr.) | .06 | 73 T Vance Law | .06 | 102 T Luis Salazar | .06 | 131 T Herm Winningham | .20 |
| 45 T Terry Harper | .06 | 74 T Johnnie LeMaster | .06 | 103 T Joe Sambito | .08 | 132 T Traded Checklist | .10 |

## 1986 Topps.... Complete Set of 792 Cards—Value $25.00

Features the rookie cards of Vince Coleman, Chris Brown and Len Dykstra. Topps printed 16 cards on the bottom of gum pack display boxes (not part of the set). There are four cards on each box—four different boxes. These 16 cards are identified by a letter code—A through P.

VINCE COLEMAN

CHRIS BROWN

ROGER McDOWELL

MARIANO DUNCAN

FLOYD YOUMANS

| NO. PLAYER | MINT | NO. PLAYER | MINT | NO. PLAYER | MINT | NO. PLAYER | MINT |
|---|---|---|---|---|---|---|---|
| 1 Pete Rose | 1.25 | 28 Eric Davis | .06 | 53 Len Dykstra (R) | 2.00 | 80 Darryl Strawberry | .50 |
| 2 Rose (Years 1963-66) | .40 | 29 Tony Phillips | .04 | 54 John Franco | .08 | 81 Gene Mauch (Mgr.) | .08 |
| 3 Rose (Years 1967-70) | .40 | 30 Eddie Murray | .40 | 55 Fred Lynn | .20 |   Angels Checklist |  |
| 4 Rose (Years 1971-74) | .40 | 31 Jamie Easterly | .04 | 56 Tom Niedenfuer | .08 | 82 Tippy Martinez | .04 |
| 5 Rose (Years 1975-78) | .40 | 32 Steve Yeager | .06 | 57 Bill Doran | .08 | 83 Phil Garner | .04 |
| 6 Rose (Years 1979-82) | .40 | 33 Jeff Lahti | .04 | 58 Bill Krueger | .04 | 84 Curt Young | .04 |
| 7 Rose (Years 1983-85) | .40 | 34 Ken Phelps | .04 | 59 Andre Thornton | .04 | 85 Tony Perez | .15 |
| 8 Dwayne Murphy | .08 | 35 Jeff Reardon | .05 | 60 Dwight Evans | .12 | 86 Tom Waddell | .04 |
| 9 Roy Smith | .04 | 36 Tigers Leaders: | .15 | 61 Karl Best | .12 | 87 Candy Maldonado | .04 |
| 10 Tony Gwynn | .25 |   Lance Parrish |  | 62 Bob Boone | .04 | 88 Tom Nieto | .04 |
| 11 Bob Ojeda | .05 | 37 Mark Thurmond | .04 | 63 Ron Roenicke | .04 | 89 Randy St. Claire | .08 |
| 12 Jose Uribe | .15 | 38 Glenn Hoffman | .04 | 64 Floyd Bannister | .04 | 90 Garry Templeton | .15 |
| 13 Bob Kearney | .04 | 39 Dave Rucker | .04 | 65 Dan Driessen | .04 | 91 Steve Crawford | .04 |
| 14 Julio Cruz | .04 | 40 Ken Griffey | .10 | 66 Cardinals Leaders: | .08 | 92 Al Cowens | .04 |
| 15 Eddie Whitson | .06 | 41 Brad Wellman | .04 |   Bob Forsch |  | 93 Scot Thompson | .04 |
| 16 Rick Schu | .10 | 42 Geoff Zahn | .04 | 67 Carmelo Martinez | .04 | 94 Rich Bordi | .04 |
| 17 Mike Stenhouse | .04 | 43 Dave Engle | .04 | 68 Ed Lynch | .04 | 95 Ozzie Virgil | .04 |
| 18 Brent Gaff | .04 | 44 Lance McCullers (R) | .40 | 69 Luis Aguayo | .04 | 96 Blue Jays Leaders: | .06 |
| 19 Rich Hebner | .04 | 45 Damaso Garcia | .12 | 70 Dave Winfield | .30 |   Jim Clancy |  |
| 20 Lou Whitaker | .15 | 46 Billy Hatcher | .08 | 71 Ken Schrom | .04 | 97 Gary Gaetti | .04 |
| 21 G. Bamberger (Mgr.) | .04 | 47 Juan Berenguer | .04 | 72 Shawon Dunston | .06 | 98 Dick Ruthven | .04 |
|   Brewers Checklist |  | 48 Bill Almon | .04 | 73 Randy O'Neal | .08 | 99 Buddy Biancalana | .04 |
| 22 Duane Walker | .08 | 49 Rick Manning | .04 | 74 Rance Mulliniks | .04 | 100 Nolan Ryan | .30 |
| 23 Manny Lee | .15 | 50 Dan Quisenberry | .15 | 75 Jose DeLeon | .04 | 101 Dave Bergman | .04 |
| 24 Len Barker | .06 | 51 Bobby Wine (Mgr.) | .08 | 76 Dion James | .04 | 102 Joe Orsulak (R) | .30 |
| 25 Willie Wilson | .20 |   Braves Checklist |  | 77 Charlie Leibrandt | .06 | 103 Luis Salazar | .04 |
| 26 Frank DiPino | .04 |   Error-reads card no. 57 |  | 78 Bruce Benedict | .04 | 104 Sid Fernandez | .12 |
| 27 Ray Knight | .06 | 52 Chris Welsh | .04 | 79 Dave Schmidt | .04 | 105 Gary Ward | .04 |

Card values from this set fluctuate considerably.

| NO. | PLAYER | MINT |
|---|---|---|
| 106 | Ray Burris | .04 |
| 107 | Rafael Ramirez | .04 |
| 108 | Ted Power | .04 |
| 109 | Len Matuszek | .04 |
| 110 | Scott McGregor | .06 |
| 111 | Roger Craig (Mgr.) | .08 |
| | Giants Checklist | |
| 112 | Bill Campbell | .04 |
| 113 | U.L. Washington | .04 |
| 114 | Mike Brown | .04 |
| 115 | Jay Howell | .04 |
| 116 | Brook Jacoby | .10 |
| 117 | Bruce Kison | .04 |
| 118 | Jerry Royster | .04 |
| 119 | Barry Bonnell | .04 |
| 120 | Steve Carlton | .30 |
| 121 | Nelson Simmons | .20 |
| 122 | Pete Filson | .04 |
| 123 | Greg Walker | .10 |
| 124 | Luis Sanchez | .04 |
| 125 | Dave Lopes | .06 |
| 126 | Mets Leaders: | .08 |
| | Mookie Wilson | |
| 127 | Jack Howell (R) | .30 |
| 128 | John Wathan | .04 |
| 129 | Jeff Dedmon | .04 |
| 130 | Alan Trammell | .20 |
| 131 | Checklist No. 1 | .08 |
| 132 | Razor Shines | .08 |
| 133 | Andy McGaffigan | .04 |
| 134 | Carney Lansford | .08 |
| 135 | Joe Niekro | .08 |
| 136 | Mike Hargrove | .04 |
| 137 | Charlie Moore | .04 |
| 138 | Mark Davis | .04 |
| 139 | Daryl Boston | .10 |
| 140 | John Candelaria | .08 |
| 141 | Chuck Cottier (Mgr.) | .08 |
| | Mariners Checklist | |
| | see card 171 | |
| 142 | Bob Jones | .04 |
| 143 | Dave Van Gorder | .04 |
| 144 | Doug Sisk | .04 |
| 145 | Pedro Guerrero | .25 |
| 146 | Jack Perconte | .04 |
| 147 | Larry Sheets | .15 |
| 148 | Mike Heath | .04 |
| 149 | Brett Butler | .10 |
| 150 | Joaquin Andujar | .08 |
| 151 | Dave Stapleton | .04 |
| 152 | Mike Morgan | .04 |
| 153 | Ricky Adams | .04 |
| 154 | Bert Roberge | .04 |
| 155 | Bob Grich | .08 |
| 156 | White Sox Leaders: | .08 |
| | Richard Dotson | |
| 157 | Ron Hassey | .04 |
| 158 | Derrel Thomas | .04 |
| 159 | Orel Hershiser | .40 |
| 160 | Chet Lemon | .06 |
| 161 | Lee Tunnell | .04 |
| 162 | Greg Gagne | .04 |
| 163 | Pete Ladd | .04 |
| 164 | Steve Balboni | .08 |
| 165 | Mike Davis | .06 |
| 166 | Dickie Thon | .04 |
| 167 | Zane Smith | .10 |
| 168 | Jeff Burroughs | .04 |
| 169 | George Wright | .04 |
| 170 | Gary Carter | .30 |
| 171 | Bob Rodgers (Mgr.) | .08 |
| | Expo Checklist | |
| | error—reads #141 | |
| 172 | Jerry Reed | .15 |
| 173 | Wayne Gross | .04 |
| 174 | Brian Snyder | .15 |
| 175 | Steve Sax | .15 |
| 176 | Jay Tibbs | .04 |
| 177 | Joel Youngblood | .04 |
| 178 | Ivan DeJesus | .04 |
| 179 | Stu Cliburn | .20 |
| 180 | Don Mattingly | 4.00 |
| 181 | Al Nipper | .04 |
| 182 | Bobby Brown | .04 |
| 183 | Larry Andersen | .04 |

| NO. | PLAYER | MINT |
|---|---|---|
| 184 | Tim Laudner | .04 |
| 185 | Rollie Fingers | .15 |
| 186 | Astros Leaders: | .08 |
| | Jose Cruz | |
| 187 | Scott Fletcher | .04 |
| 188 | Bob Dernier | .04 |
| 189 | Mike Mason | .04 |
| 190 | George Hendrick | .08 |
| 191 | Wally Backman | .04 |
| 192 | Milt Wilcox | .04 |
| 193 | Daryl Sconiers | .04 |
| 194 | Craig McMurtry | .04 |
| 195 | Dave Concepcion | .08 |
| 196 | Doyle Alexander | .04 |
| 197 | Enos Cabell | .04 |
| 198 | Ken Dixon | .08 |
| 199 | Dick Howser (Mgr.) | .08 |
| | (Royals Checklist) | |
| 200 | Mike Schmidt | .40 |
| 201 | Record—V. Coleman | .30 |
| | Most Stolen Bases— | |
| | Season, Rookie | |
| 202 | Record—D. Gooden | .60 |
| | Youngest 20-Game Winner | |
| 203 | Rec.—K. Hernandez | .20 |
| | Most Game Winning RBI, | |
| | Season | |
| 204 | Record—Phil Niekro | .15 |
| | Oldest Shutout Pitcher | |
| 205 | Record—Tony Perez | .12 |
| | Oldest to Hit Grand Slam | |
| 206 | Record—Pete Rose | .50 |
| | Most Hits, Career | |
| 207 | Record—F. Valenzuela | .15 |
| | Most Consecutive Innings, | |
| | No Earned Runs | |
| 208 | Ramon Romero | .15 |
| 209 | Randy Ready | .10 |
| 210 | Calvin Schiraldi | .25 |
| 211 | Ed Wojna | .15 |
| 212 | Chris Speier | .04 |
| 213 | Bob Shirley | .04 |
| 214 | Randy Bush | .04 |
| 215 | Frank White | .04 |
| 216 | A's Leaders: | .08 |
| | Dwayne Murphy | |
| 217 | Bill Scherrer | .04 |
| 218 | Randy Hunt | .12 |
| 219 | Dennis Lamp | .04 |
| 220 | Bob Horner | .15 |
| 221 | Dave Henderson | .04 |
| 222 | Craig Gerber | .15 |
| 223 | Atlee Hammaker | .06 |
| 224 | Cesar Cedeno | .08 |
| 225 | Ron Darling | .20 |
| 226 | Lee Lacy | .04 |
| 227 | Al Jones | .04 |
| 228 | Tom Lawless | .04 |
| 229 | Bill Gullickson | .04 |
| 230 | Terry Kennedy | .06 |
| 231 | Jim Frey (Mgr.) | .08 |
| | Cubs Checklist | |
| 232 | Rick Rhoden | .04 |
| 233 | Steve Lyons | .10 |
| 234 | Doug Corbett | .04 |
| 235 | Butch Wynegar | .06 |
| 236 | Frank Eufemia | .15 |
| 237 | Ted Simmons | .15 |
| 238 | Larry Parrish | .06 |
| 239 | Joel Skinner | .04 |
| 240 | Tommy John | .15 |
| 241 | Tony Fernandez | .08 |
| 242 | Rich Thompson | .12 |
| 243 | Johnny Grubb | .04 |
| 244 | Craig Lefferts | .04 |
| 245 | Jim Sundberg | .04 |
| 246 | Phillies Leaders: | .15 |
| | Steve Carlton | |
| 247 | Terry Harper | .04 |
| 248 | Spike Owen | .04 |
| 249 | Rob Deer | .40 |
| 250 | Dwight Gooden | 2.50 |
| 251 | Rich Dauer | .04 |
| 252 | Bobby Castillo | .04 |
| 253 | Dann Bilardello | .04 |

| NO. | PLAYER | MINT |
|---|---|---|
| 254 | Ozzie Guillen (R) | .50 |
| 255 | Tony Armas | .10 |
| 256 | Kurt Kepshire | .04 |
| 257 | Doug DeCinces | .08 |
| 258 | Tim Burke (R) | .25 |
| 259 | Dan Pasqua | 1.00 |
| 260 | Tony Pena | .10 |
| 261 | Bobby Valentine (Mgr.) | .08 |
| | Rangers Checklist | |
| 262 | Mario Ramirez | .04 |
| 263 | Checklist No. 2 | .08 |
| 264 | Darren Daulton (R) | .25 |
| 265 | Ron Davis | .04 |
| 266 | Keith Moreland | .04 |
| 267 | Paul Molitor | .12 |
| 268 | Mike Scott | .04 |
| 269 | Dane Iorg | .04 |
| 270 | Jack Morris | .15 |
| 271 | Dave Collins | .04 |
| 272 | Tim Tolman | .15 |
| 273 | Jerry Willard | .04 |
| 274 | Ron Gardenhire | .04 |
| 275 | Charlie Hough | .04 |
| 276 | Yankees Leaders: | .10 |
| | Willie Randolph | |
| 277 | Jaime Cocanower | .04 |
| 278 | Sixto Lezcano | .04 |
| 279 | Al Pardo | .15 |
| 280 | Tim Raines | .15 |
| 281 | Steve Mura | .04 |
| 282 | Jerry Mumphrey | .04 |
| 283 | Mike Fischlin | .04 |
| 284 | Brian Dayett | .04 |
| 285 | Buddy Bell | .10 |
| 286 | Luis DeLeon | .04 |
| 287 | John Christensen | .15 |
| 288 | Don Aase | .04 |
| 289 | Johnnie LeMaster | .04 |
| 290 | Carlton Fisk | .15 |
| 291 | Tom Lasorda (Mgr.) | .12 |
| | Dodgers Checklist | |
| 292 | Chuck Porter | .04 |
| 293 | Chris Chambliss | .06 |
| 294 | Danny Cox | .10 |
| 295 | Kirk Gibson | .20 |
| 296 | Geno Petralli | .04 |
| 297 | Tim Lollar | .04 |
| 298 | Craig Reynolds | .04 |
| 299 | Bryn Smith | .04 |
| 300 | George Brett | .50 |
| 301 | Dennis Rasmussen | .04 |
| 302 | Greg Gross | .04 |
| 303 | Curt Wardle | .15 |
| 304 | Mike Gallego | .15 |
| 305 | Phil Bradley | .20 |
| 306 | Padres Leaders: | .08 |
| | Terry Kennedy | |
| 307 | Dave Sax | .04 |
| 308 | Ray Fontenot | .04 |
| 309 | John Shelby | .04 |
| 310 | Greg Minton | .04 |
| 311 | Dick Schofield | .04 |
| 312 | Tom Filer | .04 |
| 313 | Joe De Sa | .15 |
| 314 | Frank Pastore | .04 |
| 315 | Mookie Wilson | .06 |
| 316 | Sammy Khalifa | .15 |
| 317 | Ed Romero | .04 |
| 318 | Terry Whitfield | .04 |
| 319 | Rick Camp | .04 |
| 320 | Jim Rice | .25 |
| 321 | Earl Weaver (Mgr.) | .12 |
| | Orioles Checklist | |
| 322 | Bob Forsch | .04 |
| 323 | Jerry Davis | .08 |
| 324 | Dan Schatzeder | .04 |
| 325 | Juan Beniquez | .04 |
| 326 | Kent Tekulve | .04 |
| 327 | Mike Pagliarulo | .08 |
| 328 | Pete O'Brien | .04 |
| 329 | Kirby Puckett | .75 |
| 330 | Rick Sutcliffe | .12 |
| 331 | Alan Ashby | .04 |
| 332 | Darryl Motley | .04 |
| 333 | Tom Henke | .06 |

| NO. | PLAYER | MINT |
|---|---|---|
| 334 | Ken Oberkfell | .04 |
| 335 | Don Sutton | .15 |
| 336 | Indians Leaders: | .08 |
| | Andre Thornton | |
| 337 | Darnell Coles | .04 |
| 338 | Jorge Bell | .10 |
| 339 | Bruce Berenyi | .04 |
| 340 | Cal Ripken | .40 |
| 341 | Frank Williams | .04 |
| 342 | Gary Redus | .04 |
| 343 | Carlos Diaz | .04 |
| 344 | Jim Wohlford | .04 |
| 345 | Donnie Moore | .04 |
| 346 | Bryan Little | .04 |
| 347 | Teddy Higuera (R) | 1.00 |
| 348 | Cliff Johnson | .04 |
| 349 | Mark Clear | .04 |
| 350 | Jack Clark | .20 |
| 351 | Chuck Tanner (Mgr.) | .08 |
| | Pirates Checklist | |
| 352 | Harry Spilman | .04 |
| 353 | Keith Atherton | .04 |
| 354 | Tony Bernazard | .04 |
| 355 | Lee Smith | .06 |
| 356 | Mickey Hatcher | .04 |
| 357 | Ed VandeBerg | .04 |
| 358 | Rick Dempsey | .04 |
| 359 | Mike LaCoss | .04 |
| 360 | Lloyd Moseby | .15 |
| 361 | Shane Rawley | .04 |
| 362 | Tom Paciorek | .04 |
| 363 | Terry Forster | .06 |
| 364 | Reid Nichols | .04 |
| 365 | Mike Flanagan | .06 |
| 366 | Reds Leaders: | .10 |
| | Dave Concepcion | |
| 367 | Aurelio Lopez | .04 |
| 368 | Greg Brock | .06 |
| 369 | Al Holland | .04 |
| 370 | Vince Coleman (R) | 2.00 |
| 371 | Bill Stein | .04 |
| 372 | Ben Ogilvie | .06 |
| 373 | Urbano Lugo | .15 |
| 374 | Terry Francona | .06 |
| 375 | Rich Gedman | .06 |
| 376 | Bill Dawley | .04 |
| 377 | Joe Carter | .04 |
| 378 | Bruce Bochte | .04 |
| 379 | Bobby Meacham | .04 |
| 380 | LaMarr Hoyt | .10 |
| 381 | Ray Miller (Mgr.) | .08 |
| | Twins Checklist | |
| 382 | Ivan Calderon (R) | .25 |
| 383 | Chris Brown (R) | 1.75 |
| 384 | Steve Trout | .04 |
| 385 | Cecil Cooper | .15 |
| 386 | Cecil Fielder (R) | .25 |
| 387 | Steve Kemp | .06 |
| 388 | Dickie Noles | .04 |
| 389 | Glenn Davis | 1.75 |
| 390 | Tom Seaver | .25 |
| 391 | Julio Franco | .10 |
| 392 | John Russell | .08 |
| 393 | Chris Pittaro | .15 |
| 394 | Checklist No. 3 | .08 |
| 395 | Scott Garrelts | .04 |
| 396 | Red Sox Leaders: | .08 |
| | Dwight Evans | |
| 397 | Steve Buechele (R) | .20 |
| 398 | Earnie Riles (R) | .40 |
| 399 | Bill Swift | .04 |
| 400 | Rod Carew | .30 |
| 401 | Turn Back the Clock: | .15 |
| | F. Valenzuela (1981) | |
| 402 | Turn Back the Clock: | .15 |
| | Tom Seaver (1976) | |
| 403 | Turn Back the Clock: | .15 |
| | Willie Mays (1971) | |
| 404 | Turn Back the Clock: | .15 |
| | Frank Robinson (1966) | |
| 405 | Turn Back the Clock: | .15 |
| | Roger Maris (1961) | |
| 406 | Scott Sanderson | .04 |
| 407 | Sal Butera | .04 |
| 408 | Dave Smith | .04 |

Card values from this set fluctuate considerably.

| NO. PLAYER | MINT |
|---|---|
| 409 Paul Runge (R) | .15 |
| 410 Dave Kingman | .10 |
| 411 Sparky Anderson (Mgr.) | .10 |
| Tigers Checklist | |
| 412 Jim Clancy | .04 |
| 413 Tim Flannery | .04 |
| 414 Tom Gorman | .04 |
| 415 Hal McRae | .04 |
| 416 Denny Martinez | .04 |
| 417 R.J. Reynolds | .04 |
| 418 Alan Knicely | .04 |
| 419 Frank Wills | .15 |
| 420 Von Hayes | .15 |
| 421 Dave Palmer | .04 |
| 422 Mike Jorgensen | .04 |
| 423 Dan Spillner | .04 |
| 424 Rick Miller | .04 |
| 425 Larry McWilliams | .04 |
| 426 Brewers Leaders: | .04 |
| Charlie Moore | |
| 427 Joe Cowley | .04 |
| 428 Max Venable | .04 |
| 429 Greg Booker | .04 |
| 430 Kent Hrbek | .25 |
| 431 George Frazier | .04 |
| 432 Mark Bailey | .04 |
| 433 Chris Codiroli | .04 |
| 434 Curt Wilkerson | .04 |
| 435 Bill Caudill | .04 |
| 436 Doug Flynn | .04 |
| 437 Rick Mahler | .04 |
| 438 Clint Hurdle | .04 |
| 439 Rick Honeycutt | .04 |
| 440 Alvin Davis | .20 |
| 441 Whitey Herzog (Mgr.) | .10 |
| Cardinals Checklist | |
| 442 Ron Robinson | .04 |
| 443 Bill Buckner | .08 |
| 444 Alex Trevino | .04 |
| 445 Bert Blyleven | .10 |
| 446 Lenn Sakata | .04 |
| 447 Jerry Don Gleaton | .04 |
| 448 Herm Winningham | .15 |
| 449 Rod Scurry | .04 |
| 450 Graig Nettles | .15 |
| 451 Mark Brown | .15 |
| 452 Bob Clark | .04 |
| 453 Steve Jeltz | .10 |
| 454 Burt Hooton | .04 |
| 455 Willie Randolph | .08 |
| 456 Braves Leaders: | .20 |
| Dale Murphy | |
| 457 Mickey Tettleton | .12 |
| 458 Kevin Bass | .04 |
| 459 Luis Leal | .04 |
| 460 Leon Durham | .15 |
| 461 Walt Terrell | .04 |
| 462 Domingo Ramos | .04 |
| 463 Jim Gott | .04 |
| 464 Ruppert Jones | .04 |
| 465 Jesse Orosco | .04 |
| 466 Tom Foley | .04 |
| 467 Bob James | .04 |
| 468 Mike Scioscia | .04 |
| 469 Storm Davis | .08 |
| 470 Bill Madlock | .15 |
| 471 Bobby Cox (Mgr.) | .08 |
| Blue Jays Checklist | |
| 472 Joe Hesketh | .15 |
| 473 Mark Brouhard | .04 |
| 474 John Tudor | .15 |
| 475 Juan Samuel | .15 |
| 476 Ron Mathis | .12 |
| 477 Mike Easler | .04 |
| 478 Andy Hawkins | .08 |
| 479 Bob Melvin | .12 |
| 480 Oddibe McDowell | .50 |
| 481 Scott Bradley | .10 |
| 482 Rick Lysander | .04 |
| 483 George Vukovich | .04 |
| 484 Donnie Hill | .04 |
| 485 Gary Matthews | .06 |
| 486 Angels Leaders: | .08 |
| Bob Grich | |
| 487 Bret Saberhagen | .30 |
| 488 Lou Thornton | .12 |
| 489 Jim Winn | .04 |
| 490 Jeff Leonard | .04 |
| 491 Pascual Perez | .04 |
| 492 Kelvin Chapman | .04 |
| 493 Gene Nelson | .04 |
| 494 Garry Roenicke | .04 |
| 495 Mark Langston | .08 |
| 496 Jay Johnstone | .04 |
| 497 John Stuper | .04 |
| 498 Tito Landrum | .04 |
| 499 Bob Gibson | .04 |
| 500 Rickey Henderson | .45 |
| 501 Dave Johnson (Mgr.) | .12 |
| Mets Checklist | |
| 502 Glen Cook | .12 |
| 503 Mike Fitzgerald | .04 |
| 504 Denny Walling | .04 |
| 505 Jerry Koosman | .08 |
| 506 Bill Russell | .04 |
| 507 Steve Ontiveros (R) | .20 |
| 508 Alan Wiggins | .08 |
| 509 Ernie Camacho | .04 |
| 510 Wade Boggs | 2.00 |
| 511 Ed Nunez | .04 |
| 512 Thad Bosley | .04 |
| 513 Ron Washington | .04 |
| 514 Mike Jones | .04 |
| 515 Darrell Evans | .08 |
| 516 Giants Leaders: | .08 |
| Greg Minton | |
| 517 Milt Thompson (R) | .25 |
| 518 Buck Martinez | .04 |
| 519 Danny Darwin | .04 |
| 520 Keith Hernandez | .25 |
| 521 Nate Snell | .12 |
| 522 Bob Bailor | .04 |
| 523 Joe Price | .04 |
| 524 Darrell Miller | .08 |
| 525 Marvel Wynne | .04 |
| 526 Charlie Lea | .04 |
| 527 Checklist No. 4 | .08 |
| 528 Terry Pendleton | .08 |
| 529 Marc Sullivan | .12 |
| 530 Rich Gossage | .15 |
| 531 Tony LaRussa (Mgr.) | .08 |
| White Sox Checklist | |
| 532 Don Carman (R) | .25 |
| 533 Billy Sample | .04 |
| 534 Jeff Calhoun | .12 |
| 535 Toby Harrah | .04 |
| 536 Jose Rijo | .04 |
| 537 Mark Salas | .15 |
| 538 Dennis Eckersley | .08 |
| 539 Glenn Hubbard | .04 |
| 540 Dan Petry | .15 |
| 541 Jorge Orta | .04 |
| 542 Don Schulze | .04 |
| 543 Jerry Narron | .04 |
| 544 Eddie Milner | .04 |
| 545 Jimmy Key | .08 |
| 546 Mariners Leaders: | .06 |
| Dave Henderson | |
| 547 Roger McDowell (R) | .45 |
| 548 Mike Young | .20 |
| 549 Bob Welch | .06 |
| 550 Tom Herr | .10 |
| 551 Dave LaPoint | .04 |
| 552 Marc Hill | .04 |
| 553 Jim Morrison | .04 |
| 554 Paul Householder | .04 |
| 555 Hubie Brooks | .08 |
| 556 John Denny | .06 |
| 557 Gerald Perry | .04 |
| 558 Tim Stoddard | .04 |
| 559 Tommy Dunbar | .04 |
| 560 Dave Righetti | .10 |
| 561 Bob Lillis (Mgr.) | .06 |
| Astros Checklist | |
| 562 Joe Beckwith | .04 |
| 563 Alejandro Sanchez | .08 |
| 564 Warren Brusstar | .04 |
| 565 Tom Brunansky | .12 |
| 566 Alfredo Griffin | .04 |
| 567 Jeff Barkley | .12 |
| 568 Donnie Scott | .04 |
| 569 Jim Acker | .04 |
| 570 Rusty Staub | .08 |
| 571 Mike Jeffcoat | .04 |
| 572 Paul Zuvella | .08 |
| 573 Tom Hume | .04 |
| 574 Ron Kittle | .10 |
| 575 Mike Boddicker | .10 |
| 576 Expos Leaders: | .08 |
| Andre Dawson | |
| 577 Jerry Reuss | .06 |
| 578 Lee Mazzilli | .04 |
| 579 Jim Slaton | .04 |
| 580 Willie McGee | .25 |
| 581 Bruce Hurst | .04 |
| 582 Jim Gantner | .04 |
| 583 Al Bumbry | .04 |
| 584 Brian Fisher (R) | .30 |
| 585 Garry Maddox | .04 |
| 586 Greg Harris | .04 |
| 587 Rafael Santana | .04 |
| 588 Steve Lake | .04 |
| 589 Sid Bream | .04 |
| 590 Bob Knepper | .04 |
| 591 Jackie Moore (Mgr.) | .08 |
| A's Checklist | |
| 592 Frank Tanana | .06 |
| 593 Jesse Barfield | .20 |
| 594 Chris Bando | .04 |
| 595 Dave Parker | .20 |
| 596 Onix Concepcion | .04 |
| 597 Sammy Stewart | .04 |
| 598 Jim Presley | .75 |
| 599 Rick Aguilera (R) | .40 |
| 600 Dale Murphy | .40 |
| 601 Gary Lucas | .04 |
| 602 Mariano Duncan (R) | .50 |
| 603 Bill Laskey | .04 |
| 604 Gary Pettis | .08 |
| 605 Dennis Boyd | .06 |
| 606 Royals Leaders: | .10 |
| Hal McRae | |
| 607 Ken Dayley | .04 |
| 608 Bruce Bochy | .04 |
| 609 Barbaro Garbey | .04 |
| 610 Ron Guidry | .15 |
| 611 Gary Woods | .04 |
| 612 Richard Dotson | .06 |
| 613 Roy Smalley | .04 |
| 614 Rick Waits | .04 |
| 615 Johnny Ray | .08 |
| 616 Glenn Brummer | .04 |
| 617 Lonnie Smith | .08 |
| 618 Jim Pankovits | .06 |
| 619 Danny Heep | .04 |
| 620 Bruce Sutter | .15 |
| 621 John Felske (Mgr.) | .08 |
| Phillies Checklist | |
| 622 Gary Lavelle | .04 |
| 623 Floyd Rayford | .04 |
| 624 Steve McCatty | .04 |
| 625 Bob Brenly | .04 |
| 626 Roy Thomas | .04 |
| 627 Ron Oester | .04 |
| 628 Kirk McCaskill (R) | .75 |
| 629 Mitch Webster (R) | .60 |
| 630 Fernando Valenzuela | .30 |
| 631 Steve Braun | .04 |
| 632 Dave Von Ohlen | .04 |
| 633 Jackie Gutierrez | .04 |
| 634 Roy Lee Jackson | .04 |
| 635 Jason Thompson | .06 |
| 636 Cubs Leaders: | .10 |
| Lee Smith | |
| 637 Rudy Law | .04 |
| 638 John Butcher | .04 |
| 639 Bo Diaz | .04 |
| 640 Jose Cruz | .08 |
| 641 Wayne Tolleson | .04 |
| 642 Ray Searage | .04 |
| 643 Tom Brookens | .04 |
| 644 Mark Gubicza | .06 |
| 645 Dusty Baker | .06 |
| 646 Mike Moore | .04 |
| 647 Mel Hall | .06 |
| 648 Steve Bedrosian | .06 |
| 649 Ronn Reynolds | .10 |
| 650 Dave Stieb | .15 |
| 651 Billy Martin (Mgr.) | .10 |
| Yankees Checklist | |
| 652 Tom Browning | .25 |
| 653 Jim Dwyer | .04 |
| 654 Ken Howell | .10 |
| 655 Manny Trillo | .04 |
| 656 Brian Harper | .04 |
| 657 Juan Agosto | .04 |
| 658 Rob Wilfong | .04 |
| 659 Checklist No. 5 | .08 |
| 660 Steve Garvey | .30 |
| 661 Roger Clemens | 2.00 |
| 662 Bill Schroeder | .04 |
| 663 Neil Allen | .04 |
| 664 Tim Corcoran | .04 |
| 665 Alejandro Pena | .06 |
| 666 Rangers Leaders: | .06 |
| Charlie Hough | |
| 667 Tim Tuefel | .08 |
| 668 Cecilio Guante | .04 |
| 669 Ron Cey | .10 |
| 670 Willie Hernandez | .12 |
| 671 Lynn Jones | .04 |
| 672 Rob Picciolo | .04 |
| 673 Ernie Whitt | .04 |
| 674 Pat Tabler | .04 |
| 675 Claudell Washington | .06 |
| 676 Matt Young | .04 |
| 677 Nick Esasky | .06 |
| 678 Dan Gladden | .06 |
| 679 Britt Burns | .06 |
| 680 George Foster | .15 |
| 681 Dick Williams (Mgr.) | .08 |
| Padres Checklist | |
| 682 Junior Ortiz | .04 |
| 683 Andy Van Slyke | .06 |
| 684 Bob McClure | .04 |
| 685 Tim Wallach | .08 |
| 686 Jeff Stone | .06 |
| 687 Mike Trujillo | .12 |
| 688 Larry Herndon | .04 |
| 689 Dave Stewart | .04 |
| 690 Ryne Sandberg | .30 |
| 691 Mike Madden | .04 |
| 692 Dale Berra | .04 |
| 693 Tom Tellmann | .04 |
| 694 Garth Iorg | .04 |
| 695 Mike Smithson | .04 |
| 696 Dodgers Leaders: | .10 |
| Bill Russell | |
| 697 Bud Black | .04 |
| 698 Brad Komminsk | .06 |
| 699 Pat Corrales (Mgr.) | .08 |
| Indians Checklist | |
| 700 Reggie Jackson | .40 |
| 701 Keith Hernandez (AS) | .15 |
| 702 Tom Herr (AS) | .08 |
| 703 Tim Wallach (AS) | .08 |
| 704 Ozzie Smith (AS) | .08 |
| 705 Dale Murphy (AS) | .30 |
| 706 Pedro Guerrero (AS) | .20 |
| 707 Willie McGee (AS) | .20 |
| 708 Gary Carter (AS) | .20 |
| 709 Dwight Gooden (AS) | .75 |
| 710 John Tudor (AS) | .08 |
| 711 Jeff Reardon (AS) | .08 |
| 712 Don Mattingly (AS) | 1.00 |
| 713 Damaso Garcia (AS) | .08 |
| 714 George Brett (AS) | .35 |
| 715 Cal Ripken (AS) | .30 |
| 716 Rickey Henderson (AS) | .30 |
| 717 Dave Winfield (AS) | .25 |
| 718 Jorge Bell (AS) | .08 |
| 719 Carlton Fisk (AS) | .10 |
| 720 Bret Saberhagen (AS) | .25 |
| 721 Ron Guidry (AS) | .10 |
| 722 Dan Quisenberry (AS) | .10 |
| 723 Marty Bystrom | .04 |
| 724 Tim Hulett | .08 |
| 725 Mario Soto | .08 |
| 726 Orioles Leaders: | .08 |
| Rick Dempsey | |

Card values from this set fluctuate considerably.

| NO. PLAYER | MINT | NO. PLAYER | MINT | NO. PLAYER | MINT | NO. PLAYER | MINT |
|---|---|---|---|---|---|---|---|
| 727 David Green | .04 | 748 Steve Henderson | .04 | 769 Harold Reynolds (R) | .15 | 789 Kurt Bevacqua | .04 |
| 728 Mike Marshall | .15 | 749 Ed Jurak | .04 | 770 Vida Blue | .08 | 790 Phil Niekro | .15 |
| 729 Jim Beattie | .04 | 750 Gorman Thomas | .08 | 771 John McNamara (Mgr.) | .08 | 791 Checklist No. 6 | .08 |
| 730 Ozzie Smith | .10 | 751 Howard Johnson | .04 | Red Sox Checklist | | 792 Charles Hudson | .06 |
| 731 Don Robinson | .04 | 752 Mike Krukow | .04 | 772 Brian Downing | .04 | | |
| 732 Floyd Youmans (R) | 1.00 | 753 Dan Ford | .04 | 773 Greg Pryor | .04 | **Cards Printed on Gum Boxes** | |
| 733 Ron Romanick | .06 | 754 Pat Clements (R) | .20 | 774 Terry Leach | .04 | A Jorge Bell | .20 |
| 734 Marty Barrett | .04 | 755 Harold Baines | .20 | 775 Al Oliver | .10 | B Wade Boggs | 1.50 |
| 735 Dave Dravecky | .04 | 756 Pirates Leaders: | .06 | 776 Gene Garber | .04 | C George Brett | .60 |
| 736 Glenn Wilson | .08 | Rick Rhoden | | 777 Wayne Krenchicki | .04 | D Vince Coleman | .60 |
| 737 Pete Vuckovich | .04 | 757 Darrell Porter | .04 | 778 Jerry Hairston | .04 | E Carlton Fisk | .20 |
| 738 Andre Robertson | .04 | 758 Dave Anderson | .04 | 779 Rick Reuschel | .04 | F Dwight Gooden | 1.50 |
| 739 Dave Rozema | .04 | 759 Moose Haas | .04 | 780 Robin Yount | .20 | G Pedro Guerrero | .30 |
| 740 Lance Parrish | .20 | 760 Andre Dawson | .20 | 781 Joe Nolan | .04 | H Ron Guidry | .25 |
| 741 Pete Rose (Mgr.) | .40 | 761 Don Slaught | .04 | 782 Ken Landreaux | .04 | I Reggie Jackson | .75 |
| Reds Checklist | | 762 Eric Show | .04 | 783 Ricky Horton | .04 | J Don Mattingly | 2.50 |
| 742 Frank Viola | .04 | 763 Terry Puhl | .04 | 784 Alan Bannister | .04 | K Oddibe McDowell | .40 |
| 743 Pat Sheridan | .04 | 764 Kevin Gross | .04 | 785 Bob Stanley | .04 | L Willie McGee | .40 |
| 744 Lary Sorensen | .04 | 765 Don Baylor | .15 | 786 Twins Leaders: | .06 | M Dale Murphy | .75 |
| 745 Willie Upshaw | .08 | 766 Rick Langford | .04 | Mickey Hatcher | | N Pete Rose | 1.00 |
| 746 Denny Gonzalez | .08 | 767 Jody Davis | .08 | 787 Vance Law | .04 | O Bret Saberhagen | .30 |
| 747 Rick Cerone | .04 | 768 Vern Ruhle | .04 | 788 Marty Castillo | .04 | P Fernando Valenzuela | .30 |

Card values from this set fluctuate considerably.

## 1986 Topps Traded.... Complete Set of 132 Cards—Value $16.00

Updates the main 1986 card set with players who changed teams during the season, and rookies. Features the first Topps card of Wally Joyner, Kevin Mitchell, Pete Incaviglia, and Andres Galarraga. The set was packaged in a printed box and distributed exclusively through card hobby dealers.

| NO. PLAYER | MINT | NO. PLAYER | MINT | NO. PLAYER | MINT | NO. PLAYER | MINT |
|---|---|---|---|---|---|---|---|
| 1T Andy Allanson | .15 | 34T Mark Eichhorn (RR) | .60 | 67T Steve Lyons | .06 | 100T Ken Schrom | .06 |
| 2T Neil Allen | .06 | 35T Steve Farr | .06 | 68T Mickey Mahler | .06 | 101T Tom Seaver | .35 |
| 3T Joaquin Andujar | .06 | 36T Scott Fletcher | .06 | 69T Candy Maldonado | .10 | 102T Ted Simmons | .06 |
| 4T Paul Assenmacher | .10 | 37T Terry Forster | .06 | 70T Roger Mason | .10 | 103T Sammy Stewart | .06 |
| 5T Scott Bailes | .15 | 38T Terry Francona | .06 | 71T Bob McClure | .06 | 104T Kurt Stillwell | .15 |
| 6T Don Baylor | .20 | 39T Jim Fregosi | .06 | 72T Andy McGaffigan | .06 | 105T Franklin Stubbs | .50 |
| 7T Steve Bedrosian | .06 | 40T Andres Galarraga (RR) | .50 | 73T Gene Michael | .06 | 106T Dale Sveum | .15 |
| 8T Juan Beniquez | .06 | 41T Ken Griffey | .06 | 74T Kevin Mitchell (RR) | 1.50 | 107T Chuck Tanner | .06 |
| 9T Juan Berenguer | .06 | 42T Bill Gullickson | .06 | 75T Omar Moreno | .06 | 108T Danny Tartabull | .60 |
| 10T Mike Bielecki | .12 | 43T Jose Guzman | .20 | 76T Jerry Mumphrey | .06 | 109T Tim Teufel | .06 |
| 11T Barry Bonds (RR) | .85 | 44T Moose Haas | .06 | 77T Phil Niekro | .20 | 110T Bob Tewksbury | .30 |
| 12T Bobby Bonilla | .20 | 45T Billy Hatcher | .06 | 78T Randy Niemann | .06 | 111T Andres Thomas | .25 |
| 13T Juan Bonilla | .06 | 46T Mike Heath | .06 | 79T Juan Nieves | .50 | 112T Milt Thompson | .06 |
| 14T Rich Bordi | .06 | 47T Tom Hume | .06 | 80T Otis Nixon | .15 | 113T Robby Thompson | .35 |
| 15T Steve Boros | .06 | 48T Pete Incaviglia (RR) | 2.00 | 81T Bob Ojeda | .06 | 114T Jay Tibbs | .06 |
| 16T Rick Burleson | .06 | 49T Dane Iorg | .06 | 82T Jose Oquendo | .10 | 115T Wayne Tolleson | .06 |
| 17T Bill Campbell | .06 | 50T Bo Jackson (RR) | 3.00 | 83T Tom Paciorek | .06 | 116T Alex Trevino | .06 |
| 18T Tom Candiotti | .06 | 51T Wally Joyner (RR) | 3.50 | 84T Dave Palmer | .06 | 117T Manny Trillo | .06 |
| 19T John Cangelosi | .30 | 52T Charlie Kerfeld | .40 | 85T Frank Pastore | .06 | 118T Ed VandeBerg | .06 |
| 20T Jose Canseco (RR) | 4.00 | 53T Eric King | .30 | 86T Lou Piniella | .08 | 119T Ozzie Virgil | .06 |
| 21T Carmen Castillo | .10 | 54T Bob Kipper | .06 | 87T Dan Plesac | .25 | 120T Bob Walk | .06 |
| 22T Rick Cerone | .06 | 55T Wayne Krenchicki | .06 | 88T Darrell Porter | .06 | 121T Gene Walter | .10 |
| 23T John Cerutti | .40 | 56T John Kruk | .35 | 89T Rey Quinones | .20 | 122T C. Washington | .06 |
| 24T Will Clark (RR) | 1.50 | 57T Mike LaCoss | .06 | 90T Gary Redus | .06 | 123T Bill Wegman | .35 |
| 25T Mark Clear | .06 | 58T Pete Ladd | .06 | 91T Bip Roberts | .25 | 124T Dick Williams | .06 |
| 26T Darnell Coles | .15 | 59T Mike Laga | .06 | 92T Billy Jo Robidoux | .40 | 125T Mitch Williams | .20 |
| 27T Dave Collins | .06 | 60T Hal Lanier | .06 | 93T Jeff Robinson | .06 | 126T Bobby Witt (RR) | .60 |
| 28T Tim Conroy | .06 | 61T Dave LaPoint | .06 | 94T Gary Roenicke | .06 | 127T Todd Worrell (RR) | 1.00 |
| 29T Joe Cowley | .10 | 62T Rudy Law | .06 | 95T Ed Romero | .06 | 128T George Wright | .06 |
| 30T Joel Davis | .15 | 63T Rick Leach | .06 | 96T Argenis Salazar | .06 | 129T Ricky Wright | .06 |
| 31T Rob Deer | .50 | 64T Tim Leary | .06 | 97T Joe Sambito | .06 | 130T Steve Yeager | .06 |
| 32T John Denny | .06 | 65T Dennis Leonard | .06 | 98T Billy Sample | .06 | 131T Paul Zuvella | .06 |
| 33T Mike Easler | .06 | 66T Jim Leyland | .06 | 99T Dave Schmidt | .06 | 132T Checklist | .06 |

# 1987 Topps....Complete Set of 792 Cards—Value $20.00

Features the rookie cards of Wally Joyner, Bo Jackson, Ruben Sierra and Pete Incaviglia. Topps printed 8 cards on the bottom of gum pack display boxes (not part of the set). There are two cards on each box—four different boxes. These 8 cards are identified by a letter code—A through H.

| NO. PLAYER | MINT | NO. PLAYER | MINT | NO. PLAYER | MINT | NO. PLAYER | MINT |
|---|---|---|---|---|---|---|---|
| 1 '86 Record: Clemens | .30 | 67 Bill Swift | .04 | 133 Jose Oquendo | .04 | 199 Mariano Duncan | .10 |
| 2 '86 Record: Deshaies | .08 | 68 Tony LaRussa (Mgr.) | .04 | 134 Rich Yett (R) | .15 | 200 Pete Rose | .75 |
| 3 '86 Record: Evans | .10 | 69 Lonnie Smith | .04 | 135 Mike Easler | .04 | 201 John Cangelosi (R) | .30 |
| 4 '86 Record: Lopes | .10 | 70 Charlie Hough | .04 | 136 Ron Romanick | .04 | 202 Ricky Wright | .04 |
| 5 '86 Record: Righetti | .08 | 71 Mike Aldrete (R) | .20 | 137 Jerry Willard | .04 | 203 Mike Kingery (R) | .25 |
| 6 '86 Record: Sierra | .15 | 72 Walt Terrell | .04 | 138 Roy Lee Jackson | .04 | 204 Sammy Stewart | .04 |
| 7 '86 Record: Worrell | .15 | 73 Dave Anderson | .04 | 139 Devon White (R) | .25 | 205 Graig Nettles | .08 |
| 8 Terry Pendleton | .04 | 74 Dan Pasqua | .20 | 140 Bret Saberhagen | .15 | 206 Twins Leaders | .06 |
| 9 Jay Tibbs | .04 | 75 Ron Darling | .20 | 141 Herm Winningham | .04 | 207 George Frazier | .04 |
| 10 Cecil Cooper | .08 | 76 Rafael Ramirez | .04 | 142 Rick Sutcliffe | .06 | 208 John Shelby | .04 |
| 11 Indians Leaders | .06 | 77 Bryan Oelkers | .04 | 143 Steve Boros (Mgr.) | .04 | 209 Rick Schu | .04 |
| 12 Jeff Sellers (R) | .15 | 78 Tom Foley | .04 | 144 Mike Scioscia | .04 | 210 Lloyd Moseby | .12 |
| 13 Nick Esasky | .04 | 79 Juan Nieves | .15 | 145 Charlie Kerfeld | .15 | 211 John Morris | .04 |
| 14 Dave Stewart | .04 | 80 Wally Joyner (R) | 2.50 | 146 Tracy Jones (R) | .20 | 212 Mike Fitzgerald | .04 |
| 15 Claudell Washington | .04 | 81 Padres Leaders | .06 | 147 Randy Niemann | .04 | 213 Randy Myers (R) | .45 |
| 16 Pat Clements | .04 | 82 Rob Murphy (R) | .15 | 148 Dave Collins | .04 | 214 Omar Moreno | .04 |
| 17 Pete O'Brien | .10 | 83 Mike Davis | .04 | 149 Ray Searage | .04 | 215 Mark Langston | .04 |
| 18 Dick Howser (Mgr.) | .04 | 84 Steve Lake | .04 | 150 Wade Boggs | 1.00 | 216 B.J. Surhoff (R) | .75 |
| 19 Matt Young | .04 | 85 Kevin Bass | .04 | 151 Mike LaCoss | .04 | 217 Chris Codiroli | .04 |
| 20 Gary Carter | .25 | 86 Nate Snell | .04 | 152 Toby Harrah | .04 | 218 S. Anderson (Mgr.) | .04 |
| 21 Mark Davis | .04 | 87 Mark Salas | .04 | 153 Duane Ward (R) | .15 | 219 Cecillo Guante | .04 |
| 22 Doug DeCinces | .06 | 88 Ed Wojna | .04 | 154 Tom O'Malley | .04 | 220 Joe Carter | .25 |
| 23 Lee Smith | .04 | 89 Ozzie Guillen | .08 | 155 Eddie Whitson | .04 | 221 Vern Ruhle | .04 |
| 24 Tony Walker (R) | .15 | 90 Dave Stieb | .10 | 156 Mariners Leaders | .06 | 222 Denny Walling | .04 |
| 25 Bert Blyleven | .08 | 91 Harold Reynolds | .08 | 157 Danny Darwin | .04 | 223 Charlie Leibrandt | .04 |
| 26 Greg Brock | .04 | 92 Urbano Lugo | .04 | 158 Tim Teufel | .04 | 224 Wayne Tolleson | .04 |
| 27 Joe Cowley | .04 | 93 Jim Leyland (Mgr.) | .04 | 159 Ed Olwine (R) | .15 | 225 Mike Smithson | .04 |
| 28 Rick Dempsey | .04 | 94 Calvin Schiraldi | .08 | 160 Julio Franco | .10 | 226 Max Venable | .04 |
| 29 Jimmy Key | .04 | 95 Oddibe McDowell | .15 | 161 Steve Ontiveros | .04 | 227 Jamie Moyer (R) | .20 |
| 30 Tim Raines | .30 | 96 Frank Williams | .04 | 162 Mike LaValliere (R) | .15 | 228 Curt Wilkerson | .04 |
| 31 Braves Leaders | .06 | 97 Glenn Wilson | .04 | 163 Kevin Gross | .04 | 229 Mike Birkbeck (R) | .15 |
| 32 Tim Leary | .04 | 98 Bill Scherrer | .04 | 164 Sammy Khalifa | .04 | 230 Don Baylor | .12 |
| 33 Andy Van Slyke | .04 | 99 Darryl Motley | .04 | 165 Jeff Reardon | .04 | 231 Giants Leaders | .06 |
| 34 Jose Rijo | .04 | 100 Steve Garvey | .25 | 166 Bob Boone | .04 | 232 Reggie Williams (R) | .25 |
| 35 Sid Bream | .04 | 101 Carl Willis (R) | .15 | 167 Jim Deshaies (R) | .35 | 233 Russ Morman (R) | .20 |
| 36 Eric King (R) | .25 | 102 Paul Zuvella | .04 | 168 Lou Piniella (Mgr.) | .06 | 234 Pat Sheridan | .04 |
| 37 Marvell Wynne | .04 | 103 Rick Aguilera | .04 | 169 Ron Washington | .04 | 235 Alvin Davis | .12 |
| 38 Dennis Leonard | .04 | 104 Billy Sample | .04 | 170 Bo Jackson (R) | 1.25 | 236 Tommy John | .08 |
| 39 Marty Barrett | .06 | 105 Floyd Youmans | .15 | 171 Chuck Cary (R) | .15 | 237 Jim Morrison | .04 |
| 40 Dave Righetti | .08 | 106 Blue Jays Leaders | .06 | 172 Ron Oester | .04 | 238 Bill Krueger | .04 |
| 41 Bo Diaz | .04 | 107 John Butcher | .04 | 173 Alex Trevino | .04 | 239 Juan Espino | .04 |
| 42 Gary Redus | .04 | 108 Jim Gantner | .04 | 174 Henry Cotto | .04 | 240 Steve Balboni | .08 |
| 43 Gene Michael (Mgr.) | .04 | 109 R. J. Reynolds | .04 | 175 Bob Stanley | .04 | 241 Danny Heep | .04 |
| 44 Greg Harris | .04 | 110 John Tudor | .04 | 176 Steve Buechele | .04 | 242 Rick Mahler | .04 |
| 45 Jim Presley | .20 | 111 Alfredo Griffin | .04 | 177 Keith Moreland | .04 | 243 Whitey Herzog (Mgr.) | .04 |
| 46 Danny Gladden | .04 | 112 Alan Ashby | .04 | 178 Cecil Fielder | .04 | 244 Dickie Noles | .04 |
| 47 Dennis Powell | .12 | 113 Neil Allen | .04 | 179 Bill Wegman | .04 | 245 Willie Upshaw | .04 |
| 48 Wally Backman | .04 | 114 Billy Beane | .04 | 180 Chris Brown | .10 | 246 Jim Dwyer | .04 |
| 49 Terry Harper | .04 | 115 Donnie Moore | .04 | 181 Cardinals Leaders | .06 | 247 Jeff Reed | .04 |
| 50 Dave Smith | .04 | 116 Bill Russell | .04 | 182 Lee Lacy | .04 | 248 Gene Walter | .10 |
| 51 Mel Hall | .04 | 117 Jim Beattie | .04 | 183 Andy Hawkins | .04 | 249 Jim Pankovits | .04 |
| 52 Keith Atherton | .04 | 118 Bobby Valentine (Mgr.) | .04 | 184 Bobby Bonilla (R) | .15 | 250 Teddy Higuera | .20 |
| 53 Ruppert Jones | .04 | 119 Ron Robinson | .04 | 185 Roger McDowell | .10 | 251 Rob Wilfong | .04 |
| 54 Bill Dawley | .04 | 120 Eddie Murray | .30 | 186 Bruce Benedict | .04 | 252 Denny Martinez | .04 |
| 55 Tim Wallach | .04 | 121 Kevin Romine (R) | .15 | 187 Mark Huismann | .04 | 253 Eddie Milner | .04 |
| 56 Brewers Leaders | .06 | 122 Jim Clancy | .04 | 188 Tony Phillips | .04 | 254 Bob Tewksbury (R) | .25 |
| 57 Scott Nielsen (R) | .15 | 123 John Kruk (R) | .20 | 189 Joe Hesketh | .04 | 255 Juan Samuel | .10 |
| 58 Thad Bosley | .04 | 124 Ray Fontenot | .04 | 190 Jim Sundberg | .04 | 256 Royals Leaders | .06 |
| 59 Ken Dayley | .04 | 125 Bob Brenly | .04 | 191 Charles Hudson | .04 | 257 Bob Forsch | .04 |
| 60 Tony Pena | .04 | 126 Mike Loynd (R) | .15 | 192 Cory Snyder | .75 | 258 Steve Yeager | .04 |
| 61 Bobby Thigpen (R) | .25 | 127 Vance Law | .04 | 193 Roger Craig (Mgr.) | .04 | 259 Mike Greenwell (R) | .10 |
| 62 Bobby Meacham | .04 | 128 Checklist: 1-132 | .06 | 194 Kirk McCaskill | .10 | 260 Vida Blue | .06 |
| 63 Fred Tollver | .12 | 129 Rick Cerone | .04 | 195 Mike Pagliarulo | .20 | 261 Ruben Sierra (R) | 1.25 |
| 64 Harry Spilman | .04 | 130 Dwight Gooden | .75 | 196 Randy O'Neal | .04 | 262 Jim Winn | .04 |
| 65 Tom Browning | .08 | 131 Pirates Leaders | .06 | 197 Mark Bailey | .04 | 263 Stan Javier | .08 |
| 66 Marc Sullivan | .04 | 132 P. Assenmacher (R) | .15 | 198 Lee Mazzilli | .08 | 264 Checklist: 133-264 | .06 |

Card values from this set fluctuate considerably.

| NO. | PLAYER | MINT |
|---|---|---|
| 265 | Darrell Evans | .04 |
| 266 | Jeff Hamilton (R) | .15 |
| 267 | Howard Johnson | .04 |
| 268 | Pat Corrales (Mgr.) | .04 |
| 269 | Cliff Speck (R) | .15 |
| 270 | Jody Davis | .04 |
| 271 | Mike Brown | .04 |
| 272 | Andres Galarraga (R) | .15 |
| 273 | Gene Nelson | .04 |
| 274 | Jeff Hearron (R) | .15 |
| 275 | LaMarr Hoyt | .04 |
| 276 | Jackie Gutierrez | .04 |
| 277 | Juan Agosto | .04 |
| 278 | Gary Pettis | .04 |
| 279 | Dan Plesac (R) | .20 |
| 280 | Jeffrey Leonard | .04 |
| 281 | Reds Leaders | .12 |
| 282 | Jeff Calhoun | .04 |
| 283 | Doug Drabek (R) | .20 |
| 284 | John Moses | .10 |
| 285 | Dennis Boyd | .12 |
| 286 | Mike Woodard | .10 |
| 287 | Dave Von Ohlen | .04 |
| 288 | Tito Landrum | .04 |
| 289 | Bob Kipper | .04 |
| 290 | Leon Durham | .10 |
| 291 | Mitch Williams (R) | .30 |
| 292 | Franklin Stubbs | .12 |
| 293 | Bob Rodgers (Mgr.) | .04 |
| 294 | Steve Jeltz | .04 |
| 295 | Len Dykstra | .25 |
| 296 | Andres Thomas (R) | .04 |
| 297 | Don Schulze | .04 |
| 298 | Larry Herndon | .04 |
| 299 | Joel Davis | .10 |
| 300 | Reggie Jackson | .30 |
| 301 | Luis Aquino | .10 |
| 302 | Bill Schroeder | .04 |
| 303 | Juan Berenguer | .04 |
| 304 | Phil Garner | .04 |
| 305 | John Franco | .04 |
| 306 | Red Sox Leaders | .10 |
| 307 | Lee Guetterman (R) | .15 |
| 308 | Don Slaught | .04 |
| 309 | Mike Young | .04 |
| 310 | Frank Viola | .04 |
| 311 | Turn Back—1982 | .15 |
| 312 | Turn Back-1977 | .15 |
| 313 | Turn Back—1972 | .15 |
| 314 | Turn Back—1967 | .15 |
| 315 | Turn Back—1962 | .15 |
| 316 | Brian Fisher | .04 |
| 317 | Clint Hurdle | .04 |
| 318 | Jim Fregosi (Mgr.) | .04 |
| 319 | Greg Swindell (R) | .60 |
| 320 | Barry Bonds (R) | .40 |
| 321 | Mike Laga | .04 |
| 322 | Chris Bando | .04 |
| 323 | Al Newman (R) | .15 |
| 324 | Dave Palmer | .04 |
| 325 | Garry Templeton | .04 |
| 326 | Mark Gubicza | .04 |
| 327 | Dale Sveum (R) | .25 |
| 328 | Bob Welch | .04 |
| 329 | Ron Roenicke | .04 |
| 330 | Mike Scott | .20 |
| 331 | Mets Leaders | .20 |
| 332 | Joe Price | .04 |
| 333 | Ken Phelps | .04 |
| 334 | Ed Correa (R) | .35 |
| 335 | Candy Maldonado | .06 |
| 336 | Allan Anderson (R) | .15 |
| 337 | Darrell Miller | .04 |
| 338 | Tim Conroy | .04 |
| 339 | Donnie Hill | .04 |
| 340 | Roger Clemens | 1.00 |
| 341 | Mike Brown | .04 |
| 342 | Bob James | .04 |
| 343 | Hal Lanier (Mgr.) | .04 |
| 344 | Joe Niekro | .06 |
| 345 | Andre Dawson | .15 |
| 346 | Shawon Dunston | .15 |
| 347 | Mickey Brantley | .15 |
| 348 | Carmelo Martinez | .04 |
| 349 | Storm Davis | .06 |
| 350 | Keith Hernandez | .25 |
| 351 | Gene Garber | .04 |
| 352 | Mike Felder | .12 |
| 353 | Ernie Camacho | .04 |
| 354 | Jamie Quick | .04 |
| 355 | Don Carman | .04 |
| 356 | White Sox Leaders | .06 |
| 357 | Steve Fireovid (R) | .15 |
| 358 | Sal Butera | .04 |
| 359 | Doug Corbett | .04 |
| 360 | Pedro Guerrero | .20 |
| 361 | Mark Thurmond | .04 |
| 362 | Luis Quinones (R) | .15 |
| 363 | Jose Guzman | .15 |
| 364 | Randy Bush | .04 |
| 365 | Rick Rhoden | .04 |
| 366 | Mark McGwire (R) | .20 |
| 367 | Jeff Lahti | .04 |
| 368 | J. McNamara (Mgr.) | .04 |
| 369 | Brian Dayett | .04 |
| 370 | Fred Lynn | .15 |
| 371 | Mark Eichhorn (R) | .30 |
| 372 | Jerry Mumphrey | .04 |
| 373 | Jeff Dedmon | .04 |
| 374 | Glenn Hoffman | .04 |
| 375 | Ron Guidry | .15 |
| 376 | Scott Bradley | .04 |
| 377 | John Henry Johnson | .04 |
| 378 | Rafael Santana | .04 |
| 379 | John Russell | .04 |
| 380 | Rich Gossage | .12 |
| 381 | Expos Leaders | .06 |
| 382 | Rudy Law | .04 |
| 383 | Ron Davis | .04 |
| 384 | Johnny Grubb | .04 |
| 385 | Orel Hershiser | .12 |
| 386 | Dickie Thon | .04 |
| 387 | T. R. Bryden (R) | .20 |
| 388 | Geno Petralli | .04 |
| 389 | Jeff Robinson | .04 |
| 390 | Gary Matthews | .04 |
| 391 | Jay Howell | .04 |
| 392 | Checklist: 265-396 | .06 |
| 393 | Pete Rose (Mgr.) | .40 |
| 394 | Mike Bielecki | .04 |
| 395 | Damaso Garcia | .04 |
| 396 | Tim Lollar | .04 |
| 397 | Greg Walker | .04 |
| 398 | Brad Havens | .04 |
| 399 | Curt Ford | .04 |
| 400 | George Brett | .35 |
| 401 | Billy Jo Robidoux | .15 |
| 402 | Mike Trujillo | .04 |
| 403 | Jerry Royster | .04 |
| 404 | Doug Sisk | .04 |
| 405 | Brook Jacoby | .10 |
| 406 | Yankees Leaders | .25 |
| 407 | Jim Acker | .04 |
| 408 | John Mizerock | .04 |
| 409 | Milt Thompson | .04 |
| 410 | Fernando Valenzuela | .20 |
| 411 | Darnell Coles | .04 |
| 412 | Eric Davis | .35 |
| 413 | Moose Haas | .04 |
| 414 | Joe Orsulak | .04 |
| 415 | Bobby Witt (R) | .60 |
| 416 | Tom Nieto | .04 |
| 417 | Pat Perry | .08 |
| 418 | Dick Williams (Mgr.) | .04 |
| 419 | Mark Portugal (R) | .15 |
| 420 | Will Clark (R) | 1.00 |
| 421 | Jose DeLeon | .04 |
| 422 | Jack Howell | .04 |
| 423 | Jaime Cocanower | .04 |
| 424 | Chris Speier | .04 |
| 425 | Tom Seaver | .25 |
| 426 | Floyd Rayford | .04 |
| 427 | Ed Nunez | .04 |
| 428 | Bruce Bochy | .04 |
| 429 | Tim Pyznarski (R) | .20 |
| 430 | Mike Schmidt | .30 |
| 431 | Dodgers Leaders | .15 |
| 432 | Jim Slaton | .04 |
| 433 | Ed Hearn (R) | .12 |
| 434 | Mike Fischlin | .04 |
| 435 | Bruce Sutter | .10 |
| 436 | Andy Allanson (R) | .15 |
| 437 | Ted Power | .04 |
| 438 | Kelly Downs (R) | .20 |
| 439 | Karl Best | .04 |
| 440 | Willie McGee | .15 |
| 441 | Dave Leiper | .15 |
| 442 | Mitch Webster | .04 |
| 443 | John Felske (Mgr.) | .04 |
| 444 | Jeff Russell | .04 |
| 445 | Dave Lopes | .08 |
| 446 | Chuck Finley (R) | .15 |
| 447 | Bill Almon | .04 |
| 448 | Chris Bosio (R) | .12 |
| 449 | Pat Dodson (R) | .20 |
| 450 | Kirby Puckett | .30 |
| 451 | Joe Sambito | .04 |
| 452 | Dave Henderson | .04 |
| 453 | Scott Terry (R) | .15 |
| 454 | Luis Salazar | .04 |
| 455 | Mike Boddicker | .04 |
| 456 | A's Leaders | .06 |
| 457 | Len Matuszek | .04 |
| 458 | Kelly Gruber | .04 |
| 459 | Dennis Eckersley | .06 |
| 460 | Darryl Strawberry | .30 |
| 461 | Craig McMurtry | .04 |
| 462 | Scott Fletcher | .04 |
| 463 | Tom Candiotti | .04 |
| 464 | Butch Wynegar | .04 |
| 465 | Todd Worrell (R) | .50 |
| 466 | Kal Daniels | .15 |
| 467 | Randy St. Claire | .04 |
| 468 | G. Bamberger (Mgr.) | .04 |
| 469 | Mike Diaz (R) | .15 |
| 470 | Dave Dravecky | .04 |
| 471 | Ronn Reynolds | .04 |
| 472 | Bill Doran | .04 |
| 473 | Steve Farr | .04 |
| 474 | Jerry Narron | .04 |
| 475 | Scott Garrelts | .04 |
| 476 | Danny Tartabull | .30 |
| 477 | Ken Howell | .04 |
| 478 | Tim Laudner | .04 |
| 479 | Bob Sebra (R) | .15 |
| 480 | Jim Rice | .25 |
| 481 | Phillies Leaders | .06 |
| 482 | Daryl Boston | .04 |
| 483 | Dwight Lowry (R) | .15 |
| 484 | Jim Traber | .10 |
| 485 | Tony Fernandez | .12 |
| 486 | Otis Nixon | .08 |
| 487 | Dave Gumpert | .04 |
| 488 | Ray Knight | .04 |
| 489 | Bill Gullickson | .04 |
| 490 | Dale Murphy | .35 |
| 491 | Ron Karkovice (R) | .25 |
| 492 | Mike Heath | .04 |
| 493 | Tom Lasorda | .04 |
| 494 | Barry Jones (R) | .15 |
| 495 | Gorman Thomas | .04 |
| 496 | Bruce Bochte | .04 |
| 497 | Dale Mohorcic (R) | .15 |
| 498 | Bob Kearney | .04 |
| 499 | Bruce Ruffin (R) | .35 |
| 500 | Don Mattingly | 2.00 |
| 501 | Craig Lefferts | .04 |
| 502 | Dick Schofield | .04 |
| 503 | Larry Andersen | .04 |
| 504 | Mickey Hatcher | .04 |
| 505 | Bryn Smith | .04 |
| 506 | Orioles Leaders | .08 |
| 507 | Dave Stapleton | .04 |
| 508 | Scott Bankhead (R) | .15 |
| 509 | Enos Cabell | .04 |
| 510 | Tom Henke | .04 |
| 511 | Steve Lyons | .04 |
| 512 | Dave Magadan (R) | .75 |
| 513 | Carmen Castillo | .04 |
| 514 | Orlando Mercado | .04 |
| 515 | Willie Hernandez | .04 |
| 516 | Ted Simmons | .04 |
| 517 | Mario Soto | .04 |
| 518 | Gene Mauch (Mgr.) | .04 |
| 519 | Curt Young | .04 |
| 520 | Jack Clark | .12 |
| 521 | Rick Reuschel | .04 |
| 522 | Checklist: 397-528 | .06 |
| 523 | Earnie Riles | .04 |
| 524 | Bob Shirley | .04 |
| 525 | Phil Bradley | .12 |
| 526 | Roger Mason | .08 |
| 527 | Jim Wohlford | .04 |
| 528 | Ken Dixon | .04 |
| 529 | Alvaro Espinoza (R) | .10 |
| 530 | Tony Gwynn | .30 |
| 531 | Astros Leaders | .06 |
| 532 | Jeff Stone | .04 |
| 533 | Argenis Salazar | .04 |
| 534 | Scott Sanderson | .04 |
| 535 | Tony Armas | .06 |
| 536 | Terry Mulholland (R) | .15 |
| 537 | Rance Mulliniks | .04 |
| 538 | Tom Niedenfuer | .04 |
| 539 | Reid Nichols | .04 |
| 540 | Terry Kennedy | .04 |
| 541 | Rafael Belliard (R) | .12 |
| 542 | Ricky Horton | .04 |
| 543 | Dave Johnson (Mgr.) | .04 |
| 544 | Zane Smith | .04 |
| 545 | Buddy Bell | .04 |
| 546 | Mike Morgan | .04 |
| 547 | Rob Deer | .20 |
| 548 | Bill Mooneyham (R) | .15 |
| 549 | Bob Melvin | .04 |
| 550 | Pete Incaviglia (R) | 1.00 |
| 551 | Frank Wills | .04 |
| 552 | Larry Sheets | .04 |
| 553 | Mike Maddux (R) | .15 |
| 554 | Buddy Biancalana | .04 |
| 555 | Dennis Rasmussen | .10 |
| 556 | Angels Leaders | .06 |
| 557 | John Cerutti (R) | .20 |
| 558 | Greg Gagne | .04 |
| 559 | Lance McCullers | .04 |
| 560 | Glenn Davis | .50 |
| 561 | Rey Quinones (R) | .15 |
| 562 | B. Clutterbuck (R) | .15 |
| 563 | John Stefero | .04 |
| 564 | Larry McWilliams | .04 |
| 565 | Dusty Baker | .04 |
| 566 | Tim Hulett | .04 |
| 567 | Greg Mathews (R) | .25 |
| 568 | Earl Weaver (Mgr.) | .04 |
| 569 | Wade Rowdon | .15 |
| 570 | Sid Fernandez | .20 |
| 571 | Ozzie Virgil | .04 |
| 572 | Pete Ladd | .04 |
| 573 | Hal McRae | .04 |
| 574 | Manny Lee | .04 |
| 575 | Pat Tabler | .04 |
| 576 | Frank Pastore | .04 |
| 577 | Dann Bilardello | .04 |
| 578 | Billy Hatcher | .04 |
| 579 | Rick Burleson | .04 |
| 580 | Mike Krukow | .04 |
| 581 | Cubs Leaders | .08 |
| 582 | Bruce Berenyi | .04 |
| 583 | Junior Ortiz | .04 |
| 584 | Ron Kittle | .08 |
| 585 | Scott Bailes (R) | .15 |
| 586 | Ben Oglivie | .04 |
| 587 | Eric Plunk | .06 |
| 588 | Wallace Johnson | .04 |
| 589 | Steve Crawford | .04 |
| 590 | Vince Coleman | .30 |
| 591 | Spike Owen | .04 |
| 592 | Chris Welsh | .04 |
| 593 | Chuck Tanner (Mgr.) | .04 |
| 594 | Rick Anderson (R) | .15 |
| 595 | Keith Hernandez (AS) | .15 |
| 596 | Steve Sax (AS) | .10 |
| 597 | Mike Schmidt (AS) | .25 |
| 598 | Ozzie Smith (AS) | .10 |
| 599 | Tony Gwynn (AS) | .20 |
| 600 | Dave Parker (AS) | .15 |
| 601 | Darryl Strawberry (AS) | .25 |
| 602 | Gary Carter (AS) | .20 |
| 603 | Dwight Gooden (AS) | .35 |

Card values from this set fluctuate considerably.

| NO. | PLAYER | MINT |
|-----|--------|------|
| 604 | F. Valenzuela (AS) | .15 |
| 605 | Todd Worrell (AS) | .15 |
| 606 | Don Mattingly (AS) | .50 |
| 607 | Tony Bernazard (AS) | .08 |
| 608 | Wade Boggs (AS) | .40 |
| 609 | Cal Ripken (AS) | .15 |
| 610 | Jim Rice (AS) | .15 |
| 611 | Kirby Puckett (AS) | .20 |
| 612 | George Bell (AS) | .08 |
| 613 | Lance Parrish (AS) | .10 |
| 614 | Roger Clemens (AS) | .40 |
| 615 | Teddy Higuera (AS) | .10 |
| 616 | Dave Righetti (AS) | .10 |
| 617 | Al Nipper | .04 |
| 618 | Tom Kelly (Mgr.) | .04 |
| 619 | Jerry Reed | .04 |
| 620 | Jose Canseco | 2.50 |
| 621 | Danny Cox | .04 |
| 622 | Glenn Braggs (R) | .50 |
| 623 | Kurt Stillwell (R) | .20 |
| 624 | Tim Burke | .04 |
| 625 | Mookie Wilson | .04 |
| 626 | Joel Skinner | .04 |
| 627 | Ken Oberkfell | .04 |
| 628 | Bob Walk | .04 |
| 629 | Larry Parrish | .04 |
| 630 | John Candelaria | .04 |
| 631 | Tigers Leaders | .15 |
| 632 | Rob Woodward | .08 |
| 633 | Jose Uribe | .04 |
| 634 | Rafael Palmeiro (R) | .40 |
| 635 | Ken Schrom | .04 |
| 636 | Darren Daulton | .04 |
| 637 | Bip Roberts (R) | .15 |
| 638 | Rich Bordi | .04 |
| 639 | Gerald Perry | .04 |
| 640 | Mark Clear | .04 |
| 641 | Domino Ramos | .04 |
| 642 | Al Pulido | .04 |
| 643 | Ron Shepherd (R) | .15 |
| 644 | John Denny | .04 |
| 645 | Dwight Evans | .04 |
| 646 | Mike Mason | .04 |
| 647 | Tom Lawless | .04 |
| 648 | Barry Larkin (R) | .25 |
| 649 | Mickey Tettleton | .04 |
| 650 | Hubie Brooks | .04 |
| 651 | Benny Distefano | .04 |
| 652 | Terry Forster | .04 |
| 653 | Kevin Mitchell (R) | .50 |

| NO. | PLAYER | MINT |
|-----|--------|------|
| 654 | Checklist: 529-660 | .06 |
| 655 | Jesse Barfield | .15 |
| 656 | Rangers Leaders | .06 |
| 657 | Tom Waddell | .04 |
| 658 | Robby Thompson (R) | .35 |
| 659 | Aurelio Lopez | .04 |
| 660 | Bob Horner | .10 |
| 661 | Lou Whitaker | .10 |
| 662 | Frank DiPino | .04 |
| 663 | Cliff Johnson | .04 |
| 664 | Mike Marshall | .08 |
| 665 | Rod Scurry | .04 |
| 666 | Von Hayes | .10 |
| 667 | Ron Hassey | .04 |
| 668 | Juan Bonilla | .04 |
| 669 | Bud Black | .04 |
| 670 | Jose Cruz | .04 |
| 671 | Ray Soff (R) | .12 |
| 672 | Chili Davis | .04 |
| 673 | Don Sutton | .10 |
| 674 | Bill Campbell | .04 |
| 675 | Ed Romero | .04 |
| 676 | Charlie Moore | .04 |
| 677 | Bob Grich | .04 |
| 678 | Carney Lansford | .04 |
| 679 | Kent Hrbek | .15 |
| 680 | Ryne Sandberg | .20 |
| 681 | George Bell | .15 |
| 682 | Jerry Reuss | .04 |
| 683 | Gary Roenicke | .04 |
| 684 | Kent Tekulve | .04 |
| 685 | Jerry Hairston | .04 |
| 686 | Doyle Alexander | .04 |
| 687 | Alan Trammell | .12 |
| 688 | Juan Beniquez | .04 |
| 689 | Darrell Porter | .04 |
| 690 | Dane Iorg | .04 |
| 691 | Dave Parker | .20 |
| 692 | Frank White | .04 |
| 693 | Terry Puhl | .04 |
| 694 | Phil Niekro | .15 |
| 695 | Chico Walker (R) | .20 |
| 696 | Gary Lucas | .04 |
| 697 | Ed Lynch | .04 |
| 698 | Ernie Whitt | .04 |
| 699 | Ken Landreaux | .04 |
| 700 | Dave Bergman | .04 |
| 701 | Willie Randolph | .08 |
| 702 | Greg Gross | .04 |
| 703 | Dave Schmidt | .04 |

| NO. | PLAYER | MINT |
|-----|--------|------|
| 704 | Jesse Orosco | .06 |
| 705 | Bruce Hurst | .04 |
| 706 | Rick Manning | .04 |
| 707 | Bob McClure | .04 |
| 708 | Scott McGregr | .04 |
| 709 | Dave Kingman | .10 |
| 710 | Gary Gaetti | .10 |
| 711 | Ken Griffey | .08 |
| 712 | Don Robinson | .04 |
| 713 | Tom Brookens | .04 |
| 714 | Don Quisenberry | .12 |
| 715 | Bob Dernier | .04 |
| 716 | Rick Leach | .04 |
| 717 | Ed Vande Berg | .04 |
| 718 | Steve Carlton | .25 |
| 719 | Tom Hume | .04 |
| 720 | Richard Dotson | .04 |
| 721 | Tom Herr | .04 |
| 722 | Bob Knepper | .08 |
| 723 | Brett Butler | .04 |
| 724 | Greg Minton | .04 |
| 725 | George Hendrick | .04 |
| 726 | Frank Tanana | .04 |
| 727 | Mike Moore | .04 |
| 728 | Tippy Martinez | .04 |
| 729 | Tom Paciorek | .04 |
| 730 | Eric Show | .06 |
| 731 | Dave Concepcion | .08 |
| 732 | Manny Trillo | .04 |
| 733 | Bill Caudill | .04 |
| 734 | Bill Madlock | .12 |
| 735 | Rickey Henderson | .35 |
| 736 | Steve Bedrosian | .04 |
| 737 | Floyd Bannister | .04 |
| 738 | Jorge Orta | .04 |
| 739 | Chet Lemon | .06 |
| 740 | Rich Gedman | .04 |
| 741 | Paul Molitor | .06 |
| 742 | Andy McGaffigan | .04 |
| 743 | Dwayne Murphy | .04 |
| 744 | Roy Smalley | .04 |
| 745 | Glenn Hubbard | .04 |
| 746 | Bob Ojeda | .12 |
| 747 | Johnny Ray | .04 |
| 748 | Mike Flanagan | .06 |
| 749 | Ozzie Smith | .15 |
| 750 | Steve Trout | .04 |
| 751 | Garth Iorg | .04 |
| 752 | Dan Petry | .04 |
| 753 | Rick Honeycutt | .04 |

| NO. | PLAYER | MINT |
|-----|--------|------|
| 754 | Dave LaPoint | .04 |
| 755 | Luis Aguayo | .04 |
| 756 | Carlton Fisk | .15 |
| 757 | Nolan Ryan | .15 |
| 758 | Tony Bernazard | .04 |
| 759 | Joel Youngblood | .04 |
| 760 | Mike Witt | .10 |
| 761 | Greg Pryor | .04 |
| 762 | Gary Ward | .04 |
| 763 | Tim Flannery | .04 |
| 764 | Bill Buckner | .04 |
| 765 | Kirk Gibson | .15 |
| 766 | Don Aase | .04 |
| 767 | Ron Cey | .04 |
| 768 | Dennis Lamp | .04 |
| 769 | Steve Sax | .10 |
| 770 | Dave Winfield | .25 |
| 771 | Shane Rawley | .04 |
| 772 | Harold Baines | .15 |
| 773 | Robin Yount | .25 |
| 774 | Wayne Krenchicki | .04 |
| 775 | Joaquin Andujar | .04 |
| 776 | Tom Brunansky | .08 |
| 777 | Chris Chambliss | .04 |
| 778 | Jack Morris | .15 |
| 779 | Craig Reynolds | .04 |
| 780 | Andre Thornton | .04 |
| 781 | Atlee Hammaker | .04 |
| 782 | Brian Downing | .04 |
| 783 | Willie Wilson | .04 |
| 784 | Cal Ripken | .15 |
| 785 | Terry Francona | .04 |
| 786 | Jimy Williams (Mgr.) | .04 |
| 787 | Alejandro Pena | .04 |
| 788 | Tim Stoddard | .04 |
| 789 | Dan Schatzeder | .04 |
| 790 | Julio Cruz | .04 |
| 791 | Lance Parris | .15 |
| 792 | Checklist: 661-792 | .06 |

**Cards Printed on Gum Boxes**

| A | Don Baylor | .15 |
|---|------------|-----|
| B | Steve Carlton | .20 |
| C | Ron Cey | .15 |
| D | Cecil Cooper | .15 |
| E | Rickey Henderson | .40 |
| F | Jim Rice | .30 |
| G | Don Sutton | .15 |
| H | Dave Winfield | .20 |

Card values from this set fluctuate considerably.

# 1981 Donruss.... Complete Set of 605 Cards (1st printing)—Value $25.00; Complete Set of 605 Cards (2nd printing)—Value $20.00

This was Donruss' *first* baseball card set. Over 35 cards contained *errors;* they were corrected in the 2nd printing run. There is very little interest by collectors in the *variety* (error) cards; none are scarce or worth much more than ordinary cards. If a *variety* (error) is significant, it is listed and explained; if it is *minor*, it is noted by an *asterisk*. This set features the rookie cards of Tim Raines and Leon Durham. The 2½"x3½" cards were printed on thinner than usual paper stock. The checklist *cards* are *not* numbered.

LAMARR HOYT PITCHER — White Sox

CHARLIE LEIBRANDT PITCHER — Reds

LEON DURHAM INFIELD/O.F. — Cardinals

JOHN TUDOR PITCHER — Red Sox

TIM RAINES SECOND BASE — Expos

| NO. PLAYER | MINT |
|---|---|
| 1 Ozzie Smith | .30 |
| 2 Rollie Fingers | .30 |
| 3 Rick Wise | .05 |
| 4 Gene Richards | .05 |
| 5 Alan Trammell | .35 |
| 6 Tom Brookens | .05 |
| 7 Duffy Dyer* | .05 |
| 8 Mark Fidrych | .08 |
| 9 Dave Rozema | .05 |
| 10 Ricky Peters | .05 |
| 11 Mike Schmidt | .90 |
| 12 Willie Stargell | .30 |
| 13 Tim Foli | .05 |
| 14 Manny Sanguillen | .05 |
| 15 Grant Jackson | .05 |
| 16 Eddie Solomon | .05 |
| 17 Omar Moreno | .05 |
| 18 Joe Morgan | .35 |
| 19 Rafael Landestoy | .05 |
| 20 Bruce Bochy | .05 |
| 21 Joe Sambito | .05 |
| 22 Manny Trillo | .05 |
| 23 Dave Smith* | .10 |
| 24 Terry Puhl | .05 |
| 25 Bump Wills | .05 |
| 26 John Ellis (error) | .40 |
| (Photo of Danny Walton) | |
| 26 John Ellis (correct) | .10 |
| 27 Jim Kern | .05 |
| 28 Richie Zisk | .05 |
| 29 John Mayberry | .05 |
| 30 Bob Davis | .05 |
| 31 Jackson Todd | .05 |
| 32 Al Woods | .05 |
| 33 Steve Carlton | .60 |
| 34 Lee Mazzilli | .05 |
| 35 John Stearns | .05 |
| 36 Roy Jackson | .05 |
| 37 Mike Scott | .50 |
| 38 Lamar Johnson | .05 |
| 39 Kevin Bell | .05 |
| 40 Ed Farmer | .05 |
| 41 Ross Baumgarten | .05 |
| 42 Leo Sutherland | .05 |
| 43 Danny Meyer | .05 |
| 44 Ron Reed | .05 |
| 45 Mario Mendoza | .05 |
| 46 Rick Honeycutt | .05 |
| 47 Glenn Abbott | .05 |
| 48 Leon Roberts | .05 |
| 49 Rod Carew | .50 |
| 50 Bert Campaneris | .05 |
| 51 Tom Donohue* | .10 |
| 52 Dave Frost | .05 |
| 53 Ed Halicki | .05 |
| 54 Dan Ford | .05 |
| 55 Garry Maddox | .05 |
| 56 Steve Garvey* | .65 |
| 57 Bill Russell | .05 |
| 58 Don Sutton | .15 |
| 59 Reggie Smith | .10 |
| 60 Rick Monday | .05 |
| 61 Ray Knight | .05 |
| 62 Johnny Bench | .50 |
| 63 Mario Soto | .15 |
| 64 Doug Bair | .05 |

| NO. PLAYER | MINT |
|---|---|
| 65 George Foster | .25 |
| 66 Jeff Burroughs | .05 |
| 67 Keith Hernandez | .40 |
| 68 Tommy Herr | .15 |
| 69 Bob Forsch | .05 |
| 70 John Fulgham | .05 |
| 71 Bobby Bonds* | .12 |
| 72 Rennie Stennett* | .10 |
| 73 Joe Strain | .05 |
| 74 Ed Whitson | .10 |
| 75 Tom Griffin | .05 |
| 76 Bill North | .05 |
| 77 Gene Garber | .05 |
| 78 Mike Hargrove | .05 |
| 79 Dave Rosello | .05 |
| 80 Ron Hassey | .05 |
| 81 Sid Monge | .05 |
| 82 Joe Charboneau* | .10 |
| 83 Cecil Cooper | .25 |
| 84 Sal Bando | .05 |
| 85 Moose Haas | .05 |
| 86 Mike Caldwell | .05 |
| 87 Larry Hisle* | .10 |
| 88 Luis Gomez | .05 |
| 89 Larry Parrish | .10 |
| 90 Gary Carter | .50 |
| 91 Bill Gullickson (R) | .35 |
| 92 Fred Norman | .05 |
| 93 Tom Hutton | .05 |
| 94 Carl Yastrzemski | .75 |
| 95 Glenn Hoffman | .05 |
| 96 Dennis Eckersley | .05 |
| 97 Tom Burgmeier* | .10 |
| 98 Win Remmerswaal | .05 |
| 99 Bob Horner | .25 |
| 100 George Brett | 1.00 |
| 101 Dave Chalk | .05 |
| 102 Dennis Leonard | .05 |
| 103 Renie Martin | .05 |
| 104 Amos Otis | .05 |
| 105 Graig Nettles | .15 |
| 106 Eric Soderholm | .05 |
| 107 Tommy John | .20 |
| 108 Tom Underwood | .05 |
| 109 Lou Piniella | .15 |
| 110 Mickey Klutts | .05 |
| 111 Bobby Murcer | .10 |
| 112 Eddie Murray | .75 |
| 113 Rick Dempsey | .05 |
| 114 Scott McGregor | .05 |
| 115 Ken Singleton | .05 |
| 116 Gary Roenicke | .05 |
| 117 Dave Revering | .05 |
| 118 Mike Norris | .05 |
| 119 Rickey Henderson | .75 |
| 120 Mike Heath | .05 |
| 121 Dave Cash | .05 |
| 122 Randy Jones | .05 |
| 123 Eric Rasmussen | .05 |
| 124 Jerry Mumphrey | .05 |
| 125 Richie Hebner | .05 |
| 126 Mark Wagner | .05 |
| 127 Jack Morris | .30 |
| 128 Dan Petry | .25 |
| 129 Bruce Robbins | .05 |
| 130 Champ Summers | .05 |

| NO. PLAYER | MINT |
|---|---|
| 131 Pete Rose* | 1.50 |
| 132 Willie Stargell | .30 |
| 133 Ed Ott | .05 |
| 134 Jim Bibby | .05 |
| 135 Bert Blyleven | .10 |
| 136 Dave Parker | .40 |
| 137 Bill Robinson | .05 |
| 138 Enos Cabell | .05 |
| 139 Dave Bergman | .05 |
| 140 J.R. Richard | .05 |
| 141 Ken Forsch | .05 |
| 142 Larry Bowa | .05 |
| 143 Frank LaCorte | .05 |
| 144 Dennis Walling | .05 |
| 145 Buddy Bell | .10 |
| 146 Ferguson Jenkins | .10 |
| 147 Danny Darwin | .05 |
| 148 Johnny Grubb | .05 |
| 149 Alfredo Griffin | .05 |
| 150 Jerry Garvin | .05 |
| 151 Paul Mirabella | .05 |
| 152 Rick Bosetti | .05 |
| 153 Dick Ruthven | .05 |
| 154 Frank Taveras | .05 |
| 155 Craig Swan | .05 |
| 156 Jeff Reardon (R) | .40 |
| 157 Steve Henderson | .05 |
| 158 Jim Morrison | .05 |
| 159 Glenn Borgmann | .05 |
| 160 LaMarr Hoyt | .40 |
| 161 Rich Wortham | .05 |
| 162 Thad Bosley | .05 |
| 163 Julio Cruz | .05 |
| 164 Del Unser* | .05 |
| 165 Jim Anderson | .05 |
| 166 Jim Beattie | .05 |
| 167 Shane Rawley | .05 |
| 168 Joe Simpson | .05 |
| 169 Rod Carew | .50 |
| 170 Freddie Patek | .05 |
| 171 Frank Tanana | .05 |
| 172 Alfredo Martinez | .05 |
| 173 Chris Knapp | .05 |
| 174 Joe Rudi | .05 |
| 175 Greg Luzinski | .10 |
| 176 Steve Garvey | .50 |
| 177 Joe Ferguson | .05 |
| 178 Bob Welch | .05 |
| 179 Dusty Baker | .10 |
| 180 Rudy Law | .05 |
| 181 Dave Concepcion | .15 |
| 182 Johnny Bench | .50 |
| 183 Mike LaCoss | .05 |
| 184 Ken Griffey | .10 |
| 185 Dave Collins | .05 |
| 186 Brian Asselstine | .05 |
| 187 Garry Templeton | .10 |
| 188 Mike Phillips | .05 |
| 189 Pete Vuckovich | .08 |
| 190 John Urrea | .05 |
| 191 Tony Scott | .05 |
| 192 Darrell Evans | .10 |
| 193 Milt May | .05 |
| 194 Bob Knepper | .05 |
| 195 Randy Moffitt | .05 |
| 196 Larry Herndon | .05 |

| NO. PLAYER | MINT |
|---|---|
| 197 Rick Camp | .05 |
| 198 Andre Thornton | .10 |
| 199 Tom Veryzer | .05 |
| 200 Gary Alexander | .05 |
| 201 Rick Waits | .05 |
| 202 Rick Manning | .05 |
| 203 Paul Molitor | .25 |
| 204 Jim Gantner | .05 |
| 205 Paul Mitchell | .05 |
| 206 Reggie Cleveland | .05 |
| 207 Sixto Lezcano | .05 |
| 208 Bruce Benedict | .05 |
| 209 Rodney Scott | .05 |
| 210 John Tamargo | .05 |
| 211 Bill Lee | .05 |
| 212 Andre Dawson | .30 |
| 213 Rowland Office | .05 |
| 214 Carl Yastrzemski | .75 |
| 215 Jerry Remy | .05 |
| 216 Mike Torrez | .05 |
| 217 Skip Lockwood | .05 |
| 218 Fred Lynn | .25 |
| 219 Chris Chambliss | .08 |
| 220 Willie Aikens | .05 |
| 221 John Wathan | .05 |
| 222 Dan Quisenberry | .30 |
| 223 Willie Wilson | .30 |
| 224 Clint Hurdle | .05 |
| 225 Bob Watson | .05 |
| 226 Jim Spencer | .05 |
| 227 Ron Guidry | .40 |
| 228 Reggie Jackson | .75 |
| 229 Oscar Gamble | .05 |
| 230 Jeff Cox | .05 |
| 231 Luis Tiant | .05 |
| 232 Rich Dauer | .05 |
| 233 Dan Graham | .05 |
| 234 Mike Flanagan | .05 |
| 235 John Lowenstein | .05 |
| 236 Benny Ayala | .05 |
| 237 Wayne Gross | .05 |
| 238 Rick Langford | .05 |
| 239 Tony Armas | .20 |
| 240 Bob Lacey* | .10 |
| 241 Gene Tenace | .05 |
| 242 Bob Shirley | .05 |
| 243 Gary Lucas | .05 |
| 244 Jerry Turner | .05 |
| 245 John Wockenfuss | .05 |
| 246 Stan Papi | .05 |
| 247 Milt Wilcox | .05 |
| 248 Dan Schatzeder | .05 |
| 249 Steve Kemp | .08 |
| 250 Jim Lentine | .05 |
| 251 Pete Rose | 1.25 |
| 252 Bill Madlock | .25 |
| 253 Dale Berra | .05 |
| 254 Kent Tekulve | .05 |
| 255 Enrique Romo | .05 |
| 256 Mike Easler | .05 |
| 257 Chuck Tanner (Mgr.) | .05 |
| 258 Art Howe | .05 |
| 259 Alan Ashby | .05 |
| 260 Nolan Ryan | .50 |
| 261 Vern Ruhle (error) | .40 |
| (Photo of Ken Forsch) | |

| NO. | PLAYER | MINT |
|---|---|---|
| 261 | Vern Ruhle (correct) | .10 |
| 262 | Bob Boone | .05 |
| 263 | Cesar Cedeno | .08 |
| 264 | Jeff Leonard | .05 |
| 265 | Pat Putnam | .05 |
| 266 | John Matlack | .05 |
| 267 | Dave Rajsich | .05 |
| 268 | Billy Sample | .05 |
| 269 | Damaso Garcia (R) | .50 |
| 270 | Tom Buskey | .05 |
| 271 | Joey McLaughlin | .05 |
| 272 | Barry Bonnell | .05 |
| 273 | Tug McGraw | .08 |
| 274 | Mike Jorgensen | .05 |
| 275 | Pat Zachry | .05 |
| 276 | Neil Allen | .05 |
| 277 | Joel Youngblood | .05 |
| 278 | Greg Pryor | .05 |
| 279 | Britt Burns (R) | .50 |
| 280 | Rich Dotson (R) | .30 |
| 281 | Chet Lemon | .05 |
| 282 | Rusty Kuntz | .05 |
| 283 | Ted Cox | .05 |
| 284 | Sparky Lyle | .05 |
| 285 | Larry Cox | .05 |
| 286 | Floyd Bannister | .05 |
| 287 | Byron McLaughlin | .05 |
| 288 | Rodney Craig | .05 |
| 289 | Bob Grich | .05 |
| 290 | Dickie Thon | .05 |
| 291 | Mark Clear | .05 |
| 292 | Dave Lemanczyk | .05 |
| 293 | Jason Thompson | .05 |
| 294 | Rick Miller | .05 |
| 295 | Lonnie Smith | .08 |
| 296 | Ron Cey | .15 |
| 297 | Steve Yeager | .05 |
| 298 | Bobby Castillo | .05 |
| 299 | Manny Mota | .05 |
| 300 | Jay Johnstone | .05 |
| 301 | Dan Driessen | .05 |
| 302 | Joe Nolan | .05 |
| 303 | Paul Householder | .05 |
| 304 | Harry Spilman | .05 |
| 305 | Cesar Geronimo | .05 |
| 306 | Gary Matthews* | .10 |
| 307 | Ken Reitz | .05 |
| 308 | Ted Simmons | .10 |
| 309 | John Littlefield | .05 |
| 310 | George Frazier | .05 |
| 311 | Dane Iorg | .05 |
| 312 | Mike Ivie | .05 |
| 313 | Dennis Littlejohn | .05 |
| 314 | Gary LaVelle | .05 |
| 315 | Jack Clark | .30 |
| 316 | Jim Wohlford | .05 |
| 317 | Rick Matula | .05 |
| 318 | Toby Harrah | .05 |
| 319 | Duane Kuiper* | .10 |
| 320 | Len Barker | .05 |
| 321 | Victor Cruz | .05 |
| 322 | Dell Alston | .05 |
| 323 | Robin Yount | .50 |
| 324 | Charlie Moore | .05 |
| 325 | Lary Sorensen | .05 |
| 326 | Gorman Thomas* | .15 |
| 327 | Bob Rodgers | .05 |
| 328 | Phil Niekro | .30 |
| 329 | Chris Speier | .05 |
| 330 | Steve Rogers* | .10 |
| 331 | Woodie Fryman | .05 |
| 332 | Warren Cromartie | .05 |
| 333 | Jerry White | .05 |
| 334 | Tony Perez | .20 |
| 335 | Carlton Fisk | .30 |
| 336 | Dick Drago | .05 |
| 337 | Steve Renko | .05 |
| 338 | Jim Rice | .50 |
| 339 | Jerry Royster | .05 |
| 340 | Frank White | .05 |
| 341 | Jamie Quirk | .05 |
| 342 | Paul Splittorff* | .05 |
| 343 | Marty Pattin | .05 |
| 344 | Pete LaCock | .05 |
| 345 | Willie Randolph | .10 |
| 346 | Rick Cerone | .05 |
| 347 | Rich Gossage | .25 |
| 348 | Reggie Jackson | .75 |
| 349 | Ruppert Jones | .05 |
| 350 | Dave McKay | .05 |
| 351 | Yogi Berra | .20 |
| 352 | Doug DeCinces | .15 |
| 353 | Jim Palmer | .30 |
| 354 | Tippy Martinez | .05 |
| 355 | Al Bumbry | .05 |
| 356 | Earl Weaver (Mgr.) | .10 |
| 357 | Rob Picciolo* | .10 |
| 358 | Matt Keough | .05 |
| 359 | Dwayne Murphy | .05 |
| 360 | Brian Kingman | .05 |
| 361 | Bill Fahey | .05 |
| 362 | Steve Mura | .05 |
| 363 | Dennis Kinney | .05 |
| 364 | Dave Winfield | .60 |
| 365 | Lou Whitaker | .30 |
| 366 | Lance Parrish | .40 |
| 367 | Tim Corcoran | .05 |
| 368 | Pat Underwood | .05 |
| 369 | Al Cowens | .05 |
| 370 | Sparky Anderson (Mgr.) | .05 |
| 371 | Pete Rose | 1.25 |
| 372 | Phil Garner | .05 |
| 373 | Steve Nicosia | .05 |
| 374 | John Candelaria | .05 |
| 375 | Don Robinson | .05 |
| 376 | Lee Lacy | .05 |
| 377 | John Milner | .05 |
| 378 | Craig Reynolds | .05 |
| 379 | Luis Pujols* | .10 |
| 380 | Joe Niekro | .10 |
| 381 | Joaquin Andujar | .25 |
| 382 | Keith Moreland (R) | .40 |
| 383 | Jose Cruz | .15 |
| 384 | Bill Virdon (Mgr.) | .05 |
| 385 | Jim Sundberg | .05 |
| 386 | Doc Medich | .05 |
| 387 | Al Oliver | .20 |
| 388 | Jim Norris | .05 |
| 389 | Bob Bailor | .05 |
| 390 | Ernie Whitt | .05 |
| 391 | Otto Velez | .05 |
| 392 | Roy Howell | .05 |
| 393 | Bob Walk | .05 |
| 394 | Doug Flynn | .05 |
| 395 | Pete Falcone | .05 |
| 396 | Tom Hausman | .05 |
| 397 | Elliott Maddox | .05 |
| 398 | Mike Squires | .05 |
| 399 | Marvis Foley | .05 |
| 400 | Steve Trout | .05 |
| 401 | Wayne Nordhagen | .05 |
| 402 | Tony LaRussa (Mgr.) | .05 |
| 403 | Bruce Bochte | .05 |
| 404 | Bake McBride | .05 |
| 405 | Jerry Narron | .05 |
| 406 | Rob Dressler | .05 |
| 407 | Dave Heaverlo | .05 |
| 408 | Tom Paciorek | .05 |
| 409 | Carney Lansford | .15 |
| 410 | Brian Downing | .05 |
| 411 | Don Aase | .05 |
| 412 | Jim Barr | .05 |
| 413 | Don Baylor | .25 |
| 414 | Jim Fregosi (Mgr.) | .05 |
| 415 | Dallas Green (Mgr.) | .05 |
| 416 | Dave Lopes | .10 |
| 417 | Jerry Reuss | .05 |
| 418 | Rick Sutcliffe | .40 |
| 419 | Derrel Thomas | .05 |
| 420 | Tommy Lasorda (Mgr.) | .15 |
| 421 | Charlie Leibrandt (R) | .40 |
| 422 | Tom Seaver | .40 |
| 423 | Ron Oester | .05 |
| 424 | Junior Kennedy | .05 |
| 425 | Tom Seaver | .40 |
| 426 | Bobby Cox (Mgr.) | .05 |
| 427 | Leon Durham (R) | 1.00 |
| 428 | Terry Kennedy | .10 |
| 429 | Silvio Martinez | .05 |
| 430 | George Hendrick | .05 |
| 431 | R. Schoendienst (Mgr.) | .05 |
| 432 | John LeMaster | .05 |
| 433 | Vida Blue | .05 |
| 434 | John Montefusco | .05 |
| 435 | Terry Whitfield | .05 |
| 436 | Dave Bristol (Mgr.) | .05 |
| 437 | Dale Murphy | 1.25 |
| 438 | Jerry Dybzinski | .05 |
| 439 | Jorge Orta | .05 |
| 440 | Wayne Garland | .05 |
| 441 | Miguel Dilone | .05 |
| 442 | Dave Garcia (Mgr.) | .05 |
| 443 | Don Money | .05 |
| 444 | Buck Martinez* | .10 |
| 445 | Jerry Augustine | .05 |
| 446 | Ben Oglivie | .10 |
| 447 | Jim Slaton | .05 |
| 448 | Doyle Alexander | .05 |
| 449 | Tony Bernazard | .05 |
| 450 | Scott Sanderson | .05 |
| 451 | Dave Palmer | .05 |
| 452 | Stan Bahnsen | .05 |
| 453 | Dick Williams (Mgr.) | .05 |
| 454 | Rick Burleson | .05 |
| 455 | Gary Allenson | .05 |
| 456 | Bob Stanley | .05 |
| 457 | John Tudor* | .60 |
| 458 | Dwight Evans | .15 |
| 459 | Glenn Hubbard | .05 |
| 460 | U.L. Washington | .05 |
| 461 | Larry Gura | .05 |
| 462 | Rich Gale | .05 |
| 463 | Hal McRae | .05 |
| 464 | Jim Frey (Mgr.) | .05 |
| 465 | Bucky Dent | .05 |
| 466 | Dennis Werth | .05 |
| 467 | Ron Davis | .05 |
| 468 | Reggie Jackson | .65 |
| 469 | Bobby Brown | .05 |
| 470 | Mike Davis (R) | .30 |
| 471 | Gaylord Perry | .30 |
| 472 | Mark Belanger | .05 |
| 473 | Jim Palmer | .30 |
| 474 | Sammy Stewart | .05 |
| 475 | Tim Stoddard | .05 |
| 476 | Steve Stone | .05 |
| 477 | Jeff Newman | .05 |
| 478 | Steve McCatty | .05 |
| 479 | Billy Martin (Mgr.) | .15 |
| 480 | Mitchell Page | .05 |
| 481 | S. Carlton (Cy Young) | .40 |
| 482 | Bill Buckner | .15 |
| 483 | Ivan DeJesus* | .10 |
| 484 | Cliff Johnson | .05 |
| 485 | Lenny Randle | .05 |
| 486 | Larry Milbourne | .05 |
| 487 | Roy Smalley | .05 |
| 488 | John Castino | .05 |
| 489 | Ron Jackson | .05 |
| 490 | Dave Roberts* | .05 |
| 491 | George Brett (MVP) | .60 |
| 492 | Mike Cubbage | .05 |
| 493 | Rob Wilfong | .05 |
| 494 | Danny Goodwin | .05 |
| 495 | Jose Morales | .05 |
| 496 | Mickey Rivers | .05 |
| 497 | Mike Edwards | .05 |
| 498 | Mike Sadek | .05 |
| 499 | Lenn Sakata | .05 |
| 500 | Gene Michael (Mgr.) | .05 |
| 501 | Dave Roberts | .05 |
| 502 | Steve Dillard | .05 |
| 503 | Jim Essian | .05 |
| 504 | Rance Mulliniks | .05 |
| 505 | Darrell Porter | .10 |
| 506 | Joe Torre (Mgr.) | .05 |
| 507 | Terry Crowley | .05 |
| 508 | Bill Travers | .05 |
| 509 | Nelson Norman | .05 |
| 510 | Bob McClure | .05 |
| 511 | Steve Howe (R) | .25 |
| 512 | Dave Rader | .05 |
| 513 | Mick Kelleher | .05 |
| 514 | Kiko Garcia | .05 |
| 515 | Larry Biittner | .05 |
| 516 | Willie Norwood* | .05 |
| 517 | Bo Diaz | .10 |
| 518 | Juan Beniqez | .05 |
| 519 | Scot Thompson | .05 |
| 520 | Jim Tracy | .05 |
| 521 | Carlos Lezcano | .05 |
| 522 | Joe Amalfitano | .05 |
| 523 | Preston Hanna | .05 |
| 524 | Ray Burris* | .10 |
| 525 | Broderick Perkins | .05 |
| 526 | Mickey Hatcher | .05 |
| 527 | John Goryl (Mgr.) | .05 |
| 528 | Dick Davis | .05 |
| 529 | Butch Wynegar | .05 |
| 530 | Sal Butera | .05 |
| 531 | Jerry Koosman | .05 |
| 532 | Jeff Zahn* | .10 |
| 533 | Dennis Martinez | .05 |
| 534 | Gary Thomasson | .05 |
| 535 | Steve Macko | .05 |
| 536 | Jim Kaat | .15 |
| 537 | Best Hitters: | 1.00 |
|  | George Brett, Rod Carew |  |
| 538 | Tim Raines (R) | 3.50 |
| 539 | Keith Smith | .05 |
| 540 | Ken Macha | .05 |
| 541 | Burt Hooton | .05 |
| 542 | Butch Hobson | .05 |
| 543 | Bill Stein | .05 |
| 544 | Dave Stapleton (R) | .15 |
| 545 | Bob Pate | .05 |
| 546 | Doug Corbett | .05 |
| 547 | Darrell Jackson | .05 |
| 548 | Pete Redfern | .05 |
| 549 | Roger Erickson | .05 |
| 550 | Al Hrabosky | .05 |
| 551 | Dick Tidrow | .05 |
| 552 | Dave Ford | .05 |
| 553 | Dave Kingman | .15 |
| 554 | Mike Vail* | .10 |
| 555 | Jerry Martin* | .10 |
| 556 | Jesus Figueroa* | .10 |
| 557 | Don Stanhouse | .05 |
| 558 | Barry Foote | .05 |
| 559 | Tim Blackwell | .05 |
| 560 | Bruce Sutter | .35 |
| 561 | Rick Reuschel | .05 |
| 562 | Lynn McGlothen | .05 |
| 563 | Bob Owchinko* | .10 |
| 564 | John Verhoeven | .05 |
| 565 | Ken Landreaux | .05 |
| 566 | Glenn Adams* | .10 |
| 567 | Hosken Powell | .05 |
| 568 | Dick Noles | .05 |
| 569 | Danny Ainge (R) | .30 |
| 570 | Bobby Mattick (Mgr.) | .05 |
| 571 | Joe LeFebvre (R) | .15 |
| 572 | Bobby Clark | .05 |
| 573 | Dennis Lamp | .05 |
| 574 | Randy Lerch | .05 |
| 575 | Mookie Wilson (R) | .35 |
| 576 | Ron LeFlore | .05 |
| 577 | Jim Dwyer | .05 |
| 578 | Bill Castro | .05 |
| 579 | Greg Minton | .05 |
| 580 | Mark Littell | .05 |
| 581 | Andy Hassler | .05 |
| 582 | Dave Stieb | .25 |
| 583 | Ken Oberkfell | .05 |
| 584 | Larry Bradford | .05 |
| 585 | Fred Stanley | .05 |
| 586 | Bill Caudill | .10 |
| 587 | Doug Capilla | .05 |
| 588 | George Riley | .05 |
| 589 | Willie Hernandez | .25 |
| 590 | Mike Schmidt* | .50 |
| 591 | Steve Stone (Cy Young) | .10 |
| 592 | Rick Sofield | .05 |
| 593 | Bombo Rivera | .05 |
| 594 | Gary Ward | .05 |
| 595 | Dave Edwards* | .10 |
| 596 | Mike Proly | .05 |
| 597 | Tommy Boggs | .05 |
| 598 | Greg Gross | .05 |
| 599 | Elias Sosa | .05 |
| 600 | Pat Kelly | .05 |
| — | Checklist No. 1* | .10 |
| — | Checklist No. 2 | .10 |
| — | Checklist No. 3* | .10 |
| — | Checklist No. 4* | .10 |
| — | Checklist No. 5* | .10 |

# 1982 Donruss....Complete Set of 660 Cards—Value $22.00

Features the rookie cards of Cal Ripken and Kent Hrbek. Several errors were corrected; none are scarce or worth much more than ordinary cards. If a *variety* (error) is significant, it is listed and explained; if it is minor, it is noted by an *asterisk*. The *checklist* cards are *not* numbered.

| NO. PLAYER | MINT | NO. PLAYER | MINT | NO. PLAYER | MINT | NO. PLAYER | MINT |
|---|---|---|---|---|---|---|---|
| **No. 1 to 26—Diamond Kings** | | 66 Bruce Kison | .05 | 132 Gorman Thomas | .15 | 198 Duane Kuiper | .05 |
| 1 Pete Rose (DK) | 1.25 | 67 Wayne Nordhagen | .05 | 133 Dan Petry | .15 | 199 Rick Cerone | .05 |
| 2 Gary Carter (DK) | .50 | 68 Woodie Fryman | .05 | 134 Bob Stanley | .05 | 200 Jim Rice | .40 |
| 3 Steve Garvey (DK) | .50 | 69 Billy Sample | .05 | 135 Lou Piniella | .10 | 201 Steve Yeager | .05 |
| 4 Vida Blue (DK) | .10 | 70 Amos Otis | .05 | 136 Pedro Guerrero | .35 | 202 Tom Brookens | .05 |
| 5 Alan Trammell* (DK) | .30 | 71 Matt Keough | .05 | 137 Len Barker | .05 | 203 Jose Morales | .05 |
| 6 Len Barker (DK) | .10 | 72 Toby Harrah | .05 | 138 Richard Gale | .05 | 204 Roy Howell | .05 |
| 7 Dwight Evans (DK) | .15 | 73 Dave Righetti (R) | 1.00 | 139 Wayne Gross | .05 | 205 Tippy Martinez | .05 |
| 8 Rod Carew (DK) | .40 | 74 Carl Yastrzemski | .75 | 140 Tim Wallach (R) | .50 | 206 Moose Haas | .05 |
| 9 George Hendrick (DK) | .10 | 75 Bob Welch | .05 | 141 Gene Mauch | .05 | 207 Al Cowens | .05 |
| 10 Phil Niekro (DK) | .25 | 76 Alan Trammell* | .35 | 142 Doc Medich | .05 | 208 Dave Stapleton | .05 |
| 11 Richie Zisk (DK) | .10 | 77 Rick Dempsey | .05 | 143 Tony Bernazard | .05 | 209 Bucky Dent | .05 |
| 12 Dave Parker (DK) | .30 | 78 Paul Molitor | .20 | 144 Bill Virdon (Mgr.) | .05 | 210 Ron Cey | .15 |
| 13 Nolan Ryan (DK) | .40 | 79 Dennis Martinez | .05 | 145 John Littlefield | .05 | 211 Jorge Orta | .05 |
| 14 Ivan DeJesus (DK) | .10 | 80 Jim Slaton | .05 | 146 Dave Bergman | .05 | 212 Jamie Quirk | .05 |
| 15 George Brett (DK) | .75 | 81 Champ Summers | .05 | 147 Dick Davis | .05 | 213 Jeff Jones | .05 |
| 16 Tom Seaver (DK) | .35 | 82 Carney Lansford | .10 | 148 Tom Seaver | .40 | 214 Tim Raines | .40 |
| 17 Dave Kingman (DK) | .10 | 83 Barry Foote | .05 | 149 Matt Sinatro | .05 | 215 Jon Matlack | .05 |
| 18 Dave Winfield (DK) | .50 | 84 Steve Garvey | .50 | 150 Chuck Tanner (Mgr.) | .05 | 216 Rod Carew | .45 |
| 19 Mike Norris (DK) | .10 | 85 Rick Manning | .05 | 151 Leon Durham | .25 | 217 Jim Kaat | .10 |
| 20 Carlton Fisk (DK) | .30 | 86 John Wathan | .05 | 152 Gene Tenace | .05 | 218 Joe Pittman | .05 |
| 21 Ozzie Smith (DK) | .15 | 87 Brian Kingman | .05 | 153 Al Bumbry | .05 | 219 Larry Christenson | .05 |
| 22 Roy Smalley (DK) | .10 | 88 Andre Dawson | .30 | 154 Mark Brouhard | .05 | 220 Juan Bonilla | .05 |
| 23 Buddy Bell (DK) | .10 | 89 Jim Kern | .05 | 155 Rick Peters | .05 | 221 Mike Easler | .05 |
| 24 Ken Singleton (DK) | .10 | 90 Bobby Grich | .05 | 156 Jerry Remy | .05 | 222 Vida Blue | .05 |
| 25 John Mayberry (DK) | .10 | 91 Bob Forsch | .05 | 157 Rick Reuschel | .05 | 223 Rick Camp | .05 |
| 26 Gorman Thomas (DK) | .10 | 92 Art Howe | .05 | 158 Steve Howe | .05 | 224 Mike Jorgensen | .05 |
| 27 Earl Weaver (Mgr.) | .10 | 93 Marty Bystrom | .05 | 159 Alan Bannister | .05 | 225 Jody Davis (R) | .40 |
| 28 Rollie Fingers | .20 | 94 Ozzie Smith | .15 | 160 U.L. Wasington | .05 | 226 Mike Parrott | .05 |
| 29 Sparky Anderson (Mgr.) | .10 | 95 Dave Parker | .30 | 161 Rick Langford | .05 | 227 Jim Clancy | .05 |
| 30 Dennis Eckersley | .05 | 96 Doyle Alexander | .05 | 162 Bill Gullickson | .05 | 228 Hosken Powell | .05 |
| 31 Dave Winfield | .50 | 97 Al Hrabosky | .05 | 163 Mark Wagner | .05 | 229 Tom Hume | .05 |
| 32 Burt Hooton | .05 | 98 Frank Taveras | .05 | 164 Geoff Zahn | .05 | 230 Britt Burns | .05 |
| 33 Rick Waits | .05 | 99 Tim Blackwell | .05 | 166 Ron LeFlore | .05 | 231 Jim Palmer | .30 |
| 34 George Brett | .75 | 100 Floyd Bannister | .05 | 166 Dane Iorg | .05 | 232 Bob Rodgers (Mgr.) | .05 |
| 35 Steve McCatty | .05 | 101 Alfredo Griffin | .05 | 167 Joe Niekro | .05 | 233 Milt Wilcox | .05 |
| 36 Steve Rogers | .05 | 102 Dave Engle | .05 | 168 Pete Rose | 1.00 | 234 Dave Revering | .05 |
| 37 Bill Stein | .05 | 103 Mario Soto | .15 | 169 Dave Collins | .05 | 235 Mike Torrez | .05 |
| 38 Steve Renko | .05 | 104 Ross Baumgarten | .05 | 170 Rick Wise | .05 | 236 Bobby Castillo | .05 |
| 39 Mike Squires | .05 | 105 Ken Singleton | .10 | 171 Jim Bibby | .05 | 237 Von Hayes (R) | .75 |
| 40 George Hendrick | .08 | 106 Ted Simmons | .15 | 172 Larry Herndon | .05 | 238 Renie Martin | .05 |
| 41 Bob Knepper | .05 | 107 Jack Morris | .25 | 173 Bob Horner | .25 | 239 Dwayne Murphy | .05 |
| 42 Steve Carlton | .50 | 108 Bob Watson | .05 | 174 Steve Dillard | .05 | 240 Rodney Scott | .05 |
| 43 Larry Biittner | .05 | 109 Dwight Evans | .15 | 175 Mookie Wilson | .10 | 241 Freddie Patek | .05 |
| 44 Chris Welsh | .05 | 110 Tommy LaSorda (Mgr.) | .10 | 176 Danny Meyer | .05 | 242 Mickey Rivers | .05 |
| 45 Steve Nicosia | .05 | 111 Bert Blyleven | .15 | 177 Fernando Arroyo | .05 | 243 Steve Trout | .05 |
| 46 Jack Clark | .25 | 112 Dan Quisenberry | .25 | 178 Jackson Todd | .05 | 244 Jose Cruz | .10 |
| 47 Chris Chambliss | .05 | 113 Rickey Henderson | .75 | 179 Darrell Jackson | .05 | 245 Manny Trillo | .05 |
| 48 Ivan DeJesus | .05 | 114 Gary Carter | .50 | 180 Al Woods | .05 | 246 Lary Sorensen | .05 |
| 49 Lee Mazzilli | .05 | 115 Brian Downing | .05 | 181 Jim Anderson | .05 | 247 Dave Edwards | .05 |
| 50 Julio Cruz | .05 | 116 Al Oliver | .15 | 182 Dave Kingman | .15 | 248 Dan Driessen | .05 |
| 51 Pete Redfern | .05 | 117 LaMarr Hoyt | .15 | 183 Steve Henderson | .05 | 249 Tommy Boggs | .05 |
| 52 Dave Stieb | .25 | 118 Cesar Cedeno | .10 | 184 Brian Asselstine | .05 | 250 Dale Berra | .05 |
| 53 Doug Corbett | .05 | 119 Keith Moreland | .05 | 185 Rod Scurry | .05 | 251 Ed Whitson | .05 |
| 54 Jorge Bell (R) | 1.25 | 120 Bob Shirley | .05 | 186 Fred Breining | .05 | 252 Lee Smith (R) | .40 |
| 55 Joe Simpson | .05 | 121 Terry Kennedy | .10 | 187 Danny Boone | .05 | 253 Tom Paciorek | .05 |
| 56 Rusty Staub | .10 | 122 Frank Pastore | .05 | 188 Junior Kennedy | .05 | 254 Pat Zachry | .05 |
| 57 Hector Cruz | .05 | 123 Gene Garber | .05 | 189 Sparky Lyle | .05 | 255 Luis Leal | .05 |
| 58 Claudell Washington | .10 | 124 Tony Pena | .15 | 190 Whitey Herzog (Mgr.) | .05 | 256 John Castino | .05 |
| 59 Enrique Romo | .05 | 125 Allen Ripley | .05 | 191 Dave Smith | .05 | 257 Rich Dauer | .05 |
| 60 Gary Lavelle | .05 | 126 Randy Martz | .05 | 192 Ed Ott | .05 | 258 Cecil Cooper | .20 |
| 61 Tim Flannery | .05 | 127 Richie Zisk | .05 | 193 Greg Luzinski | .10 | 259 Dave Rozema | .05 |
| 62 Joe Nolan | .05 | 128 Mike Scott | .05 | 194 Bill Lee | .05 | 260 John Tudor | .10 |
| 63 Larry Bowa | .05 | 129 Lloyd Moseby | .15 | 195 Don Zimmer (Mgr.) | .05 | 261 Jerry Mumphrey | .05 |
| 64 Sixto Lezcano | .05 | 130 Rob Wilfong | .05 | 196 Hal McRae | .05 | 262 Jay Johnstone | .05 |
| 65 Joe Sambito | .05 | 131 Tim Stoddard | .05 | 197 Mike Norris | .05 | 263 Bo Diaz | .05 |

| NO. | PLAYER | MINT |
|---|---|---|
| 264 | Dennis Leonard | .05 |
| 265 | Jim Spencer | .05 |
| 266 | John Milner | .05 |
| 267 | Don Aase | .05 |
| 268 | Jim Sundberg | .05 |
| 269 | Lamar Johnson | .05 |
| 270 | Frank LaCorte | .05 |
| 271 | Barry Evans | .05 |
| 272 | Enos Cabell | .05 |
| 273 | Del Unser | .05 |
| 274 | George Foster | .20 |
| 275 | Brett Butler | .40 |
| 276 | Lee Lacy | .05 |
| 277 | Ken Reitz | .05 |
| 278 | Keith Hernandez | .40 |
| 279 | Doug DeCinces | .10 |
| 280 | Charlie Moore | .05 |
| 281 | Lance Parrish | .30 |
| 282 | Ralph Houk (Mgr.) | .05 |
| 283 | Rich Gossage | .20 |
| 284 | Jerry Reuss | .05 |
| 285 | Mike Stanton | .05 |
| 286 | Frank White | .05 |
| 287 | Bob Owchinko | .05 |
| 288 | Scott Sanderson | .05 |
| 289 | Bump Wills | .05 |
| 290 | Dave Frost | .05 |
| 291 | Chet Lemon | .05 |
| 292 | Tito Landrum | .05 |
| 293 | Vern Ruhle | .05 |
| 294 | Mike Schmidt | .60 |
| 295 | San Mejias | .05 |
| 296 | Gary Lucas | .05 |
| 297 | John Candelaria | .05 |
| 298 | Jerry Martin | .05 |
| 299 | Dale Murphy | 1.00 |
| 300 | Mike Lum | .05 |
| 301 | Tom Hausman | .05 |
| 302 | Glenn Abbott | .05 |
| 303 | Roger Erickson | .05 |
| 304 | Otto Velez | .05 |
| 305 | Danny Goodwin | .05 |
| 306 | John Mayberry | .05 |
| 307 | Lenny Randle | .05 |
| 308 | Bob Bailor | .05 |
| 309 | Jerry Morales | .05 |
| 310 | Rufino Linares | .05 |
| 311 | Kent Tekulve | .05 |
| 312 | Joe Morgan | .20 |
| 313 | John Urrea | .05 |
| 314 | Paul Householder | .05 |
| 315 | Garry Maddox | .05 |
| 316 | Mike Ramsey | .05 |
| 317 | Alan Ashby | .05 |
| 318 | Bob Clark | .05 |
| 319 | Tony LaRussa (Mgr.) | .05 |
| 320 | Charlie Lea | .05 |
| 321 | Danny Darwin | .05 |
| 322 | Cesar Geronimo | .05 |
| 323 | Tom Underwood | .05 |
| 324 | Andre Thornton | .10 |
| 325 | Rudy May | .05 |
| 326 | Frank Tanana | .05 |
| 327 | Davey Lopes | .05 |
| 328 | Richie Hebner | .05 |
| 329 | Mike Flanagan | .08 |
| 330 | Mike Caldwell | .05 |
| 331 | Scott McGregor | .05 |
| 332 | Jerry Augustine | .05 |
| 333 | Stan Papi | .05 |
| 334 | Rick Miller | .05 |
| 335 | Graig Nettles | .15 |
| 336 | Dusty Baker | .10 |
| 337 | Dave Garcia (Mgr.) | .05 |
| 338 | Larry Gura | .05 |
| 339 | Cliff Johnson | .05 |
| 340 | Warren Cromartie | .05 |
| 341 | Steve Comer | .05 |
| 342 | Rick Burleson | .05 |
| 343 | John Martin | .05 |
| 344 | Craig Reynolds | .05 |
| 345 | Mike Proly | .05 |
| 346 | Ruppert Jones | .05 |
| 347 | Omar Moreno | .05 |
| 348 | Greg Minton | .05 |
| 349 | Rick Mahler (R) | .25 |
| 350 | Alex Trevino | .05 |
| 351 | Mike Krukow | .05 |
| 352 | Shane Rawley | .50 |
| | (photo of Jim Anderson) | |
| 352 | Shane Rawley (correct) | .10 |
| 353 | Garth Iorg | .05 |
| 354 | Pete Mackanin | .05 |
| 355 | Paul Moskau | .05 |
| 356 | Rich Dotson | .05 |
| 357 | Steve Stone | .05 |
| 358 | Larry Hisle | .05 |
| 359 | Aurelio Lopez | .05 |
| 360 | Oscar Gamble | .05 |
| 361 | Tom Burgmeier | .05 |
| 362 | Terry Forster | .08 |
| 363 | Joe Charboneau | .05 |
| 364 | Ken Brett | .05 |
| 365 | Tony Armas | .15 |
| 366 | Chris Speier | .05 |
| 367 | Fred Lynn | .20 |
| 368 | Buddy Bell | .10 |
| 369 | Jim Essian | .05 |
| 370 | Terry Puhl | .05 |
| 371 | Greg Gross | .05 |
| 372 | Bruce Sutter | .25 |
| 373 | Joe LeFebvre | .05 |
| 374 | Ray Knight | .05 |
| 375 | Bruce Benedict | .05 |
| 376 | Tim Foli | .05 |
| 377 | Al Holland | .05 |
| 378 | Ken Kravec | .05 |
| 379 | Jeff Burroughs | .05 |
| 380 | Pete Falcone | .05 |
| 381 | Ernie Whitt | .05 |
| 382 | Brad Havens | .05 |
| 383 | Terry Crowley | .05 |
| 384 | Don Money | .05 |
| 385 | Dan Schatzeder | .05 |
| 386 | Gary Allenson | .05 |
| 387 | Yogi Berra | .15 |
| 388 | Ken Landreaux | .05 |
| 389 | Mike Hargrove | .05 |
| 390 | Darryl Motley | .25 |
| 391 | Dave McKay | .05 |
| 392 | Stan Bahnsen | .05 |
| 393 | Ken Forsch | .05 |
| 394 | Mario Mendoza | .05 |
| 395 | Jim Morrison | .05 |
| 396 | Mike Ivie | .05 |
| 397 | Broderick Perkins | .05 |
| 398 | Darrell Evans | .10 |
| 399 | Ron Reed | .05 |
| 400 | Johnny Bench | .40 |
| 401 | Steve Bedrosian (R) | .30 |
| 402 | Bill Robinson | .05 |
| 403 | Bill Buckner | .15 |
| 404 | Ken Oberkfell | .05 |
| 405 | Cal Ripken Jr. (R) | 4.50 |
| 406 | Jim Gantner | .05 |
| 407 | Kirk Gibson | .35 |
| 408 | Tony Perez | .15 |
| 409 | Tommy John | .15 |
| 410 | Dave Stewart | .10 |
| 411 | Dan Spillner | .05 |
| 412 | Willie Aikens | .05 |
| 413 | Mike Heath | .05 |
| 414 | Ray Burris | .05 |
| 415 | Leon Roberts | .05 |
| 416 | Mike Witt (R) | .75 |
| 417 | Bobby Molinaro | .05 |
| 418 | Steve Braun | .05 |
| 419 | Nolan Ryan | .35 |
| 420 | Tug McGraw | .10 |
| 421 | Dave Concepcion | .10 |
| 422 | Juan Eichelberger | .45 |
| | (photo of Gary Lucas) | |
| 422 | J. Eichelberger (correct) | .05 |
| 423 | Rick Rhoden | .05 |
| 424 | Frank Robinson (Mgr.) | .15 |
| 425 | Eddie Miller | .05 |
| 426 | Bill Caudill | .05 |
| 427 | Doug Flynn | .05 |
| 428 | Larry Andersen | .05 |
| 429 | Al Williams | .05 |
| 430 | Jerry Garvin | .05 |
| 431 | Glenn Adams | .05 |
| 432 | Barry Bonnell | .05 |
| 433 | Jerry Narron | .05 |
| 434 | John Stearns | .05 |
| 435 | Mike Tyson | .05 |
| 436 | Glenn Hubbard | .05 |
| 437 | Eddie Solomon | .05 |
| 438 | Jeff Leonard | .05 |
| 439 | Randy Bass | .05 |
| 440 | Mike LaCoss | .05 |
| 441 | Gary Matthews | .10 |
| 442 | Mark Littell | .05 |
| 443 | Don Sutton | .15 |
| 444 | John Harris | .05 |
| 445 | Vada Pinson | .05 |
| 446 | Elias Sosa | .05 |
| 447 | Charlie Hough | .05 |
| 448 | Willie Wilson | .20 |
| 449 | Fred Stanley | .05 |
| 450 | Tommy Veryzer | .05 |
| 451 | Ron Davis | .05 |
| 452 | Mark Clear | .05 |
| 453 | Bill Russell | .05 |
| 454 | Lou Whitaker | .20 |
| 455 | Dan Graham | .05 |
| 456 | Reggie Cleveland | .05 |
| 457 | Sammy Stewart | .05 |
| 458 | Pete Vuckovich | .10 |
| 459 | John Wockenfuss | .05 |
| 460 | Glenn Hoffman | .05 |
| 461 | Willie Randolph | .05 |
| 462 | Fernando Valenzuela | .40 |
| 463 | Ron Hassey | .05 |
| 464 | Paul Splittorff | .05 |
| 465 | Rob Picciolo | .05 |
| 466 | Larry Parrish | .05 |
| 467 | John Grubb | .05 |
| 468 | Dan Ford | .05 |
| 469 | Silvio Martinez | .05 |
| 470 | Kiko Garcia | .05 |
| 471 | Bob Boone | .05 |
| 472 | Luis Salazar | .05 |
| 473 | Randy Niemann | .05 |
| 474 | Tom Griffin | .05 |
| 475 | Phil Niekro | .20 |
| 476 | Hubie Brooks | .05 |
| 477 | Dick Tidrow | .05 |
| 478 | Jim Beattie | .05 |
| 479 | Damaso Garcia | .10 |
| 480 | Mickey Hatcher | .05 |
| 481 | Joe Price | .05 |
| 482 | Ed Farmer | .05 |
| 483 | Eddie Murray | .75 |
| 484 | Ben Oglivie | .10 |
| 485 | Kevin Saucier | .05 |
| 486 | Bobby Murcer | .10 |
| 487 | Bill Campbell | .05 |
| 488 | Reggie Smith | .10 |
| 489 | Wayne Garland | .05 |
| 490 | Jim Wright | .05 |
| 491 | Billy Martin (Mgr.) | .20 |
| 492 | Jim Fanning (Mgr.) | .05 |
| 493 | Don Baylor | .15 |
| 494 | Rick Honeycutt | .05 |
| 495 | Carlton Fisk | .20 |
| 496 | Denny Walling | .05 |
| 497 | Bake McBride | .05 |
| 498 | Darrell Porter | .05 |
| 499 | Gene Richards | .05 |
| 500 | Ron Oester | .05 |
| 501 | Ken Dayley | .15 |
| 502 | Jason Thompson | .10 |
| 503 | Milt May | .05 |
| 504 | Doug Bird | .05 |
| 505 | Bruce Bochte | .05 |
| 506 | Neil Allen | .05 |
| 507 | Joey McLaughlin | .05 |
| 508 | Butch Wynegar | .06 |
| 509 | Gary Roenicke | .05 |
| 510 | Robin Yount | .50 |
| 511 | Dave Tobik | .05 |
| 512 | Rich Gedman (R) | .50 |
| 513 | Gene Nelson | .05 |
| 514 | Rick Monday | .05 |
| 515 | Miguel Dilone | .05 |
| 516 | Clint Hurdle | .05 |
| 517 | Jeff Newman | .05 |
| 518 | Grant Jackson | .05 |
| 519 | Andy Hassler | .05 |
| 520 | Pat Putnam | .05 |
| 521 | Greg Pryor | .05 |
| 522 | Tony Scott | .05 |
| 523 | Steve Mura | .05 |
| 524 | John LeMaster | .05 |
| 525 | Dick Ruthven | .05 |
| 526 | John McNamara (Mgr.) | .05 |
| 527 | Larry McWilliams | .05 |
| 528 | Johnny Ray (R) | .50 |
| 529 | Pat Tabler | .40 |
| 530 | Tom Herr | .10 |
| 531 | San Diego Chicken* | 1.00 |
| 532 | Sal Butera | .05 |
| 533 | Mike Griffin | .05 |
| 534 | Kelvin Moore | .05 |
| 535 | Reggie Jackson | .50 |
| 536 | Ed Romero | .05 |
| 537 | Derrel Thomas | .05 |
| 538 | Mike O'Berry | .05 |
| 539 | Jack O'Connor | .05 |
| 540 | Bob Ojeda (R) | .75 |
| 541 | Roy Lee Jackson | .05 |
| 542 | Lynn Jones | .05 |
| 543 | Gaylord Perry | .25 |
| 544 | Phil Garner* | .10 |
| 545 | Garry Templeton | .10 |
| 546 | Rafael Ramirez | .05 |
| 547 | Jeff Reardon | .05 |
| 548 | Ron Guidry | .20 |
| 549 | Tim Laudner | .15 |
| 550 | John Henry Johnson | .05 |
| 551 | Chris Bando | .05 |
| 552 | Bobby Brown | .05 |
| 553 | Larry Bradford | .05 |
| 554 | Scott Fletcher | .05 |
| 555 | Jerry Royster | .05 |
| 556 | Shooty Babbitt | .05 |
| 557 | Kent Hrbek (R) | 2.50 |
| 558 | Yankee Winners: Ron Guidry, Tommy John | .15 |
| 559 | Mark Bomback | .05 |
| 560 | Julio Valdez | .05 |
| 561 | Buck Martinez | .05 |
| 562 | Mike Marshall (R) | 1.00 |
| 563 | Rennie Stennett | .05 |
| 564 | Steve Crawford | .05 |
| 565 | Bob Babcock | .05 |
| 566 | Johnny Podres | .05 |
| 567 | Paul Serna | .05 |
| 568 | Harold Baines | .25 |
| 569 | Dave LaRoche | .05 |
| 570 | Lee May | .05 |
| 571 | Gary Ward | .05 |
| 572 | John Denny | .05 |
| 573 | Roy Smalley | .05 |
| 574 | Bob Brenly (R) | .30 |
| 575 | Bronx Bombers: R. Jackson, D. Winfield | .45 |
| 576 | Luis Pujols | .05 |
| 577 | Butch Hobson | .05 |
| 578 | Harvey Kuenn (Mgr.) | .05 |
| 579 | Cal Ripken, Sr. | .05 |
| 580 | Juan Berenguer | .05 |
| 581 | Benny Ayala | .05 |
| 582 | Vance Law | .05 |
| 583 | Rick Leach | .05 |
| 584 | George Frazier | .05 |
| 585 | Phillies Finest: Pete Rose, Mike Schmidt | .60 |
| 586 | Joe Rudi | .05 |
| 587 | Juan Beniquez | .05 |
| 588 | Luis DeLeon (R) | .15 |
| 589 | Craig Swan | .05 |
| 590 | Dave Chalk | .05 |
| 591 | Billy Gardner (Mgr.) | .05 |
| 592 | Sal Bando | .05 |
| 593 | Bert Campaneris | .05 |
| 594 | Steve Kemp | .05 |
| 595 | Randy Lerch' (Braves) | .35 |
| 595 | Randy Lerch (Brewers) | .08 |

# 1982 Donruss (Continued)

| NO. PLAYER | MINT | NO. PLAYER | MINT | NO. PLAYER | MINT | NO. PLAYER | MINT |
|---|---|---|---|---|---|---|---|
| 596 Bryan Clark | .05 | 613 Joel Youngblood | .05 | 629 Paul Mirabella | .05 | 646 Jesse Orosco | .10 |
| 597 Dave Ford | .05 | 614 Larry Milbourne | .05 | 630 Rance Mulliniks | .05 | 647 Jerry Dybzinski | .05 |
| 598 Mike Scioscia | .05 | 615 Phil Roof | .05 | 631 Kevin Hickey | .05 | 648 Tommy Davis | .05 |
| 599 John Lowenstein | .05 | 616 Keith Drumright | .05 | 632 Reid Nichols | .05 | 649 Ron Gardenhire | .10 |
| 600 Rene Lachmann (Mgr.) | .05 | 617 Dave Rosello | .05 | 633 Dave Geisel | .05 | 650 Felipe Alou | .05 |
| 601 Mick Kelleher | .05 | 618 Rickey Keeton | .05 | 634 Ken Griffey | .10 | 651 Harvey Haddix | .05 |
| 602 Ron Jackson | .05 | 619 Dennis Lamp | .05 | 635 Bob Lemon (Mgr.) | .10 | 652 Willie Upshaw | .10 |
| 603 Jerry Koosman | .05 | 620 Sid Monge | .05 | 636 Orlando Sanchez | .05 | 653 Bill Madlock | .15 |
| 604 Dave Goltz | .05 | 621 Jerry White | .05 | 637 Bill Almon | .05 | — DK Checklist* | .10 |
| 605 Ellis Valentine | .05 | 622 Luis Aguayo | .05 | 638 Danny Ainge | .05 | — Checklist No. 1 | .08 |
| 606 Lonnie Smith | .10 | 623 Jamie Easterly | .05 | 639 Willie Stargell | .30 | — Checklist No. 2 | .08 |
| 607 Joaquin Andujar | .15 | 624 Steve Sax (R) | 1.00 | 640 Bob Sykes | .05 | — Checklist No. 3 | .08 |
| 608 Garry Hancock | .05 | 625 Dave Roberts | .05 | 641 Ed Lynch (R) | .10 | — Checklist No. 4 | .08 |
| 609 Jerry Turner | .05 | 626 Rick Bosetti | .05 | 642 John Ellis | .05 | — Checklist No. 5 | .08 |
| 610 Bob Bonner | .05 | 627 Terry Francona (R) | .30 | 643 Fergie Jenkins | .10 | — Checklist No. 6 | .08 |
| 611 Jim Dwyer | .05 | 628 Pride of Reds: | .35 | 644 Lenn Sakata | .05 | | |
| 612 Terry Bulling | .05 | Tom Seaver, Johnny Bench | | 645 Julio Gonzalez | .05 | | |

## 1983 Donruss....Complete Set of 660 Cards—Value $25.00

Features the rookie cards of Wade Boggs, Ryne Sandberg, Willie McGee and Tony Gwynn. There were a few errors, but unlike previous years they were not corrected. The *checklist* cards are *not* numbered.

| NO. PLAYER | MINT | NO. PLAYER | MINT | NO. PLAYER | MINT | NO. PLAYER | MINT |
|---|---|---|---|---|---|---|---|
| **No. 1 to 26—Diamond Kings** | | 41 Jose Cruz | .10 | 82 Rick Miller | .05 | 123 Chris Chambliss | .05 |
| 1 F. Valenzuela (DK) | .50 | 42 Pete Rose | 1.00 | 83 Graig Nettles | .10 | 124 Chuck Tanner (Mgr.) | .05 |
| 2 Rollie Fingers (DK) | .25 | 43 Cesar Cedeno | .10 | 84 Ron Cey | .15 | 125 Johnnie LeMaster | .05 |
| 3 Reggie Jackson (DK) | .50 | 44 Floyd Chiffer | .05 | 85 Miguel Dilone | .05 | 126 Mel Hall (R) | .50 |
| 4 Jim Palmer (DK) | .30 | 45 Larry McWilliams | .05 | 86 John Wathan | .05 | 127 Bruce Bochte | .05 |
| 5 Jack Morris (DK) | .30 | 46 Alan Fowlkes | .05 | 87 Kelvin Moore | .05 | 128 Charlie Puleo | .05 |
| 6 George Foster (DK) | .20 | 47 Dale Murphy | .75 | 88 Bryn Smith | .05 | 129 Luis Leal | .05 |
| 7 Jim Sundberg (DK) | .10 | 48 Doug Bird | .05 | 89 Dave Hostetler | .05 | 130 John Pacella | .05 |
| 8 Willie Stargell (DK) | .25 | 49 Hubie Brooks | .08 | 90 Rod Carew | .40 | 131 Glenn Gulliver | .05 |
| 9 Dave Stieb (DK) | .30 | 50 Floyd Bannister | .05 | 91 Lonnie Smith | .07 | 132 Don Money | .05 |
| 10 Joe Niekro (DK) | .10 | 51 Jack O'Connor | .05 | 92 Bob Knepper | .05 | 133 Dave Rozema | .05 |
| 11 Rickey Henderson (DK) | .60 | 52 Steve Senteney | .05 | 93 Marty Bystrom | .05 | 134 Bruce Hurst | .05 |
| 12 Dale Murphy (DK) | .75 | 53 Gary Gaetti (R) | .75 | 94 Chris Welsh | .05 | 135 Rudy May | .05 |
| 13 Toby Harrah (DK) | .10 | 54 Damaso Garcia | .10 | 95 Jason Thompson | .07 | 136 Tom LaSorda (Mgr.) | .10 |
| 14 Bill Buckner (DK) | .15 | 55 Gene Nelson | .05 | 96 Tom O'Malley | .05 | 137 Dan Spillner | .10 |
| 15 Willie Wilson (DK) | .25 | 56 Mookie Wilson | .08 | 97 Phil Niekro | .20 | (photo of Ed Whitson) | |
| 16 Steve Carlton (DK) | .40 | 57 Neil Allen | .05 | 98 Neil Allen | .05 | 138 Jerry Martin | .05 |
| 17 Ron Guidry (DK) | .30 | 58 Bob Horner | .25 | 99 Bill Buckner | .10 | 139 Mike Norris | .05 |
| 18 Steve Rogers (DK) | .10 | 59 Tony Pena | .15 | 100 Ed VandeBerg | .10 | 140 Al Oliver | .10 |
| 19 Kent Hrbek (DK) | .35 | 60 Tony LaValle | .05 | 101 Jim Clancy | .05 | 141 Daryl Sconiers | .05 |
| 20 Keith Hernandez (DK) | .35 | 61 Tim Lollar | .05 | 102 Robert Castillo | .05 | 142 Lamar Johnson | .05 |
| 21 Floyd Bannister (DK) | .10 | 62 Frank Pastore | .05 | 103 Bruce Berenyi | .05 | 143 Harold Baines | .20 |
| 22 Johnny Bench (DK) | .40 | 63 Garry Maddox | .05 | 104 Carlton Fisk | .20 | 144 Alan Ashby | .05 |
| 23 Britt Burns (DK) | .10 | 64 Bob Forsch | .05 | 105 Mike Flanagan | .05 | 145 Garry Templeton | .10 |
| 24 Joe Morgan (DK) | .25 | 65 Harry Spilman | .05 | 106 Cecil Cooper | .15 | 146 Al Holland | .05 |
| 25 Carl Yastrzemski (DK) | .60 | 66 Geoff Zahn | .05 | 107 Jack Morris | .20 | 147 Bo Diaz | .05 |
| 26 Terry Kennedy (DK) | .10 | 67 Salome Barojas | .05 | 108 Mike Morgan | .05 | 148 Dave Concepcion | .10 |
| 27 Gary Roenicke | .05 | 68 David Palmer | .05 | 109 Luis Aponte | .05 | 149 Rick Camp | .05 |
| 28 Dwight Bernard | .05 | 69 Charlie Hough | .05 | 110 Pedro Guerrero | .30 | 150 Jim Morrison | .05 |
| 29 Pat Underwood | .05 | 70 Dan Quisenberry | .20 | 111 Len Barker | .05 | 151 Randy Martz | .05 |
| 30 Gary Allenson | .05 | 71 Tony Armas | .15 | 112 Willie Wilson | .20 | 152 Keith Hernandez | .30 |
| 31 Ron Guidry | .20 | 72 Rick Sutcliffe | .20 | 113 Dave Beard | .05 | 153 John Lowenstein | .05 |
| 32 Burt Hooton | .05 | 73 Steve Balboni | .10 | 114 Mike Gates | .05 | 154 Mike Caldwell | .05 |
| 33 Chris Bando | .05 | 74 Jerry Remy | .05 | 115 Reggie Jackson | .45 | 155 Milt Wilcox | .05 |
| 34 Vida Blue | .05 | 75 Mike Scioscia | .05 | 116 George Wright | .15 | 156 Rich Gedman | .05 |
| 35 Rickey Henderson | .50 | 76 John Wockenfuss | .05 | 117 Vance Law | .05 | 157 Rich Gossage | .20 |
| 36 Ray Burris | .05 | 77 Jim Palmer | .25 | 118 Nolan Ryan | .30 | 158 Jerry Reuss | .05 |
| 37 John Butcher | .05 | 78 Rollie Fingers | .25 | 119 Mike Krukow | .05 | 159 Ron Hassey | .05 |
| 38 Don Aase | .05 | 79 Joe Nolan | .05 | 120 Ozzie Smith | .10 | 160 Larry Gura | .05 |
| 39 Jerry Koosman | .05 | 80 Pete Vuckovich | .05 | 121 Broderick Perkins | .05 | 161 Dwayne Murphy | .05 |
| 40 Bruce Sutter | .20 | 81 Rick Leach | .05 | 122 Tom Seaver | .30 | 162 Woodie Fryman | .05 |

101

| NO. | PLAYER | MINT | NO. | PLAYER | MINT | NO. | PLAYER | MINT | NO. | PLAYER | MINT |
|---|---|---|---|---|---|---|---|---|---|---|---|
| 163 | Steve Comer | .05 | 247 | Joe Pittman | .10 | 330 | Jim Slaton | .05 | 414 | Charlie Lea | .05 |
| 164 | Ken Forsch | .05 | | (photo of Juan Eichelberger) | | 331 | Benny Ayala | .05 | 415 | Rick Honeycutt | .05 |
| 165 | Dennis Lamp | .05 | 248 | Mario Soto | .10 | 332 | Ted Simmons | .10 | 416 | Mike Witt | .10 |
| 166 | David Green (R) | .20 | 249 | Claudell Washington | .10 | 333 | Lou Whitaker | .20 | 417 | Steve Trout | .05 |
| 167 | Terry Puhl | .05 | 250 | Rick Rhoden | .05 | 334 | Chuck Rainey | .05 | 418 | Glenn Brummer | .05 |
| 168 | Mike Schmidt | .50 | 251 | Darrell Evans | .10 | 335 | Lou Piniella | .10 | 419 | Denny Walling | .05 |
| 169 | Eddie Milner (R) | .15 | 252 | Steve Henderson | .05 | 336 | Steve Sax | .15 | 420 | Gary Matthews | .10 |
| 170 | John Curtis | .05 | 253 | Manny Castillo | .05 | 337 | Toby Harrah | .05 | 421 | Charlie Leibrandt | .05 |
| 171 | Don Robinson | .05 | 254 | Craig Swan | .05 | 338 | George Brett | .50 | 422 | Juan Eichelberger | .05 |
| 172 | Richard Gale | .05 | 255 | Joey McLaughlin | .05 | 339 | Davey Lopes | .05 | 423 | Matt Guante | .05 |
| 173 | Steve Bedrosian | .05 | 256 | Pete Redfern | .05 | 340 | Gary Carter | .40 | 424 | Bill Laskey (R) | .15 |
| 174 | Willie Hernandez | .20 | 257 | Ken Singleton | .08 | 341 | John Grubb | .05 | 425 | Jerry Royster | .05 |
| 175 | Ron Gardenhire | .05 | 258 | Robin Yount | .30 | 342 | Tim Foli | .05 | 426 | Dickie Noles | .05 |
| 176 | Jim Beattie | .05 | 259 | Elias Sosa | .05 | 343 | Jim Kaat | .05 | 427 | George Foster | .20 |
| 177 | Tim Laudner | .05 | 260 | Bob Ojeda | .05 | 344 | Mike LaCoss | .05 | 428 | Mike Moore (R) | .25 |
| 178 | Buck Martinez | .05 | 261 | Bobby Murcer | .10 | 345 | Larry Christenson | .05 | 429 | Gary Ward | .05 |
| 179 | Kent Hrbek | .40 | 262 | Candy Maldonado (R) | .35 | 346 | Juan Bonilla | .05 | 430 | Barry Bonnell | .05 |
| 180 | Alfredo Griffin | .05 | 263 | Rick Waits | .05 | 347 | Omar Moreno | .05 | 431 | Ron Washington | .05 |
| 181 | Larry Andersen | .05 | 264 | Greg Pryor | .05 | 348 | Chili Davis | .10 | 432 | Rance Mulliniks | .05 |
| 182 | Pete Falcone | .05 | 265 | Bob Owchinko | .05 | 349 | Tommy Boggs | .05 | 433 | Mike Stanton | .05 |
| 183 | Jody Davis | .08 | 266 | Chris Speier | .05 | 350 | Rusty Staub | .10 | 434 | Jesse Orosco | .10 |
| 184 | Glenn Hubbard | .05 | 267 | Bruce Kison | .05 | 351 | Bump Wills | .05 | 435 | Larry Bowa | .05 |
| 185 | Dale Berra | .05 | 268 | Mark Wagner | .05 | 352 | Rick Sweet | .05 | 436 | Biff Pocoroba | .05 |
| 186 | Greg Minton | .05 | 269 | Steve Kemp | .05 | 353 | Jim Gott | .05 | 437 | Johnny Ray | .08 |
| 187 | Gary Lucas | .05 | 270 | Phil Garner | .05 | 354 | Terry Felton | .05 | 438 | Joe Morgan | .20 |
| 188 | Dave Van Gorder | .05 | 271 | Gene Richards | .05 | 355 | Jim Kern | .05 | 439 | Eric Show (R) | .15 |
| 189 | Bob Dernier | .05 | 272 | Renie Martin | .05 | 356 | Bill Almon | .05 | 440 | Larry Biittner | .05 |
| 190 | Willie McGee (R) | 2.50 | 273 | Dave Roberts | .05 | 357 | Tippy Martinez | .05 | 441 | Greg Gross | .05 |
| 191 | Dickie Thon | .07 | 274 | Dan Driessen | .05 | 358 | Roy Howell | .05 | 442 | Gene Tenace | .05 |
| 192 | Bob Boone | .05 | 275 | Rufino Linares | .05 | 359 | Dan Petry | .20 | 443 | Danny Heep | .05 |
| 193 | Britt Burns | .05 | 276 | Lee Lacy | .05 | 360 | Jerry Mumphrey | .05 | 444 | Bobby Clark | .05 |
| 194 | Jeff Reardon | .05 | 277 | Ryne Sandberg (R) | 3.50 | 361 | Mark Clear | .05 | 445 | Kevin Hickey | .05 |
| 195 | Jon Matlack | .05 | 278 | Darrell Porter | .05 | 362 | Mike Marshall | .20 | 446 | Scott Sanderson | .05 |
| 196 | Don Slaught (R) | .25 | 279 | Cal Ripken | .75 | 363 | Lary Sorensen | .05 | 447 | Frank Tanana | .05 |
| 197 | Fred Stanley | .05 | 280 | Jamie Easterly | .05 | 364 | Amos Otis | .08 | 448 | Cesar Geronimo | .05 |
| 198 | Rick Manning | .05 | 281 | Bill Fahey | .05 | 365 | Rick Langford | .05 | 449 | Jimmy Sexton | .05 |
| 199 | Dave Righetti | .15 | 282 | Glenn Hoffman | .05 | 366 | Brad Mills | .05 | 450 | Mike Hargrove | .05 |
| 200 | Dave Stapleton | .05 | 283 | Willie Randolph | .05 | 367 | Brian Downing | .05 | 451 | Doyle Alexander | .05 |
| 201 | Steve Yeager | .05 | 284 | Fernando Valenzuela | .40 | 368 | Mike Richardt | .05 | 452 | Dwight Evans | .10 |
| 202 | Enos Cabell | .05 | 285 | Alan Bannister | .05 | 369 | Aurelio Rodriguez | .05 | 453 | Terry Forster | .05 |
| 203 | Sammy Stewart | .05 | 286 | Paul Splittorff | .05 | 370 | Dave Smith | .05 | 454 | Tom Brookens | .05 |
| 204 | Moose Haas | .05 | 287 | Joe Rudi | .05 | 371 | Tug McGraw | .08 | 455 | Rich Dauer | .05 |
| 205 | Lenn Sakata | .05 | 288 | Bill Gullickson | .05 | 372 | Doug Bair | .05 | 456 | Rob Picciolo | .05 |
| 206 | Charlie Moore | .05 | 289 | Danny Darwin | .05 | 373 | Ruppert Jones | .05 | 457 | Terry Crowley | .05 |
| 207 | Alan Trammell | .25 | 290 | Andy Hassler | .05 | 374 | Alex Trevino | .05 | 458 | Ned Yost | .05 |
| 208 | Jim Rice | .35 | 291 | Ernesto Escarrega | .05 | 375 | Ken Dayley | .05 | 459 | Kirk Gibson | .25 |
| 209 | Roy Smalley | .05 | 292 | Steve Mura | .05 | 376 | Rod Scurry | .05 | 460 | Reid Nichols | .05 |
| 210 | Bill Russell | .05 | 293 | Tony Scott | .05 | 377 | Bob Brenly | .05 | 461 | Oscar Gamble | .05 |
| 211 | Andre Thornton | .07 | 294 | Manny Trillo | .05 | 378 | Scot Thompson | .05 | 462 | Dusty Baker | .10 |
| 212 | Willie Aikens | .05 | 295 | Greg Harris | .05 | 379 | Julio Cruz | .05 | 463 | Jack Perconte | .05 |
| 213 | Dave McKay | .05 | 296 | Luis DeLeon | .05 | 380 | John Stearns | .05 | 464 | Frank White | .05 |
| 214 | Tim Blackwell | .05 | 297 | Kent Tekulve | .05 | 381 | Dale Murray | .05 | 465 | Mickey Klutts | .05 |
| 215 | Buddy Bell | .10 | 298 | Atlee Hammaker | .05 | 382 | Frank Viola (R) | .40 | 466 | Warren Cromartie | .05 |
| 216 | Doug DeCinces | .15 | 299 | Bruce Benedict | .05 | 383 | Al Bumbry | .05 | 467 | Larry Parrish | .05 |
| 217 | Tom Herr | .10 | 300 | Fergie Jenkins | .10 | 384 | Ben Oglivie | .10 | 468 | Bobby Grich | .08 |
| 218 | Frank LaCorte | .05 | 301 | Dave Kingman | .10 | 385 | Dave Tobik | .05 | 469 | Dane Iorg | .05 |
| 219 | Steve Carlton | .30 | 302 | Bill Caudill | .05 | 386 | Bob Stanley | .05 | 470 | Joe Niekro | .10 |
| 220 | Terry Kennedy | .10 | 303 | John Castino | .05 | 387 | Andre Robertson | .05 | 471 | Ed Farmer | .05 |
| 221 | Mike Easler | .05 | 304 | Ernie Whitt | .05 | 388 | Jorge Orta | .05 | 472 | Tim Flannery | .05 |
| 222 | Jack Clark | .25 | 305 | Randy Johnson | .05 | 389 | Ed Whitson | .05 | 473 | Dave Parker | .30 |
| 223 | Gene Garber | .05 | 306 | Garth Iorg | .05 | 390 | Don Hood | .05 | 474 | Jeff Leonard | .05 |
| 224 | Scott Holman | .05 | 307 | Gaylord Perry | .20 | 391 | Tom Underwood | .05 | 475 | Al Hrabosky | .05 |
| 225 | Mike Proly | .05 | 308 | Ed Lynch | .05 | 392 | Tim Wallach | .10 | 476 | Ron Hodges | .05 |
| 226 | Terry Bulling | .05 | 309 | Keith Moreland | .05 | 393 | Steve Renko | .05 | 477 | Leon Durham | .20 |
| 227 | Jerry Garvin | .05 | 310 | Rafael Ramirez | .05 | 394 | Mickey Rivers | .05 | 478 | Jim Essian | .05 |
| 228 | Ron Davis | .05 | 311 | Bill Madlock | .15 | 395 | Greg Luzinski | .10 | 479 | Roy Lee Jackson | .05 |
| 229 | Tom Hume | .05 | 312 | Milt May | .05 | 396 | Art Howe | .05 | 480 | Brad Havens | .05 |
| 230 | Marc Hill | .05 | 313 | John Montefusco | .05 | 397 | Alan Wiggins (R) | .25 | 481 | Joe Price | .05 |
| 231 | Dennis Martinez | .05 | 314 | Wayne Krenchicki | .05 | 398 | Jim Barr | .05 | 482 | Tony Bernazard | .05 |
| 232 | Jim Gantner | .05 | 315 | George Vukovich | .05 | 399 | Ivan DeJesus | .05 | 483 | Scott McGregor | .08 |
| 233 | Larry Pashnick | .05 | 316 | Joaquin Andujar | .10 | 400 | Tom Lawless | .05 | 484 | Paul Molitor | .15 |
| 234 | Dave Collins | .05 | 317 | Craig Reynolds | .05 | 401 | Bob Walk | .05 | 485 | Mike Ivie | .05 |
| 235 | Tom Burgmeier | .05 | 318 | Rick Burleson | .05 | 402 | Jimmy Smith | .05 | 486 | Ken Griffey | .10 |
| 236 | Ken Landreaux | .05 | 319 | Richard Dotson | .05 | 403 | Lee Smith | .10 | 487 | Dennis Eckersley | .08 |
| 237 | John Denny | .10 | 320 | Steve Rogers | .05 | 404 | George Hendrick | .10 | 488 | Steve Garvey | .40 |
| 238 | Hal McRae | .05 | 321 | Dave Schmidt | .05 | 405 | Eddie Murray | .60 | 489 | Mike Fischlin | .05 |
| 239 | Matt Keough | .05 | 322 | Bud Black (R) | .30 | 406 | Marshall Edwards | .05 | 490 | U.L. Washington | .05 |
| 240 | Doug Flynn | .05 | 323 | Jeff Burroughs | .05 | 407 | Lance Parrish | .30 | 491 | Steve McCatty | .05 |
| 241 | Fred Lynn | .20 | 324 | Von Hayes | .25 | 408 | Carney Lansford | .10 | 492 | Roy Johnson | .05 |
| 242 | Billy Sample | .05 | 325 | Butch Wynegar | .05 | 409 | Dave Winfield | .40 | 493 | Don Baylor | .10 |
| 243 | Tom Paciorek | .05 | 326 | Carl Yastrzemski | .50 | 410 | Bob Welch | .05 | 494 | Bobby Johnson | .05 |
| 244 | Joe Sambito | .05 | 327 | Ron Roenicke | .05 | 411 | Larry Milbourne | .05 | 495 | Mike Squires | .05 |
| 245 | Sid Monge | .05 | 328 | Howard Johnson (R) | .15 | 412 | Dennis Leonard | .05 | 496 | Bert Roberge | .05 |
| 246 | Ken Oberkfell | .05 | 329 | Rick Dempsey | .05 | 413 | Dan Meyer | .05 | 497 | Dick Ruthven | .05 |

| NO. PLAYER | MINT | NO. PLAYER | MINT | NO. PLAYER | MINT | NO. PLAYER | MINT |
|---|---|---|---|---|---|---|---|
| 498 Tito Landrum | .05 | 540 Tim Raines | .30 | 581 Tim Stoddard | .05 | 621 John Stuper | .10 |
| 499 Sixto Lezcano | .05 | 541 Paul Mirabella | .05 | 582 Bob McClure | .05 | 622 Matt Sinatro | .05 |
| 500 Johnny Bench | .35 | 542 Luis Tiant | .05 | 583 Jim Dwyer | .05 | 623 Gene Petralli | .05 |
| 501 Larry Whisenton | .05 | 543 Ron LeFlore | .05 | 584 Ed Romero | .05 | 624 Duane Walker (R) | .15 |
| 502 Manny Sarmiento | .05 | 544 Dave LaPoint (R) | .20 | 585 Larry Herndon | .05 | 625 Dick Williams (Mgr.) | .05 |
| 503 Fred Breining | .05 | 545 Randy Moffitt | .05 | 586 Wade Boggs (R) | 12.00 | 626 Pat Corrales (Mgr.) | .05 |
| 504 Bill Campbell | .05 | 546 Luis Aguayo | .05 | 587 Jay Howell | .05 | 627 Vern Ruhle | .05 |
| 505 Todd Cruz | .05 | 547 Brad Lesley | .10 | 588 Dave Stewart | .05 | 628 Joe Torre (Mgr.) | .05 |
| 506 Bob Bailor | .05 | 548 Luis Salazar | .05 | 589 Bert Blyleven | .10 | 629 Anthony Johnson | .05 |
| 507 Dave Stieb | .20 | 549 John Candelaria | .05 | 590 Dick Howser (Mgr.) | .05 | 630 Steve Howe | .05 |
| 508 Al Williams | .05 | 550 Dave Bergman | .05 | 591 Wayne Gross | .05 | 631 Gary Woods | .05 |
| 509 Dan Ford | .05 | 551 Bob Watson | .05 | 592 Terry Francona | .08 | 632 LaMarr Hoyt | .15 |
| 510 Gorman Thomas | .10 | 552 Pat Tabler | .05 | 593 Don Werner | .05 | 633 Steve Swisher | .05 |
| 511 Chet Lemon | .10 | 553 Brent Gaff | .05 | 594 Bill Stein | .05 | 634 Terry Leach | .05 |
| 512 Mike Torrez | .05 | 554 Al Cowens | .05 | 595 Jesse Barfield | .10 | 635 Jeff Newman | .05 |
| 513 Shane Rawley | .05 | 555 Tom Brunansky | .25 | 596 Bobby Molinaro | .05 | 636 Brett Butler | .10 |
| 514 Mark Belanger | .05 | 556 Lloyd Moseby | .15 | 597 Mike Vail | .05 | 637 Gary Gray | .05 |
| 515 Rodney Craig | .05 | 557 Pascual Perez | .05 | 598 Tony Gwynn (R) | 5.00 | 638 Lee Mazzilli | .05 |
| 516 Onix Concepcion (R) | .10 | 558 Willie Upshaw | .10 | 599 Gary Rajsich | .05 | 639 Ron Jackson | .05 |
| 517 Mike Heath | .05 | 559 Richie Zisk | .05 | 600 Jerry Ujdur | .05 | 640 Juan Beniquez | .05 |
| 518 Andre Dawson | .20 | 560 Pat Zachry | .05 | 601 Cliff Johnson | .05 | 641 Dave Rucker | .05 |
| 519 Luis Sanchez | .05 | 561 Jay Johnstone | .05 | 602 Jerry White | .05 | 642 Luis Pujols | .05 |
| 520 Terry Bogener | .05 | 562 Carlos Diaz | .10 | 603 Bryan Clark | .05 | 643 Rick Monday | .05 |
| 521 Rudy Law | .05 | 563 John Tudor | .10 | 604 Joe Ferguson | .05 | 644 Hosken Powell | .05 |
| 522 Ray Knight | .05 | 564 Frank Robinson (Mgr.) | .15 | 605 Guy Sularz | .05 | 645 The Chicken | .30 |
| 523 Joe LeFebvre | .05 | 565 Dave Edwards | .05 | 606 Ozzie Virgil | .05 | 646 Dave Engle | .05 |
| 524 Jim Wohlford | .05 | 566 Paul Householder | .05 | 607 Terry Harper | .05 | 647 Dick Davis | .05 |
| 525 Julio Franco (R) | 1.00 | 567 Ron Reed | .05 | 608 Harvey Kuenn (Mgr.) | .05 | 648 MVP's: Frank Robinson, | .15 |
| 526 Ron Oester | .05 | 568 Mike Ramsey | .05 | 609 Jim Sundberg | .05 |   Vida Blue, Joe Morgan | |
| 527 Rick Mahler | .05 | 569 Kiko Garcia | .05 | 610 Willie Stargell | .20 | 649 Al Chambers | .10 |
| 528 Steve Nicosia | .05 | 570 Tommy John | .10 | 611 Reggie Smith | .10 | 650 Jesus Vega | .05 |
| 529 Junior Kennedy | .05 | 571 Tony LaRussa (Mgr.) | .05 | 612 Rob Wilfong | .05 | 651 Jeff Jones | .05 |
| 530 Whitey Herzog (Mgr.) | .05 | 572 Joel Youngblood | .05 | 613 Niekro Brothers | .15 | 652 Marvis Foley | .05 |
| 531 Don Sutton | .15 | 573 Wayne Tolleson | .05 |   Joe and Phil | | 653 Ty Cobb Puzzle | .20 |
| 532 Mark Brouhard | .05 | 574 Keith Creel | .05 | 614 Lee Elia (Mgr.) | .05 | — Checklist (DK) | .08 |
| 533 Sparky Anderson (Mgr.) | .05 | 575 Billy Martin (Mgr.) | .15 | 615 Mickey Hatcher | .05 | — Checklist No. 1 | .08 |
| 534 Roger LaFrancois | .05 | 576 Jerry Dybzinski | .05 | 616 Jerry Hairston | .05 | — Checklist No. 2 | .08 |
| 535 George Frazier | .05 | 577 Rick Cerone | .05 | 617 John Martin | .05 | — Checklist No. 3 | .08 |
| 536 Tom Niedenfuer | .07 | 578 Tony Perez | .15 | 618 Wally Backman | .05 | — Checklist No. 4 | .08 |
| 537 Ed Glynn | .05 | 579 Greg Brock (R) | .50 | 619 Storm Davis (R) | .40 | — Checklist No. 5 | .08 |
| 538 Lee May | .05 | 580 Glen Wilson (R) | .60 | 620 Alan Knicely | .05 | — Checklist No. 6 | .08 |
| 539 Bob Kearney | .10 | | | | | | |

# 1984 Donruss....Complete Set of 658 Cards—Value $225.00

Features the rookie cards of Don Mattingly and Darryl Strawberry. For the first time Donruss limited production of its main card set, creating a serious shortage. *Living Legends* cards "A" and "B" could only be found in wax packs, and are not considered to be part of the set. The *checklist* cards are *not* numbered. Cards 29 and 30 exist with the numbers deleted.

| NO. PLAYER | MINT | NO. PLAYER | MINT | NO. PLAYER | MINT | NO. PLAYER | MINT |
|---|---|---|---|---|---|---|---|
| **No. 1 to 26—Diamond Kings** | | 18 Ron Kittle (DK) | .25 | 31 Dion James (R) | .25 | 49 Lance Parrish | .40 |
| 1 Robin Yount (DK) | .60 | 19 Jim Clancy (DK) | .15 | 32 Tony Fernandez (R) | 2.25 | 50 Jim Rice | .60 |
| 2 Dave Concepcion (DK) | .20 | 20 Bill Madlock (DK) | .20 | 33 Angel Salazar (R) | .15 | 51 Dave Winfield | .50 |
| 3 Dwayne Murphy (DK) | .15 | 21 Larry Parrish (DK) | .20 | 34 Kevin McReynolds (R) | 2.50 | 52 Fernando Valenzuela | .50 |
| 4 John Castino (DK) | .15 | 22 Eddie Murray (DK) | .75 | 35 Dick Schofield (R) | .60 | 53 George Brett | .75 |
| 5 Leon Durham (DK) | .30 | 23 Mike Schmidt (DK) | 1.00 | 36 Brad Komminsk (R) | .30 | 54 Rickey Henderson | .75 |
| 6 Rusty Staub (DK) | .15 | 24 Pedro Guerrero (DK) | .50 | 37 Tim Teufel (R) | .40 | 55 Gary Carter | .60 |
| 7 Jack Clark (DK) | .30 | 25 Andre Thornton (DK) | .15 | 38 Doug Frobel (R) | .15 | 56 Buddy Bell | .15 |
| 8 Dave Dravecky (DK) | .15 | 26 Wade Boggs (DK) | 2.00 | 39 Greg Gagne (R) | .30 | 57 Reggie Jackson | .60 |
| 9 Al Oliver (DK) | .20 | **No. 27 to 46—(Rated Rookies)** | | 40 Mike Fuentes (R) | .15 | 58 Harold Baines | .25 |
| 10 Dave Righetti (DK) | .25 | 27 Joel Skinner (R) | .30 | 41 Joe Carter (R) | 4.00 | 59 Ozzie Smith | .20 |
| 11 Hal McRae (DK) | .15 | 28 Tommy Dunbar (R) | .15 | 42 Mike Brown (R) | .25 | 60 Nolan Ryan | .75 |
| 12 Ray Knight (DK) | .15 | 29 Mike Stenhouse (R) | .25 | 43 Mike Jeffcoat (R) | .15 | 61 Pete Rose | 2.00 |
| 13 Bruce Sutter (DK) | .25 |   (no number on back) | | 44 Sid Fernandez (R) | 5.00 | 62 Ron Oester | .10 |
| 14 Bob Horner (DK) | .25 | 29 Mike Stenhouse (R) | 1.00 | 45 Brian Dayett (R) | .20 | 63 Steve Garvey | .75 |
| 15 Lance Parrish (DK) | .30 | 30 Ron Darling (R) | 4.00 | 46 Chris Smith (R) | .15 | 64 Jason Thompson | .15 |
| 16 Matt Young (DK) | .15 |   (no number on back) | | 47 Eddie Murray | .75 | 65 Jack Clark | .25 |
| 17 Fred Lynn (DK) | .25 | 30 Ron Darling (R) | 6.00 | 48 Robin Yount | .50 | 66 Dale Murphy | 1.00 |

Card values from this set fluctuate considerably.

| NO. | PLAYER | MINT | NO. | PLAYER | MINT | NO. | PLAYER | MINT | NO. | PLAYER | MINT |
|---|---|---|---|---|---|---|---|---|---|---|---|
| 67 | Leon Durham | .30 | 152 | Don Baylor | .20 | 237 | Mike Caldwell | .08 | 322 | Jim Morrison | .08 |
| 68 | Darryl Strawberry (R) | 7.50 | 153 | Bob Welch | .08 | 238 | Keith Hernandez | .40 | 323 | Max Venable | .08 |
| 69 | Richie Zisk | .08 | 154 | Alan Bannister | .08 | 239 | Larry Bowa | .10 | 324 | Tony Gwynn | 2.00 |
| 70 | Kent Hrbek | .40 | 155 | Willie Aikens | .08 | 240 | Tony Bernazard | .08 | 325 | Duane Walker | .08 |
| 71 | Dave Stieb | .25 | 156 | Jeff Burroughs | .08 | 241 | Damaso Garcia | .15 | 326 | Ozzie Virgil | .08 |
| 72 | Ken Schrom | .08 | 157 | Bryan Little | .08 | 242 | Tom Brunansky | .25 | 327 | Jeff Lahti | .08 |
| 73 | George Bell | .10 | 158 | Bob Boone | .08 | 243 | Dan Driessen | .15 | 328 | Bill Dawley | .25 |
| 74 | Jon Moses | .08 | 159 | Dave Hostetler | .08 | 244 | Ron Kittle | .25 | 329 | Rob Wilfong | .08 |
| 75 | Ed Lynch | .08 | 160 | Jerry Dybzinski | .08 | 245 | Tim Stoddard | .08 | 330 | Marc Hill | .08 |
| 76 | Chuck Rainey | .08 | 161 | Mike Madden | .15 | 246 | Bob Gibson | .10 | 331 | Ray Burris | .08 |
| 77 | Biff Pocoroba | .08 | 162 | Luis DeLeon | .08 | 247 | Marty Castillo | .08 | 332 | Allan Ramirez | .08 |
| 78 | Cecilio Guante | .08 | 163 | Willie Hernandez | .25 | 248 | Don Mattingly (R) | 75.00 | 333 | Chuck Porter | .08 |
| 79 | Jim Barr | .08 | 164 | Frank Pastore | .08 | 249 | Jeff Newman | .08 | 334 | Wayne Krenchicki | .08 |
| 80 | Kurt Bevacqua | .08 | 165 | Rick Camp | .08 | 250 | Alejandro Pena | .25 | 335 | Gary Allenson | .08 |
| 81 | Tom Foley | .08 | 166 | Lee Mazzilli | .08 | 251 | Toby Harrah | .08 | 336 | Bob Meacham | .25 |
| 82 | Joe LeFebvre | .08 | 167 | Scot Thompson | .08 | 252 | Cesar Geronimo | .08 | 337 | Joe Beckwith | .08 |
| 83 | Andy Van Slyke (R) | .40 | 168 | Bob Forsch | .08 | 253 | Tom Underwood | .08 | 338 | Rick Sutcliffe | .25 |
| 84 | Bob Lillis (Mgr.) | .08 | 169 | Mike Flanagan | .08 | 254 | Doug Flynn | .08 | 339 | Mark Huismann | .15 |
| 85 | Rick Adams | .08 | 170 | Rick Manning | .08 | 255 | Andy Hassler | .08 | 340 | Tim Conroy | .08 |
| 86 | Jerry Hairston | .08 | 171 | Chet Lemon | .15 | 256 | Odell Jones | .08 | 341 | Scott Sanderson | .08 |
| 87 | Bob James | .25 | 172 | Jerry Remy | .08 | 257 | Rudy Law | .08 | 342 | Larry Biittner | .08 |
| 88 | Joe Altobelli (Mgr.) | .08 | 173 | Ron Guidry | .30 | 258 | Harry Spilman | .08 | 343 | Dave Stewart | .08 |
| 89 | Ed Romero | .08 | 174 | Pedro Guerrero | .40 | 259 | Marty Bystrom | .08 | 344 | Darryl Motley | .08 |
| 90 | John Grubb | .08 | 175 | Willie Wilson | .25 | 260 | Dave Rucker | .08 | 345 | Chris Codiroli | .08 |
| 91 | John H. Johnson | .08 | 176 | Carney Lansford | .15 | 261 | Ruppert Jones | .08 | 346 | Rich Behenna | .08 |
| 92 | Juan Espino | .08 | 177 | Al Oliver | .15 | 262 | Jeff Jones | .08 | 347 | Andre Robertson | .08 |
| 93 | Candy Maldonado | .08 | 178 | Jim Sundberg | .08 | 263 | Gerald Perry | .30 | 348 | Mike Marshall | .20 |
| 94 | Andre Thornton | .15 | 179 | Bobby Grich | .08 | 264 | Gene Tenace | .08 | 349 | Larry Herndon | .08 |
| 95 | Onix Concepcion | .08 | 180 | Richard Dotson | .08 | 265 | Brad Wellman | .08 | 350 | Rich Dauer | .08 |
| 96 | Don Hill | .08 | 181 | Joaquin Andujar | .15 | 266 | Dickie Noles | .08 | 351 | Cecil Cooper | .15 |
| 97 | Andre Dawson | .30 | 182 | Jose Cruz | .10 | 267 | Jamie Allen | .08 | 352 | Rod Carew | .50 |
| 98 | Frank Tanana | .08 | 183 | Mike Schmidt | .75 | 268 | Jim Gott | .08 | 353 | Willie McGee | .50 |
| 99 | Curt Wilkerson | .08 | 184 | Gary Redus (R) | .40 | 269 | Ron Davis | .08 | 354 | Phil Garner | .08 |
| 100 | Larry Gura | .08 | 185 | Garry Templeton | .15 | 270 | Benny Ayala | .08 | 355 | Joe Morgan | .30 |
| 101 | Dwayne Murphy | .15 | 186 | Tony Pena | .15 | 271 | Ned Yost | .08 | 356 | Luis Salazar | .08 |
| 102 | Tom Brennan | .08 | 187 | Greg Minton | .08 | 272 | Dave Rozema | .08 | 357 | John Candelaria | .08 |
| 103 | Dave Righetti | .30 | 188 | Phil Niekro | .30 | 273 | Dave Stapleton | .08 | 358 | Bill Laskey | .08 |
| 104 | Steve Sax | .25 | 189 | Ferguson Jenkins | .15 | 274 | Lou Piniella | .10 | 359 | Bob McClure | .08 |
| 105 | Dan Petry | .20 | 190 | Mookie Wilson | .15 | 275 | Jose Morales | .08 | 360 | Dave Kingman | .15 |
| 106 | Cal Ripken | .75 | 191 | Jim Beattie | .08 | 276 | Brod Perkins | .08 | 361 | Ron Cey | .15 |
| 107 | Paul Molitor | .20 | 192 | Gary Ward | .08 | 277 | Butch Davis | .10 | 362 | Matt Young (R) | .20 |
| 108 | Fred Lynn | .25 | 193 | Jesse Barfield | .40 | 278 | Tony Phillips | .08 | 363 | Lloyd Moseby | .20 |
| 109 | Neil Allen | .08 | 194 | Pete Filson | .08 | 279 | Jeff Reardon | .08 | 364 | Frank Viola | .08 |
| 110 | Joe Niekro | .08 | 195 | Roy Lee Jackson | .08 | 280 | Ken Forsch | .08 | 365 | Eddie Milner | .08 |
| 111 | Steve Carlton | .50 | 196 | Rick Sweet | .08 | 281 | Pete O'Brien (R) | 1.50 | 366 | Floyd Bannister | .08 |
| 112 | Terry Kennedy | .15 | 197 | Jesse Orosco | .15 | 282 | Tom Paciorek | .08 | 367 | Dan Ford | .08 |
| 113 | Bill Madlock | .20 | 198 | Steve Lake | .08 | 283 | Frank LaCorte | .08 | 368 | Moose Haas | .08 |
| 114 | Chili Davis | .15 | 199 | Ken Dayley | .08 | 284 | Tim Lollar | .08 | 369 | Doug Bair | .08 |
| 115 | Jim Gantner | .08 | 200 | Manny Sarmiento | .08 | 285 | Greg Gross | .08 | 370 | Ray Fontenot (R) | .15 |
| 116 | Tom Seaver | .60 | 201 | Mark Davis | .08 | 286 | Alex Trevino | .08 | 371 | Luis Aponte | .08 |
| 117 | Bill Buckner | .15 | 202 | Tim Flannery | .08 | 287 | Gene Garber | .08 | 372 | Jack Fimple | .08 |
| 118 | Bill Caudill | .08 | 203 | Bill Scherrer | .08 | 288 | Dave Parker | .40 | 373 | Neal Heaton | .15 |
| 119 | Jim Clancy | .08 | 204 | Al Holland | .08 | 289 | Lee Smith | .15 | 374 | Greg Pryor | .08 |
| 120 | John Castino | .08 | 205 | Dave Von Ohlen | .08 | 290 | Dave LaPoint | .08 | 375 | Wayne Gross | .08 |
| 121 | Dave Concepcion | .15 | 206 | Mike LaCoss | .08 | 291 | John Shelby | .15 | 376 | Charlie Lea | .08 |
| 122 | Greg Luzinski | .15 | 207 | Juan Beniquez | .08 | 292 | Charlie Moore | .08 | 377 | Steve Lubratich | .08 |
| 123 | Mike Boddicker | .15 | 208 | Juan Agosto | .08 | 293 | Alan Trammell | .40 | 378 | Jon Matlack | .08 |
| 124 | Pete Ladd | .08 | 209 | Bobby Ramos | .08 | 294 | Tony Armas | .15 | 379 | Julio Cruz | .08 |
| 125 | Juan Berenguer | .08 | 210 | Al Bumbry | .08 | 295 | Shane Rawley | .08 | 380 | John Mizerock | .08 |
| 126 | John Montefusco | .08 | 211 | Mark Brouhard | .08 | 296 | Greg Brock | .08 | 381 | Kevin Gross (R) | .30 |
| 127 | Ed Jurak | .08 | 212 | Howard Bailey | .08 | 297 | Hal McRae | .08 | 382 | Mike Ramsey | .08 |
| 128 | Tom Niedenfuer | .08 | 213 | Bruce Hurst | .08 | 298 | Mike Davis | .10 | 383 | Doug Gwosdz | .08 |
| 129 | Bert Blyleven | .15 | 214 | Bob Shirley | .08 | 299 | Tim Raines | .50 | 384 | Kelly Paris | .08 |
| 130 | Bud Black | .08 | 215 | Pat Zachry | .08 | 300 | Bucky Dent | .08 | 385 | Pete Falcone | .08 |
| 131 | Gorman Heimueller | .08 | 216 | Julio Franco | .15 | 301 | Tommy John | .20 | 386 | Milt May | .08 |
| 132 | Dan Schatzeder | .08 | 217 | Mike Armstrong | .08 | 302 | Carlton Fisk | .25 | 387 | Fred Breining | .08 |
| 133 | Ron Jackson | .08 | 218 | Dave Beard | .08 | 303 | Darrell Porter | .08 | 388 | Craig Lefferts (R) | .15 |
| 134 | Tom Henke (R) | .40 | 219 | Steve Rogers | .08 | 304 | Dickie Thon | .08 | 389 | Steve Henderson | .08 |
| 135 | Kevin Hickey | .08 | 220 | John Butcher | .08 | 305 | Garry Maddox | .08 | 390 | Randy Moffitt | .08 |
| 136 | Mike Scott | .08 | 221 | Mike Smithson | .15 | 306 | Cesar Cedeno | .08 | 391 | Ron Washington | .08 |
| 137 | Bo Diaz | .08 | 222 | Frank White | .25 | 307 | Gary Lucas | .08 | 392 | Gary Roenicke | .08 |
| 138 | Glenn Brummer | .08 | 223 | Mike Heath | .08 | 308 | Johnny Ray | .15 | 393 | Tom Candiotti | .12 |
| 139 | Sid Monge | .08 | 224 | Chris Bando | .08 | 309 | Andy McGaffigan | .08 | 394 | Larry Pashnick | .08 |
| 140 | Rich Gale | .08 | 225 | Roy Smalley | .08 | 310 | Claudell Washington | .15 | 395 | Dwight Evans | .20 |
| 141 | Brett Butler | .15 | 226 | Dusty Baker | .10 | 311 | Ryne Sandberg | 2.00 | 396 | Goose Gossage | .20 |
| 142 | Brian Harper | .08 | 227 | Lou Whitaker | .25 | 312 | George Foster | .20 | 397 | Derrel Thomas | .08 |
| 143 | John Rabb | .08 | 228 | John Lowenstein | .08 | 313 | Spike Owen (R) | .40 | 398 | Juan Eichelberger | .08 |
| 144 | Gary Woods | .08 | 229 | Ben Ogilvie | .08 | 314 | Gary Gaetti | .08 | 399 | Leon Roberts | .08 |
| 145 | Pat Putnam | .08 | 230 | Doug DeCinces | .15 | 315 | Willie Upshaw | .15 | 400 | Davey Lopes | .10 |
| 146 | Jim Acker | .15 | 231 | Lonnie Smith | .15 | 316 | Al Williams | .08 | 401 | Bill Gullickson | .08 |
| 147 | Mickey Hatcher | .08 | 232 | Ray Knight | .08 | 317 | Jorge Orta | .08 | 402 | Geoff Zahn | .08 |
| 148 | Todd Cruz | .08 | 233 | Gary Matthews | .15 | 318 | Orlando Mercado | .08 | 403 | Billy Sample | .08 |
| 149 | Tom Tellmann | .08 | 234 | Juan Bonilla | .08 | 319 | Junior Ortiz | .08 | 404 | Mike Squires | .08 |
| 150 | John Wockenfuss | .08 | 235 | Rod Scurry | .08 | 320 | Mike Proly | .08 | 405 | Craig Reynolds | .08 |
| 151 | Wade Boggs | 5.00 | 236 | Atlee Hammaker | .08 | 321 | Randy Johnson | .08 | 406 | Eric Show | .08 |

Card values from this set fluctuate considerably.

| NO. | PLAYER | MINT |
|-----|--------|------|
| 407 | John Denny | .08 |
| 408 | Dann Bilardello | .08 |
| 409 | Bruce Benedict | .08 |
| 410 | Kent Tekulve | .08 |
| 411 | Mel Hall | .15 |
| 412 | John Stuper | .08 |
| 413 | Rick Dempsey | .08 |
| 414 | Don Sutton | .20 |
| 415 | Jack Morris | .30 |
| 416 | John Tudor | .15 |
| 417 | Willie Randolph | .15 |
| 418 | Jerry Reuss | .08 |
| 419 | Don Slaught | .08 |
| 420 | Steve McCatty | .08 |
| 421 | Tim Wallach | .10 |
| 422 | Larry Parrish | .08 |
| 423 | Brian Downing | .08 |
| 424 | Britt Burns | .08 |
| 425 | David Green | .08 |
| 426 | Jerry Mumphrey | .08 |
| 427 | Ivn DeJesus | .08 |
| 428 | Mario Soto | .12 |
| 429 | Gene Richards | .08 |
| 430 | Dale Berra | .08 |
| 431 | Darrell Evans | .15 |
| 432 | Glenn Hubbard | .08 |
| 433 | Jody Davis | .12 |
| 434 | Danny Heep | .08 |
| 435 | Ed Nunez | .30 |
| 436 | Bobby Castillo | .08 |
| 437 | Ernie Whitt | .08 |
| 438 | Scott Ullger | .08 |
| 439 | Doyle Alexander | .08 |
| 440 | Domingo Ramos | .08 |
| 441 | Craig Swan | .08 |
| 442 | Warren Brusstar | .08 |
| 443 | Len Barker | .10 |
| 444 | Mike Easler | .10 |
| 445 | Renie Martin | .08 |
| 446 | Dennis Rasmussen (R) | .60 |
| 447 | Ted Power | .08 |
| 448 | Charlie Hudson (R) | .20 |
| 449 | Danny Cox (R) | .50 |
| 450 | Kevin Bass | .08 |
| 451 | Daryl Sconiers | .08 |
| 452 | Scott Fletcher | .08 |
| 453 | Bryn Smith | .08 |
| 454 | Jim Dwyer | .08 |
| 455 | Rob Picciolo | .08 |
| 456 | Enos Cabell | .08 |
| 457 | "Oil Can" Boyd (R) | 1.50 |
| 458 | Butch Wynegar | .08 |
| 459 | Burt Hooton | .08 |
| 460 | Ron Hassey | .08 |
| 461 | Danny Jackson (R) | .65 |
| 462 | Bob Kearney | .08 |
| 463 | Terry Francona | .08 |
| 464 | Wayne Tolleson | .08 |
| 465 | Mickey Rivers | .08 |
| 466 | John Wathan | .08 |
| 467 | Bill Almon | .08 |
| 468 | George Vukovich | .08 |
| 469 | Steve Kemp | .08 |
| 470 | Ken Landreaux | .08 |
| 471 | Milt Wilcox | .08 |

| NO. | PLAYER | MINT |
|-----|--------|------|
| 472 | Tippy Martinez | .08 |
| 473 | Ted Simmons | .10 |
| 474 | Tim Foli | .08 |
| 475 | George Hendrick | .10 |
| 476 | Terry Puhl | .08 |
| 477 | Von Hayes | .20 |
| 478 | Bobby Brown | .08 |
| 479 | Lee Lacy | .08 |
| 480 | Joel Youngblood | .08 |
| 481 | Jim Slaton | .08 |
| 482 | Mike Fitzgerald | .10 |
| 483 | Keith Moreland | .08 |
| 484 | Ron Roenicke | .08 |
| 485 | Luis Leal | .08 |
| 486 | Bryan Oelkers | .08 |
| 487 | Bruce Berenyi | .08 |
| 488 | LaMarr Hoyt | .15 |
| 489 | Joe Nolan | .08 |
| 490 | Marshall Edwards | .08 |
| 491 | Mike Laga | .08 |
| 492 | Rick Cerone | .08 |
| 493 | Rick Miller | .08 |
| 494 | Rick Honeycutt | .08 |
| 495 | Mike Hargrove | .08 |
| 496 | Joe Simpson | .08 |
| 497 | Keith Atherton | .08 |
| 498 | Chris Welsh | .08 |
| 499 | Bruce Kison | .08 |
| 500 | Bobby Johnson | .08 |
| 501 | Jerry Koosman | .08 |
| 502 | Frank DiPino | .08 |
| 503 | Tony Perez | .15 |
| 504 | Ken Oberkfell | .08 |
| 505 | Mark Thurmond (R) | .25 |
| 506 | Joe Price | .08 |
| 507 | Pascual Perez | .08 |
| 508 | Marvell Wynne | .15 |
| 509 | Mike Krukow | .08 |
| 510 | Dick Ruthven | .08 |
| 511 | Al Cowens | .08 |
| 512 | Cliff Johnson | .08 |
| 513 | Randy Bush | .08 |
| 514 | Sammy Stewart | .08 |
| 515 | Bill Schroeder (R) | .25 |
| 516 | Aurelio Lopez | .08 |
| 517 | Mike Brown | .08 |
| 518 | Graig Nettles | .20 |
| 519 | Dave Sax | .08 |
| 520 | Gerry Willard | .15 |
| 521 | Paul Splittorff | .08 |
| 522 | Tom Burgmeier | .08 |
| 523 | Chris Speier | .08 |
| 524 | Bobby Clark | .08 |
| 525 | George Wright | .08 |
| 526 | Dennis Lamp | .08 |
| 527 | Tony Scott | .08 |
| 528 | Ed Whitson | .08 |
| 529 | Ron Reed | .08 |
| 530 | Charlie Puleo | .08 |
| 531 | Jerry Royster | .08 |
| 532 | Don Robinson | .08 |
| 533 | Steve Trout | .08 |
| 534 | Bruce Sutter | .20 |
| 535 | Bob Horner | .20 |
| 536 | Pat Tabler | .08 |

| NO. | PLAYER | MINT |
|-----|--------|------|
| 537 | Chris Chambliss | .08 |
| 538 | Bob Ojeda | .08 |
| 539 | Alan Ashby | .08 |
| 540 | Jay Johnstone | .08 |
| 541 | Bob Dernier | .08 |
| 542 | Brook Jacoby (R) | 1.50 |
| 543 | U.L. Washington | .08 |
| 544 | Danny Darwin | .08 |
| 545 | Kiko Garcia | .08 |
| 546 | Vance Law | .08 |
| 547 | Tug McGraw | .10 |
| 548 | Dave Smith | .08 |
| 549 | Len Matuszek | .08 |
| 550 | Tom Hume | .08 |
| 551 | Dave Dravecky | .08 |
| 552 | Rick Rhoden | .08 |
| 553 | Duane Kuiper | .08 |
| 554 | Rusty Staub | .15 |
| 555 | Bill Campbell | .08 |
| 556 | Mike Torrez | .08 |
| 557 | Dave Henderson | .08 |
| 558 | Len Whitehouse | .08 |
| 559 | Barry Bonnell | .08 |
| 560 | Rick Lysander | .08 |
| 561 | Garth Iorg | .08 |
| 562 | Bryan Clark | .08 |
| 563 | Brian Giles | .08 |
| 564 | Vern Ruhle | .08 |
| 565 | Steve Bedrosian | .08 |
| 566 | Larry McWilliams | .08 |
| 567 | Jeff Leonard | .08 |
| 568 | Alan Wiggins | .08 |
| 569 | Jeff Russell | .08 |
| 570 | Salome Barojas | .08 |
| 571 | Dane Iorg | .08 |
| 572 | Bob Knepper | .08 |
| 573 | Gary Lavelle | .08 |
| 574 | Gorman Thomas | .15 |
| 575 | Manny Trillo | .08 |
| 576 | Jim Palmer | .25 |
| 577 | Dale Murray | .08 |
| 578 | Tom Brookens | .08 |
| 579 | Rich Gedman | .08 |
| 580 | Bill Doran (R) | 1.00 |
| 581 | Steve Yeager | .08 |
| 582 | Dan Spillner | .08 |
| 583 | Dan Quisenberry | .25 |
| 584 | Rance Mulliniks | .08 |
| 585 | Storm Davis | .15 |
| 586 | Dave Schmidt | .08 |
| 587 | Bill Russell | .08 |
| 588 | Pat Sheridan | .15 |
| 589 | Rafael Ramirez | .08 |
| 590 | Bud Anderson | .08 |
| 591 | George Frazier | .08 |
| 592 | Lee Tunnell | .08 |
| 593 | Kirk Gibson | .30 |
| 594 | Scott McGregor | .08 |
| 595 | Bob Bailor | .08 |
| 596 | Tom Herr | .15 |
| 597 | Luis Sanchez | .08 |
| 598 | Dave Engle | .08 |
| 599 | Craig McMurtry (R) | .15 |
| 600 | Carlos Diaz | .08 |
| 601 | Tom O'Malley | .08 |

| NO. | PLAYER | MINT |
|-----|--------|------|
| 602 | Nick Esasky (R) | .35 |
| 603 | Ron Hodges | .08 |
| 604 | Ed Vande Berg | .08 |
| 605 | Alfredo Griffin | .08 |
| 606 | Glenn Hoffman | .08 |
| 607 | Hubie Brooks | .10 |
| 608 | Richard Barnes | .08 |
| 609 | Greg Walker (R) | 1.25 |
| 610 | Ken Singleton | .08 |
| 611 | Mark Clear | .08 |
| 612 | Buck Martinez | .08 |
| 613 | Ken Griffey | .08 |
| 614 | Reid Nichols | .08 |
| 615 | Doug Sisk (R) | .15 |
| 616 | Bob Brenly | .08 |
| 617 | Joey McLaughlin | .08 |
| 618 | Glenn Wilson | .10 |
| 619 | Bob Stoddard | .08 |
| 620 | Len Sakata | .08 |
| 621 | Mike Young (R) | 1.00 |
| 622 | John Stefero | .08 |
| 623 | Carmelo Martinez (R) | .40 |
| 624 | Dave Bergman | .08 |
| 625 | Runnin' Redbirds: | .25 |
|  | David Green, Willie McGee, Lonnie Smith, Ozzie Smith |  |
| 626 | Rudy May | .08 |
| 627 | Matt Keough | .08 |
| 628 | Jose DeLeon (R) | .35 |
| 629 | Jim Essian | .08 |
| 630 | Darnell Coles | .75 |
| 631 | Mike Warren | .15 |
| 632 | Del Crandall (Mgr.) | .08 |
| 633 | Dennis Martinez | .08 |
| 634 | Mike Moore | .08 |
| 635 | Lary Sorensen | .08 |
| 636 | Ricky Nelson | .15 |
| 637 | Omar Moreno | .08 |
| 638 | Charlie Hough | .08 |
| 639 | Dennis Eckersley | .08 |
| 640 | Walt Terrell (R) | .35 |
| 641 | Denny Walling | .08 |
| 642 | Dave Anderson | .15 |
| 643 | Jose Oquendo | .08 |
| 644 | Bob Stanley | .08 |
| 645 | Dave Geisel | .08 |
| 646 | Scott Garrelts (R) | .40 |
| 647 | Gary Pettis (R) | .75 |
| 648 | Duke Snider Puzzle | .15 |
| 649 | Johnnie LeMaster | .08 |
| 650 | Dave Collins | .08 |
| 651 | The Chicken | .50 |
| — | Checklist (DK) | .12 |
| — | Checklist No. 1 | .10 |
| — | Checklist No. 2 | .10 |
| — | Checklist No. 3 | .10 |
| — | Checklist No. 4 | .10 |
| — | Checklist No. 5 | .10 |
| — | Checklist No. 6 | .10 |

**Cards From Wax Packs**

| | | |
|---|---|---|
| A | Living Legends: | 2.00 |
|  | G. Perry, R. Fingers |  |
| B | Living Legends: | 3.00 |
|  | C. Yastrzemski, J. Bench |  |

## 1985 Donruss....Complete Set of 660 Cards—Value $95.00

Features the rookie cards of Dwight Gooden, Roger Clemens, Alvin Davis, Orel Hershiser, Bret Saberhagen and Kirby Puckett. As in 1984, Donruss limited the quantity of cards printed. The *checklist* cards are *not* numbered. Four cards are printed on the bottom of gum pack display boxes; they are not part of the set. Errors found on cards 424 and 534 were corrected.

OREL HERSHISER P

KIRBY PUCKETT OF

ROGER CLEMENS P

DWIGHT GOODEN P

ALVIN DAVIS 1B

| NO. PLAYER | MINT |
|---|---|
| **No. 1 to 26 (Diamond Kings)** | |
| 1 Ryne Sandberg (DK) | .40 |
| 2 Doug DeCinces (DK) | .10 |
| 3 Rich Dotson (DK) | .10 |
| 4 Bert Blyleven (DK) | .10 |
| 5 Lou Whitaker (DK) | .20 |
| 6 Dan Quisenberry (DK) | .20 |
| 7 Don Mattingly (DK) | 5.00 |
| 8 Carney Lansford (DK) | .10 |
| 9 Frank Tanana (DK) | .10 |
| 10 Willie Upshaw (DK) | .10 |
| 11 C. Washington (DK) | .10 |
| 12 Mike Marshall (DK) | .15 |
| 13 Joaquin Andujar (DK) | .10 |
| 14 Cal Ripken (DK) | .50 |
| 15 Jim Rice (DK) | .35 |
| 16 Don Sutton (DK) | .10 |
| 17 Frank Viola (DK) | .10 |
| 18 Alvin Davis (DK) (R) | .65 |
| 19 Mario Soto (DK) | .10 |
| 20 Jose Cruz (DK) | .10 |
| 21 Charlie Lea (DK) | .10 |
| 22 Jesse Orosco (DK) | .10 |
| 23 Juan Samuel (DK) | .30 |
| 24 Tony Pena (DK) | .10 |
| 25 Tony Gwynn (DK) | .35 |
| 26 Bob Brenly (DK) | .10 |
| **No. 27 to 46 (Rated Rookies)** | |
| 27 Danny Tartabull (R) | 3.00 |
| 28 Mike Bielecki (R) | .15 |
| 29 Steve Lyons (R) | .25 |
| 30 Jeff Reed (R) | .15 |
| 31 Tony Brewer (R) | .15 |
| 32 John Morris (R) | .15 |
| 33 Daryl Boston (R) | .25 |
| 34 Alfonso Pulido (R) | .15 |
| 35 Steve Kiefer (R) | .15 |
| 36 Larry Sheets (R) | .40 |
| 37 Scott Bradley (R) | .30 |
| 38 Calvin Schiraldi (R) | 1.25 |
| 39 Shawon Dunston (R) | 1.25 |
| 40 Charlie Mitchell (R) | .15 |
| 41 Billy Hatcher (R) | .50 |
| 42 Russ Stephans (R) | .15 |
| 43 Alejandro Sanchez (R) | .15 |
| 44 Steve Jeltz (R) | .15 |
| 45 Jim Traber (R) | .40 |
| 46 Doug Loman (R) | .30 |
| 47 Eddie Murray | .50 |
| 48 Robin Yount | .30 |
| 49 Lance Parrish | .20 |
| 50 Jim Rice | .35 |
| 51 Dave Winfield | .35 |
| 52 Fernando Valenzuela | .30 |
| 53 George Brett | .60 |
| 54 Dave Kingman | .10 |
| 55 Gary Carter | .30 |
| 56 Buddy Bell | .10 |
| 57 Reggie Jackson | .40 |
| 58 Harold Baines | .20 |
| 59 Ozzie Smith | .10 |
| 60 Nolan Ryan | .25 |
| 61 Mike Schmidt | .40 |
| 62 Dave Parker | .20 |
| 63 Tony Gwynn | .50 |
| 64 Tony Pena | .15 |
| 65 Jack Clark | .25 |
| 66 Dale Murphy | .75 |
| 67 Ryne Sandberg | .50 |
| 68 Keith Hernandez | .30 |
| 69 Alvin Davis (R) | 3.00 |
| 70 Kent Hrbek | .40 |
| 71 Willie Upshaw | .10 |
| 72 Dave Engle | .05 |
| 73 Alfredo Griffin | .05 |
| 74 Jack Perconte | .05 |
| 75 Jesse Orosco | .05 |
| 76 Jody Davis | .05 |
| 77 Bob Horner | .15 |
| 78 Larry McWilliams | .05 |
| 79 Joel Youngblood | .05 |
| 80 Alan Wiggins | .10 |
| 81 Ron Oester | .05 |
| 82 Ozzie Virgil | .05 |
| 83 Ricky Horton (R) | .20 |
| 84 Bill Doran | .05 |
| 85 Rod Carew | .35 |
| 86 LaMarr Hoyt | .10 |
| 87 Tim Wallach | .10 |
| 88 Mike Flanagan | .05 |
| 89 Jim Sundberg | .05 |
| 90 Chet Lemon | .05 |
| 91 Bob Stanley | .05 |
| 92 Willie Randolph | .05 |
| 93 Bill Russell | .05 |
| 94 Julio Franco | .15 |
| 95 Dan Quisenberry | .20 |
| 96 Bill Claudill | .05 |
| 97 Bill Gullickson | .05 |
| 98 Danny Darwin | .05 |
| 99 Curt Wilkerson | .05 |
| 100 Bud Black | .05 |
| 101 Tony Phillips | .05 |
| 102 Tony Bernazard | .05 |
| 103 Jay Howell | .05 |
| 104 Burt Hooton | .05 |
| 105 Milt Wilcox | .05 |
| 106 Rich Dauer | .05 |
| 107 Don Sutton | .10 |
| 108 Mike Witt | .10 |
| 109 Bruce Sutter | .15 |
| 110 Enos Cabell | .05 |
| 111 John Denny | .05 |
| 112 Dave Dravecky | .05 |
| 113 Marvell Wynne | .05 |
| 114 John LeMaster | .05 |
| 115 Chuck Porter | .05 |
| 116 John Gibbons | .10 |
| 117 Keith Moreland | .05 |
| 118 Darnell Coles | .05 |
| 119 Dennis Lamp | .05 |
| 120 Ron Davis | .05 |
| 121 Nick Esasky | .05 |
| 122 Vance Law | .05 |
| 123 Gary Roenicke | .05 |
| 124 Bill Schroeder | .05 |
| 125 Dave Rozema | .05 |
| 126 Bobby Meacham | .05 |
| 127 Marty Barrett | .10 |
| 128 R.J. Reynolds (R) | .40 |
| 129 Ernie Camacho | .05 |
| 130 Jorge Orta | .05 |
| 131 Lary Sorensen | .05 |
| 132 Terry Francona | .05 |
| 133 Fred Lynn | .20 |
| 134 Bobby Jones | .05 |
| 135 Jerry Hairston | .05 |
| 136 Kevin Bass | .05 |
| 137 Garry Maddox | .05 |
| 138 Dave LaPoint | .05 |
| 139 Kevin McReynolds | .15 |
| 140 Wayne Krenchicki | .05 |
| 141 Rafael Ramirez | .05 |
| 142 Rod Scurry | .05 |
| 143 Greg Minton | .05 |
| 144 Tim Stoddard | .05 |
| 145 Steve Henderson | .05 |
| 146 George Bell | .10 |
| 147 Dave Meier | .10 |
| 148 Sammy Stewart | .05 |
| 149 Mark Brouhard | .05 |
| 150 Larry Herndon | .05 |
| 151 Oil Can Boyd | .05 |
| 152 Brian Dayett | .05 |
| 153 Tom Niedenfuer | .05 |
| 154 Brook Jacoby | .10 |
| 155 Onix Concepcion | .05 |
| 156 Tim Conroy | .05 |
| 157 Joe Hesketh (R) | .30 |
| 158 Brian Downing | .05 |
| 159 Tom Dunbar | .05 |
| 160 Marc Hill | .05 |
| 161 Phil Garner | .05 |
| 162 Jerry Davis | .10 |
| 163 Bill Campbell | .05 |
| 164 John Franco (R) | .40 |
| 165 Len Barker | .05 |
| 166 Benny Distefano | .10 |
| 167 George Frazier | .05 |
| 168 Tito Landrum | .05 |
| 169 Cal Ripken, Jr. | .45 |
| 170 Cecil Cooper | .15 |
| 171 Alan Trammell | .20 |
| 172 Wade Boggs | 3.00 |
| 173 Don Baylor | .15 |
| 174 Pedro Guerrero | .25 |
| 175 Frank White | .05 |
| 176 Rickey Henderson | .50 |
| 177 Charlie Lea | .05 |
| 178 Pete O'Brien | .05 |
| 179 Doug DeCinces | .10 |
| 180 Ron Kittle | .10 |
| 181 George Hendrick | .05 |
| 182 Joe Niekro | .08 |
| 183 Juan Samuel | .25 |
| 184 Mario Soto | .10 |
| 185 Goose Gossage | .15 |
| 186 Johnny Ray | .10 |
| 187 Bob Brenly | .05 |
| 188 Craig McMurtey | .05 |
| 189 Leon Durham | .15 |
| 190 Dwight Gooden (R) | 10.00 |
| 191 Barry Bonnell | .05 |
| 192 Tim Teufel | .05 |
| 193 Dave Stieb | .15 |
| 194 Mickey Hatcher | .05 |
| 195 Jesse Barfield | .10 |
| 196 Al Cowens | .05 |
| 197 Hubie Brooks | .10 |
| 198 Steve Trout | .05 |
| 199 Glenn Hubbard | .05 |
| 200 Bill Madlock | .10 |
| 201 Jeff Robinson | .10 |
| 202 Eric Show | .05 |
| 203 Dave Concepcion | .10 |
| 204 Ivan DeJesus | .05 |
| 205 Neil Allen | .05 |
| 206 Jerry Mumphrey | .05 |
| 207 Mike Brown | .05 |
| 208 Carlton Fisk | .15 |
| 209 Bryn Smith | .05 |
| 210 Tippy Martinez | .05 |
| 211 Dion James | .05 |
| 212 Willie Hernandez | .15 |
| 213 Mike Easler | .05 |
| 214 Ron Guidry | .20 |
| 215 Rick Honeycutt | .05 |
| 216 Brett Butler | .08 |
| 217 Larry Gura | .05 |
| 218 Ray Burris | .05 |
| 219 Steve Rogers | .05 |
| 220 Frank Tanana | .05 |
| 221 Ned Yost | .05 |
| 222 Bret Saberhagen (R) | 1.25 |
| 223 Mike Davis | .05 |
| 224 Bert Blyleven | .10 |
| 225 Steve Kemp | .05 |
| 226 Jerry Reuss | .05 |
| 227 Darrell Evans | .10 |
| 228 Wayne Gross | .05 |
| 229 Jim Gantner | .05 |
| 230 Bob Boone | .05 |
| 231 Lonnie Smith | .05 |
| 232 Frank DiPino | .05 |
| 233 Jerry Koosman | .05 |
| 234 Graig Nettles | .10 |
| 235 John Tudor | .10 |
| 236 John Rabb | .05 |
| 237 Rick Manning | .05 |
| 238 Mike Fitzgerald | .05 |
| 239 Gary Matthews | .05 |
| 240 Jim Presley (R) | 1.50 |
| 241 Dave Collins | .05 |
| 242 Gary Gaetti | .05 |
| 243 Dann Bilardello | .05 |
| 244 Rudy Law | .05 |
| 245 John Lowenstein | .05 |
| 246 Tom Tellman | .05 |
| 247 Howard Johnson | .05 |
| 248 Ray Fontenot | .05 |
| 249 Tony Armas | .10 |
| 250 Candy Maldonado | .05 |
| 251 Mike Jeffcoat | .05 |
| 252 Dane Iorg | .05 |
| 253 Bruce Bochte | .05 |
| 254 Pete Rose | 1.25 |
| 255 Don Aase | .05 |
| 256 George Wright | .05 |
| 257 Britt Burns | .05 |
| 258 Mike Scott | .05 |
| 259 Len Matuszek | .05 |
| 260 Dave Rucker | .05 |
| 261 Craig Lefferts | .05 |
| 262 Jay Tibbs | .25 |
| 263 Bruce Benedict | .05 |
| 264 Don Robinson | .05 |
| 265 Gary Lavelle | .05 |
| 266 Scott Sanderson | .05 |
| 267 Matt Young | .05 |
| 268 Ernie Whitt | .05 |
| 269 Houston Jimenez | .05 |
| 270 Ken Dixon | .20 |
| 271 Peter Ladd | .05 |
| 272 Juan Berenguer | .05 |
| 273 Roger Clemens (R) | 8.00 |
| 274 Rick Cerone | .05 |
| 275 Dave Anderson | .05 |
| 276 George Vukovich | .05 |
| 277 Greg Pryor | .05 |
| 278 Mike Warren | .05 |
| 279 Bob James | .05 |
| 280 Bobby Grich | .07 |
| 281 Mike Mason | .10 |
| 282 Ron Reed | .05 |
| 283 Alan Ashby | .05 |
| 284 Mark Thurmond | .05 |
| 285 Joe Lefebvre | .05 |
| 286 Ted Power | .05 |
| 287 Chris Chambliss | .05 |
| 288 Lee Tunnell | .05 |
| 289 Rich Bordi | .05 |
| 290 Glenn Brummer | .05 |
| 291 Mike Boddicker | .10 |
| 292 Rollie Fingers | .15 |
| 293 Lou Whitaker | .15 |
| 294 Dwight Evans | .15 |
| 295 Don Mattingly | 9.00 |
| 296 Mike Marshall | .15 |
| 297 Willie Wilson | .12 |
| 298 Mike Heath | .05 |
| 299 Tim Raines | .20 |
| 300 Larry Parrish | .05 |
| 301 Geoff Zahn | .05 |
| 302 Rich Dotson | .05 |
| 303 David Green | .05 |
| 304 Jose Cruz | .10 |
| 305 Steve Carlton | .25 |
| 306 Gary Redus | .05 |
| 307 Steve Garvey | .35 |
| 308 Jose DeLeon | .05 |
| 309 Randy Lerch | .05 |
| 310 Claudell Washington | .10 |
| 311 Lee Smith | .05 |
| 312 Darryl Strawberry | 1.50 |
| 313 Jim Beattie | .05 |
| 314 John Butcher | .05 |
| 315 Damaso Garcia | .07 |
| 316 Mike Smithson | .05 |
| 317 Luis Leal | .05 |
| 318 Ken Phelps | .05 |
| 319 Wally Backman | .05 |
| 320 Ron Cey | .10 |
| 321 Brad Komminsk | .10 |
| 322 Jason Thompson | .08 |
| 323 Frank Williams | .10 |
| 324 Tim Lollar | .05 |
| 325 Eric Davis (R) | 5.00 |
| 326 Von Hayes | .15 |
| 327 Andy Van Slyke | .05 |
| 328 Craig Reynolds | .05 |
| 329 Dick Schofield | .05 |
| 330 Scott Fletcher | .05 |
| 331 Jeff Reardon | .05 |
| 332 Rick Dempsey | .05 |
| 333 Ben Oglivie | .05 |
| 334 Dan Petry | .15 |
| 335 Jackie Gutierrez | .10 |
| 336 Dave Righetti | .15 |
| 337 Alejandro Pena | .05 |
| 338 Mel Hall | .05 |

Card values from this set fluctuate considerably.

| NO. PLAYER | MINT |
|---|---|
| 339 Pat Sheridan | .05 |
| 340 Keith Atherton | .05 |
| 341 David Palmer | .05 |
| 342 Gary Ward | .05 |
| 343 Dave Stewart | .05 |
| 344 Mark Gubicza (R) | .20 |
| 345 Carney Lansford | .10 |
| 346 Jerry Willard | .05 |
| 347 Ken Griffey | .05 |
| 348 Franklin Stubbs (R) | .75 |
| 349 Aurelio Lopez | .05 |
| 350 Al Bumbry | .05 |
| 351 Charlie Moore | .05 |
| 352 Luis Sanchez | .05 |
| 353 Darrell Porter | .05 |
| 354 Bill Dawley | .05 |
| 355 Charlie Hudson | .05 |
| 356 Garry Templeton | .10 |
| 357 Cecilio Guante | .05 |
| 358 Jeff Leonard | .05 |
| 359 Paul Molitor | .15 |
| 360 Ron Gardenhire | .05 |
| 361 Larry Bowa | .05 |
| 362 Bob Kearney | .05 |
| 363 Garth Iorg | .05 |
| 364 Tom Brunansky | .15 |
| 365 Brad Gulden | .05 |
| 366 Greg Walker | .10 |
| 367 Mike Young | .20 |
| 368 Rick Waits | .05 |
| 369 Doug Bair | .05 |
| 370 Bob Shirley | .05 |
| 371 Bob Ojeda | .05 |
| 372 Bob Welch | .05 |
| 373 Neal Heaton | .05 |
| 374 Dan Jackson | .05 |
| 375 Donnie Hill | .05 |
| 376 Mike Stenhouse | .05 |
| 377 Bruce Kison | .05 |
| 378 Wayne Tolleson | .05 |
| 379 Floyd Bannister | .05 |
| 380 Vern Ruhle | .05 |
| 381 Tim Corcoran | .05 |
| 382 Kurt Kepshire (R) | .15 |
| 383 Bobby Brown | .05 |
| 384 Dave Van Gorder | .05 |
| 385 Rick Mahler | .05 |
| 386 Lee Mazzilli | .05 |
| 387 Bill Laskey | .05 |
| 388 Thad Bosley | .05 |
| 389 Al Chambers | .05 |
| 390 Tony Fernandez | .05 |
| 391 Ron Washington | .05 |
| 392 Bill Swaggerty (R) | .15 |
| 393 Bob L. Gibson | .05 |
| 394 Marty Castillo | .05 |
| 395 Steve Crawford | .05 |
| 396 Clay Christiansen (R) | .15 |
| 397 Bob Bailor | .05 |
| 398 Mike Hargrove | .05 |
| 399 Charlie Leibrandt | .05 |
| 400 Tom Burgmeier | .05 |
| 401 Razor Shines (R) | .15 |
| 402 Rob Wilfong | .05 |
| 403 Tom Henke | .05 |
| 404 Al Jones (R) | .15 |
| 405 Mike LaCoss | .05 |
| 406 Luis DeLeon | .05 |
| 407 Greg Gross | .05 |
| 408 Tom Hume | .05 |
| 409 Rick Camp | .05 |
| 410 Milt May | .05 |
| 411 Henry Cotto (R) | .15 |
| 412 David Von Ohlen | .05 |
| 413 Scott McGregor | .10 |
| 414 Ted Simmons | .10 |
| 415 Jack Morris | .15 |
| 416 Bill Buckner | .10 |
| 417 Butch Wynegar | .05 |
| 418 Steve Sax | .10 |
| 419 Steve Balboni | .05 |
| 420 Dwayne Murphy | .05 |
| 421 Andre Dawson | .15 |

| NO. PLAYER | MINT |
|---|---|
| 422 Charlie Hough | .05 |
| 423 Tommy John | .10 |
| 424 Tom Seaver | 1.00 |
| (photo of Floyd Bannister) | |
| 424 Tom Seaver | 5.00 |
| 425 Tom Herr | .10 |
| 426 Terry Puhl | .05 |
| 427 Al Holland | .05 |
| 428 Eddie Milner | .05 |
| 429 Terry Kennedy | .05 |
| 430 John Candelaria | .05 |
| 431 Manny Trillo | .05 |
| 432 Ken Oberkfell | .05 |
| 433 Rick Sutcliffe | .15 |
| 434 Ron Darling | .60 |
| 435 Spike Owen | .05 |
| 436 Frank Viola | .05 |
| 437 Lloyd Moseby | .10 |
| 438 Kirby Puckett (R) | 5.00 |
| 439 Jim Clancy | .05 |
| 440 Mike Moore | .05 |
| 441 Doug Sisk | .05 |
| 442 Dennis Eckersley | .05 |
| 443 Gerald Perry | .05 |
| 444 Dale Berra | .05 |
| 445 Dusty Baker | .05 |
| 446 Ed Whitson | .05 |
| 447 Cesar Cedeno | .08 |
| 448 Rick Schu (R) | .25 |
| 449 Joaquin Andujar | .10 |
| 450 Mark Bailey (R) | .15 |
| 451 Ron Romanick (R) | .30 |
| 452 Julio Cruz | .05 |
| 453 Miguel Dilone | .05 |
| 454 Storm Davis | .05 |
| 455 Jaime Cocanower (R) | .15 |
| 456 Barbaro Garbey (R) | .15 |
| 457 Rich Gedman | .05 |
| 458 Phil Niekro | .15 |
| 459 Mike Scioscia | .05 |
| 460 Pat Tabler | .05 |
| 461 Darryl Motley | .05 |
| 462 Chris Codorili | .05 |
| 463 Doug Flynn | .05 |
| 464 Billy Sample | .05 |
| 465 Mickey Rivers | .05 |
| 466 John Wathan | .05 |
| 467 Bill Krueger | .05 |
| 468 Andre Thornton | .10 |
| 469 Rex Hudler (R) | .15 |
| 470 Sid Bream (R) | .25 |
| 471 Kirk Gibson | .20 |
| 472 John Shelby | .05 |
| 473 Moose Haas | .05 |
| 474 Doug Corbett | .05 |
| 475 Willie McGee | .30 |
| 476 Bob Knepper | .05 |
| 477 Kevin Gross | .05 |
| 478 Carmelo Martinez | .10 |
| 479 Kent Tekulve | .05 |
| 480 Chili Davis | .10 |
| 481 Bobby Clark | .05 |
| 482 Mookie Wilson | .05 |
| 483 Dave Owen (R) | .15 |
| 484 Ed Nunez | .05 |
| 485 Rance Mulliniks | .05 |
| 486 Ken Schrom | .05 |
| 487 Jeff Russell | .05 |
| 488 Tom Paciorek | .05 |
| 489 Dan Ford | .05 |
| 490 Mike Caldwell | .05 |
| 491 Scottie Earl (R) | .15 |
| 492 Jose Rijo (R) | .20 |
| 493 Bruce Hurst | .05 |
| 494 Ken Landreaux | .05 |
| 495 Mike Fischlin | .05 |
| 496 Don Slaught | .05 |
| 497 Steve McCatty | .05 |
| 498 Gary Lucas | .05 |
| 499 Gary Pettis | .10 |
| 500 Marvis Foley | .05 |
| 501 Mike Squires | .05 |
| 502 Jim Pankovitz | .10 |

| NO. PLAYER | MINT |
|---|---|
| 503 Luis Aguayo | .05 |
| 504 Ralph Citarella | .10 |
| 505 Bruce Bochy | .05 |
| 506 Bob Owchinko | .05 |
| 507 Pascual Perez | .05 |
| 508 Lee Lacy | .05 |
| 509 Atlee Hammaker | .05 |
| 510 Bob Dernier | .05 |
| 511 Ed Vande Berg | .05 |
| 512 Cliff Johnson | .05 |
| 513 Len Whitehouse | .05 |
| 514 Dennis Martinez | .05 |
| 515 Ed Romero | .05 |
| 516 Rusty Kuntz | .05 |
| 517 Rick Miller | .05 |
| 518 Dennis Rasmussen | .05 |
| 519 Steve Yeager | .05 |
| 520 Chris Bando | .05 |
| 521 U.L. Washington | .05 |
| 522 Curt Young (R) | .15 |
| 523 Angel Salazar | .05 |
| 524 Curt Kaufman (R) | .15 |
| 525 Odell Jones | .05 |
| 526 Juan Agosto | .05 |
| 527 Denny Walling | .05 |
| 528 Andy Hawkins | .05 |
| 529 Sixto Lezcano | .05 |
| 530 Skeeter Barnes | .10 |
| 531 Randy Johnson | .05 |
| 532 Jim Morrison | .05 |
| 533 Warren Brusstar | .05 |
| 534 Jeff Pendleton | .60 |
| (incorrect first name) | |
| 534 Terry Pendleton | 2.00 |
| 535 Vic Rodriguez (R) | .15 |
| 536 Bob McClure | .05 |
| 537 Dave Bergman | .05 |
| 538 Mark Clear | .05 |
| 539 Mike Pagliarulo (R) | 2.50 |
| 540 Terry Whitfield | .05 |
| 541 Joe Beckwith | .05 |
| 542 Jeff Burroughs | .05 |
| 543 Dan Schatzeder | .05 |
| 544 Donnie Scott | .10 |
| 545 Jim Slaton | .05 |
| 546 Greg Luzinski | .10 |
| 547 Mark Salas (R) | .40 |
| 548 Dave Smith | .05 |
| 549 John Wockenfuss | .05 |
| 550 Frank Pastore | .05 |
| 551 Tim Flannery | .05 |
| 552 Rick Rhoden | .05 |
| 553 Mark Davis | .05 |
| 554 Jeff Dedmon (R) | .10 |
| 555 Gary Woods | .05 |
| 556 Danny Heep | .05 |
| 557 Mark Langston (R) | .45 |
| 558 Darrell Brown | .05 |
| 559 Jimmy Key (R) | .40 |
| 560 Rick Lysander | .05 |
| 561 Doyle Alexander | .05 |
| 562 Mike Stanton | .05 |
| 563 Sid Fernandez | .75 |
| 564 Richie Hebner | .05 |
| 565 Alex Trevino | .05 |
| 566 Brian Harper | .05 |
| 567 Dan Gladden (R) | .30 |
| 568 Luis Salazar | .05 |
| 569 Tom Foley | .05 |
| 570 Larry Andersen | .05 |
| 571 Danny Cox | .10 |
| 572 Joe Sambito | .05 |
| 573 Juan Beniquez | .05 |
| 574 Joel Skinner | .05 |
| 575 Randy St. Claire | .10 |
| 576 Floyd Rayford | .05 |
| 577 Roy Howell | .05 |
| 578 John Grubb | .05 |
| 579 Ed Jurak | .05 |
| 580 John Montefusco | .05 |
| 581 Orel Hershiser (R) | 1.50 |
| 582 Tom Waddell (R) | .15 |
| 583 Mark Huismann | .05 |

| NO. PLAYER | MINT |
|---|---|
| 584 Joe Morgan | .15 |
| 585 Jim Wohlford | .05 |
| 586 Dave Schmidt | .05 |
| 587 Jeff Kunkel | .15 |
| 588 Hal McRae | .05 |
| 589 Bill Almon | .05 |
| 590 Carmen Castillo | .05 |
| 591 Omar Moreno | .05 |
| 592 Ken Howell (R) | .20 |
| 593 Tom Brookens | .05 |
| 594 Joe Nolan | .05 |
| 595 Willie Lozado | .10 |
| 596 Tom Nieto | .10 |
| 597 Walt Terrell | .05 |
| 598 Al Oliver | .10 |
| 599 Shane Rawley | .05 |
| 600 Denny Gonzalez | .10 |
| 601 Mark Grant | .10 |
| 602 Mike Armstrong | .05 |
| 603 George Foster | .15 |
| 604 Davey Lopes | .05 |
| 605 Salome Barojas | .05 |
| 606 Roy Lee Jackson | .05 |
| 607 Pete Filson | .05 |
| 608 Duane Walker | .05 |
| 609 Glenn Wilson | .10 |
| 610 Rafael Santana | .10 |
| 611 Roy Smith | .15 |
| 612 Ruppert Jones | .05 |
| 613 Joe Cowley | .05 |
| 614 Al Nipper (R) | .20 |
| 615 Gene Nelson | .05 |
| 616 Joe Carter | .60 |
| 617 Ray Knight | .05 |
| 618 Chuck Rainey | .05 |
| 619 Dan Driessen | .05 |
| 620 Daryl Sconiers | .05 |
| 621 Bill Stein | .05 |
| 622 Roy Smalley | .05 |
| 623 Ed Lynch | .05 |
| 624 Jeff Stone (R) | .30 |
| 625 Bruce Berenyi | .05 |
| 626 Kelvin Chapman (R) | .15 |
| 627 Joe Price | .05 |
| 628 Steve Bedrosian | .05 |
| 629 Vic Mata | .15 |
| 630 Mike Krukow | .05 |
| 631 Phil Bradley (R) | 1.25 |
| 632 Jim Gott | .05 |
| 633 Randy Bush | .05 |
| 634 Tom Browning (R) | 1.00 |
| 635 Lou Gehrig Puzzle | .10 |
| 636 Reid Nichols | .05 |
| 637 Dan Pasqua (R) | 2.50 |
| 638 German Rivera | .10 |
| 639 Don Schulze | .10 |
| 640 Mike Jones | .10 |
| 641 Pete Rose (Mgr.) | .75 |
| 642 Wade Rowdon | .10 |
| 643 Jerry Narron | .05 |
| 644 Darrell Miller | .15 |
| 645 Tim Hulett (R) | .20 |
| 646 Andy McGaffigan | .05 |
| 647 Kurt Bevacqua | .05 |
| 648 John Russell (R) | .20 |
| 649 Ron Robinson | .15 |
| 650 Donnie Moore | .05 |
| 651 Two For the Title: D. Winfield, D. Mattingly | 2.00 |
| 652 Tim Laudner | .05 |
| 653 Steve Farr | .10 |
| — Checklist (DK) | .10 |
| — Checklist No. 1 | .08 |
| — Checklist No. 2 | .08 |
| — Checklist No. 3 | .08 |
| — Checklist No. 4 | .08 |
| — Checklist No. 5 | .08 |
| — Checklist No. 6 | .08 |
| **Gum Pack "Display Box" Cards** | |
| PC1 Dwight Gooden | 4.00 |
| PC2 Ryne Sandberg | .50 |
| PC3 Ron Kittle | .25 |
| — Lou Gehrig Puzzle | .15 |

Card values from this set fluctuate considerably.

# 1985 Donruss Highlights....Complete Set of 56 Cards—Value $25.00

Features special events and milestones of the 1985 season from Opening Day to the last day of the regular season. Cards are numbered in chronological order. Donruss limited production, causing speculation by dealers and investors. The price of the set skyrocketed from $5 to $40 within a few months after it was issued. The entire set was packaged in a printed box, and distributed exclusively through card dealers.

| NO. PLAYER | MINT |
|---|---|
| 1 Tom Seaver | .60 |
|    Opening Day Record | |
| 2 Rollie Fingers: | .25 |
|    Establishes AL Save Mark | |
| 3 Mike Davis: | .20 |
|    AL Player of the Month | |
| 4 Charlie Leibrandt: | .20 |
|    AL Pitcher of the Month | |
| 5 Dale Murphy: | 1.25 |
|    NL Player of the Month | |
| 6 Fernando Valenzuela: | .50 |
|    NL Pitcher of the Month | |
| 7 Larry Bowa: | .20 |
|    NL Shortstop Record | |
| 8 Dave Concepcion: | .20 |
|    Joins Reds 2000 Hit Club | |
| 9 Tony Perez: | .20 |
|    Eldest Grand Slammer | |
| 10 Pete Rose: | 2.00 |
|    NL Career Run Leader | |
| 11 George Brett: | 1.35 |
|    AL Player of the Month | |
| 12 Dave Stieb: | .20 |
|    AL Pitcher of the Month | |
| 13 Dave Parker: | .50 |
|    NL Player of the Month | |
| 14 Andy Hawkins: | .20 |
|    NL Pitcher of the Month | |

| NO. PLAYER | MINT |
|---|---|
| 15 Andy Hawkins: | .20 |
|    11th Straight Win | |
| 16 Von Hayes: | .20 |
|    Two Homers in First Inning | |
| 17 Rickey Henderson: | 1.25 |
|    AL Player of the Month | |
| 18 Jay Howell: | .20 |
|    AL Pitcher of the Month | |
| 19 Pedro Guerero: | .40 |
|    NL Player of the Month | |
| 20 John Tudor: | .20 |
|    NL Pitcher of the Month | |
| 21 Hernandez/Carter | .40 |
|    Marathon Game Iron Men | |
| 22 Nolan Ryan: | .40 |
|    Records 4000th K | |
| 23 LaMarr Hoyt: | .20 |
|    All-Star Game MVP | |
| 24 Oddibe McDowell: | 1.00 |
|    1st Ranger to Hit for Cycle | |
| 25 George Brett: | 1.35 |
|    AL Player of the Month | |
| 26 Bret Saberhagen: | .50 |
|    AL Pitcher of the Month | |
| 27 Keith Hernandez: | .40 |
|    NL Player of the Month | |
| 28 Fernando Valenzuela: | .50 |
|    NL Pitcher of the Month | |

| NO. PLAYER | MINT |
|---|---|
| 29 McGee/Coleman: | 1.50 |
|    Record Base Stealers | |
| 30 Tom Seaver: | .50 |
|    300th Career Win | |
| 31 Rod Carew: | .50 |
|    Strokes 3000th Hit | |
| 32 Dwight Gooden: | 2.50 |
|    Establishes Met Record | |
| 33 Dwight Gooden: | 2.50 |
|    Strikeout Milestone | |
| 34 Eddie Murray | .75 |
|    Explodes for 9 RBI | |
| 35 Don Baylor: | .20 |
|    Al Career HBP Leader | |
| 36 Don Mattingly: | 4.00 |
|    AL Player of the Month | |
| 37 Dave Righetti: | .20 |
|    AL Pitcher of the Month | |
| 38 Willie McGee | .50 |
|    NL Player of the Month | |
| 39 Shane Rawley: | .20 |
|    NL Pitcher of the Month | |
| 40 Pete Rose: | 2.50 |
|    Ty-Breaking Hit | |
| 41 Andre Dawson: | .40 |
|    Hits 3 HR's, Drives in 8 Runs | |
| 42 Rickey Henderson: | 1.25 |
|    Sets Yankee Theft Mark | |

| NO. PLAYER | MINT |
|---|---|
| 43 Tom Browning: | .60 |
|    20 Wins in Rookie Season | |
| 44 Don Mattingly: | 4.00 |
|    Yankee Milestone for Hits | |
| 45 Don Mattingly: | 4.00 |
|    AL Player of the Month | |
| 46 Charlie Leibrandt: | .20 |
|    AL Pitcher of the Month | |
| 47 Gary Carter: | .50 |
|    NL Player of the Month | |
| 48 Dwight Gooden: | 3.00 |
|    NL Pitcher of the Month | |
| 49 Wade Boggs: | 3.00 |
|    Record Setter | |
| 50 Phil Niekro: | .30 |
|    Hurls Shutout for 300th Win | |
| 51 Darrell Evans: | .20 |
|    Venerable HR King | |
| 52 Willie McGee: | .50 |
|    NL Switch-Hitting Record | |
| 53 Dave Winfield: | .50 |
|    Equals DiMaggio Feat | |
| 54 Vince Coleman: | 3.00 |
|    Donruss—National League Rookie of the Year | |
| 55 Ozzie Guillen: | .50 |
|    Donruss—American League Rookie of the Year | |
| 56 Highlights Checklist | .20 |

# 1986 Donruss....Complete Set of 660 Cards—Value $60.00

Features the rookie cards of Jose Canseco and Vince Coleman. Donruss limited production. Three cards (PC-4 to PC-6) and an Aaron puzzle card were printed on the bottom of gum pack display boxes. Three other cards (PC-7 to PC-9) and the Aaron puzzle card were printed on the bottom of display boxes of 1986 All-Star cards. These cards are not part of the set. The *checklist* cards are *not* numbered.

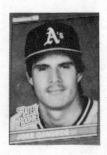 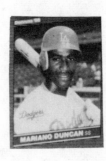   

# 1986 Donruss (Continued)

| NO. | PLAYER | MINT |
|-----|--------|------|
| **No. 1 to 26—Diamond Kings** | | |
| 1 | Kirk Gibson (DK) | .25 |
| 2 | Goose Gossage (DK) | .15 |
| 3 | Willie McGee (DK) | .30 |
| 4 | George Bell (DK) | .10 |
| 5 | Tony Armas (DK) | .10 |
| 6 | Chili Davis (DK) | .10 |
| 7 | Cecil Cooper (DK) | .15 |
| 8 | Mike Boddicker (DK) | .10 |
| 9 | Davey Lopes (DK) | .10 |
| 10 | Bill Doran (DK) | .10 |
| 11 | Bret Saberhagen (DK) | .30 |
| 12 | Brett Butler (DK) | .10 |
| 13 | Harold Baines (DK) | .20 |
| 14 | Mike Davis (DK) | .10 |
| 15 | Tony Perez (DK) | .15 |
| 16 | Willie Randolph (DK) | .10 |
| 17 | Bob Boone (DK) | .10 |
| 18 | Orel Hershiser (DK) | .35 |
| 19 | Johnny Ray (DK) | .10 |
| 20 | Gary Ward (DK) | .10 |
| 21 | Rick Mahler (DK) | .10 |
| 22 | Phil Bradley (DK) | .20 |
| 23 | Jerry Koosman (DK) | .10 |
| 24 | Tom Brunansky (DK) | .10 |
| 25 | Andre Dawson (DK) | .20 |
| 26 | Dwight Gooden (DK) | 1.25 |
| **No. 27 to 46 (Rated Rookies)** | | |
| 27 | Kal Daniels | .25 |
| 28 | Fred McGriff (R) | .15 |
| 29 | Cory Snyder (R) | 2.00 |
| 30 | Jose Guzman (R) | .25 |
| 31 | Ty Gainey (R) | .20 |
| 32 | Johnny Abrego (R) | .15 |
| 33 | Andres Galarraga (R) | .75 |
| 34 | Dave Shipanoff (R) | .15 |
| 35 | Mark McLemore (R) | .15 |
| 36 | Marty Clary (R) | .15 |
| 37 | Paul O'Neill (R) | .15 |
| 38 | Danny Tartabull (R) | .60 |
| 39 | Jose Canseco (R) | 9.00 |
| 40 | Juan Nieves (R) | .75 |
| 41 | Lance McCullers (R) | .25 |
| 42 | Rick Surhoff (R) | .15 |
| 43 | Todd Worrell (R) | 1.50 |
| 44 | Bob Kipper (R) | .20 |
| 45 | John Habyan (R) | .15 |
| 46 | Mike Woodard (R) | .15 |
| 47 | Mike Boddicker | .10 |
| 48 | Robin Yount | .30 |
| 49 | Lou Whitaker | .15 |
| 50 | Oil Can Boyd | .05 |
| 51 | Rickey Henderson | .35 |
| 52 | Mike Marshall | .10 |
| 53 | George Brett | .50 |
| 54 | Dave Kingman | .10 |
| 55 | Hubie Brooks | .10 |
| 56 | Oddibe McDowell | .40 |
| 57 | Doug DeCinces | .10 |
| 58 | Britt Burns | .05 |
| 59 | Ozzie Smith | .10 |
| 60 | Jose Cruz | .10 |
| 61 | Mike Schmidt | .35 |
| 62 | Pete Rose | .75 |
| 63 | Steve Garvey | .35 |
| 64 | Tony Pena | .10 |
| 65 | Chili Davis | .10 |
| 66 | Dale Murphy | .50 |
| 67 | Ryne Sandberg | .30 |
| 68 | Gary Carter | .30 |
| 69 | Alvin Davis | .15 |
| 70 | Kent Hrbek | .15 |
| 71 | George Bell | .10 |
| 72 | Kirby Puckett | .75 |
| 73 | Lloyd Moseby | .10 |
| 74 | Bob Kearney | .05 |
| 75 | Dwight Gooden | 2.50 |
| 76 | Gary Matthews | .05 |
| 77 | Rick Mahler | .05 |
| 78 | Benny Distefano | .05 |
| 79 | Jeff Leonard | .05 |
| 80 | Kevin McReynolds | .05 |
| 81 | Ron Oester | .05 |
| 82 | John Russell | .05 |
| 83 | Tommy Herr | .10 |

| NO. | PLAYER | MINT |
|-----|--------|------|
| 84 | Jerry Mumphrey | .05 |
| 85 | Ron Romanick | .05 |
| 86 | Daryl Boston | .05 |
| 87 | Andre Dawson | .20 |
| 88 | Eddie Murray | .40 |
| 89 | Dion James | .05 |
| 90 | Chet Lemon | .05 |
| 91 | Bob Stanley | .05 |
| 92 | Willie Randolph | .05 |
| 93 | Mike Scioscia | .05 |
| 94 | Tom Waddell | .05 |
| 95 | Danny Jackson | .05 |
| 96 | Mike Davis | .05 |
| 97 | Mike Fitzgerald | .05 |
| 98 | Gary Ward | .05 |
| 99 | Pete O'Brien | .05 |
| 100 | Bret Saberhagen | .30 |
| 101 | Alfredo Griffin | .05 |
| 102 | Brett Butler | .05 |
| 103 | Ron Guidry | .15 |
| 104 | Jerry Reuss | .05 |
| 105 | Jack Morris | .15 |
| 106 | Rick Dempsey | .05 |
| 107 | Ray Burris | .05 |
| 108 | Brian Downing | .05 |
| 109 | Willie McGee | .20 |
| 110 | Bill Doran | .05 |
| 111 | Kent Tekulve | .05 |
| 112 | Tony Gwynn | .25 |
| 113 | Marvell Wynne | .05 |
| 114 | David Green | .05 |
| 115 | Jim Gantner | .05 |
| 116 | George Foster | .15 |
| 117 | Steve Trout | .05 |
| 118 | Mark Langston | .05 |
| 119 | Tony Fernandez | .10 |
| 120 | John Butcher | .05 |
| 121 | Ron Robinson | .05 |
| 122 | Dan Spillner | .05 |
| 123 | Mike Young | .15 |
| 124 | Paul Molitor | .10 |
| 125 | Kirk Gibson | .20 |
| 126 | Ken Griffey | .05 |
| 127 | Tony Armas | .10 |
| 128 | Mariano Duncan (R) | .50 |
| 129 | Pat Tabler | .05 |
| 130 | Frank White | .05 |
| 131 | Carney Lansford | .10 |
| 132 | Vance Law | .05 |
| 133 | Dick Schofield | .05 |
| 134 | Wayne Tolleson | .05 |
| 135 | Greg Walker | .10 |
| 136 | Denny Walling | .05 |
| 137 | Ozzie Virgil | .05 |
| 138 | Ricky Horton | .05 |
| 139 | LaMarr Hoyt | .10 |
| 140 | Wayne Krenchicki | .05 |
| 141 | Glenn Hubbard | .05 |
| 142 | Cecilio Guante | .05 |
| 143 | Mike Krukow | .05 |
| 144 | Lee Smith | .05 |
| 145 | Ed Nunez | .05 |
| 146 | Dave Stieb | .15 |
| 147 | Mike Smithson | .05 |
| 148 | Ken Dixon | .05 |
| 149 | Danny Darwin | .05 |
| 150 | Chris Pittaro | .15 |
| 151 | Bill Buckner | .10 |
| 152 | Mike Pagliarulo | .05 |
| 153 | Bill Russell | .05 |
| 154 | Brook Jacoby | .10 |
| 155 | Pat Sheridan | .05 |
| 156 | Mike Gallego | .05 |
| 157 | Jim Wohlford | .05 |
| 158 | Gary Pettis | .10 |
| 159 | Toby Harrah | .05 |
| 160 | Rich Dotson | .05 |
| 161 | Bob Knepper | .05 |
| 162 | Dave Dravecky | .05 |
| 163 | Greg Gross | .05 |
| 164 | Eric Davis | .60 |
| 165 | Gerald Perry | .05 |
| 166 | Rick Rhoden | .05 |
| 167 | Keith Moreland | .05 |

| NO. | PLAYER | MINT |
|-----|--------|------|
| 168 | Jack Clark | .15 |
| 169 | Storm Davis | .05 |
| 170 | Cecil Cooper | .15 |
| 171 | Alan Trammell | .15 |
| 172 | Roger Clemens | 2.50 |
| 173 | Don Mattingly | 3.00 |
| 174 | Pedro Guerrero | .25 |
| 175 | Willie Wilson | .15 |
| 176 | Dwayne Murphy | .05 |
| 177 | Tim Raines | .20 |
| 178 | Larry Parrish | .05 |
| 179 | Mike Witt | .10 |
| 180 | Harold Baines | .20 |
| 181 | Vince Coleman (R) | 2.00 |
| 182 | Jeff Heathcock (R) | .15 |
| 183 | Steve Carlton | .30 |
| 184 | Mario Soto | .10 |
| 185 | Goose Gossage | .15 |
| 186 | Johnny Ray | .10 |
| 187 | Dan Gladden | .05 |
| 188 | Bob Horner | .10 |
| 189 | Rick Sutcliffe | .15 |
| 190 | Keith Hernandez | .25 |
| 191 | Phil Bradley | .20 |
| 192 | Tom Brunansky | .10 |
| 193 | Jesse Barfield | .10 |
| 194 | Frank Viola | .05 |
| 195 | Willie Upshaw | .10 |
| 196 | Jim Beattie | .05 |
| 197 | Darryl Strawberry | .50 |
| 198 | Ron Cey | .10 |
| 199 | Steve Bedrosian | .05 |
| 200 | Steve Kemp | .05 |
| 201 | Manny Trillo | .05 |
| 202 | Garry Templeton | .05 |
| 203 | Dave Parker | .20 |
| 204 | John Denny | .05 |
| 205 | Terry Pendleton | .05 |
| 206 | Terry Puhl | .05 |
| 207 | Bobby Grich | .05 |
| 208 | Ozzie Guillen (R) | .50 |
| 209 | Jeff Reardon | .05 |
| 210 | Cal Ripken, Jr. | .40 |
| 211 | Bill Schroeder | .05 |
| 212 | Dan Petry | .10 |
| 213 | Jim Rice | .25 |
| 214 | Dave Righetti | .10 |
| 215 | Fernando Valenzuela | .25 |
| 216 | Julio Franco | .10 |
| 217 | Darryl Motley | .05 |
| 218 | Dave Collins | .05 |
| 219 | Tim Wallach | .05 |
| 220 | George Wright | .05 |
| 221 | Tommy Dunbar | .05 |
| 222 | Steve Balboni | .05 |
| 223 | Jay Howell | .05 |
| 224 | Joe Carter | .05 |
| 225 | Ed Whitson | .05 |
| 226 | Orel Hershiser | .30 |
| 227 | Willie Hernandez | .15 |
| 228 | Lee Lacy | .05 |
| 229 | Rollie Fingers | .10 |
| 230 | Bob Boone | .05 |
| 231 | Joaquin Andujar | .10 |
| 232 | Craig Reynolds | .05 |
| 233 | Shane Rawley | .05 |
| 234 | Eric Show | .05 |
| 235 | Jose DeLeon | .05 |
| 236 | Jose Uribe (R) | .15 |
| 237 | Moose Haas | .05 |
| 238 | Wally Backman | .05 |
| 239 | Dennis Eckersley | .05 |
| 240 | Mike Moore | .05 |
| 241 | Damaso Garcia | .05 |
| 242 | Tim Teufel | .05 |
| 243 | Dave Concepcion | .05 |
| 244 | Floyd Bannister | .05 |
| 245 | Fred Lynn | .15 |
| 246 | Charlie Moore | .05 |
| 247 | Walt Terrell | .05 |
| 248 | Dave Winfield | .30 |
| 249 | Dwight Evans | .10 |
| 250 | Dennis Powell | .10 |
| 251 | Andre Thornton | .05 |

| NO. | PLAYER | MINT |
|-----|--------|------|
| 252 | Onix Concepcion | .05 |
| 253 | Mike Heath | .05 |
| 254 | David Palmer | .05 |
| 255 | Donnie Moore | .05 |
| 256 | Curtis Wilkerson | .05 |
| 257 | Julio Cruz | .05 |
| 258 | Nolan Ryan | .25 |
| 259 | Jeff Stone | .05 |
| 260 | John Tudor | .15 |
| 261 | Mark Thurmond | .05 |
| 262 | Jay Tibbs | .05 |
| 263 | Rafael Ramirez | .05 |
| 264 | Larry McWilliams | .05 |
| 265 | Mark Davis | .05 |
| 266 | Bob Dernier | .05 |
| 267 | Matt Young | .05 |
| 268 | Jim Clancy | .05 |
| 269 | Mickey Hatcher | .05 |
| 270 | Sammy Stewart | .05 |
| 271 | Bob Gibson | .05 |
| 272 | Nelson Simmons (R) | .30 |
| 273 | Rich Gedman | .05 |
| 274 | Butch Wynegar | .05 |
| 275 | Ken Howell | .05 |
| 276 | Mel Hall | .05 |
| 277 | Jim Sundberg | .05 |
| 278 | Chris Codiroli | .05 |
| 279 | H. Winningham (R) | .15 |
| 280 | Rod Carew | .25 |
| 281 | Don Slaught | .05 |
| 282 | Scott Fletcher | .05 |
| 283 | Bill Dawley | .05 |
| 284 | Andy Hawkins | .05 |
| 285 | Glenn Wilson | .10 |
| 286 | Nick Esasky | .05 |
| 287 | Claudell Washington | .05 |
| 288 | Lee Mazzilli | .05 |
| 289 | Jody Davis | .05 |
| 290 | Darrell Porter | .05 |
| 291 | Scott McGregor | .05 |
| 292 | Ted Simmons | .10 |
| 293 | Aurelio Lopez | .05 |
| 294 | Marty Barrett | .05 |
| 295 | Dale Berra | .05 |
| 296 | Greg Brock | .05 |
| 297 | Charlie Leibrandt | .05 |
| 298 | Bill Krueger | .05 |
| 299 | Bryn Smith | .05 |
| 300 | Burt Hooton | .05 |
| 301 | Stu Cliburn (R) | .20 |
| 302 | Luis Salazar | .05 |
| 303 | Ken Dayley | .05 |
| 304 | Frank DiPino | .05 |
| 305 | Von Hayes | .15 |
| 306 | Gary Redus | .05 |
| 307 | Craig Lefferts | .05 |
| 308 | Sam Khalifa | .15 |
| 309 | Scott Garrelts | .05 |
| 310 | Rick Cerone | .05 |
| 311 | Shawon Dunston | .05 |
| 312 | Howard Johnson | .05 |
| 313 | Jim Presley | .35 |
| 314 | Gary Gaetti | .05 |
| 315 | Luis Leal | .05 |
| 316 | Mark Salas | .05 |
| 317 | Bill Caudill | .05 |
| 318 | Dave Henderson | .05 |
| 319 | Rafael Santana | .05 |
| 320 | Leon Durham | .15 |
| 321 | Bruce Sutter | .15 |
| 322 | Jason Thompson | .05 |
| 323 | Bob Brenly | .05 |
| 324 | Carmelo Martinez | .05 |
| 325 | Eddie Milner | .05 |
| 326 | Juan Samuel | .10 |
| 327 | Tom Nieto | .05 |
| 328 | Dave Smith | .05 |
| 329 | Urbano Lugo (R) | .15 |
| 330 | Joel Skinner | .05 |
| 331 | Bill Gullickson | .05 |
| 332 | Floyd Rayford | .05 |
| 333 | Ben Oglivie | .05 |
| 334 | Lance Parrish | .15 |
| 335 | Jackie Gutierrez | .05 |
| 336 | Dennis Rasmussen | .05 |

Card values from this set fluctuate considerably.

| NO. | PLAYER | MINT |
|-----|--------|------|
| 337 | Terry Whitfield | .05 |
| 338 | Neal Heaton | .05 |
| 339 | Jorge Orta | .05 |
| 340 | Donnie Hill | .05 |
| 341 | Joe Hesketh | .10 |
| 342 | Charlie Hough | .05 |
| 343 | Dave Rozema | .05 |
| 344 | Greg Pryor | .05 |
| 345 | Mickey Tettleton (R) | .10 |
| 346 | George Vukovich | .05 |
| 347 | Don Baylor | .10 |
| 348 | Carlos Diaz | .05 |
| 349 | Barbaro Garbey | .05 |
| 350 | Larry Sheets | .05 |
| 351 | Teddy Higuera (R) | 1.25 |
| 352 | Juan Beniquez | .05 |
| 353 | Bob Forsch | .05 |
| 354 | Mark Bailey | .05 |
| 355 | Larry Andersen | .05 |
| 356 | Terry Kennedy | .05 |
| 357 | Don Robinson | .05 |
| 358 | Jim Gott | .05 |
| 359 | Earnest Riles (R) | .50 |
| 360 | John Christensen | .15 |
| 361 | Ray Fontenot | .05 |
| 362 | Spike Owen | .05 |
| 363 | Jim Acker | .05 |
| 364 | Ron Davis | .05 |
| 365 | Tom Hume | .05 |
| 366 | Carlton Fisk | .15 |
| 367 | Nate Snell (R) | .15 |
| 368 | Rick Manning | .05 |
| 369 | Darrell Evans | .10 |
| 370 | Ron Hassey | .05 |
| 371 | Wade Boggs | 2.50 |
| 372 | Rick Honeycutt | .05 |
| 373 | Chris Bando | .05 |
| 374 | Bud Black | .05 |
| 375 | Steve Henderson | .05 |
| 376 | Charlie Lea | .05 |
| 377 | Reggie Jackson | .30 |
| 378 | Dave Schmidt | .05 |
| 379 | Bob James | .05 |
| 380 | Glenn Davis | 1.50 |
| 381 | Tim Corcoran | .05 |
| 382 | Danny Cox | .10 |
| 383 | Tim Flannery | .05 |
| 384 | Tom Browning | .15 |
| 385 | Rick Camp | .05 |
| 386 | Jim Morrison | .05 |
| 387 | Dave LaPoint | .05 |
| 388 | Davey Lopes | .05 |
| 389 | Al Cowens | .05 |
| 390 | Doyle Alexander | .05 |
| 391 | Tim Laudner | .05 |
| 392 | Don Aase | .05 |
| 393 | Jaime Cocanower | .05 |
| 394 | Randy O'Neal | .05 |
| 395 | Mike Easler | .05 |
| 396 | Scott Bradley | .05 |
| 397 | Tom Niedenfuer | .05 |
| 398 | Jerry Willard | .05 |
| 399 | Lonnie Smith | .07 |
| 400 | Bruce Bochte | .05 |
| 401 | Terry Francona | .05 |
| 402 | Jim Slaton | .05 |
| 403 | Bill Stein | .05 |
| 404 | Timmy Hulett | .05 |
| 405 | Alan Ashby | .05 |
| 406 | Tim Stoddard | .05 |
| 407 | Garry Maddox | .05 |
| 408 | Ted Power | .05 |
| 409 | Len Barker | .05 |
| 410 | Denny Gonzalez | .05 |
| 411 | George Frazier | .05 |
| 412 | Andy Van Slyke | .05 |
| 413 | Jim Dwyer | .05 |
| 414 | Paul Householder | .05 |
| 415 | Alejandro Sanchez | .05 |
| 416 | Steve Crawford | .05 |
| 417 | Dan Pasqua | .25 |
| 418 | Enos Cabell | .05 |
| 419 | Mike Jones | .05 |
| 420 | Steve Kiefer | .05 |
| 421 | Tim Burke (R) | .25 |

| NO. | PLAYER | MINT |
|-----|--------|------|
| 422 | Mike Mason | .05 |
| 423 | Ruppert Jones | .05 |
| 424 | Jerry Hairston | .05 |
| 425 | Tito Landrum | .05 |
| 426 | Jeff Calhoun (R) | .10 |
| 427 | Don Carman (R) | .25 |
| 428 | Tony Perez | .10 |
| 429 | Jerry Davis | .05 |
| 430 | Bob Walk | .05 |
| 431 | Brad Wellman | .05 |
| 432 | Terry Forster | .05 |
| 433 | Billy Hatcher | .05 |
| 434 | Clint Hurdle | .05 |
| 435 | Ivan Calderon (R) | .20 |
| 436 | Pete Filson | .05 |
| 437 | Tom Henke | .05 |
| 438 | Dave Engle | .05 |
| 439 | Tom Filer | .05 |
| 440 | Gorman Thomas | .10 |
| 441 | Rick Aguilera (R) | .25 |
| 442 | Scott Sanderson | .05 |
| 443 | Jeff Dedmon | .05 |
| 444 | Joe Orsulak (R) | .25 |
| 445 | Atlee Hammaker | .05 |
| 446 | Jerry Royster | .05 |
| 447 | Buddy Bell | .10 |
| 448 | Dave Rucker | .05 |
| 449 | Ivan DeJesus | .05 |
| 450 | Jim Pankovits | .05 |
| 451 | Jerry Narron | .05 |
| 452 | Bryan Little | .05 |
| 453 | Gary Lucas | .05 |
| 454 | Dennis Martinez | .05 |
| 455 | Ed Romero | .05 |
| 456 | Bob Melvin (R) | .10 |
| 457 | Glenn Hoffman | .05 |
| 458 | Bob Shirley | .05 |
| 459 | Bob Welch | .05 |
| 460 | Carmen Castillo | .05 |
| 461 | Dave Leeper (R) | .10 |
| 462 | Tim Birtsas (R) | .15 |
| 463 | Randy St. Claire | .05 |
| 464 | Chris Welsh | .05 |
| 465 | Greg Harris | .05 |
| 466 | Lynn Jones | .05 |
| 467 | Dusty Baker | .05 |
| 468 | Roy Smith | .05 |
| 469 | Andre Robertson | .05 |
| 470 | Ken Landreaux | .05 |
| 471 | Dave Bergman | .05 |
| 472 | Gary Roenicke | .05 |
| 473 | Pete Vuckovich | .05 |
| 474 | Kirk McCaskill (R) | .90 |
| 475 | Jeff Lahti | .05 |
| 476 | Mike Scott | .35 |
| 477 | Darren Daulton (R) | .25 |
| 478 | Graig Nettles | .10 |
| 479 | Bill Almon | .05 |
| 480 | Greg Minton | .05 |
| 481 | Randy Ready | .05 |
| 482 | Len Dykstra (R) | 1.50 |
| 483 | Thad Bosley | .05 |
| 484 | Harold Reynolds (R) | .15 |
| 485 | Al Oliver | .10 |
| 486 | Roy Smalley | .05 |
| 487 | John Franco | .05 |
| 488 | Juan Agosto | .05 |
| 489 | Al Pardo | .15 |
| 490 | Bill Wegman (R) | .15 |
| 491 | Frank Tanana | .05 |
| 492 | Brian Fisher (R) | .30 |
| 493 | Mark Clear | .05 |
| 494 | Len Matuszek | .05 |
| 495 | Ramon Romero (R) | .10 |
| 496 | John Wathan | .05 |
| 497 | Rob Picciolo | .05 |
| 498 | U.L. Washington | .05 |
| 499 | John Candelaria | .05 |
| 500 | Duane Walker | .05 |
| 501 | Gene Nelson | .05 |
| 502 | John Mizerock | .05 |
| 503 | Luis Aguayo | .05 |
| 504 | Kurt Kepshire | .05 |
| 505 | Ed Wojna (R) | .15 |
| 506 | Joe Price | .05 |

| NO. | PLAYER | MINT |
|-----|--------|------|
| 507 | Milt Thompson (R) | .25 |
| 508 | Junior Ortiz | .05 |
| 509 | Vida Blue | .05 |
| 510 | Steve Engel (R) | .10 |
| 511 | Karl Best (R) | .10 |
| 512 | Cecil Fielder (R) | .25 |
| 513 | Frank Eufemia (R) | .15 |
| 514 | Tippy Martinez | .05 |
| 515 | Billy Robidoux (R) | .50 |
| 516 | Bill Scherrer | .05 |
| 517 | Bruce Hurst | .05 |
| 518 | Rich Bordi | .05 |
| 519 | Steve Yeager | .05 |
| 520 | Tony Bernazard | .05 |
| 521 | Hal McRae | .05 |
| 522 | Jose Rijo | .05 |
| 523 | Mitch Webster (R) | .60 |
| 524 | Jack Howell (R) | .35 |
| 525 | Alan Bannister | .05 |
| 526 | Ron Kittle | .10 |
| 527 | Phil Garner | .05 |
| 528 | Kurt Bevacqua | .05 |
| 529 | Kevin Gross | .05 |
| 530 | Bo Diaz | .05 |
| 531 | Ken Oberkfell | .05 |
| 532 | Rick Reuschel | .05 |
| 533 | Ron Meridith (R) | .10 |
| 534 | Steve Braun | .05 |
| 535 | Wayne Gross | .05 |
| 536 | Ray Searage | .05 |
| 537 | Tom Brookens | .05 |
| 538 | Al Nipper | .05 |
| 539 | Billy Sample | .05 |
| 540 | Steve Sax | .10 |
| 541 | Dan Quisenberry | .15 |
| 542 | Tony Phillips | .05 |
| 543 | Floyd Youmans (R) | 1.00 |
| 544 | Steve Buechele (R) | .15 |
| 545 | Craig Gerber (R) | .10 |
| 546 | Joe DeSa (R) | .15 |
| 547 | Brian Harper | .05 |
| 548 | Kevin Bass | .05 |
| 549 | Tom Foley | .05 |
| 550 | Dave Van Gorder | .05 |
| 551 | Bruce Bochy | .05 |
| 552 | R.J. Reynolds | .05 |
| 553 | Chris Brown (R) | 1.25 |
| 554 | Bruce Benedict | .05 |
| 555 | Warren Brusstar | .05 |
| 556 | Danny Heep | .05 |
| 557 | Darnell Coles | .05 |
| 558 | Greg Gagne | .05 |
| 559 | Ernie Whitt | .05 |
| 560 | Ron Washington | .05 |
| 561 | Jimmy Key | .05 |
| 562 | Billy Swift | .05 |
| 563 | Ron Darling | .25 |
| 564 | Dick Ruthven | .05 |
| 565 | Zane Smith | .05 |
| 566 | Sid Bream | .05 |
| 567 | Joel Youngblood | .05 |
| 568 | Mario Ramirez | .05 |
| 569 | Tom Runnells (R) | .10 |
| 570 | Rick Schu | .05 |
| 571 | Bill Campbell | .05 |
| 572 | Dickie Thon | .05 |
| 573 | Al Holland | .05 |
| 574 | Reid Nichols | .05 |
| 575 | Bert Roberge | .05 |
| 576 | Mike Flanagan | .05 |
| 577 | Tim Leary | .05 |
| 578 | Mike Laga | .05 |
| 579 | Steve Lyons | .05 |
| 580 | Phil Niekro | .15 |
| 581 | Gilberto Reyes (R) | .15 |
| 582 | Jamie Easterly | .05 |
| 583 | Mark Gubicza | .05 |
| 584 | Stan Javier (R) | .30 |
| 585 | Bill Laskey | .05 |
| 586 | Jeff Russell | .05 |
| 587 | Dickie Noles | .05 |
| 588 | Steve Farr | .05 |
| 589 | Steve Ontiveros (R) | .20 |
| 590 | Mike Hargrove | .05 |
| 591 | Marty Bystrom | .05 |

| NO. | PLAYER | MINT |
|-----|--------|------|
| 592 | Franklin Stubbs | .05 |
| 593 | Larry Herndon | .05 |
| 594 | Bill Swaggerty | .05 |
| 595 | Carlos Ponce (R) | .10 |
| 596 | Pat Perry (R) | .10 |
| 597 | Ray Knight | .05 |
| 598 | Steve Lombardozzi (R) | .20 |
| 599 | Brad Havens | .05 |
| 600 | Pat Clements (R) | .20 |
| 601 | Joe Niekro | .05 |
| 602 | Hank Aaron Puzzle | .15 |
| 603 | Dwayne Henry (R) | .10 |
| 604 | Mookie Wilson | .05 |
| 605 | Buddy Biancalana | .05 |
| 606 | Rance Mulliniks | .05 |
| 607 | Alan Wiggins | .07 |
| 608 | Joe Cowley | .05 |
| 609 | Tom Seaver | .25 |
| 610 | Neil Allen | .05 |
| 611 | Don Sutton | .10 |
| 612 | Fred Toliver (R) | .15 |
| 613 | Jay Baller (R) | .15 |
| 614 | Marc Sullivan (R) | .10 |
| 615 | John Grubb | .05 |
| 616 | Bruce Kison | .05 |
| 617 | Bill Madlock | .10 |
| 618 | Chris Chambliss | .05 |
| 619 | Dave Stewart | .05 |
| 620 | Tim Lollar | .05 |
| 621 | Gary Lavelle | .05 |
| 622 | Charles Hudson | .05 |
| 623 | Joel Davis (R) | .20 |
| 624 | Joe Johnson (R) | .20 |
| 625 | Sid Fernandez | .05 |
| 626 | Dennis Lamp | .05 |
| 627 | Terry Harper | .05 |
| 628 | Jack Lazorko | .05 |
| 629 | Roger McDowell (R) | .50 |
| 630 | Mark Funderburk (R) | .25 |
| 631 | Ed Lynch | .05 |
| 632 | Rudy Law | .05 |
| 633 | Roger Mason (R) | .15 |
| 634 | Mike Felder (R) | .15 |
| 635 | Ken Schrom | .05 |
| 636 | Bob Ojeda | .05 |
| 637 | Ed Vande Berg | .05 |
| 638 | Bobby Meacham | .05 |
| 639 | Cliff Johnson | .05 |
| 640 | Garth Iorg | .05 |
| 641 | Dan Driessen | .05 |
| 642 | Mike Brown | .05 |
| 643 | John Shelby | .05 |
| 644 | Pete Rose Ty-Breaking Hit #4192: | .30 |
| 645 | Knuckle Brothers: Phil and Joe Niekro | .10 |
| 646 | Jesse Orosco | .05 |
| 647 | Billy Beane (R) | .25 |
| 648 | Cesar Cedeno | .05 |
| 649 | Bert Blyleven | .10 |
| 650 | Max Venable | .05 |
| 651 | Fleet Feet: W. McGee, V. Coleman | .30 |
| 652 | Calvin Schiraldi | .05 |
| 653 | King of Kings: Pete Rose (DK) | .75 |
| — | Checklist (DK) | .08 |
| — | Checklist No. 1 | .08 |
| — | Checklist No. 2 | .08 |
| — | Checklist No. 3 | .08 |
| — | Checklist No. 4 | .08 |
| — | Checklist No. 5 | .08 |
| — | Checklist No. 6 | .08 |

**Gum Pack Display Box Cards**

| NO. | PLAYER | MINT |
|-----|--------|------|
| PC4 | Kirk Gibson | .50 |
| PC5 | Willie Hernandez | .25 |
| PC6 | Doug DeCinces | .15 |
| — | Aaron Puzzle | .15 |

**All-Star Display Box Cards**

| NO. | PLAYER | MINT |
|-----|--------|------|
| PC7 | Wade Boggs | 2.00 |
| PC8 | Lee Smith | .15 |
| PC9 | Cecil Cooper | .15 |
| — | Aaron Puzzle | .15 |

Card values from this set fluctuate considerably.

# 1986 Donruss Rookies....Complete Set of 56 Cards—Value $25.00

Features the outstanding rookies of the 1986 season. The cards are coated with a glossy finish. The entire set was packaged in a printed box, and distributed exclusively through card hobby dealers.

| NO. PLAYER | MINT |
|---|---|
| 1 Wally Joyner (RR) | 5.00 |
| 2 Tracy Jones | .25 |
| 3 Allan Anderson | .15 |
| 4 Ed Correa | .30 |
| 5 Reggie Williams | .25 |
| 6 Charlie Kerfeld | .30 |
| 7 Andres Galarraga | .20 |
| 8 Bob Tewksbury | .35 |
| 9 Al Newman | .20 |
| 10 Andres Thomas | .25 |
| 11 Barry Bonds (RR) | .75 |
| 12 Juan Nieves | .20 |
| 13 Mark Eichhorn | .50 |
| 14 Dan Plesac | .20 |

| NO. PLAYER | MINT |
|---|---|
| 15 Cory Snyder | 1.50 |
| 16 Kelly Gruber | .20 |
| 17 Kevin Mitchell (RR) | 1.00 |
| 18 Steve Lombardozzi | .20 |
| 19 Mitch Williams | .20 |
| 20 John Cerutti | .25 |
| 21 Todd Worrell | .60 |
| 22 Jose Canseco | 3.00 |
| 23 Pete Incaviglia (RR) | 2.00 |
| 24 Jose Guzman | .25 |
| 25 Scott Bailes | .20 |
| 26 Greg Mathews | .30 |
| 27 Eric King | .35 |
| 28 Paul Assenmacher | .25 |

| NO. PLAYER | MINT |
|---|---|
| 29 Jeff Sellers | .20 |
| 30 Bobby Bonilla | .20 |
| 31 Doug Drabek | .25 |
| 32 Will Clark (RR) | 2.00 |
| 33 Leon "Bip" Roberts | .30 |
| 34 Jim Deshaies | .20 |
| 35 Mike Lavalliere | .25 |
| 36 Scott Bankhead | .30 |
| 37 Dale Sveum | .30 |
| 38 Bo Jackson (RR) | 2.00 |
| 39 Rob Thompson | .50 |
| 40 Eric Plunk | .25 |
| 41 Bill Bathe | .25 |
| 42 John Kruk | .40 |

| NO. PLAYER | MINT |
|---|---|
| 43 Andy Allanson | .20 |
| 44 Mark Portugal | .20 |
| 45 Danny Tartabull | 1.00 |
| 46 Bob Kpper | .20 |
| 47 Gene Walter | .25 |
| 48 Rey Quinonez | .25 |
| 49 Bobby Witt | .50 |
| 50 Bill Mooneyham | .30 |
| 51 John Cangelosi | .35 |
| 52 Ruben Sierra (RR) | 1.50 |
| 53 Rob Woodward | .20 |
| 54 Ed Hearn | .20 |
| 55 Joel McKeon | .20 |
| 56 Checklist | .20 |

# 1986 Donruss Highlights....Complete Set of 56 Cards—Value $12.00

Features special events and milestones of the 1986 season from Opening Day to the last day of the regular season. Cards are numbered in chronological order. The entire set was packaged in a printed box, and distributed exclusively through card dealers.

| NO. PLAYER | MINT |
|---|---|
| 1 Will Clark: Homers in First At-Bat | .35 |
| 2 Jose Rijo: Milestone Strikeouts | .08 |
| 3 George Brett: Royals' All-Time Hit Man | .30 |
| 4 Mike Schmidt: Phillies RBI Leader | .30 |
| 5 Roger Clemens: 20 Strike Outs | .75 |
| 6 Roger Clemens (AL): Pitcher of the Month | .60 |
| 7 Kirby Puckett (AL): Player of the Month | .25 |
| 8 Dwight Gooden (NL): Pitcher of the Month | .75 |
| 9 Johnny Ray (NL): Player of the Month | .10 |
| 10 Reggie Jackson: Eclipses HR Record | .30 |
| 11 Wade Boggs: Five Hit Game | .60 |
| 12 Don Aase (AL): Pitcher of the Month | .10 |
| 13 Wade Boggs (AL): Player of the Month | .60 |
| 14 Jeff Reardon (NL): Pitcher of the Month | .10 |

| NO. PLAYER | MINT |
|---|---|
| 15 Hubie Brooks (NL): Player of the Month | .10 |
| 16 Don Sutton: Notches 300th Win | .10 |
| 17 Roger Clemens: Starts Season 14-0 | .75 |
| 18 Roger Clemens (AL): Pitcher of the Month | .60 |
| 19 Kent Hrbek (AL): Player of the Month | .15 |
| 20 Rick Rhoden (NL): Pitcher of the Month | .10 |
| 21 Kevin Bass (NL): Player of the Month | .15 |
| 22 Bob Horner: Blasts 4 HRs in 1 Game | .10 |
| 23 Wally Joyner: Starting All Star Rookie | 1.50 |
| 24 Darryl Strawberry: 3rd Straight All Star | .50 |
| 25 Fernando Valenzuela: Ties All Star Record | .25 |
| 26 Roger Clemens: All Star Game MVP | .60 |
| 27 Jack Morris (AL): Pitcher of the Month | .10 |
| 28 Scott Fletcher (AL): Player of the Month | .10 |

| NO. PLAYER | MINT |
|---|---|
| 29 Todd Worrell (NL): Pitcher of the Month | .50 |
| 30 Eric Davis (NL): Player of the Month | .60 |
| 31 Bert Blyleven: 3000th Strikeout | .10 |
| 32 Bobby Doerr: 1986 Hall of Fame | .10 |
| 33 Ernie Lombardi: 1986 Hall of Fame | .10 |
| 34 Willie McCovey: 1986 Hall of Fame | .25 |
| 35 Steve Carlton: Notches 4000th K | .25 |
| 36 Mike Schmidt: Surpasses DiMaggio | .30 |
| 37 Juan Samuel: 3rd "Quadruple Double" | .10 |
| 38 Mike Witt (AL): Pitcher of the Month | .10 |
| 39 Doug DeCinces (AL): Player of the Month | .10 |
| 40 Bill Gullickson (NL): Pitcher of the Month | .10 |
| 41 Dale Murphy (NL): Player of the Month | .60 |
| 42 Joe Carter: Offensive Record | .30 |

| NO. PLAYER | MINT |
|---|---|
| 43 Bo Jackson: Longest Royals HR | 1.25 |
| 44 Joe Cowley: 1st No-Hitter in 2 Years | .10 |
| 45 Jim Deshaies: Strikeout Record | .20 |
| 46 Mike Scott: No Hitter | .20 |
| 47 Bruce Hurst (AL): Pitcher of the Month | .15 |
| 48 Don Mattingly (AL): Player of the Month | 1.50 |
| 49 Mike Krukow (NL): Pitcher of the Month | .10 |
| 50 Steve Sax (NL): Player of the Month | .10 |
| 51 John Cangelosi (AL): Steals by a Rookie | .20 |
| 52 Dave Righetti: Shatters Save Mark | .20 |
| 53 Don Mattingly: Yankee Record for Hits & Doubles | 1.50 |
| 54 Todd Worrell: Donruss NL Rookie of the Year | .40 |
| 55 Jose Canseco: Donruss AL Rookie of the Year | 1.50 |
| 56 Checklist | .10 |

# 1987 Donruss....Complete Set of 660 Cards—Value $40.00

Features the rookie cards of Bo Jackson, Wally Joyner, Ruben Sierra and Pete Incaviglia. Donruss limited production. Three cards (PC10 to PC12) and a Clemente puzzle card were printed on the bottom of gum display boxes. These cards are not part of the set.

| NO. | PLAYER | MINT |
|---|---|---|
| **No. 1 to 26—Diamond Kings** | | |
| 1 | Wally Joyner (DK) | 1.50 |
| 2 | Roger Clemens (DK) | .50 |
| 3 | Dale Murphy (DK) | .40 |
| 4 | Darryl Strawberry (DK) | .40 |
| 5 | Ozzie Smith (DK) | .10 |
| 6 | Jose Canseco (DK) | 1.25 |
| 7 | Charlie Hough (DK) | .10 |
| 8 | Brook Jacoby (DK) | .10 |
| 9 | Fred Lynn (DK) | .15 |
| 10 | Rick Rhoden (DK) | .10 |
| 11 | Chris Brown (DK) | .15 |
| 12 | Von Hayes (DK) | .10 |
| 13 | Jack Morris (DK) | .15 |
| 14 | K. McReynolds (DK) | .10 |
| 15 | George Brett (DK) | .35 |
| 16 | Ted Higuera (DK) | .15 |
| 17 | Hubie Brooks (DK) | .10 |
| 18 | Mike Scott (DK) | .20 |
| 19 | Kirby Puckett (DK) | .30 |
| 20 | Dave Winfield (DK) | .20 |
| 21 | Lloyd Moseby (DK) | .10 |
| 22 | Eric Davis (DK) | .35 |
| 23 | Jim Presley (DK) | .20 |
| 24 | Keith Moreland (DK) | .10 |
| 25 | Greg Walker (DK) | .10 |
| 26 | Steve Sax (DK) | .15 |
| 27 | Checklist (DK) | .10 |
| **No. 28 to 47—Rated Rookies** | | |
| 28 | B.J. Surhoff (RR) | .60 |
| 29 | Randy Myers (RR) | .60 |
| 30 | Ken Gerhart (RR) | .25 |
| 31 | Benito Santiago (RR) | .20 |
| 32 | Greg Swindell (RR) | .60 |
| 33 | Mike Birkbeck (RR) | .15 |
| 34 | Terry Steinbach (RR) | .25 |
| 35 | Bo Jackson (RR) | 1.25 |
| 36 | Greg Maddux (RR) | .15 |
| 37 | Jim Lindeman (RR) | .15 |
| 38 | Devon White (RR) | .25 |
| 39 | Eric Bell (RR) | .15 |
| 40 | Will Fraser (RR) | .15 |
| 41 | Jerry Browne (RR) | .15 |
| 42 | Chris James (RR) | .20 |
| 43 | Rafael Palmeiro (RR) | .30 |
| 44 | Pat Dodson (RR) | .20 |
| 45 | Duane Ward (RR) | .15 |
| 46 | Mark McGwire (RR) | .20 |
| 47 | Bruce Fields (RR) | .15 |
| 48 | Eddie Murray | .30 |
| 49 | Ted Higuera | .15 |
| 50 | Kirk Gibson | .15 |
| 51 | Oil Can Boyd | .10 |
| 52 | Don Mattingly | 1.50 |
| 53 | Pedro Guerrero | .15 |
| 54 | George Brett | .40 |
| 55 | Jose Rijo | .05 |
| 56 | Tim Raines | .25 |
| 57 | Ed Correa (R) | .35 |
| 58 | Mike Witt | .10 |
| 59 | Greg Walker | .05 |
| 60 | Ozzie Smith | .12 |
| 61 | Glenn Davis | .50 |
| 62 | Glenn Wilson | .05 |
| 63 | Tom Browning | .05 |
| 64 | Tony Gwynn | .30 |

| NO. | PLAYER | MINT |
|---|---|---|
| 65 | R.J. Reynolds | .05 |
| 66 | Will Clark (R) | 1.00 |
| 67 | Ozzie Virgil | .05 |
| 68 | Rick Sutcliffe | .05 |
| 69 | Gary Carter | .30 |
| 70 | Mike Moore | .05 |
| 71 | Bert Blyleven | .05 |
| 72 | Tony Fernandez | .05 |
| 73 | Kent Hrbek | .15 |
| 74 | Lloyd Moseby | .10 |
| 75 | Alvin Davis | .10 |
| 76 | Keith Hernandez | .25 |
| 77 | Ryne Sandberg | .20 |
| 78 | Dale Murphy | .40 |
| 79 | Sid Bream | .05 |
| 80 | Chris Brown | .20 |
| 81 | Steve Garvey | .30 |
| 82 | Mario Soto | .05 |
| 83 | Shane Rawley | .05 |
| 84 | Willie McGee | .20 |
| 85 | Jose Cruz | .05 |
| 86 | Brian Downing | .05 |
| 87 | Ozzie Guillen | .10 |
| 88 | Hubie Brooks | .05 |
| 89 | Cal Ripken | .30 |
| 90 | Juan Nieves | .20 |
| 91 | Lance Parrish | .20 |
| 92 | Jim Rice | .30 |
| 93 | Ron Guidry | .15 |
| 94 | Fernando Valenzuela | .25 |
| 95 | Andy Allanson (R) | .20 |
| 96 | Willie Wilson | .15 |
| 97 | Jose Canseco | 2.00 |
| 98 | Jeff Reardon | .05 |
| 99 | Bobby Witt (R) | .50 |
| 100 | Checklist: 28 to 133 | .10 |
| 101 | Jose Guzman | .20 |
| 102 | Steve Balboni | .10 |
| 103 | Tony Phillips | .05 |
| 104 | Brook Jacoby | .05 |
| 105 | Dave Winfield | .25 |
| 106 | Orel Hershiser | .15 |
| 107 | Lou Whitaker | .15 |
| 108 | Fred Lynn | .15 |
| 109 | Bill Wegman | .05 |
| 110 | Donnie Moore | .05 |
| 111 | Jack Clark | .10 |
| 112 | Bob Knepper | .05 |
| 113 | Von Hayes | .10 |
| 114 | "Bip" Roberts (R) | .15 |
| 115 | Tony Pena | .05 |
| 116 | Scott Garrelts | .05 |
| 117 | Paul Molitor | .15 |
| 118 | Darryl Strawberry | .40 |
| 119 | Shawon Dunston | .05 |
| 120 | Jim Presley | .20 |
| 121 | Jesse Barfield | .15 |
| 122 | Gary Gaetti | .05 |
| 123 | Kurt Stillwell (R) | .15 |
| 124 | Joel Davis | .05 |
| 125 | Mike Boddicker | .05 |
| 126 | Robin Yount | .25 |
| 127 | Alan Trammell | .15 |
| 128 | Dave Righetti | .15 |
| 129 | Dwight Evans | .10 |
| 130 | Mike Scioscia | .05 |

| NO. | PLAYER | MINT |
|---|---|---|
| 131 | Julio Franco | .05 |
| 132 | Bret Saberhagen | .15 |
| 133 | Mike Davis | .05 |
| 134 | Joe Hesketh | .05 |
| 135 | Wally Joyner (R) | 2.50 |
| 136 | Don Slaught | .05 |
| 137 | Daryl Boston | .05 |
| 138 | Nolan Ryan | .30 |
| 139 | Mike Schmidt | .35 |
| 140 | Tommy Herr | .05 |
| 141 | Garry Templeton | .05 |
| 142 | Kal Daniels | .15 |
| 143 | Billy Sample | .05 |
| 144 | Johnny Ray | .05 |
| 145 | Rob Thompson (R) | .30 |
| 146 | Bob Dernier | .05 |
| 147 | Danny Tartabull | .30 |
| 148 | Ernie Whitt | .05 |
| 149 | Kirby Puckett | .30 |
| 150 | Mike Young | .05 |
| 151 | Ernest Riles | .15 |
| 152 | Frank Tanana | .05 |
| 153 | Rich Gedman | .05 |
| 154 | Willie Randolph | .08 |
| 155 | Bill Madlock | .15 |
| 156 | Joe Carter | .15 |
| 157 | Danny Jackson | .05 |
| 158 | Carney Lansford | .05 |
| 159 | Bryn Smith | .05 |
| 160 | Gary Pettis | .05 |
| 161 | Oddibe McDowell | .20 |
| 162 | John Cangelosi (R) | .20 |
| 163 | Mike Scott | .20 |
| 164 | Eric Show | .05 |
| 165 | Juan Samuel | .12 |
| 166 | Nick Esasky | .05 |
| 167 | Zane Smith | .05 |
| 168 | Mike Brown | .05 |
| 169 | Keith Moreland | .05 |
| 170 | John Tudor | .05 |
| 171 | Ken Dixon | .05 |
| 172 | Jim Gantner | .05 |
| 173 | Jack Morris | .15 |
| 174 | Bruce Hurst | .05 |
| 175 | Dennis Rasmussen | .12 |
| 176 | Mike Marshall | .05 |
| 177 | Dan Quisenberry | .12 |
| 178 | Eric Plunk | .05 |
| 179 | Tim Wallach | .05 |
| 180 | Steve Buechele | .05 |
| 181 | Don Sutton | .15 |
| 182 | Dave Schmidt | .05 |
| 183 | Terry Pendleton | .05 |
| 184 | Jim Deshaies (R) | .15 |
| 185 | Steve Bedrosian | .05 |
| 186 | Pete Rose (Mgr.) | .50 |
| 187 | Dave Dravecky | .05 |
| 188 | Rick Reuschel | .05 |
| 189 | Dan Gladden | .05 |
| 190 | Rick Mahler | .05 |
| 191 | Thad Bosley | .05 |
| 192 | Ron Darling | .20 |
| 193 | Matt Young | .05 |
| 194 | Tom Brunansky | .08 |
| 195 | Dave Stieb | .15 |
| 196 | Frank Viola | .05 |

| NO. | PLAYER | MINT |
|---|---|---|
| 197 | Tom Henke | .05 |
| 198 | Karl Best | .05 |
| 199 | Dwight Gooden | 1.00 |
| 200 | Checklist: 134-209 | .08 |
| 201 | Steve Trout | .05 |
| 202 | Rafael Ramirez | .05 |
| 203 | Bob Walk | .05 |
| 204 | Roger Mason | .05 |
| 205 | Terry Kennedy | .05 |
| 206 | Ron Oester | .05 |
| 207 | John Russell | .05 |
| 208 | Gerg Mathews (R) | .15 |
| 209 | Charlie Kerfeld | .05 |
| 210 | Reggie Jackson | .35 |
| 211 | Floyd Bannister | .05 |
| 212 | Vance Law | .05 |
| 213 | Rich Bordi | .05 |
| 214 | Dan Plesac (R) | .15 |
| 215 | Dave Collins | .05 |
| 216 | Bob Stanley | .05 |
| 217 | Joe Niekro | .08 |
| 218 | Tom Niedenfuer | .05 |
| 219 | Brett Butler | .05 |
| 220 | Charlie Leibrandt | .05 |
| 221 | Steve Ontiveros | .05 |
| 222 | Tim Burke | .05 |
| 223 | Curtis Wilkerson | .05 |
| 224 | Pete Incaviglia (R) | 1.00 |
| 225 | Lonnie Smith | .05 |
| 226 | Chris Codiroli | .05 |
| 227 | Scott Bailes (R) | .15 |
| 228 | Rickey Henderson | .35 |
| 229 | Ken Howell | .05 |
| 230 | Darnell Coles | .08 |
| 231 | Don Aase | .05 |
| 232 | Tim Leary | .05 |
| 233 | Bob Boone | .05 |
| 234 | Ricky Horton | .05 |
| 235 | Mark Bailey | .05 |
| 236 | Kevin Gross | .05 |
| 237 | Lance McCullers | .10 |
| 238 | Cecilio Guante | .05 |
| 239 | Bob Melvin | .05 |
| 240 | Billy Jo Robidoux | .12 |
| 241 | Roger McDowell | .15 |
| 242 | Leon Durham | .10 |
| 243 | Ed Nunez | .05 |
| 244 | Jimmy Key | .05 |
| 245 | Mike Smithson | .05 |
| 246 | Bo Diaz | .05 |
| 247 | Carlton Fisk | .15 |
| 248 | Larry Sheets | .05 |
| 249 | Juan Castillo | .10 |
| 250 | Eric King (R) | .15 |
| 251 | Doug Drabek (R) | .15 |
| 252 | Wade Boggs | 1.25 |
| 253 | Mariano Duncan | .10 |
| 254 | Pat Tabler | .05 |
| 255 | Frank White | .05 |
| 256 | Alfredo Griffin | .05 |
| 257 | Floyd Youmans | .15 |
| 258 | Rob Wilfong | .05 |
| 259 | Pete O'Brien | .08 |
| 260 | Tim Hulett | .05 |
| 261 | Dickie Thon | .05 |
| 262 | Darren Daulton | .05 |

Card values from this set fluctuate considerably.

| NO. | PLAYER | MINT |
|---|---|---|
| 263 | Vince Coleman | .35 |
| 264 | Andy Hawkins | .05 |
| 265 | Eric Davis | .40 |
| 266 | Andres Thomas (R) | .25 |
| 267 | Mike Diaz (R) | .15 |
| 268 | Chili Davis | .10 |
| 269 | Jody Davis | .05 |
| 270 | Phil Bradley | .10 |
| 271 | George Bell | .12 |
| 272 | Keith Atherton | .05 |
| 273 | Storm Davis | .08 |
| 274 | Rob Deer | .20 |
| 275 | Walt Terrell | .05 |
| 276 | Roger Clemens | 1.00 |
| 277 | Mike Easler | .05 |
| 278 | Steve Sax | .15 |
| 279 | Andre Thornton | .05 |
| 280 | Jim Sundberg | .05 |
| 281 | Bill Bathe (R) | .15 |
| 282 | Jay Tibbs | .05 |
| 283 | Dick Schofield | .05 |
| 284 | Mike Mason | .05 |
| 285 | Jerry Hairston | .05 |
| 286 | Bill Doran | .05 |
| 287 | Tim Flannery | .05 |
| 288 | Gary Redus | .05 |
| 289 | John Franco | .05 |
| 290 | P. Assenmacher (R) | .15 |
| 291 | Joe Orsulak | .05 |
| 292 | Lee Smith | .05 |
| 293 | Mike Laga | .05 |
| 294 | Rick Dempsey | .05 |
| 295 | Mike Felder | .05 |
| 296 | Tom Brookens | .05 |
| 297 | Al Nipper | .05 |
| 298 | Mike Pagliarulo | .25 |
| 299 | Franklin Stubbs | .15 |
| 300 | Checklist: 240-345 | .08 |
| 301 | Steve Farr | .05 |
| 302 | Bill Mooneyham (R) | .15 |
| 303 | Andres Galarraga | .15 |
| 304 | Scott Fletcher | .05 |
| 305 | Jack Howell | .05 |
| 306 | Russ Morman (R) | .25 |
| 307 | Todd Worrell | .35 |
| 308 | Dave Smith | .05 |
| 309 | Jeff Stone | .05 |
| 310 | Ron Robinson | .05 |
| 311 | Bruce Bochy | .05 |
| 312 | Jim Winn | .05 |
| 313 | Mark Davis | .05 |
| 314 | Jeff Dedmon | .05 |
| 315 | Jamie Moyer (R) | .15 |
| 316 | Wally Backman | .05 |
| 317 | Ken Phelps | .05 |
| 318 | Steve Lombardozzi | .12 |
| 319 | Rance Mulliniks | .05 |
| 320 | Tim Laudner | .05 |
| 321 | Mark Eichhorn (R) | .30 |
| 322 | Lee Guetterman (R) | .15 |
| 323 | Sid Fernandez | .25 |
| 324 | Jerry Mumphrey | .05 |
| 325 | David Palmer | .05 |
| 326 | Bill Almon | .05 |
| 327 | Candy Maldonado | .05 |
| 328 | John Kruk (R) | .25 |
| 329 | John Denny | .05 |
| 330 | Milt Thompson | .05 |
| 331 | Mike LaValliere (R) | .15 |
| 332 | Alan Ashby | .05 |
| 333 | Doug Corbett | .05 |
| 334 | Ron Karkovice (R) | .25 |
| 335 | Mitch Webster | .05 |
| 336 | Lee Lacy | .05 |
| 337 | Glenn Braggs (R) | .35 |
| 338 | Dwight Lowry (R) | .15 |
| 339 | Don Baylor | .15 |
| 340 | Brian Fisher | .05 |
| 341 | Reggie Williams (R) | .25 |
| 342 | Tom Candiotti | .05 |
| 343 | Rudy Law | .05 |
| 344 | Curt Young | .05 |
| 345 | Mike Fitzgerald | .05 |
| 346 | Ruben Sierra (R) | 1.00 |

| NO. | PLAYER | MINT |
|---|---|---|
| 347 | Mitch Williams (R) | .25 |
| 348 | Jorge Orta | .05 |
| 349 | Mickey Tettleton | .05 |
| 350 | Ernie Camacho | .05 |
| 351 | Ron Kittle | .10 |
| 352 | Ken Landreaux | .05 |
| 353 | Chet Lemon | .08 |
| 354 | John Shelby | .05 |
| 355 | Mark Clear | .05 |
| 356 | Doug DeCinces | .08 |
| 357 | Ken Kayley | .05 |
| 358 | Phil Garner | .05 |
| 359 | Steve Jeltz | .05 |
| 360 | Ed Whitson | .05 |
| 361 | Barry Bonds (R) | .45 |
| 362 | Vida Blue | .08 |
| 363 | Cecil Cooper | .10 |
| 364 | Bob Ojeda | .15 |
| 365 | Dennis Eckersley | .08 |
| 366 | Mike Morgan | .05 |
| 367 | Willie Upshaw | .05 |
| 368 | Allan Anderson (R) | .15 |
| 369 | Bill Gullickson | .05 |
| 370 | Bobby Thigpen (R) | .15 |
| 371 | Juan Beniquez | .05 |
| 372 | Charlie Moore | .05 |
| 373 | Dan Petry | .08 |
| 374 | Rod Scurry | .05 |
| 375 | Tom Seaver | .35 |
| 376 | Ed Vande Berg | .05 |
| 377 | Tony Bernazard | .05 |
| 378 | Greg Pryor | .05 |
| 379 | Dwayne Murphy | .05 |
| 380 | Andy McGaffigan | .05 |
| 381 | Kirk McCaskill | .10 |
| 382 | Greg Harris | .05 |
| 383 | Rich Dotson | .05 |
| 384 | Craig Reynolds | .05 |
| 385 | Greg Gross | .05 |
| 386 | Tito Landrum | .05 |
| 387 | Craig Lefferts | .05 |
| 388 | Dave Parker | .20 |
| 389 | Bob Horner | .15 |
| 390 | Pat Clements | .05 |
| 391 | Jeff Leonard | .05 |
| 392 | Chris Speier | .05 |
| 393 | John Moses | .15 |
| 394 | Garth Iorg | .05 |
| 395 | Greg Gagne | .05 |
| 396 | Nate Snell | .05 |
| 397 | Bryan Clutterbuck (R) | .15 |
| 398 | Darrell Evans | .05 |
| 399 | Steve Crawford | .05 |
| 400 | Checklist: 346-451 | .08 |
| 401 | Phil Lombardi (R) | .20 |
| 402 | Rick Honeycutt | .05 |
| 403 | Ken Schrom | .05 |
| 404 | Bud Black | .05 |
| 405 | Donnie Hill | .05 |
| 406 | Wayne Krenchicki | .05 |
| 407 | Chuck Finley (R) | .15 |
| 408 | Toby Harrah | .05 |
| 409 | Steve Lyons | .05 |
| 410 | Kevin Bass | .05 |
| 411 | Marvell Wynne | .05 |
| 412 | Ron Roenicke | .05 |
| 413 | Tracy Jones (R) | .20 |
| 414 | Gene Garber | .05 |
| 415 | Mike Bielecki | .05 |
| 416 | Frank DiPino | .05 |
| 417 | Andy Van Slyke | .05 |
| 418 | Jim Dwyer | .05 |
| 419 | Ben Oglivie | .05 |
| 420 | Dave Bergman | .05 |
| 421 | Joe Sambito | .05 |
| 422 | Bob Tewksbury (R) | .25 |
| 423 | Len Matuszek | .05 |
| 424 | Mike Kingery (R) | .15 |
| 425 | Dave Kingman | .10 |
| 426 | Al Newman (R) | .15 |
| 427 | Gary Ward | .05 |
| 428 | Ruppert Jones | .05 |
| 429 | Harold Baines | .12 |
| 430 | Pat Perry | .05 |

| NO. | PLAYER | MINT |
|---|---|---|
| 431 | Terry Puhl | .05 |
| 432 | Don Carman | .05 |
| 433 | Eddie Milner | .05 |
| 434 | LaMarr Hoyt | .05 |
| 435 | Rick Rhoden | .05 |
| 436 | Jose Uribe | .05 |
| 437 | Ken Oberkfell | .05 |
| 438 | Ron Davis | .05 |
| 439 | Jesse Orosco | .08 |
| 440 | Scott Bradley | .05 |
| 441 | Randy Bush | .05 |
| 442 | John Cerutti (R) | .20 |
| 443 | Roy Smalley | .05 |
| 444 | Kelly Gruber | .05 |
| 445 | Bob Kearney | .05 |
| 446 | Ed Hearn (R) | .15 |
| 447 | Scott Sanderson | .05 |
| 443 | Bruce Benedict | .05 |
| 449 | Junior Ortiz | .05 |
| 450 | Mike Aldrete (R) | .15 |
| 451 | Kevin McReynolds | .12 |
| 452 | Rob Murphy (R) | .15 |
| 453 | Kent Tekulve | .05 |
| 454 | Curt Ford | .15 |
| 455 | Davey Lopes | .08 |
| 456 | Bobby Grich | .05 |
| 457 | Jose DeLeon | .05 |
| 458 | Andre Dawson | .15 |
| 459 | Mike Flanagan | .05 |
| 460 | Joey Meyer (R) | .20 |
| 461 | Chuck Cary (R) | .15 |
| 462 | Bill Buckner | .08 |
| 463 | Bob Shirley | .05 |
| 464 | Jeff Hamilton (R) | .15 |
| 465 | Phil Niekro | .12 |
| 466 | Mark Gubicza | .05 |
| 467 | Jerry Willard | .05 |
| 468 | Bob Sebra (R) | .15 |
| 469 | Larry Parrish | .05 |
| 470 | Charlie Hough | .05 |
| 471 | Hal McRae | .05 |
| 472 | Dave Leiper | .05 |
| 473 | Mel Hall | .05 |
| 474 | Dan Pasqua | .15 |
| 475 | Bob Welch | .05 |
| 476 | Johnny Grubb | .05 |
| 477 | Jim Traber | .12 |
| 478 | Chris Bosio (R) | .15 |
| 479 | Mark McLemore | .08 |
| 480 | John Morris | .05 |
| 481 | Billy Hatcher | .05 |
| 482 | Dan Schatzeder | .05 |
| 483 | Rich Gossage | .12 |
| 484 | Jim Morrison | .05 |
| 485 | Bob Brenly | .05 |
| 486 | Bill Schroeder | .05 |
| 487 | Mookie Wilson | .05 |
| 488 | Dave Martinez | .15 |
| 489 | Harold Reynolds | .05 |
| 490 | Jeff Hearron (R) | .15 |
| 491 | Mickey Hatcher | .05 |
| 492 | Barry Larkin (R) | .25 |
| 493 | Bob James | .05 |
| 494 | John Habyan | .05 |
| 495 | Jim Adduci (R) | .15 |
| 496 | Mike Heath | .05 |
| 497 | Tim Stoddard | .05 |
| 498 | Tony Armas | .08 |
| 499 | Dennis Powell | .05 |
| 500 | Checklist: 452-557 | .08 |
| 501 | Chris Bando | .05 |
| 502 | David Cone (R) | .15 |
| 503 | Jay Howell | .05 |
| 504 | Tom Foley | .05 |
| 505 | Ray Chadwick (R) | .15 |
| 506 | Mike Loynd (R) | .15 |
| 507 | Neil Allen | .05 |
| 508 | Danny Darwin | .05 |
| 509 | Rick Schu | .05 |
| 510 | Jose Oquendo | .05 |
| 511 | Gene Walter | .10 |
| 512 | Terry McGriff (R) | .15 |
| 513 | Ken Griffey | .08 |
| 514 | Benny Distefano | .05 |

| NO. | PLAYER | MINT |
|---|---|---|
| 515 | Terry Mulholland (R) | .15 |
| 516 | Ed Lynch | .05 |
| 517 | Bill Swift | .05 |
| 518 | Manny Lee | .05 |
| 519 | Andre David | .05 |
| 520 | Scott McGregor | .05 |
| 521 | Rick Manning | .05 |
| 522 | Willie Hernandez | .05 |
| 523 | Marty Barrett | .05 |
| 524 | Wayne Tolleson | .05 |
| 525 | Jose Gonzalez (R) | .20 |
| 526 | Cory Snyder | .60 |
| 527 | Buddy Biancalana | .05 |
| 528 | Moose Haas | .05 |
| 529 | Wilfredo Tejada (R) | .15 |
| 530 | Stu Cliburn | .05 |
| 531 | Dale Mohorcic (R) | .15 |
| 532 | Ron Hassey | .05 |
| 533 | Ty Gainey | .05 |
| 534 | Jerry Royster | .05 |
| 535 | Mike Maddux (R) | .15 |
| 536 | Ted Power | .05 |
| 537 | Ted Simmons | .08 |
| 538 | Rafael Belliard (R) | .15 |
| 539 | Chico Walker (R) | .15 |
| 540 | Bob Forsch | .05 |
| 541 | John Stefero | .05 |
| 542 | Dale Sveum (R) | .15 |
| 543 | Mark Thurmond | .05 |
| 544 | Jeff Sellers (R) | .15 |
| 545 | Joel Skinner | .05 |
| 546 | Alex Trevino | .05 |
| 547 | Randy Kutcher (R) | .15 |
| 548 | Joaquin Andujar | .05 |
| 549 | Casey Candaele (R) | .15 |
| 550 | Jeff Russell | .05 |
| 551 | John Candelaria | .08 |
| 552 | Joe Cowley | .05 |
| 553 | Danny Cox | .05 |
| 554 | Denny Walling | .05 |
| 555 | Bruce Ruffin (R) | .30 |
| 556 | Buddy Bell | .05 |
| 557 | Jimmy Jones (R) | .15 |
| 558 | Bobby Bonilla (R) | .15 |
| 559 | Jeff Robinson | .05 |
| 560 | Ed Olwine (R) | .15 |
| 561 | Glenallen Hill (R) | .15 |
| 562 | Lee Mazzilli | .08 |
| 563 | Mike Brown | .05 |
| 564 | George Frazier | .05 |
| 565 | Mike Sharperson (R) | .15 |
| 566 | Mark Portugal (R) | .15 |
| 567 | Rick Leach | .05 |
| 568 | Mark Langston | .05 |
| 569 | Rafael Santana | .05 |
| 570 | Manny Trillo | .05 |
| 571 | Cliff Speck (R) | .15 |
| 572 | Bob Kipper | .05 |
| 573 | Kelly Downs (R) | .15 |
| 574 | Randy Asadoor (R) | .15 |
| 575 | Dave Magadan (R) | .50 |
| 576 | Marvin Freeman (R) | .15 |
| 577 | Jeff Lahti | .05 |
| 578 | Jeff Calhoun | .05 |
| 579 | Gus Polidor | .05 |
| 580 | Gene Nelson | .05 |
| 581 | Tim Teufel | .05 |
| 582 | Odell Jones | .05 |
| 583 | Mark Ryal (R) | .15 |
| 584 | Randy O'Neal | .05 |
| 585 | Mike Greenwell (R) | .15 |
| 586 | Ray Knight | .05 |
| 587 | Ralph Bryant (R) | .25 |
| 588 | Carmen Castillo | .05 |
| 589 | Ed Wojna | .05 |
| 590 | Stan Javier | .05 |
| 591 | Jeff Musselman (R) | .15 |
| 592 | Mike Stanley (R) | .15 |
| 593 | Darrell Porter | .05 |
| 594 | Drew Hall (R) | .15 |
| 595 | Rob Nelson (R) | .15 |
| 596 | Bryan Oelkers | .05 |
| 597 | Scott Nielsen (R) | .15 |
| 598 | Brian Holton (R) | .15 |

Card values from this set fluctuate considerably.

# 1987 Donruss (Continued)

| NO. | PLAYER | MINT |
|-----|--------|------|
| 599 | Kevin Mitchell (R) | .50 |
| 600 | Checklist: 558-660 | .08 |
| 601 | Jackie Gutierrez | .05 |
| 602 | Barry Jones (R) | .15 |
| 603 | Jerry Narron | .05 |
| 604 | Steve Lake | .05 |
| 605 | Jim Pankovits | .05 |
| 606 | Ed Romero | .05 |
| 607 | Dave LaPoint | .05 |
| 608 | Don Robinson | .05 |
| 609 | Mike Krukow | .05 |
| 610 | Dave Valle | .05 |
| 611 | Len Dykstra | .25 |
| 612 | "Puzzle"—Clemente | .08 |
| 613 | Mike Trujillo | .05 |
| 614 | Damaso Garcia | .05 |
| 615 | Neal Heaton | .05 |

| NO. | PLAYER | MINT |
|-----|--------|------|
| 616 | Juan Berenguer | .05 |
| 617 | Steve Carlton | .25 |
| 618 | Gary Lucas | .05 |
| 619 | Geno Petralli | .05 |
| 620 | Rick Aguilera | .08 |
| 621 | Fred McGriff | .08 |
| 622 | Dave Henderson | .05 |
| 623 | Dave Clark (R) | .15 |
| 624 | Angel Salazar | .05 |
| 625 | Randy Hunt | .05 |
| 626 | John Gibbons | .05 |
| 627 | Kevin Brown (R) | .15 |
| 628 | Bill Dawley | .05 |
| 629 | Aurelio Lopez | .05 |
| 630 | Charlie Hudson | .05 |
| 631 | Ray Soff (R) | .15 |
| 632 | Ray Hayward (R) | .15 |

| NO. | PLAYER | MINT |
|-----|--------|------|
| 633 | Spike Owen | .05 |
| 634 | Glenn Hubbard | .05 |
| 635 | Kevin Elster (R) | .15 |
| 636 | Mike LaCoss | .05 |
| 637 | Dwayne Henry | .05 |
| 638 | Rey Quinones (R) | .15 |
| 639 | Jim Clancy | .05 |
| 640 | Larry Anderson | .05 |
| 641 | Calvin Schiraldi | .08 |
| 642 | Stan Jefferson (R) | .15 |
| 643 | Marc Sullivan | .05 |
| 644 | Mark Grant (R) | .15 |
| 645 | Cliff Johnson | .05 |
| 646 | Howard Johnson | .05 |
| 647 | Dave Sax | .05 |
| 648 | Dave Stewart | .05 |
| 649 | Danny Heep | .05 |

| NO. | PLAYER | MINT |
|-----|--------|------|
| 650 | Joe Johnson | .05 |
| 651 | Bob Brower (R) | .15 |
| 652 | Rob Woodward | .05 |
| 653 | John Mizerock | .05 |
| 654 | Tim Pyznarski (R) | .15 |
| 655 | Luis Aquino | .05 |
| 656 | Mickey Brantley | .05 |
| 657 | Doyle Alexander | .05 |
| 658 | Sammy Stewart | .05 |
| 659 | Jim Acker | .05 |
| 660 | Pete Ladd | .05 |

**Cards Printed on Gum Boxes**

| NO. | PLAYER | MINT |
|-----|--------|------|
| PC10 | Dale Murphy | .50 |
| PC11 | Jeff Reardon | .15 |
| PC12 | Jose Canseco | .75 |
| — | Clemente Puzzle | .10 |

Card values from this set fluctuate considerably.

# 1981 Fleer....Complete Set of 660 Cards (1st printing, with corrected "Graig" Nettles)—Value $20.00; Complete Set of 660 Cards (1st printing, with error "Craig" Nettles)—Value $30.00; Complete Set of 660 Cards (2nd printing)—Value $18.00; Complete Set of 660 Cards (3rd printing)— Value $22.00

This was Fleer's first baseball card set since 1963. Over 30 cards contained errors; they were corrected in the 2nd and 3rd printing runs. The "Craig" Nettles error was corrected during the first printing. There is very little interest by collectors in the *variety* (error) cards; none are scarce or worth much more than ordinary cards, except card 87, "Craig" Nettles. If a *variety* (error) is significant, it is listed and explained; if it is *minor*, it is noted by an *asterisk*. This set features the rookie cards of Fernando Valenzuela, Kirk Gibson and Harold Baines.

| NO. PLAYER | MINT |
|---|---|
| **PHILADELPHIA PHILLIES** | |
| 1 Pete Rose | 1.50 |
| 2 Larry Bowa | .07 |
| 3 Manny Trillo | .05 |
| 4 Bob Boone | .05 |
| 5 Mike Schmidt | .75 |
| (MVP) Third Base | |
| See No. 640 | |
| 6 Steve Carlton | .50 |
| (Pitcher of Year) | |
| See No. 660 | |
| Error—"1066" | |
| Cardinals" on Back | |
| 6 Steve Carlton | 1.00 |
| Corrected "1966" Cardinals | |
| 7 Tug McGraw | .07 |
| See No. 657 | |
| 8 Larry Christenson | .05 |
| 9 Bake McBride | .05 |
| 10 Greg Luzinski | .10 |
| 11 Ron Reed | .05 |
| 12 Dickie Noles | .05 |
| 13 Keith Moreland (R) | .40 |
| 14 Bob Walk | .05 |
| 15 Lonnie Smith | .08 |
| 16 Dick Ruthven | .05 |
| 17 Sparky Lyle | .07 |
| 18 Greg Gross | .05 |
| 19 Garry Maddox | .05 |
| 20 Nino Espinosa | .05 |
| 21 George Vukovich | .05 |
| 22 John Vukovich | .05 |
| 23 Ramon Aviles | .05 |
| 24 Ken Saucier* | .08 |
| 25 Randy Lerch | .05 |
| 26 Del Unser | .05 |
| 27 Tim McCarver | .08 |
| **KANSAS CITY ROYALS** | |
| 28 George Brett—MVP | .75 |
| See No. 655 | |
| 29 Willie Wilson | .25 |
| See No. 653 | |
| 30 Paul Splittorff | .05 |
| 31 Dan Quisenberry | .30 |
| 32 Amos Otis* | .10 |
| 33 Steve Busby | .05 |
| 34 U.L. Washington | .05 |
| 35 Dave Chalk | .05 |
| 36 Darrell Porter | .08 |
| 37 Marty Pattin | .05 |
| 38 Larry Gura | .05 |
| 39 Renie Martin | .05 |
| 40 Rich Gale | .05 |
| 41 Hal McRae* | .40 |
| 42 Dennis Leonard | .05 |
| 43 Willie Aikens | .05 |
| 44 Frank White | .08 |
| 45 Clint Hurdle | .05 |
| 46 John Wathan | .05 |
| 47 Pete LaCock | .05 |
| 48 Rance Mulliniks | .05 |

| NO. PLAYER | MINT |
|---|---|
| 49 Jeff Twitty | .05 |
| 50 Jamie Quirk | .05 |
| **HOUSTON ASTROS** | |
| 51 Art Howe | .05 |
| 52 Ken Forsch | .05 |
| 53 Vern Ruhle | .05 |
| 54 Joe Niekro | .08 |
| 55 Frank LaCorte | .05 |
| 56 J.R. Richard | .08 |
| 57 Nolan Ryan | .40 |
| 58 Enos Cabell | .05 |
| 59 Cesar Cedeno | .08 |
| 60 Jose Cruz | .15 |
| 61 Bill Virdon (Mgr.) | .05 |
| 62 Terry Puhl | .05 |
| 63 Joaquin Andujar | .10 |
| 64 Alan Ashby | .05 |
| 65 Joe Sambito | .05 |
| 66 Denny Walling | .05 |
| 67 Jeff Leonard | .05 |
| 68 Luis Pujols | .05 |
| 69 Bruce Bochy | .05 |
| 70 Rafael Landestoy | .05 |
| 71 Dave Smith | .10 |
| 72 Danny Heep | .10 |
| 73 Julio Gonzalez | .05 |
| 74 Craig Reynolds | .05 |
| 75 Gary Woods | .05 |
| 76 Dave Bergman | .05 |
| 77 Randy Niemann | .05 |
| 78 Joe Morgan | .30 |
| **NEW YORK YANKEES** | |
| 79 Reggie Jackson | .60 |
| See No. 650 | |
| 80 Bucky Dent | .07 |
| 81 Tommy John | .15 |
| 82 Luis Tiant | .05 |
| 83 Rick Cerone | .05 |
| 84 Dick Howser (Mgr.) | .05 |
| 85 Lou Piniella | .10 |
| 86 Ron Davis | .05 |
| 87 Graig Nettles | 11.00 |
| Error—"Craig" on Back | |
| 87 Graig Nettles | .30 |
| Corrected—"Graig" | |
| 88 Ron Guidry | .25 |
| 89 Rich Gossage | .20 |
| 90 Rudy May | .05 |
| 91 Gaylord Perry | .30 |
| 92 Eric Soderholm | .05 |
| 93 Bob Watson | .05 |
| 94 Bobby Murcer | .08 |
| 95 Bobby Brown | .05 |
| 96 Jim Spencer | .05 |
| 97 Tom Underwood | .05 |
| 98 Oscar Gamble | .05 |
| 99 Johnny Oates | .05 |
| 100 Fred Stanley | .05 |
| 101 Ruppert Jones | .05 |
| 102 Dennis Werth | .05 |
| 103 Joe LeFebvre | .12 |

| NO. PLAYER | MINT |
|---|---|
| 104 Brian Doyle | .05 |
| 105 Aurelio Rodriguez | .05 |
| 106 Doug Bird | .05 |
| 107 Mike Griffin | .05 |
| 108 Tim Lollar (R) | .20 |
| 109 Willie Randolph | .08 |
| **LOS ANGELES DODGERS** | |
| 110 Steve Garvey | .50 |
| 111 Reggie Smith | .08 |
| 112 Don Sutton | .20 |
| 113 Burt Hooton | .05 |
| 114 Dave Lopes* | .08 |
| 115 Dusty Baker | .10 |
| 116 Tom Lasorda (Mgr.) | .08 |
| 117 Bill Russell | .05 |
| 118 Jerry Reuss | .08 |
| 119 Terry Forster | .05 |
| 120 Robert Welch* | .15 |
| 121 Don Stanhouse | .05 |
| 122 Rick Monday | .08 |
| 123 Derrel Thomas | .05 |
| 124 Joe Ferguson | .05 |
| 125 Rick Sutcliffe | .30 |
| 126 Ron Cey* | .15 |
| 127 Dave Goltz | .05 |
| 128 Jay Johnstone | .05 |
| 129 Steve Yeager | .05 |
| 130 Gary Weiss | .05 |
| 131 Mike Scioscia (R) | .25 |
| 132 Vic Davalillo | .05 |
| 133 Doug Rau | .05 |
| 134 Pepe Frias | .05 |
| 135 Mickey Hatcher | .05 |
| 136 Steve Howe (R) | .25 |
| 137 Robert Castillo | .05 |
| 138 Gary Thomasson | .05 |
| 139 Rudy Law | .05 |
| 140 F. Valenzuela (R) | 4.00 |
| 141 Manny Mota | .08 |
| **MONTREAL EXPOS** | |
| 142 Gary Carter | .40 |
| 143 Steve Rogers | .08 |
| 144 Warren Cromartie | .05 |
| 145 Andre Dawson | .30 |
| 146 Larry Parrish | .05 |
| 147 Rowland Office | .05 |
| 148 Ellis Valentine | .05 |
| 149 Dick Williams (Mgr.) | .05 |
| 150 Bill Gullickson (R) | .25 |
| 151 Elias Sosa | .05 |
| 152 John Tamargo | .05 |
| 153 Chris Speier | .05 |
| 154 Ron LeFlore | .05 |
| 155 Rodney Scott | .05 |
| 156 Stan Bahnsen | .05 |
| 157 Bill Lee | .05 |
| 158 Fred Norman | .05 |
| 159 Woodie Fryman | .05 |
| 160 Dave Palmer | .05 |
| 161 Jerry White | .05 |
| 162 Roberto Ramos | .05 |

| NO. PLAYER | MINT |
|---|---|
| 163 John D'Acquisto | .05 |
| 164 Tommy Hutton | .05 |
| 165 Charlie Lea (R) | .25 |
| 166 Scott Sanderson | .05 |
| 167 Ken Macha | .05 |
| 168 Tony Bernazard | .05 |
| **BALTIMORE ORIOLES** | |
| 169 Jim Palmer | .35 |
| 170 Steve Stone | .05 |
| 171 Mike Flanagan | .08 |
| 172 Al Bumbry | .05 |
| 173 Doug DeCinces | .12 |
| 174 Scott McGregor | .08 |
| 175 Mark Belanger | .05 |
| 176 Tim Stoddard | .05 |
| 177 Rick Dempsey* | .10 |
| 178 Earl Weaver (Mgr.) | .10 |
| 179 Tippy Martinez | .05 |
| 180 Dennis Martinez | .05 |
| 181 Sammy Stewart | .05 |
| 182 Rich Dauer | .05 |
| 183 Lee May | .05 |
| 184 Eddie Murray | .60 |
| 185 Benny Ayala | .05 |
| 186 John Lowenstein | .05 |
| 187 Gary Roenicke | .05 |
| 188 Ken Singleton | .08 |
| 189 Dan Graham | .05 |
| 190 Terry Crowley | .05 |
| 191 Kiko Garcia | .05 |
| 192 Dave Ford | .05 |
| 193 Mark Corey | .05 |
| 194 Lenn Sakata | .05 |
| 195 Doug DeCinces | .08 |
| **CINCINNATI REDS** | |
| 196 Johnny Bench | .50 |
| 197 Dave Concepcion | .15 |
| 198 Ray Knight | .08 |
| 199 Ken Griffey | .08 |
| 200 Tom Seaver | .40 |
| 201 Dave Collins | .07 |
| 202 George Foster | .25 |
| (Slugger) Error—No. 216 | |
| 202 George Foster | .25 |
| (Slugger) Correct No. 202 | |
| 203 Junior Kennedy | .05 |
| 204 Frank Pastore | .05 |
| 205 Dan Driessen | .05 |
| 206 Hector Cruz | .05 |
| 207 Paul Moskau | .05 |
| 208 Charlie Leibrandt (R) | .40 |
| 209 Harry Spilman | .05 |
| 210 Joe Price | .05 |
| 211 Tom Hume | .05 |
| 212 Joe Nolan | .05 |
| 213 Doug Bair | .05 |
| 214 Mario Soto | .05 |
| 215 Bill Bonham* | .08 |
| 216 George Foster | .20 |
| See No. 202 | |
| 217 Paul Householder | .08 |

| NO. | PLAYER | MINT |
|---|---|---|
| 218 | Ron Oester | .05 |
| 219 | Sam Mejias | .05 |
| 220 | Sheldon Burnside | .05 |

**BOSTON RED SOX**

| NO. | PLAYER | MINT |
|---|---|---|
| 221 | Carl Yastrzemski | .75 |
| 222 | Jim Rice | .50 |
| 223 | Fred Lynn | .25 |
| 224 | Carlton Fisk | .25 |
| 225 | Rick Burleson | .05 |
| 226 | Dennis Eckersley | .05 |
| 227 | Butch Hobson | .05 |
| 228 | Tom Burgmeier | .05 |
| 229 | Garry Hancock | .05 |
| 230 | Don Zimmer (Mgr.) | .05 |
| 231 | Steve Renko | .05 |
| 232 | Dwight Evans | .20 |
| 233 | Mike Torrez | .05 |
| 234 | Bob Stanley | .08 |
| 235 | Jim Dwyer | .05 |
| 236 | Dave Stapleton | .14 |
| 237 | Glenn Hoffman | .07 |
| 238 | Jerry Remy | .05 |
| 239 | Dick Drago | .05 |
| 240 | Bill Campbell | .05 |
| 241 | Tony Perez | .15 |

**ATLANTA BRAVES**

| NO. | PLAYER | MINT |
|---|---|---|
| 242 | Phil Niekro | .25 |
| 243 | Dale Murphy | .75 |
| 244 | Bob Horner | .20 |
| 245 | Jeff Burroughs | .05 |
| 246 | Rick Camp | .05 |
| 247 | Bob Cox (Mgr.) | .05 |
| 248 | Bruce Benedict | .05 |
| 249 | Gene Garber | .05 |
| 250 | Jerry Royster | .05 |
| 251 | Gary Matthews* | .10 |
| 252 | Chris Chambliss | .08 |
| 253 | Luis Gomez | .05 |
| 254 | Bill Nahorodny | .05 |
| 255 | Doyle Alexander | .05 |
| 256 | Brian Asselstine | .05 |
| 257 | Biff Pocoroba | .05 |
| 258 | Mike Lum | .05 |
| 259 | Charlie Spikes | .05 |
| 260 | Glenn Hubbard | .05 |
| 261 | Tommy Boggs | .05 |
| 262 | Al Hrabosky | .05 |
| 263 | Rick Matula | .05 |
| 264 | Preston Hanna | .05 |
| 265 | Larry Bradford | .05 |
| 266 | Rafael Ramirez | .20 |
| 267 | Larry McWilliams | .05 |

**CALIFORNIA ANGELS**

| NO. | PLAYER | MINT |
|---|---|---|
| 268 | Rod Carew | .40 |
| 269 | Bobby Grich | .08 |
| 270 | Carney Lansford | .10 |
| 271 | Don Baylor | .20 |
| 272 | Joe Rudi | .05 |
| 273 | Dan Ford | .05 |
| 274 | Jim Fregosi | .05 |
| 275 | Dave Frost | .05 |
| 276 | Frank Tanana | .05 |
| 277 | Dickie Thon | .07 |
| 278 | Jason Thompson | .08 |
| 279 | Rick Miller | .05 |
| 280 | Bert Campaneris | .05 |
| 281 | Tom Donohue | .05 |
| 282 | Brian Downing | .05 |
| 283 | Fred Patek | .05 |
| 284 | Bruce Kison | .05 |
| 285 | Dave LaRoche | .05 |
| 286 | Don Aase | .05 |
| 287 | Jim Barr | .05 |
| 288 | Alfredo Martinez | .05 |
| 289 | Larry Harlow | .05 |
| 290 | Andy Hassler | .05 |

**CHICAGO CUBS**

| NO. | PLAYER | MINT |
|---|---|---|
| 291 | Dave Kingman | .12 |
| 292 | Bill Buckner | .10 |
| 293 | Rick Reuschel | .05 |
| 294 | Bruce Sutter | .25 |
| 295 | Jerry Martin | .05 |
| 296 | Scot Thompson | .05 |
| 297 | Ivan DeJesus | .05 |
| 298 | Steve Dillard | .05 |

| NO. | PLAYER | MINT |
|---|---|---|
| 299 | Dick Tidrow | .05 |
| 300 | Randy Martz | .05 |
| 301 | Lenny Randle | .05 |
| 302 | Lynn McGlothen | .05 |
| 303 | Cliff Johnson | .05 |
| 304 | Tim Blackwell | .05 |
| 305 | Dennis Lamp | .05 |
| 306 | Bill Caudill | .08 |
| 307 | Carlos Lezcano | .05 |
| 308 | Jim Tracy | .05 |
| 309 | Doug Capilla | .05 |
| 310 | Willie Hernandez | .25 |
| 311 | Mike Vail | .05 |
| 312 | Mike Krukow | .05 |
| 313 | Barry Foote | .05 |
| 314 | Larry Biittner | .05 |
| 315 | Mike Tyson | .05 |

**NEW YORK METS**

| NO. | PLAYER | MINT |
|---|---|---|
| 316 | Lee Mazzilli | .05 |
| 317 | John Stearns | .05 |
| 318 | Alex Trevino | .05 |
| 319 | Craig Swan | .05 |
| 320 | Frank Taveras | .05 |
| 321 | Steve Henderson | .05 |
| 322 | Neil Allen | .05 |
| 323 | Mark Bomback | .05 |
| 324 | Mike Jorgensen | .05 |
| 325 | Joe Torre | .07 |
| 326 | Elliott Maddox | .05 |
| 327 | Pete Falcone | .05 |
| 328 | Ray Burris | .05 |
| 329 | Claudell Washington | .08 |
| 330 | Doug Flynn | .05 |
| 331 | Joel Youngblood | .05 |
| 332 | Bill Almon | .05 |
| 333 | Tom Hausman | .05 |
| 334 | Pat Zachry | .05 |
| 335 | Jeff Reardon (R) | .40 |
| 336 | Wally Backman (R) | .40 |
| 337 | Dan Norman | .05 |
| 338 | Jerry Morales | .05 |

**CHICAGO WHITE SOX (Except 351)**

| NO. | PLAYER | MINT |
|---|---|---|
| 339 | Ed Farmer | .05 |
| 340 | Bob Molinaro | .05 |
| 341 | Todd Cruz | .05 |
| 342 | Britt Burns* | .35 |
| 343 | Kevin Bell | .05 |
| 344 | Tony LaRussa (Mgr.) | .05 |
| 345 | Steve Trout | .05 |
| 346 | Harold Baines (R) | 1.50 |
| 347 | Richard Wortham | .05 |
| 348 | Wayne Nordhagen | .05 |
| 349 | Mike Squires | .05 |
| 350 | Lamar Johnson | .05 |
| 351 | Rickey Henderson | .75 |
| | Most Stolen Bases, AL | |
| 352 | Francisco Barrios | .05 |
| 353 | Thad Bosley | .05 |
| 354 | Chet Lemon | .08 |
| 355 | Bruce Kimm | .05 |
| 356 | Richard Dotson (R) | .30 |
| 357 | Jim Morrison | .05 |
| 358 | Mike Proly | .05 |
| 359 | Greg Pryor | .05 |

**PITTSBURGH PIRATES**

| NO. | PLAYER | MINT |
|---|---|---|
| 360 | Dave Parker | .30 |
| 361 | Omar Moreno | .05 |
| 362 | Kent Tekulve* | .10 |
| 363 | Willie Stargell | .30 |
| 364 | Phil Garner | .05 |
| 365 | Ed Ott | .05 |
| 366 | Don Robinson | .05 |
| 367 | Chuck Tanner (Mgr.) | .05 |
| 368 | Jim Rooker | .05 |
| 369 | Dale Berra | .05 |
| 370 | Jim Bibby | .05 |
| 371 | Steve Nicosia | .05 |
| 372 | Mike Easler | .05 |
| 373 | Bill Robinson | .05 |
| 374 | Lee Lacy | .05 |
| 375 | John Candelaria | .08 |
| 376 | Manny Sanguillen | .05 |
| 377 | Rick Rhoden | .05 |
| 378 | Grant Jackson | .05 |
| 379 | Tim Foli | .05 |

| NO. | PLAYER | MINT |
|---|---|---|
| 380 | Rod Scurry | .05 |
| 381 | Bill Madlock | .20 |
| 382 | Kurt Bevacqua* | .08 |
| 383 | Bert Blyleven | .12 |
| 384 | Eddie Solomon | .05 |
| 385 | Enrique Romo | .05 |
| 386 | John Milner | .05 |

**CLEVELAND INDIANS**

| NO. | PLAYER | MINT |
|---|---|---|
| 387 | Mike Hargrove | .05 |
| 388 | Jorge Orta | .05 |
| 389 | Toby Harrah | .05 |
| 390 | Tom Veryzer | .05 |
| 391 | Miguel Dilone | .05 |
| 392 | Dan Spillner | .05 |
| 393 | Jack Brohamer | .05 |
| 394 | Wayne Garland | .05 |
| 395 | Sid Monge | .05 |
| 396 | Rick Waits | .05 |
| 397 | Joe Charboneau | .12 |
| 398 | Gary Alexander | .05 |
| 399 | Jerry Dybzinski | .05 |
| 400 | Mike Stanton | .05 |
| 401 | Mike Paxton | .05 |
| 402 | Gary Gray | .05 |
| 403 | Rick Manning | .05 |
| 404 | Bo Diaz | .08 |
| 405 | Ron Hassey | .05 |
| 406 | Ross Grimsley | .05 |
| 407 | Victor Cruz | .05 |
| 408 | Len Barker | .08 |

**TORONTO BLUE JAYS**

| NO. | PLAYER | MINT |
|---|---|---|
| 409 | Bob Bailor | .05 |
| 410 | Otto Velez | .05 |
| 411 | Ernie Whitt | .05 |
| 412 | Jim Clancy | .05 |
| 413 | Barry Bonnell | .05 |
| 414 | Dave Stieb | .30 |
| 415 | Damaso Garcia (R) | .75 |
| 416 | John Mayberry | .05 |
| 417 | Roy Howell | .05 |
| 418 | Dan Ainge | .25 |
| 419 | Jesse Jefferson* | .08 |
| 420 | Joey McLaughlin | .05 |
| 421 | Lloyd Moseby (R) | 1.25 |
| 422 | Al Woods | .05 |
| 423 | Garth Iorg | .05 |
| 424 | Doug Ault | .05 |
| 425 | Ken Schrom | .05 |
| 426 | Mike Willis | .05 |
| 427 | Steve Braun | .05 |
| 428 | Bob Davis | .05 |
| 429 | Jerry Garvin | .05 |
| 430 | Alfredo Griffin | .08 |
| 431 | Bob Mattick (Mgr.) | .05 |

**SAN FRANCISCO GIANTS**

| NO. | PLAYER | MINT |
|---|---|---|
| 432 | Vida Blue | .08 |
| 433 | Jack Clark | .30 |
| 434 | Willie McCovey | .35 |
| 435 | Mike Ivie | .05 |
| 436 | Darrell Evans* | .15 |
| 437 | Terry Whitfield | .05 |
| 438 | Rennie Stennett | .05 |
| 439 | John Montefusco | .05 |
| 440 | Jim Wohlford | .05 |
| 441 | Bill North | .05 |
| 442 | Milt May | .05 |
| 443 | Max Venable | .05 |
| 444 | Ed Whitson | .05 |
| 445 | Al Holland | .20 |
| 446 | Randy Moffitt | .05 |
| 447 | Bob Knepper | .05 |
| 448 | Gary Lavelle | .05 |
| 449 | Greg Minton | .05 |
| 450 | Johnnie LeMaster | .05 |
| 451 | Larry Herndon | .05 |
| 452 | Rich Murray | .05 |
| 453 | Joe Pettini | .05 |
| 454 | Allen Ripley | .05 |
| 455 | Dennis Littlejohn | .05 |
| 456 | Tom Griffin | .05 |
| 457 | Alan Hargesheimer | .05 |
| 458 | Joe Strain | .05 |

**DETROIT TIGERS**

| NO. | PLAYER | MINT |
|---|---|---|
| 459 | Steve Kemp | .08 |
| 460 | Sparky Anderson (Mgr.) | .08 |

| NO. | PLAYER | MINT |
|---|---|---|
| 461 | Alan Trammell | .30 |
| 462 | Mark Fidrych | .08 |
| 463 | Lou Whitaker | .35 |
| 464 | Dave Rozema | .05 |
| 465 | Milt Wilcox | .05 |
| 466 | Champ Summers | .05 |
| 467 | Lance Parrish | .35 |
| 468 | Dan Petry | .25 |
| 469 | Pat Underwood | .05 |
| 470 | Rick Peters | .05 |
| 471 | Al Cowens | .05 |
| 472 | John Wockenfuss | .05 |
| 473 | Tom Brookens | .05 |
| 474 | Richie Hebner | .05 |
| 475 | Jack Morris | .35 |
| 476 | Jim Lentine | .05 |
| 477 | Bruce Robbins | .05 |
| 478 | Mark Wagner | .05 |
| 479 | Tim Corcoran | .05 |
| 480 | Stan Papi* | .08 |
| 481 | Kirk Gibson (R) | 1.50 |
| 482 | Dan Schatzeder | .05 |
| 483 | Amos Otis | .08 |
| | See card No. 32 | |

**SAN DIEGO PADRES**

| NO. | PLAYER | MINT |
|---|---|---|
| 484 | Dave Winfield | .50 |
| 485 | Rollie Fingers | .30 |
| 486 | Gene Richards | .05 |
| 487 | Randy Jones | .05 |
| 488 | Ozzie Smith | .20 |
| 489 | Gene Tenace | .05 |
| 490 | Bill Fahey | .05 |
| 491 | John Curtis | .05 |
| 492 | Dave Cash | .05 |
| 493 | Tim Flannery* | .12 |
| 494 | Jerry Mumphrey | .05 |
| 495 | Bob Shirley | .05 |
| 496 | Steve Mura | .05 |
| 497 | Eric Rasmussen | .05 |
| 498 | Broderick Perkins | .05 |
| 499 | Barry Evans | .05 |
| 500 | Chuck Baker | .05 |
| 501 | Luis Salazar | .05 |
| 502 | Gary Lucas | .10 |
| 503 | Mike Armstrong | .05 |
| 504 | Jerry Turner | .05 |
| 505 | Dennis Kinney | .05 |
| 506 | Willie Montanez | .05 |

**MILWAUKEE BREWERS**

| NO. | PLAYER | MINT |
|---|---|---|
| 507 | Gorman Thomas | .15 |
| 508 | Ben Oglivie | .08 |
| 509 | Larry Hisle | .05 |
| 510 | Sal Bando | .05 |
| 511 | Robin Yount | .45 |
| 512 | Mike Caldwell | .05 |
| 513 | Sixto Lezcano | .05 |
| 514 | Bill Travers | .15 |
| | Error—Jerry Augustine photo and back | |
| 514 | Bill Travers | .08 |
| 515 | Paul Molitor | .20 |
| 516 | Moose Haas | .05 |
| 517 | Bill Castro | .05 |
| 518 | Jim Slaton | .05 |
| 519 | Lary Sorensen | .05 |
| 520 | Bob McClure | .05 |
| 521 | Charlie Moore | .05 |
| 522 | Jim Gantner | .05 |
| 523 | Reggie Cleveland | .05 |
| 524 | Don Money | .05 |
| 525 | Bill Travers | .05 |
| 526 | Buck Martinez | .05 |
| 527 | Dick Davis | .05 |

**ST. LOUIS CARDINALS**

| NO. | PLAYER | MINT |
|---|---|---|
| 528 | Ted Simmons | .12 |
| 529 | Garry Templeton | .12 |
| 530 | Ken Reitz | .05 |
| 531 | Tony Scott | .05 |
| 532 | Ken Oberkfell | .05 |
| 533 | Bob Sykes | .05 |
| 534 | Keith Smith | .05 |
| 535 | John Littlefield | .05 |
| 536 | Jim Kaat | .10 |
| 537 | Bob Forsch | .05 |
| 538 | Mike Phillips | .05 |

# 1981 Fleer (Continued)

| NO. | PLAYER | MINT |
|---|---|---|
| 539 | Terry Landrum | .08 |
| 540 | Leon Durham (R) | .75 |
| 541 | Terry Kennedy | .08 |
| 542 | George Hendrick | .08 |
| 543 | Dane Iorg | .05 |
| 544 | Mark Littell | .05 |
| 545 | Keith Hernandez | .30 |
| 546 | Silvio Martinez | .05 |
| 547 | Don Hood | .25 |
| | Error—Pete Vuckovich photo and back | |
| 547 | Don Hood | .10 |
| 548 | Bobby Bonds | .08 |
| 549 | Mike Ramsey | .05 |
| 550 | Tom Herr | .15 |

**MINNESOTA TWINS**

| NO. | PLAYER | MINT |
|---|---|---|
| 551 | Roy Smalley | .05 |
| 552 | Jerry Koosman | .07 |
| 553 | Ken Landreaux | .05 |
| 554 | John Castino | .05 |
| 555 | Doug Corbett | .12 |
| 556 | Bombo Rivera | .05 |
| 557 | Ron Jackson | .05 |
| 558 | Butch Wynegar | .05 |
| 559 | Hosken Powell | .05 |
| 560 | Pete Redfern | .05 |
| 561 | Roger Erickson | .05 |
| 562 | Glenn Adams | .08 |
| 563 | Rick Sofield | .05 |
| 564 | Geoff Zahn | .05 |
| 565 | Pete Mackanin | .05 |
| 566 | Mike Cubbage | .05 |
| 567 | Darrell Jackson | .05 |
| 568 | Dave Edwards | .05 |
| 569 | Rob Wilfong | .05 |
| 570 | Sal Butera | .05 |
| 571 | Jose Morales | .05 |

**OAKLAND A'S**

| NO. | PLAYER | MINT |
|---|---|---|
| 572 | Rick Langford | .05 |
| 573 | Mike Norris | .05 |
| 574 | Rickey Henderson | .75 |
| 575 | Tony Armas | .15 |
| 576 | Dave Revering | .05 |
| 577 | Jeff Newman | .05 |
| 578 | Bob Lacey | .05 |
| 579 | Brian Kingman | .05 |
| 580 | Mitchell Page | .05 |
| 581 | Billy Martin (Mgr.) | .12 |
| 582 | Rob Picciolo | .05 |
| 583 | Mike Heath | .05 |
| 584 | Mickey Klutts | .05 |
| 585 | Orlando Gonzalez | .05 |
| 586 | Mike Davis (R) | .40 |
| 587 | Wayne Gross | .05 |
| 588 | Matt Keough | .05 |
| 589 | Steve McCatty | .05 |
| 590 | Dwayne Murphy | .08 |
| 591 | Mario Guerrero | .05 |
| 592 | Dave McKay | .05 |
| 593 | Jim Essian | .05 |
| 594 | Dave Heaverlo | .05 |

**SEATTLE MARINERS (Except 606)**

| NO. | PLAYER | MINT |
|---|---|---|
| 595 | Maury Wills (Mgr.) | .10 |
| 596 | Juan Beniquez | .05 |
| 597 | Rodney Craig | .05 |
| 598 | Jim Anderson | .05 |
| 599 | Floyd Bannister | .08 |
| 600 | Bruce Bochte | .05 |
| 601 | Julio Cruz | .05 |
| 602 | Ted Cox | .05 |
| 603 | Dan Meyer | .05 |
| 604 | Larry Cox | .05 |
| 605 | Bill Stein | .05 |
| 606 | Steve Garvey | .50 |
| | Most Hits, NL | |
| 607 | Dave Roberts | .05 |
| 608 | Leon Roberts | .05 |
| 609 | Reggie Walton | .05 |
| 610 | Dave Edler | .05 |

| NO. | PLAYER | MINT |
|---|---|---|
| 611 | Larry Milbourne | .05 |
| 612 | Kim Allen | .05 |
| 613 | Mario Mendoza | .05 |
| 614 | Tom Paciorek | .05 |
| 615 | Glenn Abbott | .05 |
| 616 | Joe Simpson | .05 |

**TEXAS RANGERS**

| NO. | PLAYER | MINT |
|---|---|---|
| 617 | Mickey Rivers | .08 |
| 618 | Jim Kern | .05 |
| 619 | Jim Sundberg | .05 |
| 620 | Richie Zisk | .05 |
| 621 | Jon Matlack | .05 |
| 622 | Ferguson Jenkins | .12 |
| 623 | Pat Corrales (Mgr.) | .05 |
| 624 | Ed Figueroa | .05 |
| 625 | Buddy Bell | .15 |
| 626 | Al Oliver | .20 |
| 627 | Doc Medich | .05 |
| 628 | Bump Wills | .05 |
| 629 | Rusty Staub | .08 |
| 630 | Pat Putnam | .05 |
| 631 | John Grubb | .05 |
| 632 | Danny Darwin | .05 |
| 633 | Ken Clay | .05 |
| 634 | Jim Norris | .05 |
| 635 | John Butcher | .20 |
| 636 | Dave Roberts | .05 |
| 637 | Billy Sample | .05 |
| 638 | Carl Yastrzemski | .75 |
| | 400 Home Run Club | |
| 639 | Cecil Cooper | .25 |
| 640 | Mike Schmidt | .75 |
| | (Third Base) Error—No. 5 | |
| 640 | Mike Schmidt | .75 |
| | (Home Run King) | |
| 641 | Checklist (1 to 50)* | .08 |
| 642 | Checklist (51 to 109) | .08 |
| 643 | Checklist (110 to 168) | .08 |

| NO. | PLAYER | MINT |
|---|---|---|
| 644 | Checklist (169 to 220)* | .08 |
| 645 | Triple Threat:* | 1.75 |
| | Schmidt, Rose, Bowa | |
| 646 | Checklist (221 to 267) | .08 |
| 647 | Checklist (268 to 315) | .08 |
| 648 | Checklist (316 to 359) | .08 |
| 649 | Checklist (360 to 408) | .08 |
| 650 | Reggie Jackson | .75 |
| | Mr. Baseball Error—No. 79 | |
| 650 | Reggie Jackson | .50 |
| | Mr. Baseball | |
| 651 | Checklist (409 to 458) | .08 |
| 652 | Checklist (459 to 506)* | .08 |
| 653 | Willie Wilson | .25 |
| | Most Hits, Most Runs Error—No. 29 | |
| 653 | Willie Wilson | .25 |
| | Most Hits, Most Runs | |
| 654 | Checklist (507 to 550)* | .08 |
| 655 | G. Brett (.390 Avg.) | .75 |
| | Error—No. 28* | |
| 656 | Checklist (551 to 593) | .08 |
| 657 | Tug McGraw | .08 |
| | Game Saver, Error—No. 7 | |
| 657 | Tug McGraw | .08 |
| | Game Saver | |
| 658 | Checklist (594 to 637) | .08 |
| 659 | Checklist (Specials)* | .08 |
| 660 | Steve Carlton | .50 |
| | "Lefty"—The Golden Arm Errors—Card No.6 and "1066" Cardinals | |
| 660 | Steve Carlton | .50 |
| | "Lefty"—The Golden Arm Error—"1066" Cardinals | |
| 660 | Steve Carlton | 1.50 |
| | "Lefty"—The Golden Arm Corrected—"1966" Cardinals | |

# 1982 Fleer.... Complete Set of 660 Cards—Value $20.00

Features the rookie card of Cal Ripken. Several errors were corrected; none are scarce or worth much more than ordinary cards, except cards 438 and 576. If a *variety* (error) is significant, it is listed and explained; if it is minor it is noted by an *asterisk*.

**LOS ANGELES DODGERS**

| NO. | PLAYER | MINT |
|---|---|---|
| 1 | Dusty Baker | .10 |
| 2 | Robert Castillo | .05 |
| 3 | Roy Cey | .15 |
| 4 | Terry Forster | .05 |
| 5 | Steve Garvey | .40 |
| 6 | Dave Goltz | .05 |
| 7 | Pedro Guerrero | .30 |
| 8 | Burt Hooton | .05 |
| 9 | Steve Howe | .05 |
| 10 | Jay Johnstone | .05 |
| 11 | Ken Landreaux | .05 |
| 12 | Davey Lopes | .05 |
| 13 | Mike Marshall (R) | .90 |
| 14 | Bobby Mitchell | .05 |
| 15 | Rick Monday | .05 |
| 16 | Tom Niedenfuer (R) | .50 |
| 17 | Ted Power (R) | .25 |

| NO. | PLAYER | MINT |
|---|---|---|
| 18 | Jerry Reuss | .05 |
| 19 | Ron Roenicke | .05 |
| 20 | Bill Russell | .05 |
| 21 | Steve Sax (R) | 1.00 |
| 22 | Mike Scioscia | .05 |
| 23 | Reggie Smith | .10 |
| 24 | Dave Stewart (R) | .15 |
| 25 | Rick Sutcliffe | .25 |
| 26 | Derrel Thomas | .05 |
| 27 | Fernando Valenzuela | .40 |
| 28 | Bob Welch | .05 |
| 29 | Steve Yeager | .05 |

**NEW YORK YANKEES**

| NO. | PLAYER | MINT |
|---|---|---|
| 30 | Bobby Brown | .05 |
| 31 | Rick Cerone | .05 |
| 32 | Ron Davis | .05 |
| 33 | Bucky Dent | .05 |
| 34 | Barry Foote | .05 |

| NO. | PLAYER | MINT |
|---|---|---|
| 35 | George Frazier | .05 |
| 36 | Oscar Gamble | .05 |
| 37 | Rich Gossage | .20 |
| 38 | Ron Guidry | .20 |
| 39 | Reggie Jackson | .40 |
| 40 | Tommy John | .15 |
| 41 | Rudy May | .05 |
| 42 | Larry Milbourne | .05 |
| 43 | Jerry Mumphrey | .05 |
| 44 | Bobby Murcer | .05 |
| 45 | Gene Nelson (R) | .15 |
| 46 | Graig Nettles | .15 |
| 47 | Johnny Oates | .05 |
| 48 | Lou Piniella | .10 |
| 49 | Willie Randolph | .05 |
| 50 | Rick Reuschel | .05 |
| 51 | Dave Revering | .05 |
| 52 | Dave Righetti (R) | 1.00 |

| NO. | PLAYER | MINT |
|---|---|---|
| 53 | Aurelio Rodriguez | .05 |
| 54 | Bob Watson | .05 |
| 55 | Dennis Werth | .05 |
| 56 | Dave Winfield | .50 |

**CINCINNATI REDS**

| NO. | PLAYER | MINT |
|---|---|---|
| 57 | Johnny Bench | .45 |
| 58 | Bruce Berenyi | .05 |
| 59 | Larry Biittner | .05 |
| 60 | Scott Brown | .05 |
| 61 | Dave Collins | .05 |
| 62 | Geoff Combe | .05 |
| 63 | Dave Concepcion | .10 |
| 64 | Dan Driessen | .05 |
| 65 | Joe Edelen | .05 |
| 66 | George Foster | .20 |
| 67 | Ken Griffey | .10 |
| 68 | Paul Householder | .05 |
| 69 | Tom Hume | .05 |

| NO. | PLAYER | MINT |
|---|---|---|
| 70 | Junior Kennedy | .05 |
| 71 | Ray Knight | .05 |
| 72 | Mike LaCoss | .05 |
| 73 | Rafael Landestoy | .05 |
| 74 | Charlie Leibrandt | .05 |
| 75 | Sam Mejias | .05 |
| 76 | Paul Moskau | .05 |
| 77 | Joe Nolan | .05 |
| 78 | Mike O'Berry | .05 |
| 79 | Ron Oester | .05 |
| 80 | Frank Pastore | .05 |
| 81 | Joe Price | .05 |
| 82 | Tom Seaver | .30 |
| 83 | Mario Soto | .10 |
| 84 | Mike Vail | .05 |

**OAKLAND A'S**

| NO. | PLAYER | MINT |
|---|---|---|
| 85 | Tony Armas | .10 |
| 86 | Shooty Babitt | .05 |
| 87 | Dave Beard | .05 |
| 88 | Rick Bosetti | .05 |
| 89 | Keith Drumright | .05 |
| 90 | Wayne Gross | .05 |
| 91 | Mike Heath | .05 |
| 92 | Rickey Henderson | .60 |
| 93 | Cliff Johnson | .05 |
| 94 | Jeff Jones | .05 |
| 95 | Matt Keough | .05 |
| 96 | Brian Kingman | .05 |
| 97 | Mickey Klutts | .05 |
| 98 | Rick Langford | .05 |
| 99 | Steve McCatty | .05 |
| 100 | Dave McKay | .05 |
| 101 | Dwayne Murphy | .07 |
| 102 | Jeff Newman | .05 |
| 103 | Mike Norris | .05 |
| 104 | Bob Owchinko | .05 |
| 105 | Mitchell Page | .05 |
| 106 | Rob Picciolo | .05 |
| 107 | Jim Spencer | .05 |
| 108 | Fred Stanley | .05 |
| 109 | Tom Underwood | .05 |

**ST. LOUIS CARDINALS**

| NO. | PLAYER | MINT |
|---|---|---|
| 110 | Joaquin Andujar | .15 |
| 111 | Steve Braun | .05 |
| 112 | Bob Forsch | .05 |
| 113 | George Hendrick | .08 |
| 114 | Keith Hernandez | .30 |
| 115 | Tom Herr | .15 |
| 116 | Dane Iorg | .05 |
| 117 | Jim Kaat | .10 |
| 118 | Tito Landrum | .05 |
| 119 | Sixto Lezcano | .05 |
| 120 | Mark Littell | .05 |
| 121 | John Martin | .05 |
| 122 | Silvio Martinez | .05 |
| 123 | Ken Oberkfell | .05 |
| 124 | Darrell Porter | .05 |
| 125 | Mike Ramsey | .05 |
| 126 | Orlando Sanchez | .05 |
| 127 | Bob Shirley | .05 |
| 128 | Lary Sorensen | .05 |
| 129 | Bruce Sutter | .25 |
| 130 | Bob Sykes | .05 |
| 131 | Garry Templeton | .15 |
| 132 | Gene Tenace | .05 |

**MILWAUKEE BREWERS**

| NO. | PLAYER | MINT |
|---|---|---|
| 133 | Jerry Augustine | .05 |
| 134 | Sal Brando | .05 |
| 135 | Mark Brouhard | .05 |
| 136 | Mike Caldwell | .05 |
| 137 | Reggie Cleveland | .05 |
| 138 | Cecil Cooper | .20 |
| 139 | Jamie Easterly | .05 |
| 140 | Marshall Edwards | .05 |
| 141 | Rollie Fingers | .20 |
| 142 | Jim Gantner | .05 |
| 143 | Moose Haas | .05 |
| 144 | Larry Hisle | .05 |
| 145 | Roy Howell | .05 |
| 146 | Rickey Keeton | .05 |
| 147 | Randy Lerch | .05 |
| 148 | Paul Molitor | .15 |
| 149 | Don Money | .05 |
| 150 | Charlie Moore | .05 |
| 151 | Ben Oglivie | .10 |

| NO. | PLAYER | MINT |
|---|---|---|
| 152 | Ted Simmons | .10 |
| 153 | Jim Slaton | .05 |
| 154 | Gorman Thomas | .10 |
| 155 | Robin Yount | .45 |
| 156 | Pete Vuckovich | .10 |

**BALTIMORE ORIOLES**

| NO. | PLAYER | MINT |
|---|---|---|
| 157 | Benny Ayala | .05 |
| 158 | Mark Belanger | .05 |
| 159 | Al Bumbry | .05 |
| 160 | Terry Crowley | .05 |
| 161 | Rich Dauer | .05 |
| 162 | Doug DeCinces | .10 |
| 163 | Rick Dempsey | .05 |
| 164 | Jim Dwyer | .05 |
| 165 | Mike Flanagan | .10 |
| 166 | Dave Ford | .05 |
| 167 | Dan Graham | .05 |
| 168 | Wayne Krenchicki | .05 |
| 169 | John Lowenstein | .05 |
| 170 | Dennis Martinez | .05 |
| 171 | Tippy Martinez | .05 |
| 172 | Scott McGregor | .10 |
| 173 | Jose Morales | .05 |
| 174 | Eddie Murray | .60 |
| 175 | Jim Palmer | .30 |
| 176 | Cal Ripken, Jr. (R) | 4.50 |
| 177 | Gary Roenicke | .05 |
| 178 | Lenn Sakata | .05 |
| 179 | Ken Singleton | .10 |
| 180 | Sammy Stewart | .05 |
| 181 | Tim Stoddard | .05 |
| 182 | Steve Stone | .05 |

**MONTREAL EXPOS**

| NO. | PLAYER | MINT |
|---|---|---|
| 183 | Stan Bahnsen | .05 |
| 184 | Ray Burris | .05 |
| 185 | Gary Carter | .50 |
| 186 | Warren Cromartie | .05 |
| 187 | Andre Dawson | .25 |
| 188 | Terry Francona (R) | .35 |
| 189 | Woodie Fryman | .05 |
| 190 | Bill Gullickson | .05 |
| 191 | Grant Jackson | .05 |
| 192 | Wallace Johnson | .05 |
| 193 | Charlie Lea | .05 |
| 194 | Bill Lee | .05 |
| 195 | Jerry Manuel | .05 |
| 196 | Brad Mills | .05 |
| 197 | John Milner | .05 |
| 198 | Rowland Office | .05 |
| 199 | David Palmer | .05 |
| 200 | Larry Parrish | .05 |
| 201 | Mike Phillips | .05 |
| 202 | Tim Raines | .40 |
| 203 | Bobby Ramos | .05 |
| 204 | Jeff Reardon | .05 |
| 205 | Steve Rogers | .10 |
| 206 | Scott Sanderson | .05 |
| 207 | Rodney Scott | .05 |
| 208 | Elias Sosa | .05 |
| 209 | Chris Speier | .05 |
| 210 | Tim Wallach (R) | .50 |
| 211 | Jerry White | .05 |

**HOUSTON ASTROS**

| NO. | PLAYER | MINT |
|---|---|---|
| 212 | Alan Ashby | .05 |
| 213 | Cesar Cedeno | .10 |
| 214 | Jose Cruz | .15 |
| 215 | Kiko Garcia | .05 |
| 216 | Phil Garner | .05 |
| 217 | Danny Heep | .05 |
| 218 | Art Howe | .05 |
| 219 | Bob Knepper | .05 |
| 220 | Frank LaCorte | .05 |
| 221 | Joe Niekro | .05 |
| 222 | Joe Pittman | .05 |
| 223 | Terry Puhl | .05 |
| 224 | Luis Pujols | .05 |
| 225 | Craig Reynolds | .05 |
| 226 | J.R. Richard | .10 |
| 227 | Dave Roberts | .05 |
| 228 | Vern Ruhle | .05 |
| 229 | Nolan Ryan | .30 |
| 230 | Joe Sambito | .05 |
| 231 | Tony Scott | .05 |
| 232 | Dave Smith | .05 |
| 233 | Harry Spilman | .05 |

| NO. | PLAYER | MINT |
|---|---|---|
| 234 | Don Sutton | .15 |
| 235 | Dickie Thon | .10 |
| 236 | Denny Walling | .05 |
| 237 | Gary Woods | .05 |

**PHILADELPHIA PHILLIES**

| NO. | PLAYER | MINT |
|---|---|---|
| 238 | Luis Aguayo | .05 |
| 239 | Ramon Aviles | .05 |
| 240 | Bob Boone | .05 |
| 241 | Larry Bowa | .10 |
| 242 | Warren Brusstar | .05 |
| 243 | Steve Carlton | .50 |
| 244 | Larry Christenson | .05 |
| 245 | Dick Davis | .05 |
| 246 | Greg Gross | .05 |
| 247 | Sparky Lyle | .08 |
| 248 | Garry Maddox | .05 |
| 249 | Gary Matthews | .10 |
| 250 | Bake McBride | .05 |
| 251 | Tug McGraw | .10 |
| 252 | Keith Moreland | .05 |
| 253 | Dickie Noles | .05 |
| 254 | Mike Proly | .05 |
| 255 | Ron Reed | .05 |
| 256 | Pete Rose | 1.00 |
| 257 | Dick Ruthven | .05 |
| 258 | Mike Schmidt | .60 |
| 259 | Lonnie Smith | .10 |
| 260 | Manny Trillo | .05 |
| 261 | Del Unser | .05 |
| 262 | George Vukovich | .05 |

**DETROIT TIGERS**

| NO. | PLAYER | MINT |
|---|---|---|
| 263 | Tom Brookens | .05 |
| 264 | George Cappuzzello | .05 |
| 265 | Marty Castillo | .05 |
| 266 | Al Cowens | .05 |
| 267 | Kirk Gibson | .30 |
| 268 | Richie Hebner | .05 |
| 269 | Ron Jackson | .05 |
| 270 | Lynn Jones | .05 |
| 271 | Steve Kemp | .10 |
| 272 | Rick Leach | .05 |
| 273 | Aurelio Lopez | .05 |
| 274 | Jack Morris | .30 |
| 275 | Kevin Saucier | .05 |
| 276 | Lance Parrish | .30 |
| 277 | Rick Peters | .05 |
| 278 | Dan Petry | .20 |
| 279 | David Rozema | .05 |
| 280 | Stan Papi | .05 |
| 281 | Dan Schatzeder | .05 |
| 282 | Champ Summers | .05 |
| 283 | Alan Trammell | .30 |
| 284 | Lou Whitaker | .30 |
| 285 | Milt Wilcox | .05 |
| 286 | John Wockenfuss | .05 |

**BOSTON RED SOX**

| NO. | PLAYER | MINT |
|---|---|---|
| 287 | Gary Allenson | .05 |
| 288 | Tom Burgmeier | .05 |
| 289 | Bill Campbell | .05 |
| 290 | Mark Clear | .05 |
| 291 | Steve Crawford | .05 |
| 292 | Dennis Eckersley | .05 |
| 293 | Dwight Evans | .15 |
| 294 | Rich Gedman (R) | .60 |
| 295 | Garry Hancock | .05 |
| 296 | Glenn Hoffman | .05 |
| 297 | Bruce Hurst | .05 |
| 298 | Carney Lansford | .15 |
| 299 | Rick Miller | .05 |
| 300 | Reid Nichols | .05 |
| 301 | Bob Ojeda (R) | .60 |
| 302 | Tony Perez | .15 |
| 303 | Chuck Rainey | .05 |
| 304 | Jerry Remy | .05 |
| 305 | Jim Rice | .40 |
| 306 | Joe Rudi | .05 |
| 307 | Bob Stanley | .05 |
| 308 | Dave Stapleton | .05 |
| 309 | Frank Tanana | .05 |
| 310 | Mike Torrez | .05 |
| 311 | John Tudor | .10 |
| 312 | Carl Yastrzemski | .60 |

**TEXAS RANGERS**

| NO. | PLAYER | MINT |
|---|---|---|
| 313 | Buddy Bell | .15 |
| 314 | Steve Comer | .05 |

| NO. | PLAYER | MINT |
|---|---|---|
| 315 | Danny Darwin | .05 |
| 316 | John Ellis | .05 |
| 317 | John Grubb | .05 |
| 318 | Rick Honeycutt | .05 |
| 319 | Charlie Hough | .05 |
| 320 | Ferguson Jenkins | .10 |
| 321 | John Henry Johnson | .05 |
| 322 | Jim Kern | .05 |
| 323 | Jon Matlack | .05 |
| 324 | Doc Medich | .05 |
| 325 | Mario Mendoza | .05 |
| 326 | Al Oliver | .15 |
| 327 | Pat Putnam | .05 |
| 328 | Mickey Rivers | .05 |
| 329 | Leon Roberts | .05 |
| 330 | Billy Sample | .05 |
| 331 | Bill Stein | .05 |
| 332 | Jim Sundberg | .05 |
| 333 | Mark Wagner | .05 |
| 334 | Bump Wills | .05 |

**CHICAGO WHITE SOX**

| NO. | PLAYER | MINT |
|---|---|---|
| 335 | Bill Almon | .05 |
| 336 | Harold Baines | .30 |
| 337 | Ross Baumgarten | .05 |
| 338 | Tony Bernazard | .05 |
| 339 | Britt Burns | .10 |
| 340 | Richard Dotson | .10 |
| 341 | Jim Essian | .05 |
| 342 | Ed Farmer | .05 |
| 343 | Carlton Fisk | .20 |
| 344 | Kevin Hickey | .05 |
| 345 | LaMarr Hoyt | .10 |
| 346 | Lamar Johnson | .05 |
| 347 | Jerry Koosman | .05 |
| 348 | Rusty Kuntz | .05 |
| 349 | Dennis Lamp | .05 |
| 350 | Ron LeFlore | .05 |
| 351 | Chet Lemon | .08 |
| 352 | Greg Luzinski | .10 |
| 353 | Bob Molinaro | .05 |
| 354 | Jim Morrison | .05 |
| 355 | Wayne Nordhagen | .05 |
| 356 | Greg Pryor | .05 |
| 357 | Mike Squires | .05 |
| 358 | Steve Trout | .05 |

**CLEVELAND INDIANS**

| NO. | PLAYER | MINT |
|---|---|---|
| 359 | Alan Bannister | .05 |
| 360 | Len Barker | .05 |
| 361 | Bert Blyleven | .15 |
| 362 | Joe Charboneau | .05 |
| 363 | John Denny | .10 |
| 364 | Bo Diaz | .05 |
| 365 | Miguel Dilone | .05 |
| 366 | Jerry Dybzinski | .05 |
| 367 | Wayne Garland | .05 |
| 368 | Mike Hargrove | .05 |
| 369 | Toby Harrah | .05 |
| 370 | Ron Hassey | .05 |
| 371 | Von Hayes (R) | .90 |
| 372 | Pat Kelly | .05 |
| 373 | Duane Kuiper | .05 |
| 374 | Rick Manning | .05 |
| 375 | Sid Monge | .05 |
| 376 | Jorge Orta | .05 |
| 377 | Dave Rosello | .05 |
| 378 | Dan Spillner | .05 |
| 379 | Mike Stanton | .05 |
| 380 | Andre Thornton | .10 |
| 381 | Tom Veryzer | .05 |
| 382 | Rick Waits | .05 |

**SAN FRANCISCO GIANTS**

| NO. | PLAYER | MINT |
|---|---|---|
| 383 | Doyle Alexander | .05 |
| 384 | Vida Blue | .05 |
| 385 | Fred Breining | .05 |
| 386 | Enos Cabell | .05 |
| 387 | Jack Clark | .25 |
| 388 | Darrell Evans | .10 |
| 389 | Tom Griffin | .05 |
| 390 | Larry Herndon | .05 |
| 391 | Al Holland | .05 |
| 392 | Gary Lavelle | .05 |
| 393 | Johnnie LeMaster | .05 |
| 394 | Jerry Martin | .05 |
| 395 | Milt May | .05 |
| 396 | Greg Minton | .05 |

| NO. | PLAYER | MINT |
|---|---|---|
| 397 | Joe Morgan | .25 |
| 398 | Joe Pettini | .05 |
| 399 | Alan Ripley | .05 |
| 400 | Billy Smith | .05 |
| 401 | Rennie Stennett | .05 |
| 402 | Ed Whitson | .05 |
| 403 | Jim Wohlford | .05 |

**KANSAS CITY ROYALS**

| NO. | PLAYER | MINT |
|---|---|---|
| 404 | Willie Aikens | .05 |
| 405 | George Brett | .75 |
| 406 | Ken Brett | .05 |
| 407 | Dave Chalk | .05 |
| 408 | Rich Gale | .05 |
| 409 | Cesar Geronimo | .05 |
| 410 | Larry Gura | .05 |
| 411 | Clint Hurdle | .05 |
| 412 | Mike Jones | .05 |
| 413 | Dennis Leonard | .05 |
| 414 | Renie Martin | .05 |
| 415 | Lee May | .05 |
| 416 | Hal McRae | .05 |
| 417 | Darryl Motley (R) | .25 |
| 418 | Rance Mulliniks | .05 |
| 419 | Amos Otis | .05 |
| 420 | Ken Phelps (R) | .25 |
| 421 | Jamie Quirk | .05 |
| 422 | Dan Quisenberry | .25 |
| 423 | Paul Splittorff | .05 |
| 424 | U.L. Washington | .05 |
| 425 | John Wathan | .05 |
| 426 | Frank White | .05 |
| 427 | Willie Wilson | .25 |

**ATLANTA BRAVES**

| NO. | PLAYER | MINT |
|---|---|---|
| 428 | Brian Asselstine | .05 |
| 429 | Bruce Benedict | .05 |
| 430 | Tom Boggs | .05 |
| 431 | Larry Bradford | .05 |
| 432 | Rick Camp | .05 |
| 433 | Chris Chambliss | .05 |
| 434 | Gene Garber | .05 |
| 435 | Preston Hanna | .05 |
| 436 | Bob Horner | .25 |
| 437 | Glenn Hubbard | .05 |
| 438 | "All" Hrabosky (error) | 10.00 |
| | "Al" misspelled | |
| 438 | Al Hrabosky | .50 |
| | (height 5'1"—error) | |
| 438 | Al Hrabosky | .07 |
| | (height 5'10" correct) | |
| 439 | Rufino Linares | .05 |
| 440 | Rick Mahler (R) | .25 |
| 441 | Ed Miller | .05 |
| 442 | John Montefusco | .05 |
| 443 | Dale Murphy | 1.00 |
| 444 | Phil Niekro | .20 |
| 445 | Gaylord Perry | .20 |
| 446 | Biff Pocoroba | .05 |
| 447 | Rafael Ramirez | .05 |
| 448 | Jerry Royster | .05 |
| 449 | Claudell Washington | .08 |

**CALIFORNIA ANGELS**

| NO. | PLAYER | MINT |
|---|---|---|
| 450 | Don Aase | .05 |
| 451 | Don Baylor | .15 |
| 452 | Juan Beniquez | .05 |
| 453 | Rick Burleson | .05 |
| 454 | Bert Campaneris | .05 |
| 455 | Rod Carew | .50 |
| 456 | Bob Clark | .05 |
| 457 | Brian Downing | .05 |
| 458 | Dan Ford | .05 |
| 459 | Ken Forsch | .05 |
| 460 | Dave Frost* | .05 |
| 461 | Bobby Grich | .10 |
| 462 | Larry Harlow | .05 |
| 463 | John Harris | .05 |
| 464 | Andy Hassler | .05 |
| 465 | Butch Hobson | .05 |
| 466 | Jesse Jefferson | .05 |
| 467 | Bruce Kison | .05 |
| 468 | Fred Lynn | .25 |
| 469 | Angel Moreno | .05 |
| 470 | Ed Ott | .05 |
| 471 | Fred Patek | .05 |
| 472 | Steve Renko | .05 |
| 473 | Mike Witt (R) | .75 |
| 474 | Geoff Zahn | .05 |

**PITTSBURGH PIRATES**

| NO. | PLAYER | MINT |
|---|---|---|
| 475 | Gary Alexander | .05 |
| 476 | Dale Berra | .05 |
| 477 | Kurt Bevacqua | .05 |
| 478 | Jim Bibby | .05 |
| 479 | John Candelaria | .05 |
| 480 | Victor Cruz | .05 |
| 481 | Mike Easler | .05 |
| 482 | Tim Foli | .05 |
| 483 | Lee Lacy | .05 |
| 484 | Vance Law | .05 |
| 485 | Bill Madlock | .15 |
| 486 | Willie Montanez | .05 |
| 487 | Omar Moreno | .05 |
| 488 | Steve Nicosia | .05 |
| 489 | Dave Parker | .25 |
| 490 | Tony Pena | .15 |
| 491 | Pascual Perez | .05 |
| 492 | Johnny Ray (R) | .60 |
| 493 | Rick Rhoden | .05 |
| 494 | Bill Robinson | .05 |
| 495 | Don Robinson | .05 |
| 496 | Enrique Romo | .05 |
| 497 | Rod Scurry | .05 |
| 498 | Eddie Solomon | .05 |
| 499 | Willie Stargell | .25 |
| 500 | Kent Tekulve | .05 |
| 501 | Jason Thompson | .05 |

**SEATTLE MARINERS**

| NO. | PLAYER | MINT |
|---|---|---|
| 502 | Glenn Abbott | .05 |
| 503 | Jim Anderson | .05 |
| 504 | Floyd Bannister | .05 |
| 505 | Bruce Bochte | .05 |
| 506 | Jeff Burroughs | .05 |
| 507 | Bryan Clark | .05 |
| 508 | Ken Clay | .05 |
| 509 | Julio Cruz | .05 |
| 510 | Dick Drago | .05 |
| 511 | Gary Gray | .05 |
| 512 | Dan Meyer | .05 |
| 513 | Jerry Narron | .05 |
| 514 | Tom Paciorek | .05 |
| 515 | Casey Parsons | .05 |
| 516 | Lenny Randle | .05 |
| 517 | Shane Rawley | .05 |
| 518 | Joe Simpson | .05 |
| 519 | Richie Zisk | .05 |

**NEW YORK METS**

| NO. | PLAYER | MINT |
|---|---|---|
| 520 | Neil Allen | .05 |
| 521 | Bob Bailor | .05 |
| 522 | Hubie Brooks | .10 |
| 523 | Mike Cubbage | .05 |
| 524 | Pete Falcone | .05 |
| 525 | Doug Flynn | .05 |
| 526 | Tom Hausman | .05 |
| 527 | Ron Hodges | .05 |
| 528 | Randy Jones | .05 |
| 529 | Mike Jorgensen | .05 |
| 530 | Dave Kingman | .15 |
| 531 | Ed Lynch | .10 |
| 532 | Mike Marshall | .05 |
| 533 | Lee Mazzilli | .05 |
| 534 | Dyar Miller | .05 |
| 535 | Mike Scott | .05 |
| 536 | Rusty Staub | .10 |
| 537 | John Stearns | .05 |
| 538 | Craig Swan | .05 |
| 539 | Frank Taveras | .05 |
| 540 | Alex Trevino | .05 |
| 541 | Ellis Valentine | .05 |
| 542 | Mookie Wilson | .05 |
| 543 | Joel Youngblood | .05 |
| 544 | Pat Zachry | .05 |

**MINNESOTA TWINS**

| NO. | PLAYER | MINT |
|---|---|---|
| 545 | Glenn Adams | .05 |
| 546 | Fernando Arroyo | .05 |
| 547 | John Verhoeven | .05 |
| 548 | Sal Butera | .05 |
| 549 | John Castino | .05 |
| 550 | Don Cooper | .05 |
| 551 | Doug Corbett | .05 |
| 552 | Dave Engle | .05 |
| 553 | Roger Erickson | .05 |
| 554 | Danny Goodwin | .05 |
| 555 | Darrell Jackson | 1.50 |
| | (error—black hat) | |
| 555 | Darrell Jackson | .10 |
| | (correct—red hat) | |
| 556 | Pete Mackanin | .05 |
| 557 | Jack O'Connor | .05 |
| 558 | Hosken Powell | .05 |
| 559 | Pete Redfern | .05 |
| 560 | Roy Smalley | .05 |
| 561 | Chuck Baker | .05 |
| 562 | Gary Ward | .05 |
| 563 | Rob Wilfong | .05 |
| 564 | Al Williams | .05 |
| 565 | Butch Wynegar | .05 |

**SAN DIEGO PADRES**

| NO. | PLAYER | MINT |
|---|---|---|
| 566 | Randy Bass | .05 |
| 567 | Juan Bonilla | .05 |
| 568 | Danny Boone | .05 |
| 569 | John Curtis | .05 |
| 570 | Juan Eichelberger | .05 |
| 571 | Barry Evans | .05 |
| 572 | Tim Flannery | .05 |
| 573 | Ruppert Jones | .05 |
| 574 | Terry Kennedy | .10 |
| 575 | Joe LeFebvre | .05 |
| 576 | John Littlefield | 40.00 |
| | (left handed—error) | |
| 576 | John Littlefield | .10 |
| | (right handed—corrected) | |
| 577 | Gary Lucas | .05 |
| 578 | Steve Mura | .05 |
| 579 | Broderick Perkins | .05 |
| 580 | Gene Richards | .05 |
| 581 | Luis Salazar | .05 |
| 582 | Ozzie Smith | .10 |
| 583 | John Urrea | .05 |
| 584 | Chris Welsh | .05 |
| 585 | Rick Wise | .05 |

**CHICAGO CUBS**

| NO. | PLAYER | MINT |
|---|---|---|
| 586 | Doug Bird | .05 |
| 587 | Tim Blackwell | .05 |
| 588 | Bobby Bonds | .10 |
| 589 | Bill Buckner | .10 |
| 590 | Bill Caudill | .05 |
| 591 | Hector Cruz | .05 |
| 592 | Jody Davis (R) | .55 |
| 593 | Ivan DeJesus | .05 |
| 594 | Steve Dillard | .05 |
| 595 | Leon Durham | .25 |
| 596 | Rawly Eastwick | .05 |
| 597 | Steve Henderson | .05 |
| 598 | Mike Krukow | .05 |
| 599 | Mike Lum | .05 |
| 600 | Randy Martz | .05 |
| 601 | Jerry Morales | .05 |
| 602 | Ken Reitz | .05 |
| 603 | Lee Smith (R)* | .50 |
| 604 | Dick Tidrow | .05 |
| 605 | Jim Tracy | .05 |
| 606 | Mike Tyson | .05 |
| 607 | Ty Waller | .05 |

**TORONTO BLUE JAYS**

| NO. | PLAYER | MINT |
|---|---|---|
| 608 | Danny Ainge | .10 |
| 609 | Jorge Bell (R) | 1.25 |
| 610 | Mark Bomback | .05 |
| 611 | Barry Bonnell | .05 |
| 612 | Jim Clancy | .05 |
| 613 | Damaso Garcia | .10 |
| 614 | Jerry Garvin | .05 |
| 615 | Alfredo Griffin | .10 |
| 616 | Garth Iorg | .05 |
| 617 | Luis Leal | .05 |
| 618 | Ken Macha | .05 |
| 619 | John Mayberry | .05 |
| 620 | Joey McLaughlin | .05 |
| 621 | Lloyd Moseby | .15 |
| 622 | Dave Stieb | .20 |
| 623 | Jackson Todd | .05 |
| 624 | Willie Upshaw | .15 |
| 625 | Otto Velez | .05 |
| 626 | Ernie Whitt | .05 |
| 627 | Al Woods | .05 |
| 628 | All-Star Game | .05 |
| 629 | All-Star Infielders: | .05 |
| | Frank White, Bucky Dent | |
| 630 | Big Red Machine: | .10 |
| | Driessen, Concepcion, Foster | |
| 631 | Bruce Sutter | .10 |
| | "Top NL Relief Pitcher" | |
| 632 | "Steve and Carlton" | .20 |
| | Steve Carlton, Carlton Fisk | |
| 633 | Carl Yastrzemski | .30 |
| | "3000th Game" | |
| 634 | "Dynamic Duo" | .25 |
| | Johnny Bench, Tom Seaver | |
| 635 | "West Meets East" | .25 |
| | Valenzuela, Carter | |
| 636 | Fernando Valenzuela:* | .30 |
| | "NL Strikeout King" | |
| 637 | Mike Schmidt | .30 |
| | "Home Run King" | |
| 638 | "NL All Stars" | .20 |
| | Gary Carter, Dave Parker | |
| 639 | "Perfect Game" | .10 |
| | Len Barker, Bo Diaz | |
| 640 | "Pete & Re-Pete" | 1.00 |
| | Pete Rose and Son | |
| 641 | "Phillies' Finest" | .30 |
| | Carlton, Smith, Schmidt | |
| 642 | "Red Sox Reunion" | .10 |
| | Fred Lynn, Dwight Evans | |
| 643 | Rickey Henderson | .30 |
| | "Most Hits, Most Runs" | |
| 644 | Rollie Fingers | .10 |
| | "Most 'Saves AL" | |
| 645 | Tom Seaver | .20 |
| | "Most 1981 Wins" | |
| 646 | "Yankee Powerhouse"* | .50 |
| | R. Jackson, D. Winfield | |
| 647 | Checklist No. 1 | .08 |
| 648 | Checklist No. 2 | .08 |
| 649 | Checklist No. 3 | .08 |
| 650 | Checklist No. 4 | .08 |
| 651 | Checklist No. 5 | .08 |
| 652 | Checklist No. 6 | .08 |
| 653 | Checklist No. 7 | .08 |
| 654 | Checklist No. 8 | .08 |
| 655 | Checklist No. 9 | .08 |
| 656 | Checklist No. 10 | .08 |
| 657 | Checklist No. 11 | .08 |
| 658 | Checklist No. 12 | .08 |
| 659 | Checklist No. 13 | .08 |
| 660 | Checklist No. 14 | .08 |

# 1983 Fleer....Complete Set of 660 Cards—Value $25.00
Features the rookie cards of Wade Boggs, Tony Gwynn, Willie McGee and Ryne Sandberg.

Willie McGee
OUTFIELD

Storm Davis
PITCHER

Wade Boggs
THIRD BASE

Tony Gwynn
OUTFIELD

Ryne Sandberg
THIRD BASE

| NO. PLAYER | MINT |
|---|---|
| **ST. LOUIS CARDINALS** | |
| 1 Joaquin Andujar | .15 |
| 2 Doug Bair | .05 |
| 3 Steve Braun | .05 |
| 4 Glenn Brummer | .05 |
| 5 Bob Forsch | .05 |
| 6 David Green (R) | .20 |
| 7 George Hendrick | .10 |
| 8 Keith Hernandez | .30 |
| 9 Tom Herr | .15 |
| 10 Dane Iorg | .05 |
| 11 Jim Kaat | .10 |
| 12 Jeff Lahti | .05 |
| 13 Tito Landrum | .05 |
| 14 Dave LaPoint (R) | .20 |
| 15 Willie McGee (R) | 2.50 |
| 16 Steve Mura | .05 |
| 17 Ken Oberkfell | .05 |
| 18 Darrell Porter | .05 |
| 19 Mike Ramsey | .05 |
| 20 Gene Roof | .05 |
| 21 Lonnie Smith | .10 |
| 22 Ozzie Smith | .10 |
| 23 John Stuper | .10 |
| 24 Bruce Sutter | .20 |
| 25 Gene Tenace | .05 |
| **MILWAUKEE BREWERS** | |
| 26 Jerry Augustine | .05 |
| 27 Dwight Bernard | .05 |
| 28 Mark Brouhard | .05 |
| 29 Mike Caldwell | .05 |
| 30 Cecil Cooper | .15 |
| 31 Jamie Easterly | .05 |
| 32 Marshall Edwards | .05 |
| 33 Rollie Fingers | .20 |
| 34 Jim Gantner | .05 |
| 35 Moose Haas | .05 |
| 36 Roy Howell | .05 |
| 37 Peter Ladd | .05 |
| 38 Bob McClure | .05 |
| 39 Doc Medich | .05 |
| 40 Paul Molitor | .15 |
| 41 Don Money | .05 |
| 42 Charlie Moore | .05 |
| 43 Ben Oglivie | .07 |
| 44 Ed Romero | .05 |
| 45 Ted Simmons | .10 |
| 46 Jim Slaton | .05 |
| 47 Don Sutton | .10 |
| 48 Gorman Thomas | .10 |
| 49 Pete Vuckovich | .05 |
| 50 Ned Yost | .05 |
| 51 Robin Yount | .30 |
| **BALTIMORE ORIOLES** | |
| 52 Benny Ayala | .05 |
| 53 Bob Bonner | .05 |
| 54 Al Bumbry | .05 |
| 55 Terry Crowley | .05 |
| 56 Storm Davis (R) | .50 |
| 57 Rich Dauer | .05 |
| 58 Rick Dempsey | .05 |
| 59 Jim Dwyer | .05 |
| 60 Mike Flanagan | .10 |
| 61 Dan Ford | .05 |
| 62 Glenn Gulliver | .05 |
| 63 John Lowenstein | .05 |

| NO. PLAYER | MINT |
|---|---|
| 64 Dennis Martinez | .05 |
| 65 Tippy Martinez | .05 |
| 66 Scott McGregor | .10 |
| 67 Eddie Murray | .60 |
| 68 Joe Nolan | .05 |
| 69 Jim Palmer | .25 |
| 70 Cal Ripken Jr. | .75 |
| 71 Gary Roenicke | .05 |
| 72 Lenn Sakata | .05 |
| 73 Ken Singleton | .05 |
| 74 Sammy Stewart | .05 |
| 75 Tim Stoddard | .05 |
| **CALIFORNIA ANGELS** | |
| 76 Don Aase | .05 |
| 77 Don Baylor | .10 |
| 78 Juan Beniquez | .05 |
| 79 Bob Boone | .05 |
| 80 Rick Burleson | .05 |
| 81 Rod Carew | .40 |
| 82 Bobby Clark | .05 |
| 83 Doug Corbett | .05 |
| 84 John Curtis | .05 |
| 85 Doug DeCinces | .10 |
| 86 Brian Downing | .05 |
| 87 Joe Ferguson | .05 |
| 88 Tim Foli | .05 |
| 89 Ken Forsch | .05 |
| 90 Dave Goltz | .05 |
| 91 Bobby Grich | .05 |
| 92 Andy Hassler | .05 |
| 93 Reggie Jackson | .45 |
| 94 Ron Jackson | .05 |
| 95 Tommy John | .15 |
| 96 Bruce Kison | .05 |
| 97 Fred Lynn | .20 |
| 98 Ed Ott | .05 |
| 99 Steve Renko | .05 |
| 100 Luis Sanchez | .05 |
| 101 Rob Wilfong | .05 |
| 102 Mike Witt | .10 |
| 103 Geoff Zahn | .05 |
| **KANSAS CITY ROYALS** | |
| 104 Willie Aikens | .05 |
| 105 Mike Armstrong | .05 |
| 106 Vida Blue | .10 |
| 107 Bud Black (R) | .35 |
| 108 George Brett | .50 |
| 109 Bill Castro | .05 |
| 110 Onix Concepcion | .10 |
| 111 Dave Frost | .05 |
| 112 Cesar Geronimo | .05 |
| 113 Larry Gura | .05 |
| 114 Steve Hammond | .05 |
| 115 Don Hood | .05 |
| 116 Dennis Leonard | .05 |
| 117 Jerry Martin | .05 |
| 118 Lee May | .05 |
| 119 Hal McRae | .05 |
| 120 Amos Otis | .05 |
| 121 Greg Pryor | .05 |
| 122 Dan Quisenberry | .20 |
| 123 Don Slaught (R) | .25 |
| 124 Paul Splittorff | .05 |
| 125 U.L. Washington | .05 |
| 126 John Wathan | .05 |
| 127 Frank White | .07 |

| NO. PLAYER | MINT |
|---|---|
| 128 Willie Wilson | .20 |
| **ATLANTA BRAVES** | |
| 129 Steve Bedrosian | .05 |
| 130 Bruce Benedict | .05 |
| 131 Tommy Boggs | .05 |
| 132 Brett Butler | .05 |
| 133 Rick Camp | .05 |
| 134 Chris Chambliss | .05 |
| 135 Ken Dayley | .05 |
| 136 Gene Garber | .05 |
| 137 Terry Harper | .05 |
| 138 Bob Horner | .20 |
| 139 Glenn Hubbard | .05 |
| 140 Rufino Linares | .05 |
| 141 Rick Mahler | .05 |
| 142 Dale Murphy | .75 |
| 143 Phil Niekro | .20 |
| 144 Pascual Perez | .10 |
| 145 Biff Pocoroba | .05 |
| 146 Rafael Ramirez | .05 |
| 147 Jerry Royster | .05 |
| 148 Ken Smith | .05 |
| 149 Bob Walk | .05 |
| 150 Claudell Washington | .10 |
| 151 Bob Watson | .05 |
| 152 Larry Whisenton | .05 |
| **PHILADELPHIA PHILLIES** | |
| 153 Porfirio Altamirano | .05 |
| 154 Marty Bystrom | .05 |
| 155 Steve Carlton | .40 |
| 156 Larry Christenson | .05 |
| 157 Ivan DeJesus | .05 |
| 158 John Denny | .10 |
| 159 Bob Dernier | .05 |
| 160 Bo Diaz | .05 |
| 161 Ed Farmer | .05 |
| 162 Greg Gross | .05 |
| 163 Mike Krukow | .05 |
| 164 Garry Maddox | .05 |
| 165 Gary Matthews | .10 |
| 166 Tug McGraw | .08 |
| 167 Bob Molinaro | .05 |
| 168 Sid Monge | .05 |
| 169 Ron Reed | .05 |
| 170 Bill Robinson | .05 |
| 171 Pete Rose | 1.00 |
| 172 Dick Ruthven | .05 |
| 173 Mike Schmidt | .50 |
| 174 Manny Trillo | .05 |
| 175 Ozzie Virgil | .05 |
| 176 George Vuckovich | .05 |
| **BOSTON RED SOX** | |
| 177 Gary Allenson | .05 |
| 178 Luis Aponte | .05 |
| 179 Wade Boggs (R) | 12.00 |
| 180 Tom Burgmeier | .05 |
| 181 Mark Clear | .05 |
| 182 Dennis Eckersley | .05 |
| 183 Dwight Evans | .15 |
| 184 Rich Gedman | .05 |
| 185 Glenn Hoffman | .05 |
| 186 Bruce Hurst | .05 |
| 187 Carney Lansford | .10 |
| 188 Rick Miller | .05 |
| 189 Reid Nichols | .05 |
| 190 Bob Ojeda | .05 |

| NO. PLAYER | MINT |
|---|---|
| 191 Tony Perez | .15 |
| 192 Chuck Rainey | .05 |
| 193 Jerry Remy | .05 |
| 194 Jim Rice | .40 |
| 195 Bob Stanley | .05 |
| 196 Dave Stapleton | .05 |
| 197 Mike Torrez | .05 |
| 198 John Tudor | .15 |
| 199 Julio Valdez | .05 |
| 200 Carl Yastrzemski | .60 |
| **LOS ANGELES DODGERS** | |
| 201 Dusty Baker | .10 |
| 202 Joe Beckwith | .05 |
| 203 Greg Brock (R) | .50 |
| 204 Roy Cey | .15 |
| 205 Terry Forster | .05 |
| 206 Steve Garvey | .40 |
| 207 Pedro Guerrero | .30 |
| 208 Burt Hooton | .05 |
| 209 Steve Howe | .05 |
| 210 Ken Landreaux | .05 |
| 211 Mike Marshall | .20 |
| 212 Candy Maldonado (R) | .30 |
| 213 Rick Monday | .05 |
| 214 Tom Niedenfuer | .05 |
| 215 Jorge Orta | .05 |
| 216 Jerry Reuss | .05 |
| 217 Ron Roenicke | .05 |
| 218 Vicente Romo | .05 |
| 219 Bill Russell | .05 |
| 220 Steve Sax | .15 |
| 221 Mike Scioscia | .05 |
| 222 Dave Stewart | .05 |
| 223 Derrel Thomas | .05 |
| 224 Fernando Valenzuela | .30 |
| 225 Bob Welch | .05 |
| 226 Ricky Wright | .05 |
| 227 Steve Yeager | .05 |
| **CHICAGO WHITE SOX** | |
| 228 Bill Almon | .05 |
| 229 Harold Baines | .25 |
| 230 Salome Barojas | .05 |
| 231 Tony Bernazard | .05 |
| 232 Britt Burns | .05 |
| 233 Richard Dotson | .05 |
| 234 Ernesto Escarrega | .05 |
| 235 Carlton Fisk | .20 |
| 236 Jerry Hairston | .05 |
| 237 Kevin Hickey | .05 |
| 238 LaMarr Hoyt | .15 |
| 239 Steve Kemp | .05 |
| 240 Jim Kern | .05 |
| 241 Ron Kittle (R) | .75 |
| 242 Jerry Koosman | .05 |
| 243 Dennis Lamp | .05 |
| 244 Rudy Law | .05 |
| 245 Vance Law | .05 |
| 246 Ron LeFlore | .05 |
| 247 Greg Luzinski | .10 |
| 248 Tom Paciorek | .05 |
| 249 Aurelio Rodriguez | .05 |
| 250 Mike Squires | .05 |
| 251 Steve Trout | .05 |
| **SAN FRANCISCO GIANTS** | |
| 252 Jim Barr | .05 |
| 253 Dave Bergman | .05 |

| NO. | PLAYER | MINT |
|---|---|---|
| 254 | Fred Breining | .05 |
| 255 | Bob Brenly | .05 |
| 256 | Jack Clark | .25 |
| 257 | Chili Davis | .15 |
| 258 | Darrell Evans | .10 |
| 259 | Alan Fowlkes | .05 |
| 260 | Rich Gale | .05 |
| 261 | Atlee Hammaker | .05 |
| 262 | Al Holland | .05 |
| 263 | Duane Kuiper | .05 |
| 264 | Bill Laskey (R) | .15 |
| 265 | Gary Lavelle | .05 |
| 266 | Johnnie LeMaster | .05 |
| 267 | Renie Martin | .05 |
| 268 | Milt May | .05 |
| 269 | Greg Minton | .05 |
| 270 | Joe Morgan | .20 |
| 271 | Tom O'Malley | .05 |
| 272 | Reggie Smith | .10 |
| 273 | Guy Sularz | .05 |
| 274 | Champ Summers | .05 |
| 275 | Max Venable | .05 |
| 276 | Jim Wohlford | .05 |
| **MONTREAL EXPOS** | | |
| 277 | Ray Burris | .05 |
| 278 | Gary Carter | .50 |
| 279 | Warren Cromartie | .05 |
| 280 | Andre Dawson | .25 |
| 281 | Terry Francona | .05 |
| 282 | Doug Flynn | .05 |
| 283 | Woody Fryman | .05 |
| 284 | Bill Gullickson | .05 |
| 285 | Wallace Johnson | .05 |
| 286 | Charlie Lea | .05 |
| 287 | Randy Lerch | .05 |
| 288 | Brad Mills | .05 |
| 289 | Dan Norman | .05 |
| 290 | Al Oliver | .20 |
| 291 | David Palmer | .05 |
| 292 | Tim Raines | .30 |
| 293 | Jeff Reardon | .05 |
| 294 | Steve Rogers | .10 |
| 295 | Scott Sanderson | .05 |
| 296 | Dan Schatzeder | .05 |
| 297 | Bryn Smith | .05 |
| 298 | Chris Speier | .05 |
| 299 | Tim Wallach | .10 |
| 300 | Jerry White | .05 |
| 301 | Joel Youngblood | .05 |
| **PITTSBURGH PIRATES** | | |
| 302 | Ross Baumgarten | .05 |
| 303 | Dale Berra | .05 |
| 304 | John Candelaria | .05 |
| 305 | Dick Davis | .05 |
| 306 | Mike Easler | .05 |
| 307 | Richie Hebner | .05 |
| 308 | Lee Lacy | .05 |
| 309 | Bill Madlock | .15 |
| 310 | Larry McWilliams | .05 |
| 311 | John Milner | .05 |
| 312 | Omar Moreno | .05 |
| 313 | Jim Morrison | .05 |
| 314 | Steve Nicosia | .05 |
| 315 | Dave Parker | .20 |
| 316 | Tony Pena | .15 |
| 317 | Johnny Ray | .15 |
| 318 | Rick Rhoden | .05 |
| 319 | Don Robinson | .05 |
| 320 | Enrique Romo | .05 |
| 321 | Manny Sarmiento | .05 |
| 322 | Rod Scurry | .05 |
| 323 | Jim Smith | .05 |
| 324 | Willie Stargell | .20 |
| 325 | Jason Thompson | .10 |
| 326 | Kent Tekulve | .05 |
| **DETROIT TIGERS** | | |
| 327 | Tom Brookens | .05 |
| 328 | Enos Cabell | .05 |
| 329 | Kirk Gibson | .25 |
| 330 | Larry Herndon | .05 |
| 331 | Mike Ivie | .05 |
| 332 | Howard Johnson (R) | .15 |
| 333 | Lynn Jones | .05 |
| 334 | Rick Leach | .05 |
| 335 | Chet Lemon | .07 |
| 336 | Jack Morris | .20 |
| 337 | Lance Parrish | .25 |
| 338 | Larry Pashnick | .05 |
| 339 | Dan Petry | .15 |
| 340 | Dave Rozema | .05 |
| 341 | Dave Rucker | .05 |
| 342 | Elias Sosa | .05 |
| 343 | Dave Tobik | .05 |
| 344 | Alan Trammell | .25 |
| 345 | Jerry Turner | .05 |
| 346 | Jerry Ujdur | .05 |
| 347 | Pat Underwood | .05 |
| 348 | Lou Whitaker | .25 |
| 349 | Milt Wilcox | .05 |
| 350 | Glenn Wilson (R) | .60 |
| 351 | John Wockenfuss | .05 |
| **SAN DIEGO PADRES** | | |
| 352 | Kurt Bevacqua | .05 |
| 353 | Juan Bonilla | .05 |
| 354 | Floyd Chiffer | .05 |
| 355 | Luis DeLeon | .05 |
| 356 | Dave Dravecky (R) | .40 |
| 357 | Dave Edwards | .05 |
| 358 | Juan Eichelberger | .05 |
| 359 | Tim Flannery | .05 |
| 360 | Tony Gwynn (R) | 5.00 |
| 361 | Ruppert Jones | .05 |
| 362 | Terry Kennedy | .10 |
| 363 | Joe Lefebvre | .05 |
| 364 | Sixto Lezcano | .05 |
| 365 | Tim Lollar | .05 |
| 366 | Gary Lucas | .05 |
| 367 | John Montefusco | .05 |
| 368 | Broderick Perkins | .05 |
| 369 | Joe Pittman | .05 |
| 370 | Gene Richards | .05 |
| 371 | Luis Salazar | .05 |
| 372 | Eric Show (R) | .15 |
| 373 | Garry Templeton | .10 |
| 374 | Chris Welsh | .05 |
| 375 | Alan Wiggins (R) | .30 |
| **NEW YORK YANKEES** | | |
| 376 | Rick Cerone | .05 |
| 377 | Dave Collins | .05 |
| 378 | Roger Erickson | .05 |
| 379 | George Frazier | .05 |
| 380 | Oscar Gamble | .05 |
| 381 | Goose Gossage | .20 |
| 382 | Ken Griffey | .10 |
| 383 | Ron Guidry | .20 |
| 384 | Dave LaRoche | .05 |
| 385 | Rudy May | .05 |
| 386 | John Mayberry | .05 |
| 387 | Lee Mazzilli | .05 |
| 388 | Mike Morgan | .05 |
| 389 | Jerry Mumphrey | .05 |
| 390 | Bobby Murcer | .10 |
| 391 | Graig Nettles | .15 |
| 392 | Lou Piniella | .10 |
| 393 | Willie Randolph | .05 |
| 394 | Shane Rawley | .05 |
| 395 | Dave Righetti | .15 |
| 396 | Andre Robertson | .05 |
| 397 | Roy Smalley | .05 |
| 398 | Dave Winfield | .40 |
| 399 | Butch Wynegar | .05 |
| **CLEVELAND INDIANS** | | |
| 400 | Chris Bando | .05 |
| 401 | Alan Bannister | .05 |
| 402 | Len Barker | .05 |
| 403 | Tom Brennan | .05 |
| 404 | Carmelo Castillo (R) | .10 |
| 405 | Miguel Dilone | .05 |
| 406 | Jerry Dybzinski | .05 |
| 407 | Mike Fischlin | .05 |
| 408 | Ed Glynn | .05 |
| 409 | Mike Hargrove | .05 |
| 410 | Toby Harrah | .05 |
| 411 | Ron Hassey | .05 |
| 412 | Von Hayes | .15 |
| 413 | Rick Manning | .05 |
| 414 | Bake McBride | .05 |
| 415 | Larry Milbourne | .05 |
| 416 | Bill Nahorodny | .05 |
| 417 | Jack Perconte | .05 |
| 418 | Lary Sorensen | .05 |
| 419 | Dan Spillner | .05 |
| 420 | Rick Sutcliffe | .20 |
| 421 | Andre Thornton | .10 |
| 422 | Rick Waits | .05 |
| 423 | Eddie Whitson | .05 |
| **TORONTO BLUE JAYS** | | |
| 424 | Jesse Barfield | .10 |
| 425 | Barry Bonnell | .05 |
| 426 | Jim Clancy | .05 |
| 427 | Damaso Garcia | .10 |
| 428 | Jerry Garvin | .05 |
| 429 | Alfredo Griffin | .05 |
| 430 | Garth Iorg | .05 |
| 431 | Roy Lee Jackson | .05 |
| 432 | Luis Leal | .05 |
| 433 | Buck Martinez | .05 |
| 434 | Joey McLaughlin | .05 |
| 435 | Lloyd Moseby | .15 |
| 436 | Rance Mulliniks | .05 |
| 437 | Dale Murray | .05 |
| 438 | Wayne Nordhagen | .05 |
| 439 | Gene Petralli | .05 |
| 440 | Hosken Powell | .05 |
| 441 | Dave Stieb | .20 |
| 442 | Willie Upshaw | .10 |
| 443 | Ernie Whitt | .05 |
| 444 | Al Woods | .05 |
| **HOUSTON ASTROS** | | |
| 445 | Alan Ashby | .05 |
| 446 | Jose Cruz | .15 |
| 447 | Kiko Garcia | .05 |
| 448 | Phil Garner | .05 |
| 449 | Danny Heep | .05 |
| 450 | Art Howe | .05 |
| 451 | Bob Knepper | .05 |
| 452 | Alan Knicely | .05 |
| 453 | Ray Knight | .05 |
| 454 | Frank LaCorte | .05 |
| 455 | Mike LaCoss | .05 |
| 456 | Randy Moffitt | .05 |
| 457 | Joe Niekro | .05 |
| 458 | Terry Puhl | .05 |
| 459 | Luis Pujols | .05 |
| 460 | Craig Reynolds | .05 |
| 461 | Bert Roberge | .05 |
| 462 | Vern Ruhle | .05 |
| 463 | Nolan Ryan | .25 |
| 464 | Joe Sambito | .05 |
| 465 | Tony Scott | .05 |
| 466 | Dave Smith | .05 |
| 467 | Harry Spilman | .05 |
| 468 | Dickie Thon | .05 |
| 469 | Denny Walling | .05 |
| **SEATTLE MARINERS** | | |
| 470 | Larry Andersen | .05 |
| 471 | Floyd Bannister | .08 |
| 472 | Jim Beattie | .05 |
| 473 | Bruce Bochte | .05 |
| 474 | Manny Castillo | .05 |
| 475 | Bill Caudill | .05 |
| 476 | Bryan Clark | .05 |
| 477 | Al Cowens | .05 |
| 478 | Julio Cruz | .05 |
| 479 | Todd Cruz | .05 |
| 480 | Gary Gray | .05 |
| 481 | Dave Henderson | .05 |
| 482 | Mike Moore (R) | .25 |
| 483 | Gaylord Perry | .20 |
| 484 | Dave Revering | .05 |
| 485 | Joe Simpson | .05 |
| 486 | Mike Stanton | .05 |
| 487 | Rick Sweet | .05 |
| 488 | Ed VandeBerg (R) | .15 |
| 489 | Richie Zisk | .05 |
| **CHICAGO CUBS** | | |
| 490 | Doug Bird | .05 |
| 491 | Larry Bowa | .10 |
| 492 | Bill Buckner | .10 |
| 493 | Bill Campbell | .05 |
| 494 | Jody Davis | .10 |
| 495 | Leon Durham | .20 |
| 496 | Steve Henderson | .05 |
| 497 | Willie Hernandez | .20 |
| 498 | Ferguson Jenkins | .15 |
| 499 | Jay Johnstone | .05 |
| 500 | Junior Kennedy | .05 |
| 501 | Randy Martz | .05 |
| 502 | Jerry Morales | .05 |
| 503 | Keith Moreland | .05 |
| 504 | Dickie Noles | .05 |
| 505 | Mike Proly | .05 |
| 506 | Allen Ripley | .05 |
| 507 | Ryne Sandberg | 3.50 |
| 508 | Lee Smith | .10 |
| 509 | Pat Tabler | .05 |
| 510 | Dick Tidrow | .05 |
| 511 | Bump Wills | .05 |
| 512 | Gary Woods | .05 |
| **OAKLAND A'S** | | |
| 513 | Tony Armas | .15 |
| 514 | Dave Beard | .05 |
| 515 | Jeff Burroughs | .05 |
| 516 | John D'Acquisto | .05 |
| 517 | Wayne Gross | .05 |
| 518 | Mike Heath | .05 |
| 519 | Rickey Henderson | .60 |
| 520 | Cliff Johnson | .05 |
| 521 | Matt Keough | .05 |
| 522 | Brian Kingman | .05 |
| 523 | Rick Langford | .05 |
| 524 | Davey Lopes | .05 |
| 525 | Steve McCatty | .05 |
| 526 | Dave McKay | .05 |
| 527 | Dan Meyer | .05 |
| 528 | Dwayne Murphy | .05 |
| 529 | Jeff Newman | .05 |
| 530 | Mike Norris | .05 |
| 531 | Bob Owchinko | .05 |
| 532 | Joe Rudi | .05 |
| 533 | Jimmy Sexton | .05 |
| 534 | Fred Stanley | .05 |
| 535 | Tom Underwood | .05 |
| **NEW YORK METS** | | |
| 536 | Neil Allen | .05 |
| 537 | Wally Backman | .05 |
| 538 | Bob Bailor | .05 |
| 539 | Hubie Brooks | .10 |
| 540 | Carlos Diaz (R) | .15 |
| 541 | Pete Falcone | .05 |
| 542 | George Foster | .15 |
| 543 | Ron Gardenhire | .05 |
| 544 | Brian Giles | .05 |
| 545 | Ron Hodges | .05 |
| 546 | Randy Jones | .05 |
| 547 | Mike Jorgensen | .05 |
| 548 | Dave Kingman | .15 |
| 549 | Ed Lynch | .05 |
| 550 | Jesse Orosco | .10 |
| 551 | Rick Ownbey | .10 |
| 552 | Charlie Puleo | .05 |
| 553 | Gary Rajsich | .05 |
| 554 | Mike Scott | .05 |
| 555 | Rusty Staub | .10 |
| 556 | John Stearns | .05 |
| 557 | Craig Swan | .05 |
| 558 | Ellis Valentine | .05 |
| 559 | Tom Veryzer | .05 |
| 560 | Mookie Wilson | .10 |
| 561 | Pat Zachry | .05 |
| **TEXAS RANGERS** | | |
| 562 | Buddy Bell | .15 |
| 563 | John Butcher | .05 |
| 564 | Steve Comer | .05 |
| 565 | Danny Darwin | .05 |
| 566 | Bucky Dent | .05 |
| 567 | John Grubb | .05 |
| 568 | Rick Honeycutt | .05 |
| 569 | Dave Hostetler | .10 |
| 570 | Charlie Hough | .05 |
| 571 | Lamar Johnson | .05 |
| 572 | Jon Matlack | .05 |
| 573 | Paul Mirabella | .05 |
| 574 | Larry Parrish | .05 |
| 575 | Mike Richardt | .05 |
| 576 | Mickey Rivers | .05 |
| 577 | Billy Sample | .05 |
| 578 | Dave Schmidt | .05 |
| 579 | Bill Stein | .05 |
| 580 | Jim Sundberg | .05 |

| NO. PLAYER | MINT |
|---|---|
| 581 Frank Tanana | .05 |
| 582 Mark Wagner | .05 |
| 583 George Wright (R) | .15 |
| **CINCINNATI REDS** | |
| 584 Johnny Bench | .40 |
| 585 Bruce Berenyi | .05 |
| 586 Larry Biittner | .05 |
| 587 Cesar Cedeno | .10 |
| 588 Dave Concepcion | .10 |
| 589 Dan Driessen | .05 |
| 590 Greg Harris | .05 |
| 591 Ben Hayes | .05 |
| 592 Paul Householder | .05 |
| 593 Tom Hume | .05 |
| 594 Wayne Krenchicki | .05 |
| 595 Rafael Landestoy | .05 |
| 596 Charlie Leibrandt | .05 |
| 597 Eddie Milner | .10 |
| 598 Ron Oester | .05 |
| 599 Frank Pastore | .05 |
| 600 Joe Price | .05 |
| 601 Tom Seaver | .30 |
| 602 Bob Shirley | .05 |
| 603 Mario Soto | .10 |
| 604 Alex Trevino | .05 |
| 605 Mike Vail | .05 |

| NO. PLAYER | MINT |
|---|---|
| 606 Duane Walker (R) | .15 |
| **MINNESOTA TWINS** | |
| 607 Tom Brunansky | .20 |
| 608 Bobby Castillo | .05 |
| 609 John Castino | .05 |
| 610 Ron Davis | .05 |
| 611 Lenny Gaetti | .05 |
| 612 Terry Felton | .05 |
| 613 Gary Gaetti (R) | .75 |
| 614 Mickey Hatcher | .05 |
| 615 Brad Havens | .05 |
| 616 Kent Hrbek | .40 |
| 617 Randy Johnson | .05 |
| 618 Tim Laudner | .05 |
| 619 Jeff Little | .05 |
| 620 Bob Mitchell | .05 |
| 621 Jack O'Connor | .05 |
| 622 John Pacella | .05 |
| 623 Pete Redfern | .05 |
| 624 Jesus Vega | .05 |
| 625 Frank Viola | .50 |
| 626 Ron Washington | .10 |
| 627 Gary Ward | .05 |
| 628 Al Williams | .05 |
| 629 Red Sox All-Stars: | .20 |
|     Eckersley, Yaz, Clear | |

| NO. PLAYER | MINT |
|---|---|
| 630 "300 Career Wins" | .15 |
|     Perry and Bulling | |
| 631 Pride of Venezuela: | .10 |
|     Concepcion, Trillo | |
| 632 All-Star Infielders: | .15 |
|     Yount and Bell | |
| 633 Mr. Vet & Mr. Rookie: | .25 |
|     Winfield, Hrbek | |
| 634 Fountain of Youth: | .60 |
|     Stargell, Rose | |
| 635 Big Chiefs: | .10 |
|     Harrah, Thornton | |
| 636 Smith Brothers: | .10 |
|     Ozzie and Lonnie | |
| 637 Base Stealers' Threat: | .10 |
|     Diaz and Carter | |
| 638 All-Star Catchers: | .15 |
|     Fisk, Carter | |
| 639 The Silver Shoe: | .35 |
|     Rickey Henderson | |
| 640 Home Run Threats: | .15 |
|     Oglivie, Jackson | |
| 641 Two Teams on the | |
|     Same Day: | .08 |
|     Joel Youngblood 8/4/82 | |

| NO. PLAYER | MINT |
|---|---|
| 642 Last Perfect Game: | .08 |
|     Hassey, Barker | |
| 643 Black and Blue: | .08 |
|     Vida Blue | |
| 644 Black and Blue: | .08 |
|     Bud Black | |
| 645 Speed and Power: | .35 |
|     Reggie Jackson | |
| 646 Speed and Power: | .35 |
|     Rickey Henderson | |
| 647 Checklist No. 1 | .08 |
| 648 Checklist No. 2 | .08 |
| 649 Checklist No. 3 | .08 |
| 650 Checklist No. 4 | .08 |
| 651 Checklist No. 5 | .08 |
| 652 Checklist No. 6 | .08 |
| 653 Checklist No. 7 | .08 |
| 654 Checklist No. 8 | .08 |
| 655 Checklist No. 9 | .08 |
| 656 Checklist No. 10 | .08 |
| 657 Checklist No. 11 | .08 |
| 658 Checklist No. 12 | .08 |
| 659 Checklist No. 13 | .08 |
| 660 Checklist No. 14 | .08 |

# 1984 Fleer....Complete Set of 660 Cards—Value $60.00

Features the rookie cards of Don Mattingly and Darryl Strawberry. For the first time a traded update set was issued later in the year.

| NO. PLAYER | MINT |
|---|---|
| **BALTIMORE ORIOLES** | |
| 1 Mike Boddicker | .20 |
| 2 Al Bumbry | .05 |
| 3 Todd Cruz | .05 |
| 4 Rich Dauer | .05 |
| 5 Storm Davis | .10 |
| 6 Rick Dempsey | .05 |
| 7 Jim Dwyer | .05 |
| 8 Mike Flanagan | .10 |
| 9 Dan Ford | .05 |
| 10 John Lowenstein | .05 |
| 11 Dennis Martinez | .05 |
| 12 Tippy Martinez | .05 |
| 13 Scott McGregor | .10 |
| 14 Eddie Murray | .50 |
| 15 Joe Nolan | .05 |
| 16 Jim Palmer | .25 |
| 17 Cal Ripken, Jr. | .60 |
| 18 Gary Roenicke | .05 |
| 19 Lenn Sakata | .05 |
| 20 John Shelby | .10 |
| 21 Ken Singleton | .10 |
| 22 Sammy Stewart | .05 |
| 23 Tim Stoddard | .05 |
| **PHILADELPHIA PHILLIES** | |
| 24 Marty Bystrom | .05 |
| 25 Steve Carlton | .25 |
| 26 Ivan DeJesus | .05 |
| 27 John Denny | .10 |
| 28 Bob Dernier | .05 |
| 29 Bo Diaz | .05 |
| 30 Kiko Garcia | .05 |
| 31 Greg Gross | .05 |
| 32 Kevin Gross (R) | .20 |

| NO. PLAYER | MINT |
|---|---|
| 33 Von Hayes | .15 |
| 34 Willie Hernandez | .20 |
| 35 Al Holland | .05 |
| 36 Charles Hudson (R) | .15 |
| 37 Joe Lefebvre | .05 |
| 38 Sixto Lezcano | .05 |
| 39 Garry Maddox | .05 |
| 40 Gary Matthews | .10 |
| 41 Len Matuszek | .05 |
| 42 Tug McGraw | .05 |
| 43 Joe Morgan | .15 |
| 44 Tony Perez | .15 |
| 45 Ron Reed | .05 |
| 46 Pete Rose | .75 |
| 47 Juan Samuel (R) | 2.25 |
| 48 Mike Schmidt | .45 |
| 49 Ozzie Virgil | .05 |
| **CHICAGO WHITE SOX** | |
| 50 Juan Agosto | .05 |
| 51 Harold Baines | .20 |
| 52 Floyd Bannister | .10 |
| 53 Salome Barojas | .05 |
| 54 Britt Burns | .05 |
| 55 Julio Cruz | .05 |
| 56 Richard Dotson | .10 |
| 57 Jerry Dybzinski | .05 |
| 58 Carlton Fisk | .15 |
| 59 Scott Fletcher | .05 |
| 60 Jerry Hairston | .05 |
| 61 Kevin Hickey | .05 |
| 62 Marc Hill | .05 |
| 63 LaMarr Hoyt | .10 |
| 64 Ron Kittle | .15 |
| 65 Jerry Koosman | .05 |

| NO. PLAYER | MINT |
|---|---|
| 66 Dennis Lamp | .05 |
| 67 Rudy Law | .05 |
| 68 Vance Law | .05 |
| 69 Greg Luzinski | .10 |
| 70 Tom Paciorek | .05 |
| 71 Mike Squires | .05 |
| 72 Dick Tidrow | .05 |
| 73 Greg Walker (R) | .60 |
| **DETROIT TIGERS** | |
| 74 Glenn Abbott | .05 |
| 75 Howard Bailey | .05 |
| 76 Doug Bair | .05 |
| 77 Juan Berenguer | .05 |
| 78 Tom Brookens | .05 |
| 79 Enos Cabell | .05 |
| 80 Kirk Gibson | .25 |
| 81 John Grubb | .05 |
| 82 Larry Herndon | .05 |
| 83 Wayne Krenchicki | .05 |
| 84 Rick Leach | .05 |
| 85 Chet Lemon | .10 |
| 86 Aurelio Lopez | .05 |
| 87 Jack Morris | .25 |
| 88 Lance Parrish | .25 |
| 89 Dan Petry | .15 |
| 90 Dave Rozema | .05 |
| 91 Alan Trammell | .25 |
| 92 Lou Whitaker | .20 |
| 93 Milt Wilcox | .05 |
| 94 Glenn Wilson | .10 |
| 95 John Wockenfuss | .05 |
| **LOS ANGELES DODGERS** | |
| 96 Dusty Baker | .05 |
| 97 Joe Beckwith | .05 |

| NO. PLAYER | MINT |
|---|---|
| 98 Greg Brock | .10 |
| 99 Jack Fimple | .05 |
| 100 Pedro Guerrero | .25 |
| 101 Rick Honeycutt | .05 |
| 102 Burt Hooton | .05 |
| 103 Steve Howe | .05 |
| 104 Ken Landreaux | .05 |
| 105 Mike Marshall | .15 |
| 106 Rick Monday | .05 |
| 107 Jose Morales | .05 |
| 108 Tom Niedenfuer | .05 |
| 109 Alejandro Pena (R) | .25 |
| 110 Jerry Reuss | .05 |
| 111 Bill Russell | .05 |
| 112 Steve Sax | .15 |
| 113 Mike Scioscia | .05 |
| 114 Derrel Thomas | .05 |
| 115 Fernando Valenzuela | .30 |
| 116 Bob Welch | .10 |
| 117 Steve Yeager | .05 |
| 118 Pat Zachry | .05 |
| **NEW YORK YANKEES** | |
| 119 Don Baylor | .10 |
| 120 Bert Campaneris | .05 |
| 121 Rick Cerone | .05 |
| 122 Ray Fontenot (R) | .15 |
| 123 George Frazier | .05 |
| 124 Oscar Gamble | .05 |
| 125 Goose Gossage | .15 |
| 126 Ken Griffey | .10 |
| 127 Ron Guidry | .15 |
| 128 Jay Howell | .05 |
| 129 Steve Kemp | .05 |
| 130 Matt Keough | .05 |

| NO. | PLAYER | MINT |
|---|---|---|
| 131 | Don Mattingly (R) | 30.00 |
| 132 | John Montefusco | .05 |
| 133 | Omar Moreno | .05 |
| 134 | Dale Murray | .05 |
| 135 | Graig Nettles | .10 |
| 136 | Lou Piniella | .10 |
| 137 | Willie Randolph | .10 |
| 138 | Shane Rawley | .05 |
| 139 | Dave Righetti | .15 |
| 140 | Andre Robertson | .05 |
| 141 | Bob Shirley | .05 |
| 142 | Roy Smalley | .05 |
| 143 | Dave Winfield | .35 |
| 144 | Butch Wynegar | .05 |

**TORONTO BLUE JAYS**

| NO. | PLAYER | MINT |
|---|---|---|
| 145 | Jim Acker (R) | .15 |
| 146 | Doyle Alexander | .05 |
| 147 | Jesse Barfield | .15 |
| 148 | Jorge Bell | .10 |
| 149 | Barry Bonnell | .05 |
| 150 | Jim Clancy | .05 |
| 151 | Dave Collins | .05 |
| 152 | Tony Fernandez (R) | .80 |
| 153 | Damaso Garcia | .10 |
| 154 | Dave Geisel | .05 |
| 155 | Jim Gott | .05 |
| 156 | Alfredo Griffin | .05 |
| 157 | Garth Iorg | .05 |
| 158 | Roy Lee Jackson | .05 |
| 159 | Cliff Johnson | .05 |
| 160 | Luis Leal | .05 |
| 161 | Buck Martinez | .05 |
| 162 | Joey McLaughlin | .05 |
| 163 | Randy Moffitt | .05 |
| 164 | Lloyd Moseby | .15 |
| 165 | Rance Mulliniks | .05 |
| 166 | Jorge Orta | .05 |
| 167 | Dave Stieb | .20 |
| 168 | Willie Upshaw | .15 |
| 169 | Ernie Whitt | .05 |

**ATLANTA BRAVES**

| NO. | PLAYER | MINT |
|---|---|---|
| 170 | Len Barker | .05 |
| 171 | Steve Bedrosian | .05 |
| 172 | Bruce Benedict | .05 |
| 173 | Brett Butler | .10 |
| 174 | Rick Camp | .05 |
| 175 | Chris Chambliss | .05 |
| 176 | Ken Dayley | .05 |
| 177 | Pete Falcone | .05 |
| 178 | Terry Forster | .05 |
| 179 | Gene Garber | .05 |
| 180 | Terry Harper | .05 |
| 181 | Bob Horner | .20 |
| 182 | Glenn Hubbard | .05 |
| 183 | Randy Johnson | .05 |
| 184 | Craig McMurtry | .10 |
| 185 | Donnie Moore | .05 |
| 186 | Dale Murphy | .75 |
| 187 | Phil Niekro | .15 |
| 188 | Pascual Perez | .05 |
| 189 | Biff Pocoroba | .05 |
| 190 | Rafael Ramirez | .05 |
| 191 | Jerry Royster | .05 |
| 192 | Claudell Washington | .10 |
| 193 | Bob Watson | .05 |

**MILWAUKEE BREWERS**

| NO. | PLAYER | MINT |
|---|---|---|
| 194 | Jerry Augustine | .05 |
| 195 | Mark Brouhard | .05 |
| 196 | Mike Caldwell | .05 |
| 197 | Tom Candiotti | .05 |
| 198 | Cecil Cooper | .15 |
| 199 | Rollie Fingers | .15 |
| 200 | Jim Gantner | .05 |
| 201 | Bob Gibson | .05 |
| 202 | Moose Haas | .05 |
| 203 | Roy Howell | .05 |
| 204 | Pete Ladd | .05 |
| 205 | Rick Manning | .05 |
| 206 | Bob McClure | .05 |
| 207 | Paul Molitor | .10 |
| 208 | Don Money | .05 |
| 209 | Charlie Moore | .05 |
| 210 | Ben Oglivie | .10 |
| 211 | Chuck Porter | .05 |
| 212 | Ed Romero | .05 |

| NO. | PLAYER | MINT |
|---|---|---|
| 213 | Ted Simmons | .10 |
| 214 | Jim Slaton | .05 |
| 215 | Don Sutton | .10 |
| 216 | Tom Tellmann | .05 |
| 217 | Pete Vuckovich | .05 |
| 218 | Ned Yost | .05 |
| 219 | Robin Yount | .30 |

**HOUSTON ASTROS**

| NO. | PLAYER | MINT |
|---|---|---|
| 220 | Alan Ashby | .05 |
| 221 | Kevin Bass | .05 |
| 222 | Jose Cruz | .10 |
| 223 | Bill Dawley (R) | .20 |
| 224 | Frank DiPino | .05 |
| 225 | Bill Doran (R) | .40 |
| 226 | Phil Garner | .05 |
| 227 | Art Howe | .05 |
| 228 | Bob Knepper | .05 |
| 229 | Ray Knight | .05 |
| 230 | Frank LaCorte | .05 |
| 231 | Mike LaCoss | .05 |
| 232 | Mike Madden (R) | .15 |
| 233 | Jerry Mumphrey | .05 |
| 234 | Joe Niekro | .05 |
| 235 | Terry Puhl | .05 |
| 236 | Luis Pujols | .05 |
| 237 | Craig Reynolds | .05 |
| 238 | Vern Ruhle | .05 |
| 239 | Nolan Ryan | .25 |
| 240 | Mike Scott | .05 |
| 241 | Tony Scott | .05 |
| 242 | Dave Smith | .05 |
| 243 | Dickie Thon | .08 |
| 244 | Denny Walling | .05 |

**PITTSBURGH PIRATES**

| NO. | PLAYER | MINT |
|---|---|---|
| 245 | Dale Berra | .05 |
| 246 | Jim Bibby | .05 |
| 247 | John Candelaria | .05 |
| 248 | Jose DeLeon (R) | .25 |
| 249 | Mike Easler | .08 |
| 250 | Cecilio Guante | .05 |
| 251 | Richie Hebner | .05 |
| 252 | Lee Lacy | .05 |
| 253 | Bill Madlock | .15 |
| 254 | Milt May | .05 |
| 255 | Lee Mazzilli | .05 |
| 256 | Larry McWilliams | .05 |
| 257 | Jim Morrison | .05 |
| 258 | Dave Parker | .25 |
| 259 | Tony Pena | .15 |
| 260 | Johnny Ray | .15 |
| 261 | Rick Rhoden | .05 |
| 262 | Don Robinson | .05 |
| 263 | Manny Sarmiento | .05 |
| 264 | Rod Scurry | .05 |
| 265 | Kent Tekulve | .05 |
| 266 | Gene Tenace | .05 |
| 267 | Jason Thompson | .10 |
| 268 | Lee Tunnell (R) | .15 |
| 269 | Marvell Wynne (R) | .15 |

**MONTREAL EXPOS**

| NO. | PLAYER | MINT |
|---|---|---|
| 270 | Ray Burris | .05 |
| 271 | Gary Carter | .40 |
| 272 | Warren Cromartie | .05 |
| 273 | Andre Dawson | .20 |
| 274 | Doug Flynn | .05 |
| 275 | Terry Francona | .05 |
| 276 | Bill Gullickson | .05 |
| 277 | Bob James (R) | .25 |
| 278 | Charlie Lea | .05 |
| 279 | Bryan Little | .05 |
| 280 | Al Oliver | .15 |
| 281 | Tim Raines | .25 |
| 282 | Bobby Ramos | .05 |
| 283 | Jeff Reardon | .25 |
| 284 | Steve Rogers | .05 |
| 285 | Scott Sanderson | .05 |
| 286 | Dan Schatzeder | .05 |
| 287 | Bryn Smith | .05 |
| 288 | Chris Speier | .05 |
| 289 | Manny Trillo | .05 |
| 290 | Mike Vail | .05 |
| 291 | Tim Wallach | .10 |
| 292 | Chris Welsh | .05 |
| 293 | Jim Wohlford | .05 |

**SAN DIEGO PADRES**

| NO. | PLAYER | MINT |
|---|---|---|
| 294 | Kurt Bevacqua | .05 |
| 295 | Juan Bonilla | .05 |
| 296 | Bobby Brown | .05 |
| 297 | Luis DeLeon | .05 |
| 298 | Dave Dravecky | .10 |
| 299 | Tim Flannery | .05 |
| 300 | Steve Garvey | .40 |
| 301 | Tony Gwynn | .60 |
| 302 | Andy Hawkins (R) | .60 |
| 303 | Ruppert Jones | .05 |
| 304 | Terry Kennedy | .10 |
| 305 | Tim Lollar | .05 |
| 306 | Gary Lucas | .05 |
| 307 | Kevin McReynolds (R) | 1.00 |
| 308 | Sid Monge | .05 |
| 309 | Mario Ramirez | .05 |
| 310 | Gene Richards | .05 |
| 311 | Luis Salazar | .05 |
| 312 | Eric Show | .05 |
| 313 | Elias Sosa | .05 |
| 314 | Garry Templeton | .10 |
| 315 | Mark Thurmond (R) | .20 |
| 316 | Ed Whitson | .05 |
| 317 | Alan Wiggins | .10 |

**ST. LOUIS CARDINALS**

| NO. | PLAYER | MINT |
|---|---|---|
| 318 | Neil Allen | .05 |
| 319 | Joaquin Andujar | .10 |
| 320 | Steve Braun | .05 |
| 321 | Glenn Brummer | .05 |
| 322 | Bob Firsch | .05 |
| 323 | David Green | .05 |
| 324 | George Hendrick | .08 |
| 325 | Tom Herr | .10 |
| 326 | Dane Iorg | .05 |
| 327 | Jeff Lahti | .05 |
| 328 | Dave LaPoint | .05 |
| 329 | Willie McGee | .35 |
| 330 | Ken Oberkfell | .05 |
| 331 | Darrell Porter | .05 |
| 332 | Jamie Quirk | .05 |
| 333 | Mike Ramsey | .05 |
| 334 | Floyd Rayford | .05 |
| 335 | Lonnie Smith | .10 |
| 336 | Ozzie Smith | .10 |
| 337 | John Stuper | .05 |
| 338 | Bruce Sutter | .15 |
| 339 | And Van Slyke (R) | .40 |
| 340 | Dave Von Ohlen | .05 |

**KANSAS CITY ROYALS**

| NO. | PLAYER | MINT |
|---|---|---|
| 341 | Willie Aikens | .05 |
| 342 | Mike Armstrong | .05 |
| 343 | Bud Black | .05 |
| 344 | George Brett | .50 |
| 345 | Onix Concepcion | .05 |
| 346 | Keith Creel | .05 |
| 347 | Larry Gura | .05 |
| 348 | Don Hood | .05 |
| 349 | Dennis Leonard | .05 |
| 350 | Hal McRae | .05 |
| 351 | Amos Otis | .05 |
| 352 | Gaylord Perry | .15 |
| 353 | Greg Pryor | .05 |
| 354 | Dan Quisenberry | .20 |
| 355 | Steve Renko | .05 |
| 356 | Leon Roberts | .05 |
| 357 | Pat Sheridan (R) | .15 |
| 358 | Joe Simpson | .05 |
| 359 | Don Slaught | .05 |
| 360 | Paul Splittorff | .05 |
| 361 | U.L. Washington | .05 |
| 362 | John Wathan | .05 |
| 363 | Frank White | .05 |
| 364 | Willie Wilson | .15 |

**SAN FRANCISCO GIANTS**

| NO. | PLAYER | MINT |
|---|---|---|
| 365 | Jim Barr | .05 |
| 366 | Dave Bergman | .05 |
| 367 | Fred Breining | .05 |
| 368 | Bob Brenly | .05 |
| 369 | Jack Clark | .20 |
| 370 | Chili Davis | .15 |
| 371 | Mark Davis | .05 |
| 372 | Darrell Evans | .10 |
| 373 | Atlee Hammaker | .05 |
| 374 | Mike Krukow | .05 |

| NO. | PLAYER | MINT |
|---|---|---|
| 375 | Duane Kuiper | .05 |
| 376 | Bill Laskey | .05 |
| 377 | Gary Lavelle | .05 |
| 378 | Johnnie LeMaster | .05 |
| 379 | Jeff Leonard | .05 |
| 380 | Randy Lerch | .05 |
| 381 | Renie Martin | .05 |
| 382 | Andy McGaffigan | .05 |
| 383 | Greg Minton | .05 |
| 384 | Tom O'Malley | .05 |
| 385 | Max Venable | .05 |
| 386 | Brad Wellman | .05 |
| 387 | Joel Youngblood | .05 |

**BOSTON RED SOX**

| NO. | PLAYER | MINT |
|---|---|---|
| 388 | Gary Allenson | .05 |
| 389 | Luis Aponte | .05 |
| 390 | Tony Armas | .15 |
| 391 | Doug Bird | .05 |
| 392 | Wade Boggs | 2.50 |
| 393 | Dennis Boyd (R) | .60 |
| 394 | Mike Brown | .05 |
| 395 | Mark Clear | .05 |
| 396 | Dennis Eckersley | .05 |
| 397 | Dwight Evans | .15 |
| 398 | Rich Gedman | .05 |
| 399 | Glenn Hoffman | .05 |
| 400 | Bruce Hurst | .05 |
| 401 | John Henry Johnson | .05 |
| 402 | Ed Jurak | .05 |
| 403 | Rick Miller | .05 |
| 404 | Jeff Newman | .05 |
| 405 | Reid Nichols | .05 |
| 406 | Bob Ojeda | .05 |
| 407 | Jerry Remy | .05 |
| 408 | Jim Rice | .35 |
| 409 | Bob Stanley | .05 |
| 410 | Dave Stapleton | .05 |
| 411 | John Tudor | .10 |
| 412 | Carl Yastrzemski | .40 |

**TEXAS RANGERS**

| NO. | PLAYER | MINT |
|---|---|---|
| 413 | Buddy Bell | .15 |
| 414 | Larry Biittner | .05 |
| 415 | John Butcher | .05 |
| 416 | Danny Darwin | .05 |
| 417 | Bucky Dent | .05 |
| 418 | Dave Hostetler | .05 |
| 419 | Charlie Hough | .05 |
| 420 | Bobby Johnson | .05 |
| 421 | Odell Jones | .05 |
| 422 | Jon Matlack | .05 |
| 423 | Pete O'Brien (R) | .50 |
| 424 | Larry Parrish | .05 |
| 425 | Mickey Rivers | .05 |
| 426 | Billy Sample | .05 |
| 427 | Dave Schmidt | .05 |
| 428 | Mike Smithson (R) | .15 |
| 429 | Bill Stein | .05 |
| 430 | Dave Stewart | .05 |
| 431 | Jim Sundberg | .05 |
| 432 | Frank Tanana | .05 |
| 433 | Dave Tobik | .05 |
| 434 | Wayne Tolleson | .05 |
| 435 | George Wright | .05 |

**OAKLAND A'S**

| NO. | PLAYER | MINT |
|---|---|---|
| 436 | Bill Almon | .05 |
| 437 | Keith Atherton | .05 |
| 438 | Dave Beard | .05 |
| 439 | Tom Burgmeier | .05 |
| 440 | Jeff Burroughs | .05 |
| 441 | Chris Codiroli | .10 |
| 442 | Tim Conroy | .05 |
| 443 | Mike Davis | .10 |
| 444 | Wayne Gross | .05 |
| 445 | Garry Hancock | .05 |
| 446 | Mike Heath | .05 |
| 447 | Rickey Henderson | .50 |
| 448 | Don Hill | .10 |
| 449 | Bob Kearney | .05 |
| 450 | Bill Krueger | .05 |
| 451 | Rick Langford | .05 |
| 452 | Carney Lansford | .10 |
| 453 | Davey Lopes | .05 |
| 454 | Steve McCatty | .05 |
| 455 | Dan Meyer | .05 |
| 456 | Dwayne Murphy | .05 |

# 1984 Fleer (Continued)

| NO. | PLAYER | MINT |
|---|---|---|
| 457 | Mike Norris | .05 |
| 458 | Ricky Peters | .05 |
| 459 | Tony Phillips | .05 |
| 460 | Tom Underwood | .05 |
| 461 | Mike Warren (R) | .15 |

**CINCINNATI REDS**

| NO. | PLAYER | MINT |
|---|---|---|
| 462 | Johnny Bench | .40 |
| 463 | Bruce Berenyi | .05 |
| 464 | Dann Bilardello | .05 |
| 465 | Cesar Cedeno | .05 |
| 466 | Dave Concepcion | .10 |
| 467 | Dan Driessen | .05 |
| 468 | Nick Esasky (R) | .30 |
| 469 | Rich Gale | .05 |
| 470 | Ben Hayes | .05 |
| 471 | Paul Householder | .05 |
| 472 | Tom Hume | .05 |
| 473 | Alan Knicely | .05 |
| 474 | Eddie Milner | .05 |
| 475 | Ron Oester | .05 |
| 476 | Kelly Paris | .10 |
| 477 | Frank Pastore | .05 |
| 478 | Ted Power | .05 |
| 479 | Joe Price | .05 |
| 480 | Charlie Puleo | .05 |
| 481 | Gary Redus (R) | .25 |
| 482 | Bill Scherrer | .05 |
| 483 | Mario Soto | .10 |
| 484 | Alex Trevino | .05 |
| 485 | Duane Walker | .05 |

**CHICAGO CUBS**

| NO. | PLAYER | MINT |
|---|---|---|
| 486 | Larry Bowa | .05 |
| 487 | Warren Brusstar | .05 |
| 488 | Bill Buckner | .10 |
| 489 | Bill Campbell | .05 |
| 490 | Ron Cey | .15 |
| 491 | Jody Davis | .05 |
| 492 | Leon Durham | .15 |
| 493 | Mel Hall | .10 |
| 494 | Ferguson Jenkins | .10 |
| 495 | Jay Johnstone | .05 |
| 496 | Craig Lefferts (R) | .15 |
| 497 | Carmelo Martinez (R) | .30 |
| 498 | Jerry Morales | .05 |
| 499 | Keith Moreland | .05 |
| 500 | Dickie Noles | .05 |
| 501 | Mike Proly | .05 |
| 502 | Chuck Rainey | .05 |
| 503 | Dick Ruthven | .05 |
| 504 | Ryne Sandberg | .60 |
| 505 | Lee Smith | .05 |
| 506 | Steve Trout | .05 |
| 507 | Gary Woods | .05 |

**CALIFORNIA ANGELS**

| NO. | PLAYER | MINT |
|---|---|---|
| 508 | Juan Beniquez | .05 |
| 509 | Bob Boone | .05 |
| 510 | Rick Burleson | .05 |
| 511 | Rod Carew | .30 |
| 512 | Bobby Clark | .05 |
| 513 | John Curtis | .05 |
| 514 | Doug DeCinces | .10 |
| 515 | Brian Downing | .05 |
| 516 | Tim Foli | .05 |
| 517 | Ken Forsch | .05 |
| 518 | Bobby Grich | .05 |
| 519 | Andy Hassler | .05 |
| 520 | Reggie Jackson | .40 |
| 521 | Ron Jackson | .05 |
| 522 | Tommy John | .10 |
| 523 | Bruce Kison | .05 |
| 524 | Steve Lubratich | .05 |
| 525 | Fred Lynn | .15 |
| 526 | Gary Pettis (R) | .45 |
| 527 | Luis Sanchez | .05 |
| 528 | Daryl Sconiers | .05 |
| 529 | Ellis Valentine | .05 |
| 530 | Rob Wilfong | .05 |
| 531 | Mike Witt | .10 |
| 532 | Geoff Zahn | .05 |

**CLEVELAND INDIANS**

| NO. | PLAYER | MINT |
|---|---|---|
| 533 | Bud Anderson | .05 |
| 534 | Chris Bando | .05 |
| 535 | Alan Bannister | .05 |
| 536 | Bert Blyleven | .10 |
| 537 | Tom Brennan | .05 |
| 538 | Jamie Easterly | .05 |
| 539 | Juan Eichelberger | .05 |
| 540 | Jim Essian | .05 |
| 541 | Mike Fischlin | .05 |
| 542 | Julio Franco | .10 |
| 543 | Mike Hargrove | .05 |
| 544 | Toby Harrah | .05 |
| 545 | Ron Hassey | .05 |
| 546 | Neal Heaton (R) | .15 |
| 547 | Bake McBride | .05 |
| 548 | Broderick Perkins | .05 |
| 549 | Lary Sorensen | .05 |
| 550 | Dan Spillner | .05 |
| 551 | Rick Sutcliffe | .20 |
| 552 | Pat Tabler | .05 |
| 553 | Gorman Thomas | .10 |
| 554 | Andre Thornton | .10 |
| 555 | George Vukovich | .05 |

**MINNESOTA TWINS**

| NO. | PLAYER | MINT |
|---|---|---|
| 556 | Darrell Brown | .05 |
| 557 | Tom Brunansky | .15 |
| 558 | Randy Bush | .05 |
| 559 | Bobby Castillo | .05 |
| 560 | John Castino | .05 |
| 561 | Ron Davis | .05 |
| 562 | Dave Engle | .05 |
| 563 | Lenny Faedo | .05 |
| 564 | Pete Filson | .05 |
| 565 | Gary Gaetti | .05 |
| 566 | Mickey Hatcher | .05 |
| 567 | Kent Hrbek | .30 |
| 568 | Rusty Kuntz | .05 |
| 569 | Tim Laudner | .05 |
| 570 | Rick Lysander | .05 |
| 571 | Bobby Mitchell | .05 |
| 572 | Ken Schrom | .05 |
| 573 | Ray Smith | .05 |
| 574 | Tim Teufel (R) | .50 |
| 575 | Frank Viola | .05 |
| 576 | Gary Ward | .05 |
| 577 | Ron Washington | .05 |
| 578 | Len Whitehouse | .05 |
| 579 | Al Williams | .05 |

**NEW YORK METS**

| NO. | PLAYER | MINT |
|---|---|---|
| 580 | Bob Bailor | .05 |
| 581 | Mark Bradley | .10 |
| 582 | Hubie Brooks | .10 |
| 583 | Carlos Diaz | .05 |
| 584 | George Foster | .15 |
| 585 | Brian Giles | .05 |
| 586 | Danny Heep | .05 |
| 587 | Keith Hernandez | .30 |
| 588 | Ron Hodges | .05 |
| 589 | Scott Holman | .05 |
| 590 | Dave Kingman | .15 |
| 591 | Ed Lynch | .05 |
| 592 | Jose Oquendo | .10 |
| 593 | Jesse Orosco | .10 |
| 594 | Junior Ortiz | .10 |
| 595 | Tom Seaver | .30 |
| 596 | Doug Sisk | .15 |
| 597 | Rusty Staub | .10 |
| 598 | John Stearns | .05 |
| 599 | Darryl Strawberry (R) | 5.00 |
| 600 | Craig Swan | .05 |
| 601 | Walt Terrell (R) | .35 |
| 602 | Mike Torrez | .05 |
| 603 | Mookie Wilson | .10 |

**SEATTLE MARINERS**

| NO. | PLAYER | MINT |
|---|---|---|
| 604 | Jamie Allen | .05 |
| 605 | Jim Beattie | .05 |
| 606 | Tony Bernazard | .05 |
| 607 | Manny Castillo | .05 |
| 608 | Bill Caudill | .05 |
| 609 | Bryan Clark | .05 |
| 610 | Al Cowens | .05 |
| 611 | Dave Henderson | .05 |
| 612 | Steve Henderson | .05 |
| 613 | Orlando Mercado | .05 |
| 614 | Mike Moore | .05 |
| 615 | Ricky Nelson | .05 |
| 616 | Spike Owen (R) | .20 |
| 617 | Pat Putnam | .05 |
| 618 | Ron Roenicke | .05 |
| 619 | Mike Stanton | .05 |
| 620 | Bob Stoddard | .05 |
| 621 | Rick Sweet | .05 |
| 622 | Roy Thomas | .05 |
| 623 | Ed Vande Berg | .05 |
| 624 | Matt Young (R) | .15 |
| 625 | Richie Zisk | .05 |
| 626 | Fred Lynn: | .15 |
| | All-Star Record Breaker | |
| 627 | Manny Trillo: | .05 |
| | "All-Star Record Breaker" | |
| 628 | Steve Garvey | .25 |
| | "NL Iron Man" | |
| 629 | Rod Carew: | .20 |
| | "AL Batting Runner-Up" | |
| 630 | Wade Boggs: | .50 |
| | "AL Batting Champion" | |
| 631 | Tim Raines: | .15 |
| | "Letting Go Of The Raines" | |
| 632 | Al Oliver: | .15 |
| | "Double Trouble" | |
| 633 | Steve Sax: | .10 |
| | "All-Star Second Base" | |
| 634 | Dickie Thon: | .10 |
| | "All-Star Shortstop" | |
| 635 | Quisenberry & Martinez | .10 |
| | "Ace Fireman" | |
| 636 | Perez, Rose, & Morgan | .40 |
| | "Reds Reunited" | |
| 637 | Parrish & Boone: | .10 |
| | "Backstop Stars" | |
| 638 | Brett & Perry: | .25 |
| | "Pine Tar Incident" | |
| 639 | Forsch, Warren & Righetti | .10 |
| | "1983 No-Hitters" | |
| 640 | Bench and Yaz: | .25 |
| | "Retiring Superstars" | |
| 641 | Gaylord Perry: | .15 |
| | "Going Out In Style" | |
| 642 | Steve Carlton: | .20 |
| | 300 Club and Strikeout Record | |
| 643 | Altobelli and Owens: | .05 |
| | "World Series Managers" | |
| 644 | Rick Dempsey: | .05 |
| | "World Series MVP" | |
| 645 | Mike Boddicker: | .10 |
| | "Rookie Winner" | |
| 646 | Scott McGregor: | .10 |
| | "The Clincher" | |
| 647 | Checklist No. 1 | .08 |
| 648 | Checklist No. 2 | .08 |
| 649 | Checklist No. 3 | .08 |
| 650 | Checklist No. 4 | .08 |
| 651 | Checklist No. 5 | .08 |
| 652 | Checklist No. 6 | .08 |
| 653 | Checklist No. 7 | .08 |
| 654 | Checklist No. 8 | .08 |
| 655 | Checklist No. 9 | .08 |
| 656 | Checklist No. 10 | .08 |
| 657 | Checklist No. 11 | .08 |
| 658 | Checklist No. 12 | .08 |
| 659 | Checklist No 13 | .08 |
| 660 | Checklist No. 14 | .08 |

# 1984 Fleer Traded Update....Complete Set of 132 Cards—Value $275.00

This was Fleer's first traded update set. It updates the main 1984 card set with players who had changed teams during the season and rookies. This set features Fleer's first card of Dwight Gooden, Roger Clemens, Bret Saberhagen and Kirby Puckett. Production was extremely limited. The complete set was packaged in its own printed box and distributed exclusively through card hobby dealers.

Card values shown here fluctuate considerably.

| NO. | PLAYER | MINT | NO. | PLAYER | MINT | NO. | PLAYER | MINT | NO. | PLAYER | MINT |
|---|---|---|---|---|---|---|---|---|---|---|---|
| U1 | Willie Aikens | .20 | U34 | Dennis Eckersley | .15 | U67 | Frank LaCorte | .15 | U100 | Jeff Robinson | .25 |
| U2 | Luis Aponte | .15 | U35 | Jim Essian | .15 | U68 | Dennis Lamp | .15 | U101 | R. Romanick (RR) | 1.50 |
| U3 | Mark Bailey | .30 | U36 | Darrell Evans | .35 | U69 | Tito Landrum | .15 | U102 | Pete Rose | 17.50 |
| U4 | Bob Bailor | .15 | U37 | Mike Fitzgerald | .25 | U70 | Mark Langston (RR) | 2.50 | U103 | B. Saberhagen (RR) | 6.00 |
| U5 | Dusty Baker | .20 | U38 | Tim Foli | .15 | U71 | Rick Leach | .15 | U104 | Scott Sanderson | .25 |
| U6 | Steve Balboni | .20 | U39 | John Franco (RR) | 2.00 | U72 | Craig Lefferts | .15 | U105 | Dick Schofield | .75 |
| U7 | Alan Bannister | .15 | U40 | George Frazier | .15 | U73 | Gary Lucas | .15 | U106 | Tom Seaver | 5.00 |
| U8 | Marty Barrett (RR) | 5.00 | U41 | Rich Gale | .15 | U74 | Jerry Martin | .15 | U107 | Jim Slaton | .15 |
| U9 | Dave Beard | .15 | U42 | Barbaro Garbey | .25 | U75 | Carmelo Martinez | .20 | U108 | Mike Smithson | .15 |
| U10 | Joe Beckwith | .15 | U43 | Dwight Gooden (RR) | .75.00 | U76 | Mike Mason | .25 | U109 | Lary Sorensen | .15 |
| U11 | Dave Bergman | .15 | U44 | Goose Gossage | .50 | U77 | Gary Matthews | .15 | U110 | Tim Stoddard | .15 |
| U12 | Tony Bernazard | .15 | U45 | Wayne Gross | .15 | U78 | Andy McGaffigan | .15 | U111 | Jeff Stone (RR) | .75 |
| U13 | Bruce Bochte | .15 | U46 | Mark Gubicza | .75 | U79 | Joey McLaughlin | .15 | U112 | Champ Summers | .15 |
| U14 | Barry Bonnell | .15 | U47 | Jackie Gutierrez | .30 | U80 | Joe Morgan | 2.50 | U113 | Jim Sundberg | .15 |
| U15 | Phil Bradley (RR) | 7.50 | U48 | Toby Harrah | .15 | U81 | Darryl Motley | .25 | U114 | Rick Sutcliffe | .75 |
| U16 | Fred Breining | .15 | U49 | Ron Hassey | .15 | U82 | Graig Nettles | .75 | U115 | Craig Swan | .15 |
| U17 | Mike Brown | .25 | U50 | Richie Hebner | .15 | U83 | Phil Niekro | 1.50 | U116 | Derrel Thomas | .15 |
| U18 | Bill Buckner | .20 | U51 | Willie Hernandez | .60 | U84 | Ken Oberkfell | .15 | U117 | Gorman Thomas | .25 |
| U19 | Ray Burris | .15 | U52 | Ed Hodge | .15 | U85 | Al Oliver | .60 | U118 | Alex Trevino | .15 |
| U20 | John Butcher | .15 | U53 | Ricky Horton | .60 | U86 | Jorge Orta | .15 | U119 | Manny Trillo | .15 |
| U21 | Brett Butler | .40 | U54 | Art Howe | 1.25 | U87 | Amos Otis | .15 | U120 | John Tudor | .25 |
| U22 | Enos Cabell | .15 | U55 | Dane Iorg | .15 | U88 | Bob Owchinko | .15 | U121 | Tom Underwood | .15 |
| U23 | Bill Campbell | .15 | U56 | Brook Jacoby (RR) | 3.00 | U89 | Dave Parker | 2.00 | U122 | Mike Vail | .15 |
| U24 | Bill Caudill | .15 | U57 | Dion James | .50 | U90 | Jack Perconte | .15 | U123 | Tom Waddell | .15 |
| U25 | Bobby Clark | .15 | U58 | Mike Jeffcoat | .20 | U91 | Tony Perez | 1.00 | U124 | Gary Ward | .15 |
| U26 | Bryan Clark | .15 | U59 | Ruppert Jones | .15 | U92 | Gerald Perry | .25 | U125 | Terry Whitfield | .15 |
| U27 | R. Clemens (RR) | 70.00 | U60 | Bob Kearney | .15 | U93 | Kirby Puckett (RR) | 30.00 | U126 | Curtis Wilkerson | .15 |
| U28 | Jaime Cocanower | .25 | U61 | Jimmy Key (RR) | 2.50 | U94 | Shane Rawley | .20 | U127 | Frank Williams | .15 |
| U29 | Ron Darling (RR) | 10.00 | U62 | Dave Kingman | .25 | U95 | Floyd Rayford | .15 | U128 | Glenn Wilson | .25 |
| U30 | Alvin Davis (RR) | 8.00 | U63 | B. Komminsk (RR) | .75 | U96 | Ron Reed | .15 | U129 | John Wockenfuss | .15 |
| U31 | Bob Dernier | .20 | U64 | Jerry Koosman | .15 | U97 | R.J. Reynolds (RR) | 2.00 | U130 | Ned Yost | .15 |
| U32 | Carlos Diaz | .15 | U65 | Wayne Krenchicki | .15 | U98 | Gene Richards | .15 | U131 | Mike Young (RR) | 2.00 |
| U33 | Mike Easler | .15 | U66 | Rusty Kuntz | .15 | U99 | Jose Rijo | .75 | U132 | Checklist | .25 |

# 1985 Fleer....Complete Set of 660 Cards—Value $45.00

Features the rookie cards of Dwight Gooden, Roger Clemens, Bret Saberhagen, Alvin Davis, Orel Hershiser and Kirby Puckett.

| NO. | PLAYER | MINT | NO. | PLAYER | MINT | NO. | PLAYER | MINT | NO. | PLAYER | MINT |
|---|---|---|---|---|---|---|---|---|---|---|---|
| **DETROIT TIGERS** | | | 7 | Barbaro Garbey (R) | .20 | 14 | Rusty Kuntz | .05 | 21 | Dave Rozema | .05 |
| 1 | Doug Bair | .10 | 8 | Kirk Gibson | .20 | 15 | Chet Lemon | .05 | 22 | Bill Scherrer | .05 |
| 2 | Juan Berenguer | .05 | 9 | John Grubb | .05 | 16 | Aurelio Lopez | .05 | 23 | Alan Trammell | .20 |
| 3 | Dave Bergman | .05 | 10 | Willie Hernandez | .15 | 17 | Sid Monge | .05 | 24 | Lou Whitaker | .20 |
| 4 | Tom Brookens | .05 | 11 | Larry Herndon | .05 | 18 | Jack Morris | .20 | 25 | Milt Wilcox | .05 |
| 5 | Marty Castillo | .05 | 12 | Howard Johnson | .05 | 19 | Lance Parrish | .20 | **SAN DIEGO PADRES** | | |
| 6 | Darrell Evans | .10 | 13 | Ruppert Jones | .05 | 20 | Dan Petry | .15 | 26 | Kurt Bevacqua | .05 |

Card values shown here fluctuate considerably.

# 1985 Fleer (Continued)

| NO. | PLAYER | MINT |
|---|---|---|
| 27 | Greg Booker (R) | .10 |
| 28 | Bobby Brown | .05 |
| 29 | Luis DeLeon | .05 |
| 30 | Dave Dravecky | .05 |
| 31 | Tim Flannery | .05 |
| 32 | Steve Garvey | .40 |
| 33 | Goose Gossage | .15 |
| 34 | Tony Gwynn | .50 |
| 35 | Greg Harris | .05 |
| 36 | Andy Hawkins | .05 |
| 37 | Terry Kennedy | .05 |
| 38 | Craig Lefferts | .05 |
| 39 | Tim Lollar | .05 |
| 40 | Carmelo Martinez | .05 |
| 41 | Kevin McReynolds | .15 |
| 42 | Graig Nettles | .10 |
| 43 | Luis Salazar | .05 |
| 44 | Eric Show | .05 |
| 45 | Garry Templeton | .08 |
| 46 | Mark Thurmond | .05 |
| 47 | Ed Whitson | .05 |
| 48 | Alan Wiggins | .10 |

**CHICAGO CUBS**

| NO. | PLAYER | MINT |
|---|---|---|
| 49 | Rich Bordi | .05 |
| 50 | Larry Bowa | .05 |
| 51 | Warren Brusstar | .05 |
| 52 | Ron Cey | .15 |
| 53 | Henry Cotto (R) | .15 |
| 54 | Jody Davis | .10 |
| 55 | Bob Dernier | .05 |
| 56 | Leon Durham | .15 |
| 57 | Dennis Eckersley | .05 |
| 58 | George Frazier | .05 |
| 59 | Richie Hebner | .05 |
| 60 | Dave Lopes | .05 |
| 61 | Gary Matthews | .10 |
| 62 | Keith Moreland | .05 |
| 63 | Rick Reuschel | .05 |
| 64 | Dick Ruthven | .05 |
| 65 | Ryne Sandberg | .40 |
| 66 | Scott Sanderson | .05 |
| 67 | Lee Smith | .10 |
| 68 | Tim Stoddard | .05 |
| 69 | Rick Sutcliffe | .20 |
| 70 | Steve Trout | .05 |
| 71 | Gary Woods | .05 |

**NEW YORK METS**

| NO. | PLAYER | MINT |
|---|---|---|
| 72 | Wally Backman | .05 |
| 73 | Bruce Berenyi | .05 |
| 74 | Hubie Brooks | .10 |
| 75 | Kelvin Chapman (R) | .15 |
| 76 | Ron Darling | .45 |
| 77 | Sid Fernandez | .50 |
| 78 | Mike Fitzgerald | .05 |
| 79 | George Foster | .15 |
| 80 | Brent Gaff | .05 |
| 81 | Ron Gardenhire | .05 |
| 82 | Dwight Gooden (R) | 6.00 |
| 83 | Tom Gorman | .05 |
| 84 | Danny Heep | .05 |
| 85 | Keith Hernandez | .30 |
| 86 | Ray Knight | .05 |
| 87 | Ed Lynch | .05 |
| 88 | Jose Oquendo | .05 |
| 89 | Jesse Orosco | .10 |
| 90 | Rafael Santana (R) | .15 |
| 91 | Doug Sisk | .05 |
| 92 | Rusty Staub | .10 |
| 93 | Darryl Strawberry | .60 |
| 94 | Walt Terrell | .05 |
| 95 | Mookie Wilson | .05 |

**TORONTO BLUE JAYS**

| NO. | PLAYER | MINT |
|---|---|---|
| 96 | Jim Acker | .05 |
| 97 | Willie Aikens | .05 |
| 98 | Doyle Alexander | .05 |
| 99 | Jesse Barfield | .20 |
| 100 | George Bell | .10 |
| 101 | Jim Clancy | .05 |
| 102 | Dave Collins | .05 |
| 103 | Tony Fernandez | .10 |
| 104 | Damaso Garcia | .10 |
| 105 | Jim Gott | .05 |
| 106 | Alfredo Griffin | .05 |
| 107 | Garth Iorg | .05 |
| 108 | Roy Lee Jackson | .05 |
| 109 | Cliff Johnson | .05 |

| NO. | PLAYER | MINT |
|---|---|---|
| 110 | Jimmy Key (R) | .35 |
| 111 | Dennis Lamp | .05 |
| 112 | Rick Leach | .05 |
| 113 | Luis Leal | .05 |
| 114 | Buck Martinez | .05 |
| 115 | Lloyd Moseby | .15 |
| 116 | Rance Mulliniks | .05 |
| 117 | Dave Stieb | .15 |
| 118 | Willie Upshaw | .10 |
| 119 | Ernie Whitt | .05 |

**NEW YORK YANKEES**

| NO. | PLAYER | MINT |
|---|---|---|
| 120 | Mike Armstrong | .05 |
| 121 | Don Baylor | .10 |
| 122 | Marty Bystrom | .05 |
| 123 | Rick Cerone | .05 |
| 124 | Joe Cowley | .05 |
| 125 | Brian Dayett | .05 |
| 126 | Tim Foli | .05 |
| 127 | Ray Fontenot | .05 |
| 128 | Ken Griffey | .05 |
| 129 | Ron Guidry | .15 |
| 130 | Toby Harrah | .05 |
| 131 | Jay Howell | .05 |
| 132 | Steve Kemp | .05 |
| 133 | Don Mattingly | 5.00 |
| 134 | Bobby Meacham | .05 |
| 135 | John Montefusco | .05 |
| 136 | Omar Moreno | .05 |
| 137 | Dale Murray | .05 |
| 138 | Phil Niekro | .15 |
| 139 | Mike Pagliarulo (R) | 1.50 |
| 140 | Willie Randolph | .05 |
| 141 | Dennis Rasmussen | .05 |
| 142 | Dave Righetti | .10 |
| 143 | Jose Rijo (R) | .25 |
| 144 | Andre Robertson | .05 |
| 145 | Bob Shirley | .05 |
| 146 | Dave Winfield | .35 |
| 147 | Butch Wynegar | .05 |

**BOSTON RED SOX**

| NO. | PLAYER | MINT |
|---|---|---|
| 148 | Gary Allenson | .05 |
| 149 | Tony Armas | .10 |
| 150 | Marty Barrett | .05 |
| 151 | Wade Boggs | 2.00 |
| 152 | Dennis Boyd | .05 |
| 153 | Bill Buckner | .05 |
| 154 | Mark Clear | .05 |
| 155 | Roger Clemens (R) | 7.00 |
| 156 | Steve Crawford | .05 |
| 157 | Mike Easler | .05 |
| 158 | Dwight Evans | .10 |
| 159 | Rich Gedman | .05 |
| 160 | Jackie Gutierrez (R) | .15 |
| 161 | Bruce Hurst | .05 |
| 162 | John H. Johnson | .05 |
| 163 | Rick Miller | .05 |
| 164 | Reid Nichols | .05 |
| 165 | Al Nipper (R) | .20 |
| 166 | Bob Ojeda | .05 |
| 167 | Jerry Remy | .05 |
| 168 | Jim Rice | .35 |
| 169 | Bob Stanley | .05 |

**BALTIMORE ORIOLES**

| NO. | PLAYER | MINT |
|---|---|---|
| 170 | Mike Boddicker | .10 |
| 171 | Al Bumbry | .05 |
| 172 | Todd Cruz | .05 |
| 173 | Rich Dauer | .05 |
| 174 | Storm Davis | .05 |
| 175 | Rick Dempsey | .05 |
| 176 | Jim Dwyer | .05 |
| 177 | Mike Flanagan | .05 |
| 178 | Dan Ford | .05 |
| 179 | Wayne Gross | .05 |
| 180 | John Lowenstein | .05 |
| 181 | Dennis Martinez | .05 |
| 182 | Tippy Martinez | .05 |
| 183 | Scott McGregor | .05 |
| 184 | Eddie Murray | .50 |
| 185 | Joe Nolan | .05 |
| 186 | Floyd Rayford | .05 |
| 187 | Cal Ripken, Jr. | .50 |
| 188 | Gary Roenicke | .05 |
| 189 | Lenn Sakata | .05 |
| 190 | John Shelby | .05 |
| 191 | Ken Singleton | .05 |

| NO. | PLAYER | MINT |
|---|---|---|
| 192 | Sammy Stewart | .05 |
| 193 | Bill Swaggerty (R) | .15 |
| 194 | Tom Underwood | .05 |
| 195 | Mike Young | .25 |

**KANSAS CITY ROYALS**

| NO. | PLAYER | MINT |
|---|---|---|
| 196 | Steve Balboni | .10 |
| 197 | Joe Beckwith | .05 |
| 198 | Bud Black | .05 |
| 199 | George Brett | .50 |
| 200 | Onix Concepcion | .05 |
| 201 | Mark Gubicza (R) | .20 |
| 202 | Larry Gura | .05 |
| 203 | Mark Huismann | .05 |
| 204 | Dane Iorg | .05 |
| 205 | Danny Jackson | .05 |
| 206 | Charlie Leibrandt | .05 |
| 207 | Hal McRae | .05 |
| 208 | Darryl Motley | .05 |
| 209 | Jorge Orta | .05 |
| 210 | Greg Pryor | .05 |
| 211 | Dan Quisenberry | .15 |
| 212 | Bret Saberhagen (R) | 1.00 |
| 213 | Pat Sheridan | .05 |
| 214 | Don Slaught | .05 |
| 215 | U.L. Washington | .05 |
| 216 | John Wathan | .05 |
| 217 | Frank White | .05 |
| 218 | Willie Wilson | .15 |

**ST. LOUIS CARDINALS**

| NO. | PLAYER | MINT |
|---|---|---|
| 219 | Neil Allen | .05 |
| 220 | Joaquin Andujar | .10 |
| 221 | Steve Braun | .05 |
| 222 | Danny Cox | .05 |
| 223 | Bob Forsch | .05 |
| 224 | David Green | .05 |
| 225 | George Hendrick | .08 |
| 226 | Tom Herr | .10 |
| 227 | Ricky Horton (R) | .25 |
| 228 | Art Howe | .05 |
| 229 | Mike Jorgensen | .05 |
| 230 | Kurt Kepshire (R) | .15 |
| 231 | Jeff Lahti | .05 |
| 232 | Tito Landrum | .05 |
| 233 | Dave LaPoint | .05 |
| 234 | Willie McGee | .30 |
| 235 | Tom Nieto (R) | .15 |
| 236 | Terry Pendleton (R) | .50 |
| 237 | Darrell Porter | .05 |
| 238 | Dave Rucker | .05 |
| 239 | Lonnie Smith | .05 |
| 240 | Ozzie Smith | .10 |
| 241 | Bruce Sutter | .15 |
| 242 | Andy Van Slyke | .10 |
| 243 | Dave Von Ohlen | .05 |

**PHILADELPHIA PHILLIES**

| NO. | PLAYER | MINT |
|---|---|---|
| 244 | Larry Andersen | .05 |
| 245 | Bill Campbell | .05 |
| 246 | Steve Carlton | .30 |
| 247 | Tim Corcoran | .05 |
| 248 | Ivan DeJesus | .05 |
| 249 | John Denny | .05 |
| 250 | Bo Diaz | .05 |
| 251 | Greg Gross | .05 |
| 252 | Kevin Gross | .05 |
| 253 | Von Hayes | .15 |
| 254 | Al Holland | .05 |
| 255 | Charles Hudson | .05 |
| 256 | Jerry Koosman | .05 |
| 257 | Joe Lefebvre | .05 |
| 258 | Sixto Lezcano | .05 |
| 259 | Garry Maddox | .05 |
| 260 | Len Matuszek | .05 |
| 261 | Tug McGraw | .05 |
| 262 | Al Oliver | .10 |
| 263 | Shane Rawley | .05 |
| 264 | Juan Samuel | .30 |
| 265 | Mike Schmidt | .35 |
| 266 | Jeff Stone (R) | .30 |
| 267 | Ozzie Virgil | .05 |
| 268 | Glenn Wilson | .10 |
| 269 | John Wockenfuss | .05 |

**MINNESOTA TWINS**

| NO. | PLAYER | MINT |
|---|---|---|
| 270 | Darrell Brown | .05 |
| 271 | Tom Brunansky | .10 |
| 272 | Randy Bush | .05 |

| NO. | PLAYER | MINT |
|---|---|---|
| 273 | John Butcher | .05 |
| 274 | Bobby Castillo | .05 |
| 275 | Ron Davis | .05 |
| 276 | Dave Engle | .05 |
| 277 | Pete Filson | .05 |
| 278 | Gary Gaetti | .05 |
| 279 | Mickey Hatcher | .05 |
| 280 | Ed Hodge (R) | .15 |
| 281 | Kent Hrbek | .35 |
| 282 | Houston Jimenez | .05 |
| 283 | Tim Laudner | .05 |
| 284 | Rick Lysander | .05 |
| 285 | Dave Meier (R) | .15 |
| 286 | Kirby Puckett (R) | 4.50 |
| 287 | Pat Putnam | .05 |
| 288 | Ken Schrom | .05 |
| 289 | Mike Smithson | .05 |
| 290 | Tim Teufel | .05 |
| 291 | Frank Viola | .05 |
| 292 | Ron Washington | .05 |

**CALIFORNIA ANGELS**

| NO. | PLAYER | MINT |
|---|---|---|
| 293 | Don Aase | .05 |
| 294 | Juan Beniquez | .05 |
| 295 | Bob Boone | .05 |
| 296 | Mike Brown | .05 |
| 297 | Rod Carew | .30 |
| 298 | Doug Corbett | .05 |
| 299 | Doug DeCinces | .05 |
| 300 | Brian Downing | .05 |
| 301 | Ken Forsch | .05 |
| 302 | Bobby Grich | .05 |
| 303 | Reggie Jackson | .40 |
| 304 | Tommy John | .10 |
| 305 | Curt Kaufman (R) | .15 |
| 306 | Bruce Kison | .05 |
| 307 | Fred Lynn | .15 |
| 308 | Gary Pettis | .10 |
| 309 | Ron Romanick (R) | .30 |
| 310 | Luis Sanchez | .05 |
| 311 | Dick Schofield | .05 |
| 312 | Daryl Sconiers | .05 |
| 313 | Jim Slaton | .05 |
| 314 | Derrel Thomas | .05 |
| 315 | Rob Wilfong | .05 |
| 316 | Mike Witt | .10 |
| 317 | Geoff Zahn | .05 |

**ATLANTA BRAVES**

| NO. | PLAYER | MINT |
|---|---|---|
| 318 | Len Barker | .05 |
| 319 | Steve Bedrosian | .05 |
| 320 | Bruce Benedict | .05 |
| 321 | Rick Camp | .05 |
| 322 | Chris Chambliss | .05 |
| 323 | Jeff Dedmon (R) | .10 |
| 324 | Terry Forster | .05 |
| 325 | Gene Garber | .05 |
| 326 | Albert Hall (R) | .15 |
| 327 | Terry Harper | .05 |
| 328 | Bob Horner | .15 |
| 329 | Glenn Hubbard | .05 |
| 330 | Randy Johnson | .05 |
| 331 | Brad Komminsk | .05 |
| 332 | Rick Mahler | .05 |
| 333 | Craig McMurtry | .05 |
| 334 | Donnie Moore | .05 |
| 335 | Dale Murphy | .60 |
| 336 | Ken Oberkfell | .05 |
| 337 | Pascual Perez | .05 |
| 338 | Gerald Perry | .05 |
| 339 | Rafael Ramirez | .05 |
| 340 | Jerry Royster | .05 |
| 341 | Alex Trevino | .05 |
| 342 | Claudell Washington | .08 |

**HOUSTON ASTROS**

| NO. | PLAYER | MINT |
|---|---|---|
| 343 | Alan Ashby | .05 |
| 344 | Mark Bailey | .05 |
| 345 | Kevin Bass | .05 |
| 346 | Enos Cabell | .05 |
| 347 | Jose Cruz | .10 |
| 348 | Bill Dawley | .05 |
| 349 | Frank DiPino | .05 |
| 350 | Bill Doran | .05 |
| 351 | Phil Garner | .05 |
| 352 | Bob Knepper | .05 |
| 353 | Mike LaCoss | .05 |
| 354 | Jerry Mumphrey | .05 |
| 355 | Joe Niekro | .05 |

Card values shown here fluctuate considerably.

| NO. | PLAYER | MINT |
|---|---|---|
| 356 | Terry Puhl | .05 |
| 357 | Craig Reynolds | .05 |
| 358 | Vern Ruhle | .05 |
| 359 | Nolan Ryan | .25 |
| 360 | Joe Sambito | .05 |
| 361 | Mike Scott | .25 |
| 362 | Dave Smith | .05 |
| 363 | Julio Solano (R) | .10 |
| 364 | Dickie Thon | .05 |
| 365 | Denny Walling | .05 |

**LOS ANGELES DODGERS**

| NO. | PLAYER | MINT |
|---|---|---|
| 366 | Dave Anderson | .05 |
| 367 | Bob Bailor | .05 |
| 368 | Greg Brock | .05 |
| 369 | Carlos Diaz | .05 |
| 370 | Pedro Guerrero | .25 |
| 371 | Orel Hershiser (R) | 1.00 |
| 372 | Rick Honeycutt | .05 |
| 373 | Burt Hooton | .05 |
| 374 | Ken Howell (R) | .20 |
| 375 | Ken Landreaux | .05 |
| 376 | Candy Maldonado | .05 |
| 377 | Mike Marshall | .10 |
| 378 | Tom Niedenfuer | .05 |
| 379 | Alejandro Pena | .05 |
| 380 | Jerry Reuss | .05 |
| 381 | R.J. Reynolds (R) | .30 |
| 382 | German Rivera (R) | .15 |
| 383 | Bill Russell | .05 |
| 384 | Steve Sax | .10 |
| 385 | Mike Scioscia | .05 |
| 386 | Franklin Stubbs (R) | .75 |
| 387 | Fernando Valenzuela | .35 |
| 388 | Bob Welch | .05 |
| 389 | Terry Whitfield | .05 |
| 390 | Steve Yeager | .05 |
| 391 | Pat Zachry | .05 |

**MONTREAL EXPOS**

| NO. | PLAYER | MINT |
|---|---|---|
| 392 | Fred Breining | .05 |
| 393 | Gary Carter | .30 |
| 394 | Andre Dawson | .20 |
| 395 | Miguel Dilone | .05 |
| 396 | Dan Driessen | .05 |
| 397 | Doug Flynn | .05 |
| 398 | Terry Francona | .05 |
| 399 | Bill Gullickson | .05 |
| 400 | Bob James | .05 |
| 401 | Chrlie Lea | .05 |
| 402 | Bryan Little | .05 |
| 403 | Gary Lucas | .05 |
| 404 | David Palmer | .05 |
| 405 | Tim Raines | .20 |
| 406 | Mike Ramsey | .05 |
| 407 | Jeff Reardon | .05 |
| 408 | Steve Rogers | .05 |
| 409 | Dan Schatzeder | .05 |
| 410 | Bryn Smith | .05 |
| 411 | Mike Stenhouse | .05 |
| 412 | Tim Wallach | .08 |
| 413 | Jim Wohlford | .05 |

**OAKLAND A'S**

| NO. | PLAYER | MINT |
|---|---|---|
| 414 | Bill Almon | .05 |
| 415 | Keith Atherton | .05 |
| 416 | Bruce Bochte | .05 |
| 417 | Tom Burgmeier | .05 |
| 418 | Ray Burris | .05 |
| 419 | Bill Caudill | .05 |
| 420 | Chris Codiroli | .05 |
| 421 | Tim Conroy | .05 |
| 422 | Mike Davis | .05 |
| 423 | Jim Essian | .05 |
| 424 | Mike Heath | .05 |
| 425 | Rickey Henderson | .50 |
| 426 | Donnie Hill | .05 |
| 427 | Dave Kingman | .10 |
| 428 | Bill Krueger | .05 |
| 429 | Carney Lansford | .10 |
| 430 | Steve McCatty | .05 |
| 431 | Joe Morgan | .15 |
| 432 | Dwayne Murphy | .05 |
| 433 | Tony Phillips | .05 |
| 434 | Lary Sorensen | .05 |
| 435 | Mike Warren | .05 |
| 436 | Curt Young (R) | .15 |

**CLEVELAND INDIANS**

| NO. | PLAYER | MINT |
|---|---|---|
| 437 | Luis Aponte | .05 |
| 438 | Chris Bando | .05 |
| 439 | Tony Bernazard | .05 |
| 440 | Bert Blyleven | .10 |
| 441 | Brett Butler | .05 |
| 442 | Ernie Camacho | .05 |
| 443 | Joe Carter | .05 |
| 444 | Carmelo Castillo | .05 |
| 445 | Jamie Easterly | .05 |
| 446 | Steve Farr (R) | .15 |
| 447 | Mike Fischlin | .05 |
| 448 | Julio Franco | .15 |
| 449 | Mel Hall | .10 |
| 450 | Mike Hargrove | .05 |
| 451 | Neal Heaton | .05 |
| 452 | Brook Jacoby | .10 |
| 453 | Mike Jeffcoat | .05 |
| 454 | Don Schulze (R) | .15 |
| 455 | Roy Smith (R) | .15 |
| 456 | Pat Tabler | .05 |
| 457 | Andre Thornton | .05 |
| 458 | George Vukovich | .05 |
| 459 | Tom Waddell (R) | .15 |
| 460 | Jerry Willard | .05 |

**PITTSBURGH PIRATES**

| NO. | PLAYER | MINT |
|---|---|---|
| 461 | Dale Berra | .05 |
| 462 | John Candelaria | .05 |
| 463 | Jose DeLeon | .05 |
| 464 | Doug Frobel | .05 |
| 465 | Cecilio Guante | .05 |
| 466 | Brian Harper | .05 |
| 467 | Lee Lacy | .05 |
| 468 | Bill Madlock | .10 |
| 469 | Lee Mazzilli | .05 |
| 470 | Larry McWilliams | .05 |
| 471 | Jim Morrison | .05 |
| 472 | Tony Pena | .10 |
| 473 | Johnny Ray | .10 |
| 474 | Rick Rhoden | .05 |
| 475 | Don Robinson | .05 |
| 476 | Rod Scurry | .05 |
| 477 | Kent Tekulve | .05 |
| 478 | Jason Thompson | .05 |
| 479 | John Tudor | .10 |
| 480 | Lee Tunnell | .05 |
| 481 | Marvell Wynne | .05 |

**SEATTLE MARINERS**

| NO. | PLAYER | MINT |
|---|---|---|
| 482 | Salome Barojas | .05 |
| 483 | Dave Beard | .05 |
| 484 | Jim Beattie | .05 |
| 485 | Barry Bonnell | .05 |
| 486 | Phil Bradley (R) | 1.25 |
| 487 | Al Cowens | .05 |
| 488 | Alvin Davis (R) | 2.00 |
| 489 | Dave Henderson | .05 |
| 490 | Steve Henderson | .05 |
| 491 | Bob Kearney | .05 |
| 492 | Mark Langston (R) | .50 |
| 493 | Larry Milbourne | .05 |
| 494 | Paul Mirabella | .05 |
| 495 | Mike Moore | .05 |
| 496 | Edwin Nunez | .05 |
| 497 | Spike Owen | .05 |
| 498 | Jack Perconte | .05 |
| 499 | Ken Phelps | .05 |
| 500 | Jim Presley (R) | 1.50 |
| 501 | Mike Stanton | .05 |
| 502 | Bob Stoddard | .05 |
| 503 | Gorman Thomas | .10 |
| 504 | Ed VandeBerg | .05 |
| 505 | Matt Young | .05 |

**CHICAGO WHITE SOX**

| NO. | PLAYER | MINT |
|---|---|---|
| 506 | Juan Agosto | .05 |
| 507 | Harold Baines | .20 |
| 508 | Floyd Bannister | .05 |
| 509 | Britt Burns | .05 |
| 510 | Julio Cruz | .05 |
| 511 | Richard Dotson | .05 |
| 512 | Jerry Dybzinski | .05 |
| 513 | Carlton Fisk | .15 |
| 514 | Scott Fletcher | .05 |
| 515 | Jerry Hairston | .05 |
| 516 | Marc Hill | .05 |
| 517 | LaMarr Hoyt | .10 |
| 518 | Ron Kittle | .15 |

| NO. | PLAYER | MINT |
|---|---|---|
| 519 | Rudy Law | .05 |
| 520 | Vance Law | .05 |
| 521 | Greg Luzinski | .10 |
| 522 | Gene Nelson | .05 |
| 523 | Tom Paciorek | .05 |
| 524 | Ron Reed | .05 |
| 525 | Bert Roberge | .05 |
| 526 | Tom Seaver | .25 |
| 527 | Roy Smalley | .05 |
| 528 | Dan Spillner | .05 |
| 529 | Mike Squires | .05 |
| 530 | Greg Walker | .10 |

**CINCINNATI REDS**

| NO. | PLAYER | MINT |
|---|---|---|
| 531 | Cesar Cedeno | .05 |
| 532 | Dave Concepcion | .10 |
| 533 | Eric Davis (R) | 4.00 |
| 534 | Nick Esasky | .05 |
| 535 | Tom Foley | .05 |
| 536 | John Franco (R) | .35 |
| 537 | Brad Guden | .05 |
| 538 | Tom Hume | .05 |
| 539 | Wayne Krenchicki | .05 |
| 540 | Andy McGaffigan | .05 |
| 541 | Eddie Milner | .05 |
| 542 | Ron Oester | .05 |
| 543 | Bob Owchinko | .05 |
| 544 | Dave Parker | .15 |
| 545 | Frank Pastore | .05 |
| 546 | Tony Perez | .10 |
| 547 | Ted Power | .05 |
| 548 | Joe Price | .05 |
| 549 | Gary Redus | .05 |
| 550 | Pete Rose | .75 |
| 551 | Jeff Russell | .05 |
| 552 | Mario Soto | .10 |
| 553 | Jay Tibbs (R) | .20 |
| 554 | Duane Walker | .05 |

**TEXAS RANGERS**

| NO. | PLAYER | MINT |
|---|---|---|
| 555 | Alan Bannister | .05 |
| 556 | Buddy Bell | .10 |
| 557 | Danny Darwin | .05 |
| 558 | Charlie Hough | .05 |
| 559 | Bobby Jones | .05 |
| 560 | Odell Jones | .05 |
| 561 | Jeff Kunkel (R) | .15 |
| 562 | Mike Mason (R) | .15 |
| 563 | Pete O'Brien | .05 |
| 564 | Larry Parrish | .05 |
| 565 | Mickey Rivers | .05 |
| 566 | Billy Sample | .05 |
| 567 | Dave Schmidt | .05 |
| 568 | Donnie Scott (R) | .15 |
| 569 | Dave Stewart | .05 |
| 570 | Frank Tanana | .05 |
| 571 | Wayne Tolleson | .05 |
| 572 | Gary Ward | .05 |
| 573 | Curtis Wilkerson | .05 |
| 574 | George Wright | .05 |
| 575 | Ned Yost | .05 |

**MILWAUKEE BREWERS**

| NO. | PLAYER | MINT |
|---|---|---|
| 576 | Mark Brouhard | .05 |
| 577 | Mike Caldwell | .05 |
| 578 | Bobby Clark | .05 |
| 579 | Jaime Cocanower (R) | .15 |
| 580 | Cecil Cooper | .10 |
| 581 | Rollie Fingers | .15 |
| 582 | Jim Gantner | .05 |
| 583 | Moose Haas | .05 |
| 584 | Dion James | .05 |
| 585 | Pete Ladd | .05 |
| 586 | Rick Manning | .05 |
| 587 | Bob McClure | .05 |
| 588 | Paul Molitor | .10 |
| 589 | Charlie Moore | .05 |
| 590 | Ben Oglivie | .05 |
| 591 | Chuck Porter | .05 |
| 592 | Randy Ready (R) | .20 |
| 593 | Ed Romero | .05 |
| 594 | Bill Schroeder | .05 |
| 595 | Ray Searage | .05 |
| 596 | Ted Simmons | .10 |
| 597 | Jim Sundberg | .05 |
| 598 | Don Sutton | .10 |
| 599 | Tom Tellmann | .05 |
| 600 | Rick Waits | .05 |

| NO. | PLAYER | MINT |
|---|---|---|
| 601 | Robin Yount | .25 |

**SAN FRANCISCO GIANTS**

| NO. | PLAYER | MINT |
|---|---|---|
| 602 | Dusty Baker | .05 |
| 603 | Bob Brenly | .05 |
| 604 | Jack Clark | .15 |
| 605 | Chili Davis | .10 |
| 607 | Dan Gladden (R) | .25 |
| 608 | Atlee Hammaker | .05 |
| 609 | Mike Krukow | .05 |
| 610 | Duane Kuiper | .05 |
| 611 | Bob Lacey | .05 |
| 612 | Bill Laskey | .05 |
| 613 | Gary Lavelle | .05 |
| 614 | Johnnie LeMaster | .05 |
| 615 | Jeff Leonard | .05 |
| 616 | Randy Lerch | .05 |
| 617 | Greg Minton | .05 |
| 618 | Steve Nicosia | .05 |
| 619 | Gene Richards | .05 |
| 620 | Jeff Robinson (R) | .15 |
| 621 | Scot Thompson | .05 |
| 622 | Manny Trillo | .05 |
| 623 | Brad Wellman | .05 |
| 624 | Frank Williams (R) | .15 |
| 625 | Joel Youngblood | .05 |
| 626 | Ripken-In-Action | .25 |
| 627 | Schmidt-In-Action | .25 |
| 628 | Giving The Signs: Sparky Anderson | .05 |
| 629 | AL Pitcher's Nightmare: Henderson & Winfield | .25 |
| 630 | NL Pitcher's Nightmare: Schmidt & Sandberg | .25 |
| 631 | NL All-Stars: Strawberry, Carter, Garvey, Smith | .25 |
| 632 | All-Star Game Winning Battery: Carter, Lea | .10 |
| 633 | NL Pennant Clinchers: Garvey, Gossage | .15 |
| 634 | NL Rookie Phenoms: Samuel, Gooden | 1.50 |
| 635 | Toronto's Big Guns: Willie Upshaw | .10 |
| 636 | Toronto's Big Guns: Lloyd Moseby | .10 |
| 637 | Al Holland | .05 |
| 638 | Lee Tunnell | .05 |
| 639 | 500th Homer: Reggie Jackson | .25 |
| 640 | 4,000th Hit: Pete Rose | .50 |
| 641 | Father and Son: Cal Ripken & Cal, Jr. | .25 |
| 642 | Cubs: Division Champs | .05 |
| 643 | Two Perfect Games and One No-Hitter: Witt, Palmer, Morris | .10 |
| 644 | Willie Lozado (R), Vic Mata (R) | .15 |
| 645 | Kelly Gruber (R), Randy O'Neal (R) | .25 |
| 646 | Jose Roman (R), Joel Skinner (R) | .20 |
| 647 | Steve Kiefer (R), Danny Tartabull (R) | 2.00 |
| 648 | Rob Deer (R), Alejandro Sanchez (R) | 1.00 |
| 649 | Bill Hatcher (R), Shawon Dunston (R) | 1.00 |
| 650 | Ron Robinson (R), Mike Bielecki (R) | .25 |
| 651 | Zane Smith (R), Paul Zuvella (R) | .25 |
| 652 | Joe Hesketh (R), Glenn Davis (R) | 5.00 |
| 653 | John Russell (R), Steve Jeltz (R) | .25 |
| 654 | Checklist No. 1 | .08 |
| 655 | Checklist No. 2 | .08 |
| 656 | Checklist No. 3 | .08 |
| 657 | Checklist No. 4 | .08 |
| 658 | Checklist No. 5 | .08 |
| 659 | Checklist No. 6 | .08 |
| 660 | Checklist No. 7 | .08 |

Card values shown here fluctuate considerably.

# 1985 Fleer Traded Update....Complete Set of 132 Cards—Value $20.00

This set updates the main 1985 card set with players who had changed teams during the season, and rookies. This set features Fleer's first card of Vince Coleman, Chris Brown and Oddibe McDowell. The set was packaged in a printed box and distributed exclusively through card hobby dealers.

| NO. PLAYER | MINT | NO. PLAYER | MINT | NO. PLAYER | MINT | NO. PLAYER | MINT |
|---|---|---|---|---|---|---|---|
| U1 Don Aase | .07 | U34 Jerry Davis | .15 | U67 Lee Lacy | .07 | U100 Rick Schu | .25 |
| U2 Bill Almon | .07 | U35 Brian Dayett | .15 | U68 Dave LaPoint | .07 | U101 Larry Sheets | .40 |
| U3 Dusty Baker | .10 | U36 Ken Dixon (RR) | .25 | U69 Gary Lavelle | .07 | U102 Ron Shephard | .15 |
| U4 Dale Berra | .07 | U37 Tommy Dunbar | .12 | U70 Vance Law | .07 | U103 Nelson Simmons | .25 |
| U5 Karl Best | .12 | U38 M. Duncan (RR) | .80 | U71 Manny Lee | .15 | U104 Don Slaught | .07 |
| U6 Tim Birtsas | .25 | U39 Bob Fallon | .12 | U72 Sixto Lezcano | .07 | U105 Roy Smalley | .07 |
| U7 Vida Blue | .07 | U40 Brian Fisher (RR) | .35 | U73 Tim Lollar | .07 | U106 Lonnie Smith | .07 |
| U8 Rich Bordi | .07 | U41 Mike Fitzgerald | .07 | U74 Urbano Lugo | .12 | U107 Nate Snell | .20 |
| U9 Daryl Boston | .20 | U42 Ray Fontenot | .07 | U75 Fred Lynn | .20 | U108 Lary Sorensen | .07 |
| U10 Hubie Brooks | .15 | U43 Greg Gagne | .15 | U76 Steve Lyons | .30 | U109 Chris Speier | .07 |
| U11 Chris Brown (RR) | 2.00 | U44 Oscar Gamble | .07 | U77 Mickey Mahler | .07 | U110 Mike Stenhouse | .07 |
| U12 T. Browning | 1.00 | U45 Jim Gott | .07 | U78 Ron Mathis | .15 | U111 Tim Stoddard | .07 |
| U13 Al Bumbry | .07 | U46 David Green | .07 | U79 Len Matuszek | .10 | U112 John Stuper | .07 |
| U14 Tim Burke | .25 | U47 Alfredo Griffin | .07 | U80 O. McDowell (RR) | 1.50 | U113 Jim Sundberg | .07 |
| U15 Ray Burris | .07 | U48 Ozzie Guillen (RR) | .75 | U81 R. McDowell (RR) | .90 | U114 Bruce Sutter | .25 |
| U16 Jeff Burroughs | .07 | U49 Toby Harrah | .07 | U82 Donnie Moore | .10 | U115 Don Sutton | .25 |
| U17 Ivan Calderon | .25 | U50 Ron Hassey | .07 | U83 Ron Musselman | .12 | U116 Bruce Tanner | .15 |
| U18 Jeff Calhoun | .15 | U51 Rickey Henderson | .75 | U84 Al Oliver | .15 | U117 Kent Tekulve | .07 |
| U19 Bill Campbell | .07 | U52 Steve Henderson | .07 | U85 Joe Orsulak | .25 | U118 Walt Terrell | .07 |
| U20 Don Carman | .25 | U53 George Hendrick | .07 | U86 Dan Pasqua | 1.50 | U119 Mickey Tettleton | .12 |
| U21 Gary Carter | .60 | U54 Teddy Higuera (RR) | 1.50 | U87 Chris Pittaro | .15 | U120 Rich Thompson | .10 |
| U22 Bobby Castillo | .07 | U55 Al Holland | .07 | U88 Rick Reuschel | .12 | U121 Louis Thornton | .10 |
| U23 Bill Caudill | .07 | U56 Burt Hooton | .07 | U89 Earnie Riles (RR) | .60 | U122 Alex Trevino | .07 |
| U24 Rick Cerone | .07 | U57 Jay Howell | .15 | U90 Jerry Royster | .07 | U123 John Tudor | .20 |
| U25 Jack Clark | .30 | U58 LaMarr Hoyt | .12 | U91 Dave Rozema | .07 | U124 Jose Uribe | .12 |
| U26 Pat Clements | .25 | U59 Tim Hulett | .15 | U92 Dave Rucker | .07 | U125 Dave Valle | .12 |
| U27 Stewart Cliburn | .20 | U60 Bob James | .07 | U93 Vern Ruhle | .07 | U126 Dave Von Ohlen | .07 |
| U28 V. Coleman (RR) | 3.00 | U61 Cliff Johnson | .07 | U94 Mark Salas | .40 | U127 Curt Wardle | .07 |
| U29 Dave Collins | .07 | U62 Howard Johnson | .07 | U95 Luis Salazar | .07 | U128 U.L. Washington | .07 |
| U30 Fritz Connally | .15 | U63 Ruppert Jones | .07 | U96 Joe Sambito | .07 | U129 Ed Whitson | .07 |
| U31 Henry Cotto | .07 | U64 Steve Kemp | .07 | U97 Billy Sample | .07 | U130 Herm Winningham | .20 |
| U32 Danny Darwin | .07 | U65 Bruce Kison | .07 | U98 Alex Sanchez | .07 | U131 Rich Yett | .12 |
| U33 Darren Daulton | .25 | U66 Mike LaCoss | .07 | U99 Calvin Schiraldi | .60 | U132 Update Checklist | .07 |

# 1986 Fleer....Complete Set of 660 Cards—Value $35.00

Features the rookie cards of Vince Coleman, Jose Canseco, Andres Galarraga and Cory Snyder. Eight different cards (C1 to C8) were printed on the bottom of gum pack display boxes or cello pack display boxes; each box contained four cards, either C1 to C4 or C5 to C8. These cards are not part of the set. *Future Hall of Famer* cards and *All-Star* cards were used as *inserts* inside gum packs and cello packs.

| NO. PLAYER | MINT | NO. PLAYER | MINT | NO. PLAYER | MINT | NO. PLAYER | MINT |
|---|---|---|---|---|---|---|---|
| **KANSAS CITY ROYALS** | | 8 Mark Gubicza | .05 | 16 Darryl Motley | .05 | 24 Frank White | .05 |
| 1 Steve Balboni | .10 | 9 Dane Iorg | .05 | 17 Jorge Orta | .05 | 25 Willie Wilson | .15 |
| 2 Joe Beckwith | .05 | 10 Danny Jackson | .05 | 18 Dan Quisenberry | .15 | **ST. LOUIS CARDINALS** | |
| 3 Buddy Biancalana | .05 | 11 Lynn Jones | .05 | 19 Bret Saberhagen | .25 | 26 Joaquin Andujar | .10 |
| 4 Bud Black | .05 | 12 Mike Jones | .05 | 20 Pat Sheridan | .05 | 27 Steve Braun | .05 |
| 5 George Brett | .45 | 13 Charlie Leibrandt | .05 | 21 Lonnie Smith | .05 | 28 Bill Campbell | .05 |
| 6 Onix Concepcion | .05 | 14 Hal McRae | .05 | 22 Jim Sundberg | .05 | 29 Cesar Cedeno | .05 |
| 7 Steve Farr | .05 | 15 Omar Moreno | .05 | 23 John Wathan | .05 | 30 Jack Clark | .15 |

Card values from this set fluctuate considerably.

| NO. | PLAYER | MINT |
|----|--------|------|
| 31 | Vince Coleman (R) | 1.50 |
| 32 | Danny Cox | .10 |
| 33 | Ken Dayley | .05 |
| 34 | Ivan DeJesus | .05 |
| 35 | Bob Forsch | .05 |
| 36 | Brian Harper | .05 |
| 37 | Tom Herr | .10 |
| 38 | Ricky Horton | .05 |
| 39 | Kurt Kepshire | .05 |
| 40 | Jeff Lahti | .05 |
| 41 | Tito Landrum | .05 |
| 42 | Willie McGee | .20 |
| 43 | Tom Nieto | .05 |
| 44 | Terry Pendleton | .05 |
| 45 | Darrell Porter | .05 |
| 46 | Ozzie Smith | .10 |
| 47 | John Tudor | .10 |
| 48 | Andy Van Slyke | .05 |
| 49 | Todd Worrell (R) | .75 |

**TORONTO BLUE JAYS**

| NO. | PLAYER | MINT |
|----|--------|------|
| 50 | Jim Acker | .05 |
| 51 | Doyle Alexander | .05 |
| 52 | Jesse Barfield | .10 |
| 53 | George Bell | .10 |
| 54 | Jeff Burroughs | .05 |
| 55 | Bill Caudill | .05 |
| 56 | Jim Clancy | .05 |
| 57 | Tony Fernandez | .10 |
| 58 | Tom Filer | .05 |
| 59 | Damaso Garcia | .10 |
| 60 | Tom Henke | .05 |
| 61 | Garth Iorg | .05 |
| 62 | Cliff Johnson | .05 |
| 63 | Jimmy Key | .05 |
| 64 | Dennis Lamp | .05 |
| 65 | Gary Lavelle | .05 |
| 66 | Buck Martinez | .05 |
| 67 | Lloyd Moseby | .10 |
| 68 | Rance Mulliniks | .05 |
| 69 | Al Oliver | .10 |
| 70 | Dave Stieb | .15 |
| 71 | Louis Thornton | .15 |
| 72 | Willie Upshaw | .10 |
| 73 | Ernie Whitt | .05 |

**NEW YORK METS**

| NO. | PLAYER | MINT |
|----|--------|------|
| 74 | Rick Aguilera (R) | .30 |
| 75 | Wally Backman | .05 |
| 76 | Gary Carter | .30 |
| 77 | Ron Darling | .30 |
| 78 | Len Dykstra (R) | 1.50 |
| 79 | Sid Fernandez | .05 |
| 80 | George Foster | .15 |
| 81 | Dwight Gooden | 2.00 |
| 82 | Tom Gorman | .05 |
| 83 | Danny Heep | .05 |
| 84 | Keith Hernandez | .25 |
| 85 | Howard Johnson | .05 |
| 86 | Ray Knight | .05 |
| 87 | Terry Leach | .05 |
| 88 | Ed Lynch | .05 |
| 89 | Roger McDowell (R) | .50 |
| 90 | Jesse Orosco | .05 |
| 91 | Tom Paciorek | .05 |
| 92 | Ronn Reynolds | .05 |
| 93 | Rafael Santana | .05 |
| 94 | Doug Sisk | .05 |
| 95 | Rusty Staub | .10 |
| 96 | Darryl Strawberry | .50 |
| 97 | Mookie Wilson | .05 |

**NEW YORK YANKEES**

| NO. | PLAYER | MINT |
|----|--------|------|
| 98 | Neil Allen | .05 |
| 99 | Don Baylor | .10 |
| 100 | Dale Berra | .05 |
| 101 | Rich Bordi | .05 |
| 102 | Marty Bystrom | .05 |
| 103 | Joe Cowley | .05 |
| 104 | Brian Fisher (R) | .40 |
| 105 | Ken Griffey | .15 |
| 106 | Ron Guidry | .15 |
| 107 | Ron Hassey | .05 |
| 108 | Rickey Henderson | .45 |
| 109 | Dan Mattingly | 2.50 |
| 110 | Bobby Meacham | .05 |
| 111 | John Montefusco | .05 |
| 112 | Phil Niekro | .15 |
| 113 | Mike Pagliarulo | .05 |

| NO. | PLAYER | MINT |
|----|--------|------|
| 114 | Dan Pasqua | .15 |
| 115 | Willie Randolph | .05 |
| 116 | Dave Righetti | .10 |
| 117 | Andre Robertson | .05 |
| 118 | Billy Sample | .05 |
| 119 | Bob Shirley | .05 |
| 120 | Ed Whitson | .05 |
| 121 | Dave Winfield | .30 |
| 122 | Butch Wynegar | .05 |

**LOS ANGELES DODGERS**

| NO. | PLAYER | MINT |
|----|--------|------|
| 123 | Dave Anderson | .05 |
| 124 | Bob Bailor | .05 |
| 125 | Greg Brock | .05 |
| 126 | Enos Cabell | .05 |
| 127 | Bobby Castillo | .05 |
| 128 | Carlos Diaz | .05 |
| 129 | Mariano Duncan (R) | .50 |
| 130 | Pedro Guerrero | .25 |
| 131 | Orel Hershiser | .30 |
| 132 | Rick Honeycutt | .05 |
| 133 | Ken Howell | .05 |
| 134 | Ken Landreaux | .05 |
| 135 | Bill Madlock | .10 |
| 136 | Candy Maldonado | .05 |
| 137 | Mike Marshall | .10 |
| 138 | Len Matuszek | .05 |
| 139 | Tom Niedenfuer | .05 |
| 140 | Alejandro Pena | .05 |
| 141 | Jerry Reuss | .05 |
| 142 | Bill Russell | .05 |
| 143 | Steve Sax | .10 |
| 144 | Mike Scioscia | .05 |
| 145 | Fernando Valenzuela | .30 |
| 146 | Bob Welch | .05 |
| 147 | Terry Whitfield | .05 |

**CALIFORNIA ANGELS**

| NO. | PLAYER | MINT |
|----|--------|------|
| 148 | Juan Beniquez | .05 |
| 149 | Bob Boone | .05 |
| 150 | John Candelaria | .05 |
| 151 | Rod Carew | .30 |
| 152 | Stewart Cliburn (R) | .25 |
| 153 | Doug DeCinces | .10 |
| 154 | Brian Downing | .05 |
| 155 | Ken Forsch | .05 |
| 156 | Craig Gerber (R) | .15 |
| 157 | Bobby Grich | .10 |
| 158 | George Hendrick | .05 |
| 159 | Al Holland | .05 |
| 160 | Reggie Jackson | .30 |
| 161 | Ruppert Jones | .05 |
| 162 | Urbano Lugo (R) | .15 |
| 163 | Kirk McCaskill (R) | .50 |
| 164 | Donnie Moore | .05 |
| 165 | Gary Pettis | .05 |
| 166 | Ron Romanick | .05 |
| 167 | Dick Schofield | .05 |
| 168 | Daryl Sconiers | .05 |
| 169 | Jim Slaton | .05 |
| 170 | Don Sutton | .10 |
| 171 | Mike Witt | .10 |

**CINCINNATI REDS**

| NO. | PLAYER | MINT |
|----|--------|------|
| 172 | Buddy Bell | .10 |
| 173 | Tom Browning | .15 |
| 174 | Dave Concepcion | .10 |
| 175 | Eric Davis | .60 |
| 176 | Bo Diaz | .05 |
| 177 | Nick Esasky | .05 |
| 178 | John Franco | .05 |
| 179 | Tom Hume | .05 |
| 180 | Wayne Krenchicki | .05 |
| 181 | Andy McGaffigan | .05 |
| 182 | Eddie Milner | .05 |
| 183 | Ron Oester | .05 |
| 184 | Dave Parker | .15 |
| 185 | Frank Pastore | .05 |
| 186 | Tony Perez | .10 |
| 187 | Ted Power | .05 |
| 188 | Joe Price | .05 |
| 189 | Gary Redus | .05 |
| 190 | Ron Robinson | .05 |
| 191 | Pete Rose | .60 |
| 192 | Mario Soto | .10 |
| 193 | John Stuper | .05 |
| 194 | Jay Tibbs | .05 |
| 195 | Dave Van Gorder | .05 |
| 196 | Max Venable | .05 |

**CHICAGO WHITE SOX**

| NO. | PLAYER | MINT |
|----|--------|------|
| 197 | Juan Agosto | .05 |
| 198 | Harold Baines | .15 |
| 199 | Floyd Bannister | .05 |
| 200 | Britt Burns | .05 |
| 201 | Julio Cruz | .05 |
| 202 | Joel Davis (R) | .25 |
| 203 | Richard Dotson | .05 |
| 204 | Carlton Fisk | .15 |
| 205 | Scott Fletcher | .05 |
| 206 | Ozzie Guillen (R) | .50 |
| 207 | Jerry Hairston | .05 |
| 208 | Tim Hulett | .05 |
| 209 | Bob James | .05 |
| 210 | Ron Kittle | .10 |
| 211 | Rudy Law | .05 |
| 212 | Bryan Little | .05 |
| 213 | Gene Nelson | .05 |
| 214 | Reid Nichols | .05 |
| 215 | Luis Salazar | .05 |
| 216 | Tom Seaver | .25 |
| 217 | Dan Spillner | .05 |
| 218 | Bruce Tanner (R) | .15 |
| 219 | Greg Walker | .10 |
| 220 | Dave Wehrmeister | .05 |

**DETROIT TIGERS**

| NO. | PLAYER | MINT |
|----|--------|------|
| 221 | Juan Berenguer | .05 |
| 222 | Dave Bergman | .05 |
| 223 | Tom Brookens | .05 |
| 224 | Darrell Evans | .10 |
| 225 | Barbaro Garbey | .05 |
| 226 | Kirk Gibson | .15 |
| 227 | John Grubb | .05 |
| 228 | Willie Hernandez | .15 |
| 229 | Larry Herndon | .05 |
| 230 | Chet Lemon | .05 |
| 231 | Aurelio Lopez | .05 |
| 232 | Jack Morris | .15 |
| 233 | Randy O'Neal | .05 |
| 234 | Lance Parrish | .15 |
| 235 | Dan Petry | .15 |
| 236 | Alex Sanchez | .05 |
| 237 | Bill Scherrer | .05 |
| 238 | Nelson Simmons (R) | .25 |
| 239 | Frank Tanana | .05 |
| 240 | Walt Terrell | .05 |
| 241 | Alan Trammell | .15 |
| 242 | Lou Whitaker | .15 |
| 243 | Milt Wilcox | .05 |

**MONTREAL EXPOS**

| NO. | PLAYER | MINT |
|----|--------|------|
| 244 | Hubie Brooks | .10 |
| 245 | Tim Burke (R) | .20 |
| 246 | Andre Dawson | .20 |
| 247 | Mike Fitzgerald | .05 |
| 248 | Terry Francona | .05 |
| 249 | Bill Gullickson | .05 |
| 250 | Joe Hesketh | .10 |
| 251 | Bill Laskey | .05 |
| 252 | Vance Law | .05 |
| 253 | Charlie Lea | .05 |
| 254 | Gary Lucas | .05 |
| 255 | David Palmer | .05 |
| 256 | Tim Raines | .20 |
| 257 | Jeff Reardon | .05 |
| 258 | Bert Roberge | .05 |
| 259 | Dan Schatzeder | .05 |
| 260 | Bryn Smith | .05 |
| 261 | Randy St. Claire | .05 |
| 262 | Scot Thompson | .05 |
| 263 | Tim Wallach | .10 |
| 264 | U.L. Washington | .05 |
| 265 | Mitch Webster (R) | .35 |
| 266 | Herm Winningham (R) | .15 |
| 267 | Floyd Youmans (R) | .75 |

**BALTIMORE ORIOLES**

| NO. | PLAYER | MINT |
|----|--------|------|
| 268 | Don Aase | .05 |
| 269 | Mike Boddicker | .10 |
| 270 | Rich Dauer | .05 |
| 271 | Storm Davis | .05 |
| 272 | Rick Dempsey | .05 |
| 273 | Ken Dixon | .05 |
| 274 | Jim Dwyer | .05 |
| 275 | Mike Flanagan | .05 |
| 276 | Wayne Gross | .05 |
| 277 | Lee Lacy | .05 |
| 278 | Fred Lynn | .15 |

| NO. | PLAYER | MINT |
|----|--------|------|
| 279 | Tippy Martinez | .05 |
| 280 | Dennis Martinez | .05 |
| 281 | Scott McGregor | .05 |
| 282 | Eddie Murray | .40 |
| 283 | Floyd Rayford | .05 |
| 284 | Cal Ripken, Jr. | .35 |
| 285 | Gary Roenicke | .05 |
| 286 | Larry Sheets | .05 |
| 287 | John Shelby | .05 |
| 288 | Nate Snell (R) | .15 |
| 289 | Sammy Stewart | .05 |
| 290 | Alan Wiggins | .05 |
| 291 | Mike Young | .20 |

**HOUSTON ASTROS**

| NO. | PLAYER | MINT |
|----|--------|------|
| 292 | Alan Ashby | .05 |
| 293 | Mark Bailey | .05 |
| 294 | Kevin Bass | .05 |
| 295 | Jeff Calhoun (R) | .15 |
| 296 | Jose Cruz | .10 |
| 297 | Glenn Davis | 1.00 |
| 298 | Bill Dawley | .05 |
| 299 | Frank DiPino | .05 |
| 300 | Bill Doran | .05 |
| 301 | Phil Garner | .05 |
| 302 | Jeff Heathcock (R) | .15 |
| 303 | Charlie Kerfeld (R) | .35 |
| 304 | Bob Knepper | .05 |
| 305 | Ron Mathis (R) | .15 |
| 306 | Jerry Mumphrey | .05 |
| 307 | Jim Pankovits | .05 |
| 308 | Terry Puhl | .05 |
| 309 | Craig Reynolds | .05 |
| 310 | Nolan Ryan | .25 |
| 311 | Mike Scott | .25 |
| 312 | Dave Smith | .05 |
| 313 | Dickie Thon | .05 |
| 314 | Denny Walling | .05 |

**SAN DIEGO PADRES**

| NO. | PLAYER | MINT |
|----|--------|------|
| 315 | Kurt Bevacqua | .05 |
| 316 | Al Bumbry | .05 |
| 317 | Jerry Davis | .05 |
| 318 | Luis DeLeon | .05 |
| 319 | Dave Dravecky | .05 |
| 320 | Tim Flannery | .05 |
| 321 | Steve Garvey | .35 |
| 322 | Goose Gossage | .15 |
| 323 | Tony Gwynn | .30 |
| 324 | Andy Hawkins | .05 |
| 325 | LaMarr Hoyt | .05 |
| 326 | Roy Lee Jackson | .05 |
| 327 | Terry Kennedy | .05 |
| 328 | Craig Lefferts | .05 |
| 329 | Carmelo Martinez | .05 |
| 330 | Lance McCullers (R) | .40 |
| 331 | Kevin McReynolds | .10 |
| 332 | Graig Nettles | .10 |
| 333 | Jerry Royster | .05 |
| 334 | Eric Show | .05 |
| 335 | Tim Stoddard | .05 |
| 336 | Garry Templeton | .08 |
| 337 | Mark Thurmond | .05 |
| 338 | Ed Wojna (R) | .15 |

**BOSTON RED SOX**

| NO. | PLAYER | MINT |
|----|--------|------|
| 339 | Tony Armas | .10 |
| 340 | Marty Barrett | .05 |
| 341 | Wade Boggs | 1.50 |
| 342 | Dennis Boyd | .05 |
| 343 | Bill Buckner | .05 |
| 344 | Mark Clear | .05 |
| 345 | Roger Clemens | 1.50 |
| 346 | Steve Crawford | .05 |
| 347 | Mike Easler | .05 |
| 348 | Dwight Evans | .12 |
| 349 | Rich Gedman | .08 |
| 350 | Jackie Gutierrez | .05 |
| 351 | Glenn Hoffman | .05 |
| 352 | Bruce Hurst | .05 |
| 353 | Bruce Kison | .05 |
| 354 | Tim Lollar | .05 |
| 355 | Steve Lyons | .05 |
| 356 | Al Nipper | .05 |
| 357 | Bob Ojeda | .05 |
| 358 | Jim Rice | .30 |
| 359 | Bob Stanley | .05 |
| 360 | Mike Trujillo (R) | .15 |

Card values from this set fluctuate considerably.

| NO. | PLAYER | MINT |
|---|---|---|
| | **CHICAGO CUBS** | |
| 361 | Thad Bosley | .05 |
| 362 | Warren Brusstar | .05 |
| 363 | Ron Cey | .10 |
| 364 | Jody Davis | .07 |
| 365 | Bob Dernier | .05 |
| 366 | Shawon Dunston | .05 |
| 367 | Leon Durham | .15 |
| 368 | Dennis Eckersley | .05 |
| 369 | Ray Fontenot | .05 |
| 370 | George Frazier | .05 |
| 371 | Bill Hatcher | .05 |
| 372 | Dave Lopes | .05 |
| 373 | Gary Matthews | .05 |
| 374 | Ron Meredith (R) | .15 |
| 375 | Keith Moreland | .05 |
| 376 | Reggie Patterson | .05 |
| 377 | Dick Ruthven | .05 |
| 378 | Ryne Sandberg | .30 |
| 379 | Scott Sanderson | .05 |
| 380 | Lee Smith | .05 |
| 381 | Lary Sorensen | .05 |
| 382 | Chris Speier | .05 |
| 383 | Rick Sutcliffe | .15 |
| 384 | Steve Trout | .05 |
| 385 | Gary Woods | .05 |
| | **MINNESOTA TWINS** | |
| 386 | Bert Blyleven | .10 |
| 387 | Tom Brunansky | .10 |
| 388 | Randy Bush | .05 |
| 389 | John Butcher | .05 |
| 390 | Ron Davis | .05 |
| 391 | Dave Engle | .05 |
| 392 | Frank Eufemia | .15 |
| 393 | Pete Filson | .05 |
| 394 | Gary Gaetti | .05 |
| 395 | Greg Gagne | .05 |
| 396 | Mickey Hatcher | .05 |
| 397 | Kent Hrbek | .20 |
| 398 | Tim Laudner | .05 |
| 399 | Rick Lysander | .05 |
| 400 | Dave Meier | .05 |
| 401 | Kirby Puckett | .25 |
| 402 | Mark Salas | .05 |
| 403 | Ken Schrom | .05 |
| 404 | Roy Smalley | .05 |
| 405 | Mike Smithson | .05 |
| 406 | Mike Stenhouse | .05 |
| 407 | Tim Teufel | .05 |
| 408 | Frank Viola | .05 |
| 409 | Ron Washington | .05 |
| | **OAKLAND A'S** | |
| 410 | Keith Atherton | .05 |
| 411 | Dusty Baker | .05 |
| 412 | Tim Birtsas (R) | .20 |
| 413 | Bruce Bochte | .05 |
| 414 | Chris Codiroli | .05 |
| 415 | Dave Collins | .05 |
| 416 | Mike Davis | .05 |
| 417 | Alfredo Griffin | .05 |
| 418 | Mike Heath | .05 |
| 419 | Steve Henderson | .05 |
| 420 | Donnie Hill | .05 |
| 421 | Jay Howell | .05 |
| 422 | Tommy John | .10 |
| 423 | Dave Kingman | .10 |
| 424 | Bill Krueger | .05 |
| 425 | Rick Langford | .05 |
| 426 | Carney Lansford | .10 |
| 427 | Steve McCatty | .05 |
| 428 | Dwayne Murphy | .05 |
| 429 | Steve Ontiveros (R) | .20 |
| 430 | Tony Phillips | .05 |
| 431 | Jose Rijo | .05 |
| 432 | Mickey Tettleton (R) | .15 |
| | **PHILADELPHIA PHILLIES** | |
| 433 | Luis Aguayo | .05 |
| 434 | Larry Andersen | .05 |
| 435 | Steve Carlton | .30 |
| 436 | Don Carman (R) | .15 |
| 437 | Tim Corcoran | .05 |
| 438 | Darren Daulton (R) | .25 |
| 439 | John Denny | .08 |
| 440 | Tom Foley | .05 |
| 441 | Greg Gross | .05 |
| 442 | Kevin Gross | .05 |
| 443 | Von Hayes | .15 |

| NO. | PLAYER | MINT |
|---|---|---|
| 444 | Charles Hudson | .05 |
| 445 | Garry Maddox | .05 |
| 446 | Shane Rawley | .05 |
| 447 | Dave Rucker | .05 |
| 448 | John Russell | .05 |
| 449 | Juan Samuel | .10 |
| 450 | Mike Schmidt | .30 |
| 451 | Rick Schu | .05 |
| 452 | Dave Shipanoff (R) | .15 |
| 453 | Dave Stewart | .05 |
| 454 | Jeff Stone | .05 |
| 455 | Kent Tekulve | .05 |
| 456 | Ozzie Virgil | .05 |
| 457 | Glenn Wilson | .10 |
| | **SEATTLE MARINERS** | |
| 458 | Jim Beattie | .05 |
| 459 | Karl Best | .10 |
| 460 | Barry Bonnell | .05 |
| 461 | Phil Bradley | .20 |
| 462 | Ivan Calderon (R) | .25 |
| 463 | Al Cowens | .05 |
| 464 | Alvin Davis | .20 |
| 465 | Dave Henderson | .05 |
| 466 | Bob Kearney | .05 |
| 467 | Mark Langston | .05 |
| 468 | Bob Long | .05 |
| 469 | Mike Moore | .05 |
| 470 | Edwin Nunez | .05 |
| 471 | Spike Owen | .05 |
| 472 | Jack Perconte | .05 |
| 473 | Jim Presley | .25 |
| 474 | Donnie Scott | .05 |
| 475 | Bill Swift | .05 |
| 476 | Danny Tartabull | .20 |
| 477 | Gorman Thomas | .10 |
| 478 | Roy Thomas | .05 |
| 479 | Ed VandeBerg | .05 |
| 480 | Frank Wills (R) | .15 |
| 481 | Matt Young | .05 |
| | **MILWAUKEE BREWERS** | |
| 482 | Ray Burris | .05 |
| 483 | Jaime Cocanower | .05 |
| 484 | Cecil Cooper | .15 |
| 485 | Danny Darwin | .05 |
| 486 | Rollie Fingers | .15 |
| 487 | Jim Gantner | .05 |
| 488 | Bob Gibson | .05 |
| 489 | Moose Haas | .05 |
| 490 | Teddy Higuera (R) | .65 |
| 491 | Paul Householder | .05 |
| 492 | Pete Ladd | .05 |
| 493 | Rick Manning | .05 |
| 494 | Bob McClure | .05 |
| 495 | Paul Molitor | .10 |
| 496 | Charlie Moore | .05 |
| 497 | Ben Oglivie | .05 |
| 498 | Randy Ready | .05 |
| 499 | Earnie Riles (R) | .40 |
| 500 | Ed Romero | .05 |
| 501 | Bill Schroeder | .05 |
| 502 | Ray Searage | .05 |
| 503 | Ted Simmons | .10 |
| 504 | Pete Vuckovich | .05 |
| 505 | Rick Waits | .05 |
| 506 | Robin Yount | .25 |
| | **ATLANTA BRAVES** | |
| 507 | Len Barker | .05 |
| 508 | Steve Bedrosian | .05 |
| 509 | Bruce Benedict | .05 |
| 510 | Rick Camp | .05 |
| 511 | Rick Cerone | .05 |
| 512 | Chris Chambliss | .05 |
| 513 | Jeff Dedmon | .05 |
| 514 | Terry Forster | .05 |
| 515 | Gene Garber | .05 |
| 516 | Terry Harper | .05 |
| 517 | Bob Horner | .15 |
| 518 | Glenn Hubbard | .05 |
| 519 | Joe Johnson (R) | .20 |
| 520 | Brad Komminsk | .05 |
| 521 | Rick Mahler | .05 |
| 522 | Dale Murphy | .50 |
| 523 | Ken Oberkfell | .05 |
| 524 | Pascual Perez | .05 |
| 525 | Gerald Perry | .05 |
| 526 | Rafael Ramirez | .05 |

| NO. | PLAYER | MINT |
|---|---|---|
| 527 | Steve Shields (R) | .15 |
| 528 | Zane Smith | .05 |
| 529 | Bruce Sutter | .15 |
| 530 | Milt Thompson (R) | .25 |
| 531 | Claudell Washington | .05 |
| 532 | Paul Zuvella | .05 |
| | **S.F. GIANTS** | |
| 533 | Vida Blue | .05 |
| 534 | Bob Brenly | .05 |
| 535 | Chris Brown (R) | 1.00 |
| 536 | Chili Davis | .10 |
| 537 | Mark Davis | .05 |
| 538 | Rob Deer | .05 |
| 539 | Dan Driessen | .05 |
| 540 | Scott Garrelts | .05 |
| 541 | Dan Gladden | .05 |
| 542 | Jim Gott | .05 |
| 543 | David Green | .05 |
| 544 | Atlee Hammaker | .05 |
| 545 | Mike Jeffcoat | .05 |
| 546 | Mike Krukow | .05 |
| 547 | Dave LaPoint | .05 |
| 548 | Jeff Leonard | .05 |
| 549 | Greg Minton | .05 |
| 550 | Alex Trevino | .05 |
| 551 | Manny Trillo | .05 |
| 552 | Jose Uribe (R) | .15 |
| 553 | Brad Wellman | .05 |
| 554 | Frank Williams | .05 |
| 555 | Joel Youngblood | .05 |
| | **TEXAS RANGERS** | |
| 556 | Alan Bannister | .05 |
| 557 | Glenn Brummer | .05 |
| 558 | Steve Buechele (R) | .25 |
| 559 | Jose Guzman (R) | .15 |
| 560 | Toby Harrah | .05 |
| 561 | Greg Harris | .05 |
| 562 | Dwayne Henry (R) | .15 |
| 563 | Burt Hooton | .05 |
| 564 | Charlie Hough | .05 |
| 565 | Mike Mason | .05 |
| 566 | Oddibe McDowell | .30 |
| 567 | Dickie Noles | .05 |
| 568 | Pete O'Brien | .05 |
| 569 | Larry Parrish | .05 |
| 570 | Dave Rozema | .05 |
| 571 | Dave Schmidt | .05 |
| 572 | Don Slaught | .05 |
| 573 | Wayne Tolleson | .05 |
| 574 | Duane Walker | .05 |
| 575 | Gary Ward | .05 |
| 576 | Chris Welsh | .05 |
| 577 | Curtis Wilkerson | .05 |
| 578 | George Wright | .05 |
| | **CLEVELAND INDIANS** | |
| 579 | Chris Bando | .05 |
| 580 | Tony Bernazard | .05 |
| 581 | Brett Butler | .10 |
| 582 | Ernie Camacho | .05 |
| 583 | Joe Carter | .05 |
| 584 | Carmello Castillo | .05 |
| 585 | Jamie Easterly | .05 |
| 586 | Julio Franco | .10 |
| 587 | Mel Hall | .05 |
| 588 | Mike Hargrove | .05 |
| 589 | Neal Heaton | .05 |
| 590 | Brook Jacoby | .10 |
| 591 | Otis Nixon (R) | .20 |
| 592 | Jerry Reed (R) | .15 |
| 593 | Vern Ruhle | .05 |
| 594 | Pat Tabler | .05 |
| 595 | Rich Thompson (R) | .15 |
| 596 | Andre Thornton | .05 |
| 597 | Dave Von Ohlen | .05 |
| 598 | George Vuckovich | .05 |
| 599 | Tom Waddell | .05 |
| 600 | Curt Wardle (R) | .15 |
| 601 | Jerry Willard | .05 |
| | **PITTSBURGH PIRATES** | |
| 602 | Bill Almon | .05 |
| 603 | Mike Bielecki | .05 |
| 604 | Sid Bream | .05 |
| 605 | Mike Brown | .05 |
| 606 | Pat Clements (R) | .25 |
| 607 | Jose DeLeon | .05 |
| 608 | Denny Gonzalez | .05 |

| NO. | PLAYER | MINT |
|---|---|---|
| 609 | Cecilio Guante | .05 |
| 610 | Steve Kemp | .05 |
| 611 | Sam Khalifa (R) | .15 |
| 612 | Lee Mazzilli | .05 |
| 613 | Larry McWilliams | .05 |
| 614 | Jim Morrison | .05 |
| 615 | Joe Orsulak (R) | .25 |
| 616 | Tony Pena | .10 |
| 617 | Johnny Ray | .10 |
| 618 | Rick Reuschel | .05 |
| 619 | R.J. Reynolds | .05 |
| 620 | Rick Rhoden | .05 |
| 621 | Don Robinson | .05 |
| 622 | Jason Thompson | .05 |
| 623 | Lee Tunnell | .05 |
| 624 | Jim Winn | .05 |
| 625 | Marvell Wynne | .05 |
| 626 | Gooden in Action | .75 |
| 627 | Mattingly in Action | 1.00 |
| 628 | Pete Rose—4,192 | .50 |
| 629 | 3,000 Career Hits: Rod Carew | .25 |
| 630 | 300 Career Wins: Tom Seaver, Phil Niekro | .20 |
| 631 | Ouch: Don Baylor | .15 |
| 632 | Instant Offense: Raines and Strawberry | .30 |
| 633 | Shortstops Supreme: Trammell & Ripken | .25 |
| 634 | Boggs and "Hero": Wade Boggs, George Brett | .50 |
| 635 | Braves Dynamic Duo: Horner and Murphy | .30 |
| 636 | Cardinal Ignitors: Coleman & McGee | .50 |
| 637 | Terror on Basepaths: Vince Coleman | .40 |
| 638 | Charlie Hustle and Dr. K: Rose and Gooden | 1.00 |
| 639 | 1984 and 1985 AL Batting Champs: Mattingly and Boggs | 1.50 |
| 640 | NL West Sluggers: Murphy, Garvey, Parker | .30 |
| 641 | Staff Aces: Valenzuela & Gooden | .60 |
| 642 | Blue Jay Stoppers: Key and Stieb | .10 |
| 643 | AL All-Star Backstops Fisk & Gedman | .10 |
| 644 | Benito Santiago (R) and Gene Walter (R) | .20 |
| 645 | Mike Woodard (R) and Colin Ward (R) | .15 |
| 646 | Kal Daniels (R) and Paul O'Neill (R) | .30 |
| 647 | Fred Toliver (R) and Andres Galarraga (R) | .75 |
| 648 | Bob Kipper (R) and Curt Ford (R) | .20 |
| 649 | Eric Plunk (R) and Jose Canseco (R) | 5.00 |
| 650 | Gus Polidor (R) and Mark McLemore (R) | .20 |
| 651 | Rob Woodward (R) and Mickey Brantley (R) | .20 |
| 652 | Billy Joe Robidoux (R) and Mark Funderburk (R) | .40 |
| 653 | Cecil Fielder (R) and Cory Snyder (R) | 2.50 |
| 654 | Checklist No. 1 | .08 |
| 655 | Checklist No. 2 | .08 |
| 656 | Checklist No. 3 | .08 |
| 657 | Checklist No. 4 | .08 |
| 658 | Checklist No. 5 | .08 |
| 659 | Checklist No. 6 | .08 |
| 660 | Checklist No. 7 | .08 |
| | **Gum Box Display Cards** | |
| C1 | K.C. Royals Logo | .12 |
| C2 | George Brett | .75 |
| C3 | Ozzie Guillen | .30 |
| C4 | Dale Murphy | .75 |
| C5 | St. L. Cardinals Logo | .12 |
| C6 | Tom Browning | .25 |
| C7 | Gary Carter | .30 |
| C8 | Carlton Fisk | .20 |

Card values shown here fluctuate considerably.

# 1986 Fleer Traded Update. . . Complete Set of 132 Cards—Value $20.00

This set updates the main 1986 card set with players who had changed teams during the season, and rookies. This set features Fleer's first card of Wally Joyner, Ruben Sierra, and Will Clark. The set was packaged in a printed box and distributed exclusively through card hobby dealers.

| NO. | PLAYER | MINT |
|---|---|---|
| U1 | Mike Aldrete | .15 |
| U2 | Andy Allanson | .20 |
| U3 | Nell Allen | .07 |
| U4 | Joaquin Andujar | .07 |
| U5 | Paul Assenmacher | .25 |
| U6 | Scott Bailes | .20 |
| U7 | Jay Baller | .15 |
| U8 | Scott Bankhead | .15 |
| U9 | Bill Bathe | .15 |
| U10 | Don Baylor | .12 |
| U11 | Billy Beane | .15 |
| U12 | Steve Bedrosian | .07 |
| U13 | Juan Beniquez | .10 |
| U14 | Barry Bonds (RR) | .75 |
| U15 | Bobby Bonilla | .20 |
| U16 | Rich Bordi | .07 |
| U17 | Bill Campbell | .07 |
| U18 | Tom Candiotti | .10 |
| U19 | John Cangelosi | .25 |
| U20 | Jose Canseco (RR) | 3.00 |
| U21 | Chuck Cary | .07 |
| U22 | Juan Castillo | .15 |
| U23 | Rick Cerone | .07 |
| U24 | John Cerutti | .15 |
| U25 | Will Clark (RR) | 1.00 |
| U26 | Mark Clear | .07 |
| U27 | Darnell Coles | .15 |
| U28 | Dave Collins | .07 |
| U29 | Tim Conroy | .07 |
| U30 | Ed Correa | .25 |
| U31 | Joe Cowley | .07 |
| U32 | Bill Dawley | .07 |
| U33 | Rob Deer | .25 |
| U34 | John Denny | .07 |
| U35 | Jim DeShaies | .40 |
| U36 | Doug Drabek | .15 |
| U37 | Mike Easler | .07 |
| U38 | Mark Eichhorn | .35 |
| U39 | Dave Engle | .07 |
| U40 | Mike Fischlin | .07 |
| U41 | Scott Fletcher | .07 |
| U42 | Terry Forster | .07 |
| U43 | Terry Francona | .07 |
| U44 | Andres Galarraga | .25 |
| U45 | Lee Guetterman | .15 |
| U46 | Bill Gullickson | .07 |
| U47 | Jackie Gutierrez | .07 |
| U48 | Moose Haas | .07 |
| U49 | Bily Hatcher | .12 |
| U50 | Mike Heath | .10 |
| U51 | Guy Hoffman | .07 |
| U52 | Tom Hume | .07 |
| U53 | Pete Incaviglia | 2.25 |
| U54 | Dane Iorg | .07 |
| U55 | Chris James | .25 |
| U56 | Stan Javier | .15 |
| U57 | Tommy John | .07 |
| U58 | Tracy Jones | .20 |
| U59 | Wally Joyner (RR) | 3.00 |
| U60 | Wayne Krenchicki | .07 |
| U61 | John Kruk | .25 |
| U62 | Mike LaCoss | .07 |
| U63 | Pete Ladd | .07 |
| U64 | Dave LaPoint | .07 |
| U65 | Mike LaValliere | .07 |
| U66 | Rudy Law | .07 |
| U67 | Dennis Leonard | .07 |
| U68 | Steve Lombardozzi | .07 |
| U69 | Aurelio Lopez | .07 |
| U70 | Miceky Mahler | .07 |
| U71 | Candy Maldonado | .07 |
| U72 | Roger Mason | .15 |
| U73 | Greg Mathews | .20 |
| U74 | Andy McGaffigan | .10 |
| U75 | Joel McKeon | .15 |
| U76 | Kevin Mitchell (RR) | .75 |
| U77 | Bill Mooneyham | .12 |
| U78 | Omar Moreno | .07 |
| U79 | Jerry Mumphrey | .07 |
| U80 | Al Newman | .12 |
| U81 | Phil Niekro | .25 |
| U82 | Randy Niemann | .07 |
| U83 | Juan Nieves | .25 |
| U84 | Bob Ojeda | .25 |
| U85 | Rick Ownbey | .07 |
| U86 | Tom Paciorek | .07 |
| U87 | David Palmer | .07 |
| U88 | Jeff Parrett | .15 |
| U89 | Pat Perry | .10 |
| U90 | Dan Plesac | .15 |
| U91 | Darrell Porter | .07 |
| U92 | Luis Quinones | .15 |
| U93 | Rey Quinonez | .15 |
| U94 | Gary Redus | .12 |
| U95 | Jeff Reed | .12 |
| U96 | Bip Roberts | .25 |
| U97 | Billy Joe Robidoux | .25 |
| U98 | Gary Roenicke | .07 |
| U99 | Ron Roenicke | .07 |
| U100 | Angel Salazar | .07 |
| U101 | Joe Sambito | .07 |
| U102 | Billy Sample | .07 |
| U103 | Dave Schmidt | .07 |
| U104 | Ken Schrom | .07 |
| U105 | Ruben Sierra | 1.50 |
| U106 | Ted Simmons | .10 |
| U107 | Sammy Stewart | .07 |
| U108 | Kurt Stillwell | .15 |
| U109 | Dale Sveum | .07 |
| U110 | Tim Teufel | .07 |
| U111 | Bob Tewksbury | .30 |
| U112 | Andres Thomas | .20 |
| U113 | Jason Thompson | .12 |
| U114 | Milt Thompson | .07 |
| U115 | Rob Thompson | .25 |
| U116 | Jay Tibbs | .07 |
| U117 | Fred Toliver | .07 |
| U118 | Wayne Tolleson | .07 |
| U119 | Alex Trevino | .07 |
| U120 | Manny Trillo | .07 |
| U121 | Ed Vande Berg | .07 |
| U122 | Ozzie Virgil | .07 |
| U123 | Tony Walker | .20 |
| U124 | Gene Walter | .15 |
| U125 | Duane Ward | .20 |
| U126 | Jerry Willard | .07 |
| U127 | Mitch Williams | .20 |
| U128 | Reggie Williams | .25 |
| U129 | Bobby Witt | .50 |
| U130 | Marvell Wynne | .07 |
| U131 | Steve Yeager | .10 |
| U132 | Checklist | .07 |

# 1987 Fleer....Complete Set of 660 Cards—Value $40.00

Features the rookie cards of Bo Jackson, Wally Joyner, Ruben Sierra and Pete Incaviglia. The back of each card features a *scouting report*. Sixteen different cards (C1 to C16) were printed on the bottom of gum boxes. These cards are not part of the set.

| NO. | PLAYER | MINT |
|---|---|---|
| **NEW YORK METS** | | |
| 1 | Rick Aguilera | .15 |
| 2 | R. Anderson (R) | .15 |
| 3 | Wally Backman | .07 |
| 4 | Gary Carter | .25 |
| 5 | Ron Darling | .20 |
| 6 | Len Dykstra | .25 |
| 7 | Kevin Elster (R) | .20 |
| 8 | Sid Fernandez | .20 |
| 9 | Dwight Gooden | .75 |
| 10 | Ed Hearn (R) | .15 |
| 11 | Danny Heep | .05 |
| 12 | Keith Hernandez | .25 |
| 13 | Howard Johnson | .07 |
| 14 | Ray Knight | .07 |
| 15 | Lee Mazzilli | .07 |
| 16 | Roger McDowell | .15 |
| 17 | Kevin Mitchell (R) | .60 |
| 18 | Randy Niemann | .05 |
| 19 | Bob Ojeda | .15 |
| 20 | Jesse Orosco | .07 |
| 21 | Rafael Santana | .07 |
| 22 | Doug Sisk | .07 |
| 23 | Darryl Strawberry | .35 |
| 24 | Tim Teufel | .07 |
| 25 | Mookie Wilson | .07 |
| **BOSTON RED SOX** | | |
| 26 | Tony Armas | .07 |
| 27 | Marty Barrett | .07 |
| 28 | Don Baylor | .12 |
| 29 | Wade Boggs | 1.50 |
| 30 | Oil Can Boyd | .12 |
| 31 | Bill Buckner | .08 |
| 32 | Roger Clemens | 1.25 |
| 33 | Steve Crawford | .07 |
| 34 | Dwight Evans | .10 |
| 35 | Rich Gedman | .07 |
| 36 | Dave Henderson | .07 |
| 37 | Bruce Hurst | .07 |
| 38 | Tim Lollar | .07 |

Card values from this set fluctuate considerably.

| NO. | PLAYER | MINT |
|---|---|---|
| 39 | Al Nipper | .07 |
| 40 | Spike Owen | .07 |
| 41 | Jim Rice | .30 |
| 42 | Ed Romero | .07 |
| 43 | Joe Sambito | .07 |
| 44 | Calvin Schiraldi | .15 |
| 45 | Tom Seaver | .30 |
| 46 | Jeff Sellers (R) | .15 |
| 47 | Bob Stanley | .07 |
| 48 | Sammy Stewart | .07 |
| **HOUSTON ASTROS** | | |
| 49 | Larry Andersen | .05 |
| 50 | Alan Ashby | .05 |
| 51 | Kevin Bass | .05 |
| 52 | Jeff Calhoun | .05 |
| 53 | Jose Cruz | .05 |
| 54 | Danny Darwin | .05 |
| 55 | Glenn Davis | .60 |
| 56 | Jim Deshaies (R) | .35 |
| 57 | Bill Doran | .05 |
| 58 | Phil Garner | .05 |
| 59 | Billy Hatcher | .05 |
| 60 | Charlie Kerfeld | .12 |
| 61 | Bob Knepper | .08 |
| 62 | Dave Lopes | .08 |
| 63 | Aurelio Lopez | .05 |
| 64 | Jim Pankovits | .05 |
| 65 | Terry Puhl | .08 |
| 66 | Craig Reynolds | .08 |
| 67 | Nolan Ryan | .30 |
| 68 | Mike Scott | .20 |
| 69 | Dave Smith | .05 |
| 70 | Dickie Thon | .05 |
| 71 | Tony Walker (R) | .15 |
| 72 | Denny Walling | .05 |
| **CALIFORNIA ANGELS** | | |
| 73 | Bob Boone | .05 |
| 74 | Rick Burleson | .05 |
| 75 | John Candelaria | .08 |
| 76 | Doug Corbett | .05 |
| 77 | Doug DeCinces | .08 |
| 78 | Brian Downing | .05 |
| 79 | Chuck Finley (R) | .15 |
| 80 | Terry Forster | .05 |
| 81 | Bobby Grich | .05 |
| 82 | George Hendrick | .05 |
| 83 | Jack Howell | .05 |
| 84 | Reggie Jackson | .35 |
| 85 | Ruppert Jones | .05 |
| 86 | Wally Joyner (R) | 2.50 |
| 87 | Gary Lucas | .05 |
| 88 | Kirk McCaskill | .12 |
| 89 | Donnie Moore | .05 |
| 90 | Gary Pettis | .05 |
| 91 | Vern Ruhle | .05 |
| 92 | Dick Schofield | .05 |
| 93 | Don Sutton | .12 |
| 94 | Rob Wilfong | .05 |
| 95 | Mike Witt | .12 |
| **NEW YORK YANKEES** | | |
| 96 | Doug Drabek (R) | .40 |
| 97 | Mike Easler | .07 |
| 98 | Mike Fischlin | .07 |
| 99 | Brian Fisher | .07 |
| 100 | Ron Guidry | .15 |
| 101 | Rickey Henderson | .35 |
| 102 | Tommy John | .10 |
| 103 | Ron Kittle | .10 |
| 104 | Don Mattingly | 2.00 |
| 105 | Bobby Meacham | .07 |
| 106 | Joe Niekro | .07 |
| 107 | Mike Pagliarulo | .25 |
| 108 | Dan Pasqua | .20 |
| 109 | Willie Randolph | .07 |
| 110 | Dennis Rasmussen | .07 |
| 111 | Dave Righetti | .15 |
| 112 | Gary Roenicke | .07 |
| 113 | Rod Scurry | .07 |
| 114 | Bob Shirley | .07 |
| 115 | Joel Skinner | .07 |
| 116 | Tim Stoddard | .07 |
| 117 | Bob Tewksbury (R) | .25 |
| 118 | Wayne Tolleson | .07 |
| 119 | C. Washington | .07 |
| 120 | Dave Winfield | .30 |
| **TEXAS RANGERS** | | |
| 121 | Steve Buechele | .05 |

| NO. | PLAYER | MINT |
|---|---|---|
| 122 | Ed Correa (R) | .40 |
| 123 | Scott Fletcher | .05 |
| 124 | Joe Guzman | .15 |
| 125 | Toby Harrah | .05 |
| 126 | Greg Harris | .05 |
| 127 | Charlie Hough | .05 |
| 128 | Pete Incaviglia (R) | 1.25 |
| 129 | Mike Mason | .05 |
| 130 | Oddibe McDowell | .25 |
| 131 | Dale Mohorcic (R) | .15 |
| 132 | Pete O'Brien | .10 |
| 133 | Tom Paciorek | .05 |
| 134 | Larry Parrish | .05 |
| 135 | Geno Petralli | .05 |
| 136 | Darrell Porter | .05 |
| 137 | Jeff Russell | .05 |
| 138 | Ruben Sierra (R) | 1.25 |
| 139 | Don Slaught | .05 |
| 140 | Gary Ward | .05 |
| 141 | Curtis Wilkerson | .05 |
| 142 | Mitch Williams (R) | .25 |
| 143 | Bobby Witt (R) | .50 |
| **DETROIT TIGERS** | | |
| 144 | Dave Bergman | .05 |
| 145 | Tom Brookens | .05 |
| 146 | Bill Campbell | .05 |
| 147 | Chuck Cary (R) | .20 |
| 148 | Darnell Coles | .05 |
| 149 | Dave Collins | .05 |
| 150 | Darrell Evans | .05 |
| 151 | Kirk Gibson | .20 |
| 152 | John Grubb | .05 |
| 153 | Willie Hernandez | .05 |
| 154 | Larry Herndon | .05 |
| 155 | Eric King (R) | .30 |
| 156 | Chet Lemon | .07 |
| 157 | Dwight Lowry (R) | .20 |
| 158 | Jack Morris | .15 |
| 159 | Randy O'Neal | .05 |
| 160 | Lance Parrish | .20 |
| 161 | Dan Petry | .05 |
| 162 | Pat Sheridan | .05 |
| 163 | Jim Slaton | .05 |
| 164 | Frank Tanana | .05 |
| 165 | Walt Terrell | .05 |
| 166 | Mark Thurmond | .05 |
| 167 | Alan Trammell | .10 |
| 168 | Lou Whitaker | .12 |
| **PHILADELPHIA PHILLIES** | | |
| 169 | Luis Aguayo | .05 |
| 170 | Steve Bedrosian | .05 |
| 171 | Don Carman | .05 |
| 172 | Darren Daulton | .05 |
| 173 | Greg Gross | .05 |
| 175 | Von Hayes | .12 |
| 176 | Charles Hudson | .05 |
| 177 | Tom Hume | .05 |
| 178 | Steve Jeltz | .05 |
| 179 | Mike Maddux (R) | .15 |
| 180 | Shane Rawley | .05 |
| 181 | Gary Redus | .05 |
| 182 | Ron Roenicke | .05 |
| 183 | Bruce Ruffin (R) | .40 |
| 184 | John Russell | .05 |
| 185 | Juan Samuel | .10 |
| 186 | Dan Schatzeder | .05 |
| 187 | Mike Schmidt | .30 |
| 188 | Rick Schu | .05 |
| 189 | Jeff Stone | .05 |
| 190 | Kent Tekulve | .05 |
| 191 | Milt Thompson | .05 |
| 192 | Glenn Wilson | .05 |
| **CINCINNATI REDS** | | |
| 193 | Buddy Bell | .05 |
| 194 | Tom Browning | .07 |
| 195 | Sal Butera | .05 |
| 196 | Dave Concepcion | .07 |
| 197 | Kal Daniels | .05 |
| 198 | Eric Davis | .50 |
| 199 | John Denny | .05 |
| 200 | Bo Diaz | .05 |
| 201 | Nick Esasky | .05 |
| 202 | John Franco | .05 |
| 203 | Bill Gullickson | .05 |
| 204 | Barry Larkin (R) | .25 |
| 205 | Eddie Milner | .05 |
| 206 | Rob Murphy (R) | .20 |

| NO. | PLAYER | MINT |
|---|---|---|
| 207 | Ron Oester | .05 |
| 208 | Dave Parker | .15 |
| 209 | Tony Perez | .12 |
| 210 | Ted Power | .05 |
| 211 | Joe Price | .05 |
| 212 | Ron Robinson | .05 |
| 213 | Pete Rose (Mgr.) | .50 |
| 214 | Mario Soto | .05 |
| 215 | Kurt Stillwell | .15 |
| 216 | Max Venable | .05 |
| 217 | Chris Welsh | .05 |
| 218 | Carl Willis (R) | .15 |
| **TORONTO BLUE JAYS** | | |
| 219 | Jesse Barfield | .12 |
| 220 | George Bell | .12 |
| 221 | Bill Caudill | .05 |
| 222 | John Cerutti (R) | .30 |
| 223 | Jim Clancy | .05 |
| 224 | Mark Eichhorn (R) | .30 |
| 225 | Tony Fernandez | .05 |
| 226 | Damaso Garcia | .07 |
| 227 | Kelly Gruber | .05 |
| 228 | Tom Henke | .05 |
| 229 | Garth Iorg | .05 |
| 230 | Joe Johnson | .07 |
| 231 | Cliff Johnson | .05 |
| 232 | Jimmy Key | .05 |
| 233 | Dennis Lamp | .05 |
| 234 | Rick Leach | .05 |
| 235 | Buck Martinez | .05 |
| 236 | Lloyd Moseby | .07 |
| 237 | Rance Mulliniks | .05 |
| 238 | Dave Stieb | .10 |
| 239 | Willie Upshaw | .05 |
| 240 | Ernie Whitt | .05 |
| **CLEVELAND INDIANS** | | |
| 241 | Andy Allanson (R) | .15 |
| 242 | Scott Bailes (R) | .15 |
| 243 | Chris Bando | .05 |
| 244 | Tony Bernazard | .05 |
| 245 | John Butcher | .05 |
| 246 | Brett Butler | .05 |
| 247 | Ernie Camacho | .05 |
| 248 | Tom Candiotti | .05 |
| 249 | Joe Carter | .15 |
| 250 | Carmen Castillo | .05 |
| 251 | Julio Franco | .05 |
| 252 | Mel Hall | .05 |
| 253 | Brook Jacoby | .05 |
| 254 | Phil Niekro | .15 |
| 255 | Otis Nixon | .05 |
| 256 | Dickie Noles | .05 |
| 257 | Bryan Oelkers | .05 |
| 258 | Ken Schrom | .05 |
| 259 | Don Schulze | .05 |
| 260 | Cory Snyder | .50 |
| 261 | Pat Tabler | .05 |
| 262 | Andre Thornton | .05 |
| 263 | Rich Yett (R) | .05 |
| **SAN FRANCISCO GIANTS** | | |
| 264 | Mike Aldrete (R) | .15 |
| 265 | Juan Berenguer | .05 |
| 266 | Vida Blue | .05 |
| 267 | Bob Brenly | .05 |
| 268 | Chris Brown | .15 |
| 269 | Will Clark (R) | .75 |
| 270 | Chili Davis | .05 |
| 271 | Mark Davis | .05 |
| 272 | Kelly Downs (R) | .15 |
| 273 | Scott Garrelts | .05 |
| 274 | Dan Gladden | .05 |
| 275 | Mike Krukow | .05 |
| 276 | Randy Kutcher (R) | .15 |
| 277 | Mike LaCoss | .05 |
| 278 | Jeff Leonard | .05 |
| 279 | Candy Maldonado | .05 |
| 280 | Roger Mason | .05 |
| 281 | Bob Melvin | .05 |
| 282 | Greg Minton | .05 |
| 283 | Jeff Robinson | .05 |
| 284 | Harry Spilman | .05 |
| 285 | Rob Thompson (R) | .40 |
| 286 | Jose Uribe | .05 |
| 287 | Frank Williams | .05 |
| 288 | Joel Youngblood | .05 |
| **ST. LOUIS CARDINALS** | | |
| 289 | Jack Clark | .05 |

| NO. | PLAYER | MINT |
|---|---|---|
| 290 | Vince Coleman | .35 |
| 291 | Tim Conroy | .05 |
| 292 | Danny Cox | .05 |
| 293 | Ken Dayley | .05 |
| 294 | Curt Ford | .15 |
| 295 | Bob Forsch | .05 |
| 296 | Tom Herr | .05 |
| 297 | Ricky Horton | .05 |
| 298 | Clint Hurdle | .05 |
| 299 | Jeff Lahti | .05 |
| 300 | Steve Lake | .05 |
| 301 | Tito Landrum | .05 |
| 302 | Mike LaValliere (R) | .05 |
| 303 | Greg Mathews (R) | .05 |
| 304 | Willie McGee | .15 |
| 305 | Jose Oquendo | .05 |
| 306 | Terry Pendleton | .05 |
| 307 | Pat Perry | .10 |
| 308 | Ozzie Smith | .10 |
| 309 | Ray Soff (R) | .15 |
| 310 | John Tudor | .05 |
| 311 | Andy Van Slyke | .05 |
| 312 | Todd Worrell | .30 |
| **MONTREAL EXPOS** | | |
| 313 | Dann Bilardello | .05 |
| 314 | Hubie Brooks | .05 |
| 315 | Tim Burke | .05 |
| 316 | Andre Dawson | .15 |
| 317 | Mike Fitzgerald | .05 |
| 318 | Tom Foley | .05 |
| 319 | Andres Galarraga | .15 |
| 320 | Joe Hesketh | .05 |
| 321 | Wallace Johnson | .05 |
| 322 | Wayne Krenchicki | .05 |
| 323 | Vance Law | .05 |
| 324 | Dennis Martinez | .05 |
| 325 | Bob McClure | .05 |
| 326 | Andy McGaffigan | .05 |
| 327 | Al Newman (R) | .15 |
| 328 | Tim Raines | .30 |
| 329 | Jeff Reardon | .05 |
| 330 | Luis Rivera (R) | .15 |
| 331 | Bob Sebra (R) | .15 |
| 332 | Bryn Smith | .05 |
| 333 | Jay Tibbs | .05 |
| 334 | Tim Wallach | .05 |
| 335 | Mitch Webster | .12 |
| 336 | John Wohlford | .05 |
| 337 | Floyd Youmans | .25 |
| **MILWAUKEE BREWERS** | | |
| 338 | Chris Bosio (R) | .15 |
| 339 | Glenn Braggs (R) | .35 |
| 340 | Rick Cerone | .05 |
| 341 | Mark Clear | .05 |
| 342 | B. Clutterbuck (R) | .15 |
| 343 | Cecil Cooper | .15 |
| 344 | Rob Deer | .20 |
| 345 | Jim Gantner | .05 |
| 346 | Ted Higuera | .20 |
| 347 | J.H. Johnson | .05 |
| 348 | Tim Leary | .05 |
| 349 | Rick Manning | .05 |
| 350 | Paul Molitor | .05 |
| 351 | Charlie Moore | .05 |
| 352 | Juan Nieves | .15 |
| 353 | Ben Oglivie | .05 |
| 354 | Dan Plesac (R) | .25 |
| 355 | Ernest Riles | .05 |
| 356 | Billy Joe Robidoux | .15 |
| 357 | Bill Schroeder | .05 |
| 358 | Dale Sveum (R) | .20 |
| 359 | Gorman Thomas | .07 |
| 360 | Bill Wegman | .05 |
| 361 | Robin Yount | .25 |
| **KC ROYALS** | | |
| 362 | Steve Balboni | .07 |
| 363 | Scott Bankhead (R) | .20 |
| 364 | Buddy Biancalana | .05 |
| 365 | Bud Black | .05 |
| 366 | George Brett | .40 |
| 367 | Steve Farr | .05 |
| 368 | Mark Gubicza | .05 |
| 369 | Bo Jackson (R) | 1.50 |
| 370 | Danny Jackson | .05 |
| 371 | Mike Kingery (R) | .20 |
| 372 | Rudy Law | .05 |
| 373 | Charlie Leibrandt | .05 |

Card values from this set fluctuate considerably.

| NO. PLAYER | MINT |
|---|---|
| 374 Dennis Leonard | .05 |
| 375 Hal McRae | .05 |
| 376 Jorge Orta | .05 |
| 377 Jamie Quirk | .05 |
| 378 Dan Quisenberry | .10 |
| 379 Bret Saberhagen | .12 |
| 380 Angel Salazar | .05 |
| 381 Lonnie Smith | .05 |
| 382 Jim Sundberg | .05 |
| 383 Frank White | .05 |
| 384 Willie Wilson | .12 |
| **OAKLAND A's** | |
| 385 Joaquin Andujar | .05 |
| 386 Doug Bair | .05 |
| 387 Dusty Baker | .05 |
| 388 Bruce Bochte | .05 |
| 389 Jose Canseco | 2.00 |
| 390 Chris Codiroli | .05 |
| 391 Mike Davis | .05 |
| 392 Alfredo Griffin | .05 |
| 393 Moose Haas | .05 |
| 394 Donnie Hill | .05 |
| 395 Jay Howell | .05 |
| 396 Dave Kingman | .12 |
| 397 Carney Lansford | .05 |
| 398 David Leiper | .12 |
| 399 B. Mooneyham (R) | .15 |
| 400 Dwayne Murphy | .05 |
| 401 Steve Ontiveros | .05 |
| 402 Tony Phillips | .05 |
| 403 Eric Plunk | .05 |
| 404 Jose Rijo | .05 |
| 405 Terry Steinbach (R) | .20 |
| 406 Dave Stewart | .05 |
| 407 Mickey Tettleton | .05 |
| 408 Dave Von Ohlen | .05 |
| 409 Jerry Willard | .05 |
| 410 Curt Young | .05 |
| **SAN DIEGO PADRES** | |
| 411 Bruce Bochy | .05 |
| 412 Dave Dravecky | .05 |
| 413 Tim Flannery | .05 |
| 414 Steve Garvey | .30 |
| 415 Goose Gossage | .12 |
| 416 Tony Gwynn | .30 |
| 417 Andy Hawkins | .05 |
| 418 LaMarr Hoyt | .05 |
| 419 Terry Kennedy | .05 |
| 420 John Kruk (R) | .25 |
| 421 Dave LaPoint | .05 |
| 422 Craig Letters | .05 |
| 423 Carmelo Martinez | .05 |
| 424 Lance McCullers | .12 |
| 425 Kevin McReynolds | .12 |
| 426 Graig Nettles | .10 |
| 427 Bip Roberts (R) | .15 |
| 428 Jerry Royster | .05 |
| 429 Benito Santiago | .20 |
| 430 Eric Show | .07 |
| 431 Bob Stoddard | .05 |
| 432 Garry Templeton | .05 |
| 433 Gene Walter | .10 |
| 434 Ed Whitson | .05 |
| 435 Marvell Wynne | .05 |
| **LA DODGERS** | |
| 436 Dave Anderson | .05 |
| 437 Greg Brock | .05 |
| 438 Enos Cabell | .05 |
| 439 Mariano Duncan | .12 |
| 440 Pedro Guerrero | .20 |
| 441 Orel Hershiser | .15 |
| 442 Rick Honeycutt | .05 |
| 443 Ken Howell | .05 |
| 444 Ken Landreaux | .05 |
| 445 Bill Madlock | .08 |
| 446 Mike Marshall | .08 |
| 447 Len Matuszek | .05 |
| 448 Tom Niedenfuer | .05 |
| 449 Alejandro Pena | .05 |
| 450 Dennis Powell | .05 |
| 451 Jerry Reuss | .05 |
| 452 Bill Russell | .05 |
| 453 Steve Sax | .12 |
| 454 Mike Scioscia | .05 |
| 455 Franklin Stubbs | .05 |
| 456 Alex Trevino | .05 |
| 457 F. Valenzuela | .25 |
| 458 Ed Vande Berg | .05 |

| NO. PLAYER | MINT |
|---|---|
| 459 Bob Welch | .05 |
| 460 Reggie Williams (R) | .25 |
| **BALTIMORE ORIOLES** | |
| 461 Don Aase | .05 |
| 462 Juan Beniquez | .05 |
| 463 Mike Boddicker | .05 |
| 464 Juan Bonilla | .05 |
| 465 Rich Bordi | .05 |
| 466 Storm Davis | .05 |
| 467 Rick Dempsey | .05 |
| 468 Ken Dixon | .05 |
| 469 Jim Dwyer | .05 |
| 470 Mike Flanagan | .05 |
| 471 Jackie Gutierrez | .05 |
| 472 Brad Havens | .05 |
| 473 Lee Lacy | .05 |
| 474 Fred Lynn | .15 |
| 475 Scott McGregor | .08 |
| 476 Eddie Murray | .30 |
| 477 Tom O'Malley | .05 |
| 478 Cal Ripken, Jr. | .30 |
| 479 Larry Sheets | .05 |
| 480 John Shelby | .05 |
| 481 Nate Snell | .05 |
| 482 Jim Traber | .10 |
| 483 Mike Young | .05 |
| **CHICAGO WHITE SOX** | |
| 484 Neil Allen | .05 |
| 485 Harold Baines | .15 |
| 486 Floyd Bannister | .05 |
| 487 Daryl Boston | .05 |
| 488 Ivan Calderon | .05 |
| 489 John Cangelosi (R) | .25 |
| 490 Steve Carlton | .25 |
| 491 Joe Cowley | .05 |
| 492 Julio Cruz | .05 |
| 493 Bill Dawley | .05 |
| 494 Jose DeLeon | .05 |
| 495 Richard Dotson | .05 |
| 496 Carlton Fisk | .10 |
| 497 Ozzie Guillen | .12 |
| 498 Jerry Hairston | .05 |
| 499 Ron Hassey | .05 |
| 500 Tim Hulett | .05 |
| 501 Bob James | .05 |
| 502 Steve Lyons | .05 |
| 503 Joel McKeon (R) | .15 |
| 504 Gene Nelson | .05 |
| 505 Dave Schmidt | .05 |
| 506 Ray Searage | .05 |
| 507 Bobby Thigpen (R) | .20 |
| 508 Greg Walker | .05 |
| **ATLANTA BRAVES** | |
| 509 Jim Acker | .05 |
| 510 Doyle Alexander | .05 |
| 511 P. Assenmacher (R) | .15 |
| 512 Bruce Benedict | .05 |
| 513 Chris Chambliss | .08 |
| 514 Jeff Dedmon | .05 |
| 515 Gene Garber | .05 |
| 516 Ken Griffey | .08 |
| 517 Terry Harper | .05 |
| 518 Bob Horner | .15 |
| 519 Glenn Hubbard | .05 |
| 520 Rick Mahler | .05 |
| 521 Omar Moreno | .05 |
| 522 Dale Murphy | .40 |
| 523 Ken Oberkfell | .05 |
| 524 Ed Olwine (R) | .15 |
| 525 David Palmer | .05 |
| 526 Rafael Ramirez | .05 |
| 527 Billy Sample | .05 |
| 528 Ted Simmons | .05 |
| 529 Zane Smith | .05 |
| 530 Bruce Sutter | .12 |
| 531 Andres Thomas (R) | .25 |
| 532 Ozzie Virgil | .05 |
| **MINNESOTA TWINS** | |
| 533 A. Anderson (R) | .15 |
| 534 Keith Atherton | .05 |
| 535 Billy Beane | .05 |
| 536 Bert Blyleven | .05 |
| 537 Tom Brunansky | .10 |
| 538 Randy Bush | .05 |
| 539 George Frazier | .05 |
| 540 Gary Gaetti | .05 |
| 541 Greg Gagne | .05 |
| 542 Mickey Hatcher | .05 |

| NO. PLAYER | MINT |
|---|---|
| 543 Neal Heaton | .05 |
| 544 Kent Hrbek | .15 |
| 545 Roy Lee Jackson | .05 |
| 546 Tim Laudner | .05 |
| 547 Steve Lombardozzi | .05 |
| 548 Mark Portugal (R) | .15 |
| 549 Kirby Puckett | .25 |
| 550 Jeff Reed | .05 |
| 551 Mark Salas | .05 |
| 552 Roy Smalley | .05 |
| 553 Mike Smithson | .05 |
| 554 Frank Viola | .05 |
| **CHICAGO CUBS** | |
| 555 Thad Bosley | .05 |
| 556 Ron Cey | .05 |
| 557 Jody Davis | .05 |
| 558 Ron Davis | .05 |
| 559 Bob Dernier | .05 |
| 560 Frank DiPino | .05 |
| 561 Shawon Dunston | .07 |
| 562 Leon Durham | .10 |
| 563 Dennis Eckersley | .05 |
| 564 Terry Francona | .05 |
| 565 Dave Gumpert | .05 |
| 566 Guy Hoffman | .05 |
| 567 Ed Lynch | .05 |
| 568 Gary Matthews | .05 |
| 569 Keith Moreland | .05 |
| 570 Jamie Moyer (R) | .15 |
| 571 Jerry Mumphrey | .05 |
| 572 Ryne Sandberg | .20 |
| 573 Scott Sanderson | .05 |
| 574 Lee Smith | .05 |
| 575 Chris Speier | .05 |
| 576 Rick Sutcliffe | .07 |
| 577 Manny Trillo | .05 |
| 578 Steve Trout | .05 |
| **SEATTLE MARINERS** | |
| 579 Karl Best | .05 |
| 580 Scott Bradley | .10 |
| 581 Phil Bradley | .05 |
| 582 Mickey Brantley | .05 |
| 583 Mike Brown | .05 |
| 584 Alvin Davis | .10 |
| 585 L. Guetterman (R) | .15 |
| 586 Mark Huismann | .05 |
| 587 Bob Kearney | .05 |
| 588 Pete Ladd | .05 |
| 589 Mark Langston | .05 |
| 590 Mike Moore | .05 |
| 591 Mike Morgan | .05 |
| 592 John Moses | .05 |
| 593 Ken Phelps | .05 |
| 594 Jim Presley | .20 |
| 595 Rey Quinonez (R) | .15 |
| 596 Harold Reynolds | .05 |
| 597 Billy Swift | .05 |
| 598 Danny Tartabull | .20 |
| 599 Steve Yeager | .05 |
| 600 Matt Young | .05 |
| **PITTSBURGH PIRATES** | |
| 601 Bill Almon | .05 |
| 602 Rafael Belliard (R) | .15 |
| 603 Mike Bielecki | .05 |
| 604 Barry Bonds (R) | .40 |
| 605 Bobby Bonilla (R) | .15 |
| 606 Sid Bream | .05 |
| 607 Mike Brown | .05 |
| 608 Pat Clements | .05 |
| 609 Mike Diaz (R) | .20 |
| 610 Cecilio Guante | .05 |
| 611 Barry Jones (R) | .15 |
| 612 Bob Kipper | .05 |
| 613 Larry McWilliams | .05 |
| 614 Jim Morrison | .05 |
| 615 Joe Orsulak | .05 |
| 616 Junior Ortiz | .05 |
| 617 Tony Pena | .05 |
| 618 Johnny Ray | .05 |
| 619 Rick Reuschel | .05 |
| 620 R.J. Reynolds | .05 |
| 621 Rick Rhoden | .05 |
| 622 Don Robinson | .05 |
| 623 Bob Walk | .05 |
| 624 Jim Winn | .05 |
| 625 Youthful Power: | .60 |
| P. Incaviglia, J. Canseco | |

| NO. PLAYER | MINT |
|---|---|
| 626 300 Game Winners: | .15 |
| D. Sutton, P. Niekro | |
| 627 A.L. Firemen: | .15 |
| D. Righetti, D. Asse | |
| 628 Rookie All-Stars: | 1.25 |
| W. Joyner, J. Canseco | |
| 629 Magic Mets: | 1.00 |
| G. Carter, S. Fernandez, | |
| D. Gooden, K. Hernandez, | |
| D. Strawberry | |
| 630 N.L. Best Righties: | .15 |
| M. Scott, M. Krukow | |
| 631 Sensational Southpaws: | .15 |
| F. Venezuela, J. Franco | |
| 632 4 HR's in Game: | .15 |
| Bob Horner | |
| 633 Pitcher's Nightmare: | .75 |
| J. Canseco, J. Rice, | |
| K. Puckett | |
| 634 All-Star Battery: | .50 |
| G. Carter, R. Clemens | |
| 635 4,000 Strikeouts: | .25 |
| S. Carlton | |
| 636 Big Bats at First Sack: | .25 |
| G. Davis, E. Murray | |
| 637 On Base: | .50 |
| W. Boggs, K. Hernandez | |
| 638 Sluggers from Left Side: | 1.00 |
| D. Mattingly, | |
| D. Strawberry | |
| 639 Former MVP's: | .25 |
| D. Parker, R. Sandberg | |
| 640 Dr. K. & Super K: | 1.00 |
| D. Gooden, R. Clemens | |
| 641 A.L. West Stoppers: | .15 |
| M. Witt, C. Hough | |
| 642 Doubles & Triples: | .15 |
| J. Samuel, T. Raines | |
| 643 Outfielders with Punch: | .15 |
| H. Baines, J. Barfield | |
| **No. 644 to 653—Major League Prospects** | |
| 644 D. Clark (R) and | |
| G. Swindell (R) | .50 |
| 645 Ron Karkovice (R) and | |
| Russ Morman (R) | .25 |
| 646 Devon White (R) and | |
| Willie Fraser (R) | .25 |
| 647 Mike Stanley (R) and | |
| Jerry Browne (R) | .20 |
| 648 Dave Magadan (R) and | |
| Phil Lombardi (R) | .75 |
| 649 Jose Gonzalez (R) and | |
| Ralph Bryant (R) | .50 |
| 650 Jimmy Jones (R) and | |
| Randy Asadoor (R) | .25 |
| 651 Tracy Jones (R) and | |
| Marvin Freeman (R) | .25 |
| 652 John Stefero (R) and | |
| Kevin Seitzer (R) | .25 |
| 653 Rob Nelson (R) and | |
| Steve Fireovid (R) | .25 |
| 654 Checklist No. 1 | .08 |
| 655 Checklist No. 2 | .08 |
| 656 Checklist No. 3 | .08 |
| 657 Checklist No. 4 | .08 |
| 658 Checklist No. 5 | .08 |
| 659 Checklist No. 6 | .08 |
| 660 Checklist No. 7 | .08 |
| **Cards Printed on Gum Boxes** | |
| C 1 Mets logo | .10 |
| C 2 Jesse Barfield | .15 |
| C 3 George Brett | .40 |
| C 4 Dwight Gooden | .50 |
| C 5 Red Sox logo | .10 |
| C 6 Keith Hernandez | .15 |
| C 7 Wally Joyner | .75 |
| C 8 Dale Murphy | .40 |
| C 9 Astros logo | .10 |
| C10 Dave Parker | .15 |
| C11 Kirby Puckett | .35 |
| C12 Dave Righetti | .15 |
| C13 Angels logo | .15 |
| C14 Ryne Sandberg | .15 |
| C15 Mike Schmidt | .35 |
| C16 Robin Yount | .20 |

Card values from this set fluctuate considerably.

# 1986 Sportflics.... Complete Set of 200 Cards —Value $40.00

Sportflics entered the baseball card market in 1986. Each 2½″x3½″ card could be tilted to show three different photos. The set included 139 cards, each featuring three poses of the same player; 50 "Tri-Stars"—each card featuring three players; 10 "Big Six" cards—each featuring six players; 1 World Series card—featuring 12 players. 133 question and answer trivia cards were also issued. The complete set was packaged in a printed box for distribution through card hobby dealers. Wax packs were sold through mass market outlets. In addition to its main card set, Sportflics issued two other sets in 1986—50-card set of "Rookies" and 75-card set of "Decade Greats."

Dwight Gooden—Phase 1

Dwight Gooden—Phase 2

Dwight Gooden—Phase 3

| NO. PLAYER | MINT |
|---|---|
| 1 George Brett | 2.00 |
| 2 Don Mattingly | 3.50 |
| 3 Wade Boggs | 2.50 |
| 4 Eddie Murray | 1.00 |
| 5 Dale Murphy | 2.00 |
| 6 Rickey Henderson | 1.50 |
| 7 Harold Baines | .40 |
| 8 Cal Ripken, Jr. | 1.25 |
| 9 Orel Hershiser | .50 |
| 10 Bret Saberhagen | .50 |
| 11 Tim Raines | .50 |
| 12 Fernando Valenzuela | .50 |
| 13 Tony Gwynn | .50 |
| 14 Pedro Guerrero | .45 |
| 15 Keith Hernandez | .45 |
| 16 Ernest Riles | .45 |
| 17 Jim Rice | .50 |
| 18 Ron Guidry | .45 |
| 19 Willie McGee | .50 |
| 20 Ryne Sandberg | .75 |
| 21 Kirk Gibson | .50 |
| 22 Ozzie Guillen (R) | .75 |
| 23 Dave Parker | .50 |
| 24 Vince Coleman (R) | 2.00 |
| 25 Tom Seaver | .75 |
| 26 Brett Butler | .25 |
| 27 Steve Carlton | .60 |
| 28 Gary Carter | .75 |
| 29 Cecil Cooper | .40 |
| 30 Jose Cruz | .25 |
| 31 Alvin Davis | .30 |
| 32 Dwight Evans | .25 |
| 33 Julio Franco | .30 |
| 34 Damaso Garcia | .25 |
| 35 Steve Garvey | .75 |
| 36 Kent Hrbek | .40 |
| 37 Reggie Jackson | .75 |
| 38 Fred Lynn | .40 |
| 39 Paul Molitor | .25 |
| 40 Jim Presley | .30 |
| 41 Dave Righetti | .25 |
| 42 Robin Yount | .45 |
| 43 Nolan Ryan | .60 |
| 44 Mike Schmidt | .75 |
| 45 Lee Smith | .25 |
| 46 Rick Sutcliffe | .25 |
| 47 Bruce Sutter | .40 |
| 48 Lou Whitaker | .30 |
| 49 Dave Winfield | .75 |
| 50 Pete Rose | 3.00 |

**No. 51 to 75—TRI-STARS**

| NO. PLAYER | MINT |
|---|---|
| 51 Nat'l. League MVPs: | 1.00 |
| Ryne Sandberg, Steve Garvey, Pete Rose | |
| 52 Slugging Stars: | .75 |
| Harold Baines, George Brett, Jim Rice | |
| 53 No-Hitters: | .30 |
| Mike Witt, Phil Niekro, Jerry Reuss | |
| 54 Big Hitters: | 1.25 |
| Robin Yount, Don Mattingly, Cal Ripken, Jr. | |

| NO. PLAYER | MINT |
|---|---|
| 55 Bullpen Aces: | .35 |
| Dan Quisenberry, Lee Smith, Goose Gossage | |
| 56 Rookies of The Year: | 1.25 |
| Pete Rose, Steve Sax, Darryl Strawberry | |
| 57 Am. League MVP's: | .75 |
| Cal Ripken, Jr., Don Baylor, Reggie Jackson | |
| 58 Batting Champs: | .75 |
| Bill Madlock, Pete Rose, Dave Parker | |
| 59 Cy Young Winners: | .30 |
| LaMarr Hoyt, Mike Flanagan, Ron Guidry | |
| 60 Double Award Winners: | .40 |
| Fernando Valenzuela, Rick Sutcliffe, Tom Seaver | |
| 61 Home Run Champs: | .75 |
| Tony Armas, Reggie Jackson, Jim Rice | |
| 62 Nat'l League MVP's: | 1.00 |
| Keith Hernandez, Mike Schmidt, Dale Murphy | |
| 63 Am. League MVP's | .75 |
| George Brett, Robin Yount, Fred Lynn | |
| 64 Comeback Players: | .25 |
| Bert Blyleven, Jerry Koosman, John Denny | |
| 65 Cy Young Relievers: | .25 |
| Willie Hernandez, Rollie Fingers, Bruce Sutter | |
| 66 Rookies of The Year: | .25 |
| Bob Horner, Andre Dawson, G. Matthews | |
| 67 Rookies of The Year: | .35 |
| Ron Kittle, Carlton Fisk, Tom Seaver | |
| 68 Home Run Champs: | .40 |
| Dave Kingman, Mike Schmidt, George Foster | |
| 69 Dbl. Award Winners: | 1.25 |
| Cal Ripken, Jr., Pete Rose, Rod Carew | |
| 70 Cy Young Winners: | .40 |
| Rick Sutcliffe, Steve Carlton, Tom Seaver | |
| 71 Top Sluggers: | .50 |
| Reggie Jackson, Fred Lynn, Robin Yount | |
| 72 Rookies of The Year: | .30 |
| Rick Sutcliffe, Dave Righetti, F. Valenzuela | |
| 73 Rookies of The Year: | 1.00 |
| Fred Lynn, Eddie Murray, Cal Ripken, Jr. | |
| 74 Rookies of The Year: | .40 |
| Alvin Davis, Lou Whitaker, Rod Carew | |
| 75 Batting Champs: | 2.00 |
| Don Mattingly, Carney Lansford, Wade Boggs | |

| NO. PLAYER | MINT |
|---|---|
| 76 Jesse Barfield | .25 |
| 77 Phil Bradley | .40 |
| 78 Chris Brown (R) | 1.00 |
| 79 Tom Browning | .40 |
| 80 Tom Brunansky | .25 |
| 81 Bill Buckner | .25 |
| 82 Chili Davis | .25 |
| 83 Mike Davis | .25 |
| 84 Rich Gedman | .25 |
| 85 Willie Hernandez | .25 |
| 86 Ron Kittle | .25 |
| 87 Lee Lacy | .25 |
| 88 Bill Madlock | .25 |
| 89 Mike Marshall | .25 |
| 90 Keith Moreland | .25 |
| 91 Graig Nettles | .25 |
| 92 Lance Parrish | .35 |
| 93 Kirby Puckett | .75 |
| 94 Juan Samuel | .25 |
| 95 Steve Sax | .25 |
| 96 Dave Stieb | .35 |
| 97 Darryl Strawberry | 1.50 |
| 98 Willie Upshaw | .25 |
| 99 Frank Viola | .25 |
| 100 Dwight Gooden | 2.50 |
| 101 Joaquin Andujar | .25 |
| 102 George Bell | .25 |
| 103 Bert Blyleven | .25 |
| 104 Mike Boddicker | .25 |
| 105 Britt Burns | .25 |
| 106 Rod Carew | .75 |
| 107 Jack Clark | .40 |
| 108 Danny Cox | .25 |
| 109 Ron Darling | .40 |
| 110 Andre Dawson | .45 |
| 111 Leon Durham | .25 |
| 112 Tony Fernandez | .25 |
| 113 Tom Herr | .25 |
| 114 Teddy Higuera (R) | .85 |
| 115 Bob Horner | .25 |
| 116 Dave Kingman | .25 |
| 117 Jack Morris | .35 |
| 118 Dan Quisenberry | .40 |
| 119 Jeff Reardon | .25 |
| 120 Bryn Smith | .25 |
| 121 Ozzie Smith | .25 |
| 122 John Tudor | .25 |
| 123 Tim Wallach | .25 |
| 124 Willie Wilson | .35 |
| 125 Carlton Fisk | .40 |

**No. 126 to 150—TRI-STARS**

| NO. PLAYER | MINT |
|---|---|
| 126 RBI Sluggers: | .35 |
| George Foster, Gary Carter, Al Oliver | |
| 127 Run Scorers: | .50 |
| Keith Hernandez, Tim Raines, Ryne Sandberg | |
| 128 Run Scorers: | .50 |
| Willie Wilson, Paul Molitor, Cal Ripken, Jr. | |
| 129 No-Hitters: | .25 |
| J. Candelaria, B. Forsch, D. Eckersley | |

| NO. PLAYER | MINT |
|---|---|
| 130 World Series MVP's: | 1.00 |
| Rollie Fingers, Pete Rose, Ron Cey | |
| 131 All-Star Game MVP's: | .25 |
| George Foster, Dave Concepcion, Bill Madlock | |
| 132 Cy Young Winners: | .30 |
| Vida Blue, John Denny, Fernando Valenzuela | |
| 133 Comeback Players: | .25 |
| Richard Dotson, Joaquin Andujar, Doyle Alexander | |
| 134 Big Winners: | .40 |
| Rick Sutcliffe, Tom Seaver, John Denny | |
| 135 Veteran Pitchers: | .40 |
| Tom Seaver, Phil Niekro, Don Sutton | |
| 136 Rookies of The Year: | 1.50 |
| Dwight Gooden, Vince Coleman, Alfredo Griffin | |
| 137 All-Star Game MVP's | .50 |
| Steve Garvey, Gary Carter, Fred Lynn | |
| 138 Veteran Hitters: | 1.00 |
| Tony Perez, Pete Rose, Rusty Staub | |
| 139 Power Hitters: | .50 |
| Mike Schmidt, Jim Rice, George Foster | |
| 140 Batting Champs: | .35 |
| Tony Gwynn, Al Oliver, Bill Buckner | |
| 141 No-Hitters: | .30 |
| Jack Morris, Dave Righetti, Nolan Ryan | |
| 142 No-Hitters: | .30 |
| Tom Seaver, Bert Blyleven, Vida Blue | |
| 143 Strikeout Kings: | 1.50 |
| Nolan Ryan, Fernando Valenzuela, Dwight Gooden | |
| 144 Base Stealers: | .40 |
| Willie Wilson, Tim Raines, Davey Lopes | |
| 145 RBI Sluggers: | .60 |
| Tony Armas, Cecil Cooper, Eddie Murray | |
| 146 Am. League MVP's: | .40 |
| Rod Carew, Jim Rice, Rollie Fingers | |
| 147 World Series MVP's: | .40 |
| Alan Trammell, Rick Dempsey, Reggie Jackson | |
| 148 World Series MVP's: | .40 |
| Darrell Porter, Mike Schmidt, Pedro Guerrero | |
| 149 ERA Leaders: | .30 |
| Mike Boddicker, Rick Sutcliffe, Ron Guidry | |
| 150 Comeback Players: | .60 |
| Reggie Jackson, Dave Kingman, Fred Lynn | |

# 1986 Sportflics (Continued)

| NO. PLAYER | MINT |
|---|---|
| 151 Buddy Bell | .25 |
| 152 Dennis Boyd | .25 |
| 153 Dave Concepcion | .25 |
| 154 Brian Downing | .25 |
| 155 Shawon Dunston | .25 |
| 156 John Franco | .25 |
| 157 Scott Garrelts | .25 |
| 158 Bob James | .25 |
| 159 Charlie Leibrandt | .25 |
| 160 Oddibe McDowell | .75 |
| 161 Roger McDowell (R) | .60 |
| 162 Mike Moore | .25 |
| 163 Phil Niekro | .45 |
| 164 Al Oliver | .25 |
| 165 Tony Pena | .25 |
| 166 Ted Power | .25 |
| 167 Mike Scioscia | .25 |
| 168 Mario Soto | .25 |
| 169 Bob Stanley | .25 |
| 170 Gary Templeton | .25 |
| 171 Andre Thornton | .25 |
| 172 Alan Trammell | .40 |
| 173 Doug DeCinces | .25 |
| 174 Greg Walker | .25 |
| 175 Don Sutton | .40 |

**No. 176 to 185—THE BIG SIX**

| NO. PLAYER | MINT |
|---|---|
| 176 1985 Award Winners: | 1.50 |
| Vince Coleman, Ozzie Guillen, Bret Saberhagen, Don Mattingly, Dwight Gooden, Willie McGee | |
| 177 1985 Hot Rookies: | .60 |
| Mark Salas, Stew Cliburn, Brian Fisher, Joe Hesketh, Joe Orsulak, Larry Sheets | |
| 178 Future Stars: | 5.00 |
| Steve Lombardozzi, Jose Canseco, Mark Funderburk, Mike Greenwell, Billy Joe Robidoux, Dan Tartabull | |
| 179 1985 Gold Glovers: | 1.00 |
| George Brett, Don Mattingly, Ron Guidry, Keith Hernandez, Willie McGee, Dale Murphy | |
| 180 Active .300 Hitters | 1.00 |
| Wade Boggs, George Brett, Rod Carew, Cecil Cooper, Don Mattingly, W. Wilson | |

| NO. PLAYER | MINT |
|---|---|
| 181 Active .300 Hitters | 1.00 |
| Tony Gwynn, Bill Madlock, Pedro Guerrero, Dave Parker, Pete Rose, Keith Hernandez | |
| 182 1985 Milestones: | 1.00 |
| Rod Carew, Phil Niekro, Pete Rose, Tom Seaver, Nolan Ryan, Matt Tallman | |
| 183 1985 Triple Crown: | 1.00 |
| Willie McGee, Dave Parker, Wade Boggs, Darrell Evans, D. Mattingly, D. Murphy | |
| 184 1985 Highlights: | 1.50 |
| Wade Boggs, Rickey Henderson, Don Mattingly, Willie McGee, Dwight Gooden, John Tudor | |
| 185 20 Game Winners: | 1.25 |
| Dwight Gooden, Ron Guidry, John Tudor, Joaquin Andujar, Bret Saberhagen, Tom Browning | |

| NO. PLAYER | MINT |
|---|---|
| 186 W. Series Champions: | 1.00 |
| D. Iorg, W. Wilson, C. Leibrandt, L. Smith, G. Brett, B. Saberhagen, D. Motley, D. Quisenberry, J. Sundberg, S. Balboni, F. White, D. Jackson | |
| 187 Hubie Brooks | .25 |
| 188 Glenn Davis | .25 |
| 189 Darrell Evans | .25 |
| 190 Rich Gossage | .40 |
| 191 Andy Hawkins | .25 |
| 192 Jay Howell | .25 |
| 193 LaMarr Hoyt | .25 |
| 194 Davey Lopes | .25 |
| 195 Mike Scott | .25 |
| 196 Ted Simmons | .25 |
| 197 Gary Ward | .25 |
| 198 Bob Welch | .25 |
| 199 Mike Young | .50 |
| 200 Buddy Blancalana | .25 |

# 1986 Sportflics Decade Greats....Complete Set of 75 Cards—Value $20.00

The set features outstanding players by position, from the 1930's to the 1980's, by decades. Each 2½" x 3½" card can be tilted to show three different photos. 59 cards feature one player; 16 are multi-player cards. The players from the 1930's and 1940's are printed in sepia tones and the other cards are in color. The complete set was packaged in a printed box and sold exclusively through card hobby dealers.

Mel Ott—Phase 1

Mel Ott—Phase 2

Mel Ott—Phase 3

| NO. PLAYER | MINT |
|---|---|
| **1930's** | |
| 1 Babe Ruth | 2.00 |
| 2 Jimmie Foxx | .40 |
| 3 Lefty Grove | .25 |
| 4 Hank Greenberg | 1.00 |
| 5 Al Simmons | .20 |
| 6 Carl Hubbell | .20 |
| 7 Joe Cronin | .20 |
| 8 Mel Ott | .20 |
| 9 Lefty Gomez | .20 |
| 10 Player of the Decade Lou Gehrig | 1.50 |
| 11 Pie Traynor | .20 |
| 12 Charlie Gehringer | .30 |
| 13 Catchers: | .50 |
| B. Dickey, M. Cochrane, G. Hartnett | |
| 14 Pitchers: | .20 |
| R. Ruffing, D. Dean, P. Derringer | |
| 15 Outfielders: | .20 |
| P. Waner, J. Medwick, E. Averill | |
| **1940's** | |
| 16 Bob Feller | .40 |
| 17 Lou Boudreau | .20 |
| 18 Enos Slaughter | .50 |
| 19 Hal Newhouser | .20 |
| 20 Joe DiMaggio | 1.50 |

| NO. PLAYER | MINT |
|---|---|
| 21 Pee Wee Reese | .40 |
| 22 Phil Rizzuto | .75 |
| 23 Ernie Lombardi | .40 |
| 24 Infielders: | .20 |
| J. Mize, J. Gordon, G. Kell | |
| 25 Player of the Decade Ted Williams | 1.50 |
| **1950's and 60's** | |
| 26 Mickey Mantle | 2.50 |
| 27 Warren Spahn | .20 |
| 28 Jackie Robinson | .60 |
| 29 Ernie Banks | .50 |
| 30 Player of the Decade Stan Musial | .75 |
| 31 Yogi Berra | .75 |
| 32 Duke Snider | .50 |
| 33 Roy Campanella | .75 |
| 34 Eddie Mathews | .20 |
| 35 Ralph Kiner | .75 |
| 36 Early Wynn | .20 |
| 37 Double Play Duo: | .20 |
| N. Fox, L. Aparicio | |
| 38 First Basemen: | .20 |
| G. Hodges, M. Vernon, T. Kluszewski | |
| 39 Pitchers: | .20 |
| B. Lemon, D. Newcombe, R. Roberts | |

| NO. PLAYER | MINT |
|---|---|
| 40 Henry Aaron | 1.00 |
| 41 Frank Robinson | .40 |
| 42 Bob Gibson | .30 |
| 43 Roberto Clemente | 1.00 |
| 44 Whitey Ford | .40 |
| 45 Brooks Robinson | .50 |
| 46 Juan Marichal | .20 |
| 47 Carl Yastrzemski | 1.00 |
| 48 First Basemen: | .20 |
| W. McCovey, O. Cepeda, H. Killebrew | |
| 49 Catchers: | .20 |
| J. Torre, E. Howard, B. Freehan | |
| 50 Player of the Decade Willie Mays | .50 |
| 51 Outfielders: | .20 |
| A. Kaline, T. Oliva, B. Williams | |
| **1970's** | |
| 52 Tom Seaver | .75 |
| 53 Reggie Jackson | .75 |
| 54 Steve Carlton | .50 |
| 55 Mike Schmidt | .50 |
| 56 Joe Morgan | .20 |
| 57 Jim Rice | .50 |
| 58 Jim Palmer | .20 |
| 59 Lou Brock | .20 |

| NO. PLAYER | MINT |
|---|---|
| 60 Player of the Decade Pete Rose | 1.50 |
| 61 Steve Garvey | .50 |
| 62 Catchers: | .40 |
| T. Munson, C. Fisk, T. Simmons | |
| 63 Pitchers: | .20 |
| V. Blue, C. Hunter, N. Ryan | |
| **1980's** | |
| 64 George Brett | .75 |
| 65 Don Mattingly | 2.00 |
| 66 Fernando Valenzuela | .50 |
| 67 Dale Murphy | .75 |
| 68 Wade Boggs | 1.50 |
| 69 Rickey Henderson | .60 |
| 70 Player of the Decade Eddie Murray | .20 |
| 71 Ron Guidry | .20 |
| 72 Catchers: | .20 |
| G. Carter, Tony Pena, L. Parrish | |
| 73 Infielders: | .20 |
| C. Ripken, L. Whitaker, R. Yount | |
| 74 Outfielders: | .20 |
| P. Guerrero, T. Raines, D. Winfield | |
| 75 Dwight Gooden | 1.50 |

# 1986 Sportflics Rookies....Complete Set of 50 Cards—Value $18.00

Features the outstanding rookies of the 1986 season. The set was packaged in a printed box, and distributed exclusively through card hobby dealers.

| NO. PLAYER | MINT | NO. PLAYER | MINT | NO. PLAYER | MINT | NO. PLAYER | MINT |
|---|---|---|---|---|---|---|---|
| 1 John Kruk | .25 | 15 Jim Deshaies | .35 | 29 Bruce Ruffin (RR) | .40 | 43 Kal Daniels | .25 |
| 2 Edwin Correa | .25 | 16 Ruben Sierra (RR) | 1.50 | 30 Greg Swindell (RR) | .60 | 44 Calvin Schiraldi | .35 |
| 3 Pete Incaviglia (RR) | 1.50 | 17 Steve Lombardozzi | .20 | 31 John Cangelosi | .30 | 45 Mickey Brantley | .25 |
| 4 Dale Sveum | .25 | 18 Cory Snyder | 1.25 | 32 Jim Traber | .20 | 46 "Tri-Stars"—W. Mays, | |
| 5 Juan Nieves | .30 | 19 Reggie Williams | .20 | 33 Russ Morman | .25 | P. Rose, F. Lynn | .75 |
| 6 Will Clark (RR) | 1.00 | 20 Mitch Williams | .30 | 34 Barry Larkin | .40 | 47 "Tri-Stars"—T. Seaver, | |
| 7 Wally Joyner (RR) | 3.00 | 21 Glenn Braggs | .40 | 35 Todd Worrell (RR) | .60 | F. Valenzuela, | |
| 8 Lance McCullers | .25 | 22 Danny Tartabull | .50 | 36 John Cerutti | .20 | D. Gooden | .75 |
| 9 Scott Bailes | .20 | 23 Charlie Kerfeld | .25 | 37 Mike Kingery | .25 | 48 "Big Six"—E. Murray, | |
| 10 Dan Plesac | .25 | 24 Paul Assenmacher | .20 | 38 Mark Eichhorn | .35 | L. Whitaker, D. Righetti, | |
| 11 Jose Canseco | 2.00 | 25 Robby Thompson | .40 | 39 Scott Bankhead | .20 | S. Sax, C. Ripken, | |
| 12 Bobby Witt (RR) | .60 | 26 Bobby Bonilla | .25 | 40 Bo Jackson (RR) | 1.75 | D. Stawberry | 1.00 |
| 13 Barry Bonds (RR) | .60 | 27 Andres Galarraga | .25 | 41 Greg Mathews | .25 | 49 Kevin Mitchell (RR) | .75 |
| 14 Andres Thomas | .25 | 28 Billy Jo Robidoux | .20 | 42 Eric King | .25 | 50 Mike Diaz | .25 |

# 1987 Sportflics....Complete Set of 200 Cards—Value $40.00

Features the rookie cards of Bo Jackson, Wally Joyner, Will Clark and Pete Incaviglia.

| NO. PLAYER | MINT | NO. PLAYER | MINT | NO. PLAYER | MINT | NO. PLAYER | MINT |
|---|---|---|---|---|---|---|---|
| 1 Don Mattingly | 2.50 | 46 Robby Thompson | .25 | 87 Jack Morris | .25 | 120 Tri-Stars: | .75 |
| 2 Wade Boggs | 1.50 | 47 Dennis Boyd | .15 | 88 Ray Knight | .15 | Valenzuela, Scott, Gooden | |
| 3 Dale Murphy | .60 | 48 Kirk Gibson | .25 | 89 Phil Bradley | .20 | 121 Johnny Ray | .15 |
| 4 Rickey Henderson | .50 | 49 Fred Lynn | .20 | 90 Jose Canseco | 2.50 | 122 Keith Moreland | .15 |
| 5 George Brett | .60 | 50 Gary Carter | .40 | 91 Gary Ward | .15 | 123 Juan Samuel | .15 |
| 6 Eddie Murray | .50 | 51 George Bell | .20 | 92 Mike Easler | .15 | 124 Wally Backman | .15 |
| 7 Kirby Puckett | .50 | 52 Pete O'Brien | .20 | 93 Tony Pena | .15 | 125 Nolan Ryan | .40 |
| 8 Ryne Sandberg | .35 | 53 Ron Darling | .25 | 94 Dave Smith | .15 | 126 Greg Harris | .15 |
| 9 Cal Ripken Jr. | .40 | 54 Paul Molitor | .15 | 95 Will Clark (R) | 1.00 | 127 Kirk McCaskill | .20 |
| 10 Roger Clemens | 1.25 | 55 Mike Pagliarulo | .30 | 96 Lloyd Moseby | .15 | 128 Dwight Evans | .15 |
| 11 Teddy Higuera | .25 | 56 Mike Boddicker | .15 | 97 Jim Rice | .40 | 129 Rick Rhoden | .15 |
| 12 Steve Sax | .25 | 57 Dave Righetti | .20 | 98 Shawon Dunston | .15 | 130 Bill Madlock | .15 |
| 13 Chris Brown | .25 | 58 Len Dykstra | .40 | 99 Don Sutton | .20 | 131 Oddibe McDowell | .25 |
| 14 Jesse Barfield | .25 | 59 Mike Witt | .15 | 100 Dwight Gooden | 1.00 | 132 Darrell Evans | .15 |
| 15 Kent Hrbek | .20 | 60 Tony Bernazard | .15 | 101 Lance Parrish | .20 | 133 Keith Hernandez | .30 |
| 16 Robin Yount | .30 | 61 John Kruk | .30 | 102 Mark Langston | .15 | 134 Tom Brunansky | .15 |
| 17 Glenn Davis | .50 | 62 Mike Krukow | .15 | 103 Floyd Youmans | .20 | 135 Kevin McReynolds | .25 |
| 18 Hubie Brooks | .15 | 63 Sid Fernandez | .20 | 104 Lee Smith | .15 | 136 Scott Fletcher | .15 |
| 19 Mike Scott | .25 | 64 Gary Gaetti | .15 | 105 Willie Hernandez | .15 | 137 Lou Whitaker | .15 |
| 20 Darryl Strawberry | .50 | 65 Vince Coleman | .30 | 106 Doug DeCinces | .15 | 138 Carney Lansford | .15 |
| 21 Alvin Davis | .20 | 66 Pat Tabler | .15 | 107 Ken Schrom | .15 | 139 Andre Dawson | .25 |
| 22 Eric Davis | .50 | 67 Mike Scioscia | .15 | 108 Don Carman | .15 | 140 Carlton Fisk | .25 |
| 23 Danny Tartabull | .45 | 68 Scott Garrelts | .15 | 109 Brook Jacoby | .15 | 141 Buddy Bell | .15 |
| 24 Cory Snyder | .75 | 69 Brett Butler | .15 | 110 Steve Bedrosian | .15 | 142 Ozzie Smith | .25 |
| 25 Pete Rose | 1.00 | 70 Bill Buckner | .15 | 111 Tri-Stars: | .50 | 143 Dan Pasqua | .25 |
| 26 Wally Joyner (R) | 2.50 | 71 Dennis Rasmussen | .15 | Clemens, Morris, Higuera | | 144 Kevin Mitchell (R) | .50 |
| 27 Pedro Guerrero | .25 | 72 Tim Wallach | .15 | 112 Tri-Stars: | .20 | 145 Bret Saberhagen | .25 |
| 28 Tom Seaver | .50 | 73 Bob Horner | .25 | Barrett, Bernazard, Whitaker | | 146 Charlie Kerfeld | .15 |
| 29 Bob Knepper | .20 | 74 Willie McGee | .30 | 113 Tri-Stars: | .25 | 147 Phil Niekro | .20 |
| 30 Mike Schmidt | .50 | 75 Tri-Stars: | 1.25 | Ripken, Fletcher, Fernandez | | 148 John Candelaria | .15 |
| 31 Tony Gwynn | .50 | Mattingly, Joyner, Murray | | 114 Tri-Stars: | .75 | 149 Rich Gedman | .15 |
| 32 Don Slaught | .15 | 76 Jesse Orosco | .20 | Boggs, Brett, Gaetti | | 150 Fernando Valenzuela | .35 |
| 33 Todd Worrell | .35 | 77 Tri-Stars: | .25 | 115 Tri-Stars: | .35 | 151 Tri-Stars: | .15 |
| 34 Tim Raines | .25 | Worrell, Reardon, Smith | | Schmidt, Brown, Wallach | | Carter, Scioscia, Pena | |
| 35 Dave Parker | .15 | 78 Candy Maldonado | .15 | 116 Tri-Stars: | .25 | 152 Tri-Stars: | .50 |
| 36 Bob Ojeda | .20 | 79 Tri-Stars: | .25 | Sandberg, Ray, Doran | | Raines, Cruz, Coleman | |
| 37 Pete Incaviglia (R) | 1.00 | Smith, Brooks, Dunston | | 117 Tri-Stars: | .25 | 153 Tri-Stars: | .25 |
| 38 Bruce Hurst | .20 | 80 Tri-Stars: | 1.25 | Parker, Gwynn, Bass | | Barfield, Baines, Winfield | |
| 39 Bobby Witt (R) | .50 | Bell, Canseco, Rice | | 118 Big 6 Rookies: | 1.00 | 154 Tri-Stars: | .25 |
| 40 Steve Garvey | .30 | 81 Bert Blyleven | .20 | Ty Gainey, Terry Steinbach, | | Parrish, Slaught, Gedman | |
| 41 Dave Winfield | .50 | 82 Mike Marshall | .20 | David Clark, Pat Dodson, | | 155 Tri-Stars: | .50 |
| 42 Jose Cruz | .15 | 83 Ron Guidry | .20 | Phil Lombardi, B. Santiago | | Murphy, McReynolds, Davis | |
| 43 Orel Hershiser | .15 | 84 Julio Franco | .20 | 119 Hi-Lite Tri-Stars: | .35 | 156 Hi-Lite Tri-Stars: | .35 |
| 44 Reggie Jackson | .75 | 85 Willie Wilson | .20 | Righetti, Valenzuela, Scott | | Sutton, Schmidt, Deshaies | |
| 45 Chili Davis | .20 | 86 Lee Lacy | .15 | | | | |

| NO. PLAYER | MINT |
|---|---|
| 157 Speedburners: | .35 |
| Henderson, Cangelosi, Pettis | |
| 158 Big 6 Rookies: | 1.00 |
| Randy Asadoor, C. Candaele, | |
| K. Seitzer, Rafael Palmeiro, | |
| Tim Pyznarski, D. Cochrane | |
| 159 Big 6: | 1.50 |
| Mattingly, Henderson, | |
| Clemens, Murphy, | |
| Murray, Gooden | |
| 160 Roger McDowell | .15 |
| 161 Brian Downing | .15 |
| 162 Bill Doran | .15 |
| 163 Don Baylor | .15 |
| 164 Alfredo Griffin | .15 |

| NO. PLAYER | MINT |
|---|---|
| 165 Don Aase | .15 |
| 166 Glenn Wilson | .15 |
| 167 Dan Quisenberry | .20 |
| 168 Frank White | .15 |
| 169 Cecil Cooper | .20 |
| 170 Jody Davis | .15 |
| 171 Harold Baines | .25 |
| 172 Rob Deer | .20 |
| 173 John Tudor | .15 |
| 174 Larry Parrish | .15 |
| 175 Kevin Bass | .15 |
| 176 Joe Carter | .30 |
| 177 Mitch Webster | .15 |
| 178 Dave Kingman | .25 |

| NO. PLAYER | MINT |
|---|---|
| 179 Jim Presley | .35 |
| 180 Mel Hall | .15 |
| 181 Shane Rawley | .15 |
| 182 Marty Barrett | .15 |
| 183 Damaso Garcia | .15 |
| 184 Bobby Grich | .15 |
| 185 Leon Durham | .15 |
| 186 Ozzie Guillen | .15 |
| 187 Tony Fernandez | .15 |
| 188 Alan Trammell | .25 |
| 189 Jim Clancy | .15 |
| 190 Bo Jackson (R) | 1.50 |
| 191 Bob Forsch | .15 |
| 192 John Franco | .15 |

| NO. PLAYER | MINT |
|---|---|
| 193 Von Hayes | .20 |
| 194 Tri-Stars: | .25 |
| Aase, Righetti, Eichhorn | |
| 195 Tri-Stars: | .35 |
| Hernandez, Clark, Davis | |
| 196 Hi-Lite Tri-Stars: | .50 |
| Clemens, Cowley, Horner | |
| 197 Big 6: | 1.00 |
| Brett, Brooks, Gwynn, | |
| Sandberg, Raines, Bogg | |
| 198 Tri-Stars: | .35 |
| Puckett, Henderson, Lynn | |
| 199 Speedburners: | .50 |
| Raines, Coleman, Davis | |
| 200 Steve Carlton | .30 |

## 1985 McCrory (Fleer) "Limited Edition" Superstars.... Complete Set of 44 Cards—Value $6.00

Distributed exclusively through the McCrory chain store group, which includes McLellan, Green, J.J. Newbury, and T.G. & Y. This was the first of many card sets produced by Fleer for McCrorys. The set was packaged in a printed box, with a *checklist* printed on the back of the box.

| NO. | PLAYER | MINT | NO. | PLAYER | MINT | NO. | PLAYER | MINT |
|---|---|---|---|---|---|---|---|---|
| 1 | Buddy Bell | .08 | 16 | Ron Kittle | .08 | 31 | Ryne Sandberg | .30 |
| 2 | Bert Blyleven | .08 | 17 | Mark Langston | .08 | 32 | Steve Sax | .15 |
| 3 | Wade Boggs | 1.00 | 18 | Jeff Leonard | .08 | 33 | Mike Schmidt | .40 |
| 4 | George Brett | .60 | 19 | Bill Madlock | .08 | 34 | Tom Seaver | .25 |
| 5 | Rod Carew | .30 | 20 | Don Mattingly | 1.00 | 35 | Ozzie Smith | .15 |
| 6 | Steve Carlton | .25 | 21 | Jack Morris | .08 | 36 | Mario Soto | .08 |
| 7 | Alvin Davis | .15 | 22 | Dale Murphy | .75 | 37 | Dave Stieb | .08 |
| 8 | Andre Dawson | .15 | 23 | Eddie Murray | .50 | 38 | Darryl Strawberry | .50 |
| 9 | Steve Garvey | .30 | 24 | Tony Pena | .08 | 39 | Rick Sutcliffe | .08 |
| 10 | Goose Gossage | .15 | 25 | Dan Quisenberry | .08 | 40 | Alan Trammell | .20 |
| 11 | Tony Gwynn | .30 | 26 | Tim Raines | .15 | 41 | Willie Upshaw | .08 |
| 12 | Keith Hernandez | .25 | 27 | Jim Rice | .20 | 42 | F. Valenzuela | .20 |
| 13 | Kent Hrbek | .20 | 28 | Cal Ripken Jr. | .35 | 43 | Dave Winfield | .20 |
| 14 | Reggie Jackson | .30 | 29 | Pete Rose | 1.00 | 44 | Robin Yount | .25 |
| 15 | Dave Kingman | .08 | 30 | Nolan Ryan | .25 | | | |

## 1986 McCrory (Fleer) "Limited Edition" Superstars.... Complete Set of 44 Cards—Value $6.00

Distributed exclusively through the McCrory chain store group, which includes McLellan, Green, J.J. Newbury, and T.G. & Y. The complete set was packaged in a printed box, with a *checklist* printed on the back of the box.

| NO. | PLAYER | MINT | NO. | PLAYER | MINT | NO. | PLAYER | MINT |
|---|---|---|---|---|---|---|---|---|
| 1 | Doyle Alexander | .05 | 16 | Julio Franco | .05 | 31 | Dale Murphy | .75 |
| 2 | Joaquin Andujar | .10 | 17 | Damaso Garcia | .05 | 32 | Eddie Murray | .25 |
| 3 | Harold Baines | .25 | 18 | Rich Gedman | .05 | 33 | Dave Parker | .15 |
| 4 | Wade Boggs | 1.00 | 19 | Kirk Gibson | .30 | 34 | Tony Pena | .05 |
| 5 | Phil Bradley | .15 | 20 | Dwight Gooden | 2.00 | 35 | Jeff Reardon | .05 |
| 6 | George Brett | .50 | 21 | Pedro Guerrero | .25 | 36 | Cal Ripken, Jr. | .30 |
| 7 | Hubie Brooks | .05 | 22 | Tony Gwynn | .25 | 37 | Pete Rose | .75 |
| 8 | Chris Brown | .15 | 23 | Rickey Henderson | .50 | 38 | Bret Saberhagen | .50 |
| 9 | Tom Brunansky | .05 | 24 | Orel Hershiser | .30 | 39 | Juan Samuel | .05 |
| 10 | Gary Carter | .25 | 25 | LaMarr Hoyt | .05 | 40 | Ryne Sandberg | .25 |
| 11 | Vince Coleman | 1.00 | 26 | Reggie Jackson | .25 | 41 | Mike Schmidt | .30 |
| 12 | Cecil Copper | .05 | 27 | Don Mattingly | 1.00 | 42 | Lee Smith | .05 |
| 13 | Jose Cruz | .05 | 28 | Oddibe McDowell | .25 | 43 | Don Sutton | .05 |
| 14 | Mike Davis | .05 | 29 | Willie McGee | .15 | 44 | Lou Whitaker | .25 |
| 15 | Carlton Fisk | .05 | 30 | Paul Molitor | .05 | | | |

## 1986 McCrory (Fleer) Sluggers vs. Pitchers.... Complete Set of 44 Cards—Value $6.00

Distributed exclusively through the McCrory chain store group, which includes McLellan, Green, J.J. Newbury, and T.G. & Y. The set features 22 of baseball's best hitters and 22 of the top pitchers. The complete set was packaged in a printed box, with a *checklist* printed on the back of the box.

| NO. | PLAYER | MINT | NO. | PLAYER | MINT | NO. | PLAYER | MINT |
|---|---|---|---|---|---|---|---|---|
| 1 | Bert Blyleven | .08 | 16 | Orel Hershiser | .20 | 31 | Bret Saberhagen | .20 |
| 2 | Wade Boggs | .50 | 17 | Kent Hrbek | .15 | 32 | Ryne Sandberg | .15 |
| 3 | George Brett | .30 | 18 | Reggie Jackson | .15 | 33 | Mike Schmidt | .15 |
| 4 | Tom Browning | .08 | 19 | Wally Joyner | 2.50 | 34 | Tom Seaver | .10 |
| 5 | Jose Canseco | 2.00 | 20 | Charlie Leibrandt | .08 | 35 | Bryn Smith | .08 |
| 6 | Will Clark | 1.00 | 21 | Don Mattingly | .75 | 36 | Mario Soto | .08 |
| 7 | Roger Clemens | .50 | 22 | Willie McGee | .20 | 37 | Dave Stieb | .15 |
| 8 | Alvin Davis | .15 | 23 | Jack Morris | .08 | 38 | Darryl Strawberry | .40 |
| 9 | Julio Franco | .08 | 24 | Dale Murphy | .40 | 39 | Rick Sutcliffe | .08 |
| 10 | Kirk Gibson | .15 | 25 | Eddie Murray | .15 | 40 | John Tudor | .15 |
| 11 | Dwight Gooden | 1.00 | 26 | Jeff Reardon | .08 | 41 | F. Valenzuela | .15 |
| 12 | Goose Gossage | .08 | 27 | Rick Reuschel | .08 | 42 | Bobby Witt | .15 |
| 13 | Pedro Guerrero | .15 | 28 | Cal Ripken, Jr. | .20 | 43 | Mike Witt | .25 |
| 14 | Ron Guidry | .08 | 29 | Pete Rose | .50 | 44 | Robin Yount | .15 |
| 15 | Tony Gwynn | .15 | 30 | Nolan Ryan | .08 | | | |

## 1986 Walgreen (Fleer) "Limited Edition" League Leaders....Complete Set of 44 Cards—Value $6.00

Distributed exclusively through Walgreen drug stores. The set was packaged in a printed box, with a *checklist* printed on the back of the box.

| NO. PLAYER | MINT | NO. PLAYER | MINT | NO. PLAYER | MINT |
|---|---|---|---|---|---|
| 1 Wade Boggs | 1.00 | 16 Dwight Gooden | 1.50 | 31 Lance Parrish | .05 |
| 2 George Brett | .50 | 17 Ozzie Guillen | .10 | 32 Kirby Puckett | 1.00 |
| 3 Jose Canseco | 2.00 | 18 Willie Hernandez | .05 | 33 Tim Raines | .05 |
| 4 Rod Carew | .10 | 19 Bob Horner | .05 | 34 Earnie Riles | .15 |
| 5 Gary Carter | .15 | 20 Kent Hrbek | .05 | 35 Cal Ripken, Jr. | .20 |
| 6 Jack Clark | .10 | 21 Charlie Leibrandt | .05 | 36 Pete Rose | 1.00 |
| 7 Vince Coleman | 1.00 | 22 Don Mattingly | 1.50 | 37 Bret Saberhagen | .25 |
| 8 Jose Cruz | .05 | 23 Oddibe McDowell | .15 | 38 Juan Samuel | .05 |
| 9 Alvin Davis | .15 | 24 Willie McGee | .10 | 39 Ryne Sandberg | .25 |
| 10 Mariano Duncan | .10 | 25 Keith Moreland | .05 | 40 Tom Seaver | .10 |
| 11 Leon Durham | .10 | 26 Lloyd Moseby | .05 | 41 Lee Smith | .05 |
| 12 Carlton Fisk | .05 | 27 Dale Murphy | .50 | 42 Ozzie Smith | .05 |
| 13 Julio Franco | .05 | 28 Phil Niekro | .05 | 43 Dave Stieb | .05 |
| 14 Scott Garrelts | .05 | 29 Joe Orsulak | .05 | 44 Robin Yount | .10 |
| 15 Steve Garvey | .15 | 30 Dave Parker | .10 | | |

## 1986 Woolworth (Topps) Champion Superstars....Complete Set of 33 Cards—Value $5.00

Distributed exclusively through Woolworth stores. The cards are coated with a super gloss. The complete set was packaged in a printed box, with a *checklist* printed on the back or the box.

| NO. PLAYER | MINT | NO. PLAYER | MINT | NO. PLAYER | MINT |
|---|---|---|---|---|---|
| 1 Tony Armas | .05 | 12 Bob Grich | .05 | 23 Dale Murphy | .50 |
| 2 Don Baylor | .05 | 13 Tony Gwynn | .15 | 24 Eddie Murray | .30 |
| 3 Wade Boggs | .60 | 14 Keith Hernandez | .10 | 25 Ben Oglivie | .05 |
| 4 George Brett | .50 | 15 Reggie Jackson | .20 | 26 Al Oliver | .05 |
| 5 Bill Buckner | .05 | 16 Dave Kingman | .05 | 27 Dave Parker | .10 |
| 6 Rod Carew | .08 | 17 Carney Lansford | .05 | 28 Jim Rice | .15 |
| 7 Gary Carter | .15 | 18 Fred Lynn | .05 | 29 Pete Rose | .75 |
| 8 Cecil Cooper | .05 | 19 Bill Madlock | .05 | 30 Mike Schmidt | .50 |
| 9 Darrell Evans | .05 | 20 Don Mattingly | 1.00 | 31 Gorman Thomas | .05 |
| 10 Dwight Evans | .05 | 21 Willie McGee | .20 | 32 Willie Wilson | .05 |
| 11 George Foster | .05 | 22 Hal McRae | .05 | 33 Dave Winfield | .10 |

## 1986 Kaybee (Topps) Young Superstars of Baseball....Complete Set of 33 Cards—Value $4.50

Distributed exclusively through Kay Bee toy stores. The cards are coated with a super gloss. The complete set was packaged in a printed box, with a *checklist* printed on the back of the box.

| NO. PLAYER | MINT | NO. PLAYER | MINT | NO. PLAYER | MINT |
|---|---|---|---|---|---|
| 1 Rick Aguilera | .15 | 12 Brian Fisher | .15 | 23 Terry Pendleton | .10 |
| 2 Chris Brown | .30 | 13 John Franco | .10 | 24 Jim Presley | .40 |
| 3 Tom Browning | .20 | 14 Julio Franco | .10 | 25 Kirby Puckett | .50 |
| 4 Tom Brunansky | .15 | 15 Dwight Gooden | 1.00 | 26 Earnie Riles | .15 |
| 5 Vince Coleman | .75 | 16 Ozzie Guillen | .15 | 27 Bret Saberhagen | .20 |
| 6 Ron Darling | .30 | 17 Tony Gwynn | .15 | 28 Mark Salas | .10 |
| 7 Alvin Davis | .25 | 18 Jimmy Key | .10 | 29 Juan Samuel | .10 |
| 8 Mariano Duncan | .20 | 19 Don Mattingly | 1.50 | 30 Jeff Stone | .10 |
| 9 Shawon Dunston | .20 | 20 Oddibe McDowell | .40 | 31 Darryl Strawberry | .40 |
| 10 Sid Fernandez | .20 | 21 Roger McDowell | .10 | 32 Andy Van Slyke | .10 |
| 11 Tony Fernandez | .10 | 22 Dan Pasqua | .25 | 33 Frank Viola | .10 |

# SPECIAL CARD SETS

## TOPPS® SPECIAL CARD SETS

| Year | Description | Cards in Set | Value Mint |
|---|---|---|---|
| 1986 | Limited Edition-Glossy | 792 | $150.00 |
| 1986 | Update Glossy | 132 | 35.00 |
| 1986 | All-Star-Glossy (mail-in) | 60 | 18.00 |
| 1986 | Mini | 66 | 10.00 |
| 1986 | Three Dimensional | 30 | 15.00 |
| 1986 | All-Star-Glossy (insert) | 22 | 5.00 |
| 1986 | Super | 60 | 10.00 |
| 1985 | Limited Edition-Glossy | 792 | 225.00 |
| 1985 | Update Glossy | 132 | 50.00 |
| 1985 | Three-Dimensional | 30 | 15.00 |
| 1985 | All-Star-Glossy (mail-in) | 40 | 12.00 |
| 1985 | All-Star-Glossy (insert) | 22 | 5.00 |
| 1985 | Super | 60 | 14.00 |
| 1984 | Limited Edition-Glossy | 792 | 300.00 |
| 1984 | Update Glossy | 132 | 150.00 |
| 1984 | All-Star Glossy (mail-in) | 40 | 12.00 |
| 1984 | All-Star-Glossy (insert) | 22 | 6.00 |
| 1984 | Super | 30 | 8.00 |
| 1983 | All-Star-Glossy (mail-in) | 40 | 12.00 |
| 1981 | Star Photo | 15 | 5.00 |

| Year | Description | Cards in Set | Value Mint |
|---|---|---|---|
| 1981 | Team Photo | 102 | 30.00 |
| 1980 | Star Photo | 60 | 6.00 |
| 1977 | Cloth Stickers | 73 | 50.00 |
| 1975 | Mini | 660 | 550.00 |
| 1974 | Team Checklist | 24 | 8.00 |
| 1974 | Deckle Edge | 72 | 1,350.00 |
| 1971 | Greatest Moments | 55 | 900.00 |
| 1971 | Super | 63 | 150.00 |
| 1970 | Super | 42 | 150.00 |
| 1969 | Deckle Edge | 33 | 50.00 |
| 1969 | Super | 66 | 2,000.00 |
| 1968 | Three-Dimensional | 12 | 3,000.00 |
| 1968 | Game Cards | 33 | 45.00 |
| 1965 | Gold Foil Embossed | 72 | 60.00 |
| 1964 | Die-Cut | 77 | 700.00 |
| 1964 | Giant | 60 | 60.00 |
| 1955 | Double Header | 66 | 1,500.00 |
| 1951 | Connie Mack All-Stars | 11 | 3,000.00 |
| 1951 | Team Cards | 9 | 1,000.00 |
| 1951 | Major-League All-Stars | 11 | 13,500.00 |

## DONRUSS® SPECIAL CARD SETS

| Year | Description | Cards in Set | Value Mint |
|---|---|---|---|
| 1986 | Rookies | 56 | $25.00 |
| 1986 | Pop-Ups | 18 | 7.00 |
| 1986 | Action All-Stars | 60 | 7.00 |
| 1986 | Highlights | 56 | 10.00 |
| 1985 | Super Diamond Kings | 28 | 9.00 |
| 1985 | Action All-Stars | 60 | 7.00 |
| 1985 | Highlights | 56 | 30.00 |
| 1984 | Champions | 60 | 7.00 |
| 1984 | Action All-Stars | 60 | 7.00 |
| 1983 | Hall of Fame Heroes | 44 | 3.00 |
| 1983 | Action All-Stars | 60 | 7.00 |

## FLEER® SPECIAL CARD SETS

| Year | Description | Cards in Set | Value Mint |
|---|---|---|---|
| 1987 | Fleer Glossy (tin) | 660 | $140.00 |
| 1986 | Classic Mini | 120 | 12.00 |
| 1986 | All-Star Team | 12 | 6.00 |
| 1986 | Future Hall of Famers | 6 | 8.00 |
| 1986 | McCrory Superstars | 44 | 6.00 |
| 1986 | McCrory Sluggers vs. Pitchers | 44 | 6.00 |
| 1986 | Walgreen League Leaders | 44 | 6.00 |
| 1985 | McCrory Superstars | 44 | 6.00 |

# FACTORY SEALED BOXES

Note—Due to high demand, the value of factory-sealed boxes fluctuates considerably.

## TOPPS® VENDING BOXES

| Year | Description | Value |
|---|---|---|
| 1987 | Vending Box of 500 cards | $11.00 |
| 1986 | Vending Box of 500 cards | 12.50 |
| 1985 | Vending Box of 500 cards | 40.00 |
| 1984 | Vending Box of 500 cards | 40.00 |
| 1983 | Vending Box of 500 cards | 45.00 |
| 1982 | Vending Box of 500 cards | 40.00 |
| 1981 | Vending Box of 500 cards | 35.00 |
| 1980 | Vending Box of 500 cards | 55.00 |
| 1979 | Vending Box of 500 cards | 55.00 |
| 1978 | Vending Box of 500 cards | 80.00 |
| 1977 | Vending Box of 500 cards | 140.00 |

## TOPPS® GUM BOXES

| Year | Description | Value |
|---|---|---|
| 1987 | Gum Box of 36 Packs | $15.00 |
| 1986 | Gum Box of 36 Packs | 17.50 |
| 1985 | Gum Box of 36 Packs | 50.00 |
| 1984 | Gum Box of 36 Packs | 50.00 |
| 1983 | Gum Box of 36 Packs | 55.00 |
| 1982 | Gum Box of 36 Packs | 50.00 |
| 1981 | Gum Box of 36 Packs | 45.00 |
| 1980 | Gum Box of 36 Packs | 105.00 |
| 1979 | Gum Box of 36 Packs | 110.00 |
| 1978 | Gum Box of 36 Packs | 150.00 |
| 1977 | Gum Box of 36 Packs | 250.00 |

## TOPPS® RACK BOXES

| Year | Description | Value |
|---|---|---|
| 1987 | Box of 24 Rack Packs | $25.00 |
| 1986 | Box of 24 Rack Packs | 30.00 |
| 1985 | Box of 24 Rack Packs | 80.00 |
| 1984 | Box of 24 Rack Packs | 80.00 |
| 1983 | Box of 24 Rack Packs | 90.00 |
| 1982 | Box of 24 Rack Packs | 80.00 |
| 1981 | Box of 24 Rack Packs | 70.00 |
| 1980 | Box of 24 Rack Packs | 120.00 |
| 1979 | Box of 24 Rack Packs | 120.00 |
| 1978 | Box of 24 Rack Packs | 150.00 |

## TOPPS® CELLO BOXES

| Year | Description | Value |
|---|---|---|
| 1987 | Box of 24 Cello Packs | $15.00 |
| 1986 | Box of 24 Cello Packs | 20.00 |
| 1985 | Box of 24 Cello Packs | 50.00 |
| 1984 | Box of 24 Cello Packs | 50.00 |
| 1983 | Box of 24 Cello Packs | 55.00 |
| 1982 | Box of 24 Cello Packs | 50.00 |
| 1981 | Box of 24 Cello Packs | 50.00 |
| 1980 | Box of 24 Cello Packs | 80.00 |
| 1979 | Box of 24 Cello Packs | 75.00 |
| 1978 | Box of 24 Cello Packs | 90.00 |

## DONRUSS GUM BOXES

| Year | Description | Value |
|---|---|---|
| 1987 | Gum Box of 36 Packs | $25.00 |
| 1986 | Gum Box of 36 Packs | 40.00 |
| 1985 | Gum Box of 36 Packs | 90.00 |
| 1984 | Gum Box of 36 Packs | 175.00 |
| 1983 | Gum Box of 36 Packs | 25.00 |
| 1982 | Gum Box of 36 Packs | 20.00 |
| 1981 | Gum Box of 36 Packs | 20.00 |

## FLEER GUM BOXES

| Year | Description | Value |
|---|---|---|
| 1987 | Gum Box of 36 Packs | $25.00 |
| 1986 | Gum Box of 36 Packs | 40.00 |
| 1985 | Gum Box of 36 Packs | 70.00 |
| 1984 | Gum Box of 36 Packs | 75.00 |
| 1983 | Gum Box of 36 Packs | 25.00 |
| 1982 | Gum Box of 36 Packs | 20.00 |
| 1981 | Gum Box of 36 Packs | 20.00 |

## DONRUSS RACK BOXES

| Year | Description | Value |
|---|---|---|
| 1987 | Rack Box of 24 Packs | $45.00 |
| 1986 | Rack Box of 24 Packs | 90.00 |
| 1985 | Rack Box of 24 Packs | 160.00 |
| 1984 | Rack Box of 24 Packs | 425.00 |

(Rack Packs were not produced from 1981 to 1983)

## FLEER RACK BOXES

| Year | Description | Value |
|---|---|---|
| 1987 | Rack Box of 24 Packs | $45.00 |

CELLO PACK

VENDING BOX

RACK PACK

GUM BOX